Fodor's 2016

FRANCE

TIGRE D'OR
LONDON
L'IMPRESSIONNISTE
L'IMPRESSIONNISTE

WELCOME TO FRANCE

Famed artists, writers, gourmands, and bon vivants have all been put under France's intoxicating spell. And travelers can still relish the same enchanting attractions, from Matisse's coastal villages to Hemingway's Parisian cafés to Marie-Antoinette's pastoral escape inside Versailles. France is a gastronomic wonderland, an artistic mecca, and a historical pop-up book. Vineyards blanket the wine regions, cathedrals crown the cities, and sandy beaches drape the coastline. With all these riches, you may start plotting your return visit before you even return home.

TOP REASONS TO GO

★ **Marvelous Food:** From the humble café to haute cuisine, the French know how to eat.

★ **Fairy-Tale Castles and Châteaux:** The elegance and majesty of France's past endure.

★ **Shopping:** Parisian luxuries, famed street markets, and handicrafts all beckon.

★ **Wineries and Vineyards:** White to red, you can sip your way across the countryside.

★ **Awesome Art:** From the grand, sprawling Louvre to the intimate Atelier Cézanne.

★ **Charming Villages:** Countryside hamlets with pretty cottages are plentiful.

Fodor's FRANCE 2016

Publisher: Amanda D'Acierno, *Senior Vice President*

Editorial: Arabella Bowen, *Editor in Chief*; Linda Cabasin, *Editorial Director*

Design: Tina Malaney, *Associate Art Director*; Chie Ushio, *Senior Designer*

Photography: Jennifer Arnow, *Senior Photo Editor*; Mary Robnett, *Photo Researcher*

Production: Linda Schmidt, *Managing Editor*; Evangelos Vasilakis, *Associate Managing Editor*; Angela L. McLean, *Senior Production Manager*

Maps: Rebecca Baer, *Senior Map Editor*; Mark Stroud (Moon Street Cartography), David Lindroth, Ed Jacobus, *Cartographers*

Sales: Jacqueline Lebow, *Sales Director*

Marketing & Publicity: Heather Dalton, *Marketing Director*; Katherine Punia, *Publicity Director*

Business & Operations: Susan Livingston, *Vice President, Strategic Business Planning*; Sue Daulton, *Vice President, Operations*

Fodors.com: Megan Bell, *Executive Director, Revenue & Business Development*; Yasmin Marinaro, *Senior Director, Marketing & Partnerships*

Writers: Linda Hervieux, Nancy Heslin, Sean Hillen, Jennifer Ladonne, Lyn Parry, Virginia Power, Avery Sumner, Jack Vermee

Editors: Mark Sullivan, Amanda Sadlowski, Sue MacCallum-Whitcomb

Production Editor: Carolyn Roth

ISBN 978-1-101-87841-5

ISSN 0532–5692

SPECIAL SALES

This book is available at special discounts for bulk purchases for sales promotions or premiums. For more information, e-mail specialmarkets@penguinrandomhouse.com.

PRINTED IN THE UNITED STATES OF AMERICA

10 9 8 7 6 5 4 3 2 1

CONTENTS

Fodor's Features

MAPS

ABOUT THIS GUIDE

Fodor's Recommendations

Everything in this guide is worth doing—we don't cover what isn't—but exceptional sights, hotels, and restaurants are recognized with additional accolades. Fodor's Choice★ indicates our top recommendations. Care to nominate a new place? Visit Fodors.com/contact-us.

Trip Costs

We list prices wherever possible to help you budget well. Hotel and restaurant price categories from **$** to **$$$$** are noted alongside each recommendation. For hotels, we include the lowest cost of a standard double room in high season. For restaurants, we cite the average price of a main course at dinner or, if dinner isn't served, at lunch. For attractions, we always list adult admission fees; discounts are usually available for children, students, and senior citizens.

Hotels

Our local writers vet every hotel to recommend the best overnights in each price category, from budget to expensive. Unless otherwise specified, you can expect private bath, phone, and TV in your room. For expanded hotel reviews, facilities, and deals visit Fodors.com.

Top Picks

★ Fodor's Choice

Listings

- ✉ Address
- Branch address
- Telephone
- Fax
- Website
- E-mail
- Admission fee
- Open/closed times
- Ⓜ Subway
- Directions or Map coordinates

Hotels & Restaurants

- Hotel
- Number of rooms
- Meal plans
- ✕ Restaurant
- Reservations
- Dress code
- No credit cards
- $ Price

Other

- ⇨ See also
- ☞ Take note
- Golf facilities

Restaurants

Unless we state otherwise, restaurants are open for lunch and dinner daily. We mention dress code only when there's a specific requirement and reservations only when they're essential or not accepted. To make restaurant reservations, visit Fodors.com.

Credit Cards

The hotels and restaurants in this guide typically accept credit cards. If not, we'll say so.

EUGENE FODOR

Hungarian-born Eugene Fodor (1905–91) began his travel career as an interpreter on a French cruise ship. The experience inspired him to write *On the Continent* (1936), the first guidebook to receive annual updates and discuss a country's way of life as well as its sights. Fodor later joined the U.S. Army and worked for the OSS in World War II. After the war, he kept up his intelligence work while expanding his guidebook series. During the Cold War, many guides were written by fellow agents who understood the value of insider information. Today's guides continue Fodor's legacy by providing travelers with timely coverage, insider tips, and cultural context.

EXPERIENCE FRANCE

FRANCE TODAY

It may be a cliché to say the French fret over their place in the world, but they do. Faced with the ever-dominant Anglo-American axis and hobbled by the global economic crisis, the French are rallying to protect their institutions, their language, and, above all, *la vie française*—their treasured lifestyle. Still, polls show the French are optimistic about the future—and there's plenty of good news.

Tourism is thriving, with France maintaining its rank as the world's top tourist destination, with more than 86 million visitors each year. The French remain leaders in science and technology. France is the world's leading producer of luxury goods, and fashion remains the nation's birthright. Dining in Paris has never been better, with the city experiencing a vibrant emergence of smaller, lower-priced bistros concentrating on quality and terroir, the local bounty that France is famous for.

Turning in Their Stars

Several of France's acclaimed chefs, including Yannick Alléno, and Olivier Roellinger, have handed in their Michelin stars and bowed out of the fast track in favor of smaller, less formal settings. The global crisis and changing lifestyles have deeply influenced a new generation of chefs seeking a more modern approach to cooking, yet still eager to strut their stuff for an educated, ever-appreciative audience. All of these trends have culminated in a movement that's taken France by storm—*bistronomie.*

Well under way since the late 1990s, the bistronomie movement is now in full swing, with exciting new restaurants opening in Paris every month. A hybrid of "bistrot" and "gastronomy," bistronomie broadly defines a new breed of bistro, run by ambitious young chefs who combine rigorous haute cuisine training with a more laid-back, individual, and creative approach. As the irreverent foodie publications *Omnivore* and *Le Fooding*—viewed as little more than cheeky upstarts when they appeared a decade ago—have evolved into major forces behind the movement, people have taken notice.

Bistronomie dovetails with other popular movements—like the locavores, who advocate the use of fresh, local ingredients, and the trend toward natural and biodynamic wines, which are grown without the use of chemical fertilizers and produced with less sulfites. An international roster of passionate young chefs has also invigorated the movement, with no single approach stealing the limelight.

Marriage Equality

After a national discussion that had lasted more than a decade, France passed a law allowing same-sex marriage in 2013. In a country where most people believe the government should stay out of personal relationships, the debate was particularly acrimonious. A group called La Manif Pour Tous staged massive, colorful demonstrations in Paris, Lyon, and other major cities.

François Hollande's Socialist government easily won passage of the law, and changed many minds in the process. At the time the law passed, polls found that about 53% of French adults favored same-sex marriage. In 2014, less than a year later, that number had jumped to 61%.

But Hollande also burned a lot of bridges along the way. In 2014, after another round of protests, his government announced that it would not push ahead with legislation to give joint parenting

rights to gay couples who had a child together.

Madame–Mademoiselle

The French government made a long-overdue concession to French feminists, finally enforcing a law that excises the honorific Mademoiselle from official forms, and advising that all women now be referred to as Madame regardless of marital status. What took France so long?

A deep ambivalence on the part of both men and women regarding gender roles certainly plays a part. As does the kind of entrenched inequality with men still earning wages an average of 14% to 28% higher than women, although France has been working on closing the gender pay gap, following EU directives. Attitudes here are slow to change, and with so few female legislators, another area where France lags behind other nations, it seems that French women have their work cut out for them.

Pity the Rich

French millionaires can relax—for now. France's prime minister Manuel Valls announced that president Francois Hollande's proposed 75% tax on individuals earning more than €1 million would be abandoned in 2015. The threat of this tax alone is said to have caused wealthy people to leave the country. Gérard Depardieu, France's most famous actor, has already jumped ship. Depardieu, courted by none other than Russia's Vladimir Putin, put his 20,000-square-foot mansion in Paris's elegant 7th arrondissement up for sale. Ex-president Nicholas Sarkozy set France abuzz when his plan to vacate Paris and start up a hedge fund with a group of wealthy investors in London was uncovered during a police raid on the scandal-ridden former president's property.

From a distance, an income tax this steep may seem like madness. But the French have long reconciled themselves to higher taxes in the interest of a fundamental French value, *égalité,* reaping the benefits in the form of one of the world's best health care systems, low-cost education, universal child care, and a plethora of social safety nets. With the global crisis, however, preserving the French quality of life is an ever more delicate balancing act. Whether President Hollande is up to the task remains to be seen, and this battle may be a decisive one.

Driving Smart

Paris has taken another big step toward mitigating the noise, pollution, and congestion caused by the city's automobile traffic. The dapper four-seat, fully electric Bluecar has finished its test run and is now available at 2,000 stations around the city. Similar programs have been launched in Lyon and Bordeaux.

Based on the successful Vélib' bicycle exchange, which boasts more than 20,000 bicycles and is still growing, the Autolib' program allows cars to be taken from one of the semicircular metal-and-glass stations to any point in Paris, and 56 suburban destinations. After a nominal subscription rate, each ride is paid for in half-hour increments, costing €5.50 to €9.

WHAT'S WHERE

Numbers refer to chapters.

2 Paris. A quayside vista that takes in the Seine, a passing boat, Notre-Dame, the Eiffel Tower, and mansard roofs all in one generous sweep is enough to convince you that Paris is indeed the most beautiful city on Earth.

3 Side Trips from Paris. Appearing like all France in miniature, the Ile-de-France region is the nation's heartland. Here Louis XIV built vainglorious Versailles, Chartres brings the faithful to their knees, and Monet's Giverny enchants all.

4 Loire Valley. Chenonceaux, Chambord, and Saumur—the parade of royal and near-royal châteaux magnificently captures France's golden age of monarchy in an idyllic region threaded by the Loire River.

5 Normandy. Sculpted with cliff-lined coasts, Normandy has been home to saints and sculptors, painters and poets, with a dramatic past marked by Mont-St-Michel's majestic abbey, Rouen's towering cathedral, and the D-Day beaches.

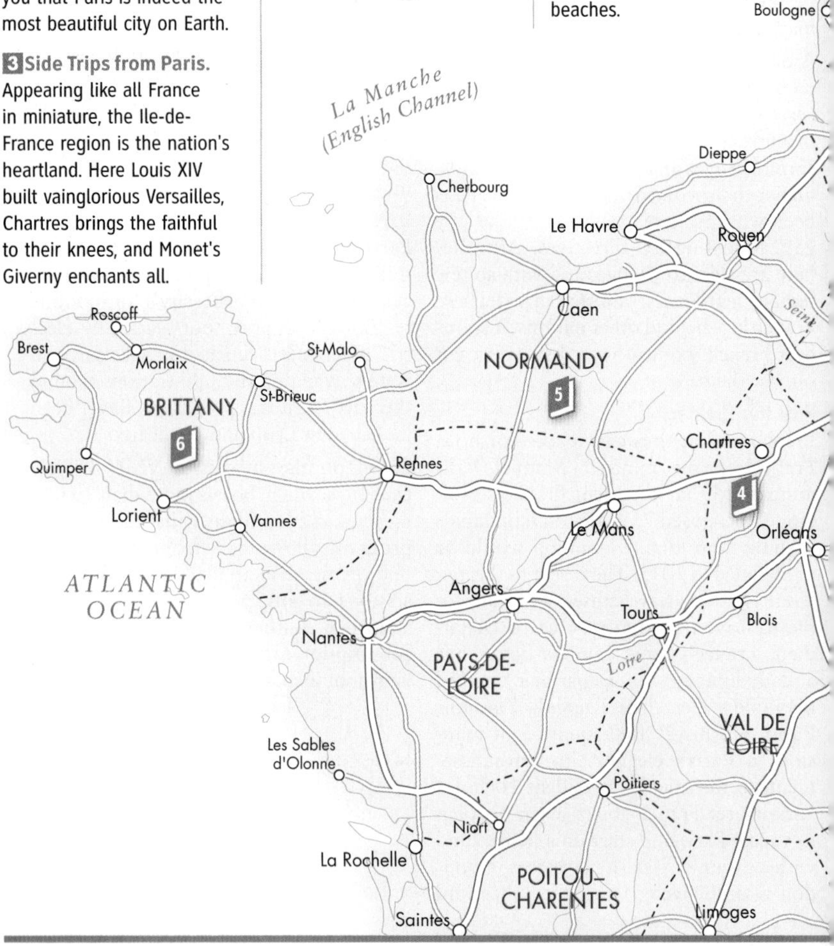

6 Brittany. A long arm of rocky land stretching into the Atlantic, Brittany is a place unto itself, with its own language, customs, and time-defying towns such as Gauguin's Pont-Aven and the pirate haven of St-Malo.

7 Champagne Country. The capital of bubbly is Reims, set near four great Gothic cathedrals and the beginning of the scenic Route de Champagne.

8 Alsace-Lorraine. Although this region bordered by the Rhine often looks German and sounds German, its main sights—18th-century Nancy, medieval Strasbourg, and the lovely Route du Vin—remain proudly French.

WHAT'S WHERE

9 Burgundy. Hallowed ground for wine lovers, Burgundy hardly needs to be beautiful—but it is. Around the gastronomic hub of Dijon, the region is famed for its verdant vineyards and Romanesque churches.

10 Lyon and the Alps. Local chefs rival their Parisian counterparts in treasure-filled Lyon, heart of a diverse region where you ski down Mont Blanc or take a heady trip along the Beaujolais Wine Road.

11 Provence. Famed for its Lavender Route, the honey-gold hill towns of the Luberon, and vibrant cities like Aix and Marseilles, this region was dazzlingly abstracted into vivid daubs of paint by Van Gogh and Cézanne.

12 French Riviera (Côte d'Azur). From glamorous St-Tropez through beauteous Antibes to sophisticated Nice, this sprawl of pebble beaches and zillion-dollar houses has always captivated sun lovers and socialites.

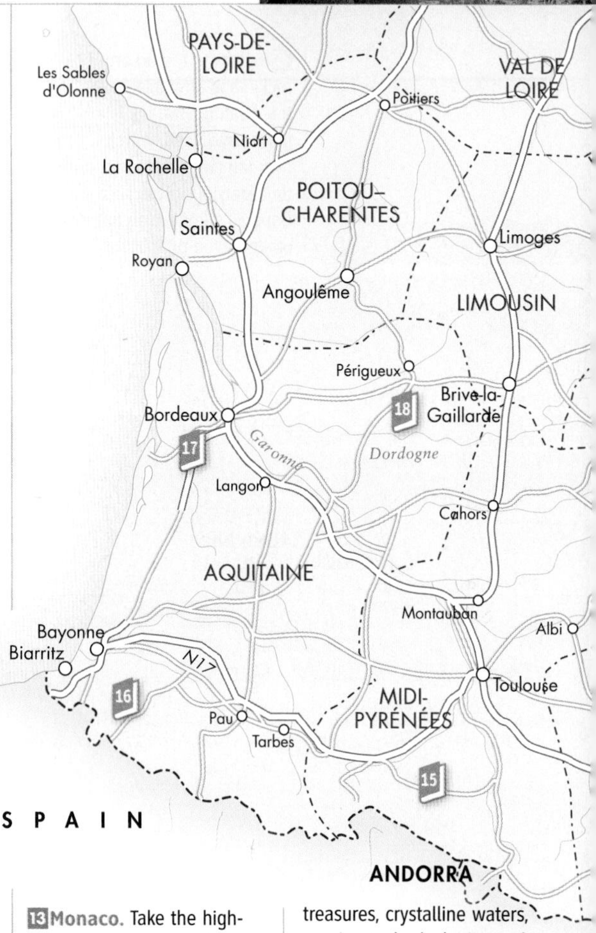

13 Monaco. Take the high-rises of Hong Kong, add the amusement-park feel of Disneyland, and mix in a royal touch, and there you have Monte Carlo—all 473 acres of it. Monaco remains the playground of royalty.

14 Corsica. Corsica's gifts of artistic and archaeological treasures, crystalline waters, granite peaks, lush vineyards, and pine forests add up to one of France's most unspoiled sanctuaries.

15 Midi-Pyrénées and Languedoc-Roussillon. Rose-hue Toulouse, once-upon-a-time-ified Carcassone, and the

Matisse-beloved Vermillion Coast are among southwest France's most colorful sights.

16 Basque Country, Gascony, and the Hautes-Pyrénées. Whether you head for Bay of Biscay resorts like Biarritz, coastal villages such as St-Jean-de-Luz, or the Pyrenean peaks, this region will cast a spell.

17 Bordeaux and the Wine Country. The wines of Bordeaux tower as a standard against which others are measured, and they made the city of Bordeaux rich and owners of its vineyards—like Château Lafite-Rothschild—even richer.

18 The Dordogne. One of the hottest destinations in France, the Dordogne is a stone-cottage pastorale studded with fairy-tale castles, storybook villages, and France's top prehistoric sights.

NEED TO KNOW

AT A GLANCE

Capital: Paris

Population: 63,460,000

Currency: Euro

Money: ATMs are common; credit cards widely accepted

Language: French

Country Code: 33

Emergencies: 112

Driving: On the right

Electricity: 220v/50 cycles; electrical plugs have two round prongs

Time: Six hours ahead of New York

Documents: Up to 90 days with valid passport; Schengen rules apply

Mobile Phones: GSM (900 and 1800 bands)

Major Mobile Companies: Bouygues, Orange, Free

WEBSITES

France: 🌐 *us.franceguide.com*

Paris: 🌐 *www.paris.fr/english* 🌐 *www.parisinfo.com*

GETTING AROUND

Air Travel: The major airports are Paris, Lyon, Nice, and Marseille.

Bus Travel: Good for smaller regional towns and the only direct public transit to Giverny from Paris.

Car Travel: Renting a car is the best way to explore at your own pace, but never in Paris, and beware of unmanned gas stations and toll booths on major highways. Gas is very expensive.

Train Travel: Fast TGV trains link Paris with major cities like Rouen, Avignon, and Nice; switch to local trains for smaller places.

PLAN YOUR BUDGET

	HOTEL ROOM	MEAL	ATTRACTIONS
Low Budget	€105	€17	Stairs to Eiffel Tower, Level 2, €5
Mid Budget	€160	€30	Louvre ticket with temp. exhibitions, €16
High Budget	€300	€120	Opera ticket, €135

WAYS TO SAVE

Eat lunch picnic-style. Take advantage of France's wonderful outdoor markets and shops, then eat picnic-style indoors or out.

Book a rental apartment. For more space and a kitchen, consider a furnished rental—a good bet for families.

Book rail tickets in advance. For the cheapest rail fares, book online 90 days before travel at the website for the French railway. 🌐 *www.sncf.com.*

Look for free museum days. Most museums are free on the first Sunday of the month, and often one afternoon or evening a week.

PLAN YOUR TIME

Hassle Factor	Low. Flights to Paris are frequent, and France has great transport elsewhere.
3 days	You can see some of the magic of Paris and take a half-day trip out to Versailles or Chartres.
1 week	Combine a short trip to Paris with a day trip to Normandy or Giverny, as well as an additional day or two in a place within easy reach by high-speed train (TGV) like Lyons or Marseille.
2 weeks	You have time to move around and for the highlights, including a stop in Paris, excursions to Normandy, and a trip to see the highlights of atmospheric Provence and the ritzy French Riviera.

WHEN TO GO

High Season: June through August is the most expensive and popular time to visit France. June and July in Paris are especially crowded; August is quieter in Paris but is the busiest month in the south. Famously fickle weather means you never know what to expect in the north.

Low Season: Unless you are skiing, winter offers the least appealing weather, though it's the best time for airfares and hotel deals—and to escape the crowds. Particularly in the south, the famous mistral winds make travel uncomfortable.

Value Season: September is lovely, with temperate weather, saner airfares, and cultural events. October has great weather, though temperatures drop by late November. Late April or May is a great time to visit, before the masses arrive but when cafés are abuzz. March and early April weather can be varied and wet.

BIG EVENTS

May: The French Open kicks off the last week of May in Paris. 🌐 *www.rolandgarros.com*

July: Every town celebrates le quatorze juillet (Bastille Day).

September: The Journée du Patrimoine opens France's most beautiful buildings on the third Sunday. 🌐 *www.journeesdupatrimoine.culture.fr*

February: Carnival rocks Lent for three weeks. 🌐 *www.nicecarnaval.com*

READ THIS

- ***A Food Lover's Guide to France,*** Patricia Wells. For lovers of food and wine.
- ***A Year in Provence,*** Peter Mayle. Satirical introduction to French country life.
- ***France Today,*** John Ardagh. The best primer on modern France.

WATCH THIS

- ***Amelie.*** A quirky and romantic view of Paris.
- ***The Untouchables.*** A touching tale of an unlikely friendship.
- ***Jean de Florette.*** A view of rural Provençal life.

EAT THIS

- ***Boeuf bourgignon***: the famous French stew
- ***Confit de canard***: tender and delicious duck leg
- ***Crêpes***: savory or sweet, streetside or in a café
- ***Croissant or pain au chocolat***: from a café
- ***Fromage***: French cheese comes in seemingly endless varieties.
- ***Salade Niçoise***: a classic French Riviera lunch (with a glass of rosé)

FRANCE TOP ATTRACTIONS

Louvre, Paris

(A) Home to art's most photogenic beauties—the *Venus de Milo*, the *Winged Victory*, and the *Mona Lisa*—this is not only the largest palace in France but also the most important museum in the world.

Chartres, Side Trips from Paris

(B) Triply famous for its peerless stained-glass windows, as the resting place for an important relic of the Virgin Mary, and as the birthplace of High Gothic, Chartres is more than a cathedral—it's a spiritual experience.

Versailles, Side Trips from Paris

(C) A palace and then some, this prime example of royals-gone-wild Baroque style served as backdrop for the rise to power of King Louis XIV. To escape all his bicep-flexing grandeur visit the park to see Marie-Antoinette's fairy-tale farm.

Monet's Garden, Giverny, Side Trips from Paris

(D) An 8-acre "Monet," these lush gardens were works of art the Impressionist master spent years perfecting before he began re-creating them on canvas. The colors radiate best on sunny spring days.

Chenonceau, Loire Valley

Half bridge, half pleasure palace, this "queen of the châteaux" was presided over by six remarkable women. It was Catherine de' Medici who brilliantly enlarged it to span the River Cher in homage to the Ponte Vecchio of her native Florence.

Lyon, Rhône-Alps

The second-largest city in France, Lyon vies with Paris as the country's true gastronomic capital—gourmands flock here for its galaxy of multistar superchefs and cozy *bouchons* (taverns).

Mont-St-Michel, Normandy

(E) Once seen, never forgotten, this Romanesque abbey rises from its bay like a shimmering apparition, becoming an island at high tide. French and English fought to dominate the "rock" until the 13th century, when it was crowned with a splendid Gothic church.

Strasbourg, Alsace-Lorraine

(F) The cosmopolitan seat of Europe's Parliament, this fascinating mix of half-timber houses and modern glass buildings was fought over by France and Germany—a battle that resulted in a rich intertwining of cultures.

Beaune, Burgundy

At the heart of some of the world's most esteemed vineyards, this atmospheric town is inextricably linked with the wine trade, especially during the annual auction at Beaune's beautiful 15th-century Hôtel-Dieu.

Èze, the French Riviera

Spectacularly perched atop a rocky promontory, this watercolor-pretty village has some of the most breathtaking views in la belle France.

St-Tropez, the French Riviera

(G) Single-handedly propelled from sleepy hamlet to glamorous resort by Brigitte Bardot, St-Trop today heaves with crowds of petulant glitterati. Chill out in the quiet pastel-hue alleys of La Ponche quarter.

Aix-en-Provence, Provence

(H) With sun-dappled squares, luxuriant fountains, and Paul Cézanne's hallowed studio, this captivating town is just the spot for those who consider café-sitting, people-watching, and boutique shopping a way of life.

TOP EXPERIENCES

How will you experience France? Will you while away the hours in the shops and cafés of Paris? Will you dine at the temples of gastronomy in Lyon? Will you play feudal lord among the châteaux of the Loire Valley? Or will you simply throw away your map and chance upon nestled-away villages of the Côte d'Azur or fairy-tale hamlets of the Dordogne? These suggestions, and the following, await you as memorable experiences for your next trip to France.

Walk Like a Parisian

Paris was made for wandering, and the French have coined a lovely word for a person who strolls, usually without a destination in mind: *le flâneur*. In Paris, no matter how aimlessly you wander, chances are you'll end up somewhere magical. Why not first head to the most beautiful spot on the Right Bank: the Palais Royal gardens?

Go Glam in Paris

Break out your bling in this capital of luxury with a stroll down Rue Saint-Honoré to window-shop—the French call it *lèche-vitrine* (or "window-licking")—from Chanel and Hermès to Chloé. Then do some real feasting at one of Paris's gastronomic temples, L'Arpège (lunch main courses are around €160) or L'Astrance.

Rendezvous with the Phantom

Want to feel like one of the aristocrats from the Second Empire? Promenade the fabulously opulent lobby and theater of the 19th-century Palais Garnier—haunt of the Phantom and Degas's immortal dancers—or get tickets for an evening performance.

Pique-Nique at Place des Vosges

No restaurant can beat the "decor" of Paris's most beautiful square, the 17th-century place des Vosges, so pull up a bench and enjoy your own foodie fixings. Get them at the nearby Marché d'Aligre market (Tuesday to Sunday), off rue du Faubourg Saint-Antoine.

Step into an 8-Acre Monet

It doesn't matter how many posters, photos, or T-shirts you've seen emblazoned with Monet's famous water lilies, nothing beats a visit to Giverny. Savor the Impressionist painter's famous house and gardens in person.

Trip the Light Fantastique at Versailles

Exquisitely choreographed pyrotechnical shows are held each summer and fall in Versailles's immense château gardens. Accompanied by son-et-lumière music and dance performances, these evenings are fit for the Sun King himself.

Plan an Ascent on Heaven at Mont-St-Michel

Keep the faith with a climb to the top and get a God's View of this fabled Benedictine abbey, whose fortified medieval village is the crowning glory of the Normandy coastline.

Become Scott and Zelda on the Riviera

Channel F. Scott Fitzgerald and his wife at their old haunts and discover their side of paradise: stay at Les Belles Rives hotel in Juan-les-Pins, visit hangouts like the Villa Eilenroc at Cap d'Antibes, or dine with superstars at the Hôtel du Cap-Eden Roc.

Rate the Best of Alsace's Würsts

As you head down Alsace's famous Wine Road, Hansel and Gretel villages pop up every few miles, and each has *winstubs* (wine bistros) that cook up delicious dishes of *choucroute garnie*. The inns in Riquewihr and Ribeauvillé are supposed to serve the best.

Pop Your Cork along the Champagne Road

The famous Route du Champagne leads fans of the famous bubbly to the prestigious Champagne houses of Épernay and Reims (including Mumm and Taittinger) plus smaller, family-run estates for tours and tastings.

Que la Fête Commence at Nice's Carnaval

February is festival time on the Côte d'Azur, with boisterous street processions and a celebratory bonfire for the Mardi-Gras Carnaval de Nice. Or march along the citrus-decked parade floats of Menton's Fête du Citron.

Go Castle-Hopping on a Loire Valley Bike Tour

From Blois to Azay-le-Rideau, bike with VBT Tours (🌐 *www.vbt.com*) along the meandering Loire River past royal châteaux and bountiful gardens, and discover quirky cliff-side troglodyte dwellings that house wine caves and mushroom growers.

Submerge Yourself in Hip-Deep Purple along the Lavender Route

Join the lavender-happy crowds from June to mid-July and travel the Route de la Lavande, a wide blue-purple swath that connects major sights like the Abbaye Notre-Dame de Sènaque, Coustellet's Musée de la Lavande, and Forcalquier's famous market.

Après-Ski the Day Away in the French Alps

As home to the first Winter Olympic games in 1924, the ski station of Chamonix, set at the foot of Mont Blanc, provides an ideal backdrop for all winter outdoor activities.

Ride Shotgun on Picasso's Road to St-Paul-de-Vence

Use Aix-en-Provence, Arles, or Antibes as a base for touring the Modern Art Road. Explore picture-perfect villages immortalized by Cézanne and Van Gogh and pose under the Picassos on view at the Colombe d'Or inn (🌐 *www.la-colombe-dor.com*).

Play Once-Upon-a-Time in Carcassonne

Protected by a double ring of ramparts and 53 towers, this perfectly preserved fortified city of the Languedoc-Roussillon region is considered to be one of the most romantic medieval settings in France.

Attend the Festival d'Avignon

This internationally renowned summer theater festival features well more than a thousand performances throughout the city, plus hundreds more in the "unofficial" Avignon Off festival.

Track the Tour de France

No tickets are required to watch this famed cycling competition as it winds through some of the country's most dramatic scenery. Why not enjoy a picnic anywhere along the route as the riders race past?

QUINTESSENTIAL FRANCE

If you want to get a sense of contemporary French culture, and indulge in some of its pleasures, start by familiarizing yourself with the rituals of daily life. These are a few highlights—things you can take part in with relative ease.

Café Society

Along with air, water, and wine, the café remains one of the basic necessities of life in France. You may prefer a posh perch at a renowned Paris spot such as the Deux Magots on boulevard St-Germain or opt for a tiny *café du coin* (corner café) in Lyon or Marseilles, where you can have a quick cup of coffee at the counter. Those on Paris's major boulevards (such as boulevard St-Michel and the Champs-Élysées) will almost always be the most expensive and the least interesting.

In effect, the more modest establishments (look for nonchalant locals) are the places to really get a feeling for French café culture.

And we do mean culture—not only the practical rituals of the experience (perusing the posted menu, choosing a table, unwrapping your sugar cube) but an intellectual spur as well.

You'll see businesspeople, students, and pensive types pulling out notebooks for intent scribblings. In fact, some Paris landmarks like the Café de Flore host readings, while several years ago a trend for *cafés philos* (philosophy cafés) took off.

And there's always the frisson of history available at places like La Closerie des Lilas, where an expensive drink allows you to rest your derrière on the spots once favored by Apollinaire, Picasso, and Henry Miller.

Finally, there's people-watching, which goes hand in glove with the café lifestyle—what better excuse to linger over your *café crème* or Lillet? So get ready to settle in, sip your *pastis*, and pretend your

travel notebook is a Hemingway story in the making.

Street Markets

Browsing through the street markets and *marchés couverts* (covered markets) of France is enough to make you regret all the tempting restaurants. But even though their seafood, free-range poultry, olives, and produce cry out to be gathered in a basket and cooked in their purest forms, you can also enjoy them as a simple visual feast.

Over at flea and *brocante* (collectibles) markets, food plays second fiddle. With any luck, you'll find a little 18th-century engraving that makes your heart go *trottinant*.

Bistros and Brasseries

The choice of restaurants in France is a feast in itself. Of course, at least once during your trip you'll want to indulge in a luxurious meal at a great haute-cuisine restaurant—but there's no need to get knee-deep in white truffles at Paris's Pierre Gagnaire to savor the France the French eat. You can discover the most delicious and indulgent food with a quick visit to a city neighborhood bistro.

History tells us that bistros served the world's first fast food—after the fall of Napoléon, the Russian soldiers who occupied Paris were known to cry *bistro* ("quickly" in Russian) when ordering.

Here, at zinc-top tables, you'll find the great delights of *cuisine traditionelle,* like *grand-mère's* lamb with white beans.

Brasseries, with few exceptions, remain unchanged—great bustling places with white-aproned waiters and hearty, mainly Alsatian, food, such as pork-based dishes, *choucroute* (sauerkraut), and beer (*brasserie* also means brewery).

IF YOU LIKE

Great Food

Forget the Louvre or the Château de Chenonceau—the real reason for a visit to France is to dine at its famous temples of gastronomy. Once you dive into Taillevent's lobster soufflé, you'll quickly realize that food in France is far more than fuel. The French regard gastronomy as essential to the art of living, so don't feel guilty if your meal at Paris's L'Ambroisie takes as long as your visit to the Musée d'Orsay: two hours for a three-course menu is par, and you may, after relaxing into the routine, feel pressured at less than three. Gastronomads—those who travel to eat—won't want to miss a pilgrimage to L'Assiette Champenoise in Reims to witness the culinary fireworks of chef Arnaud Lallement, or farther afield at the revered Maison Lameloise in the heart of Bourgogne wine country. So plan on treating dining as religiously as the French do—at least once.

Epicure, Paris. Eric Frechon's masterful cuisine is *extraordinaire* and the garden-side setting *très elegante*.

L'Assiette Champenois, Reims. Master chef Arnaud Lallement marries grand cuisine with humble Provençal touches—don't be surprised to find octopus in your bouillabaisse.

L'Auberge de L'Ill, Illhaeusern, near Ribeauville, Alsace. Gourmands worship at this culinary temple where the Haeberline family create a brave nouvelle world by fusing Alsatian and Asian fixings to the hautest cuisine.

Le Louis XV, Monaco. If you're going to feast like a king, this Alain Ducasse outpost is the place to do it.

La Vie de Châteaux

From the humblest feudal ruin to the most delicate Loire Valley spires to the grandest of Sun King spreads, the châteaux of France evoke the history of Europe as no museum can. It is easy to slip into the role of a feudal lord standing on his castellated ramparts and scrambling to protect his patchwork of holdings from kings and dukes. The lovely landscape takes on a strategic air and you find yourself role-playing thus, whether swanning aristocratically over Chenonceau's bridgelike *galerie de bal* spanning the River Cher or curling a revolutionary lip at the splendid excesses of Versailles. These are, after all, the castles that inspired Charles Perrault's "Sleeping Beauty" and "Beauty and the Beast," and their fairy-tale magic—rich with history and Disney-free—still holds true. Better yet, enjoy a "queen-for-a-stay" night at one of France's many châteaux-hotels. Many are surprisingly affordable.

Chambord, Loire Valley. This French Renaissance extravaganza—all 440 rooms and 365 chimneys—will take your breath away. Be sure to go up the down staircase designed by Leonardo da Vinci.

Château de la Bourdaisière, Loire Valley. Not one but *two* princes de Broglie welcome you to this idyllic and elegant neo-Renaissance hotel.

Château d'Ussé, Loire Valley. Step into a fairy tale at Sleeping Beauty's legendary home.

Vaux-le-Vicomte, Side Trips from Paris. Louis XIV was so jealous when he saw this 17th-century Xanadu that he promptly imprisoned its owner and commissioned Versailles.

Beautiful Villages

Nearly everyone has a mind's-eye view of the perfect French village. Oozing half-timber houses and rose bowers, these once-upon-a-time villages have a sense of tranquillity not even tour buses can ruin. The Loire Valley's prettiest village, Saché, is so small it seems your own personal property—an eyebrow of cottages, a Romanesque church, a 17th-century *auberge* (inn), and a modest château. Little wonder Honoré de Balzac came here to write some of his greatest novels. Auvers-sur-Oise, the pretty riverside village in the Ile-de-France, inspired some of Van Gogh's finest landscapes. In the Dordogne region, hamlets have a Disney-like quality, right down to Rapunzel windows, flocks of geese, and storks'-nest towers. Along the Côte d'Azur you'll find the sky-kissing, hilltop *villages perchés,* like Èze. All in all, France has an *embarras de richesses* of nestled-away treasures—so just throw away the map. After all, no penciled itinerary is half as fun as stumbling upon some half-hidden Brigadoon.

Haut-de-Cagnes, French Riviera. This perfect example of the eagle's-nest village near the coast is nearly boutique-free, was once adored by Renoir, and remains ancient in atmosphere.

La Roque-Gageac, Dordogne. Lorded over by its immense rock cliff, this centuries-old riverside village is the perfect backdrop for a beautiful *pique-nique.*

Riquewihr, Alsace. Full of storybook buildings, cul-de-sac courtyards, and stone gargoyles, this is the showpiece of the Alsatian Wine Route.

Monet, Manet, and Matisse

It is through the eyes of its artists that many first get to know France. No wonder people from across the globe come to search for Gauguin's bobbing boats at Pont-Aven, Monet's bridge at Giverny, and the gaslit Moulin Rouge of Toulouse-Lautrec—not hung in a museum but alive in all their three-dimensional glory. In Arles you can stand on the spot where Van Gogh painted and compare his perspective to a placard with his finished work; in Paris you can climb into the garret-atelier where Delacroix created his epic canvases, or wander the redolent streets of Montmartre, once haunted by Renoir, Utrillo, and Modigliani. A short visit to any major museum can transport the viewer—by way of the paintings of Pisarro, Millet, Poussin, Cézanne, Van Gogh, Sisley, and Matisse—to its legendary landscapes. But what could be better than entering the real landscapes that inspired these famed artists?

Aix-en-Provence, Route de Cézanne. Follow in Cézanne's footsteps through elegant, arts-loving Aix then up to the artist's favorite muse, the incomparable Mont Ste-Victoire.

Céret, Languedoc-Roussillon. Pack your crayons for a trip to Matisse Country, for this is where the artist fell in love with the *fauve* (savage) hues found only in Mother Nature.

Giverny, Side Trips from Paris. Replacing paint and water with earth and water, Monet transformed his 8-acre garden into a veritable live-in Impressionist painting.

St-Paul-de-Vence, Côte d'Azur. Pose under the Picassos at the famed Colombe d'Or inn, once favored by Signac, Modigliani, and Bonnard.

Le Shopping

Although it's somewhat disconcerting to see Gap stores gracing major street corners in Paris and other urban areas in France, if you take the time to peruse smaller specialty shops, you can find rare original gifts—be it an antique brooch from the 1890s or a modern vase crafted from Parisian rooftop-tile zinc. It's true that the traditional gifts of silk scarves, perfume, and wine can often be purchased for less in the shopping mall back home, but you can make an interesting twist by purchasing a vintage Hermès scarf, or a unique perfume from an artisan perfumer. Bargaining is traditional in outdoor and flea markets, antiques stores, small jewelry shops, and craft galleries, for example. If you're thinking of buying several items, or if you're simply in love with something a little bit too expensive, you've nothing to lose by cheerfully suggesting to the proprietor, "Vous me faites un prix?" ("How about a discount?") The small businessperson will immediately size you up, and you'll have some good-natured fun.

Colette, Paris. Wiggle into something sleek and chic at this fashionista shrine.

Grain de Vanille, Cancale. These sublime tastes of Brittany—salted butter caramels and rare honeys—make great gifts, *non*?

L'Isle-sur-la-Sorgue, Provence. This canal-laced antiques town becomes a Marrakech of marketeers on weekends, when dazzling *brocante* (collectibles) dealers set up shop.

Gothic Churches and Cathedrals

Their extraordinary permanence, their everlasting relevance even in a secular world, and their transcendent beauty make the Gothic churches and cathedrals of France a lightning rod if you are in search of the essence of French culture. The product of a peculiarly Gallic mix of mysticism, exquisite taste, and high technology, France's 13th- and 14th-century "heavenly mansions" provide a thorough grounding in the history of architecture (some say there was nothing new in the art of building between France's Gothic arch and Frank Lloyd Wright's cantilevered slab). Each cathedral imparts its own monumental experience—knee-weakening grandeur, a mighty resonance that touches a chord of awe, and humility in the unbeliever. Even cynics will find satisfaction in these edifices' social history—the anonymity of the architects, the solidarity of the artisans, and the astonishing bravery of experiments in suspended stone.

Chartres, Ile-de-France. Get enlightened with France's most exquisite stained-glass windows and famous labyrinth.

Mont-St-Michel, Normandy. From its silhouette against the horizon to the abbey and gardens at the peak of the rock, you'll never forget this awe-inspiring sight.

Notre-Dame, Paris. Make a face back at the gargoyles high atop Quasimodo's home.

Reims, Champagne. Tally up the 34 VIPs crowned at this magnificent edifice, the age-old setting for the coronations of French kings.

L'Esprit Sportif

Though the physically inclined would consider walking across Scotland or bicycling across Holland, they often misconstrue France as a sedentary country where one plods from museum to château to restaurant. But it's possible to take a more active approach: imagine pedaling past barges on the Saône River or along slender poplars on a *route départementale* (provincial road); hiking over Alpine meadows near Megéve; or sailing the historic ports of Honfleur or Antibes. Experiencing this side of France will take you off the beaten path and into the countryside. As you bike along French country roads or along the extensive network of *Grandes Randonnées* (Lengthy Trails) crisscrossing the country, you will have time to tune into the landscape—to study crumbling garden walls, smell the honeysuckle, and chat with a farmer in his *potager* (vegetable garden).

Sentier des Cascades, Haute-Pyrénées. Near Cauterets is the GR10 walk, which features stunning views of the famous waterfalls and abundant *marmottes* (Pyrenean groundhogs).

Tracking the Camargue Reserve, Provence. Take an unforgettable *promenade équestre* (horseback tour) of this amazing nature park, home to bulls and birds—50,000 flamingos, that is.

The VBT Loire Biking Tour. Stunning châteaux-hotels, Pissarro-worthy riverside trails, and 20 new best friends make this a *fantastique* way to go "around the whirl."

Clos Encounters

Bordeaux or Burgundy, Sauternes or Sancerre, Romanée-Conti or Côte du Rhône—wherever you turn in France, you'll find famous Gallic wine regions and vineyards, born of the country's curvaceous landscape. Speckled unevenly with hills, canals, forests, vineyards, châteaux, and the occasional cow clinging to 30-degree inclines, the great wine regions of France attract hordes of travelers more interested in shoving their noses deep into wineglasses than staring high into the stratosphere of French cathedral naves. Fact is, you can buy the bottles of the fabled regions—the Côte d'Or, the Rhône Valley, or that oenophile's nirvana, Bordeaux—anywhere, so why not taste the lesser-known local crus from, say, the lovely vineyards in the Loire Valley. Explore the various *clos* (enclosures) and *côtes* (hillsides) that grow golden by October, study the *vendangeur* (grape pickers), then drive along the wine routes looking for those "Dégustation" signs, promising free sips from the local vintner. Pretty soon you'll be an expert on judging any wine's aroma, body, and backwash.

The Alsace Route de Vin. Between Mulhouse and Strasbourg, many picture-book villages entice with top vintners.

Clos de Vougeot, Burgundy. A historic winemaking barn, 13th-century grape presses, and its verdant vineyard make this a must-do.

Lafite-Rothschild, Route de Médoc. Baron Philippe perfected one of the great five premiers crus here—and there's an excellent visitor center.

HISTORY YOU CAN SEE

France has long been the standard-bearer of Western civilization—without her, neither English liberalism nor the American Constitution would exist today. It has given us Notre-Dame, Loire châteaux, Versailles, Stendhal, Chardin, Monet, Renoir, and the most beautiful city in the world, Paris. So it is no surprise that France unfolds like a gigantic historical pop-up book. To help you understand the country's masterful mélange of old and new, here's a quick overview of La Belle France's stirring historical pageant.

Ancient France

France's own "Stonehenge"—the megalithic stone complexes at Carnac in Brittany (circa 3500 BC)—were created by the Celts, who inhabited most of northwest Europe during the last millennia BC. In the 1st century BC, Julius Caesar conquered Gaul, and the classical civilizations of the Mediterranean soon made artistic inroads. The Greek trading colonies at Marseille eventually gave way to the Roman Empire, with the result that ancient Roman aesthetics left a lasting impression: it is no accident that the most famous modern example of a Roman triumphal arch—the **Arc de Triomphe**—should have been built in Paris.

What to See: France possesses examples of ancient Roman architecture that even Italy cannot match: Provence, whose name comes from the Latin, had been one of the most popular places to holiday for the ancient Romans. The result is that you can find the best-preserved **Roman arena in Nîmes** (along with the **Maison Carrée**), the best preserved **Roman theater at Orange**, and the best preserved Roman bridge aqueduct, the **Pont du Gard**.

The Middle Ages: From Romanesque to Gothic

By the 7th century AD, Christianity was well established throughout France. Its interaction with an inherited classical tradition produced the first great indigenous French culture, the Frankish or Merovingian, created by the Franks (who gave their name to the new nation), Germanic tribes who expelled the Romans from French soil. Various French provinces began to unite as part of Charlemagne's new Holy Roman Empire and, as a central core of European Catholicism, France now gave rise to great monastic centers—**Tours, Auxerre, Reims, and Chartres**—that were also cultural powerhouses. After the Crusades, more settled conditions led to the flowering of the Romanesque style developed by reformist monastic orders like the Benedictines at Cluny. This then gave way to the Gothic, which led to the construction of many cathedrals—perhaps the greatest architectural achievement created in France—during the biggest building spree of the Middle Ages. Under the Capetian kings, French government became more centralized. The most notable king was Louis IX (1226–70), known as Saint Louis, who left important monuments in the Gothic style, which lasted some 400 years and gained currency throughout Europe.

What to See: The Romanesque style sprang out of the forms of classical art left by the Romans; its top artistic landmarks adorn Burgundy: the giant transept of **Cluny,** the sculptures of Gislebertus at **Autun's Cathèdrale St-Lazare,** and the amazing tympanum of the **Basilique Ste-Madeleine at Vézelay.** Another top Romanesque artwork is in Normandy: the **Bayeux Tapestry** on view in Bayeux. The desire to span greater area with stone and to admit

more light led to the development of the new Gothic style. This became famed for its use of the pointed arch and the rib vault, resulting in an essentially skeletal structure containing large areas of glass. First fully developed at **Notre-Dame,** Paris (from 1163), **Chartres** (from 1200), **Reims** (from 1211), and **Amiens** (from 1220), the Gothic cathedral contains distinctive Gothic forms: delicate filigree-like rose windows of stained glass, tall lancet windows, elaborately sculpted portails, and flying buttresses. King Louis IV commissioned **Paris's Sainte-Chapell** chapel in the 1240s and it remains the most beautiful artistic creation of the Middle Ages.

The Renaissance

France nationalism came to the fore once the tensions and wars fomented by the Houses of Anjou and Capet climaxed in the Hundred Years' War (1328–1453). During this time, Joan of Arc helped drive English rulers from France with the Valois line of kings taking the throne. From the late 15th century into the 16th, the golden light of the Italian Renaissance dawned over France. This was due, in large measure, to King François I (accession 1515), who returned from wars in Italy with many Italian artists and craftsmen, among them Leonardo da Vinci (who lived in Amboise from 1507). With decades of peace, fortresses soon became châteaux and the picture palaces of the Loire Valley came into being. The grandest of these, Fontainebleau and Chambord, reflected the growing centralization of the French court and were greatly influenced by the new Italian styles.

What to See: An earnest desire to rival and outdo Italy in cultural pursuits dominated French culture during the 15th and 16th centuries. For the decoration of the new **Palace of Fontainebleau** (from 1528) artists like **Cellini, Primaticcio,** and **Rosso** used rich colors, elongated forms, and a concentration on allegory and eroticism to help cement the Mannerist style. Gothic and vernacular forms of architecture were now rejected in favor of classical models, as could be seen in the châteaux in the Loire Valley such as **Blois** (from 1498), **Chambord** (from 1519, where design elements were created by **Leonardo**), and **Chenonceau,** which was commissioned by the king's mother, Catherine de' Medici. The rebuilding of Paris's **Louvre,** begun in 1546, marked the final assimilation of Italian classical architecture into France.

Royal Absolutism and the Baroque Style

Rising out of the conflicts between Catholics and Protestants (thousands of Huguenots were murdered in the St. Bartholomew's Day massacre of 1572), King Henry IV became the first Bourbon king and fomented religious tolerance with the Edict of Nantes (1598). By the 17th century architecture still had an Italianate flavor, as seen in the Roman Baroque forms adorning Parisian churches. The new Baroque architectural taste for large-scale town planning gave rise to the many squares that formed focal points within cities. King Louis XIV, the Sun King, came to the throne in 1643, but he chose to rule from a new power base he built outside Paris: Versailles soon became a symbol of the absolutist court of the Sun King and the new insatiable national taste for glory. But with Louis XIV, XV, and XVI going for broke, a reaction against extravagance and for logic and empirical reason took over. Before long, writers like Jean-Jacques Rousseau argued for social and political reform—the need for revolution.

What to See: To create a more carefully ordered aristocratic bureaucracy, courtiers were commanded to leave their family châteaux and take up residence in the massive new **Versailles** palace. A golden age for art began. The palaces of the **Louvre** (1545–1878) and **Versailles** (1661–1756) bear witness to this in their sheer scale. "After me, the deluge," Louis XIV said, and early-18th-century France was on the verge of bankruptcy. In turn, the court turned away from the over-the-top splendor of Versailles and Paris's **Luxembourg Palace** to retreat to smaller, more domestic houses in Paris, seen in such hôtel particuliers as the **Musée Nissim de Camondo** and the charming **Hameau** farm created for Marie-Antoinette in Versailles's park. Bombastic Baroque gave way to the rococo style, as the charming, feminine paintings of **Watteau, Boucher,** and **Fragonard** provided cultural diversions for an aristocracy withdrawn from the stage of power politics. Find their masterpieces at the Louvre, **Carnavalet,** and other museums.

Revolution and Romanticism

The end of Bourbon rule came with the execution of **Louis XVI and Marie-Antoinette.** The French Revolution ushered in the First Republic (1792–1804). After a backlash to the Terror (1793–94), in which hundreds were guillotined, **Napoléon** rose to power from the ashes of the Revolutionary **Directoire.** With him a new intellectual force and aesthetic mode came to the fore—**Romanticism.** This new style focused on inner emotions and the self, leading to the withdrawal of the artists from politics, growing industrialization, and urbanization into a more subjective world. Napoléon's First Empire (1804–14) conquered most of Europe, but after the disastrous Russian invasion the Bourbon dynasty was restored with the rule of Charles X and Louis-Philippe. The latter, known as the Citizen King, abdicated in 1848 and made way for the Second Republic and the return of Napoleonic forces with Napoléon III's Second Empire (1852–70).

What to See: As often happens, art is one step ahead of history. The design of Paris's **Panthéon** by Soufflot, Gabriel's refined **Petit Trianon** at Versailles (1762), and the paintings of **Greuze** (1725–1805) and **David** (1745–1825), on view at the Louvre, display a conceit for moral order in great contrast to the flippancies of Fragonard. A renewed taste for classicism was

58–51 BC	Caesar's conquest of Gaul
800 AD	Charlemagne made Holy Roman Emperor
1066	William of Normandy invades England with victory at the Battle of Hastings
12th–13th century	Cathedrals of Notre-Dame and Chartres
1431	Joan of Arc burned; from lowest point, French nation revived
1572 St.	Bartholomew Massacre of Protestants
1580–87	Montaigne's *Essays*
1678	Louis XIV adds the Hall of Mirrors to Versailles
18th	Zenith of French enlightenment century and influence, thanks to Molière, Racine, Voltaire, Diderot, and Rousseau
1789–92	The French Revolution
1793	Queen Marie-Antoinette is guillotined on Paris's place de la Concorde

seen in the Empire style promulgated by Napoléon; see the emperor's Paris come alive at the Left Bank's charming **Cour du Commerce St-André** and his shrine, **Les Invalides.** But the rigidly formal neoclassical style soon gave way to Romanticism, whose touchstones are immediacy of technique, emotionalism, and the ability to convey the uncertainties of the human condition. Go to Paris's **Musée Delacroix** to get an up-close look at this expressive, emotive master of Romanticism.

The Modern Age Begins

Napoléon III's Second Empire lead to the vast aggrandizement of France on the world stage, with colonies set up across the globe, a booming economy, and the capital city of Paris remade into Europe's showplace thanks to **Baron Haussmann.** After the Prussians invaded, France was defeated and culture was shattered and reformed. Romanticism became **Realism,** often carrying strong social overtones, as seen in the works of **Courbet.** The closer reexamination of reality by the **Barbizon School** of landscape painters led to **Impressionism,** whose masters approached their subjects with a fresh eye, using clear, bright colors to create atmospheric effects and naturalistic observation. By 1870 French rule was reinstated with the **Third Republic,** which lasted until 1940.

What to See: Thanks to Haussmann, Paris became the City of Light, with new large boulevards opening up the dark urban city, an outlook culminating in the **Eiffel Tower,** built for the Paris Exposition of 1889. Taking modern life as their subject matter, great Impressionist masters like **Monet** (1840–1926), **Renoir** (1841–1919), and **Degas** (1834–1917) proceeded to break down visual perceptions in terms of light and color, culminating in the late series of *Water Lilies*paintings (from 1916) done at **Monet's Giverny estate.** Along with masterpieces by **Degas, Gauguin, Van Gogh,** and **Cézanne,** the most famous Impressionist and Postimpressionist paintings can be seen at Paris's famed **Musée d'Orsay.** These artists began the myth of the Parisian bohemian artist, the disaffected idealist kicking at the shins of tradition, and they forged the path then boldly trod by the greatest artist of the 20th century, **Picasso,** whose works can be seen at Paris's **Musée Picasso** and **Centre Beaubourg.**

1799–1804	Napoléon rules as First Consul of the Consulate
1805–12	Napoléon conquers large parts of Europe but is defeated in Russia
1815	Napoléon loses battle at Waterloo to England's Duke of Wellington
1848–70	The Second Empire, ruled by Emperor Napoléon III, with colonial expansion into Indochina, Syria, and Mexico
1863	Impressionists show at the Salon des Refusés in Paris
1870	Franco-Prussian War; France defeated, but Flaubert's and Baudelaire's writings soar
1871	Alsace-Lorraine ceded to Germany
1940	France surrenders to Germany during World War II: Paris falls
1958	General de Gaulle elected president
1969	Student riots in Paris; government is subsequently stabilized through presidents including Georges Pompidou, François Mitterand, and Nicolas Sarkozy

GREAT ITINERARIES

THE GOOD LIFE

Beginning in château country, head south and west, through Cognac country into wine country around Bordeaux. Then lose yourself in the Dordogne, a landscape of rolling hills peppered with medieval villages, fortresses, and prehistoric caves.

Loire Valley Châteaux

3 or 4 days. Base yourself at the crossroads of Blois, starting with its multi-era château. Then head for the huge château in Chambord. Amboise's château echoes with history, and the neighboring manor, Clos Lucé, was Leonardo da Vinci's final home—or instead of this "town" château, head west to the tiny village of Rigny-Ussé for the Sleeping Beauty castle of Ussé. Heading southeast, finish up at Chenonceau—the most magical one of all—then return to the transportation hub city of Tours.

Bordeaux Wine Country

2 days. Pay homage to the great names of Médoc, north of the city of Bordeaux, though the hallowed villages of Margaux, St-Julien, Pauillac, and St-Estèphe aren't much to look at. East of Bordeaux, via the prettier Pomerol vineyards, the village of St-Émilion is everything you'd want a wine town to be, with ramparts and medieval streets.

Dordogne and Périgord

2 or 3 days. Follow the famous Dordogne River east to the half-timber market town of Bergerac. Wind through the green, wooded countryside into the region where humans' earliest ancestors left their mark, in the caves in Les Eyzies-de-Tayac and the famous Grotte de Lascaux. Be sure to sample the region's culinary specialties: truffles, foie gras, and preserved duck. Then travel south to the stunning and sky-high pilgrimage village of Rocamadour.

By Public Transportation

It's easy to get to Blois and Chenonceaux by rail, but you'll need to take a bus to visit other Loire châteaux. Forays farther into Bordeaux country and the Dordogne are difficult by train, involving complex and frequent changes (Limoges is a big railway hub). Further exploration requires a rental car or sometimes-unreliable bus routes.

FRANCE FROM NORTH TO SOUTH

Zoom from Paris to the heart of historic Burgundy, its rolling green hills traced with hedgerows and etched with vineyards. From here, plunge into the arid beauty of Provence and toward the spectacular coastline of the Côte d'Azur.

Burgundy Wine Country

2 to 3 days. Base yourself in the market town of Beaune and visit its famous hospices and surrounding vineyards. Make a day trip to the ancient hill town of Vézelay, with its incomparable basilica, stopping in Autun to explore Roman ruins and its celebrated Romanesque cathedral. For more vineyards, follow the Côte d'Or from Beaune to Dijon. Or make a beeline to Dijon, with its charming Vieille Ville and fine museums. From here it's a two-hour drive to Lyon, where you can feast on this city's famous earthy cuisine. Another three hours' push takes you deep into the heart of Provence.

Arles and Provence

2 to 3 days. Arles is the atmospheric, sun-drenched southern town that inspired Van Gogh and Gauguin. Make a day trip into grand old Avignon, home to the

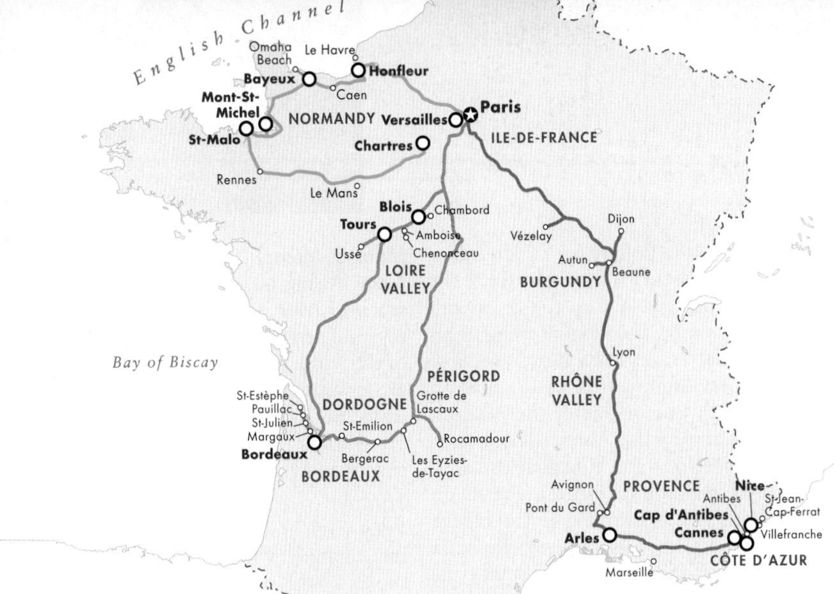

14th-century rebel popes, to view their imposing palace. And make a pilgrimage to the Pont du Gard, the famous triple-tiered Roman aqueduct west of Avignon. From here, two hours' drive will bring you to the glittering Côte d'Azur.

Antibes and the French Riviera

2 to 3 days. This historic and atmospheric port town is well positioned for day trips. First, head west to glamorous Cannes. The next day head east into Nice, with its exotic Vieille Ville and its bounty of modern art. There are ports to explore in Villefranche and St-Jean-Cap-Ferrat, east of Nice. Allow time for a walk out onto the tropical paradise peninsula of Cap d'Antibes, or for an hour or two lolling on the coast's famous pebble beaches.

By Public Transportation

The high-speed TGV travels from Paris through Burgundy and Lyon, then zips through the south to Marseille. Train connections to Beaune from the TGV are easy; getting to Autun from Beaune takes up to two hours, with a change at Chagny. Vézelay can be reached by bus excursion from Dijon or Beaune. Rail connections are easy between Arles and Avignon; you'll need a bus to get to the Pont du Gard from Avignon. Antibes, Cannes, and Nice are easily reached by the scenic rail line, as are most of the resorts and ports along the coast. To squeeze the most daytime out of your trip, take a night train or a plane from Nice back to Paris.

FRANCE AVEC FAMILLE

Make your way through Normandy and Brittany, with enough wonders and evocative topics to inspire any child to put down the iPhone games and gawk.

Paris

2 days. Paris's major museums, like the Louvre, can be as engaging as they are educational—as long as you keep your visits short. Start out your Paris stay by giving your kids an idea of how the city was planned by climbing to the top of the Arc de Triomphe. From here work your way down the Champs-Élysées toward place de la Concorde. Stop for a puppet show at the Marionettes des Champs-Élysées (Wednesday, Saturday, or Sunday), at avenues Matignon and Gabriel, halfway down the Champs. Continue walking down the Champs to the Jardin des Tuileries, where kids can sail boats on a small pond. Then taxi or

hike over to the Louvre for an afternoon visit. Your reward? A famously thick hot chocolate at Angélina on rue de Rivoli, across the street. The next morning, head to the Eiffel Tower for a bird's-eye view of the city. After you descend, ride on the Bateaux Bus or one of the Bateaux Mouches at place de l'Alma, nearby. Then take the métro to the hunchback's hangout, Notre-Dame Cathedral. Finish up your Paris visit by walking several blocks over, through the center of the Ile de la Cité, to Paris's most storybook sight—the Saint-Chapelle, a fairy-tale, stained-glass chapel that looks like a stage set for Walt Disney's *Sleeping Beauty.*

Versailles

1 day. Here's an opportunity for a history lesson: with its amazing Baroque extravagance, no other monument so succinctly illustrates what inspired the rage of the French Revolution. Louis XIV's eye-popping château of Versailles pleases the secret monarch in most of us.

Honfleur

1 day. From this picture-book seaport lined with skinny half-timber row houses and salt-dampened cobblestones, the first French explorers set sail for Canada in the 15th century.

Bayeux

2 days. William the Conqueror's extraordinary invasion of England in 1066 was launched from the shores of Normandy. The famous Bayeux tapestry, showcased in a state-of-the-art museum, spins the tale of the Battle of Hastings. From this home base you can introduce the family to the modern saga of 1944's Allied landings with a visit to the Museum of the Battle of Normandy, then make a pilgrimage to Omaha Beach.

Mont-St-Michel

1 day. Rising majestically in a shroud of sea mist over vacillating tidal flats, this mystical peninsula is Gothic in every sense of the word. Though its tiny, steep streets are crammed with visitors and tourist traps, no sight gives a stronger sense of the worldly power of medieval monasticism than Mont-St-Michel.

St-Malo

1 day. Even in winter you'll want to brave the Channel winds to beachcomb the shores of this onetime pirate base. (Yes, kids, *pirates!*) In summer, of course, it's mobbed with sun seekers who stroll the old streets, restored to quaintness after World War II.

Chartres

1 day. Making a beeline on the autoroute back to Paris, stop in Chartres to view the loveliest of all of France's cathedrals.

By Public Transportation

Coordinating a sightseeing tour like this with a limited local train schedule isn't easy, and connections to Mont-St-Michel are especially complicated. Versailles, Chartres, and St-Malo are easy to reach, and Bayeux and Honfleur are doable, if inconvenient. But you'll spend a lot of vacation time waiting along train tracks.

PARIS

WELCOME TO PARIS

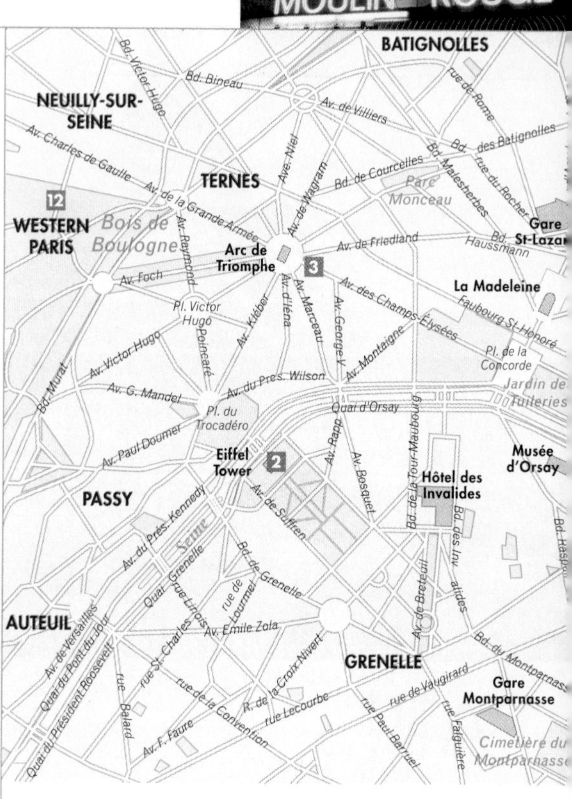

TOP REASONS TO GO

★ **Museum masterpieces:** There will always be something new to see at the Louvre—after all, the *Mona Lisa* is just one of 800,000 treasures.

★ **Feasting at Le Grand Véfour:** Back when Napoléon dined here, this was the most beautiful restaurant in Paris. It remains among the best.

★ **Quasimodo's Notre-Dame:** Get to know the stone gargoyles high atop this playground of Victor Hugo's hunchback, then savor the splendor inside this great Gothic cathedral.

★ **Café society:** Whether you prefer a posh perch at Les Deux Magots or just the corner café, be sure to Hemingway an afternoon away over two café crèmes.

★ **Spend time on the Seine:** Take a leisurely stroll along the Rive Droite and the Rive Gauche, making sure to carve out time to visit the oldest part of Paris—Ile de la Cité and Ile St-Louis.

1 The Islands. This is where you can find Notre-Dame and Sainte-Chapelle.

2 Around the Eiffel Tower. With the Champs de Mars, Invalides, and the Seine nearby, many lovely strolls give you striking views.

3 Champs-Élysées. The Champs-Élysées and Arc de Triomphe attract the tourists, but there are also several excellent museums here.

4 Around the Louvre. The Faubourg St-Honoré, with its well-established shops and cafés, has always been chic, and probably always will be.

5 Les Grands Boulevards. Use the Opéra Garnier as your landmark and set out to do some power shopping.

6 Montmartre. It feels distinctly separate from the rest of Paris—but Montmartre is prime tourist territory,

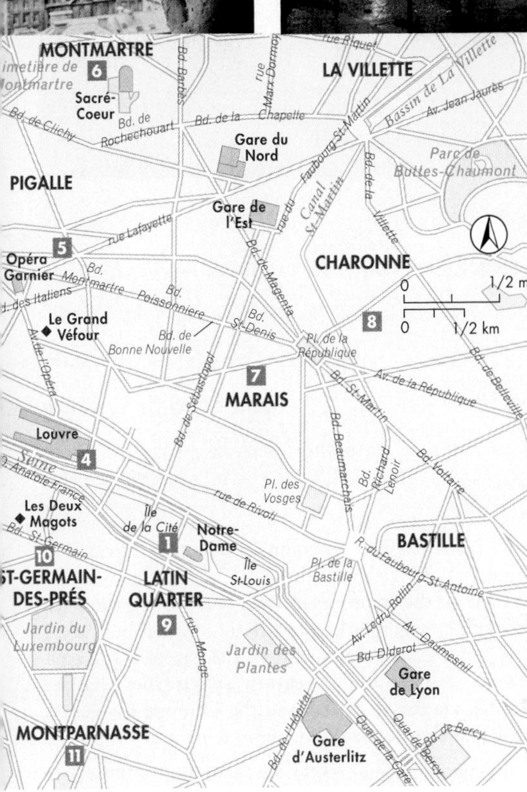

with Sacré-Coeur as its main attraction.

7 Marais. While away the afternoon at the Place des Vosges or shop to your heart's content.

8 Eastern Paris. If it's new and happening in Paris, you'll find it out here.

9 The Latin Quarter. Leave yourself time to wander the Latin Quarter, known for its vibrant student life.

10 St-Germain-des-Prés. The Musée d'Orsay is here, but make sure to also wander the Jardin du Luxembourg.

11 Montparnasse. This neighborhood is known for its contemporary-art scene.

12 Western Paris. The Bois de Boulogne, a popular park, is one great reason to trek here.

GETTING ORIENTED

Paris is divided into 20 *arrondissements* (neighborhoods) spiraling out from the center of the city. The number reveals the neighborhood's location, and its age: the 1st arrondissement at the city's heart is the oldest. The arrondissements in central Paris—the 1st to 8th—are the most visited. If you want to figure out what arrondissement something is in, check the zip code. The first three digits are always 750 for Paris, and the last two identify the arrondissement.

It's worth picking up a copy of *Paris Pratique,* the essential map guide, available at bookstores, newsstands, and souvenir shops.

Updated By Jennifer Ladonne, Linda Hervieux, Nancy Heslin, Virginia Power, and Jack Vermee

If there's a problem with a trip to Paris, it's the embarrassment of riches that faces you. No matter which aspect of Paris you choose—touristy, historic, fashion-conscious, pretentious-bourgeois, thrifty, or the legendary bohemian arty Paris of undying attraction—one thing is certain: you will carve out your own Paris, one that is vivid, exciting, ultimately unforgettable.

As world capitals go, Paris is surprisingly compact. The city is divided in two by the River Seine, with two islands (Ile de la Cité and Ile St-Louis) in the middle. Each bank of the Seine has its own personality; the Rive Droite (Right Bank), with its spacious boulevards and formal buildings, generally has a more genteel, dignified feel than the carefree and chic Rive Gauche (Left Bank), to the south. The east–west axis from Châtelet to the Arc de Triomphe, via rue de Rivoli and the Champs-Élysées, is the Right Bank's principal thoroughfare for sightseeing and shopping.

If this is your first trip, you may want to take a guided tour of the city—a good introduction that will help you get your bearings and provide you with a general impression before you return to explore the sights that particularly interest you. *To help track those down, this chapter's exploration of Paris is divided into eight neighborhood walks.* Each *quartier,* or neighborhood, has its own personality, which is best discovered by foot power. Ultimately, your route will be marked by your preferences, your curiosity, and your energy level. You can wander for hours without getting bored—though not, perhaps, without getting lost. By the time you have seen only a few neighborhoods, drinking in the rich variety they have to offer, you should not only be culturally replete but downright exhausted—and hungry, too. Again, take your cue from Parisians and think out your next move in a sidewalk café.

PLANNING

WHEN TO GO

The City of Light is magical all year round, but it's particularly gorgeous in June, when the long days (the sun doesn't set until 10 pm) stretch sightseeing hours and make it ideal to linger in the cafés practicing the city's favorite pastime—people-watching. Winter can be dark and chilly, but it's also the best time to find cheap airfares and hotel deals. April in Paris, despite what the song says, is often rainy. Keep in mind that, like some other European cities, Paris somewhat shuts down in August—some restaurants are closed for the entire month, for example—though there are still plenty of fun things to do, namely, free open-air movies and concerts, and the popular Paris *plage,* the "beach" on the right bank of the Seine.

SAVING TIME AND MONEY

Paris is one of the world's most visited cities—with crowds to prove it—so it pays to be prepared. Buy tickets online when you can: most cultural centers and museums offer advance-ticket sales, and the small service fee you'll pay is worth the time saved waiting in line. Also, national museums are free the first Sunday of each month. There are many within Paris, including the Louvre, Musée d'Orsay, and Centre Pompidou.

A Paris Museum Pass (🌐 *www.parismuseumpass.com*) can save you money if you're planning serious sightseeing, but it might be even more valuable because it allows you to bypass the lines. It's sold at the destinations it covers and at airports, major métro stations, and the tourism office in the Carrousel du Louvre. The two-, four-, or six-day passes are €39, €54, or €69, respectively.

GETTING HERE AND AROUND

Addresses in Paris are fairly straightforward: there's the number, the street name, and the zip code designating one of Paris's 20 *arrondissements* (districts); for instance, in Paris 75010, the last two digits ("10") indicate that the address is in the 10e. The large 16e arrondissement has two numbers assigned to it: 75016 and 75116.

The arrondissements are laid out in a spiral, beginning from the area around the Louvre (1er arrondissement), then moving clockwise through the Marais, the Latin Quarter, St-Germain, and then out from the city center to the outskirts to Ménilmontant/Père-Lachaise (20e arrondissement). Occasionally you may see an address with a number plus bis—for instance, 20 bis, rue Vavin. This indicates the next entrance or door down from 20 rue Vavin.

AIR TRAVEL

The major airports are Charles de Gaulle (CDG, also known as Roissy), 26 km (16 miles) northeast of Paris, and Orly (ORY), 16 km (10 miles) south of Paris. Both are easily accessible from the city. Whether you take a car or bus to travel from Paris to the airport on your departure, always allot an extra hour because of the often horrendous traffic tie-ups in the airports themselves (especially in peak seasons and at peak times). Free light-rail connections (Orlyval and CDGval) available between the major terminals are one option for avoiding some of the traffic mess, but still give yourself enough time to navigate through these busy airports.

BUS TRAVEL

With dedicated bus lanes now in place throughout the city—allowing buses and taxis to whiz past other traffic mired in tedious jams—taking the bus is an appealing option. Although nothing can beat the métro for speed, buses offer great city views, and the newer ones are equipped with air-conditioning—a real perk on those sweltering August days.

Paris buses are green and white; the route number and destination are marked in front, major stopping places along the sides. Glass-covered bus shelters contain timetables and route maps; note that buses must be hailed at these larger bus shelters, as they service multiple lines and routes. Smaller stops are designated simply by a pole bearing bus numbers.

When buying tickets, your best bet is a *carnet* of 10 tickets, available for €13.30 at any métro station, or a single ticket, which can be bought onboard for €1.70 (exact change appreciated).

CAR TRAVEL

Driving is not recommended within Paris. Parisian drivers are aggressive behind the wheel and it's often very difficult to park. Should you be driving into the city from elsewhere in Ile-de-France, the major ring road encircling the city is called the *périférique,* with the *périférique intérieur* going counterclockwise around the city, and the *périférique extérieur,* or the outside ring, going clockwise. Five lanes wide, the périférique is a highway from which *portes* (gates) connect Paris to the major highways of France. The highway names function on the same principle as the métro, with the final destination used as the route "name."

MÉTRO TRAVEL

Taking the métro is the most efficient way to get around Paris. Métro stations are recognizable either by a large yellow M within a circle or by the distinctive curly green Art Nouveau railings and archway bearing the full title (Métropolitain).

It's essential to know the name of the last station on the line you take, as this name appears on all signs. A connection (you can make as many as you like on one ticket) is called a *correspondance*. At junction stations, illuminated orange signs bearing the name of the line terminus appear over the correct corridors for each correspondance. Illuminated blue signs marked *sortie* indicate the station exit. Note that tickets are valid only inside the gates, or *limites*.

Access to métro platforms is through an automatic ticket barrier. Slide your ticket in and pick it up as it pops out. Keep your ticket during your journey; you'll need it in case you run into any green-clad ticket inspectors, who will impose a hefty fine if you can't produce your ticket (they even accept credit cards!). Métro service starts at 5:30 am and continues until 12:40 am Sunday through Thursday, and until 2:15 am on Friday, Saturday, and nights before holidays.

TAXI TRAVEL

On weekend nights after 11 pm, and during the morning rush, it's nearly impossible to find a taxi—you're best off asking hotel or restaurant staff to call you one. If you want to hail a cab on your own, look for the taxis with their signs lighted up—their signs will be glowing green (white for older taxis) as opposed to the taxis that are already taken whose signs will glow red (dull orange for older taxis). Taxi stands are marked by a square dark blue sign with a white T in the middle.

Taxi rates are based on location and time. Monday to Saturday, daytime rates (10 am–5 pm) within Paris are €1.04 per km (½ mile); nighttime rates (5 pm–10 am) are €1.27 per km. On Sunday, you'll pay €1.54 per km from midnight to 7 am and €1.27 from 7 am to midnight within Paris. Rates to suburban zones and airports are a flat €1.54 per km. There's a basic hire charge of €2.60 for all rides, and a €1 supplement per piece of luggage (stroller, skis, etc.).

RESTAURANTS

Restaurants follow French mealtimes, serving lunch from noon to 2:30 pm and dinner from 7:30 or 8 pm. Some cafés serve food all day long. Always reserve a table for dinner, as top restaurants book up months in advance. When it comes to the check, you must ask for it (it's considered rude to bring it unbidden). In cafés you'll get a register receipt with your order. *Servis* (gratuity) is always included in the bill, but it's good form to leave something extra if you're satisfied with the service.

Brasseries often have nonstop service; some are open 24 hours. Assume a restaurant is open every day, unless otherwise indicated. Surprisingly, many prestigious restaurants close on weekends and sometimes Monday. July and August are the most common months for annual closings, although Paris in August is no longer the wasteland it once was.

HOTELS

Unless stated in the review, hotels have elevators, and all guest rooms have TV, telephone, and a private bathroom. Recently, more and more hotels have standard air-conditioning, something that makes a summer stay much more bearable. Tubs don't always have shower curtains or showerheads. (How the French manage to scrub up without flooding the bathroom remains a cultural mystery.) If you book a budget hotel, be sure to confirm whether the bathroom is shared or not. *Hotel reviews have been shortened. For full information, visit Fodors.com.*

WHAT IT COSTS IN EUROS

	$	$$	$$$	$$$$
Restaurants	under €18	€18–€24	€25–€32	over €32
Hotels	under €120	€120–€174	€175–€250	over €250

Restaurant prices are the average cost of a main course at dinner or, if dinner is not served, at lunch. Hotel prices are the lowest cost of a standard double room in high season.

VISITOR INFORMATION

Paris is without question best explored on foot and, thanks to Baron Haussmann's mid-19th-century redesign, the City of Light is a compact wonder of wide boulevards, gracious parks, and leafy squares. Happily and conveniently, there are a half-dozen branches of the Paris tourist office located at key points in the capital.

Office du Tourisme de la Ville de Paris Pyramides. ✉ *25 rue des Pyramides, Pyramides* 🌐 *www.parisinfo.com* Ⓜ *Pyramides.*

WHAT TO WEAR

When it comes to clothing, the standard French look is dressier than the American equivalent. Athletic clothes are reserved for sports. Sneakers are not usually worn by adults but if you pack yours, keep them for daytime only. Neat jeans are acceptable everywhere except at higher-end restaurants; check to see whether there's a dress code.

EXPLORING PARIS

THE ISLANDS

At the heart of Paris, linked to the banks of the Seine by a series of bridges, are two small islands: Ile St-Louis and Ile de la Cité. They're the perfect places to begin your visit, with postcard-worthy views all around. The Ile de la Cité is anchored by mighty Notre-Dame; farther east, the atmospheric Ile St-Louis is dotted with charming hotels, cozy restaurants, and small specialty shops.

TOP ATTRACTIONS

Fodor's Choice ★ **Ancien Cloître Quartier.** Hidden in the shadows of Notre-Dame is an evocative, often-overlooked tangle of medieval streets. Through the years lucky folks, including Ludwig Bemelmans (who created the beloved *Madeleine* books) and the Aga Khan have called this area home, but back in the Middle Ages it was the domain of cathedral seminary students. One of them was the celebrated Peter Abélard (1079–1142)—philosopher, questioner of the faith, and renowned declaimer of love poems. Abélard boarded with Notre-Dame's clergyman, Fulbert, whose 17-year-old niece, Héloïse, was seduced by the compelling Abélard, 39 years her senior. She became pregnant and the vengeful clergyman had Abélard castrated; amazingly, he survived and fled to a monastery, while Héloïse took refuge in a nunnery. The poetic, passionate letters between the two cemented their fame as thwarted lovers, and their story inspired a devoted following during the romantic 19th century. They still draw admirers to the Père Lachaise Cemetery, where they're interred *ensemble*. The clergyman's house at 10 rue Chanoinesse was redone in 1849; a plaque at the back of the building at 9-11 quai aux Fleurs commemorates the lovers. ✉ *Rue du Cloître-Notre-Dame north to Quai des Fleurs, Ile de la Cité* Ⓜ *Cité.*

Fodor's Choice ★ **Notre-Dame.** ✉ *Pl. du Parvis* ☎ *01–42–34–56–10* 🌐 *www.notredamedeparis.fr* 🎫 *Cathedral free, towers €8.50, crypt €6, treasury €4* ⏲ *Cathedral weekdays 8–6:45, weekends 8–7:15. Towers Apr.–June and*

Sept., daily 10–6:30; July and Aug., Sun.–Thurs. 10–6:30, Fri. and Sat. 10 am–11 pm; Oct.–Mar., daily 10–5:30. Treasury weekdays 9:30–6, Sat. 9:30–6:30, Sun. 1:30–6:30. Crypt Tues.–Sun. 10–6 ⇨ *See highlighted listing in this chapter for more information.*

Fodor's Choice ★ **Sainte-Chapelle.** Built by the obsessively pious Louis IX (1214–70), this Gothic jewel is home to the oldest stained-glass windows in Paris. The chapel was constructed over three years, at phenomenal expense, to house the king's collection of relics acquired from the impoverished emperor of Constantinople. These included Christ's Crown of Thorns, fragments of the Cross, and drops of Christ's blood—though even in Louis's time these were considered of questionable authenticity. Some of the relics have survived and can be seen in the treasury of Notre-Dame, but most were lost during the Revolution.

The narrow spiral staircase by the entrance takes you to the upper chapel where the famed beauty of Sainte-Chapelle comes alive: 6,458 square feet of stained glass is delicately supported by painted stonework that seems to disappear in the colorful light streaming through the windows. Deep reds and blues dominate the background, noticeably different from later, lighter medieval styles such as those of Notre-Dame's rose windows.

The chapel is essentially an enormous magic lantern illuminating 1,130 biblical figures. Its 15 windows—each 50 feet high—were dismantled and cleaned with laser technology during a 40-year restoration, completed in 2014 to coincide with the 800th anniversary of St. Louis's birth. Besides the dazzling glass, observe the detailed carvings on the columns and the statues of the apostles. The lower chapel is gloomy and plain, but take note of the low, vaulted ceiling decorated with fleurs-de-lis and cleverly arranged *L*s for Louis.

■ TIP→ **Sunset is the optimal time to see the rose window; however, to avoid waiting in killer lines, plan your visit for a weekday morning, the earlier the better.** Come on a sunny day to appreciate the full effect of the light filtering through all that glorious stained glass.

You can buy a joint ticket with the Conciergerie: lines are shorter if you purchase it there or online, though you'll still have to go through a longish metal-detector line to get into Sainte-Chapelle itself.

The chapel makes a divine setting for classical concerts; check the schedule at *www.infoconcert.com.* ✉ *4 bd. du Palais, Ile de la Cité* ☎ *01–53–40–60–97* 🌐 *www.sainte-chapelle.monuments-nationaux.fr* 🎫 *€8.50; joint ticket with Conciergerie €12.50* ⏲ *Mar.–mid-May and mid-Sept.–Oct., daily 9:30–6; mid-May–mid-Sept., Thurs.–Tues. 9:30–6, Wed. 9:30 am–9:30 pm; Nov.–Feb., daily 9–5* ☞ *Ticket window closes 30 mins before closing* Ⓜ *Cité.*

WORTH NOTING

FAMILY **Conciergerie.** Most of the Ile de la Cité's medieval structures fell victim to wunderkind urban planner Baron Haussmann's ambitious rebuilding program of the 1860s. Among the rare survivors are the jewel-like Sainte-Chapelle, a vision of shimmering stained glass, and the Conciergerie, the cavernous former prison where Marie-Antoinette and other victims of the French Revolution spent their final days.

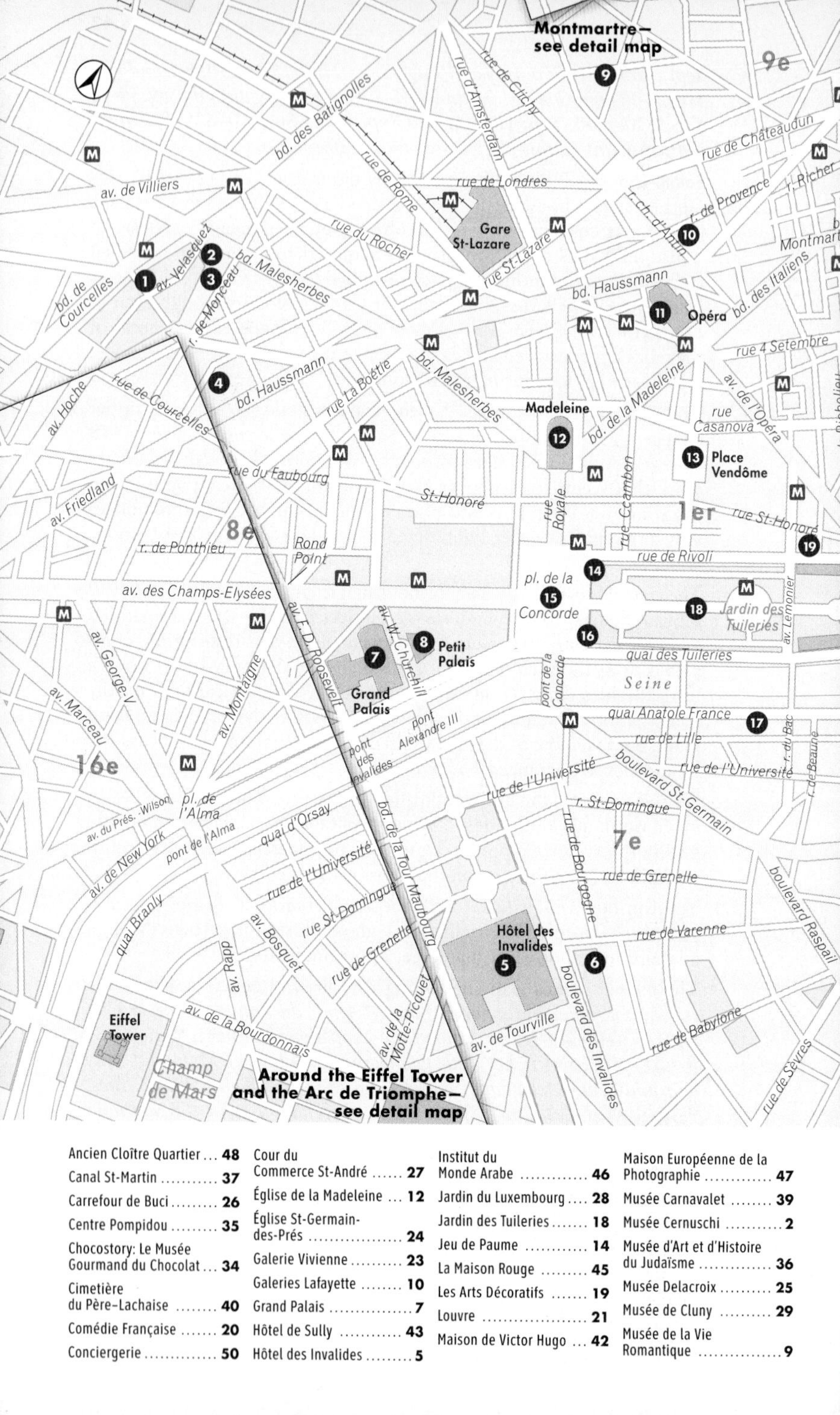

Montmartre—
see detail map
9e
bd. des Batignolles
rue d'Amsterdam
rue de Clichy
rue de Rome
rue de Londres
rue de Châteaudun
av. de Villiers
Gare
St-Lazare
rue du Rocher
rue St-Lazare
r. ch. d'Antin
r. de Provence
r. Richer
Montmartre
bd. des Italiens
bd. Haussmann
Opéra
rue 4 Septembre
bd. de
Courcelles
av. Velasquez
r. de Monceau
bd. Malesherbes
bd. Haussmann
rue La Boétie
bd. Malesherbes
Madeleine
bd. de la Madeleine
av. de l'Opéra
rue
Casanova
rue de Richelieu
av. Hoche
rue de Courcelles
rue du Faubourg
St-Honoré
Place
Vendôme
rue Royale
rue Cambon
1er
rue St-Honoré
av. Friedland
8e
r. de Ponthieu
Rond
Point
rue de Rivoli
pl. de la
Concorde
av. des Champs-Elysées
Jardin des
Tuileries
av. Lemonier
av. George-V
av. F. D. Roosevelt
av. W. Churchill
Petit
Palais
quai des Tuileries
Grand
Palais
Seine
pont de la Concorde
av. Marceau
av. Montaigne
pont
Alexandre III
quai Anatole France
rue de Lille
r. du Bac
r. de Beaune
16e
pont
des
Invalides
boulevard St-Germain
rue de l'Université
av. du Prés. Wilson
pl. de
l'Alma
r. St-Dominique
rue de Bourgogne
av. de New York
pont de l'Alma
quai d'Orsay
bd. de la Tour Maubourg
7e
rue de l'Université
rue de Grenelle
quai Branly
rue St-Dominique
boulevard Raspail
av. Bosquet
rue de Grenelle
Hôtel des
Invalides
rue de Varenne
av. Rapp
boulevard des Invalides
av. de la Bourdonnais
av. de la Motte-Picquet
av. de Tourville
rue de Babylone
Eiffel
Tower
Champ
de Mars
rue de Sèvres
Around the Eiffel Tower
and the Arc de Triomphe—
see detail map

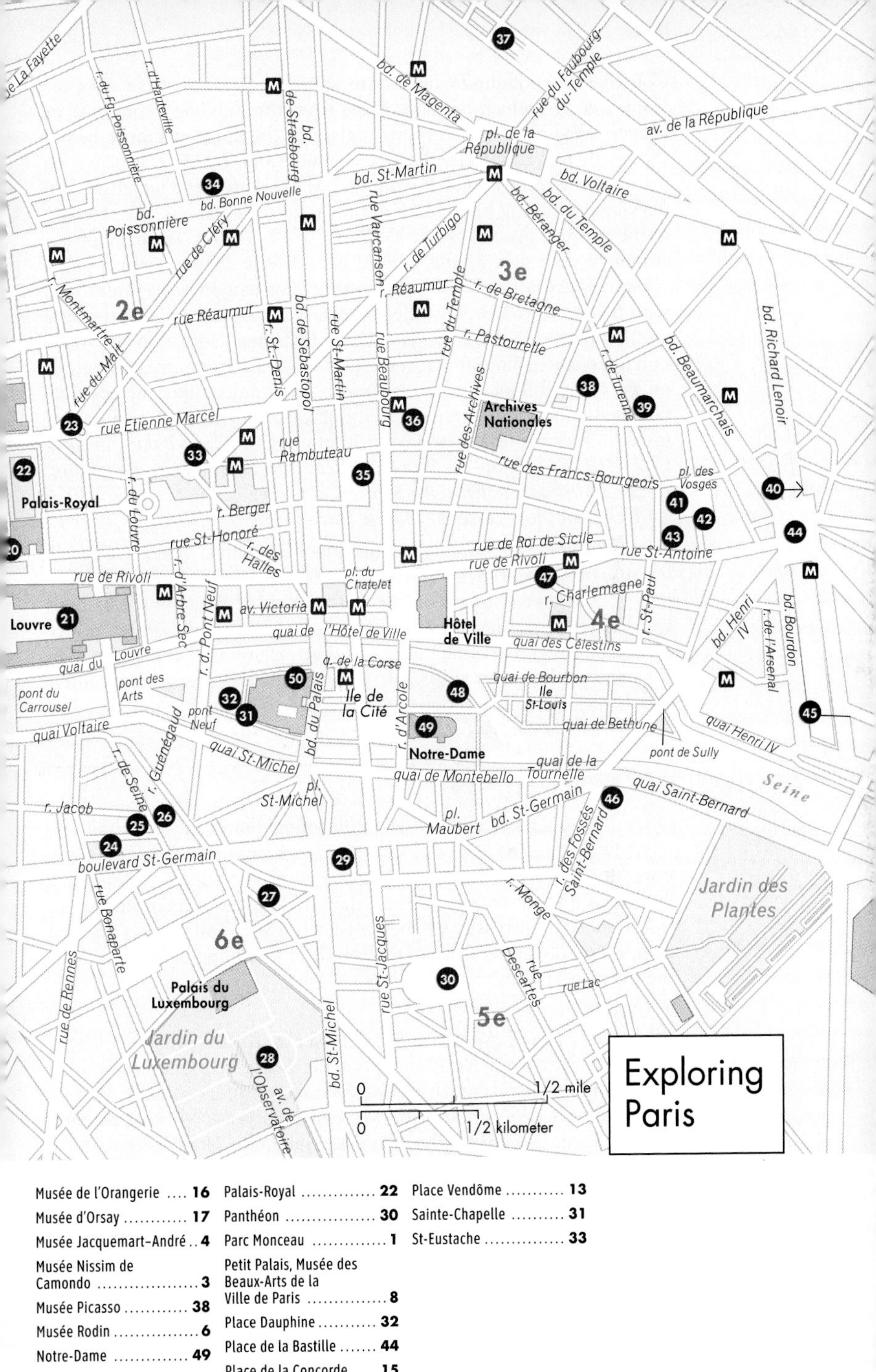

Musée de l'Orangerie **16**
Musée d'Orsay **17**
Musée Jacquemart-André .. **4**
Musée Nissim de Camondo **3**
Musée Picasso **38**
Musée Rodin **6**
Notre-Dame **49**
Opéra Garnier **11**
Palais-Royal **22**
Panthéon **30**
Parc Monceau **1**
Petit Palais, Musée des Beaux-Arts de la Ville de Paris **8**
Place Dauphine **32**
Place de la Bastille **44**
Place de la Concorde **15**
Place des Vosges **41**
Place Vendôme **13**
Sainte-Chapelle **31**
St-Eustache **33**

Constructed by Philip IV in the late 13th and early 14th centuries, the Conciergerie—which takes its name from the building's concierge or keeper—was part of the original palace of the kings of France before the royals moved into the Louvre around 1364. In 1391, it became a prison. During the French Revolution, Marie-Antoinette languished 76 days here awaiting her date with the guillotine. There is a re-creation of the doomed queen's sad little cell—plus others that are far smaller—complete with wax figures behind bars. In the chapel, stained glass, commissioned after the queen's death by her daughter, is emblazoned with the initials M. A. Outside you can see the small courtyard where women prisoners took meals and washed their clothes in the fountain (men enjoyed no similar respite). Well-done temporary exhibitions on the ground floor aim to please kids and adults alike; themes have included enchanted forests and Gothic castles. There are free guided tours (in French only) most days at 11 and 3. ✉ *2 bd. du Palais, Ile de la Cité* ☎ *01–53–40–60–80* 🌐 *www.conciergerie.monuments-nationaux.fr* 🎫 *€8.50; joint ticket with Sainte-Chapelle €12.50* ⏲ *Daily 9:30–6* ☞ *Ticket window closes at 5:30* Ⓜ *Cité.*

Place Dauphine. The Surrealists called Place Dauphine "le sexe de Paris" because of its suggestive V shape; however, its origins were much more proper. The pretty square on the western side of Pont Neuf was built by Henry IV, who named it as a homage to his son the crown prince (or dauphin) who became Louis XIII when Henry was assassinated. In warmer weather, treat yourself to a romantic meal on a restaurant terrace here—the square is one of the best places in Paris to dine *en plein air.* ✉ *Ile de la Cité* Ⓜ *Cité.*

AROUND THE EIFFEL TOWER

One of Paris's most upscale neighborhoods, the posh 7e arrondissement (where nearly every block affords a view of La Tour Eiffel) is home to the French bourgeoisie and well-heeled expats. Commanding the southwestern end of Paris, the Eiffel Tower was considered an iron-latticed monstrosity when it opened in 1889. Today it is a beloved icon, especially at night when thousands of twinkling lights sparkle at the top of every hour.

TOP ATTRACTIONS

FAMILY Fodor's Choice ★ **Eiffel Tower** (*Tour Eiffel*). The Eiffel Tower is to Paris what the Statue of Liberty is to New York and what Big Ben is to London: the ultimate civic emblem. French engineer Gustave Eiffel—already famous for building viaducts and bridges—spent two years working to erect this iconic monument for the World Exhibition of 1889.

Because its colossal bulk exudes such a feeling of permanence, you may have trouble believing that the tower nearly became 7,000 tons of scrap (it contains 12,000 pieces of metal and 2.5 million rivets) when the concession expired in 1909. Only its potential use as a radio antenna saved the day; and it still bristles with a forest of radio and television transmitters. Given La Tour's landmark status, it is equally hard to believe that so many Parisians—including arbiters of taste like Guy de

Continued on page 51

NOTRE-DAME

Notre-Dame is the symbolic heart of Paris and, for many, of France itself. Napoléon was crowned here, and kings and queens exchanged marriage vows before its altar. There are a few things worth seeing inside the Gothic cathedral, but the real highlights are the exterior architectural details and the unforgettable view of Paris, framed by stone gargoyles, from the top of the south tower.

THE STONE GARGOYLES

Notre-Dame's gargoyles were designed by Eugène Viollet-le-Duc, the architect who oversaw the cathedral's 19th-century renovations. Technically they're chimeras, not gargoyles, as they're purely ornamental; a true "gargoyle" is a carved sculpture that functions as a waterspout.

OUTSIDE NOTRE-DAME

Begun in 1163, completed in 1345, badly damaged during the Revolution, and restored by the architect Eugène Viollet-le-Duc in the 19th century, Notre-Dame may not be France's oldest or largest cathedral, but in beauty and architectural harmony it has few peers. The front entranceways seem like hands joined in prayer, the sculpted kings on the facade form a noble procession, and the west (front) rose window gleams with what seems like divine light.

The most dramatic approach to Notre-Dame is from the Rive Gauche, crossing at the Pont au Double from quai de Montebello, at the St-Michel métro or RER stop. This bridge will take you to the open square, place du Parvis, in front of the cathedral. (The more direct metro stop is Cité.)

THE WEST (FRONT) FACADE

The three front entrances are, left to right: the Portal of the Virgin, the Portal of the Last Judgment (above), and the Portal of St. Anne, the oldest of the three. Above the three front entrances are the 28 restored statues of the kings of Israel, the Galerie des Rois.

INSIDE THE CATHEDRAL

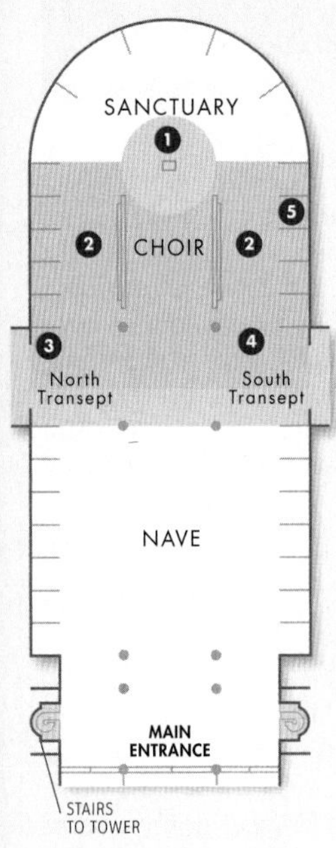

❶ **The Pietà,** behind the choir, represents the Virgin Mary mourning over the dead body of Christ.

❷ **The biblical scenes** on the north and south screens of the choir represent the life of Christ and the apparitions of Christ after the Resurrection.

❸ **The north rose window** is one of the cathedral's original stained-glass panels; at the center is an image of Mary holding a young Jesus.

❹ At the south (right) entrance to the choir, you'll glimpse the haunting 12th-century statue of **Notre-Dame de Paris,** "Our Lady of Paris," the Virgin, for whom the cathedral is named.

❺ **The treasury**, on the south side of the choir, holds a small collection of religious garments, reliquaries, and silver- and gold-plate.

MAKING THE CLIMB A separate entrance, to the left of the front facade if you're facing it, leads to the 387 stone steps of the south tower. These steps take you to the bell of Notre-Dame (as tolled by the fictional Quasimodo). Looking out from the tower, you can see how Paris—like the trunk of a tree developing new rings—has grown outward from the Ile de la Cité. To the north is Montmartre; to the west is the Arc de Triomphe, at the top of the Champs-Elysées; and to the south are the towers of St-Sulpice.

Place du Parvis

Notre-Dame was one of the first Gothic cathedrals in Europe and one of the first buildings to make use of **flying buttresses**—exterior supports that spread out the weight of the building and roof. At first people thought they looked like scaffolding that the builders forgot to remove. ■ TIP→ **The most tranquil place to appreciate the architecture of Notre-Dame is from the lovely garden behind the cathedral, Square Jean-XXIII. By night, take a boat ride on the Seine for the best view—the lights at night are magnificent.**

Place du Parvis is *kilomètre zéro,* the spot from which all distances to and from the city are officially measured. A polished brass circle set in the ground, about 20 yards from the cathedral's main entrance, marks the exact spot.

The Crypt Archéologique (entrance down the stairs in front of the cathedral) offers a fascinating subterranean view of this busy area from the 1st century when Paris was a Roman city called Lutetia, with ruins of houses, baths and even a quay, through medieval times when the former rue Neuve-Notre-Dame that passed through here was packed with houses and shops. A 2012 renovation cleaned the remains and added 3-D video touch screen panels that bring the ruins to life.

SOMETHING TO PONDER

Do Notre-Dame's hunchback and its gargoyles have anything in common other than bad posture? Quasimodo was created by Victor Hugo in the novel *Notre-Dame de Paris,* published in 1831. The incredible popularity of the book made Parisians finally take notice of the cathedral's state of disrepair and spurred Viollet-le-Duc's renovations. These included the addition of the gargoyles, among other things, and resulted in the structure we see today.

Detail of the Gallery of Kings, over the front entrance.

■ TIP→ **The best time to visit Notre-Dame is early in the morning, when the cathedral is at its brightest and least crowded.**

■ TIP→ **There are free guided tours in English several times a week; check website for times.**

Maupassant and Alexandre Dumas—initially derided the 1,063-foot structure. (De Maupassant reputedly had lunch in the tower's restaurant every day because it was the only place in Paris from which the tower wasn't visible.)

Gradually, though, the Tour Eiffel became part of the city's topography, entering the hearts and souls of residents and visitors alike. Today it is most breathtaking at night, when every girder is highlighted in a sparkling display originally conceived to celebrate the turn of the millennium. The glittering light show was so popular that the 20,000 lights were reinstalled for permanent use in 2003. The tower does its electric dance for five minutes every hour on the hour until 1 am.

More recent enhancements are also noteworthy. A two-year, €30 million renovation of the first floor, completed in 2014, has added a vertigo-inducing "transparent" floor 187 feet above the esplanade, plus a pair of glass-facade pavilions that hug the side of the tower and house interactive educational areas. A new mini-turbine plant, four vertical-turbine windmills, and eco-friendly solar panels will minimize the tower's carbon footprint over time, too.

You can stride up 1,700 steps as far as the third floor, but if you want to go to the top you'll have to take the elevator. (Be sure to look closely at the fantastic ironwork.) Although the view of the flat sweep of Paris at 1,000 feet may not beat the one from the Tour Montparnasse skyscraper, the setting makes it considerably more romantic—especially if you come in the late evening, after the crowds have dispersed. Beat the crushing lines by reserving your ticket online. You can also book a guided tour. ✉ *Quai Branly, Trocadéro/Tour Eiffel* ☎ *08–92–70–12–39 €0.34 per min* 🌐 *www.tour-eiffel.fr* 🎫 *By elevator: 1st and 2nd levels €9; top €15.50. By stairs: 1st and 2nd levels only, €5* ⏲ *Mid-June–early Sept., daily 9 am–12:45 am (11 pm for summit); early Sept.–mid-June, daily 9:30 am–11:45 pm (10:30 pm for summit)* ☞ *Stairs close at 6 pm in off-season* Ⓜ *Bir-Hakeim, Trocadéro, École Militaire; RER: Champ de Mars.*

Fodor's Choice ★ **Hôtel des Invalides.** The Baroque complex known as Les Invalides (pronounced *lehz-ahn-vah-leed*) is the eternal home of Napoléon Bonaparte (1769–1821) or, more precisely, the little dictator's remains, which lie entombed under the towering golden dome.

Louis XIV ordered the facility built in 1670 to house disabled soldiers (hence the name), and at one time 4,000 military men lived here. Today, a portion of it still serves as a veterans' residence and hospital. The Musée de l'Armée, containing an exhaustive collection of military artifacts from antique armor to weapons, is also here.

If you see only a single sight, make it the Église du Dome (one of Les Invalides' two churches) at the back of the complex. Napoléon's tomb was moved here in 1840 from the island of Saint Helena, where he died in forced exile. The emperor's body is protected by a series of no fewer than six coffins—one set inside the next, sort of like a Russian nesting doll—which is then encased in a sarcophagus of red quartzite. The bombastic tribute is ringed by statues symbolizing Napoléon's campaigns of conquest. To see more Napoléoniana, check out the collection in the Musée de l'Armée featuring his trademark gray frock coat and huge bicorne hat. Look for the figurines reenacting the famous coronation scene when Napoléon crowns his empress, Josephine. You can see a grander version of this scene hanging in the Louvre by the painter David.

The Esplanade des Invalides, the great lawns in front of the building, are favorite spots for pickup soccer, Frisbee games, sunbathing, and dog walking—despite signs asking you to stay off the grass. **■ TIP→ The best entrance to use is at the southern end, on Place Vauban (Avenue de Tourville). The ticket office is here, as is Napoléon's Tomb. There are automatic ticket machines at the main entrance on the Place des Invalides.** ✉ *Pl. des Invalides, Tour Eiffel* ☎ *01–44–42–38–77* 🌐 *www.musee-armee.fr* 🎫 *€9.50* 🕓 *Église du Dôme and museums Apr.–Oct., daily 10–6; Nov.–Mar., daily 10–5; closed 1st Mon. of every month Oct.–June* ☞ *Ticket window closes 30 mins before museum* Ⓜ *La Tour–Maubourg/Invalides.*

FAMILY Fodor's Choice ★ **Musée Rodin.** Auguste Rodin (1840–1917) briefly made his home and studio in the Hôtel Biron, a grand 18th-century mansion that now houses a museum dedicated to his work. He died rich and famous, but many of the sculptures that earned him a place in art history were originally greeted with contempt by the general public, which was unprepared for his powerful brand of sexuality and raw physicality. During a much-needed, multiyear renovation that has closed parts of the Hôtel Biron (it's set to finish in the second half of 2015), the museum is showcasing a pared-down, "greatest hits" selection of Rodin's works.

Most of his best-known sculptures are in the gardens. The front garden is dominated by *The Gates of Hell* (circa 1880). Inspired by the monumental bronze doors of Italian Renaissance churches, Rodin set out to illustrate stories from Dante's *Divine Comedy.* He worked on the sculpture for more than 30 years, and it served as a "sketch pad" for many of his later works. Look carefully and you can see miniature versions of *The Kiss* (bottom right), *The Thinker* (top center), and *The Three Shades* (top center).

Inside the museum, look for *The Bronze Age,* which was inspired by the sculptures of Michelangelo: this piece was so realistic that critics accused Rodin of having cast a real body in plaster. There's also a room (condensed during the renovation) of works by Camille Claudel (1864–1943), Rodin's student and longtime mistress, who was a remarkable sculptor in her own right. Her torturous relationship with Rodin eventually drove her out of his studio—and out of her mind. In 1913 she was packed off to an asylum, where she remained until her death.

If you want to linger, the Café du Musée Rodin serves meals and snacks in the shade of the garden's linden trees. As you enter, a gallery on the right houses temporary exhibitions. An English audioguide (€6) is available for the permanent collection and for temporary exhibitions. Buy your ticket online for priority access (€1.80 extra fee). ✉ *79 rue de Varenne, Trocadéro/Tour Eiffel* ☎ *01–44–18–61–10* 🌐 *www.musee-rodin.fr* 🎫 *€9; €2 gardens only; free 1st Sun. of month* 🕓 *Tues. and Thurs.–Sun. 10–5:45, Wed. 10–8:45* Ⓜ *Varenne.*

DID YOU KNOW?

The Eiffel Tower did not begin life as the beloved icon it is today. Gustave Eiffel's iron creation for the 1889 World's Fair was greeted with disgust by Parisians, who dubbed it the Giant Asparagus.

WORTH NOTING

FAMILY **Musée du Quai Branly.** This eye-catching museum overlooking the Seine was built by star architect Jean Nouvel to house the state-owned collection of "non-Western" art, culled from the Musée National des Arts d'Afrique et d'Océanie and the Musée de l'Homme. Exhibits mix artifacts from antiquity to the modern age, such as funeral masks from Melanesia, Siberian shaman drums, Indonesian textiles, and African statuary. A corkscrew ramp leads from the lobby to a cavernous exhibition space, which is color coded to designate sections from Asia, Africa, and Oceania. The lighting is dim—sometimes too dim to read the information panels (which makes investing in the €5 audioguide a good idea).

Renowned for his bold modern designs, Nouvel has said he wanted the museum to follow no rules; however, many critics gave his vision a thumbs-down when it was unveiled in 2006. The exterior resembles a massive, rust-color rectangle suspended on stilts, with geometric shapes cantilevered to the facade facing the Seine and louvered panels on the opposite side. The colors (dark reds, oranges, and yellows) are meant to evoke the tribal art within. A "living wall" comprised of some 150 species of exotic plants grows on the exterior, which is surrounded by a wild jungle garden with swampy patches—an impressive sight after dark when scores of cylindrical colored lights are illuminated. The trendy Les Ombres restaurant on the museum's fifth floor (separate entrance) has prime views of the Tour Eiffel—and prices to match. The budget-conscious can enjoy the garden at Le Café Branly on the ground floor. ✉ *37 quai Branly, Trocadéro/Tour Eiffel* ☎ *01–56–61–70–00* 🌐 *www.quaibranly.fr* 🎫 *€9; €11 with temporary exhibits* ⏲ *Tues., Wed., and Sun. 11–7; Thurs.–Sat. 11–9* ☞ *Ticket office closes 1 hr before museum* Ⓜ *Alma-Marceau.*

CHAMPS-ÉLYSÉES

Make no mistake: the Champs-Élysées, while ceding some of its elegance in recent times, remains the most famous avenue in Paris—and, perhaps, the world. Like New York's Times Square or London's Piccadilly Circus, it is a mecca for travelers and locals alike. Some Parisians complain that fast-food joints and chain stores have cheapened the Avenue des Champs-Élysées, but others are more philosophical, noting that there is something here for everyone. If you can't afford lunch at Ladurée, there's always McDonald's (and the view from its second floor is terrific).

TOP ATTRACTIONS

Fodor's Choice ★ **Arc de Triomphe.** Inspired by Rome's Arch of Titus, this colossal, 164-foot triumphal arch was ordered by Napoléon—who liked to consider himself the heir to Roman emperors—to celebrate his military successes. Unfortunately, Napoléon's strategic and architectural visions were not entirely on the same plane, and the Arc de Triomphe proved something of an embarrassment. Although the emperor wanted the monument completed in time for an 1810 parade in honor of his new bride, Marie-Louise, it was still only a few feet high, and a dummy arch of painted canvas was strung up to save face. Empires come and go, but Napoléon's had been gone for more than 20 years before the Arc was finally finished in 1836. A small museum halfway up recounts its history.

The Arc de Triomphe is notable for magnificent sculptures by François Rude, including *The Departure of the Volunteers in 1792*, better known as *La Marseillaise*, to the right of the arch when viewed from the Champs-Élysées. Names of Napoléon's generals are inscribed on the stone facades—the underlined names identify the hallowed figures who fell in battle.

The traffic circle around the Arc is named for Charles de Gaulle, but it's known to Parisians as "L'Étoile," or the Star—a reference to the streets that fan out from it. Climb the stairs to the top of the arch and you can see the star effect of the 12 radiating avenues and the vista down the Champs-Élysées toward Place de la Concorde and the distant Musée du Louvre.

■ TIP→ France's Unknown Soldier is buried beneath the arch, and a commemorative flame is rekindled every evening at 6:30. That's the most atmospheric time to visit, but, to beat the crowds, come early in the morning or buy your ticket online (€1.60 service fee). ✉ *Pl. Charles-de-Gaulle, Champs-Élysées* ☎ *01–55–37–73–77* 🌐 *arc-de-triomphe.monuments-nationaux.fr* 🎫 *€9.50* ⏲ *Apr.–Sept., daily 10 am–11 pm; Oct.–Mar., daily 10 am–10:30 pm* ☞ *Last admission 45 mins before closing* Ⓜ *Métro or RER: Étoile.*

FAMILY **Avenue des Champs-Élysées.** Marcel Proust lovingly described the genteel elegance of the storied Champs-Élysées (pronounced chahnz- *eleezay*, with an "n" sound instead of "m" and no "p") during its Belle Époque heyday, when its cobblestones resounded with the clatter of horses and carriages. Today, despite unrelenting traffic and the intrusion of chain stores and fast-food franchises, the avenue still sparkles. There's always something happening here: stores are open late (and many are open on Sunday, a rarity in Paris); nightclubs remain top destinations; and cafés offer prime people-watching, though you'll pay for the privilege—after all, this is Europe's most expensive piece of real estate. Along the 2-km (1¼-mile) stretch, you can find marquee names in French luxury, like Cartier, Guerlain, and Louis Vuitton. Car manufacturers lure international visitors with space-age showrooms. Old stalwarts, meanwhile, are still going strong—including the Lido cabaret and Fouquet's, whose celebrity clientele extends back to James Joyce. The avenue is also the setting for the last leg of the Tour de France bicycle race (the third or fourth Sunday in July), as well as Bastille Day (July 14) and Armistice Day (November 11) ceremonies. The Champs-Élysées, which translates to "Elysian Fields" (the resting place of the blessed in Greek mythology), began life as a cow pasture and in 1666 was transformed into a park by the royal landscape architect André Le Nôtre. Traces of its green origins are visible towards the Concorde, where elegant 19th-century park pavilions house the historic restaurants Ledoyen, Laurent, and the more recent Lenôtre. ✉ *Champs-Élysée* Ⓜ *Champs-Élysées–Clemenceau, Franklin-D.-Roosevelt, George V, Étoile.*

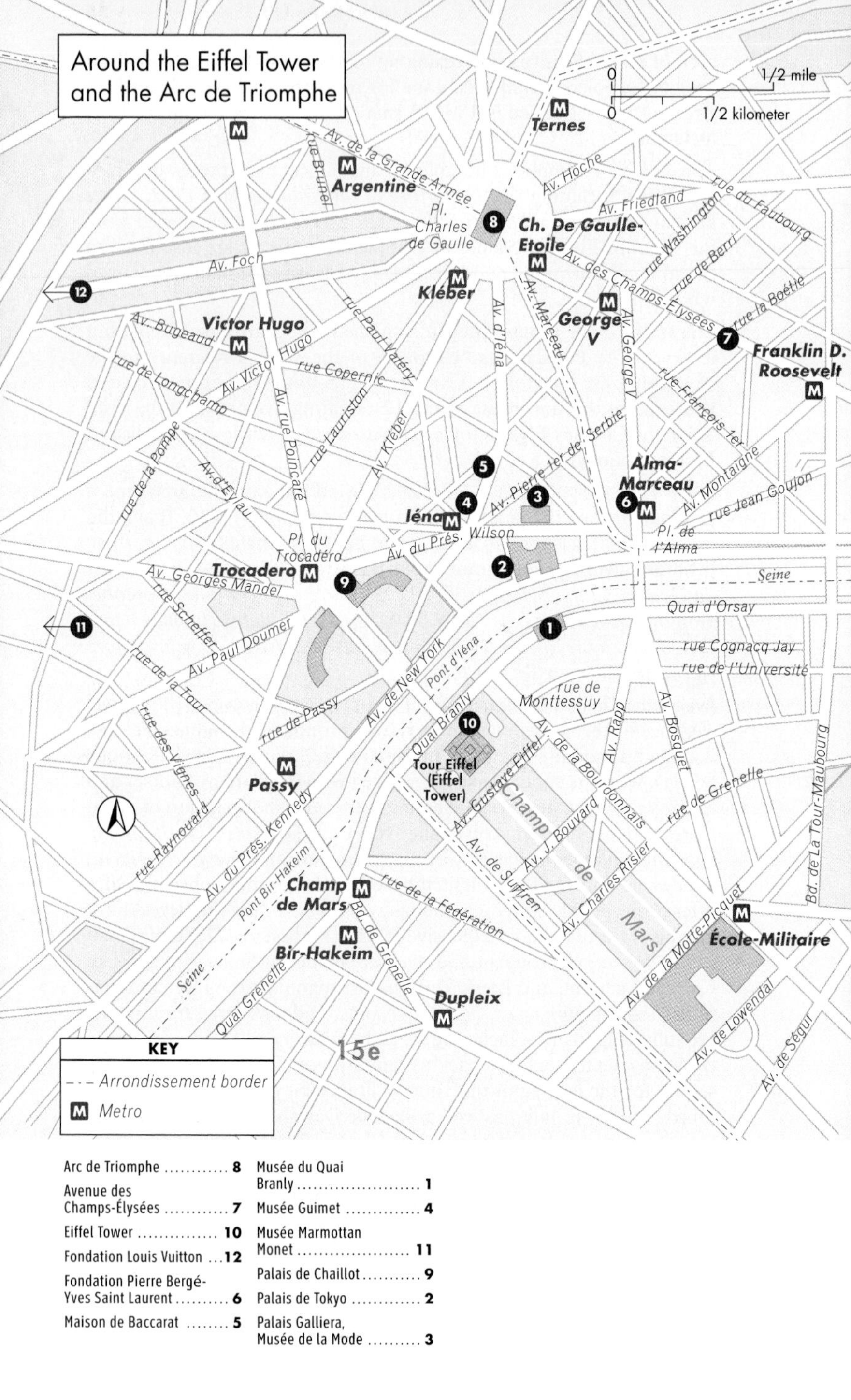

Arc de Triomphe 8
Avenue des Champs-Élysées 7
Eiffel Tower 10
Fondation Louis Vuitton ...12
Fondation Pierre Bergé-Yves Saint Laurent 6
Maison de Baccarat 5
Musée du Quai Branly 1
Musée Guimet 4
Musée Marmottan Monet 11
Palais de Chaillot 9
Palais de Tokyo 2
Palais Galliera, Musée de la Mode 3

Grand Palais. With its curved-glass roof and gorgeously restored Belle Époque ornamentation, you can't miss the Grand Palais whether you're approaching from the Seine or the Champs-Élysées. It forms an elegant duo with the Petit Palais across Avenue Winston Churchill: both stone buildings, adorned with mosaics and sculpted friezes, were built for the 1900 World's Fair, and, like the Eiffel Tower, were not intended to be permanent. The exquisite main exhibition space called le Nef (or nave) plays host to large-scale shows that might focus on anything from jewelry to cars. The art-oriented shows staged here—including the annual FIAC, Paris's contemporary-art fair—are some of the hottest tickets in town. Previous must-sees included an Edward Hopper retrospective and "Picasso and the Masters." To skip the long queue, book an advance ticket online for an extra euro. ✉ *Av. Winston Churchill, Champs-Élysées* ☎ *01–44–13–17–17* 🌐 *www.grandpalais.fr* 🎫 *€14 (can vary)* ⏲ *Wed.–Mon. 10–8 or 10–10, depending on exhibit* Ⓜ *Champs-Élysées–Clemenceau.*

Fodor's Choice ★ **Musée Guimet.** The outstanding Musée Guimet boasts the western world's biggest collection of Asian art, thanks to the 19th-century wanderings of Lyonnaise industrialist Émile Guimet. Exhibits, enriched by the state's vast holdings, are laid out geographically in airy, light-filled rooms. Just past the entry, you can find the largest assemblage of Khmer sculpture outside Cambodia. The second floor has statuary and masks from Nepal, ritual funerary art from Tibet, and jewelry and fabrics from India. Peek into the library rotunda, where Monsieur Guimet once entertained the city's notables under the gaze of eight carytids atop ionic columns; Mata Hari danced here in 1905. The much-heralded Chinese collection, made up of 20,000-odd objects, covers seven millennia. Pick up a free English-language audioguide and brochure at the entrance. If you need a pick-me-up, stop at the Salon des Porcelaines café on the lower level for a ginger milk shake. Don't miss the Guimet's impressive Buddhist Pantheon, with two floors of Buddhas from China and Japan, and a Japanese garden; it's just up the street at 19 avenue d'Iéna, and admission is free with a Musée Guimet ticket. ✉ *6 pl. d'Iéna, Trocadéro/Tour Eiffel* ☎ *01–56–52–53–00* 🌐 *www.guimet.fr* 🎫 *€7.50; €9.50 with temporary exhibition* ⏲ *Wed.–Mon. 10–6* Ⓜ *Iéna, Boissiére.*

Petit Palais, Musée des Beaux-Arts de la Ville de Paris. The "little" palace has a small, overlooked collection of excellent painting, sculpture, and objets d'art, with works by Monet, Gauguin, and Courbet, among others. Temporary exhibitions, beefed up in recent years (and often free), are particularly good—especially those dedicated to photography. The building, like the Grand Palais across the street, is an architectural marvel of marble, glass, and gilt built for the 1900 World's Fair, with impressive entry doors and huge windows overlooking the river. Search directly above the main galleries for 16 plaster busts set into the wall representing famous artists. Outside, note two eye-catching sculptures: French World War I hero Georges Clemenceau faces the Champs-Élysées, while a resolute Winston Churchill faces the Seine. In warmer weather, head to the garden café with terrace seating. ✉ *Av. Winston Churchill, Champs-Élysées* ☎ *01–53–43–40–00* 🌐 *www.petitpalais.paris.fr* 🎫 *Permanent collection free; temporary exhibits*

€5–€11 ⏲ Tues.–Sun. 10–6 (Thurs. until 8 for temporary exhibits) Ⓜ Champs-Élysées–Clemenceau.

NEED A BREAK?

Le Jardin du Petit Palais. The quiet little café hidden in the lush garden inside the Petit Palais is one of this quarter's best-kept secrets. ✉ *Av. Winston Churchill, Champs-Élysées ☎ 01–53–43–40–00 🌐 www.petitpalais.paris.fr ⏲ Tues.–Sun. 10–5:15 (Thurs. until 7:30 during temporary exhibitions) Ⓜ Champs-Élysées–Clemenceau.*

WORTH NOTING

Fondation Pierre Bergé–Yves Saint Laurent. With his longtime business and life partner Pierre Bergé, the late fashion designer Yves Saint Laurent reopened his former atelier as a gallery and archive of his work in 2004. Unfortunately, YSL's private collection of dresses can be viewed only on private group tours booked in advance. What you can see here are exhibitions staged twice annually. Themes include painting, photography and, of course, fashion—such as a retrospective on couture maven Nan Kempner. ✉ *3 rue Léonce Reynaud, Trocadéro/Tour Eiffel ☎ 01–44–31–64–31 🌐 www.fondation-pb-ysl.net 🎫 €7 ⏲ Tues.–Sun. 11–6 during temporary exhibitions only ☞ Last entry at 5:15 Ⓜ Alma-Marceau.*

Maison de Baccarat. Playing on the building's Surrealist legacy, designer Philippe Starck brought an irreverent *Alice in Wonderland* approach to the HQ and museum of the venerable Baccarat crystal firm: Cocteau, Dalí, Buñuel, and Man Ray were all frequent guests of the mansion's onetime owner, Countess Marie-Laure de Noailles. At the entrance, talking heads are projected onto giant crystal urns, and a lighted chandelier is submerged in an aquarium. Upstairs, the museum features masterworks created by Baccarat since 1764, including soaring candlesticks made for Czar Nicholas II and the perfume flacon Dalí designed for Schiaparelli. Don't miss the rotunda's "Alchemy" section by Gérard Garouste, showcasing the technical history of cutting, wheel engraving, enamelling, and gilding. If you're in the mood for shopping, contemporary crystal by top-name designers as well as stemware, vases, tableware, jewelry, chandeliers, and even furniture are sold in the on-site shop. Set aside a few moments to enjoy the little park just outside in the Place des États-Unis with impressive statues of Washington and Lafayette. ✉ *11 pl. des États-Unis, Champs-Élysées ☎ 01–40–22–11–00 🌐 www.baccarat.fr 🎫 €7 ⏲ Mon. and Wed.–Sat. 10–6:30 Ⓜ Iéna.*

FAMILY **Palais de Chaillot.** This honey-color Art Deco cultural center on Place du Trocadéro was built in the 1930s to replace a Moorish-style building constructed for the 1878 World's Fair. Its esplanade is a top draw for camera-toting visitors intent on snapping the perfect shot of the Eiffel Tower. In the building to the left is the Cité de l'Architecture et du Patrimoine—an excellent architecture museum—and the Théâtre National de Chaillot, which occasionally stages plays in English. Also here is the Institut Français d'Architecture, an organization and school. The twin building to the right contains the Musée National de la Marine, a charming small museum showcasing nautical history; and the Musée de l'Homme, a natural history museum that's closed for renovation until late 2015. Sculptures

DID YOU KNOW?

The magnificent Grand Palais, with its enormous glass roof, is known for its provocative and crowd-pleasing temporary art exhibits.

and fountains adorn the garden leading to the Seine. ⊠ *Pl. du Trocadéro, Trocadéro/Tour Eiffel* Ⓜ *Trocadéro.*

Palais de Tokyo. The go-to address for some of the city's funkiest exhibitions, the Palais de Tokyo is a stripped-down venue that spotlights provocative, ambitious contemporary art. There is no permanent collection: instead, cutting-edge temporary shows are staged in a cavernous space reminiscent of a light-filled industrial loft. The programming extends to performance art, concerts, readings, and fashion shows. Night owls will appreciate the midnight closing. The museum's Tokyo Eat restaurant—serving an affordable French–Asian-fusion menu—is a haunt of hip locals, especially at lunch. Visit the offbeat gift shop for souvenirs that are as edgy and subversive as the exhibits. ⊠ *13 av. du Président Wilson, Trocadéro/Tour Eiffel* ☎ *01–81–97–35–88* 🌐 *www.palaisdetokyo.com* 🎫 *€10* 🕒 *Wed.–Mon. noon–midnight* Ⓜ *Iéna.*

Fodor's Choice ★ **Palais Galliera, Musée de la Mode.** The city's Museum of Fashion occupies a suitably fashionable mansion—the 19th-century residence of Marie Brignole-Sale, Duchess of Galliera; and, having emerged from an extensive makeover in 2013, it is now more stylish than ever. Inside, temporary exhibitions focus on costume and clothing design (a reopening retrospective, for instance, honored the visionary Azzedine Alaïa). Covering key moments in fashion history and showcasing iconic French designers, the museum's collection includes 100,000 dresses and accessories that run the gamut from basic streetwear to haute couture. Details on shows (there are no permanent displays) are available on the museum website. Don't miss the lovely 19th-century garden that encircles the palace. ⊠ *10 av. Pierre-1er-de-Serbie, Trocadéro/Tour Eiffel* ☎ *01–56–52–86–00* 🌐 *palaisgalliera.paris.fr* 🎫 *€9* 🕒 *Tues., Wed., and Fri–Sun. 10–6, Thurs. 10–9* Ⓜ *Iéna.*

AROUND THE LOUVRE

Between Faubourg St-Honoré and Les Halles, you can find some of Paris's top draws—namely the mighty Musée du Louvre and, next door, the majestic Jardin des Tuileries. The garden is home to the Musée de l'Orangerie, with its curved galleries showcasing Monet's Water Lilies, while the nearby Jeu De Paume and Les Arts Décoratifs are musts for design buffs. Hidden just off Place Colette is the Palais-Royal, a romantic garden ringed by arcades with boutiques selling everything from old-fashioned music boxes to fashion-forward frocks.

TOP ATTRACTIONS

Galerie Vivienne. Considered the grande dame of Paris's 19th-century *passages couverts*—the world's first shopping malls—this graceful covered arcade evokes an age of gaslights and horse-drawn carriages. Once Parisians came to passages like this one to tred tiled floors instead of muddy streets and to see and be seen browsing boutiques under the glass-and-iron roofs. Today, the Galerie Vivienne still attracts top-flight retailers such as Jean-Paul Gaultier (6 rue Vivienne) and the high-quality secondhand clothes seller La Marelle (No. 21), as well as shops selling accessories, housewares, and fine wine. The Place des Victoires, a few steps away, is one of Paris's most picturesque squares. In the center is a statue of an outsized Louis XIV (1643–1715), the Sun King, who appears almost as large as his horse. ✉ *Main entrance at 4 rue des Petits-Champs, Louvre/Tuileries* Ⓜ *Palais-Royal/Bourse.*

FAMILY Fodor's Choice ★ **Jardin des Tuileries.** The quintessential French garden, with its verdant lawns, manicured rows of trees, and gravel paths, was designed by André Le Nôtre for Louis XIV. After the king moved his court to Versailles in 1682, the Tuileries became *the* place for stylish Parisians to stroll. (Ironically, the name derives from the decidedly unstylish factories which once occupied this area: they produced *tuiles,* or roof tiles, fired in kilns called *tuileries.*) Monet and Renoir captured the garden with paint and brush, and it's no wonder the Impressionists loved it—the gray, austere light of Paris's famously overcast days make the green trees appear even greener.

The garden still serves as a setting for one of the city's loveliest walks. Laid out before you is a vista of must-see monuments, with the Louvre at one end and the Place de la Concorde at the other. The Eiffel Tower is on the Seine side, along with the Musée d'Orsay, reachable across a footbridge in the center of the garden. A good place to begin is at the Louvre end, at the Arc du Carrousel, a stone-and-marble arch ordered by Napoléon to showcase the bronze horses he stole from St. Mark's Cathedral in Venice. The horses were eventually returned and replaced here with a statue of a *quadriga,* a four-horse chariot. On the Place de la Concorde end, twin buildings bookend the garden. On the Seine side, the former royal greenhouse is now the exceptional Musée de l'Orangerie, home to the largest display of Monet's lovely *Water Lilies* series, as well as a sizable collection of early-20th-century paintings. On the opposite end is the Jeu de Paume, which has some of the city's best temporary photography exhibits.

■ TIP→ Garden buffs will enjoy the small bookstore at the Place de la Concorde entrance, open 10 am to 7 pm. Aside from volumes on gardening and plants (including some titles in English), it has gift items, knickknacks, and toys for the junior gardener. The Tuileries is one of the best places in Paris to take kids if they're itching to run around. There's a carousel (€2.50), trampolines (€2.50) and, in summer, an amusement park.

If you're hungry, look for carts serving gelato from Amorino or sandwiches from the chain bakery Paul at the eastern end near the Louvre. Within the gated part of the gardens are lovely cafés with terraces. Le Médicis near Place de la Concorde is a good place to stop for late-afternoon tea or apéritif. ✉ *Bordered by Quai des Tuileries, Pl. de la Concorde, Rue de Rivoli, and the Louvre, Louvre/Tuileries* ☎ *01–40–20–90–43* 🎫 *Free* ⏲ *June–Aug., daily 7 am–11 pm; Apr., May, and Sept., daily 7:30 am–9 pm; Oct.–Mar., daily 7:30–7:30* Ⓜ *Tuileries or Concorde.*

Fodor's Choice ★ **The Louvre.** The most recognized symbol of Paris is the Tour Eiffel, but the ultimate traveler's prize is the Louvre. This is the world's greatest art museum—and the largest, with 675,000 square feet of works from almost every civilization on earth. The three most popular pieces here are, of course, the *Mona Lisa*, the Venus de Milo, and Winged Victory.

Beyond these must-sees, your best bet is to focus on whatever interests you the most—and don't despair about getting lost, for you're bound to stumble on something memorable. Pick up an excellent color-coded map at the information desk. There are slick Nintendo 3DS multimedia guides at the entrance to each wing; for €5 you get four self-guided tours and details about 250 works of art, plus a function to help you find your bearings. There are also 90-minute guided tours (€12) in English daily at 11:15 and 2. Thematic leaflets (including some for kids) are available at the information desk.

Bear in mind that the Louvre is much more than a museum—it represents a saga that started centuries ago, having been a fortress at the turn of the 13th century, and later a royal residence. It was not until the 16th century, under François I, that today's Louvre began to take shape, and through the years Henry IV, Louis XIII, Louis XV, Napoléon I, and Napoléon III all contributed to its construction. Napoléon Bonaparte's military campaigns at the turn of the 19th century brought a new influx of holdings, as his soldiers carried off treasures from each invaded country. During World War II the most precious artworks were hidden, while the remainder was looted. Most of the stolen pieces were recovered, though, after the liberation of Paris. No large-scale changes were made until François Mitterrand was elected president in 1981, when he kicked off the Grand Louvre project to expand and modernize the museum.

Mitterrand commissioned I.M. Pei's Pyramide, the giant glass pyramid surrounded by three smaller pyramids that opened in 1989 over the new entrance in the Cour Napoléon. In 2012, the Louvre's newest architectural wonder debuted—the 30,000-square-foot **Arts of Islam wing.** Built into the Cour Visconti in the Denon wing and topped with an undulating golden roof evoking a veil blowing in the wind, the two-level galleries house one of the world's largest collections of art from all corners of the Islamic world.

The Louvre comprises three wings—the Richelieu, the Sully, and the Denon—arranged like a horseshoe, with the Pyramide nestled outside in the middle. Entering from it, head upstairs to the sculpture courtyards in the Richelieu wing, where you'll find the *Marly Horses,* four equine sculptures—two carved for Louis XIV and two for Louis XV—in Cour Marly. The ground floor and underground rooms in this wing contain 5th- to 19th-century French sculpture, and the Near East Antiquities Collection, including the Lamassu, carved 8th-century winged beasts. On the first floor of this wing you'll find the Royal Apartments of Napoléon III, a dozen elaborately decorated reception rooms. Continue to the second floor for the French and Northern School paintings, including Vermeer's *The Lacemaker.*The entrance to the Sully wing is the most impressive, as you can walk around the 12th-century foundations and vestiges of the original medieval moat. Belowground is also the largest display of Egyptian antiques in the world after that of the Cairo museum, featuring such artifacts as Ramses II, a beautifully proportioned statue from the site of Tanis. Upstairs in Salle 16 is the armless **Venus de Milo** , a 2nd-century representation of the goddess Aphrodite. She was cleaned and restored over six months in 2010, the work taking place after hours and on Tuesday, when the museum is closed.

The first and second floors of the Sully Wing boast decorative arts from all over Europe, as well as 17th-century French paintings, including the *Turkish Bath* by Jean-August-Dominique Ingres. Don't miss one of the newest additions, the contemporary ceiling in Salle 32 on the first floor by American Cy Twombly, unveiled in 2010. On the first floor, period rooms (reopened in 2014 after a multiyear renovation) contain 18th-century furnishings and objets d'art. To the south and east of the Pyramide entrance are galleries displaying early Renaissance sculpture in the Denon Wing. Don't skip the coat checks on the ground floor of the Denon or Richelieu wings—much of the museum is hot and stuffy. Walk up the marble Escalier Daru to discover the sublime (and newly cleaned) **Winged Victory of Samothrace,** a statue found on a tiny Greek island that was carved in 305 BC to commemorate the naval victory of Demetrius Poliocretes over the Turks. In the paintings section of the Denon Wing, you'll find three by Leonardo da Vinci, including the most famous painting in the world: the ***Mona Lisa,*** located in Salle 7. Head across to Salle 75 for the *Coronation of Napoléon,* or to Salle 77 for the graphic 1819 *Raft of the Medusa,* the first work of art based on a real news event, in this case the survivors of the wreck of a French ship.

The Louvre still hasn't mastered easy online ticket sales, which are handled by outside vendors andmust be picked up at designated locations. The city's tourism office will mail tickets worldwide or deliver them to your hotel for a fee. You can also pick them up for free at the Paris Convention and Visitors Bureau office near the museum at 25 rue des Pyramides (use métro Pyramides).

If you arrive without a ticket, shorten your wait by avoiding the main entrance at the Pyramide and head for the entrance in the underground mall, Carrousel du Louvre. Automatic ticket machines are available. Aware of how frustrating it can be to enter the musem at busy times, the Louvre in 2014 launched a two-year, $67million renovation of the Pyramide entrance intended to ease bottlenecks with a fast-track line for advance ticket holders. Note that crowds are thinner on Wednesday and Friday nights, when the museum is open late.

Need a break? Visit an on-site café (like Café Richelieu, run by upscale *confiseur* Angelina); or pop out to an open-air café in the Jardin de Tuileries.

If you have your heart set on seeing a particular work, check the website for room closings; renovations are always taking place. Remember that the Louvre is closed Tuesday. ✉ *Palais du Louvre, Louvre/Tuileries* ☎ *01–40–20–53–17 information* 🌐 *www.louvre.fr* 🎟 *€12; €13 for Napoléon Hall exhibitions; €16 with all temporary exhibits and same-day entry to Musée Eugène Delacroix; free 1st Sun. of month* ⏲ *Mon., Thurs., and weekends 9–6, Wed. and Fri. 9 am–9:45 pm* Ⓜ *Palais-Royal–Musée du Louvre.*

Jeu de Paume. This Napoleon III–era building at the north entrance of the Jardin des Tuileries began life in 1861 as a place to play *jeu de paume* (or "palm game"), a forerunner of tennis. It later served as a transfer point for art looted by the Germans during World War II. Today, it's been given another lease on life as an ultramodern, white-walled

Architect I.M. Pei's pyramid entrance reaffirms the ever-old-but-always-new vitality of the Louvre's French Baroque architecture.

showcase for excellent temporary exhibits of photography featuring up-and-comers as well as icons such as Diane Arbus, Richard Avedon, Cindy Sherman, and Robert Frank. ✉ *1 pl. de la Concorde, Louvre/Tuileries* ☎ *01–47–03–12–50* 🌐 *www.jeudepaume.org* 🎟 *€10* ⏲ *Tues. 11–9, Wed.–Sun. 11–7* Ⓜ *Concorde.*

Fodor's Choice ★ **Les Arts Décoratifs.** Sharing a wing of the Musée du Louvre, but with a separate entrance and admission charge, Les Arts Décoratifs is actually three museums in one. Spread across nine floors, it showcases a stellar array of decorative arts, design and fashion, and graphics. The collection includes altarpieces from the Middle Ages and furnishings from the Italian Renaissance to the present day. There are period rooms reflecting the ages, such as the early 1820s salon of the Duchesse de Berry (who actually lived in the building), plus several rooms reproduced from designer Jeanne Lanvin's 1920s apartment. Don't miss the gilt-and-green-velvet bed of the Parisian courtesan who inspired the boudoir in Émile Zola's novel *Nana.* You can hear Zola's description of it on the free English audioguide, which is highly recommended. The second-floor jewelry gallery is a must-see, and special events are often staged in the first-floor Nef (nave).

The center is also home to an exceptional collection of textiles, advertising posters, films, and related objects that are shown in rotating temporary exhibitions. Before leaving, take a break at Le Saut du Loup restaurant: its outdoor terrace is an ideal spot for lunch or afternoon tea. Shoppers should also browse through the tempting on-site store (107 Rivoli), which carries an interesting collection of books, paper products, toys, tableware, and jewelry. If you're combining a visit here

2

with the Musée du Louvre, note that the two close on different days, so don't come on Monday or Tuesday. If you're pairing it with the exquisite Nissim de Camondo, joint tickets are available at a reduced cost. ✉ *107 rue de Rivoli, Louvre/Tuileries* ☎ *01–44–55–57–50* 🌐 *www.lesartsdecoratifs.fr* 🎟 *€11; €15 with temporary exhibits; €13 joint ticket with Musée Nissim de Camondo* 🕓 *Tues.–Sun. 11–6 (Thurs. until 9 during exhibits)* Ⓜ *Palais-Royal.*

Musée de l'Orangerie. The lines can be long to see Claude Monet's huge, meditative *Water Lilies* (*Nymphéas*) , displayed in two curved galleries designed in 1914 by the master himself. But they are well worth the wait. These works are the highlight of the Orangerie Museum's small but excellent collection, which includes early-20th-century paintings by Renoir, Cézanne, and Matisse. Many hail from the private holdings of art dealer Paul Guillaume (1891–1934), including Guillaume's portrait by Modigliani entitled *Novo Pilota,* or "New Pilot," signaling Guillaume's status as an important presence in the arts world. Built in 1852 to shelter orange trees, the museum also includes a portion of the city's 16th-century wall (you can see remnants on the lower floor). ✉ *Jardin des Tuileries at Pl. de la Concorde, Louvre/Tuileries* ☎ *01–44–77–80–07* 🌐 *www.musee-orangerie.fr* 🎟 *€9 ($6.50 after 5); €16 joint ticket with Musée d'Orsay* 🕓 *Wed.–Mon. 9–6* Ⓜ *Concorde.*

Fodor's Choice ★ **Palais-Royal.** The quietest, most romantic Parisian garden is enclosed within the former home of Cardinal Richelieu (1585–1642). It's an ideal spot to while away an afternoon, cuddling with your sweetheart on a bench under the trees, soaking up the sunshine beside the fountain, or browsing the 400-year-old arcades that are now home to boutiques ranging from quirky (picture Anna Joliet's music boxes) to chic (think designs by Stella McCartney and Marc Jacobs). One of the city's oldest restaurants is here, the haute-cuisine Le Grand Véfour, where brass plaques recall regulars like Napoléon and Victor Hugo. Built in 1629, the *palais* became royal when Richelieu bequeathed it to Louis XIII. Other famous residents include Jean Cocteau and Colette, who wrote of her pleasurable "country" view of the *province à Paris*. Today, the garden often plays host to giant-size temporary art installations sponsored by another tenant, the Ministry of Culture. The courtyard off Place Colette is outfitted with an unusual collection of short black-and-white columns created in 1986 by artist Daniel Buren. ✉ *Pl. du Palais-Royal, Louvre/Palais-Royal* Ⓜ *Palais-Royal.*

Place de la Concorde. This square at the foot of the Champs-Élysées was originally named after Louis XV. It later became the Place de la Révolution, where crowds cheered as Louis XVI, Marie-Antoinette, and some 2,500 others lost their heads to the guillotine. Renamed Concorde in 1836, it got a new centerpiece: the 75-foot granite Obelisk of Luxor, a gift from Egypt quarried in the 8th century BC. Among the handsome 18th-century buildings facing the square is the Hôtel Crillon, which was originally built as a private home by Gabriel, the architect of Versailles's Petit Trianon. ✉ *Rue Royale, Champs-Élysées* Ⓜ *Concorde.*

Place Vendôme. Jules-Hardouin Mansart, an architect of Versailles, designed this perfectly proportioned octagonal plaza near the Tuileries in 1702; and, to maintain a uniform appearance, he gave the surrounding *hôtels particuliers* (private mansions) identical facades. It was originally called Place des Conquêtes to extoll the military conquests of Louis XIV, whose statue on horseback graced the center until Revolutionaries destroyed it in 1792. Later, Napoléon ordered his likeness erected atop a 144-foot column modestly modeled after Rome's Trajan Column. But that, too, was toppled in 1871 by painter Gustave Courbet and his band of radicals. The Third Republic raised a new column and sent Courbet the bill, though he died in exile before paying it. Chopin lived and died at No. 12, which is also where Napoléon III enjoyed trysts with his mistress; since 1902 it has been home to the high-end jeweler Chaumet. ✉ *Place Vendôme, Louvre/Tuileries* Ⓜ *Tuileries.*

WORTH NOTING

Comédie Française. Refined productions by Molière and Racine are staged regularly (though only in French) at the vintage venue where actress Sarah Bernhardt began her career. Founded in 1680 by Louis XIV, the theater finally opened its doors to the public in 1799. It nearly burned to the ground a hundred years later. The current building dates from 1900. ✉ *1 pl. Colette, Louvre/Tuileries* ☎ *08–25–10–16–80 €0.15 per minute* 🌐 *www.comedie-francaise.fr* Ⓜ *Palais-Royal.*

Église de la Madeleine. With its rows of uncompromising columns, this enormous neoclassical edifice in the center of Place de la Madeleine was consecrated as a church in 1842, nearly 78 years after construction began. Initially planned as a Baroque building, it was later razed and begun anew by an architect who had the Roman Pantheon in mind. Interrupted by the Revolution, the site was razed yet again when Napoléon decided to make it into a Greek temple dedicated to the glory of his army. Those plans changed when the army was defeated and the emperor deposed. Other ideas for the building included making it into a train station, a market, and a library. Finally, Louis XVIII decided to make it a church, which it still is today. Classical concerts are held here regularly, some of them free. ✉ *Pl. de la Madeleine, Faubourg* ☎ *01–44–51–69–00* 🌐 *www.eglise-lamadeleine.com* 🕓 *Daily 9:30–7* Ⓜ *Madeleine.*

St-Eustache. Built as the market neighborhood's answer to Notre-Dame, this massive church is decidedly squeezed into its surroundings. Constructed between 1532 and 1640 with foundations dating to 1200, the church mixes a Gothic exterior, complete with impressive flying buttresses, and a Renaissance interior. On the east end (Rue Montmartre), Dutch master Rubens's *Pilgrims of Emmaus* (1611) hangs in a small chapel. Two chapels to the left is Keith Haring's *The Life of Christ*, a triptych in bronze and white-gold patina: it was given to the church after the artist's death in 1990, in recognition of the parish's efforts to help people with AIDS. On the Rue Montmartre side of the church, look for the small door to Saint Agnes's crypt, topped with a stone plaque noting the date, 1213, below a curled fish, an indication the patron made his fortune in fish. ✉ *2 impasse St-Eustache, Beaubourg/Les Halles* 🌐 *www.saint-eustache.org for concert info* 🕓 *Weekdays 9:30–7, weekends 9–7* Ⓜ *Les Halles; RER: Châtelet Les Halles.*

LES GRANDS BOULEVARDS

In Belle Époque Paris, the Grand Boulevards were the place to see and be seen: in the cafés, at the opera, or in the ornate passages, the glass-covered arcades that were the world's first shopping malls. If you close your eyes, you can almost imagine the Grands Boulevards immortalized on canvas by the Impressionists: well-dressed Parisians strolling wide avenues dotted with shops, cafés, and horse-drawn carriages—all set against a backdrop of stately Haussmannian buildings. Today, despite the chain stores, sidewalk vendors, and fast-food joints, the Grands Boulevards remain the city's shopping epicenter, home to the most popular *grands magasins* (department stores), Galeries Lafayette and Le Printemps, near Place de l'Opéra at the heart of the long chain of avenues, which change names six times.

TOP ATTRACTIONS

Galeries Lafayette. The stunning Byzantine glass *coupole* (dome) of the city's most famous department store is not to be missed. Amble to the center of the main store, amid the perfumes and cosmetics, and look up. If you're not in the mood for shopping, sip a glass of Champagne at the Bar à Bulles at the top of the first-floor escalator; or have lunch at one of the restaurants, including a rooftop café in the main store (open in spring and summer). On your way down, the top floor of the main store is a good place to pick up interesting Parisian souvenirs. Next door, the excellent Lafayette Gourmet food hall, on the second floor of the men's store, has one of the city's best selections of delicacies. Try a green-tea éclair from Japanese–French baker Sadaharu Aoki. ✉ *40 bd. Haussmann, Opéra/Grands Boulevards* ☎ *01–42–82–34–56* 🌐 *www.galerieslafayette.com* ⏲ *Mon.–Wed., Fri., and Sat. 9:30–8, Thurs. 9:30–9* Ⓜ *Chaussée d'Antin, Opéra; RER A: Auber.*

Fodor's Choice ★ **Musée Cernuschi.** Wealthy Milanese banker and patriot Enrico (Henri) Cernuschi fled to Paris in 1850 after the new Italian government collapsed, only to be arrested during the 1871 Paris Commune. He subsequently decided to wait out the unrest by traveling and collecting Asian art. Upon his return 18 months later, he had a special mansion built on the edge of Parc Monceau to house his treasures, notably a two-story bronze Buddha from Japan. Today, this well-appointed museum contains France's second-most-important collection of Asian art, after the Musée Guimet. Cernuschi had an eye not only for the bronze pieces he adored but also for Neolithic pottery (8,000 BC), *mingqi* tomb figures (300–900 AD), and an impressive array of terra-cotta figures from various dynasties. A collection highlight is La Tigresse, a bronze wine vessel in the shape of a roaring feline (11th century BC) purchased after Cernuschi's death. Although the museum is free, there is a charge for temporary exhibitions: previous shows have featured Japanese drawings, Iranian sculpture, and Imperial Chinese bronzes. ✉ *7 av. Velasquez, Parc Monceau* ☎ *01–53–96–21–50* 🌐 *www.cernuschi.paris.fr* 🎟 *Free; temporary exhibitions €4–€11* ⏲ *Tues.–Sun. 10–6* Ⓜ *Monceau.*

Fodor's Choice ★ **Musée Jacquemart-André.** Perhaps the city's best small museum, the opulent Musée Jacquemart-André is home to a huge collection of art and furnishings lovingly assembled in the late 19th century by banking heir

CLOSE UP

Hemingway's Paris

There is a saying: "Everyone has two countries, his or her own—and France." For the Lost Generation after World War I, these words rang particularly true. Lured by favorable exchange rates, free-flowing alcohol, and a booming artistic scene, many American writers, composers, and painters moved to Paris in the 1920s and 1930s, Ernest Hemingway among them. He arrived in Paris with his first wife, Hadley, in December 1921 and made for the Rive Gauche—the Hôtel Jacob et d'Angleterre, to be exact (still operating at 44 rue Jacob). To celebrate their arrival the couple went to the Café de la Paix for a meal they nearly couldn't afford.

Hemingway worked as a journalist and quickly made friends with other expat writers such as Gertrude Stein and Ezra Pound. In 1922 the Hemingways moved to 74 rue du Cardinal Lemoine, a bare-bones apartment with no running water (his writing studio was around the corner, on the top floor of 39 rue Descartes). Then in early 1924 the couple and their baby son settled at 113 rue Notre-Dame des Champs. Much of *The Sun Also Rises,*Hemingway's first serious novel, was written at nearby café La Closerie des Lilas. These were the years in which he forged his writing style, paring his sentences down to the pith. As he noted in *A Moveable Feast,* "hunger was good discipline." There were some particularly hungry months when Hemingway gave up journalism and tried to publish short stories, and the family was "very poor and very happy."

They weren't happy for long. In 1926, just when *The Sun Also Rises* made him famous, Hemingway left Hadley and the next year wedded his mistress, Pauline Pfeiffer, across town at St-Honoré d'Eylau, then moved to 6 rue Férou, near the Musée du Luxembourg, whose collection of Cézanne landscapes (now in the Musée d'Orsay) he revered.

For gossip and books, and to pick up his mail, Papa would visit Shakespeare & Co., then at 12 rue de l'Odéon, owned by Sylvia Beach, who became a trusted friend. For cash and cocktails Hemingway usually headed to the upscale Rive Droite. He collected the former at the Guaranty Trust Company, at 1 rue des Italiens. He found the latter, when he was flush, at the bar of the Hôtel Crillon, or, when poor, at Caves Mura, at 19 rue d'Antin, or Harry's Bar, still in brisk business at 5 rue Daunou. Hemingway's legendary association with the Hotel Ritz was sealed during the Liberation in 1944, when he strode in at the head of his platoon and "liberated" the joint by ordering martinis all around. Here Hemingway asked Mary Welsh to become his fourth wife, and here also, the story goes, a trunk full of notes on his first years in Paris turned up in the 1950s, giving him the raw material to write *A Moveable Feast.*

The eye-popping atrium of the Galeries Lafayette is the subject of this entry by Elizabeth A. Millar, a Fodors.com member, to Fodor's "Show Us Your France" contest.

Edouard André and his artist wife, Nélie Jacquemart. Their midlife marriage in 1881 raised eyebrows—he was a dashing bachelor and a Protestant, and she, no great beauty, hailed from a modest Catholic family. Still, theirs was a happy union fused by a common passion for art. For six months every year, the couple traveled, most often to Italy, where they hunted down works from the Renaissance, their preferred period. Their collection also includes French painters Fragonard, Jacques-Louis David, and François Boucher, plus Dutch masters Van Dyke and Rembrandt. The Belle Époque mansion itself is a major attraction. The elegant ballroom, equipped with collapsible walls operated by then-state-of-the-art hydraulics, could hold 1,000 guests. The winter garden was a wonder of its day, spilling into the *fumoir,* where André would share cigars with the *grands hommes* (important men) of the day. You can tour the separate bedrooms—his in dusty pink, hers in pale yellow. The former dining room, now an elegant café, features a ceiling by Tiepolo. Don't forget to pick up the free audioguide in English, and do inquire about the current temporary exhibition (two per year), which is usually top-notch. Plan on a Sunday visit and enjoy the popular brunch (€29.30) in the café from 11 to 3. Reservations are not accepted, so come early or late to avoid waiting in line. ✉ *158 bd. Haussmann, Parc Monceau* ☎ *01–45–62–11–59* 🌐 *www.musee-jacquemart-andre.com* 🎟 *€12* 🕓 *Daily 10–6 (until 8:30 Mon. and Sat. during exhibitions)* Ⓜ *St-Philippe-du-Roule, Miromesnil.*

Fodor's Choice ★ **Opéra Garnier.** Haunt of the Phantom of the Opera and the real-life inspiration for Edgar Degas's dancer paintings, the gorgeous Opéra Garnier is one of two homes of the National Opera of Paris. The building, the

Palais Garnier, was begun in 1860 by then-unknown architect Charles Garnier, who finished his masterwork 15 long years later, way over budget. Festooned with (real) gold leaf, colored marble, paintings, and sculpture from the top artists of the day, the opera house was about as subtle as Versailles and sparked controversy in post-Revolutionary France. The sweeping marble staircase, in particular, drew criticism from a public skeptical of its extravagance. But Garnier, determined to make a landmark that would last forever, spared no expense. The magnificent grand foyer is one of the most exquisite salons in France. In its heyday, the cream of Paris society strolled all 59 yards of the vast hall at intermission, admiring themselves in the towering mirrors. To see the opera house, buy a ticket for an unguided visit, which allows access to most parts of the building, including a peek into the auditorium. There is also a small ballet museum with a few works by Degas and the tutu worn by prima ballerina Anna Pavlova when she danced her epic Dying Swan in 1905. To get to it, pass through the unfinished entrance built for Napoléon III and his carriage (construction was abruptly halted when the emperor abdicated in 1870). On the upper level, you can see a sample of the auditorium's original classical ceiling, which was later replaced with a modern version painted by a septuagenarian Mark Chagall. His trademark willowy figures encircling the dazzling crystal chandelier—today the world's third largest—shocked an unappreciative public upon its debut in 1964. Critics who fret that Chagall's masterpiece clashes with the fussy crimson-and-gilt decor can take some comfort in knowing that the original ceiling is preserved underneath, encased in a plastic dome.

The Opéra Garnier plays host to the Paris Ballet as well as a few operas each season (most are performed at the Opéra Bastille). If you're planning to see a performance, tickets cost €5–€230 and should be reserved as soon as they go on sale—typically a month ahead at the box office, earlier by phone or online; otherwise, try your luck last minute. To learn about the building's history, and get a taste of aristocratic life during the Second Empire, take an entertaining English-language tour. They're offered most months at 11:30 and 3:30 on Wednesday, Saturday, and Sunday; tours go at the same times daily in summer, with an extra one added at 2. To complete the experience, dine at L'Opéra, the contemporary on-site restaurant run by chef Stéphane Bidi; or browse through the Palais Garnier gift shop for ballet-inspired wares, fine Bernardaud porcelain depicting the famous Chagall ceiling, and an exceptional selection of themed DVDs and books. ✉ *Pl. de l'Opéra, Opéra/Grands Boulevards* ☎ *08–92–89–90–90 €0.34 per min* 🌐 *www.operadeparis.fr* 🎫 *€10; €14.50 for tours* ⏲ *Sept.–mid-July, daily 10–5; mid-July–Aug., daily 10–6* Ⓜ *Opéra.*

FAMILY **Parc Monceau.** This exquisitely landscaped park began in 1778 as the Duc de Chartres's private garden. Though some of the land was sold off under the Second Empire (creating the exclusive real estate that now borders the park), the refined atmosphere and some of the fanciful faux ruins have survived. Immaculately dressed children play under the watchful eye of their nannies, while lovers cuddle on the benches. In 1797 André Garnerin, the world's first-recorded parachutist, staged a

The Grand Foyer proves that Paris's Opéra Garnier is the most opulent theater in the world.

landing in the park. The rotunda—known as the Chartres Pavilion—is surely the city's grandest public restroom: it started life as a tollhouse. ✉ *Entrances on Bd. de Courcelles, Av. Velasquez, Av. Ruysdaël, Av. van Dyck, Parc Monceau* ⏲ *Oct.–May, 7 am–8 pm; June–Aug., 7 am–10 pm; Sept., 7 am–9 pm* Ⓜ *Monceau.*

WORTH NOTING

FAMILY **Chocostory: Le Musée Gourmand du Chocolat.** Considering that a daily dose of chocolate is practically obligatory in Paris, it's hard to believe that this spot (opened in 2010) is the city's first museum dedicated to the sweet stuff. Exhibits on three floors tell the story of chocolate from the earliest traces of the "divine nectar" in Mayan and Aztec cultures, through to its introduction in Europe by the Spanish, who added milk and sugar to the spicy dark brew and launched a Continental craze. There are detailed explanations in English, with many for the kids. While the production of chocolate is a major topic, there is also a respectable collection of some 1,000 chocolate-related artifacts, such as terra-cotta Mayan sipping vessels (they blew into straws to create foam) and delicate chocolate pots in fine porcelain that were favored by the French royal court. Frequent chocolate-making demonstrations finish with a free tasting. ✉ *28 bd. de Bonne Nouvelle, Opéra/Grands Boulevards* ☎ *01–42–29–68–60* 🌐 *www.museeduchocolat.fr* 🎫 *€9.50, €12.50 with a cup of hot chocolate* ⏲ *Daily 10–6* ☞ *Last entry at 5* Ⓜ *Bonne-Nouvelle, Strasbourg, St-Denis.*

Musée de la Vie Romantique. A visit to the charming Museum of the Romantic Life, dedicated to novelist George Sand (1804–76), will transport you to the countryside. Occupying a pretty 1830s mansion in a tree-lined courtyard, the small permanent collection features drawings by Delacroix and Ingres, among others, though Sand is the undisputed star. Displays include glass cases stuffed with her jewelry and even a mold of the hand of composer Frédéric Chopin—one of her many lovers. The museum, about a five-minute walk from the Musée National Gustave-Moreau, is in a picturesque neighborhood once called New Athens, a reflection of the architectural tastes of the writers and artists who lived there. There is usually an interesting temporary exhibit here, too. The garden café (open March to October) is a lovely spot for lunch or afternoon tea. ✉ *16 rue Chaptal, Opéra/Grands Boulevards* ☎ *01–55–31–95–67* 🌐 *www.vie-romantique.paris.fr* 🎫 *Free; €7 temporary exhibits* ⏲ *Tues.–Sun. 10–6* Ⓜ *Blanche, Pigalle, St-Georges.*

Musée Nissim de Camondo. The story of the Camondo family is steeped in tragedy, and it's all recorded within the walls of this superb museum. Patriarch Moïse de Camondo, born in Istanbul to a successful banking family, built his showpiece mansion in 1911 in the style of the Petit Trianon at Versailles, and stocked it with some of the most exquisite furniture, wainscoting, and bibelots of the mid-to-late 18th century. Despite his vast wealth and purported charm, his wife left him five years after their marriage. Then his son, Nissim, was killed in World War I. Upon Moïse's death in 1935, the house and its contents were left to the state as a museum named for his lost son. A few years later, daughter Béatrice, her husband, and two children were murdered at Auschwitz. No heirs remained and the Camondo name died out. Today, the house remains an impeccable tribute to Moïse's life, from the gleaming salons to the refined private rooms. ✉ *63 rue de Monceau, Parc Monceau* ☎ *01–53–89–06–50* 🌐 *www.lesartsdecoratifs.fr* 🎫 *€9; €13 joint ticket with Les Arts Décoratifs* ⏲ *Wed.–Sun. 10–5:30* Ⓜ *Villiers, Monceau.*

MONTMARTRE

Montmartre has become almost too charming for its own good. Yes, it feels like a village (if you wander off the beaten path); yes, there are working artists here (though far fewer than there used to be); and yes, the best view of Paris is yours for free from the top of the hill (if there's no haze). That's why on any weekend day, year-round, you can find scores of visitors crowding these cobbled alleys, scaling the staircases that pass for streets, and queuing to see Sacré-Coeur, the "sculpted cloud," at the summit.

TOP ATTRACTIONS

Fodor's Choice ★ **Basilique du Sacré-Coeur.** It's hard to not feel as though you're climbing up to heaven when you visit Sacred Heart Basilica, the white castle in the sky, perched atop Montmartre. The French government commissioned it in 1873 to symbolize the return of self-confidence after the devastating years of the Commune and Franco-Prussian War, and architect Paul Abadie employed elements from Romanesque and Byzantine styles when designing it—a mélange many critics dismissed as gaudy. Construction lasted until World War I, and the church was finally consecrated in 1919.

Many people come to Sacré-Coeur to admire the superlative view from the top of its 271-foot-high dome. If you opt to skip the climb up the spiral staircase, the view from the front steps is still ample compensation for the trip.

Inside, expect another visual treat—namely the massive golden mosaic set high above the choir. Created in 1922 by Luc-Olivier Merson, *Christ in Majesty* depicts Christ with a golden heart and outstretched arms, surrounded by various figures, including the Virgin Mary and Joan of Arc. It remains one of the largest mosaics of its kind. Also worth noting are the seemingly endless vaulted arches in the basilica's crypt; the portico's bronze doors, decorated with biblical scenes; and the stained-glass windows, which were installed in 1922, destroyed by a bombing during World War II (there were miraculously no deaths), and later rebuilt in 1946. In the basilica's 262-foot-high campanile hangs La Savoyarde, one of the world's heaviest bells, weighing about 19 tons.

■ TIP→ The best time to visit Sacré-Coeur is early morning or early evening, and preferably not on a Sunday, when the crowds are thick. If you're coming to worship, there are daily Masses. Photographers angling for the perfect shot of the church should aim for a clear blue-sky day or arrive at dusk, when the pink sky plays nicely with the lights of the basilica.

To avoid the steps, take the funicular, which costs one métro ticket each way. ✉ *Pl. du Parvis-du-Sacré-Coeur, Montmartre* ☎ *01–53–41–89–00* 🌐 *www.sacre-coeur-montmartre.com* 🎫 *Basilica free; dome €6; crypt €2* ⏲ *Basilica daily 6 am–10:30 pm; dome Oct.–Apr., daily 9–5; May.–Sept., daily 8:30–8; crypt Thurs.–Mon., daily 10–5* Ⓜ *Anvers, plus funicular; Jules Joffrin plus Montmartrobus.*

Moulin de la Galette. Of the 14 windmills (*moulins*) that used to sit atop this hill, only two remain. They're known collectively as Moulin de la Galette—the name being taken from the bread that the owners used to produce. The more storied of the two is Le Blute-Fin. In the late 1800s there was a dance hall on the site, famously captured by Renoir (you can see the painting in the Musée d'Orsay). A face-lift restored the windmill to its 19th-century glory; however, it is on private land and can't be visited. Down the street is the other moulin, Le Radet. ✉ *Le Blute-Fin, corner of Rue Lepic and Rue Tholozé, Montmartre* Ⓜ *Abbesses.*

Place des Abbesses. This triangular square is typical of the countrified style that has made Montmartre famous. Now a hub for shopping and people-watching, the *place* is surrounded by hip boutiques, sidewalk cafés, and shabby-chic restaurants—a prime habitat for the young, neo-bohemian crowd and a sprinkling of expats. Trendy streets like Rue Houdon and Rue des Martyrs have attracted small designer shops, an international beer seller, and even a cupcake shop. Some retailers remain open on Sunday afternoon. ✉ *Intersection of Rue des Abbesses and Rue la Vieuville, Montmartre* Ⓜ *Abbesses.*

WORTH NOTING

Bateau-Lavoir (*Wash-barge*). The birthplace of Cubism isn't open to the public, but a display in the front window details this unimposing spot's rich history. Montmartre poet Max Jacob coined the name because the

Residents of Montmartre often talk about "going down into Paris," and after climbing the many steps to get here you'll understand why.

original structure here reminded him of the laundry boats that used to float in the Seine, and he joked that the warren of paint-splattered artists' studios needed a good hosing down (wishful thinking, since the building had only one water tap). It was in the Bateau-Lavoir that, early in the 20th century, Pablo Picasso, Georges Braque, and Juan Gris made their first bold stabs at Cubism, and Picasso painted the groundbreaking *Les Demoiselles d'Avignon* in 1906–07. The experimental works of the artists weren't met with open arms, even in liberal Montmartre. All but the facade was rebuilt after a fire in 1970. Like the original building, though, the current incarnation houses artists and their studios. ✉ *13 pl. Émile-Goudeau, Montmartre* Ⓜ *Abbesses.*

Moulin Rouge. When this world-famous cabaret opened in 1889, aristocrats, professionals, and the working classes all flocked in to ogle the scandalous performers (the cancan was considerably more kinky in Toulouse-Lautrec's day, when girls kicked off their knickers). There's not much to see from the outside except for tourist buses and sex shops; souvenir seekers should check out the Moulin Rouge gift shop (around the corner at 11 rue Lepic), which sells better-quality official merchandise, from jewelry to sculpture, by reputable French makers. ✉ *82 bd. de Clichy, Montmartre* ☎ *01–53–09–82–82* 🌐 *www.moulinrouge.fr* Ⓜ *Blanche.*

Musée de Montmartre. During its turn-of-the-20th-century heyday, this building—now home to Montmartre's historical museum—was occupied by painters, writers, and cabaret artists. Foremost among them was Auguste Renoir, who painted *Le Moulin de la Galette* (an archetypal scene of sun-drenched revelers) while living here. Recapping the

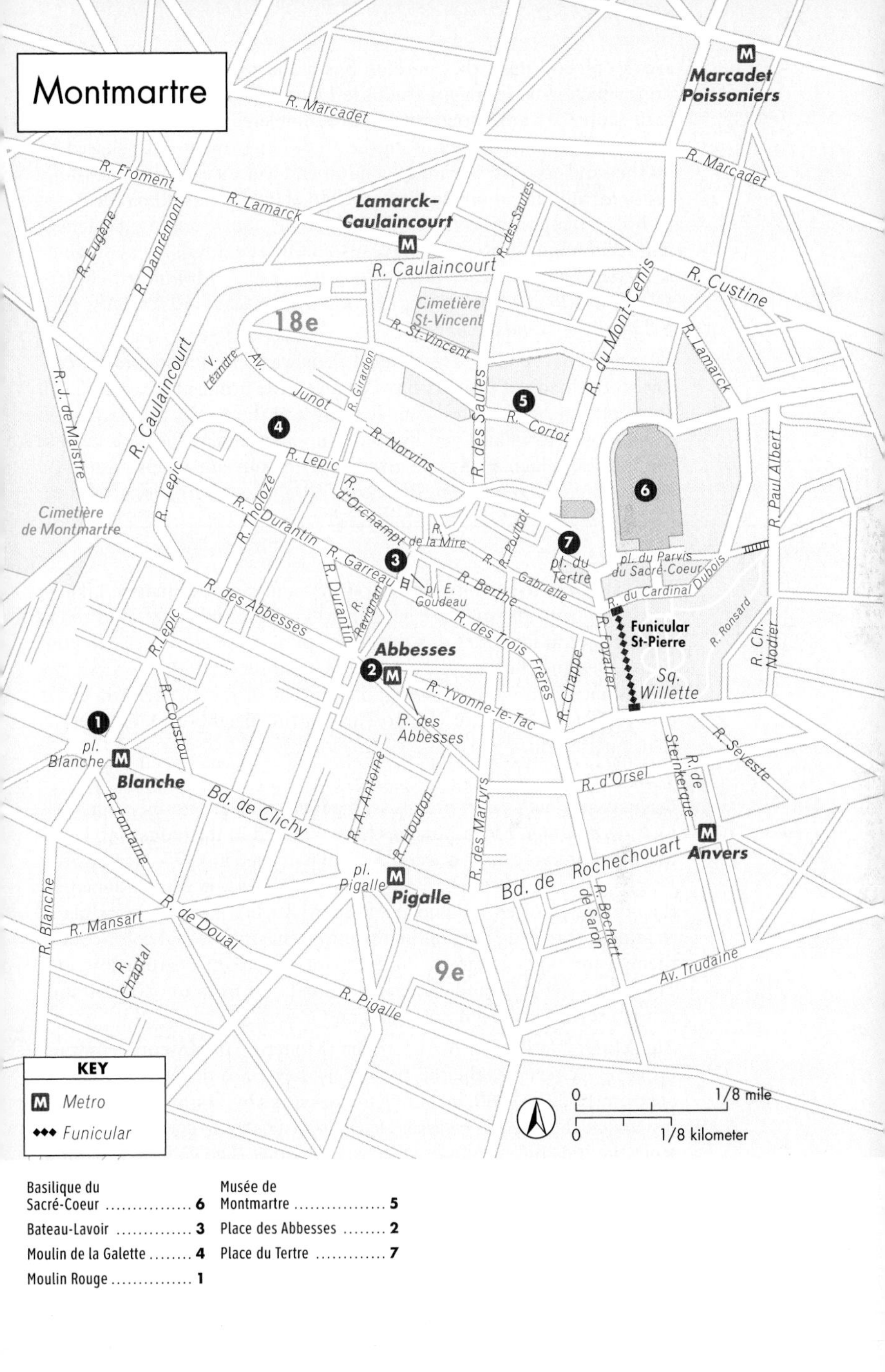

Basilique du Sacré-Coeur **6**	Musée de Montmartre **5**
Bateau-Lavoir **3**	Place des Abbesses **2**
Moulin de la Galette **4**	Place du Tertre **7**
Moulin Rouge **1**	

area's colorful past, the museum has a charming permanent collection, which includes many Toulouse-Lautrec posters and original Eric Satie scores. An ambitious renovation, completed in late 2014, doubled its space by incorporating both the studio-apartment once shared by mother-and-son duo Suzanne Valadon and Maurice Utrillo (now fully restored) and the adjoining Demarne Hotel (which has been redesigned to house temporary exhibitions). The lovely surrounding gardens—named in honor of Renoir—have also been revitalized. An audioguide is included in the ticket price. ✉ *12 rue Cortot, Montmartre* ☎ *01–49–25–89–39* 🌐 *www.museedemontmartre.fr* 🎟 *€9.50* ⏲ *Daily 10–6* Ⓜ *Lamarck—Caulaincourt.*

Place du Tertre. Artists have peddled their wares in this square for centuries. Busloads of tourists have changed the atmosphere, but if you come off-season—when the air is chilly and the streets are bare—you can almost feel what is was like when up-and-coming Picassos lived in the houses, which today are given over to souvenir shops and cafés. ✉ *East end of Rue Norvin, Place du Tertre, Montmartre* Ⓜ *Abbesses.*

MARAIS

From swampy to swanky, the Marais has a fascinating history. Like an aging pop star, the *quartier* has remade itself many times, and today retains several identities. It's the city's epicenter of cool with hip boutiques, designer hotels, and art galleries galore; the hub of Paris's gay community; and, though fading, the nucleus of Jewish life. You could easily spend your entire visit to Paris in this neighborhood—there is that much to do.

TOP ATTRACTIONS

FAMILY Fodor's Choice ★ **Centre Pompidou.** Love it or hate it, the Pompidou is certainly a unique-looking building. Most Parisians have warmed to the industrial, Lego-like exterior that caused a scandal when it opened in 1977. Named after French president Georges Pompidou (1911–74), it was designed by then-unknowns Renzo Piano and Richard Rogers. The architects' claim to fame was putting the building's guts on the outside and color-coding them: water pipes are green, air ducts are blue, electrics are yellow, and things like elevators and escalators are red. Art from the 20th century to the present day is what you can find inside.

The Musée National d'Art Moderne (Modern Art Museum, entrance on Level 4) occupies the top two levels. Level 5 is devoted to modern art from 1905 to 1960, including major works by Matisse, Modigliani, Marcel Duchamp, and Picasso; Level 4 is dedicated to contemporary art from the '60s on, including video installations. The Galerie d'Enfants (Children's Gallery) on the mezzanine level has interactive exhibits designed to keep the kids busy. Outside, next to the museum's sloping plaza—where throngs of teenagers hang out (and where there's free Wi-Fi)—is the Atelier Brancusi. This small, airy museum contains four rooms reconstituting Brancusi's Montparnasse studios with works from all periods of his career. On the opposite side, in Place Igor-Stravinsky, is the Stravinsky fountain, which has 16 gyrating mechanical figures in primary colors, including a giant pair of ruby red lips. On the opposite side of Rue Rambuteau, on the wall at the corner of Rue Clairvaux and Passage Brantôme, is the appealingly bizarre mechanical brass-and-steel clock, *Le Défenseur de Temps*.

The Pompidou's permanent collection takes up a relatively small amount of the space when you consider this massive building's other features: temporary exhibition galleries, with a special wing for design and architecture; a highly regarded free reference library (there's often a queue of university students on Rue Renard waiting to get in); and the basement, which includes two cinemas, a theater, a dance space, and a small, free exhibition space.

On your way up the escalator, you'll have spectacular views of Paris, ranging from the Tour Montparnasse, to the left, around to the hilltop Sacré-Coeur on the right. The rooftop restaurant, Georges, is a romantic spot for dinner. Be sure to reserve a table near the window. ⊠ *Pl. Georges-Pompidou, Beaubourg/Les Halles* ☎ *01–44–78–12–33* 🌐 *www.centrepompidou.fr* 🎫 *€11–€13; free first Sun. of month* ⏲ *Wed.–Mon. 11–9* Ⓜ *Rambuteau.*

Fodor's Choice ★ **Musée Carnavalet.** If it has to do with Parisian history, it's here. A fascinating hodgepodge of artifacts and art, the collection ranges from the prehistoric canoes used by Parisii tribes to the furniture of the cork-lined bedroom where Marcel Proust labored over his evocative novels. Thanks to scores of paintings, nowhere else in Paris can you get such a precise picture of the city's evolution through the ages. The museum fills two adjacent mansions, the Hôtel Le Peletier de St-Fargeau and the Hôtel Carnavalet. The latter is a Renaissance jewel that in the mid-1600s became the home of writer Madame de Sévigné. Throughout her long life, Sévigné wrote hundreds of frank and funny letters to her daughter, giving an incomparable view of both public and private life during the time of Louis XIV. The museum offers a glimpse into her world, but the collection covers far more than just the 17th century. The exhibits on the Revolution are especially interesting, with scale models of guillotines and a replica of the Bastille prison carved from one of its stones. Louis XVI's prison cell is reconstructed along with mementos of his life, even medallions containing locks of his family's hair. Other impressive interiors are reconstructed from the Middle Ages through the rococo period and into Art Nouveau—showstoppers include the Fouquet jewelry shop and the Café de Paris's original furnishings. The sculpted garden at 16 rue des Francs-Bourgeois is open from April to the end of October. Extensive renovations, begun in 2013, may be ongoing; be prepared for room closures. ⊠ *23 rue de Sévigné, Marais* ☎ *01–44–59–58–58* 🌐 *www.carnavalet.paris.fr* 🎫 *Free; around €7 for temporary exhibitions* ⏲ *Tues.–Sun. 10–6* Ⓜ *St-Paul.*

Fodor's Choice ★ **Musée Picasso Paris.** This immensely popular museum rose phoenix-like in late 2014, when it finally reopened after an ambitious (and often controversial) five-year makeover that cost an estimated €52 million. Home to the world's largest public collection of Picasso's inimitable oeuvre, it now covers almost 54,000 square feet in two buildings: the regal 17th-century Hôtel Salé and a sprawling new structure in the back

One of the most beautiful examples of 17th-century town planning, Place des Vosges is a Parisian jewel constructed by King Henri IV.

garden that's dedicated to temporary exhibitions. Diego Giacometti's exclusively designed furnishings in the former are an added bonus.

The collection of 200,000-plus paintings, sculptures, drawings, documents, and other archival materials (much of it previously in storage for lack of space) spans the artist's entire career; and while it doesn't include his most recognizable works, it does contain many of the pieces treasured most by Picasso himself. The renovated museum (which now has more than double the dedicated public space) is split into three distinct areas. The first two floors cover Picasso's work from 1895 to 1972. The top floor illustrates his relationship to his favorite artists; landscapes, nudes, portraits, and still lifes taken from his private collection detail his "artistic dialogue" with Cézanne, Gauguin, Degas, Rousseau, Matisse, Braque, Renoir, Modigliani, Miró, and others. The basement centers around Picasso's workshops, with photographs and engravings, paintings, and sculptures that document or evoke key pieces created at the Bateau Lavoir, Château de Boisgeloup, Grands-Augustins, the Villa La Californie, and his farmhouse, Notre-Dame-de-Vie, in Mougins. With plenty of multimedia components and special activities that cater to kids, this is ideal for both children and adult art lovers alike.

■ TIP→ Try to avoid visiting on weekends, when the crowds are thickest. Buy tickets online (there's no extra charge) well in advance of your planned visit. ✉ *5 rue de Thorigny, Marais* ☎ *01–85–56–00–36* 🌐 *www.musee-picasso.fr* 🎫 *€11; free 1st Sun. of the month* 🕒 *Tues.–Fri. 11:30–6 (until 9 every 3rd Fri.), weekends 9:30–6* Ⓜ *St-Sébastien–Froissart.*

FAMILY Fodor's Choice ★ **Place des Vosges.** The oldest square in Paris and—dare we say it?—the most beautiful, Place des Vosges represents an early stab at urban planning. The precise proportions offer a placid symmetry, but things weren't always so calm here. Four centuries ago this was the site of the Palais des Tournelles, home to King Henry II and Queen Catherine de' Medici. The couple staged regular jousting tournaments, and Henry was fatally lanced in the eye during one of them in 1559. Catherine fled for the Louvre, abandoning her palace and ordering it destroyed. In 1612 it became Place Royal on the occasion of Louis XIII's engagement to Anne of Austria. Napoléon renamed it Place des Vosges to honor the northeast region of Vosges, the first in the country to pony up taxes to the Revolutionary government.

At the base of the 36 redbrick-and-stone houses—nine on each side of the square—is an arcaded, covered walkway lined with art galleries, shops, and cafés. There's also an elementary school, a synagogue (whose barrel roof was designed by Gustav Eiffel), and several chic hotels. The formal, gated garden's perimeter is lined with chestnut trees; inside are a children's play area and a fountain.

Aside from hanging out in the park, people come here to see the house of the man who once lived at No. 6—Victor Hugo, the author of *Les Misérables* and *Notre-Dame de Paris* (aka *The Hunchback of Notre-Dame*).

■ **TIP→ One of the best things about this park is that you're actually allowed to sit—or snooze or snack—on the grass during spring and summer.** There is no better spot in the Marais for a picnic: you can pick up fixings at the nearby street market on Thursday and Saturday mornings (it's on Boulevard Richard Lenoir between rues Amelot and St-Sabin). The most likely approach to Place des Vosges is from Rue de Francs-Bourgeois, the main shopping street. However, for a grander entrance walk along Rue St-Antoine until you get to Rue de Birague, which leads directly into the square. ✉ *Off Rue des Francs-Bourgeois, near Rue de Turenne, Marais* Ⓜ *Bastille, St-Paul.*

WORTH NOTING

Hôtel de Sully (*Hôtel de Béthune-Sully*). This early Baroque gem, built in 1624, is one of the city's loveliest *hôtels particuliers*. Like much of the area, it fell into ruin until the 1950s, when it was rescued by the administration of French historic monuments (the Centre des Monuments Nationaux), which is based here. The recently renovated headquarters aren't open to the public; however, you are welcome to enjoy the equally lovely garden. Stroll through it, past the Orangerie, to find a small passage into nearby Place des Vosges: Sully's best buddy, King Henri IV, would have lived there had he not been assassinated in 1610. An on-site bookstore (with a 17th-century ceiling of exposed wooden beams) sells specialized English-language guides to Paris. ✉ *62 rue St-Antoine, Marais* ☎ *01–44–61–21–50* 🌐 *www.sully.monuments-nationaux.fr* ⏲ *Garden and bookstore daily 9–7* Ⓜ *St-Paul.*

Maison de Victor Hugo. France's most famous scribe lived in this house on the northeast corner of Place des Vosges between 1832 and 1848. It's now a museum dedicated to the multitalented author of *Les Misérables*.

In Hugo's apartment on the second floor, you can see the tall desk, next to the short bed, where he began writing his masterwork *Les Miz* (as always, standing up). There are manuscripts and early editions of the novel on display, as well as others such as *The Hunchback of Notre-Dame*. You can see illustrations of Hugo's writings by other artists, including Bayard's rendering of the impish Cosette holding her giant broom (which has graced countless *Les Miz* T-shirts). The collection includes many of Hugo's own, sometimes macabre, ink drawings (he was a fine artist) and furniture from several of his homes. Particularly impressive is the room of carved and painted Chinese-style wooden panels that Hugo designed for the house of his mistress, Juliet Drouet, on the island of Guernsey, when he was exiled there for agitating against Napoléon III. Try to spot the intertwined Vs and Js (hint: look for the angel's trumpet in the left corner). The first floor is dedicated to temporary exhibitions that often have modern ties to Hugo's work. ✉ *6 pl. des Vosges, Marais* ☎ *01–42–72–10–16* 🌐 *www.musee-hugo.paris.fr* 🎫 *Free; €5–€7 for temporary exhibitions* ⏲ *Tues.–Sun. 10–6* Ⓜ *St-Paul.*

Maison Européenne de la Photographie (*Center for European Photography*). Much of the credit for the city's ascendancy as a hub of international photography goes to MEP and its director, Jean-Luc Monterosso, who also founded Paris's hugely successful Mois de la Photo festival (a biennial event held in November of even-numbered years). The MEP hosts up to four simultaneous exhibitions, changing about every three months. Shows feature the work of an international crop of photographers and video artists. Works by superstar Annie Leibovitz or designer-photographer Karl Lagerfeld may overlap with a collection of self-portraits by an up-and-coming Japanese artist. MEP often stages retrospectives of the classics (by Doisneau, Cartier-Bresson, Man Ray, and others) from its vast private collection. Programs are available in English, and English-language tours are sometimes given; check the website for details. ✉ *5 rue de Fourcy, Marais* ☎ *01–44–78–75–00* 🌐 *www.mep-fr.org* 🎫 *€8, free Wed. after 5* ⏲ *Wed.–Sun. 11–8* Ⓜ *St-Paul.*

Musée d'Art et d'Histoire du Judaïsme. This excellent museum traces the tempestuous history of French and European Jews through art and history. Housed in the refined 17th-century Hôtel St-Aignan, exhibits have good explanatory texts in English, but the free English audioguide adds another layer of insight; guided tours in English are also available on request. Highlights include 13th-century tombstones excavated in Paris; a wooden model of a destroyed Eastern European synagogue; a roomful of early paintings by Marc Chagall; and Christian Boltanski's stark, two-part tribute to Shoah (Holocaust) victims in the form of plaques on an outer wall naming the (mainly Jewish) inhabitants of the Hôtel St-Aignan in 1939, and canvas hangings with the personal data of the 13 residents who were deported and died in concentration camps. The rear-facing windows offer a view of the Jardin Anne Frank. To visit it, use the entrance on Impasse Berthaud, off Rue Beaubourg, just north of Rue Rambuteau. ✉ *71 rue du Temple, Marais* ☎ *01–53–01–86–60* 🌐 *www.mahj.org* 🎫 *€8; €10 with temporary exhibitions* ⏲ *Weekdays 11–6, Sun. 10–6* Ⓜ *Rambuteau, Hôtel de Ville.*

EASTERN PARIS

The Bastille used to be the star of this area, and a stop here—at the epicenter of the French Revolution—was a must. The small streets forking off Place de la Bastille still buzz at night, thanks to bars, music clubs, and the top-flight Opéra Bastille. But today the neighborhoods farther afield are the real draw, having evolved into some of Paris's top destinations. Canal St-Martin, once the down-and-out cousin on the northeastern border, is now trend-spotting central, brimming with funky bars, cafés, art galleries, and boutiques. The scene is similar to the south, on rues Oberkampf, St-Maur, and Jean-Pierre-Timbaud, where artists and small designers have set up shop, and where a substantial slice of the city's *bobo* (bourgeois-bohemian) contingent is buying up the no-longer-so-affordable apartments.

TOP ATTRACTIONS

Fodor's Choice ★ **Canal St-Martin.** This once-forgotten canal has morphed into one of the city's trendiest places to wander. A good time to come is Sunday afternoon, when the Quai de Valmy is closed to cars and some of the shops are open. Rent a bike at any of the many Vélib' stations, stroll along the banks, or go native and cuddle quai-side in the sunshine with someone special.

In 1802 Napoléon ordered the 4.3-km (2.7-mile) canal dug as a source of clean drinking water after cholera and other epidemics swept the city. When it finally opened 23 years later, it extended north from the Seine at Place de la Bastille to the Canal de l'Ourcq, near La Villette. Baron Haussmann later covered a 1.6-km (1-mile) stretch of it, along today's Boulevard Richard Lenoir. It nearly became a highway in the 1970s, before the city's urban planners regained their senses. These days you can take a boat tour from end to end through the canal's nine locks: along the way, the bridges swing or lift open. The drawbridge with four giant pulleys at Rue de Crimée, near La Villette, was a technological marvel when it debuted in 1885.

In recent years gentrification has transformed the once-dodgy canal, with artists taking over former industrial spaces and creating studios and galleries. The bar and restaurant scene is hipster central, and small designers have arrived, fleeing expensive rents in the Marais. To explore this evolving *quartier,* set out on foot: Start on the Quai de Valmy at Rue Faubourg du Temple (use the République métro stop). Here, at Square Frédéric Lemaître facing north, there is a good view of one of the locks (behind you the canal disappears underground). As you head north, detour onto side streets like Rue Beaurepaire, a fashionista destination with several "stock" (or surplus) shops for popular brands, some open on Sunday. Rues Lancry and Vinaigriers are lined with bars, restaurants, and small shops.

A swing bridge across the canal connects Lancry to the Rue de la Grange aux Belles, where you'll find the entrance to the massive Hôpital Saint-Louis, built in 1607 to accommodate plague victims and still a working hospital today. In front of you is the entrance to the chapel, which held its first Mass in July 1610, two months after the assassination of the hospital's patron, Henry IV. Stroll the grounds, flanked by the original brick-and-stone buildings with steeply sloping roofs. The peaceful courtyard garden is a neighborhood secret.

Back on Quai Valmy, browse more shops near the Rue des Récollets. Nearby is the Jardin Villemin, the 10e arrondissement's largest park (4.5 acres) on the former site of another hospital. The nighttime scene, especially in summer, is hopping with twentysomethings spilling out of cafés and bars and onto the canal banks. If you've made it this far, reward yourself with a fresh taco or burrito at the tiny and authentically Mexican El Nopal taqueria at 3 rue Eugène Varlin. Farther up, just past Place Stalingrad, is the Rotonde de la Villette, a lively square with restaurants and twin MK2 cinemas on either side of the canal, with a boat to ferry ticket holders across. **Canauxrama** (*www.canauxrama.com*) offers 2½-hour boat cruises through the locks (€17). Embarkation is at each end of canal: at Bassin de la Villette (*13 quai de la Loire, La Villette*) or Marina Arsenal (*50 bd. de la Bastille, Bastille*). ✉ *Canal St-Martin* Ⓜ *Jaurès (northern end) or République (southern end).*

Fodor's Choice ★ **Cimetière du Père-Lachaise.** Bring a red rose for "the Little Sparrow" Edith Piaf when you visit the cobblestone avenues and towering trees that make this 118-acre oasis of green perhaps the world's most famous cemetery. Named for Père François de la Chaise, Louis XIV's confessor, Père-Lachaise is more than just a who's who of celebrities. The Paris Commune's final battle took place here on May 28, 1871, when 147 rebels were lined up and shot against the Mur des Fédérés (Federalists' Wall) in the southeast corner.

Aside from the sheer aesthetic beauty of the cemetery, the main attraction is what (or who, more accurately) is belowground.

Two of the biggest draws are Jim Morrison's grave (with its own guard to keep Doors fans under control) and the life-size bronze figure of French journalist Victor Noir, whose alleged fertility-enhancing power accounts for the patches rubbed smooth by hopeful hands. Other significant grave sites include those of 12th-century French philosopher Pierre Abélard and his lover Héloïse; French writers Colette, Honoré de Balzac, and Marcel Proust; American writers Richard Wright, Gertrude Stein, and Alice B. Toklas; Irish writer Oscar Wilde; French actress Sarah Bernhardt; French composer Georges Bizet; Greek-American opera singer Maria Callas; Franco-Polish composer Frédéric Chopin; painters of various nationalities including Georges-Pierre Seurat, Camille Pissaro, Jean Auguste Dominique Ingres, Jacques-Louis David, Eugène Delacroix, Théodore Géricault, Amedeo Clemente Modigliani, and Max Ernst; French jazz violinist Stephane Grappelli; French civic planner Baron Haussmann; French playwright and actor Molière; and French singer Edith Piaf.

■ **TIP→ Pinpoint grave sites on the website before you come, but buy a map anyway outside the entrances—you'll still get lost, but that's part of the fun.** One of the best days to visit is on All Saints' Day (November 1), when Parisians bring flowers to adorn the graves of loved ones or favorite celebrities. ✉ *Entrances on Rue des Rondeaux, Bd. de Ménilmontant, and Rue de la Réunion, Père Lachaise* ☎ *01–55–25–82–10*

🌐 *www.pere-lachaise.com* ⏲ *Weekdays 8–6, Sat. 8:30–6, Sun. 9–6 (closes at 5:30 in winter)* Ⓜ *Gambetta, Philippe-Auguste, Père-Lachaise.*

Place de la Bastille. Almost nothing remains of the infamous Bastille prison, destroyed more than 225 years ago, though tourists still ask bemused Parisians where to find it. Until the late 1980s, there was little more to see here than a busy traffic circle ringing the Colonne de Juillet (July Column), a memorial to the victims of later uprisings in 1830 and 1848. The opening of the Opéra Bastille in 1989 rejuvenated the area, however, drawing art galleries, bars, and restaurants to the narrow streets, notably along Rue de Lappe—once a haunt of Edith Piaf—and Rue de la Roquette.

Before it became a prison, the Bastille St-Antoine was a defensive fortress with eight immense towers and a wide moat. It was built by Charles V in the late 14th century and transformed into a prison during the reign of Louis XIII (1610–43). Famous occupants included Voltaire, the Marquis de Sade, and the Man in the Iron Mask. On July 14, 1789, it was stormed by an angry mob that dramatically freed all of the remaining prisoners (there were only seven, including one lunatic), thereby launching the French Revolution. The roots of the revolt ran deep. Resentment toward Louis XVI and Marie-Antoinette had been building amid a severe financial crisis. There was a crippling bread shortage, and the free-spending monarch was blamed. When the king dismissed the popular finance minister, Jacques Necker, enraged Parisians took to the streets. They marched to Les Invalides, helping themselves to stocks of arms, then continued on to the Bastille. A few months later, what was left of the prison was razed—and 83 of its stones were carved into miniature Bastilles and sent to the provinces as a memento (you can see one of them in the Musée Carnavalet). The key to the prison was given to George Washington by Lafayette and has remained at Mount Vernon ever since. Today, nearly every major street demonstration in Paris—and there are many—passes through this square. ✉ *Bastille* Ⓜ *Bastille.*

WORTH NOTING

La Maison Rouge. One of the city's premier spaces for contemporary art, La Maison Rouge art foundation was established by former gallery owner Antoine de Galbert to fill a hole in the Parisian art world. Always edgy, often provocative, the foundation stages several temporary exhibitions each year in a cleverly renovated industrial space anchored by a central courtyard building that's painted bright red on the outside (hence the name). Past shows have included "*Tous Cannibales*," themed around cannibalism, and "Memories of the Future," a death-obsessed display featuring artists from Hieronymus Bosch to Damien Hirst. Check the website to see what's on. Stop by the Rose Bakery near the entrance: it's the latest Parisian outpost of the popular English café. ✉ *10 bd. de la Bastille, Bastille* ☎ *01–40–01–08–81* 🌐 *www.lamaisonrouge.org* 🎟 *€9* ⏲ *Wed. and Fri.–Sun. 11–7, Thurs. 11–9* Ⓜ *Quai de la Rapée/Bastille.*

THE LATIN QUARTER

The Quartier Latin is the heart of student Paris—and has been for more than 800 years. France's oldest university, La Sorbonne, was founded here in 1257, and the neighborhood takes its name from the fact that Latin was the common language of the students, who came from all over Europe. Today the area is full of cheap and cheerful cafés, bars, and shops.

TOP ATTRACTIONS

Fodor's Choice ★ **Musée de Cluny** (*Musée National du Moyen-Age [National Museum of the Middle Ages]*). Built on the ruins of Roman baths, the Hôtel de Cluny has been a museum since medievalist Alexandre Du Sommerard established his collection here in 1844. The ornate 15th-century mansion was created for the abbot of Cluny, leader of the mightiest monastery in France. Symbols of the abbot's power surround the building, from the crenellated walls that proclaimed his independence from the king, to the carved Burgundian grapes twining up the entrance that symbolize his valuable vineyards. The scallop shells (*coquilles St-Jacques*) covering the facade are a symbol of religious pilgrimage, another important source of income for the abbot; the well-traveled pilgrimage route to Spain once ran around the corner along Rue St-Jacques. The highlight of the museum's collection is the world-famous *Dame à la Licorne* (*Lady and the Unicorn*) tapestry series, woven in the 16th century, probably in Belgium, and now presented in refurbished surroundings. The vermillion tapestries (Room 13) are an allegorical representation of the five senses. In each, a unicorn and a lion surround an elegant young woman against an elaborate millefleur (literally, 1,000 flowers) background. The enigmatic sixth tapestry is thought to be either a tribute to a sixth sense, perhaps intelligence, or a renouncement of the other senses. "To my only desire" is inscribed at the top. The collection also includes the original sculpted heads of the *Kings of Israel and Judah* from Notre-Dame, decapitated during the Revolution and discovered in 1977 in the basement of a French bank. The *frigidarium* (Room 9) is a stunning reminder of the city's cold-water Roman baths; the soaring space, painstakingly renovated, houses temporary exhibits. Also notable is the pocket-size chapel (Room 20) with its elaborate Gothic ceiling. Outside, in Place Paul Painlevé, is a charming medieval-style garden where you can see flora depicted in the unicorn tapestries. The free audioguide in English is highly recommended. ✉ *6 pl. Paul-Painlevé, Latin Quarter* ☎ *01–53–73–78–00* 🌐 *www.musee-moyenage.fr* 🎫 *€8; €9 during temporary exhibitions; free first Sun. of month* ⏲ *Wed.–Mon. 9:15–5:45* Ⓜ *Cluny–La Sorbonne.*

WORTH NOTING

FAMILY **Institut du Monde Arabe.** This eye-catching metal-and-glass tower by architect Jean Nouvel cleverly uses metal diaphragms in the shape of square Arabic-style screens to work like a camera lens, opening and closing to control the flow of sunlight. The vast cultural center's layout is intended to reinterpret the traditional enclosed Arab courtyard. Inside, there are various spaces—among them a museum, inaugurated in 2012, that explores the culture and religion of the 22 Arab League member nations. With the addition of elements from the Louvre's holdings and private donors, the museum's impressive collection includes Islamic art, artifacts, ceramics, and textiles, which are displayed on four floors. There is also a performance space, a sound-and-image center, a library, and a bookstore. Temporary exhibitions usually have information and an audioguide in English. Glass elevators whisk you to the ninth floor, where you can sip mint tea in the rooftop café, Le Zyriab, while feasting on one of the best views in Paris. ✉ *1 rue des Fossés-St-Bernard, Latin Quarter* ☎ *01–40–51–38–38* 🌐 *www.imarabe.org* 🎫 *€8* ⏲ *Tues.–Thurs. 10–6, Fri. 10–9:30, weekends 10–7* Ⓜ *Cardinal Lemoine.*

Panthéon. Rome has St. Peter's, London has St. Paul's, and Paris has the Panthéon, whose enormous dome dominates the Left Bank. Built as the church of Ste-Geneviève, the patron saint of Paris, it was later converted to an all-star mausoleum for some of France's biggest names, including Voltaire, Zola, Dumas, Rousseau, and Hugo. Pierre and Marie Curie were reinterred here together in 1995. Begun in 1764, the building was almost complete when the French Revolution erupted. By then, architect Jacques-German Soufflot had died—supposedly from worrying that the 220-foot-high dome would collapse. He needn't have fretted: the dome was so perfect that Foucault used it in his famous pendulum test to prove the Earth rotates on its axis. Time, however, has taken its toll on the Panthéon, and the structure is now in the midst of an extensive, multiyear overhaul. The crypt and nave remain accessible to the public, but the pendulum won't return to its place of honor until 2016. ✉ *Pl. du Panthéon, Latin Quarter* ☎ *01–44–32–18–00* 🌐 *www.pantheon.monuments-nationaux.fr* 🎫 *€7.50* ⏲ *Apr.–Sept., daily 10–6:30; Oct.–Mar., daily 10–6* Ⓜ *Cardinal Lemoine; RER: Luxembourg.*

ST-GERMAIN-DES-PRÉS

If you had to choose the most classically Parisian neighborhood in Paris, this would be it. St-Germain-des-Prés has it all: genteel blocks lined with upscale art galleries, storied cafés, designer boutiques, and a fine selection of museums. Cast your eyes upward after dark and you may spy a frescoed ceiling in a tony apartment. These historic streets can get quite crowded, so mind your elbows and plunge in.

At the southern end of this district is the city's poshest park, the Jardin du Luxembourg, which is also home to the Musée du Luxembourg. This small museum plays host to excellent temporary exhibitions. The Musée Delacroix, in lovely Place Furstenburg, is home to a small collection of the Romantic master's works. Not far away is the stately Église St-Sulpice, where you can see two impressive Delacroix frescoes. Nearby in the 7e arrondissement, the star attraction is the Musée d'Orsay, home to a world-class collection of Impressionist paintings in a converted Belle Époque rail station on the Seine.

TOP ATTRACTIONS

FAMILY Fodor's Choice ★ **Carrefour de Buci.** Just behind the neighborhood's namesake St-Germain church, this colorful crossroads (*carrefour* means "intersection") was once a notorious Rive Gauche landmark. During the French Revolution, the army enrolled its first volunteers here. It was also here that thousands of royalists and priests lost their heads during the 10-month wave of public executions known as the Reign of Terror. There's certainly nothing sinister about the area today, though; brightly colored flowers are for sale alongside take-out ice cream and other sweet treats. Devotees of the superb, traditional bakery Carton (at 6 rue de Buci) line up for fresh breads and pastries (try the *pain aux raisins, tuiles* cookies, and *tarte de citron*). ✉ *Intersection of rues Mazarine, Dauphine, and de Buci, St-Germain-des-Prés* Ⓜ *Mabillon.*

Cour du Commerce St-André. Like an 18th-century engraving come to life, this charming street arcade is a remnant of *ancien* Paris with its uneven cobblestones, antique roofs, and old-world facades. Famed for its rabble-rousing inhabitants—journalist Jean-Paul Marat ran the Revolutionary newspaper *L'Ami du Peuple* at No. 8, and the agitator Georges Danton lived at No. 20—it is also home to Le Procope, Paris's oldest café. The passageway contains a turret from the 12th-century wall of Philippe-Auguste, which is visible through the windows of Un Dimanche à Paris, a chocolate shop–pastry atelier at No. 4. ✉ *Linking Bd. St-Germain and Rue St-André-des-Arts, St-Germain-des-Prés* Ⓜ *Odéon.*

Église St-Germain-des-Prés. Paris's oldest church was built to shelter a simple shard of wood, said to be a relic of Jesus' cross brought back from Spain in AD 542. Vikings came down the Seine and sacked the sanctuary, and Revolutionaries used it to store gunpowder. Yet the elegant building has defied history's abuses: its 11th-century Romanesque tower continues to be the central symbol of the neighborhood. The colorful 19th-century frescoes in the nave are by Hippolyte Flandrin, a pupil of the classical master Ingres; and the Saint Benoit chapel contains the tomb of philosopher René Descartes. Step inside for spiritual nourishment, or pause in the square to people-watch—there's usually a street musician tucked against the church wall, out of the wind. The church stages superb organ concerts and recitals. See the website for details. ✉ *Pl. St-Germain-des-Prés, St-Germain-des-Prés* ☎ *01–55–42–81–10* 🌐 *www.eglise-sgp.org* ⏲ *Daily 8–7:45* Ⓜ *St-Germain-des-Prés.*

FAMILY Fodor's Choice ★ **Jardin du Luxembourg.** Everything that is charming, unique, and befuddling about Parisian parks can be found in the Luxembourg Gardens: cookie-cutter trees, ironed-and-pressed walkways, sculpted flower beds, and immaculate emerald lawns meant for admiring, not necessarily for lounging. The tree- and bench-lined paths are a marvelous reprieve from the bustle of the two neighborhoods it borders: the Quartier Latin and St-Germain-des-Prés. Beautifully austere during the winter months, the garden grows intoxicating as spring brings blooming beds of daffodils, tulips, and hyacinths, and the circular pool teems with boats nudged along by children. The park's northern boundary is dominated by the Palais du Luxembourg, which houses the Sénat (Senate), one of two chambers that make up the Parliament.

The original inspiration for the gardens came from Marie de Medici, nostalgic for the Boboli Gardens of her native Florence. She is commemorated by the Fontaine de Medicis.

Continued on page 92

THE SEINE

No matter how you approach Paris—historically, geographically, or emotionally—the Seine flows through its heart, dividing the City of Light into two banks, the *Rive Droite* (Right Bank) and the *Rive Gauche* (Left Bank).

The Seine has long been used as a means for transportation and commerce and although there are no longer any factories along its banks, all manner of boats still ply the water. You'll see tugboats, fire and police boats, the occasional bobbing houseboat, and many kinds of tour boats; it might sound hokey, but there's really no better introduction to the City of Light than a boat cruise, and there are several options, depending on whether you want commentary on the sights or not. Many of the city's most famous attractions can be seen from the river, and are especially spectacular at dusk, as those celebrated lights of Paris glint against the sky.

FROM ILE DES CYGNES TO THE LOUVRE

Musée d'Orsay clock

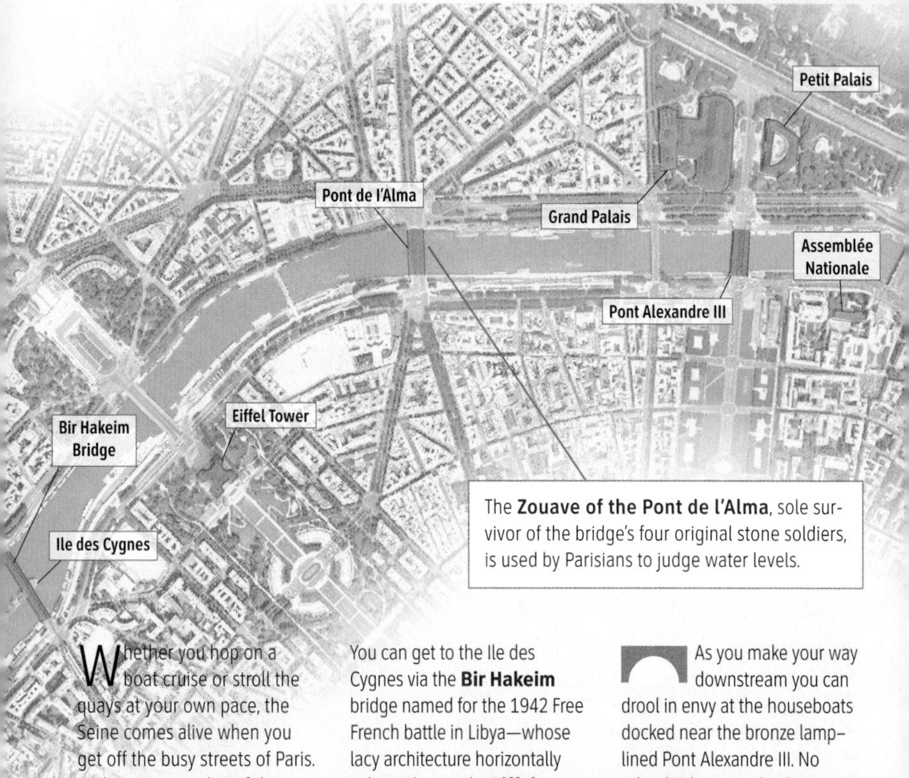

Petit Palais

Pont de l'Alma

Grand Palais

Assemblée Nationale

Pont Alexandre III

Eiffel Tower

Bir Hakeim Bridge

Ile des Cygnes

The **Zouave of the Pont de l'Alma**, sole survivor of the bridge's four original stone soldiers, is used by Parisians to judge water levels.

Whether you hop on a boat cruise or stroll the quays at your own pace, the Seine comes alive when you get off the busy streets of Paris. At the western edge of the city on the **Ile des Cygnes** (literally the Isle of Swans), a small version of the Statue of Liberty stands guard. Auguste Bartholdi designed the original statue, given as a gift from France to America in 1886, and in 1889 a group of Americans living in Paris installed this ¼ scale bronze replica—it's 37 feet, 8 inches tall.

You can get to the Ile des Cygnes via the **Bir Hakeim** bridge named for the 1942 Free French battle in Libya—whose lacy architecture horizontally echoes the nearby **Eiffel Tower**. You might recognize the view of the bridge from the movie *Last Tango in Paris.*

As you make your way downstream you can drool in envy at the houseboats docked near the bronze lamp-lined Pont Alexandre III. No other bridge over the Seine epitomizes the fin-de-siècle frivolity of the Belle Epoque: It seems as much created of cake frosting and sugar sculptures as of stone and iron, and makes quite the backdrop for fashion shoots and weddings. The elaborate decorations include Art Nouveau lamps, cherubs, nymphs, and winged horses at either end. The bridge was built, like the Grand Palais and Petit Palais nearby, for the 1900 World's Fair.

Along the banks of the Seine

Bouquinistes

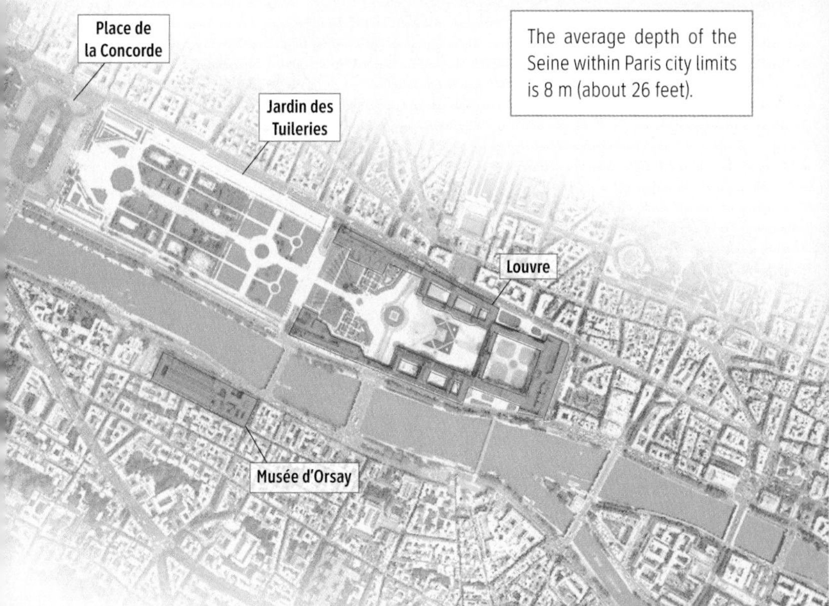

Place de la Concorde

Jardin des Tuileries

Louvre

Musée d'Orsay

The average depth of the Seine within Paris city limits is 8 m (about 26 feet).

Past the dome of the Église du Dôme is the 18th-century neoclassical façade of the **Assemblée Nationale**, the palace that houses the French Parliament. Across the river stands the **Place de la Concorde.** Also look for the great railway station clocks of the Musée d'Orsay that once allowed writer Anaïs Nin to co-ordinate her lovers' visits to her houseboat, moored below the Tuileries. The palatial **Louvre** museum, on the Right Bank, seems to go on and on as you continue up the Seine.

PERFECT PICNIC PLACES

Paris abounds with romantic spots to pause for a picnic or a bottle of wine, but the Seine has some of the best.

Try scouting out a place on the point of Ile St-Louis; at sunset you can watch the sun slip beneath receding arches of stone bridges.

The long, low quays of the Left Bank, with its public sculpture work, are perfect for an alfresco lunch.

FROM PONT DES ARTS TO JARDIN DES PLANTES

At the water's edge.

Pont des Arts
Pont Neuf
Châtelet Theatres
Hotel de Ville
Institut de France
Ile de la Cité
Conciergerie
Notre-Dame

The Institut de France

Parisians love to linger on the elegant **Pont des Arts** footbridge that streches between the palatial Louvre museum and the Institut de France. Napoléon commissioned the original cast-iron bridge with nine arches; it was rebuilt in 1984 with seven arches.

Five carved stone arches of the **Pont Neuf**—the name means "new bridge" but it actually dates from 1605 and is the oldest bridge in Paris—connect the Left Bank to the Ile de la Cité. Another seven arches connect the Ile and the Right Bank. The pale gray curving balustrades include a row of stone heads; some say they're caricatures of King Henry IV's ministers, glaring down at the river.

On the Right Bank at the end of the Ile de la Cité is the **Hôtel de Ville (City Hall)**—this area was once the main port of Paris, crowded with boats delivering everything from wood and produce to visitors and slaves.

Medieval turrets rise up from **Ile de la Cité,** part of the original royal palace; the section facing the Right Bank includes the **Conciergerie**, where Marie Antoinette was imprisoned in 1793 before her execution.

PARIS PLAGE

Paris Plage, literally Paris Beach, is Mayor Bertrand Delanoë's summer gift to Parisians and visitors. In August the roads along the Seine are closed, tons of sand are brought in and decorated with palm trees, and a slew of activities are organized, from free early-morning yoga classes to evening samba and swimming (not in the Seine, but in the fabulous Josephine Baker swimming pool). Going topless is discouraged, but hammocks, kids' playgrounds, rock-climbing, and cafés keep everyone entertained.

View of the Seine and the Pont des Arts

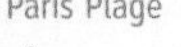

Paris Plage

Notre-Dame

Also on the Ile de la Cité is the cathedral of **Notre-Dame,** a stunning sight from the water. From the side it looks almost like a great boat sailing down the Seine.

As you pass the end of the island, you'll notice a small grated window: this is the evocative Deportation Memorial.

Next to the Ile de la Cite is the lovely residential **Ile St-Louis**; keep an eye out for the "proper" depth measuring stick on Ile St-Louis, near the Tour d'Argent restaurant.

Sightseeing boats turn near the public sculpture garden at the **Jardin des Plantes**, where you'll get a view of the huge national library, **Bibliothèque François Mitterrand**—the four towers look like opened books. Moored in the Seine near the bibliothèque is the Josephine Baker swimming pool with its retractable roof. Paris used to have several floating pools, including the elaborate Piscine Deligny, which was used in the Paris Olympics in 1924; it inexplicably sank in 1993.

Ile St-Louis

Jardin des Plantes

Bibliothéque Francois Mitterand

Les Marionettes du Théâtre du Luxembourg is a timeless attraction, where, on weekends at 11 and 3:15 and Wednesday at 3:15 (hours may vary), you can catch classic *guignols* (marionette shows) for €4.80. The wide-eyed kids might be the real attraction—their expressions of utter surprise, despair, and glee have fascinated the likes of Henri Cartier-Bresson and François Truffaut. The park also has a merry-go-round, swings, and pony rides; the bandstand hosts free concerts on summer afternoons.

Check out the rotating photography exhibits hanging on the perimeter fence near the entrance on the Boulevard St-Michel and Rue Vaugirard.

■TIP→ If the grass is en repos, a nice way of saying "stay off," feel free to move the green chairs around to create a picnic spot or people-watching perch.

If you want to burn off that breakfast *pain au chocolat,* there's a well-maintained trail around the perimeter that is frequented by gentrified joggers. If you're looking for a familiar face, one of the original (miniature) casts of the Statue of Liberty was installed in the gardens in 1906.

Gendarmes regularly walk the grounds to ensure park rules are enforced; follow guidelines posted on entry gates. ✉ *Bordered by Bd. St-Michel and Rues de Vaugirard, de Medicis, Guynemer, and Auguste-Comte, St-Germain-des-Prés* 🎫 *Free* 🕒 *Daily 7:30–dusk (depending on season)* Ⓜ *Odéon; RER: B Luxembourg.*

FAMILY
Fodor's Choice ★

Musée d'Orsay. Opened in 1986, this gorgeously renovated Belle Époque train station displays a world-famous collection of Impressionist and Postimpressionist paintings on three floors. To visit the exhibits in a roughly chronologic manner, start on the first floor, take the escalators to the top, and end on the second. If you came to see the biggest names here, head straight for the top floor and work your way down. English audioguides and free color-coded museum maps (both available just past the ticket booths) will help you plot your route.

Ground floor: Galleries off the main alley feature early works by Manet and Cézanne in addition to pieces by masters such as Delacroix and Ingres. Later works by the likes of Toulouse-Lautrec are found in Salle 10. The Pavillon Amont has Courbet's masterpieces *L'Enterrement à Ornans* and *Un Atelier du Peintre*. Hanging in Salle 14 is Édouard Manet's *Olympia*, a painting that pokes fun at the fashion for all things Greek and Roman (his nubile subject is a 19th-century courtesan, not a classical goddess).

Top floor: Impressionism gets going here, with iconic works by Degas, Pissarro, Sisley, and Renoir. Don't miss Monet's series on the cathedral at Rouen and, of course, samples of his water lilies. Other selections by these artists are housed in galleries on the ground floor.

Second floor: An exquisite collection of sculpture as well as Art Nouveau furniture and decorative objects is housed here. There are rare surviving works by Hector Guimard (designer of the swooping green Paris métro entrances), plus Lalique and Tiffany glassware. Postimpressionist galleries include work by van Gogh and Gauguin, while Neo-Impressionist galleries highlight Seurat and Signac.

■ TIP→ Lines here are among the worst in Paris. Book ahead online or buy a Museum Pass, then go directly to entrance C. Otherwise, go early. Thursday evening the museum is open until 9:45 pm and less crowded. The elegant Musée d'Orsay Restaurant once served patrons of the 1900 World's Fair; Café du Lion offers quick fare on the ground floor by the entrance; there's also a café and a self-service cafeteria on the top floor just after the Cézanne galleries. Don't miss the views of Sacré-Coeur from the balcony—this is the Paris that inspired the Impressionists. The d'Orsay is closed Monday, unlike the Pompidou and the Louvre, which are closed Tuesday. ✉ *1 rue de la Légion d'Honneur, St-Germain-des-Prés* ☎ *01–40–49–48–14* 🌐 *www.musee-orsay.fr* 🎟 *€11; €8.50 after 4:30, except Thurs. after 6* ⏲ *Tues., Wed., and Fri.–Sun. 9:30–6, Thurs. 9:30 am–9:45 pm* Ⓜ *Solférino; RER: Musée d'Orsay.*

WORTH NOTING

Musée Delacroix. The final home of artist Eugène Delacroix (1798–1863) contains only a small collection of his sketches and drawings. But you can check out the lovely studio he had built in the large garden at the back to work on frescoes he created for St-Sulpice Church, where they remain on display today. The museum also plays host to temporary exhibitions, such as Delacroix's experiments with photography. France's foremost Romantic painter had the good luck to live on Place Furstenberg, one of the smallest, most romantic squares in Paris: seeing it is reason enough to come. ✉ *6 rue Furstenberg, St-Germain-des-Prés* ☎ *01–44–41–86–50* 🌐 *www.musee-delacroix.fr* 🎟 *€6; €7.50 with temporary exhibitions; €12 with same-day admission to the Louvre* ⏲ *Wed.–Mon. 9:30–5* Ⓜ *St-Germain-des-Prés.*

WESTERN PARIS

Meet Paris at its most prim and proper. This genteel area is a study in smart urban planning, with classical architecture and newer construction cohabitating as easily as the haute bourgeoisie inhabitants mix with their expat neighbors. There's no shortage of celebrities seeking some peace and quiet here, but you're just as likely to find well-heeled families who decamped from the center of the city in search of a spacious apartment. Passy, once a separate village and home to American ambassadors Benjamin Franklin and Thomas Jefferson, was incorporated into the city in 1860 under Napoléon III.

TOP ATTRACTIONS

Fodor's Choice ★ **Fondation Louis Vuitton.** Rising up out of the Bois de Boulogne like a magnificent ship sporting billowing crystal sails, Frank Gehry's new contemporary-art museum and cultural center is the most captivating addition to the Parisian skyline since the unveiling of the Centre Pompidou in 1977. Commissioned by Bernard Arnault (chairman and CEO of luxury-goods conglomerate LVMH), it houses Arnault's substantial private collection, including pieces by Pierre Huyghe, Gerhard Richter, Thomas Schütte, Ellsworth Kelly, Bertrand Lavier, Taryn Simon, Sarah Morris, and Christian Boltanski, among others. La Fondation Louis Vuitton also hosts extensive temporary exhibitions, like the mesmerizing light installations of Danish-Icelandic artist Olafur Eliasson.

Le Frank, the pricey on-site restaurant overseen by Michelin-starred chef Jean-Louis Nomicos, is rapidly gaining fans for its mix of French and international cuisine. The museum is a 12-minute walk from Les Sablons métro on Line 1; alternatively, you can catch the Fondation shuttle (€1), which leaves every 10 to 15 minutes from Avenue de Friedland at Place de l'Étoile. ✉ *8 av. du Mahatma Gandhi, Western Paris* ☎ *01–40–69–96–00* 🌐 *www.fondationlouisvuitton.fr* 🎫 *€9, €14 during temporary exhibitions. includes entrance to Jardin d'Acclimatation* ⏲ *Mon., Wed., and Thurs. noon–7, Fri. noon–11, weekends 11–8* Ⓜ *Les Sablons.*

Fodor's Choice ★ **Musée Marmottan Monet.** A few years ago the underrated Marmottan tacked "Monet" onto its official name—and justly so, as this is the largest collection of the artist's works anywhere. More than 100 pieces, donated by his son Michel, occupy a specially built basement gallery in an elegant 19th-century mansion, which was once the hunting lodge of the Duke de Valmy. Among them you can find such works as the *Cathédrale de Rouen* series (1892–96) and *Impression: Soleil Levant* (*Impression: Sunrise,* 1872), the painting that helped give the Impressionist movement its name. Other exhibits include letters exchanged by Impressionist painters Berthe Morisot and Mary Cassatt. Upstairs, the mansion still feels like a graciously decorated private home. Empire furnishings fill the salons overlooking the Jardin du Ranelagh on one side and the private yard on the other. There's also a captivating room of illuminated medieval manuscripts. To best understand the collection's context, buy an English-language catalog in the museum shop on your way in. ✉ *2 rue Louis-Boilly, Passy-Auteuil* ☎ *01–44–96–50–33* 🌐 *www.marmottan.fr* 🎫 *€11* ⏲ *Wed. and Fri.–Sun. 10–6, Thurs. 10–9* Ⓜ *La Muette.*

WHERE TO EAT

A new wave of culinary confidence has been running through one of the world's great food cities and spilling over both banks of the Seine. Whether cooking up *grand-mère*'s roast chicken and *riz au lait* or placing a whimsical hat of cotton candy atop wild-strawberry-and-rose ice cream, Paris chefs have been breaking free from the tyranny of tradition and following their passions.

Emblematic of this movement is the proliferation of trained bistro chefs who have opened their own restaurants. Among the newcomers to the *bistronomique* scene are David Rathgeber, who left Benoît to take over the chic Montparnasse bistro L'Assiette; Mickaël Gaignon, a veteran of Pierre Gagnaire and Le Pré Catelan who now runs the Marais bistro Le Gaigne; and Stéphane Marcouzzi, who was maître d'hôtel at Guy Savoy's Le Cap Vernet before opening L'Epigramme in St-Germain with chef Aymeric Kräml, and now L'Epicuriste, in the 15th arrondissement.

But self-expression is not the only driving force behind the current changes. A traditional high-end restaurant can be prohibitively expensive to operate. As a result, more casual bistros and cafés, which often have lower operational costs and higher profit margins, have become attractive businesses for even top chefs.

Use the coordinate (1:B3) at the end of each listing to locate a site on the corresponding map.

AROUND THE EIFFEL TOWER

$$ MODERN FRENCH Fodor's Choice ★

Abri. This tiny storefront restaurant's well-deserved popularity has much to do with chef Katsuaki Okiyama's fresh and imaginative food, the friendly servers, and great prices. A veteran of Taillevent and Robuchon, Okiyama works from a small open kitchen behind a zinc bar, putting forth skillfully prepared dishes, like lemon-marinated mackeral topped with micro-thin slices of beet with honey vinaigrette, succulent duck breast with vegetables au jus, or a scrumptious pumpkin soup with fragrant coffee cream. With food this good, and prices to match (€25 at lunch, €40 for a four-course dinner) be sure to reserve early. *Average main: €22 92 rue du Faubourg-Poissonnière, 10e, Canal St-Martin 01–83–97–00–00 Closed Sun. and Mon. Reservations essential Poissonnière, Cadet 1:F2.*

$$$$ FRENCH FUSION Fodor's Choice ★

Hiramatsu. In this Art Deco dining room near Trocadéro, Yoshiaki Ito continues his variations on the subtly Japanese-inspired French cuisine of restaurant namesake Hiroyuki Hiramatsu, who still sometimes works the kitchen. Luxury ingredients feature prominently in dishes such as thin slices of lamb with onion jam and thyme-and-truffle-spiked jus, or an unusual pot-au-feu of oysters with foie gras and black truffle. For dessert, a mille-feuille of caramelized apples comes with rosemary sorbet. Helpful sommeliers will guide you through the staggering wine list, with more than 1,000 different bottles to choose from. There's no way to get away cheaply, so save this for a special occasion, when you might be tempted to order a carte-blanche menu for €115 (lunch menus at €48). *Average main: €50 52 rue de Longchamp, 16e, Trocadéro 01–56–81–08–80 www.hiramatsu.co.jp/fr Closed weekends, Aug., and 1 wk at Christmas Reservations essential Trocadéro 1:A3.*

$$$$ FRENCH FUSION

Il Vino. It might seem audacious to present hungry diners with nothing more than a wine list, but the gamble is paying off for Enrico Bernardo at his wine-centric restaurant with a branch in Courchevel, in the French Alps. This charismatic Italian left the George V to oversee a dining room where food plays second fiddle (in status, not quality). The hip decor—plum-color banquettes, body-hugging white chairs, a few high tables—attracts a mostly young clientele that's happy to play the game by ordering one of the blind, multicourse tasting menus. The €95 menu, with four dishes and four wines, is a good compromise that might bring you a white Mâcon with saffron risotto, crisp Malvasia with crabmeat and black radish, a full-bodied red from Puglia with Provençal-style lamb, sherry-like *vin jaune* d'Arbois with aged Comté cheese, and sweet Jurançon with berry crumble. You can also order individual wine-food combinations à la carte or pick a bottle straight from the cellar and ask for a meal to match. *Average main: €40 13 bd. de la Tour-Maubourg, 7e, Invalides 01–44–11–72–00 www.*

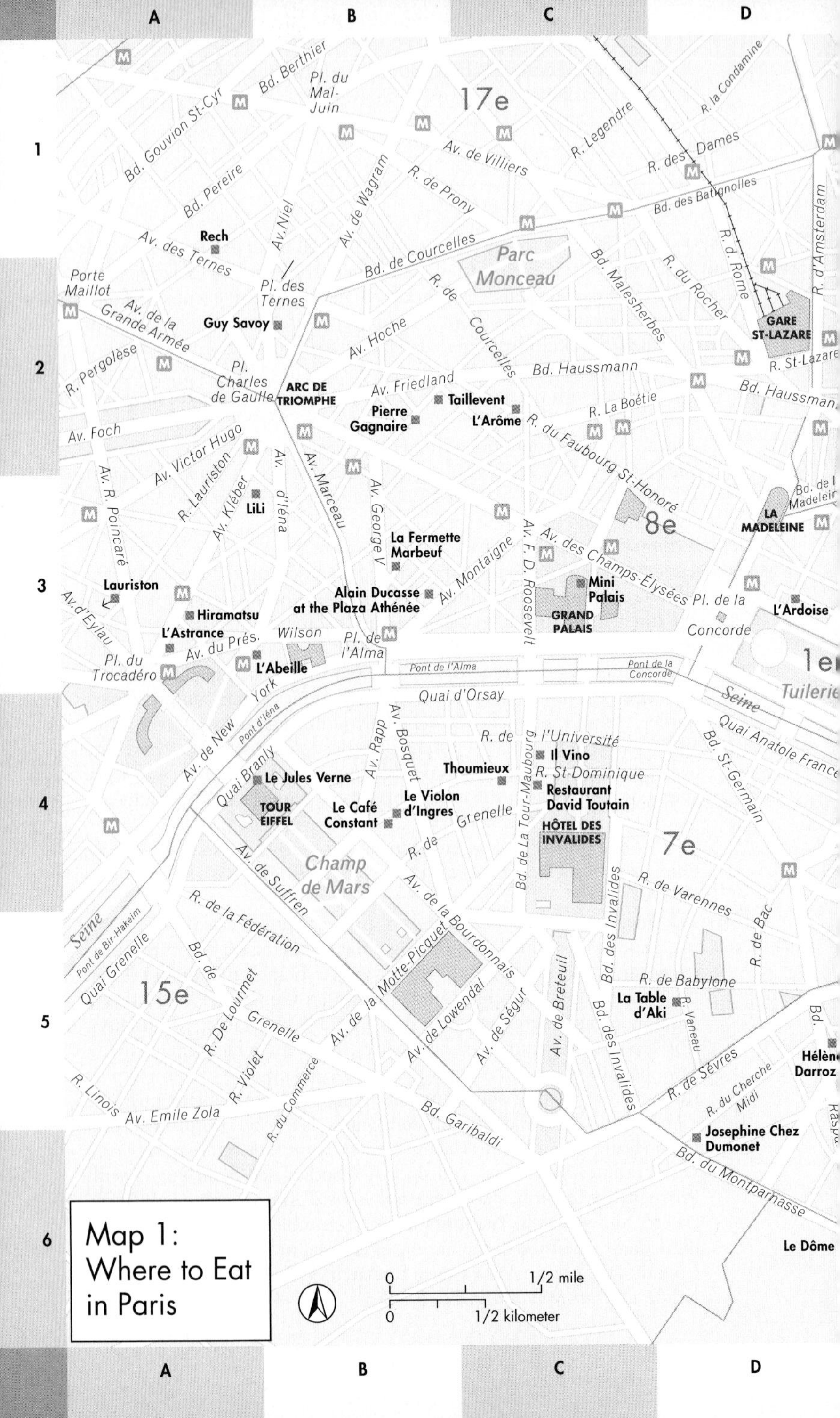

Map 1: Where to Eat in Paris

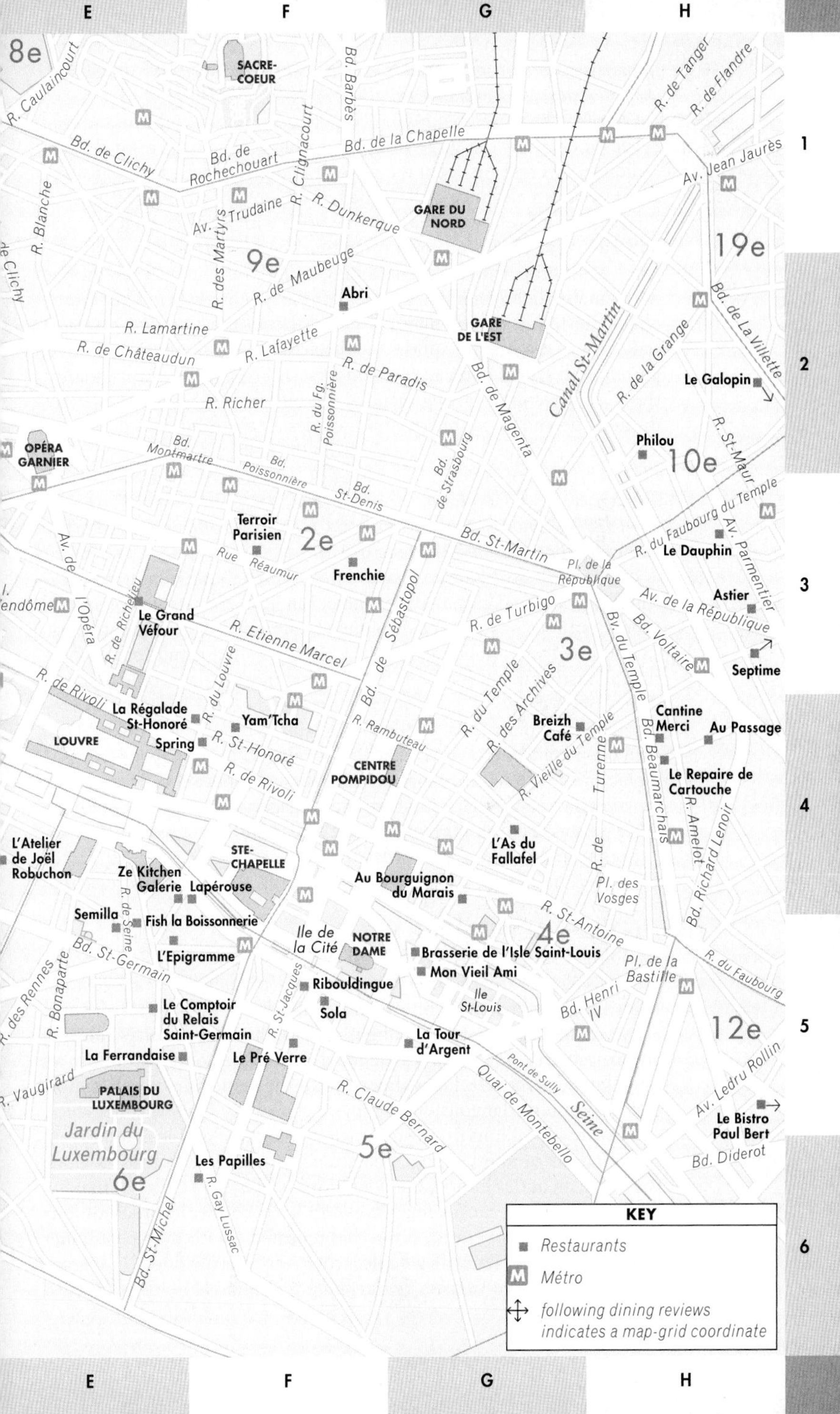

E
F
G
H
1
2
3
4
5
6
8e
9e
19e
10e
2e
3e
4e
12e
5e
6e
SACRE-COEUR
GARE DU NORD
GARE DE L'EST
OPÉRA GARNIER
LOUVRE
CENTRE POMPIDOU
STE-CHAPELLE
NOTRE DAME
PALAIS DU LUXEMBOURG
Jardin du Luxembourg
Ile de la Cité
Ile St-Louis
Seine
Canal St-Martin
Abri
Le Galopin
Philou
Terroir Parisien
Frenchie
Le Dauphin
Astier
Septime
Le Grand Véfour
La Régalade St-Honoré
Yam'Tcha
Spring
Breizh Café
Cantine Merci
Au Passage
Le Repaire de Cartouche
L'As du Fallafel
L'Atelier de Joël Robuchon
Ze Kitchen Galerie
Lapérouse
Au Bourguignon du Marais
Semilla
Fish la Boissonnerie
L'Epigramme
Brasserie de l'Isle Saint-Louis
Mon Vieil Ami
Ribouldingue
Sola
Le Comptoir du Relais Saint-Germain
La Ferrandaise
Le Pré Verre
La Tour d'Argent
Le Bistro Paul Bert
Les Papilles
R. Caulaincourt
Bd. de Clichy
R. Blanche
Bd. de Rochechouart
Bd. Barbès
R. Clignancourt
Bd. de la Chapelle
R. de Tanger
R. de Flandre
Av. Jean Jaurès
Av. Trudaine
R. Dunkerque
R. des Martyrs
R. de Maubeuge
R. Lamartine
R. de Châteaudun
R. Lafayette
R. de Paradis
R. du Fg. Poissonnière
R. Richer
Bd. de Magenta
R. de la Grange
Bd. de La Villette
R. St-Maur
Bd. Montmartre
Bd. Poissonnière
Bd. St-Denis
Bd. de Strasbourg
Bd. St-Martin
Pl. de la République
R. du Faubourg du Temple
Av. Parmentier
Av. de l'Opéra
Rue Réaumur
R. de Richelieu
R. Etienne Marcel
Bd. de Sébastopol
R. de Turbigo
Av. de la République
Bd. Voltaire
Bv. du Temple
R. de Rivoli
R. du Louvre
R. St-Honoré
R. Rambuteau
R. du Temple
R. des Archives
R. Vieille du Temple
R. de Turenne
Bd. Beaumarchais
R. Amelot
Bd. Richard Lenoir
Pl. des Vosges
R. St-Antoine
Pl. de la Bastille
R. du Faubourg
Bd. Henri IV
R. de Seine
Bd. St-Germain
R. des Rennes
R. Bonaparte
R. St-Jacques
R. Vaugirard
R. Claude Bernard
Pont de Sully
Quai de Montebello
Av. Ledru Rollin
Bd. Diderot
Bd. St-Michel
R. Gay Lussac
KEY
Restaurants
Métro
following dining reviews indicates a map-grid coordinate

ilvinobyenricobernardo.com ⏲ *Closed Sun. and Mon. No lunch Sat.* ✍ *Reservations essential* Ⓜ *Invalides* ✥ *1:C4.*

$$$$ MODERN FRENCH Fodor's Choice ★

✕ **L'Abeille.** The name conjures up Napoléon's imperial emblem, the honeybee (adopted by the emperor's grandnephew, who once resided in the building). Everything, from the dove-gray decor to the sparkling silver, speaks of quiet elegance—all the better to highlight a masterful cuisine: "harlequin" of yellow, red, and white beets with a ginger-tinged yogurt and aloe vera emulsion; Breton langoustine in a cinnamon-perfumed gelée, with grapefruit pulp and a ginger- and Tahitian vanilla–infused mayonnaise; lightly caramelized scallops in an ethereal cloud of white-chocolate foam; tender fillet of wild duck with a tart-sweet apricot reduction. Desserts are subtle and surprising, like the apple Reinette, paired with fennel and candied lemon zest. For cuisine of this quality, the €225 six-course tasting menu is not outlandish. Service is friendly, discrete, devoid of snobbery, and includes all the flourishes that make a dining experience unforgettable, from the first flute of Champagne to the parting gift of—what else?—a jar of honey. Ⓢ *Average main: €100* ✉ *Paris Shangri-La Hotel, 10 av. d'Iéna, 16e, Trocadéro* ☎ *01–53–67–19–90* 🌐 *www.shangri-la.com* ⏲ *Closed Sun. and Mon. No lunch* ✍ *Reservations essential* Ⓜ *Iéna* ✥ *1:B3.*

$$$$ MODERN FRENCH Fodor's Choice ★

✕ **L'Astrance.** Pascal Barbot rose to fame thanks to his restaurant's reasonable prices and casual atmosphere, but after the passage of several years, Astrance has become resolutely haute. There's no à la carte; you can choose from a lunch menu for €70, a seasonal menu for €150, or the full tasting menu for €230 (this is what most people come for). His dishes often draw on Asian ingredients, as in grilled lamb with miso-lacquered eggplant and a palate-cleansing white sorbet spiked with chili pepper and lemongrass. Each menu also comes at a (considerably) higher price with wines to match each course. Barbot's cooking has such an ethereal quality that it's worth the considerable effort of booking a table—you should start trying at least two months in advance. Ⓢ *Average main: €120* ✉ *4 rue Beethoven, 16e, Trocadéro* ☎ *01–40–50–84–40* ⏲ *Closed Sat.–Mon., 1 wk in Nov., and Aug.* ✍ *Reservations essential* Ⓜ *Passy* ✥ *1:A3.*

$$$ MODERN FRENCH Fodor's Choice ★

✕ **La Table d'Aki.** Did the stars align during our meal, or could it be that La Table d'Aki actually *is* the most perfect restaurant in Paris? Set in a quiet, aristocratic *quartier* near the Musée Rodin, its pale celadon walls, crisp white linen, and restrained lighting add up to a simple elegance, all the better to highlight chef Akihiro Horikoshi's thrilling cuisine centered on the sea. Amazingly, Horikoshi works all alone in an open kitchen while 16 lucky diners await the next course: lush, simple dishes like plump langoustine shimmering in a silky shallot-fennel sauce, or delicate medallions of sole in a mellow red-wine-and-leek reduction. In the hands of another chef, the attempt to create these feasts alone would be an act of hubris, but chef Horikoshi is only guilty of making more unrepentant fans: some have even been known to order all four entrées at one sitting or toast the chef repeatedly with their postdinner cognac, and all practically genuflect their way out the door. Ⓢ *Average main: €32* ✉ *49 rue Vaneau, 7e, Invalides* ☎ *01–45–44–43–48* ⏲ *Closed*

Sun., Mon., 2 wks in Feb., and Aug. *Reservations essential* M *Saint Francis–Xavier* ⊕ *1:D5.*

$ BISTRO

Le Café Constant. Parisians are a nostalgic bunch, which explains the popularity of this down-to-earth venue from esteemed chef Christian Constant. This is a relatively humble bistro with cream-color walls, red banquettes, and wooden tables, and you'll often see Constant himself perched at the bar at the end of lunch service. The menu reads like a French cookbook from the 1970s—who cooks veal *cordon bleu* these days?—but with Constant overseeing the kitchen, the dishes taste even better than before. There's delicious and creamy lentil soup with morsels of foie gras, and the artichoke salad comes with fresh—not bottled or frozen—hearts. A towering *vacherin* (meringue layered with ice cream) might bring this delightfully retro meal to a close. On weekdays there is a bargain lunch menu for €16 (two courses) or €23 (three courses). $ *Average main: €16* ✉ *139 rue St-Dominique, 7e, Around the Eiffel Tower* ☎ *01–47–53–73–34* 🌐 *www.cafeconstant.com* *Reservations not accepted* M *Métro École Militaire; Métro or RER: Pont de l'Alma* ⊕ *1:B4.*

$$$$ MODERN FRENCH

Le Jules Verne. Alain Ducasse doesn't set his sights low, so it was no real surprise when he took over this prestigious dining room on the second floor of the Eiffel Tower and had designer Patrick Jouin give the room a neo-futuristic look in shades of brown. Sauces and pastries are prepared in a kitchen below the Champ de Mars before being whisked up the elevator to the kitchen, which is overseen by young chef Pascal Féraud. Most accessible is the €98 lunch menu (weekdays only), which brings you à la carte dishes in slightly smaller portions. Spend more (about €185 to €230 per person without drinks) and you'll be entitled to more lavish dishes such as lobster with celery root and black truffle, and fricassee of Bresse chicken with crayfish. For dessert the kitchen reinterprets French classics, as in an unsinkable pink grapefruit soufflé with grapefruit sorbet. Book months ahead or try your luck at the last minute. $ *Average main: €82* ✉ *Tour Eiffel, south pillar, Av. Gustave Eiffel, 7e, Around the Eiffel Tower* ☎ *01–45–55–61–44* 🌐 *www.lejulesverne-paris.com* *Reservations essential* *Jacket and tie* M *Bir-Hakeim* ⊕ *1:B4.*

$$$$ MODERN FRENCH

Le Violon d'Ingres. Following in the footsteps of Joël Robuchon and Alain Senderens, Christian Constant gave up the Michelin-star chase in favor of relatively accessible prices and a packed dining room (book at least a week ahead). And with Grégory Gbiorczyk in charge of the kitchen here, Constant can dash among his four restaurants on this street, making sure the hordes are happy. Why wouldn't they be? The food is sophisticated and the atmosphere is lively; you can even find signature dishes like the almond-crusted sea bass with rémoulade (a buttery caper sauce), alongside game and scallops (in season), and comforting desserts like *pots de crème* and chocolate tart. With wines starting at around €35 (and a €49 lunch menu on weekdays) this is a wonderful place for a classic yet informal French meal. $ *Average main: €36* ✉ *135 rue St-Dominique, 7e, Around the Eiffel Tower* ☎ *01–45–55–15–05* 🌐 *www.leviolondingres.com* *Reservations essential* M *École Militaire* ⊕ *1:B4.*

$$$$ FRENCH FUSION Fodor's Choice ★ **Restaurant David Toutain.** Youthful David Toutain is often called a prodigy, a status applied sparingly in Paris and in this case well deserved. Although his approach may be exasperatingly conceptual for some, others find his earthy, surprising, and inspired concoctions utterly thrilling. Each dish is a lesson in contrasts—of temperature, texture, and flavor—as well as a feat of composition: briny oysters, brussels sprouts, and foie gras in a warm potato consommé; creamy raw oysters with tart kiwi and yuzu; crispy pork chips alongside velvety smoked potato puree. Toutain has a particular soft spot for root vegetables and truffles, which he sprinkles liberally throughout dishes like salsify broth with lardo and black truffle. The €42 lunch menu is a great way to sample a unique and challenging cuisine that changes daily. *Average main: €40 29 rue Surcouf, 7e, Around the Eiffel Tower 01–45–50–11–10 www.davidtoutain.com Closed weekends Reservations essential M Invalides, La Tour–Maubourg 1:C4.*

$$$$ BRASSERIE **Thoumieux.** Former Crillon chef Jean-François Piège and Thierry Costes, of the fashionable brasserie clan that created Café Marly and Le Georges, are behind the revival of this old-world bistro. The space has thankfully preserved much of its vintage character, with globe lights and etched mirrors. Despite its location in the sedate 7e arrondissement, this has quickly become the place to be seen, with food that's a good notch above brasserie fare. A juicy Angus beef hamburger comes with a superfluous shower of Parmesan and ultraskinny fries, while the more sophisticated slow-cooked salmon is accompanied by vegetables from star market gardener Joël Thiébault. For dessert, try the piping-hot churros with chocolate sauce. The new restaurant *gastronomique* upstairs is ever so chic and a good bit pricier, yet proffers an experience commensurate with the top bistros in town (there's a €154 set menu at lunch and dinner and a €99 three-course menu at lunch). Reservations are taken exactly six days ahead. *Average main: €40 79 rue St-Dominique, 7e, Invalides 01–47–05–49–75 www.thoumieux.fr Reservations essential M La Tour–Maubourg 1:C4.*

CHAMPS-ÉLYSÉES

$$$$ MODERN FRENCH Fodor's Choice ★ **Alain Ducasse at the Plaza Athénée.** After a 10-month interlude during the Plaza's top-to-toe renovation, Alain Ducasse's flagship Paris restaurant reopened with a dazzling new look and a menu that totally redefines French haute cuisine. Arguably the world's most visible chef, Ducassee surprises here, devoting himself entirely to vegetables, grains, and fish; on second thought, maybe only a chef of this stature could pull it off to a success of this magnitude. From the moment you enter the glittering dining room, alight with thousands of crystals reflected in sinuous mirrored banquettes, you know you've entered a parallel universe entirely devoted to pleasure and well-being. Chef Romain Meder executes Ducasse's recipes,which mix the most luxe with the humblest ingredients, to sublime effect: caviar over tender langoustine in a lemongrass-infused broth; a stack of lacy buckwheat blini accompanied by lentils and caviar in a smoked gelée topped with ethereal truffle cream. Vegetables from the queen's gardens at Versailles are featured in a masterful dish of brioche-encased cauliflower served with buttery

scallops and a generous shaving of white truffles, or earthy black Camargue rice punctuated with razor clams and cockles. Desserts like lemon ice with candied lemon and silky kombu seaweed take the notion of dining for pleasure and health to vertiginous new heights. *$ Average main: €120 ✉ Hôtel Plaza Athénée, 25 av. Montaigne, 8e, Champs-Élysées ☎ 01–53–67–65–00 🌐 www.alain-ducasse.com ⏲ Closed weekends. No lunch Mon.–Wed. Reservations essential Jacket required M Alma-Marceau ✥ 1:B3.*

$$$$ MODERN FRENCH Fodor's Choice ★

Guy Savoy. With dark African wood, rich leather, cream-color marble, and the chef's own art collection, Guy Savoy's luxury restaurant doesn't dwell on the past. Come here for a perfectly measured haute-cuisine experience, since Savoy's several bistros have not lured him away from the kitchen. The artichoke soup with black truffles, sea bass with spices, and veal kidneys in mustard-spiked jus reveal the magnitude of his talent, and his mille-feuille is an instant classic. If the waiters see you're relishing a dish, they won't hesitate to offer second helpings. Generous half portions allow you to graze your way through the menu—unless you choose a blowout feast for set menus ranging from €360 to €490 for the 18-course menu—and reasonably priced wines are available (though beware the cost of wines by the glass). The €170 "discovery" menu at noon or after 10:30 pm is a good way to sample some of this fine chef's inspired cooking. Best of all, the atmosphere is joyful, because Savoy knows that having fun is just as important as eating well. *$ Average main: €120 ✉ 18 rue Troyon, 17e, Champs-Élysées ☎ 01–43–80–40–61 🌐 www.guysavoy.com ⏲ Closed Sun., Mon., and 1 wk at Christmas. No lunch Sat. Reservations essential Jacket required M Charles-de-Gaulle–Étoile ✥ 1:B2.*

$$$$ MODERN FRENCH

L'Arôme. Eric Martins ran a popular bistro in the far reaches of the 15e arrondissement before opening this contemporary restaurant off the Champs-Élysées, and his background in haute cuisine—he worked at Ledoyen and Hélène Darroze, among others—makes this ambitious restaurant an easy transition. The chef, Thomas Boullaut, turns out seasonal dishes with a touch of finesse from the open kitchen: dishes like foie gras confit with rosemary-poached quince and wild rose jam, or scallops *à la plancha* (from the grill) with vanilla and spaghetti squash might be featured. There is no à la carte, and if the dinner menus seem steep at €99 (€159 with wine pairing), try the lunch menu for €79. Watch out for the pricey wines by the glass. *$ Average main: €45 ✉ 3 rue St-Philippe du Roule, 8e, Champs-Élysées ☎ 01–42–25–55–98 🌐 www.larome.fr ⏲ Closed weekends and Aug. Reservations essential M St-Philippe du Roule ✥ 1:C2.*

$$$ BRASSERIE

La Fermette Marbeuf. Graced with one of the most mesmerizing Belle Époque rooms in town—accidentally rediscovered during renovations in the 1970s—this is a favorite haunt of French celebrities, who adore the sunflowers, peacocks, and dragonflies of the Art Nouveau mosaic. The menu rolls out updated classics: try the snails in puff pastry, beef fillet with pepper sauce, and the Grand Marnier soufflé—but ignore the limited-choice €30 prix fixe unless you're on a budget: the options are a notch below what you get à la carte. Popular with tourists and business executives at lunch, La Fermette becomes truly animated around 9 pm. $ *Average main: €28* ✉ *5 rue Marbeuf, 8e, Champs-Élysées* ☎ *01–53–23–08–00* 🌐 *www.fermettemarbeuf.com* Ⓜ *Franklin-D.-Roosevelt* ✣ *1:B3.*

$$$$ CANTONESE Fodor's Choice ★

✕ **LiLi.** The operatically beautiful LiLi, in the newly unveiled Peninsula Hotel, places sophisticated Cantonese cuisine in its rightful place—the gastronomic center of the world. Sheathed in cascades of red silk, the glamorous dining room, especially romantic in the evening, shimmers with ebony and gold damask under indigo-blue chandeliers. As alluring as the decor, the menu—presided over by Michelin-starred chef Tang Chi Keung—features all the classics, raised to the status of haute cuisine: small plates of dim sum (seafood, vegetable, or pork dumplings) alongside more substantial fare like fried rice studded with market-fresh vegetables, succulent Sichuan shrimp, and barbecued suckling pig. For the pièce de résistance, black-gloved waiters carve tender-crisp slices from a lacquered Peking duck that are folded in warm crepes with a mellow plum sauce. The chef's signature *crème de mangue* laced with pomelo pearls is an ethereal ending to an exceptional meal. At €59, the prix-fixe lunch menu is a wonderful introduction to this timeless cuisine. $ *Average main: €35* ✉ *The Peninsula Paris, 19 rue Kléber, 16e, Champs-Élysée* ☎ *01–58–12–67–50* 🌐 *paris.peninsula.com* ✍ *Reservations essential* Ⓜ *Kléber, Charles de Gaulle–Étoile* ✣ *1:B3.*

$$$ MODERN FRENCH

✕ **Mini Palais.** Inside the Grand Palais, Mini Palais has gotten things smashingly right. With silvery ceilings, dark wood, and faux classical marble, it's among Paris's most stylish dining rooms, but the menu—designed by superchef Eric Frechon of Le Bristol and executed by protegé Stephane d'Aboville—is the real draw. The burger *de magret et foie gras,* a flavorful mélange of tender duckling breast and duck foie gras drizzled with truffled jus on a buttery brioche bun underscores what's best about this place: a thoroughly modern cuisine with an old-fashioned extravagance. For a summer meal or a cocktail, the majestically pillared terrace overlooking Pont d'Alexandre III must be the most beautiful in Paris. What's more, it's open nonstop from 10 am till 2 am, an oasis in a neighborhood short on conveniences. $ *Average main: €25* ✉ *3 av. Winston Churchill, 8e, Champs-Élysées* ☎ *01–42–56–42–42* 🌐 *www.minipalais.com* ✍ *Reservations essential* Ⓜ *Champs-Élysées–Clemenceau* ✣ *1:C3.*

$$$$ MODERN FRENCH Fodor's Choice ★

✕ **Pierre Gagnaire.** If you want to venture to the frontier of contemporary cooking—and if money is no object—dinner here is a must. Chef Pierre Gagnaire's work is at once intellectual and poetic, often blending three or four unexpected tastes and textures in a single dish. Just taking in the menu requires concentration (ask the waiters for help), so complex are the multiline descriptions about each dish's six or seven ingredients. The Grand Dessert, a seven-dessert marathon, will leave you breathless, though it's not as overwhelming as it sounds. The businesslike gray-and-wood dining room feels refreshingly informal, especially at lunch, but it also lacks the grandeur expected at this level. The uninspiring prix-fixe lunch (€115) and occasional ill-judged dishes (Gagnaire is a big risk taker, but also one of France's top chefs) linger as drawbacks, and prices keep shooting skyward, so Pierre Gagnaire is an experience best saved for the financial elite. $ *Average main: €110* ✉ *6 rue de Balzac,*

8e, Champs-Élysées ☎ *01–58–36–12–50* 🌐 *www.pierre-gagnaire.com* ⏲ *Closed weekends, Aug., and at Christmas* ✍ *Reservations essential* Ⓜ *Charles-de-Gaulle–Étoile* ✧ *1:B2.*

$$$ SEAFOOD Fodor's Choice ★ **Rech.** Having restored the historic Paris bistros Aux Lyonnais and Benoît to their former glory, star chef Alain Ducasse turned his piercing attention to this seafood brasserie founded in 1925. His wisdom lies in knowing what not to change: the original Art Deco chairs in the main floor dining room; seafood shucker Malec, who has been a fixture on this chic stretch of sidewalk since 1982; and the XL éclair (it's supersize) that's drawn in locals for decades. Original owner Auguste Rech believed in serving a limited selection of high-quality products—a principle that suits Ducasse perfectly—and Adrien Trouilloud is now in the kitchen, turning out Med-inspired dishes such as tomato cream with crayfish and fresh almonds or Niçoise-style sea bass with thyme fritters. Save room for the whole farmer's Camembert, another Rech tradition. A great-value €42 menu is available at lunch; the dinner menu is €54. 💲 *Average main: €32* ✉ *62 av. des Ternes, 17e, Champs-Élysées* ☎ *01–45–72–29–47* 🌐 *www.restaurant-rech.fr* ⏲ *Closed Sun., Mon., late July–late Aug., and 1 wk at Christmas* ✍ *Reservations essential* Ⓜ *Ternes* ✧ *1:A1.*

$$$$ MODERN FRENCH **Taillevent.** Perhaps the most traditional—for many diners this is only high praise—of all Paris luxury restaurants, this grande dame basks in renewed freshness under brilliant chef Alain Solivérès, who draws inspiration from the Basque country, Bordeaux, and Languedoc for his daily menu. Traditional dishes such as scallops meunière (with butter and lemon) are matched with contemporary choices like a splendid spelt risotto with truffles and frogs' legs or panfried duck liver with caramelized fruits and vegetables. One of the 19th-century paneled salons has been turned into a winter garden, and contemporary paintings adorn the walls. The service is flawless, and the exemplary wine list is well priced. All in all, a meal here comes as close to the classic haute-cuisine experience as you can find in Paris. There's an €88 lunch menu and special wine "degustation" evenings, pairing food with exceptional wines from the legendary cave for €180. 💲 *Average main: €110* ✉ *15 rue Lamennais, 8e, Champs-Élysées* ☎ *01–44–95–15–01* 🌐 *www.taillevent.com* ⏲ *Closed weekends and Aug.* ✍ *Reservations essential* 👔 *Jacket and tie* Ⓜ *Charles-de-Gaulle–Étoile* ✧ *1:B2.*

AROUND THE LOUVRE

$$$ BISTRO Fodor's Choice ★ **L'Ardoise.** A minuscule storefront decorated with enlargements of old sepia postcards of Paris, L'Ardoise is a model of the kind of contemporary bistro making waves in Paris. Chef Pierre Jay's first-rate three-course dinner menu for €38 tempts with such original dishes as mushroom-and-foie-gras ravioli with smoked duck; farmer's pork with porcini mushrooms; and red mullet with creole sauce (you can also order à la carte, but it's less of a bargain). Just as enticing are the desserts, such as a superb *feuillantine au citron*—caramelized pastry leaves filled with lemon cream and lemon slices—and a boozy baba au rhum. With friendly waiters and a small but well-chosen wine list, L'Ardoise would be perfect if it weren't so popular (meaning noisy and crowded).

Average main: €27 28 rue du Mont Thabor, 1er, Louvre/Tuileries 01–42–96–28–18 www.lardoise-paris.com No lunch Sun. Reservations essential Concorde 1:D3.

$$ MODERN FRENCH Fodor's Choice ★

La Régalade St. Honoré. When Bruno Doucet bought the original La Régalade from bistro-wizard Yves Camdeborde, some feared the end of an era. How wrong they were. While Doucet kept some of what made the old dining room so popular (country terrines, reasonably priced wines, convivial atmosphere), he had a few tricks under his toque, creating a brilliantly successful haute-cuisine-meets-comfort-food destination with dishes like earthy morel mushrooms in a frothy cream for a starter, followed by the chef's signature succulent caramelized pork belly over tender Puy lentils, and a perfectly cooked fillet of cod, crispy on the outside and buttery within, served in a rich shrimp bouillon. For dessert, don't skip the updated take on grand-mère's creamy rice pudding or the house Grand Marnier soufflé. With an excellent price-to-value ratio (€37 for the prix-fixe menu at lunch and dinner), this chic bistro and its elder sister in the 14th have evolved into staples for Paris gastronomes. *Average main: €24 123 rue Saint-Honoré, 1er, Faubourg St-Honoré 01–42–21–92–40 Closed weekends and Aug. Reservations essential Louvre-Rivoli 1:F4.*

$$$$ MODERN FRENCH

Le Grand Véfour. Victor Hugo could stride in and still recognize this restaurant, which was in his day, as now, a contender for the title of most beautiful restaurant in Paris. Originally built in 1784, it has welcomed everyone from Napoléon to Colette to Jean Cocteau under its mirrored ceiling, and amid the early-19th-century glass paintings of goddesses and muses that create an air of restrained seduction. The rich and fashionable gather here to enjoy chef Guy Martin's unique blend of sophistication and rusticity, as seen in dishes such as frogs' legs with sorrel sauce, and oxtail *parmentier* (a kind of shepherd's pie) with truffles. There's an outstanding cheese trolley, and for dessert try the house specialty, *palet aux noisettes* (meringue cake with chocolate mousse, hazelnuts, and salted caramel ice cream). Prices are as extravagant as the decor, but there is a €98 lunch menu. *Average main: €120 17 rue de Beaujolais, 1er, Louvre/Tuileries 01–42–96–56–27 www.grand-vefour.com Closed weekends, Aug., and Christmas holidays Reservations essential Palais-Royal 1:E3.*

$$$$ MODERN FRENCH Fodor's Choice ★

Spring. The private-party atmosphere in this intimate, elegantly modern space may be exuberance at having finally snagged a table, but most likely it's chef Daniel Rose's inspired cuisine. Though firmly rooted in technique, Rose sets himself the task of improvising two different menus each day, one for lunch and one for dinner, from whatever strikes his fancy that morning. His insistence on fresh, top-quality ingredients sourced from every corner of France is evident in dishes that are both refined and deeply satisfying: you might have an updated parmentier with a velvety layer of deboned pig's foot topped with lemon-infused whipped potatoes or buttery venison with tart-sweet candied kumquats. For dessert, there's a sublime combo of whiskey-and-vanilla-infused pineapple, crunchy toasted coconut biscuits, and lime-zest-sprinkled vanilla ice cream. A four-course dinner menu will run you €84. The 17th-century vaulted dining room is an intimate spot

Just across the street from famed Café de Flore, legendary Les Deux Magots was once the favorite of Hemingway, Joyce, and Sartre.

yet can accommodate larger groups. $ *Average main: €45* ✉ *6 rue Bailleul, 1er, Louvre/Tuileries* ☎ *01–45–96–05–72* 🌐 *www.springparis.fr* ⏲ *Closed Sun. and Mon. No lunch* ✍ *Reservations essential* Ⓜ *Louvre-Rivoli* ✛ *1:F4.*

THE GRANDS BOULEVARDS

$$$ BISTRO Fodor's Choice ★ ✕ **Frenchie.** The prodigiously talented Grégory Marchand worked with Jamie Oliver in London before opening this brick-and-stone-walled bistro on a pedestrian street near Rue Montorgueil. Word of mouth and bloggers quickly made this one of the most packed bistros in town, with tables booked months in advance, despite two seatings each evening. Marchand owes a large part of his success to the good-value €65 five-course menu at dinner (prix fixe only)—boldly flavored dishes such as calamari gazpacho with squash blossoms, and melt-in-the-mouth braised lamb with roasted eggplant and spinach are excellent options. Service can be, shall we say, a tad brusque, but for some that's a small price to pay for food this good. If you can't get a reservation, nearby Frenchie Bar à Vins will fix you right up. $ *Average main: €31* ✉ *5 rue du Nil, 2e, Les Halles* ☎ *01–40–39–96–19* 🌐 *www.frenchie-restaurant.com* ⏲ *Closed weekends, 2 wks in Aug., and 10 days at Christmas. No lunch* ✍ *Reservations essential* Ⓜ *Sentier* ✛ *1:F3.*

$$ BISTRO Fodor's Choice ★ ✕ **Terroir Parisien–Palais Brongniart.** Yannick Alléno's departure from Le Meurice, where he'd earned three Michelin stars, may have stunned the culinary world, but it's good news for diners. Besides taking the helm at august Ledoyen, Alléno presides over this warm, modern space under the Paris Bourse, the city's stock exchange. The star chef's dishes achieve

an ephemeral balance, allowing top-notch ingredients to shine through while combining flavors and textures in unexpected and delightful ways. Tender roasted leeks are sprinkled with eggs, shallots, chives, and sprigs of chervil. A perfectly prepared steak with crispy matchstick fries and tender boudin blanc sausage with truffled celery root purée are comfort food at its best. Desserts like a velvety chocolate tart with a layer of salted caramel or a roasted apple filled with raspberry jam are not to be missed. There's also a "rillette bar," where you can take out traditional French charcuterie: *rillettes de lapin* (rabbit terrine) and *paté de campagne* (country terrine). A big plus here is the welcoming, helpful service. *Average main: €22 28 pl. de la Bourse, 2e, Opéra/Grands Boulevards 01–83–92–20–30 www.yannick-alleno.com/restaurant/paris-terroir-parisien-palais-brongniart Closed Sun. No lunch Sat. Reservations essential M Bourse 1:F3.*

MONTPARNASSE

$$$$
BRASSERIE

Le Dôme. Now a fancy fish brasserie serving seafood delivered fresh from Normandy every day, this restaurant began as a dingy meeting place for exiled artists and intellectuals like Lenin and Picasso. Try the sole meunière or the bouillabaisse, the ingredients of which are on display in their raw form in the restaurant's sparkling fish shop next door. You can still drop by the covered terrace for a cup of coffee or a drink. *Average main: €36 108 bd. Montparnasse, 14e, Montparnasse 01–43–35–25–81 Closed Sun. and Mon. in July and Aug. M Vavin 1:D6.*

MARAIS

$$
BISTRO

Au Bourguignon du Marais. The handsome, contemporary look of this Marais bistro and wine bar is the perfect backdrop for traditional fare and excellent Burgundies served by the glass and bottle. Unusual for Paris, food is served nonstop from noon to 11 pm, and you can drop by just for a glass of wine in the afternoon. Always on the menu are Burgundian classics such as *jambon persillé* (ham in parsleyed aspic jelly), escargots, and *boeuf bourguignon* (beef stewed in red wine). More up-to-date picks include a cèpe-mushroom velouté with poached oysters, though the fancier dishes are generally less successful. The terrace is busy in warmer months. *Average main: €22 52 rue François-Miron, 3e, Marais 01–48–87–15–40 Closed Sun. and Mon., 3 wks in Aug., and 2 wks in Feb. M St-Paul 1:G4.*

$$
BRASSERIE

Brasserie de l'Isle Saint-Louis. With so much going for it, including a dream location on the tip of Ile St-Louis overlooking the Seine and Notre-Dame, you'd think this charming brasserie, like so many before it, would have succumbed to its own success. Yet it remains exactly what a decent neighborhood brasserie should be, with an authentic decor, efficiently friendly service, and solid brassiere fare—classic leeks vinaigrette, country terrine, and a savory onion tarte *à la maison* for starters, followed by tender sole meuniere, classic choucroute, or buttered entrecôte. The outdoor terrace simply can't be beat. *Average main: €19 55 quai de Bourbon, 4e, Ile St-Louis 01–43–54–02–59* *www.labrasserie-isl.fr* *Closed Wed.* *Reservations not accepted* *Pont Marie, Maubert-Mutualité, Sully-Morland* *1:G5.*

$ FRENCH FAMILY Fodor's Choice ★ **Breizh Café.** Eating a crêpe in Paris might seem a bit clichéd, until you venture into this modern offshoot of a Breton crêperie. The pale-wood, almost Japanese-style decor is refreshing, but what really makes the difference are the ingredients—farmers' eggs, unpasteurized Gruyère, shiitake mushrooms, Valrhona chocolate, homemade caramel, and extraordinary butter from Breton dairy farmer Jean-Yves Bordier. You'll find all the classics among the galettes (buckwheat crêpes), but it's worth choosing something more adventurous like the *cancalaise* (traditionally smoked herring, potato, crème fraîche, and herring roe). You might also slurp a few Cancale oysters, a rarity in Paris, and try one of the 20 artisanal ciders on offer. The nonstop serving hours from noon to 11 pm can be a lifesaver if you're shopping in the Marais. Weekends are hectic, so be sure to reserve. *Average main: €12* *109 rue Vieille du Temple, 3e, Marais* *01–42–72–13–77* *www.breizhcafe.com* *Closed Mon., Tues., and Aug.* *Reservations essential* *St-Sébastien–Froissart* *1:G4.*

$ MODERN FRENCH **Cantine Merci.** Deep inside the city's latest concept store, whose proceeds go to charities for women in India and Madagascar, lurks the perfect spot for a quick and healthy lunch between bouts of shopping. The brief menu of soups, salads, risottos, and a daily hot dish is more than slightly reminiscent of another city lunch spot, Rose Bakery—salads such as fava beans with radish and lemon wedges or melon, cherry tomato, and arugula are bright, lively, and crunchy, and you can order a freshly squeezed juice or iced tea with fresh mint to wash it all down. Delicious, homey desserts might include cherry clafouti or raspberry-and-pistachio crumble. *Average main: €17* *111 bd. Beaumarchais, 3e, Marais* *01–42–77–79–28* *www.merci-merci.com* *Closed Sun. No dinner* *St-Sébastien–Froissart* *1:H4.*

$ MIDDLE EASTERN FAMILY **L'As du Fallafel.** Look no further than the fantastic falafel stands on the pedestrian Rue de Rosiers for some of the cheapest and tastiest meals in Paris. L'As (the Ace) is widely considered the best of the bunch, which accounts for the lunchtime line that extends down the street. A falafel sandwich costs €6 to go, €8 in the dining room, and comes heaped with grilled eggplant, cabbage, hummus, tahini, and hot sauce. The shawarma (grilled, skewered meat) sandwich, made with chicken or lamb, is also one of the finest in town. Though takeout is popular, it can be more fun (and not as messy) to eat off a plastic plate in one of the two frenzied dining rooms. Fresh lemonade is the falafel's best match. *Average main: €10* *34 rue des Rosiers, 4e, Marais* *01–48–87–63–60* *Closed Sat. No dinner Fri.* *St-Paul* *1:G4.*

$$ MODERN FRENCH Fodor's Choice ★ **Mon Vieil Ami.** "Modern Alsatian" might sound like an oxymoron, but once you've tasted the food here, you'll understand. The updated medieval dining room—stone walls and dark-wood tables—provides a stylish milieu for the inventive cooking orchestrated by star Alsatian chef Antoine Westermann, which showcases heirloom vegetables (such as yellow carrots and pink-and-white beets) from star producer Joël Thiébault. Pâté *en croûte* (wrapped in pastry) with a knob of foie gras is hard to resist among the starters. Among the mains, red mullet

might come in a bouillabaisse sauce with sautéed baby artichokes, and the shoulder of lamb with white beans, preserved lemon, and cilantro has become a classic. This is not necessarily the place for a romantic dinner, since seating is a little tight, but the quality of the food never falters, and the portions are quite generous. *Average main: €24* ✉ *69 rue St-Louis-en-l'Ile, 4e, Ile St-Louis* ☎ *01–40–46–01–35* 🌐 *www.mon-vieil-ami.com* Ⓜ *Pont Marie* ✣ *1:G5.*

EASTERN PARIS

$$ BISTRO FAMILY **Astier.** There are three good reasons to go to Astier: the generous cheese platter plunked on your table atop a help-yourself wicker tray, the exceptional wine cellar with bottles dating back to the 1970s, and the French bistro fare (even if portions seem to have diminished over the years). Dishes like marinated herring with warm potato salad, sausage with lentils, and baba au rhum are classics on the frequently changing set menu for €45 (€39 at lunch), which includes a selection of no less than 20 cheeses. The vintage 1950s wood-panel dining room attracts plenty of locals and remains a fairly sure bet in the area, especially because it's open every day. *Average main: €21* ✉ *44 rue Jean-Pierre Timbaud, 11e, République* ☎ *01–43–57–16–35* 🌐 *www.restaurant-astier.com* *Reservations essential* Ⓜ *Parmentier* ✣ *1:H3.*

$ WINE BAR **Au Passage.** This *bistrot à vins* has the lived-in look of a longtime neighborhood favorite—which it was until two veterans of the raging Paris wine-bar scene reinvented the place, keeping the laid-back atmosphere and adding a serious foodie menu that's one of the best deals in town. A blackboard lists a selection of small €4 to €8 tapas dishes—including several house-made pâtés, fresh tomato or beet salad, a superb seafood carpaccio, and artisanal charcuterie and cheeses. Four or more diners can hack away at a crispy-succulent roasted lamb haunch. The excellent wine list features plenty of natural wines. It's a diverse and lively crowd of happy diners who know they've found a very good thing. *Average main: €15* ✉ *1 bis, passage Saint-Sébastien, 11e, République* ☎ *01–43–55–07–52* 🌐 *www.restaurant-aupassage.fr* *Closed Sun. No lunch* *Reservations essential* Ⓜ *Saint-Ambroise, Saint-Sebastien–Froissart, Richard Lenoir* ✣ *1:H4.*

$$ BISTRO Fodor's Choice ★ **Le Bistrot Paul Bert.** Faded 1930s decor: check. Boisterous crowd: check. Thick steak with real frites: check. Good value: check. The Paul Bert delivers everything you could want from a traditional Paris bistro, so it's no wonder its two dining rooms fill every night with a cosmopolitan crowd. Some are from the neighborhood, others have done their bistro research, but they've all come for the balance of ingredients that makes for a feel-good experience every time. The impressively stocked wine cellar helps, as does the cheese cart, the laid-back yet efficient staff, and hearty dishes such as monkfish with white beans and duck with pears. The reasonable prix fixe is three courses for €38, or you can order à la carte. If you're looking for an inexpensive wine, choose from the chalkboard rather than the wine list. *Average main: €24* ✉ *18 rue Paul Bert, 11e, Bastille/Nation* ☎ *01–43–72–24–01* *Closed Sun., Mon., and Aug.* *Reservations essential* Ⓜ *Rue des Boulets* ✣ *1:H5.*

$$ WINE BAR **Le Dauphin.** Avant-garde chef Inaki Aizpatarte has struck again, transforming (with a little help from Rem Koolhaas) a dowdy little café two doors from his acclaimed Le Chateaubriand into a sleek, if chilly, all-marble watering hole for late-night cuisinistas. Honing his ever-iconoclastic take on tapas, the dishes served here—along with a thoughtful selection of natural wines—are a great way to get an idea of what all the fuss is about. Offerings like sweetly delicate crabmeat punctuated with tart marinated radish and avocado purée, or a well-prepared lemon sole drizzled with hazelnut butter highlight what this chef can do with quality ingredients. Dishes are small, well priced, and meant to be shared to maximize exposure to the food. *Average main: €20* *131 av. Parmentier, 11e, Canal St-Martin* *01–55–28–78–88* *www.restaurantledauphin.net* *Closed Sun., Mon. and 1 wk at Christmas. No lunch Sat.* *Reservations essential* *Parmentier* *1:H3.*

$$ BISTRO Fodor's Choice ★ **Le Galopin.** Across from a pretty square on the border of two up-and-coming neighborhoods, this light-drenched spot, run by brothers Maxime and Romain Tischenko (the former a veteran of Inaki Aizpitarte's Chateaubriand and the latter a *Top Chef* winner) is one of Paris's better bistros. While the brothers adhere to a tried-and-true formula—meticulously sourced produce, natural wines, open kitchen—they've managed to make it very much their own. Dishes are small wonders of texture and flavor, like velvety Basque pork with razor-thin slices of cauliflower, briny olives, and crunchy pumpkin seeds; or crisp-moist sea bass with spring-fresh asparagus and mint. This is a great choice for diners eager to experience what this scene's all about in a hip, off-the-beaten-path locale. *Average main: €20* *34 rue Sainte-Marthe, 10e, Canal St-Martin* *01–42–06–05–03* *www.le-galopin.com* *Closed weekends. No lunch* *Reservations essential* *Goncourt, Belleville, Colonel Fabien* *1:H2.*

$$ BISTRO **Le Repaire de Cartouche.** In this split-level, dark-wood bistro between Bastille and République, chef Rodolphe Paquin applies a disciplined creativity to earthy French regional dishes. The menu changes regularly, but typical options are a salad of haricots verts topped with tender slices of squid; scallops on a bed of diced pumpkin; juicy lamb with white beans; game dishes in winter; and old-fashioned desserts like baked custard with tiny shell-shaped madeleines. In keeping with cost-conscious times, there is a bargain three-course lunch menu for €19 that doesn't skimp on ingredients—expect the likes of homemade pâté to start, followed by fried red mullet or hanger steak with french fries, and chocolate tart. The wine list is very good, too, with some bargain selections from small producers. *Average main: €24* *99 rue Amelot, 11e, Bastille/Nation* *01–47–00–25–86* *Closed Sun., Mon., and Aug.* *Reservations essential* *Filles du Calvaire* *1:H4.*

$$ BISTRO **Philou.** On a quiet street between Canal St-Martin and the historic Hôpital Saint-Louis, few places could be more pleasant than a sidewalk table at this most welcome addition to Paris's thriving bistro scene. On a cool day the red banquettes and Ingo Maurer chandelier cast a cozy glow, all the better to enjoy a hearty, well-priced selection of dishes, like slices of foie gras served atop *crème de lentilles* and sprinkled with garlicky croutons, ham clafoutis with girolle mushrooms,

or a rosy beef entrecôte with roasted baby Yukon gold potatoes and mushrooms *de Paris*. In springtime, fat white asparagus is nicely paired with salty smoked haddock and spring peas. A wine list replete with well-chosen natural wines plus the reasonable €30, two-course and €38, three-course menus at lunch and dinner make it one of more popular tables in town, so reserve ahead. *Average main: €22 12 av. Richerand, 10e, Canal St-Martin 01–42–38–00–13 www.restophilou.com Closed Sun. and Mon. Reservations essential Jacques Bonsergent 1:H2.*

$$ BISTRO **Septime.** This is the kind of bistro we'd all love in our neighborhood—good food and a convivial atmosphere where diners crane to admire each other's plates. Bertrand Grébaut, the affable young chef, can often be found chatting away with guests in the cacophonous dining room. In a neighborhood where excellent bistro fare is ridiculously plentiful—thanks to several talented young chefs who've set up shop here in the last few years—this spot stands out. Seasonal ingredients, inventive pairings, excellent natural wines, plus dishes like creamy gnochetti in an orange-rind-flecked Gouda sauce sprinkled with coriander flowers; tender fillet of Landes hen in a mustard-peanut sauce, with braised endive and cabbage perfumed with lemon; and fresh white asparagus with raspberries and blanched almonds are sophisticated and satisfying. The €30 weekday lunch menu is a good place to begin. *Average main: €22 80 rue de Charonne, 11e, Bastille/Nation 01–43–67–38–29 www.septime-charonne.fr Closed weekends. No lunch Mon. Reservations essential Ledru Rollin, Charonne 1:H3.*

LATIN QUARTER

$$$$ MODERN FRENCH **La Tour d'Argent.** La Tour d'Argent has had a rocky time in recent years with the death of owner Claude Terrail, but chef Laurent Delarbre has found his footing, and there's no denying the splendor of the setting overlooking the Seine. If you don't want to splash out on dinner, treat yourself to the three-course lunch menu for a reduced price of €85; this entitles you to succulent slices of one of the restaurant's numbered ducks (the great duck slaughter began in 1919 and is now well past the millionth mallard, as your numbered certificate will attest). Don't be too daunted by the vast wine list—with the aid of the sommelier you can splurge a little (about €85) and perhaps taste a rare vintage Burgundy from the extraordinary cellars, which survived World War II. *Average main: €105 15–17 quai de la Tournelle, 5e, Latin Quarter 01–43–54–23–31 www.latourdargent.com Closed Sun., Mon., and Aug. Reservations essential Jacket and tie Cardinal Lemoine 1:G5.*

$$$$ BISTRO **Lapérouse.** Émile Zola, George Sand, and Victor Hugo were regulars here, and the restaurant's mirrors still bear diamond scratches from the days when mistresses would double-check their jewels' value. It's hard not to fall in love with this storied 17th-century Seine-side town house with a warren of woodwork-graced salons. Anthony Germani's cuisine seeks a balance between traditional and modern, often drawing on Mediterranean inspirations. For a truly intimate meal, reserve one of the legendary private *salons* where anything can happen (and probably has). You can also sample the restaurant's magic at lunch,

when a bargain prix-fixe menu is served for €45 in both the main dining room and the private salons. *Average main: €45* *51 quai des Grands Augustins, 6e, St-Germain-des-Prés* *01–43–26–68–04* *www.laperouse.fr* *Closed Sun. No lunch Sat.* *Reservations essential* *St-Michel* *1:F4.*

$$ MODERN FRENCH **Le Pré Verre.** Chef Jean-François Paris knows his cassia bark from his cinnamon thanks to a long stint in Asia. He opened this lively bistro with its purple-gray walls and photos of jazz musicians to showcase his culinary style, rejuvenating archetypal French dishes with Asian and Mediterranean spices. His bargain prix-fixe menus (€14.50 at lunch, €32 at dinner) change constantly, but his trademark spiced suckling pig with crisp cabbage is always a winner, as is his rhubarb compote with gingered white-chocolate mousse. Ask for advice in selecting wine from a list that highlights small producers. *Average main: €20* *8 rue Thénard, 5e, Latin Quarter* *01–43–54–59–47* *www.lepreverre.com* *Closed Sun., Mon., and 1 wk at Christmas* *Reservations essential* *Maubert-Mutualité* *1:F5.*

$$ WINE BAR **Les Papilles.** Part wineshop and épicerie, part restaurant, Les Papilles has a winning formula—pick any bottle off the well-stocked shelf and pay a €7 corkage fee to drink it with your meal. You can also savor one of several superb wines by the glass at your table or around the classic zinc bar. The superb set menu—made with top-notch, seasonal ingredients—usually begins with a luscious velouté, a velvety soup served from a large tureen, and proceeds with a hearty-yet-tender meat dish alongside perfectly cooked vegetables—well worth spending a little extra time for lunch or dinner. *Average main: €18* *30 rue Gay-Lussac, 5e, Latin Quarter* *01–43–25–20–79* *www.lespapillesparis.fr* *Closed Sun., Mon., last wk of July, and 2 wks in Aug.* *Reservations essential* *Cluny–La Sorbonne* *1:F6.*

$$ BISTRO **Ribouldingue.** Find offal off-putting? Off-cuts take pride of place on the prix-fixe menu (€28 at lunch, €34 at dinner), but don't let that stop you from trying this bistro near the ancient St-Julien-le-Pauvre church. You can avoid odd animal bits completely, if you must, and still have an excellent meal—opt for dishes like marinated salmon or veal rib with fingerling potatoes—or go out on a limb with the *tétine de vache* (thin breaded and fried slices of cow's udder) and *groin de cochon* (the tip of a pig's snout). This adventurous menu is the brainchild of Nadège Varigny, daughter of a Lyonnais butcher (*quel surprise*). Veal kidney with potato gratin is a house classic, and there are always three fish dishes. Don't miss the unusual desserts, like tangy ewe's-milk ice cream. *Average main: €21* *10 rue St-Julien-le-Pauvre, 5e, Latin Quarter* *01–46–33–98–80* *www.ribouldingue-restaurant.fr* *Closed Sun. and Mon.* *St-Michel* *1:F5.*

$$$$ ECLECTIC **Sola.** Chef Hiroki Yoshitake was schooled in the kitchens of famed innovators Pascal Barbot of Astrance and William Ledeuil of Ze Kitchen Galerie before striking out on his own. Dishes like miso-lacquered foie gras or sake-glazed suckling pig—perfectly crisp on the outside and melting inside—pair traditional Japanese and French ingredients to wondrous effect. Plates are artfully arranged with a sprinkling of piquant shiso leaves or jewel-like roasted vegetables to please the eye

and the palate. Costing €48, the three-course set lunch menu offers a choice of fish or meat and finishes with Fukano Hirobu's stunning confections. Shoes stay on in the tranquil half-timbered dining room upstairs, but the vaulted room downstairs is totally traditional—and one of the loveliest in Paris. *Average main: €35 ✉ 12 rue de l'Hôtel Colbert, 5e, Latin Quarter ☎ 01–43–29–59–04 www.restaurant-sola.com Closed Sun. and Mon. Reservations essential Ⓜ Maubert—Mutualié ✥ 1:F5.*

$$$$ MODERN FRENCH Fodor's Choice ★ **Ze Kitchen Galerie.** William Ledeuil made his name at the popular Les Bouquinistes before opening this contemporary bistro in a loftlike space. The name might not be inspired, but the cooking shows creativity and a sense of fun: from a deliberately deconstructed menu featuring raw fish, soups, pastas, and à la plancha (grilled) plates, consider the roast and confit duck with a tamarind-and-sesame condiment and foie gras, or lobster with mussels, white beans, and Thai herbs. A tireless experimenter, Ledeuil buys heirloom vegetables direct from farmers and tracks down herbs and spices in Asian supermarkets. The menu changes monthly, and there are several different prix-fixe options at lunch, starting at €40. *Average main: €39 ✉ 4 rue des Grands-Augustins, 6e, Latin Quarter ☎ 01–44–32–00–32 www.zekitchengalerie.fr Closed Sun. No lunch Sat. Reservations essential Ⓜ St-Michel ✥ 1:F4.*

ST-GERMAIN-DES-PRÉS

$$ BISTRO Fodor's Choice ★ **Fish la Boissonérie.** A perennial favorite, expats and locals prize this lively, unpretentious bistro for its friendly atmosphere, consistently good food, solid wine list, and English-speaking staff—a quartet sorely lacking in the neighborhood. Dishes like velvety black squid-ink risotto, roasted cod with tender braised fennel, and crispy pumpkin tempura always hit the spot, especially when followed by decadent molten chocolate cake, honey-roasted figs, or banana-bread pudding. Everything is satisfying and reasonably priced. A big plus: it's open all day Sunday. *Average main: €22 ✉ 69 rue de Seine, 6e, St-Germain-des-Prés ☎ 01–43–54–34–69 Reservations essential Ⓜ St-Germain-des-Prés, Odéon ✥ 1:E5*

$$$$ MODERN FRENCH **Hélène Darroze.** The most celebrated female chef in Paris is now cooking at the Connaught in London, but her St-Germain dining room is an exclusive setting for her sophisticated take on southwestern French food. Darroze's intriguingly modern touch comes through in such dishes as a sublime duck-foie-gras confit served with an exotic-fruit chutney or a blowout of roast wild duck stuffed with foie gras and truffles. At its best, the food lives up to the very high prices, but for a sampling without the wallet shock, her €28 eight-course tapas lunch menu, served in the plush red salon, is one of the best deals in town. *Average main: €65 ✉ 4 rue d'Assas, 6e, St-Germain-des-Prés ☎ 01–42–22–00–11 www.helenedarroze.com Closed Sun. and Mon. Reservations essential Ⓜ Sèvres-Babylone ✥ 1:D5.*

$$$$ BISTRO **Josephine Chez Dumonet.** Theater types, politicos, and locals fill the moleskin banquettes of this venerable bistro, where the frosted-glass lamps and amber walls put everyone in a good light. Unlike most

bistros, Josephine caters to the indecisive, since generous half portions allow you to graze your way through the temptingly retro menu. Try the excellent boeuf bourguignon, roasted saddle of lamb with artichokes, top-notch steak tartare prepared table-side, or anything with truffles in season; game is also a specialty in fall and winter. For dessert, choose between a mille-feuille big enough to serve three and a Grand Marnier soufflé that simply refuses to sink, even with prodding. The wine list, like the food, is outstanding if expensive. $ *Average main: €34* ✉ *117 rue du Cherche-Midi, 6e, St-Germain-des-Prés* ☎ *01–45–48–52–40* ⏲ *Closed weekends* ✍ *Reservations essential* Ⓜ *Duroc* ✣ *1:D6.*

$$ BISTRO **La Ferrandaise.** Portraits of cows adorn the stone walls of this bistro near the Luxembourg Gardens, hinting at the kitchen's penchant for meaty cooking (Ferrandaise is a breed of cattle). Still, there's something for every taste on the market-inspired menu, which always lists three meat and three fish mains. Dill-marinated salmon with sweet mustard sauce is a typical starter, and a thick, milk-fed veal chop might come with a squash pancake and spinach. The dining room buzzes with locals who appreciate the good-value €37 prix fixe—there is no à la carte—and the brilliant bento box–style €16 lunch menu, in which three courses are served all at once. $ *Average main: €24* ✉ *8 rue de Vaugirard, 6e, St-Germain-des-Prés* ☎ *01–43–26–36–36* 🌐 *www.laferrandaise.com* ⏲ *Closed Sun. and 3 wks in Aug. No lunch Mon. and Sat.* Ⓜ *Odéon; RER: Luxembourg* ✣ *1:E5.*

$$ BISTRO **Le Comptoir du Relais Saint-Germain.** Run by legendary bistro chef Yves Camdeborde, this tiny Art Deco hotel restaurant is booked up well in advance for the single dinner sitting featuring five courses of haute-cuisine fare. On weekdays from noon to 6 and weekends until 10, a brasserie menu is served; reservations are not accepted, resulting in long lines and brisk, sometimes shockingly rude, service. Start with charcuterie or pâté, then choose from open-faced sandwiches like a smoked-salmon-and-Comté-cheese croque monsieur, gourmet salads, and a variety of hot dishes such as braised beef cheek, roast tuna, and Camdeborde's famed deboned and breaded pig's trotter. If you don't mind bus fumes, sidewalk tables make for prime people-watching in summer. Camdeborde also runs neighboring Avant Comptoir, a minuscule stand-up zinc bar with hanging hams and sausages where you can score a superb plate of charcuterie and an inky glass of Morgon. Quality crêpes and sandwiches are still served from the window out front. $ *Average main: €22* ✉ *9 carrefour de l'Odéon, 6e, St-Germain-des-Prés* ☎ *01–44–27–07–50* 🌐 *www.hotel-paris-relais-saint-germain.com* Ⓜ *Odéon* ✣ *1:E5.*

$$$$ MODERN FRENCH **L'Atelier de Joël Robuchon.** Worldwide phenomenon Joël Robuchon retired from the restaurant business for several years before opening this red-and-black-lacquer space with a bento-box-meets-tapas aesthetic. High seats surround two U-shape bars, and this novel plan encourages neighbors to share recommendations and opinions. Robuchon's devoted kitchen staff whip up small plates for grazing (€19 to €75) as well as full portions, which can turn out to be the better bargain. Highlights from the oft-changing menu have included an intense tomato jelly topped with avocado purée and the thin-crusted mackerel tart, although his

DID YOU KNOW?

Because the Latin Quarter is Student Central it is home to many reasonably priced eateries—pull up a café seat during *l'heure bleue* (twilight) to enjoy some real Parisian magic.

inauthentic (but who's complaining?) take on carbonara with cream and Alsatian bacon, and the *merlan* Colbert (fried herb butter) remain signature dishes. Reservations are taken for the first sittings only at lunch and dinner. *Average main: €40 5 rue Montalembert, 7e, St-Germain-des-Prés 01–42–22–56–56 www.atelier-robuchon-saint-germain.com Rue du Bac 1:E4.*

$$ BISTRO FAMILY **L'Epigramme.** Great bistro food is not so hard to find in Paris, but only rarely does it come in a comfortable setting. At L'Epigramme, the striped orange-and-yellow chairs are softly padded, there's space between you and your neighbors, and a big glass pane lets in plenty of light from the courtyard. Chef Karine Camcian has an almost magical touch with meat: try her stuffed suckling pig with turnip choucroute, or seared slices of pink lamb with root vegetables in a glossy reduced sauce. In winter the elaborate game dish *lièvre à la royale* (hare stuffed with goose or duck liver and cooked in wine) sometimes makes an appearance. Desserts are not quite as inspired, so try to take a peek at the plates coming out of the kitchen before making your choice. *Average main: €22 9 rue de l'Eperon, 6e, St-Germain-des-Prés 01–44–41–00–09 Closed Sun., Mon., 3 wks in Aug., and 1 wk at Christmas Reservations essential Odéon 1:E5.*

$$$ BISTRO Fodor's Choice ★ **Semilla.** The duo behind the popular neighborhood bistro Fish and the excellent La Dernière Goutte wineshop have poured their significant expertise into this laid-back new bistro in the heart of tony St-Germain-des-Prés. Its sophisticated cuisine, superb wines by the bottle or glass, and total lack of pretension has quickly made Semilla the toast of the town. A lively open kitchen produces a menu of plentiful dishes either raw, roasted, baked, or steamed, with choices that will thrill both carnivores and herbivores. Velvety chestnut soup, lentil croquettes with a light curry emulsion, beet carpaccio, and the excellent marinated salmon are good choices to start, followed by roasted coquilles St-Jacques with Jerusalem artichoke puree or venison served with celery root and quince. There are also plenty of bistro classics to choose from, like beef tartare or côte de boeuf with roasted potatoes and a fine sauce bordelaise—and it's open Sunday. *Average main: €25 54 rue de Seine, 6e, St-Germain-des-Prés 01–43–54–34–50 Reservations essential Odéon, St-Germain-des-Prés 1:E5.*

WHERE TO STAY

If your Parisian fantasy involves staying in a historic hotel with the smell of fresh-baked croissants gently rousing you in the morning, here's some good news: you need not be Ritz-rich to realize it. With more than 1,450 hotels, the City of Light gives visitors stylish options in all price ranges.

Although historic charm is a given, space to stretch out is not. Even budget travelers can sleep under 200-year-old wooden beams, but if you're looking for enough room to spread out multiple suitcases, better book a suite in a four-star palace hotel. Indoor spaces—from beds to elevators—may feel cramped to those not used to life on a European scale. A no-smoking law went into effect in all public spaces in 2008. Enforcement is not always perfect, but at least now you'll have a valid complaint if your room smells like stale smoke. Amenities have also improved, with virtually every hotel now equipped with cable TV, in-room safe, and Wi-Fi access (though not always free). A recent change is the increasing availability of air-conditioning, which can be saintly in August.

Use the coordinate (2:D4) at the end of each listing to locate a site on the corresponding map.

AROUND THE EIFFEL TOWER

$$ HOTEL **Hôtel du Champ de Mars.** Around the corner from picturesque Rue Cler, this charming, affordable hotel welcomes guests with a Provence-inspired lobby and huge picture windows overlooking a quiet street. **Pros:** good value; walking distance to Eiffel Tower, Les Invalides, and Rodin Museum; free Wi-Fi. **Cons:** small rooms compared to larger hotels; no air-conditioning; inconsistent service. *Rooms from: €150 ✉ 7 rue du Champ de Mars, 7e, Around the Eiffel Tower ☎ 01–45–51–52–30 ⊕ www.hotelduchampdemars.com 25 rooms No meals Ⓜ École Militaire ✣ 2:B4.*

$$$ HOTEL **Hôtel Eiffel Trocadéro.** A curious blend of Second Empire and rococo styling awaits guests in this hotel on a quiet corner just off Place Trocadéro. **Pros:** views of Eiffel Tower from upper floors; upscale residential district convenient to métro; organic breakfast buffet. **Cons:** no full-service restaurant; long walk to city center; basic rooms feel cramped. *Rooms from: €250 ✉ 35 rue Benjamin-Franklin, 16e, Around the Eiffel Tower ☎ 01–53–70–17–70 ⊕ www.hoteleiffeltrocadero.com 16 rooms, 1 suite No meals Ⓜ Trocadéro ✣ 2:A4.*

$$$$ HOTEL **Hôtel Le Bellechasse.** If you like eclectic modern interior design, this tiny boutique hotel right around the corner from the popular Musée d'Orsay is a good choice for its access to the major sites. **Pros:** central location near top museums; one-of-a-kind style; helpful staff. **Cons:** pricey rates; street-facing rooms can be noisy; open bathrooms lack privacy. *Rooms from: €400 ✉ 8 rue de Bellechasse, 7e, Around the Eiffel Tower ☎ 01–45–50–22–31 ⊕ www.lebellechasse.com 33 rooms No meals Ⓜ Solferino ✣ 2:D4.*

$$$ HOTEL **Hôtel Le Tourville.** This cozy, contemporary haven near the Eiffel Tower, Champs de Mars, and Invalides is a comfortable base for exploring Paris. **Pros:** convenient location near métro; friendly service; soundproof windows. **Cons:** small standard rooms; air-conditioning only during summer months; no restaurant. *Rooms from: €250 ✉ 16 av. de Tourville, 7e, Around the Eiffel Tower ☎ 01–47–05–62–62 ⊕ www.paris-hotel-tourville.com 27 rooms, 3 suites No meals Ⓜ École Militaire ✣ 2:C5.*

$$$$ HOTEL Fodor's Choice ★ **Shangri-La Hotel Paris.** Displaying French elegance at its best, this impressively restored 19th-century mansion gazing across the Seine at the Eiffel Tower was once the stately home of Prince Roland Bonaparte, grandnephew of the emperor himself, and his gilded private apartments have been transformed into La Suite Impérial. **Pros:** close to the métro and luxury shopping; varied culinary options; exceptional suites. **Cons:** astronomical rates; pool only open until 9 pm; some obstructed views.

2

WHERE SHOULD I STAY?

	NEIGHBORHOOD VIBE	PROS	CONS
St-Germain and Montparnasse (6e, 14e, 15e)	The center of café culture and the emblem of the Left Bank, the mood is leisurely, the attractions are well established, and the prices are high.	A safe, historic area with chic fashion boutiques, famous cafés and brasseries, and lovely side streets. Lively day and night.	Expensive. Noisy along the main streets. The area around the monstrous Tour Montparnasse is a soul-sucking tribute to commerce.
The Quartier Latin (5e)	The historic student quarter of the Left Bank, full of narrow, winding streets, and major parks and monuments such as the Panthéon.	Plenty of cheap eats and sleeps, discount book and music shops, and noteworthy open-air markets. Safe area for wandering walks.	Touristy. No métro stations on the hilltop around the Panthéon. Student pubs can be noisy in summer. Hotel rooms tend to be smaller.
Marais and Bastille (3e, 4e, 11e)	Cute shops, museums, and laid-back bistros line the narrow streets of the Marais, home to both the gay and Jewish communities. Farther east, ethnic eats and edgy shops.	Generally excellent shopping, sightseeing, dining, and nightlife in the super-safe Marais. Bargains aplenty at Bastille hotels. Several modern-design hotels, too.	The Marais's narrow sidewalks are always overcrowded, and rooms don't come cheap. It's noisy around the gritty boulevards of Place de la Bastille and Nation.
Montmartre and northeast Paris (18e, 19e)	The hilltop district is known for winding streets leading from the racy Pigalle district to the stark-white Sacré-Coeur Basilica.	Amazing views of Paris, romantic cobblestone streets, easy access to Roissy-Charles de Gaulle airport.	Steep staircases, few métro stations, and Pigalle can be too seedy to stomach, especially late at night, when it can also be unsafe.
Champs-Élysées and western Paris (8e, 16e, 17e)	The world-famous avenue is lively 24/7 with cinemas, high-end shops, and nightclubs, all catering to the moneyed jet set.	The home to most of the city's famous palace hotels, there's no shortage of luxurious sleeps here.	The high prices of this neighborhood, along with its Times Square tendencies, repel Parisians but lure pickpockets.
Around the Tour Eiffel (7e, 15e)	The impressive Eiffel Tower and monumental Palais de Chaillot at Trocadéro straddle the Seine River.	Safe, quiet, and relatively inexpensive area of Paris with green spaces and picture-perfect views at every turn.	With few shops and restaurants, this district is very quiet at night; long distances between métro stations.
Louvre, Les Halles, Ile de la Cité (1er, 2e, 8e)	The central Parisian district around the Tuileries gardens and Louvre museum is best known for shopping and sightseeing; Les Halles is a buzzing hub of commerce and mass transit.	Convenient for getting around Paris on foot, bus, or métro. Safe, attractive district close to the Seine and shops of all types. All the major métro and RER lines are right by Les Halles.	The main drag along Rue de Rivoli can be noisy with traffic during the day, and the restaurants cater mostly to tourists. Shops are tacky and fast food predominates around Les Halles.

$ Rooms from: €1100 ✉ 10 av. Iéna, 16e, Around the Eiffel Tower ☎ 01–53–67–19–98, 01–53–67–19–19 🌐 www.shangri-la.com ⇨ 65 rooms, 36 suites 🍽 No meals M Iéna ✥ 2:B3.

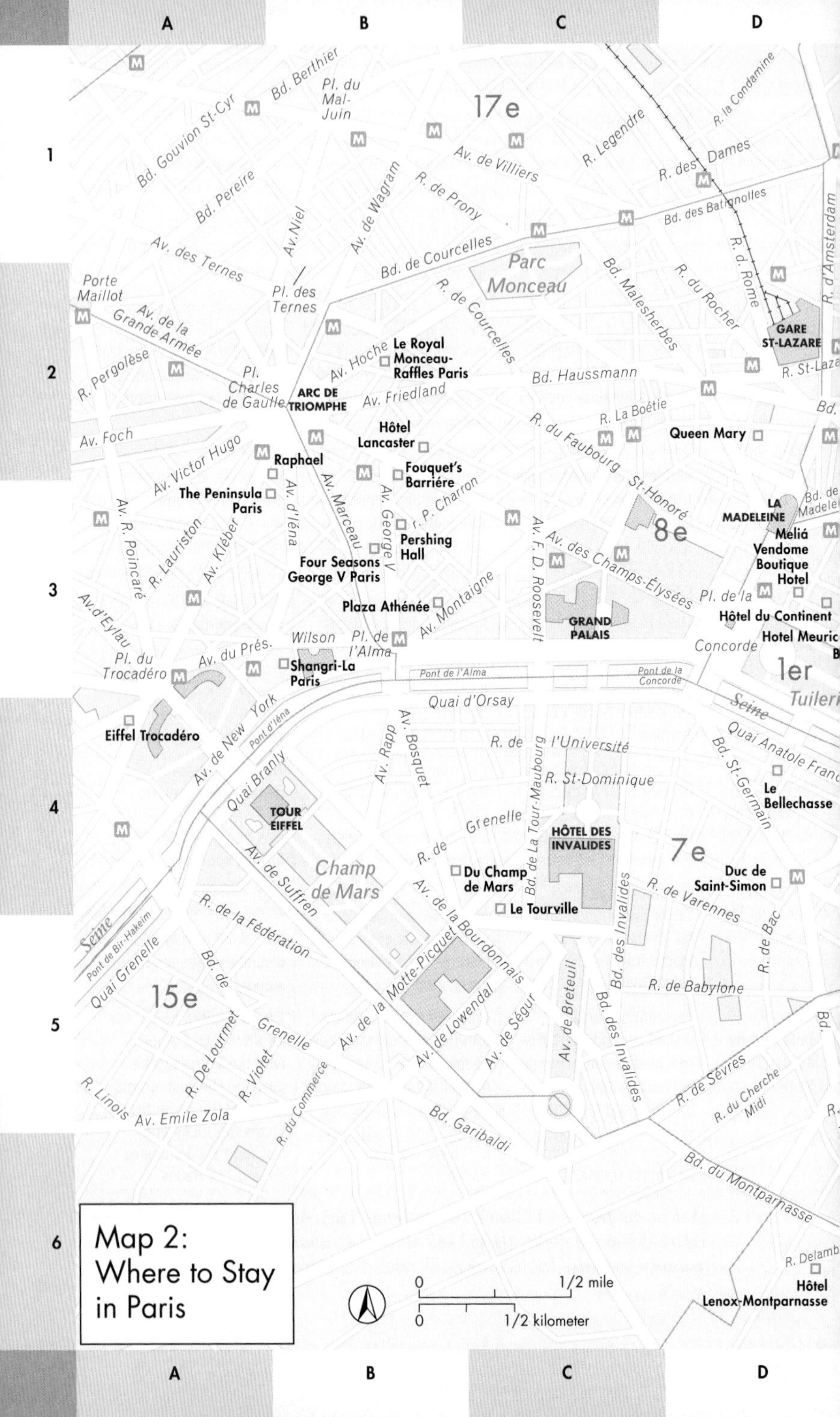
Map 2:
Where to Stay
in Paris
Le Royal Monceau-Raffles Paris
Hôtel Lancaster
Raphael
The Peninsula Paris
Fouquet's Barrière
Pershing Hall
Four Seasons George V Paris
Plaza Athénée
Shangri-La Paris
Eiffel Trocadéro
Queen Mary
Meliá Vendome Boutique Hotel
Hôtel du Continent
Hotel Meuric
Le Bellechasse
Duc de Saint-Simon
Du Champ de Mars
Le Tourville
Hôtel Lenox-Montparnasse
ARC DE TRIOMPHE
GARE ST-LAZARE
LA MADELEINE
GRAND PALAIS
TOUR EIFFEL
HÔTEL DES INVALIDES
Parc Monceau
Champ de Mars
Seine
17e
8e
7e
1er
15e
0
1/2 mile
1/2 kilometer

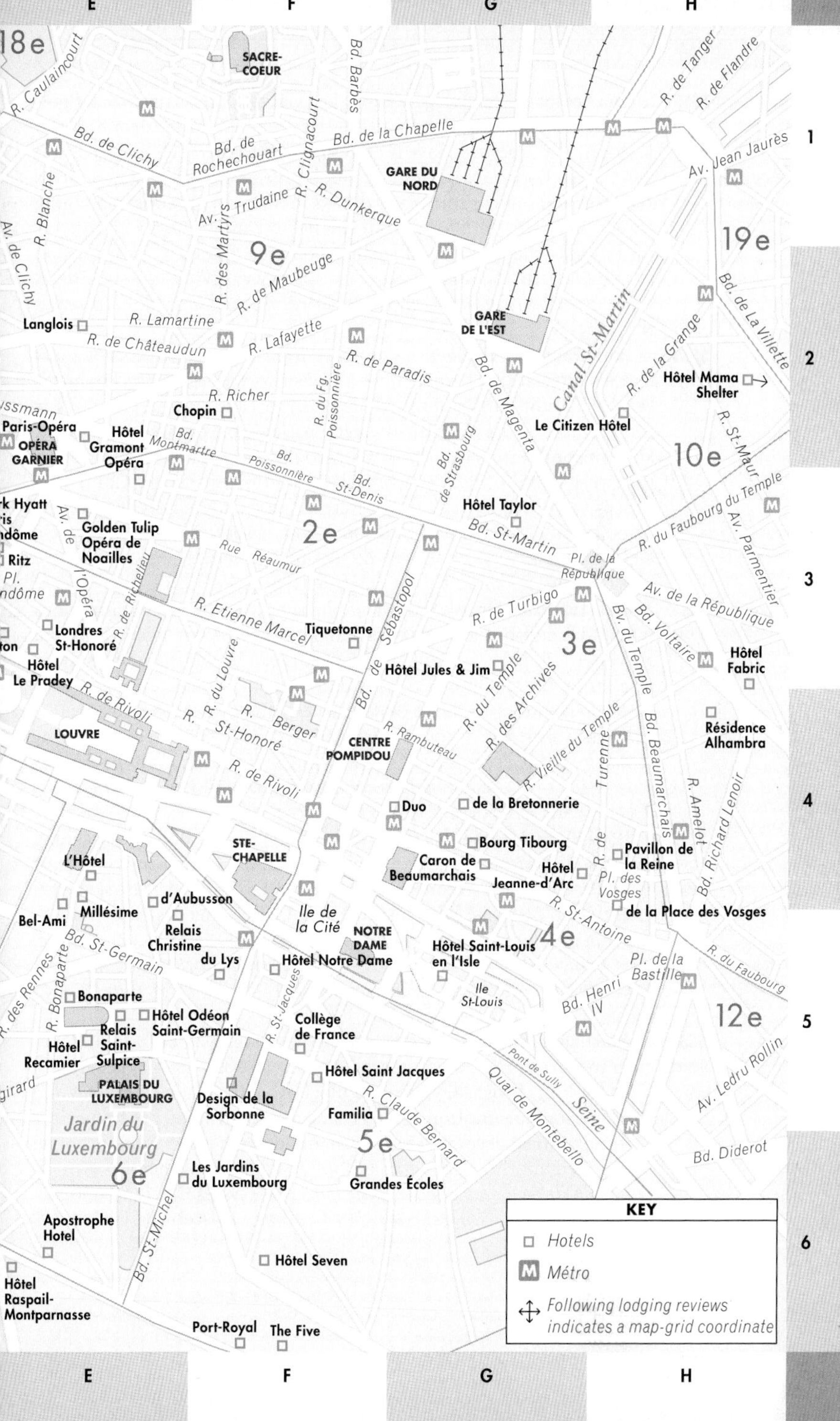

E
F
G
H
1
2
3
4
5
6
18e
SACRE-COEUR
Bd. Barbès
R. Caulaincourt
R. de Tanger
R. de Flandre
Bd. de Clichy
Bd. de Rochechouart
R. Clignancourt
Bd. de la Chapelle
Av. Jean Jaurès
GARE DU NORD
R. Blanche
Av. Trudaine
R. Dunkerque
Av. de Clichy
R. des Martyrs
9e
19e
R. de Maubeuge
Bd. de La Villette
Langlois
R. Lamartine
GARE DE L'EST
R. de Châteaudun
R. Lafayette
Canal St-Martin
R. de Paradis
R. de la Grange
R. du Fg. Poissonnière
Hôtel Mama Shelter
R. Richer
Bd. de Magenta
Chopin
Le Citizen Hôtel
Paris-Opéra
Hôtel Gramont Opéra
Bd. Montmartre
OPÉRA GARNIER
Bd. Poissonnière
Bd. de Strasbourg
10e
R. St-Maur
Bd. St-Denis
Hôtel Taylor
R. du Faubourg du Temple
Golden Tulip Opéra de Noailles
2e
Bd. St-Martin
Av. Parmentier
Ritz
Rue Réaumur
Pl. de la République
Av. de l'Opéra
R. de Richelieu
R. de Turbigo
Av. de la République
R. Etienne Marcel
Bd. Voltaire
Londres St-Honoré
Tiquetonne
Bv. du Temple
3e
Hôtel Le Pradey
Hôtel Jules & Jim
Hôtel Fabric
R. de Rivoli
R. du Louvre
R. du Temple
R. des Archives
Bd. de Sébastopol
LOUVRE
R. Berger
R. St-Honoré
R. Rambuteau
R. Vieille du Temple
Résidence Alhambra
CENTRE POMPIDOU
R. de Turenne
Bd. Beaumarchais
R. Amelot
R. de Rivoli
Duo
de la Bretonnerie
Bd. Richard Lenoir
STE-CHAPELLE
Bourg Tibourg
Pavillon de la Reine
L'Hôtel
Caron de Beaumarchais
Hôtel Jeanne-d'Arc
Pl. des Vosges
Bel-Ami
Millésime
d'Aubusson
de la Place des Vosges
Relais Christine
Ile de la Cité
R. St-Antoine
NOTRE DAME
4e
Bd. St-Germain
du Lys
Hôtel Notre Dame
Hôtel Saint-Louis en l'Isle
Pl. de la Bastille
R. du Faubourg
R. des Rennes
Ile St-Louis
Bonaparte
R. Bonaparte
R. St-Jacques
Bd. Henri IV
Hôtel Odéon Saint-Germain
Relais Saint-Sulpice
Collège de France
12e
Hôtel Recamier
Pont de Sully
Av. Ledru Rollin
PALAIS DU LUXEMBOURG
Hôtel Saint Jacques
Quai de Montebello
Design de la Sorbonne
R. Claude Bernard
Familia
Seine
Jardin du Luxembourg
5e
Bd. Diderot
6e
Les Jardins du Luxembourg
Grandes Écoles
Apostrophe Hotel
Bd. St-Michel
Hôtel Seven
Hôtel Raspail-Montparnasse
Port-Royal
The Five
KEY
Hotels
Métro
Following lodging reviews indicates a map-grid coordinate

CHAMPS-ÉLYSÉES

$$$$ HOTEL FAMILY Fodor's Choice ★ **Four Seasons Hôtel George V Paris.** The George V is as poised and polished as the day it opened in 1928—the original plaster detailing and 17th-century tapestries have been restored, the bas-reliefs regilded, and the marble-floor mosaics rebuilt tile by tile. **Pros:** privileged address near top boutiques; courtyard dining in summer; indoor swimming pool. **Cons:** several blocks from the nearest métro; extra charge for Wi-Fi; lacks the intimacy of smaller boutique hotels. *Rooms from: €1100 ✉ 31 av. George V, 8e, Champs-Élysées ☎ 01–49–52–70–00 🌐 www.fourseasons.com/paris 184 rooms, 60 suites No meals M George V ✣ 2:B3.*

$$$$ HOTEL **Hôtel Fouquet's Barrière.** Steps away from one of the world's most famous streets, this luxury hotel adjacent to the legendary Fouquet's Brasserie at the corner of the Champs-Élysées and Avenue George V is recognizable by its uniformed valets, parked sports cars, and elegant Haussmannian entryway. **Pros:** many rooms overlook the Champs-Élysées; very close to métro; beautiful spa and fitness center. **Cons:** very expensive prices; bar can get overcrowded; corporate events give the place a business-hotel feel. *Rooms from: €1000 ✉ 46 av. George V, 8e, Champs-Élysées ☎ 01–40–69–60–00 🌐 www.lucienbarriere.com 81 rooms, 33 suites No meals M George V ✣ 2:B3.*

$$$$ HOTEL **Hôtel Lancaster.** Once a Spanish nobleman's town house, this luxurious retreat dating from 1889 dazzles with its elegant decor, lush courtyard, and international restaurant led by chef Julien Roucheteau. **Pros:** steps away from the Champs-Élysées and five minutes from métro; excellent seasonal menus at La Table du Lancaster; Sunday brunch with organic produce. **Cons:** size of rooms varies greatly; pricey room service; decor looks tired. *Rooms from: €600 ✉ 7 rue de Berri, 8e, Champs-Élysées ☎ 01–40–76–40–76 🌐 www.hotel-lancaster.fr 43 rooms, 14 suites No meals M George V ✣ 2:B2.*

$$$$ HOTEL FAMILY Fodor's Choice ★ **Hôtel Plaza Athénée.** Distinguished by the scarlet flowers cascading over its elegant facade, this glamorous landmark hotel sits on one of the most expensive avenues in Paris. **Pros:** Eiffel Tower views; special attention to children; Dior Institute spa. **Cons:** some design a bit over-the-top; exorbitant prices. *Rooms from: €1100 ✉ 25 av. Montaigne, 8e, Champs-Élysées ☎ 01–53–67–66–65 🌐 www.dorchestercollection.com/fr/paris/hotel-plaza-athenee-paris 154 rooms, 54 suites No meals M Alma-Marceau ✣ 2:B3.*

$$$$ HOTEL FAMILY **Hôtel Raphael.** This discreet palace-like hotel was built in 1925 to cater to travelers spending a season in Paris, so every space is generously sized for long, lavish stays. **Pros:** a block from the Champs-Élysées and Arc de Triomphe; rooftop garden terrace; intimate hotel bar frequented by locals. **Cons:** decor can feel worn and dowdy; some soundproofing issues; neighborhood has a majestic yet cold atmosphere. *Rooms from: €650 ✉ 17 av. Kléber, 16e, Champs-Élysées ☎ 01–53–64–32–00 🌐 www.raphael-hotel.com 47 rooms, 36 suites No meals M Kléber ✣ 2:B2.*

$$$$ HOTEL FAMILY Fodor's Choice ★ **Le Royal Monceau Raffles Paris.** The glamorous Royal Monceau Raffles offers unparalleled luxury along with a hefty dose of cool. **Pros:** ethereal spa and fitness center; art and cooking ateliers for kids; gorgeous terrace garden. **Cons:** prices exceed a king's ransom. *Rooms from: €750 37 av. Hoche, 8e, Champs-Élysées 01–42–99–88–00 www.leroyalmonceau.com 85 rooms, 64 suites No meals Charles-de-Gaulle-Étoile 2:B2.*

$$$$ HOTEL FAMILY Fodor's Choice ★ **The Peninsula Paris.** After a $900 million renovation that restored the luster of this gem dating from 1908, the lavishly appointed Peninsula raises the bar for luxury hotels in Paris. **Pros:** luxurious touches abound; the city's most beautiful spa; amazing views from higher floors. **Cons:** price out of reach for most mortals; not centrally located; still working out service kinks. *Rooms from: €795 19 ave. Kléber, Champs-Élysées 01–58–12–28–88 paris.peninsula.com 166 rooms, 34 suites No meals Kléber, Etoile 2:B3.*

$$$$ HOTEL **Pershing Hall.** Built in the 18th century for French aristocracy and once serving as the American Legion Hall, this boutique hotel is a must-stay address for the dressed-in-black pack. **Pros:** prime shopping and nightlife district; excellent Sunday brunch buffet; free Wi-Fi throughout hotel. **Cons:** bar noise can be heard in some rooms; inconsistent service. *Rooms from: €500 49 rue Pierre Charron, 8e, Champs-Élysées 01–58–36–58–00 www.pershinghall.com 20 rooms, 6 suites No meals George V, Franklin-D.-Roosevelt 2:B3.*

AROUND THE LOUVRE

$$$$ HOTEL FAMILY **Hôtel Brighton.** A few of the city's most prestigious hotels face the Tuileries or Place de la Concorde, but the 19th-century Brighton occupies the same prime real estate and offers a privileged stay for a fraction of the price. **Pros:** convenient central location; friendly service; breakfast buffet (free for kids under 12). **Cons:** some areas in need of repair; variable quality in decor between rooms; no restaurant for lunch or dinner. *Rooms from: €290 218 rue de Rivoli, 1er, Louvre/Tuileries 01–47–03–61–61 www.paris-hotel-brighton.com 61 rooms No meals Tuileries 2:E3.*

$$ HOTEL Fodor's Choice ★ **Hôtel du Continent.** You'd be hard-pressed to find a budget hotel this stylish anywhere in Paris, let alone in an upscale neighborhood close to many of the top attractions. **Pros:** superfriendly staff; all modern amenities; location, location, location. **Cons:** no lobby; tiny bathrooms. *Rooms from: €135 30 rue du Mont-Thabor, 1e, Louvre/Tuileries 01–42–60–75–32 www.hotelcontinent.com 25 rooms No meals Concord, Tuileries 2:D3.*

$$$$ HOTEL **Hôtel Le Pradey.** Offering Michel Cluizel chocolates and Roger & Gallet toiletries, this compact boutique hotel near the Tuileries has a luxe feel. **Pros:** choice of copious breakfast buffet or quick coffee and croissant; designer touches throughout; double doors for soundproofing in suites. **Cons:** smaller rooms lack closet space; rooms vary greatly in style; nondescript entry and lackluster service results in lukewarm welcome. *Rooms from: €390 5 rue St-Roch, 1e, Louvre/Tuileries 01–42–60–31–70 www.lepradey.com 21 rooms, 7 suites No meals Tuileries 2:E4.*

$$ HOTEL **Hôtel Londres St-Honoré.** Smack-dab in the center of Paris, this no-frills hotel across from a 17th-century church gets points for its location—shops, restaurants, and points of interest are literally steps away. **Pros:** within walking distance of major sites; friendly service; free Wi-Fi. **Cons:** small beds with worn decor; tiny elevator doesn't go to ground floor; extremely narrow staircase. *Rooms from: €149 ✉ 13 rue St-Roch, 1er, Louvre/Tuileries ☎ 01–42–60–15–62 www.hotellondressthonore-paris.com 24 rooms, 4 suites No meals M Pyramides ⊕ 2:E3.*

$$$$ HOTEL FAMILY Fodor's Choice ★ **Hôtel Meurice.** Since 1835, the Meurice has welcomed royalty and celebrities from the Duchess of Windsor to Salvador Dalí—who both resided in the grande-dame establishment—and Paris's first palace hotel continues to please with service, style, and views. **Pros:** stunning art and architecture; views over the Tuileries gardens; central location convenient to métro and major sites. **Cons:** popularity makes the public areas not very discreet; inconsistent front-desk service at times unattentive. *Rooms from: €1295 ✉ 228 rue de Rivoli, 1er, Louvre/Tuileries ☎ 01–44–58–10–09 www.dorchestercollection.com 154 rooms, 54 suites No meals M Tuileries, Concorde ⊕ 2:E3.*

$$$$ HOTEL **Meliá Vendôme.** In a prestigious quarter a few minutes from the Jardin des Tuileries, Place de la Concorde, Opéra Garnier, and the Louvre, the Meliá Vendôme has handsome and spacious rooms in attractive contemporary tones that exude an understated elegance. **Pros:** oustanding location in the city center; near world-class shopping; elegant, immaculate rooms. **Cons:** expensive breakfast; no spa or pool; in-room cooling system unreliable. *Rooms from: €350 ✉ 8 rue Cambon, 1e, Louvre/Tuileries ☎ 01–44–77–54–00 www.melia.com/en/hotels/france/paris/melia-vendome-boutique-hotel/index.html 78 rooms, 5 suites No meals M Concorde, Madeleine ⊕ 2:D3.*

$$$$ HOTEL FAMILY **Ritz.** In novels, songs, and the common parlance, there's not a word that evokes the romance and luxury of Paris better than the Ritz, which is scheduled to reopen in late 2015 or early 2016 after a major renovation. **Pros:** spacious swimming pool; superlative selection of bars and restaurants; top-notch service. **Cons:** easy to get lost in the vast hotel; paparazzi magnet; astronomical prices. *Rooms from: €1000 ✉ 15 pl. Vendôme, 1er, Louvre/Tuileries ☎ 01–43–16–30–30 www.ritzparis.com 71 rooms, 72 suites No meals M Opéra ⊕ 2:E3.*

THE GRANDS BOULEVARDS

$$$$ HOTEL **Hôtel de Noailles.** With a nod to the work of postmodern designers like Putman and Starck, this stylish boutique hotel is both contemporary and cozy. **Pros:** 15- to 20-minute walk to the Louvre and Opéra; a block from the airport bus; free Wi-Fi. **Cons:** no interesting views; some bathrooms in need of renovation; small elevator. *Rooms from: €345 ✉ 9 rue de la Michodière, 2e, Opéra/Grands Boulevards ☎ 01–47–42–92–90 www.hoteldenoailles.com 56 rooms No meals M Opéra ⊕ 2:E3.*

$ HOTEL **Hôtel Chopin.** A unique mainstay of the district, the Chopin recalls its 1846 birth date with a creaky-floored lobby and aged woodwork. **Pros:** special location; close to major métro station; great nightlife district.

Cons: thin walls; single rooms are very small; few amenities. *Rooms from: €106 ✉ 10 bd. Montmartre, 46 passage Jouffroy, 9e, Opéra/Grands Boulevards ☎ 01–47–70–58–10 🌐 www.hotelchopin.fr 36 rooms No meals Ⓜ Grands Boulevards ⊕ 2:F2.*

$$$ HOTEL **Hôtel Gramont Opéra.** Near the Opéra Garnier and some of the city's best department stores, this family-owned boutique hotel has lots of little extras that make it a great value. **Pros:** good breakfast buffet with eggs to order; personalized and professional service; connecting rooms for families. **Cons:** singles have no desk; small bathrooms; elevator doesn't go to top floor rooms. *Rooms from: €239 ✉ 22 rue Gramont, 2e, Grands Boulevards ☎ 01–42–96–85–90 🌐 www.hotel-gramont-opera.com 25 rooms No meals Ⓜ Quatre-Septembre ⊕ 2:E3.*

$$$ HOTEL **Hôtel Langlois.** This darling hotel gained a reputation as one of the most atmospheric budget sleeps in the city. **Pros:** excellent views from the top floor; close to department stores and Opéra Garnier; historic decor. **Cons:** noisy street; off the beaten path; some sagging furniture and worn fabrics. *Rooms from: €185 ✉ 63 rue St-Lazare, 9e, Opéra/Grands Boulevards ☎ 01–48–74–78–24 🌐 www.hotel-langlois.com 24 rooms, 3 suites No meals Ⓜ Trinité ⊕ 2:E2.*

$$$ HOTEL **Hôtel Queen Mary.** Although showing its age, this cozy hotel is well situated near high-end shopping and the city's famous department stores. **Pros:** close to Place de la Madeleine; extra-attentive service; pretty garden. **Cons:** some rooms are claustrophobic; those on the ground floor and facing the street can be noisy; decor can feel somewhat old-fashioned. *Rooms from: €219 ✉ 9 rue Greffulhe, 8e, Opéra/Grands Boulevards ☎ 01–42–66–40–50 🌐 www.hotelqueenmary.com 33 rooms, 2 suites No meals Ⓜ Madeleine, St-Lazare, Havre Caumartin ⊕ 2:D2.*

$ HOTEL **Hôtel Tiquetonne.** Just off the market street of Rue Montorgueil and a short walk from Les Halles, this is one of the least expensive hotels in the city center. **Pros:** cheap rooms in the center of town; in trendy shopping and nightlife area; some views onto Sacré-Coeur. **Cons:** minimal service and no amenities; noise from the street; decor feels outdated. *Rooms from: €65 ✉ 6 rue Tiquetonne, 2e, Les Halles ☎ 01–42–36–94–58 🌐 www.hoteltiquetonne.fr 45 rooms, 33 with bath No meals Ⓜ Étienne Marcel ⊕ 2:F3.*

$$$$ HOTEL Fodor's Choice ★ **Park Hyatt Paris Vendôme.** Understated luxury with a contemporary Zen vibe differentiates this Hyatt from its more classic neighbors between Place Vendôme and Opéra Garnier. **Pros:** stylish urban-chic design; the latest technology; only in-suite spas in Paris. **Cons:** as part of the Hyatt chain, it can feel anonymous; many corporate events held here; very expensive rates. *Rooms from: €850 ✉ 3–5 rue de la Paix, 2e, Opéra/Grands Boulevards ☎ 01–58–71–12–34 🌐 www.paris.vendome.hyatt.com 124 rooms, 24 suites No meals Ⓜ Concorde, Opéra ⊕ 2:E3.*

$$$$ HOTEL Fodor's Choice ★ **W Paris-Opéra.** Located near Opéra Garnier, this 91-room hotel—the first W in France—feels part Moulin Rouge, part art gallery, with cheeky and irreverent touches strewn throughout. **Pros:** coveted location in historic 19th-century building; excellent restaurant; cutting-edge rooms with comfortable beds. **Cons:** fee for Wi-Fi; rooms and

public spaces feel claustrophobic; noisy neighborhood. *Rooms from: €450 4 rue Meyerbeer, 9e, Opéra/Grands Boulevards 01–77–48–94–94 www.wparisopera.com 72 rooms, 19 suites No meals Chaussée d'Antin–La Fayette 2:E2.*

MARAIS

$$$$ HOTEL **Hôtel Bourg Tibourg.** Scented candles and subdued lighting announce the blend of romance and contemplation designer-du-jour Jacques Garcia brought to the Hôtel Bourg Tibourg. **Pros:** in the heart of the trendy Marais; moderate prices; great nightlife district. **Cons:** rooms tend to be small and poorly lit; no hotel restaurant; lounge area gets crowded. *Rooms from: €290 19 rue du Bourg Tibourg, 4e, Marais 01–42–78–47–39 bourgtibourg.com 29 rooms, 1 suite No meals Hôtel de Ville 2:G4.*

$$ HOTEL **Hôtel Caron de Beaumarchais.** For that traditional French feeling, book a room at this intimate, affordable, romantic hotel—the theme is the work of former next-door-neighbor Pierre-Augustin Caron de Beaumarchais, a supplier of military aid to American revolutionaries and the playwright who penned *The Marriage of Figaro* and *The Barber of Seville*. **Pros:** cozy Parisian decor of yesteryear; breakfast in bed served until noon; excellent location within easy walking distance of major monuments. **Cons:** small rooms with few amenities; busy street of bars and cafés can be noisy; may feel old-fashioned for younger crowd. *Rooms from: €170 12 rue Vieille-du-Temple, 4e, Marais 01–42–72–34–12 www.carondebeaumarchais.com 19 rooms No meals Hôtel de Ville 2:G4.*

$$$ HOTEL **Hôtel de la Bretonnerie.** In a 17th-century *hôtel particulier* (town house) on a side street in the Marais, this small hotel with exposed wooden beams and traditional styling sits a few minutes from the Centre Pompidou and the numerous bars and cafés of Rue Vieille du Temple. **Pros:** typical Parisian character; moderate prices; free Wi-Fi access. **Cons:** quality and size of the rooms vary greatly; no air-conditioning; rooms facing street can be noisy. *Rooms from: €185 22 rue Ste-Croix-de-la-Bretonnerie, 4e, Marais 01–48–87–77–63 www.hotelparismaraisbretonnerie.com 22 rooms, 7 suites No meals Hôtel de Ville 2:G4.*

$$ HOTEL **Hôtel de la Place des Vosges.** Despite a Lilliputian elevator that doesn't serve all floors, this small, simple hotel just off 17th-century Place des Vosges draws a loyal clientele. **Pros:** excellent location near famous sights and public transportation; traditional ambience; reasonable rates. **Cons:** no air-conditioning; most rooms are very small; street-facing rooms can be noisy. *Rooms from: €150 12 rue de Birague, 4e, Marais 01–42–72–60–46 www.hotelplacedesvosges.com 16 rooms No meals Bastille 2:H4.*

$$$$ HOTEL **Hôtel Duo.** For this hotel in the heart of the trendy Marais district, architect Jean Philippe Nuel was commissioned to bring things up-to-date with bold colors and dramatic lighting; some rooms still have the original 16th-century beams, but the overall feel is casual urban chic. **Pros:** central location near shops and cafés; walking distance to major monuments; good amenities. **Cons:** noisy neighborhood; service not

always delivered with a smile; small standard rooms and bathrooms. *Rooms from: €290* *11 rue du Temple, 4e, Marais* *01–42–72–72–22* *www.duoparis.com* *58 rooms* *No meals* *Hôtel de Ville* *2:G4.*

$$ HOTEL **Hôtel Jeanne-d'Arc.** This hotel is prized for its unbeatable location off tranquil Place du Marché Ste-Catherine, one of the city's lesser-known pedestrian squares. **Pros:** charming street close to major attractions; good value for the Marais; lots of drinking and dining options nearby. **Cons:** noisy garbage trucks and late-night revelers on the square after midnight; dreary decor; no air-conditioning. *Rooms from: €120* *3 rue de Jarente, 4e, Marais* *01–48–87–62–11* *www.hoteljeannedarc.com* *35 rooms* *No meals* *St-Paul* *2:G4.*

$$$ HOTEL Fodor's Choice ★ **Hôtel Jules & Jim.** In the less-traveled corner of the trendy Marais district, this contemporary boutique hotel feels almost like an art gallery. **Pros:** bright and modern; stylish design; close to public transportation. **Cons:** the small "Jules" rooms are best for those traveling light or staying just one night; no restaurant. *Rooms from: €210* *11 rue des Gravilliers, 3e, Marais* *01–42–78–10–01* *www.hoteljulesetjim.com* *22 rooms, 1 duplex* *No meals* *Arts et Métiers* *2:G3.*

$$$ HOTEL **Hôtel Saint-Louis en l'Isle.** The location on the exceptionally charming Ile St-Louis is the real draw of this five-story hotel, which retains many of its original 17th-century stone walls and wooden beams. **Pros:** romantic location; ancient architectural details; friendly staff. **Cons:** location is a bit far from the sights; métro stations are not so convenient; small rooms. *Rooms from: €205* *75 rue St-Louis-en-l'Ile, 4e, Ile St-Louis* *01–46–34–04–80* *www.saintlouisenlisle.com* *20 rooms* *No meals* *Pont Marie* *2:G5.*

$$$$ HOTEL **Pavillon de la Reine.** Hidden off regal Place des Vosges behind a stunning garden courtyard, this enchanting château has gigantic beams, chunky stone pillars, and a weathered fireplace that speaks to its 1612 origins. **Pros:** historic character; quiet setting; soothing spa treatments. **Cons:** expensive for the area and the size of the rooms; the nearest métro is a few blocks away; no uniform theme in interior design. *Rooms from: €440* *28 pl. des Vosges, 3e, Marais* *01–40–29–19–19* *www.pavillon-de-la-reine.com* *31 rooms, 23 suites* *No meals* *Bastille, St-Paul* *2:H4.*

EASTERN PARIS

$$ HOTEL Fodor's Choice ★ **Hôtel Fabric.** This urban-chic hotel tucked away on an old artisan street is fully in tune with the pulse of the lively Oberkampf neighborhood, close to fabulous nightlife, cocktail bars, restaurants, bakeries, and shopping (and the Marais and Canal St-Martin). **Pros:** all-you-can-eat breakfast for €15; lots of great sightseeing within walking distance; warm and helpful staff. **Cons:** rooms can be noisy; very popular so book well in advance. *Rooms from: €153* *31 rue de la Folie Méricourt, 11e* *01–43–57–27–00* *www.hotelfabric.com* *33 rooms* *No meals* *Saint-Ambroise, Oberkampf* *2:H4.*

$$ HOTEL **Hôtel Taylor.** Tucked away on a tiny one-way street between République and Canal St-Martin, the Hôtel Taylor offers spacious rooms at an affordable price in the edgy 10e arrondissement. **Pros:** close to the

métro; Wi-Fi available; breakfast can be served in your room. **Cons:** bathrooms and some rooms need refurbishment; street can seem intimidating at night. *$ Rooms from: €136 ✉ 6 rue Taylor, 10e, Canal St-Martin ☎ 01–42–40–11–01 ⊕ www.paris-hotel-taylor.com 36 rooms No meals M République ⊕ 2:G3.*

$$$ HOTEL Fodor's Choice ★ **Le Citizen Hôtel.** Boasting direct views over the historic Canal St-Martin and a setting close to the Marais, Le Citizen features a minimalist-chic decor, high-tech touches like loaner iPads, and a cool east-Paris vibe. **Pros:** trendy neighborhood; cool perks; friendly, attentive staff. **Cons:** smallest rooms are best for one person; noisy street; about 20 minutes by métro from the main attractions. *$ Rooms from: €199 ✉ 96 quai de Jemmapes, 10e, Canal St-Martin ☎ 01–83–62–55–50 ⊕ www.lecitizenhotel.com 12 rooms Breakfast M Jacques-Bonsergent ⊕ 2:H2.*

$$ HOTEL **Hôtel Résidence Alhambra.** The gleaming white facade, enclosed garden, and flower-filled window boxes brighten this hotel in a lesser-known neighborhood between the Marais and Rue Oberkampf. **Pros:** popular nightlife district; friendly service; inexpensive rates. **Cons:** small doubles; a walk to the center of town; no air-conditioning. *$ Rooms from: €124 ✉ 13 rue de Malte, 11e, République ☎ 01–47–00–35–52 ⊕ www.hotelalhambra.fr 53 rooms No meals M Oberkampf ⊕ 2:H4.*

LATIN QUARTER

$$$$ HOTEL **The Five Hôtel.** Small is beautiful at this design hotel on a quiet street near the Rue Mouffetard market and the Latin Quarter. **Pros:** unique design; personalized welcome; quiet side street. **Cons:** most rooms are too small for excessive baggage; the nearest métro is a 15-minute walk; most rooms only have showers. *$ Rooms from: €255 ✉ 3 rue Flatters, 5e, Latin Quarter ☎ 01–43–31–74–21 ⊕ www.thefivehotel.com 24 rooms No meals M Gobelins ⊕ 2:F6.*

$ HOTEL **Hôtel Collège de France.** Exposed stone walls, wooden beams, and medieval artwork echo the style of the Musée Cluny, two blocks from this charming, family-run hotel. **Pros:** walk to Rive Gauche sights; free Wi-Fi; ceiling fans. **Cons:** thin walls between rooms; no air-conditioning. *$ Rooms from: €118 ✉ 7 rue Thénard, 5e, Latin Quarter ☎ 01–43–26–78–36 ⊕ www.hotel-collegedefrance.com 29 rooms No meals M Maubert—Mutualité, St-Michel, Cluny–La Sorbonne ⊕ 2:F5.*

$$ HOTEL FAMILY Fodor's Choice ★ **Hôtel Familia.** Owners Eric and Sylvie Gaucheron continue to update and improve this popular budget hotel—they've added custom-made wood furniture from Brittany, antique tapestries and prints, and lovely carpeting. **Pros:** attentive, friendly service; great value; lots of character. **Cons:** on a busy street; some rooms are small; some noise between rooms. *$ Rooms from: €134 ✉ 11 rue des Écoles, 5e, Latin Quarter ☎ 01–43–54–55–27 ⊕ www.familiahotel.com 30 rooms No meals M Cardinal Lemoine ⊕ 2:F5.*

$$ HOTEL **Hôtel des Grandes Écoles.** Distributed among a trio of three-story buildings, Madame Le Floch's rooms have a distinct grandmotherly vibe because of their flowery wallpaper and lace bedspreads, but they're downright spacious for this part of Paris. **Pros:** close to Latin Quarter

nightlife spots; lovely courtyard; good value. **Cons:** uphill walk from the métro; some noisy rooms; few amenities. *Rooms from: €160* *75 rue du Cardinal Lemoine, 5e, Latin Quarter* *01–43–26–79–23* *www.hotel-grandes-ecoles.com* *51 rooms* *No meals* *Cardinal Lemoine* *2:F6.*

2

$$$$ HOTEL **Hotel Design de la Sorbonne.** For what French students pay to study at the Sorbonne (tuition is inexpensive), you can stay a few nights next door at this swanky design hotel. **Pros:** centrally located; fun decor; attentive service. **Cons:** tiny rooms for the price; small breakfast room; lacks traditional French flavor. *Rooms from: €320* *6 rue Victor Cousin, 5e, Latin Quarter* *01–43–54–01–52* *www.hotelsorbonne.com* *38 rooms* *No meals* *Cluny–La Sorbonne* *2:F5.*

$$ HOTEL **Hôtel du Lys.** To jump into an inexpensive Parisian fantasy, just climb the stairway to your room in this former 17th-century royal residence. **Pros:** central location on a quiet side street; historic character; free Wi-Fi. **Cons:** old-fashioned decor; perfunctory service; no air-conditioning or elevator. *Rooms from: €150* *23 rue Serpente, 6e, Latin Quarter* *01–43–26–97–57* *www.hoteldulys.com* *22 rooms* *Breakfast* *St-Michel, Odéon* *2:F5.*

$$$$ HOTEL **Hôtel Notre Dame.** If you love the quirky and eclectic fashions of Christian Lacroix and don't mind hauling your bags up some steps, this unique boutique hotel overlooking Notre-Dame may be for you. **Pros:** decor by Christian Lacroix; views of the river; comfortable beds. **Cons:** stairs can be tricky with large bags; no minibars; some noise from busy street. *Rooms from: €280* *1 quai Saint-Michel, 4e, Latin Quarter* *01–43–54–20–43* *www.hotelnotredameparis.com* *26 rooms* *No meals* *St-Michel* *2:F5.*

$$$ HOTEL **Hôtel Saint Jacques.** Nearly every wall in this Latin Quarter hotel is bedecked with faux-marble and trompe-l'oeil murals. **Pros:** unique Parisian decor; close to Latin Quarter sights; free Wi-Fi. **Cons:** busy street makes it noisy in summer; thin walls between rooms; decor needs refurbishment. *Rooms from: €216* *35 rue des Écoles, 5e, Latin Quarter* *01–44–07–45–45* *www.paris-hotel-saintjacques.com* *38 rooms* *No meals* *Maubert—Mutualité* *2:F5.*

$$$ HOTEL **Hotel Seven.** The "seven" refers to the level of heaven you'll find at this extraordinary boutique hotel, where a team of designers and artists has created seven magnificent suites with imaginative themes like Alice in Wonderland, James Bond, and Marie-Antoinette. **Pros:** fun design elements; copious breakfast buffet; quiet location near Mouffetard market street. **Cons:** small closets; several blocks to closest métro; expensive rates for so few amenities. *Rooms from: €250* *20 rue Berthollet, 5e, Latin Quarter* *01–43–31–47–52* *www.sevenhotelparis.com* *28 rooms, 7 suites* *No meals* *Censier-Daubentin* *2:F6.*

$$$ HOTEL **Les Jardins du Luxembourg.** Blessed with a personable staff and a warm ambience, this hotel on a calm cul-de-sac puts you just a block away from the Jardin du Luxembourg. **Pros:** on a quiet street close to major attractions and transportation; hot buffet breakfast; relaxing sauna. **Cons:** some very small rooms; air-conditioning not very strong. *Rooms from: €199* *5 impasse Royer-Collard, 5e, Latin*

Quarter ☎ *01–40–46–08–88* 🌐 *www.les-jardins-du-luxembourg.com* *26 rooms* 🍴 *No meals* Ⓜ *RER: Luxembourg* ✥ *2:E6.*

$ HOTEL **Port-Royal Hôtel.** The sparkling rooms and extra-helpful staff at the Port-Royal are well above average for hotels in this price range. **Pros:** excellent value; attentive service; close to two major markets. **Cons:** not very central; on a busy street; no room air-conditioning. $ *Rooms from: €98* ✉ *8 bd. de Port-Royal, 5e, Latin Quarter* ☎ *01–43–31–70–06* 🌐 *www.port-royal-hotel.fr* *46 rooms, 20 with bath* 🍴 *No meals* Ⓜ *Les Gobelins* ✥ *2:F6.*

ST-GERMAIN-DES-PRES

$$$$ HOTEL **Hôtel Bel Ami.** A short stroll from the famous Café de Flore, the Bel Ami hides its past as an 18th-century textile factory behind low-slung furnishings, computer stations, and flat-screen TVs. **Pros:** central St-Germain-des-Prés location; feels completely up-to-date; spacious fitness center and spa. **Cons:** some guests report loud noise between rooms; some small rooms in lower price category; not suitable for families with younger kids. $ *Rooms from: €550* ✉ *7–11 rue St-Benoît, 6e, St-Germain-des-Prés* ☎ *01–42–61–53–53* 🌐 *www.hotelbelami-paris.fr* *101 rooms, 7 suites* 🍴 *No meals* Ⓜ *St-Germain-des-Prés* ✥ *2:E5.*

$$$ HOTEL FAMILY **Hôtel Bonaparte.** The service, amenities, and *petit déjeuner* (breakfast) may be far from luxurious at this unpretentious family-run hotel, but the location in the heart of St-Germain is fabulous. **Pros:** upscale shopping neighborhood; large rooms for the Rive Gauche; welcoming to families. **Cons:** outdated decor; minuscule elevator fits one person; no shower curtains. $ *Rooms from: €189* ✉ *61 rue Bonaparte, 6e, St-Germain-des-Prés* ☎ *01–43–26–97–37* 🌐 *www.hotelbonaparte.fr* *29 rooms* 🍴 *No meals* Ⓜ *St-Sulpice* ✥ *2:E5.*

$$$$ HOTEL FAMILY **Hôtel d'Aubusson.** The showpiece at this 17th-century town house in the heart of St-Germain-des-Prés is the stunning front lobby, spanned by massive beams and a gigantic stone fireplace reminiscent of French aristocratic homes of yore. **Pros:** central location near shops and a market street; spacious rooms; staff greets you warmly. **Cons:** some of the newer rooms lack character; busy street and bar can be noisy; very touristy. $ *Rooms from: €405* ✉ *33 rue Dauphine, 6e, St-Germain-des-Prés* ☎ *01–43–29–43–43* 🌐 *www.hoteldaubusson.com* *49 rooms* 🍴 *No meals* Ⓜ *Odéon* ✥ *2:E4.*

$$$$ HOTEL **Hôtel Duc de Saint-Simon.** For pure French flavor, including rooms decorated in floral chintz, head to this intimate hotel in a hidden location between Boulevard St-Germain and Rue de Bac. Four of the antiques-filled rooms have spacious terraces overlooking the courtyard. **Pros:** upscale neighborhood close to St-Germain-des-Prés; historic character; friendly service. **Cons:** rooms in the annex are smaller and have no elevator; cramped bathrooms; no room service. $ *Rooms from: €295* ✉ *14 rue St-Simon, 7e, St-Germain-des-Prés* ☎ *01–44–39–20–20* 🌐 *www.hotelducdesaintsimon.com* *29 rooms, 5 suites* 🍴 *No meals* Ⓜ *Rue du Bac* ✥ *2:D4.*

$$$$ HOTEL **Hôtel Millésime.** The beautiful stone archway of this 17th-century city mansion in St-Germain-des-Prés was the original entrance to the Saint Germain Abbey—as you enter, you'll feel transported to the sunny

2

south of France. **Pros:** upscale shopping nearby; young, friendly staff; plenty of atmosphere. **Cons:** ground-floor rooms can be noisy; smoke from courtyard when windows are open; some furnishings need repair. *Rooms from: €280 15 rue Jacob, 6e, St-Germain-des-Prés 01–44–07–97–97 www.millesimehotel.com 19 rooms, 1 suite No meals St-Germain-des-Prés 2:E4.*

$$$$ HOTEL **Hôtel Odéon Saint-Germain.** Exposed stone walls and original wooden beams give this 16th-century building typical Rive Gauche character, and designer Jacques Garcia's generous use of striped taffeta curtains, velvet upholstery, and plush carpeting imbues it with the distinct luxury of St-Germain-des-Prés. **Pros:** free Internet; luxuriously appointed rooms; in an upscale shopping district near Jardin Luxembourg. **Cons:** small rooms a challenge for those with extra-large suitcases; tiny elevator; prices high for room size and average service. *Rooms from: €260 13 rue St-Sulpice, 6e, St-Germain-des-Prés 01–43–25–70–11 www.hotelparisodeonsaintgermain.com 24 rooms, 3 junior suites No meals Odéon 2:E5.*

$$$$ HOTEL **Hôtel Recamier.** This discreet boutique hotel in a quiet corner overlooking Eglise St-Sulpice is perfect if you're seeking a romantic and cozy hideaway in the St-Germain-des-Près district. **Pros:** peaceful garden courtyard; free Wi-Fi and computer station; well-appointed bathrooms. **Cons:** small closets and bathrooms; room service only until 11 pm; no fitness area, spa, or restaurant. *Rooms from: €290 3 bis, pl. St-Sulpice, 6e, St-Germain-des-Prés 01–43–26–04–89 www.hotelrecamier.com 24 rooms No meals Mabillon 2:E5.*

$$$ HOTEL **Hôtel Relais Saint-Sulpice.** Sandwiched between St-Sulpice and the Jardin du Luxembourg, this little hotel wins accolades for its location. **Pros:** chic location; close to two métro stations; bright breakfast room and courtyard. **Cons:** some smallish rooms; noise from the street on weekend evenings; poorly designed lighting. *Rooms from: €250 3 rue Garancière, 6e, St-Germain-des-Prés 01–46–33–99–00 www.relais-saint-sulpice.com 26 rooms No meals St-Germain-des-Prés, St-Sulpice 2:E5.*

$$$$ HOTEL **L'Hôtel.** There's something just a bit naughty in the air at this eccentric and opulent boutique hotel. **Pros:** luxurious decor; elegant bar and restaurant; walking distance to the Musée d'Orsay and the Louvre. **Cons:** some rooms are very small for the price; closest métro station is a few blocks away; eclectic decoration seems mismatched. *Rooms from: €295 13 rue des Beaux-Arts, 6e, St-Germain-des-Prés 01–44–41–99–00 www.l-hotel.com 16 rooms, 4 suites No meals St-Germain-des-Prés 2:E4.*

$$$$ HOTEL **Relais Christine.** On a quiet street on the Left Bank, this exquisite *hôtel de charme* dates back to the 13th century as a former abbey of the Grands-Augustins and has an impressive stone courtyard and interior garden. **Pros:** quiet address; close to the Latin Quarter; historic character. **Cons:** thin walls in some rooms; no on-site restaurant; a bit touristy. *Rooms from: €420 3 rue Christine, 6e, St-Germain-des-Prés 01–40–51–60–80 www.relais-christine.com 44 rooms, 5 suites No meals Odéon 2:E4.*

MONTPARNASSE

$$$ HOTEL **Apostrophe Hotel.** Those enamored of the artistic and literary history of Paris's Left Bank will appreciate this whimsical family-run hotel between Montparnasse and Luxembourg Garden. **Pros:** very friendly multilingual staff; quiet street in charming area; close to métro. **Cons:** limited closet space; little privacy with bathrooms opening up directly to rooms; no restaurant or bar. *Rooms from: €230 3 rue de Chevreuse, 6e, Montparnasse 01–56–54–31–31 www.apostrophe-hotel.com 16 rooms No meals Vavin 2:E6.*

$$$ HOTEL **Hôtel Raspail-Montparnasse.** Montparnasse was the art capital of the world in the '20s and '30s, and this affordable hotel captures some of that spirit by naming its rooms after some of the illustrious neighborhood stars—Picasso, Chagall, and Modigliani. **Pros:** convenient to métro and bus; many markets and cafés nearby; friendly staff. **Cons:** traffic noise; some rooms small; dated interiors with worn fabrics. *Rooms from: €190 203 bd. Raspail, 14e, Montparnasse 01–43–20–62–86 www.hotelraspailmontparnasse.com 38 rooms No meals Vavin 2:E6.*

NIGHTLIFE AND PERFORMING ARTS

The performing-arts scene in Paris runs the gamut from highbrow to lowbrow, cheap (or free) to break-the-bank expensive. Venues are indoors and outdoors, opulent or spartan, and dress codes vary accordingly. Regardless of the performance you choose, it's unlikely to be like anything you've seen before. Parisians have an audacious sense of artistic adventure and a stunning eye for scene and staging. An added bonus in this city of classic beauty is that many of the venues themselves—from the opulent interiors of the Opéra Garnier and the Opéra Royal de Versailles to the Art Deco splendor of the Théâtre des Champs-Élysées—are a feast for the eyes.

Detailed entertainment listings in French can be found in the weekly magazines *Pariscope* and *L'Officiel des Spectacles*, available at newsstands and in bookstores; in the Wednesday entertainment insert *Figaroscope,* in the *Figaro* newspaper (*www.scope.lefigaro.fr/theatres-spectacles*); and in the weekly *À Nous Paris*, distributed free in the métro. The webzine *Paris Voice* (*www.parisvoice.com*) offers superb highlights in English. Most performing arts venues also have their own websites, and many include listings as well as other helpful information in English.

The website of the Paris Tourist Office (*www.parisinfo.com*) has theater and music listings in English.

Le Kiosque Théâtre. Half-price tickets for same-day theater performances are available at Le Kiosque Théâtre's Madeleine location. See the website for information on outlets in Place Raoul Dautry (Montparnasse) and Place des Ternes. *Across from 15 pl. de la Madeleine, 7e, Opéra/Grands Boulevards www.kiosquetheatre.com Tues.–Sat. 12:30–7:45, Sun. 12:30–3:45 Madeleine.*

PERFORMING ARTS

CLASSICAL MUSIC

Fodor'sChoice ★ **Salle Cortot.** This acoustic jewel was built in 1929 by Auguste Perret, who promised to construct "a concert hall that sounds like a Stradivarius." Tickets for the jazz and classical concerts held here can only be bought from the box office 30 minutes beforehand, otherwise go online to *www.FNAC.com* or *www.concertclassic.com*. Free student recitals are offered at 12:30 on Tuesday and Thursday from October to May, and some Wednesday afternoons from January to May. ✉ *78 rue Cardinet, 17e, Parc Monceau* ☎ *01–47–63–47–48* 🌐 *www.sallecortot.com* Ⓜ *Malesherbes*.

2

DANCE

Centre National de la Danse. Occupying a former administrative center in the suburb of Pantin, this space is dedicated to supporting professional dancers by offering classes, rehearsal studios, and a multimedia dance library. A regular program of free and reasonably priced performances, expositions, screenings, and conferences is also open to the public from October to July. ✉ *1 rue Victor Hugo, Pantin* ☎ *01–41–83–98–98* 🌐 *www.cnd.fr* Ⓜ *Hoche or RER: Pantin*.

Théâtre de la Ville. At *the* top spot for contemporary dance, you'll find French and international troupes choreographed by the world's best—like William Forsythe and Anne-Teresa de Keersmaeker's Rosas company. Concerts and theatrical performances are also part of the season. Book early; shows sell out quickly. ✉ *2 pl. du Châtelet, 4e, Beaubourg/Les Halles* ☎ *01–42–74–22–77* 🌐 *www.theatredelaville-paris.com* Ⓜ *Châtelet*.

OPERA

Paris offers some of the best opera in the world—and thousands know it. Consequently, it's best to plan ahead if you'd like to attend a performance of the **Opéra National de Paris** at its two homes, the Opéra de la Bastille and the Opéra Garnier. Tickets range from €5 (for standing room at Opéra Bastille only) to €200 and generally go on sale at the box office a month before shows, earlier by phone and online. The opera season usually runs September through July (with each opera given a minirun of a week or two), and the box office is open Monday through Saturday 11–6:30. Last-minute discount tickets, when available, are offered 15 minutes before a performance for seniors and anyone under 28. The box office is open 11 to 6:30 pm daily.

Opéra Bastille. This mammoth ultramodern facility, designed by architect Carlos Ott and inaugurated in 1989, long ago took over the role of Paris's main opera house from the Opéra Garnier (although both operate under the same Opéra de Paris umbrella). Like the building, performances tend to be on the avant-garde side—you're as likely to see a contemporary adaptation of *La Bohème* as you are to hear Kafka set to music. Tickets for Opéra de Paris productions range from €10 to €230 and generally go on sale at the box office a month before shows, earlier by phone and online. Once the doors open, "standing places" can be purchased for €5 from vending machines in the lobby, but you'll need coins or a credit card (no bills) and patience to snag one, as the lines are long. The opera season usually runs September through July; the box office is open Monday–Saturday 2:30–6:30 and one hour before curtain call. If you just want to look around inside, you can also buy tickets for a 75-minute guided tour (€12). (*See Chapter 9, Eastern Paris.*) ✉ *Pl. de la Bastille, 12e, Bastille/Nation* ☎ *08–92–89–90–90 €0.34 per minute, 01–71–25–24–23 from outside France, 01–40–01–19–70 Tours* 🌐 *www.operadeparis.fr* ☞ *Box office closed July 17 to August 24.* Ⓜ *Bastille.*

Fodor's Choice ★ **Opéra Garnier.** The magnificent, magical former haunt of the Phantom of the Opera, painter Edgar Degas, and any number of legendary opera stars still hosts performances of the Opéra de Paris, along with a fuller calendar of dance performances (the theater is the official home of the Ballet de l'Opéra National de Paris). The grandest opera productions are usually mounted at the Opéra Bastille, whereas the Garnier now presents smaller-scale works such as Mozart's *La Clemenza di Tito* and *Così Fan Tutte*. Gorgeous and intimate though the Garnier is, its tiara-shape theater means that many seats have limited visibility, so it's best to ask specifically what the sight lines are when booking (partial view in French is *visibilité partielle*). The cheaper seats are often those with partial views. Seats generally go on sale at the box office a month before any given show, earlier by phone and online; you must appear in person to buy the cheapest tickets. Last-minute returned or unsold tickets, if available, are offered an hour prior to a performance. The box office is open 11:30–6:30 Monday to Saturday and one hour before curtain call; however, you should get in line up to two hours in advance. Venue visits (€10) and guided tours in English (€14.50) are available and can be reserved online; check the website for details. (*See Chapter 6, Les Grands Boulevards.*) ✉ *Pl. de l'Opéra, 9e, Opéra/Grands Boulevards* ☎ *08–92–89–90–90 €0.34 per min, 01–71–25–24–23 from outside France* 🌐 *www.operadeparis.fr* ☞ *Box office closed July 17–Aug. 24* Ⓜ *Opéra.*

Théâtre du Châtelet. Also known as Théâtre Musical de Paris, this venue stages some of the finest opera productions in the city and regularly attracts international divas like Cecilia Bartoli and Anne-Sofie von Otter. It also hosts classical concerts, dance performances, Broadway musicals, and the occasional play. ✉ *Pl. du Châtelet, 2 rue Edouard Colonne, 1er, Beaubourg/Les Halles* ☎ *01–40–28–28–40* 🌐 *www.chatelet-theatre.com* Ⓜ *Châtelet.*

THEATER

A number of theaters line the Grands Boulevards between Opéra and République, but there's no Paris equivalent of Broadway or the West End. Shows are mostly in French. English-language theater groups playing in venues throughout Paris include the **International Players** (🌐 *www.internationalplayers.co.uk*). Broadway-scale singing-and-dancing musicals are generally staged at either the Palais des Sports or the Palais des Congrès.

Fodor's Choice ★ **Comédie Française.** Founded in 1680, Comédie Française is the most hallowed institution in French theater. It specializes in splendid classical French plays by the likes of Racine, Molière, and Marivaux. Buy tickets at the box office, by telephone, or online. If the theater is sold out, the Salle Richelieu offers steeply discounted last-minute tickets an hour before the performance. ✉ *Salle Richelieu, Pl. Colette, 1er, Louvre* ☎ *08–25–10–16–80 €0.15 per min* 🌐 *www.comedie-francaise.fr* Ⓜ *Palais-Royal–Musée du Louvre.*

Théâtre des Bouffes du Nord. Welcome to the wonderfully atmospheric, slightly decrepit home of Peter Brook. The renowned British director regularly delights with his quirky experimental productions in French and, sometimes, English. ✉ *37 bis, bd. de la Chapelle, 10e, Stalingrad/La Chapelle* ☎ *01–46–07–34–50* 🌐 *www.bouffesdunord.com* Ⓜ *La Chapelle.*

Théâtre du Palais-Royal. Located in the former residence of Cardinal Richelieu, this plush 716-seat, Italian-style theater is bedecked in gold and purple. It specializes in lighter fare, like comedies and theaterical productions aimed at the under-12 set. ✉ *38 rue de Montpensier, 1er, Louvre* ☎ *01–42–97–40–00* 🌐 *theatrepalaisroyal.com* Ⓜ *Palais-Royal.*

NIGHTLIFE

If you prefer clinking drinks with models and celebrities, check out the Champs-Élysées area, but be prepared to shell out *beaucoup* bucks and stare down surly bouncers. Easygoing, bohemian-chic revelers can be found in the northeastern districts like Canal St-Martin and Belleville, while students tend to pour into the Bastille, St-Germain-des-Prés, and the Quartier Latin. Grands Boulevards and Rue Montorgueil, just north of Les Halles, is party central for young professionals and the fashion crowd, and the Pigalle and Montmartre areas are always hopping with plenty of theaters, cabarets, bars, and concert venues. Warmer months draw the adventurous to floating clubs and bars, moored along the Seine from Bercy to the Eiffel Tower.

CHAMPS-ÉLYSÉES

BARS

Le Bar at George V. An ultraluxe, clubby hideaway in the Four Seasons Hotel, Le Bar at George V is perfect for stargazing from the plush wine-red armchairs, cognac in hand. Its charm still lures the glitterati, especially during fashion weeks. Be sure to notice the hotel's signature—and stunning—flower arrangements. ✉ *31 av. George V, 8e, Champs-Élysées* ☎ *01–49–52–70–00* 🌐 *www.fourseasons.com/paris/dining/lounges/le_bar* Ⓜ *George V.*

Pershing Hall. Pershing Hall has an überstylish lounge with muted colors and minimalist lines, plus an enormous "vertical garden" in the simply stunning indoor courtyard. The chic ambience and hip lounge music make this a popular neighborhood nightspot; starting at 10 pm there's a DJ. Try the signature Lalique cocktail—it comes in an actual Lalique crystal glass. ✉ *49 rue Pierre Charron, 8e, Champs-Élysées* ☎ *01–58–36–58–00* 🌐 *www.pershinghall.com* Ⓜ *George V.*

CABARETS

Fodor's Choice ★ **Crazy Horse.** This world-renowned cabaret has elevated the striptease to an art form. Founded in 1951, it's famous for gorgeous dancers and naughty routines characterized by lots of humor and very little clothing. What garments there are have been dazzlingly designed by the likes of Louboutin and Alaïa and shed by top divas (including Dita von Teese). ✉ *12 av. George V, 8e, Champs-Élysées* ☎ *01–47–23–32–32* 🌐 *www.lecrazyhorseparis.com* Ⓜ *Alma-Marceau.*

Lido. Celebrating its 70th anniversary in 2016, the legendary Lido has launched a new show created by Cirque du Soleil alum Franco Dragone, who adds a modern-day dose of awe-inspiring stage design to the cabaret's trademark style. The 100-minute production—still featuring those beloved Blubell Girls—runs at 9 pm and 11 pm, 365 days a year. Dinner for Two packages for the earlier show include the Soirée Etoile (€165), Soirée Champs-Elysées (€195), and the Soirée Triomphe (€300). If you're on a budget, €115 gets you a ticket plus half a bottle of bubbly. Did we mention these prices are per person? Ah yes, this is Paris nightlife as it's meant to be experienced. Although the Lido holds 1,150, it's best to your book tickets in advance by phone, online, or on-site. ✉ *116 bis, av. des Champs-Élysées, 8e, Champs-Élysées* ☎ *01–40–76–56–10* 🌐 *www.lido.fr* Ⓜ *George V.*

AROUND THE LOUVRE

BARS

Fodor's Choice ★ **Ballroom du Beef Club.** Unmarked black door, basement setting, pressed-tin ceilings, atmospheric lighting—did anyone say speakeasy? All this and luscious libations draw a sophisticated crowd that appreciates the extra touches that make this cocktail bar a standout. ✉ *58 rue Jean-Jacques-Rousseau, 1er, Les Halles* ☎ *09–54–37–13–65* Ⓜ *Les Halles, Palais Royal–Musée du Louvre.*

Bar 8. Since this monolithic marble bar at the Mandarin Oriental Hotel opened its doors, it has been the "in" game in town. There's an extensive Champagne menu, and the terrace is especially busy during fashion weeks. ✉ *251 rue Saint-Honoré, 1er, Louvre/Tuileries* ☎ *01–70–98–78–88* 🌐 *www.mandarinoriental.com* Ⓜ *Concorde, Tuileries.*

Experimental Cocktail Club. Fashioned as a speakeasy on a tiny brick-paved street, the Experimental Cocktail Club seems like it should be lighted by gas lamps. The show is all about the *alcool*; colorful, innovative cocktails like the Lemon Drop are mixed with aplomb by friendly (and attractive) bartenders. By 11 pm it's packed with a diverse mix of locals, professionals, and fashionistas, who occasionally dress up like characters from a Toulouse-Lautrec painting on special costume nights. ✉ *37 rue Saint-Sauveur, 2e, Les Halles* ☎ *01–45–08–88–09* Ⓜ *Réamur-Sébastopol.*

The Hemingway Bar & the Ritz Bar. Literature lovers, cocktail connoisseurs, and other drink-swilling devotees drew a collective sigh when the iconic Hemingway Bar & the Ritz Bar were shuttered—along with the rest of the Ritz—when the hotel closed for a top-to-bottom makeover in 2012. It's expected that libations will start being poured again in late 2015. Watch for the big reveal: this is one of the most hotly anticipated face-lifts in Paris. ✉ *15 pl. Vendôme, 1er, Louvre/Tuileries* 🌐 *www.ritzparis.com* Ⓜ *Opéra.*

Kong. Kong is glorious not only for its panoramic skyline views, but for its exquisite manga-inspired decor, the top-shelf DJs for weekend dancing, and its kooky, disco-ball-and-kid-sumo-adorned bathrooms. ✉ *1 rue du Pont-Neuf, 1er, Louvre* ☎ *01–40–39–09–00* 🌐 *www.kong.fr* Ⓜ *Pont-Neuf.*

2

THE GRANDS BOULEVARDS

BARS

Fodor's Choice ★ **Delaville Café.** With its huge, heated sidewalk terrace, Belle Époque mosaic-tile bar, graffitied walls, and swishy lounge, Delaville Café boasts a funky Baroque ambience. Hot Paris DJs ignite the scene Thursday to Saturday, so arrive early on weekends if you want a seat. ✉ *34 bd. Bonne Nouvelle, 10e, Opéra/Grands Boulevards* ☎ *01–48–24–48–09* 🌐 *delavillecafe.com* Ⓜ *Bonne Nouvelle, Grands Boulevards.*

MONTMARTRE

CABARETS

Fodor's Choice ★ **Au Lapin Agile.** An authentic survivor from the 19th century, Au Lapin Agile considers itself the doyen of cabarets. Founded in 1860, it inhabits the same modest house that was a favorite subject of painter Maurice Utrillo. It became the home-away-from-home for Braque, Modigliani, Apollinaire, and Picasso—who once paid for a meal with one of his paintings, then promptly exited and painted another that he named after this place. There are no topless dancers; this is a genuine French cabaret with songs, poetry, and humor (in French) in a pub-like setting. Entry is €28. ✉ *22 rue des Saules, 18e, Montmartre* ☎ *01–46–06–85–87* 🌐 *www.au-lapin-agile.com* Ⓜ *Lamarck Caulaincourt.*

Michou. The always-decked-out-in-blue owner, Michou, presents an over-the-top show here. It features *tranformiste* men on stage in extravagant drag, performing with high camp for a radically different cabaret experience. Dinner shows are €110 and €140, or you can watch from the bar for €40, which includes a drink. ✉ *80 rue des Martyrs, 18e, Montmartre* ☎ *01–46–06–16–04* 🌐 *www.michou.com* Ⓜ *Pigalle.*

Moulin Rouge. When it opened in 1889, the Moulin Rouge lured Parisians of all social stripes—including, of course, the famous Toulouse-Lautrec, who immortalized the venue and its dancers in his paintings. Although shows are no longer quite so exotic (no elephants or donkey rides for the ladies), you will still see the incomparable French cancan. It's the highlight of what is now a classy version of a Vegas-y revue, starring 100 dancers, acrobats, ventriloquists, and contortionists, and more than 1,000 costumes. Dinner starts at 7, revues at 9 and 11 (arrive 30 minutes early). Men are expected to wear a jacket. Prices range from €112 for just a revue to €210 for a luxe dinner and a show. ✉ *82 bd. de Clichy, 18e, Montmartre* ☎ *01–53–09–82–82* 🌐 *www.moulinrouge.fr* Ⓜ *Blanche.*

MARAIS

BARS

FodorsChoice ★ **Candelaria.** Steamy Candelaria is a tacqueria by day and a cocktail lounge by night. The tang of tequila hangs in the air at this hip hideaway, where deftly crafted drinks are poured for a contented crowd. ✉ *52 rue de Saintonge, 3e, Marais* ☎ *01–42–74–41–28* 🌐 *www.candelariaparis.com* Ⓜ *Filles du Calvaire.*

La Perle. La Perle is a bustling, buzzy Marais masterpiece, where straights, gays, and lesbians of all types come to mingle. The crowd makes this place interesting, not the neon lights, diner-style seats, or stripped-down decor. It continues to pack in some of the city's fashion movers and shakers from midafternoon on. ✉ *78 rue Vielle-du-Temple, 3e, Marais* ☎ *01–42–72–69–93* 🌐 *cafelaperle.com* Ⓜ *Chemin-Vert.*

ST-GERMAIN-DES-PRÉS

BARS

Bar du Marché. Waiters wearing red overalls and revolutionary "Gavroche" hats serve drinks every day of the week at this local institution (they demonstrate particular zeal around happy hour). With bottles of wine at about €25, it draws a quintessential Left Bank mix of expats, fashion-house interns, and even some professional rugby players. Sit outside on the terrace and enjoy the prime corner location. ✉ *75 rue de Seine, 6e, St-Germain/Buci* ☎ *01–43–26–55–15* Ⓜ *Mabillon, Odéon.*

MONTPARNASSE

BARS

La Closerie des Lilas. La Closerie's swank "American-style" bar lets you drink in the swirling action of the adjacent restaurant and brasserie at a piano bar adorned with plaques honoring former habitués like Man Ray, Jean-Paul Sartre, Samuel Beckett, and Ernest Hemingway, who talks of "the Lilas" in *A Moveable Feast.* ✉ *171 bd. du Montparnasse, 6e, Montparnasse* ☎ *01–40–51–34–50* 🌐 *www.closeriedeslilas.fr* Ⓜ *Montparnasse.*

SHOPPING

In the most beautiful city in the world, it's no surprise to discover that the local greengrocer displays his tomatoes as artistically as Cartier does its rubies. Window-shopping is one of this city's greatest spectator sports; the French call it *lèche-vitrine*—literally, "licking the windows"—which is fitting because many of the displays look good enough to eat. Most stores, excepting department stores and flea markets, stay open until 6 or 7 pm, but many take a lunch break sometime between noon and 2 pm. Many shops traditionally close on Sunday.

CHAMPS-ÉLYSÉES

BEAUTY

Guerlain. This opulent address is a fitting home for Paris's first—and most famous—perfumer. Still the only Paris outlet for legendary perfumes like Shalimar and L'Heure Blue, it has added several new signature scents (including Myrrhe et Délires and Cuir Beluga). Personalized bottles in several sizes can be filled on demand, or, for a mere €30,000, a customized scent can be blended just for you. Sybarites will also appreciate Guerlain's makeup, scented candles, and redesigned spa featuring its much-adored skin-care line. There's an elegant new gourmet restaurant for lunch or tea, too. ✉ *68 av. des Champs-Élysées, 8e, Champs-Élysées* ☎ *01–45–62–52–57* 🌐 *www.guerlain.com* Ⓜ *Franklin-D.-Roosevelt.*

2

CHILDREN'S CLOTHING

Fodor's Choice ★ **Bonpoint.** Outfit the prince or princess in your life at Bonpoint (yes, royalty *does* shop here). The prices are high, but the quality is exceptional, and the adorable mini-duds couldn't be more stylish: picture a perfect hand-smocked Liberty-print dress, a velvety lambskin vest, or a double-breasted cashmere sweater for Little Lord Fauntleroy. The Avenue Raymond Poincaré boutique is one of more than a dozen citywide. ✉ *64 av. Raymond Poincaré, 16e, Champs-Élysée* ☎ *01–47–27–60–81* 🌐 *www.bonpoint.com* Ⓜ *Trocadéro.*

CLOTHING

Fodor's Choice ★ **Balenciaga.** This venerable Paris fashion house was completely revamped under the brilliant Nicolas Ghesquière, whose singular vision electrified the runway world. With his abrupt departure in late 2012, American wunderkind Alexander Wang took charge. Today the young designer's structured-yet-feminine and freshly appealing designs draw raves each season and consistently reaffirm his stellar fashion credentials. ✉ *10 av. George V, 8e, Champs-Élysées* ☎ *01–47–20–21–11* 🌐 *www.balenciaga.com* Ⓜ *Alma-Marceau.*

Fodor's Choice ★ **Céline.** Reinvigorated by Michael Kors in the late 1990s, Céline got another much-needed jolt when Phoebe Philo arrived in 2009 and began dazzling the critics with her focused approach. Philo's characteristically refined tailoring and attention to minute details underlie the seeming simplicity of her styles, which veer from flowing pants and long, unstructured jackets to streamlined swing skirts. Along with the ready-to-wear, Céline's exquisite bags and shoes are staples for Paris's fashion cognoscenti. The new Avenue Montaigne flagship carries the full line, including eyewear and perfume. There's also a St-Germain boutique on Rue de Grenelle. ✉ *53 av. Montaigne, 8e, Champs-Élysées* ☎ *01–40–70–07–03* 🌐 *www.celine.com* Ⓜ *Franklin-D.-Roosevelt.*

Fodor's Choice ★ **Chanel.** Elegant, modern looks with sex appeal and lasting value are Chanel's stock in trade. Although the spectacular Avenue Montaigne flagship takes shoppers' breath away, the heart of this revered fashion house—helmed by Karl Lagerfeld—is still the boutique at 31 rue Cambon, where Chanel once perched high up on the mirrored staircase watching audience reactions to her collection debuts. Great investments include all of Coco's favorites: the perfectly tailored suit, a lean soigné dress, or a quilted bag with a gold chain. Handbags, jewelry, shoes, and accessories are all found at the newly refurbished 42 avenue Montaigne boutique, opposite the flagship store. ✉ *51 av. Montaigne, 8e, Champs-Élysées* ☎ *01–44–50–73–00* 🌐 *www.chanel.com* Ⓜ *Franklin-D.-Roosevelt.*

Fodor's Choice ★ **Christian Dior.** Raf Simons's modern, streamlined, and feminine looks have redefined this legendary label. Since assuming the helm in 2012 after John Galliano's inglorious fall from grace, Simons has taken an architectural approach to ready-to-wear, playing with volume and contrasting geometric forms with fluid, dimensional fabrics (sometimes pierced or transparent). His meticulously tailored clothes and steadfast vision have consistently elated the fashion press. ✉ *30 av. Montaigne, 8e, Champs-Élysées* ☎ *01–40–73–73–73* 🌐 *www.dior.com* Ⓜ *Franklin-D.-Roosevelt.*

Jean-Paul Gaultier. Jean-Paul Gaultier first made headlines by engineering that celebrated corset with the ironic iconic breasts for Madonna but now sends fashion editors into ecstasies with his sumptuous haute-couture creations. Designer Philippe Starck spun an *Alice in Wonderland* fantasy for the boutique, with quilted cream walls and Murano mirrors. Make no mistake, though, it's all about the clothes. You'll find a second shop in the gorgeous Galerie Vivienne. ✉ *44 av. George V, 8e, Champs-Élysées* ☎ *01–44–43–00–44* 🌐 *www.jeanpaulgaultier.com* Ⓜ *George V.*

Maison Ullens. A glam Golden Triangle location, a Rem Koolhaas–designed boutique, sumptuous clothes—the Belgian label's first Paris outpost hits all the marks and then some. Founded in 2013, Maison Ullens puts the focus on luxe fabrics and skins in classic-chic designs with plenty of staying power. It has everything you need for après-ski or weekends on Capri. ✉ *4 rue de Marignan, 8e, Champs-Élysées* ☎ *01–47–20–23–56* 🌐 *www.maisonullens.com* Ⓜ *Franklin-D.-Roosevelt.*

SHOES, HANDBAGS, AND LEATHER GOODS

Fodor's Choice ★ **Louis Vuitton.** Louis Vuitton has spawned a voracious fan base from Texas to Tokyo with its mix of classic leather goods and saucy revamped versions orchestrated by Marc Jacobs, who made an exit in late 2013 after 16 years with the company. Jacobs left tall boots to fill, but Nicholas Ghesquière—a daring designer who single-handedly resurrected the Balenciaga label—is the man to do it. If his latest collection is any indication, Ghesquière will be taking the legendary luxe label to new heights, mixing architecturally precise volumes with a softer, sexier look. ✉ *101 av. des Champs-Élysées, 8e, Champs-Élysées* ☎ *01–53–57–52–00* 🌐 *www.louisvuitton.com* Ⓜ *George V.*

AROUND THE LOUVRE

BOOKS AND STATIONERY

Librarie Galignani. Dating back to 1520s Venice, this venerable bookstore opened in Paris in 1801 and was the first to specialize in English-language books. Its present location, across from the Tuileries Garden on Rue de Rivoli, opened in 1856, and the wood bookshelves, creaking floors, and hushed interior provide the perfect atmosphere for perusing Paris's best collection of contemporary and classic greats in English and French, plus a huge selection of gorgeous art books. ✉ *224 rue de Rivoli, 1er, Louvre/Tuileries* ☎ *01–42–60–76–07* 🌐 *www.galignani.com* Ⓜ *Tuileries.*

South of the Champs-Élysées you'll find the posh Avenue Montaigne shopping district.

CLOTHING

Fodor's Choice ★ **Chantal Thomass.** The legendary lingerie diva is back with a *Pillow Talk*–meets–Louis XIV–inspired boutique. This is French naughtiness at its best, striking the perfect balance between playful and seductive. Sheer silk negligees edged in Chantilly lace and lascivious bra-and-corset sets punctuate the signature line. ✉ *211 rue St-Honoré, 1er, Louvre/Tuileries* ☎ *01–42–60–40–56* 🌐 *www.chantalthomass.fr* Ⓜ *Tuileries.*

Colette. This is *the* place for ridiculously cool fashion. So the staff barely deigns to make eye contact—who cares! There are ultramodern trinkets and trifles of all kinds: from Lego-link alarm clocks to snappy iPad cases and tongue in chic sportswear—and that's just on the ground floor. The first floor has wearable wares from every internationally known and unknown designer with street cred. The basement has a water bar, plus a small restaurant that's good for a quick bite. ✉ *213 rue St-Honoré, 1er, Louvre/Tuileries* ☎ *01–55–35–33–90* 🌐 *www.colette.fr* Ⓜ *Tuileries.*

Vanessa Bruno. Expect a new brew of feminine dressing from Vanessa Bruno: some androgynous pieces (skinny pants) plus delicacy (filmy tops) with a dash of whimsy (lace insets). Separates are coveted for their sleek styling, gorgeous colors, and unerring sexiness. Wardrobe staples include perfectly proportioned cotton tops and sophisticated dresses. Athé, the diffusion line, flies off the racks, so if you see something you love, grab it. Bruno's shoes and accessories are the cherry on the cake: her ultrapopular sequin-striped totes inspired an army of knock-offs. ✉ *12 rue de Castiglione, 1er, Louvre/Tuileries* ☎ *01–42–61–44–60* 🌐 *www.vanessabruno.com* Ⓜ *Pyramides.*

CLOSE UP

Notable Neighborhoods, Select Streets

Paris's legendary shopping destinations draw people from the world over, but perhaps a deeper allure lies in lesser-known attractions: the city harbors scores of hidden neighborhoods and shopping streets—some well traveled, others just emerging. Each carries its own distinct style that reflects the character of the particular *quartier*. Here are a few of Paris's most satisfying and *très branché* (very trendy) enclaves.

Rue Keller, Rue Charonne (11e). These streets are a haven for young clothing designers. Stylish housewares, jewelry, and art galleries augment the appeal. Start at the end of Rue Keller where it intersects with Rue de la Roquette: walk the length of this short street, then make a right onto Rue Charonne and meander all the way to Rue du Faubourg St-Antoine.

Rue Oberkampf (11e). At the outer edge of the Marais, this street is well known among youthful fashionistas for its eclectic atmosphere and bohemian flavor. High-end jewelry and of-the-minute boutiques are clustered amid stylish wine bars and comfy cafés.

Rue des Abbesses, Rue des Martyrs (18e and 9e). In the shadow of lofty Sacré-Coeur, Rue des Abbesses is studded with shops—from vintage jewelry and unique clothing to antiques and upscale gardening. Turn onto Rue des Martyrs and discover a burgeoning scene, with hot boutiques scattered among inviting cafés, and superb gourmet shops.

Rues Étienne Marcel, du Jour, du Louvre, and Montmartre (2e). Just around the corner from teeming Les Halles, this area is jam-packed with big names (Yohji Yamamoto, Agnès b, Barbara Bui), but it also boasts a multitude of smaller boutiques (Madame à Paris, Shine, Gas by Marie) popular with hip young Parisians.

Rue du Bac (7e). After browsing at Le Bon Marché turn the corner at the Grand Epicerie and stroll down this most bountiful of shopping streets. Old and well established, it's where the Paris *beau monde* find everything from elegant linens and home furnishings to any item of apparel a grown-up or child could possibly want.

Rue Vavin (6e). One of Paris's epicenters for outfitting those hopelessly chic Parisian children, this street is lined with boutiques for tots. If you have the kids in tow, follow up with a pony ride at the Luxembourg Garden (weekends and Wednesday afternoon only). Jewelry stores, clothing stores, and J.P. Hevin (one of Paris's top chocolatiers) give adults plenty to love, too.

Rue Pont Louis Philippe (4e). Known for a plethora of elegant paper and stationery shops, the street also has boutiques selling antiques, musical instruments, artisan jewelry, and classy clothing. It's a great spot for window-shopping en route from the Marais to Ile St-Louis.

Rue Francois Miron (from St-Paul métro to Place St-Gervais, 4e). Many overlook this lovely street at the Marais's Seine-side fringes, but there's plenty to make a wander worthwhile. Parisians in the know head here for spices, top-notch designs for the home, antiques, jewelry, pretty cafés, and much more. Bonus: Two of the oldest houses in Paris are here; they're the medieval half-timbered ones.

MALLS AND SHOPPING CENTERS

Fodor's Choice ★ **Galerie Vivienne.** Located between the Bourse and the Palais-Royal, Galerie Vivienne is the most glorious glass-capped arcade in Paris. The 19th-century beauty is home to an array of interesting luxury shops as well as a lovely tearoom (A Priori Thé) and a terrific wineshop (Cave Legrand Filles et Fils). Don't leave without checking out the Jean-Paul Gaultier boutique at 6 rue Vivienne. ✉ *4 rue des Petits-Champs, 2e, Around the Louvre* 🌐 *www.galerie-vivienne.com* Ⓜ *Bourse.*

SHOES, HANDBAGS, AND LEATHER GOODS

Goyard. These colorful totes are the choice of royals, blue bloods, and the like (clients have included Sir Arthur Conan Doyle, Gregory Peck, and the Duke and Duchess of Windsor). Parisians swear by their durability and longevity; they're copious enough for a mile-long baguette, and durable enough for a magnum of Champagne. What's more, they easily transition into ultrachic beach or diaper bags. ✉ *233 rue St-Honoré, 1er, Louvre/Tuileries* ☎ *01–42–60–57–04* 🌐 *www.goyard.com* Ⓜ *Tuileries.*

Hermès. The go-to for those who prefer their logo discrete yet still crave instant recognition, Hermès was established as a saddlery in 1837; then went on to create the eternally chic Kelly (named for Grace Kelly) and Birkin (named for Jane Birkin) handbags. The silk scarves are legendary for their rich colors and intricate designs, which change yearly. Other accessories are also extremely covetable: enamel bracelets, dashing silk-twill ties, and small leather goods. During semiannual sales, in January and July, prices are slashed up to 50%, and the crowds line up for blocks. ✉ *24 rue du Faubourg St-Honoré, 8e, Louvre/Tuileries* ☎ *01–40–17–46–00* 🌐 *www.hermes.com* Ⓜ *Concorde.*

Maison Fabre. Until you've eased into an exquisite pair of gloves handcrafted by Fabre, you probably haven't experienced the sensation of having a second skin far superior to your own. Founded in 1924, this is one of Paris's historic *gantiers*. Styles range from classic to haute: picture elbow-length croc leather, coyote-fur mittens, and peccary driving gloves. ✉ *128–129 Galerie de Valois, 1er, Louvre/Tuileries* ☎ *01–42–60–75–88* 🌐 *www.maisonfabre.com* Ⓜ *Palais-Royal–Musée du Louvre.*

Roger Vivier. Known for decades for his Pilgrim-buckle shoes and inventive heels, Roger Vivier's name is being resurrected through the creativity of über-Parisienne Inès de la Fressange and the expertise of shoe designer Bruno Frisoni. The results are easily some of the best shoes in town: leather boots that mold to the calf perfectly, towering rhinestone-encrusted or feathered platforms for evening, and vertiginous crocodile pumps. ✉ *29 rue du Faubourg St-Honoré, 8e, Louvre/Tuileries* ☎ *01–53–43–00–85* 🌐 *www.rogervivier.com* Ⓜ *Concorde.*

THE GRANDS BOULEVARDS

CLOTHING

Charvet. The Parisian equivalent of a Savile Row tailor, Charvet is a conservative, aristocratic institution. It's famed for made-to-measure shirts, exquisite ties, and accessories; for garbing John F. Kennedy, Charles de Gaulle, and the Duke of Windsor; and for its regal address. Although the exquisite silk ties, in hundreds of colors and patterns, and custom-made shirts for men are the biggest draw, refined pieces for women and girls, as well as adorable miniatures for boys, round out the collection. ✉ *28 pl. Vendôme, 1er, Opéra/Grands Boulevards* ☎ *01–42–60–30–70* 🌐 *www.charvet.com* Ⓜ *Opéra.*

FOOD AND WINE

À la Mère de Famille. This enchanting shop is well versed in French regional specialties as well as old-fashioned bonbons, chocolates, marzipan, and more. ✉ *35 rue du Faubourg-Montmartre, 9e, Opéra/Grands Boulevards* ☎ *01–47–70–83–69* 🌐 *www.lameredefamille.com* Ⓜ *Cadet.*

MONTMARTRE

MARKETS

Fodor's Choice ★ **Marché aux Puces St-Ouen** (*Clignancourt*). This picturesque market on the city's northern boundary—open Saturday and Sunday 9 to 6, Monday 10 to 5—still lures crowds, but its once-unbeatable prices are now a relic. Packed with antiques booths and *brocante* stalls, the century-old, miles-long labyrinth has been undergoing a mild renaissance lately: witness Village Vintage's newly opened warehouses filled with midcentury-modern pieces at 77 rue des Rosiers, plus other buzz-worthy shops and galleries (some of which keep weekend-only hours). Destination eateries—including Philippe Starck's hugely popular Ma Cocotte—are also attracting a hip Paris contingent. Arrive early to pick up the best loot, then linger over an excellent meal or apèro. Be warned, though: if there's one place in Paris where you need to know how to bargain, this is it! If you're arriving by métro, walk under the overpass and take the first left at the Rue de Rosiers to reach the center of the market. Note that stands selling dodgy odds and ends (think designer knockoffs and questionable gadgets) set up around the overpass. These blocks are crowded and gritty; be careful with your valuables. ✉ *18e, Montmartre* 🌐 *www.marcheauxpuces-saintouen.com* Ⓜ *Porte de Clignancourt.*

MARAIS

BOOKS

Comptoir de l'Image. This is where designers John Galliano, Marc Jacobs, and Emanuel Ungaro stock up on old copies of *Vogue*, *Harper's Bazaar,* and *The Face*. You'll also find trendy magazines like *Dutch, Purple,* and *Spoon*, plus designer catalogs from the past and rare photo books. Don't go early: whimsical opening hours tend to start after lunch. ✉ *44 rue de Sévigné, 3e, Marais* ☎ *01–42–72–03–92* Ⓜ *St-Paul.*

CLOTHING

Fodor's Choice ★ **Azzedine Alaïa.** Thanks to his perfectly proportioned "king of cling" dresses, Azzedine Alaïa is considered a master at his game. You don't have to be under 20 to look good in his garments. Tina Turner wears them well, as does every other beautiful woman with the courage and the curves. His boutique-workshop-apartment is covered with artwork by Julian Schnabel and is not the kind of place you casually wander into out of curiosity: the sales staff immediately makes you feel awkward in that distinctive Parisian way. Think $3,500 is too much for a dress? The Alaïa stock store (same building, different entrance) takes 50% off last season's styles, samples, and gently worn catwalk items. Access it at 18 rue de la Verrerie. ✉ *7 rue de Moussy, 4e, Marais* ☎ *01–42–72–30–69* 🌐 *www.alaia.fr* Ⓜ *Hôtel de Ville.*

COS. COS—which stands for Collection of Style—is the H&M group's answer to fashion sophisticates, who flock here in droves for high-concept, minimalist design with serious attention to quality tailoring and fabrics at a reasonable price. Classic accessories and shoes look more expensive than they are. ✉ *4 rue des Rosiers, 4e, Marais* ☎ *01–44–54–37–70* 🌐 *www.cosstores.com* Ⓜ *St-Paul.*

FrenchTrotters. The flagship store features an understated collection of contemporary French-made classic clothes and accessories for men and women that emphasize quality fabrics, style, and cut over trendiness. You'll also find a handpicked collection of exclusive collaborations with cutting-edge French brands (like sleek leather-and-suede booties by Avril Gau for FrenchTrotters), as well as FrenchTrotters' namesake label, and a limited selection of housewares for chic Parisian apartments. ✉ *128 rue Vieille du Temple, 3e, Marais* ☎ *01–44–61–00–14* 🌐 *www.frenchtrotters.fr* Ⓜ *St-Sébastien–Froissart, Filles du Calvaire.*

L'Eclaireur. This Rue de Sevigné boutique is Paris's touchstone for edgy, up-to-the-second styles. L'Eclaireur's knack for uncovering new talent and championing established visionaries is legendary—no surprise after 30 years in the business. Hard-to-find geniuses, like leather wizard Isaac Sellam and British prodigy Paul Harnden, cohabit with luxe labels such as Ann Demeulemeester, Haider Ackermann, and Lanvin. There's a second Marais outpost at 12 rue Mahler. ✉ *40 rue de Sevigné, 3e, Marais* ☎ *01–48–87–10–22* 🌐 *www.leclaireur.com* Ⓜ *St-Paul.*

EASTERN PARIS

CLOTHING

Isabel Marant. This rising design star is a honeypot of bohemian rock-star style. Her separates skim the body without constricting: layered miniskirts, loose peekaboo sweaters ready to slip from a shoulder, and super fox-fur jackets in lurid colors. Look for the secondary line, Étoile, for a less expensive take. ✉ *16 rue de Charonne, 11e, Bastille/Nation* ☎ *01–49–29–71–55* 🌐 *www.isabelmarant.com* Ⓜ *Ledru-Rollin.*

SHOES, HANDBAGS, AND LEATHER GOODS

Fodor's Choice ★ **Philippe Roucou.** By turns bold and dainty, these exquisitely constructed vintage-inspired bags are some of the yummiest in Paris. A python-and-calf tote is demure in storm gray: in ice blue it's a statement. Day bags in myriad shapes and sizes are always stylish; for evening, ingenious faceted clutches come in a range of colors and skins, with a sexy signature version chained to a python wristband. Other leather accessories (like iPad cases and wallets) and whimsical Polaroid-print silk scarves are also available. ✉ *30 rue de Charonne, 11e, Bastille* ☎ *01–49–29–97–35* 🌐 *www.philipperoucou.com* Ⓜ *Ledru-Rollin, Bastille.*

LATIN QUARTER

BOOKS

Shakespeare & Company. This sentimental Rive Gauche favorite is named after the bookstore whose American owner, Sylvia Beach, first published James Joyce's *Ulysses*. Nowadays it specializes in expat literature. Although the eccentric and beloved owner, George Whitman, passed away in 2011, his daughter Sylvia has taken up the torch. You can still count on a couple of characters lurking in the stacks, a sometimes spacey staff, the latest titles from British presses, and hidden secondhand treasures in the odd corners and crannies. Check the website for readings and workshops throughout the week. ✉ *37 rue de la Bûcherie, 5e, Latin Quarter* ☎ *01–43–25–40–93* 🌐 *shakespeareandcompany.com* Ⓜ *St-Michel.*

JEWELRY AND ACCESSORIES

Peggy Kingg. The minimalist accessories designed by former architect Peggy Huynh Kinh include understated totes, shoulder bags, wallets, and belts in the highest-quality leather, as well as a line of picnic bags and elegant office-oriented pieces. Look for them at her streamlined—and recently rebranded—Peggy Kingg boutique. ✉ *9 rue Coëtlogon, 6e, Latin Quarter* ☎ *01–42–84–83–84* 🌐 *www.peggykingg.com* Ⓜ *St-Sulpice.*

ST-GERMAIN-DES-PRÉS

ANTIQUES AND COLLECTIBLES

Fodor's Choice ★ **Carré Rive Gauche.** Carré Rive Gauche is where you'll unearth museum-quality pieces. Head to the streets between Rue du Bac, Rue de l'Université, Rue de Lille, and Rue des Sts-Pères to find more than 100 associated shops, marked with a small, blue square banner on their storefronts. ✉ *Between St-Germain-des-Prés and Musée d'Orsay, 6e, St-Germain-des-Prés* 🌐 *www.carrerivegauche.com* Ⓜ *St-Germain-des-Prés, Rue du Bac.*

3

SIDE TRIPS FROM PARIS

WELCOME TO SIDE TRIPS FROM PARIS

TOP REASONS TO GO

★ **Louis XIV's Versailles:** Famed as glorious testimony to the Sun King's megalomania, this is the world's most over-the-top palace and nature-tamed park.

★ **Gorgeous Chantilly:** Stately château, stellar art collection, fabulous forest, palatial stables . . . all within the same square mile.

★ **Van Gogh in Auvers:** The artist spent his last, manically productive three months here—you can see where he painted, where he got drunk, where he shot himself, and where he remains.

★ **Chartres Cathedral:** A pinnacle of Gothic achievement, this 13th-century masterpiece has peerless stained glass and a hilltop silhouette visible for miles around.

★ **Monet's water lilies:** Come to Giverny to see his lily pond—a half-acre 3-D "Monet"—then peek around his charming home and stroll the time-warped streets to the exceptional Musée des Impressionnismes.

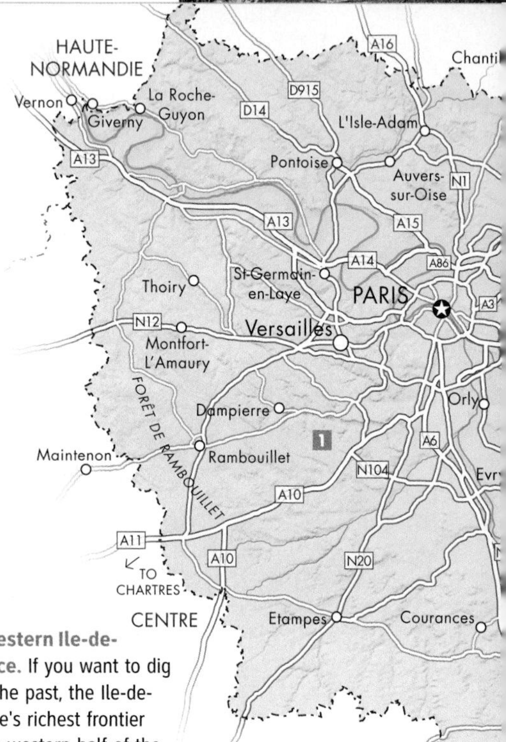

1 Western Ile-de-France. If you want to dig into the past, the Ile-de-France's richest frontier is the western half of the 60-km (35-mile) circle that rings Paris. The towns are charming and the sylvan woods are full of châteaux—including the world's grandest one, Château de Versailles. Haunt of Louis XIV, Madame de Pompadour, and Marie-Antoinette, it is a monument to splendidly wretched excess and once home to 20,000 courtiers and servants. More spiritual concerns are embodied in Chartres Cathedral, a soaring pinnacle of Gothic architecture. Nineteen kilometers (30 miles) north are landscapes of lasting impressions: Giverny and Auvers, immortalized by Monet and Van Gogh, respectively.

2 Eastern Ile-de-France. By traveling an eastward arc through the remainder of the Ile you can savor the icing on the cake. Begin with Chantilly, an opulent château noted for its royal stables, stunning gardens,

GETTING ORIENTED

The "island of France" is the poetic name for the area surrounding Paris and taking in the valleys of three rivers: the Seine, the Marne, and the Oise. Ever since the days of Julius Caesar, this has been the economic, political, and religious hub of France and, consequently, no other region boasts such a wealth of great buildings, from Chartres to Fontainebleau and Versailles. Though small, it is so rich in treasures that a whole day of fascinating exploration may take you no more than 60 km (35 miles) from the capital.

and a top-notch art collection that is rivaled only by the Louvre's. Northward lie medieval Senlis and the storybook castle of Pierrefonds. Heading east, you'll hit Disneyland Paris where Mickey Mouse and his animated friends get a French makeover. Continuing south, two more magnificent châteaux—Vaux-le-Vicomte and Fontainebleau—were built for some of France's most pampered monarchs and ministers.

Updated By Jennifer Ladonne

Just what is it that makes the Ile-de-France so attractive, so comfortingly familiar? Is it its proximity to the great city of Paris—or perhaps that it's so far removed?

Had there not been the world-class cultural hub of Paris nearby, would Monet have retreated to his Japanese gardens at Giverny? Or Paul Cézanne and Van Gogh to bucolic Auvers? Kings and courtiers to the game-rich forests of Rambouillet? Would Napoléon have truly settled at Malmaison and then abdicated at the palace of Fontainebleau? Would abbeys and cathedrals have sprung skyward in Chartres and Senlis?

If you had asked Louis XIV, he wouldn't have minced his words: the city of Paris—yawn—was simply *démodée*—out of fashion. In the 17th century the new power base was going to be Versailles, once a tiny village in the heart of the Ile-de-France, now the site of a gigantic château from which the Sun King's rays could radiate, unfettered by rebellious rabble and European arrivistes. Of course, later heirs kept the lines open and restored the grandiose palace as the governmental hub it was meant to be—and commuted to Paris, well before the high-speed RER.

That, indeed, is the dream of most Parisians today: to have a foot in both worlds. Paris may be small as capital cities go, with slightly fewer than 2 million inhabitants, but the Ile-de-France, the region around Paris, contains more than 10 million people—a sixth of France's entire population. That's why on closer inspection the once-rustic villages of the Ile-de-France reveal cosseted gardens, stylishly gentrified cottages, and extraordinary country restaurants no peasant farmer could afford to frequent.

The nation's heartland isn't really an *île* (island), of course. The green-forested buffer zone that enfolds Paris is only vaguely surrounded by the three rivers that meander through its periphery. But it nevertheless offers a rich and varied sampling of everything you expect from France—grand cathedrals, painters' villages, lavish palaces, plus the bubble gum–pink turrets of Disneyland Paris—all delightfully located within easy shooting distance of the capital.

PLANNER

WHEN TO GO

Spring and fall are the optimal times to come. The Ile's rightly renowned gardens look their best in the former, and its extensive forests are particularly beautiful in the latter. From May through June or September through early October, you can still take advantage of memorable warm-weather offerings—such as a candlelight visit to Vaux-le-Vicomte or an evening of music, dancing, and fireworks at Versailles—without having to contend with the high summer heat or the crowds that pack places like Disneyland Paris or Monet's Giverny, especially on weekends.

Be aware when making your travel plans that some places are closed one or two days a week. The château of Versailles is closed Monday (the gardens remain open), and the château of Fontainebleau is closed Tuesday. In fact, as a rule, even well-touristed towns make their *fermeture hebdomadaire* (weekly closing) on Monday or Tuesday. At these times museums, shops, and markets may be shuttered—call ahead if in doubt. During the winter months, some spots shut completely (Vaux-le-Vicomte, for one, is closed from mid-November to mid-March). So it's always best to check websites or phone ahead before venturing out in the off-season.

PLANNING YOUR TIME

A great advantage to exploring this region is that all its major monuments are within a half-day's drive from Paris, or less if you take the trains that run to many of the towns. The catch is that most of those rail lines connect Ile communities with Paris, not, in general, with neighboring towns of the region. Thus, it may be easier to plan on "touring" the Ile in a series of side trips from Paris, rather than expecting to travel through it in clockwise fashion (which, of course, can be easily done if you have a car).

This chapter is broken up into two halves. Threading the western half of the Ile, the first tour heads southwest from Paris to Versailles and Chartres, turns northwest along the Seine to Monet's Giverny, and returns to Paris after visiting Vincent van Gogh's Auvers. Exploring the eastern half of the Ile, the second tour picks up east of the Oise Valley in glamorous Chantilly, then detours north to Pierrefonds, and finishes up southward by heading to Disneyland Paris, Vaux-le-Vicomte, and Fontainebleau.

For a stimulating mix of pomp, nature, and spirituality, we suggest your three priorities should be Versailles, Giverny, and Chartres.

EXPERIENCING IMPRESSIONISM

Paris's Musée d'Orsay may have some of the most fabled Monet and Van Gogh paintings in the world, but the Ile-de-France has something (almost) better—the actual landscapes that were rendered into masterpieces by the brushes of many great Impressionist and Postimpressionist artists. At Giverny, Claude Monet's house and garden are a moving visual link to his finest daubs—its famous lily-pond garden gave rise to his legendary water-lilies series (some historians feel it was the other way around). Here, too, is the impressive Musée des Impressionnismes.

In Auvers-sur-Oise, Vincent van Gogh had a final burst of creativity before ending his life; the famous wheat field where he was attacked by crows and painted his last work is just outside town. Back then, they called him Fou-Roux (mad redhead) and derided his art; now the townspeople here love to pay tribute to the man who helped make their village famous. André Derain lived in Chambourcy, Camille Pissarro in Pontoise, and Alfred Sisley in Moret-sur-Loing: all were inspired by the silvery sunlight that tumbles over these hills and towns.

Earlier, Rousseau, Millet, and Corot paved the way for Impressionism with their penchant for outdoor landscape painting in the village of Barbizon, still surrounded by its romantic, quietly dramatic forest. A trip to any of these towns will provide lasting impressions.

GETTING HERE AND AROUND

AIR TRAVEL

Proximity to Paris means that the Ile-de-France is well served by both international and intra-continental flights. Charles de Gaulle Airport, commonly known as Roissy, is 26 km (16 miles) northeast of the capital; Orly Airport is 16 km (10 miles) south.

Air Travel Information Charles de Gaulle/Roissy and Orly Airports. ☎ *3950 €0.34 per min* 🌐 *www.aeroportsdeparis.fr.*

BUS TRAVEL

Although many of the major sights have rail lines connecting them directly to Paris, the lesser destinations pose more of a problem and require taking a local bus run by the SNCF (⇨ *see Train Travel below*) from the nearest train station (*gare*). This will be the case if you're going onward to Senlis from the Chantilly Gare, to Fontainebleau and Barbizon from the Avon Gare, to Vaux-le-Vicomte from the Melun Gare, or to Giverny from the Vernon Gare.

CAR TRAVEL

A13 links Paris (from the Porte d'Auteuil) to Versailles. You can get to Chartres on A10 from Paris (Porte d'Orléans). For Fontainebleau take A6 from Paris (Porte d'Orléans). For a slower, more scenic route through the Forest of Sénart and the northern part of the Forest of Fontainebleau, take N6 from Paris (Porte de Charenton) via Melun. A4 runs from Paris (Porte de Bercy) to Disneyland. Although a comprehensive rail network ensures that most towns in the Ile-de-France qualify as comfortable day trips from Paris, the only way to crisscross the region without returning to the capital is by car. There's no shortage of expressways or fast highways. However, you should be prepared for delays close to Paris, especially during the morning and evening rush hours.

TRAIN TRAVEL

Departing from Paris, it's easy to reach key locales in this region by rail because you can take advantage of the SNCF's main-line and Transilien networks, as well as RER routes, which are part of Paris's comprehensive RATP public transit system. Chartres and Chantilly, for example, are served by both main-line and Transilien trains; those bound for

Chartres leave from Gare Montparnasse (50–70 minutes), while those going to Chantilly leave from Gare du Nord (25–30 minutes). Versailles is best accessed via the RER-C line, which gets you within a five-minute walk of the château (45 minutes); and the RER-A line deposits you 100 yards from the entrance to Disneyland (40 minutes). Note that the Parisian station you start from is typically determined by the direction you're heading in.

Train Information **RATP.** ☎ *3246 €0.34 per min* 🌐 *www.ratp.fr.* **SNCF.** ☎ *3635 €0.34 per min* 🌐 *www.sncf.com.* **Transilien.** ☎ *3658 €0.23 per min* 🌐 *www.transilien.com.*

RESTAURANTS

The Ile-de-France's fanciest restaurants can be just as pricey as their Parisian counterparts. Close to the Channel for fresh fish, lush Normandy for beef and dairy products, and the rich agricultural regions of Picardy and the Beauce, Ile-de-France chefs have all the ingredients they could wish for, and shop for the freshest produce early each morning at the huge food market at Rungis, 18 km (10 miles) south of the capital. Traditional "local delicacies"—lamb stew, *pâté de Pantin* (pastry filled with meat), or pig's trotters—tend to be obsolete, though creamy Brie, made locally in Meaux and Coulommiers, remains queen of the cheese board.

HOTELS

In summer, hotel rooms are at a premium, and making reservations is essential; almost all accommodations in the swankier towns—Versailles, Rambouillet, and Fontainebleau—are on the costly side. Take nothing for granted; picturesque Senlis, for instance, does not have a single hotel in its historic downtown area. *Hotel reviews have been shortened. For full information, visit Fodors.com.*

WHAT IT COSTS IN EUROS

	$	$$	$$$	$$$$
Restaurants	under €18	€18–€24	€25–€32	over €32
Hotels	under €106	€106–€145	€146–€215	over €215

Restaurant prices are the average cost of a main course at dinner or, if dinner is not served, at lunch. Hotel prices are the lowest cost of a standard double room in high season.

VISITOR INFORMATION

Special *forfait* tickets, combining travel and admission, are available for several regional tourist destinations (including Versailles, Fontainebleau, and Auvers-sur-Oise). For general information on the area, check the website of Espace du Tourisme d'Ile-de-France (🌐 *www.visitparisregion.com*), or visit one of its kiosks; you'll find them at the Charles de Gaulle airport, Orly airport, Versailles, and Disneyland. Further information on Disneyland can be obtained from the Disneyland Paris reservations office. ⇨ *Local tourist offices are listed throughout by town.*

TOUR OPTIONS

Alliance Autos. Bilingual guides from Alliance Autos give private tours of the Paris area in a chauffeured luxury car or minibus; outings for three to eight people last a minimum of four hours and cost about €80 an hour. ✉ *149 rue de Charonne, Paris* ☎ *01–55–25–23–23* 🌐 *www.alliance-limousine.com.*

Euroscope. You can sign on for full-day minibus trips from Paris to Versailles (€162), Chartres (€110), and Giverny (€102), or pair up places such as Fontainebleau and Barbizon (€97). Check the Euroscope website for all the options. ✉ *46 rue de Provence, Paris* ☎ *01–56–03–56–81* 🌐 *www.euroscope.fr.*

Pariscityvision. Guided coach excursions to Giverny, Versailles, Vaux le Vicomte, and Fontainebleau—plus multiple destination combinations—can be booked through Pariscityvision (€55–€220). Some are offered year-round, but most run April through October. Half- and full-day minibus excursions for up to eight people are also available (€89–€199). ✉ *2 rue des Pyramides, Paris* ☎ *01–44–55–60–00* 🌐 *www.pariscityvision.com.*

WESTERN ILE-DE-FRANCE

Not only is majestic Versailles one of the most unforgettable sights in the Ile-de-France, it's also within easy reach of Paris—40 minutes or less by either car (using the A13 expressway from Porte d'Auteuil) or RER train. This is the starting point for a visit to the western half of the Ile-de-France, anchored by holy Chartres to the south and Vincent van Gogh's Auvers-sur-Oise to the north.

VERSAILLES

16 km (10 miles) west of Paris via A13.

It's hard to tell which is larger at **Château de Versailles**—the world-famous château that housed Louis XIV and 20,000 of his courtiers, or the mass of tour buses and visitors standing in front of it. The grandest palace in France remains one of the marvels of the world. But this edifice was not just home to the Sun King, it was also the new headquarters of the French government (from 1682 to 1789 and again from 1871 to 1879). To accompany the palace, a new city—in fact, a new capital—had to be built from scratch. Tough-thinking town planners took no prisoners, dreaming up vast mansions and avenues broader than the Champs-Élysées.

GETTING HERE

Versailles has three train stations, but its Rive Gauche gare—on the RER-C line from Paris, with trains departing from Austerlitz, St-Michel, Invalides, and Champ-de-Mars—provides the easiest access and puts you within a five-minute walk of the château (45 mins, €3.45).

Visitor Information Versailles Tourist Office. ☎ *01–39–24–88–88* 🌐 *www.versailles-tourisme.com.*

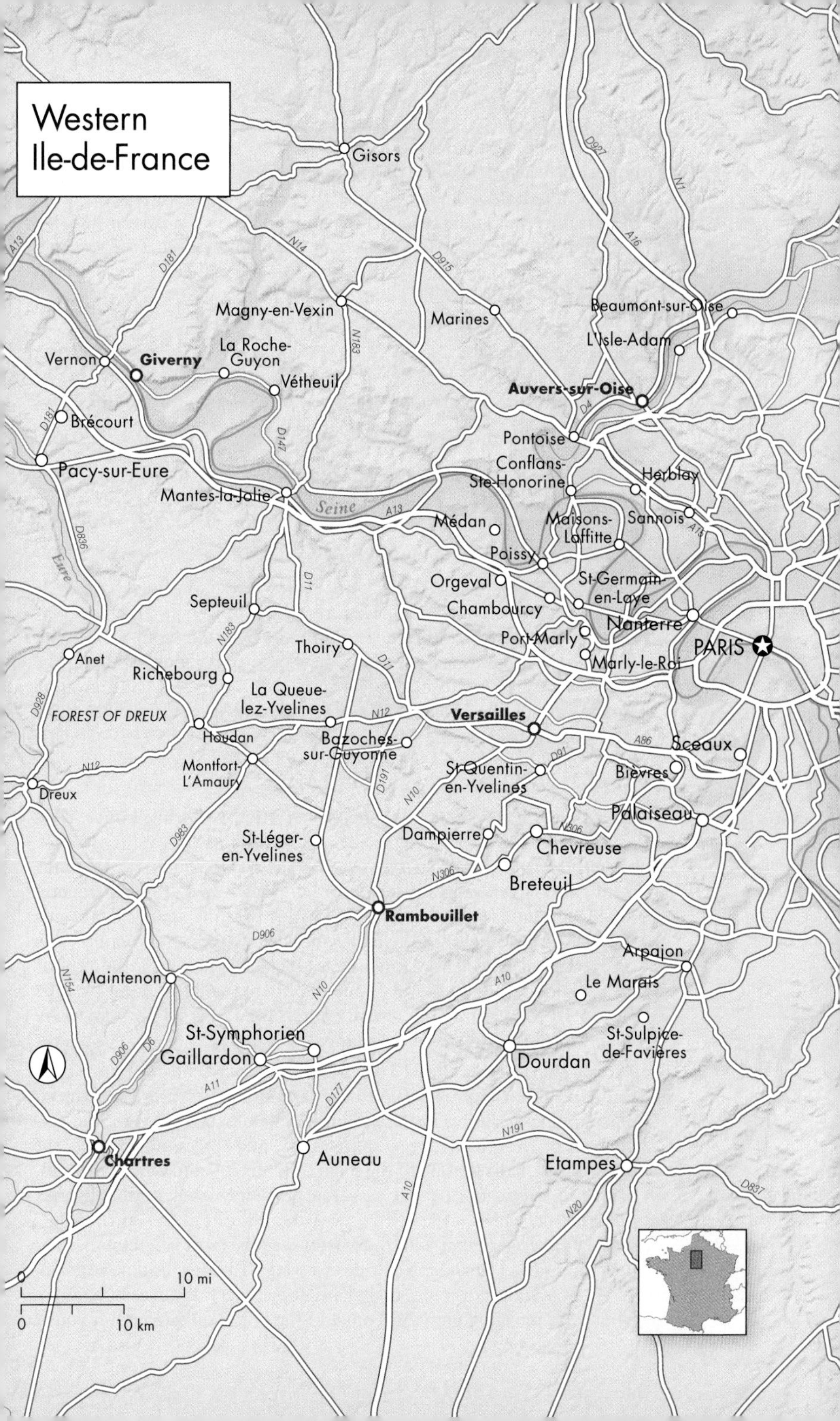
Western
Ile-de-France
Gisors
Magny-en-Vexin
Marines
Beaumont-sur-Oise
L'Isle-Adam
Vernon
Giverny
La Roche-Guyon
Vétheuil
Auvers-sur-Oise
Brécourt
Pontoise
Pacy-sur-Eure
Conflans-Ste-Honorine
Herblay
Mantes-la-Jolie
Seine
Médan
Maisons-Laffitte
Sannois
Poissy
Orgeval
St-Germain-en-Laye
Septeuil
Chambourcy
Nanterre
Port-Marly
Thoiry
PARIS
Anet
Marly-le-Roi
Richebourg
La Queue-lez-Yvelines
FOREST OF DREUX
Versailles
Houdan
Bazoches-sur-Guyonne
Sceaux
Montfort-L'Amaury
St-Quentin-en-Yvelines
Bièvres
Dreux
Palaiseau
St-Léger-en-Yvelines
Dampierre
Chevreuse
Breteuil
Rambouillet
Arpajon
Maintenon
Le Marais
St-Symphorien
St-Sulpice-de-Favières
Gaillardon
Dourdan
Chartres
Auneau
Etampes
Eure
10 mi
0
10 km
A13
D181
N14
D915
D927
N1
A16
N183
D4
D147
A13
D836
A15
D11
N183
D11
N12
D928
N12
A86
D91
D191
N10
N306
D983
N306
D906
A10
N154
N10
D906
D6
A11
D177
N191
A10
N20
D837

EXPLORING

Cathédrale St-Louis. Turn left from the Grandes Écuries stables, cross Avenue de Sceaux and Avenue de Paris, pass the imposing chancellery on the corner, and take Rue de Satory (a cute pedestrian shopping street) to the Cathédrale St-Louis. Outside, the 18th-century seat of the Bishop of Versailles is notable for its dome and twin-tower facade; inside, the sanctuary is enriched with a fine organ and paintings. On Thursday and Saturday mornings, the square in front of the cathedral hosts a classic farmers' market. ✉ *Pl. Saint-Louis, Versailles* ☎ *01–39–50–40–65* 🌐 *www.cathedrale-versailles.org.*

Fodor's Choice ★ **Château de Versailles** ✉ *Pl. d'Armes* ☎ *01–30–83–78–00* 🌐 *www.chateauversailles.fr* 🎫 *€18 general admission; €25 all-attractions pass; €10 Marie-Antoinette's Domain; park free (weekend fountain show, €9, Apr.–Oct.). On 1st Sun. of month Nov.–Mar. all palace tours are free* 🕐 *Palace Apr.–Oct., Tues.–Sun. 9–6:30; Nov.–Mar., Tues.–Sun. 9–5:30. Trianons Apr.–Oct., Tues.–Sun. noon–6:30; Nov.–Mar., Tues.–Sun. noon–5:30. Garden Apr.–Oct., daily 8 am–8:30 pm; Nov.–Mar., daily 8–6. Park Apr.–Oct., daily 7am–8:30 pm; Nov.–Mar., daily 8–6.*

⇨ *See the highlighted listing in this chapter for more information.*

Musée Lambinet. Around the back of Notre-Dame, on Boulevard de la Reine (note the regimented lines of trees), are the elegant Hôtel de Neyret and the Musée Lambinet, a sumptuous mansion from 1751, with collections of paintings, weapons, fans, and porcelain (including the Madame du Barry "Rose"). A tearoom, open Thursday, Saturday, and Sunday afternoons, provides an elegant way to refresh after an intensive round of sightseeing. ✉ *54 bd. de la Reine, Versailles* ☎ *01–39–50–30–32* 🌐 *www.versailles.fr/culture-et-patrimoine/etablissements-culturels/musee-lambinet* 🎫 *€4* 🕐 *Thurs.–Tues. 2–6.*

Notre-Dame. If you have any energy left after exploring Louis XIV's palace and park, a tour of Versailles—a textbook 18th-century town—offers a telling contrast between the majestic and the domestic. From the front gate of Versailles's palace turn left onto Rue de l'Independence-Américaine and walk over to Rue Carnot past the stately Écuries de la Reine—once the queen's stables, now the regional law courts—to octagonal place Hoche. Down Rue Hoche to the left is the powerful Baroque facade of Notre-Dame, built from 1684 to 1686 by Jules Hardouin-Mansart as the parish church for Louis XIV's new town. ✉ *Versailles* 🌐 *notredameversailles.org.*

Place du Marché-Notre-Dame. This lively square in the heart of the Notre-Dame neighborhood is home to the largest market in the region, far outstripping anything in Paris. Outdoors stalls offer a veritable cornucopia of fresh fruits, vegetables, herbs, and spices; meanwhile, the four historic halls (dating to the reign of Louis XV and rebuilt in 1841) brim with every gourmet delight—foie gras, fine wines, seafood, game, prepared delicacies, cheese from every corner of France—providing a sensory experience that will overwhelm even the most jaded foodie. The open-air market runs three half-days a week (Tuesday, Friday, and Sunday 7–2), but the covered food halls are open every day except Monday, from early morning until 7:30 pm (closing is at 2 on Sunday). If you're in the mood for more shopping, the town's marvelous antiques district begins at the northwest corner of the market square and extends along the cobbled streets to the charming Passage de la Geôle. ✉ *Versailles.*

Fodor's Choice ★ **Potager du Roi.** The King's Potager—a 6-acre, split-level fruit-and-vegetable garden—was created in 1683 by Jean-Baptiste de La Quintinye. Many rare heirloom species are painstakingly cultivated here by a team of gardeners and students studying at the famous École Nationale Supérieure d'Horticulture. You can sample their wares (which are used in some of the finest Parisian restaurants) or pick up a bottle of fruit juice or jam made from the king's produce. Perfumed "Potager du Roi" candles, sold at the delightful boutique, make a nice souvenir. ✉ *10 rue du Maréchal Joffre, Versailles* ☎ *01–39–24–62–62* 🌐 *www.potager-du-roi.fr* 🎫 *Weekends €7, other days €4.50* ⏲ *Apr.–Oct., Tues.–Sun. 10–6; Nov. and Dec., Tues. and Thurs. 10–6; Jan.–Mar., Tues. and Thurs. 10–6, Sat. 10–1.*

3

Salle du Jeu de Paume. On June 20, 1789, members of the Third Estate—the commoner's section of the three-part Estates General, which included nobles (First Estate) and clergy (Second Estate)—found themselves locked out of their regular meeting place by palace guards, so they convened in this tennis court instead to discuss their demands. The resulting Tennis Court Oath stated that the sovereignty of the people did not reside with the king but with the people themselves. It became the first draft of the French Constitution (based closely on the American Declaration of Independence) and was a major first step in the revolution and subsequent abolition of the monarchy. The members are depicted in a monumental painting on the court's far wall. A fascinating guided visit in English is available through the Versailles tourist office. ✉ *Rue du Jeu de Paume, Quartier Saint-Louis, Versailles* ☎ *01–30–83–78–00* 🎫 *Free* ⏲ *Tues.–Sun. 2–5:45.*

WHERE TO EAT

$$$$ MODERN FRENCH Fodor's Choice ★ ✕ **Gordon Ramsay au Trianon.** Gordon Ramsay—the ebullient "bad boy of *la cuisine Anglaise*"—has amassed a string of restaurants worldwide and maintained a consistent two stars for this one. Overseen by his longstanding London number two, Simone Zanoni, the dishes are predictably conversation-worthy: picture exemplary entrées like ravioli of langoustines and lobster cooked in a Riesling bisque with Petrossian caviar and lime consommé, or Périgord foie gras done "2 ways," roasted with a beetroot tart and pressed with green apple and Sauternes. Desserts are marvels, too, with chocolate meringue with vanilla ice cream, candied pear, and black currant vying for top honors with the raspberry soufflé with chocolate and tarragon ice cream. The Trianon's more casual, 60-seat Véranda restaurant is also under Ramsay's sway, and in its black-and-white contemporary setting you can opt for his "light, modern take" on such bistro novelties as radicchio and Parmesan risotto with chorizo oil or the fillet of sole in a parsley crust, cèpes, and sautéed artichokes. Teatime provides a delightful (and more reasonable) restorative for weary château-goers, with a French twist on high tea: scones, madeleines, and heavenly *macarons.* $ *Average main: €55* ✉ *1 bd. de la Reine, Versailles* ☎ *01–30–84–50–18* 🌐 *www.gordonramsay.*

Continued on page 164

VERSAILLES

By Robert I.C. Fisher

Louis XIV's Hall of Mirrors

A two-century spree of indulgence in the finest bling-bling of the age by the consecutive reigns of three French kings produced two of the world's most historic artifacts: gloriously, the Palace of Versailles and, momentously, the French Revolution.

Less a monument than an entire world unto itself, Versailles is the king of palaces. The end result of 380 million francs, 36,000 laborers, and enough paintings, if laid end to end, to equal 7 miles of canvas, it was conceived as the ne plus ultra expression of monarchy by Louis XIV. As a child, the king had developed a hatred for Paris (where he had been imprisoned by a group of nobles known as the Frondeurs), so, when barely out of his teens, he cast his cantankerous royal eye in search of a new power base. Marshy, inhospitable Versailles was the stuff of his dreams. Down came dad's modest royal hunting lodge and up, up, and along went the minion-crushing, Baroque palace we see today.

Between 1661 and 1710, architects Louis Le Vau and Jules Hardouin Mansart designed everything his royal acquisitiveness could want, including a throne room devoted to Apollo, god of the sun (Louis was known as *le roi soleil*). Convinced that his might depended upon dominating French nobility, Louis XIV summoned thousands of grandees from their own far-flung châteaux to reside at his new seat of government. In doing so, however, he unwittingly triggered the downfall of the monarchy. Like an 18th-century Disneyland, Versailles kept its courtiers so richly entertained they all but forgot the murmurs of discontent brewing back home.

As Louis XV chillingly foretold, "After me, the deluge." The royal commune was therefore shocked—shocked!—by the appearance, on October 5, 1789, of a revolutionary mob from Paris ready to sack Versailles and imprison Louis XVI. So as you walk through this awesome monument to splendor and excess, give a thought to its historic companion: the French Revolution. A tour of Versailles's grand salons inextricably mixes pathos with glory.

CROWNING GLORIES: TOP SIGHTS OF VERSAILLES

Versailles from the outside

Seducing their court with their self-assured approach to 17th- and 18th-century art and decoration, a trinity of French kings made Versailles into the most vainglorious of châteaux.

Detail of the ceiling

Galerie des Glaces (Hall of Mirrors). Of all the rooms at Versailles, none matches the magnificence of the Galerie des Glaces (Hall of Mirrors). Begun by Mansart in 1678, this represents the acme of the Louis Quatorze (Louis-XIV) style. Measuring 240 feet long, 33 feet wide, and 40 feet high, it is ornamented with gilded candlesticks, crystal chandeliers, and a coved ceiling painted with Charles Le Brun's homage to Louis XIV's reign.

Hall of Mirrors

In Louis's day, the Galerie was laid with priceless carpets and filled with orange trees in silver pots. Nighttime galas were illuminated by 3,000 candles, their blaze doubled in the 17 gigantic mirrors that precisely echo the banner of windows along the west front. Lavish balls were once held here, and you can still get the full royal treatment at the Serenade Royale. This reenacts one of Louis XIV's grand soirées with dancers in period costumes. The 45-minute spectacle is held at 6:45 and 7:45 pm, from mid-June to September. (€39, €27 ages 6–18 www.chateauversailles-spectacles.fr 01–30–83–78–98).

Inside the Apollo Chamber

The Grands Appartements (State Apartments). Virtual stages for ceremonies of court ritual and etiquette, Louis XIV's first-floor state salons were designed in the Baroque style on a biceps-flexing scale meant to one-up the lavish Vaux-le-Vicomte château recently built for Nicolas Fouquet, the king's finance minister.

Flanking the Hall of Mirrors and retaining most of their bombastic Italianate Baroque decoration, the Salon de la Guerre (Salon of War) and the Salon de la Paix (Salon of Peace) are ornately decorated with gilt stucco, painted ceilings, and marble sculpture. Perhaps the most extravagant is the Salon d'Apollon (Apollo Chamber), the former throne room.

Hall of Battles

Appartements du Roi (King's Apartments). Completed in 1701 in the Louis-XIV style, the king's state and private chambers comprise a suite of 15 rooms set in a "U" around the east facade's Marble Court. Dead center across the sprawling cobbled forecourt is Louis XIV's bedchamber—he would awake and rise (just as the sun did, from the east) attended by members of his court and the public. Holding the king's chemise when he dressed soon became a more definitive reflection of status than the possession of an entire province. Nearby is Louis XV's magnificent Cabinet Intérieur (Office of the King), shining with gold and white boiseries; in the center is the most famous piece of furniture at Versailles, Louis XV's roll-top desk, crafted by Oeben and Riesener in 1769.

Louis XIV

King's Apartments

Chambre de la Reine (Queen's Bedchamber). Probably the most opulent bedroom in the world, this was initially created for Marie Thérèse, first wife of Louis XIV, to be part of the Queen's Apartments. For Marie Antoinette, however, the entire room was glammed up with silk wall-hangings covered with Rococo motifs that reflect her love of flowers. Legend has it that the gardens directly beyond these windows were replanted daily so that the queen could enjoy a fresh assortment of blossoms each morning. The bed, decked out with white ostrich plumes *en panache*, was also redone for Louis XVI's queen. Nineteen royal children were born in this room.

VINTAGE BOURBON

Versailles was built by three great kings of the Bourbon dynasty. Louis XIV (1638–1715) began its construction in 1661. After ruling for 72 years, Louis Quatorze was succeeded by his great grandson, Louis XV (1710–74), who added the Royal Opera and the Petit Trianon to the palace. Louis XVI (1754–93) came to the throne in 1774 and was forced out of Versailles in 1789, along with Marie Antoinette, both guillotined three years later.

Queen's Bedchamber

Petits Appartements (Small Apartments). As styles of decor changed, Louis XIV's successors felt out of sync with their architectural inheritance. Louis XV exchanged the heavy red-and-gilt of Italianate Baroque for lighter, pastel-hued Rococo. On the top floor of the palace, on the right side of the central portion, are the apartments Louis XV commissioned to escape the wearisome pomp of the first-floor rooms. Here, Madame de Pompadour, mistress of Louis XV and famous patroness of the Rococo style, introduced grace notes of intimacy and refinement. In so doing, she transformed the daunting royal apartments into places to live rather than pose.

Parc de Versailles. Even Bourbon kings needed respite from Versailles's endless maze, hence the creation of one of Europe's largest parks. The sublime 250-acre grounds (☎ 01–30–83–77–88 for guided tour) is the masterpiece of André Le Nôtre, presiding genius of 17th-century classical French landscaping. Le Nôtre was famous for his "green geometries": ordered fantasies of clipped yew trees, multicolored flower beds (called *parterres*), and perspectival allées cleverly punctuated with statuary, laid out between 1661 and 1668. The spatial effect is best admired from inside the palace, views about which Le Nôtre said, "Flowers can only be walked on by the eyes."

Ultimately, at the royal command, rivers were diverted—to flow into more than 600 fountains—and entire forests were imported to ornament the park, which is centered around the mile-long Grand Canal. As for the great fountains, their operation costs a fortune in these democratic days, and so they perform only on Saturday and Sunday afternoons (🕓 3:30–5:30) from mid-April through mid-October; admission to the park during this time is €8. The park is open daily 8 AM–8:30 PM.

LIGHTING UP THE SKY

The largest fountain at Versailles, the Bassin de Neptune, becomes a spectacle of rare grandeur during the Grandes Eaux Nocturnes, a light show to the strains of Baroque music, held Saturdays from the end of June through August at 9 pm, with fireworks at 11. Tickets are €23, €19 ages 6–17, and free for children under 6. 🌐 www.chateauversailles-spectacles.fr ☎ 01–30–83–78–98.

Dauphin's Apartments

Bassin de Neptune

Chapel and Opéra Royal: In the north wing of the château are three showpieces of the palace. The solemn white-and-gold Chapelle was completed in 1710—the king and queen attended daily mass here seated in gilt boxes. The Opéra Royal (Opera House), entirely constructed of wood painted to look like marble, was designed by Jacques-Ange Gabriel for Louis XV in 1770. Connecting the two, the 17th-century Galeries have exhibits retracing the château's history.

Opéra Royal

VERSAILLES: FIRST FLOOR, GARDENS & ADJACENT PARK

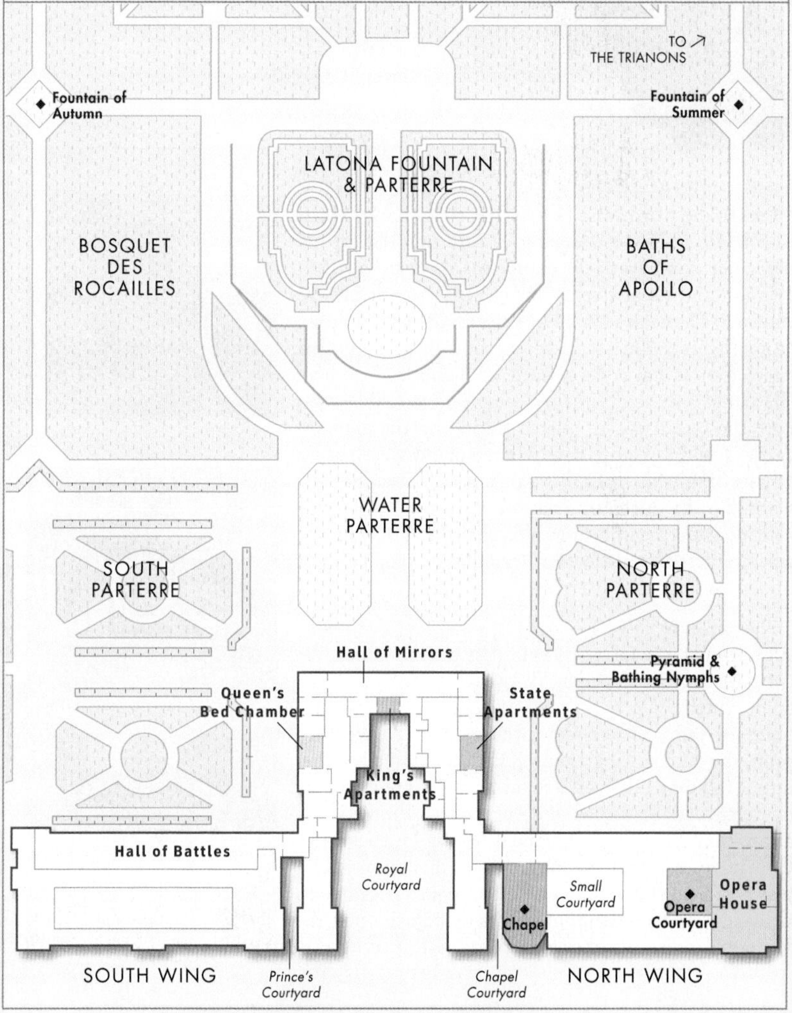

TO THE TRIANONS
Fountain of Autumn
Fountain of Summer
LATONA FOUNTAIN & PARTERRE
BOSQUET DES ROCAILLES
BATHS OF APOLLO
WATER PARTERRE
SOUTH PARTERRE
NORTH PARTERRE
Hall of Mirrors
Pyramid & Bathing Nymphs
Queen's Bed Chamber
State Apartments
King's Apartments
Hall of Battles
Royal Courtyard
Small Courtyard
Chapel
Opera Courtyard
Opera House
SOUTH WING
Prince's Courtyard
Chapel Courtyard
NORTH WING

LET THEM EAT CRÊPE: MARIE ANTOINETTE'S ROYAL LAIR

Was Marie Antoinette a luxury-mad butterfly flitting from ball to costume ball? Or was she a misunderstood queen who suffered a loveless marriage and became a prisoner of court etiquette at Versailles? Historians now believe the answer was the latter and point to her private retreats at Versailles as proof.

R.F.D. VERSAILLES?

Here, in the northwest part of the royal park, Marie Antoinette (1755–93) created a tiny universe of her own: her comparatively dainty mansion called Petit Trianon and its adjacent "farm," the relentlessly picturesque Hameau ("hamlet"). In a life that took her from royal cradle to throne of France to guillotine, her happiest days were spent at Trianon. For here she could live a life in the "simplest" possible way; here the queen could enter a salon and the game of cards would not stop; here women could wear simple gowns of muslin without a single jewel. Toinette only wanted to be queen of Trianon, not queen of France. And considering the horrible, chamber-pot-pungent, gossip-infested corridors of Versailles, you can almost understand why.

TEEN QUEEN

From the first, Maria-Antonia (her actual name) was ostracized as an outsider, "l'Autrichienne"—the Austrian "bitch." Upon arriving in France in 1770—at a mere 14 years of age—she was married to the Dauphin, the future King Louis XVI. But shamed by her initial failure to deliver a royal heir, she grew to hate overcrowded Versailles and escaped to the Petit Trianon. Built between 1763 and 1768 by Jacques-Ange Gabriel for Madame de Pompadour, this bijou palace was a radical statement: a royal residence designed to be casual and unassuming. Toinette refashioned the Trianon's interior in the sober Neoclassical style.

Hameau

Queen's House

Temple of Love

Petit Trianon

"THE SIMPLE LIFE"

Just beyond Petit Trianon lay the storybook Hameau, a mock-Norman village inspired by the peasant-luxe, simple-life daydreams caught by Boucher on canvas and by Rousseau in literature. With its water mill, thatched-roof houses, pigeon loft, and vegetable plots, this make-believe farm village was run by Monsieur Valy-Busard, a farmer, and his wife, who often helped the queen—outfitted as a Dresden shepherdess with a Sèvres porcelain crook—tend her flock of perfumed sheep.

As if to destroy any last link with reality, the queen built nearby a jewel-box theater (open by appointment). Here she acted in little plays, sometimes essaying the role of a servant girl. Only the immediate royal family, about seven or so friends, and her personal servants were permitted entry; disastrously, the entire officialdom of Versailles society was shut out—a move that only served to infuriate courtiers. This is how fate and destiny close the circle. For it was here at Trianon that a page sent by Monsieur de Saint-Priest found Marie-Antoinette on October 5, 1789, to tell her that Paris was marching on an already half-deserted Versailles.

Was Marie Antoinette a political traitor to France whose execution was well merited? Or was she the ultimate fashion victim? For those who feel that this tragic queen spent—and shopped—her way into a revolution, a visit to her relatively modest Petit Trianon and Hameau should prove a revelation.

Marie Antoinette

LES BEAUX TRIANONS

A mile from the château, the Grand Trianon was created by Hardouin Mansart in 1687 as a retreat for Louis XIV; it was restored in the early 19th century, with Empire-style salons. It's a memorable spot often missed by foot-weary tourists exhausted by the château, but well worth the effort. A special treat is Marie Antoinette's hideaway nearby, the Petit Trianon, presumably restored to how she left it before being forced to Paris by an angry mob of soon-to-be revolutionaries.

com/grautrianon ⌚ *Closed Sun., Mon., and July 27—Aug. 25. No lunch Tues.–Thurs.* ✍ *Reservations essential* 👔 *Jacket required.*

$$$ MODERN FRENCH Fodor's Choice ★ ✕ **L'Angelique.** Régis Douysset's refined yet unfussy French cuisine attracts the Versailles gourmet crowd. The dining room, in a restored 17th-century town house, is serene and comfortable, with white walls, wood-beam ceilings, dark wood paneling, and tasteful artwork—and the meals served here are among the best in town. A seasonally changing menu offers a good balance of seafood and game: picture a delicate perch fillet with spaghetti *de mer* (in a shellfish bouillon) or venison shoulder with grilled turnips and a spätzle of girolle mushrooms. Desserts alone are worth the Michelin star—the tart *feuilletée*, with candied peaches, cardamom, and peach sorbet, is ethereal. $ *Average main: €31* ✉ *27 av. de Saint-Cloud, Versailles* ☎ *01–30–84–98–85* 🌐 *www.langelique.fr* ⌚ *Closed Sun., Mon., 1 wk Christmas, 1 wk Feb., and 2 wks Aug.*

$ MODERN FRENCH FAMILY Fodor's Choice ★ ✕ **Lenôtre.** Set in the glamorous Cour des Senteurs, this handsome café (a branch of the renowned Paris pastry shop) fills a much-needed gap in Versailles dining. The warm, English-speaking staff and excellent, well-priced food—combined with a prime location amid elegant boutiques and beautiful gardens—make it a lovely choice at lunchtime, teatime, or just about any other time. The outdoor terrace is a fine spot on temperate days. Don't miss the sublime jasmine-scented *macaron*, specially created for the Cour des Senteurs. $ *Average main: €12* ✉ *8 rue de la Chancellerie, Versailles* ☎ *01–39–02–60–13* 🌐 *www.lenotre.com.*

$$ BISTRO FAMILY ✕ **Le Saint Julien.** It's not just convenience that draws a mix of locals, expats, and tourists to this pleasant corner bistro, close to the château in the old Saint Louis quarter. In terms of both decor and cuisine, Le Saint Julien mixes the traditional and the modern; hearty dishes like lamb confit and rabbit *parmentier* (a riff on the classic beef-and-potato casserole) are complemented by tender foie gras-stuffed ravioli or velvety mushroom soup. For lighter fare, the menu always includes a fish and a vegetarian dish. Helpings are generous, but try to leave room for an impressive cheese plate or one of the famously decadent desserts. $ *Average main: €22* ✉ *6 rue Saint Julien, Versailles* ☎ *01–39–50–00–97* 🌐 *www.lesaintjulien.fr* ⌚ *Closed Sun. and Mon.* ✍ *Reservations essential.*

WHERE TO STAY

$$ HOTEL 🏨 **Hôtel La Residence du Berry.** On a quiet main street in the picturesque Saint-Louis district, this 18th-century hotel with wood-beamed ceilings, antique engravings, and cozy rooms melds old-world charm with modern amenities; the bar and billiard room, with oriental rugs and a fireplace, are pleasant spots for a nightcap, and breakfast can be taken on a charming outdoor terrace. **Pros:** convenient yet quiet location; renovated lobby adds a touch of elegance. **Cons:** lovely breakfast not included in the price. $ *Rooms from: €139* ✉ *14 rue Anjou, Versailles* ☎ *01–39–49–07–07* 🌐 *www.hotel-berry.com* *38 rooms* 🍽 *No meals.*

$ HOTEL 🏨 **Le Cheval Rouge.** Built in 1676, this unpretentious option is in a corner of the market square, close to the château and strongly recommended if you plan to explore the town on foot. **Pros:** great setting in town center; good value for Versailles. **Cons:** bland public areas; some rooms need renovating. $ *Rooms from: €94* ✉ *18 rue André-Chénier, Versailles* ☎ *01–39–50–03–03* 🌐 *www.chevalrougeversailles.fr* *40 rooms* *No meals.*

$$$ HOTEL **Trianon Palace Versailles.** Like a modern-day Versailles, this deluxe turn-of-the-20th-century hotel is a creamy white creation of imposing size, filled with soaring rooms (including the historic Salle Clemenceau, site of the 1919 Versailles Peace Conference). **Pros:** palatial glamour; wonderful setting right by château park; Gordon Ramsay's on-site restaurant. **Cons:** lacks a personal touch. $ *Rooms from: €166* ✉ *1 bd. de la Reine, Versailles* ☎ *01–30–84–50–00* 🌐 *www.trianonpalace.fr* *176 rooms, 23 suites* *No meals.*

3

NIGHTLIFE AND PERFORMING ARTS

Académie du Spectacle Equestre. On most weekends (and on certain weekdays during school holidays), you can watch 28 elegant white horses and their expert riders perform balletic feats to music in a dazzling hour-long show directed by the great equine choreographer Bartabas. Fodor's Travel Talk Forum readers rave about the spectacle. If you can't make it, try catching a morning practice session. Both are held in the converted 17th-century Manège (riding school) at the aptly named Grandes Écuries (grand stables). Located opposite the palace, the structure was built for Louis XIV's royal cavalry. ✉ *Av. Rockefeller, Versailles* ☎ *01–39–02–62–75* 🌐 *www.bartabas.fr* *Shows €25; morning practice €12.*

Centre de Musique Baroque. An accomplished dancer, Louis XIV was also a great music lover who bankrolled the finest musicians and composers of the day—Lully, Charpentier, Rameau, Marais. So it's only fitting that France's foremost institute for the study and performance of French Baroque music should be based at Versailles. An excellent program of concerts is presented in the château's Opéra Royal and chapel; the latter are free of charge. ✉ *Versailles* ☎ *01–39–20–78–01* 🌐 *www.cmbv.com.*

Mois Molière. In June, Mois Molière (Molière Month) heralds a program of concerts, dramatic productions, and exhibits inspired by the famous playwright. See the website for details. ✉ *Pl. du Marché Notre-Dame, Versailles* ☎ *01–30–21–51–39* 🌐 *www.moismoliere.com.*

Fodor'sChoice ★ **Opéra Royal de Château de Versailles.** One of the most beautiful opera houses in Europe was built for 14-year-old Marie-Antoinette on the occasion of her marriage to Louis XVI, and entering this extravagantly gilded performance hall from the hewn-stone passageway can literally take your breath away. But the beauty is not just skin deep—the intimate 700-seat venue is blessed with rich acoustics. Home to the Royal Opéra, it also hosts a world-class roster of orchestral and chamber concerts, as well as modern dance and ballet performances. For arts lovers, this spot alone will justify the quick trip from Paris. ✉ *Château de Versailles, Versailles* ☎ *01–30–83–78–89* 🌐 *www.chateauversailles-spectacles.fr.*

Théâtre Montansier. The calendar here features a full program of plays in French, music, dance, and children's entertainment. ✉ *13 rue des Réservoirs, Versailles* ☎ *01–39–20–16–00* 🌐 *www.theatremontansier.com.*

SHOPPING

Aux Colonnes. This charming, highly rated *confiserie* (candy shop) offers a cornucopia of chocolates and traditional French sweets. ✉ *14 rue Hoche, Versailles* 🌐 *www.auxcolonnes.com* ⏲ *Closed Mon.*

Fodor's Choice ★ **La Cour des Senteurs.** At the threshold of Versailles's Old Town, the beautiful Cour des Senteurs—Courtyard of Fragrances—celebrates the town's status as the birthplace of the modern perfumer. Tiny **Maison des Parfums** charmingly recounts the history of perfume via a timeline and interactive displays, while the exquisite **Guerlain** boutique —only the second in the world after Paris's Champs Elysées original—carries the company's signature fragrances and cosmetics, plus a new jasmine-and-bergamot-based perfume you'll find only here. Couture glove maker **Maison Fabre** has a limited-edition perfumed glove in honor of Marie-Antoinette, along with a line of stylish handmade gloves crafted from luxury leathers; and the fabled **Diptyque** boutique sells all the scented candles, home fragrances, and perfumes that are beloved by chic Parisians. ✉ *8 rue de la Chancellerie, Versailles* ☎ *01–39–51–17–21* 🌐 *www.parfumsetsenteurs.fr.*

Les Délices du Palais. Everyone heads here to pick up homemade pâté, cold cuts, cheese, salad, and other picnic essentials. ✉ *4 rue du Maréchal-Foch, Versailles* 🌐 *www.charcuterie-lesdelicesdupalais.com* ⏲ *Closed Mon.*

RAMBOUILLET

32 km (20 miles) southwest of Versailles, 42 km (26 miles) southwest of Paris.

Haughty Rambouillet, once favored by kings and dukes, is now home to affluent gentry and, occasionally, the French president.

GETTING HERE

Frequent daily trains from Paris's Gare Montparnasse arrive at Gare de Rambouillet on place Prud'homme (35 mins, €8.20).

Visitor Information Rambouillet Tourist Office. ☎ *01–34–83–21–21* 🌐 *www.rambouillet-tourisme.fr.*

EXPLORING

FAMILY **Bergerie Nationale.** Located within Parc du Château, the Bergerie Nationale (National Sheepfold) is the site of a more serious agricultural venture: the famous Rambouillet Merinos raised here, prized for the quality and yield of their wool, are descendants of sheep imported from Spain by Louis XVI in 1786. A museum alongside tells the tale and evokes shepherd life. Don't miss the wonderful boutique—it features products from the farm, including *fromage de brebis* (sheep's milk cheese), produce, potted pâtés, jams, honey, and, of course, wool. ✉ *Rambouillet* ☎ *01–61–08–68–70* 🌐 *www.bergerie-nationale.educagri.fr* 🎫 *€6* ⏲ *Wed. and weekends 2—5:30.*

Château de Rambouillet. Surrounded by a magnificent 36,000-acre forest, this elegant château is a popular spot for biking and walking. Most of the structure dates from the early 18th century, but the brawny **Tour François-Ier** (François I Tower), named for the king who died here in

1547, was part of a fortified castle that earlier stood on this site. Highlights include the wood-panel apartments, especially the **Boudoir de la Comtesse** (Countess's Dressing Room); the marble-wall **Salle de Marbre** (Marble Hall), dating from the Renaissance; and the **Salle de Bains de Napoléon** (Napoléon's Bathroom), adorned with Pompeii-style frescoes. Compared to the muscular forecourt, the château's lakeside facade is a scene of unsuspected serenity and, as flowers spill from its balconies, cheerful informality. Guided visits in English are available on the hour (10–5) by reservation. ✉ *Rambouillet* ☎ *01–34–83–00–25* 🌐 *chateau-rambouillet.monuments-nationaux.fr* 🎫 *€8.50* ⏲ *Wed.–Mon. 10–noon and 2–6.*

Parc du Château. An extensive park—complete with island-dotted lake—stretches behind the château. Within it is the **Laiterie de la Reine** (Queen's Dairy), built for Marie-Antoinette: inspired by the writings of Jean-Jacques Rousseau, she came here to escape from the pressures of court life, pretending to be a simple milkmaid. It has a small marble temple and grotto and, nearby, the shell-lined Chaumière des Coquillages (Shell Pavilion). ✉ *Rambouillet* 🌐 *chateau-rambouillet.monuments-nationaux.fr* 🎫 *Included in château ticket* ⏲ *Wed., weekends, and holidays 2–6.*

WHERE TO EAT

$$ BISTRO

✕ **Auberge du Louvetier.** With a roaring fire in winter and an outdoor terrace in summer, this quaint, country-style restaurant specializes in the fruits of the sea. Traditional dishes—like brioche-enrobed *escargot* (snails) with Roquefort sauce, plump seafood sausage, a hearty *soupe de poisson* (fish soup), and a heaping seafood platter—are served in a wood-beamed dining room. 💲 *Average main: €22* ✉ *19 rue de l'Etang de la Tour, Rambouillet* ☎ *01–34–85–61–00* 🌐 *aubergedulouvetier.com* 💳 *No credit cards* ⏲ *Closed Mon. No lunch Sat., no dinner Sun.*

$$$ MODERN FRENCH

✕ **La Villa Marinette.** In an atmospheric 18th-century villa at the edge of the forest, husband-and-wife team Myriam and Sébastien Bourgeois welcome diners as though entertaining in their own home. Dishes such as venison with celery-root mousseline, plump langoustine baked in a pistachio and lemon crust, or veal with wild mushrooms gathered in the nearby forest are prepared with herbs fresh from the kitchen garden. Tables by the fire in winter or in the spacious garden in warm weather are at a premium, and the good-value, three-course lunch menu (€33) is a big draw, so be sure to book ahead. 💲 *Average main: €30* ✉ *20 av. du Général de Gaulle, Gazeran* ✥ *3 km (2 miles) west of Rambouillet* ☎ *01–34–83–19–01* 🌐 *villamarinette.fr* ⏲ *Closed Mon. and Tues. No dinner Sun.* ✍ *Reservations essential.*

CHARTRES

39 km (24 miles) southwest of Rambouillet via N10 and A11, 88 km (55 miles) southwest of Paris.

If Versailles is the climax of French secular architecture, Chartres is its religious apogee. All the descriptive prose and poetry that have been lavished on this supreme cathedral can only begin to suggest the glory of its 12th- and 13th-century statuary and stained glass, somehow suffused with burning mysticism and a strange sense of the numinous. Chartres is more than a church—it's a nondenominational spiritual experience. If you arrive in summer from Maintenon across the edge of the Beauce, the richest agrarian plain in France, you can see Chartres's spires rising up from oceans of wheat. The whole town, however, is worth a leisurely exploration. Ancient streets tumble down from the cathedral to the river, lined most weekends with *bouquinistes*selling old books and prints. The streets are especially busy each year on August 15, when pilgrims and tourists flock in for the Procession du Vœu de Louis XIII commemorating the French monarchy's vow to serve the Virgin Mary.

GETTING HERE

Both Transilien and main-line (Le Mans–bound) trains leave Paris's Gare Montparnasse for Chartres (50–70 mins, €15). The train station on Place Pierre-Sémard puts you within walking distance of the cathedral.

Visitor Information Chartres Tourist Office. ☎ *02–37–18–26–26* 🌐 *www.chartres-tourisme.com.*

EXPLORING

Fodor's Choice ★ **Cathédrale Notre-Dame** (*Chartres Cathedral*). Worship on the site of the Cathédrale Notre-Dame, better known as Chartres Cathedral, goes back to before the Gallo-Roman period—the crypt contains a well that was the focus of druid ceremonies. In the late 9th century Charles II (aka "the Bald") presented Chartres with what was believed to be the tunic of the Virgin Mary, a precious relic that went on to attract hordes of pilgrims. The current cathedral, the sixth church on the spot, dates mainly from the 12th and 13th centuries and was erected after the previous building, dating from the 11th century, burned down in 1194. A well-chronicled outburst of religious fervor followed the discovery that the Virgin Mary's relic had miraculously survived unsinged. Motivated by this "miracle," princes and paupers, barons and bourgeoisie gave their money and their labor to build the new cathedral. Ladies of the manor came to help monks and peasants on the scaffolding in a tremendous resurgence of religious faith that followed the Second Crusade. Just 25 years were needed for Chartres Cathedral to rise again, and it has remained substantially unchanged ever since.

The lower half of the facade survives from the earlier Romanesque church: this can be seen most clearly in the use of round arches rather than pointed Gothic-style ones. The **Royal Portal** is richly sculpted with scenes from the life of Christ—these meticulously detailed figures are among the greatest created during the Middle Ages. The taller of the two spires (380 feet versus 350 feet) was erected at the start of the 16th century, after its predecessor was destroyed by fire; its fanciful Flamboyant intricacy contrasts sharply with the stumpy solemnity of its Romanesque counterpart (access €6, open daily 9:30–noon and 2–4:30). The **rose window** above the main portal dates from the 13th century, and the three windows below it contain some of the finest examples of 12th-century stained-glass artistry in all of France.

As spiritual as Chartres is, the cathedral also had its more-earthbound uses. Look closely and you can see that the main nave floor has a

DID YOU KNOW?

Chartres's beautiful Clocher Neuf ("New Bell-tower") was completed in 1134, well before the Clocher Vieux ("Old Bell-tower"), on the right, which was originally built between 1145 and 1165, then rebuilt following a fire in the 16th century.

subtle slant. It was designed to provide drainage because this part of the church was often used as a "hostel" by thousands of overnighting pilgrims in medieval times.

Your eyes will need time to adjust to the somber interior. The reward is seeing the gem-like richness of the stained glass, with the famous deep Chartres blue predominating. The oldest window is arguably the most beautiful: **Notre-Dame de la Belle Verrière** (Our Lady of the Lovely Window), in the south choir. The cathedral's windows are gradually being cleaned and repaired—a lengthy, painstaking process—and the contrast with those still covered in the grime of centuries is staggering. It's worth taking a pair of binoculars along with you to pick out the details. If you wish to know more about stained-glass techniques and the motifs used, visit the small exhibit in the gallery opposite the north porch. Since 2008, the cathedral has been undergoing an ambitious €20-million renovation that will continue through 2017. To date, two major chapels (the chapels of the Martyrs and the Apostles) have been completely restored, as have the two bays of the nave and the lower choir and the transept windows. For those who remember these dark recesses before the restoration, the difference is nothing short of miraculous (or alarming, depending on your perspective); an estimated 160,000-square feet of original plasterwork is now visible, and many of the sublime details for which the cathedral is famous have been returned to their 13th-century state. The restoration includes a layer of creamy paint, gilding, and trompe l'oeil marble over the church's entire interior sandstone surface, but changes this sudden and drastic are inevitably accompanied by controversy. For some the transformation is transcendent, for others it's a travesty. It's best to judge for yourself. To help you do this, try to arrange a tour (in English) with local institution Malcolm Miller, whose knowledge of the cathedral's history is formidable. (He leads tours twice a day Monday through Saturday, April–October, and once a day November–March at noon. You can contact him at *02–37–28–15–58* or at *millerchartres@aol.com.*) The vast black-and-white labyrinth on the floor of the nave is one of the few to have survived from the Middle Ages; the faithful were expected to travel along its entire length (some 300 yards) on their knees. Guided tours of the **Crypte** start from the Maison de la Crypte opposite the south porch. You can also see a 4th-century Gallo-Roman wall and some 12th-century wall paintings. ✉ *16 cloître Notre-Dame, Chartres* ☎ *02–37–21–75–02* 🌐 *www.chartres-tourisme.com* 🎫 *Crypt €3; tours €7.50* ⏲ *Cathedral daily 8:30–7:30; guided tours of crypt Apr.–Oct., daily at 11, 2:15, 3:30, and 4:30; Nov.–Mar., daily at 11 and 4:15.*

Chartres en Lumieres. If you need an incentive to linger here until dusk, "Chartres en Lumieres" (Chartres's festival of lights) provides it: 28 of the city's most revered monuments, including the glorious Notre-Dame Cathedral, are transformed into vivid light canvases. Thematically based on the history and purpose of each specific site, the animated projections are organized into a city walk that covers a wide swath of the Old Town's cobbled streets and bridges. The spectacle is free and occurs nightly from mid-April through mid-October. A train tour of the illuminated city operates several times a night in summer. ✉ *Chartres* 🌐 *www.chartresenlumieres.com.*

Galerie du Vitrail. Since *vitrail* (stained glass) is the key to Chartres's fame, you may want to visit the Galerie du Vitrail, which specializes in the noble art. Pieces range from small plaques to entire windows, and there are books on the subject in English and French. ✉ *17 cloître Notre-Dame, Chartres* ☎ *02–37–36–10–03* 🌐 *www.galerie-du-vitrail.com.*

Musée des Beaux-Arts (*Fine Arts Museum*). Just behind the famed cathedral, the town art museum is housed in a handsome 18th-century building that once served as the bishop's palace. Its varied collection includes Renaissance enamels, a portrait of Erasmus by Holbein, tapestries, armor, and some fine (mainly French) paintings from the 17th, 18th, and 19th centuries. There's also a room devoted to the forceful 20th-century landscapes of Maurice de Vlaminck, who lived in the region. ✉ *29 cloître Notre-Dame, Chartres* ☎ *02–37–90–45–80* 🎟 *€3.40* 🕓 *Wed.—Sat. 10–12:30 and 2–6, Sun. 2–5.*

St-Aignan. Exquisite 17th-century stained glass can be admired at the church of St-Aignan, around the corner from St-Pierre. ✉ *Rue des Grenets, Chartres.*

St-Pierre. The Gothic church of St-Pierre, near the Eure River, has magnificent medieval windows from a period not represented at the cathedral. The oldest stained glass here, portraying Old Testament worthies, is to the right of the choir and dates from the late 13th century. ✉ *Rue St-Pierre, Chartres.*

WHERE TO EAT AND STAY

$
FRENCH
FAMILY
Fodor's Choice ★

✕ **Esprit Gourmand.** On a picturesque street close to the cathedral, this quaint bistro is a life-saver in a town sorely lacking in quality dining. The traditional French favorites it serves—like roast *poulet* with buttery potatoes, sautéed filet of dorade with grilled vegetables, and braised pork that's crisp on the outside and meltingly tender inside—are perennial crowd pleasers. The dining room, though small, doesn't feel cramped, and there's a charming garden terrace for outdoor eating in summer. It's wise to reserve ahead, as fine cuisine and excellent service assure a full house at every meal. Ⓢ *Average main: €17* ✉ *6 rue du Cheval-Blanc, Chartres* ☎ *02–37–36–97–84.*

$$
FRENCH
Fodor's Choice ★

✕ **Les Feuillantines.** The adventurous cuisine served at Les Feuillantines (one of Chartres's few gastronomic restaurants) rarely falters and very often soars. Try the superb house-made terrine with tangy cornichons to start, followed by duck risotto topped with caramelized shallots or beef ravioli perfumed with lemongrass and smoked tea. For dessert, the copious cheese plate, vanilla-flecked baba à rhum, and divine melted-chocolate cake all hit the spot. In warmer months, the garden is an added bonus, as is a good, if slightly unimaginative, wine list. The location (on a tiny street near the cathedral) is convenient, and in terms of quality for price this cozy spot can't be beat. Ⓢ *Average main: €22* ✉ *4 rue du Bourg, Chartres* ☎ *02–37–30–22–21* 🕓 *Closed Sun. and Mon.* ✍ *Reservations essential.*

$$ HOTEL

Best Western Le Grand Monarque. On Chartres's main square, not far from the cathedral, this converted coaching inn warmly evokes the 19th century; many guest rooms are outfitted with brick walls, attractive antiques, lush drapes, and modern bathrooms (the best are in a separate turn-of-the-20th-century building overlooking a garden, while the most atmospheric are tucked away in the attic). **Pros:** its old-fashioned charm still works today; the spa and fitness center offers beauty treatments and massage. **Cons:** best rooms are in an annex; uphill walk to cathedral. *Rooms from: €143 ✉ 22 pl. des Épars, Chateauneuf-de-Grasse ☎ 02–37–18–15–15 ⊕ www.bw-grand-monarque.com 50 rooms, 5 suites No meals.*

$$$ HOTEL Fodor's Choice ★

Château d'Esclimont. One of France's most spectacular château-hotels lies northeast of Chartres in the town of St-Symphorien. **Pros:** the grand style of a country château; wonderful rural setting. **Cons:** service can be pompous; off the beaten path and not easy to find. *Rooms from: €200 ✉ 2 rue du Château-d'Esclimont, St-Symphorien-le-Château ⊕ 24 km (15 miles) northeast of Chartres via N10/D18 ☎ 02–37–31–15–15 ⊕ www.grandesetapes.fr 48 rooms, 4 suites No meals.*

GIVERNY

70 km (44 miles) northwest of Paris.

The small village of Giverny (pronounced jee-vair-knee), just beyond the Epte River, which marks the boundary of the Ile-de-France, has become a place of pilgrimage for art lovers. It was here that Claude Monet lived for 43 years, until his death at the age of 86 in 1926. Although his house is now prized by connoisseurs of 19th-century interior decoration, it's his garden, with its Japanese-inspired water-lily pond and bridge, that remains the high point for many—a 5-acre, three-dimensional Impressionist painting you can stroll around at leisure. Most make this a day trip, but Giverny has some lovely lodgings, so you could also overnight here.

GETTING HERE

Frequent main-line trains connect Paris's Gare St-Lazare with Vernon (50 mins, €15); you can then cover the remaining 10 km (6 miles) to Giverny by taxi, bus, or bike (the last of these can be rented at the café opposite Vernon station). April through October, shuttle buses meet trains daily and whisk passengers to Giverny for €8.

EXPLORING

Fodor's Choice ★

Maison et Jardin Claude Monet (*Monet's House and Garden*). Monet was brought up in Normandy and, like many of the Impressionists, was captivated by the soft light of the Seine Valley. After several years in Argenteuil, just north of Paris, he moved downriver to Giverny in 1883 along with his two sons, his mistress, Alice Hoschedé (whom he later married), and her six children. By 1890 a prospering Monet was able to buy this pretty *maison*—now a museum—outright. With pink walls and green shutters, it has a warm, homey feel that may come as a welcome change after the stateliness of the French châteaux. Rooms have been returned to Monet's original designs: witness the kitchen with its blue tiles, the buttercup-yellow dining room, and Monet's bedroom on the second floor. The house was fully restored only in the 1970s, thanks to the millions contributed by fans and patrons (who were largely Americans). Reproductions of the painter's works, and some of the Japanese prints he avidly collected, crowd its walls. During his era, French culture had come under the spell of Orientalism, and these framed prints were often gifts from visiting Japanese diplomats whom Monet had befriended in Paris.

Three years after buying his house and cultivating its garden—which the family called the "Clos Normand"—Monet purchased another plot of land across the lane to continue his gardening experiments, even diverting the Epte to make a pond. The resulting garden *à la japonaise* (reached through a tunnel from the "Clos"), with flowers spilling out across the paths, contains the famous "tea-garden" bridge and water-lily pond, flanked by a mighty willow and rhododendrons. Images of the bridge and the water lilies—in French, *nymphéas*—in various seasons appear in much of Monet's later work. Looking across the pond, it's easy to conjure up the grizzled, bearded painter dabbing at his canvases—capturing changes in light and pioneering a breakdown in form that was to have a major influence on 20th-century art.

The garden—planted with nearly 100,000 annuals and even more perennials—is a place of wonder. No matter that about 500,000 visitors troop through each year; they seem to fade in the presence of beautiful roses, carnations, lady's slipper, tulips, irises, hollyhocks, poppies, daises, nasturtiums, larkspur, azaleas, and more. With that said, it still helps to visit midweek when crowds are thinner. If you want to pay your respects to the original gardener, Monet is buried in the family vault in Giverny's village church. ■ **TIP→ Although the gardens overall are most beautiful in spring, the water lilies bloom during the latter part of July and the first two weeks of August.** ✉ *84 rue Claude Monet, Giverny* ☎ *02–32–51–28–21* 🌐 *www.fondation-monet.com* 🎫 *€9.50* ⏲ *Apr.–Oct., daily 9:30–6.*

Fodor's Choice ★ **Musée des Impressionnismes.** After touring the painterly grounds of Monet's house, you may wish to see some real paintings at the Musée des Impressionnismes. Originally endowed by the late Chicago art patrons Daniel and Judith Terra, it featured a few works by the American Impressionists, including Willard Metcalf, Louis Ritter, Theodore Wendel, and John Leslie Breck, who flocked to Giverny to study at the hand of the master. But in recent years the museum has extended its scope with an exciting array of exhibitions that explore the origins, geographical diversity, and wide-ranging influences of Impressionism—in the process highlighting the importance of Giverny and the Seine Valley in the history of the movement. There's an on-site restaurant and *salon de thé* (tearoom) with a fine outdoor terrace, as well as a garden "quoting" some of Monet's plant compositions. Farther down the road, you can visit Giverny's landmark Hôtel Baudy, a restaurant that was once the preferred watering hole of many 19th-century artists. ✉ *99 rue Claude Monet, Giverny* ☎ *02–32–51–94–65* 🌐 *www.mdig.fr* 🎫 *€7* ⏲ *Apr.–Oct., daily 10–6.*

An entry to Fodor's France contest, ShutterbugBill, a Fodors.com member, sent in this entrancing view of the Japanese footbridge in Monet's Garden.

WHERE TO EAT AND STAY

$$ BRASSERIE Fodor's Choice ★

Hôtel Baudy. Back in Monet's day, this pretty-in-pink villa was the favorite hotel of the American painters' colony. Today it remains one of the most charming spots in the Ile-de-France—despite the busloads of tour groups that pull in (luckily they're channeled upstairs). Renovated to appear as it did in Monet's time, the dining room is stage-set rustic; and there's an extraordinarily pretty rose garden out back with embowered paths that lead to the studio Cézanne once used. The surroundings retain more historic charm than the simple cuisine (mainly salads large enough to count as a main course in their own right, or straightforward dishes like an omelette or *gigot d'agneau*), but a decent three-course prix-fixe menu is available at lunch and dinner. *Average main: €18 81 rue Claude-Monet, Giverny 02–32–21–10–03 www.restaurantbaudy.com No credit cards Closed Nov.–Mar.*

$ B&B/INN

La Musardière. Just a short stroll from chez Monet, this 1880 manor house (the name means "Place to Idle") has a cozy lobby, guest rooms with views overlooking a leafy garden, and its own restaurant-crêperie. **Pros:** surrounded by greenery. **Cons:** mediocre eatery attracts noisy tourist crowds in peak season. *Rooms from: €85 123 rue Claude Monet, Giverny 02–32–21–03–18 www.lamusardiere.fr Closed mid-Dec.—Jan. 10 rooms No meals.*

$ B&B/INN

Le Clos Fleuri. Giverny's hotel shortage is offset by several stylish and affordable bed-and-breakfasts—this one, located just 600 yards from Monet's estate, is among the best. **Pros:** co-owner Danielle Fouche speaks fluent English thanks to years spent in Australia and will happily give advice about touring the area; colorful oasis in the heart of the village. **Cons:** no air-conditioning; books up quickly. *Rooms from:*

€98 ✉ 5 rue de la Dîme, Giverny ☎ 02–32–21–36–51 🌐 www.giverny-leclosfleuri.fr ⏲ Closed Oct.–Mar. 3 rooms 🍽 Breakfast.

$$$ B&B/INN **Le Jardin des Plumes.** This Norman-style half-timbered inn with its lovely surrounding garden is a welcome addition to the oft-lamented Giverny lodging and dining scene. **Pros:** location, location, location; fine restaurant; stylish rooms. **Cons:** dinner on the pricey side. *$ Rooms from: €180 ✉ 1 rue du Milieu, Giverny ☎ 02–32–54–26–35 🌐 www.lejardindesplumes.fr ⏲ Closed Jan. 4 rooms, 4 suites 🍽 No meals.*

$$ HOTEL FAMILY **Les Jardins d'Epicure.** Set on 7 acres of picture-perfect parkland, this unique hotel occupies three charming 19th-century buildings: the picturesque stables, with "Gothic" brick trim, high beamed ceilings, and the delightful Unicorn Suite; the Villa Florentine (once home to famed poet Paul Éluard) whose Chambre Marquise has no less than seven windows overlooking the park and stream; and the elegant Castel Napoléon III, with six separate guest rooms featuring period antiques and oriental rugs. **Pros:** superb setting; excellent restaurant. **Cons:** a 20-minute drive from Giverny; gates close at 11 pm, sharp. *$ Rooms from: €110 ✉ 16 Grande Rue, Giverny ✥ 15 km (9 miles) northeast of Vernon on D86 ☎ 01–34–67–75–87 🌐 www.lesjardinsdepicure.com 16 rooms, 3 suites 🍽 No meals.*

AUVERS-SUR-OISE

74 km (46 miles) east of Giverny via D147, N14, and D4; 33 km (21 miles) northwest of Paris via N328.

The tranquil Oise River valley retains much of the charm that attracted Camille Pissarro, Paul Cézanne, Camille Corot, Charles-François Daubigny, and Berthe Morisot to Auvers-sur-Oise in the second half of the 19th century. Despite this lofty company, though, it's the spirit of Vincent van Gogh—who spent the last months of his life painting no fewer than 70 works here—that haunts every nook and cranny of this pretty riverside village. On July 27, 1890, the tormented artist laid his easel against a haystack, walked behind the Château d'Auvers, shot himself, then stumbled to the Auberge Ravoux. He died on July 29. The next day, using a hearse from neighboring Méry (because the priest of Auvers refused to provide his for a suicide victim), Van Gogh's body was borne up the hill to the village cemetery. His heartbroken brother Theo died the following year and, in 1914, was reburied alongside him in a simple ivy-covered grave. Today many visitors make a pilgrimage to town sites associated with Van Gogh (the tourist office has information). Short hikes outside the center will lead you to lovely rural landscapes, including the one that inspired Van Gogh's last painting, *Wheat Fields with Crows*.

GETTING HERE

Take the RER-C line from Paris (direction Pontoise) to St-Ouen l'Aumone, and then a second train (direction Creil) onward to Auvers; the total travel is 45–55 minutes, the total cost €6.10. There is no connecting public transportation from the area around Vernon.

Visitor Information Auvers-sur-Oise Tourist Office. ☎ *01–30–36–10–06* 🌐 *www.auvers-sur-oise.com.*

EXPLORING

Maison-Atelier de Daubigny. The landscape artist Charles-François Daubigny, a precursor of the Impressionists, lived in Auvers from 1861 until his death in 1878. You can visit his studio, the Maison-Atelier de Daubigny, and admire the mural and roof paintings by Daubigny and fellow artists Camille Corot and Honoré Daumier. ✉ *61 rue Daubigny, Auvers-sur-Oise* ☎ *01–34–48–03–03* 🌐 *www.atelier-daubigny.com* 🎫 *€6* ⏱ *Mid-Apr.–mid-July and mid-Aug.—Oct., Thurs.–Sun. 2–6.*

Maison de Van Gogh (*Van Gogh House*). Opposite the town hall, the Auberge Ravoux—where Van Gogh lived and died—is now the Maison de Van Gogh. The inn opened in 1876 and owes its name to Arthur Ravoux, the landlord from 1889 to 1891. He had seven lodgers in all, who paid 3.50 francs for room and board (that was cheaper than the other inns in Auvers, where 6 francs was the going rate). A dingy staircase leads up to the tiny attic where Van Gogh stored some of modern art's most iconic paintings under his bed. A short film retraces the artist's time at Auvers, and there's a well-stocked souvenir shop. Stop for a drink or for lunch in the ground-floor restaurant. ✉ *8 rue de la Sansonne, Auvers-sur-Oise* ☎ *01–30–36–60–60* 🌐 *www.maisondevangogh.fr* 🎫 *€6* ⏱ *Mar.–Oct., Wed.–Sun. 10–6.*

Maison du Dr. Gachet. The former home of Van Gogh's closest friend in Auvers, Dr. Paul Gachet, is a local landmark. Documents and mementos evoke both Van Gogh's stay and Gachet's passion for the avant-garde art of his era. The good doctor was himself the subject of one of the artist's most famous portraits (and the world's second–most expensive painting when it sold for $82 million in the late 1980s); the actual creation of it was reenacted in the 1956 biopic, *Lust for Life,* starring Kirk Douglas. Even this house was immortalized on canvas, courtesy of Cézanne. A friend and patron to many of the artists who settled in and visited Auvers in the 1880s, Gachet also contributed to their artistic education by teaching them about engraving processes. Don't overlook the garden—it provided the ivy that covers Van Gogh's grave in the cemetery across town. ✉ *78 rue du Dr-Gachet, Auvers-sur-Oise* ☎ *01–30–36–81–27* 🎫 *Free* ⏱ *Apr.–Oct., Wed.–Sun. 10:30–6.*

Musée Daubigny. You may want to visit the modest Musée Daubigny to admire the drawings, lithographs, and occasional oils by local 19th-century artists, some of which were collected by Daubigny himself. The museum is opposite the Maison de Van Gogh, above the tourist office, which shows a 15-minute film (in English on request) about life in Auvers, *From Daubigny to Van Gogh.* ✉ *Manoir des Colombières, Rue de la Sansonne, Auvers-sur-Oise* ☎ *01–30–36–80–20* 🌐 *www.museedaubigny.com* 🎫 *€4* ⏱ *Apr.–Oct., Wed.–Fri. 2–5:30, weekends 10:30–12:30 and 2–6; Nov.–Mar., Wed.–Fri. 2–5:30, weekends 10:30–12:30 and 2–5:30.*

FAMILY **Voyage au Temps des Impressionnistes** (*Journey Through the Impressionist Era*). Set above split-level gardens, this 17th-century village château (also depicted by Van Gogh) now houses the Voyage au Temps des Impressionnistes. You'll receive a set of headphones (English available), with commentary that guides you past various tableaux illustrating life during the Impressionist years. Although there are no Impressionist originals—500 reproductions pop up on screens interspersed between the tableaux—this is one of France's most imaginative, enjoyable, and innovative museums. Some of the special effects, including talking mirrors, computerized cabaret dancing girls, and a simulated train ride past Impressionist landscapes, are worthy of Disney. The on-site Impressionist Café has three dining areas: the elegant 17th-century Orangerie, the Espaces Scénographiques, and a re-creation of a 19th-century *guinguette* (café/dance hall), where more casual fare is on the menu. ✉ *Rue de Léry, Auvers-sur-Oise* ☎ *01–34–48–48–40* 🌐 *www.chateau-auvers.fr* 🎫 *€14.25* ⏲ *Apr.–Sept., Tues.–Sun. 10:30–6; Oct.–Mar., Tues.–Sun. 10:30–4:30.*

A VAN GOGH SELF-TOUR

Auvers-sur-Oise is peppered with plaques marking the spots that inspired Van Gogh. They bear reproductions of his paintings, enabling you to compare his final works with the scenes as they are today. His last abode—the Auberge Ravoux—has been turned into a shrine. You can also visit the medieval village church, subject of one of Van Gogh's most famous pieces, *L'Église d'Auvers*; admire Osip Zadkine's powerful statue of Van Gogh in the village park; and visit the restored house of Dr. Gachet, his best friend.

3

WHERE TO EAT AND STAY

$$$ BISTRO ✕ **Auberge Ravoux.** For total Van Gogh immersion, have lunch—or dinner on Friday and Saturday—in the restaurant he patronized regularly more than 100 years ago, in the building where he finally expired. A three-course prix-fixe menu is available, and saddle of lamb and homemade terrine are among Loran Gattufo's specialties. What makes eating here special, though, is the *genius loci*, complete with glasswork, lace curtains, and wall blandishments carefully modeled on the original designs. Table No. 5, the "*table des habitués*," is where Van Gogh used to sit. A magnificently illustrated book, *Van Gogh's Table*by culinary historian Alexandra Leaf and art historian Fred Leeman, recalls Vincent's stay at the auberge and describes in loving detail the dishes served here at the time. $ *Average main: €25* ✉ *52 rue Général-de-Gaulle, Auvers-sur-Oise* ☎ *01–30–36–60–63* 🌐 *www.maisondevangogh.fr* 💳 *No credit cards* ⏲ *Closed Mon. and Tues. and Dec.–Feb. No dinner Wed., Thurs., or Sun.* ✍ *Reservations essential.*

$$ HOTEL 🏨 **Hostellerie du Nord.** This sturdy mansion, which began life as a coach house in the 17th century, is now a prim hotel; its small, white-wall bedrooms are adorned with gilt-framed pictures and named after artists, including Cézanne (who stayed here in 1872) and Van Gogh (whose eponymous junior suite is the quaintest, if priciest, option). **Pros:** only hotel in Auvers; great location close to river, train station, and Van Gogh's house. **Cons:** bland interiors; small rooms. $ *Rooms from: €129* ✉ *6 rue du Général de Gaulle, Auvers-sur-Oise* ☎ *01–30–36–70–74* 🌐 *www.hostelleriedunord.fr* 🛏 *8 rooms* 🍽 *No meals.*

EASTERN ILE-DE-FRANCE

This area covers a broad arc, beginning northeast of Paris in Chantilly, one of the most popular day trips from the French capital. From the frozen-in-time medieval town of Senlis, we detour north to visit Pierrefonds, a fairy-tale 19th-century castle that may even outdo the one at Disneyland Paris, the very next stop on this tour heading south. Two of France's most spectacular châteaux—Vaux-le-Vicomte and Fontainebleau—offer a fitting grand finale.

CHANTILLY

37 km (23 miles) north of Paris via N16.

Celebrated for lace, cream, and the most beautiful medieval manuscript in the world—*Les Très Riches Heures du Duc de Berry*—romantic Chantilly has a host of other attractions. Most notable among them are a faux Renaissance château with an eye-popping art collection second only to the Louvre's, a classy racecourse, and 18th-century stables that are called *grande* for good reason.

GETTING HERE

Chantilly can be reached on both Transilien and main-line trains from Paris's Gare du Nord (25–30 mins, €8.40).

Visitor Information Chantilly Tourist Office. ☎ *03–44–67–37–37* 🌐 *www.chantilly-tourisme.com.*

EXPLORING

Fodor's Choice ★ **Château de Chantilly.** Although its lavish exterior may be 19th-century Renaissance pastiche, the Château de Chantilly, sitting snugly behind an artificial lake, houses the outstanding **Musée Condé,** with illuminated medieval manuscripts, tapestries, furniture, and paintings. The most famous room, the **Santuario** (sanctuary), contains two celebrated works by Italian painter Raphael (1483–1520)—the *Three Graces* and the *Orleans Virgin*—plus an exquisite ensemble of 15th-century miniatures by the most illustrious French painter of his time, Jean Fouquet (1420–81). Farther on, in the **Cabinet des Livres** (library), is the world-famous Book of Hours whose title translates as *The Very Rich Hours of the Duc de Berry.* It was illuminated by the Brothers Limbourg with magical pictures of early-15th-century life as lived by one of Burgundy's richest lords; unfortunately, due to their fragility, painted facsimiles of the celebrated calendar illuminations are on display, not the actual pages of the book. Other highlights of this unusual museum are the **Galerie de Psyché** (Psyche Gallery), with 16th-century stained glass and portrait drawings by Flemish artist Jean Clouet II; the **Chapelle,** with sculptures by Jean Goujon and Jacques Sarrazin; and the extensive collection of paintings by 19th-century French artists, headed by Jean-Auguste-Dominique Ingres. In addition, there are grand and smaller salons, all stuffed with palace furniture, family portraits, and Sèvres porcelains, making this a must for lovers of the decorative and applied arts. ✉ *Domaine de Chantilly, Chantilly* ☎ *03–44–27–31–80* 🌐 *www.domainedechantilly.com*

€16 Apr.–Oct., daily 10–6; Feb. and Mar., Wed.–Mon. 10:30–5 Closed last three wks of Jan.

FAMILY Fodor's Choice ★ **Grandes Écuries** (*Grand Stables*). The grandest stables in France were built by Jean Aubert in 1719 to accommodate 240 horses and 500 hounds used for stag- and boar-hunting in the forests nearby. Now with 30 breeds of horses and ponies living here in straw-lined comfort, the palatial stables function as the **Musée Vivant du Cheval** (Living Horse Museum). This fascinating facility, which reopened in 2013 after a two-year renovation, isn't just for horse lovers. Equine history is explored through an array of artifacts, prints, paintings, textiles, sculptures, equipment, and weaponry. Visitors can also enjoy the elaborate horse shows and dressage demonstrations scheduled year-round. Check the website for dates and times. *7 rue du Connétable, Chantilly 03–44–27–31–80 www.domainedechantilly.com Stables included in château ticket; horse shows €21; dressage demonstrations €11 Apr.–Oct., Wed.–Mon. 10–5; Jan.–Mar., Wed.–Mon. 1–5; Dec., Wed.–Mon. 2–5.*

Hippodrome des Princes de Condé. Chantilly, France's equestrienne epicenter, is home to the fabled Hippodrome racetrack. Established in 1834, it comes into its own each June with two of Europe's most prestigious events: the Prix du Jockey-Club (French Derby) on the first Sunday of the month, and the Prix de Diane for three-year-old fillies the Sunday after. On main race days, a free shuttle bus runs between Chantilly's train station and the track. *Rte. de la Plaine-des-Aigles, Chantilly 03–44–62–44–00 www.france-galop.com/hippodrome-de-chantilly.2828.0.html.*

Park. Le Nôtre's park is based on that familiar French royal combination of formality and romantic eccentricity. The former is represented in the neatly planned parterres and a mighty, straight-banked canal; the latter comes to the fore in the waterfall and the Hameau, a mock-Norman village that inspired Marie-Antoinette's version at Versailles. You can explore on foot or on an electric train, and, in the warmer months, take a **rowboat** for a meander down the Grand Canal. *Chantilly 03–44–27–31–80 www.domainedechantilly.com Park only €7; park and château €16 Apr.–Oct., Wed.–Mon. 10–8; Nov.–Mar., Wed.–Mon. 10:30–6.*

WHERE TO EAT AND STAY

$$ FRENCH **La Capitainerie.** Housed in the stone-vaulted kitchens of the Château de Chantilly's legendary 17th-century chef Vorace Vatel, this quaint restaurant has an open-hearth fireplace big enough for whole lambs or oxen to sizzle on the spit. Reflect at leisure on your cultural peregrinations over mouthfuls of grilled turbot or roast quail, and don't forget to add a good dollop of homemade crème de Chantilly to your dessert. Open from noon to 5, it offers à la carte options plus a €35 prix-fixe menu. *Average main: €22 Château de Chantilly, Chantilly 03–44–57–15–89 Closed Tues. Nov.—Apr. No dinner.*

$$$$ HOTEL Fodor's Choice ★ **Auberge du Jeu de Paume.** Set within the Domaine de Chantilly, the largest princely estate in France, this newcomer combines its stunning setting with old-world elegance and modern comforts to create a deluxe country retreat; all of the beautifully appointed guest rooms

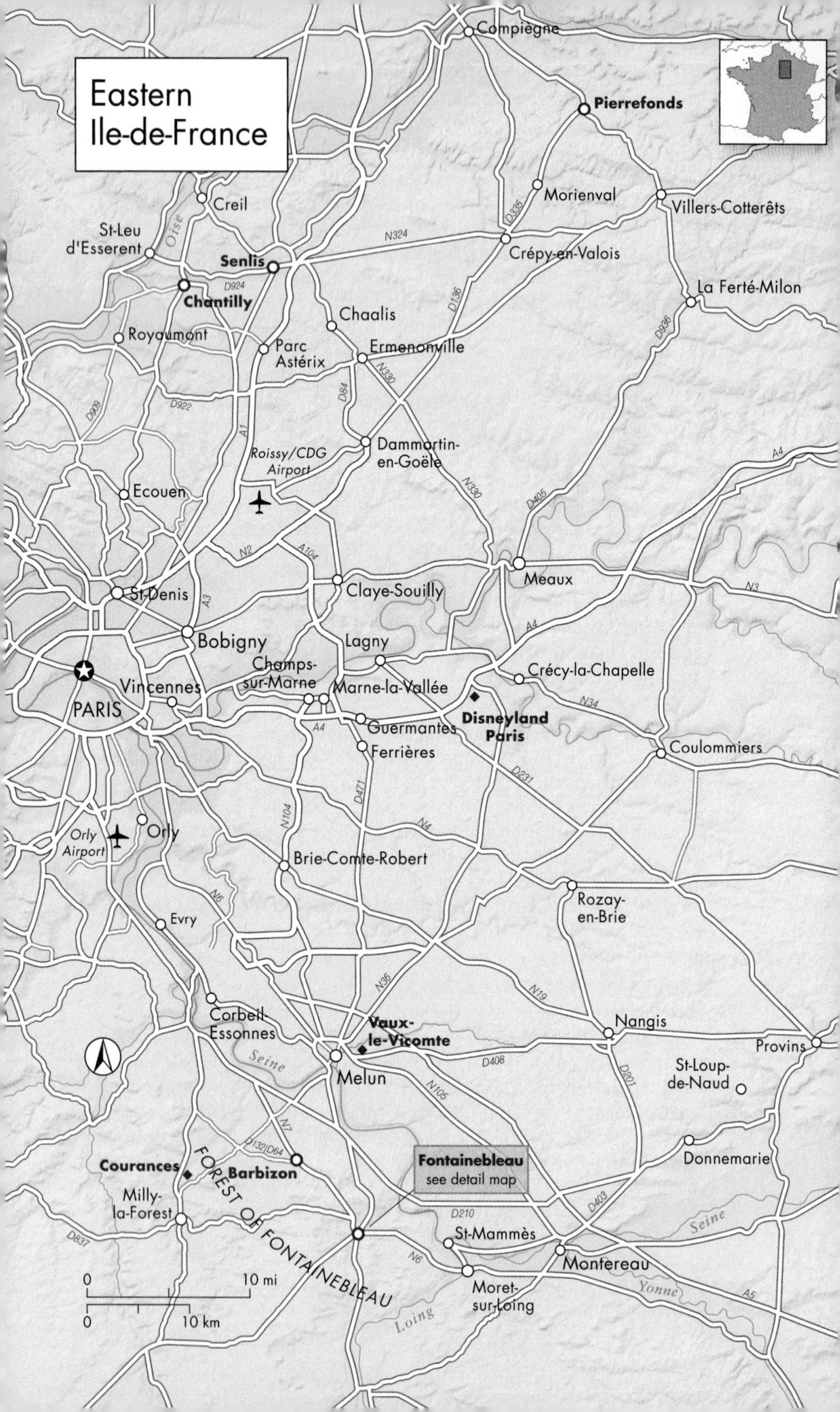
Eastern
Ile-de-France
Compiègne
Pierrefonds
Morienval
Villers-Cotterêts
Creil
Oise
St-Leu
d'Esserent
N324
D335
Crépy-en-Valois
Senlis
D924
Chantilly
D136
La Ferté-Milon
Chaalis
Royaumont
Parc
Astérix
Ermenonville
D936
N330
D84
D909
D922
A1
Dammartin-
en-Goële
Roissy/CDG
Airport
Ecouen
N330
D405
A4
N2
A104
Meaux
Claye-Souilly
N3
St-Denis
A3
Bobigny
A4
Lagny
Champs-
sur-Marne
Crécy-la-Chapelle
PARIS
Vincennes
Marne-la-Vallée
N34
Disneyland
Paris
Guermantes
A4
Ferrières
Coulommiers
D231
D471
N104
Orly
Orly
Airport
N4
Brie-Comte-Robert
Rozay-
en-Brie
N6
Evry
N36
N19
Corbeil-
Essonnes
Vaux-
le-Vicomte
Nangis
Provins
Seine
Melun
D408
St-Loup-
de-Naud
D201
N105
N7
D132|D64
Donnemarie
Courances
Barbizon
Fontainebleau
see detail map
FOREST OF FONTAINEBLEAU
D403
Milly-
la-Forest
D210
Seine
D837
St-Mammès
Montereau
N6
0
10 mi
Moret-
sur-Loing
Yonne
A5
0
10 km
Loing

have elegant furnishings, spacious marble baths, and floor-to-ceiling windows—the last being particularly appreciated because many accommodations overlook the château grounds, the historic Grand Stables, and Le Nôtre–designed gardens. **Pros:** proximity to all the sights; sublime country setting; luxe amenities. **Cons:** dining room could be more intimate. *Rooms from: €250 ✉ 4 rue du Connétable, Chantilly ☎ 03–44–65–50–00 🌐 www.aubergedujeudepaumechantilly.fr 68 rooms, 24 suites No meals.*

3

$$$ HOTEL **Dolce Chantilly.** Surrounded by forest and its own 18-hole golf course, this sleekly modern hotel—1½ km (1 mile) northeast of the château—has a glitzy marble-floor reception hall that is not quite matched by the guest rooms: in such a vast new building, these rooms seem a bit small, but they are satisfyingly functional and fit into the contemporary style of the place. **Pros:** great facilities, including fitness rooms and indoor-outdoor pool; ambitious restaurant; stylish public areas. **Cons:** rooms lack character; overall the place can feel impersonal. *Rooms from: €200 ✉ Rte. d'Apremont, Vineuil-St-Firmin ☎ 03–44–58–47–77 🌐 www.dolcechantilly.com ⏲ Closed Christmas–New Year's 175 rooms, 25 suites No meals.*

SENLIS

10 km (6 miles) east of Chantilly via D924, 40 km (26 miles) north of Paris via A1.

Senlis is an exceptionally well-preserved medieval town with a crooked maze of streets dominated by the svelte, soaring spire of its Gothic cathedral. For a glimpse into the more distant past, be sure to also inspect the superb Musée d'Art et d'Archéologie.

GETTING HERE

Take either the Transilien or main-line trains from Paris's Gare du Nord to Chantilly (25–30 mins, €8.70), then a bus onward to Senlis.

Visitor Information Senlis Tourist Office. ☎ *03–44–53–06–40* 🌐 *www.senlis-tourisme.fr.*

EXPLORING

Fodor's Choice ★ **Cathédrale Notre-Dame.** The breathtaking Cathédrale Notre-Dame, one of the country's oldest and narrowest cathedrals, dates from the second half of the 12th century. The superb spire—arguably the most elegant in France—was added around 1240, and the majestic transept, with its ornate rose windows, in the 16th century. ✉ *Pl. du Parvis, Senlis.*

Fodor's Choice ★ **Musée d'Art et d'Archéologie.** Reopened in 2013 after a stunning four-year renovation, the town's excellent Musée d'Art et d'Archéologie displays finds ranging from Gallo-Roman votive objects unearthed in the neighboring Halatte Forest to the building's own excavated foundations (visible in the basement); note the superb stone heads bathed in half light. Upstairs, paintings include works by Manet's teacher, Thomas Couture (who lived in Senlis) and charming naïve florals by the town's own Séraphine de Senlis. ✉ *Palais Épiscopal, Pl. du Parvis Notre-Dame, Senlis* ☎ *03–44–24–86–72* 🌐 *www.musees-senlis.fr/*

Musee-d-Art-et-d-Archeologie/historique-du-musee.html €4 *Mon., Thurs., and Fri. 10–noon and 2–6, weekends 11–1 and 2–6, Wed. 2–6.*

WHERE TO EAT AND STAY

$ MODERN FRENCH **Le Scaramouche.** This handsome and well-priced bistro, in an enviable spot facing the cathedral, provides a pleasant setting in which to enjoy a modern take on French classics. The focus here is more on quality than quantity, yet the menu covers all the important bases: a warm casserole of escargots with parsley butter, ravioli *Dauphiné*, hand-cut steak tartare with crispy frites, buttery scallops with lentils and a garlicky mayonnaise, and an array of tempting salads and desserts. On a warm day, diners can enjoy the outdoor terrace and unparalleled views of charming Senlis. *Average main: €14* *4 pl. Notre Dame, Senlis* *03–44–53–01–26* *www.le-scaramouche.fr* *Closed Sun. and Mon.*

$ HOTEL **L'Hostellerie de la Porte Bellon.** This old stone house, near the bus station and five minutes by foot from the cathedral, is the closest you can get to spending a night in the historic center of Senlis; the prettiest room is No. 14, which overlooks the garden and has sloping walls and exposed beams. **Pros:** only hotel close to historic town center; attractive old building. **Cons:** modest facilities; some rooms need renovating. *Rooms from: €85* *51 rue Bellon, Senlis* *03–44–53–03–05* *www.portebellon.fr* *Closed 1st 2 wks of Jan.* *18 rooms* *No meals.*

PIERREFONDS

38 km (24 miles) northeast of Senlis via N324, D335, and D973.

Dominating the attractive lakeside village of Pierrefonds, a former spa resort, is its immense ersatz medieval castle.

GETTING HERE

From Paris's Gare du Nord take the Transilien train to Compiègne (45 mins, €15); from there you can carry on to Pierrefonds by cab (€27).

EXPLORING

Château de Pierrefonds. Built on a huge mound in the 15th century, the Château de Pierrefonds was dismantled in 1620, and then re-created to reflect its imagined former glory in the 1860s at the behest of Emperor Napoléon III, who was seeking to cash in on the craze for the Middle Ages. Architect Viollet-le-Duc left a crenellated fortress with a fairy-tale silhouette, although, like the fortified town of Carcassonne (which he also restored), Pierrefonds is more a construct of what he thought it should have looked like than what it really was. A visit takes in the chapel, barracks, and the majestic keep containing the lord's bedchamber and reception hall, which is bordered by a spiral staircase—its lower and upper sections clearly reveal what is ancient and what is more recent in this former fortress. Don't miss the plaster casts of tomb sculptures from all over France in the cellars, and the **Collection Monduit**—industrially produced, larger-than-life lead decorations made by the 19th-century firm that brought the Statue of Liberty to life. *Rue Viollet-le-Duc, Pierrefonds* *03–44–42–72–72* *www.pierrefonds.*

monuments-nationaux.fr €7.50 *May–Aug., daily 9:30–6; Sept.–Apr., Tues.—Sun. 10–1 and 2–5:30.*

WHERE TO STAY

$ B&B/INN Fodor'sChoice ★ **Le Relais Brunehaut.** Crowned with a picturesque stepped gable, this tiny ensemble of flower-bedecked, stucco-and-stone buildings has a bucolic setting—it rises up from a park, next to the village's abbey church and by a small river that has its own wooden waterwheel. **Pros:** quaint, camera-ready setting; gentle rates. **Cons:** you might overdose on charm. *Rooms from: €70* *3 rue de l'Église, Chelles* *5 km (3 miles) east of Pierrefonds on D85* *03–44–42–85–05* *www.lerelaisbrunehaut.fr* *Closed mid-Jan.–mid-Feb.* *11 rooms* *No meals.*

3

DISNEYLAND PARIS

68 km (40 miles) southwest of Pierrefonds via D335, D136, N330, and A4; 38 km (24 miles) east of Paris via A4.

Disneyland Paris is probably not what you've traveled to France for. But if you have a child in tow, the promise of a day with Mickey might get you through an afternoon at Versailles or Fontainebleau. If you're a dyed-in-the-wool Disney fan, you'll also want to make a beeline here to see how the park has been molded to suit European tastes (Disney's "Imagineers" call it their most lovingly detailed one, and it simultaneously feels both decidedly foreign and eerily familiar). And if you've never experienced this particular form of Disney showmanship before, you may want to put in an appearance simply to find out what all the fuss is about.

GETTING HERE

Take the RER-A from central Paris (stations at Étoile, Auber, Les Halles, Gare de Lyon, and Nation) to Marne-la-Vallée–Chessy—the gare there is 100 yards from the Disneyland entrance; trains operate every 10–30 minutes, depending on the time of day (40 mins, €7.50). High-speed TGV train service (*www.tgv.com*) links Disneyland to Lille, Lyon, Brussels, and London (via Lille and the Channel Tunnel). Disneyland's hotel complex also offers a shuttle bus service connecting it with the Orly and Charles de Gaulle airports; in each case the trip takes about 45 minutes and tickets cost €20.

Visitor Information Disneyland Paris Reservations Office. *01–60–30–60–90, 407/939–7675 in U.S.* *www.disneylandparis.com.*

EXPLORING

FAMILY Fodor'sChoice ★ **Disneyland Paris.** A slightly downsized version of its United States counterpart, Disneyland Paris is a spectacular sight created with an acute attention to detail. Disney never had quite the following here as it did Stateside, so when the park first opened, few turned up; Walt's vision, however, eventually won them over. Today the place is jammed with families from around the world reveling in the many splendors of the Disney universe.

Some of the rides can be a bit scary for little kids, but tots adore Alice's Maze, Peter Pan's Flight, and especially the whirling Mad Hatter's

Teacups. Also getting high marks are the afternoon parades, which feature music, introductions in five languages, and huge floats swarming with all of Disney's most beloved characters—just make sure to stake your place along Main Street in advance for a good spot (check for posted times). There's a lot here, so pace yourself: kids can easily feel overwhelmed by the barrage of stimuli or frustrated by extra-long waits at the rides (also be aware that there are size restrictions for some). The older the children, the more they will enjoy Walt Disney Studios, a cinematically driven sister park, where many of the newer attractions can be found.

Disneyland Park, the original part of the complex, consists of five "lands": Main Street U.S.A., Frontierland, Adventureland, Fantasyland, and Discoveryland. The central theme of each is relentlessly echoed in everything from attractions to restaurant menus to souvenirs. The park is circled by a railroad, which stops three times along the perimeter. **Main Street U.S.A.** goes under the railroad and past shops and restaurants toward the main plaza; Disney parades are held here every afternoon and, during holiday periods, every evening.

Top attractions at **Frontierland** are the chilling Phantom Manor, haunted by holographic spooks, and the thrilling runaway mine train of Big Thunder Mountain, a roller coaster that plunges wildly through floods and avalanches in a setting meant to evoke Utah's Monument Valley. Whiffs of Arabia, Africa, and the Caribbean give **Adventureland** its exotic cachet; the spicy meals and snacks served here rank among the best food in the park. Don't miss Pirates of the Caribbean, an exciting *mise-en-scène* populated by lifelike animatronic figures, or Indiana Jones and the Temple of Doom, a rapid-fire ride that re-creates some of this hapless hero's most exciting moments.

Fantasyland charms the youngest parkgoers with familiar cartoon characters from such classic Disney films as *Snow White, Pinocchio, Dumbo, Alice in Wonderland,* and *Peter Pan.* The focal point of Fantasyland, and indeed Disneyland Paris, is Le Château de la Belle au Bois Dormant (Sleeping Beauty's Castle), a 140-foot, bubble-gum-pink structure topped with 16 blue- and gold-tipped turrets. Its design was allegedly inspired by illustrations from a medieval Book of Hours—if so, it was by way of Beverly Hills. The castle's dungeon conceals a 2-ton scaly green dragon that rumbles in its sleep and occasionally rouses to roar—an impressive feat of engineering, producing an answering chorus of shrieks from younger children. **Discoveryland** is a high-tech, futuristic eye-popper. Robots on roller skates welcome you on your way to Star Tours, a pitching, plunging, sense-confounding ride based on the *Star Wars* films; and another robot, the staggeringly realistic 9-Eye, hosts a simulated space journey in Le Visionarium. Other top Discoveryland attractions include the Jules Verne–inspired Space Mountain Mission 2, which pretends to catapult *exploronauts* on a rocket-boosted, comet-battered journey through the Milky Way; and Buzz Lightyear Laser Blast, which challenges kids to blast the villain Zurg with their own laser gun from a whirling star cruiser.

The Alice in Wonderland Labyrinth delights children—and intrigues guests of all ages—at Disneyland Paris.

As you'd expect, Disneyland Paris has lots of dining options, ranging from snack bars and fast-food joints to five full-service restaurants—all with a distinguishing theme. If your child has his or her heart set on a specifically themed restaurant, say, Pirates of the Caribbean (a dark corsair's lair that looks over the titular ride) or the Auberge de Cendrillon (Cinderella's Inn, where the nasty stepmother and sisters themselves bustle through the aisles), make sure to make advance reservations in person or online. In addition, Walt Disney Studios, Disney Village, and Disney Hotels have restaurants open to the public. But since these are outside the park, it's not recommended that you waste time traveling to them for lunch. Disneyland Paris serves wine and beer in the park's sit-down restaurants, as well as in the hotels and restaurants outside the park.

Walt Disney Studios opened next to the Disneyland Park in 2002. It's divided into four "production zones." Beneath imposing entrance gates and a 100-foot water tower inspired by the one erected in 1939 at Disney Studios in Burbank, California, **Front Lot** contains shops, a restaurant, and a studio re-creating the atmosphere of Sunset Boulevard. In **Animation Courtyard,** Disney artists demonstrate the various phases of character animation; Animagique brings to life scenes from *Pinocchio* and *The Lion King*, while the Genie from *Aladdin* pilots Flying Carpets over Agrabah. **Production Courtyard** hosts the Walt Disney Television Studios; Cinémagique, a special-effects tribute to U.S. and European cinema; and a behind-the-scenes Studio Tram tour of location sites, movie props, studio interiors, and costumes, ending with a visit to Catastrophe Canyon in the heart of a film shoot. **Back Lot**

majors in stunts. At Armageddon Special Effects you can confront a flaming meteor shower aboard the Mir space station, then complete your visit at the giant outdoor arena with a Stunt Show Spectacular involving cars, motorbikes, and Jet Skis. **La Place de Rémy**, the newest addition to Walt Disney Studios, opened in 2014. Appropriately, it's a mini-land—complete with ride and restaurant—themed around the Paris-based Pixar flick *Ratatouille.* ✉ *Marne-la-Vallée* ☎ *01–60–30–60–90* 🌐 *www.disneylandparis.com* 🎟 *€80, or €169 for 3-day Passport; includes admission to all individual attractions within Disneyland or Walt Disney Studios; tickets for Walt Disney Studios are also valid for admission to Disneyland during last 3 opening hrs of same day* ⏲ *Disneyland mid-June–mid-Sept., daily 9 am–10 pm; mid-Sept.–Dec. 19 and Jan. 5–mid-June, weekdays 10–8, weekends 9–8; Dec. 20–Jan. 4, daily 9–8. Walt Disney Studios daily 10–6.*

WHERE TO STAY

$$$$ HOTEL **Sequoia Lodge.** Ranging from superluxe to still-a-pretty-penny, Disneyland Paris has 5,000 rooms in five hotels, but your best bet on all counts may be the Sequoia Lodge—a grand re-creation of an American mountain lodge, just a few minutes' walk from the theme park. **Pros:** package deals include admission to theme park; cozy, secluded feel; great pools. **Cons:** restaurants a bit ho-hum; many rooms do not have lake view. $ *Rooms from: €300* ✉ *Marne-la-Vallée* ☎ *01–60–30–60–90, 407/939–7675 in U.S.* 🌐 *www.disneylandparis.com* 🛏 *1,020 rooms* 🍽 *No meals.*

NIGHTLIFE AND PERFORMING ARTS

Buffalo Bill's Wild West Show. One highlight within Disney Village is Buffalo Bill's Wild West Show, a two-hour dinner extravaganza with a menu of sausage, spareribs, and chili. The entertainment component includes performances by a talented troupe of stunt riders, bronco busters, tribal dancers, and musicians; plus some 50 horses, a dozen buffalo, a bull, and an Annie Oakley–style sharpshooter, with a golden-maned "Buffalo Bill" as emcee. A re-creation of a show that dazzled Parisians 100 years ago, it's corny but great fun. Tickets for shows, which start nightly at 6:30 and 9:30, cost €60. ✉ *Marne-la-Vallée* ☎ *01–60–45–71–00 for reservations* 🌐 *www.disneylandparis.fr.*

Disney Village. Nocturnal entertainment outside the park centers on Disney Village, a vast pleasure mall designed by American architect Frank Gehry. Homesick kids who've had enough of *croque-monsieur* sandwiches will be happy to hear that vintage American-style restaurants—a diner, a deli, and a steak house among them—dominate the food scene here. ✉ *Marne-la-Vallée* 🌐 *www.disneylandparis.fr.*

CHATEAU DE VAUX-LE-VICOMTE

48 km (30 miles) south of Disneyland Paris via N36, 5 km (3 miles) northeast of Melun via N36 and D215, 56 km (35 miles) southeast of Paris via A6, N104, A5, and N36.

A manifesto for French 17th-century splendor, the Château de Vaux-le-Vicomte was built between 1656 and 1661 by finance minister Nicolas

Fouquet. The construction program was monstrous. Entire villages were razed; 18,000 workmen were called in; and architect Louis Le Vau, painter Charles Le Brun, and landscape architect André Le Nôtre were recruited at vast expense to prove that Fouquet's taste was as refined as his business acumen. The housewarming party was so lavish it had star guest Louis XIV, testy at the best of times, spitting jealous curses. He hurled Fouquet in the slammer and set about building Versailles to prove just who was top banana. Poor Fouquet may be gone but his home, still privately owned, has survived to astonish and delight centuries of travelers.

GETTING HERE

Take a train from Paris's Gare de Lyon to Melun (25 mins, €8.30), then a taxi for the 7-km (4-mile) trip to the château (about €20). April through mid-November, a special Châteaubus shuttle runs from the Melun train station (€7 round-trip).

EXPLORING

Fodor's Choice ★ **Château de Vaux-le-Vicomte.** The high-roof Château de Vaux-le-Vicomte, partially surrounded by a moat, is set well back from the road behind iron railings topped with sculpted heads. A cobbled avenue stretches up to the entrance, and stone steps lead to the vestibule, which seems small given the noble scale of the exterior. Charles Le Brun's captivating decoration includes the ceiling of the Chambre du Roi (Royal Bedchamber), depicting *Time Bearing Truth Heavenward,* framed by stuccowork by sculptors François Girardon and André Legendre. Along the frieze you can make out small squirrels, the Fouquet family's emblem—squirrels are known as *fouquets* in local dialect. But Le Brun's masterpiece is the ceiling in the **Salon des Muses** (Hall of Muses), a brilliant allegorical composition painted in glowing, sensuous colors that some feel even surpasses his work at Versailles. On the ground floor the impressive **Grand Salon** (Great Hall), with its unusual oval form and 16 caryatid pillars symbolizing the months and seasons, has harmony and style even though the ceiling decoration was never finished.

The state salons are redolent of *le style louis quartorze,* thanks to the grand state beds, Mazarin desks, and Baroque marble busts—gathered together by the current owners of the château, the Comte et Comtesse de Vogüé—that replace the original pieces, which Louis XIV trundled off as booty to Versailles. In the basement, where cool, dim rooms were once used to store food and wine and house the château's kitchens, you can find rotating exhibits about the château's past and life-size wax figures illustrating its history, including the notorious 19th-century murder-suicide of two erstwhile owners, the Duc and Duchess de Choiseul-Praslin.

Le Nôtre's carefully restored **gardens**, considered by many to be the designer's masterwork, are at their best when the fountains—which function via gravity, exactly as they did in the 17th century—are turned on (the second and last Saturdays of each month from April through October, 4–6 pm). The popular illuminated evenings, when the château is dazzlingly lit with 2,000 candles, are held every Saturday from early May to early October. Open for dinner during this event only,

Louis XIV was so jealous of the splendor of Vaux-le-Vicomte that he promptly went out and built Versailles.

the formal Les Charmilles restaurant serves refined cuisine with château views (reservations essential). At other times, L'Ecureuil (a more casual eatery) is a good choice for lunch or snacks. You can also bring a picnic to enjoy in the extensive gardens. ✉ *Vaux-le-Vicomte* ☎ *01–64–14–41–90* 🌐 *www.vaux-le-vicomte.com* 🎫 *€16.50; candlelight château visits €19.50; gardens only €8.50* ⏲ *Mid-Mar.–mid-Nov., daily 10–6.*

WHERE TO EAT

$$$$ MODERN FRENCH

✕ **La Table Saint Just.** A pleasing mix of ancient and modern, this colorful, light-filled restaurant, with high-beamed ceilings and limestone walls hung with contemporary art and "candeliers," was once a farmstead on the grounds of the nearby Château de Vaux-le-Pénil. But Isabelle and Fabrice Vitu's warm welcome and Michelin-starred cuisine are the real draws; locals and Parisians alike appreciate the refined menu that includes surprising twists on French classics and plenty of delicacies from the sea. Savor scallops on a bed of Puy lentils, crisp veal foot in a smoked-eel emulsion, or succulent John Dory with truffles—but be sure to save room for the warm Grand Marnier soufflé, a house specialty. The three-course menu (€51) is the best value. $ *Average main: €36* ✉ *11 rue de la Libération, Vaux-le-Pénil* ✥ *6 km (4 miles) southwest of Vaux-leVicomte, 13 km (8 miles) northwest of Barbizon* ☎ *01–64–52–09–09* 🌐 *www.restaurant-latablesaintjust.com* ⏲ *Closed Sun. and Mon.* ✍ *Reservations essential.*

$$$$ MODERN FRENCH

✕ **Le Pouilly.** The lofty dining room of this ancient *demeure* has everything a country manor should: creamy stone walls, warm oak paneling, beamed ceilings, a giant central fireplace, and a stately balcony. In winter, hearty yet refined dishes—which have earned Le Pouilly a

Michelin star—are served before a roaring fire, and in summer the garden terrace makes a lovely spot for lunch or a candlelight dinner. Chef Nicolas Dousset works his magic in dishes like tender Challans duck with a purée of Jerusalem artichoke or grilled swordfish with bergamot-scented quinoa and avocado vinaigrette. For dessert, the locally grown glacéed peach served with a tender cookie of pistachio and raisins pairs perfectly with a sweet Montlouis from the exceptional wine list. $ *Average main: €36* ✉ *1 rue de la Fontaine Pouilly, Pouilly le Fort* ✣ *8 km (5 miles) northwest of Vaux-le-Vicomte* ☎ *01–64–09–56–64* 🌐 *www.restaurant-lepouilly.com* ⏲ *Closed Mon. and 3 wks in Aug. No dinner Sun.* ✍ *Reservations essential.*

A CANDLELIGHT TOUR

Perhaps the most beautiful time to visit the château and gardens is when they are illuminated by thousands of candles during the Candlelight Evenings, held every Saturday night from 8 to midnight, early May through early October. Readers complain, however, that at night the vast and grand gardens are nearly invisible and the low candlepower doesn't really do justice to the splendor of the salons.

BARBIZON

17 km (11 miles) southwest of Vaux-le-Vicomte via Melun and D132/ D64, 52 km (33 miles) southeast of Paris.

On the western edge of the 62,000-acre Forest of Fontainebleau, the village of Barbizon retains its time-stained allure despite the intrusion of art galleries, souvenir shops, and busloads of tourists. The group of landscape painters known as the Barbizon School—Camille Corot, Jean-François Millet, Narcisse Diaz de la Peña, and Théodore Rousseau, among others—lived here from the 1830s on. They paved the way for the Impressionists by their willingness to accept nature on its own terms rather than using it as an idealized base for carefully structured compositions. Sealed to one of the famous sandstone rocks in the forest—which starts, literally, at the far end of the main street—is a bronze medallion by sculptor Henri Chapu, paying homage to Millet and Rousseau. Threading the village is a Painters Trail (marked in yellow), which links main village landmarks to natural splendors such as the rocky waterfall once painted by Corot.

GETTING HERE

Take a Transilien train from Gare de Lyon to Melun (25 mins, €8.10) or Avon (38 mins, €8.75); you can pick up a taxi to Barbizon in either town (around €30).

Visitor Information Barbizon Tourist Office. ☎ *01–60–66–41–87* 🌐 *www.barbizon.fr.*

EXPLORING

Atelier Jean-François Millet (*Millet's Studio*). Though there are no actual Millet works, the Atelier Jean-François Millet is cluttered with photographs and mementos evoking his career. It was here that the painter produced some of his most renowned pieces, including *The Gleaners.* ✉ *27 rue Grande, Barbizon* ☎ *01–60–66–21–55* 🌐 *www.atelier-millet.fr* 🎫 *€4* 🕒 *July and Aug., daily 9:30–12:30 and 2–5:30; Sept.—June, Wed.–Mon. 9:30–12:30 and 2–5:30.*

Musée Départemental des Peintres de Barbizon (*Barbizon School Museum*). Corot and company would often repair to the Auberge Ganne after painting to brush up on their social life; the inn is now the Musée de Peintres de Barbizon. Here you can find documents detailing village life in the 19th century, as well as a few original works. The Barbizon artists painted on every available surface, and even now you can see some of their creations on the upstairs walls. Two of the ground-floor rooms have been reconstituted as they were in Ganne's time—note the trompe-l'oeil paintings on the buffet doors. There's also a video about the Barbizon School. ✉ *92 rue Grande, Barbizon* ☎ *01–60–66–22–27* 🌐 *musee-peintres-barbizon.fr* 🎫 *€3* 🕒 *Wed.–Mon. 10—12:30 and 2—5:30 (until 6 in July and Aug.).*

WHERE TO EAT AND STAY

$$$ FRENCH ✕ **Le Relais de Barbizon.** French country specialties and fish are served at this rustic restaurant with a big open fire and a large terrace shaded by lime and chestnut trees. The four-course weekday menu is a good value, but wine here is expensive and cannot be ordered by the *pichet* (pitcher). Reservations are essential on weekends. 💲 *Average main: €25* ✉ *2 av. Charles de Gaulle, Barbizon* ☎ *01–60–66–40–28* 🌐 *www.lerelaisdebarbizon.fr* 🕒 *Closed Tues. and Wed., part of Aug., and part of Dec.*

$$$ HOTEL 🏨 **Les Pléiades.** The onetime home of Barbizon-school painter Charles Daubigny started out as a humble village abode in 1830; now it's been expanded and brought sumptuously up-to-date with contemporary interiors and features. **Pros:** great location in the heart of the village; indoor-outdoor heated pools to swim in after a hike in the nearby woods; impeccable service. **Cons:** contemporary interiors can be a bit austere. 💲 *Rooms from: €189* ✉ *21 rue Grande, Barbizon* ☎ *01–60–66–40–25* 🌐 *www.hotel-les-pleiades.com* 🛏 *20 rooms* 🍽 *No meals.*

COURANCES

11 km (7 miles) west of Barbizon via the A6, Exit 13, a few miles from Milly-la-Fôret.

Set within one of the most lavish water gardens in Europe, the Château de Courances is a byword for beauty and style.

GETTING HERE

Take the train from Paris's Gare de Lyon to Fontainebleau-Avon, then a La Patache shuttle bus to Courances.

EXPLORING

Fodor's Choice ★ **Château de Courances.** Framed by majestic avenues of centuries-old plane trees, Château de Courances's style is Louis Treize, although its finishing touch—a horseshoe staircase (mirroring the one at nearby Fontainebleau)—was an opulent 19th-century statement made by Baron Samuel de Haber, a banker who bought the estate and whose daughter then married into the regal family of the de Behagués. Their descendants, the Marquises de Ganay, have made the house uniquely and famously *chez soi,* letting charming personal taste trump conventional *bon goût,* thanks to a delightful mixture of 19th-century knickknacks and grand antiques. Outside, the vast French Renaissance water gardens create stunning vistas of stonework, grand canals, and rushing cascades. The house can only be seen on a 40-minute tour. ✉ *13 rue de Chateau, Courances* ☎ *01–64–98–07–36* 🌐 *www.courances.net* 🎫 *€9.50, park only €7.50* 🕒 *Apr.–Oct., weekends and school holidays 2–6.*

FONTAINEBLEAU

9 km (6 miles) southeast of Barbizon via N7, 61 km (38 miles) southeast of Paris via A6 and N7.

Like Chambord in the Loire Valley or Compiègne to the north, Fontainebleau was a favorite spot for royal hunting parties long before the construction of one of France's grandest residences. Although not as celebrated as Versailles, this palace is almost as spectacular.

GETTING HERE

Fontainebleau—or rather, neighboring Avon—is a 38-minute train ride from Paris's Gare de Lyon (€8.75); from here, take one of the frequent shuttle buses to the château, 2 km (1½ miles) away (€4.20 round-trip).

Visitor Information Fontainebleau Tourist Office. ☎ *01–60–74–99–99* 🌐 *www.fontainebleau-tourisme.com.*

EXPLORING

Fodor's Choice ★ **Château de Fontainebleau.** The château you see today dates from the 16th century, although additions were made by various royal incumbents through the next 300 years. It was begun under the flamboyant Renaissance king François I, the French contemporary of England's Henry VIII, who hired Italian artists Il Rosso (a pupil of Michelangelo) and Primaticcio to embellish his château. In fact, they did much more: by introducing the pagan allegories and elegant lines of Mannerism to France, they revolutionized French decorative art. Their virtuoso frescoes and stuccowork can be admired in the **Galerie François-Ier** (Francis I Gallery) and in the jewel of the interior, the 100-foot-long **Salle de Bal** (Ballroom), with its luxuriant wood paneling, completed under Henri II, François's successor, and its gleaming parquet floor that reflects the patterns on the ceiling. Like the château as a whole, the room exudes a sense of elegance and style, but on a more intimate, human scale than at Versailles—this is Renaissance, not Baroque. **Napoléon's apartments** occupied the first floor. You can see a lock of his hair, his Légion d'Honneur medal, his imperial uniform, the hat he wore on his return from Elba in 1815, and one bed in which he definitely did spend a night (almost every town in France boasts a bed in which the emperor supposedly snoozed). Joséphine's **Salon Jaune** (Yellow Room) is one of the best examples of the Empire style—the austere neoclassical style promoted by the emperor. There's also a throne room—Napoléon spurned the one at Versailles, a palace he disliked, establishing his imperial seat in the former King's Bedchamber here—and the Queen's Boudoir, also known as the Room

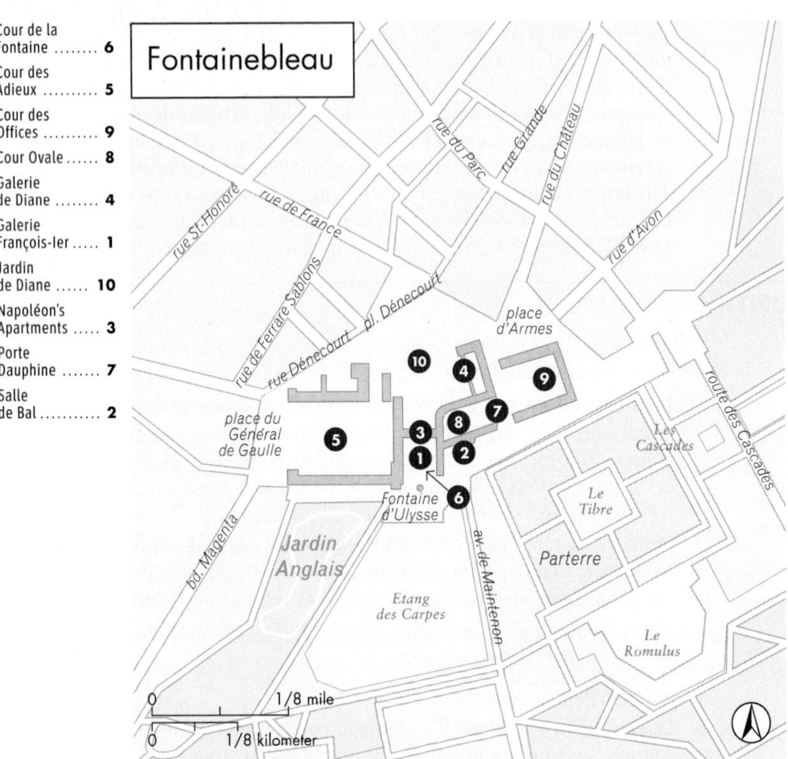

of the Six Maries (occupants included ill-fated Marie-Antoinette and Napoléon's second wife, Marie-Louise). The sweeping **Galerie de Diane,** built during the reign of Henri IV (1589–1610), was converted into a library in the 1860s. Other salons have 17th-century tapestries and paintings, and frescoes by members of the Fontainebleau School.

Although Louis XIV's architectural fancy was concentrated on Versailles, he commissioned Mansart to design new pavilions and had André Le Nôtre replant the gardens at Fontainebleau, where he and his court returned faithfully in fall for the hunting season. But it was Napoléon who spent lavishly to make a Versailles, as it were, out of Fontainebleau. He held Pope Pius VII here as a captive guest in 1812, signed the second church-state concordat here in 1813, and, in the cobbled **Cour des Adieux** (Farewell Courtyard), said good-bye to his Old Guard on April 20, 1814, as he began his brief exile on the Mediterranean island of Elba. The famous **Horseshoe Staircase** that dominates the Cour des Adieux, once the Cour du Cheval Blanc (White Horse Courtyard), was built by Androuet du Cerceau for Louis XIII (1610–43); it was down this staircase that Napoléon made his way slowly to take a final salute from his Vieille Garde. Another courtyard—the **Cour de la Fontaine** (Fountain Courtyard)—was commissioned by Napoléon in 1812 and adjoins the Étang des Carpes (Carp Pond). Across from the pond is the formal Parterre (flower garden) and, on the other side, the leafy Jardin Anglais (English Garden).

The **Porte Dauphine** is the most beautiful of the various gateways that connect the complex of buildings; its name commemorates the christening of the dauphin—the heir to the throne, later Louis XIII—under its archway in 1606. The gateway fronts the **Cour Ovale** (Oval Court), shaped like a flattened egg. Opposite the courtyard is the **Cour des Offices** (Kitchen Court), a large, severe square built at the same time as Place des Vosges in Paris (1609). Around the corner is the informal **Jardin de Diane** (Diana's Garden), with peacocks and a statue of the hunting goddess surrounded by mournful hounds. ✉ *Pl. du Général de Gaulle, Fontainebleau* ☎ *01–60–71–50–70* 🌐 *www.musee-chateau-fontainebleau.fr* 🎫 *€11, Napoléon's Apartments €6.50, €15.50 for both; gardens free* 🕒 *Palace Oct.–Mar., Wed.–Mon. 9:30–5; Apr.–Sept., Wed.–Mon. 9:30–6. Gardens May–Sept., daily 9–7; Mar., Apr., and Oct., daily 9–6; Nov.–Feb., daily 9–5.*

WHERE TO EAT AND STAY

$
MODERN FRENCH
FAMILY
Fodor's Choice ★

✕ **Frédéric Cassel.** A mandatory stop for pastry and chocolate lovers alike, this master *pâtissier* excels in classic French confections with all the bells and whistles. Light-as-air and made with the finest ingredients, Cassel's award-winning creations are as beautiful as they are scrumptious. The sinful *millefeuille* comes in five flavors, including sweet chestnut and Earl Gray tea; the *tarte duo de cerise* mixes tart and sweet cherries with almond cream; and some say his classic *macaron* is one of the best in France—high praise indeed! Chocolates are freshly made on the premises. Don't miss the lovely tea salon, where you can choose from a large selection of Dammann Frères teas, coffée, *chocolat chaud*, and pastries. $ *Average main: €9* ✉ *21 rue des Sablons, Fontainebleau* ☎ *01–60–71–00–64* 🌐 *www.frederic-cassel.com* 🕒 *Tues.–Fri. 10–7, Sat. 10–7:30, Sun. 10–1* ✍ *Reservations not accepted.*

$$$$
MODERN FRENCH

✕ **Les Prémices.** Adjoining the property of the stately 17th-century Château de Bourron, in the heart of the Forest of Fontainebleau, this lovely restaurant is well worth the short trip out of town. Bright and airy, with an open terrace in warm weather, the elegant dining room shows meticulous attention to detail—from the crisp table linens to the stylish flower arrangements—all the better to highlight Chef Dominique Maès's sophisticated French fare. A starter of piquant rabbit farci, served alongside velvety tapenade and candied tomatoes, followed by a sublimely succulent hen, fattened on the salt flats of the Mont-St-Michel bay and infused with lemon thyme and white truffles, will barely leave room for the beautifully displayed local artisanal cheeses. The six-course tasting menu—with wine pairings at an extra cost—is the best deal, allowing for a well-rounded sampling of this talented chef's inventive cuisine. $ *Average main: €35* ✉ *12 bis rue Blaise de Montesquiou, Bourron-Marlotte* ✣ *8 km (5 miles) south of Fontainebleau via D607* ☎ *01–64–78–33–00* 🌐 *www.restaurant-les-premices.com* 🕒 *Closed Mon., Tues., and Dec. 19–Jan. 5. No dinner Sun.* ✍ *Reservations essential.*

$$$
HOTEL

🏨 **Aigle Noir.** This may be Fontainebleau's costliest hotel, but it does promise old-world elegance, graceful service, and oodles of atmosphere. **Pros:** period ambience; great location opposite château. **Cons:**

no restaurant. *Rooms from: €190* *27 pl. Napoléon Bonaparte, Fontainebleau* *01–60–74–60–00* *www.hotelaiglenoir.com* *53 rooms* *No meals.*

$$ HOTEL Fodor's Choice ★ **Hôtel de Londres.** Established in 1850, the superbly located Londres has been run with pride by the same family for three generations, and guests are treated to a warm welcome by owners who go out of their way to make your stay pleasant. **Pros:** excellent value; château views from some rooms; two-minute walk to the Fontainebleau 18-hole golf course. **Cons:** not all rooms have air-conditioning; limited parking. *Rooms from: €138* *1 pl. du Général de Gaulle, Fontainebleau* *01–64–22–20–21* *www.hoteldelondres.com* *Closed 1 wk in Aug. and Christmas–early Jan.* *14 rooms, 2 suites* *No meals.*

SPORTS AND THE OUTDOORS

Club Alpin Français. The Forest of Fontainebleau is laced with hiking trails; the *Guide des Sentiers* (trail guide), available at the tourist office, has details. Bikes can be rented at La Petite Reine (14 rue de la Paroisse). The forest is also famed for its quirky rock formations, where many a novice alpinist first caught the climbing bug; for more information contact the Club Alpin Français. *24 av. Laumière, Paris* *01–60–74–57–57* *www.ffcam.fr.*

4

THE LOIRE VALLEY

WELCOME TO THE LOIRE VALLEY

TOP REASONS TO GO

★ **Step into a fairy tale at Sleeping Beauty's castle:** Play once-upon-a-time at Ussé—gleaming white against an emerald forest backdrop, it's so beautiful it inspired Perrault's immortal tale.

★ **Marvel at mighty Chambord:** The world's most impressive rooftop, with a forest of chimneys to match the game-rich woodlands extending in all directions, marks the Loire's grandest château.

★ **Find splendor in the grass at Villandry:** The Renaissance reblooms in these geometric gardens that have been lovingly restored to floricultural magnificence.

★ **Indulge in a bit of romance at Chenonceau:** Half bridge, half pleasure palace, this epitome of picturesque France extends across the Cher River, so why not row a boat under its arches?

★ **Revel in medieval magic at Fontevraud:** The majestic abbey is the resting place of English kings—and a queen.

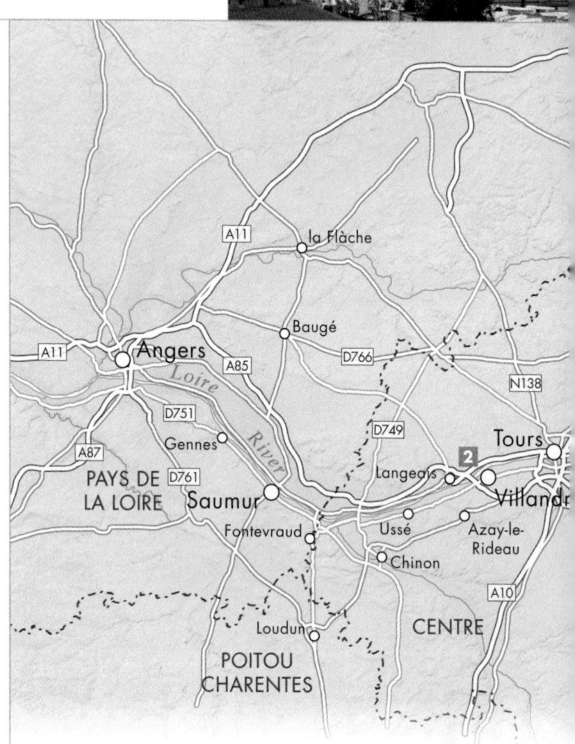

1 The Eastern Loire Valley. East from Tours, strung like precious gems along the peaceful Loire, the royal and near-royal châteaux are among the most celebrated sights in France. From magical Chenonceau—improbably suspended above the River Cher—to mighty Chambord, with its 440 rooms, to Amboise (where Leonardo da Vinci breathed his last), this architectural conveyor belt moves up along the southern bank to deposit you at Orléans, burnished to old-world splendor with its pedestrian-only *centre ville historique* (it was here that Joan of Arc had her most rousing successes against the English). Heading back to Tours on the northern bank, you'll discover the immense palace at Blois and some of the best hotels in the region.

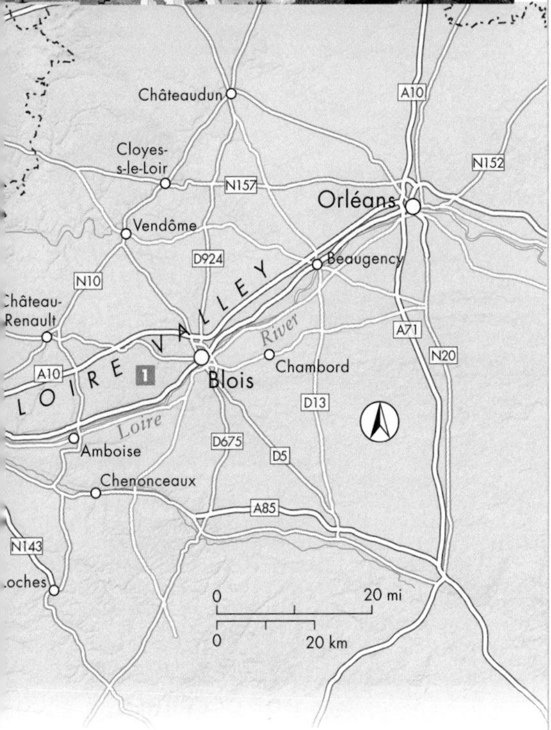

GETTING ORIENTED

The Loire Valley, which pretty much splits France in two, has been heavily traveled through the ages—once by power-hungry armies and peaceful Santiago pilgrims, now by Bordeaux-bound TGV trains. Yet it retains a relaxing backwater feel that mirrors the river's languid, meandering flow. Tours is the main gateway to the region, not only for its central position but because the TGV links it with Paris in little more than an hour. Angers (at the west end of the valley) and Orléans (at the east end) are also well connected to the capital by train. Coming to the Loire by rail and renting a car on arrival in any one of these three cities will save you the hassle of Paris traffic, while still letting you enjoy the flexibility of a châteaux driving tour.

2 The Central and Western Loire Valley. Get your fairy-tale fix by castle-hopping among the most beautiful châteaux in France, from Villandry's fabled gardens to Ussé, which seems to levitate over the unicorn-haunted Forest of Chinon. From the Renaissance jewel of Azay-le-Rideau, continue west to Chinon for a dip in the Middle Ages along its Rue Haute St-Maurice—a pop-up illuminated manuscript. Continue time traveling at the 12th-century royal abbey of Fontevraud, resting place of Richard the Lionheart and Eleanor of Aquitaine. Then fast-forward to the 15th century at Saumur's storybook castle and Angers's brooding fortress.

EATING AND DRINKING WELL IN THE LOIRE VALLEY

Pike perch in beurre-blanc sauce is the Loire's most famous dish *(above)*; goat cheeses are often paired with Loire white wines *(right, top)*; tarte Tatins are *delicieux* (*right, bottom*).

Finesse rather than fireworks marks the gastronomy of this gentle region, known for exceptional white wines, delicate fish, and France's most bountiful fruits and vegetables.

The serene Loire imposes its placid personality throughout this fertile valley. The weather, too, is calm and cool, ideal for creating the Loire's diverse and memorable wines, from the elegant and refined Savennières to the mildly sweet, pretty-in-pink rosés of the Anjou. No big, bold, heavily tannic wines here. The culinary repertoire evokes a sense of the good life, with a nod to the royal legacy of châteaux living over centuries past. Many dishes are simply presented, and they couldn't be better: a perfect pike perch, called *sandre*, from the river, bathed in a silky beurre-blanc sauce; coq au vin prepared with a fruity red Sancerre; a tender fillet of beef in a Chinon red-wine reduction. It is the wines that highlight the Loire's gastronomic scene, and these alone justify a trip here, although, of course, you could make time to visit a château or two while you're in the neighborhood.

OF CABBAGES AND KINGS

The great kitchens of the royal households that set up throughout the Loire planned menus around the magnificent produce that thrives in this fecund region, dubbed the Garden of France. Local cooks still do. There are fat white asparagus in the spring; peas, red cherries, haricots verts, artichokes, and lettuces in the summer; followed by apples, pears, cabbages, and pumpkins in the fall.

WHITE WINES (REDS, TOO!)

The Loire region spawns not only dazzling châteaux, but also some of the best wines in France—this is an important region for white-wine lovers, thanks to great chenin blanc and sauvignon blanc grapes. Top white appellations to imbibe, starting at the eastern end of the Loire and moving west, include flinty Sancerres, slightly smoky Pouilly-Fumés, vigorous and complex Vouvrays, distinguished Savennières, sparkling Champagne-style Saumurs, and finally the light, dry Muscadets, perfect with oysters on the half shell.

In the realm of reds, try the raspberry-scented reds of Touraine, the heartier Chinons and Bourgueils, and the elegant rosés of the Anjou. For tastings, just follow the "Dégustation" signs, though it's always a good idea to call ahead.

Check out Vinci Cave in Amboise (*02–47–23–41–52* ⊕ *www.vinci-cave.fr*); Charles Joguet in Chinon (*02–47–58–55–53* ⊕ *www.charlesjoguet.com*); Bouvet-Ladubay in Saumur (*02–41–83–83–83* ⊕ *www.bouvet-ladubay.fr*); and the Maison du Vin d'Angers (*02–41–88–81–13* ⊕ *www.vinsdeloire.fr*).

TARTE TATIN

This luscious "upside-down" apple tart is sometimes claimed by Normandy, but originated, so legend has it, at the Hôtel Tatin in the Loire Valley town of Beuvron-Lamotte south of Orléans.

The best tarte Tatins are made with deeply caramelized apples cooked under a buttery short-crust pastry, then inverted and served while still warm.

BEURRE BLANC

Made with a shallot, wine vinegar, and fish-stock reduction, and swirled with lots of butter, this iconic white sauce originated in the western Loire about a century ago in the kitchen of an aristocrat whose chef devised this variation on the classic Béarnaise. Beurre blanc is the perfect accompaniment to the Loire's delicate shad and pike.

CHÈVRE

With your glass of Pouilly-Fumé, there are few things better than one of the region's tangy, herby, and assertive goat cheeses.

Among the best, appellation-controlled and farmhouse-made: the squat, pyramid-shape Pouligny-Saint-Pierre; the creamy, cylindrical Sainte-Maure de Touraine; and the piquant Crottins de Chavignol from Sancerre.

Try a warmed and gooey Crottin atop a salad for a real treat.

Updated By
Jack Vermee

A fairy-tale realm par excellence, the Loire Valley is studded with storybook villages, time-burnished towns, and—*bien sûr*—the famous châteaux de la Loire. These postcard staples, like Chenonceau and Chambord, seem to be strung like a strand of pearls across a countryside so serene it could win the Nobel peace prize. With magic at every curve in the road, Cinderella's glass coach might be the optimal way to get around. If that is not available, buses and trains can carry you to the main towns of the three Loire provinces—Anjou (to the west), Orléans (to the east), and the center ring of the show, Touraine.

For centuries, the Loire River (France's longest) was the region's principal means of transportation as well as an effective barrier against invading armies—and there were a lot of the latter. The valley was hotly disputed by France and England during the Middle Ages; it belonged to England (under the Anjou Plantagenet family) between 1154 and 1216 and again during the Hundred Years' War (1337–1453). So it's understandable that towering slopes would be fortified early on and that towns would arise at strategic bridgeheads.

But why did the Loire become so prized for its châteaux? With the wars of the 15th century fading, the Loire Valley, long known as "the Garden of France," became a showplace of new and fabulous châteaux *d'agrément*, or pleasure castles. In short order, there were boxwood gardens endlessly receding toward vanishing points, moats graced with swans, parades of delicate cone-top towers, frescoes, and fancywork ceilings. The glories of the Italian Renaissance, observed by the Valois while making war on their neighbor, were brought to bear on these mega-monuments with all the elegance characteristic of antiquity.

By the time François I (the flamboyant contemporary of England's Henry VIII) took charge in 1515, extravagance knew no bounds: on a 13,000-acre forest estate, hunting parties at Chambord drew A-list crowds from the far reaches of Europe—and the availability of 430 rooms made weekend entertaining a snap. Queen Claudia hired only the most recherché Italian artisans: Chambord's famous double-helix staircase may, in fact, have been Leonardo da Vinci's design (he was a frequent houseguest there when not in residence in a manor on the Amboise grounds). From massive kennels teeming with hunting hounds at Cheverny to luxurious stables at Chaumont-sur-Loire, from endless allées of pollarded lime trees at Villandry to the fanciful towers of Ussé—worthy of Sleeping Beauty herself—the Loire Valley became the power base and social center for the New France, allowing the monarchy to go all out in strutting its stuff.

All for good reason. In 1519 Charles V of Spain, at the age of 19, inherited the Holy Roman Empire, leaving François and his New France out in the cold. It was perhaps no coincidence that in 1519 François, in a grand stab at face-saving one-upmanship, commenced construction on his gigantic Chambord. Centuries later, even the Revolution and the efforts of latter-day socialists have not totally erased a lingering gentility in the people of the region, characterized by an air of refined assurance far removed from the shoulder-shrugging, chest-tapping French stereotypes. Here life proceeds at a pleasingly genteel pace, and—despite the delights of the 1,001 châteaux that await—you should, too.

PLANNER

WHEN TO GO

The Loire Valley divides France in two, both geographically and climatically: to the north is the moist, temperate climate of northern Europe; southward lies the drier climate of the Mediterranean. July and August are peak months for tourism, but the weather then can be hot and sultry, and the top attractions can be packed. Moreover, water levels in Europe's last great undammed river can drop, revealing unsightly sandbanks in midsummer. So the best time to arrive may be in the late spring, when the river still looks like a river and the châteaux gardens are beautifully blooming; or in the fall, when the crowds have thinned and the restaurant menus are showcasing the bounty of harvest and hunt. October is a particularly good off-season option—all is mist and mellow fruitfulness along the Loire and its tributaries.

On Sunday, when most shops are closed, try to avoid the main cities—Orléans, Tours, Angers.

PLANNING YOUR TIME

More than a region in the usual sense, the Loire Valley is just that: a valley. Although most sites are close to the meandering river, it's a long way—225 km (140 miles)—between Orléans, on the eastern edge, and Angers to the west. If you have 10 days or so you can visit the majority of the destinations we cover. Otherwise we suggest you divide the valley into three segments and choose the base(s) as your time and tastes dictate. To cover the eastern Loire (Chambord, Cheverny, Chaumont), base yourself in or near Blois. For the central Loire (Amboise,

Chenonceaux, Villandry, Azay-le-Rideau), base yourself in or around Tours. For the western Loire (Ussé, Chinon, Fontevraud, Angers), opt for pretty Saumur.

GETTING HERE AND AROUND

The regional rail line along the riverbank will get you to the main destinations (Angers, Saumur, Tours, Blois, Orléans, plus 10 more towns); some other châteaux (Chenonceau, Azay, and Chinon among them) are served by branch lines. Occasionally, you may arrive at the rail station and need to take a taxi or bus to get to a site buried deep in the countryside. The bigger inconvenience with train travel is having to build your itinerary around rail routes and constraining timetables. That makes renting a car a particularly practical option. Given the flattish terrain here, hiring a bike may well appeal, too. During the tourist season, local shuttle and coach excursions are also available for day-trippers, many of them departing from Tours.

BUS TRAVEL

Local bus services can provide a link between train stations and scenic areas off the river, making it possible to reach many villages and châteaux. However, routes are often geared to schoolchildren, meaning service is less frequent in summer and sometimes all but nonexistent on Sunday, so only consider the bus if you have no other options. Inquire at tourist offices about routes and timetables, as the bus companies rarely have information available in English. The leading operators are Les Rapides du Val de Loire, based in Orléans; TLC, serving Chambord and Cheverny from Blois; Touraine Fil Vert and Fil Bleu, both of which serve the Touraine region, from Amboise in the east to Chinon in the west; and AnjouBus.

Bus Information AnjouBus. ☎ *08-20-16-00-49 €.34 per minute* 🌐 *www.anjoubus.fr.* **Fil Bleu.** ☎ *02-47-66-70-70* 🌐 *www.filbleu.fr.* **Les Rapides du Val de Loire.** ☎ *02-38-61-90-00* 🌐 *www.rvl-info.com.* **TLC (Transports du Loir-et-Cher).** ☎ *02-54-58-55-44* 🌐 *www.tlcinfo.net.* **Touraine Fil Vert.** ☎ *02-47-05-30-49* 🌐 *www.tourainefilvert.com.*

CAR TRAVEL

The Loire Valley is an easy drive from Paris. A10 runs from the capital to Orléans—a distance of around 125 km (78 miles)—and on to Tours, with exits at Meung, Blois, and Amboise. After Tours, A10 veers south toward Poitiers and Bordeaux. A11 links Paris to Angers and Saumur via Le Mans. Slower but more scenic routes run from the Channel ports down through Normandy into the Loire region. Once here, driving is also the most time-efficient way to see the Loire châteaux—and you won't have to sacrifice scenic views; D952, which hugs the riverbank, is excellent for sightseeing. Just note that road signs can be few and far between once you get off the main road, and many a traveler has stories about a 15-minute trip lasting two hours. You can rent a car in Paris, in all the large towns in the region, or at train stations in Orléans, Blois, Tours, and Angers.

TRAIN TRAVEL

Train travel is quite helpful when touring the Loire Valley, as there is one line that goes up and down the river. Be aware, though, that not all destinations are served by rail, so a quick cab or bus ride from the nearest station might be needed to complete your trip.

Tours and Angers are both served by the superfast TGV (Trains à Grande Vitesse) from Paris's Gare Montparnasse, with a travel time of about 75 and 95 minutes respectively. Loire Valley TGV trains from Charles-de-Gaulle Airport also go direct to Tours's suburban station in St-Pierre-des-Corps (just under 2 hrs) and to Angers (2 hrs, 30 mins). Traditional express trains frequently depart from Paris's Gare d'Austerlitz for Orléans (1 hr) and Blois (1 hr, 25 mins).

The main rail line follows the Loire from Orléans to Angers (2 hrs, 5 mins); there are trains every few hours to Blois, Tours, and Saumur, as well as multiple daily ones to Onzain (for Chaumont), Amboise, and Langeais. Branch lines run from Tours to Chenonceaux (30 mins), Azay-le-Rideau (30 mins), and Chinon (50 mins).

Ask the SNCF for the brochure *Les Châteaux de la Loire en Train* for more detailed information. Helpful train-schedule brochures are available at most stations.

Train Information Gare SNCF Angers. ☎ *3635 €0.34 per min.* **Gare SNCF Orléans.** ☎ *3635 €0.34 per min.* **Gare SNCF Tours.** ☎ *3635 €0.34 per min.* **SNCF.** ☎ *3635 €0.34 per min* 🌐 *www.voyages-sncf.com.* **TGV.** ☎ *3635 €.34 per min* 🌐 *www.tgv.com.*

RESTAURANTS

Considering its resplendent châteaux, you might expect that the Loire Valley would feature restaurants fit for royals. Well, it does. The main destinations—Orléans, Tours, Saumur, Chinon, and Angers—all boast top-notch eateries, which take full advantage of the bounty found here in the "Garden of France." They offer regional cuisine and local wines in venues ranging from the intimate to the intimidating. Expect to pay less than you would in Paris or Lyon, and prepare to come away smiling.

HOTELS

Even before the age of the railway, the Loire Valley drew vacationers from far afield, so there are hundreds of hotels of all types. At the higher end are sumptuous, stylishly converted châteaux, but even these are not as pricey as you might think. Note that most are in small villages, and that upscale hotels are in short supply in the major towns. At the lower end is a wide choice of gîtes, bed-and-breakfasts, and small, traditional inns, usually offering terrific value for the money. The Loire Valley is a popular destination, so make reservations well in advance—in July and August, this is essential (and we're talking weeks in advance, not days).

Be aware that from November through Easter, many properties are closed. *Hotel reviews have been shortened. For full information, visit Fodors.com.*

WHAT IT COSTS IN EUROS				
	$	$$	$$$	$$$$
Restaurants	under €18	€18–€24	€25–€32	over €32
Hotels	under €106	€106–€145	€146–€215	over €215

Restaurant prices are the average cost of a main course at dinner or, if dinner is not served, at lunch. Hotel prices are the lowest cost of a standard double room in high season.

VISITOR INFORMATION

The Loire region has four area tourist offices. For Chinon and points east, contact the Comité Régional du Tourisme du Centre or L'Agence Départementale du Tourisme de Touraine. For Fontevraud and points west, contact the Comité Départemental du Tourisme de l'Anjou or the Comité Départemental du Tourisme des Pays de la Loire. ⇨ *For specific town tourist offices, see the town entries.*

Contacts Comité Départemental du Tourisme de l'Anjou. ☎ *02-41-23-51-51* 🌐 *www.anjou-tourisme.com.* **Comité Départemental du Tourisme des Pays de la Loire.** 🌐 *www.enpaysdelaloire.com.* **Comité Régional du Tourisme du Centre.** ☎ *02-38-79-95-00* 🌐 *www.loirevalleytourism.com.* **L'Agence Départementale du Tourisme de Touraine.** ☎ *02-47-31-47-48* 🌐 *www.touraineloirevalley.com.*

TOUR OPTIONS

Bus tours of the main châteaux leave daily in summer from Tours and other hubs: tourist offices have the latest times and prices. Readers rave about Acco-Dispo van excursions, which usually include two or three top châteaux; half-day trips start at €23 and depart from Tours or Amboise. Eager for an aerial view? Jet Systems makes helicopter trips over the Loire Valley on Tuesday, Thursday, and weekends from the aerodrome at Dierre, just south of Amboise; per-person prices range from €79 (for a 10-minute flight over Chenonceau) to €580 (for a 90-minute survey of the glories of the Loire, including a stop at Chaumont or Le Rivau). France Montgolfières provides a tranquil alternative; its balloon rides over the Loire—costing €189 to €249 per person in high season—last at least 75 minutes, and the experience as a whole takes about three hours. Depending on water levels, you can also sightsee by boat. La Bélandre Crosières, for one, offers some unique outings; April through October, you can sail the Cher River on a traditional flat-bottom boat from the foot of Chenonceau for just €9.50.

Contacts Acco-Dispo Tours. ☎ *06-82-00-64-51* 🌐 *www.accodispo-tours.com.* **France Montgolfiéres.** ☎ *03-80-97-38-61* 🌐 *www.franceballoons.com.* **Jet Systems.** ☎ *08-20-82-06-98 €0.34 per min.* 🌐 *www.jet-systems.fr.* **La Bélandre Croisières.** ☎ *02-47-23-98-64* 🌐 *www.labelandre.com.*

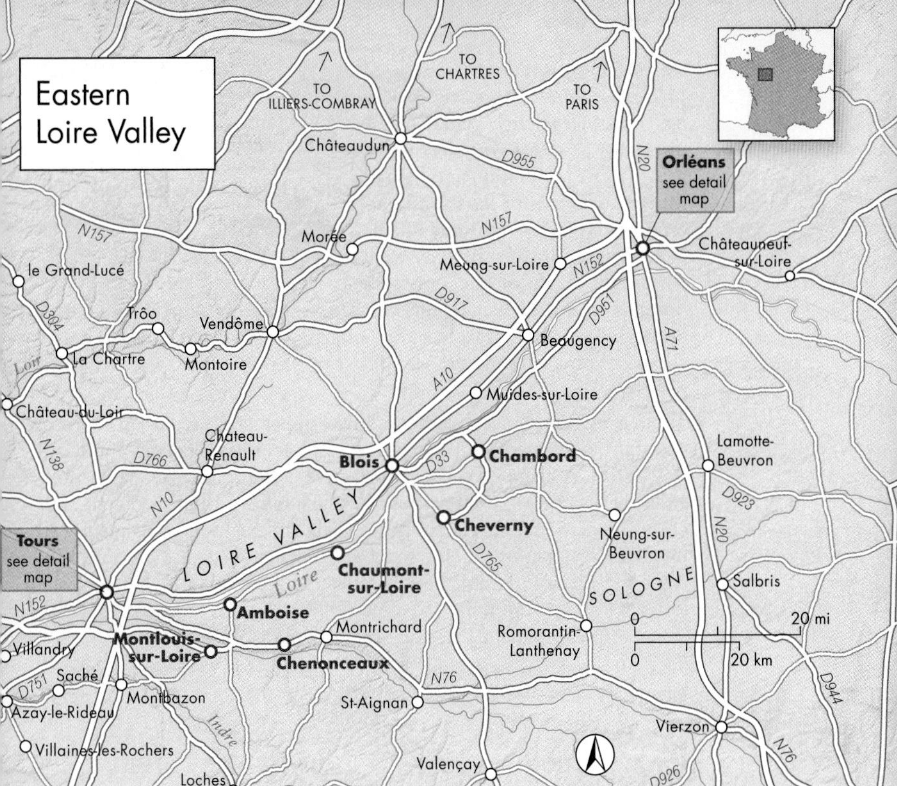

THE EASTERN LOIRE VALLEY

The city of Orléans—halfway along the river's long route—marks the beginning of the low, rich Val de Loire, the eastern part of which stretches 112 km (70 miles) to the central hub of Tours. All along it, magnificent châteaux built of local tufa (creamy white limestone) during the Middle Ages and Renaissance rise up near the water—including the mightiest of them all, show-stopping Chambord. Sigh-worthy Chenonceau sits farther west, while a storied royal château and Leonardo da Vinci's last home vie for attention in Amboise. Closer to Tours, you can enjoy royal treatment yourself by overnighting in Montlouis-sur-Loire's blissful Château de la Bourdaisière.

TOURS

240 km (150 miles) southwest of Paris.

Home to about 150,000 residents, Tours is the region's largest city and its commercial center. Vacationers concerned only with the quaint may be put off by the modern sprawl of factories, high-rise blocks, and overhead expressway junctions cluttering up the outskirts; however, Tours does have a lot to offer. Being a transportation hub, it's a practical base—trains run along the river in both directions, and the city is the starting point for many organized bus excursions. Moreover, Tours has a distinct energy, thanks to the university students who make up a fourth of its population and help to fill the many cafés, bars, and eateries in the pedestrian-only Vieille Ville. There's history here as well. Although much of the city was bombed in World War II, the attractive half-timber medieval quarter around Place Plumereau has been smartly restored, and Tours's grand cathedral ranks among France's finest.

LUSCIOUS LOIRE

If the natives of Tours are known for one thing, it's their elegant French. Paris may be the capital, but for the Tourangeaux, Parisians are the ones with the accent.

GETTING HERE

Tours is the Loire Valley rail hub. Eight direct TGVs from Paris's Gare Montparnasse arrive daily, covering 240 km (150 miles) in 75 minutes (€25–€65). A cheaper, slower alternative is the four-times-daily Intercities service from Gare d'Austerlitz, which takes around two hours but costs only €15–€28. Frequent trains also connect Tours to Langeais (20 mins, €5.70), Amboise (20 mins, €5.70), Chenonceaux (30 mins, €7), Azay-le-Rideau (30 mins, €5.90), Blois (35–45 mins, €11.20), Saumur (45 mins, €12.30), Chinon (50 mins, €9.90), Orléans (75 mins, €20.70), Angers (60–95 mins, €19), and other towns.

Visitor Information Tours Tourist Office. ☎ *02–47–70–37–37* 🌐 *www.tours-tourisme.fr.*

EXPLORING

TOP ATTRACTIONS

Cathédral St-Gatien. Built between 1239 and 1484, this noted cathedral, one of the greatest churches of the Loire Valley, reveals a mixture of architectural styles. The richly sculpted stonework of its majestic two-tower facade betrays the Renaissance influence on local château-trained craftsmen. The stained glass dates from the 13th century (if you have binoculars, bring them). Also take a look at both the little tomb with kneeling angels built in memory of Charles VIII and Anne of Brittany's two children, and the **Cloître de La Psalette** (Psalm Cloister), on the south side of the cathedral, where the canons of St-Gatien created some of the most beautiful illuminated manuscripts in medieval Europe. ✉ *Rue Lavoisier, Tours* ☎ *02–47–47–05–19* 🌐 *www.la-psalette.monuments-nationaux.fr* 🎫 *Psalm Cloister €3* ⏲ *Apr., Mon.–Sat. 10–12:30 and 2–5:30, Sun. 2–5:30; May–Aug., Mon.–Sat. 9:30–12:30 and 2–6, Sun. 2–6; Sept.–Mar., Wed.–Sat. 9:30–12:30 and 2–5, Sun.–Tues. 2–5.*

Fodor's Choice ★ **Château de Candé.** When King Edward VIII of England abdicated his throne in 1937 to marry the American divorcée Wallace Simpson, the couple chose to escape the international limelight and exchange their wedding vows at this elegant 16th-century château. Although it's decorated with period furnishings and features Art Deco bathrooms, all eyes are drawn to the mementos from the Duke and Duchess of Windsor's stay (including the famous Cecil Beaton photographs taken on their big day). Fashionistas will also appreciate the haute-couture wardrobe compiled by the stylish lady of the house, Fern Bedaux. Befitting the owners' flawless taste (if questionable politics, as the Bedauxs were known fascist sympathizers), the château is a particularly pretty example of late Gothic style. ✉ *10 km (6 miles) southwest of Tours, Monts, Tours* ☎ *02–47–34–03–70* 🌐 *www.domainecande.fr* 🎫 *€6.50* 🕓 *Mid-Apr.–June and Sept., Wed.–Sun. 10:30–12:30 and 1:30–6 (gardens until 7); July and Aug., daily 10:30–7 (gardens until 9); Oct.–mid-Nov., Wed.–Sun. 1–5 (château and gardens).*

Fodor's Choice ★ **Place Plumereau.** North from the Basilique St-Martin to the river is **Le Vieux Tours.** This lovely medieval quarter—a warren of quaint streets, wood-beam houses, and grand mansions once owned by 15th-century merchants—has been gentrified with chic apartments and pedestrianized streets. It's centered around Place Plumereau, Tours's erstwhile *carroi aux chapeaux* (hat market). Local college students and tourists alike love to linger in its cafés, and the buildings rimming the square have become postcard staples. Nos. 1 through 7 form a magnificent series of half-timber houses; note the wood carvings of royal moneylenders on Nos. 11 and 12. At the top of the square a vaulted passageway leads to medieval **Place St-Pierre-le-Puellier.** Running off Place Plumereau are other streets adorned with historic houses, notably Rue Briçonnet—at No. 16 is the **Maison de Tristan,** with a medieval staircase. ✉ *Bordered by rues du Commerce, Briçonnet, de la Monnaie, and du Grand-Marché, Tours.*

WORTH NOTING

Basilique St-Martin. Only two sturdy towers—the Tour Charlemagne and the Tour de l'Horloge (Clock Tower)—remain of the great medieval abbey built over the tomb of St. Martin, the city's 4th-century bishop and patron saint. Most of the abbey, which once dominated the heart of Tours, was razed during the French Revolution. Today the site is occupied by the bombastic neo-Byzantine Basilique St-Martin, which was completed in 1924. There's a shrine to St. Martin in the crypt. ✉ *Rue Descartes, Tours* ☎ *02–47–05–63–87* 🌐 *www.basiliquesaintmartin.fr* 🕓 *Daily 7:30–7 (until 9 in summer).*

Musée des Beaux-Arts (*Fine Arts Museum*). In what was once the archbishop's palace (built into an ancient Roman wall), this museum features an eclectic selection of furniture, sculpture, and wrought-iron work, plus art by Rubens, Rembrandt, Boucher, Degas, and Calder. A favorite is Fritz the Elephant, stuffed in 1902. ✉ *18 pl. François-Sicard, Tours* ☎ *02–47–05–68–82* 🌐 *www.mba.tours.fr* 🎫 *€5* 🕓 *Wed.–Mon. 9–12:45 and 2–6.*

Musée du Compagnonnage (*Guild Museum*). Housed in the cloisters of the 13th-century church of St-Julien, this collection honors the *Compagnonnage,* a sort of apprenticeship-cum-trade-union system. On display you'll see virtuoso 19th-century works produced by candidates for guild membership, some of them eccentric (an Eiffel Tower made of slate, for instance, and a château constructed of varnished noodles). ✉ *8 rue Nationale, Tours* ☎ *02–47–21–62–20* 🌐 *www.museecompagnonnage.fr* 🎫 *€5* 🕓 *Mid-June–mid-Sept., daily 9–12:30 and 2–6; mid-Sept.–mid-June, Wed.–Mon. 9–12:30 and 2–6.*

Basilique St-Martin 1
Cathédrale St-Gatien 4
Château de Candé 6
Musée des Beaux-Arts 5
Musée du Compagnonnage/ Musée du Vin ... 3
Place Plumereau 2

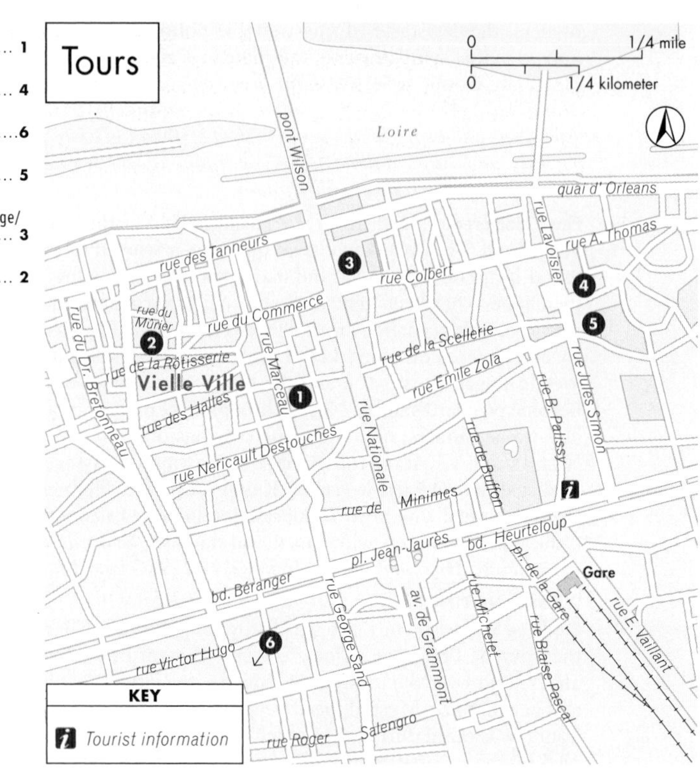

WHERE TO EAT

$$ BISTRO ✕ **Le Petit Patrimoine.** Locals in the know reserve well in advance to get a table at this tiny restaurant in Vieux Tours, which specializes in traditional regional cuisine. Don't miss Balzac's much-loved Rillons de Tours, a glazed pork dish, and the delicious St-Maure goat cheese. *Average main: €24 58 rue Colbert, Tours 02–47–66–05–81 Closed Sun. and Mon. Reservations essential.*

$$$$ MODERN FRENCH ✕ **L'Odéon.** Enjoy traditional Loire Valley haute cuisine prepared with modern flair in the heart of Tours. Flavors can be surprising, such as fresh lobster with truffle sauce and walnut oil, roast Iberian lomo in a red-onion-and- *vin-doux* (fortified wine) fricassee, or roasted sea bass with rhubarb and shrimp sauce. The Art Deco setting is not particularly romantic, so come at lunch (when you can take advantage of the great midday menus) rather than paying more for dinner. *Average main: €35 10 pl. du Général Leclerc, Tours 02–47–20–12–65 www.restaurant-lodeon.com Closed Sun. No lunch Sat. and Mon. Reservations essential.*

WHERE TO STAY

$$$ RESORT **Domaine de la Tortinière.** This was reportedly one of Audrey Hepburn's favorites, and you can immediately see why: the neo-Gothic château, sitting atop a vast, sloping lawn, features a pair of fairy-tale towers,

Louis Seize public salons, and soigné guest rooms—some in the turrets, others in the smartly converted stables and servants' quarters. **Pros:** gourmet restaurant; romantic setting; luxurious Louis XVI style. **Cons:** some rooms on the small side; a bit off the beaten track. *Rooms from: €180 10 rte. de Ballan-Miré, 12 km (7 miles) south of Tours, Veigné 02–47–34–35–00 www.tortiniere.com Closed mid-Dec.–Feb. 24 rooms, 6 suites No meals.*

$ HOTEL **L'Adresse.** These guest rooms in the heart of Tours's Old Town, a block from half-timbered Place Plumereau and the open-air market, have a fresh look and a pleasant neutral palette; some have whitewashed wood-beam ceilings, while others have Juliet balconies. **Pros:** central location in Vieux Tours; flat-screen TVs; air-conditioning. **Cons:** student district can be very noisy at night; no parking. *Rooms from: €88 12 rue de la Rôtisserie, Tours 02–47–20–85–76 www.hotel-ladresse.com 17 rooms Some meals.*

$$$$ HOTEL **Les Hautes Roches.** Far from their original role as monastic cells and even further from the Flintstone-influenced idea of cave dwellings, these luxe-troglodyte lodgings—with their limestone walls, Louis Treize seating, rich fabrics, carved fireplaces, gas-lantern lamps, finished marble steps, and riverside setting—are the epitome of quiet luxury amid the soothing elements of stone and water. **Pros:** unique troglodyte setting; river views; fabulous gourmet restaurant with terrace. **Cons:** apprentice-style service; busy road (hidden by shrubs) in front of hotel. *Rooms from: €225 86 quai de la Loire, 5 km (3 miles) east of Tours, Rochecorbon 02–47–52–88–88 www.leshautesroches.com Closed mid-Feb.–Mar. 15 rooms Some meals.*

$ HOTEL **Mondial.** These contemporary rooms, decorated in neutral tones with red or floral accents, are all on the small side, but they are nicely tucked away on a small leafy square 300 yards from the Loire and a five-minute walk from historic Place Plumereau. **Pros:** free Wi-Fi; good location; friendly service; good value. **Cons:** noise from downstairs nightclub Wednesday–Sunday nights until 5 am; restricted reception hours. *Rooms from: €74 3 pl. de la Résistance, Tours 02–47–05–62–68 www.hotelmondialtours.com 20 rooms No meals.*

MONTLOUIS-SUR-LOIRE

11 km (7 miles) east of Tours on south bank of the Loire.

Montlouis—like Vouvray, its sister town on the north side of the Loire—is noted for white wines, and you can learn all about the vintages produced here at the Cave Touristique on Place Courtemanche. Afterward, retreat to the Château de la Bourdaisière, Prince Louis-Albert de Broglie's suitably regal hotel on the eastern side of town (even day-trippers who can't spend a night can visit it on a guided tour).

GETTING HERE

Touraine Fil Vert's Line C bus runs from the Tours bus station to Montlouis-sur-Loire and the Château de la Bourdaisière (30 mins, €2.20); since the town is only 11 km (7 miles) from Tours, a taxi is a faster option.

Spend your first evening in the Loire Valley dining on gorgeous Place Plumereau, hub of the historic district of Tours, gateway to the region.

Visitor Information Montlouis-sur-Loire Tourist Office. ☎ *02–47–45–85–10* 🌐 *www.tourisme-montlouis-loire.fr.*

WHERE TO STAY

$$$ HOTEL Fodor's Choice ★ **Château de la Bourdaisière.** A 15th-century, 100-carat jewel of a castle, once the favored retreat of kings François I and Henri IV, is today the luxurious country setting for the Prince de Broglie's hotel—a magnificent place that magically distills all the grace, warmth, and élan of *la vie de châteaux* as no other. **Pros:** exquisite setting; secluded pool; stylish salons; extensive gardens. **Cons:** only offers quick and casual lunches; rooms lack air-conditioning; town is a bore. *Rooms from: €170* ✉ *25 rue de la Bourdaisière, Montlouis-sur-Loire* ☎ *02–47–45–16–31* 🌐 *www.labourdaisiere.com* *Closed mid-Nov.–Mar.* *17 rooms, 3 suites* *No meals.*

AMBOISE

13 km (8 miles) northeast of Montlouis via D751, 24 km (15 miles) east of Tours.

It is hardly surprising that this hub town is considered a must-see on any Val de Loire itinerary. Crowned by a royal château that's soaked in history (and blood), Amboise also happens to be the site of Leonardo da Vinci's final home, the pretty Clos-Lucé. As if that wasn't enough, it has bustling markets plus an enviable selection of hotels and eateries. The caveat? On hot summer days, the plethora of tour buses turns this Renaissance town into a mass of carbon monoxide.

GETTING HERE

Amboise has frequent train connections with Tours (20 mins, €5.70), Blois (20 mins, €7.20), and many other towns on the main rail route, which follows the banks of the river. From Amboise's station, follow the signs across two bridges to the *centre ville* and Place Richelieu.

Visitor Information Amboise Tourist Office. ☎ *02–47–57–09–28* ⊕ *www.amboise-valdeloire.com.*

EXPLORING

Château d'Amboise. The Château d'Amboise became a royal palace in the 15th and 16th centuries. Charles VII stayed here, as did the unfortunate Charles VIII, best remembered for banging his head on a low doorway lintel (you will be shown it) and dying as a result. The gigantic **Tour des Minimes** drops down the side of the cliff, enclosing a massive circular ramp designed to lead horses and carriages up the steep hillside. François I, whose long nose appears in so many château paintings, based his court here, inviting Leonardo da Vinci as his guest. The castle was also the stage for the Amboise Conspiracy, an ill-fated Protestant plot against François II; you're shown where the corpses of the conspirators dangled from the castle walls. Partly due to the fact that most interior furnishings have been lost, most halls here are haunted and forlorn. The maze of underground passages are opened to the public for guided visits (April–September). While exploring the grounds, don't miss the little chapel of St-Hubert; built in the 1490s, this Flamboyant Gothic gem is fronted by a glorious tympanum, adorned with carvings, and graced by a tomb that's said to contain the remains of Leonardo. Audio guides are available for €4. ✉ *Amboise* ☎ *02–47–57–00–98* ⊕ *www.chateau-amboise.com* 🎫 *€10.70* ⏲ *Feb., daily 9–12:30 and 1:30–5; Mar. and Nov. 1–15, daily 9–5:30; Apr.–June, daily 9–6:30; July and Aug., daily 9–7; Sept. and Oct., daily 9–6; mid-Nov.–Jan., daily 9–12:30 and 2–4:45.*

FAMILY **Clos Lucé.** If you want to see where "the 20th century was born"—as the curators here like to proclaim—head to the Clos Lucé, about 600 yards up Rue Victor-Hugo from the château. Leonardo da Vinci (1452–1519) spent the last four years of his life in this handsome Renaissance manor, tinkering away at inventions, amusing his patron, King François I, and gazing out over a garden that was planted in the most fashionable Italian manner. The garden was completely restored in 2008 to contain plants and trees found in his sketches, as well as a dozen full-size renderings of machines he designed. The **Halle Interactive** contains working models of some of Leonardo's extraordinary inventions, all built by IBM engineers using the artist's detailed notebooks (by this time Leonardo had put away his paint box because of arthritis). Mechanisms on display include three-speed gearboxes, a military tank, a clockwork car, and a flying machine complete with designs for parachutes. Originally called Cloux, the property was given to Anne of Brittany by Charles VIII, who built a chapel for her that is still here. Some of the house's furnishings are authentically 16th century—indeed, thanks to the artist's presence, Clos Lucé was one of the first places where the Italian Renaissance made inroads in France: Leonardo's *Mona Lisa* and *Virgin*

Continued on page 216

4

ONCE UPON A CHÂTEAU

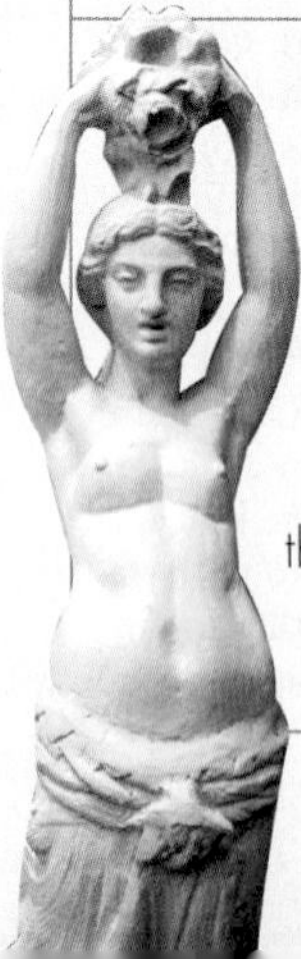

France's most famous châteaux range in style from medieval fortresses to Renaissance country homes, and they don't skip a beat in between. Today, travelers hop their way from the fairytale splendor of Ussé to the imposing dungeons at Angers to the graceful spans of Chenonceau. But to truly appreciate these spectacular structures, it helps to review their evolution from warlike stronghold to Sleeping Beauty's home.

Château de Chambord

Loire and château are almost synonymous. There may be châteaux in every region of France, but nowhere are they so thickly clustered as they are in the Loire Valley. There are several reasons for this. By the early Middle Ages, prosperous towns had already evolved due to being strategically sited on the Loire, and defensive fortresses—the first châteaux—were built by warlords to control certain key points along the route. And with good reason: the riches of this wildly fertile region drew many feuding lords; in the 12th century, the medieval Plantagenet kings of France and England had installed themselves here (at Chinon and Fontevraud, to be exact).

During this time, dukes and counts began to build châteaux, from which they could watch over the king's lands and also defend themselves from each others' invasions. Spare, cold, and uninviting (that being the point), their châteaux were fancy forts. The notion of defense extended to the décor: massive high-back chairs protected the sitter from being stabbed in the back during dinner, and the *crédence* (credenza) was a table used by a noble's official taster to test for poison in the food.

These fortifications continued to come in handy during the Hundred Years' War, during which France and England quibbled over the French crown, for 116 years. When that war came to an end, in 1453, King François I went to Italy, looking for someone else to beat up on, and came back with the Renaissance (he literally brought home Leonardo da Vinci). The king promptly built a 440-room Xanadu, Chambord, in the Italianate style.

By the 15th century, under the later medieval Valois kings, the Loire was effectively functioning as the country's capital, with new châteaux springing up apace, advertising their owners' power and riches. Many were built using a chalky local stone called *tuffeau* (tufa), whose softness and whiteness made it ideal for the sculpted details which were the pride of the new architectural style. The resulting Renaissance pleasure palaces were sumptuous both inside and out—Charles Perrault found the Château de Ussé to be so peaceful and alluring it inspired him to write "Sleeping Beauty" in 1697. A few years before, Louis XIV had started building his new seat of government. It wasn't long before it was goodbye Loire Valley, hello Versailles.

By Heather Stimmler-Hall

FROM DEFENSE TO DECORATION

13TH CENTURY

Angers

The parade of châteaux began with the medieval fortress at Angers, a brooding, muscular fort built by St. Louis to defend the gateway to the Loire against pesky English invaders. Military architecture gave birth to this château, a perfect specimen of great, massive defensiveness. Such castles were meant to look grim, advertising horrid problems for attackers—defenders shot cross-bow arrows from the slit windows—and unpleasant conditions for prisoners in the dungeons. The most important features of these fortress-châteaux were the *châtelets* (twin turrets that frame the drawbridge), the *chemin de ronde* (the machicolated passageways between towers), and the *donjon* (fortress keep).

14TH CENTURY

Saumur

When the battle cries faded and periods of peace once more beguiled the land, the château changed its appearance and the picture palaces of the Loire came into being. Elegance arrived early at Saumur, built in 1360 by Louis I of Anjou. His heir, the luxury-loving Duc de Berri, dressed up the sturdy fort with high, pointed roofs, gilded steeples, iron weather vanes, and soaring pinnacles, creating a Gothic-style castle that Walt Disney would have been proud of. Former cross-bow apertures were replaced with good-size windows, from which love-sick princesses would gaze down on chivalric tournaments, now featuring fancy cloth-of-gold trappings, and festive banquets with blaring trumpet backup became the norm.

1214 French king **Philippe Auguste** defeats English and German armies in Anjou.

1228

1238 Constructuion of **Angers Castle.**

1270 **Death of Louis IX** (St. Louis) in Tunis during the 8th Crusade.

1300

1337 **Hundred Years' War** between France and England. begins.

1348 The **Black Death** kills one third of the French population.

1360 Louis I of Anjou tranforms **Saumur** into his elegant residence.

1400

16TH CENTURY

Azay-le-Rideau

By the Renaissance—brought to France from Italy by Charles VIII at the end of the 15th century—balance, harmony, and grace were brought to the fore. Rich officials wowed the womenfolk with châteaux that were homages to the bygone days of chivalry, such as Azay-le-Rideau. The château may look Gothic from a distance, but its moat is actually the River Indre, and its purpose is to provide a pleasing reflection, thereby emphasizing the Italianate symmetry of this architectural bijou. Funded by the royal financier Berthelot but designed by his wife, Philippe, this was a fairy-tale castle. The turrets and machicolations were just for fun, and a grand staircase was added to showcase the ladies' sweeping skirts.

16TH CENTURY

Chenonceau

Its architecture is civilized, peaceful, and feminine, aptly so since it was constructed by three ladies. Catherine Briçonnet, a tax collector's wife, built the Gothic-style château; Diane de Poitiers, the mistress of Henri II, extended it by adding a bridge across the river (for easy access to her hunting grounds), before being kicked out by Henri's wife, Catherine de Medici, who tacked galleries onto the bridge in homage to the Ponte Vecchio in Florence, her home town. Although its broad facade offers a curtsey to the virtues of Baroque style, Chenonceau is actually only two rooms deep—the château had become an exquisite stage curtain and little more.

1431 After rallying the French to victory in Orléans, **Joan of Arc** is burned at the stake by the English.

1485 **Charles VIII** invades Italy, importing home the Renaissance.

1500

1518 **Azay-le-Rideau** is rebuilt with Italian influences.

1525 François I builds **Chambord.**

1547 King Henri II gives **Chenonceau** to his mistress Diane de Poitiers.

1600

of the Rocks, both of which once graced the walls here, were bought by the king, who then moved them to the Louvre. ✉ *2 rue du Clos-Lucé, Amboise* ☎ *02–47–57–00–73* 🌐 *www.vinci-closluce.com* 🎫 *€14* ⏲ *Feb.–June, Sept., and Oct., daily 9–7; July and Aug., daily 9–8; Nov. and Dec., daily 9–6; Jan., daily 10–6. Garden Mar.–Nov.*

WHERE TO STAY

$$$$ HOTEL **Château de Noizay.** Filled with the mystery of the past—this was once the fabled redoubt of the Protestant plotters in the 1559 Amboise Conspiracy—Château de Noizay is fitted out with Renaissance chimneys and salons, a parterre garden, and guest rooms so regal that you may feel like bowing or curtsying to the staff. **Pros:** historic ambience; excellent restaurant. **Cons:** some rooms have faded decor; high rates for the countryside. $ *Rooms from: €270* ✉ *Promenade de Waulsort, 8 km (5 miles) west of Tours, Noizay* ☎ *02–47–52–11–01* 🌐 *www.chateaudenoizay.com* ⏲ *Closed mid-Jan.–mid-Mar.* *14 rooms* *All meals.*

$$$ HOTEL Fodor's Choice ★ **Château de Pray.** Like a Rolls-Royce Silver Cloud, this hotel keeps purring along, decade after decade, offering many delights: a romantic twin-tower château, a Loire River vista, tranquil guest rooms (four of the less expensive are in a charming "Pavillon Renaissance"), and an excellent restaurant. **Pros:** marvelous setting; superlative restaurant; open year-round. **Cons:** service can be haughty; no bar. $ *Rooms from: €149* ✉ *Rue du Cèdre, 4 km (2 miles) east of Amboise, Chargé* ☎ *02–47–57–23–67* 🌐 *www.chateaudepray.fr* *17 rooms, 2 suites* *Some meals.*

$ HOTEL **Le Blason.** Two blocks behind Château d'Amboise and a five-minute walk from the town center, this small hotel in a 15th-century building has welcoming, English-speaking owners and the gentlest prices in town. **Pros:** quaint; families welcome; good value. **Cons:** small bathrooms; traffic noise in some rooms. $ *Rooms from: €54* ✉ *11 pl. Richelieu, Amboise* ☎ *02–47–23–22–41* 🌐 *www.leblason.fr* *27 rooms* *Some meals.*

$$ HOTEL **Le Manoir Les Minimes.** Soigné as can be, this stylish 18th-century *manoir* is lucky enough to preside over a Loire riverbank under the shadow of Amboise's great cliff-side château, offering a calm oasis in a busy town center. **Pros:** historic style; flawlessly elegant. **Cons:** overpriced breakfast (€16—€20); no outside food and drink allowed. $ *Rooms from: €142* ✉ *34 quai Charles-Guinot, Amboise* ☎ *02–47–30–40–40* 🌐 *www.manoirlesminimes.com* ⏲ *Closed last wk of Nov.–mid-Dec. and last wk of Jan.–mid-Feb.* *13 rooms, 2 suites* *No meals.*

$$$ B&B/INN Fodor's Choice ★ **Le Vieux Manoir.** Toile de Jouy screens, gilt-framed paintings, comfy Napoléon III covered-in-jute armchairs, timeworn armoires, and tables adorned with Shaker baskets make this extraordinary inn—run by native Californian owners Gloria and Bob—*House Beautiful* (and prolonged stay) worthy. **Pros:** real style; scrumptious complimentary breakfasts served in glassed-in conservatory. **Cons:** steep staircase; many "house rules". $ *Rooms from: €160* ✉ *13 rue Rabelais, Amboise* ☎ *02–47–30–41–27* 🌐 *www.le-vieux-manoir.com* *6 rooms, 2 cottages* *Breakfast.*

CHENONCEAUX

12 km (8 miles) southeast of Amboise via D81, 32 km (20 miles) east of Tours.

GETTING HERE

Eleven trains run daily between Tours and Chenonceaux (30 mins, €7). The station is a minute's walk from the front gates of the château; across the tracks is the one-road town.

HAVE THAT NIKON READY

Be sure to walk to the most distant point of Chenonceau's largest parterre garden, le Jardin de Diane de Poitiers—there you can find a tiny bridge leading to a river lookout point where you can find the most beautiful view of France's most glorious château. Sorry, no picnics allowed.

EXPLORING

Fodor's Choice ★ **Château de Chenonceau.** Achingly beautiful, the Château de Chenonceau has long been considered the "most romantic" of all the Loire châteaux, thanks in part to its showpiece—a breathtaking *galerie de bal* that spans the River Cher like a bridge. The gallery was used as an escape point for French Resistance fighters during World War II, since all other crossings had been bombed. Set in the village of Chenonceaux (spelled with an *x*) on the River Cher, this was the fabled retreat for the *dames de Chenonceau,* Diane de Poitiers, Catherine de' Medici, and Mary, Queen of Scots. Spend at least half a day wandering through the château and grounds, and you will see that this monument has an undeniable feminine touch. During the peak summer season the only drawback is the château's popularity: if you want to avoid a roomful of schoolchildren, take a stroll on the grounds and come back to the house at lunchtime.

More pleasure palace than fortress, the château was built in 1520 by Thomas Bohier, a wealthy tax collector, for his wife, Catherine Briçonnet. When he went bankrupt, it passed to François I. Later, Henri II gave it to his mistress, Diane de Poitiers. After his death, Henri's not-so-understanding widow, Catherine de' Medici, expelled Diane to nearby Chaumont and took back the château. Before this time, Diane's five-arched bridge over the River Cher was simply meant as a grand ceremonial entryway leading to a gigantic château, a building never constructed. It was to Catherine, and her architect, Philibert de l'Orme, that historians owe the audacious plan to transform the bridge itself into the most unusual château in France. Two stories were constructed over the river, including an enormous gallery that runs from one end of the château to the other. This design might seem the height of originality but, in fact, was inspired by Florence's covered Ponte Vecchio, commissioned by a Medici queen homesick for her native town.

July and August are the peak months at Chenonceau, but you can escape the madding crowds by exiting at the far end of the gallery to walk along the opposite bank (weekends only), rent a rowboat to spend an hour just drifting in the river (where Diane used to enjoy her morning dips), and enjoy the **Promenade Nocturne,** an evocative son et lumière performed in the illuminated château gardens.

Before you go inside, pick up an English-language leaflet at the gate. Then walk around to the right of the main building to see the harmonious, delicate architecture beyond the formal garden—the southern part belonged to Diane de Poitiers, the northern was Catherine's—with the river gliding under the arches (providing superb "air-conditioning" to the rooms above). Inside the château are splendid ceilings, colossal fireplaces, scattered furnishings, and paintings by Rubens, del Sarto, and Correggio. The curatorial staff have delightfully dispensed with velvet ropes and adorned some of the rooms with bouquets designed in 17th-century style. As you tour the salons, be sure to pay your respects to former owner Madame Dupin, tellingly captured in Nattier's charming portrait: Thanks to the affection she inspired among her proletarian neighbors, the château and its treasures survived the Revolution intact (her grave is enshrined near the northern embankment). The château's history is illustrated with wax figures in the **Musée des Cires** (Waxwork Museum) in one of the château's outbuildings. A cafeteria, tearoom, and the ambitious Orangerie restaurant handle the crowds' varied appetites. ✉ *Chenonceaux* ☎ *08–20–20–90–90 €.34 per minute* 🌐 *www.chenonceau.com* 🎫 *€12.50 (includes Musée des Cires); night visit of gardens €6* ⏰ *Mid-Feb.—Mar., daily 9:30–5:30; Apr. and May, daily 9–7; June and Sept., daily 9–7:30; July and Aug., daily 9–8; Oct.–mid-Nov., daily 9–6; mid-Nov.–mid-Feb., daily 9:30–5.*

WHERE TO STAY

$ HOTEL **La Roseraie.** Set around a vast pool terrace and within walking distance of the château, these delightful guest rooms designed with florals, checks, and lace are overseen by charming (and English-speaking) hosts Sabine Müller and Thierry Bellanger. **Pros:** wonderful welcome; free Wi-Fi; verdant setting. **Cons:** some rooms in separate block; street noise in some rooms. [$] *Rooms from: €75* ✉ *7 rue du Dr-Bretonneau, Chenonceaux* ☎ *02–47–23–90–09* 🌐 *www.hotel-chenonceau.com* ⏰ *Closed mid-Nov.–mid-Mar.* *13 rooms, 2 suites* 🍽 *Breakfast.*

$$ HOTEL Fodor's Choice ★ **Le Bon Laboureur.** In 1882 this ivy-covered inn won Henry James's praise, and, thanks to four generations of the Jeudi family, the author might be even more impressed today—this remains one of the Loire's most wonderful auberges, with guest rooms enchantingly accented in toile de Jouy fabrics and Redouté pink-and-blue pastels. **Pros:** charming decor; outstanding food. **Cons:** small bathrooms; some rooms overlook busy road. [$] *Rooms from: €134* ✉ *6 rue du Dr-Bretonneau, Chenonceaux* ☎ *02–47–23–90–02* 🌐 *www.bonlaboureur.com* ⏰ *Closed 1st wk of Jan.–mid-Feb.* *25 rooms* 🍽 *Some meals.*

CHAUMONT-SUR-LOIRE

26 km (16 miles) northeast of Chenonceaux via D176/D62, 21 km (13 miles) southwest of Blois.

Once belonging to Catherine de' Medici, this dramatic hilltop château combines Gothic fortifications with Renaissance style. After touring the stunning interior, be sure to explore the grounds—they're especially gorgeous during the garden show, held annually from April to November.

GETTING HERE

Fifteen trains per day travel from Tours to Onzain Chaumont-sur-Loire, just across the river from the châtéau (30 mins, €8.80); ones from Blois are even more frequent (10 mins, €3.70).

EXPLORING

Château de Chaumont. Although a favorite of Loire connoisseurs, the 16th-century Château de Chaumont is often overlooked by visitors who are content to ride the conveyor belt of big châteaux like Chambord and Chenonceau. It's their loss. Set on a dramatic bluff that towers over the river, Chaumont has always cast a spell—perhaps literally so. One of its fabled owners, Catherine de' Medici, occasionally came here with her court "astrologer," the notorious Ruggieri. In one of Chaumont's bell-tower rooms, the queen reputedly practiced sorcery. Whether or not Ruggieri still haunts the place (or Nostradamus, another on Catherine's guest list), there seem to be few castles as spirit-warm as this one.

Built by Charles II d'Amboise between 1465 and 1510, the château greets visitors with glorious, twin-tower *châtelets*—twin turrets that frame a double drawbridge. The castle became the residence of Henri II. After his death his widow Catherine de' Medici took revenge on his mistress, the fabled beauty Diane de Poitiers, and forced her to exchange Chenonceau for Chaumont. Another "refugee" was the late-18th-century writer Madame de Staël. Exiled from Paris by Napoléon, she wrote *De l'Allemagne* (*On Germany*) here, a book that helped kick-start the Romantic movement in France. In the 19th century her descendants, the Prince and Princess de Broglie, set up regal shop, as you can still see from the stone-and-brick stables, where purebred horses (and one elephant) lived like royalty in velvet-lined stalls. The couple also renovated many rooms in the glamorous neo-Gothic style of the 1870s. Today the castle retains a sense of fantasy: witness the contemporary art installations displayed in different rooms or the latest horticultural innovations showcased during the **Festival International des Jardins**, held from April to November in the extensive park. The château is a stiff walk up a long path from the little village of Chaumont-sur-Loire, but cars and taxis can also drop you off at the top of the hill. ✉ *Chaumont-sur-Loire* ☎ *02–54–20–99–22* 🌐 *www.domaine-chaumont.fr* 🎫 *€11; €17 for combined château-festival entrance; €12.50 for garden alone* ⏲ *Apr.–June and Sept., daily 10–5:45; July and Aug., daily 10–6:15; Oct., daily 10–5:15; Nov.–Mar., daily 10–4:15.*

WHERE TO STAY

$$$$ **HOTEL** **Domaine des Hauts-de-Loire.** Turreted and vine-covered, this 18th-century hunting lodge features an antiques-filled grand salon, a lovely pool, an adorable swan lake, and guest rooms that more often than not are simply beige and elegantly suave; those in the adjacent coach house can be considerably more spectacular—the best have exposed brick walls and timbered cathedral ceilings. **Pros:** kingly service; luxurious style; superb dining. **Cons:** no château architecture; pricey restaurant (appetizers begin at €36). $ *Rooms from: €250* ✉ *79 rue Gilbert Navard, Onzain* ☎ *02–54–20–72–57* 🌐 *www.domainehautsloire.com* ⏲ *Closed most of Dec.–mid-Feb.* *25 rooms, 11 suites* 🍽 *Some meals.*

DID YOU KNOW?

Catherine de' Medici commissioned Chenonceau's river-spanning design because, homesick for her hometown, she wanted to pay homage to Florence's covered Ponte Vecchio.

$ HOTEL **Hostellerie du Château.** Set on a bank of the Loire directly opposite the road leading up to Chaumont's château, this quaint edifice, built in the early 20th century as a hotel, rises four stories to its half-timber eaves in a vision that charmingly conjures up the grace of earlier days. **Pros:** handy setting; good value; free Wi-Fi. **Cons:** street-facing rooms are noisy; restaurant service can be slow. *Rooms from: €84* ✉ *2 rue Maréchal-de-Lattre-de-Tassigny, Chaumont-sur-Loire* ☎ *02–54–20–98–04* *www.hostellerie-du-chateau.com* *Closed mid-Nov.–mid-Mar.* *15 rooms* *No meals.*

CHEVERNY

24 km (15 miles) east of Chaumont, 14 km (9 miles) southeast of Blois.

GETTING HERE

TLC provides bus service from Blois (30 mins, €2); it also operates a twice-daily shuttle to Cheverny and Chambord, April through October (€6).

EXPLORING

Château de Cheverny. Perhaps best remembered as Capitaine Haddock's mansion in the Tintin comic books, the Château de Cheverny is also iconic for its restrained 17th-century elegance. One of the last in the area to be erected, it was finished in 1634, at a time when the rich and famous had mostly stopped building in the Loire Valley. By then, the taste for quaintly shaped châteaux had given way to disciplined Classicism; so here a white, elegantly proportioned, horizontally coursed, single-block facade greets you across manicured lawns. To emphasize the strict symmetry of the plan, a ruler-straight drive leads to the front entrance. The Louis XIII interior with its stridently painted and gilded rooms, splendid furniture, and rich tapestries depicting the Labors of Hercules is one of the few still intact in the Loire region. Despite the priceless Delft vases and Persian embroideries, it feels lived in. That's because it's one of the rare Loire Valley houses still occupied by a noble family. You can visit a small Tintin exhibition called *Le Secret de Moulinsart* (admission extra) and are free to contemplate the antlers of 2,000 stags in the Trophy Room: hunting, called "venery" in the leaflets, continues vigorously here, with red coats, bugles, and all. In the château's kennels, hordes of hungry hounds lounge around dreaming of their next kill. Feeding times—*la soupe aux chiens*—are posted on a notice board (usually 5 pm in summer), and you are welcome to watch the "ceremony" (delicate sensibilities beware: the dogs line up like statues and are called, one by one, to wolf down their meal from the trainer). ✉ *Cheverny* ☎ *02–54–79–96–29* *www.chateau-cheverny.fr* *€10; €14.50 with Tintin exhibition; €20 with Tintin exhibition and boat-and-buggy rides* *Apr.–Oct. daily 9:15–6:30; Nov.–Mar., daily 10–5.*

CHAMBORD

13 km (21 miles) northeast of Chaumont-sur-Loire via D33, 19 km (12 miles) east of Blois, 45 km (28 miles) southwest of Orléans.

The "Versailles" of the 16th century and the largest of the Loire châteaux, the **Château de Chambord** is the kind of place William Randolph Hearst might have built if he'd had the money. Variously dubbed "megalomaniacal" and "an enormous film-set extravaganza," this is one of the most extraordinary structures in Europe, set in the middle of a royal game forest, with just a cluster of buildings—barely a village—across the road.

GETTING HERE

There is surprisingly little public transportation to Chambord (a state-owned château, to boot). But TLC does make a twice-daily bus trip from Blois (35 mins, €2); April through October, it also runs a twice-daily shuttle that covers both Chambord and Cheverny (€6).

EXPLORING

FAMILY
Fodor's Choice ★

Château de Chambord. As you travel the gigantic, tree-shaded roadways that converge on Chambord, you first spot the château's incredible towers—19th-century novelist Henry James said they were "more like the spires of a city than the salient points of a single building"—rising above the forest. When the entire palace breaks into view, it is an unforgettable sight.

With a 420-foot long facade, 440 rooms, 365 chimneys, and a wall that extends 32 km (20 miles) to enclose a 13,000-acre forest, the Château de Chambord is one of the greatest buildings in France. Under François I, building began in 1519, a job that took 12 years and required 1,800 workers. His original grandiose idea was to divert the Loire to form a moat, but someone (perhaps his adviser, Leonardo da Vinci, who some feel may have provided the inspiration behind the entire complex) persuaded him to make do with the River Cosson. François I used the château only for short stays; yet 12,000 horses were required to transport his luggage, servants, and entourage when he came. Later kings also used Chambord as an occasional retreat, and Louis XIV, the Sun King, had Molière perform here. In the 18th century Louis XV gave the château to the Maréchal de Saxe as a reward for his victory over the English and Dutch at Fontenoy (southern Belgium) in 1745. When not indulging in wine, women, and song, the marshal planted himself on the roof to oversee the exercises of his personal regiment of 1,000 cavalry. Now, after long neglect—all the original furnishings vanished during the French Revolution—Chambord belongs to the state.

There's plenty to see inside. You can wander freely through the vast rooms, filled with exhibits (including a hunting museum)—not all concerned with Chambord, but interesting nonetheless—and lots of Ancien Régime furnishings. The enormous double-helix staircase (probably envisioned by Leonardo, who had a thing about spirals) looks like a single staircase, but an entire regiment could march up one spiral while a second came down the other, and never the twain would meet. The real high point here in more ways than one is the spectacular chimneyscape—the roof terrace whose forest of Italianate towers, turrets, cupolas, gables, and chimneys has been compared to everything from the minarets of Constantinople to a bizarre chessboard. During the year there's a packed calendar of activities on tap, from 90-minute tours of the park in a 4x4 vehicle (€18) to guided carriage tours (€11). A soaring three-story-tall hall has been fitted out to offer lunches and dinners. ✉ *Chambord* ☎ *02–54–50–40–00* 🌐 *www.chambord.org* 🎫 *€11* ⏲ *Apr.–Sept., daily 9–6; Oct.–Mar., daily 9–5.*

WHERE TO EAT AND STAY

$$$ MODERN FRENCH ✕ **La Maison d'à Côté.** Just a five-minute drive from Chambord in a tiny village, La Maison à Côté serves traditional French haute cuisine in a cozy yet contemporary dining room with a fireplace, exposed beam ceilings, and wrought-iron entry gate. Specialties, which vary with the seasons, include foie gras with fruit confit, Challans duck fillet with caramelized endive, and lacquered cod with carrots and Orléans mustard. Save room for the surprisingly creative desserts. There's plenty of free parking in the church parking lot across the street, and a handful of tastefully modern rooms are available in the adjacent inn (€80–€128; closed first three weeks of January). $ *Average main: €31* ✉ *25 Rte. de Chambord, Montlivault* ☎ *02–54–20–62–30* 🌐 *www.lamaisondacote.fr* ⏲ *Closed Tues. and Wed.* ✍ *Reservations essential.*

$$$ B&B/INN Fodor's Choice ★ **Château de Colliers.** Small enough to feel like a home, stuffed with delicious 18th-century decor, and replete with the most beautiful river terrace, this overlooked treasure proves—for a few lucky travelers—to be the most unforgettable château in the Loire. **Pros:** authentic antique furnishings; unique riverside setting. **Cons:** grounds and exterior a bit worse for wear; surrounding area fairly dull. $ *Rooms from: €146* ✉ *D951, 8 km (4 miles) northwest of Chambord, Muides-sur-Loire* ☎ *02–54–87–50–75* 🌐 *www.chateau-colliers.com* ⏲ *Closed Sun.–Thurs. Dec.–Feb.* *2 rooms, 3 suites* 🍴 *Breakfast.*

$$ HOTEL **Grand St-Michel.** A revamped hunting lodge right out of the pages of a Flaubert novel grandly sits across the lawn from Chambord's fabled château. **Pros:** wondrous location opposite Chambord; impressive, good-value restaurant; free parking. **Cons:** creeky hallways; old-fashioned decor; staff can be rather cold. $ *Rooms from: €130* ✉ *Pl. St-Louis, Chambord* ☎ *02–54–20–31–31* 🌐 *www.saintmichel-chambord.com* ⏲ *Closed 2nd wk of Dec. and last 2 wks of Jan.* *40 rooms* 🍴 *Breakfast.*

ORLÉANS

115 km (23 miles) northeast of Chambord, 112 km (70 miles) northeast of Tours, 125 km (78 miles) south of Paris.

Surrounded by locales renowned for their beauty, it's little wonder that Orléans once suffered from an inferiority complex. A century ago hamfisted urban planners razed many of its fine old buildings; then both German and Allied bombs helped finish the job during World War II. Today, though, Orléans is a thriving commercial city—and, thanks to a decade of sensitive urban renewal, its Vieille Ville (Old Town) has been gorgeously restored, thereby adding enormous charm to the streets between the Loire and the cathedral.

One thing that hasn't changed is the pride locals take in *la pucelle d'Orléans* (the Maid of Orleans); otherwise known as Joan of Arc, she arrived in 1429 intent on rallying the troops and saving the kingdom from the English during a crucial episode in the Hundred Years' War. Admittedly, there's little left here from the saintly teen's time, but the city honors her through assorted statutes, museum exhibits, and an annual festival (the Fêtes de Jeanne d'Arc).

GETTING HERE AND AROUND

Trains from Paris's Gare d'Austerlitz leave for Orléans every hour or so; the 137-km (78-mile) trip takes between 60 and 95 minutes, with a change in suburban Les Aubrais sometimes required (€10–€21.40). Multiple direct trains per day also connect Orléans with Tours (75 mins, €20.70), Blois (25–45 mins, €11.50), and Angers (2 hrs, 5 mins; €34.50). Once here, the civic tramway makes it easy to get from the rail station to the Old Town and the banks of the Loire.

Visitor Information Orléans Tourist Office. ☎ *02-38-24-05-05* 🌐 *www.tourisme-orleans.com.*

EXPLORING

Cathédrale Ste-Croix. A riot of pinnacles and gargoyles embellished with 18th-century wedding-cake towers, the Cathédrale Ste-Croix is both Gothic and pseudo-Gothic. After most of it was destroyed in the 16th century during the Wars of Religion, Henry IV and his successors rebuilt the cathedral. Novelist Marcel Proust (1871–1922) called it France's ugliest church, but most find it impressive. Inside are dramatic stained glass and 18th-century wood carvings, plus the modern **Chapelle de Jeanne d'Arc** (Joan of Arc Chapel), with plaques in memory of British and American war dead. ✉ *Pl. Ste-Croix, Orléans* 🌐 *www.orleans.catholique.fr* ⏲ *May–Sept., daily 9:15–6; Oct.–Apr., daily 9:15–noon and 2–6.*

Fodor's Choice ★ **Hôtel Groslot.** Just across the square from the cathedral is the Hôtel Groslot, a Renaissance-era extravaganza bristling with caryatids, strap work, and Flemish columns. Inside are regal salons redolent of the city's history (this used to be the Town Hall); they're done up in the most sumptuous 19th-century Gothic Troubadour style and perhaps haunted by King François II, who died here in 1560 by the side of his bride, Mary, Queen of Scots. ✉ *Pl. de l'Étape, Orléans* ☎ *02-38-79-22-30* 🎟 *Free* ⏲ *June–Aug., weekdays 9–6, Sun. 10–6; Sept.–May, Sun.–Fri. 10–noon and 2–6.*

Maison de Jeanne d'Arc (*Joan of Arc House*). During the 10-day Siege of Orléans in 1429, 17-year-old Joan of Arc stayed on the site of the Maison de Jeanne d'Arc. This faithful reconstruction of the house she knew contains exhibits about her life and costumes and weapons of her time. Several dioramas modeled by Lucien Harmey recount the main episodes in Joan's saintly saga, from the audience at Chinon to the coronation at Reims, her capture at Compiègne, and her burning at the stake at Rouen. ✉ *3 pl. du Général-de-Gaulle, Orléans* ☎ *02-38-68-32-63*

Cathédrale Ste-Croix 1
Hôtel Groslot 2
Maison de Jeanne d'Arc 5
Musée des Beaux-Arts 3
Musée Historique et Archéologique .. 4

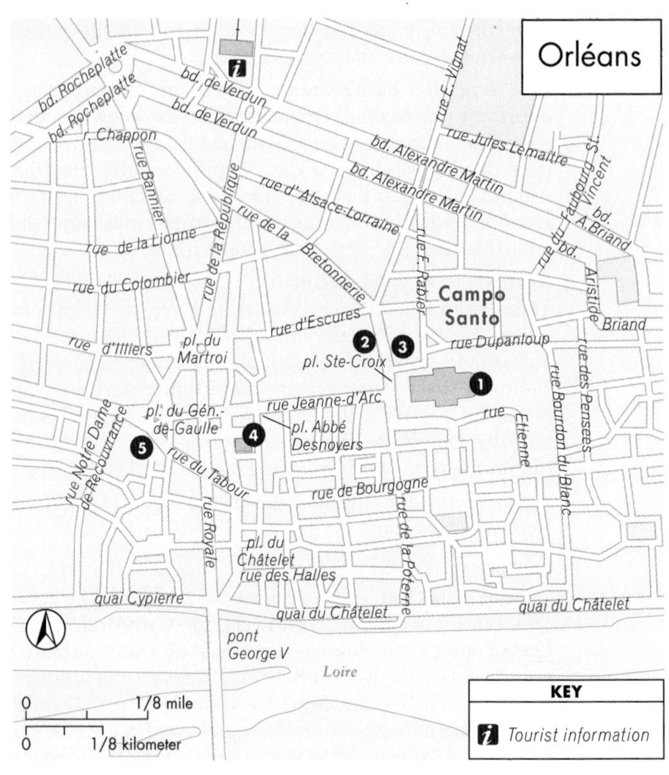

www.jeannedarc.com.fr *€4* *Apr.–Sept., Tues.–Sun. 10–6; Oct.–Mar., Tues.–Sun. 2–6.*

Musée des Beaux-Arts (*Fine Arts Museum*). Take the elevator to the top of this five-story building across from the cathedral then make your way down to see works by such artists as Tintoretto, Velázquez, Watteau, Boucher, Rodin, and Gauguin. The museum's richest collection is its 17th-century French paintings, prints, and drawings, reputedly second only to the Louvre. *1 rue Fernand-Rabier, Orléans* *02–38–79–21–55* *€4, joint ticket with History and Archaeology Museum* *Tues.–Sun. 10–6.*

Musée Historique et Archéologique (*History and Archaeology Museum*). Housed in the **Hôtel Cabu,** a Renaissance mansion restored after World War II, this history and archaeology museum contains works of both "fine" and "popular" art connected with the town's past, including a remarkable collection of pagan bronzes depicting animals and dancers. These were hidden from zealous Christian missionaries in the 4th century and discovered in a sandpit near St-Benoît in 1861. An exposition is dedicated to the life of Jeanne d'Arc. *Sq. Abbé-Desnoyers, Orléans* *02–38–79–25–60* *€4, joint ticket with Fine Arts Museum* *Tues.–Fri. 1:30–5:45 (Joan of Arc and French-Roman rooms only), Sat. 9:30–noon and 1:30–5:45, Sun. 2–6.*

WHERE TO EAT AND STAY

$$$ MODERN FRENCH **Le Lift.** Decorated with quirky contemporary statues, this is a surprisingly modern and stylish restaurant. Using only the freshest local ingredients, Chef Philippe Bardeau combines textures and flavors to create a colorfully vibrant cuisine. Large windows provide views of the leafy park across the way (and, thankfully, not of the cineplex, which sits just below the restaurant); reserve a seat on the panoramic terrace overlooking the Loire River when the weather is warm. This is an excellent choice for a night out with friends, but the noisy atmosphere doesn't lend itself to a romantic rendezvous. *Average main: €28* *Pl. de la Loire, Orléans* *02–30–98–01–47* *www.restaurant-le-lift.com* *No dinner Sun.* *Reservations essential.*

$$ B&B/INN **Château de Champvallins.** When you enter the gates of Jacqueline Létang's magnificent 18th-century estate, with its vast wooded grounds and luxurious lodgings, you'll immediately feel the outside world melt away. **Pros:** authentic antique furnishings; peaceful forest setting; breakfast included. **Cons:** no restaurant; only accessible by car. *Rooms from: €110* *1079 rue de Champvallins, 12 km (7 miles) southeast of Orléans, Sandillon* *02–38–41–16–53* *www.chateaudechampvallins.com* *5 rooms* *Breakfast.*

$ HOTEL Fodor's Choice ★ **L'Abeille.** Conveniently located on the main shopping street in Orléans, this charming family-run hotel—a block from the train/tram station—welcomes guests in rooms with fresh floral wall coverings, parquet flooring, and immaculate tiled bathrooms (many as large as the rooms). **Pros:** easily accessible by train; free Wi-Fi; extra-spacious rooms. **Cons:** rooms facing street can be noisy; pricey city parking. *Rooms from: €98* *64 rue Alsace-Lorraine, Orléans* *02–38–53–54–87* *www.hoteldelabeille.com* *28 rooms* *Some meals.*

NIGHTLIFE AND PERFORMING ARTS

Fêtes de Jeanne d'Arc (*Joan of Arc Festival*). Held in early May, the venerable Fêtes de Jeanne d'Arc celebrates the heroic Maid of Orléans with a parade, religious procession, medieval fair, and reenactments of the famous siege of Orléans. *Orléans* *www.fetesjeannedarc.com.*

4

BLOIS

54 km (34 miles) southwest of Orléans, 58 km (36 miles) northeast of Tours.

Perched on a steep hillside overlooking the Loire, the bustling big town of Blois is a convenient base, well served by train and highway. A signposted route leads you on a walking tour of the Vieille Ville (Old Town)—a romantic honeycomb of twisting alleys, cobblestone streets, and half-timber houses. Its historic highlights include Place St-Louis, where you can find the Maison des Acrobats (note the timbers carved with *jongleurs*, or jugglers), Cathédrale St-Louis, and unexpected Renaissance galleries and staircases lurking in tucked-away courtyards; most visitors, however, are understandably distracted by Blois's superlative, era-bridging château.

CLOSE UP

Bike Tour Options

With its nearly flat terrain, the Loire Valley seems custom-built for cycling, and the recently added Loire à Vélo signposted bike trails, extending 800 km (500 miles) from Orléans to the Atlantic Ocean, make it even easier to pedal between each town and village. The bigger communities all have bike rental agencies. One of the top choices is Loire Vélo Nature, which has more than a dozen outlets along the Loire, where you can rent bikes for independent exploration from €15 a day or €55 a week. The Anjou tourism offices in Angers and Saumur also rent out "Cyclopédia" GPS gadgets that attach to your bike and guide you through the paths and sights of the Anjou region. For stress-free cycling, local bike tour companies such as Biking France and Loire à Vélo offer two- to six-day self-guided vacations costing as little as €150 per day per person, for which they arrange hotels, restaurants, itineraries, maps, baggage transfers, and bike hire. They even have electric bikes for those who prefer to glide *sans* effort.

Contacts Anjou Vélo. ☎ *02-41-40-20-60 Saumur Tourist Office* 🌐 *www.anjou-velo.com.* **Biking France.** ☎ *02-54-78-62-52* 🌐 *www.biking-france.com.* **Loire à Vélo.** ☎ *02-38-79-95-28* 🌐 *www.loireavelo.fr.* **Loire Vélo Nature.** ☎ *06-03-89-23-14* 🌐 *www.loirevelonature.com.*

GETTING HERE

Multiple direct trains per day leave Paris's Gare d'Austerlitz for Blois, making the 185-km (115-mile) trip in 1 hour, 25 minutes (€10–€23.60). There are also dozens of daily trains from Tours (30–45 mins, €11.20) and Orléans (25–45 mins, €11.50), plus multiple direct ones from Angers (85 mins, €27.50).

Visitor Information Blois Tourist Office. ☎ *02-54-90-41-41* 🌐 *www.bloischambord.com.*

EXPLORING

Château de Blois. The massive Château de Blois spans several architectural periods and is among the valley's finest. Your ticket entitles you to a guided tour—given in English when there are enough visitors who don't understand French—but you're more than welcome to roam around on your own. Before entering, pause in the courtyard to admire examples of four centuries of architecture. On one side stand the 13th-century hall and tower, the latter offering a stunning view of the town and countryside. The Renaissance begins to flower in the Louis XII wing (built between 1498 and 1503), through which you enter, and comes to full bloom in the François I wing (1515–24). The masterpiece here is the openwork spiral staircase, painstakingly restored. The fourth side consists of the Classical Gaston d'Orléans wing (1635–38). Upstairs in the François I wing is a series of enormous rooms with tremendous fireplaces decorated with the gilded porcupine, emblem of Louis XII, the ermine of Anne of Brittany, and, of course, François I's salamander, breathing fire and surrounded by flickering flames. Many rooms have intricate ceilings and carved gilt paneling. In the council room the Duke of Guise was murdered by order of Henri III in 1588. Every evening mid-April through mid-September, son-et-lumière shows are staged (audio guides are provided, but the earbuds will set you back €2). ✉ *Blois* ☎ *02–54–90–33–33* 🌐 *www.chateaudeblois.fr* 🎫 *€10 château; €8 sound-and-light show; €15 joint ticket* ⏲ *Apr.–June and Sept., daily 9–6:30; July and Aug., daily 9–7; Oct., daily 9–6; Nov.–Mar., daily 9–12:30 and 1:30–5:30.*

WHERE TO EAT AND STAY

$$$$ SEAFOOD ✕ **Au Rendez-Vous des Pêcheurs.** This friendly restaurant in an old grocery near the Loire has simple decor but impressively creative cooking. Chef Christophe Cosme was an apprentice with Burgundy's late, legendary Bernard Loiseau, and his inventive dishes range from fish and seafood specialties (try the crayfish-and-parsley flan) to succulent baby pigeon on a bed of cabbage. $ *Average main: €39* ✉ *27 rue du Foix, Blois* ☎ *02–54–74–67–48* 🌐 *www.rendezvousdespecheurs.com* ⏲ *Closed Sun., Mon., last wk of Dec., and 1st wk of Jan.* ✍ *Reservations essential.*

$ B&B/INN 🏨 **16 Place Saint Louis.** In the heart of Blois's Old Town, across the square from the St-Louis Cathedral, this elegant bed-and-breakfast gives guests the experience of staying in a classic haute bourgeois home. **Pros:** convenient location in historic center; beautifully appointed; breakfast included. **Cons:** no elevator and the stairs can be a squeeze; limited space for luggage. $ *Rooms from: €100* ✉ *16 pl. Saint Louis, Blois* ☎ *02–54–74–13–61* 🌐 *www.16placesaintlouis.fr* 💳 *No credit cards* ⏲ *Closed 3 wks in Jan.* 🛏 *2 rooms, 1 suite* 🍽 *Breakfast.*

$$$ B&B/INN 🏨 **Le Clos Pasquier.** Time seems to have stood still at Claire and Laurent's snug 16th-century countryside manor set on the edge of the forest—an inviting place featuring heavy wooden beams, well-worn terra-cotta floor tiles, and welcoming stone fireplaces. **Pros:** luxurious bedding; historic building; direct bus to town center; gourmet breakfast included. **Cons:** no restaurant; away from urban amenities. $ *Rooms from: €160* ✉ *10–12 impasse de l'Orée du Bois, Blois* ☎ *02–54–58–84–08* 🌐 *www.leclospasquier.fr* 🛏 *2 rooms, 2 suites* 🍽 *Breakfast.*

$ HOTEL 🏨 **Le Médicis.** Known far and wide for its exceptional restaurant, this smart little hotel 1 km (½ mile) from the Château de Blois has guest rooms that are comfortable, air-conditioned, and soundproof; all share a joyous color scheme but are individually decorated. **Pros:** excellent Renaissance-style dining room; cheerful lodgings; welcoming staff. **Cons:** no views; no elevator; not in town center. $ *Rooms from: €79* ✉ *2 allée François-Ier, Blois* ☎ *02–54–43–94–04* 🌐 *www.le-medicis.com* ⏲ *Closed 3 wks in Jan.* 🛏 *8 rooms, 2 suites* 🍽 *Some meals.*

CENTRAL AND WESTERN LOIRE VALLEY

To the west of Tours, breathtaking châteaux dot the Indre Valley between the regional capital and the once-upon-a-time town of Chinon on the River Vienne. This is the most glamorous part of the Val de Loire—the picturesque pageant beginning in the glorious gardens of Villandry, with the fairy-tale châteaux of Azay-le-Rideaux and Ussé following in rapid succession. Continuing west, no one will want to miss the towns of Fontevraud and Saumur or the city of Angers, which collectively capture the essence of romantic medievalism. Along the way, leave time to savor such storybook delights as Saché—perhaps the Loire's prettiest village.

VILLANDRY

18 km (11 miles) west of Tours via D7.

GETTING HERE

Fil Bleu buses make frequent trips from Tours (30 mins, €2.70, round-trip).

EXPLORING

Fodor's Choice ★ **Château de Villandry.** Green-thumbers get weak in the knees at the mere mention of the Château de Villandry, a grand estate near the Cher River, thanks to its painstakingly relaid 16th-century **gardens,** now the finest example of Renaissance garden design in France. These were originally planted in 1906 by Dr. Joachim Carvallo and Anne Coleman, his American wife, whose passion resulted in three terraces planted in styles that combine the French monastic garden with Italianate models depicted in historic Du Cerceau etchings. Seen from Villandry's cliff-side walkway, the garden terraces look like flowered chessboards blown up to the nth power—a breathtaking sight.

Beyond the water garden and an ornamental garden depicting symbols of chivalric love is the famous *potager,* or vegetable garden, which stretches on for bed after bed—the pumpkins here are *les pièces de résistance.* Flower lovers will rejoice in the main *jardin à la française* (French-style garden): framed by a canal, it's a vast carpet of rare and colorful blooms planted *en broderie* ("like embroidery"), set into patterns by box hedges and paths. The aromatic and medicinal garden, its plots neatly labeled in three languages, is especially appealing. Below an avenue of 1,200 precisely pruned lime trees lies an ornamental lake that is home to swans: not a ripple is out of place. The château interior, still used by the Carvallo family, was redecorated in the mid-18th century; of particular note are the painted and gilt Moorish ceiling from Toledo and one of the finest collections of 17th-century Spanish paintings in France.

The quietest time to visit is usually during the two-hour French lunch break, while the most photogenic time is during the **Nuits des Mille Feux** (Nights of a Thousand Lights, held the first weekend in July), when paths and pergolas are illuminated with myriad lanterns and a dance troupe offers a tableau vivant. There is a gardening weekend held in late September and a music festival in October. ✉ *3 rue Principale, Villandry* ☎ *02–47–50–02–09* 🌐 *www.chateauvillandry.com* 🎫 *€10 château and gardens; €6.50 gardens only* ⏲ *Château Mar., daily 9–6; Apr.–June, Sept., and Oct., daily 9–6; July and Aug., daily 9–6:30; 1st 2 wks of Nov. and last 2 wks of Feb., daily 9–5. Gardens Apr.–June and Sept., daily 9–7; July and Aug., daily 9–7:30; Oct.–mid-Nov., daily 9–5; mid-Nov.–Feb., daily 9–5.*

DID YOU KNOW?

Almost as famed as the vegetable gardens at the Château de Villandry are its gardens *à la française*, whose hedges are strikingly shaped into symbols, including hearts, fans, and daggers.

WHERE TO STAY

$ HOTEL **Auberge Le Colombien.** Just a few steps away from the château, this humble yet cozy inn with country-style accommodations is in the heart of Villandry village. **Pros:** free Wi-Fi; historic building. **Cons:** small windows; right on main road; few amenities. *Rooms from: €82 2 rue de la Mairie, Villandry 02–47–50–07–27 www.auberge-lecolombien.com 14 rooms Some meals.*

LANGEAIS

10 km (6 miles) west of Villandry via D7, A85, and D952.

Sometimes unjustly overlooked, the Château de Langeais—a castle in the true sense of the word—will particularly delight those who dream of knights in shining armor and the chivalric days of yore.

GETTING HERE

There are nine direct trains a day from Tours (20 mins, €5.70) and five from Saumur (25 mins, €8.30). Fil Vert provides a bus link with Chinon (40 mins, €2).

EXPLORING

FAMILY **Château de Langeais.** Built in the 1460s, bearing a massive portcullis and gate, and never altered, the Château de Langeais has an interior noted for its superb collection of medieval and Renaissance furnishings: its assorted fireplaces, tapestries, chests, and beds would make Guinevere and Lancelot feel right at home. An hourly waxworks and video show (an extra €8.80 with entrance) tells the story of the secret dawn wedding of King Charles VIII with Anne of Brittany in the room where it took place in 1491. Outside, gardens nestle behind sturdy walls and battlements; kids will make a beeline for the playgrounds and tree house. The town itself has other sites, including a Renaissance church tower, but chances are you won't want to move from the delightful outdoor cafés that face the castle entrance. Do follow the road a bit to the right (when looking at the entrance) to discover the charming historic houses grouped around a waterfall and canal. *Pl. Pierre de Brosse, Langeais 02–47–96–72–60 www.chateaudelangeais.com €9 Apr.–June and Sept.–mid-Nov., daily 9:30–6:30; July and Aug., daily 9–7; mid-Nov.–Jan. daily 10–5; Feb. and Mar., daily 9:30–5:30.*

AZAY-LE-RIDEAU

11 km (7 miles) south of Villandry via D39, 27 km (17 miles) southwest of Tours.

A largish town surrounding a sylvan dell on the banks of the River Indre, pleasant Azay-le-Rideau is famed for its white-wall Renaissance pleasure palace, called "a faceted diamond set in the Indre Valley" by Honoré de Balzac.

GETTING HERE

Azay-le-Rideau is on the main rail line between Tours (30 mins, €5.90) and Chinon (20 mins, €5.30). The Fil Bleu bus network also provides regular service from Tours train station (35 mins, €2.70).

EXPLORING

Château d'Azay-le-Rideau. The 16th-century Château d'Azay-le-Rideau was created as a literal fairy-tale castle. When it was constructed, the nouveau-riche treasurer Gilles Berthelot decided he wanted to add tall corner turrets, a moat, and machicolations to conjure up the distant seigneurial past when knighthood was in flower and two families, the Azays and the Ridels, ruled this terrain. It was never a serious fortress—it certainly offered no protection to its builder when a financial scandal forced him to flee France shortly after the château's completion in 1529. For centuries the château passed from one private owner to another until it was finally bought by the state in 1905. Though the interior contains an interesting blend of furniture and artwork (one room is an homage to the Marquis de Biencourt who, in the early 20th century, led the way in renovating château interiors in sumptuous fashion—sadly, many of his elegant furnishings were later sold), you may wish to spend most of your time exploring the enchanting gardens, complete with a moat-like lake. Innovative son-et-lumière shows are held on the grounds nightly in July and August, beginning at 9:30 pm. ✉ *Azay-le-Rideau* ☎ *02–47–45–68–60* 🌐 *www.azay-le-rideau.monuments-nationaux.fr* 🎫 *€8.50 château; €10 sound-and-light show; €14 joint ticket* ⏲ *Apr.–June and Sept., daily 9:30–6; July and Aug., daily 9:30–11; Oct.–Mar., daily 10–5:15.*

THE VERSAILLES OF VEGETABLES

Organized in square patterns, Villandry's world-famous *potager* (vegetable garden) is seasonally ablaze with purple cabbages, bright pumpkins, and many other heirloom veggies. In total, there are nearly 150,000 plantings, with two seasonal shows presented—the spring show is a veritable "salad." The fall show comes to fruition in late September or early October and is the one with the pumpkins. Paging Cinderella.

OFF THE BEATEN PATH

Jardins de la Chatonnière. Situated 4 km (2½ miles) north of Azay-le-Rideau and overseen by Madame Béatrice de Andia—one of the grandes dames of the Loire—the 15-acre Jardins de la Chatonnière will make most visitors emerald-green with envy. Framing the private, turreted Renaissance château are seven spectacular visions, each garden devoted to a theme, including L'Élégance and L'Abondance, in the extraordinary shape of a gigantic leaf. ✉ *Rte. D57, direction Lignières–Langeais, Saché* ☎ *02–47–45–40–29* 🌐 *www.lachatonniere.fr* 🎫 *€8* ⏲ *Mar.–mid-Nov., daily 10–8 (last entry at 7).*

WHERE TO STAY

$ B&B/INN **Hotel de Biencourt.** Charmingly set on the pedestrian street that leads to Azay's château gates, this shuttered town house has a delightful courtyard-garden that hides an authentic 19th-century schoolhouse, now converted into lodgings cozily furnished in traditional country style (complete with the stray blackboard and school desk). **Pros:** families welcome; free Wi-Fi. **Cons:** no private parking; thin walls. $ *Rooms from: €85* ✉ *7 rue Balzac, Azay-le-Rideau* ☎ *02–47–45–20–75* 🌐 *www.hotelbiencourt.com* ⏲ *Closed mid-Nov.–Mar.* *17 rooms* *No meals.*

4

$ HOTEL **Le Grand Monarque.** Home to one of France's most beauteous châteaux, Azay should rightly have a hotel that befits the town jewel and this landmark—a three-minute walk from the château gates—nicely fits the bill. **Pros:** fine restaurant with large wine list; town-center setting; free Wi-Fi. **Cons:** some rooms need redecorating. *Rooms from: €98 ✉ 1 rue du Château, Azay-le-Rideau ☎ 02–47–45–40–08 🌐 www.legrandmonarque.com ⊗ Closed Nov.–mid-Feb. 22 rooms, 2 suites Some meals.*

SPORTS AND THE OUTDOORS

J.C. Leprovost Cycles. Rent bikes from J.C. Leprovost to ride along the Indre; the area around Azay-le-Rideau is among the most tranquil and scenic in Touraine. *✉ 13 rue Carnot, Azay-le-Rideau ☎ 02–47–45–40–94.*

SACHÉ

7 km (4½ miles) east of Azay-le-Rideau via D17.

A crook in the road, a Gothic church, the centuries-old Auberge du XIIe Siècle, an Alexander Calder stabile (the great American sculptor created a modern atelier nearby), and the country retreat of novelist Honoré de Balzac (1799–1850)—these few but choice elements all add up to Saché, one of the prettiest (and most undiscovered) nooks in the Val de Loire. If you're heading into the town from the east, you're first welcomed by the Pont-de-Ruan—a dream sequence of a flower-bedecked bridge, water mill, and lake that is so picturesque it will practically click your camera for you.

GETTING HERE

No trains serve Saché, but you can ride as far as the Azay-de-Rideau rail station and cover the remaining 7 km (4½ miles) by cab. Alternatively, you can hop Fil Vert's Line 1 bus from Tours (75 mins, €2).

EXPLORING

Fodor's Choice ★ **Château de Saché.** In the center of town, the Château de Saché houses the **Musée Balzac.** If you've never read any of Balzac's "Comédies Humaine," you might find little of interest in it; but if you have, you can return to such novels as *Cousine Bette* and *Eugénie Grandet* with fresh enthusiasm and understanding. Much of the landscape around here, and some of the people back then, found immortality by being fictionalized in many a Balzac novel. Surrounded by 6 acres of gardens, the present château, built between the 16th and the 18th century, is more of a comfortable country house than a fortress. Born in Tours, Balzac came here—to stay with his friends, the Margonnes—during the 1830s, both to write such works as *Le Père Goriot* and to escape his creditors. The château's themed exhibits range from photographs and original manuscripts to the coffee service Balzac used (the caffeine helped to keep him writing up to 16 hours a day). A few period rooms impress with 19th-century charm, including a lavish emerald-green salon and the author's own writing room. Be sure to study some of the corrected book proofs on display. Balzac had to pay for corrections and additions beyond a certain limit. Painfully in debt, he made emendations

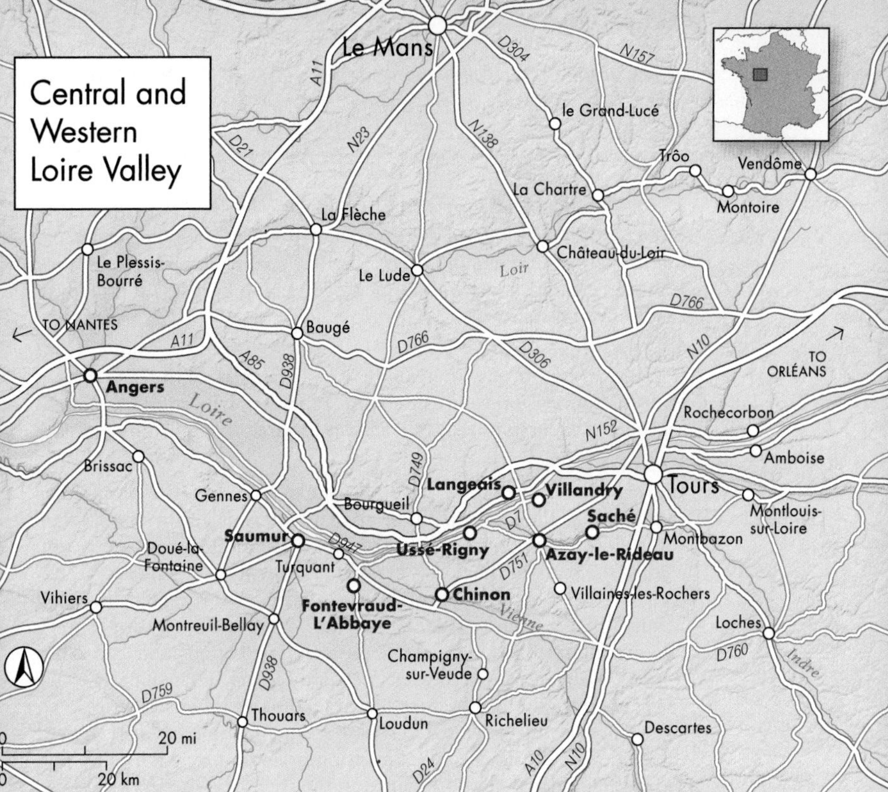

filling all the margins of his proofs, causing dismay to his printers. Their legitimate bills for extra payment meant that some of his works, best sellers for nearly two centuries, failed to bring him a centime. ✉ *2 rue de Château, Saché* ☎ *02–47–26–86–50* 🌐 *www.musee-balzac.fr* 🎫 *€5.50* ⏲ *Apr.–June and Sept., daily 10–6; July and Aug., daily 10–7; Oct.–Mar., Wed.–Mon. 10–12:30 and 2–5.*

WHERE TO EAT

$$$$ FRENCH Fodor's Choice ★

✕ **Auberge du XIIe Siècle.** You half expect Balzac himself to come strolling in the door of this delightful half-timber auberge, so little has it changed since the 19th century. Still sporting a time-stained painted sign and its original exterior staircase, and nearly opposite the great author's country retreat, this inn retains its centuries-old dining room, now warmed by a fireplace, floral bouquets, and rich wood tables. Beyond this room is a modern extension—all airy glass and white walls but not exactly what you're looking for in such historic surrounds. Balzac's ample girth attested to his great love of food, and he would no doubt enjoy the sautéed lobster or the nouvelle spins on his classic *géline* chicken favorites served here today. Dessert is excellent, and so is the coffee—a beverage Balzac drank incessantly (which may explain how he had the energy to create 2,000-plus characters). $ *Average main: €40* ✉ *1 rue du Château, Saché* ☎ *02–47–26–88–77* ⏲ *Closed Mon.,*

2 wks in Jan., and 1 wk in June, Sept., and Nov. No dinner Sun., no lunch Tues. ✍ *Reservations essential.*

USSÉ-RIGNY

14 km (9 miles) west of Azay-le-Rideau via D17 and D7.

The Loire Valley is blessed with an abundance of eye-popping châteaux, but the fairest of them all is here. The Château d'Ussé, inspiration for Charles Perrault's (and Walt Disney's) "Sleeping Beauty," continues to cast a spell on visitors.

GETTING HERE

If don't have a car, the Château d'Ussé is a hard place to reach. Check with the tourism office in Chinon or Tours for daily shuttles or high-season bus excursions that take in two or three châteaux in a day.

EXPLORING

FAMILY Fodor's Choice ★ **Château d'Ussé.** The most beautiful castle in France is first glimpsed as you approach the Château d'Ussé and an astonishing array of blue-slate roofs, dormer windows, delicate towers, and Gothic turrets greets you against the flank of the Forest of Chinon. Literature describes this château, overlooking the banks of the River Indre, as the original "Sleeping Beauty" castle; Charles Perrault—author of this beloved 17th-century tale—spent time here as a guest of the Count of Saumur, and legend has it that Ussé inspired him to write the famous story. Though parts of the castle are from the 1400s, most of it was completed two centuries later. By the 17th century, the region was so secure that one fortified wing of the castle was demolished to allow for grand vistas over the valley and the castle gardens, newly designed in the style Le Nôtre had made so fashionable at Versailles.

Only Disney could have outdone this white-tufa marvel: the château is a flamboyant mix of Gothic and Renaissance styles—romantic and built for fun, not for fighting. Its history supports this playful image: it endured no bloodbaths—no political conquests or conflicts—while a tablet in the chapel indicates that even the French Revolution passed it by. Inside, a tour leads you through several sumptuous period salons, a 19th-century French fashion exhibit, and the Salle de Roi bedchamber built for a visit by King Louis XV (the red-silk, canopied four-poster bed is the stuff of dreams). At the end of the house tour, you can go up the fun spiral staircases to the *chemin de ronde* of the lofty towers; there are pleasant views of the Indre River from the battlements, and you can also find rooms filled with waxwork effigies detailing the fable of Sleeping Beauty herself. Kids will love this.

Before you leave, visit the exquisite Gothic-becomes-Renaissance chapel in the garden, built for Charles d'Espinay and his wife in 1523–35. Note the door decorated with pleasingly sinister skull-and-crossbones carvings. Just a few steps from the chapel are two towering cedars of Lebanon—a gift from the genius-poet of Romanticism, Viscount René de Chateaubriand, to the lady of the house, the Duchess of Duras. When her famous amour died in 1848, she stopped all the clocks in the house—à la Sleeping Beauty—"so as never to hear struck the hours you will not come again." The castle then was inherited by her relations, the Comte and Comtesse de la Rochejaquelin, one of the most dashing couples of the 19th century. Today, Ussé belongs to their descendant, the Duc de Blacas, who is as soigné as his castle. If you do meet him, proffer thanks, as every night his family floodlights the entire château, a vision that is one of the Loire Valley's dreamiest sights. Long regarded as a symbol of *la vieille France,* Ussé can't be topped for fairy-tale splendor, so make this a must-do. ✉ *Rigny-Ussé, Ussé* ☎ *02–47–95–54–05* 🌐 *www.chateaudusse.fr* 🎫 *€14* ⏲ *Apr.–Sept., daily 10–7; Oct.–mid-Nov. and mid-Feb.–Mar., daily 10–6.*

WHERE TO STAY

$ HOTEL **Le Clos d'Ussé.** Thank heavens for this delightful inn—the best time to see the great Château d'Ussé is in early morning light or illuminated at night, and the easiest way to do that is to stay in the village of Rigny-Ussé at the home of the *famille* Duchemin. **Pros:** close to château; charming restaurant. **Cons:** basic guest-room facilities; you-get-what-you-pay-for bathrooms. $ *Rooms from: €60* ✉ *7 rue Principale, Rigny-Ussé* ☎ *02–47–95–55–47* 🌐 *www.leclosdusse.fr* ⏲ *Closed Nov.–mid-Feb.* *4 rooms, 1 suite* *No meals.*

4

CHINON

13 km (8 miles) southwest of Rigny-Ussé via D7 and D16, 44 km (28 miles) southwest of Tours.

Fodor's Choice ★ Chinon—the birthplace of author François Rabelais (1494–1553)—is dominated by a 12th-century castle, perched imposingly above the River Vienne. But its leading photo op is the medieval heart of town. Rue Haute St-Maurice, in particular, stretches for more than 15 wondrous, time-warped blocks, and it's virtually impossible to stroll past the half-timber houses that line it without reaching for your camera. Little wonder that Jean Cocteau used Chinon's fairy-tale allure to effectively frame Josette Day when she appeared as Beauty in his classic 1949 film *La Belle et la Bête.*

GETTING HERE

Trains from Tours pull into Chinon eight times a day (50 mins, €9.90).

Visitor Information Chinon Tourist Office. ☎ *02–47–93–17–85* 🌐 *www.chinon-valdeloire.com.*

EXPLORING

Fortresse de Chinon. This vast fortress dates from the time of Henry II of England, who died within its 400-yard long walls in 1189; another historic event occurred in 1429, when Joan of Arc recognized the disguised dauphin (later Charles VII) here. Long years of neglect, however, eventually left the fortress little more than a ruin, completely open to the elements. The good news is that sweeping restoration work has returned its majestic rooftop, ramparts, and towers to their former glory. A visitor center now welcomes guests a few steps from the glass elevator that provides direct access from the center of Chinon's Old Town. You can tour the **Logis Royal** (Royal Chambers), a section of which has been transformed into an interactive museum dedicated to

As an overnight guest, Charles Perrault was so seduced by the secluded beauty of Château d'Ussé that he was inspired to write "Sleeping Beauty."

Joan of Arc. For a bird's-eye look at the landscape, climb the **Tour Coudray** (Coudray Tower), where in 1307 leading members of the crusading Knights Templar were imprisoned before being taken to Paris, tried, and burned at the stake. The **Tour de l'Horloge** (Clock Tower), whose bell has sounded the hours since 1399, has a view over the ensemble of buildings; while the ramparts offer sensational ones over Chinon, the Vienne Valley, and (toward the back of the castle) the famous Le Clos de l'Echo vineyard. A *salon de thé* is open on the terrace from May through September. ✉ *Chinon* ☎ *02–47–93–13–45* 🌐 *www.forteressechinon.fr* 🎫 *€8.50* ⏲ *Mar., Apr., Sept., and Oct, daily 9:30–6; May–Aug., daily 9:30–7; Nov.–Feb., daily 9:30–5.*

Rue Haute St-Maurice. Once you've visited the castle, recharge your camera batteries and head for the medieval heart of town, Rue Haute St-Maurice. Block after block of storybook half-timber houses make this street a virtual open-air museum that catapults you back to the days of Rabelais. It's also home to one actual museum—the Musée d'Art et d'Histoire at No. 44, which is devoted to the arts and crafts of Chinon and surrounding area from prehistory to the 19th century. ✉ *Chinon* 🎫 *Museum €3* ⏲ *Museum Mar., Apr., and Oct.–mid-Nov., Fri.–Mon. 2–6; May–Sept., daily 2:30–6:30.*

WHERE TO EAT AND STAY

$$$ FRENCH ✕ **Les Années Trente.** Located in the heart of medieval Chinon, at the foot of the royal fortress, this spot welcomes diners with a venerable 16th-century facade. A romantic Belle Époque interior continues the historic vibe—but the food, *au contraire*, is prepared with a light, modern touch. Stéphane and Karine Charles's delicious dishes combine fish, game,

and regional specialties that melt in your mouth without weighing you down. There are three different set menus to choose from; the best might be Le 30 (€45), which comes perfectly paired with local wines and cheeses. *Average main: €30* ✉ *78 rue Haute St Maurice, Chinon* ☎ *02–47–93–37–18* 🌐 *www.lesannees30.com* ⊙ *Closed Tues. and Wed.* *Reservations essential.*

$ HOTEL Fodor's Choice ★ **Hôtel Diderot.** With its ivy-covered stone, white shutters, mansard roof, dormer windows, and rococo spiral staircase, this hotel looks like an 18th-century François Boucher painting. **Pros:** parking in the courtyard or in a free lot nearby; cozy bar and breakfast room; accessible ground-floor rooms. **Cons:** somewhat worn decor; outdated bathrooms. *Rooms from: €70* ✉ *4 rue de Buffon, Chinon* ☎ *02–47–93–18–87* 🌐 *www.hoteldiderot.com* *27 rooms* *Some meals.*

DRINK ALWAYS AND NEVER DIE

Participants in Chinon's medieval festival, the Marché à l'Ancienne (🌐 *www.chinon.com*), are fond of quoting the presiding muse of the city, Renaissance writer François Rabelais. Held on the third Saturday of August, this free wine-tasting extravaganza has stalls, displays, and costumed locals recalling the rural life of ages past. For details, contact the tourist office.

4

FONTEVRAUD-L'ABBAYE

20 km (12 miles) northwest of Chinon via D751.

A refreshing break from the worldly grandeur of châteaux, the small village of Fontevraud is crowned with the largest abbey in France—a magnificent complex of Romanesque and Renaissance buildings that featured prominently in the history of both England and France.

GETTING HERE

Buses connect Saumur and Fontevraud four times per day (30 mins, €1.40). In high season, coach tours and shuttles travel from both Saumur and Chinon—check with town tourist offices for schedules and fares.

Visitor Information Fontevraud-l'Abbaye Tourist Office. ☎ *02–41–51–79–45* 🌐 *www.ot-saumur.fr.*

EXPLORING

Fodor's Choice ★ **Abbaye Royale de Fontevraud.** Founded in 1101, the Abbaye Royale de Fontevraud (Royal Abbey) had separate churches and living quarters for nuns, monks, lepers, "repentant" female sinners, and the sick. Between 1115 and the French Revolution in 1789, a succession of 39 abbesses—among them a granddaughter of William the Conqueror—directed operations. The great 12th-century **Église Abbatiale** (Abbey Church) contains the tombs of Henry II of England, his wife Eleanor of Aquitaine, and their son, Richard Cœur de Lion (the Lionheart). Though their bones were scattered during the Revolution, their effigies still lie *en couchant* in the middle of the echoey nave. Napoléon turned the abbey church into a prison, and so it remained until 1963, when historical restoration work began. The **Salle Capitulaire** (Chapter

House), adjacent to the church, with its collection of 16th-century religious wall paintings (prominent abbesses served as models), is unmistakably Renaissance; the paving stones bear the salamander emblem of François I. Next to the long refectory is the famously octagonal **Cuisine** (Kitchen), topped by 20 scaly stone chimneys led by the **Tour d'Evrault.** ✉ *Pl. des Plantagenêts, Fontevraud* ☎ *02–41–51–73–52* 🌐 *www.fontevraud.fr* 🎟 *€10* ⏲ *Apr., May, Sept., and Oct., daily 9:30–6; June–Aug, daily 9:30–6:30; Nov. and Dec. and the last wk of Jan.–Mar., daily 10–5.*

FAITH, HOPE, AND CLARITY

With its clean-cut lines, Fontevraud's Abbey Church is a gigantic monument of the French Romanesque, the solid style of simple geometric forms eschewing ornamentation. Home to the tombs of Eleanor of Aquitaine and Richard the Lionheart, the soaring nave was intended to elevate the soul.

Allée Sainte-Catherine. After touring the Abbaye Royale, head outside the gates of the complex a block to the north to discover one of the Loire Valley's most time-burnished streets, Allée Sainte-Catherine. Bordered by the Fontevraud park, headed by a charming medieval church, and lined with a few scattered houses (which now contain the town tourist office, a gallery that sells medieval illuminated manuscript pages, and the lovely Licorne restaurant), this street still conjures up the 14th century. ✉ *Fontevraud.*

Château du Petit Thouars. Try some local wines at the stunning, Renaissance-era Château du Petit Thouars, which enjoys an enchanting hilltop setting just off the Vienne River (between Chinon and Fontevraud). The descendents of Aristide du Petit Thouars, a French naval officer who fought in the American Revolution, have created a small museum illustrating the adventures of their family members that visitors can see after a *dégustation* of still and sparkling wines from their hillside vineyard. The historic château, alas, is still a private home, only to be enjoyed from the outside. ✉ *Rte. de la Chaussee, St-Germain-sur-Vienne, Fontevraud* ☎ *02–47–95–96–40* 🌐 *www.chateaudptwines.com* 🎟 *Museum and tasting free* ⏲ *May–Sept., Tues.–Sat. 9:30–12:30 and 2:30–4:30; Oct.–Apr., weekdays 9:30–12:30 and 2:30–4:30.*

WHERE TO EAT

$$$ FRENCH ✕ **La Licorne.** A hanging shop sign adorned with a painted unicorn beckons you to this pretty-as-a-picture 18th-century town-house restaurant on Fontevraud's idyllic Allée Sainte-Catherine. Past a flowery garden and table-adorned terrace, tiny salons glow with happy folks feasting on some of the best food in the region: dishes like Loire salmon, boned quail, Triple Sec soufflé, and langoustine ravioli make most diners purr with contentment. 💲 *Average main: €32* ✉ *Allée Ste-Catherine, Fontevraud* ☎ *02–41–51–72–49* 🌐 *www.restaurant-gastronomique-licorne.fr* ⏲ *Closed Mon. and 4 wks mid-Dec.–mid-Jan. No dinner Sun. or Wed. Oct.–Easter* ✍ *Reservations essential* 👔 *Jacket required.*

$$$ HOTEL 🏨 **Fontevraud L'Hôtel.** Set within the medieval splendor of Fontevraud, this series of outbuildings was once the abbey's lepers' hospice, but you'd never know it—a gorgeous, understated redesign has made it

one of the more unusual hotels in the Loire Valley. **Pros:** unique historic setting; superb restaurant. **Cons:** rooms can be small. $ *Rooms from: €189* ✉ *Abbaye Royale, 38 rue St-Jean de l'Habit, Fontevraud* ☎ *02–46–46–10–10* 🌐 *www.fontevraud.fr* *54 rooms* 🍴 *Some meals.*

SAUMUR

15 km (9 miles) northwest of Fontevraud via D947, 68 km (43 miles) west of Tours.

You'll find putting up with the locals' legendary *snobisme* well worth it once you get a gander at Saumur's *centre historique*, a camera-ready quarter studded with elegant 19th-century town houses and anchored by the vast 12th-century church of St-Pierre. Looming over it all is an equally photogenic riverside castle, the Château de Saumur. Architecture aside, this town (one of the largest along the Loire) is known for agriculture—in particular a flourishing mushroom industry, which produces 100,000 tons per year. The same cool tunnels in which the mushrooms grow provide an ideal storage place for the local *mousseux* (sparkling wines); many of the vineyards hereabouts are open for public tours.

4

GETTING HERE

More than a dozen daily direct trains link Saumur to Tours (45 mins, €12.30) and Angers (20–30 mins, €9.10).

Visitor Information Saumur Tourist Office. ☎ *02–41–40–20–60* 🌐 *www.ot-saumur.fr.*

EXPLORING

FAMILY **Cadre Noir de Saumur** (*Riding School*). This prestigious national equestrian academy trains France's future riding stars. Unique in Europe, the Cadre Noir de Saumur has 400 horses, extensive stables, five Olympic-size riding rings, and miles of specially laid tracks. Try for a morning tour, which gives you a chance to admire the horses in training. A gala equestrian performance is put on for enthusiastic crowds during special weekends in April, June, July, and October; reservations are a must. ✉ *Av. de l'Ecole Nationale d'Equitation, Saumur* ☎ *02–41–53–50–60* 🌐 *www.cadrenoir.fr* *€8* ⏱ *Guided tours only, mid-Feb.–mid-Apr. and mid-Oct.–Nov., Mon. 2:30 and 4, Tues.–Fri. 10, 11, 2:30, and 4, Sat. 9:30 and 11; mid-Apr.–mid-Oct., Mon. 2, 2:30, 3, 3:30, and 4, Tues.–Fri. every half hr 10–4 except noon–2, Sat. every half hr 10–11:30* ☞ *Closed during performances.*

Château de Saumur. If you arrive in the evening, the sight of the floodlighted 14th-century Château de Saumur will take your breath away. Look familiar? You've probably seen the elegant white edifice in reproductions of the famous *Très Riches Heures* (Book of Hours) painted for the Duc de Berry in 1416. Inside it's bright and cheerful, with a gorgeous gateway and plentiful potted flowers. Owing to renovation of the castle walls, the **Musée des Arts Décoratifs** (Decorative Arts Museum) is now housed on the first floor, and exhibitions from the **Musée du Cheval** (Equestrian Museum) can be seen in the adjoining abbey; visitors can also access the gardens and panoramic terrace. July through August, there are temporary expositions in certain areas of the château, as well as medieval-style jousting matches during the day and a sound-and-light show at night (Thursday through Saturday, €19). From the cliff-side promenade beyond the parking lot there's a thrilling vista of the castle on its bluff against the river backdrop. ✉ *Esplanade du Château, Saumur* ☎ *02–41–40–24–40* 🌐 *www.chateau-saumur.fr* 🎫 *€7 in July and Aug.; €6 other months* 🕐 *Apr.–mid-June and mid-Sept.–Oct., Tues.–Sun. 10–1 and 2–5:30; mid-June–mid-Sept., daily 10–6.*

Les Caves Louis de Grenelle. In the center of town and easily accessible on foot or by car, Les Caves Louis de Grenelle offers a fascinating 90-minute tour through the 15th-century quarry tunnels that today serve as aging cellars; a tasting of sparkling and still wines is included. ✉ *839 rue Marceau, Saumur* ☎ *02–41–50–23–21* 🌐 *www.caves-de-grenelle.fr* 🎫 *€2.50* 🕐 *June–Aug., daily 9:30–6:30; Sept., Apr., and May, daily 9:30–noon and 1:30–6; Oct.–Dec., Feb., and Mar., Mon.–Sat. 10–noon and 1:30–6.*

Maison des Vins de Loire (*House of Wine*). Saumur is the heart of one of the finest wine regions in France. To pay a call on some of the vineyards around the city, first stop into the Maison des Vins de Loire for the full scoop on hours and directions; its English-language website is also a helpful resource. ✉ *Quai Lucien-Gautier, Saumur* ✥ *next door to the Tourism Office* ☎ *02–41–38–45–83* 🌐 *www.vinsvaldeloire.fr* 🕐 *Apr., Tues.–Sat. 10–1 and 2:30–6:30; May–Sept., Mon. 2–7, Tues.–Sat. 9:30–1 and 2–7, Sun. 9:30–1; Oct.–Mar., Tues.–Fri. 10:30–12:30 and 3–6, Sat. 10:30–12:30 and 2–6:30.*

Place St. Pierre. This atmospheric square is the focal point of the warren of streets that make up Saumur's *centre historique*. Fringed by half-timbered houses, many of which have been converted into shops and cafés, it's anchored by the grand Église St-Pierre (whose origins date back to the late 12th century) and serves as a popular destination for a refreshing summer *apéro*. ✉ *Saumur.*

Veuve Amiot. This long-established producer of Saumur wines offers guided tours of its production facilities and cellars, followed by a wine-tasting session—all free of charge. ✉ *21 rue Jean-Ackerman, St-Hilaire, Saumur* ☎ *02–41–83–14–14* 🌐 *www.veuve-amiot.com* 🕐 *Daily 10–1 and 2–6* ☞ *Closed Sun. in Jan. and Feb.*

WHERE TO STAY

$ HOTEL **Anne d'Anjou.** With a spectacular setting at the foot of Saumur castle, a flower-strewn courtyard, and views of the Loire from some of the guest rooms (the finest of which retain their original late-18th- and early-19th-century decoration), it's an understatement to describe this elegant spot as appealing. **Pros:** classic architecture; serious restaurant; free Wi-Fi. **Cons:** smallish rooms; rooms facing the river get traffic noise. $ *Rooms from: €89* ✉ *32 quai Mayaud, Saumur* ☎ *02–41–67–30–30* 🌐 *www.hotel-anneanjou.com* 🛏 *42 rooms* 🍽 *Some meals.*

$$ HOTEL Fodor's Choice ★ **Saint-Pierre.** At the very epicenter of historic Saumur, this little 15th- to 17th-century house is hidden beneath the medieval walls of the church of Saint-Pierre—look for its entrance on one of the pedestrian passages that circle the nave. **Pros:** central location; sophisticated decor.

Cons: no restaurant (but café-lined Place St-Pierre is just steps away); some rooms face busy road. *Rooms from: €120 Rue Haute-Saint-Pierre, Saumur 02–41–50–33–00 www.saintpierresaumur.com 14 rooms, 1 suite No meals.*

EN ROUTE

Le Tasting Room. Based in an ancient farmhouse between Angers and Saumur, Le Tasting Room is a small company that showcases the Loire Valley's best wines through all-inclusive tastings and tours. Run by friendly British transplants Cathy and Nigel Henton, who have more than 25 years of experience in the wine industry, the fun, informative vino-themed experiences provide you with an insider's perspective. You'll be picked up at Angers train station, given a primer on local wines, served a home-cooked meal, and then taken to see the neighboring vineyards. The Hentons can also recommend local accommodations or help plan your day trip from Paris. Prices start at €130 per person. *37 chemin du Lavoir, Cumeray 02–41–79–80–21 www.letastingroom.com.*

4

ANGERS

45 km (28 miles) northwest of Saumur, 88 km (55 miles) northeast of Nantes.

The bustling city of Angers, on the banks of the Maine River, just north of the Loire, has a fine Gothic cathedral, a tempting selection of art galleries, plus a network of pleasant, traffic-free streets lined with half-timber houses. Its focal point, though, is the imposing, tower-ringed Château d'Angers. After contemplating the massive, medieval Apocalypse Tapestry, which is beautifully displayed inside it, cap your day with a sip of Cointreau, the popular locally made liqueur.

GETTING HERE AND AROUND

TGVs from Paris's Gare Montparnasse depart for Angers every hour or so; the 290-km (180-mile) trip takes 95 minutes (€25–€55). Multiple daily direct trains connect Angers to Saumur (20–30 mins, €9.10), Tours (60–95 mins, €19), Blois (85 mins, €27.50), and Orléans (2 hrs, 5 mins; €34.50). Angers's principal sights lie within a compact square formed by the three main boulevards and the Maine, all accessible via the city tramway.

Visitor Information Angers Tourist Office. *02-41-23-50-00 www.angersloiretourisme.com.*

EXPLORING

Carré Cointreau. To learn about the heartwarming liqueur made in Angers since 1849, head to the Carré Cointreau on the east side of the city. Guided tours of the distillery start with an introductory film, move past "cointreauversial" advertising posters, through the bottling plant and alembic room with its gleaming copper-pot stills, and end with a tasting. English tours are staged at 3 pm. City bus No. 6 from the Angers train station gets you here in 17 minutes. *2 bd. des Bretonnières, St-Barthélémy d'Anjou 02–41–31–50–50 www.carre-cointreau.fr €10 Tues.–Sat. 11–6 (reservations essential).*

Cathédrale St-Maurice. This 12th- and 13th-century Gothic edifice is noted for its curious Romanesque facade and original stained-glass windows; bring binoculars to appreciate both fully. The medieval Treasury is open to the public Monday through Saturday in summer (every other Saturday off-season) from 2:30 to 6. ✉ *Pl. Monseigneur-Chappoulie, Angers* ☎ *02–41–87–58–45.*

Château d'Angers. The banded black-and-white Château d'Angers, built by St-Louis (1228–38), glowers over the town from behind turreted moats, now laid out as gardens and overrun with flowers. As you explore the grounds, note the startling contrast between the thick defensive walls, guarded by a drawbridge and 17 massive round towers in a distinctive pattern, and the formal garden, with its delicate white-tufa chapel, erected in the 15th century. For a sweeping view of the city and surrounding countryside, climb one of the castle towers. A well-integrated modern gallery on the castle grounds contains the great **Tenture de l'Apocalypse** (Apocalypse Tapestry), woven in Paris in the 1380s for the Duke of Anjou. Measuring 16-feet high and 120-yards long, its many panels show a series of 70 horrifying and humorous scenes from the Book of Revelation. In one, mountains of fire fall from heaven while boats capsize and men struggle in the water; another features the Beast with Seven Heads. ✉ *2 promenade du Bout-du-Monde, Angers* ☎ *02–41–86–48–77* 🌐 *www.angers.monuments-nationaux.fr* 🎟 *€8.50 (audio guide €4.50)* ⏲ *May–Aug., daily 9:30–6:30; Sept.–Apr., daily 10–5:30.*

Musée des Beaux-Arts (*Fine Arts Museum*). Set within the 15th-century Logis Barrault, the Musée des Beaux-Arts has an art collection spanning the 14th to the 21st century, as well as a section depicting the history of Angers through archaeological and artistic works from the Neolithic period to the present. The vast museum complex combines historic architecture with contemporary lighting and signage to optimize the experience. ✉ *14 rue du Museé, Angers* ☎ *02–41–05–38–00* 🌐 *www.musees.angers.fr* 🎟 *€4 (€6 with temporary exhibition)* ⏲ *May–mid-Sept., daily 10–6; mid-Sept.–Apr., Tues.–Sun. 10–6.*

WHERE TO STAY

$ HOTEL **Mail.** A stately lime tree stands sentinel behind wrought-iron, wisteria-framed gates outside this 17th-century mansion with a surprisingly modern interior on a calm street between the Hôtel de Ville and the river. **Pros:** calm; good value. **Cons:** small rooms; those on the top floor can get quite warm in summer; no elevator. $ *Rooms from: €73* ✉ *8 rue des Ursules, Angers* ☎ *02–41–25–05–25* 🌐 *www.hoteldumail.fr* *26 rooms* *Breakfast.*

NIGHTLIFE AND PERFORMING ARTS

Angers Tempo Rives (*Angers Summer Music Festival*). In July and August, the Tempo Rives music festival hosts free riverfront concerts on Cale de la Savatte, in the shadow of the Château d'Angers. ✉ *Cale de la Savatte, Angers* ☎ *02–41–05–41–48* 🌐 *www.angers.fr.*

NORMANDY

WELCOME TO NORMANDY

TOP REASONS TO GO

★ **Mont-St-Michel:** The spire-top silhouette of this mighty offshore mound, dubbed the Marvel of the Occident, is one of the greatest sights in Europe. Plan to arrive at high tide, when the water races across the endless sands.

★ **Bayeux:** Come not just for the splendor of the tapestry telling how William conquered England, but also for untouched medieval buildings and the beefy, bonnet-top cathedral.

★ **Honfleur:** From France's prettiest harbor, bobbing with boats and lined with beam-fronted houses, you can head to the ravishing wooden church of Ste-Catherine.

★ **Rouen:** Sanctified by the memory of Jeanne d'Arc, hallowed by its towering Gothic cathedral, and graced by a huge Renaissance clock, Rouen is the gateway to Normandy.

★ **D-Day beaches:** Contemplate the dramatic deeds of World War II by visiting Caen's Mémorial, then touring the beaches from rocky Omaha to pancake-flat Utah.

1 Upper Normandy. Haute-Normandie is anchored by Rouen. Despite being battered in World War II, this alluring gateway city retains such an overwhelming number of churches, chapels, towers, fountains, and old cross-beam houses that many visitors take two full days to soak it all in. Heading some 60 km (35 miles) northwest to the Channel shore, the Côte d'Alabâtre (Alabaster Coast) beckons. Named for the white cliffs that stretch north, it includes the spectacular rock formations at Étretat that inspired Monet to pick up his paintbrush. Nearby Fécamp bridges the sacred and secular with its noted Benedictine abbey and distillery.

GETTING ORIENTED

The Seine Valley divides Normandy in two as it flows northwest from Paris through Rouen and into the English Channel at Le Havre. To the north lies Upper Normandy and a spectacular coastline of towering chalk cliffs called the Côte d'Alabâtre (Alabaster Coast). West of the Seine lies Lower Normandy, full of lush meadows and lined with the sandy beaches of the Côte Fleurie, or Flower Coast. (These are the same beaches where the Allies landed on D-Day.) Far to the west, at the foot of the sparsely populated Cotentin Peninsula, the offshore Mont-St-Michel patrols one of the continent's biggest bays.

2 Lower Normandy. Basse-Normandie begins with the sandy Côte Fleurie (Flower Coast), announced by seaside Honfleur, an artist's paradise full of half-timber houses. Just south, Rothschilds by the Rolls arrive in season at the Belle Époque beach resort of Deauville. Modern, student-filled Caen is famed for two gigantic abbey churches begun by William the Conqueror, who is immortalized in nearby Bayeux's legendary tapestry. This town makes a great base for exploring somber D-Day sites along Utah and Omaha beaches; bus tours and moving memorials make a fitting prelude for a drive across Normandy's Cotentin Peninsula to Mont-St-Michel, whose tiny island is crowned by one of the most gorgeous Gothic abbeys in France.

EATING AND DRINKING WELL IN NORMANDY

The felicitous combination of dairy farms, apple orchards, and the sea inspire Normandy's crème de la crème cuisine, featuring voluptuous cream sauces, tender cheeses, lavish seafood platters, and head-spinning Calvados brandy.

As befits one of France's best regional cuisines, Normandy boasts many delightful kitchens *(above)*; fresh-this-very-hour oysters *(right, top)*; great cheeses make great desserts *(right, bottom)*.

Normandy's verdant landscape—a patchwork of pastures and orchards bordered by the sea—heralds a region of culinary delights. The apples feature in tarts, cakes, sauces, and *cidre bouché,* a sparkling cider sold in cork-top bottles. Brown-and-white cows—the famous *vaches normandes*—grazing beneath the apple blossoms each produce up to seven gallons of milk a day, destined to become golden butter, thick crème fraîche, and prized cheeses. Coastal waters from Dieppe to Granville are equally generous, yielding sole, turbot, and oysters. To fully appreciate Normandy's gastronomic wealth, stroll through a weekend market, such as the splendid Saturday morning affair in Honfleur on Place Ste-Catherine, sample a seafood platter at a boardwalk café in Deauville, or meet the omelet of your dreams at La Mère Poulard at Mont-Saint-Michel.

APPLE COUNTRY

One fragrance evokes Normandy—the pungent, earthy smell of apples awaiting the press in autumn. Normandy is apple country, where apples with quaint varietal names, such as Windmill and Donkey Snout, are celebrated in the region's gastronomy, along the Route du Cidre, or at Vimoutier's Foire de la Pomme (Apple Festival) in October (where they vote for the Most Beautiful Apple).

CHEESE PLATTER

Camembert is king in the dairy realm of Normandy. Invented by a farmer's wife in the late 18th century, this tangy, opulently creamy cow's-milk cheese with a worldwide reputation hails from the Auge region. The best—Véritable Camembert de Normandie—with velvety white rinds and supple, sometimes oozy interiors, are produced on small farms, such as the esteemed Moulin de Carel.

Other members of Normandy's (cheese) board are the savory, grassy Pont L'Évêque, the impressively pungent Livarot with rust-color rind, and the Pavé d'Auge, a robust cheese with a honey-hue center.

CALVADOS

There are no wines in Normandy, but the region makes its mark in the spirits world with the apple-based Calvados, a fragrant oak-aged brandy.

Like Cognac, Calvados, which is distilled from cider, gets better and more expensive with age.

Top producers, such as Dupont in Victot-Pontfol and Pierre Huet in Cambremer, sell Calvados from "Vieux," aged a minimum of three years, to "X.O." or "Napoléon," aged from 6 to 25 years.

Many producers also offer Pommeau, an aperitif blending cider with a generous dose of Calvados.

ON THE HALF SHELL

Few places in France make an oyster lover happier than Normandy's Cotentin Peninsula, where the land juts into the sea a few miles beyond the Landing Beaches.

Ports such as Blanville-sur-Mer, Granville, and particularly St-Vaast-La Hougue, are where oystermen haul in tons of plump, briny oysters distinguished by a subtle note of hazelnut.

Enjoy a dozen on the half shell at the many traditional restaurants in this region, accompanied by a saucer of shallot vinegar and brown bread.

OMELET EXTRAORDINAIRE

There is no more famous omelet in the world than the puffy, pillow-like confection offered at La Mère Poulard in Mont-Saint-Michel.

Whipped with a balloon whisk in a large copper bowl, then cooked in a long-handled skillet over a wood fire, the omelet is delicately browned and crusted on the outside, as soft and airy as a soufflé within.

Order the omelet with ham and cheese as a main course, or sugared and flambéed as a divine dessert.

Updated By Jack Vermee

Normandy—shaped roughly like a jigsaw puzzle piece—sprawls across France's northwestern corner. Due to its geographic position, this region is blessed with a stunning natural beauty that once inspired Maupassant and Monet. Little wonder today's sightseers pack into colorful Rouen, seaside Honfleur, and magnificent Mont-St-Michel. Happily, it is easy to escape all those travelers. Simply lose yourself along the spectacular cliff-lined coast or in the green spaces inland, where the closest thing to a crowd is a farmer with his herd of brown-and-white cows. Whatever road you turn down, the region is sure to enchant.

Say the name "Normandy," and which Channel-side scenario comes to mind? Are you reminded of the dramatic silhouette of Mont-St-Michel looming above the tidal flats, its cobbles echoing with the footfalls of medieval scholars? Or do you think of iron-gray convoys massing silently at dawn, lowering tailgates to pour troops of young Allied infantrymen into the line of German machine-gun fire? At Omaha Beach you may marvel at the odds faced by the handful of soldiers who in June 1944 were able to rise above the waterfront carnage to capture the cliff-top battery, paving the way for the Allies' reconquest of Europe.

Perhaps you think of Joan of Arc—imprisoned by the English yet burned at the Rouen stake by the Church she believed in? In a modern church you may light a candle on the very spot where, in 1431, the Maiden Warrior sizzled into history at the hands of panicky politicians and time-serving clerics: a dark deed that marked a turning point in the Hundred Years' War.

The destinies of England and Normandy have been intertwined ever since William, Duke of Normandy, insisted that King Edward the Confessor had promised him the succession to the English crown. When a royal council instead anointed the Anglo-Saxon Harold Godwinsson, the irate William stormed across the Channel with 7,000 well-equipped archers, well-mounted knights, and well-paid Frankish mercenaries. They landed at Pevensey Bay on September 28, 1066, and two weeks later, conquered at Hastings.

There followed nearly 400 years of Norman sovereignty in England. For generations England and Normandie (as the French spell it) blurred, merged, and diverged. Today you can still feel the strong flow of English culture over the Channel, from the Deauville horse races frequented by high-born ladies in gloves, to silver spoons mounded high with teatime cream; from the bowfront, slope-roof shops along the harbor at Honfleur to the black-and-white row houses of Rouen, which would seem just as much at home in the setting of *David Copperfield* as they are in *Madame Bovary.*

The French divide Normandy into two: Haute-Normandie and Basse-Normandie. Upper (Haute) Normandy is delineated by the Seine as it meanders northwest from the Ile-de-France between chalky cliffs and verdant hills to Rouen—the region's cultural and commercial capital—and on to the port of Le Havre. Pebbly beaches and even more impressive chalk cliffs line the Côte d'Alabâtre (Alabaster Coast) from Le Havre to Dieppe. Lower (Basse) Normandy encompasses the sandy Côte Fleurie, stretching from the resort towns of Trouville and Deauville to the D-Day landing beaches and the Cotentin Peninsula, jutting out into the English Channel.

PLANNING

WHEN TO GO

July and August are the busiest months but also the most activity-filled: Concerts are held every evening at Mont-St-Michel, and the region's most important equestrian events are held in Deauville, culminating with the Gold Cup Polo Championship and the Grand Prix race in late August. June 6, the anniversary of the Allied invasion, is the most popular time to visit the D-Day beaches. If you're trying to avoid crowds, come in late spring or early autumn, when it is still fairly temperate. May finds the apple trees in full bloom and miles of waving flaxseed fields spotted with tiny sky-blue flowers. Some of Normandy's biggest events take place during these seasons: Rouen, for example, honors Joan of Arc at a festival named for her in late May, and Deauville hosts the American Film Festival in early September.

PLANNING YOUR TIME

Normandy is a big region with lots to see. If you have 10 days or so you can do it justice; if not, you'll need to prioritize. In search of natural beauty? Head to the coastline north of Le Havre. Prefer sea and sand? Beat it to the beaches west of Trouville. Love little villages? Honfleur is one of France's most picturesque old fishing ports. Like city life? Pretty Rouen is for you. Are you a history buff? Base yourself in Caen to tour the D-Day beaches. Can't get enough of churches and cathedrals? You can go pretty much anywhere, but don't miss Bayeux, Rouen, or

Mont-St-Michel. (The last is a bit isolated, so you might want to get there directly from Paris, or at the start or end of a Brittany tour.)

GETTING HERE AND AROUND

High-speed rail service is very limited in Normandy—perhaps because it's so close to Paris or because it's not on a lucrative route to a neighboring country; depending on your destination, though, the regional rail network can be helpful. Rouen is the train hub for Upper Normandy, Caen for Lower Normandy. Unless you're driving, you'll ultimately need a bus to reach coastal locales like Honfleur and Mont-St-Michel. To visit the D-Day beaches, a guided minibus tour, leaving from Caen or Bayeux, is your best bet. For motorists, the A13 expressway is the gateway from Paris, running northwest to Rouen and then to Caen. From here the A84 takes you almost all the way to Mont-St-Michel, and the N13 brings you to Bayeux. If you're arriving from England or northern Europe, the A16/A28 from Calais to Rouen is a scenic (and near-empty) delight.

AIR TRAVEL

Air travelers will likely land at one of Paris's two major airports and proceed onward by bus, train, or car; however, Normandy does have its own regional facilities. These include Aéroport de Caen-Carpiquet, which receives regular flights from Air France (🌐 *www.airfrance.com*) and budget carrier HOP! (🌐 *www.hop.com*); and Aéroport de Deauville-Normandie, which receives twice-weekly flights from London operated by CityJet (🌐 *www.cityjet.com*). Note: If your primary goal is to see Mont-St-Michel, Ryanair (🌐 *www.ryanair.com*) flies from London to the Breton town of Dinard (*02–99–46–18–46* 🌐 *www.dinard.aeroport.fr*), putting you just 56 km (35 miles) west of the Mont.

Airport Information **Aéroport de Caen-Carpiquet.** ☎ *02–31–71–20–10* 🌐 *www.caen.aeroport.fr.* **Aéroport de Deauville-Normandie.** ☎ *02–31–65–65–65* 🌐 *www.deauville.aeroport.fr.*

BUS TRAVEL

Cars Perier runs buses from Fécamp to Le Havre, stopping in Étretat along the way. Bus Verts du Calvados covers the coast, connecting Caen with Honfleur, Bayeux, and other towns. Bus routes operated by Keolis and VTNI link many destinations, including Rouen, Fécamp, Étretat, Le Havre, Caen, Honfleur, Deauville, Trouville, and Arromanches. For Mont-St-Michel, catch buses from nearby Pontorson, or from St-Malo or Rennes in adjacent Brittany. Schedules are available at tourist offices and at the local *gare routière* (bus station).

Bus Information **Bus Verts du Calvados.** ☎ *08–10–21–42–14* 🌐 *www.busverts.fr.* **Cars Perier.** ☎ *08–00–80–87–03* 🌐 *www.cars-perier.fr.* **Keolis.** ☎ *02–99–19–70–70* 🌐 *www.keolis-emeraude.com.* **VTNI.** ☎ *02–32–08–19–75* 🌐 *www.vtni.fr.*

CAR TRAVEL

From Paris, A13 slices its way to Rouen in 1½ hours (toll €14.40) before forking to Caen (an additional 87 mins, toll €8.90) or Le Havre (45 mins on A131, toll €5.40). N13 continues from Caen to Bayeux in another two hours. At Caen, the A84 forks off southwest toward

Mont-St-Michel and Rennes. The Pont de Normandie, spanning the Seine between Le Havre and Honfleur, effectively unites Upper and Lower Normandy.

FERRY AND EUROTUNNEL TRAVEL

A number of companies sail between the United Kingdom and ports in Normandy. Brittany Ferries travels from Portsmouth to Le Havre, Caen, and Cherbourg year-round; its vessels run from Poole to Cherbourg as well. Daily ferries operated by LD lines connect Newhaven with Dieppe, and Dover with Calais or Dunkirk. The quickest crossing—a four-hour voyage between Newhaven and Dieppe—costs about €100 for a car and two passengers. If you'd rather travel under the Channel than on it, you can drive your car or motorcycle onto a Eurotunnel train at Folkestone for the 35-minute trip to Calais.

Boat Information Brittany Ferries. ☎ *08–25–82–88–28 in France (€0.15 per min), 0871–244–0744 in U.K. (£0.10 per min)* 🌐 *www.brittany-ferries.com.* **Eurotunnel Le Shuttle.** ☎ *08–10–63–03–04 in France (€0.15 per min), 0844–335–3535 in U.K.* 🌐 *www.eurotunnel.com.* **LD Lines.** ☎ *08–25–30–43–04 in France (€0.15 per min), 0844–576–8836 in U.K.* 🌐 *www.ldlines.fr.*

5

TRAIN TRAVEL

Although there is no direct TGV service from Paris, separate SNCF rail lines originating at Gare St-Lazare head to Upper Normandy (Rouen and Le Havre) and Lower Normandy (Deauville-Trouville, Caen, and Bayeux, sometimes requiring a change in Lisieux). But unless you're content to stick to the major towns, visiting Normandy by train can be frustrating. You can occasionally reach smaller ones (such as Fécamp) on snail-paced branch lines, but the irregular intricacies of what is said to be Europe's most complicated regional timetable may prove daunting. Other destinations, like Honfleur, Étretat, or Mont-St-Michel, invariably require a train/bus combination.

Train Information Gare SNCF Rouen. 🌐 *www.gares-en-mouvement.com/fr/frurd/accueil.* **SNCF.** ☎ *3635 €0.34 per min* 🌐 *www.ter-sncf.com.*

TOURING THE D-DAY BEACHES

One of modern history's landmark events—the D-Day invasion of June 1944—was enacted on the beaches of Normandy. Omaha Beach, Utah Beach, as well as many sites on the Cotentin Peninsula, all bear witness to the furious fighting that once raged in this now-peaceful corner of France. Today, as seagulls sweep over the cliffs where American rangers scrambled desperately up ropes to silence murderous German batteries, visitors wander through the blockhouses and peer into the bomb craters, the carnage of battle now a distant, if still horrifying, memory.

Unless you have a car, the D-Day beaches are best visited by bus. Public ones are relatively rare, but Bus No. 74 does go to Arromanches and Bus No. 70 heads to Omaha Beach and the American cemetery (summer only); both are operated by Bus Verts du Calvados and originate in Bayeux. The company also has a "Circuit Caen-Omaha Beach" route that connects many of the D-Day sights.

As for guided bus excursions, Normandy Tours departs twice daily from Bayeux's Hôtel de la Gare, carrying passengers in an eight-person minibus. The guides are walking encyclopedias of local war lore and may be flexible about points interesting to you. Half-day tours (€62 including museum fees) are available all year in English; full-day outings are offered as well.

Other Bayeux-based outfits include Normandy Sightseeing Tours, with half- and full-day options costing €45–€60 and €90 respectively. Paul Woodadge, the "D-Day Historian," offers highly acclaimed, customized tours for up to eight people with an all-inclusive price tag of €600 for a full-day, full-immersion experience (children under 12 not permitted).

In Caen, the stunning Mémorial museum organizes a series of English-language outings; prices (starting at €42) depend on the sites included and mode of transportation used. If you're staying in Paris—and have lots of stamina—Paris City Vision also runs 12- to 14-hour tours to key D-Day locales; the cost is €175 by coach and €252 by minivan.

D-Day Historian. ☎ *02–31–22–28–82* 🌐 *www.ddayhistorian.com* ☞ *payment via PayPal only.*

Mémorial Tours. ✉ *Esplanade General Eisenhower, Caen* ☎ *02–31–06–06–45 tour bookings* 🌐 *www.memorial-caen.fr.*

Normandy Sightseeing Tours. ✉ *6 rue St-Jean, Bayeux* ☎ *02–31–51–70–52* 🌐 *www.normandy-sightseeing-tours.com.*

Normandy Tours. ✉ *Hôtel de la Gare, 26 pl. de la Gare, Bayeux* ☎ *02–31–92–10–70* 🌐 *www.normandy-landing-tours.com.*

Paris City Vision. ✉ *2 rue des Pyramides, Opéra, Paris* ☎ *01–44–55–61–00* 🌐 *www.pariscityvision.com.*

RESTAURANTS

Most of Normandy's smaller restaurants and family-run eateries rely heavily on seasonal customers, so some close in winter. However, the region's proximity to Paris and its thriving "casino culture" ensure that the many Michelin-starred and Grand Hotel options remain open year-round. Local specialties differ from place to place. Rouen is famous for *canard à la rouennaise* (duck in blood sauce); Caen, for *tripes à la mode de Caen* (tripe cooked with carrots in a seasoned cider stock); Mont-St-Michel, for omelets Mère Poulard and *pré-salé* (salt-meadow lamb). Fish and seafood lovers can feast on oysters, lobster, shrimp, and sole *dieppoise* (poached in a sauce with cream and mussels) all along the coast.

HOTELS

Accommodations to suit every taste can be found throughout Normandy, from basic bed-and-breakfasts to luxurious hotels—although there's a slimmer selection of the latter than you might expect in the region's two largest cities (Rouen and Caen). Even in popular resort towns like Deauville and Trouville it's possible to find delightful, inexpensive vacation spots. Spending the night on Mont-St-Michel is especially memorable, but be sure to reserve your room weeks in advance. Prices are ratcheted up in summer all along the coast, and you will need to book ahead, especially on weekends. In the beach resorts the season runs from the end of April to October, and many hotels are closed in winter. *Hotel reviews have been shortened. For full information, visit Fodors.com.*

WHAT IT COSTS IN EUROS				
	$	$$	$$$	$$$$
Restaurants	under €18	€18–€24	€25–€32	over €32
Hotels	under €106	€106–€145	€146–€215	over €215

Restaurant prices are the average cost of a main course at dinner or, if dinner is not served, at lunch. Hotel prices are the lowest cost of a standard double room in high season.

VISITOR INFORMATION

The Normandy Regional Tourist Board's website is an invaluable source of information. For specifics about visiting Upper Normandy, contact Région Haute-Normandie; for Lower Normandy, contact Région Basse-Normandie. The numerous local tourist offices (listed under town names below) are also very useful.

5

Normandy Regional Tourist Board. ☎ *02–32–33–79–00* 🌐 *www.normandie-tourisme.fr.*

Région Basse-Normandie. ✉ *Abbaye-aux-Dames, Pl. Reine Mathilde, Caen* ☎ *02–31–06–98–98* 🌐 *www.region-basse-normandie.fr.*

Région Haute-Normandie. ✉ *Hôtel de Région, 5 rue Robert Schuman, Rouen* ☎ *02–35–52–56–00* 🌐 *www.hautenormandie.fr.*

UPPER NORMANDY

From Rouen to the coast, medieval castles and abbeys stand guard above rolling countryside, while seaside vacation communities and vintage fishing towns line the white cliffs of the Côte d'Alabâtre (Alabaster Coast). In the 19th century, the dramatic scenery and bathing resorts along this shore attracted creative souls like Maupassant, Monet, and Braque—and today it has the same effect on thousands of visitors.

ROUEN

130 km (80 miles) northwest of Paris, 86 km (53 miles) east of Le Havre.

Fodor's Choice ★

"O Rouen, art thou then to be my final abode!" was the agonized cry of Joan of Arc as the English dragged her out to be burned alive in the market square on May 30, 1431. The exact location of her pyre is marked by a concrete-and-metal cross in front of the modern Église Jeanne-d'Arc—and that eye-catching, flame-evoking church is just one of the many landmarks that make this sizable port city so fascinating. Once the capital of the duchy of Normandy, it was hit hard during World War II, but a wealth of medieval half-timber houses still line the tiny cobblestone streets of Vieux Rouen. The most famous of those streets—Rue du Gros-Horloge, between Place du Vieux-Marché (where Joan burned) and Cathédrale Notre-Dame—is suitably embellished halfway along

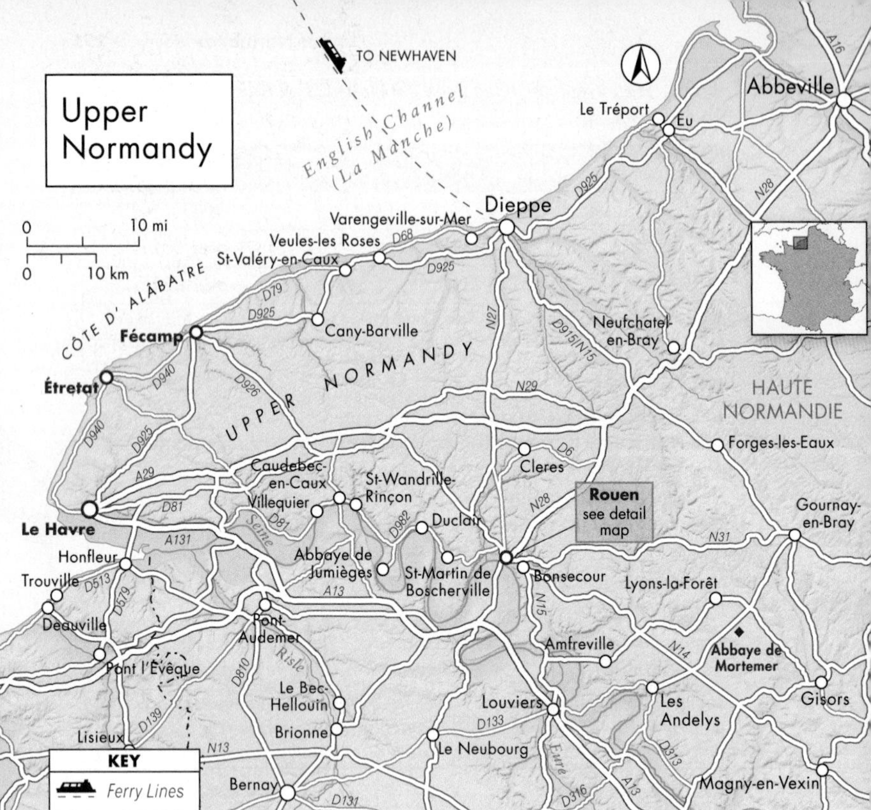

with a massive and much photographed 14th-century horloge (clock). Of course, the glorious cathedral itself is nothing to scoff at: Claude Monet immortalized it in a memorable series of paintings.

GETTING HERE

Rouen-bound trains leave Paris's Gare St-Lazare every half hour or so (85 mins, €24.10); rail links are also available from Caen (90 mins, €27.50) and Fécamp (90 mins, €15.30).

Visitor Information Rouen Tourist Office. ☎ *02–32–08–32–40* 🌐 *www.rouentourisme.com.*

EXPLORING

TOP ATTRACTIONS

Abbaye St-Ouen. Next to the imposing neoclassical City Hall, this stupendous example of high Gothic architecture is noted for its stained-glass windows, dating from the 14th to the 16th century. They are the most spectacular grace notes of the spare interior along with the 19th-century pipe organ, among the finest in France. ✉ *Portail des Marmousets, Pl. du Général-de-Gaulle, Rouen* ☎ *02–32–08–13–90* 🌐 *www.rouen.fr/abbatiale-saint-ouen* ⏲ *Apr.–Oct., Tues.–Thurs. and weekends 10–noon and 2–6; Nov.–Mar., Tues.–Thurs. and weekends 10–noon and 2–5.*

> ## MONET IN 3-D
>
> If you're familiar with the works of Impressionist artist Claude Monet, you'll immediately recognize Rouen Cathedral's immense west front, rendered in an increasingly hazy fashion in his series *Cathédrales de Rouen*. Enjoy a ringside view and a coffee at the Brasserie Paul, just opposite. The facade is illuminated by a free light show, based on Monet's canvases, for an hour every evening from June through mid-September.

5

Cathédrale Notre-Dame (*Rouen Cathedral*). Even in the so-called "City of 100 Spires" the one crowning this cathedral stands out. Erected in 1876, it's the highest in France—a cast-iron tour de force rising 490 feet above the crossing. The original 12th-century construction was replaced after a devastating fire in 1200; only the left-hand spire, the **Tour St-Romain** (St. Romanus Tower), survived the flames. Construction on the imposing 250-foot steeple on the right, known as the **Tour de Beurre** (Butter Tower), was begun in the 15th century and completed in the 17th, when a group of wealthy citizens donated large sums of money for the privilege of continuing to eat butter during Lent. Interior highlights include the 13th-century choir, with its pointed arcades; vibrant stained glass depicting the crucified Christ (restored after heavy damage during World War II); and massive stone columns topped by some intriguing carved faces. The first flight of the famous **Escalier de la Librairie** (Library Stairway), attributed to Guillaume Pontifs (also responsible for most of the 15th-century work seen in the cathedral), rises from a tiny balcony just to the left of the transept. ✉ *Pl. de la Cathédrale, St-Maclou, Rouen* ☎ *02–35–71–51–23 tour reservation* 🌐 *www.cathedrale-rouen.net* 🎫 *Tours €2* ⏲ *Apr.–Oct., Mon. 2–6, Tues.–Sat. 9–7, Sun. 8–6; Nov.–Mar., Mon. 2–6, Tues.–Sat. 9–noon and 2–6, Sun. 2–6.*

Gros-Horloge. The name of the pedestrian Rue du Gros-Horloge, Rouen's most popular street, comes from the Gros-Horloge itself, a giant Renaissance clock. In 1527 the Rouennais had a splendid arch built especially for it, and today its golden face looks out over the street. You can see the clock's inner workings from the 15th-century belfry. Though the street is crammed with stores, a few old houses dating from the 16th century remain. Wander through the surrounding **Vieux Rouen** (Old Rouen), a warren of tiny streets lined with more than 700 half-timber houses, many artfully transformed into fashionable shops. ✉ *Rue du Gros-Horloge, Vieux-Marché, Rouen* ☎ *02–32–08–01–90* 🎫 *€6* ⏲ *Apr.–June, Sept., and Oct., Tues.–Sun. 10–1 and 2–7; July and Aug., daily 9–6; Nov.–Mar., Tues.–Sun. 2–6.*

Musée des Beaux-Arts (*Fine Arts Museum*). One of Rouen's cultural mainstays, this museum is famed for its stellar collection of paintings and sculptures from the 16th to the 20th century, including works by native son Géricault as well as by David, Rubens, Caravaggio, Velasquez, Poussin, Delacroix, Degas, and Modigliani. Most popular of all, however, is the impressive Impressionist gallery, with Monet, Renoir, and Sisley, plus the Postimpressionist School of Rouen headed by Albert Lebourg and Gustave Loiseau. ✉ *Esplanade Marcel-Duchamp, Gare, Rouen* ☎ *02–35–71–28–40* 🌐 *www.mbarouen.fr* 🎫 *€5 (free first Sun.*

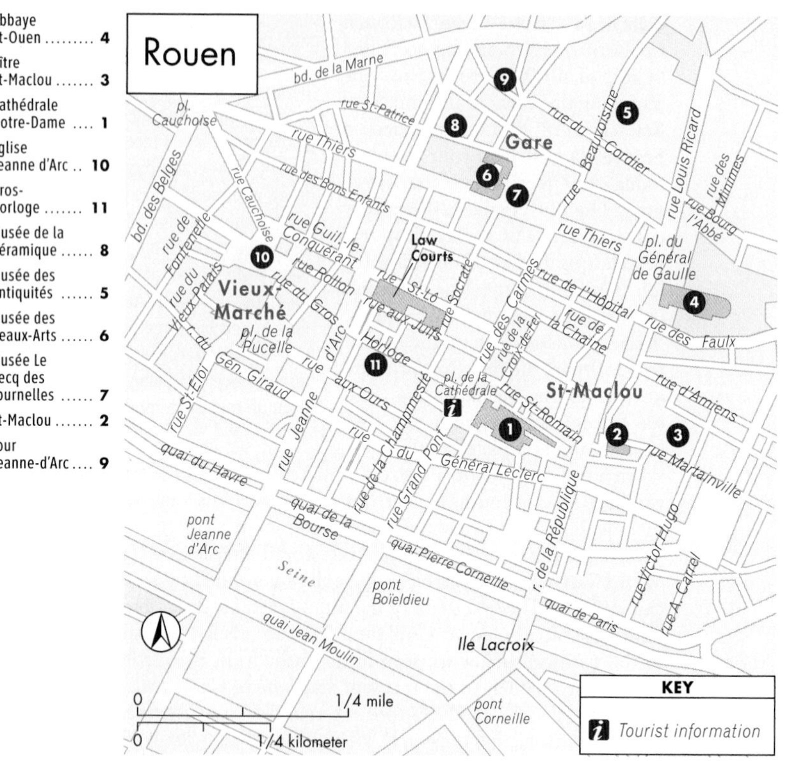

of month), €8 includes Musée Le Secq des Tournelles and Musée de la Céramique ⏲ Wed.–Mon. 10–6.

St-Maclou. A late-Gothic masterpiece, this church sits across Rue de la République behind the cathedral and bears testimony to the wild excesses of Flamboyant architecture. Take time to examine the central and left-hand portals of the main facade, covered with little bronze lion heads and pagan engravings. Inside, note the 16th-century organ, with its Renaissance wood carving, and the fine marble columns. ✉ *3 pl. Barthélémy, St-Maclou, Rouen* ☎ *02–32–08–13–90* ⏲ *Apr.–Oct., Sat.–Mon. 10–noon and 2–6; Nov.–Mar., Sat.–Mon. 10–noon and 2–5:30.*

Tour Jeanne-d'Arc. Sole remnant of the early-13th-century castle built by French king Philippe-Auguste, this beefy, pointed-top circular tower provides a fine photo op. Inside you'll find a small exhibit of documents and models charting the history of the castle where Joan of Arc was tried and held prisoner in 1430. ✉ *Rue Bouvreuil, Gare, Rouen* ☎ *02–35–98–16–21* 🌐 *www.tourjeannedarc.fr* 🎫 *€1.50* ⏲ *Apr.–Sept., Mon.–Sat. 10–12:30 and 2–6, Sun. 2–6:30; Oct.–Mar., Mon.–Sat. 10–12:30 and 2–5, Sun. 2–5:30.*

WORTH NOTING

Aître St-Maclou. This former ossuary (a charnel house used for the bodies of plague victims) is a reminder of the "Black Death" that devastated Europe during the Middle Ages; these days it holds Rouen's Fine Art Academy. French composer Camille Saint-Saëns (1835–1921) is said to have been inspired by the ossuary when he was working on his *Danse Macabre*. The half-timber courtyard, where you can wander at leisure, and perhaps see an art exhibition, contains graphic carvings of skulls, bones, and gravediggers' tools. ✉ *186 rue Martainville, St-Maclou, Rouen* ☎ *02–76–08–81–13* ⊙ *Daily 9–6.*

Église Jeanne d'Arc (*Joan of Arc Church*). Dedicated to Joan of Arc, this church was built in the 1970s on the spot where she was burned to death in 1431. The aesthetic merit of its odd cement-and-wood design is debatable—the shape of the roof is *supposed* to symbolize the flames of Joan's fire. Not all is new, however: the church showcases some remarkable 16th-century stained-glass windows taken from the former Église St-Vincent, bombed out in 1944. ✉ *Pl. du Vieux-Marché, Vieux-Marché, Rouen* ☎ *02–32–08–13–90* ⊙ *Mon.–Thurs. and Sat. 10–noon and 2–6, Fri. and Sun. 2–6.*

5

Musée de la Céramique (*Ceramics Museum*). A superb array of local pottery and European porcelain can be admired at this museum, housed in an elegant mansion near the Musée des Beaux-Arts. ✉ *1 rue Faucon, Gare, Rouen* ☎ *02–35–07–31–74* 🌐 *rouen-musees.fr* 🎫 *€3 (free first Sun. of month), €8 includes Musée Le Secq des Tournelles and Musée des Beaux-Arts* ⊙ *Wed.–Mon. 2–6.*

Musée des Antiquités. Gallo-Roman glassware and mosaics, medieval tapestries and enamels, and Moorish ceramics vie for attention inside this extensive antiquities museum. Occupying a former 17th-century monastery, it also has a display devoted to natural history, which includes some skeletons dating to prehistoric times. ✉ *198 rue Beauvoisine, Gare, Rouen* ☎ *02–35–98–55–10* 🌐 *www.museedesantiquites.fr* 🎫 *€3.50* ⊙ *Tues.–Sat. 10–12:15 (during school holidays only) and 1:30–5:30, Sun. 2–6.*

Musée Le Secq des Tournelles (*Wrought Iron Museum*). Not far from the Musée des Beaux-Arts, this museum claims to have the world's finest collection of wrought iron, with exhibits spanning the 4th through the 19th century. The displays, imaginatively housed in a converted medieval church, include the professional instruments of surgeons, barbers, carpenters, clockmakers, and gardeners. ✉ *2 rue Jacques-Villon, Gare, Rouen* ☎ *02–35–88–42–92* 🌐 *www.museelesecqdestournelles.fr* 🎫 *€3 (free first Sun. of month), €8 includes Musée des Beaux-Arts and Musée de la Céramique* ⊙ *Wed.–Mon. 2–6.*

NEED A BREAK?

Maison Hardy. The friendly Maison Hardy offers zestful service and a splendid view of the picturesque market square, scene of the burning of Joan of Arc, whose story is retraced in colorful frescoes on the café wall. ✉ ***22 pl. du Vieux-Marché, Vieux-Marché, Rouen*** ☎ ***02–35–71–81–55*** 🌐 ***www.hardy-traiteur.com*** ⊙ ***Mon.–Sat. 8:30–7:30.***

WHERE TO EAT

$$ BISTRO Fodor's Choice ★ ✕ **Gill Côté Bistro.** With two Michelin stars under his toque for his tony gastronomic Restaurant Gill, Chef Gilles Tournadre jumped at the chance to open a bistro on Rouen's storied Place du Vieux-Marché. Sleek and modern, it specializes in updated bistro fare. You can order inspired versions of beloved French classics like *tête de veau* (calf's head) with *sauce gribich* (a caper, parsley, and cornichon Hollandaise) or *andouillette* (tripe sausage), along with more contemporary dishes, including a piquant Caesar salad. Portions are ample and the small but choice menu—with a great-value €22 fixed-price option—changes monthly. Call ahead to reserve a table. *Average main: €22 ✉ 14 pl. du Vieux-Marché, Vieux-Marché, Rouen ☎ 02–35–89–88–72 ⊕ www.gill-cote-bistro.fr ✍ Reservations essential.*

THE MESSENGER

Before Joan of Arc was torched on Rouen's Place du Vieux-Marché, she asked a friar to hold a crucifix high in the air and to shout out assurances of her salvation so that she could hear him above the roar of the fire.

$$$$ MODERN FRENCH Fodor's Choice ★ ✕ **La Couronne.** If P.T. Barnum, Florenz Ziegfeld, and Cecil B. DeMille had put together a spot distilling all the charm and glamour of Normandy, this would be it. Behind a half-timber facade gushing geraniums, the "oldest inn in France," dating from 1345, is a sometimes-ersatz extravaganza crammed with stained leaded glass, sculpted wood beams, marble Norman chimneys, leather-upholstered chairs, and damask curtains. The Salon Jeanne d'Arc is the largest room and has a wonderful wall-wide sash window and quaint paintings, but the only place to sit is the adorably cozy, wood-lined Salon des Rôtisseurs, an antiquarian's delight. The star attractions on Vincent Taillefer's menu—lobster stew with chestnut, sheeps' feet, duck in blood sauce—make few modern concessions. Dine here and you'll be adding your name to a list that includes Sophia Loren, John Wayne, Jean-Paul Sartre, Salvador Dalí, and Princess Grace of Monaco. The €35 dinner menu is an excellent value. *Average main: €36 ✉ 31 pl. du Vieux-Marché, Vieux-Marché, Rouen ☎ 02–35–71–40–90 ⊕ www.lacouronne.com.fr ✍ Reservations essential.*

$ FRENCH ✕ **Le 37.** The excellent price-to-quality quotient at this sleek little eatery has made it one of Rouen's hot spots. Chef Sylvain Nouin focuses on contemporary bistro fare, and what his monthly changing menu lacks in size (it fits on a small blackboard) it more than makes up for in style. The two-course set menu—featuring dishes like an oxtail *mille-feuille* with a celeriac starter, coriander-roasted chicken with ginger-carrot mousseline, or slow-cooked lamb shank with port-infused prunes and panfried polenta—is a steal at €19.80. The solid wine list is an added bonus. *Average main: €16 ✉ 37 rue Saint-Etienne-des-Tonneliers, Vieux-Marché, Rouen ☎ 02–35–70–56–65 ⊕ www.le37.fr ⊗ Closed Sun., Mon., and 1st 3 wks of Aug.*

$$$$ FRENCH ✕ **Les Nymphéas.** Chef Alexandre Dessaux, formerly second-in-command under Patrick Kukurudz (who served Norman haute cuisine to the town's gourmands for almost 30 years), took over as head chef in 2012, thus preserving the traditions of this venerable dining room. At

DID YOU KNOW?

Dating from the 14th century, the Gros-Horloge clock is the heart of Vieux Rouen, a warren of tiny streets lined with more than 700 half-timber houses, many gorgeously transformed into shops.

the end of a cobbled courtyard in the city's Old Town, the half-timber building is a vintage charmer, and the elegant dining room is cozy and hushed. Regional flourishes—such as panfried bass with braised leeks in a Champagne sauce, squab with cabbage and duck foie gras, or duck breast doused in Bordelaise coulis—dominate the menu. There are several excellent prix-fixe dinner menus (€42–€74), but the best bargain is the weekly lunch menu (€27), which includes a glass of wine. *Average main: €35 7-9 rue de la Pie, Vieux-Marché, Rouen 02–35–89–26–69 www.lesnympheas-rouen.com Closed Mon. No lunch Tues., no dinner Sun.*

$$$$ FRENCH Fodor's Choice ★ **Restaurant Gill.** On the quay at the heart of Rouen's gastronomic epicenter, Rouen's only Michelin two-star restaurant goes to great lengths to make sure you feel pampered from start to finish. That's not hard to do when Chef Gilles Tournadre (and his charming wife Sylvie) are in charge of things. With a reputation for culinary rigor, this native son is well versed in the splendors of the Norman woods, fields, and shore: oysters, crab, scallops, lobster, and several types of fish can be found on the menu every day, year-round, along with hare, piglet, and sweetbreads. Signature dishes include pigeon *à la Rouennaise* and panfried bass with cider jus, apple-onion marmalade, and creamy Calvados foam. When ordering your dinner, remember to request the soufflé made with (what else?) a silky old Norman Calvados. Although the tasting menu is pricey (€98), it's worth the splurge for a primer in one of France's great regional cuisines. *Average main: €38 8–9 quai de la Bourse, Vieux-Marché, Rouen 02–35–71–16–14 www.gill.fr Closed Sun., Mon., 2 wks in Mar., and 1st 3 wks in Aug. Reservations essential.*

WHERE TO STAY

$$ HOTEL **Best Western–Dieppe.** Established in 1880, the Dieppe remains up-to-date thanks to resolute management by five generations of the Guéret family who welcome guests to their fine restaurant and compact accommodations; guest rooms (No. 22 is the largest) all have modern color schemes, refurbished bathrooms, and flat-screen TVs. **Pros:** personal service; helpful, English-speaking owners; convenient to train station. **Cons:** slightly corporate; street noise gets through in spite of double-glazed windows; a bit away from city center. *Rooms from: €120 Pl. Bernard Tissot, Gare, Rouen 02–35–71–96–00 www.hotel-dieppe.fr 41 rooms No meals.*

$ HOTEL **Cathédrale.** There are enough half-timber walls and beams here to fill a super-luxe hotel, but the happy news is that this is a budget option—even better, this 17th-century building is found on a narrow pedestrian street just behind Rouen's cathedral. **Pros:** storybook surroundings; can't-be-beat location. **Cons:** some small rooms; no car access. *Rooms from: €90 12 rue St-Romain, St-Maclou, Rouen 02–35–71–57–95 www.hotel-de-la-cathedrale.fr 26 rooms Breakfast.*

$$$$ HOTEL Fodor's Choice ★ **Marriott–Hotel de Bourgtheroulde.** One of Normandy's most magnificent *hôtels particuliers* (family mansions) opened its doors in 2010 to become Rouen's finest hotel. **Pros:** gorgeously Gothic; attentive staff; steps from the center of historic Rouen. **Cons:** minimalism is not for everyone. *Rooms from: €270 15 pl. de la Pucelle, Vieux-Marché,*

Rouen ☎ *02–35–14–50–50* 🌐 *www.hotelsparouen.com* *78 rooms* *Some meals.*

$$ **Mercure–Centre Cathedrale Hotel.** In the jumble of streets near Rouen's HOTEL cathedral—a navigational challenge if you arrive by car—this modern chain hotel has small, comfortable guest rooms decorated in breezy pastels. **Pros:** functional; central; breakfast (included in the price) has a gluten-free option. **Cons:** interiors lack character; hard to find. *Rooms from: €125* ✉ *7 rue de la Croix-de-Fer, St-Maclou, Rouen* ☎ *02–35–52–69–52* 🌐 *www.mercure.com* *125 rooms* *Breakfast.*

$ **Vieux Carré.** In the heart of Old Rouen, this cute hotel has practical HOTEL and comfortable rooms that, while recently refurbished, retain their taste for the exotic: picture lamps from Egypt, tables from Morocco, and 1940s English armoires. **Pros:** charming; central; exceptional prices. **Cons:** small rooms; parking 220 yards away. *Rooms from: €62* ✉ *34 rue Ganterie, Gare, Rouen* ☎ *02–35–71–67–70* 🌐 *www.hotel-vieux-carre.com* *13 rooms* *No meals.*

5

NIGHTLIFE AND PERFORMING ARTS

Bar de la Crosse. Enjoy an aperitif and a good chat with some outgoing Rouennais at this popular local haunt. You can take advantage of free Wi-Fi, too. ✉ *53 rue de l'Hôpital, St-Maclou, Rouen* ☎ *02–35–70–16–68* ⏲ *Tues.–Sat. 9–9.*

Fête Jeanne d'Arc (*Joan of Arc Festival*). Parades, street plays, concerts, exhibitions, and a medieval market are just a few of the exciting events that mark the annual homage to Rouen's fabled martyr; it takes place on the Sunday nearest to May 30th. ✉ *Rouen* ☎ *02–32–08–69–71* 🌐 *www.rouen.fr.*

Théâtre des Arts. Operas, plays, and concerts are staged at the Théâtre des Arts. ✉ *7 rue du Dr-Rambert, Vieux-Marché, Rouen* ☎ *02–35–98–74–78 ticket office* 🌐 *www.operaderouen.com.*

FÉCAMP

71 km (44 miles) northwest of Rouen, 17 km (11 miles) northeast of Étretat via D940.

Founded in the 10th century as a fishing port (the name is a Germanic form of "fish"), Fécamp still relies on the sea for its sustenance. After taking in the sights, be sure to sample the catch of the day in one of its harborside eateries; you can cap the meal with a dram of Bénédictine, the town's own herbal liqueur.

GETTING HERE

Multiple train-bus combinations arrive from Rouen daily via Breaute (90 mins, €15.30); and Cars Perier's No. 24 bus comes in from Le Havre via Étretat (90 mins, €2).

Visitor Information Fécamp Tourist Office. ☎ *02–35–28–51–01* 🌐 *www.fecamptourisme.com.*

EXPLORING

Abbaye de La Trinité. The ancient cod-fishing port of Fécamp was once a major pilgrimage site, and this magnificent abbey church bears witness to its religious past. Founded by the Duke of Normandy in the 11th century, the Benedictine abbey became the home of the monastic order of the Précieux Sang de la Trinité (Precious Blood of the Trinity—referring to Christ's blood, which supposedly arrived here in the 7th century in a reliquary from the Holy Land). ✉ *Pl. des Ducs Richard, Fécamp* ⏲ *Daily, except during services.*

Palais de la Bénédictine (*Benedictine Palace*). Fécamp is also the home of Benedictine liqueur. The Palais de la Bénédictine, across from the tourist office, is a florid building dating from 1892 that mixes neo-Gothic and Renaissance styles. Watery pastiche or taste-tingling architectural cocktail? Whether you're shaken or stirred, this remains one of Normandy's most popular attractions. The interior is just as exhausting as the facade. Paintings, sculptures, ivories, advertising posters, and fake bottles of Bénédictine compete for attention with a display of the ingredients used for the liqueur, and a chance to sample it. There's also a shop selling Bénédictine products and souvenirs. ✉ *110 rue Alexandre-le-Grand, Fécamp* ☎ *02–35–10–26–10* 🌐 *www.benedictine.fr* 🎟 *€8, €12 with guide* ⏲ *Mid-Apr.–early July and early Sept.—mid-Oct., daily 10–1 and 2–6.30; early July–early Sept., daily 10–7; times vary other months, so check website before visiting.*

WHERE TO EAT AND STAY

$ SEAFOOD ✕ **La Marée.** Overlooking Fécamp's lively harbor, this popular seafood restaurant makes up in conviviality what it lacks in charm. Considering the number of copious seafood *plateaux* that breeze by, it seems no one pays much attention to style anyway. For sheer volume, the dishes will please even the most insatiable gourmand; factor in variety and freshness (most everything is caught locally) and you've got a winning combo. Gigantic langoustine, plump crabs, and the renowned Fécamp herring are standouts. Other good choices include the whole grilled sole and the salt cod poached in Normandy cream, a hearty local specialty. The lunch *formule* (€17.50) is a good bargain. $ *Average main: €17* ✉ *77 quai Bérigny, Fécamp* ☎ *02–35–29–39–15* 🌐 *www.restaurant-maree-fecamp.fr* ⏲ *Closed Jan. No dinner Sun. and Thurs.*

$$ FRENCH ✕ **Le Vicomté.** Market-fresh ingredients grace a daily-changing set menu (€19) at this friendly and inexpensive Fécamp favorite. On it, you might find grilled scallops or celeriac rémoulade to start, and a rich dogfish stew or guinea fowl in cider sauce for mains, all followed by cheese, a choice of homemade desserts, and coffee. Popular with locals and visitors alike, the limited space brings guests well within elbow reach to share simple fare, dished up with aplomb and humor by *le patron.* $ *Average main: €19* ✉ *4 rue du Président-René-Coty, Fécamp* ☎ *02–35–28–47–63* ⏲ *Closed Sun. and Wed., 1st wk of May, last 2 wks of Aug., and Dec. 20–Jan. 4* ✍ *Reservations essential.*

$ B&B/INN 🏨 **Auberge de la Rouge.** The Enderlins welcome you to this little inn just south of Fécamp, where you can enjoy guest rooms overlooking a pretty garden and also savor local specialties in the fine on-site restaurant. **Pros:** spacious rooms; family feel. **Cons:** away from town center; busy road outside. *Rooms from: €69 ✉ 445 rte. du Havre, St-Léonard, Fécamp ☎ 02–35–28–07–59 🌐 www.auberge-rouge.com ⏲ Closed Christmas wk 🛏 8 rooms 🍽 Breakfast.*

$ HOTEL **La Ferme de la Chapelle.** The charm of this former priory lies neither in the simple, comfortable guest rooms around the courtyard nor in the restaurant with its no-frills menu, but rather in its breathtaking location high atop the cliffs overlooking Fécamp. **Pros:** spectacular setting; good-value meals. **Cons:** not central; often fully booked for conferences; decidedly rustic. *Rooms from: €95 ✉ Côte de la Vierge, Fécamp ☎ 02–35–10–12–12 🌐 www.fermedelachapelle.fr ⏲ Closed 1st 2 wks. of Jan., 2nd wk. of Nov. 🛏 17 rooms, 5 studios 🍽 Some meals.*

ÉTRETAT

17 km (11 miles) southwest of Fécamp via D940, 88 km (55 miles) northwest of Rouen.

Fodor's Choice ★ Midway along Normandy's Alabaster Coast, Étretat might not at first seem worthy of a detour. However, its end-of-the-world location, its spectacular stone formations famously immortalized by the Impressionists, and the community itself—a Fisher-Price toy town lined with houses covered in picturesque 19th-century figural carvings—all add up to one of France's most unforgettable destinations. No matter there are no museums here—Étretat itself could be an exhibit.

GETTING HERE

Your best bet is to take Cars Perier's No. 24 bus from either Fécamp (30 mins, €2) or Le Havre (60 mins, €2).

Visitor Information Étretat Tourist Office. *☎ 02–35–27–05–21 🌐 www.etretat.net.*

EXPLORING

Falaises d'Étretat. This large village, with its promenade running the length of the pebble beach, is renowned for the magnificent tall rock formations that extend out into the sea. The Falaises d'Étretat are white cliffs that are as famous in France as Dover's are in England—and have been painted by many artists, Claude Monet chief among them.

A stunning white-sand beach and white-chalk rocks, such as the "Manneporte"—a limestone portal likened by author Guy de Maupassant to an elephant dipping its trunk into water—are major elements in the composition. Here Monet became a pictorial rock climber with the help of his famous "slotted box," built with compartments for six different canvases, allowing him to switch midstream from painting to painting, as weather patterns momentarily changed. With storms and sun alternating hour by the hour, you'll quickly understand why they say, "Just wait: in Normandy we have great weather several times a day!"—it was yet another reason why the Impressionists, intent on capturing the ephemeral, so loved this town.

At low tide it's possible to walk through the huge archways formed by the rocks to neighboring beaches. The biggest arch is at the **Falaise d'Aval,** to the south, and for a breathtaking view of the whole bay be sure to climb the easy path up to the top. From here you can hike for

5

miles across the Manneporte Hills, or play a round of golf on one of Europe's windiest and most scenic courses, overlooking **L'Aiguille** (The Needle), a 300-foot spike of rock jutting out of the sea just offshore. To the north towers the **Falaise d'Amont,** topped by the gloriously picturesque chapel of Notre-Dame de la Garde.

The plunging chalk cliffs of Étretat are so gorgeous and strange that they seem surreal at first—the hordes of camera-toting visitors, however, can bring you back to reality quickly. So plan on heading for the cliffs in early morning or early evening. ✉ *Étretat* 🌐 *www.etretat.net.*

WHERE TO EAT AND STAY

$ SEAFOOD **Les Roches Blanches.** The exterior of this family-owned restaurant off the beach is a post–World War II concrete eyesore. But take a table by the window with a view of the cliffs, order the superb fresh seafood (try the tuna steak or sea bass roasted in Calvados), and you'll be glad you came. Reservations are essential for Sunday lunch. *Average main: €12* ✉ *Front de Mer, Rue de l'Abbé-Cochet, Étretat* ☎ *02–35–27–07–34* 🌐 *www.les-roches-blanches.com* *Closed Jan.*

$$$ HOTEL **Domaine Saint Clair Le Donjon.** From the look of this charming, ivy-covered, Anglo-Norman château—complete with storybook tower, private park, and lovely sea vistas—it is easy to understand why Monet, Proust, Offenbach, and other greats accepted invitations here. **Pros:** grand architecture; gorgeous setting; outdoor swimming pool; massage relaxation center. **Cons:** pricey; strident decoration in some rooms. *Rooms from: €200* ✉ *Chemin de St-Clair, Étretat* ☎ *02–35–27–08–23* 🌐 *www.hoteletretat.com* *21 rooms* *Some meals.*

$ HOTEL **Dormy House.** Ideally located halfway up the Étretat cliffs, this smart, modernish hotel is perched amid acres of manicured cliffside parkland. **Pros:** grand views; fine restaurant; breakfast included. **Cons:** small rooms; those in annex lack character; you'll pay a premium for one with sea view (they start at €150). *Rooms from: €105* ✉ *Rte. du Havre, Étretat* ☎ *02–35–27–07–88* 🌐 *www.dormy-house.com* *Closed 1st 3 wks of Jan.* *60 rooms, 3 suites* *Some meals.*

$ HOTEL **La Résidence.** A picturesque 16th-century house in the heart of town, La Résidence is noted for its organic eatery and young, energetic staff; the cheapest rooms (€45) are pretty basic—both the bathroom and the shower are in the hallway—but the more expensive options are en suite and one even has a hot tub. **Pros:** great value; close to beach; breakfast included. **Cons:** spartan facilities; can be noisy. *Rooms from: €75* ✉ *4 bd. du Président René Coty, Étretat* ☎ *02–35–27–02–87* 🌐 *www.hotellaresidenceetretat.com* *15 rooms* *Breakfast.*

SPORTS AND THE OUTDOORS

Golf d'Étretat. Don't miss the chance to play at Golf d'Étretat, where the stupendous 6,580-yard, par-72 course drapes across the cliff tops of the Falaise d'Aval. Green fees range from €44 to €72. ✉ *Rte. du Havre, Étretat* ☎ *02–35–27–04–89* 🌐 *www.golfetretat.com* *Green Fees: Low season, weekdays €44, weekends €62; High season, weekdays €62, weekends €72* *Closed Tues. Check for weekend access during summer.*

LE HAVRE

28 km (18 miles) southwest of Étretat via D940, 86 km (53 miles) west of Rouen, 200 km (125 miles) northwest of Paris.

Considering it was bombarded 146 times during World War II, you might think there'd be little left to see in Le Havre—France's second-largest port (after Marseille). Think again. The rebuilt city, with its uncompromising recourse to reinforced concrete and open spaces, is admittedly short on old-school charm; on the flip side, it is home to some of France's most spectacular 20th-century edifices. The rational planning and audacious architecture of Auguste Perret (1874–1954) have now earned the city UNESCO World Heritage status. His unforgettable **Église St-Joseph**—half rocket ship, half church—is alone worth the trip.

GETTING HERE

Direct trains from Paris's Gare St-Lazare arrive here 13 times a day (2 hrs, 15 mins; €35.40). If you're coming from the United Kingdom, Brittany Ferries provides sea links between Portsmouth and Le Havre. Buses operated by Cars Perier connect it to Fécamp and other communities in Upper Normandy; while Bus Verts du Calvados routes go to Deauville, Honfleur, and Caen.

Visitor Information Le Havre Tourist Office. ☎ *02–32–74–04–04* 🌐 *www.lehavretourisme.com.*

EXPLORING

5

Fodor's Choice ★ **Église St-Joseph.** Perhaps the most eye-popping piece of 20th-century architecture anywhere, and one of the most impressive modernist churches in France, is the Église St-Joseph, built to the plans of Auguste Perret in the 1950s. The 350-foot tower powers into the sky like a fat rocket. The interior is just as thrilling. No frills here: the 270-foot octagonal lantern soars above the crossing, filled almost to the top with abstract stained glass that hurls colored light over the bare concrete walls. *Star Wars* had nothing on this! ✉ *Bd. François-Ier, Le Havre* ⏲ *Daily 9–5:30, except during services.*

Musée d'Art Moderne André-Malraux. Occupying an innovative 1960s glass-and-metal building, the city's art museum has soaring plate-glass window that bathe the interior in the famous sea light that drew scores of artists to Le Havre. Two local painters who gorgeously immortalized the Normandy coast are showcased here—Raoul Dufy (1877–1953), through a remarkable collection of his brightly colored oils, watercolors, and sketches; and Eugène Boudin (1824–98), a forerunner of Impressionism, whose compelling beach scenes and landscapes tellingly evoke the Normandy sea and skyline. ✉ *2 bd. Clemenceau, Le Havre* ☎ *02–35–19–62–62* 🌐 *www.muma-lehavre.fr* 🎫 *€5* ⏲ *Mon. and Wed.–Fri. 11–6, weekends 11–7.*

WHERE TO EAT AND STAY

$$ SEAFOOD ✕ **L'Orchidée.** With the port and fish market within netting distance, seafood is guaranteed to be fresh here. Decor-wise, L'Orchidée is a no-frills place—the visual appeal is on your plate: picture homemade fish terrine with smoked salmon and avocado sauce, or scallops with

a leek and white truffle fricassee. Meat lovers should note that Chef Stéphane Lamotte's excellent €29 set menu also features dishes such as duck breast with foie gras cream sauce. Mouthwatering desserts, like the rice pudding with candied orange peel and Grand Marnier, will make you opt for the extra course. *Average main: €18 41 rue du Général-Faidherbe, Le Havre 02–76–25–38–03 Closed Mon. No dinner Tues., no lunch Sat. Reservations essential.*

$ HOTEL **Best Western–ART Hotel.** Designed by the famed architect Auguste Perret, and located by the soothing waters of the Bassin de Commerce, this hotel's light, airy rooms have contemporary furniture, and a few—like No. 63—have balconies and views of the port. **Pros:** modernist panache; functional; central. **Cons:** some street noise; few rooms have a balcony. *Rooms from: €89 147 rue Louis-Brindeau, Le Havre 02–35–22–69–44 www.art-hotel.fr 31 rooms Breakfast.*

LOWER NORMANDY

Basse-Normandie begins to the west of the Seine Estuary, near the Belle Époque resort towns of Trouville and Deauville, extending out to the sandy Côte Fleurie (Flower Coast), stretching northwest from the D-Day landing sites past Omaha Beach and on to Utah Beach and the Cotentin Peninsula, which juts out into the English Channel. After the World War II D-Day landings, some of the fiercest fighting took place around Caen and Bayeux, as many monuments and memorials testify. Heading south, in the prosperous Pays d'Auge, dairy farms produce the region's famous cheeses. Rising to the west is the fabled Mont-St-Michel. Inland, heading back toward central France, lush green meadows and apple orchards cover the countryside that is the heart of Calvados country.

HONFLEUR

35 km (22 miles) southwest of Étretat via D940, A131, and D579; 80 km (50 miles) west of Rouen.

Honfleur, the most picturesque of the Côte Fleurie's seaside towns, is a time-burnished place with a surplus of half-timber houses and cobbled streets that are lined with a stunning selection of stylish boutiques. Much of its Renaissance architecture remains intact—especially around the 17th-century Vieux Bassin harbor, where the water is fronted on one side by two-story stone houses with low, sloping roofs and on the other by tall slate-topped houses with wooden facades. Maritime expeditions (including some of the first voyages to Canada) departed from here; later, Impressionists were inspired to capture it on canvas. But the town as a whole has become increasingly crowded since the Pont de Normandie opened in 1995. Providing a direct link with Upper Normandy, the world's sixth-largest cable-stayed bridge is supported by two concrete pylons taller than the Eiffel Tower and designed to resist winds of 257 kph (160 mph).

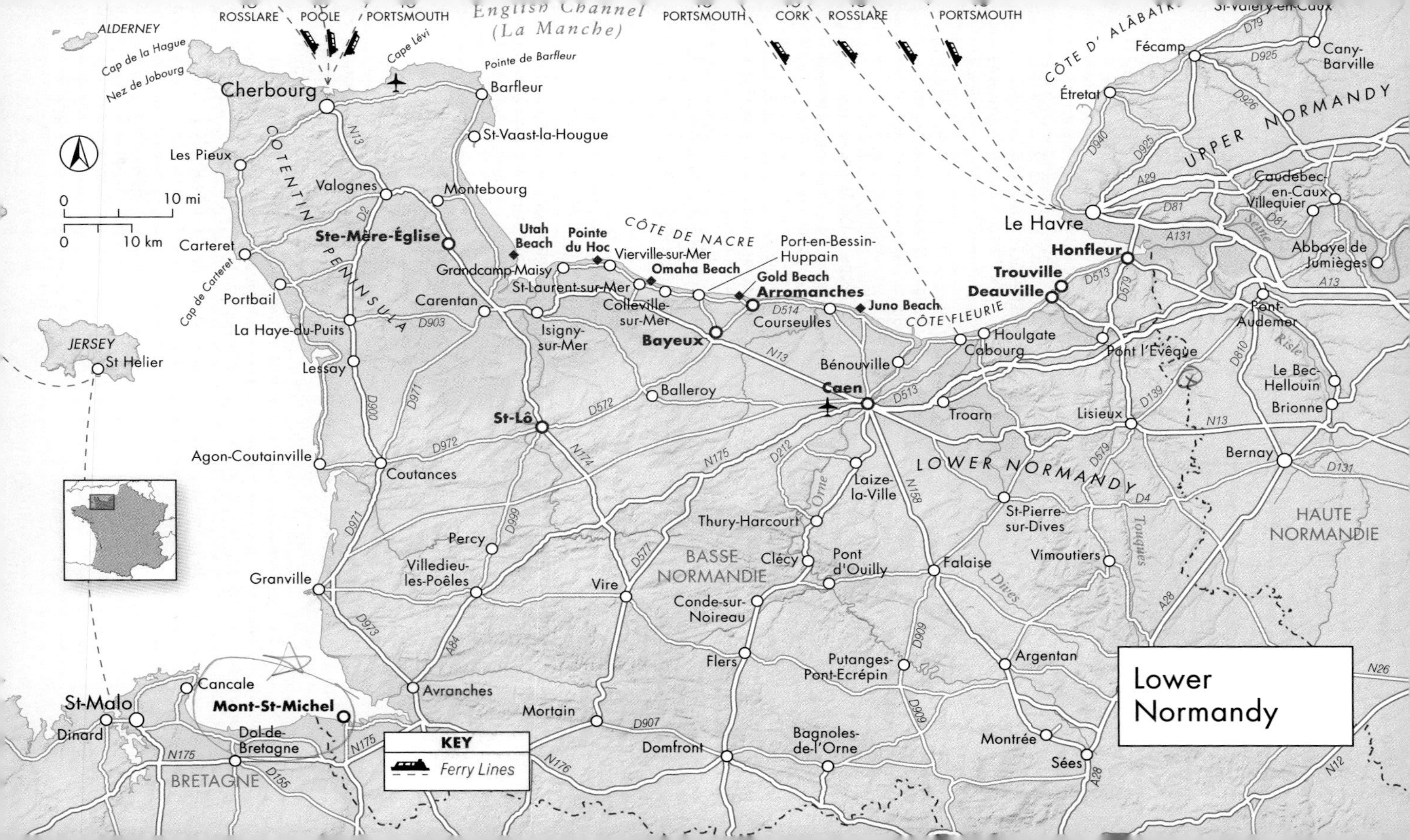

Lower Normandy
KEY
Ferry Lines
English Channel
(La Manche)
ROSSLARE
POOLE
PORTSMOUTH
CORK
ALDERNEY
JERSEY
St Helier
Cap de la Hague
Nez de Jobourg
Cape Lévi
Pointe de Barfleur
Cherbourg
Barfleur
St-Vaast-la-Hougue
Les Pieux
COTENTIN PENINSULA
Valognes
Montebourg
Ste-Mère-Église
Carteret
Cap de Carteret
Portbail
La Haye-du-Puits
Lessay
Carentan
Utah Beach
Pointe du Hoc
Vierville-sur-Mer
Omaha Beach
Grandcamp-Maisy
St-Laurent-sur-Mer
Colleville-sur-Mer
Isigny-sur-Mer
CÔTE DE NACRE
Port-en-Bessin-Huppain
Gold Beach
Arromanches
Juno Beach
Courseulles
Bayeux
Bénouville
Caen
Balleroy
St-Lô
Agon-Coutainville
Coutances
Percy
Villedieu-les-Poêles
Granville
Vire
Avranches
Mortain
Domfront
Cancale
Mont-St-Michel
St-Malo
Dinard
Dol-de-Bretagne
BRETAGNE
BASSE NORMANDIE
Thury-Harcourt
Clécy
Pont d'Ouilly
Conde-sur-Noireau
Flers
Putanges-Pont-Ecrépin
Bagnoles-de-l'Orne
Laize-la-Ville
Orne
Falaise
Argentan
Montrée
Sées
Troarn
LOWER NORMANDY
St-Pierre-sur-Dives
Vimoutiers
Dives
Touques
Lisieux
Bernay
HAUTE NORMANDIE
Cabourg
Houlgate
CÔTE FLEURIE
Deauville
Trouville
Honfleur
Pont l'Evêque
Le Havre
Étretat
Fécamp
CÔTE D' ALÂBATRE
St-Valery-en-Caux
Cany-Barville
UPPER NORMANDY
Caudebec-en-Caux
Villequier
Seine
Abbaye de Jumièges
Pont-Audemer
Risle
Le Bec-Hellouin
Brionne
0
10 mi
10 km
N13
D2
D903
D900
D971
D972
D572
N174
N175
D212
N158
D513
D514
D999
D577
D973
A84
D907
N176
D909
D155
D579
D139
D810
D131
D4
A28
N12
N26
D940
D925
D926
A29
D81
A131
A13
D79

NORMANDY ON CANVAS

Long before Claude Monet created his Giverny lily pond by diverting the Epte River that marks the boundary with the Ile-de-France, artists had been scudding into Normandy for two watery reasons: the Seine and the sea. Just downstream from Vernon, where the Epte joins the Seine, Richard the Lionheart's ruined castle at Les Andelys was committed to canvas by Paul Signac and Félix Vallotton, while the soft-lighted, cliff-lined Seine Valley was impressionistically reproduced by Albert Lebourg and Gustave Loiseau. Their pieces grace the Musée des Beaux-Arts in Rouen—where Camille Corot once studied, and whose mighty cathedral Monet painted until he was pink, purple, and blue in the face.

The Seine joins the sea at Le Havre, where Monet grew up. His mentor Eugène Boudin would boat across the estuary from Honfleur, where he hobnobbed with Gustave Courbet, Charles Daubigny, and Alfred Sisley at the Ferme St-Siméon. Le Havre in the 1860s was the base from which Monet and his pals Frédéric Bazille and Johan Barthold Jongkind explored the rugged coast up to Dieppe, often opening their easels beneath the cliffs of Étretat.

The railroad from Gare St-Lazare (also smokily evoked by Monet) put Dieppe within easy reach of Paris. Eugène Delacroix daubed seascapes here in 1852. Auguste Renoir visited Dieppe from 1878 to 1885; Paul Gauguin and Edgar Degas clinked glasses here in 1885; Camille Pissarro painted his way from Gisors to Dieppe in the 1890s. As the nearest port to Paris, Dieppe wowed the English, too. Walter Sickert moved in from 1898 to 1905, and other artists from the Camden Town Group he founded back in London often painted in Dieppe before World War I.

GETTING HERE

With departures every few hours, Bus Verts du Calvados can get you here from Deauville (37 mins, €2.50), Le Havre (30 mins, €4.85), and Caen (2 hrs, €8.55; or 1 hr express, €12). If you're driving, keep in mind that parking can be a problem—your best bet is the lot just beyond the Vieux-Bassin (Old Harbor) on the left as you approach from the land side.

Visitor Information Honfleur Tourist Office. ☎ *02–31–89–23–30* 🌐 *en.ot-honfleur.fr.*

EXPLORING

Ste-Catherine. Soak up the seafaring atmosphere by strolling around the old harbor and paying a visit to the ravishing wooden church of Ste-Catherine, which dominates a tumbling square. The sanctuary and ramshackle belfry across the way—note the many touches of marine engineering in their architecture—were built by townspeople to show their gratitude for the departure of the English at the end of the Hundred Years' War, in 1453. ✉ *Rue des Lingots, Honfleur* ☎ *02–31–89–11–83* ⏲ *Daily 9–7.*

Relentlessly picturesque Honfleur has been immortalized by many painters, most famously by J.M.W. Turner and Eugène Boudin.

WHERE TO EAT AND STAY

$$ MODERN FRENCH

Le Fleur de Sel. A low-beamed 16th-century fisherman's house provides the cozy setting for Chef Vincent's Guyon's locally influenced cuisine. Centered on the daily catch, the ambitious menu usually includes at least five different fish dishes—all presented with artistic panache—along with plenty of grilled meats, like salt-marsh lamb or duck. Three fixed-price menus (€30–€60) assure a splendid meal on any budget. Be sure to save room for one of the masterful desserts or an informed cheese course. *Average main: €21* *17 rue Haute, Honfleur* *02–31–89–01–92* *www.lafleurdesel-honfleur.com* *Closed Mon., Tues., and Jan.* *Reservations essential.*

$$$$ MODERN FRENCH Fodor's Choice ★

SaQuaNa. Chef Alexandre Bourdas earned his second Michelin star in 2010, after putting Honfleur on the gastronomic map with his first in 2008. From the small but ravishing dining room to the impeccable presentation, his restaurant is a study in getting it right down to the smallest detail. Surprising combinations—like sea bream with nori and marinated sanshō, or cabbage tempura with a truffle crust—attest to Bourdas's far-flung influences: including his native Midi-Pyrénées, Japan (where he cooked for three years), and the local bounty he seeks out daily from farmers and fishermen. For dessert, *patissierre par excellence* Justine Rethore creates sweet masterpieces, among them an apple-marmalade crumble laced with butter, double-cream, yuzu, and Calvados. In addition to a pair of sublime tasting menus (€75 and €115), there's a "surprise menu" for kids (€25). *Bien sûr*, reserve well in advance. *Average main: €75* *22 pl. Hamelin, Honfleur* *02–31–89–40–80* *saquana-alexandre-bourdas.com* *Closed Mon.–Wed.* *Reservations essential.*

$$$$ HOTEL **Ferme St-Siméon.** The story goes that this 19th-century manor house was the birthplace of Impressionism, and that its park inspired Monet and Sisley—neither of whom would have dismissed the welcoming mix of elegance and down-home Norman delights inside, where rich fabrics, grand paintings, and Louis Seize chairs are married with rustic antiques, ancient beams, and half-timbered walls; the result casts a deliciously cozy spell. **Pros:** famed historic charm. **Cons:** expensive; bland annex rooms. *Rooms from: €340 ✉ Rue Adolphe-Marais, on D513 to Trouville, Honfleur ☎ 02–31–81–78–00 ⊕ www.fermesaintsimeon.fr 32 rooms, 3 suites Some meals.*

$$$ B&B/INN Fodor's Choice ★ **La Petite Folie.** Charming simply doesn't suffice to describe this beautifully renovated 1830s town house, a stone's throw from Honfleur's old port. **Pros:** gracious welcome; a good value, with generous breakfast included and secure parking optional. **Cons:** no-children-under-10 policy; no elevator. *Rooms from: €150 ✉ 44 rue Haute, Honfleur ☎ 06–74–39–46–46 ⊕ www.lapetitefolie-honfleur.com Closed 1st. wk. Jan. and Feb. 4 rooms, 7 apartments, 1 suite Breakfast.*

$$$ HOTEL **Le Manoir des Impressionnistes.** Set atop a small wooded hill 200 yards from the sea, this gorgeous half-timber, dormer-roof manor has a pretty green-and-white facade in the Anglo-Norman style, plus accommodations that promise sweeping views. **Pros:** exquisitely decorated and furnished; sea views; stylish bathrooms. **Cons:** away from town center; no elevator. *Rooms from: €190 ✉ Phare du Butin, Rte. de Trouville, Honfleur ☎ 02–31–81–63–00 ⊕ www.manoirdesimpressionnistes.eu 10 rooms Some meals.*

NIGHTLIFE AND PERFORMING ARTS

Fête des Marins (*Marine Festival*). The two-day Fête des Marins is held on Pentecost Sunday and Monday (50 days after Easter). On the first day all the boats in the harbor are decked out in flags and paper roses, and a priest bestows his blessing at high tide. The next day, model boats and local children head a musical procession to the small chapel of Notre-Dame de Grâce. *✉ St. Catherine, Honfleur.*

Fête du Jazz (*Jazz Festival*). There's a five-day Fête du Jazz in mid-August, with performances in the streets and venues throughout the town center. *✉ Honfleur ☎ 06–08–81–68–76 ⊕ www.jazzauxgreniers.com.*

DEAUVILLE-TROUVILLE

16 km (10 miles) southwest of Honfleur via D513, 92 km (57 miles) west of Rouen.

Divided only by the River Touques, the twin beach towns of Deauville and Trouville are distinctly different in character. The latter, arguably France's oldest seaside resort, was discovered by artists and the upper crust in the days of Louis-Philippe; by the mid-1800s, it was the beach à la mode and painters like Eugène Boudin captured its beauty. Then the Duc de Mornay (half-brother of Napoléon III) and other aristocrats on the hunt for something more exclusive began building their villas along the deserted beach across the river. Thus was launched Deauville, a vigorous grande dame who started kicking up her heels in the Second Empire, kept swinging through the Belle Époque, and is still frequented by Rothschilds, princes, and movie stars. Few of them ever actually get in the water, though, because other attractions (including a gilt-edge casino and a fabled racecourse—to say nothing of the extravagant shops along Rue Eugène-Colas) prove so distracting. But perhaps Deauville is known best for its promenade des Planches—a boardwalk extending along the seafront that's lined with deck chairs, bars, striped cabanas, elegant hotels, plus an array of lovely half-timber Norman villas and block after block of prewar apartment houses.

Overbuilding has diminished the charm of both towns, yet the two maintain their popularity. Deauville is sometimes jokingly referred to as Paris's 21st arrondissement; while Trouville is a more of a family resort, harboring few pretensions. Moreover, shuttling between them is still easy by means of a five-minute drive or boat crossing.

GETTING HERE

Trains from Paris's Gare St-Lazare to Deauville-Trouville (the station between the two towns) often require a change at Lisieux (2 hrs, €34.50). Bus Verts du Calvados runs multiple buses per day to Deauville from Le Havre (1 hr, €8.25), Honfleur (37 mins, €2.50), and Caen (75 mins, €5.15).

Visitor Information Deauville-Trouville Tourist Office. *02–31–14–40–00* *www.deauville.org.*

5

WHERE TO EAT AND STAY

$$$ FRENCH **L'Essentiel.** A nice change from the grand, overly formal hotel dining rooms that dominate Deauville, the relaxed atmosphere and sensational, seasonal cuisine at this contemporary eatery have made it extremely popular. Chef Charles Thuillant, whose pedigree includes stints at two top Paris restaurants, focuses on lighter Asian-inspired dishes with European influences. The menu—which might include foie gras in duck broth with Thai herbs or Wagyu beef with grilled vegetables—brings his talents to the forefront. A capacious terrace, a selection of excellent wines by the glass, and a bargain weekday lunch menu (€19) make L'Essentiel an ideal place to linger. *Average main: €26* *29 rue Mirabeau, Deauville* *02–31–87–22–11* *www.lessentieldeauville.com* *Closed Mon. and Tues.* *Reservations essential.*

$$ HOTEL **81 L'Hôtel.** While this boutique hotel pours on the gloss, the nicer original features of the 1906 mansion—parquet floors, stained-glass windows, impossibly high ceilings—remain to complement the added postmodern touches (think faux crocodile chairs, silver furniture, shrouded chandeliers, and ersatz-Baroque beds); the top-floor "Hippodrome" suite offers a nice view of the famous racetrack, and others have terraces. **Pros:** rooms outfitted with air-conditioning, free Wi-Fi, and flat-screen TVs; easy parking. **Cons:** no restaurant; a walk to the beach. *Rooms from: €125* *81 av. de la République, Deauville* *02–31–14–01–50* *www.81lhotel.com* *Closed 1st 3 wks of Jan.* *21 rooms, 8 studios, 1 apartment* *Breakfast.*

$$ HOTEL **Continental.** Vintage daguerreotypes prove that this is one of Deauville's oldest establishments. **Pros:** cheap; convenient to train station. **Cons:** not close to the beach; lacks character. *Rooms from: €130*

✉ *1 rue Désiré-Le-Hoc, Deauville* ☎ *02–31–88–21–06* 🌐 *www.hotel-continental-deauville.com* *42 rooms* 🍽 *Breakfast.*

$$$$ HOTEL Fodor's Choice ★ **Normandy-Barrière.** This hotel—its facade a riot of pastel-green timbering, checkerboard walls, and Anglo-Norman balconies—has been a town landmark since it opened in 1912, and crowds still pack the place. **Pros:** grand interiors; luxurious amenities; Deauville's place to be seen. **Cons:** some elements of kitschy bombast; patronizing service; can be steamy in summer. $ *Rooms from: €385* ✉ *38 rue Jean-Mermoz, Deauville* ☎ *02–31–98–66–22, 800/223–5652 for U.S. reservations* 🌐 *www.lucienbarriere.com* *259 rooms, 31 suites* 🍽 *Some meals.*

NIGHTLIFE AND PERFORMING ARTS

American Film Festival. One of the biggest cultural events on the Norman calendar is the 10-day American Film Festival, held in Deauville in early September. ✉ *Centre International de Deauville, 1 av. Lucien Barrière, Deauville* ☎ *02–31–14–14–14* 🌐 *www.festival-deauville.com.*

Casino de Deauville. Formal attire is required at the Casino de Deauville. ✉ *2 rue Edmond-Blanc, Deauville-Trouville* ☎ *02–31–14–31–14* 🌐 *www.lucienbarriere.com/fr/Casino/Deauville/accueil.html.*

Casino de Trouville. Trouville's Casino de Trouville is slightly less highbrow than Deauville's. ✉ *Pl. du Maréchal-Foch, Trouville* ☎ *02–31–87–75–00* 🌐 *www.lucienbarriere.com/fr/Casino/Trouville/accueil.html.*

Le Chic. Open nightly from 11 pm to 5 am, Le Chic is *the* place to dance, according to some natives. ✉ *14 rue Désiré Le Hoc, Deauville* ☎ *02–31–88–30–91* 🌐 *www.lechicdeauville.fr.*

Le Seven. Night owls enjoy Le Seven; it's open until 6 am. ✉ *13 rue Albert-Fracasse, Deauville* ☎ *07–87–91–01–94 02–31–88–40–50 after 11 pm* 🌐 *www.lesevendeauville.com.*

SPORTS AND THE OUTDOORS

Club Nautique de Trouville. Sailing boats large and small can be rented from the Club Nautique de Trouville. ✉ *Digue des Roches Noires, Deauville-Trouville* ☎ *02–31–88–13–59* 🌐 *www.cnth.org.*

Hippodrome de Deauville Clairefontaine. Horse races and polo matches can be seen most summer afternoons at the Hippodrome de Deauville Clairefontaine. ✉ *Rte. de Clairefontaine, Tourgéville, Deauville* ☎ *02–31–14–69–00* 🌐 *www.hippodrome-deauville-clairefontaine.com.*

Hippodrome de Deauville–La Touques. Deauville becomes Europe's horse capital in August, when breeders jet in from around the world for its yearling auctions and the races at its two attractive hippodromes. Afternoon horse races are held in the heart of Deauville at the Hippodrome de Deauville—La Touques. It hosts the Gold Cup Polo Championship (the final is held on the last Sunday of August), and the summer season closes with the course's signature event, the Grand Prix de Deauville. ✉ *45 av. Hocquart de Turtot, Deauville* ☎ *02–31–14–20–00* 🌐 *www.france-galop.com.*

Poney Club. Head for the Poney Club for a wonderful horseback ride on the beach (the sunsets can be spectacular). It's open weekends and holidays, but be sure to call early to reserve a horse, or a pony for your little

Even in the 19th century, elegant Parisians flocked to Deauville to enjoy a promenade along its beautiful seafront boardwalk.

one. ✉ *Rue Reynoldo-Hahn, Deauville-Trouville* ☎ *02–31–98–56–24* 🌐 *poney-club-deauville.ffe.com.*

CAEN

54 km (35 miles) southwest of Deauville-Trouville, 28 km (17 miles) southeast of Bayeux, 120 km (75 miles) west of Rouen.

Fodor's Choice ★ Basically a modern commercial and administrative center with a vibrant student scene, Caen—the capital of Lower Normandy—is very different from the coastal resorts. Atmospheric castles and abbeys remain from the 11th-century glory days when William of Normandy ruled here before heading across the Channel to conquer England. During the two-month Battle of Caen in 1944, however, a fire raged for 11 days, devastating much of the town. The Caen Mémorial, an impressive museum devoted to World War II, is considered a must-see by travelers interested in 20th-century history; and many avail themselves of the excellent bus tours the museum sponsors to the nearby D-Day beaches.

GETTING HERE

Frequent daily trains arrive from Paris's Gare St-Lazare (2 hrs, €36.70); some continue to Bayeux (2 hrs, €30.30). Daily trains also link Caen to Rouen (90 mins, €27.50) and St-Lô (50 mins, €14.10). Bus Verts du Calvados connects the city with Deauville (75 mins, €5.15), Le Havre (90 mins, €16.85 express), and Honfleur (1 hr, €12 express).

Visitor Information Caen Tourist Office. ☎ *02–31–27–14–14* 🌐 *www.tourisme.caen.fr.*

EXPLORING

TOP ATTRACTIONS

Fodor's Choice ★ **Abbaye aux Hommes** (*Men's Abbey*). Caen's finest church, of cathedral proportions, is part of the Abbaye aux Hommes, built by William the Conqueror from local Caen stone (which was also used for England's Canterbury Cathedral, Westminster Abbey, and the Tower of London). The abbey was begun in Romanesque style in 1066 and expanded in the 18th century; its elegant buildings are now part of City Hall, and some rooms are brightened by the city's fine collection of paintings. Note the magnificent yet spare facade of the abbey church of **St-Étienne,** enhanced by two 11th-century towers topped by octagonal spires. Inside, what had been William the Conqueror's tomb was destroyed by 16th-century Huguenots during the Wars of Religion. However, the choir still stands; it was the first to be built in Norman Gothic style, and many subsequent choirs were modeled after it. To get the full historical scoop, sign up for one of the special tours: English-language ones are offered in July and August at 11, 1:30, and 4. ✉ *Esplanade Jean-Marie Louve, Caen* ☎ *02–31–30–42–81* 🌐 *caen.fr/decouvrir-patrimoine* 🎫 *Tours €4.50–€7* ⏲ *Daily 9–6.*

Château Ducal. The ruins of William the Conqueror's fortress, built in 1060 and sensitively restored after the war, loom on a mound ahead of St-Étienne. The château gardens are a perfect spot for strolling, and the ramparts afford good views of the city. Inside, you'll discover two museums—the Musée des Beaux-Arts and the Musée de Normandie—plus the medieval church of **St-Georges,** which is used for exhibitions. ✉ *Caen* 🌐 *www.chateau.caen.fr.*

Mémorial de Caen. An imaginative museum erected in 1988 on the north side of the city, the Mémorial is a must-see if you're interested in World War II history. The stark, flat facade, with a narrow doorway symbolizing the Allies' breach in the Nazi's supposedly impregnable Atlantic Wall, opens onto an immense foyer with British Typhoon aircraft suspended overhead. The museum itself is down a spiral ramp, lined with photos and documents charting the Nazi's rise to power in the 1930s. The idea—hardly subtle but visually effective—is to suggest a descent into the hell of war. The extensive displays range from wartime plastic jewelry to scale models of battleships, with scholarly sections on how the Nazis tracked down radios used by the French Resistance and on the development of the atomic bomb. A room commemorating the Holocaust, with flickering candles and twinkling overhead lights, sounds a jarring note. The D-Day landings are evoked by a tabletop map of the theater of war and by a spectacular split-screen presentation of the D-Day invasion from both the Allied and Nazi standpoints. Softening the effect of the modern structure are tranquil gardens, including a British one inaugurated by Prince Charles. Fittingly, the museum is located 10 minutes away from the Pegasus Bridge and 15 minutes from the D-Day beaches. ✉ *Esplanade Dwight-D.-Eisenhower, Caen* ☎ *02–31–06–06–44* 🌐 *www.memorial-caen.fr* 🎫 *€19* ⏲ *Early Feb.–Oct., daily 9–7; Nov., Dec., and late Jan.–early Feb., Tues.–Sun. 9:30–6.*

WORTH NOTING

Abbaye aux Dames (*Ladies' Abbey*). Founded in 1059 by William the Conqueror's wife, Matilda, the Abbaye aux Dames was rebuilt in the 18th century; it then served as a hospital and nursing home before being fully restored in the 1980s by the Regional Council, which promptly requisitioned it for office space. The abbey's elegant arcaded courtyard and ground-floor reception rooms can, however, still be admired during free guided tours. You can also visit the squat **Église de la Trinité** (Trinity Church), a fine example of 11th-century Romanesque architecture, though its original spires were replaced by timid balustrades in the early 18th century. Note the intricate carvings on columns and arches in the chapel; the 11th-century crypt; and, in the choir, the marble slab commemorating Queen Matilda, who was buried here in 1083. ✉ *Pl. de la Reine-Mathilde, Caen* ☎ *02–31–06–98–98* 🌐 *www.region-basse-normandie.fr* 🎫 *Free* ⏲ *Daily 2–6; tours at 2:30 and 4.*

5

Hôtel d'Escoville. A good place to begin exploring Caen is the Hôtel d'Escoville, a stately mansion in the city center built by wealthy merchant Nicolas Le Valois d'Escoville in the 1530s. The building was badly damaged during the war but has since been restored; the austere facade conceals an elaborate inner courtyard, reflecting the Italian influence on early Renaissance Norman architecture. The on-site city **tourist office** is an excellent resource. ✉ *Pl. St-Pierre, Caen* ☎ *02–31–27–14–14 tourist office* 🌐 *www.tourisme.caen.fr.*

Musée de Normandie (*Normandy Museum*). Set in a mansion built for the castle governor, this museum is dedicated to regional arts such as ceramics and sculpture. Some local archaeological finds are also on display. ✉ *Château Ducal, Entrance by château gateway, Caen* ☎ *02–31–30–47–60* 🌐 *musee-de-normandie.caen.fr* 🎫 *€3.20; €5.30 for 48-hr pass to both Beaux-Arts and Normandy museums* ⏲ *June–Oct., daily 9:30–6; Nov.–May, Wed.–Mon. 9:30–6.*

Musée des Beaux-Arts. Within the castle's walls, the Musée des Beaux-Arts is a heavyweight among France's provincial fine arts museums. Its old-masters collection includes works by Poussin, Perugino, Rembrandt, Titian, Tintoretto, and Veronese; there's also a wide range of 20th-century art on view. ✉ *Château Ducal, entrance by château gateway, Caen* ☎ *02–31–30–47–70* 🌐 *www.mba.caen.fr* 🎫 *€3.10; €5.30 for 48-hr pass to both Beaux-Arts and Normandy museums* ⏲ *Wed.–Mon. 9:30–6.*

St-Pierre. Across the square, beneath a 240-foot spire, the late-Gothic church of St-Pierre is a riot of ornamental stonework. It's open for visits despite extensive, ongoing restoration work. ✉ *Pl. St-Pierre, Caen.*

WHERE TO EAT AND STAY

$ FRENCH ✕ **Le P'tit B.** On one of Caen's oldest streets near the castle, this half-timber 17th-century dining room—complete with stone walls, beam ceilings, and a large fireplace—showcases the regional cuisine of David Schiebold. The three-course prix-fixe menu (€20) is a great value: options might include grilled duck, cannelloni with goat cheese, or king-prawn risotto, and, to finish, red berries in flaky pastry with coconut milk. [$] *Average main: €15* ✉ *15 rue de Vaugueux, Caen* ☎ *02–31–93–50–76* *www.leptitb.fr* *Reservations essential.*

$ WINE BAR **Le Verre à Soi.** Smack in the city center, overlooking the river, this convivial *cave à manger* has everything necessary for a satisfying, affordable dining experience. Opt for small plates of artisanal charcuterie and cheese, or go for a satisfying main course—like chicken breast served with cream and chorizo sauce or marinated sardines, a local specialty. The prix-fixe lunch menus are a bargain (€13–€16); and you can choose from an impressive selection of wines by the bottle or glass. Friendly service and a lively clientele are an added bonus. *Average main: €13* *23 Quai Eugene Meslin, Caen* *02–31–83–08–77* *www.le-verreasoi.fr* *Closed Sun. and Mon.* *Reservations not accepted.*

$$$ HOTEL **Best Western–Le Dauphin.** Despite being in the heart of the city, this hotel, in a restored 12th-century priory, is surprisingly quiet; some of the smallish guest rooms have exposed beams, those overlooking the street are soundproof, and the ones in back look out on the courtyard. **Pros:** quiet, historic building; spa and fitness center. **Cons:** small rooms; excellent but pricey restaurant. *Rooms from: €150* *29 rue Gémare, Caen* *02–31–86–22–26* *www.le-dauphin-normandie.com* *32 rooms, 5 suites* *Some meals.*

$$ HOTEL **Hotel Ivan Vautier.** A bastion of modern luxury, this quiet hotel is Caen's go-to spot for stylish lodging and dining: handsome, spacious rooms are decorated in jewel and earth tones and feature sleek, sparkling bathrooms; splendid food options include an elegant, Michelin-star restaurant. **Pros:** well maintained; on-site spa and gastronomic restaurant; good packages. **Cons:** not central; no meals included. *Rooms from: €135* *3 av. Henry Chéron, Caen* *02–31–73–32–71* *www.ivanvautier.com* *15 rooms, 4 suites* *No meals.*

FROM WAR TO PEACE

Normandy war museums are legion, but the Mémorial de Caen, its one and only *peace* museum, is special. Even better, readers rave about the museum's five-hour minibus tours of the D-Day beaches, run daily. You can even make a day trip from Paris for this by catching a morning train out of Gare St-Lazare to Caen (tours start at 1 or 2 pm) and returning on the 8:13 pm train. In addition to the tour, this €115 trip includes pickup at the station and lunch.

SHOPPING

Open Air Markets (*Farmers' markets*). Farmers' markets (which often include clothing and household goods) run every day except Monday, but the largest are held Friday morning on Place St-Sauveur and Sunday morning on Place Courtonne. In May, collectors and dealers flock to Caen's bric-a-brac and **antiques fair** at the Parc des Expositions. *Caen* *02–31–27–14–14.*

SPORTS AND THE OUTDOORS

Boëdic. Take a barge trip along the canal that leads from Caen to the sea on the *Boëdic*. The boat runs every day except Saturday in July and August, and every day except Monday in the shoulder seasons (mid-April through June and September through mid-October). All departures are at 3 pm, and tickets are sold onboard. Arromanches/Omaha Beach sorties are also available in summer. ✉ *Bassin Saint-Pierre, Quai Vendeuvre, Caen* ☎ *02–31–43–86–12* 🎫 *€14 round-trip, €11 one-way.*

EN ROUTE

Pegasus Bridge. Early on June 6, 1944, the British 6th Airborne Division landed by glider and captured Pegasus Bridge (named for the division's emblem, showing Bellerophon astride his winged horse). This proved to be the first step toward liberating France from Nazi occupation, and the structure itself became a symbol of the Allied invasion. To see it, take D514 north from Caen for 13 km (8 miles) and turn right at Bénouville. The original bridge—erected in 1935—has been replaced by a similar, slightly wider one; but the older span can be seen at the adjacent **Mémorial Pegasus** visitor center. **Café Gondrée** by the bridge—the first building recaptured on French soil—is still standing and still serving; it also houses a small museum. A 40-minute son-et-lumière show lights up the bridge and café at nightfall between June and September. ✉ *Av. du Major Howard, Ranville* ☎ *02–31–78–19–44 Mémorial Pegasus, 02–31–44–62–25 Café Gondrée* 🌐 *www.memorial-pegasus.org; pegasus-bridge-cafe-gondree.com* 🎫 *Mémorial Pegasus €7* 🕒 *Apr.–Sept., daily 9:30–6:30; Oct.–Mar., daily 10–5.*

5

ARROMANCHES-LES-BAINS

31 km (19 miles) northwest of Caen, 10 km (6 miles) northeast of Bayeux.

Now a tourist-friendly beach town, Arromanches played a pivotal role during the D-Day invasion. Vestiges of the great artificial ports called "mulberries" remain and local attractions—including a landing-themed museum and a 360-degree movie theater—conjure up those desperate June days in 1944.

GETTING HERE

Bus Verts du Calvados's No. 74 and 75 routes link Arromanches-le-Bains to Bayeux (30 mins, €2.10).

Visitor Information Arromanches Tourist Office. ☎ *02–31–22–36–45* 🌐 *www.ot-arromanches.fr.*

EXPLORING

Arromanches 360. This striking movie theater has a circular screen—actually nine curved screens synchronized to show an 18-minute film titled *Le Prix de la Liberté* (*The Price of Freedom*), which tells the story of the D-Day landings through a mix of archival and more recent footage from major sites and cemeteries. Evocative music and sound effects serve as dramatic substitutes for spoken commentary. The film is screened at 10 past and 40 past the hour. ✉ *Chemin du Calvaire, Arromanches-les-Bains* ☎ *02–31–06–06–44* 🌐 *www.arromanches360.com* 🎫 *€5* 🕒 *Apr., May, and Sept., daily 10:10–6:10; June–Aug., daily 9:40–6:40; Oct.–Mar., Tues.–Sun. 10:10–5:10.*

Musée du Débarquement. Little remains to mark the furious fighting waged hereabouts after D-Day. In the bay off Arromanches, however, some elements of the floating harbor are still visible. As you contemplate the seemingly insignificant hunks of concrete that form a broken offshore semicircle, try to imagine the extraordinary feat involved in towing them across the Channel from England. General Eisenhower said that victory would have been impossible without this prefabricated harbor, which was nicknamed "Winston." The Musée du Débarquement, on the seafront, has models, mock-ups, and photographs depicting the creation of this technical marvel. *Pl. du 6-Juin, Arromanches-les-Bains 02–31–22–34–31 www.musee-arromanches.fr €7.90 Apr., daily 9–12:30 and 1:30–6; May–Aug., daily 9–7; Sept., daily 9–6; Oct. and Mar., daily 9:30–12:30 and 1:30–5:30; Nov., Dec., and late-Jan–Feb., daily 10–12:30 and 1:30–5.*

WHERE TO STAY

$ HOTEL **Le Mulberry.** This little hotel, one block back from the seafront, is cheerfully run by Sophie and Christian Le Blanc. **Pros:** warm welcome; breakfast included; tasty home cooking and natural wines. **Cons:** small, basic rooms. *Rooms from: €82 6 rue Maurice-Lithare, Arromanches-les-Bains 02–31–22–36–05 www.lemulberry.fr Closed Jan.–mid-Feb. 9 rooms Breakfast.*

BAYEUX

28 km (17 miles) northwest of Caen.

Bayeux makes a fine starting point for excursions to nearby World War II sites. Despite being close to scenes of such destruction, Bayeux itself was never bombed by either side (without factories or military bases, it served no strategic purpose); hence, its Norman Gothic cathedral and beautiful Old Town emerged intact. The highlight here for most visitors is the world's most celebrated piece of needlework: the Bayeux Tapestry, which vividly conjures up life circa 1066. For a different take on the past, plan to come for the boisterous Fêtes Médiévales, a market-cum-carnival held in the streets around the cathedral on the first weekend of July. A more conventional market is held every Saturday morning.

GETTING HERE

Bus Verts du Calvados's No. 30 route, originating at Caen's rail station, runs to Bayeux (€4.15) and other towns in the vicinity. Trains also arrive regularly from Caen (2 hrs, €30.30).

Visitor Information Bayeux Tourist Office. *02–31–51–28–28 bayeux-bessin-tourisme.com.*

EXPLORING

Fodor's Choice ★ **Bayeux Tapestry.** Essentially a 225-foot-long embroidered scroll stitched in 1067, the Bayeux Tapestry, known in French as the *Tapisserie de la Reine Mathilde* (Queen Matilda's Tapestry), depicts, in 58 comic strip–type scenes, the epic story of William of Normandy's conquest of England, narrating Will's trials and victory over his cousin Harold, culminating in the Battle of Hastings on October 14, 1066. The tapestry was probably commissioned from Saxon embroiderers by the count of Kent—who was also the bishop of Bayeux—to be displayed in his newly built Cathédrale Notre-Dame. Despite its age, the tapestry is in remarkably good condition; the extremely detailed, often homey scenes provide an unequaled record of the clothes, weapons, ships, and lifestyles of the day. It's showcased in the **Musée de la Tapisserie** (Tapestry Museum; free audio guides let you listen to an English commentary about the tapestry). ✉ *Centre Guillaume-le-Conquérant, 13 bis rue de Nesmond, Bayeux* ☎ *02–31–51–25–50* 🌐 *www.tapisserie-bayeux.fr* 🎫 *€9* 🕒 *Mid-Mar.–Oct., daily 9–5:45 (until 6:15 in summer); Nov., Dec., and Feb., daily 9:30–11:45 and 2–5:15.*

Cathédrale Notre-Dame. Bayeux's mightiest edifice, the Cathédrale Notre-Dame, is a harmonious mixture of Norman and Gothic architecture. Note the portal on the south side of the transept that depicts the assassination of English archbishop Thomas à Becket in Canterbury Cathedral in 1170, following his courageous opposition to King Henry II's attempts to control the church. On weekdays in July and August, a guided tour is offered at 3. ✉ *Rue du Bienvenu, Bayeux* ☎ *02–31–92–01–85* 🌐 *cathedraledebayeux.voila.net* 🎫 *Tour €4* 🕒 *July–Sept., daily 8:30–7; Oct.–June, daily 8:30–6.*

5

Conservatoire de la Dentelle. Handmade lace is a specialty of Bayeux. The best place to learn about it—and buy some to take home—is the Conservatoire de la Dentelle near the cathedral. ✉ *6 rue du Bienvenu, Bayeux* ☎ *02–31–92–73–80* 🌐 *dentelledebayeux.free.fr* 🎫 *Free* 🕒 *Mon.–Sat. 9:30–12:30 and 2:30–5.*

Musée Baron-Gérard. Housed in the Bishop's Palace beneath the cathedral, the Musée Baron-Gérard (also known as the Musée d'Art et d'Histoire de Baron Gérard or MAHB) was completely renovated in 2013. It displays a fine collection of Bayeux porcelain and lace, plus ceramics from Rouen, vintage pharmaceutical jars, 16th- to 19th-century furniture, and paintings by local artists. Note the magnificent plane tree out front—dubbed the Tree of Liberty, it was planted in 1797. ✉ *1 pl. de la Liberté, Bayeux* ☎ *02–31–92–14–21* 🌐 *www.mairie-bayeux.fr/index.php?id=229* 🎫 *€7* 🕒 *May–Sept., daily 9:30–6:30; Oct.–Dec. and mid-Feb.–Apr., daily 10–12:30 and 2–6.*

Musée de la Bataille de Normandie (*Battle of Normandy Museum*). Exhibits at the Musée de la Bataille de Normandie trace the story of the struggle from June 6 to August 22, 1944. Located near the moving British War Cemetery, it contains some impressive war paraphernalia. ✉ *Bd. du Général-Fabian-Ware, Bayeux* ☎ *02–31–51–46–90* 🌐 *www.normandiememoire.com/en/visit/view/id-315-musee-memorial-de-la-bataille-de-normandie-* 🎫 *€6* 🕒 *May–Sept., daily 9:30–6:30; Oct.–Dec., Mar., and Apr., daily 10–12:30 and 2–6.*

WHERE TO STAY

$$$$ HOTEL **Château d'Audrieu.** Princely opulence, overstuffed chairs, wall sconces, antiques—this family-owned château with an elegant 18th-century facade and grand restaurant fulfills the Hollywood notion of a palatial property. **Pros:** grandiose building; magnificent gardens. **Cons:** out of the way; bland interiors in some rooms. 💲 *Rooms from: €228* ✉ *Off D82, 13 km (8 miles) southeast of Bayeux, Audrieu* ☎ *02–31–80–21–52* 🌐 *www.chateaudaudrieu.com* 🕒 *Closed Dec. and Jan.* 🛏 *25 rooms, 4 suites* 🍽 *Some meals.*

$ HOTEL **Grand Hôtel du Luxembourg.** Don't be misled by the name—the small guest rooms here are more bland than grand, but they do have updated comforts and all but two face a courtyard garden; the on-site restaurant, one of the best in town, is another perk. **Pros:** quiet; central; fine restaurant. **Cons:** unprepossessing lobby; some rooms are on the dark side. *Rooms from: €100 ✉ 25 rue des Bouchers, Bayeux ☎ 02–31–92–00–04 ⊕ www.hotel-luxembourg-bayeux.com ⊗ Closed mid-Jan.–Feb. 25 rooms, 3 suites Some meals.*

THE D-DAY BEACHES

History focused its sights along the coasts of Normandy at 6:30 am on June 6, 1944, as the 135,000 men and 20,000 vehicles of the Allied forces made land in their first incursion in Europe in World War II. The entire operation on this "Longest Day" was called Operation Overlord—the code name for the invasion of Normandy. Five beachheads (dubbed Utah, Omaha, Gold, Juno, and Sword) were established along the coast to either side of Arromanches. Preparations started in mid-1943, and British shipyards worked furiously through the following winter and spring building two artificial harbors (called "mulberries"), boats, and landing equipment. The British and Canadian troops that landed on Sword, Juno, and Gold on June 6, 1944, quickly pushed inland and joined with parachute regiments previously dropped behind German lines, before encountering fierce resistance at Caen, which did not fall until July 9.

GETTING HERE

Since public buses from Bayeux are infrequent, it's best to take a guided bus tour or drive yourself on a DIY excursion through the area.

Mémorial Tours. Guided, English-language excursions to the D-Day landing beaches are organized by Mémorial. You can opt to travel by tour bus (€42) or, for a more personalized experience, by minivan (€115). *✉ Esplanade General Eisenhower, Caen ☎ 02–31–06–06–44 ⊕ www.memorial-caen.fr.*

Normandy Sightseeing Tours. Normandy Sightseeing Tours runs a number of trips to the D-Day beaches; a full-day outing (8:30–6) costs €90. *✉ 6 rue St-Jean, Bayeux ☎ 02–31–51–70–52 ⊕ www.normandy-sightseeing-tours.com.*

EXPLORING

Musee du Débarquement Utah Beach. In La Madeleine, inspect the sleek Musee du Débarquement Utah Beach (Utah Beach Landing Museum)—a stunning facility, located right on the beachhead, where exhibits include vintage aircraft and a W5 Utah scale model detailing the German defenses. Continue north to the **Dunes de Varreville**, where you'll find a monument to French hero General Leclerc, who landed here. Offshore you can see the fortified **Iles St-Marcouf.** Carry on to Quinéville, at the far end of Utah Beach, to visit the **Memorial de la Liberte** at 18 avenue de la Plage (*02–33–95–95–95, www.memorial-quineville.com*): open daily from April to September, this small museum evokes life during the German Occupation (€6.50). *✉ Plage de La Madeleine, Ste Marie du Mont ☎ 02–33–71–53–35 Utah Beach Landing Museum ⊕ www.utah-beach.com €8 ⊗ June–Sept., daily 9:30–7; Oct.–May, daily 10–6.*

Omaha Beach. You won't be disappointed by the rugged terrain and windswept sand of Omaha Beach, 16 km (10 miles) northwest of Bayeux. Here you can find the **Monument du Débarquement** (Monument to the Normandy Landings) and the **Musée-Mémorial d'Omaha Beach,** a large shedlike structure packed with tanks, dioramas, and archival photographs that stand silent witness to "Bloody Omaha." Nearby, in Vierville-sur-Mer, is the **U.S. National Guard Monument.** Throughout June 6, Allied forces battled a hailstorm of German bullets and bombs, but by the end of the day they had taken the Omaha Beach sector—suffering grievous losses in the process. In Colleville-sur-Mer, overlooking Omaha Beach, is the hilltop **American Cemetery and Memorial,** designed by landscape architect Markley Stevenson; you can look out to sea across the landing beach from a platform on its north side. ✉ *Les Moulins, Av. de la Libération, Saint-Laurent-sur-Mer* ☎ *02–31–21–97–44* 🌐 *www.musee-memorial-omaha.com* 🎟 *€6.20* ⏲ *Mid-Feb.–mid-Mar., daily 10–12:30 and 2:30–6; mid-Mar.–mid-May and mid-Sept.–mid-Nov., daily 9:30–6:30; mid-May–mid-Sept., daily 9:30–7 (until 7:30 July and Aug.).*

5

Pointe du Hoc. The most spectacular scenery along the coast is at the Pointe du Hoc, 13 km (8 miles) west of St-Laurent. Wildly undulating grassland leads past ruined blockhouses to a cliff-top observatory and a German machine-gun post whose intimidating mass of reinforced concrete merits chilly exploration. Despite Spielberg's cinematic genius, it remains hard to imagine just how Colonel Rudder and his 225 Rangers—only 90 survived—managed to scale the jagged cliffs with rope ladders and capture the German defenses in one of the most heroic and dramatic episodes of the war. A granite memorial pillar now stands on top of a concrete bunker, but the site otherwise remains as the Rangers left it—look down through the barbed wire at the jutting cliffs the troops ascended and see the huge craters left by exploded shells. ✉ *Cricqueville-en-Bessin.*

Utah Beach. Head east on D67 from Sainte-Mère to Utah Beach, which, being sheltered from the Atlantic winds by the Cotentin Peninsula and surveyed by lowly sand dunes rather than rocky cliffs, proved easier to attack than Omaha. Allied troops stormed the beach at dawn, and just a few hours later had managed to conquer the German defenses, heading inland to join up with the airborne troops. ✉ *Utah Beach, Ste Marie du Mont.*

WHERE TO STAY

$ HOTEL **Hotel du Casino.** You can't get closer to the action than this—the handsome, triangular-gabled stone hotel, run by the same family since it was built in the 1950s, looks directly onto Omaha Beach. **Pros:** calm; right by the beach. **Cons:** small bathrooms; slow service in restaurant. *Rooms from: €100* ✉ *Rue de la Percée, Vierville-sur-Mer* ☎ *02–31–22–41–02* 🌐 *www.hotel-omaha-beach.fr* ⏲ *Closed mid-Nov.–Mar.* *12 rooms* *Some meals.*

$$$$ HOTEL **La Chenevière.** Occupying an elegant 18th-century mansion that's topped by an impressive mansard roof and surrounded by cheerful gardens, this is a true oasis of peace—although located only a few miles inland from World War II sites like Omaha Beach, it feels

Continued on page 288

MONT-ST-MICHEL

A magnetic beacon to millions of travelers each year, this "Wonder of the Western World"—a 264-foot mound of rock topped by a history-shrouded abbey—remains the crowning glory of medieval France.

by Jennifer Ladonne

Wrought by nature and centuries of tireless human toil, this mass of granite surmounted by the soul-lifting silhouette of the **Abbaye du Mont-St-Michel** is Normandy's most enduring image. Its fame stems not just from the majesty of its geographical situation but even more from its impressive history. Perched on the border between Normandy and Brittany, the medieval Mont (or Mount) was a political football between English conquerors and French kings for centuries. Mont-St-Michel was designed to be as much a fortress as it was a shrine, so it looks as tough as it is beautiful.

Legend has it that the Archangel Michael appeared in 709 to Aubert, Bishop of Avranches, inspiring him to build an oratory on what was then called Mont Tombe. The original church was completed in 1144, but further buildings were added in the 13th century to accommodate the hordes of pilgrims—known as *miquelots*—who flocked here even during the Hundred Years' War (1337–1453), when the region was in English hands.

Out of the French rulers' desire to protect Brittany from subjugation by the Normans (whose leader, William the Conqueror, had assumed the English throne in 1066) came the clever strategy of what we would call propaganda. Because of St. Michel's legendary role as dragon slayer and leader of the Heavenly Army, the French lords transformed him, and the Mont, into a major rallying force. During this period the abbey remained a symbol, both physical and emotional, of French independence.

By 1203, King Philippe-Auguste of France had succeeded in wresting the Mont back from the Normans and to shore up French popularity in Normandy he provided funds to restore the abbey. The resulting, greatly expanded, three-level Gothic abbey (1203–1228) became known as *La Merveille* (The Marvel).

During the French Revolution, the abbey was converted into a prison, but shortly after Victor Hugo (of *Hunchback of Notre Dame* fame) declaimed "A toad in a reliquary! When will we understand in France the sanctity of monuments?," the prison was converted into a museum in 1874 and, fittingly, Emmanuel Frémiet's great gilt statute of St. Michael was added to the spire in 1897.

Only at high tide is the Mont transformed into an island.

CLIMB EVERY MONT

Mont-St-Michel is the result of more than 500 years of construction, from 1017 to 1521, and traces the history of French medieval architecture, from earliest Romanesque to its last flowering, Flamboyant Gothic.

HOW TO TOUR THE MONT

There are two basic options for touring the abbey of Mont-St-Michel: guided tours and exploring on your own (which you can do with the aid of an excellent audioguide tour in English). Realistically, a visit to Mont-St-Michel's abbey and village needs a half a day but an entire day at least is needed if you do several of the museums, go on one of the abbey's guided tours, and fit in a walk on the surrounding expanses of sand.

General admission to the abbey includes an optional hour-long guided tour in English, offered twice a day and night in high season. A more extensive, two-hour-long guided tour in French costs an extra 4 euros. The English-language tour takes you throughout the spectacular **Église Abbatiale,** the abbey church that crowns the rock, as well as the **Merveille,** a 13th-century, three-story collection of rooms and passageways built by King Philippe-Auguste. The French tour also includes the celebrated **Escalier de Dentelle** (Lace Staircase) and other highlights. Invest in at least one tour while you are here—each of them gets you on top of or into things you can't see alone.

If you do go it alone, stop halfway up Grande-Rue at the church of St-Pierre to admire its richly carved side chapel with its dramatic statue of St. Michael slaying the dragon. The famous **Grand Degré** staircase leads to the abbey entrance, from which a wider flight of steps climbs to the **Saut Gautier Terrace** outside the sober, dignified church. After visiting the arcaded cloisters alongside, you can wander at leisure, and probably get lost, among the maze of vaulted halls.

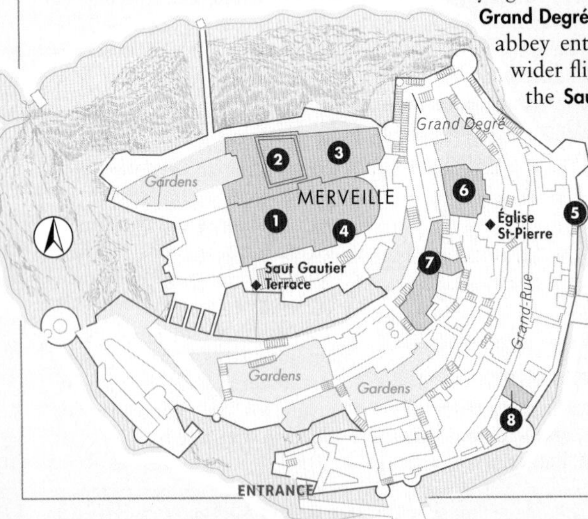

(above) Watchtower at Mont-Saint-Michel

DON'T MISS

❶ **Église Abbatiale** (above). Crowning the mount, the Abbey Church is in two different styles. The main nave and transepts (1020–1135) were built in the Norman Romanesque style; after the collapse of the original chancel in 1421, it was rebuilt in Flamboyant Gothic with seven Rayonnant-style chapels.

❷ **La Cloitre de l'Abbatiale** (above). The main cloister was the only part of the abbey complex open to "heaven"—the sky. Its southern gallery contains the lavabos (washing stands) of the monks. Look for the column capitals beautifully chiseled with flower and vine motifs.

❸ **Salle des Chevaliers** (above). Part of the triple-tiered "La Merveille"—the complex of state chambers, refectory, and cloister that surrounds the main church—the Knights' Hall was originally a scriptorium for copying manuscripts. It was the only heated room on the Mont.

❹ **Escalier de Dentelle** Set atop one of the "flying buttresses" (top right) of the main church, the famous perforated Lace Staircase is a bravura Gothic showpiece of carved stone. It leads to a parapet—adorned with stone gargoyles—390 feet above the sea.

MUSEUMS

Scattered through the Mont are four mini-museums. The most popular is the ❺ **Archéoscope** whose sound-and-light show, *L'Eau et La Lumiere* (Water and Light), offers the best introduction to the Mont. Some exhibits use wax figures garbed in the most elegant 15th-century–style clothes. ❻ **The Logis Tiphaine** is the home that Bertrand Duguesclin, a general fierce in his allegiance to the cause of French independence, built for his wife Tiphaine in 1365. ❼ **The Musée Historique** traces the 1,000-year history of the Mont in one of its former prisons. ❽ **The Musée Maritime** explores the science of the Mont's tidal bay and has a vast collection of model ships.

INFORMATION

☎ 02–33–89–80–00.
🌐 www.ot-montsaintmichel.com

light-years away. **Pros:** magnificent architecture; luxurious rooms. **Cons:** three different buildings; no air-conditioning in the château. *Rooms from: €260* ✉ *Les Escures-Commes, off the D6, Port-en-Bessin-Huppain* ☎ *02–31–51–25–25* *www.lacheneviere.com* *Closed Dec.–Mar.* *26 rooms, 3 suites* *Some meals.*

OÙ EST PRIVATE RYAN?

The American Cemetery is a moving tribute to the fallen, with its Wall of the Missing, drumlike chapel, and avenues of holly oaks trimmed to resemble open parachutes. The crisply mowed lawns are studded with 9,386 marble tombstones; this is where Stephen Spielberg's fictional hero Captain John Miller was supposed to have been buried in *Saving Private Ryan*.

SAINTE-MÈRE ÉGLISE

59 km (22 miles) northwest of Bayeux.

Sainte-Mère's symbolic importance as the first French village to be liberated from the Nazis is commemorated by the Borne 0 (Zero) outside the town hall—a large dome milestone marking the start of the Voie de la Liberté (Freedom Way), charting the Allies' progress across France. The main reason to visit, especially if you're here for the D-Day Beaches, is the fascinating Musée Airborne.

GETTING HERE

The nearest train station is in neigbhoring Carentan. Otherwise, the town is a short drive from the D-Day Beaches or Bayeux.

EXPLORING

Musée Airborne (*Airborne Museum*). Constructed behind the town church in 1964 in the form of an open parachute, this fascinating museum houses documents, maps, mementos, and one of the Waco CG4A gliders used to drop troops. ✉ *14 rue Eisenhower, St Mere L'Eglise* ☎ *02–33–41–41–35* *www.musee-airborne.com* *€8* *May–Aug., daily 9–7; Apr. and Sept., daily 9–6:30; Oct.–Mar., daily 10–6.*

Sainte-Mère Église. At 2:30 am on June 6, 1944, the 82nd Airborne Division was dropped over Sainte-Mère, heralding the start of D-Day operations. After securing their position, U.S. forces pushed north, then west, cutting off the Cotentin Peninsula on June 18 and taking Cherbourg on June 26. German defenses proved fiercer farther south, and St-Lô was not liberated until July 19. ✉ *Saint-Mère Eglise* ☎ *02–33–21–00–33 tourist office* *www.ot-baieducotentin.fr.*

ST-LÔ

36 km (22 miles) southwest of Bayeux.

St-Lô, perched dramatically on a rocky spur above the Vire Valley, was a key communications center that suffered so badly in World War II it became known as the "capital of ruins." The medieval Église Notre-Dame bears mournful witness to those dark days: its imposing, spire-top west front was never rebuilt, merely shored up with a wall of greenish stone. Reconstruction elsewhere, though, was wholesale. Some of it was spectacular, like the slender, spiral-staircase tower outside the Mairie (Town Hall); the circular theater; or the openwork belfry of the church of Ste-Croix. The town was freed by American troops, and its rebuilding was financed with U.S. support, notably from the city of Baltimore. The Hôpital Mémorial France–États-Unis (France–United States Memorial Hospital), designed by Paul Nelson and featuring a giant mosaic by Fernand Léger, was named to honor those links.

GETTING HERE

Several trains daily come from Caen (50 mins, €14.10). Another 11 per day, departing from Gare St-Lazare, connect St-Lô and the capital; the trip requires a change in either Caen or Lison (3 hrs, €46).

Visitor Information St-Lô Tourist Office. ☎ *02–14–29–00–17* 🌐 *www.saint-lo-agglo.fr/Decouvrir-et-Visiter.*

EXPLORING

Haras National (*National Stud*). St-Lô, the capital of the Manche *département* (province), also considers itself France's horse capital. Hundreds of breeders are based in its environs, and the Haras National stud farm was established here in 1886. It can be visited by guided tour only—call the tourist office at least a month in advance to book one. ✉ *Rue du Maréchal Juin, St-Lô* ☎ *08–11–90–21–31 €0.34 per min, 02–14–29–00–17 tourist office* 🌐 *www.haras-nationaux.fr* 🎫 *€6* ⏲ *Tours mid-Apr.–June and Sept., daily 2:30, 3:30, and 4:30; July and Aug., daily 11, 2, 3, 4, and 5.*

Musée des Beaux-Arts et d'Histoire. St-Lô has the perfect French provincial art museum. Its halls are airy, seldom busy, and not too big, yet full of varied exhibits—including an unexpected masterpiece: *Gombault et Macée,* a set of nine silk-and-wool tapestries woven in Bruges around 1600 relating a tale about a shepherd couple, exquisitely showcased in a special circular room. Other highlights include brash modern tapestries by Jean Lurçat; paintings by Corot, Boudin, and Géricault; and court miniatures by Daniel Saint. Photographs, models, and documents evoke St-Lô's wartime devastation. ✉ *Centre Culturel, Pl. du Champ-de-Mars, St-Lô* ☎ *02–33–72–52–55* 🌐 *www.musees-basse-normandie.fr* 🎫 *€2.75* ⏲ *Wed.–Sun. 2–6.*

MONT-ST-MICHEL

61 km (39 miles) southwest of St-Lô via D999 and N175, 123 km (77 miles) southwest of Caen, 67 km (42 miles) north of Rennes, 325 km (202 miles) west of Paris.

Fodor's Choice ★ Mont-St-Michel is the third-most-visited sight in France, after the Eiffel Tower and the Louvre. This beached mass of granite, rising some 400 feet, was begun in 709 and is crowned with the "Marvel," or great monastery, which was built during the 13th century.

GETTING HERE

There are two routes to Mont-St-Michel, depending on whether you arrive from Caen or from Paris. From Caen you can take either an early-morning or an afternoon train to Pontorson, the nearest rail station (2 hrs, €28.80), and then hop a cab or bus for the 15-minute drive to the foot of the abbey (both leave from in front of the station). From Paris, take the TGV from Gare Montparnasse to Rennes, in adjacent Brittany, and proceed onward by bus; the total journey costs €74.30. There are several early-morning choices that allow you a full day on the Mont, including one train leaving at 7 am and arriving at 10:50 am, and another leaving at 7:34 am and arriving at 11:10 am. Paris City Vision (*www.pariscityvision.com*) also runs full-day bus excursions from the capital to Mont-St-Michel for €175, meals and admissions included. But this is definitely not for the faint of heart—buses leave Paris at 7:15 am and return around 9:15 pm.

Visitor Information Mont-St-Michel Tourist Office. *02–33–60–14–30* *www.ot-montsaintmichel.com.*

EXPLORING

Abbaye du Mont-St-Michel. *02–33–89–80–00* *www.mont-saint-michel.monuments-nationaux.fr* *€9, €13.50 with audio guide* *May–Aug., daily 9–7; Sept.–Apr., daily 9:30–6.*

See highlighted feature for more information.

WHERE TO STAY

$$$$ HOTEL **Auberge St-Pierre.** This inn is a popular spot due to the fact that it's in a half-timber 15th-century building adjacent to the ramparts and has its own garden restaurant (half-board rates are available). **Pros:** great location; interesting building; good dining options. **Cons:** not all rooms have views. *Rooms from: €217* *Grande-Rue, Mont-St-Michel* *02–33–60–14–03* *www.auberge-saint-pierre.fr* *21 rooms* *Some meals.*

$$$ HOTEL **La Mère Poulard.** Mont-St-Michel's most famous hostelry can be tough to book: after all, its historic restaurant is the birthplace of Mère Poulard's legendary soufflé-like omelet. **Pros:** right at the entrance to the abbey; one of the city's best restaurants; full of history. **Cons:** breakfast is extra; some rooms are small. *Rooms from: €171* *Grande-Rue, Mont-St-Michel* *02–33–89–68–68* *www.merepoulard.com* *27 rooms* *No meals.*

$ HOTEL **Les Terrasses Poulard.** Run by the same folks who own the noted Mère Poulard hotel, this charming ensemble of buildings is clustered around a small garden in the middle of the Mont. **Pros:** lots of elbow room; affordable rates; great setting. **Cons:** a long way to the parking lot; steps to climb. *Rooms from: €99* *Grande-Rue, Mont-St-Michel* *02–33–89–02–02* *www.terrasses-poulard.com* *29 rooms* *No meals.*

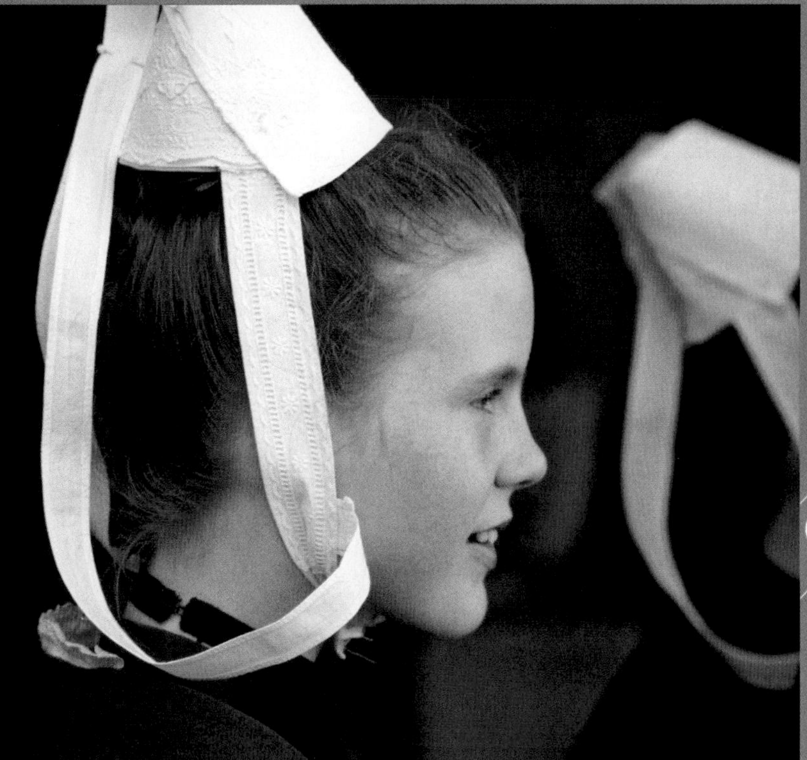

6

BRITTANY

WELCOME TO BRITTANY

TOP REASONS TO GO

★ **Waterworld:** Experience the extreme drama of the Granite Coast, with its crazy-shape outcrops, or the rippling waters of the Bay of Morbihan, snuggling in the Gulf Stream behind the angry Atlantic.

★ **The wild isle:** Venture down the untamed Quiberon Peninsula and catch a boat to rugged, unspoiled Belle-Ile-en-Mer, Brittany's wildest island.

★ **Gauguin's Pont-Aven:** A *cité des artistes*, Pont-Aven and its colorful folkloric ways helped ignite the painter's interest in Tahiti.

★ **Unidentical twins:** A ferry ride across the Rance River links two delightfully contrasting towns: romantic, once pirate-ridden St-Malo and genteel, Edwardian Dinard.

★ **Ancient wonders:** Contemplate the solemn majesty of row upon row of *anciens* menhirs at Carnac, the "French Stonehenge."

1 Northeast Brittany and the Channel Coast. The northern half of Brittany is demarcated by its 240-km (150-mile) Channel Coast, which stretches from Cancale, just west of Normandy's Mont-St-Michel, to Morlaix. This can be loosely divided into two parts: the Côte d'Emeraude (Emerald Coast), with cliffs punctuated by golden, curving beaches; and the Côte de Granit Rose (Pink Granite Coast), including the astonishing area around Trébeurden, where Brittany's granite takes amazing forms that glow an otherworldly pink. On the road heading there are the gateway city of Rennes; the oyster mecca of Cancale; and the great port of St-Malo, where stone ramparts conjure up the days of marauding corsairs.

GETTING ORIENTED

Bretons like to say they are Celtic, not Gallic, and other French people sometimes feel they are in a foreign land when they visit this jagged triangle perched on the northwest tip of mainland Europe. Two sides of the triangle are defined by the sea. Brittany's northern coast faces the English Channel; its western coast defies the Atlantic Ocean. The north of Brittany tends to be wilder than the south, or Basse Bretagne, where the countryside becomes softer as it descends toward Nantes and the Loire. But wherever you go, "Côtes d'Armor"—the Land of the Sea—is never too far away.

2 The Atlantic Coast. Bypassing the lobster-claw of Brittany's Finistère ("Land's End"), this westernmost region tempts with folkloric treasures like Ste-Anne-la-Palud (famed for its *pardon* festival); Quimper, noted for its signature ceramics; and cheerful riverside villages like Pont-Aven, which Gauguin immortalized in many paintings. Here, the 320-km (200-mile) Atlantic coast zigzags southeast, its frenzied, cliff-bashing surf alternating with sprawling beaches and busy harbors. Belle-Ile is a jewel off the Morbihan coast, another beautiful stretch of shoreline. Enjoy its away-from-it-all atmosphere, because the bustling city of Nantes lies just to the southeast.

EATING AND DRINKING WELL IN BRITTANY

One taste and you'll know why Cancale oysters are so prized *(above)*; who can resist those Breton dessert crêpes? *(right, top)*; Plougastel strawberries are red as rubies *(right, bottom)*.

Bounded on two of its three sides by water, Brittany is blessed with an abundance of fresh seafood. Aquatic delights, not surprisingly, dominate Breton cuisine, but crêpes, lamb, and butter also play starring roles.

Maritime headliners include *coquilles St-Jacques* (scallops); langoustines, which are something between a large shrimp and a lobster; and oysters, prized for their balance of briny and sweet. Perhaps the most famous regional seafood dishes are *homard à l'armoricaine*, lobster with cream, and *cotriade*, fish soup with potatoes, onions, garlic, and butter.

Beyond the sea, the lamb that hails from farms on the little island of Ouessant is well known. Called *pré-salé,* or "salt meadow," lambs feed on sea-salted grass, which tenderizes their meat while their hearts are still pumping. Try the regional *ragoût de mouton* and you can taste the difference. Of all its culinary treasures, however, Brittany is best known as home of the humble crêpe—a large, delicate pancake served warm with a variety of sweet or savory fillings.

CELTIC ELIXIR

Chouchen, Brittany's classic meadlike beverage made from honey, dates back to Celtic times, when it was considered an aphrodisiac and an *elixir d'immortalité*. This delicious drink is traditionally served cold as an aperitif to highlight its refreshing qualities and its soft, earthy flavor.

CRÊPES

Brittany's most illustrious contribution to French cuisine is the crêpe and its heartier sibling the *galette*. What's the difference between the two? The darker galette is made with tender buckwheat called *blé noir* or *blé sarrasin,* and has a deeper flavor that's best paired with savory fillings—like lobster, mushrooms, or the traditional ham and cheese. A crêpe is wafer-thin and made with a lighter batter. It is typically served with sweet fillings like strawberries and cream, apples in brandy, or chocolate. Accompanied by a glass of local cider, galettes and crêpes make an ideal light, inexpensive meal. Traditionally, crêpes are eaten from the tails toward the center point to save the most flavorful, buttery part for last.

CANCALE OYSTER

At around €8 a dozen, you simply can't do better than a plate of freshly shucked Cancale oysters and half a lemon from a seafood stand along the quay. Best enjoyed atop the breezy sea wall overlooking the Mont-St-Michel bay, you can just toss the shells into the water after slurping the succulent insides. Cancale's oyster beds benefit from some of the world's highest tides and strongest currents, which keep the oysters oxygen- and plankton-rich, resulting in a large, firm, yet tender specimen.

PLOUGASTEL STRAWBERRY AND CAMUS DE BRETAGNE ARTICHOKE

Together, the four regions of Brittany make up France's highest-yielding farmland. Among the more prosaic crops grown here are two standouts: the large, fleshy camus artichoke and the plump Plougastel strawberry. Come spring, the markets of Brittany (and Paris, for that matter) are teeming with enthusiastic cooks just itching to get their hands on the first produce of the season. The juicy Plougastel strawberries only appear for a few weeks in June, while artichoke season runs into the fall.

LE BEURRE

Temperate Brittany's lush grazing lands make for exceptional milk products and, like wine, they are discussed in terms of *élévages* (maturity) and *terroir* (origin). Butter your roll at a four-star Paris restaurant and you're likely getting a taste of Brittany's finest—*le beurre Bordier.* Jean-Yves Bordier, headquartered in St-Malo's Vieille Ville, sets the gold standard for butter, and his luscious sweet cream version is exported daily to top restaurants throughout France. Other flavors include a pungent purple- and green-flecked algae butter (best slathered on sourdough bread and eaten with oysters), and the *beurre fleur de sel de Guérande,* laced with crunchy grains of the prized gray-hued salt hand-harvested in the salt marshes of Guérande, near La Baule.

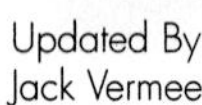

Updated By Jack Vermee

Wherever you wander in Brittany—along jagged coastal cliffs, through cobbled seaport streets, into time-burnished cider pubs—you'll hear the primal pulse of Celtic music. Made up of bagpipes, drums, and the thin, haunting filigree of a tin whistle, these folkloric tunes tell you that you are in the land of the Bretons, where Celtic bloodlines run as deep as a druid's roots into the rocky, sea-swept soil.

France's most fiercely and determinedly ethnic people, the Bretons delight in celebrating their ancient culture—circle dancing at street fairs, the women donning starched lace-bonnet *coiffes,* and the men in striped fishermen's shirts at the least sign of a regional celebration. They name their children Erwan and Edwige, carry sacred statues in ceremonial religious processions called pardons and pray in hobbit-scale stone churches decked with elfin, moonfaced gargoyles. Scattered over the mossy hillsides stand Stonehenge-like dolmens and menhirs (prehistoric standing stones), eerie testimony to a primordial culture that predated and has long outlived Frankish France.

Similarities in character, situation, or culture to certain islands across the Channel are by no means coincidental. Indeed, the Celts that migrated to this westernmost outcrop of the French landmass spent much of the Iron Age on the British Isles, where they introduced the indigenes to innovations like the potter's wheel, the rotary millstone, and the compass. This first influx of Continental culture to Great Britain was greeted with typically mixed feelings, and by the late 5th century AD the Saxon hordes had sent these Celtic "Brits" packing southward, to the peninsula that became Brittany. So completely did they dominate their new, Cornwall-like peninsula (appropriately named Finistère, from *finis terrae,* or "land's end") that when in 496 they allied themselves with Clovis, the king of the Franks, he felt as if he'd just claimed a little bit of England.

Needless to say, the cultural exchange flowed both ways over the Channel. From their days on the British Isles the Bretons brought a folklore that shares with England the bittersweet legend of Tristan and Iseult, and that weaves mystical tales of the Cornwall—Cornouaille—of King Arthur and Merlin. They brought a language that still renders village names unpronounceable: Aber-Wrac'h, Tronoën, Locmariaquer, Pouldreuzic, Kerhornaouen. They brought a way of life with them, too: half-timber seaside cider bars, their blackened-oak tables softened with prim bits of lace; stone cottages fringed with clumps of hollyhock, hydrangea, and foxglove; bearded fishermen in yellow oilskins heaving the day's catch into weather-beaten boats as terns and seagulls wheel in their wake. It's a way of life that feels deliciously exotic to the Frenchman and—like the ancient drone of the bagpipes—comfortably, delightfully, even innately familiar to the Anglo-Saxon.

PLANNING

WHEN TO GO

The tourist season is short in Brittany: late June through early September. Long, damp winters keep visitors away, and many hotels are closed until Easter. Brittany is particularly crowded in July and August, when most French people are on vacation, so why not opt for crowd-free June or September? Some say early October, with autumnal colors and crisp evenings, is even better and truly makes for an invigorating visit. But if you want to sample local folklore, late summer is the most festive time to come.

PLANNING YOUR TIME

If you have just a few days here, choose your coast: Channel or Atlantic! Cliffs and beaches, culture and history—both shorelines offer all these and more. St-Malo makes a good base if you're Channel-bound. Dinard, the elegant Belle Époque resort once favored by British aristocrats, is nearby; and the lively, student-filled city of Rennes offers an urban respite.

Pretty Vannes is a good base for exploring the Atlantic coast. Highlights hereabouts include lively Quimper, with its fine cathedral and coveted pottery; the painters' village of Pont-Aven, made famous by Gauguin; the prehistoric menhirs of Carnac; the rugged island of Belle-Ile-en Mer; and the picturesque Bay of Morbihan. The third side of the Brittany triangle is its verdant, unhurried hinterland. Charming—but forget it unless you're here for a month.

FESTIVALS AND PARDONS

It has been said that there are as many Breton saints as there are stones in the ground. One of the great attractions of Brittany, therefore, remains its many festivals, pardons (religious processions), and folklore events. Banners and saintly statues are borne in colorful parades, accompanied by hymns, and the events are often capped by a feast. In February, the great Pardon de Terre-Neuve takes place at St-Malo. Nantes prepares for Easter with a pre-Lenten carnival procession, and then follows up in June with a ceremonial Feux de Saint-Jean (bonfire honoring St. John). July sees Quimper's Celtic Festival de Cornouaille, while August brings Pont-Aven's Festival of the Golden Gorse and a big

DID YOU KNOW?

Elaborately half-timbered houses (called *colombage* in French) are everywhere in Brittany, relics of the medieval days when this region, along with Normandy, was colonized by the English.

pardon in Ste-Anne-la-Palud. Another pardon held in Le Folgoët during September is one of the most extraordinary, with flocks of bishops, Bretons in traditional costumes, and devout pilgrims.

GETTING HERE AND AROUND

In just over two hours the TGV train from Paris can whisk you to Rennes, the hub of Brittany. Once in the region, you'll find that the rail network can take you onward to many popular places. You'll need to combine a train ride with a short bus jaunt, though, to reach others; and a car will be required if you want to see some of the most sublime (and secluded) landscapes. If you're driving from Paris, you're best to approach Brittany via the A11 expressway.

AIR TRAVEL

The closest major airports are Paris's Charles de Gaulle (Roissy) and Orly; however, Brittany does have several regional airports. The Aéroport Nantes Atlantique and the Aéroport Rennes Bretagne are both served by big players like Air France (🌐 *www.airfrance.com*), as well as assorted low-cost airlines—including Flybe (🌐 *www.flybe.com*) and HOP! (🌐 *www.hop.fr*)—which provide air links to other European cities, sometimes on a seasonal basis. The Aéroport de Dinard-Pleurtuit-Saint-Malo, meanwhile, has four weekly connections to London (Stansted) operated by Ryanair (🌐 *www.ryanair.com*).

Airport Information Aéroport de Dinard-Pleurtuit-Saint-Malo. ☎ *02-99-46-18-46* 🌐 *www.dinard.aeroport.fr.* **Aéroport Nantes Atlantique.** ☎ *08-92-56-88-00 €.34 per minute* 🌐 *www.nantes-aeroport.fr.* **Aéroport Rennes Bretagne.** ☎ *02-99-29-60-00* 🌐 *www.rennes.aeroport.fr.*

6

BOAT TRAVEL

Brittany Ferries is the leading company for maritime transportation between this region and the United Kingdom. It offers daily overnight crossings from Portsmouth to St-Malo in high season (11 hrs; from €160 for a car and two passengers). Vessels also make the crossing from Plymouth to Roscoff, on Brittany's westernmost tip, up to two times daily: daytime trips take six hours, nighttime ones take nine (from €215 for a car and two passengers).

Boat Information Brittany Ferries. ☎ *0871/244-0744 in U.K., 08-25-82-88-28 in France (€0.34 per min)* 🌐 *www.brittanyferries.com.*

BUS TRAVEL

Brittany is serviced by a bewildering number of bus companies. Generally speaking, routes in each part of it are coordinated through an umbrella organization: for travel in the Ille-et-Vilaine region around Rennes, Illenoo is a good bet; for the Morbihan region around Vannes use CTM or Keolis Atlantique; for Finistère and coastal towns near Quimper, arrange your trip through CAT; and for the Côtes d'Armor region around St-Malo, check out Tibus or Keolis Emeraude.

Bus Information CAT. ☎ *02-98-44-60-60* 🌐 *www.cat29.fr.* **CTM.** ☎ *02-97-01-22-01 for Vannes* 🌐 *www.lactm.com.* **Illenoo.** ☎ *08-10-35-10-35 €0.34 per min* 🌐 *www.illenoo-services.fr.* **Keolis Atlantique.** ☎ *02-97-47-29-64* 🌐 *www.keolis-atlantique.com.* **Keolis Emeraude.** ☎ *02-99-19-70-70* 🌐 *www.keolis-emeraude.com.* **Tibus.** ☎ *08-10-22-22-22 €0.34 per min* 🌐 *www.tibus.fr.*

CAR TRAVEL

Rennes, the gateway to Brittany, is 347 km (215 miles) west of Paris. It can be reached in about three hours via Le Mans using A11 then A81 (A11 continues southwest from Le Mans to Nantes). Rennes is also linked by good roads to Quimper (N24/N165), Vannes (N24/N166), and several other key locales. A car is pretty much essential if you want to see out-of-the-way places; when planning a coastal road trip, just remember to allocate plenty of time—winding roads make for slow (albeit scenic) driving.

TRAIN TRAVEL

High-speed TGVs from Paris's Gare Montparnasse travel multiple times a day to Rennes (2 hrs, 10 mins), Nantes (2 hrs, 15 mins), Vannes (3 hrs, 20 mins), La Baule (3 hrs, 15 mins), Lorient (3 hrs, 50 mins), and Quimper (4 hrs, 30 mins). The region as a whole is nicely threaded by train lines, making most Breton towns accessible by rail; however, some communities—like Cancale and Carnac—can be reached by car or bus only.

Train Information SNCF. ☎ *3635 €0.34 per min* 🌐 *www.voyages-sncf.com.*
TGV. 🌐 *www.tgv.com.*

RESTAURANTS

Crêpes, galettes, and seafood, seafood, seafood are the star attractions at restaurants throughout Brittany. From the fresh oyster stands along the seafront in Cancale to the finer restaurants of St-Malo and Rennes, you will find ample opportunity to indulge in these delicious offerings—all of which can be washed down by a bottle of locally produced *cidre* (cider). Other regional specialties include the Breton version of pot-au-feu (called *kig ha farz*), featuring tender pork or beef surrounded by buckwheat dumplings, and the legendary *kouign amann*, a divine butter cake.

HOTELS

Aside from the usual selection of hotels in the main cities (Rennes and Nantes), Brittany has plenty of small and appealing family-run accommodations that cater to seasonal visitors. Note that many close for one or more months between October and March. Booking ahead is strongly advised for the Easter period. This is also the case for midsummer, when prices are routinely ratcheted up by 30% to 50%. Dinard, on the English Channel, and La Baule, on the Atlantic, are the area's two most expensive resorts. *Hotel reviews have been shortened. For full information, visit Fodors.com.*

WHAT IT COSTS IN EUROS

	$	$$	$$$	$$$$
Restaurants	under €18	€18–€24	€25–€32	over €32
Hotels	under €106	€106–€145	€146–€215	over €215

Restaurant prices are the average cost of a main course at dinner or, if dinner is not served, at lunch. Hotel prices are the lowest cost of a standard double room in high season.

VISITOR INFORMATION

Different Breton regions have their own tourist offices, as do many individual communities (the latter are listed under specific destinations below); however, your single best source for trip-planning information in English is the Brittany Tourism website.

Brittany Tourism. *www.brittanytourism.com.*

Comité Départemental du Tourisme de Loire-Atlantique. *11 rue du Château de l'Eraudière, Nantes 02–51–72–95–30 www.ohlaloireatlantique.com.*

Côtes-d'Armor Tourisme. *7 rue St-Benoît, St-Brieuc 02–96–58–06–58 www.cotesdarmor.com.*

Finistère Tourisme. *4 rue du 19 mars 1962, Quimper 02–98–76–25–64 www.finisteretourisme.com.*

Maison de la Bretagne. *8 rue de l'Arrivée, Paris 01–53–63–11–50 www.maisondelabretagne.fr.*

PARLEZ-VOUS BRETON?

Most place names in Brittany are in the Breton language; the popular term *plou* means "parish"—this is where the French got the word *plouc,* meaning "hick." Other common geographical names are *coat* (forest), *mor* (sea), *aber* or *aven* (estuary), *ster* (river), and *enez* (island). *Ty* and *ti,* like the French *chez,* mean "at the house of." Traditional Breton folkways are an integral part of France's cultural patrimony—and a priceless boost to tourism—so preserving the Breton language is a goal shared by many.

NORTHEAST BRITTANY AND THE CHANNEL COAST

It's useful to know that Brittany is divided into two nearly equal parts—Upper Brittany, along the Channel Coast, and Lower Brittany. The latter (called Basse-Bretagne or Bretagne Bretonnante in French) is, generally speaking, the more interesting. But the Channel Coast of Upper Brittany has its share of marvels. The rolling farmland around Rennes is strewn with mighty castles, remnants of Brittany's ceaseless efforts to repel invaders during the Middle Ages and a testimony to the wealth derived from pirate and merchant ships. The beautiful Côte d'Émeraude (Emerald Coast) stretches west from Cancale to St-Brieuc, and the dramatic Côte de Granit Rose (Pink Granite Coast) extends from Paimpol to Trébeurden and the Corniche Bretonne. Follow the coastal routes D786 and D10—winding, narrow roads that total less than 100 km (62 miles) but can take five hours to drive; the spectacular views that unfold en route make the journey worthwhile.

VITRÉ

42 km (26 miles) east of Rennes via N157 and D777.

There's still a feel of the Middle Ages about the formidable castle, tightly packed half-timber houses, remaining ramparts, and dark alleyways of

Vitré (pronounced vee- *tray*). Built high above the Vilaine Valley, the small medieval walled town that spreads out from the castle's gates is the best-preserved in Brittany and utterly beguiling.

GETTING HERE

Several trains traveling from Paris through Rennes stop daily in Vitré. The trip from Rennes takes 30 minutes (€8.20).

Visitor Information Vitré Tourist Office. ☎ *02–99–75–04–46* 🌐 *www.ot-vitre.fr.*

EXPLORING

Château de Vitré. Rebuilt in the 14th and 15th centuries to protect Brittany from invasion, the fairy-tale, 11th-century Château de Vitré—shaped in an imposing triangle with fat, round towers—proved to be one of the province's most successful fortresses: during the Hundred Years' War (1337–1453) the English repeatedly failed to take it, even when they occupied the rest of the town. It's a splendid sight, especially from the vantage point of Rue de Fougères across the river valley below. Time, not foreigners, came closest to ravaging the castle, which has been heavily though tastefully restored during the past century.

The **Hôtel de Ville** (town hall), however, is an unfortunate 1913 accretion to the castle courtyard. Visit the wing to the left of the entrance, beginning with the **Tour St-Laurent** and its museum, which contains 15th- and 16th-century sculptures, Aubusson tapestries, and engravings. Continue along the walls via the **Tour de l'Argenterie**—which contains a macabre collection of stuffed frogs and reptiles preserved in glass jars—to the **Tour de l'Oratoire** (Oratory Tower). ✉ *Pl. du Château, Vitré* ☎ *02–99–75–04–54* 🌐 *www.mairie-vitre.com* 🎫 *€4* ⏲ *Apr.–June and Sept., daily 10–12:30 and 2–6; July and Aug., daily 10–6; Oct.–Mar., Mon. and Wed.–Fri. 10:30–12:30 and 2–5, weekends 2–5.*

Notre-Dame. The church of Notre-Dame, with its fine, pinnacled south front, was built in the 15th and 16th centuries. This is a good starting point to visit the 10 or so other picturesque historical sites, from medieval postern gateways to the 14th-century St. Nicolas hospital chapel (now a museum of religious art) within town; other jewels, such as Madame de Sévigné's Château-Musée des Roches-Sévigné, are set in the nearby countryside. Inquire at the tourist office for details. ✉ *Pl. Notre-Dame, Vitré.*

Tour de la Bridole. Fragments of the town's medieval ramparts include the 15th-century Tour de la Bridole, five blocks up from Vitré's castle. ✉ *Rue de la Bridole, near Pl. de la République, Vitré.*

WHERE TO STAY

$ HOTEL **Le Petit Billot.** Faded pastel tones and carved paneling in the breakfast room give this small family-run hotel a delightful French provincial air; when you retire you'll find that the guest rooms may not be spacious but they are spic-and-span—and a steal at the price. **Pros:** family ambience; great value. **Cons:** rooms are small; most bathrooms have only showers, not tubs. $ *Rooms from: €65* ✉ *5 bis, pl. du Général-Leclerc, Vitré* ☎ *02–99–75–02–10* 🌐 *www.hotel-vitre.com* *21 rooms* 🍽 *No meals.*

RENNES

347 km (215 miles) west of Paris, 107 km (66 miles) north of Nantes.

Rennes (pronounced wren) is the capital of and traditional gateway to this region. It's also one of Brittany's liveliest cities, thanks to the 40,000-odd students who set a youthful tone during the school year. Place Ste-Anne, where bars and cafés are housed in medieval buildings with character to spare, is particularly packed. Although summer seems to happen elsewhere for most Rennais, it is still a pleasant time for visitors. United with the Kingdom of France in 1532, Rennes has long been the political center of Brittany, and its stature is reflected in grand public edifices—many of them erected after fire swept through the city in 1720. The remaining cobbled streets and 15th-century half-timber houses form an interesting contrast to the classical feel of the cathedral and Jacques Gabriel's disciplined 18th-century granite buildings, broad avenues, and spacious squares.

GETTING HERE AND AROUND

The TGV *Atlantique*arrives from Paris's Gare Montparnasse 22 times daily (2 hrs, 10 mins; €30–€50). Rennes's train station (a 20-minute walk from the heart of the city) can also be reached from Nantes (1 hr, 30 mins; €26.30) and St-Malo (55 mins; €15). Buses from Nantes (2 hrs, €2), St-Malo (2 hrs, €5.70), and Mont-St-Michel (70 mins, €11) pull into the *gare routière* next door, though it's not the safest place to hang out. Within the city, buses and subways operated by STAR (🌐 *www.metro-rennes-metropole.fr*) will get you anywhere you want to go. If you'd prefer to cycle, try the Vélo STAR rental scheme (🌐 *www.levelostar.fr*); you'll pay €1 for an hour of pedaling.

Visitor Information Rennes Tourist Office. ☎ *02–99–67–11–11* 🌐 *www.tourisme-rennes.com.*

6

EXPLORING

Cathédrale St-Pierre. A late-18th-century building in Classical style that took 57 years to construct, the Cathédrale St-Pierre looms above Rue de la Monnaie at the west end of the Vieille Ville (Old Town), bordered by the Rance River. Stop in to admire its richly decorated interior and outstanding 16th-century Flemish altarpiece. ✉ *Carrefour de la Cathédrale, Rennes* 🌐 *www.tourisme-rennes.com* ⏲ *Daily 9:30–noon and 3–6.*

Musée de Bretagne (*Museum of Brittany*). Designed by superstar architect Christian de Portzamparc, this museum occupies a vast three-part space that it shares with the Rennes municipal library and Espaces des Sciences. Portzamparc's layout harmonizes nicely with the organization of the museum's extensive ethnographic and archaeological collection, which depicts the everyday life of Bretons from prehistoric times to the present. There's also a space devoted to the famous Dreyfus Affair; Alfred Dreyfus, an army captain who was wrongly accused of espionage and whose case was championed by Émile Zola, was tried a second time in Rennes in 1899. ✉ *10 cours des Allies, Rennes* ☎ *02–23–40–66–00* 🌐 *www.musee-bretagne.fr* 🎟 *€5 museum, €9 with exhibitions and planetarium* ⏲ *Tues. noon–9, Wed.–Fri. noon–7, weekends 2–7.*

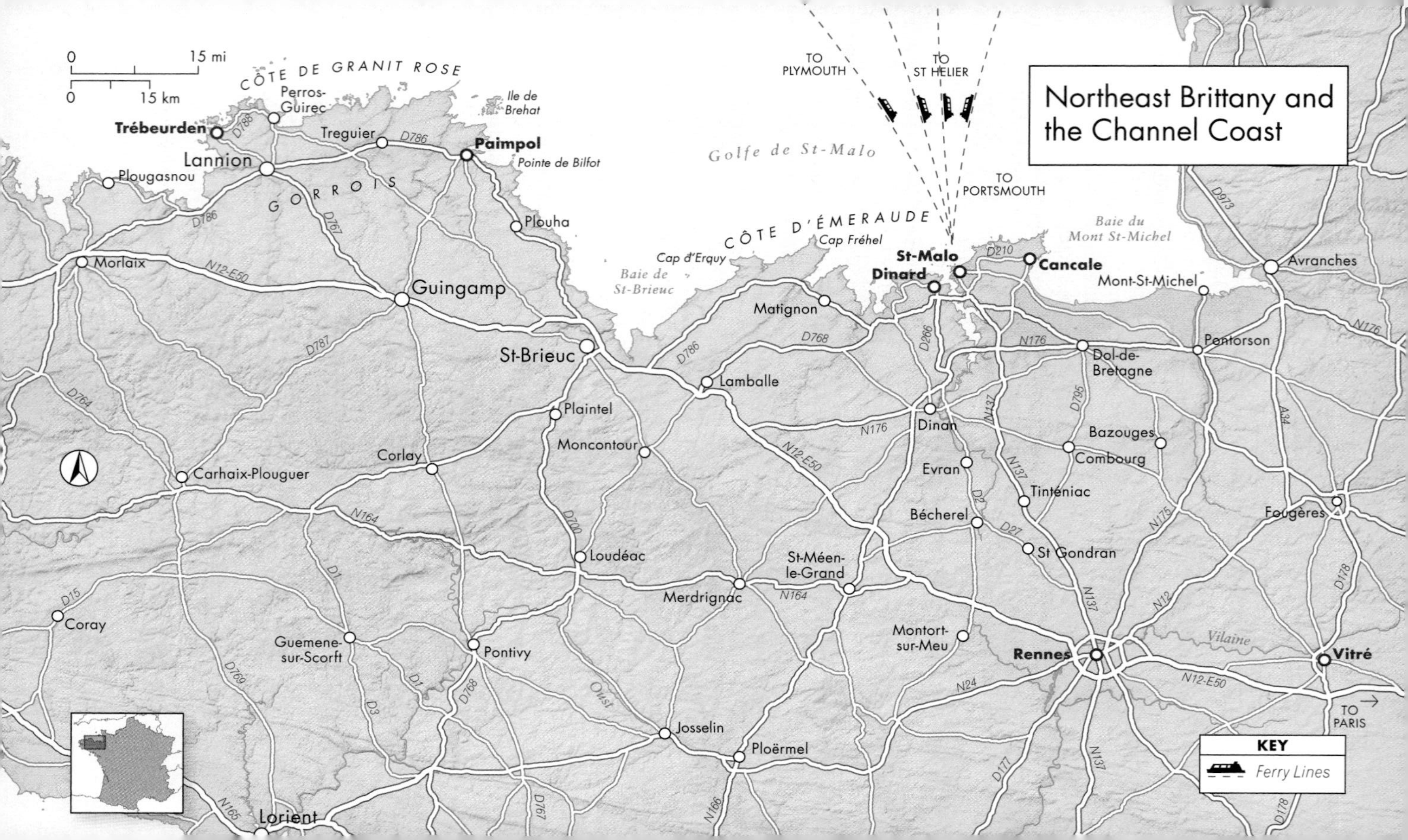

Northeast Brittany and the Channel Coast
0
15 mi
0
15 km
CÔTE DE GRANIT ROSE
Perros-Guirec
Ile de Brehat
Trébeurden
Treguier
Paimpol
Pointe de Bilfot
Lannion
Plougasnou
GORROIS
Plouha
Morlaix
Guingamp
St-Brieuc
TO PLYMOUTH
TO ST HELIER
TO PORTSMOUTH
Golfe de St-Malo
CÔTE D'ÉMERAUDE
Cap Fréhel
Cap d'Erquy
Baie de St-Brieuc
St-Malo
Dinard
Cancale
Baie du Mont St-Michel
Mont-St-Michel
Avranches
Matignon
Lamballe
Pontorson
Dol-de-Bretagne
Plaintel
Moncontour
Dinan
Evran
Bazouges
Combourg
Tinténiac
Corlay
Carhaix-Plouguer
Bécherel
St Gondran
Fougères
Loudéac
St-Méen-le-Grand
Merdrignac
Coray
Guemene-sur-Scorft
Pontivy
Montort-sur-Meu
Rennes
Vilaine
Vitré
Oust
Josselin
Ploërmel
TO PARIS
Lorient
KEY
Ferry Lines
D788
D786
D767
N12-E50
D787
D764
N164
D700
D15
D1
D769
D3
D768
D767
N165
N166
D786
D768
D266
N176
D210
D973
N176
N137
D795
A34
N175
D27
D2
N12
D178
N24
D177
N137

One delightful lunch on a Rennes square and all your troubles will melt away.

Musée des Beaux-Arts (*Fine Arts Museum*). Containing works by Georges de La Tour, Jean-Baptiste Chardin, Camille Corot, Paul Gauguin, and Maurice Utrillo, to name a few, this museum is particularly strong on French 17th-century paintings and drawings, and has an interesting collection of works by modern French artists. ✉ *20 quai Émile Zola, Rennes* ☎ *02–23–62–17–45* 🌐 *www.mbar.org* 🎫 *€5, free the 1st Sun. of each month* ⏲ *Wed.–Sun. 10–noon and 2–6, Tues. 10–6.*

Parlement de Bretagne. Originally the palatial home of the Breton Parliament and now of the Rennes law courts, the Parlement de Bretagne was designed in 1618 by Salomon de Brosse, architect of the Luxembourg Palace in Paris. It was the most important building in Rennes to escape the 1720 flames; however, in 1994, following a massive demonstration by Breton fishermen demanding state subsidies, another disastrous fire broke out that left it a charred shell. Fortunately, much of the artwork—though damaged—was saved by firefighters, who arrived at the scene after the building was already engulfed in flames. It was a case of the alarm that cried "fire" once too often; a faulty bell, which rang regularly for no reason, had led the man on duty to ignore the signal. It has been completely restored. Call the tourist office (*02–99–67–11–11*) to book a 90-minute guided tour. ✉ *Rue Nationale, Rennes* 🌐 *www.tourisme-rennes.com* 🎫 *€7.20, by guided tour only (reservation required)* ⏲ *Weekdays 8:45–noon, and 1:45–5.*

WHERE TO STAY

$ HOTEL **Garden.** With all rooms overlooking a picturesque, stone-lined, treillage-bedecked garden, this hotel likes to welcome visitors to "silent nights"—and cheerful ones, too, thanks to the *charmant* guest rooms, which are stylishly wrought in pink and orange pastels, with wickerwood headboards and fetching wood-trim furniture. **Pros:** pretty architecture; handy for sights. **Cons:** small rooms; difficult parking. *Rooms from: €75 3 rue Jean-Marie Duhamel, Rennes 02–99–65–45–06 www.hotel-garden.fr 25 rooms Breakfast.*

$$ HOTEL **Le Coq-Gadby.** A 19th-century mansion with huge fireplaces and fine antiques sets the stage for this cozy retreat, which gets serious about pampering its guests, thanks to handsome accommodations and Julien Lemarié's celebrated cuisine—French presidents have dined here on such delicacies as langoustine *au sake* with *crème de riz* (restaurant closed Sunday and Monday; no lunch Wednesday). **Pros:** manorial surroundings; great organic cuisine; cute shop. **Cons:** hotel rooms often booked solid; can be expensive if not booked six months in advance. *Rooms from: €120 156 rue d'Antrain, Rennes 02–99–38–05–55 www.lecoq-gadby.com 11 rooms Some meals.*

$$ HOTEL **Mercure Rennes Place de Bretagne.** Ranging in style from rococo revisited to severe neoclassical, these three side-by-side 19th-century buildings add up to one centrally located hotel; it's a good option, on a quiet, narrow backstreet close to the cathedral and a few blocks from the town's main museums and theaters. **Pros:** city-center location; quiet rooms. **Cons:** interiors a bit bland; no restaurant. *Rooms from: €119 6 rue Lanjuinais, Rennes 02–99–79–12–36 www.mercure.com 48 rooms Breakfast.*

NIGHTLIFE AND PERFORMING ARTS

Top spots for nightlife are on the streets around place Ste-Anne.

L'Espace. If you feel like dancing the night away, head to L'Espace. It's open Thursday through Saturday. *45 bd. de la Tour d'Auvergne, Rennes 02–99–23–00–00 www.discotheque-espace.com.*

Les Tombées de la Nuit. During the first three weekends in July, Les Tombées de la Nuit (or "Nightfalls" Festival) features Celtic music, dance, and theater performances staged in the streets and in churches around town. *Rennes 02–99–32–56–56 www.lestombeesdelanuit.com.*

Les Trans Musicales. The famous annual international rock-and-roll festival, Les Trans Musicales, happens the first half of December in bars around town and at the Théâtre National de Bretagne. *Rennes 02–99–31–12–10 www.lestrans.com.*

FAMILY **Opéra de Rennes.** Brittany's top classical music venue is the Opéra de Rennes. *Pl. de la Mairie, Rennes 02–23–62–28–28 ticket office www.opera-rennes.fr.*

Pym's Club. With three dance floors, Pym's Club stays open all night, every night. *27 pl. du Colombier, Rennes 02–99–67–30–00 www.pyms.fr.*

FAMILY **Théâtre National de Bretagne.** A range of performances are staged at the Théâtre National de Bretagne. *1 rue Saint-Hélier, Rennes 02–99–31–55–33 www.t-n-b.fr.*

CANCALE

86 km (54 miles) northwest of Rennes via N137 and D210.

Nothing says Brittany like seafood and nothing says seafood like this fishing village, one of the most picturesque in the region. Renowned for its offshore *bancs d'huîtres* (oyster beds), Cancale has countless quayside eateries where you can slurp down these magnificent mollusks, and at the Château Richeux (a nearby culinary mecca) you can enjoy them as part of a full-on seafood feast. If your interest is more academic, learn how oysters are "farmed" at the Musée de la Ferme Marine.

GETTING HERE

Trains from Rennes (50 mins, €13.60) travel to La Gouesnière, and from there you can proceed by bus to Cancale; buses from St-Malo also make the 30-minute trip multiple times per day (€1.25).

Visitor Information Cancale Tourist Office. ☎ *02–99–89–63–72* 🌐 *www.cancale-tourisme.fr.*

EXPLORING

Musée de la Ferme Marine (*Sea Farm Museum*). Just south of town, this museum explains everything you ever wanted to know about farming oysters and has a display of 1,500 different types of shells. ✉ *L'Aurore, Cancale* ☎ *02–99–89–69–99* 🌐 *www.ferme-marine.com* 🎫 *€7* ⏲ *July–mid-Sept., daily 10–6; mid-Sept.–Oct., weekdays 2–5. Guided 1-hr tours in English, July–mid-Sept., daily at 2.*

6

WHERE TO STAY

$$$$ HOTEL Fodor's Choice ★ **Château Richeux.** Retired superstar-chef Olivier Roellinger and his wife Jane still preside over their family's luxurious hotel empire, which includes the beautiful, castellated, 1920s waterfront Château Richeux. **Pros:** famous cuisine; picturesque and quiet setting. **Cons:** isolated for those seeking crowds; breakfast is an additional €24. $ *Rooms from: €220* ✉ *Le Point du Jour, St-Méloir des Ondes, Cancale* ☎ *02–99–89–64–76* 🌐 *www.maisons-de-bricourt.com* ⏲ *Closed mid-Jan.–Feb.* *13 rooms* *No meals.*

SHOPPING

Grain de Vanille. Sublime tastes of Brittany—salted butter caramels, fruity sorbets, rare honeys, and heirloom breads—are sold in upper Cancale at the Roellingers's Grain de Vanille. Tables beckon, so why not sit a spell and enjoy a cup of Mariage Frères tea and—Brittany in a bite—some cinnamon-orange-flavored *malouine* cookies? ✉ *12 pl. de la Victoire, Cancale* ☎ *02–23–15–12–70* 🌐 *www.maisons-de-bricourt.com.*

Les Entrepôts Épices-Roellinger. Monsieur Roellinger's newest addition to his culinary empire, Les Entrepôts Épices-Roellinger, is dedicated to the exotic spices he personally searches the world to find. In addition to individual spices, it stocks exotic peppers, fleur de sel, choice vanillas, and the acclaimed owner's signature spice blends—such as Poudre Curry Corsaire (for mussels and shellfish) and Poudre du Vent (for squab or cream sauces). There's now a branch in St-Malo and another in Paris. ✉ *1 rue Duguesclin, Cancale* ☎ *02–23–15–13–91* 🌐 *www.maisons-de-bricourt.com.*

ST-MALO

23 km (14 miles) west of Cancale via coastal D201.

Thrust out into the sea and bound to the mainland only by tenuous man-made causeways, romantic St-Malo has built a reputation as a breeding ground for phenomenal sailors. Many were fishermen, but others—most notably Jacques Cartier, who claimed Canada for Francis I in 1534—were New World explorers. Still others were corsairs, "sea dogs" paid by the French crown to harass the Limeys across the Channel: legendary ones like Robert Surcouf and Duguay-Trouin helped make St-Malo rich through their pillaging, in the process earning it the nickname "the pirates' city." The St-Malo you see today isn't quite the one they called home because a weeklong fire in 1944, kindled by retreating Nazis, wiped out nearly all of the old buildings. Restoration work was more painstaking than brilliant, but the narrow streets and granite houses of the Vieille Ville were satisfactorily recreated, enabling St-Malo to regain its role as a busy fishing port, seaside resort, and tourist destination. The ramparts that help define this city figuratively and literally are authentic, and the flames also spared houses along Rue de Pelicot in the Vieille Ville. Battalions of tourists invade this quaint part of town in summer, so arrive off-season if you want to avoid crowds.

GETTING HERE

The rail station (a 15-minute walk from the Old Town walls) receives more than 15 daily trains from Rennes (55 mins; €15). Buses based at the gare routière, immediately outside the walls, link St-Malo to Dinard (30 mins, €2.50), Cancale (30 mins, €1.25), Dinan (55 mins, €2), Rennes (2 hrs, €5.70), and Mont-St-Michel in Normandy (75 mins, €11). April through October, ferries operated by the Compagnie Corsaire (🌐 *www.compagniecorsaire.com*) also carry passengers to Dinard (10 mins, €7.60 return).

Visitor Information St-Malo Tourist Office. ☎ *08–25–13–52–00 €0.15 per min* 🌐 *www.saint-malo-tourisme.com.*

EXPLORING

Cathédrale St-Vincent (*Saint-Malo Cathedral*). Originally founded in the 12th century, the Cathédrale St-Vincent represents an eclectic range of architectural styles. Inside you can pay homage to Jacques Cartier—who set sail from St-Malo in 1534 on a voyage during which he would discover the St. Lawrence River and claim what is now Québec in his King's name—at his tomb. ✉ *12 rue Saint-Benoist, St-Malo* ☎ *02–99–40–82–31* 🌐 *rennes.catholique.fr/Cathedrale-St-Vincent-de-St-Malo,106.html* ⏲ *Daily 9–6.*

Château (*Town History Museum*). At the edge of the ramparts sits a 15th-century château, its keep and watchtowers commanding an impressive view of the harbor and coastline. It contains the **Musée d'Histoire de la Ville,** devoted to great figures who have touched local history (like the founder of French Canada, Jacques Cartier, and Châteaubriand, the

"Father of Romanticism"); plus the **Galerie Quic-en-Grogne,** a tower museum that uses waxworks to conjure up various episodes from St-Malo's past. ✉ *Hôtel de Ville, Quai St-Vincent, St-Malo* ☎ *02–99–40–71–57* 🌐 *www.ville-saint-malo.fr* 🎫 *€6* 🕑 *Apr.–Sept., daily 10–12:30 and 2–6; Oct.–Mar., Tues.–Sun. 10–noon and 2–6.*

Fort National. Lying offshore and accessible by causeway at low tide only, the "Bastille of Brittany" is a massive fortress with a dungeon constructed in 1689 by military-engineering genius Sébastien de Vauban. Thirty-five-minute tours commence at the drawbridge (an English text is available). ✉ *St-Malo* ☎ *06–72–46–66–26* 🌐 *www.fortnational.com* 🎫 *€5* 🕑 *Mid-Apr.–Sept., Wed.–Mon. 10–1 and 2–6 (depending on tides; see website).*

Ramparts. St-Malo's imposing stone ramparts have withstood the pounding of the Atlantic since the 12th century. They were considerably enlarged and modified in the 18th century, and now extend from the château for almost 2 km (1 mile) around the Vieille Ville—known as *intra-muros* (within walls). The views from them are stupendous, especially at high tide. Look for the statues of celebrated explorer Jacques Cartier and swashbuckling corsair Robert Surcouf; the latter, a hero of many daring 18th-century raids on the British navy, is eternally wagging an angry finger over the waves at England. ✉ *St-Malo.*

6

WHERE TO EAT AND STAY

$$$ SEAFOOD ✕ **Le Chalut.** The reputation of this small Michelin-starred restaurant with a nautical theme has grown since Chef Jean-Philippe Foucat decided to emphasize fresh seafood. A favorite with French vacationers for its ample portions, the succinct menus change as frequently as the catch of the day. Try the sautéed John Dory with langoustines and asparagus, or the scallops and white truffles in walnut oil. [$] *Average main: €29* ✉ *8 rue de la Corne-de-Cerf, St-Malo* ☎ *02–99–56–71–58* 🕑 *Closed Mon. and Tues.* ✍ *Reservations essential.*

$$$$ MODERN FRENCH ✕ **Le Saint-Placide.** This sleek, modern dining room has managed to garner serious accolades—not to mention a Michelin star—in a town where culinary talent is in no short supply. Chef Luc Mobihan's cuisine brilliantly blends flavors to draw out the intrinsic qualities of local meat and seafood without overpowering it. Lobster and bacon risotto is both rich and light, and langoustine ravioli with coriander and Parmesan literally melts in the mouth. With three prix-fixe menus to choose from, diners have the pleasure of sampling a range of dishes. [$] *Average main: €38* ✉ *6 pl. du Poncel, St-Malo* ☎ *02–99–81–70–73* 🌐 *www.st-placide.com* 🕑 *Closed Mon., Tues., and 3rd wk of Feb.* ✍ *Reservations essential.*

$$ HOTEL 🏨 **Beaufort.** A gracious welcome and infinite sea views greet you at this beachfront hotel, handsomely accented with a terra-cotta facade and stylish mansard roof. **Pros:** lovely facade; a few minutes' ride to the intra-muros Old Town and walking distance to good restaurants and shops. **Cons:** rooms are on the small side and not all face the water. [$] *Rooms from: €120* ✉ *25 Chaussée du Sillon, St-Malo* ☎ *02–99–40–99–99* 🌐 *www.hotel-beaufort.com* 🛏 *22 rooms* 🍽 *No meals.*

$ HOTEL 🏨 **Elizabeth.** Done up with impressive style, this 17th-century town house, built into the ancient city walls and near the Porte St-Louise, is a little gem of sophistication in touristy St-Malo. **Pros:** central; good value; free Wi-Fi. **Cons:** hard to park; big difference between bland rooms and stylish suites. $ *Rooms from: €91* ✉ *2 rue des Cordiers, St-Malo* ☎ *02–99–56–24–98* 🌐 *www.saintmalo-hotel-elizabeth.com* *17 rooms* *No meals.*

NIGHTLIFE AND PERFORMING ARTS

Bar de l'Univers. If you ever wanted to sip a drink in a pirate's-lair setting, this is your chance. ✉ *12 pl. Chateaubriand, St-Malo* ☎ *02–99–40–89–52* 🌐 *www.hotel-univers-saintmalo.com.*

Festival de Musique Sacrée. July and August bring a two-month-long religious music festival, the Festival de Musique Sacrée. ✉ *St-Malo* ☎ *06–08–31–99–93* 🌐 *www.festivaldemusiquesacree-stmalo.com.*

Folklores du Monde. The city hosts a weeklong festival of world folk music and dance in July. ✉ *St-Malo* ☎ *02–99–40–42–50* 🌐 *www.saint-malo-tourisme.com.*

La Belle Époque. A popular hangout for all ages, La Belle Époque rages until the wee hours. ✉ *11 rue de Dinan, St-Malo* ☎ *02–99–40–82–23.*

L'Éscalier Club. Ask town residents and many will say this is the best place for dancing the night away. ✉ *Rue de la Buzardière, St-Malo* ☎ *02–99–81–65–56* 🌐 *www.escalier.fr.*

Théâtre Chateaubriand. In summer, assorted performances are staged at the Théâtre Chateaubriand. ✉ *6 rue du Grout-de-St-Georges, St-Malo* ☎ *02–99–40–18–30* 🌐 *www.theatresaintmalo.com.*

DINARD

13 km (8 miles) west of St-Malo via Rance Bridge.

The most elegant resort town on this stretch of the Brittany coast, Dinard enjoys a picture-book perch on the Rance Estuary opposite the walled town of St-Malo. Toward the end of the 19th century, when sea air became a fashionable "cure," the English aristocracy arrived en masse. As a result, what started out as a small fishing port soon became a seaside mecca with lavish Belle Époque villas (more than 400 still dot the town and shoreline), grand hotels, and a bustling casino. Although a number of modern establishments punctuate the landscape, Dinard still retains something of an Edwardian tone. The town's natural beauty remains intact, too: make the most it by strolling along the narrow promenade or heading down to the pointe de la Vicomté, at Dinard's southern tip, where the cliffs offer panoramic views across the Baie du Prieuré and Rance Estuary.

GETTING HERE

April through October, a ferry operated by Compagnie Corsaire (🌐 *www.compagniecorsaire.com*) links St-Malo and Dinard (10 mins, €7.60 return); the towns are 30 minutes apart by bus (€2.50).

Visitor Information Dinard Tourist Office. ☎ *08–21–23–55–00 €0.12 per min* 🌐 *www.dinardtourisme.com.*

EXPLORING

Promenade du Clair de Lune. Hugging the seacoast on its way toward the English Channel, the Promenade du Clair de Lune passes in front of the small jetty used by boats crossing to St-Malo. In Dinard, the road weaves along the shore and is adorned with luxuriant palm trees and mimosa blooms, which, from July to the end of September, are illuminated at dusk by spotlights; strollers are serenaded with recorded music. The promenade really hits its stride as it rounds the **Pointe du Moulinet** and heads toward the sandy **Plage du Prieuré,** named after a priory that once stood here. River meets sea in a foaming mass of rock-pounding surf: use caution as you walk along the slippery path to the calm shelter of the **Plage de l'Écluse,** an inviting sandy beach bordered by the casino and numerous stylish hotels. The coastal path picks up on the west side of Plage de l'Écluse, ringing the Pointe de la Malouine and the Pointe des Êtêtés before arriving at the **Plage de St-Énogat.** ✉ *Dinard.*

WHERE TO EAT AND STAY

$$$ MODERN FRENCH ✕ **Didier Méril.** Nudging right up to the beach in Dinard's historic center, this chic restaurant has both gourmet fare and fabulous water views. Chef Méril takes his inspiration from the local bounty: fresh-from-the-sea dishes, such as salty-sweet Cancale oysters, fricassée de langoustines, and *trilogie de poisson noble* with lobster coulis vie with Breton specialties, like deboned squab dressed in foie gras. An impressive wine list, with 450 wines and *digestifs* from every region imaginable, satisfies the most discerning connoisseur. In warm weather, the seaside terrace is a fine place to enjoy a frosty glass of Champagne or an *apéro*. If you feel inclined to linger, on-site lodging is available in six stylish rooms that come with some endearing quirks. For example, the top floor's room No. 6 offers spectacular ocean vistas from the bathtub, which is smack in the center of the room. Ⓢ *Average main: €31* ✉ *1 pl. du Général de Gaulle, Dinard* ☎ *02–99–46–95–74* 🌐 *www.restaurant-didier-meril.com* ⏲ *Closed mid-Nov.–mid-Dec.* ✍ *Reservations essential.*

$ B&B/INN **Manoir de Rigourdaine.** Between Dinard and St-Malo on the beautiful Rance Estuary, Patrick Van Valenberg's renovated country estate provides exceptional comfort inside and great views outside, courtesy of its promontory perch. **Pros:** wonderful view; great ambience and friendly service; above-average breakfast (€9.50). **Cons:** no restaurant; two-night minimum stay. Ⓢ *Rooms from: €97* ✉ *Rigourdaine, Plouër-sur-Rance* ☎ *02–96–86–89–96* 🌐 *www.hotel-rigourdaine.fr* ⏲ *Closed Nov.–Mar.* *19 rooms* 🍽 *Breakfast.*

$ HOTEL **Printania.** Replete with verandas, charming Breton wood carvings, and a low-key Napoléon III vibe, Le Printania boasts a sweet location right on Dinard's Clair de Lune promenade. **Pros:** friendly staff; tasteful rooms; enticing food (meal plans available). **Cons:** some rooms lack a view. Ⓢ *Rooms from: €95* ✉ *5 av. George V, Dinard* ☎ *02–99–46–13–07* 🌐 *www.printaniahotel.com* *55 rooms* 🍽 *No meals.*

$$$ HOTEL **Villa Reine-Hortense.** All the Napoléon III glamour of 19th-century-resort France is yours when you stay at this *folie*—a villa built by the Russian Prince Vlassov in homage to his "queen," Hortense de Beauharnais (daughter of Napoléon's beloved Joséphine and mother to Emperor Napoléon III). **Pros:** high-style paradise; intimate; quirky.

6

A Belle Époque beauty, Dinard adds a big dollop of 19th-century elegance to the natural splendor of the Breton coast.

Cons: a bit "de trop". $ *Rooms from: €152* ✉ *19 rue de la Malouine, Dinard* ☎ *02–99–46–54–31* 🌐 *www.villa-reine-hortense.com* ⊗ *Closed Oct.–mid-Apr.* *8 rooms* *Some meals.*

NIGHTLIFE

Casino. The main nightlife activity in town is at the casino. ✉ *4 bd. du Président-Wilson, Dinard* ☎ *02–99–16–30–30* 🌐 *www.lucienbarriere.com.*

Clair de Lune. During July and August, stretches of the Clair de Lune promenade become a nighttime son-et-lumière wonderland, thanks to spotlights and recorded music. ✉ *Dinard.*

SPORTS AND THE OUTDOORS

Wishbone Club. For windsurfing, wander over to the Wishbone Club. ✉ *Plage de l'Écluse, Dinard* ☎ *02–99–88–15–20* 🌐 *www.wishbone-club-dinard.com.*

Yacht Club. Boats can be rented from the Yacht Club. ✉ *Promenade du Clair de Lune, Dinard* ☎ *02–99–46–14–32* 🌐 *www.ycdinard.wordpress.com.*

TRÉBEURDEN

46 km (27 miles) west of Paimpol via D786 and D65.

Fodor's Choice ★

Trébeurden is one of the highlights of the Côtes d'Armor. A pleasant fishing village that's popular with summer vacationers, it offers access to the rosy-hue cliffs of the Corniche Bretonne. Look at the profile of dramatic rocks off the coast near Trégastel and Perros-Guirec and use your imagination to see La Tête de Mort (Death's Head), La Tortoise, Le Sentinel, and Le Chapeau de Wellington (Wellington's Hat). The coastal scene changes with the sunlight and with the ebb and flow of tides that are strong enough to leave formerly floating boats stranded on the dry sea floor.

GETTING HERE

Buses from Lannion, a town 12 km (7 miles) inland, travel to Trébeurden several times a day, with stops in Perros-Guirec, Trestraou beach, and neighboring Ploumanac'h (45 mins, €2).

Visitor Information Trébeurden Tourist Office. ☎ *02–96–23–51–64* 🌐 *www.tourisme-trebeurden.com.*

EXPLORING

FAMILY **Sentier des Douaniers.** The famous seaside footpath, the Sentier des Douaniers, starts up at the west end of the Trestraou beach in the resort town of **Perros-Guirec,** 3 km (2 miles) east of Trébeurden; from there this beautifully manicured, fence-lined, and gorgeously scenic path provides a two-hour walk eastward, through fern forests, past cliffs and pink granite boulders to the pretty beach at Ploumanac'h. If you keep an eye out, you might even spot one of the mythical, 900-year-old Korrigans—native sprites with pointed ears, beards, and hooves, who come out at night from seaside grottoes to dance around fires. From Perros-Guirec you can take a boat trip out to the Sept Iles, a group of seven islets that are bird sanctuaries. On a hillside perch above **Ploumanac'h** is the village of La Clarté, home to the little Chapelle Notre-Dame de la Clarté, built of local pink granite and decorated with 14 stations of the cross painted by the master of the Pont-Aven school, Maurice Denis. During the **Pardon of la Clarté** (August 15), a bishop preaches an outdoor Mass for the Virgin Mary, village girls wear Trégor costumes, and the statue of the Virgin Mary wears a gold crown (she wears a fake one for the rest of the year). On Ploumanac'h's pleasant beach, Plage de la Bastille, you'll find the Oratoire de St-Guirec, a rose-granite chapel lodged in the sand with other rocks; facing the beach is the neo-medieval, 19th-century **Château de Costaeres,** where Henryk Sienkiewicz wrote *Quo Vadis.* Unfortunately, the magical castle-by-the-sea—whose image graces many postcards—is private property (you can, however, rent it for €15,000 per week.) ✉ *Trébeurden* 🌐 *www.perros-guirec.fr.*

WHERE TO STAY

$$$ HOTEL **Manoir de Lan Kerellec.** The beauty of the coastline is embraced by this Relais & Châteaux hotel, where guest rooms are far more than just comfortable; long and cruise-liner-low, the renovated 19th-century Breton manor house has been outfitted with dramatic windows—plate-glass, round, panoramic—so as to frame stirring vistas of the endless sea and the cliffs of the Côte de Granit Rose (all rooms have sea views and some have terraces). **Pros:** great views; comfy rooms. **Cons:** restaurant only serves lunch Thursday to Sunday. *Rooms from: €195* ✉ *11 allée Centrale, Trébeurden* ☎ *02–96–15–00–00* 🌐 *www.lankerellec.com* *Closed Nov.–mid-Mar.* *19 rooms* *Some meals.*

THE ATLANTIC COAST

What Brittany offers in the way of the sea handsomely makes up for its shortage of mountain peaks and passes. Hundreds of miles of sawtooth coastline reveal the Atlantic Ocean in every mood and form—from the peaceful cove where waders collect seashells to the treacherous bay with unpredictable crosscurrents; from the majestic serenity of the breakers rolling across La Baule's miles of golden-sand beaches to the savage fury of the gigantic waves that fling their force against jagged rocks 340 dizzy feet below the cliffs of Pointe du Raz.

Consisting of the territory lying west of Saint-Brieuc to the Atlantic coast a short distance east of Vannes, Lower Brittany contains in abundance all things Breton, including many of the pardons and other colorful religious ceremonies that take place hereabouts. As for bright lights, Rennes (the student-fueled mind of Brittany) gives way to poets and painters, bringing a refreshing breeze to the historical heaviness of the region. On the Atlantic coast, Nantes—part of Brittany until regional boundaries were redrawn in the 1940s, placing it in the Pays de la Loire—is an industrial port that pumps the economy of the region and provides a bracing swig of daily life. Head inland to find a landscape studded with bent trees and craggy rocks that look like they've been bewitched by Merlin in a bad mood.

STE-ANNE-LA-PALUD

136 km (82 miles) southwest of Trébeurden via D767 and D787.

Fodor's Choice ★ One of the biggest draws on the Breton events calendar is the celebration of a religious festival known as a village pardon, replete with banners, saintly statues, a procession, women in folk costume, a feast, and hundreds of attendees. Each year, the seaside village of Ste-Anne-la-Palud hosts one of the finest and most authentic on the last Sunday in August.

GETTING HERE

More than a dozen trains daily go from Vannes to Quimper (1 hr, 20 mins; €21.20); from there, catch a bus onward to Ste-Anne-la-Palud (30 mins, €2).

WHERE TO STAY

$$$$ HOTEL **Hôtel de la Plage.** Nestled in a cove on a quiet strip of sandy beach on the Bay of Douarnenez, this mansion, with its sturdy round tower, is a remote retreat perfect for long, restorative walks; some of the comfortably furnished guest rooms face the water, as does the glass-front restaurant, where reservations are essential. **Pros:** Relais & Châteaux taste; waterfront setting; spa facilities; top-rank restaurant. **Cons:** very expensive; rather formal. *Rooms from: €240 ✉ Ste-Anne-la-Palud ☎ 02–98–92–50–12 ⊕ www.plage.com ⊗ Closed Jan.–Mar. 24 rooms, 4 suites Some meals.*

Brittany's
Atlantic Coast
KEY
Ferry Lines
Atlantic Ocean
Brest
Camaret-sur-Mer
Crozon
Rostudel
Baie de Douarnenez
Pointe du Van
Plogoff
Douarnenez
Audierne
Plozévet
Baie d'Audierne
Pont-l'Abbé
St-Guénolé
Pointe de Penmarc'h
Penmarc'h
Ste-Anne-la-Palud
Châteaulin
Plonévez-Porzay
Locronan
Quimper
Concarneau
Pont-Aven
Riec-sur-Belon
Pointe de Trévignon
Iles de Glénan
Pleyben
Carhaix-Plouguer
Gourin
Coray
Rosporden
Quimperlé
Lorient
Port-Louis
Hennebont
Ile de Groix
Groix
Guemene-sur-Scorft
Corlay
Plaintel
Moncontour
Loudéac
Pontivy
Josselin
Ploërmel
La Chapelle
Elven
Auray
Carnac
La Trinité-sur-Mer
Vannes
Golfe du Morbihan
Baie de Quiberon
Quiberon
Pointe du Conguel
Ile Houat
Ile Hoëdic
Sauzon
le Palais
Belle-Ile-en-Mer
Muzillac
Billiers
Rochefort-en-Terre
Redon
Vilaine
Missillac
St-Lyphard
St-Joachim
Parc Régional De Brière
Guérande
le Croisic
Pointe du Croisic
La Baule
St-Nazaire
St-Brévin-les-Pins
Pointe de St-Gildas
Nantes see detail map
Guémené Penfao
Plessé
Bain-de-Bretagne
Plélan-le-Grand
Mauron
Merdrignac
St-Méen-le-Grand
Montort-sur-Meu
Rennes
Dinan
Evran
Bécherel
Château de Caradeuc
Combourg
Tinténiac
St Gondran
Oust
Aulne
N176
N12-E50
N164
N137
N12
N175
N24
N166
N165
N171
D795
D2
D27
D700
D1
D3
D768
D767
D778
D769
D15
D764
D107
D765
D784
D783
D22
D28
D20
D114
D773
D164
D774
D47
D177

DOUARNENEZ

14 km (8 miles) south of Ste-Anne-la-Palud.

Douarnenez is a quaint old fishing town with quayside paths and zigzagging narrow streets. Boats come in from the Atlantic to unload their catches of mackerel, sardines, and tuna. Just offshore is the Ile Tristan, which is accessible on foot at low tide (guided tours only, €5.50), and across the Port-Rhu channel is Tréboul, a seaside resort town favored by French families.

GETTING HERE

Douarnenez is served by buses from Quimper (30 mins, €2).

Visitor Information Douarnenez Tourist Office. *02-98-92-13-35 www.douarnenez-tourisme.com.*

EXPLORING

FAMILY **Port-Musée** (*Port Museum*). The unique Port-Musée combines maritime-themed museum displays with open-air exhibits. Along the wharves you can visit the workshops of boatbuilders, sailmakers, and other old-time craftspeople, then go aboard the historic trawlers, lobster boats, and barges anchored beside them. On the first weekend in May you can even sail on an antique fishing boat. *Pl. de l'Enfer, Douarnenez 02-98-92-65-20 www.port-musee.org €7.50 (€5.50 Quai museum only, Feb. and Mar.) July and Aug., daily 10-7; Apr.-June, Sept., and Oct., Tues.-Sun. 10-12:30 and 2-6; Feb. and Mar. (Quai museum only), Tues.-Sun. 10-12:30 and 2-6.*

WHERE TO STAY

$ HOTEL **Manoir de Moëllien.** Surrounded by extensive forested grounds, this textbook 17th-century granite manor, landmarked by a sturdy tower and filled with precious antiques, offers enviable lodgings; guest rooms vary greatly in size, but most have terraces overlooking the peaceful country garden. **Pros:** charming setting; historic atmosphere. **Cons:** out of the way; restaurant service can be offhand. *Rooms from: €96 12 km (7 miles) northeast of Douarnenez, Plonévez-Porzay 02-98-92-50-40 www.manoirmoellien.fr 18 rooms All meals.*

$$ HOTEL **Ty Mad.** This landmark hotel—frequented by artists and writers such as Picasso and Breton native Max Jacob in the 1920s—has been completely refitted with cool, light, modern furnishings that blend perfectly with its cove and beach setting. **Pros:** delightful seaside setting; stylish modern interior. **Cons:** rooms are small and modestly equipped. *Rooms from: €120 Plage St-Jean, Douarnenez 02-98-74-00-53 www.hoteltymad.com Closed mid-Nov.-mid-Mar. 15 rooms Some meals.*

QUIMPER

22 km (14 miles) southeast of Douarnenez via D765.

Quimper (pronounced cam-pair) owes its strange name to its site at the confluence (kemper in Breton) of the Odet and Steir rivers. A traditional crowd-puller, its twisting streets and tottering medieval houses supply rich postcard material; lovers of decorative arts, however, head here because this is the home of Quimperware, one of the more famous variants of French hand-painted pottery. After learning about the prized collectibles at the Musée de la Faïence, you can stroll through the Vieille Ville, ogle its immense 15th-century cathedral, then wander the surrounding shop-lined streets. Keep your camera handy—the ancient capital of the Cornouaille province is very photogenic.

GETTING HERE

The TGV travels here direct from Paris's Gare Montparnasse five times per day (4 hrs, 30 mins; €30–€67). Multiple daily trains also connect Quimper with Lorient (40 mins, €12.90), Vannes (1 hr, 15 mins; €21.20), and Nantes (2 hrs, 40 mins; €38.60). Frequent buses run to Concarneau (40 mins, €2).

Visitor Information Quimper Tourist Office. ☎ *02–98–53–04–05* 🌐 *www.quimper-tourisme.com.*

EXPLORING

Cathédrale St-Corentin. Brittany's second-largest cathedral (surpassed sizewise only by the one in Dol-de-Bretagne) is a masterpiece of Gothic architecture enlivened by luminous 15th-century stained glass. Legendary King Gradlon is represented on horseback just below the base of the spires, which are harmonious mid-19th-century additions to the medieval ensemble. The church interior remains very much in use by fervent Quimperois, giving the candlelit vaults a meditative air. Behind the cathedral is the stately **Jardin de l'Évêché** (Bishop's Garden). ✉ *Pl. St-Corentin, Quimper* ⏲ *Mon.–Sat. 8:30–noon, Sun. 8:30–noon and 2–6.*

6

Musée de la Faïence (*Earthenware Museum*). In the mid-18th century Quimper sprang to nationwide attention as a pottery manufacturing center. Normands, whose distinctive Rouennaise faïence was already famous, imported the techniques. But the Quimpérois customized them by replacing the pottery's usual blue-and-white patterns with brighter Breton scenes depicting local life. Today's colorful designs, based on floral arrangements and marine fauna, are still often hand-painted. To understand Quimper's pottery-making past—and see more than 500 examples of *style Quimper*—take one of the guided tours at the Musée de la Faïence. ✉ *14 rue Jean-Baptiste-Bousquet, Quimper* ☎ *02–98–90–12–72* 🌐 *www.musee-faience-quimper.com* 🎟 *€5* ⏲ *Mid-Apr.–Sept., Mon.–Sat. 10–6.*

Musée Départemental Breton (*Brittany Regional Museum*). Local furniture, ceramics, and folklore top the bill at the Musée Départemental Breton. ✉ *1 rue du Roi-Gradlon, Quimper* ☎ *02–98–95–21–60* 🌐 *www.museedepartementalbreton.fr* 🎟 *€5* ⏲ *Mid-June–Sept., daily 9–6; Oct.–mid-June, Tues.–Sat. 9–12:30 and 1:30–5, Sun. 2–5.*

Musée des Beaux-Arts (*Fine Arts Museum*). More than 400 works by such masters as Rubens, Corot, and Picasso mingle with pretty landscapes from the local Gauguin-inspired Pont-Aven school in the Musée des Beaux-Arts, next to the cathedral. Of particular note is a fascinating series of paintings depicting traditional life in Breton villages. ✉ *40 pl. St-Corentin, Quimper* ☎ *02–98–95–45–20* 🌐 *www.mbaq.fr* 🎟 *€5* ⏲ *July and Aug., daily 10–7; Apr.–June, Sept., and Oct., Wed.–Mon.*

Quimper hosts many parades but the largest is reserved for the six-day Celtic extravaganza known as the Festival de Cornouaille.

9:30–noon and 2–6; Nov.–Mar., Mon. and Wed.–Sat. 9:30–noon and 2–5:30, Sun. 2–5:30.

WHERE TO EAT AND STAY

$$$ MODERN FRENCH

L'Ambroisie. This cozy little Michelin-star restaurant has soft-yellow walls, huge contemporary paintings, and different settings at every table. Chef Gilbert Guyon's traditional yet nouvelle menu is seasonal; local products are chosen by hand or come from the restaurant's garden. Highlights include a buckwheat-galette stuffed with crab, grapefruit, and avocado; curried lobster with asparagus "cappuccino"; and xocopili-spiced roast pigeon. The homemade desserts—like the omelet *Norvégienne* with warm chocolate and nougat ice cream in meringue—are delicious. Weekday lunch menus are a bargain. *Average main: €29* *49 rue Élie-Fréron, Quimper* *02–98–95–00–02* *www.ambroisie-quimper.com* *Closed Mon. No dinner Sun.* *Reservations essential.*

$ WINE BAR

Le Comptoir des Tapas. Xavier Hamon, the owner of this compact *épicerie* and tapas bar in Quimper's old covered market, had the novel idea of pairing delicacies from Spain and Brittany. An auspicious match, it turns out, as small plates of artisanal cured meats, like Iberico and chorizo, served *à la planche* with bread and spicy olive oil, go nicely with local specialties such as a velvety langoustine flan. With Spanish or French regional wines by the glass for as little as €3—and small plates starting at €4—it's a great opportunity to experiment with pairings. Drop by for lunch or a *very* early dinner (it closes at 7:15). *Average main: €12* *16 quai de Steir, Halles St-François, Quimper* *02–98–98–00–81* *Closed Sun. and Mon.* *Reservations not accepted.*

$ HOTEL **Hôtel Gradlon.** This authentically Breton *hôtel particulier* has a mild (bordering on nondescript) facade that thoroughly disguises the charms that lie within. **Pros:** good breakfast (€12); free Wi-Fi. **Cons:** no restaurant; no elevator. *Rooms from: €98 ✉ 30 rue de Brest, Quimper ☎ 02–98–95–04–39 🌐 www.hotel-gradlon.fr 20 rooms No meals.*

ANCIENT EVENINGS

During the second half of July, Quimper hosts the Celtic-themed Festival de Cornouaille (*02–98–55–53–53 🌐 www.festival-cornouaille.com*). More than 250 artists, dancers, and musicians fill streets already packed with the 4,000 people who come each year to enjoy the exuberant six-day street fair.

SHOPPING

Maison Breton. Faïence and a wide selection of hand-painted pottery can be purchased at the Maison Breton. *✉ 16 bis, rue du Parc, Quimper ☎ 02–98–95–34–13.*

Rue du Parc. The streets around the cathedral, especially Rue du Parc, are full of shops selling woolen goods (notably thick marine sweaters). Also keep an eye out for such typical Breton products as woven and embroidered cloth, brass and wood objects, puppets, dolls, and locally designed jewelry. When it comes to distinctive Breton folk costumes, Quimper is the best place to look. *✉ Quimper.*

6

CONCARNEAU

22 km (14 miles) southeast of Quimper via D783.

Concarneau may be an industrial town known for sardine packaging, but its 17th-century Vauban-designed Ville Close ranks among the most picturesque sites in Brittany.

GETTING HERE

Buses run here multiple times per day from Quimper (40 mins, €2) and Pont-Aven (45 mins, €2).

Visitor Information Concarneau Tourist Office. *☎ 02–98–97–01–44 🌐 www.tourismeconcarneau.fr.*

EXPLORING

Fodor's Choice ★ **Château de Keriolet.** The village of Beuzec-Conq, just outside Concarneau, is home to the Château de Keriolet—a fairy-tale, neo-Gothic extravaganza dating from the 19th century that Walt Disney would have adored. Replete with gargoyles, storybook towers, and Flamboyant Gothic—style windows, this showpiece was constructed by the Comtesse de Chauveau, born Zenaide Narishkine Youssoupov, an imperial Russian princess who was niece to Czar Nicholas II (and related to Prince Youssoupov, famed assassin of Rasputin). Take one of the four daily guided tours through the Arms Room, folkloric kitchen, and grand salons. *✉ 2 km (1 mile) southeast of Concarneau, Beuzec-Conq, Concarneau ☎ 02–98–97–36–50 🌐 www.chateaudekeriolet.com €5.50 June–Sept., Sun.–Fri. 10:30–1 and 2–6, Sat. 10:30–1.*

Fodor's Choice ★ **Ville Close.** Sitting in the middle of Concarneau's harbor, topped by a cupola-clock tower, and entered by way of a quaint drawbridge, the fortress-islet of the Ville Close is a particularly photogenic relic of medieval days. Its fortifications were further strengthened by the English under John de Montfort during the Breton War of Succession (1341–64). Three hundred years later Sébastien de Vauban remodeled the ramparts into what you see today: a kilometer-long (half-mile) expanse, with splendid views across the two harbors on either side. The Fête des Filets Bleus (Blue Net Festival), a weeklong folk celebration in which costumed Bretons whirl and dance to the wail of bagpipes, is held here in the middle of August. It is also home to the Musée de la Pêche (Maritime Museum). ✉ *Ramparts, Concarneau* ☎ *02–98–97–10–20 Museum* 🌐 *www.musee-peche.fr* 🎫 *Museum €5* ⏲ *Museum July and Aug., daily 9:30–7; Apr.–June and Sept., daily 10–6; Oct. and mid-Dec.–Mar., daily 10–12:30 and 2–6.*

WHERE TO STAY

$$ HOTEL **Les Sables Blancs.** One of the fine-white-sand beaches that distinguish the Morbihan coast serves as the perfect backdrop for this spare, modern hotel, which calls to mind a cruise ship. **Pros:** miles of paths on the cliffs overlooking the water make for lovely walks; open year-round. **Cons:** the relentless crashing of waves can disturb light sleepers. $ *Rooms from: €132* ✉ *45 rue des Sables Blancs, Concarneau* ☎ *02–98–50–10–12* 🌐 *www.hotel-les-sables-blancs.com* *16 rooms, 4 suites* *No meals.*

PONT-AVEN

37 km (23 miles) east of Quimper via D783.

Fodor's Choice ★ This lovely village sits astride the Aven River as it descends from the Montagnes Noires to the sea, turning the town's mills along the way (there were once 14; now just a handful remain). A former artists' colony, Pont-Aven is where Paul Gauguin lived before he headed off to the South Seas—and where he left dewy, sunlit Impressionism behind for a stronger, more linear style. After exploring the town, you can seek inspiration (as so many painters did) in the Bois d'Amour or cool off on a boat trip down the estuary.

GETTING HERE

There are no direct trains, but you can ride the rails to nearby Quimperlé and transfer to a bus for the 20-minute drive into town (€7). Buses also arrive from Quimper (70 mins, €17) and Concarneau (45 mins, €2) several times a day. The last buses leave early in the evening, and service is limited on Sunday.

Visitor Information Pont-Aven Tourist Office. ☎ *02–98–06–04–70* 🌐 *www.pontaven.com.*

EXPLORING

Bois d'Amour. One glance at these leafy, light-dappled woods, a bit north of Pont-Aven's town center, will make you realize why artists continue to come here. Past some meadows, just outside the Bois d'Amour, you can find Gauguin's inspiration for his famous painting *The Yellow*

CLOSE UP

Gauguin and the Pont-Aven School

Surrounded by some of Brittany's most beautiful countryside, Pont-Aven was a natural to become a "cité des artistes" in the heady days of Impressionism and Postimpressionism. It was actually the introduction of the railroad in the 19th century that put travel to Brittany in vogue, and it was here that Gauguin and other like-minded artists founded the noted Pont-Aven School. Inspired by the vibrant light, vivid colors, and lovely vistas to be found here, they created *Synthétisme*, a painting style characterized by broad patches of pure color and strong symbolism, in revolt against the dominant Impressionist school back in Paris. Gauguin arrived in the summer of 1886, happy to find a place "where you can live on nothing" (Paris's stock market had crashed and cost Gauguin his job). At Madame Gloanec's boardinghouse, he welcomed a circle of painters to join him in his artistic quest for monumental simplicity and striking color.

Today Pont-Aven seems content to rest on its laurels. Although it's labeled a "city of artists," the galleries that line its streets display paintings that lack the unifying theme and common creative energy of the earlier works of art.

6

Christ—a wooden crucifix in the secluded **Chapelle de Trémalo**: it's privately owned but usually open from 10 to 5 (until 6 in summer). ✉ *330 ft from town center, along the opposite bank of the river, Pont-Aven.*

Moulin du Grand Poulguin. Now housing a restaurant, this pretty mill was built in the early 1600s. It's a delightful place to dine on a terrace directly beside the flowing waters of the Aven River, in view of the footbridge. ✉ *2 quai Théodore Botrel, Pont-Aven* ☎ *02–98–06–02–67* 🌐 *www.moulin-pontaven.com.*

Musée de Beaux-Arts. The town's art museum captures some of the history of the Pont-Aven School, whose adherents painted Breton landscapes in a bold yet dreamy style called *Synthétisme*. In addition to works by "member" artists—Paul Gauguin, Paul Sérusier, Maurice Denis, and Émile Bernard among them—the Musée de Beaux-Arts has a photography exhibit documenting the Pont-Aven School. Following extensive renovations, it is slated to reopen at the end of 2015. ✉ *Pl. de l'Hôtel-de-Ville, Pont-Aven* ☎ *02–98–06–14–43* 🌐 *www.museepontaven.fr.*

WHERE TO EAT AND STAY

$$$$ MODERN FRENCH

✕ **La Taupinière.** At an airy roadside inn with an attractive garden, Guy Guilloux turns out a range of Breton specialties. Since the chef places a special emphasis on seafood, options might include a galette stuffed with spider crab, a langoustine flan, or a *brochette de coquilles Saint-Jacques* that's been grilled on the large hearth in his open kitchen. For dessert, indulge without guilt on the light homemade rhubarb-and-strawberry compote. $ *Average main: €38* ✉ *Croissant St-André, 3 km (2 miles) west on Rte. de Concarneau, Pont-Aven* ☎ *02–98–06–03–12* 🌐 *www.la-taupiniere.fr* ⏲ *Closed Mon., Tues., and 1st half of Oct.* ✍ *Reservations essential.*

$$$ HOTEL Fodor's Choice ★ **Domaine de Kerbastic.** This beautiful gated estate—a hotel since 2008—served as the country getaway for generations of Princesses de Polignac and their eminent friends, including Stravinsky, Colette, and Proust. **Pros:** everything done with exquisite taste; enormous marble bathrooms; historic vibe. **Cons:** somewhat off the beaten path; you can't stay forever. *Rooms from: €190 ✉ Rte. de Locmaria, 28 km (17 miles) southeast of Pont-Aven, off Rte. E60, Guidel ☎ 02–97–65–98–01 ⊕ www.domaine-de-kerbastic.com ⊗ Closed Jan.–mid-Feb. 15 rooms Some meals.*

$ HOTEL **La Chaumière Roz-Aven.** Partly built into a rock face on a bank of the Aven, this efficiently run hotel is a perfect blend of antique and modern—offering simple, clean rooms with 18th- and 19th-century-style touches. **Pros:** families welcome; rooms tastefully modernized. **Cons:** small rooms; rooms in annex lack character. *Rooms from: €78 ✉ 11 quai Théodore-Botrel, Pont-Aven ☎ 02–98–06–13–06 ⊕ www.hotelpontaven.com ⊗ Closed Jan. 14 rooms No meals.*

$ HOTEL Fodor's Choice ★ **Le Moulin de Rosmadec.** This pretty-as-a-picture, 15th-century stone watermill juts out above the rushing, rocky Aven River. **Pros:** great setting; great value. **Cons:** attic rooms can be stuffy in midsummer; restaurant reservations are essential. *Rooms from: €98 ✉ Venelle de Rosmadec, Pont-Aven ☎ 02–98–06–00–22 ⊕ www.moulinderosmadec.com 4 rooms Some meals.*

BELLE-ILE-EN-MER

45 mins by boat from Quiberon, 78 km (52 miles) southeast of Pont-Aven.

Covering 84-square km (32-square miles), Belle-Ile is the largest of Brittany's islands; and, as its name implies, it is beautiful. Being less commercialized than its mainland counterpart, Quiberon (a spa town with pearl-like beaches on the eastern side of the Quiberon Peninsula), Belle-Ile maintains a natural appeal. Monet created several famous paintings on the island, and the pristine terrain may tempt you to set up an easel yourself.

GETTING HERE AND AROUND

Ferries, which run hourly in July and August, connect Belle-Ile's Le Palais with Quiberon's Gare Maritime (45 mins, from €30 round-trip). Because of the cost and inconvenience involved in taking a vehicle over, it's best to make the crossing as a foot passenger; you can then rent a car or (if you don't mind hilly terrain) a bike on arrival.

Visitor Information Belle-Ile-en-Mer Tourist Office. *☎ 02–97–31–81–93 ⊕ www.belle-ile.com.*

EXPLORING

Citadelle Vauban. Your first stop on Belle-Ile will most likely be Le Palais, the island's largest community. As you enter the port, it's impossible to miss the star-shaped Citadelle Vauban, named for the famous military engineer who, in the early 1700s, oversaw a redesign of the original fort here (which dated back to the 11th century). Stroll the grounds, savor the views, and then bone up on local lore at the on-site Musée de la

Citadelle Vauban. ✉ *Le Palais, Belle-Ile-en-Mer* €7.50 ⏲ *Apr.–June, Sept., and Oct., daily 9:30–6; July and Aug., daily 9–7; Nov., Dec., Feb., and Mar., daily 9:30 –5.*

Grand Phare (*Great Lighthouse*). Built in 1835, the Grand Phare at Port Goulphar rises 275 feet above sea level and has one of the most powerful beacons in Europe, visible from 120 km (75 miles) across the Atlantic. If the keeper is available and you are feeling well rested, you may be able to climb to the top. ✉ *Belle-Ile-en-Mer.*

Grotte de l'Apothicairerie. Continue on to the Grotte de l'Apothicairerie, which derives its name from the local cormorants' nests, said to resemble apothecary bottles. ✉ *Belle-Ile-en-Mer.*

Sauzon. Northwest of Le Palais, you'll discover the prettiest fishing harbor on the island; from here you can see across to the Quiberon Peninsula, with its dramatic coastal cliffs and sea-lashed coves. ✉ *Belle-Ile-en-Mer.*

WHERE TO STAY

$$$$ RESORT **Castel Clara.** Perched on a cliff overlooking the surf and the narrow Anse de Goulphar Bay, this '70s-era hotel was François Mitterrand's address when he vacationed on Belle-Ile and it still retains presidential glamour, with its renowned spa, saltwater pool, and spectacular views. **Pros:** great facilities; spectacular setting. **Cons:** impersonal service; hard to get to. *Rooms from: €290* ✉ *Port-Goulphar, Bangor* ☎ *02–97–31–84–21* *www.castel-clara.com* ⏲ *Closed mid-Nov.–mid-Dec.* *59 rooms, 4 suites* *Some meals.*

$$$ B&B/INN **Château Bordeneo.** More of a large-scale house than a château, this imposing residence has been transformed by Françoise and Jean-Luc Duplessy into a handsome, fully modernized *chambres d'hôtes* within walking distance of the beach. **Pros:** excellent breakfast included; good value. **Cons:** pool open April to October only. *Rooms from: €174* ✉ *Le Palais* ☎ *02–97–31–80–77* *www.chateau-bordeneo.fr* *5 rooms* *Breakfast.*

SPORTS AND THE OUTDOORS

Roue Libre. The ideal way to get around to the island's 90 spectacular beaches is by bike. The best place to rent two-wheelers (and cars—this is also the island's Avis outlet) is at Roue Libre in Le Palais. ✉ *6 quai Jacques Le Blanc, Le Palais, Belle-Ile-en-Mer* ☎ *02–97–31–49–81* *www.velobelleile.fr.*

CARNAC

19 km (12 miles) northeast of Quiberon via D768/D781.

Fodor's Choice ★ At the north end of Quiberon Bay, Carnac is known for its expansive beaches and its ancient stone monuments—"standing stones," called menhirs, that were erected by Brittany's pre-Celtic people 6,500 years ago.

One of France's prettiest islands, Belle-Ile-en-Mer casts an especially potent spell at sunset.

GETTING HERE

Catch a bus from Quiberon (35 mins, €2) or take advantage of the SNCF's rail-road combination, which involves a train from Vannes to Auray followed by a bus to Carnac (1 hr, 15 mins; €8.30).

Visitor Information Carnac Tourist Office. ☎ *02–97–52–13–52* 🌐 *www.ot-carnac.fr.*

EXPLORING

Menhirs. Dating from around 4500 BC, Carnac's menhirs remain as mysterious in origin as their English contemporaries at Stonehenge, although religious beliefs and astronomy were doubtless an influence. The 2,395 monuments that make up the three *alignements*—Kermario, Kerlescan, and Ménec—form the largest megalithic site in the world, and are positioned with astounding astronomical accuracy in semicircles and parallel lines over about a kilometer (half a mile). The site, just north of the town, is fenced off for protection, and you can examine the menhirs up close only from October through March; in summer you must join a €6 guided tour (some are in English). This visitor center explains the menhirs' history and significance, plus it offers an excellent selection of interesting books in all languages, as well as DVDs and regional gifts. ✉ *D196, Carnac* ☎ *02–97–52–29–81 Maison des Mégalithes* 🌐 *www.carnac.monuments-nationaux.fr* 🕒 *July and Aug., daily 9:30–7:30; May and June, daily 9–6; Sept.–Apr., daily 10–5.*

Tumulus de St-Michel. Carnac also has smaller-scale dolmen ensembles and three *tumuli* (mounds or barrows), including the 390-foot-long, 38-foot-high Tumulus de St-Michel, topped by a small chapel with views of the rock-strewn countryside. ✉ *Carnac.*

WHERE TO STAY

$$$ HOTEL Fodor's Choice ★ **Château de Locguénolé.** According to legend, Saint-Guénolé (for whom the 19th-century château was named) took refuge on this spot while fleeing the devil, and it remains a grand retreat—after all, it's part of a sweeping 250-acre estate with lush garden and stunning water views. **Pros:** peace and quiet reign; lovely setting; large bathrooms are all in marble. **Cons:** out of the way (but well worth the detour). *Rooms from: €189 ✉ Rte. de Port-Louis, 25 km (16 miles) south of Carnac, Kervignac, Carnac ☎ 02–97–76–76–76 ⊕ www.chateau-de-locguenole.com ⊙ Closed Jan.–mid-Feb. 18 rooms, 4 suites All meals.*

$$$ HOTEL **Hôtel Tumulus.** Dramatic views over Carnac and Quiberon Bay, coupled with a prime location just beneath the famous Tumulus de St-Michel, have been big draws for this modest, family-run hotel from its inception in the 1930s. **Pros:** close to Carnac's menhirs; tasteful interiors. **Cons:** some rooms on the small side; some with less-than-pristine carpets. *Rooms from: €185 ✉ Chemin de Tumulus, Carnac ☎ 02–97–52–08–21 ⊕ www.hotel-tumulus.com ⊙ Closed mid-Nov.–mid-Feb. 23 rooms Breakfast.*

VANNES

35 km (20 miles) east of Carnac via D768, 108 km (67 miles) southwest of Rennes.

Scene of the declaration of unity between France and Brittany in 1532, Vannes is one of the few towns in the region to have been spared damage during World War II. That makes its Vielle Ville (Old Town), where many of the prettiest sights are concentrated, particularly appealing. The ramparts crumble evocatively under ivy blankets, and each gateway has a character all its own. Visit the 16th-century cathedral; browse the antiques shops in the pedestrian streets around pretty place Henri-IV; and then take a boat trip around the scenic Golfe du Morbihan.

GETTING HERE

Direct TGVs from Paris's Gare Montparnasse leave for Vannes six times daily (3 hrs, 20 mins; €30–€65). Ten trains daily (many with a change at Redon) link Vannes to Nantes (1 hr, 30 mins; €23.40); frequent trains also link it to Lorient (35 mins, €10.60) and Quimper (1 hr, 15 mins; €21.20). Buses to Quiberon (2 hrs, €2) and Nantes (1 hr, 45 mins; €12) are available as well.

Visitor Information **Vannes Tourist Office.** ☎ *02–97–47–24–34* ⊕ *www.tourisme-vannes.com.*

EXPLORING

Cathédrale St-Pierre. A panoply of medieval art, St-Pierre boasts a 1537 Renaissance chapel, a Flamboyant Gothic transept portal, and a treasury. *✉ 22 rue des Chanoines, Vannes ☎ 02–97–47–10–88 ⊕ www.cathedrale-vannes.cef.fr ⊙ Daily 8:30–7.*

WHERE TO EAT AND STAY

$$$$ MODERN FRENCH **Le Roscanvec.** On a pedestrian street in the charming old city, this modern gastronomic restaurant ditches stuffiness in favor of a relaxed, contemporary approach to food. What it doesn't dispense with is

Brittany's version of Stonehenge, this stone menhir at Carnac is just one of the area's impressive megalithic sights.

seriousness in the kitchen. Chef Thierry Seychelles seeks out top-quality ingredients from a wealth of local suppliers for his seasonal, meticulously presented cuisine. Start with oysters from the nearby Bay of Pénerf, cocotte of asparagus with lime hollandaise, tender foie gras–stuffed ravioli, or smoked eel with lemon confit in a parsley reduction, followed up by monkfish served with French caviar (depending on market availability and the chef's mood, of course). His take on the traditional kouign aman pastry is made with apples and served warm with salty caramel ice cream. Three-course lunch or dinner menus (€25–€70) are the way to go. *Average main: €36 ✉ 17 rue des Halles, Vannes ☎ 02–97–47–15–96 🌐 www.roscanvec.com ⏲ Closed Mon. year-round, Tues. Sept.–June, last wk of June–1st wk of July, and mid-Jan.–early Feb. No dinner Sun. Reservations essential.*

$$$$ RESORT Fodor's Choice ★ **Domaine de Rochevilaine.** At the tip of the magical Pen Lan Peninsula, this luxurious collection of 15th- and 16th-century Breton stone buildings resembles a tiny village—albeit one surrounded by terraced gardens that promise grand vistas of the Baie de Vilaine (Vilaine Bay). **Pros:** stylish interiors; ocean views; superb spa facilities. **Cons:** the staff seems to favor French guests; tons of steps from one house to another. *Rooms from: €290 ✉ Pointe de Pen-Lan, 30 km (19 miles) southeast of Vannes, Billiers ☎ 02–97–41–61–61 🌐 www.domainerochevilaine.com 35 rooms, 3 suites All meals.*

$ HOTEL **Kyriad.** In an old but thoroughly modernized building, this hotel attracts a varied foreign clientele, drawn by homey guest rooms that are clean, bright, and simple, with check-pattern quilts and warm yellow walls. **Pros:** tastefully modernized; friendly, efficient staff. **Cons:** some rooms on the small side; some a bit noisy. *Rooms from: €79 ✉ 8 pl.*

de la Libération, Vannes ☎ *02–97–63–27–36* 🌐 *www.kyriad-vannes.fr* *33 rooms* 🍽 *No meals.*

LORIENT

50 km (30 miles) west of Vannes via N165.

France's most exotically named town was founded by Jean-Baptiste Colbert in 1666 as a base for the Compagnie des Indes, which sent ships from here to the Orient in search of spices. Now a major fishing port, Lorient was smashed into semi-oblivion during World War II (a massive submarine base—Base de Sous-Marins Keroman—attests to its wartime importance); however, you can still see a handful of Art Deco mansions, explore the mile-long quay, and enjoy nearby beaches. Lorient is at its liveliest during the Festival Interceltique in August.

GETTING HERE

Direct TGVs from Paris's Gare Montparnasse leave for Lorient five times per day (3 hrs, 50 mins; €30–€68). Trains also run frequently from Nantes (2 hrs, €30.30), Vannes (35 mins, €10.60), and Quimper (40 mins, €12.90). For trips by bus or boat to any of the surrounding towns, contact the Compagnie des Transports de la Région Lorientaise (🌐 *www.ctrl.fr*).

Visitor Information Lorient Tourist Office. ☎ *02–97–84–78–00* 🌐 *www.lorientbretagnesudtourisme.fr.*

EXPLORING

Base de Sous-Marins Keroman. Built by the Nazis during World War II, this submarine base is the world's largest 20th-century fort. Thirty submarines could be comfortably housed in the squat concrete bunker—and its 27-foot-thick roof withstood intensive Allied bombing virtually intact. Ninety-minute tours begin at 3 pm daily in summer and during school vacations; they run at the same time on Sunday year-round. ✉ *Port de Keroman, Lorient* ☎ *02–97–02–23–29* 🌐 *www.lorient.fr* *€6* ⏲ *Closed last 3 wks of Jan.*

FAMILY **Festival Interceltique.** Held in the first half of August, this festival focuses on Celtic culture—music, drama, poetry, dance—and fellow Celts from Cornwall, Wales, Ireland, Scotland, Galicia, and other Western European locales pour in to celebrate. ✉ *Lorient* ☎ *02–97–21–24–29* 🌐 *www.festival-interceltique.com.*

Larmor-Plage. There's a good beach, Larmor-Plage, 5 km (3 miles) south of Lorient. You can also take a ferry to the rocky yet utterly charming Ile de Groix or cross the bay to Port-Louis to see its 17th-century fort and ramparts. ✉ *D29, Lorient.*

LA BAULE

72 km (45 miles) southeast of Vannes via N165 and D774.

La Baule is a popular resort town that once rivaled Biarritz. Today it leans toward the tacky rather than the sophisticated, but you still can't beat its breathtaking 5-km (3-mile) beach or the lovely, long seafront promenade lined with hotels. Like Dinard, La Baule is a 19th-century creation, founded in 1879 to make the most of the sandy strands that extend around the broad, sheltered bay between Pornichet and Le Pouliguen. A pine forest helps keep shifting dunes in place. All in all, this can offer an idyllic stay for those who like the idea of a day at the beach and an evening at the casino.

GETTING HERE

Three TGVs per day arrive direct from Paris (3 hrs, 15 mins; €30–€68); six more make the trip with a transfer in Nantes. Direct trains from Nantes run almost hourly (55 mins, €15.30).

Visitor Information La Baule Tourist Office. *02–40–24–34–44 www.labaule.fr.*

WHERE TO EAT AND STAY

$ FRENCH **La Ferme du Grand Clos.** At this lively restaurant in an old farmhouse, 325 yards from the sea, you should understand the difference between *crêpe* and *galette* before ordering because the menu showcases both in all their many forms. Alternately, you can opt for the simple, straightforward menu featuring food that owner Christophe Mercy likes to call *la cuisine de grand-mère* (grandma's cooking). Come early for a table; it's a very friendly and popular place. *Average main: €9 52 av. de Lattre-de-Tassigny, La Baule 02–40–60–03–30 www.lafermedugrandclos.com Closed Mon. Sept.–July, Tues. and Wed. Oct.–Mar., and mid-Nov.–mid-Dec.*

$ HOTEL **Concorde.** This bright-blue-shuttered, white-walled establishment ranks among the least expensive "good" hotels in pricey La Baule. **Pros:** just a short block from the beach; some rooms flaunt sea views; good value. **Cons:** no restaurant; lengthy annual closure. *Rooms from: €98 1 bis, av. de la Concorde, La Baule 02–40–60–23–09 www.hotel-la-concorde.com Closed Oct.–Mar. 47 rooms Breakfast.*

$$ HOTEL FAMILY **Hôtel de la Plage.** One of the few hotels on the beach in St-Marc-sur-Mer, southeast of La Baule, this comfortable lodging was the celebrated setting for Jacques Tati's classic comedy *Mr. Hulot's Holiday.* It has been updated since and, *hélas,* the swinging door to the dining room is no longer there. **Pros:** silver-screen claim to fame; beachside setting. **Cons:** old-fashioned; overrun by French families in midsummer. *Rooms from: €109 37 rue du Commandant-Charcot, 10 km (6 miles) southeast of La Baule, St-Marc-sur-Mer 02–40–91–99–01 www.hotel-delaplage.fr 30 rooms Some meals.*

NIGHTLIFE

Casino. Occasionally you see high stakes on the tables at La Baule's casino. *24 esplanade Lucien Barrière, La Baule 02–40–11–48–28 www.lucienbarriere.com.*

NANTES

72 km (45 miles) east of La Baule via N171 and N165, 108 km (67 miles) south of Rennes.

The writer Stendhal remarked of 19th-century Nantes, "I hadn't taken 20 steps before I recognized a great city." Since then, the river that flowed around the upper-crust Ile Feydeau neighborhood has been filled in and replaced with a rushing torrent of cars on the major highways that now cut through the heart of town. Still, Nantes is more than the sum of its traffic jams, and even the bureaucratic severance of the city from Brittany—it's now the capital of the Pays de la Loire region—has not robbed it of its historic Breton character. Stay a spell to discover its many sights, among them an evocative 15th-century château and a cathedral from the same period that seems to float heavenward. Across the broad boulevard, Cours des 50-Otages, sits the 19th-century city.

GETTING HERE AND AROUND

Frequent Nantes-bound TGVs depart from Paris's Gare Montparnasse (2 hrs, 15 minutes; €30-€72). The city is also well served by trains from La Baule (55 mins, €15.30), Vannes (1 hr, 30 mins; €23.40), Rennes (1 hr, 30 mins; €26.30), Lorient (2 hrs, €30.30), and Quimper (2 hrs, 40 mins; €38.60). Nantes's train station, on Boulevard Stalingrad, is a 10-minute walk from the Vieille Ville. Regional bus service to nearby towns is available. Civic trams and buses operated by TAN (🌐 *www.tan.fr*) provide efficient public transit within the city.

Visitor Information Nantes Tourist Office. ☎ *08–92–46–40–44 €0.34 min* 🌐 *www.nantes-tourisme.com.*

6

EXPLORING

TOP ATTRACTIONS

Cathédrale St-Pierre–St-Paul. One of France's last Gothic cathedrals, this was begun in 1434—well after most other medieval cathedrals had been completed. The facade is ponderous and austere, in contrast to the light, wide, limestone interior, whose vaults rise higher (120 feet) than those of Notre-Dame in Paris. ✉ *Pl. St-Pierre, Nantes* ☎ *02–40–47–84–64* 🌐 *www.cathedrale-nantes.cef.fr* ⏲ *Daily 8:30–7 (6 in winter).*

Château des Ducs de Bretagne. Built by the dukes of Brittany, who had no doubt that Nantes belonged in their domain, this moated 15th-century château looks well preserved, despite having lost an entire tower during a gunpowder explosion in 1800. François II, the duke responsible for building most of the massive structure, led a hedonistic life here, surrounded by ministers, chamberlains, and an army of servants. Numerous monarchs later stayed in the castle, where in 1598 Henri IV signed the famous Edict of Nantes advocating religious tolerance. ✉ *4 pl. Marc-Elder, Nantes* ☎ *02–51–17–49–48* 🌐 *www.chateau-nantes.fr* 🎫 *€5 (€8 with temporary exhibition)* ⏲ *July and Aug., daily 10–7; Sept.–June, Tues.–Sun. 10–6.*

Fodor's Choice ★ **Grand Eléphant et Galerie de les Machines de l'île.** Had Jules Verne (a son of Nantes) and Leonardo da Vinci somehow got together when they were both in a particularly whimsical frame of mind, they may well have established this unique and engaging workshop-gallery. Their spirit certainly lives on in the imaginative, artistic, and mechanically brilliant creations that are built and displayed here. The Grand Eléphant gets most attention—hardly surprising, since the 50-ton giant, just short of 40-feet high, regularly "ambles" along the quay carrying 49 passengers. Inside the gallery are works in many shapes and sizes—some of them interactive—and you can watch more being made in the workshop on weekdays. The *Carrousel des Mondes Marins* (Marine Worlds

Cathédrale St-Pierre—St-Paul 2

Château des Ducs de Bretagne 1

Grand Eléphant et Galerie de les Machines de l'île 6

Musée des Beaux-Arts 3

Musée Thomas-Dobrée 5

Passage Pommeraye 4

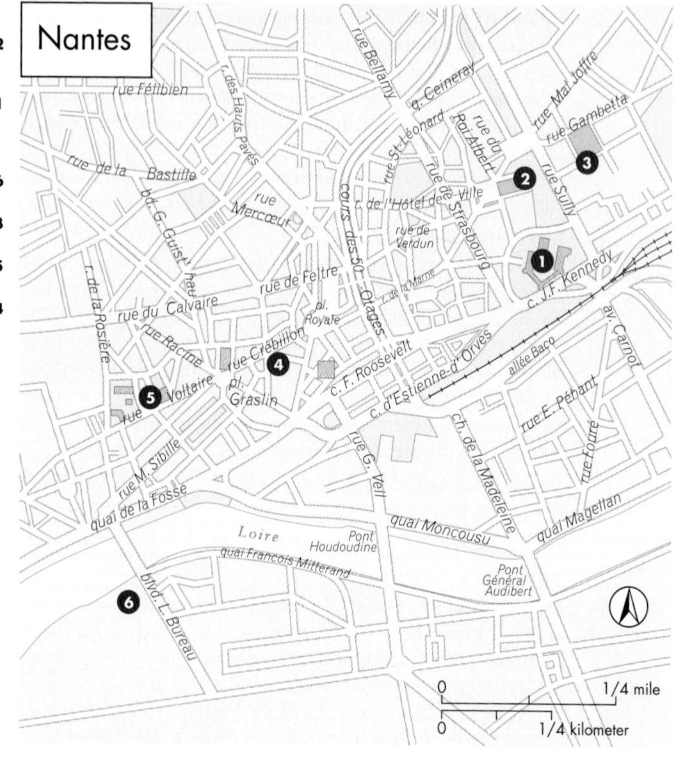

Carousel), the newest eye-popping addition, is located just outside the gallery on the banks of the Loire. ✉ *Les Chantiers, Bd. Léon Bureau, Ile de Nantes, Nantes* ☎ *08–10–12–12–25* 🌐 *www.lesmachines-nantes.fr* 🎫 *Gallery €8.50; elephant ride €8.50; carousel €8.50* 🕒 *July and Aug., daily 10–7; Sept.–early Jan. and mid-Feb.–June, hrs vary (see website).*

WORTH NOTING

Musée des Beaux-Arts (*Museum of Fine Arts*). Designed by Clément-Marie Josso, this noted museum was opened in 1900. Inside, skylights cast their glow over a fine array of paintings, extending from the Renaissance period onward, including works by Jacopo Tintoretto, Georges de La Tour, Jean-Auguste-Dominique Ingres, and Gustave Courbet. To go from the sublime to the ridiculous, look for the famous late-19th-century painting of a gorilla running amok with a maiden. The main *palais* is closed for renovations until the end of 2016, but the Chapelle de l'Oratoire (on Place de l'Oratoire) hosts temporary exhibitions of the permanent collection in the interim. ✉ *10 rue Georges-Clemenceau, Nantes* ☎ *02–51–17–45–00 Museum, 02–51–17–45–00* 🌐 *www.museedesbeauxarts.nantes.fr* 🎫 *€2 (free Thurs. after 6 and the 1st Sun. of each month, except July and Aug.)* 🕒 *Wed.–Mon. 10–6, Thurs. 10–8.*

Musée Thomas-Dobrée. Across from the medieval Manoir de la Touche, this mansion was built by arts connoisseur Thomas Dobrée in the 19th century. On the mock-Romanesque facade he had chiseled the old Breton saying, *Ann dianaf a rog ac'hanoun* ("The Unknown devours me"), and his vast collection offers proof, as it ranges from old-master paintings to tapestries, from medieval manuscripts to Gothic goldwork— including the *coffret* reliquary containing the heart of Anne de Bretagne. Anne, the last independent ruler of Brittany, married the region away to King Charles VIII of France in 1491, and Bretons have never quite recovered from the shock. Currently in the midst of a renovation, the museum will be closed to the public until the end of 2015. ✉ *18 rue Voltaire, Nantes* ☎ *02–40–71–03–50.*

Passage Pommeraye. Erected in 1843, this is an elegant shopping gallery in the 19th-century part of town. ✉ *Rue Crébillon, Nantes* 🌐 *www.passagepommeraye.fr.*

WHERE TO EAT AND STAY

$$ BRASSERIE ✕ **La Cigale.** Palm trees, gleaming woodwork, colorful enamel tiles, and painted ceilings have led to the official recognition of La Cigale brasserie (built in 1895) as a *monument historique.* You can savor its Belle Époque blandishments without spending a fortune—the prix-fixe lunch menus are a good value. But the banks of fresh oysters and well-stacked dessert cart may tempt you to order à la carte. Best of all, it's open every day from early morning till after midnight, a rare convenience in France. [$] *Average main: €19* ✉ *4 pl. Graslin, Nantes* ☎ *02–51–84–94–94* 🌐 *www.lacigale.com* ✍ *Reservations essential.*

$$ MODERN FRENCH ✕ **L'Embellie.** Sweet and simple L'Embellie lures diners with its inventive attitude and friendly service. Chef Nicolas Lewandowsky has brought renewed vigor to the creative regional cuisine that has been a staple of this bright, elegant eatery. The menu, dependent on his daily trips to markets, might include fresh fish specials (like the thickly sliced sturgeon fillet with a dill-and-verbena cream sauce) or roasted and deboned, locally raised pigeon in a simple au jus. A delicious crème brûlée flavored with tonka beans is a fitting twist on a classic finale. [$] *Average main: €22* ✉ *14 rue Armand-Brossard, Nantes* ☎ *02–40–48–20–02* 🌐 *www.restaurantlembellie.com* ⏲ *Closed Wed. No lunch Thurs.* ✍ *Reservations essential.*

$$ BISTRO ✕ **Les Chants d'Avril.** It may not be the fanciest restaurant in Nantes, but Les Chants d'Avril is where the locals go for affordable "bistronomic" fare. Murals, dark-wood paneling, and leather banquettes lend a warm, traditional look; the attention to market-driven ingredients and interesting wines, however, puts it on par with the best modern *bistrôts à vin.* Labels aside, dishes like the excellent homemade foie gras, white-peach gazpacho, or lobster consommé speak for themselves. For dessert, the luscious caramel clafouti (when on offer) is a must. Although dinner is served on Thursday and Friday, it's best to come at lunch for the three-course menu—a great deal at €22.50. [$] *Average main: €19* ✉ *2 rue Laënnec, Nantes* ☎ *02–40–89–34–76* 🌐 *www.leschantsdavril.fr* ⏲ *No dinner Mon.–Wed. Closed weekends.*

$ HOTEL 🏨 **La Pérouse.** Bare parquet floors, plain off-white walls, simple high-tech lighting, and minimal contemporary furnishings by celebrated modernist designers all helped earn La Pérouse the accolade of Europe's Design Hotel of the Year back in 1995—shortly after this big white cube of a hotel opened its doors. **Pros:** stylish interiors; friendly staff; organic breakfasts included. **Cons:** hard to park; no restaurant; noisy bar. *Rooms from: €95 3 allée Dusquesne, Nantes 02–40–89–75–00 www.hotel-laperouse.fr 46 rooms Breakfast.*

NIGHTLIFE AND PERFORMING ARTS

Le Lieu Unique. This is the place to go for an impressive selection of cutting-edge cultural and leisure events, including music, dance, art exhibitions, and creative "happenings." The contemporary space includes a bar, restaurant, boutique, and, yes, a hammam, too. *2 quai Ferdinand-Favre, Nantes 02–40–12–14–34 www.lelieuunique.com.*

Théâtre Graslin. Nantes's principal concert hall was built in 1788, ravaged by fire in 1796, and rebuilt by the grace of Emperor Napoléon I in 1811. Today it's home to the acclaimed Angers Nantes Opéra. *1 rue Molière, Nantes 02–40–69–77–18 www.angers-nantes-opera.com.*

Univers. An informal "speakeasy," Univers has live jazz concerts the first and third Tuesday of the month—and 50 brands of whiskey every day. *16 rue Jean-Jacques-Rousseau, Nantes 02–40–73–49–55 www.univers-cafe.com.*

SPORTS AND THE OUTDOORS

FAMILY **Bateaux Nantais.** Take a 100-minute cruise along the pretty Erdre River, past a string of gardens and châteaux, on the Bateaux Nantais. There are also four-course lunch and dinner cruises that last about 2½ hours (€51–€86). *Quai de la Motte Rouge, Nantes 02–40–14–51–14 www.bateaux-nantais.fr €12.50 Mar.–Apr. and Oct.–Nov., Sun. and holidays at 3:30; May–June and Sept., daily at 3:30; July–Aug., Mon.–Sat. at 3:30 and 5:30, Sun. and holidays 10:30, 3:30, and 5:30; Dec.–Feb. call for info.*

SHOPPING

The commercial quarter of Nantes stretches from Place Royale to Place Graslin. Various antiques shops can be found on Rue Voltaire.

Devineau. Since 1803, the Devineau family has been selling handmade candles of every imaginable size and color, as well as wax fruit and vegetables, various *objets d'art,* and wildflower honey. *4 rue Belle Image, Nantes 02–40–47–19–59 www.bougies-devineau.fr.*

Gautier-Debotté. For chocolate, head to Gautier-Debotté; try the local Muscadet grapes macerated in the local Muscadet wine and enrobed in chocolate. *9 rue de la Fosse, Nantes 02–40–48–23–19 www.debotte.fr.*

7

CHAMPAGNE COUNTRY

WELCOME TO CHAMPAGNE COUNTRY

TOP REASONS TO GO

★ **Drink Champagne—what else!:** Sample some bubbly, see the vineyards, and visit the cavernous chalk cellars where bottles are stored by the million.

★ **Bask in Gothic glory:** No fewer than 10 Gothic cathedrals dot the region—don't miss the biggest (Amiens) or the tallest (neighboring Beauvais).

★ **Look up in Laon:** With its cathedral towers patrolling the hilly horizon, the "Crowned Mountain" has a site whose grandeur rivals Mont-St-Michel.

★ **Drink now, pray later in Reims:** Beyond being a center for Champagne production, regal Reims is also home to France's great coronation cathedral.

★ **Exercise your options:** Hiking on one of Champagne's fabulous, forested *sentiers de Grandes Randonnées*can be an intoxicating outdoor activity.

1 Champagne. The local obsession with Champagne is especially evident in Reims, the region's hub, which is home to the great Champagne houses and site of one of the most historically important cathedrals in France. Once you've paid tribute to the 34 VIPs who have been crowned here and toured some Champagne cellars to bone up on the backstory behind this noble beverage, you can head south. Smack-dab in the middle of the 280 square kilometers (108 square miles) that make up the entire Champagne-producing area, Épernay lives and dies for the bubbly brew. Continue on the Route du Champagne to other wine villages.

2 The Cathedral Cities. To the west of Champagne lies a region where the popping of Champagne corks is only a distant murmur, and not just because Reims is 160 km (100 miles) away. Here you'll find some of the most gargantuan Gothic hulks of architectural harmony—namely the cathedrals of Beauvais, Amiens, Laon, and Soissons. Beauvais is positively dizzying from within (it features the highest choir in France, and you nearly keel over craning your neck back to see it); Amiens, the largest church in the land, is fantastically ornate in places; while Laon is notable for its majestic towers; and Soissons shows Gothic at its most restrained.

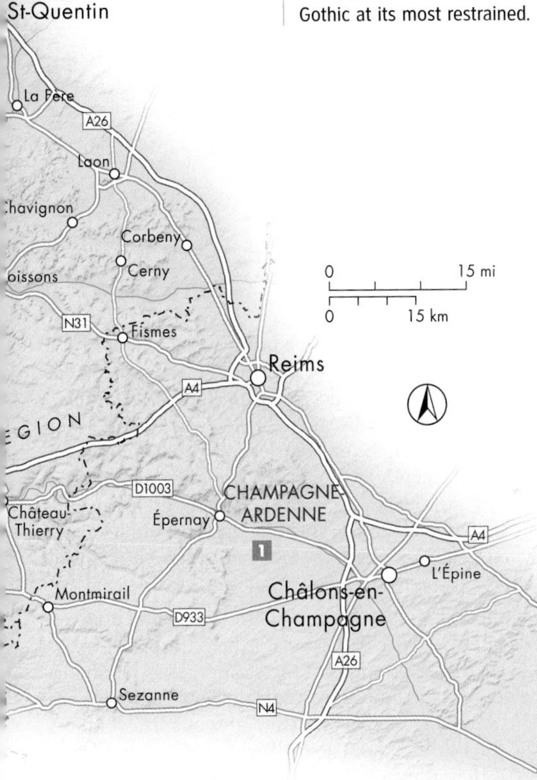

GETTING ORIENTED

As you head toward Reims, the landscape loosens and undulates, and the hills tantalize with vineyards that—thanks to *la méthode champenoise*—produce the world's antidote to gloom. Each year, millions of bottles of bubbly mature in hundreds of kilometers of chalk tunnels carved under the streets of Reims and Épernay, both of which fight for the title "The Champagne City." Long before a drink put it on the map, though, this area of northern France was marked by marvelous architecture, and it contains many of France's greatest medieval cathedrals.

7

Updated By
Lyn Parry

Few drinks in the world have such a pull on the imagination as Champagne, yet surprisingly few tourists visit the pretty vineyards south of Reims. Perhaps it's because the Champagne region is seen as a bit of a backwater, halfway between Paris and Luxembourg. The arrival of the TGV line serving eastern France and Germany has helped to change this perception.

Champagne, a place-name that has become a universal synonym for joy and festivity, actually began as a word of humble meaning. Like *campagna*, its Italian counterpart, it's derived from the Latin *campus*, or "open field." In French *campus* became *champ*, with the old language extending this to *champaign*, for "battlefield," and *champaine*, for "district of plains." The gentle vine-covered slopes of the hillsides rising from vast chalky plains here have been the center of Champagne production for more than two centuries, stocking the cellars of its many conquerors (Napoléon, Czar Nicholas I, the Duke of Wellington) as well as those of contemporary case-toting bubblyphiles.

Meanwhile, great cathedrals testify to the wealth this region enjoyed thanks to its prime location between Paris and northern Europe. The flying buttresses and heaven-seeking spires of these sanctuaries remind us that medieval stoneworkers sought to raise radically new Gothic arches to improbable heights, running for cover if their ambitious efforts failed. Most have stood the test of time, though you might want to hover near the exits at Beauvais, the tallest cathedral in France—its height still makes some engineers nervous.

The region's crossroads status also exacted a heavy toll, and it paid heavily for its role as a battleground for the bickering British, German, and French. From pre-Roman times to the armistice of 1945, some of Europe's costliest wars were fought on northern French soil. World War I and World War II were especially unkind: epic cemeteries cover the plains of Picardy, and you can still see bullet-pocked buildings in

Amiens. These days, happily, the vineyards of Champagne attract tourists interested in less sobering events.

PLANNER

WHEN TO GO

Of course, the optimal time to visit vineyards is around the fall harvest, when the weather is usually at its best. Summer also has its advantages. Compared to many other regions of France, Champagne remains relatively uncrowded in July and August; and the coolness of the chalk cellars makes it a pleasure to tour the Champagne houses then (note that many close after the busy winter holidays for the first few months of the year, as do some of the smaller hotels and restaurants). Spring is generally unpredictable weather-wise, but on the dry and sunny days it can be idyllic. Whatever you plan to do, be sure to come between May and October; the ubiquitous vineyards are a dismal, leafless sight the rest of the year.

MAKING THE MOST OF YOUR TIME

Threading the triangle between Reims, Épernay, and Château-Thierry are the famous Routes Touristique du Champagne (Champagne Roads), which divvy up the region into four fabulous itineraries. These follow the main four côtes of the Champagne vineyards. Northwest of Reims (use the Tinqueux exit) is the Massif de Saint-Thierry—a vineyard-rich region once hallowed by kings. Heading south of Reims to Épernay, veer west along the Vallée de la Marne through the Hauteurs d'Épernay, traveling west on the right bank of the river and east on the left. To the east of Épernay lies the most beautiful stretch of Champagne Country: the Montagne de Reims. To the south of Épernay is the Côte de Blancs, the "cradle of Chardonnay." More than 80 producers of Champagne are scattered along these roads, and you can guarantee a better reception if you call the ones you'd like to visit in advance.

The two main centers to the Champagne Wine Road are Reims and Épernay, which are about 64 km (40 miles) apart if you work your way through the wine villages that dot the slopes of the Montagne de Reims. Start in Reims, with its host of major Champagne houses, then go south on D951 and east on D26 through pretty Rilly-la-Montagne, Mailly-Champagne, and Verzy, where you can visit local producers Étienne and Anne-Laure Lefevre at 30 rue de Villers (*03–26–97–96–99* 🌐 *www.champagne-etienne-lefevre.com*). Continue south to Ambonnay, then track back west to Bouzy, Ay, and Hautvillers—where Dom Pérignon is buried in the village church—before crossing the Marne River to Épernay, whose main street is home to several producers.

From Épernay, spear south along the Côte de Blanc to Vertus, 19 km (12 miles) away, where Pierre and Sophie Larmandier will sell and tell you all about their organic bio-Champagne at 19 avenue du General-de-Gaulle (*03–26–52–13–24* 🌐 *www.larmandier.fr*). If you're heading back to Paris, take D1 from Épernay west along the banks of the Marne to Château-Thierry 50 km (30 miles) away. The steep-climbing vineyards

7

hugging the river are the most scenic in Champagne. For maps of the four Routes Touristique du Champagne, stop at the Marne Regional Tourist Office in Châlons-en-Champagne or the tourist offices in Reims or Épernay.

GETTING HERE AND AROUND

Reims remains the natural hub—especially now that it's just 50 minutes from Paris by TGV. It's easy to get to major towns in the region by rail; as always in France, intercity buses are less frequent than trains, and much slower. If you're driving, Reims is linked to Laon by the A26 expressway and to Châlons-en-Champagne by the A4 expressway arriving from Paris. The west, Amiens and Beauvais, are connected by the A16. Épernay, south of Reims, can be reached from Reims by the twisting wine road or quicker D951. Only Soissons, 32 km (20 miles) southwest of Laon, is a bit off the beaten track.

AIR TRAVEL

If you're coming from the United States or most other locales, count on arriving at Paris's Charles de Gaulle or Orly airport. The former offers easy access to the northbound A16 and A1 for Beauvais and Amiens, and the eastbound A4 for Reims. If coming from within the European Union, consider the direct flights into Beauvais operated by several budget carriers.

Airport Information Aéroport de Beauvais-Tillé. ☎ *08-92-68-20-66* 🌐 *www.aeroportbeauvais.com.*

BUS TRAVEL

As train travel is so much more efficient and dependable, we don't recommend relying on bus service outside Paris. There are more than a dozen different bus operators in the Champagne and Picardy regions, but since few of them have websites, reliable schedules, or any personnel who speak English, it's best to contact the local tourism office if you're looking into bus options. In Picardy the main bus hub is at the Gare Routière in Amiens, next to the train station. In the Champagne region, the main hub is Châlons-en-Champagne, with routes from Reims to Troyes, Épernay to Châlons, and Reims to Laon. In Reims, municipal buses depart from the train station.

CAR TRAVEL

The A4 heads east from Paris to Reims; allow 90 minutes to two hours, depending on traffic. The A16 leads from L'Isle-Adam, north of Paris, up to Beauvais and Amiens.

If you're arriving by car via the Channel Tunnel, you'll disembark at Coquelles, near Calais, and join A16 not far from its junction with A26, which heads to Reims (2 hrs, 30 mins).

TRAIN TRAVEL

Most sites can be reached by regular service, except for the Champagne vineyards, which require a car. There are frequent daily trains from Paris (Gare du Nord) to Beauvais (1 hr, 15 mins), Amiens (1 hr, 20 mins), Soissons (1 hr, 5 mins), and Laon (1 hr, 40 mins). The super-express TGV service covers the 170 km (105 miles) from Paris (Gare de l'Est) to Reims in 50 minutes. Trains departing from Gare de l'Est regularly travel to Châlons as well, making the 174-km (108-mile) trip in 1 hour, 30 minutes—1 hour, 6 minutes if you take the TGV. From the same station you can travel to Épernay (1 hr, 21 mins) or to Château-Thierry (46 mins). Within the Champagne region, trains also connect Reims and Épernay (30 mins).

Train Information Gare SNCF Reims. ☎ *09–69–36–66–69.* **SNCF.** ☎ *3635 €0.34 per min* 🌐 *www.voyages-sncf.com.* **TGV.** 🌐 *www.tgv.com.*

RESTAURANTS

This region is less dependent on tourism than many in France, and most restaurants are open year-round. However, in the largest cities, Reims and Amiens, many do close for two to three weeks in July and August.

Smoked ham, pigs' feet, gingerbread, and Champagne-based mustard are specialties of the Reims area, along with sautéed chicken, kidneys, stuffed trout, pike, and snails.

One particularly hearty dish is *potée champenoise,* consisting of smoked ham, bacon, sausage, and cabbage. Rabbit (often cooked with prunes) is common, while boar and venison are specialties in fall and winter, when vegetable soups are high on the menu.

In Picardy, the popular *ficelle picarde* is a pancake stuffed with cheese, mushrooms, and ham.

Apart from Champagne, try drinking the region's *hydromel* (mead, made from honey) and Ratafia, a sweet aperitif made from grape juice and brandy.

HOTELS

The Champagne Region has a mix of old, rambling hotels, often simple rather than pretentious. In addition, there are a handful of stylish hostelries catering to those with more discerning tastes, including a large contingent of staffers who work in the Champagne industry. ⇨ *Be warned, though, that few of the destinations mentioned in this chapter have much in the way of upscale choice.* Many of the region's most character-filled establishments are in the countryside and require a car to reach. *Hotel reviews have been shortened. For full information, visit Fodors.com.*

WHAT IT COSTS IN EUROS

	$	$$	$$$	$$$$
Restaurants	under €18	€18–€24	€25–€32	over €32
Hotels	under €106	€106–€145	€146–€215	over €215

Restaurant prices are the average cost of a main course at dinner or, if dinner is not served, at lunch. Hotel prices are the lowest cost of a standard double room in high season.

VISITOR INFORMATION

The regional tourist offices are goldmines of information. Reims, Amiens, and many smaller locales also operate their own helpful tourist offices; these are listed in this chapter under the destination's names. If traveling extensively by public transportation, you can load up on brochures, maps, and such upon arrival at the ticket counter or help desk of larger train and bus stations.

Picardy Regional Tourist Office. ✉ *3 rue Vincent Auriol, Amiens* ☎ *03–22–22–33–66* 🌐 *www.picardietourisme.com.*

CHAMPAGNE

An uplifting landscape tumbles about Reims and Épernay, perhaps because its inhabitants treat themselves to a regular infusion of the local, world-prized elixir. But unlike the great vineyards of Bordeaux and Burgundy, there are few country châteaux to go with the fabled names of this region—Mumm, Taittinger, Pommery, and Veuve-Clicquot. Most of the glory is to be found in *caves* (wine cellars), not to mention the fascinating guided tours offered by the most famous producers.

Despite its glamorous image as the home of Champagne, the region in fact has a laid-back rustic charm where "life in the fast lane" refers strictly to the Paris-bound A4 expressway. On the map, Champagne encompasses Reims and the surrounding vineyards and chalky plains. The province starts just beyond Château-Thierry, 96 km (60 miles) northeast of Paris, and continues along the towering Marne Valley to Épernay. Cheerful villages line the Routes Touristique du Champagne *(Champagne Road; for details, see our chapter Planner section)*, which twines north to Reims, the largest city in Champagne. To the southeast the grapes of Champagne flourish on the steep slopes of the Marne Valley and the Montagne de Reims, really more of a mighty hill than a mountain. For a handy online resource covering many of the great Champagne houses in the region, log on to 🌐 *www.maisons-champagne.com.*

REIMS

161 km (100 miles) northeast of Paris.

Behind a facade of austerity, Champagne's largest city remains one of France's richest tourist sites, thanks especially to the fact that it sparkles with some of the biggest names in Champagne production. This thriving industry has conferred wealth and sometimes an arrogant reserve on the region's inhabitants. The maze of Champagne cellars constitutes a leading attraction here. Several of these producers organize visits to their cellars, combining video presentations with guided tours of their cavernous, hewn-chalk underground warehouses. The city's tourist office will provide you with a complete list of Champagne cellars. While there, you can also get information on other standout sights. Although many of Reims's historic buildings were flattened in World War I and replaced by drab, modern architecture, those that do remain are of royal magnitude. Topping the list is the magnificent cathedral, in which the kings of France were crowned until 1825.

Champagne and Picardy
Amiens
Péronne
St-Quentin
Guise
Vervins
Grandvilliers
Ham
Roye
Breteuil
Montdidier
Marle
Rozoy-s-Serre
Montcornet
La Fère
Chauny
Marseille-en-Beauvaisis
Noyon
St-Just-en-Chaussée
Laon
Blérancourt
Beauvais
Chavignon
Rethel
Compiègne
PICARDIE
Corbeny
Cerny
Asfeld
Soissons
Pierrefonds
Reims
see detail map
Fismes
Crépy-en-Valois
Chantilly
Senlis
Nanteuil-le-Haudouin
CHAMPAGNE REGION
ÎLE-DE-FRANCE
CHAMPAGNE-ARDENNE
Château-Thierry
Épernay
Meaux
PARIS
L'Épine
Châlons-en-Champagne
Montmirail
0
10 mi
0
10 km
A29
D1001
A1
D1
A26
A16
D934
D1016
N1
N31
N2
A4
N51
A15
A14
A13
A6
A104
D1003
D933
A26

GETTING HERE

You can make it to Reims in 50 minutes on the TGV express from Gare de l'Est: trains depart 10 times daily and cost €34–€59. Several SNCF trains per day connect Reims to Épernay (30 mins, €7), and there is also regular daily train service to Châlons-en-Champagne (40 mins, €11.10) and Laon (50 mins, €10.20). Les Courriers de L'Aube runs seven daily buses to Reims from Châlons-en-Champagne (Line 140; 1 hr, €10).

Visitor Information Reims Tourist Office. ☎ *08–21–61–01–60 €0.09min* 🌐 *www.reims-tourisme.com.*

EXPLORING

TOP ATTRACTIONS

Basilique St-Rémi. This 11th-century Romanesque-Gothic basilica honors the 5th-century saint who gave his name to the city and baptized Clovis (the first king of France) in 498. The interior seems to stretch into the endless distance, an impression created by its relative murk and lowness. The airy four-story Gothic choir contains some fine stained glass from the 12th century. The holy phial used in the crowning of monarchs was formerly kept alongside the basilica in the Abbaye Royale; today that building houses an interesting museum that highlights the history of the abbey, the Gallo-Roman history of the town, and the military history of the region. ✉ *Pl. Chandoine Ladame, Reims* ☎ *03–26–85–06–69* 🌐 *stremi-reims.cef.fr* 🎫 *Museum, €4* 🕒 *Basilica Mar.–Sept., daily 7:30–7:30; Oct.–Feb., daily 8–5. Museum weekdays 2–6:30, weekends 2–7.*

Fodor's Choice ★ **Cathédrale Notre-Dame de Reims.** Recently restored for its 800th birthday, this magnificent Gothic cathedral provided the setting for the coronations of French kings. The great historical saga began with Clovis, king of the Franks, who was baptized in an early structure on this site at the end of the 5th century; Joan of Arc led her recalcitrant Dauphin here to be crowned King Charles VII; Charles X's coronation, in 1825, was the last. The east-end windows have stained glass by Marc Chagall and Imi Knoebel. Admire the vista toward the west end, with an interplay of narrow pointed arches. The glory of Reims's cathedral is its facade: it's so skillfully proportioned that initially you have little idea of its monumental size. Above the north (left) door hovers the *Laughing Angel,* a delightful statue whose famous smile threatens to melt into an acid-rain scowl now that pollution has succeeded war as the ravager of the building's fabric. With the exception of the 15th-century towers, most of the original building went up in the 100 years after 1211. You can climb to the top of the towers and peek inside the breathtaking timber-and-concrete roof (reconstructed in the 1920s with Rockefeller money) for €7.50. A stroll around the outside reinforces the impression of harmony, discipline, and decorative richness. The east end presents an idyllic sight across well-tended lawns. ✉ *Pl. du Cardinal-Luçon, Reims* ☎ *03–26–47–81–79* 🌐 *www.cathedrale-reims.monuments-nationaux.fr* 🎫 *€7.50* 🕒 *Cathedral daily 7:30–7:30. Towers mid-Mar.–early May, Sept., and Oct., Sat. at 10, 11, 2, 3, and 4, Sun. at 2, 3, and 4; early May–Aug., Tues.– Sat. at 10, 11, 2, 3, 4, and 5, Sun. at 2, 3, 4, and 5.*

Tally up the 34 kings who were crowned at Notre-Dame de Reims, one of the largest and greatest of French cathedrals.

Musée des Beaux-Arts (*Museum of Fine Arts*). Two blocks southwest of Reims's massive cathedral, this noted museum has an outstanding collection of paintings, which includes no fewer than 27 Corots, as well as Jacques-Louis David's unforgettable *Death of Marat* (the portrait shows the revolutionary polemicist Jean-Paul Marat stabbed to death in his bath—a deed committed by Charlotte Corday, in 1793). Unfortunately, the museum is only open for temporary exhibitions at the moment, and the main collection is already packed away in preparation for a major move. In 2018 the museum is set to open in new premises, designed by David Chipperfield, near Les Halles du Boulingrin on the Rue de Mars. ✉ *8 rue Chanzy, Reims* ☎ *03–26–35–36–00* 🌐 *www.ville-reims.fr* 🎫 *€4* ⏲ *Wed.–Mon. 10–noon and 2–6.*

Fodor's Choice ★ **Ruinart.** Founded back in 1729, just a year after Louis XV's decision to allow wine to be transported by bottle (previously it could only be moved by cask), Ruinart effectively kick-started the Champagne industry. Four of its huge, church-sized chalk galleries (24 in all) are listed as historic monuments. This is the costliest visit in the area; if you're willing to shell out €70, you can taste a vintage Champagne. ✉ *4 rue des Crayères, Reims* ☎ *03–26–77–51–21* 🌐 *www.ruinart.com* 🎫 *€70–€100* ⏲ *Feb.–mid-Dec., Tues.–Sat. Call or book for times.*

Fodor's Choice ★ **Taittinger.** Cavernous chalk cellars, first used by monks for wine storage, house 15 million bottles and partly occupy the crypt of the 13 century abbey that used to stand on this spot. You can see a model of the abbey and its elegant church, both demolished during the French Revolution. ✉ *9 pl. St-Nicaise, Reims* ☎ *03–26–51–19–11* 🌐 *www.taittinger.com*

Basilique St-Rémi 1
Cathédrale Notre-Dame 4
Cryptoportique .. 6
Hôtel Le Vergeur Museum 5
Musée des Beaux-Arts 3
Musée de la Reddition 7
Palais du Tau 2

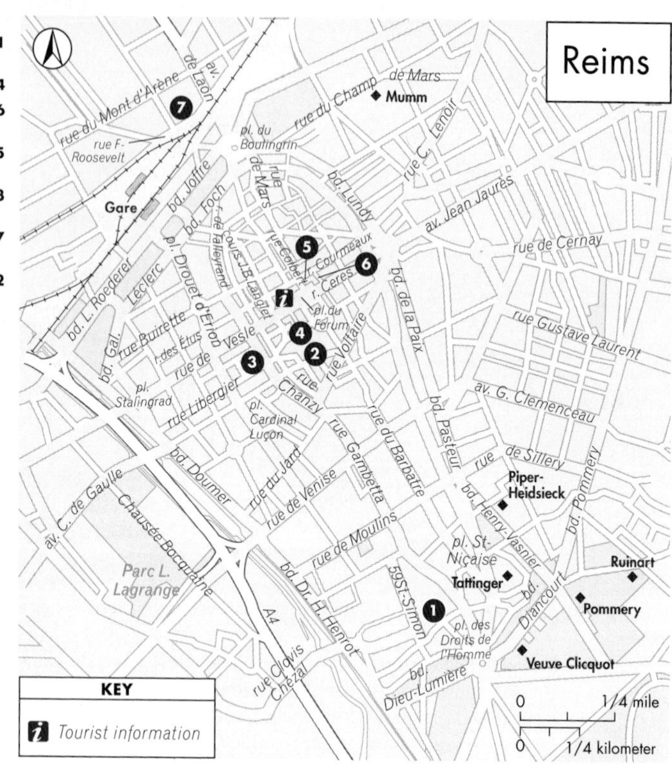

€16.50 By appointment only: mid-Mar.–mid-Nov., daily 9:30–1 and 2–5:30; mid-Nov.–mid-Mar., weekdays only.

WORTH NOTING

Cryptoportique. A Gallo-Roman underground gallery and crypt, now a semi-subterranean venue for municipal expositions, was initially constructed around AD 200 beneath the forum of Reims's predecessor, the Roman town of Durocortorum. *Pl. du Forum, Reims 03–26–77–45–03 Free June–Sept., daily 2–6.*

Hôtel Le Vergeur Museum. One of the best examples of late medieval and early Renaissance architecture in Reims was built during the 13th century. Originally overlooking the historic linen-and-wheat market in the center of town, this noble town house changed hands between aristocrats and Champagne traders before being acquired in 1910 by Hugues Kraft—a man whose sole passion was preserving the city's historic buildings. It was completely restored after the WWI bombings and today houses an impressive collection of historical prints, paintings, and furnishings from the region, as well as an original, complete series of 15th-century Albert Dürer prints of the "Apocalypse" and "Large Passion." There are guided tours of the collection Tuesday through Sunday, from 2 to 5. *36 pl. du Forum, Reims 03–26–47–20–75 www.museelevergeur.com €5 Tues.–Sun. 2–6.*

Mumm. Not the most spectacular cellars but a practical option if you have little time: you can walk to it from the cathedral and the train station. Mumm was confiscated by the French state in World War I because it had always remained under German ownership. The visit starts with a 10-minute film and ends with your choice of three dégustations. ✉ *29 rue du Champ-de-Mars, Reims* ☎ *03–26–49–59–70* 🌐 *www.ghmumm.com* 🎫 *€20–€39* 🕑 *Mar.–Oct., daily 9–1 and 2–6 (last tours at 11:30 and 4:30); Nov.–Feb., Mon.–Sat. 9:30–noon and 2–6 (last tours 10:50 and 4:15).*

Musée de la Reddition (*Museum of the Surrender*). Also known as the Salle du 8-Mai-1945 or the "little red school house," this museum is a well-preserved map-covered room used by General Eisenhower as Allied headquarters at the end of World War II. It was here that General Alfred Jodl signed the German surrender at 2:41 am on May 7, 1945. Fighting officially ceased at midnight the next day. The museum also presents a collection of local photos, documents, uniforms, and artifacts recounting the fighting, occupation, and liberation of Reims. Guided tours begin with a short film in English and French. ✉ *12 rue Franklin-Roosevelt, Reims* ☎ *03–26–47–84–19* 🎫 *€4* 🕑 *Wed.–Mon. 10–noon and 2–6.*

Palais du Tau. Formerly the Archbishop's Palace, this UNESCO World Heritage List museum has an impressive display of tapestries and coronation robes of 32 French kings, as well as several statues rescued from the cathedral facade. The second-floor views of the cathedral, which stands alongside it, are terrific. ✉ *2 pl. du Cardinal-Luçon, Reims* ☎ *03–26–47–81–79* 🌐 *www.palais-tau.monuments-nationaux.fr* 🎫 *€7.50* 🕑 *May–Aug., Tues.–Sun. 9:30–6:30; Sept.–Apr., Tues.–Sun. 9:30–12:30 and 2–5:30.*

7

Pommery. This turreted wedding-cake extravaganza on the city outskirts was designed by Jeanne-Alexandrine Pommery (1819–1890), another formidable Champagne widow. The 11 miles of cellars (about a hundred feet underground) are reached by a grandiose 116-step staircase. Visit the Art Nouveau Villa Demoiselle across the street (owned by Pommery). ✉ *5 pl. du General-Gouraud, Reims* ☎ *03–26–61–62–56* 🌐 *www.visite-vrankenpommery.fr* 🎫 *€13* 🕑 *Daily 10–6.*

WHERE TO EAT

$$$ MODERN FRENCH

Anna-S. La Table Amoureuse. About a five-minute walk from Reims's cathedral, this small room features creative, contemporary French cuisine in charming pastel-toned surroundings. Try fillet of roe deer with red cabbage and cranberries, sea bass with smashed potatoes, or smoked salmon served on potato waffles with horseradish sauce—just be sure to leave room for the desserts, which are almost too pretty to eat. A vegetarian menu is available on request. $ *Average main: €27* ✉ *6 rue Gambetta, Reims* ☎ *03–26–89–12–12* 🌐 *www.annas-latableamoureuse.com* 🕑 *Closed Mon. No dinner Sun. and Wed.*

$$$ BRASSERIE

Brasserie Flo. This authentic brasserie, part of the Flo chain, has polished wood floors, Art Nouveau glass windows, and mirrored walls. The food is sophisticated and dependable, the service sleek. Signature dishes—like foie gras terrine with seasonal fruit chutney, or roast monkfish with cèpe mushrooms—are just some of the delicious choices. There are also good fixed-price menus, which change on a weekly basis. The terrace is an added bonus in the summer. *Average main: €25 96 pl. Drouet d'Erlon, Reims 03-26-91-40-50 www.floreims.com.*

$$ BISTRO **Café du Palais.** Walls at this 1930s eatery are crammed with gilt-edged mirrors, golden cherubs, and old paintings, while crystal chandeliers hang from the ceiling, which itself is topped by a magnificent Art Deco glass roof signed by Jacques Simon. Bistro-style dishes like quail breast or poached salmon in a creamy leek sauce top the menu. Desserts are regional favorites (such as ice cream with the famous *biscuits roses de Reims*), and the selection of Champagnes is extensive—there's a good choice of red Coteaux Champenois wines, too. The café is popular among locals, so reserve a table in advance (request one inside as the terrace looks out over a tramline). Note that this is primarily a lunch spot and serves dinner on Saturday only. *Average main: €23 14 pl. Myron T-Herrick, Reims 03-26-47-52-54 www.cafedupalais.fr Closed Sun. and Mon. No dinner Tues.–Fri.*

$$ SEAFOOD **Le Bocal.** Freshness is guaranteed at this tiny treasure, hidden at the back of a fishmonger's shop across from the old food court (les Halles du Boulingrin). Everything is just off the boat, but most of the dozen lucky diners automatically go with the catch of the day. Tempting as that is, no one should pass up the divine cooked oysters in season. Tables in the bright, contemporary room are in demand, so it's best to reserve ahead. *Average main: €20 27 rue de Mars, Reims 03-26-47-02-51 www.restaurantlebocal.fr Closed Sun. and Mon.*

$$$$ MODERN FRENCH **Le Millénaire.** Appearances deceive at this traditional town house just off Place Royale, a few feet from the cathedral. Inside, it has an updated Art Deco feel with plush eggplant-hued carpets and sleek, chic chairs. Chef Laurent Laplaige, seconded by Frédéric Dupont, finds an outlet for his decorative artistry in colorful food presented on elegant white plates. Stunning specialties range from John Dory panfried in hazelnut butter and served with sweet potato, snails, and an aniseed sauce, to fillet of beef accompanied by stuffed zucchini flowers and celery puree. Dessert dazzlers include a chocolate sphere filled with chocolate cream and orange compote. *Average main: €50 4 rue Bertin, Reims 03-26-08-26-62 www.lemillenaire.com Closed Sun. No lunch Sat.*

WHERE TO STAY

$$$$ HOTEL **Château Les Crayères.** In a grand park with towering trees planted by Champagne legend Madame Pommery, this celebrated hotel remains the showplace of Reims—a stylish, late-19th-century château featuring guest rooms bedecked with antiques, boiseries, and couture fabrics, plus the finest Champenoise restaurant of them all, Le Parc. **Pros:** hotel and two restaurants in same luxurious setting; innovative food and Champagne pairings; glorious salons are gilt trimmed and bouquet laden. **Cons:** outside the center of town. *Rooms from: €395 64 bd. Henry-Vasnier, Reims 03-26-24-90-00 www.lescrayeres.com Closed 3 wks in late Dec.–early Jan. 16 rooms, 4 suites No meals.*

$ HOTEL **Grand Hôtel Continental.** Centrally located on the main pedestrian street, this hotel was originally a private 19th-century mansion, and the lobby still exudes old-world charm with worn leather couches, low-level lighting, and a grand staircase; in contrast the smart guest rooms, individually decorated in either classic or contemporary styles, have flat-screen TVs and modern bathrooms. **Pros:** central location; air-conditioning. **Cons:** some rooms lack charm. *Rooms from: €82 ✉ 93 pl. Drouet d'Erlon, Reims ☎ 03–26–40–39–35 www.grandhotelcontinental.com Closed 2 wks late Dec.–early Jan. 61 rooms, 2 suites No meals.*

$ HOTEL **Hôtel Azur.** At this comfortable, friendly spot on a residential street in the center of Reims, rooms are simply furnished and decorated in cheerful primary colors with modern white tile bathrooms. **Pros:** free Wi-Fi; near train station and 10-minute walk to cathedral; secure parking. **Cons:** few rooms have bathtubs; limited reception hours. *Rooms from: €89 ✉ 9 rue des Ecrevées, Reims ☎ 03–26–47–43–39 www.hotel-azur-reims.com Closed 2 wks late Dec.–early Jan. 19 rooms No meals.*

$$$ HOTEL **La Paix.** An antidote to historical overload, this contemporary eight-story Best Western—branded property, 10 minutes on foot from the cathedral, has modern furnishings, dramatic artworks, plus an up-to-date color palette (think mustard, aubergine, pomegranate, and cocoa). **Pros:** central location; stylish hotel bar; free Wi-Fi. **Cons:** often hosts corporate groups. *Rooms from: €180 ✉ 9 rue Buirette, Reims ☎ 03–26–40–04–08 www.bestwestern-lapaix-reims.com 164 rooms, 1 suite No meals.*

7

L'ÉPINE

56 km (35 miles) southeast of Reims via A4/D933, 7 km (4½ miles) east of Châlons via D933.

Legend has it that in the Middle Ages some shepherds herding their flock down from pasture found a statue of the Virgin in a burning thorn bush (épine). Their discovery triggered the building of a church—Basilique de Notre-Dame de l'Épine—which today looms over this otherwise uninspiring village.

GETTING HERE

Lying east of Châlons, L'Épine is best reached by car. If you don't have your own, expect to pay about €20 for cab fare.

EXPLORING

Basilique de Notre-Dame de l'Épine. Tiny L'Épine is dominated by its twin-tower church, the Flamboyant Gothic Basilique de Notre-Dame de l'Épine. Decorated with a multitude of leering gargoyles, the facade is a magnificent creation of intricate patterns and spires. The interior, conversely, exudes elegance and restraint; note the sculptures depicting the Entombment of Christ and the stone rood screen, carved in the late-15th century. *✉ Rue de l'Église, L'Épine ☎ 03–26–66–96–98 Free Oct.–Mar., daily 9–7; Apr.–Sept., daily 8:30–7:30.*

Continued on page 352

Champagne Uncorked

Dom Pierre Pérignon was the first to discover the secret of Champagne's production by combining the still wines of the region and storing the beverage in bottles. oday, the world's most famous sparkling vine comes from the very same vineyards, along the towering Marne Valley between pernay and Château-Thierry and on the lopes of the Montagne de Reims between pernay and Reims.

Vhen you take a Champagne tasting tour, ou won't be at the vineyards—it's all done ide the various houses, miles away from here the grapes are grown. Champagne irms—Veuve-Clicquot, Mumm, Pommery, aittinger, and others—give travelers tours of their chalky, mazelike *caves* (cellars). he quality of the tours is inconsistent, ranging from hilarious to despairingly tedious, hough a glass of Champagne at the end nakes even the most mediocre worth it (some vould say). On the tours, you'll discover that Champagne is not made so differently from he way the Dom did it three centuries ago.

By Heather Stimmler-Hall

A view along the Routes du Champagne; for details on e Champagne Roads see this chapter's Planner section.

7

IN FOCUS CHAMPAGNE UNCORKED

BUBBLY BASICS

ALL ABOUT GRAPES

Three types of grape are used to make Champagne: pinot noir, chardonnay, and pinot meunier. The two pinots, which account for 75% of production, are black grapes with white juice. Rosé Champagne is made either by leaving pinot noir juice in contact with the grape skins just long enough to turn it pink, or by mixing local red wine with Champagne prior to bottling.

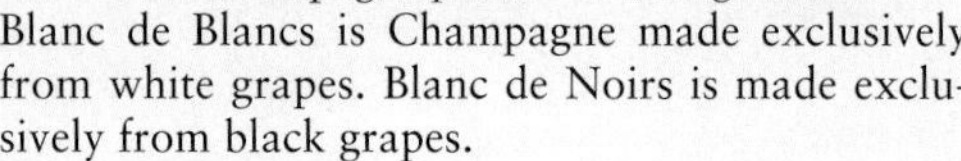

Blanc de Blancs is Champagne made exclusively from white grapes. Blanc de Noirs is made exclusively from black grapes.

HOW SWEET IT IS

The amount of residual sugar determines the category—ranging from Demi-Sec (literally half-dry, actually sweet) with 33–55 grams of residual sugar per liter, to Extra-Brut (very dry) at less than 6 grams of residual sugar per liter. Classifications in between include Sec at 17 to 35 grams, Extra Dry at 12–20 grams, and Brut, under 15 grams.

VINTAGE VS. NONVINTAGE

Vintage Champagne is named for a specific year, on the premise that the grapes harvested in that year were of extraordinary quality to produce a Champagne by themselves without being blended with wine from other years. Cuvées de Prestige are the finest and most expensive Champagnes that a firm has to offer.

LABEL KNOW-HOW

Along with specific descriptors—such as Blanc de Blancs, Blanc de Noirs, Vintage, etc.—the label carries the following information:

1. The Champagne appellation
2. The brand or name of the producer
3. The level of alcohol volume. Champagne is permitted to vary between 10 and 13%. The amount of sugar (dosage) added results in the styles of Brut, Extra Brut, and Demi-Sec.

THE MERRY WIDOW & THE STARSTRUCK MONK

MADAME CLICQUOT (1777–1866)

WHY THE NICKNAME? Born Nicole-Barbe Ponsardin and married into the Clicquot family, Madame Clicquot was widowed just seven years after she married François Clicquot (in French, *veuve* means widow).

I'M A HOTSHOT BECAUSE . . . : After her husband's death, she took over the firm and was one of France's earliest female entrepreneurs and the smartest marketer of the Napoléonic era. During her 60 years in control of the firm, business soared.

GREATEST CONTRIBUTION: She invented the *table de remuage*—the slanted rack used for "riddling," a method for capturing and releasing sediment that collects in the wine—a process that is still used today.

BRAGGING RIGHTS: She persuaded Czar Alexander I to toast Napoléon's demise with Champagne rather than vodka, and other royal courts were soon in bubbly pursuit.

DOM PIERRE PÉRIGNON (1638–1715)

WHY THE NICKNAME? When Dom Pierre first tasted his creation, he is quoted as saying that he was drinking stars.

I'M A HOTSHOT BECAUSE . . . : He discovered Champagne when he was about 30 years old while he was the cellarmaster at the Abbey of Hautvillers, just north of Épernay.

GREATEST CONTRIBUTION: He blended wines from different vats and vineyards (now a common practice but then a novelty), reintroduced corks—forgotten since Roman times—and used thicker glass bottles to prevent them from exploding during fermentation.

BRAGGING RIGHTS: Who else can claim the title Father of Champagne?

"Brother, come quickly! I'm drinking stars!"
–Dom Pierre Pérignon

WHAT YOU'LL PAY

Champagne relentlessly markets itself as a luxury product—the sippable equivalent of perfume and haute couture—so it's no surprise that two of the top Champagne brands, Krug and Dom Pérignon, are owned by a luxury goods conglomerate (Louis Vuitton-Moët Hennessy). Sure, at small local producers, or in giant French hypermarkets, you can find a bottle of nonvintage bubbly for $15. But it's more likely to be nearer $40 and, if you fancy something special—say a bottle of vintage Dom Perignon Rose—be prepared to fork out $350. One of the priciest Blanc de Noirs is Bollinger's Vieilles Vignes—tagged at around $500. At the very top of the line is Krug's single-vineyard Clos du Mesnil, with the stellar 2000 vintage retailing at around $1,220. Just 12,624 bottles were ever produced of this golden elixir.

CHÂLONS-EN-CHAMPAGNE

7 km (4½ miles) west of L'Épine via D933, 34 km (21 miles) southeast of Épernay via D1003.

The administrative capital of the Marne and the Champagne region is famous for its Blanc de Blancs vineyards. The town center, crisscrossed with canals and streams, is a charming mix of half-timbered houses and riverside gardens; and several major churches bear eloquent testimony to Châlons's medieval importance.

GETTING HERE

Trains from Paris (Gare de l'Est) leave for Châlons every 2 hours or so (€27); the 174-km (108-mile) trip takes around 1 hour, 30 minutes (€28). There's also limited TGV service from Paris: one train in the afternoon, one in the evening (1 hr, 6 mins; €43). Sixteen direct trains a day arrive here from Reims (40 mins, €11.10), and Les Courriers de L'Aube (*03–25–71–28–42* 🌐 *www.courriersdelaube.fr*) runs regular buses from the same city (1 hr, €10). A great way to explore the town itself is by boat; tours are organized by the tourist office.

Visitor Information Châlons-en-Champagne Tourist Office. ☎ *03–26–65–35–65* 🌐 *www.chalons-tourisme.com.*

EXPLORING

Cathédrale St-Étienne. The 13th-century Cathédrale St-Étienne is a harmonious structure with large nave windows and tidy flying buttresses; the exterior effect is marred only by the bulky 17th-century Baroque west front. ✉ *Rue de la Marne, Châlons-en-Champagne* ⏲ *July and Aug., Tues.–Sat. 10–noon and 2–6, Sun. 2:30–6; Sept.–June, weekends 2–6.*

Notre-Dame-en-Vaux. With its twin spires, Romanesque nave, and early Gothic choir and vaults, the church of Notre-Dame-en-Vaux is one of the most imposing in Champagne. The small **museum** beside the excavated cloister contains outstanding medieval statuary. ✉ *Rue Nicolas-Durand, Châlons-en-Champagne* ☎ *03–26–69–99–61* 🎫 *Museum €3.50* ⏲ *Church: Mon.–Sat. 10–noon and 2–6. Museum: Apr.–Sept., Wed.–Mon. 10–noon and 2–6; Oct.–Mar., Wed.–Fri. 10–noon and 2–5, weekends 10–noon and 2–6.*

WHERE TO EAT AND STAY

$$$ FRENCH FAMILY ✕ **Les Caudalies.** This elegant, semiformal restaurant has a pair of stylish Art Deco dining rooms: one with mosaic floors, sleek contemporary table settings, and a glass ceiling; the other with wood-paneling and parquet floors. The menu focuses on creative French dishes like snails in a two-cheese sauce, seared tuna with panfried foie gras, and duck breast with pear and Roquefort sauce. Don't miss out on daring desserts like the upside-down fig tart with licorice ice cream. There's a pretty walled terrace for summer dining, too. $ *Average main: €28* ✉ *2 Rue de L'Abbé Lambert, Châlons-en-Champagne* ☎ *03–26–65–07–87* 🌐 *www.les-caudalies.com* ⏲ *Closed Sun., late Dec.–early Jan., 2 wks in Feb., and 2 wks late Aug. No dinner Tues. and Thurs.*

CLOSE UP

Hiking Champagne: Lift Your Spirits!

There's nothing like getting out into Mother Nature to send the spirits soaring and, as it turns out, the region of Champagne is custom-made for easy and scenic hiking.

Just south of Reims rises the Montagne de Reims, a vast forested plateau on whose slopes grow the Pinot Noir and Pinot Meunier grapes used to make Champagne.

Several *sentiers de Grandes Randonnées* (long hiking trails; also known as GRs) run across the top of the plateau, burrowing through dense forest and looping around the edges.

For example, the GR141 and the GR14 form a loop more than 50 km (30 miles) long around the plateau's eastern half, passing by several train stations en route.

You can access some of these hiking trails from the Rilly-la-Montagne, Avenay, and Ay stops on the Reims-Épernay rail line.

If you're a serious hiker, make for the Ardennes region, which lies just to the northeast of Champagne.

$$$ HOTEL **Hôtel d'Angleterre.** Guests at this stylish spot in central Châlons can enjoy well-appointed rooms (think modern furniture, marble bathrooms, and either wood floors or plush carpets) along with outstanding dining options. **Pros:** finely modernized rooms; inventive cuisine. **Cons:** the hotel and restaurants are all closed Sundays; dinner service ends early. *Rooms from: €150* *19 pl. Monseigneur-Tissier, Châlons-en-Champagne* *03–26–68–21–51* *www.hotel-dangleterre.fr* *Closed late July–mid-Aug., late Dec.–early Jan., and Sun.* *25 rooms* *No meals.*

7

ÉPERNAY

28 km (18 miles) south of Reims via D951, 35 km (24 miles) west of Châlons-en-Champagne via D1003, 50 km (31 miles) east of Château-Thierry via D1003.

Although Reims loudly proclaims itself to be the last word in Champagne production, Épernay—on the south bank of the Marne—is really the center of the bubbly drink's spirit. It was here in 1741 that the first full-blown Champagne house, Moët (now Moët et Chandon), took the lifetime passion of Dom Pérignon and turned it into an industry. Unfortunately, no relation exists between the fabulous wealth of Épernay's illustrious wine houses and the drab, dreary appearance of the town as a whole. Most Champagne firms—Moët et Chandon (*20 av. de Champagne*); Mercier (*68–70 av. de Champagne*); and De Castellane (*57 rue de Verdun*)—are spaced out along the long, straight Avenue de Champagne, and although their names may provoke sighs of wonder, their facades are either functional or overly dressy.

GETTING HERE

Trains from Paris (Gare de l'Est) leave for Épernay every hour or so (€24); the 145-km (90-mile) trip takes 1 hour, 21 minutes (€24). Several trains daily also link Épernay to Reims (30 mins, €7) and Châlons (15 mins, €6.60).

Visitor Information Épernay Tourist Office. ☎ *03-26-53-33-00* 🌐 *www.ot-epernay.fr.*

EXPLORING

Fodor's Choice ★ **Castellane.** Above the Champagne cellars here, there's a museum with an intriguing display of old tools, bottles, labels, and posters. There's also a chance to see the bottling and labeling plant, and climb to the top of a 200-foot tower for a great view over Épernay and the surrounding Marne vineyards. ✉ *57 rue de Verdun, Épernay* ☎ *03-26-51-19-11* 🌐 *www.castellane.com* 🎟 *€12 (includes museum)* ⏲ *Mar.-Dec., daily 10–11 and 2–5.*

Hautvillers. To understand how the region's still wine became sparkling Champagne, head across the Marne to Hautvillers. Here Dom Pérignon (1638–1715)—a blind monk who was reputedly blessed with exceptional taste buds and a heightened sense of smell—invented Champagne as everyone knows it by using corks for stoppers and blending wines from different vineyards. Legend has it that upon his first sip he cried out, "Come quickly, I am drinking the stars." Dom Pérignon's simple tomb, in a damp, dreary Benedictine abbey church (now owned by Moët et Chandon), is a forlorn memorial to the man behind one of the world's most exalted libations. ✉ *Épernay.*

Mercier. At these high-tech cellars, you can ride an electric train and admire the giant 200,000-bottle oak barrel it took 24 oxen three weeks to cart to the Exposition Universelle in Paris in 1889. An elevator down to (and up from) the cellars is a welcome plus. ✉ *68-70 av. de Champagne, Épernay* ☎ *03-26-51-22-22* 🌐 *www.champagnemercier.fr* 🎟 *€13-€25* ⏲ *Feb.–mid-Nov., daily 9:30–11 and 2–4.*

Fodor's Choice ★ **Moët & Chandon.** Foreign royalty from Czar Alexander I to Queen Elizabeth II have visited this most prestigious of all Champagne houses, founded by Charles Moët in 1743. The chalk-cellar galleries run for a mind-blowing 17 miles. The visit includes a glass of Brut Imperial. ✉ *20 av. de Champagne, Épernay* ☎ *03-26-51-20-20* 🌐 *www.moet.com* 🎟 *€22–€35* ⏲ *Late Jan.–late Mar., weekdays 9:30–11:30 and 2:30–4:30; late Mar.–late Jan., daily 9:30–11:30 and 2:30–4:30.*

WHERE TO EAT AND STAY

$$ FRENCH ✕ **La Cave à Champagne.** This convivial little restaurant in the center of Épernay serves authentic regional dishes with a refined twist at reasonable prices. Chef Bernard Ocio executes a perfect marriage of flavors by highlighting the local wines; classics include homemade foie gras cooked in *ratafia de Champagne*, rump steak served with a Pinot Noir sauce, salmon accompanied by a Champagne sauce, and the quintessential *potée à la champenoise*. There are also more rustic choices for the daring, such as snails in parsley butter and *tête de veau*. The desserts hold no surprises, so expect to see old favorites like pear poached in red wine and crème brûlée. Reservations are essential on weekends.

$ Average main: €22 ✉ 16 rue Gambetta, Épernay ☎ 03–26–55–50–70 🌐 www.la-cave-a-champagne.com ⏲ Closed Wed. No dinner Tues.

$$$$ HOTEL **La Briqueterie.** Épernay is short on good hotels, so it's worth driving south to Vinay and booking into this luxurious manor, which has spacious accommodations, wonderful gardens, an indoor pool, plus a well-equipped spa. **Pros:** pool has garden view; spa includes sauna and hammam facilities. **Cons:** rooms can be small; corporate feel (it hosts frequent business seminars). *$ Rooms from: €235 ✉ 4 rte. de Sézanne, Vinay ✣ 6 km (4 miles) south of Épernay ☎ 03–26–59–99–99 🌐 www.labriqueterie.fr ⏲ Closed late Dec.–late Jan. 36 rooms, 4 suites No meals.*

CHÂTEAU-THIERRY

37 km (23 miles) east of Épernay via D1003.

Château-Thierry is best known as the birthplace of the French fabulist Jean de La Fontaine (1621–95). Built along the Marne River beneath the ruins of a hilltop castle that dates from the time of Joan of Arc, it's within sight of the American **Belleau Wood** War Cemetery (open daily 9–5), which commemorates the 2,300 American soldiers slain here in 1918.

GETTING HERE

Château-Thierry is easily reached by train from Paris; 11 direct ones depart daily from Gare de l'Est (46 mins, €16.50).

EXPLORING

Musée Jean de La Fontaine. Recently restored, the 16th-century mansion where La Fontaine was born and lived until 1676 is now a museum, furnished in the style of the 17th century. It contains La Fontaine's bust, portrait, and baptism certificate, plus editions of his fables magnificently illustrated by Jean-Baptiste Oudry (1755) and Gustave Doré (1868). *✉ 12 rue Jean-de-La-Fontaine, Château-Thierry ☎ 03–23–69–05–60 🌐 www.musee-jean-de-la-fontaine.fr €3.70 ⏲ Tues.–Sun. 9:30–noon and 2–5:30.*

THE CATHEDRAL CITIES

Champagne's neighbor, the province of Picardy, located to the northeast of the region, is traversed by the Aisne and Oise rivers, and remains home to some of France's greatest cathedrals. The hundreds of kilometers of chalk tunnels throughout northern France, some dug by the ancient Romans as quarries, may serve as the damp and moldy berth for millions of bottles of Champagne, but they also gave up tons of blocks to create other treasures of the region: the magical and magnificent Gothic cathedrals.

Here, in the wake of regal Reims, lie four more of the most superlative: Amiens, the largest; Beauvais, the tallest; Laon, with the most towers and fantastic hilltop setting; and Soissons, beloved by Rodin. Add in those at St-Omer, St-Quentin, and Châlons-en-Champagne, along with the Flamboyant Gothic masterpieces in St-Riquier and L'Épine *(above)*,

Rumor has it that even the air is 30-proof in Champagne—discover whether this is true or not on the many hiking trails in the region.

and aficionados of medieval architecture may wish to explore the region more extensively, following the development of Gothic architecture from its debut at Noyon to its flamboyant finale at Abbeville, where, according to the 19th-century English essayist John Ruskin, Gothic "lay down and died."

LAON

66 km (41 miles) north of Château-Thierry via D1/N2, 52 km (32 miles) northwest of Reims.

Thanks to its awe-inducing hilltop site and the forest of towers sprouting from its ancient cathedral, lofty Laon basks in the title of the "Crowned Mountain." The medieval ramparts, virtually undisturbed by passing traffic, provide a ready-made itinerary for a tour of old Laon. Panoramic views, sturdy gateways, and intriguing glimpses of the cathedral lurk around every bend. There's even a funicular, which makes frequent trips (except on Sunday in winter) up and down the hillside between the station and the Vieille Ville (Old Town).

GETTING HERE

There are regular direct trains from Paris (Gare du Nord) to Laon; the 145-km (90-mile) journey takes 1 hour, 40 minutes and costs €23.50. Trains departing nearly every hour also link Reims to Laon (50 mins, €10.20), and eight direct trains arrive daily from Amiens (1 hr, 45 mins; €18.50).

Visitor Information Laon Tourist Office. ☎ *03–23–20–28–62* 🌐 *www.tourisme-paysdelaon.com.*

EXPLORING

Fodor's Choice ★ **Cathédrale Notre-Dame.** Constructed between 1150 and 1230, the Cathédrale Notre-Dame is a superb example of early Gothic. The light interior gives the impression of order and immense length, and the first flourishing of Gothic architecture is reflected in the harmony of the four-tier nave: from the bottom up, observe the wide arcades, the double windows of the tribune, the squat windows of the triforium, and, finally, the upper windows of the clerestory. Medieval stained glass includes the rose window dedicated to the liberal arts in the left transept, and the windows in the flat east end, an unusual feature for France although common in England. The majestic towers can be explored during guided visits; these depart from the tourist office, which occupies a 12th-century hospital on the cathedral square. Audioguides can be rented for €5. ✉ *Pl. du Parvis, Laon* 🎫 *Tours €5* ⏲ *Cathedral daily 8:30–6:30. Tours July and Aug., daily 11:30; Sept.–June, Fri.–Sun. 11:30.*

Musée d'Art et d'Archéologie. Laon's art and archeology museum has a collection of Mediterranean finds from the Bronze Age through the Gallo-Roman era that is second in importance only to that at the Louvre. Other highlights include fine 17th- and 18th-century paintings by celebrated local artists Mathieu Le Nain and Jean-Simon Berthélemy, as well as the chilling effigy of Guillaume de Harcigny, doctor to the insane Charles VI. The **Chapelle des Templiers** in the garden—a small, octagonal 12th-century chapel topped by a shallow dome—houses fragments of the cathedral's gable. ✉ *32 rue Georges-Ermant, Laon* ☎ *03–23–22–87–00* 🌐 *www.ville-laon.fr* 🎫 *€4* ⏲ *June–Sept., Tues.–Sun. 11–6; Oct.–May, Tues.–Sun. 2–6.*

WHERE TO STAY

$ HOTEL **Bannière de France.** In business since 1685, this ancient hostelry is five minutes from the cathedral and welcomes visitors with its cozy accommodations and venerable dining room. **Pros:** comfy rooms; free breakfast and Wi-Fi. **Cons:** some rooms need modernizing; short on parking space. *Ⓢ Rooms from: €102* ✉ *11 rue Franklin-Roosevelt, Laon* ☎ *03–23–23–21–44* 🌐 *www.hoteldelabannieredefrance.com* ⏲ *Closed mid-Dec.–mid-Jan.* *17 rooms* *Breakfast.*

$ B&B/INN FAMILY **La Maison des 3 Rois.** Within walking distance of the cathedral, this centuries-old town house blends modern comforts with timbered ceilings, creaky stairs, and either wood or terra-cotta tiled floors. **Pros:** centrally located. **Cons:** steep staircase to attic rooms; parking hard to find on street in front. *Ⓢ Rooms from: €95* ✉ *17 rue Saint Martin, Laon* ☎ *03–23–20–74–24* 🌐 *www.lamaisondes3rois.com* *5 rooms* *Breakfast.*

SOISSONS

38 km (22 miles) southwest of Laon.

Although this was a major city in medieval times, the ravages of the French Revolution and World War I left little of it intact. Nowadays only the magnificent cathedral and the evocative ruins of its onetime abbey bear witness to Soissons's illustrious past.

GETTING HERE

Trains from Paris Gare du Nord take at least 65 minutes (€14.70), while those from Laon take about 30 (€6.10).

Visitor Information **Soissons Tourist Office.** ☎ *03–23–53–17–37* 🌐 *www.tourisme-soissons.fr.*

EXPLORING

Cathédrale Saint-Gervais Saint-Protais. Rodin famously declared that "there are no hours in this cathedral, but rather eternity." The Gothic interior, with its pure lines and restrained ornamentation, creates a more harmonious impression than the asymmetrical, one-tower facade. The most remarkable feature, however, is the rounded four-story southern transept, an element more frequently found in the German Rhineland than in France. Rubens's *Adoration of the Shepherds* hangs on the other side of the transept. ✉ *Pl. Fernand-Marquigny, Soissons* 🎫 *Tours €5* ⏲ *Cathedral daily 9:30–noon and 2:30–5:30. Tours mid-June–mid-Sept., daily at 2:30.*

Musée de Soissons. Partly housed in the medieval abbey of St-Léger, the town museum has a varied collection of local archaeological finds and paintings, with fine 19th-century works by Gustave Courbet and Eugène Boudin. ✉ *2 rue de la Congrégation, Soissons* ☎ *03–23–55–94–73* 🌐 *www.musee-soissons.org* 🎫 *€2* ⏲ *Apr.–Sept., Tues.–Fri. 9–noon and 2–6, weekends 2–7; Oct.–Mar., Tues.–Fri. 9–noon and 2–5, weekends 2–5.*

St-Jean-des-Vignes. The twin-spire facade, arcaded cloister, and airy refectory are all that remain of this hilltop abbey church. Constructed between the 14th and 16th century, St-Jean-des-Vignes was largely dismantled just after the Revolution, and its fallen stones were used to restore the Cathédrale Saint-Gervais Saint-Potrais. Nevertheless, the church is still the most impressive sight in Soissons, the hollow of what was once its rose window peering out over the town like the eye of some giant Cyclops. ✉ *Cours St-Jean-des-Vignes, Soissons* 🌐 *www.musee-soissons.org* 🎫 *Free* ⏲ *Daily 8–6.*

WHERE TO STAY

$$$$ HOTEL **Château de Courcelles.** Loaded with charm, this refined château by the Vesles River has a Louis XIV facade, and the classic exterior somehow harmonizes nicely with the sweeping brass main staircase attributed to Jean Cocteau. **Pros:** verdant setting; historic decor; welcomes families. **Cons:** accommodations vary in size and grandeur; no elevator. 💲 *Rooms from: €255* ✉ *8 rue du Château, 20 km (12 miles) east of Soissons via N31, Courcelles-sur-Vesles* ☎ *03–23–74–13–53* 🌐 *www.chateau-de-courcelles.fr* *12 rooms, 6 suites* 🍽 *Some meals.*

AMIENS

112 km (70 miles) northwest of Soissons via N31/D935, 58 km (36 miles) north of Beauvais via A16.

Although Amiens showcases some pretty brazen postwar reconstruction, epitomized by Auguste Perret's 340-foot Tour Perret (a soaring concrete stump by the train station), the city is well worth exploring.

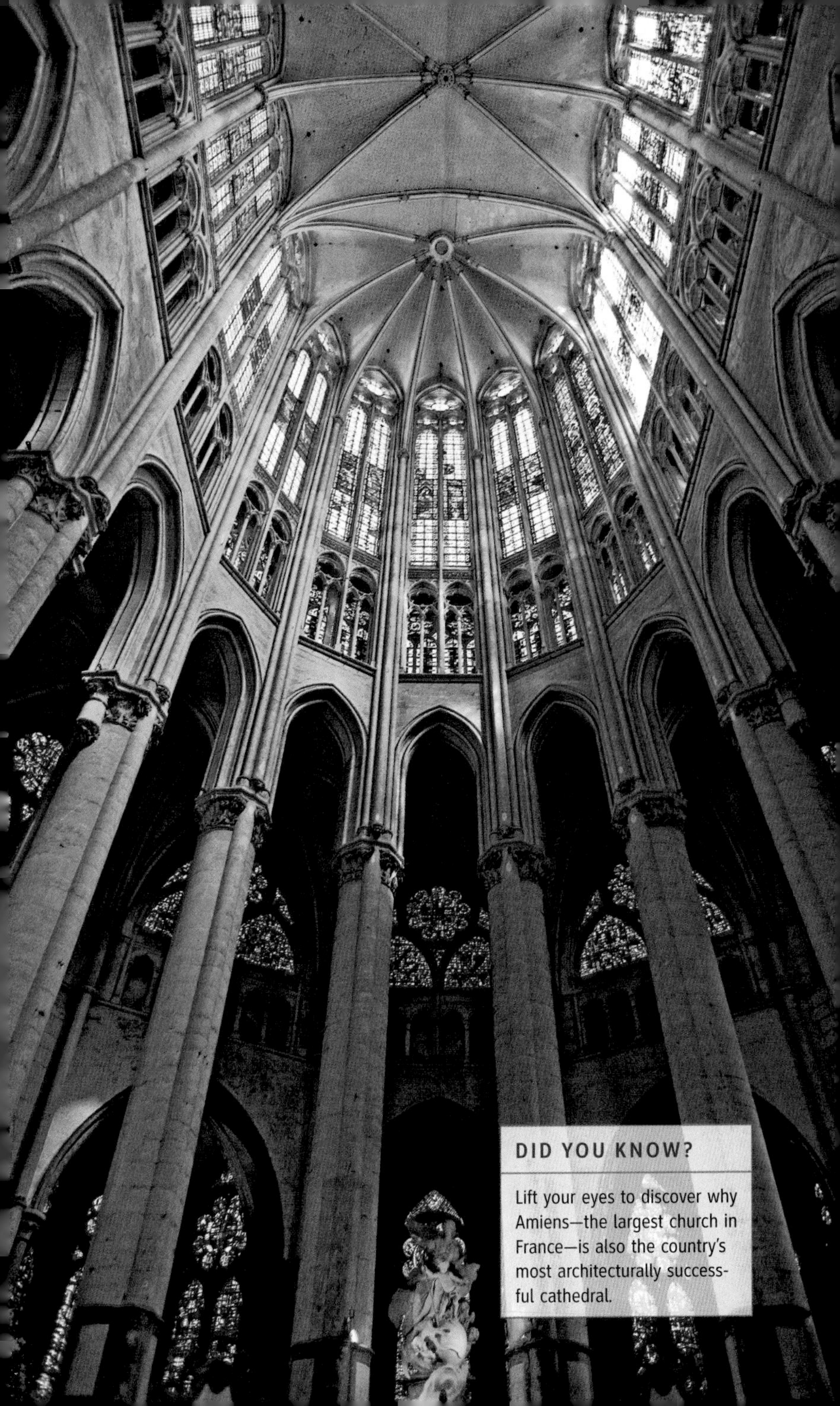

DID YOU KNOW?

Lift your eyes to discover why Amiens—the largest church in France—is also the country's most architecturally successful cathedral.

It has lovely Art Deco buildings in its traffic-free center, as well as elegant, older stone structures like the 18th-century Beffroi (Belfry) and neoclassical prefecture. Crowning the city is its great Gothic cathedral, which has survived the ages intact. Nearby is the waterfront quarter of St-Leu—with its small, colorful houses—rivaling the squares of Arras and streets of old Lille as the cutest city district north of Paris.

GETTING HERE

Trains from Paris (Gare du Nord) leave for Amiens every hour or so; the 129-km (80-mile) trip takes 1 hour, 20 minutes and costs €22.20. There are eight direct trains daily from Laon to Amiens (1 hr, 45 mins; €18.50). Buses operated by Oisemobilité (*08–10–60–00–60* 🌐 *www.cabaro.fr*) run between Beauvais and Amiens throughout the day (1 hr, 20 mins; €11.90). Note that the TGV Haute Picardie train station is a 50-minute bus ride away; from here trains go to all major destinations, including Charles de Gaulle airport.

Visitor Information Amiens Tourist Office. ☎ *03–22–71–60–50* 🌐 *www.amiens-tourisme.com.*

EXPLORING

Fodor'sChoice ★ **Cathédrale Notre-Dame d'Amiens.** By far the largest church in France, the Cathédrale Notre-Dame d'Amiens could enclose Paris's Notre-Dame twice. It may lack the stained glass of Chartres or the sculpture of Reims, but for architectural harmony, engineering proficiency, and sheer size, it's without peer. The soaring, asymmetrical facade has a notable Flamboyant Gothic rose window and is brought to life on summer evenings when a sophisticated 45-minute light show recreates its original color scheme. Inside, there's no stylistic disunity to mar the perspective, creating an overwhelming sensation of pure space. Construction took place between 1220 and 1264, a remarkably short period in cathedral-building terms. One of the highlights of a visit here is hidden from the eye, at least until you lift up some of the 110 choir-stall seats and admire the humorous, skillful misericord seat carvings executed between 1508 and 1518 (access with guide only). ✉ *Pl. Notre-Dame, Amiens* ☎ *03–22–92–03–32 cathedral, 03–22–80–03–41 tours* 🌐 *cathedrale-amiens.monuments-nationaux.fr* 🎟 *Tours €5.50* ⏲ *Church daily 9–6:30; tours Wed.–Mon. 8:30–6:15 (5:15 Oct.–Mar.).*

Hortillonnages. Situated on the east side of town, the Hortillonnages are commercial water gardens—covering more than 700 acres—where vegetables have been cultivated since Roman times. Every Saturday the products grown here are sold at the water market in the St-Leu district. There's a 45-minute boat tour of these aquatic jewels. ✉ *Boats leave from 54 bd. de Beauvillé, Amiens* ☎ *03–22–92–12–18* 🌐 *www.hortillonnages-amiens.fr* 🎟 *€5.90* ⏲ *Apr.–Oct., daily 9–noon and 1:30–5.*

Maison Jules-Verne. Jules Verne (1828–1905) spent his last 35 years in Amiens, and his former home contains some 15,000 documents about his life as well as original furniture and a reconstruction of the writing studio where he created his science-fiction classics. If you're a true Jules Verne fan, you might also want to visit his final resting place in the Cimetière de la Madeleine (*2 rue de la Poudrière*), where he is melodramatically portrayed pushing up his tombstone as if enacting his own sci-fi resurrection. *2 rue Charles-Dubois, Amiens 03–22–45–45–75 maisondejulesverne.amiens.fr €7.50 Mid-Apr.–mid-Oct., Mon., and Wed.–Fri. 10–12:30 and 2–6:30, Tues. 2–6:30, weekends 11–6:30; mid-Oct.–mid-Apr., Mon. and Wed.–Fri. 10–12:30 and 2–6, weekends 2–6.*

Musée de Picardie. Behind an opulent columned facade, the Musée de Picardie, built 1855–67, looks like a pompous offering from the Second Empire. Initial impressions are hardly challenged by the grand staircase lined with marouflaged murals by local-born Puvis de Chavannes, or the Grand Salon hung with huge canvases like Gérôme's 1855 *Siècle d'Auguste* and Maignan's 1892 *La Mort de Carpeaux*. One step beyond, though, and you're in a rotunda painted top to bottom in modern minimalist fashion by Sol LeWitt. The basement, notable for its masterly brick vaulting, is filled with subtly lighted archaeological finds and Egyptian artifacts. The ground floor houses 18th- and 19th-century paintings by artists such as Fragonard and Boucher. Major renovations are underway, so parts of the museum may be closed to the public until 2018. *48 rue de la République, Amiens 03–22–97–14–00 www.amiens.fr/musees €5.50 Tues., Fri., and Sat. 10–noon and 2–6, Wed. 10–6, Thurs. 10–noon and 2–9, Sun. 2–7.*

WHERE TO EAT AND STAY

$$ FRENCH FAMILY

Chez Lafleur. Unassuming and modern, this restaurant near the cathedral features a seasonal menu inspired by locally sourced ingredients—think vegetables from the Hortillonnages, Antan pork, salicorne (samphire greens) from the Baie de Somme, and regional Corbie beers. The specialties are spit-roasted chicken and freshwater char with saffron butter. Decked out with traditional puppetry memorabilia, Chez Lafleur is named after a Picardy puppet hero. *Average main: €19 6 rue Cormont, Amiens 03–22–91–98–12 www.chezlafleur.fr.*

$$$ MODERN FRENCH

Les Marissons. This picturesque waterside restaurant occupies an elegantly transformed boatbuilding shed in the scenic St-Leu section of Amiens. Chef Guillaume Grain showcases regional ingredients—including Amiens duck (delectably rendered in a homemade pâté) and lamb raised at the Baie de Somme. There's also a special Picardie truffle menu in season. To avoid pricey à la carte dining, order from the prix-fixe menus. *Average main: €32 Pont de la Dodone, 68 rue des Marissons, Amiens 03–22–92–96–66 www.les-marissons.fr No lunch Wed. and Sat. Closed Sun. and 3 wks in May.*

$$$ HOTEL FAMILY

Marotte Hotel. Built as a private mansion in the 19th century, this five-star boutique hotel has a dead-center location, an eco-friendly attitude, plus style to spare. **Pros:** centrally located; gentle prices; parking. **Cons:** no restaurant; no air-conditioning (rooms in original building can get stuffy in hot weather); no 24-hour reception. *Rooms from: €165 3 rue Marotte, Amiens 03–60–12–50–00 www.hotel-marotte.com 10 rooms, 2 suites No meals.*

PERFORMING ARTS

Théâtre de Marionnettes. Come to Théâtre de Marionnettes for a rare glimpse at traditional Picardy puppetry—known locally as Chés Cabotans d'Amiens. Shows are performed in French, with plot synopses printed in English; they're usually held on Sunday afternoons at 3, September through mid-July, and Tuesday to Sunday at 6, from mid-July through August. Expect to pay €5–€10 for tickets. ✉ *31 rue Edouard-David, Amiens* ☎ *03–22–22–30–90* 🌐 *www.ches-cabotans-damiens.com.*

BEAUVAIS

56 km (35 miles) south of Amiens via A16, 96 km (60 miles) west of Soissons.

Beauvais and its neighbor Amiens have been rivals since the 13th century, when they locked horns over who could build the bigger cathedral. Beauvais lost—gloriously.

GETTING HERE

Flights land at the Aéroport de Beauvais-Tillé; an airport bus (municipal line No. 12) stops in the town center and train station (20 mins, €4.50 for a 48-hour ticket). Trains from Paris (Gare du Nord) leave for Beauvais every 30 minutes; the 80-km (50-mile) trip takes 1 hour, 15 minutes and costs €14.20. Buses operated by the Oisemobilité (*08–10–60–00–60* 🌐 *www.cabaro.fr*) offer frequent daily service between Amiens and Beauvais (1 hr, 20 mins; €11.90).

Visitor Information Beauvais Tourist Office. ☎ *03–44–15–30–30* 🌐 *www.beauvaistourisme.fr.*

EXPLORING

Fodor's Choice ★ **Cathédrale St-Pierre.** Soaring above the town center is the tallest cathedral in France: the Cathédrale St-Pierre. You may have an attack of vertigo just gazing up at its vaults, 153 feet above the ground. Despite its grandeur, the cathedral has a shaky past. The choir collapsed in 1284, shortly after completion, and was rebuilt with extra pillars. This engineering fiasco, paid for by the riches of Beauvais's wool industry, proved so costly that the transept was not attempted until the 16th century. It was worth the wait: an outstanding example of Flamboyant Gothic, with ornate rose windows flanked by pinnacles and turrets. However, a megalomaniacal 450-foot spire erected at the same time came crashing down after just four years, and Beauvais's dream of having the largest church in Christendom vanished forever. Now the cathedral is starting to lean, and cracks have appeared in the choir vaults because of shifting water levels in the soil. No such problems bedevil the **Basse Oeuvre** (Lower Edifice; closed to the public), which juts out impertinently where the nave should have been. It has been there for 1,000 years. Fittingly donated to the cathedral by the canon Étienne Musique, the oldest surviving **chiming clock** in the world—a 1302 model with a 15th-century painted wooden face and most of its original clockwork—is built into the wall of the cathedral. Perhaps Auguste Vérité drew his inspiration from this humbler timepiece when, in 1868, he made a gift to his hometown of the gilded, temple-like **astrological clock** (*€4; displays at 10:40, 11:40, 2:40, 3:40, and 4:40*), which features animated religious figurines representing the Last Judgment. ✉ *Rue St-Pierre, Beauvais* 🌐 *www.cathedrale-beauvais.fr* ⏲ *May and Oct., daily 9–12:30 and 2–6:30; June–Sept., daily 9–6:30; Nov.–Apr., daily 9–12:30 and 2–5:30.*

Musée de l'Oise (*Regional Museum*). One of the few remaining testaments to Beauvais's glorious past, the old Bishop's Palace is now the Musée de l'Oise. Don't miss Thomas Couture's epic canvas depicting the French Revolution, the 14th-century frescoes of instrument-playing sirens on a section of the palace's vaults, or the first-century brass *Guerrier Gaulois* (Gallic Warrior). ✉ *1 rue du Musée, Beauvais* ☎ *03–44–10–40–50* 🌐 *www.mudo.oise.fr* 🎫 *Free* ⏲ *Wed.–Mon. 11–6.*

WHERE TO EAT AND STAY

$$$ FRENCH FAMILY

✕ **Le Palais d'Antan.** Facing the cathedral, Le Palais d'Antan is popular among savvy locals and well-informed tourists (be sure to reserve ahead on weekend evenings). The interior is crammed with an eclectic collection of tea pots, theatrical candelabras, and reclaimed furniture; the menu, meanwhile, offers creative takes on traditional French and Picard dishes. Duck parmentier with truffles, foie gras with fig chutney, and seared monkfish with Camembert sauce are just some of the succulent dishes you can sample. $ *Average main: €28* ✉ *75 rue Saint Pierre, Beauvais* ☎ *03–44–45–06–52* 🌐 *www.palais-dantan.fr* ⏲ *Closed Tues., Wed., and late July–early Aug.*

$$ BRASSERIE

✕ **Le Zinc Bleu.** This lively brasserie opposite Beauvais Cathedral offers sturdy if unadventurous lunch fare (duck, steak, and the like) along with a wide variety of fresh seafood. There is a good selection of copiously sized salads and warming soups, too. The dining room has light wooden tables and bright modern pictures. Ask for a seat under the glass-capped veranda or on the sidewalk terrace if the weather's good. $ *Average main: €18* ✉ *61 rue St-Pierre, Beauvais* ☎ *03–44–45–18–30* ⏲ *No dinner.*

$ HOTEL

Chenal Hotel. This foursquare street-corner establishment—close to the train station, a 10-minute walk from the cathedral, and served by a shuttle bus from the airport—is perhaps the most convenient choice in central Beauvais. **Pros:** free Wi-Fi; convenient location; private parking. **Cons:** small rooms; lacks charm. $ *Rooms from: €98* ✉ *63 bd. Général-de-Gaulle, Beauvais* ☎ *03–44–06–04–60* 🌐 *www.chenalhotel.fr* *29 rooms* 🍴 *No meals.*

$ HOTEL FAMILY

Hôtel de la Cathédrale. There's a shortage of hotels in central Beauvais, but this small one is close to key sights, and you'll find a friendly welcome behind its heavily-tinted glass doors. **Pros:** hard-to-beat location; courtyard terrace at the rear. **Cons:** pricey city parking; limited closet space; bar doubles as the reception area. $ *Rooms from: €85* ✉ *11–13 rue Chambiges, Beauvais* ☎ *03–44–04–10–22* 🌐 *www.hoteldelacathedrale.fr* *12 rooms* 🍴 *No meals.*

8

ALSACE-LORRAINE

WELCOME TO ALSACE-LORRAINE

TOP REASONS TO GO

★ **Follow the wine road:** Ribeauvillé and Riquewihr, a pair of medieval villages filled with "Hansel and Gretel" houses and bottle-laden cellars, are at the heart of the Alsatian wine route.

★ **Be enchanted by Colmar:** After two world wars Colmar rebuilt itself—today the mazelike cobblestone streets and Petite Venise waterways of its Vieille Ville are as atmospheric as ever.

★ **Get an architectural eyeful in Nancy:** Classic 18th-century elegance and fanciful Art Nouveau innovation meet reminders of the medieval past in this city.

★ **Pay tribute to Joan of Arc:** If you're a fan of Jeanne d'Arc, you've come to the right place; she was born right here in Domrémy-la-Pucelle.

★ **Discover the charms of Strasbourg, capital of Alsace:** The symbolic capital of Europe is a cosmopolitan French city rivaled only by Paris in its medieval allure, history, and haute cuisine.

1 Nancy. When Stanislas Leszczynski, ex-king of Poland, succeeded in marrying his daughter to Louis XV, he paid homage to the monarch by transforming Nancy into another Versailles, embellishing it with elegant showstoppers like Place Stanislas. Elsewhere in the city, you can sate your appetite for the best Art Nouveau at the Musée École de Nancy and the Villa Majorelle—after all, the style originated here.

2 Lorraine. In long-neglected Lorraine, many make the pilgrimage to Joan of Arc Country. The faithful, feisty teen, who went on to become one of France's patron saints, was born in Domrémy in the early 1400s; and nearby spots like Vaucouleurs featured prominently in her short but inspiring life story. If you listen carefully, you might hear the church bells in which Joan discerned voices challenging her to save France.

3 Strasbourg. An appealing combination of medieval alleys, international think tanks, and the European Parliament, Strasbourg is best loved for the village-like atmosphere of La Petite France, the looming presence of the Cathédrale de Notre-Dame, the rich museums, and the local libations served in its *winstubs* (wine-bistros, pronounced *veen*-shtoob).

4 Alsace. Tinged with a German flavor, Alsace is a never-ending procession of colorful towns and villages, many fitted out with spires, gabled houses, and storks' nests in chimney pots. Here you can find the Route du Vin, the famous Alsatian Wine Road, with its vineyards of Riesling and Gewurztraminer. This conveniently heads south to Colmar, where the half-timber buildings of the *centre ville* seem cut out of a child's coloring book. The town's main treasure is Grünewald's unforgettable 16th-century Issenheim Altarpiece.

LUXEMBOURG
Luxembourg
Thionville
Saarbrücken
GERMANY
A4
Metz
Bitche
D674
D955
LORRAINE
2
A4
ALSACE
4
Hagenau
N4
Saverne
A35
Strasbourg
3
A5
N4
Lunéville
D1420
N59
D1083
A35
D657
Route de Vin
St Dié
Sélestat
Épinal
Ribeauvillé
River
GERMANY
N57
Riquewihr
Colmar
Freiburg
VOSGES
N57
D1083
Rhine
N66
FRANCHE COMTE
A35
Mulhouse
A36
Basel
SWITZERLAND
0 20 mi
0 20 km

GETTING ORIENTED

Bordered by Germany, Alsace-Lorraine has often changed hands between the two countries in the past 350 years. This back-and-forth has left a mark—you'll find that Germanic half-timber houses sometimes clash with a very French café scene. Art also pays homage to both nations, as you can see in the museums of Strasbourg, Alsace's hub. Westward lies Lorraine, birthplace of Joan of Arc (and the famous quiche). Due west of Strasbourg on the other side of the Vosges Mountains, the main city of Nancy entices with Art Nouveau and grand 18th-century architecture.

EATING AND DRINKING WELL IN ALSACE-LORRAINE

Quiches on parade in Obernai in a photo submitted by Klondike for Fodor's France contest *(above)*; luxurious fois gras *(right, top)*; the best of the würsts *(right bottom)*.

Bountiful is the watchword in this region where lush vineyards flourish, vintage winstubs serve heaping platters of *choucroute garnie* (sauerkraut, meat, and potatoes), and Michelin-starred restaurants abound.

A visit to the proud region of Alsace promises sensory overload: gorgeous vistas, antique walled towns, satisfying meals—from farm-style to richly gastronomic—and, of course, superb wines. The predominantly white varietals, such as Riesling and Pinot Gris, complement the rich and varied old-school cooking. It's not for nouvelle-style or fusion dishes that you come to Alsace: tradition is king here, and copious is an understatement. Rustic regional fare includes hearty stews, custardy quiches, sauerkraut platters, and the thin-crusted onion tarts known as *flammekueche*. Also to be savored are some of the best restaurants in France—among them the noble, romantic L'Auberge de L'Ill in Illhausern, where a salmon soufflé with a Riesling reduction might catch your fancy.

FOLLOW THE WINES

Alsace is one of France's most important but least-known wine-producing regions, where vintners designate wines by varietals, not by town or château. Look for distinctive whites, like full-bodied Pinot Gris, citrusy Riesling, and spicy Gewurztraminer. In reds, Pinot Noir stands alone. Top producers include Hugel et Fils, de Ribeauvillé, and Zind-Humbrecht.

KOUGELHOPF

This tall, fluted, crown-shape cake, dusted with sugar and studded with raisins and almonds, beckons invitingly from every pastry-shop window in the region. You won't resist. The delicately sweet, yeast-based dough is kneaded and proofed, baked in a Bundt-style mold, and traditionally served, sometimes sprinkled with kirsch, at Sunday breakfast. Locals say it's even better on the second day, when it achieves a perfect, slightly dry texture.

CHOUCROUTE GARNIE

Daunting in size, a heaping platter of choucroute garnie, laden with fermented sauerkraut, smoked bacon, ham, pork shoulder, sausages, and potatoes, is the signature dish of the region. The best places serving it, usually winstubs such as the atmospheric Zum Pfifferhüs in Ribeauvillé, are worth a detour. You've never had sauerkraut like this, tender and delicate, dotted with juniper berries and often cooked with a splash of Riesling or Sylvaner white wine. Complement your choucroute with the region's own sweet white mustard.

MUNSTER CHEESE

This round, semisoft cow's-milk cheese with the orange rind, distinctive nutty aroma, and pungent flavor is Alsace's only claim to cheese fame, but it's a standout. The cheese, which is aged from five weeks to three months,

originated in the Vosges valley town of Munster, just west of Colmar, and the best—farm produced—come from this area. Sample it with fresh cherries or pears, thin-sliced rye bread, and a glass of Gewurztraminer.

FOIE GRAS

The production sure ain't pretty, but the product is sublime—satiny, opulent goose foie gras. Many gastronomes believe that Alsace produces the best in the world. The meltingly tender, fattened livers of plump Alsatian geese are prepared in a number of luscious ways: wrapped in a towel and gently poached—the classic *à la torchon* method; panfried and served on a slice of toasted gingerbread; wrapped in puff pastry and baked; or pressed into terrines and pâtés.

BAECKEOFFE

You can't get much heartier or homier than this baked casserole of pork, lamb, and beef marinated in white wine and slow-cooked in a terra-cotta pot with potatoes, onions, garlic, and herbs. The name—pronounced "bake-eh oaf-eh"—means "baker's oven" in the Germanic Alsatian dialect. It was so named because this was a dish traditionally assembled at home, then carried to the local baker to cook in his hot ovens. It's soul-warming fare for a chilly evening.

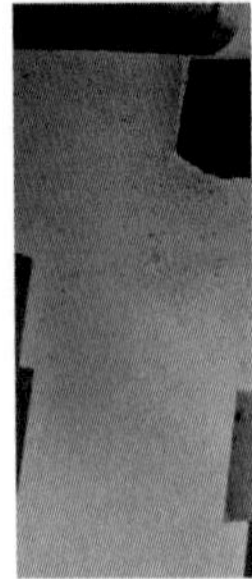

Updated By Lyn Parry

Only the Rhine separates Germany from Alsace-Lorraine, a region that often looks German and even sounds German. But its heart—just to prove how deceptive appearances can be—is passionately French. One has only to remember that Strasbourg was the birthplace of the Marseillaise national anthem to appreciate why Alsace and Lorraine remain among the most intensely French of all France's provinces.

No matter how forcefully the French tout its Frenchness, though, Alsace's German roots do run deep, as one look at its storybook medieval architecture reveals. Gabled, half-timber houses, ornate wells and fountains, oriels (upstairs bay windows), storks' nests, and carved-wood balustrades—all calling to mind the Brothers Grimm—will satisfy a visitor's deepest craving for Old World Germanic atmosphere. Strasbourg, perhaps France's most fascinating city outside Paris, offers this and urban sophistication as well.

Lorraine, on the other hand, has suffered a decline in its northern industry and the miseries of its small farmers have left much of it tarnished and neglected—or, as others might say, kept it unspoiled. Yet Lorraine's rich caches of verdure, its rolling countryside dotted with *mirabelle* (plum) orchards and crumbling-stucco villages, abbeys, fortresses, and historic cities, such as Art Nouveau–ed Nancy, offer a truly French view of life in the north. Its borders flank Belgium, Luxembourg, and Germany's mellow Mosel (Moselle in French). Home of Baccarat and St-Louis crystal (thanks to limitless supplies of firewood from the Vosges Forest), the birthplace of Gregorian chant, Art Nouveau, and Joan of Arc, Lorraine-the-underdog has much of its own to contribute.

The question remains: Who put the hyphen in Alsace-Lorraine? Alsace's strip of vine-covered hills squeezed between the Rhine and the Vosges Mountains started out being called Prima Germania by the Romans, and belonged to the fiercely Germanic Holy Roman Empire for more than 700 years. West of the Vosges, Lorraine served under French and Burgundian lords as well as the Holy Roman Empire, coming into its own under the powerful and influential dukes of Lorraine in the Middle Ages and Renaissance. Stanislas, the duke of Lorraine who transformed Nancy into a cosmopolitan Paris of the East, was Louis XV's father-in-law. Thus Lorraine's culture evolved as decidedly less German than its neighbor to the southeast.

But then, in the late 19th century, Kaiser Wilhelm sliced off the Moselle chunk of Lorraine and sutured it, à la Dr. Frankenstein, to Alsace, claiming the unfortunate graft as German turf—a concession after France's 1871 surrender in the Franco-Prussian War. At that point the region was systematically Teutonized—architecturally, linguistically, culinarily ("Ve haff our own vays of cookink sauerkraut!")—and the next two generations grew up culturally torn. Until 1918, that is, when France undid its defeat and reclaimed its turf. Until 1940, when Hitler snatched it back and reinstated German textbooks in the primary schools. Until 1945, when France once again triumphantly raised the *bleu-blanc-rouge* over Strasbourg. Today, the regions remain both officially and proudly French.

PLANNER

WHEN TO GO

Alsace is blessed with four distinct seasons and one of the lowest rainfalls in all of France—so anytime at all is the right time to visit. Snow in winter adds magic to the Christmas markets; spring brings forth the scent of burgeoning grape flowers as the world turns green with life; summer can be warm, which rhymes with swarm; autumn is nature's symphony of color—the leaves of tree and vine become a riot of golden yellows and oranges, as the bountiful grapes are harvested.

PLANNING YOUR TIME

If an overall experience is what you're after, setting up headquarters in Strasbourg or Colmar will give you the best access to the greatest number of sites, either by public transport or car, while also residing in one. If wine tasting and vineyards are your priority, setting up in either Riquewihr or Ribeauvillé will put you at the heart of the action. Remember that many of the region's towns and villages stage summer festivals—among them the spectacular pagan-inspired burning of the three pine trees in Thann (late June), the Flower Carnival in Sélestat (mid-August), and the wine fair in Colmar (first half of August). And although Lorraine is a lusterless place in winter, Strasbourg pays tribute to the Germanic tradition with a Christmas fair.

GETTING HERE AND AROUND

Alsace is a small region and fairly well interconnected with bus and train routes, making it possible to travel extensively by public transportation. Be sure to stock up on information (schedules, the best taxi-for-call companies, etc.) upon arriving at the ticket counter or help desk of the bigger train and bus stations in the area, such as Nancy, Strasbourg, and Colmar. In Alsace, trains are the way to go. In Lorraine you may need to take short bus jaunts to the smaller towns. If you're relying on trains, download the handy widgets from the TER website at 🌐 *www.*

DID YOU KNOW?

As this fountain on Place Stanislas proves, the city of Nancy is a spectacular showcase of the 18th-century rococo style.

ter-sncf.com .A useful up-to-date website with details on buses and trams is 🌐 *www.vialsace.eu*. Unfortunately, schedules change rather frequently in Alsace-Lorraine.

AIR TRAVEL

Air France (🌐 *www.airfrance.com*) and assorted budget carriers serve Aéroport International Strasbourg, located 15 km (9½ miles) southwest of the city in Entzheim. Train service from the main line station in Strasbourg runs to the airport every 15 minutes on weekdays, every half hour on weekends (€2.50).

Aéroport International Strasbourg. ✉ *Rte. de Strasbourg, Entzheim* ✣ *15 km (9½ miles) southwest of city* ☎ *03–88–64–67–67* 🌐 *www.strasbourg.aeroport.fr.*

BUS TRAVEL

The two main bus companies are **Les Rapides de Lorraine,** based in Metz, and **Compagnie des Transports Strasbourgeois,** based in Strasbourg. Nancy, Strasbourg, and Colmar all have civic transit systems, too.

Compagnie des Transports Strasbourgeois (*CTS*). ✉ *Strasbourg* ☎ *03–88–77–70–70* 🌐 *www.cts-strasbourg.eu.*

Les Rapides de Lorraine. ✉ *Metz* ☎ *03–87–63–65–65, 03–87–75–26–62 Agence TIM for ticket information and tariffs* 🌐 *www.rapidesdelorraine.fr.*

CAR TRAVEL

A4 heads east from Paris to Strasbourg, via Verdun, Metz, and Saverne. It's met by A26, descending from the English Channel, at Reims. A31 links Metz to Nancy, continuing south to Burgundy and Lyon. D1083/D83/A35 connects Strasbourg, Colmar, and Mulhouse. A36 continues to Belfort and Besançon. A4, linking Paris to Strasbourg, passes through Lorraine via Metz, linking Lorraine and Alsace. Picturesque secondary roads lead from Nancy through Joan of Arc country. Several scenic roads climb switchbacks over forested mountain passes through the Vosges, connecting Lorraine to Alsace. A quicker alternative is the tunnel *under* the Vosges at Ste-Marie-aux-Mines, linking Sélestat to Lunéville. Alsace's Route du Vin, winding from Marlenheim in the north all the way south to Thann, is the ultimate in scenic driving.

TRAIN TRAVEL

Fourteen direct high-speed TGVs per day leave Paris's Gare de l'Est for Strasbourg, making the journey in 2 hours, 20 minutes; another dozen direct ones depart daily from the same station bound for Nancy, with a travel time of about 90 minutes. Four daily direct TGVs head to Colmar, arriving in just under 3 hours, and two travel to Épinal in 2 hours, 20 minutes. A network of regional trains and buses links popular locales (like Ribeauvillé or Obernai), but you'll need a car to visit the smallest villages.

Train Information Gare SNCF Colmar. ☎ *3635 €0.34 per min.* **Gare SNCF Nancy.** ☎ *3635 €0.34 per min.* **Gare SNCF Strasbourg.** ☎ *3635 €0.34 per min.* **SNCF.** ☎ *3635 €0.34 per min* 🌐 *www.voyages-sncf.com.* **TGV.** 🌐 *www.tgv.com.*

RESTAURANTS

Strasbourg and Nancy may be two of France's more expensive cities, but you wouldn't know it judging by all the down-to-earth eating spots with down-to-earth prices—most notably winstubs, which are cozier and more wine-oriented than the usual French brasserie. In Strasbourg and Nancy, as well as the villages along Alsace's wine road, you'll need to arrive early (soon after noon for lunch, before 8 for dinner) to be sure of a restaurant table in July and August. Out-of-season is a different matter throughout.

HOTELS

Alsace-Lorraine is well served in terms of accommodations. From the picturesque village inns of the Route du Vin and the "Fermes Auberges" of the Vosges to four-star palaces or international-style hotels in the main cities of Nancy and Strasbourg, the range is vast. Since much of Alsace is in the "countryside" there's also a range of *gîtes*, self-catering cottages or houses that provide a base for longer stays (🌐 *www.gites-de-france.com*). *Hotel reviews have been shortened. For full information, visit Fodors.com.*

WHAT IT COSTS IN EUROS

	$	$$	$$$	$$$$
Restaurants	under €18	€18–€24	€25–€32	over €32
Hotels	under €106	€106–€145	€146–€215	over €215

Restaurant prices are the average cost of a main course at dinner or, if dinner is not served, at lunch. Hotel prices are the lowest cost of a standard double room in high season.

VISITOR INFORMATION

The Alsace-Lorraine region has three main area tourist offices, all of which can be contacted by telephone, mail, or email. For the Alsace area, contact Access Alsace. For Lorraine, contact the Comité Régional du Tourisme de Lorraine. For the city of Strasbourg and its environs, contact the Office de Tourisme de Strasbourg et Sa Region. ⇨ *For specific town tourist offices, see the town entries in this chapter.*

Contacts Access Alsace. ☎ *03–89–29–81–00* 🌐 *www.tourisme-alsace.com.* **Comité Régional du Tourisme de Lorraine.** ☎ *03–83–80–01–80* 🌐 *www.tourisme-lorraine.fr.* **Office de Tourisme de Strasbourg et Sa Région.** ☎ *03–88–52–28–28* 🌐 *www.otstrasbourg.fr.*

NANCY

For architectural variety, few French locales match this one in the heart of Lorraine, 300 km (190 miles) east of Paris. Medieval ornamentation, 18th-century grandeur, and Belle Époque fluidity rub shoulders in the city center, where the bustle of commerce mingles with stately elegance. Nancy's majesty derives from its long history as the domain of the powerful dukes of Lorraine, whose double-barred crosses figure prominently on local statues and buildings. Never having fallen under

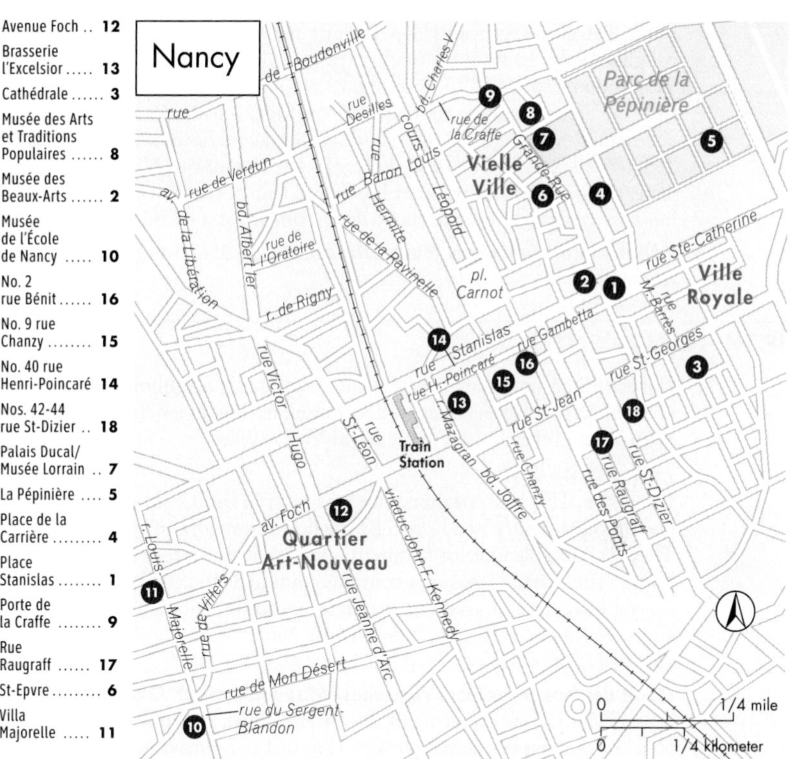

the rule of the Holy Roman Empire or the Germans, the city retains an eminently Gallic charm that's exemplified by harmoniously constructed squares and buildings. Vestiges of the 18th century, these have the quiet refinement associated with the best in French architecture.

Ironically, a Pole was responsible for most of them. Stanislas Leszczynski, the ex-king of Poland and father of Maria Leszczynska (who married Louis XV of France) was given the Duchy of Lorraine by his royal son-in-law on the understanding that it would revert to France when he died. Stanislas installed himself in Nancy and devoted himself to the glorious embellishment of the city. Today Place Stanislas remains one of the loveliest and most perfectly proportioned squares in the world, with Place de la Carrière—reached through Stanislas's Arc de Triomphe—with its elegant, homogeneous 18th-century houses, being a close rival for this honor.

GETTING HERE AND AROUND

Nancy, the jewel in Lorraine's tourism crown, has benefited greatly from the introduction of the TGV Est European service. Twelve direct TGVs depart daily from Paris's Gare de l'Est, arriving about 90 minutes later. Four others take over an hour longer; three involve a change in Metz and one in Bar Le Duc. One-way fares vary from €48.70 to €82.70 depending on the train type, time of day, and how far in advance you book. Eleven direct trains depart daily for Strasbourg (€25.50), and roughly every 20 minutes one leaves for Metz (€10.90). Two-dozen TER trains also travel to Épinal (€13.60). Once in Nancy, you'll find that the central core is manageable on foot, but it still helps to get acquainted with Stan (*03–83–30–08–08* ⊕ *www.reseau-stan.com*) and Ted (*08–20–20–54–54* ⊕ *www.ted.cg54.fr*). The former, Nancy's public transit system, has convenient buses and trams; the latter is a 40-line bus service that covers the entire *département* for a €3.40 flat rate.

Visitor Information Nancy Tourist Office. ☎ *03–83–35–22–41* ⊕ *www.nancy-tourisme.fr.*

THE HISTORIC CENTER

Concentrated northeast of the train station, this neighborhood—rich in architectural treasures as well as museums—includes classical Place Stanislas and the shuttered, medieval Vieille Ville.

TOP ATTRACTIONS

Cathédrale. This vast, frigid edifice was built in the 1740s in a ponderous Baroque style, eased in part by the florid ironwork of Jean Lamour. The most notable interior feature is a murky 19th-century fresco in the dome. The **Trésor** (Treasury) contains minute 10th-century splendors carved of ivory and gold but is only open to the public on rare occasions. ✉ *Rue St-Georges, Ville Neuve, Nancy* ⊙ *Daily 7–11:20 and 12:40–7.*

Musée des Arts et Traditions Populaires (*Museum of Folk Arts and Traditions*). Just up the street from the Palais Ducal, this quirky museum is in the **Couvent des Cordeliers** (Convent of the Franciscans, who were known as Cordeliers until the Revolution). Displays re-create how local people lived in preindustrial times, using a series of evocative rural interiors. Craftsmen's tools, colorful crockery, somber stone fireplaces, and dark waxed-oak furniture accent the tableaulike settings. The dukes of Lorraine are buried in the crypt of the adjoining **Église des Cordeliers,** a Flamboyant Gothic church; the detailed *gisant* (reclining statue) of Philippa de Gueldra, second wife of René II, is executed in limestone and serves as a moving example of Renaissance portraiture. The octagonal Ducal Chapel was begun in 1607 in the Renaissance style, modeled on the Medici Chapel in Florence. ✉ *64 Grande-Rue, Vieille Ville, Nancy* ☎ *03–83–32–18–74* ⊕ *www.musee-lorrain.nancy.fr* 🎟 *€3.50* ⊙ *Tues.–Sun. 10–12:30 and 2–6.*

Musée des Beaux-Arts (*Fine Arts Museum*). In a splendid building that now spills over into a spectacular modern wing, a broad and varied collection of art treasures lives up to the noble white facade designed by Emmanuel Héré. The showpiece is Rubens's massive *Transfiguration,* and among the most striking works are the freeze-the-moment realist tableaux painted by native son Émile Friant at the turn of the 20th century. A sizable collection of Lipschitz sculptures includes portrait busts of Gertrude Stein, Jean Cocteau, and Coco Chanel. You'll also find 19th- and 20th-century paintings by Monet, Manet, Utrillo, and Modigliani; a Caravaggio *Annunciation*; and a wealth of other old masters

CLOSE UP

Nancy 1900

History has a curious way of having similar events take place at the same time in different places. The creation of the Art Nouveau movement is one such event. Simultaneously emerging from the Pre-Raphaelite, High Victorian, and Arts and Crafts movements in England, it was also a synthesis of the Jugenstil (Youth style) movement in Germany; the Skonvirke movement in Denmark; the Mloda Polska (Young Poland) movement in Poland; Secessionism in Vienna, exemplified by the paintings of Gustav Klimt; and Modernism in Spain, centered around Gaudi's outlandish architectural achievements in Barcelona. Its fluid, undulating, organic forms drawn from the natural world (picture seaweed, grasses, flowers, birds, and insects) also drew inspiration from Symbolism, Japanese woodcuts, and assorted other sources.

One of its founding centers was Nancy, which at the time was drawing the wealthy French bourgeoisie of Alsace, recently invaded by Germany, who refused to become German. Proud of their opulence, they had sublime houses built that were entirely furnished—from simple vases and wrought-iron beds to bathtubs in the shape of lily pads—in the pure Art Nouveau style.

Emile Gallé (1846–1904), the driving force behind Nancy's Art Nouveau movement, called on his fellow artists to follow examples in nature (as opposed to the Greek or Roman models then in favor) and aim for innovation. Working primarily in glass and inventing new, patented techniques, Gallé brought luxury craftsmanship to a whole range of everyday products, thus reestablishing the link between the ordinary and the exceptional. This was a major advance on the bourgeois bad taste for mass-produced pieces of dubious quality that imitated styles of the past.

Everywhere stylized flowers suddenly became the preferred motif. The tree and its leaves, and plants with their flowers, were modified, folded, and curled to the artist's demand. Among the main Art Nouveau emblems figure the lily, the iris, morning glory, bracken fern, poppies, peacocks, birds that feed on flowers, ivy, dragonflies, butterflies, and anything that evokes the immense poetry of the seasons. It reveals a world that is as fragile as it is precious.

By giving an artistic quality to manufactured objects, Gallé and the other creators of the École de Nancy accomplished a dream that had been growing since the romantic generation of Victorian England of making an alliance between art and industry. As a meeting point for the hopes and interests of artists, intellectuals, industrials, and merchants, the École de Nancy was a thoroughly global phenomenon. From Chicago to Turin, Munich to Brussels, and on to London, the industries of Nancy went on to conquer the world.

from the Italian, Dutch, Flemish, and French schools; and impressive glassworks by Nancy native Antonin Daum. Audioguides in English are available at reception. ✉ *3 pl. Stanislas, Ville Royale, Nancy* ☎ *03–83–85–30–72* 🌐 *mban.nancy.fr* 🎫 *€6* 🕙 *Wed.–Mon. 10–6.*

EVERYONE LOVES A LAMOUR

A fitting showpiece on the southern flank of the square is the 18th-century Hôtel de Ville, Nancy's Town Hall, where the handiwork of Jean Lamour can be seen to stunning effect on the wrought-iron handrail of the *grand escalier* (grand staircase) leading off the lobby. You can get a closer view when the building is open to the public (July and August, see the tourist office for exact dates); mounting the staircase to the Grands Salons lets you survey the full beauty of Place Stanislas.

Palais Ducal (*Ducal Palace*). Built in the 13th century, completely restored in the 15th century and again after a fire at the end of the 19th century, this palace originally housed the Dukes of Lorraine. Now it is home to the Musée Lorrain. A major renovation project means the museum is closed to the public until 2018; however, you can still admire the palace's stunning architecture from the outside. One wing is a spectacular example of Flamboyant Gothic. ✉ *64 Grande-Rue, Vieille Ville, Nancy* ☎ *03–83–32–18–74.*

Place Stanislas. With its severe, gleaming-white Classical facades given a touch of rococo jollity by fanciful wrought gilt-iron railings, this perfectly proportioned square may remind you of Versailles. It is named for Stanislas Leszczynski, twice dethroned as king of Poland but offered the Duchy of Lorraine by Louis XV (his son-in-law) in 1736. Stanislas left a legacy of spectacular buildings, undertaken between 1751 and 1760 by architect Emmanuel Héré and ironwork genius Jean Lamour. The sculpture of Stanislas dominating the square went up in the 1830s. Framing the exit, and marking the divide between the Vieille Ville and the Ville Neuve (New Town), is the **Arc de Triomphe,** erected in the 1750s to honor Louis XV. The facade trumpets the gods of war and peace; Louis's portrait is here. ✉ *Ville Royale, Nancy.*

WORTH NOTING

FAMILY **Parc de la Pépinière.** This picturesque, landscaped city park has labeled ancient trees, a rose garden, playgrounds, a carousel, and a small zoo. ✉ *Entrance off pl. de la Carrière, Vieille Ville, Nancy* 🕙 *Apr., May, Sept., and Oct, daily 6:30 am–9 pm; June–Aug., daily 6:30—10:30 pm; Nov.–Mar., daily 6:30 am–8 pm.*

Place de la Carrière. Lined with pollarded trees and handsome 18th-century mansions (another successful collaboration between King Stanislas and Emmanuel Héré), this UNESCO World Heritage Site's elegant rectangle leads from Place Stanislas to the colonnaded facade of the **Palais du Gouvernement** (Government Palace), former home of the governors of Lorraine. ✉ *Vieille Ville, Nancy.*

Porte de la Craffe. A fairy-tale vision out of the late Middle Ages, this 14th- and 15th-century gate is all that remains of Nancy's medieval fortifications. With its twin turrets looming at one end of the Grande-Rue, the arch served as a prison through the Revolution. Above the main portal is the Lorraine Cross, comprising a thistle and cross. ✉ *Vieille Ville, Nancy.*

St-Epvre. A 275-foot spire towers over this splendid neo-Gothic church, completed in 1451 and rebuilt in the 1860s. Most of the 2,800 square yards of stained glass were created by the Geyling workshop in Vienna; the chandeliers were made in Liège, Belgium; many carvings are the work of Margraff of Munich; the heaviest of the eight bells was cast in Budapest; and the organ, though manufactured by Merklin of Paris, was inaugurated in 1869 by Austrian composer Anton Bruckner. ✉ *Pl. St-Epvre, Vieille Ville, Nancy* ⏲ *Daily 10–6.*

ART NOUVEAU NANCY

Think *Art Nouveau*, and many will conjure up the rich salons of Paris's Maxim's restaurant, the lavender-hue Prague posters of Alphonse Mucha, or the stained-glass dragonflies and opalescent vases that, to this day, remain the darlings of such collectors as Barbra Streisand. All of that beauty was born, to a great extent, in 19th-century Nancy. Inspired and coordinated by the glass master Émile Gallé, the local movement was formalized in 1901 as L'École de Nancy—from here, it spread like wildfire through Europe, from Naples to Monte-Carlo to Prague. The ensuing flourish encompassed the floral *pâte de verre* (literally, "glass dough") works of Gallé and Antonin Daum; the Tiffany-esque stained-glass windows of Jacques Gruber; the fluidity of Louis Majorelle's furniture designs; and the sinuous architecture of Lucien Weissenburger, Émile André, and Eugène Vallin. Thanks to these artists, Nancy's downtown architecture gives the impression of a living garden suspended above the sidewalks. ⇨ *For more on Art Nouveau's birthplace, see our Close-Up box in this chapter, "Nancy 1900."*

8

TOP ATTRACTIONS

Fodor's Choice ★ **Musée de l'École de Nancy** (*School of Nancy Museum*). France's only museum devoted to Art Nouveau is in an airy turn-of-the-last-century garden–town house built by Eugène Corbin, an early patron of the School of Nancy. Re-created rooms show off original works by local Art Nouveau glassmakers Emile Gallé, Antonin and Auguste Daum, Amalric Walter, and other artisans. Immerse yourself in the fanciful, highly stylized, curlicue style that crept into interiors and exteriors throughout Nancy in the early 20th century, then became a sensation around the world. ✉ *36 rue du Sergent-Blandan, Quartier Art-Nouveau, Nancy* ☎ *03–83–40–14–86* 🌐 *www.ecole-de-nancy.com* 🎫 *€6* ⏲ *Wed.–Sun. 10–6.*

Villa Majorelle. In this villa, built in 1902 by Paris architect Henri Sauvage for Art Nouveau furniture designer Louis Majorelle, sinuous metal supports seem to sneak up on the unsuspecting balcony like swaying cobras. The two grand windows are by Jacques Gruber: one lights the staircase (visible from the street) and the other is set in the dining room on the south side of the villa (peek around from the garden side). ✉ *1 rue Louis-Majorelle, Quartier Art-Nouveau, Nancy.*

Place Stanislas—the crown jewel of the city—is a huge public square enclosed by gold-and-black gates and gorgeous neoclassical buildings.

WORTH NOTING

Avenue Foch. This busy boulevard lined with mansions was laid out for Nancy's affluent 19th- and early 20th-century middle class. At No. 69, built in 1902 by Émile André, the occasional pinnacle suggests Gothic influence; André designed the neighboring No. 71 two years later. No. 41, built by Paul Charbonnier in 1905, bears ironwork by Louis Majorelle. ✉ *Quartier Art-Nouveau, Nancy.*

Brasserie l'Excelsior. This bustling brasserie has a severely rhythmic facade that is invitingly illuminated at night. Inside, the decor continues to evoke the Belle Époque. ✉ *50 rue Henri-Poincaré, Quartier Art-Nouveau, Nancy.*

No. 2 rue Bénit. This elaborately worked metal exoskeleton, the first in Nancy (1901), exudes functional beauty. The floral decoration is reminiscent of the building's past as a seed supply store. Windows were worked by Jacques Gruber; the building was designed by Henry-Barthélemy Gutton, while Victor Schertzer conceived the metal frame. ✉ *2 rue Bénit, Quartier Art-Nouveau, Nancy.*

No. 9 rue Chanzy. Designed by architect Émile André, this lovely structure—now a bank—can be visited during business hours. You can still see the cabinetry of Louis Majorelle, the decor of Paul Charbonnier, and the stained-glass windows of Jacques Gruber. ✉ *9 rue Chanzy, Quartier Art-Nouveau, Nancy.*

No. 40 rue Henri-Poincaré. The Lorraine thistle (a civic emblem) and brewing hops weave through this undulating exterior, designed by architects Émile Toussaint and Louis Marchal. Victor Schertzer conceived the metal structure in 1908, after the success of No. 2 rue Bénit. Gruber's windows are enhanced by the curving metalwork of Louis Majorelle. ✉ *40 rue Henri-Poincaré, Quartier Art-Nouveau, Nancy.*

Nos. 42–44 rue St-Dizier. Furniture maker Eugène Vallin and architect Georges Biet left their mark on this graceful 1903 bank. ✉ *42–44 rue St-Dizier, Quartier Art-Nouveau, Nancy* ⏲ *Weekdays 9–5:30.*

Rue Raugraff. Once there were two stores here—Vaxelaire and Pignot, both built in 1901. The facade is the last vestige of the work of Émile André and Eugène Vallin. ✉ *13 rue Raugraff, Quartier Art-Nouveau, Nancy.*

WHERE TO EAT AND STAY

$$$ BRASSERIE ✕ **Brasserie l'Excelsior.** Above all, you'll want to eat in this 1911 restaurant, part of the dependable Flo group, for its sensational Art Nouveau stained glass, mosaics, Daum lamps, and sinuous Majorelle furniture. But the food is stylish, too, with succulent choices ranging from duck fois gras served with Mirabelle plum chutney to grilled steak served with Choron sauce. Don't miss out on regional desserts like *kouglof* (a distinctively shaped Alsatian cake). The waiters are attentive and exude Parisian chic. $ *Average main: €27* ✉ *50 rue Henri-Poincaré, Quartier Art-Nouveau, Nancy* ☎ *03–83–35–24–57* 🌐 *www.brasserie-excelsior.com.*

$$$$ FRENCH ✕ **Le Capu.** Barely a stone's throw from Place Stanislas, this stylish landmark puts its best foot forward under Chef Hervé Fourrière. The menu includes revisited favorites, such as *preskopf* of langoustines with a creamy herb sauce. Desserts—like warm chestnut crème with vanilla, accompanied by *boules de Berlin* (Alsatian doughnuts)—are also noteworthy. A buffet brunch is served Sunday between 11 and 3, and cooking lessons are offered Wednesday afternoons and Saturday mornings. The choice of Toul wines is extensive. $ *Average main: €34* ✉ *31 rue Gambetta, Ville Royale, Nancy* ☎ *03–83–35–26–98* 🌐 *www.lecapu.com* ⏲ *No lunch Sat., no dinner Sun.* ✍ *Reservations essential.*

$ BISTRO ✕ **Les Frères Marchand.** If you were inspired by the rustic exhibits at the Musée des Arts et Traditions Populaires, cross the street and sink your teeth into authentic Lorraine cuisine in the form of mouthwatering choucroutes, *tête de veau* (calf's head), or foie gras-stuffed pig's trotter. Tables inside are tight, creating a bustling, canteen-like atmosphere, and the quality of the service seems to vary with the weather, but the hearty food is irreproachable. $ *Average main: €17* ✉ *97 Grande-Rue, Vieille Ville, Nancy* ☎ *03–83–32–85–94* 🌐 *www.restaurant-marchand.com.*

$$ HOTEL **Grand Hôtel de la Reine.** Every bit as grand as Place Stanislas, on which it stands, this magnificent 18th-century building is officially classified as a historic monument with an interior that is just as regal: guest rooms are decorated in Louis XV style (the most luxurious overlook the square). **Pros:** sumptuous location; old-world atmosphere. **Cons:** rooms get street noise; indifferent staff. $ *Rooms from: €115* ✉ *2 pl. Stanislas, Ville Royale, Nancy* ☎ *03–83–35–03–01* 🌐 *www.hoteldelareine.com* *49 rooms, 2 suites* 🍽 *No meals.*

$ HOTEL **Hôtel de Guise.** Deep in the shuttered Vieille Ville, this quiet, convivial hotel occupies an 18th-century nobleman's mansion with a magnificent stone-floor entry and a delightful walled garden; some guest rooms

8

are furnished with period pieces and charmingly incongruous floral patterns, while others have been redecorated in a sleek contemporary style. **Pros:** tidy rooms; central location; helpful staff. **Cons:** no air-conditioning; overheated, stuffy rooms. *Rooms from: €102 18 rue de Guise, Vieille Ville, Nancy 03–83–32–24–68 www.hoteldeguise.com 46 rooms, 4 suites No meals.*

NIGHTLIFE AND PERFORMING ARTS

Ballet de Lorraine. Created in 1978 to assume the mission of a national ballet, it stages performances in the Opéra de Nancy on Place Stanislas. *1 rue Ste-Catherine, Vieille Ville, Nancy 03–83–85–69–01 www.ballet-de-lorraine.eu.*

Le Chat Noir. The "Black Cat" is a hit with thirtysomethings who enjoy retro-themed dance parties. *63 rue Jeanne-d'Arc, Ville Neuve, Nancy 03–83–28–49–29 www.lechatnoir.fr.*

Les Caves du Roy. A young upscale crowd comes to dance at Les Caves du Roy. *9 pl. Stanislas, Ville Royale, Nancy 03–83–35–24–14.*

Opéra National de Lorraine. The musical repertoire of this opera company ranges from ancient to contemporary. *1 rue Ste-Catherine, Vieille Ville, Nancy 03–83–85–30–60 www.opera-national-lorraine.fr.*

Orchestre Symphonique et Lyrique. Established in 1884, the Orchestre Symphonique et Lyrique organizes concerts from fall through spring. *1 rue Ste-Catherine, Vieille Ville, Nancy 03–83–85–30–60 www.opera-national-lorraine.fr.*

SHOPPING

Daum Boutique. This boutique sells deluxe crystal and examples of the city's traditional Art Nouveau *pâte de verre*, in which crushed glass is mixed with a binding material to form a decorative surface. *14 pl. Stanislas, Vieille Ville, Nancy 03–83–32–21–65 www.daum.fr.*

Librairie Ancienne Dornier. Located near the Musée des Arts et Traditions Populaires, Librairie Ancienne Dornier is an excellent bookstore that sells engravings as well as old and new books devoted to local history. *74 Grande-Rue, Vieille Ville, Nancy 03–83–36–50–62.*

LORRAINE: JOAN OF ARC COUNTRY

Lorraine is the land of Joan of Arc, one of France's patron saints and an iconic figure worldwide. Following D64, which winds between Contrexéville and Void, puts you on her home turf; almost unchanged since the Middle Ages, it's a landscape that Joan would probably find familiar today. Certainly the names of some local communities will be familiar to her fans. Domrémy was the place where she was born in 1411 or 1412; Neufchâteau, then a fortified town guarding the region, was where a teenage Joan and her fellow villagers sought refuge from the menacing English armies; and Vaucouleurs was where she went in 1428 to enlist the aid of the governor and prepare for a mission that would take her onward to the king—and her destiny.

VAUCOULEURS

73 km (41 miles) southwest of Nancy on N4 and D964.

Above the modest main street in the market town of Vaucouleurs, you can see ruins of Robert de Baudricourt's medieval castle and the Porte de France. The barefoot Maid of Orléans spent several months here, arriving on May 13, 1428 to ask Governor de Baudricourt for help. After wheedling an audience at the castle, she convinced him of the necessity of her mission, learning to ride and to wield a sword. Won over finally by her conviction and by popular sentiment, de Baudricourt offered to give her an escort to seek out the king. On February 23, 1429, clad in page's garb and with her hair cut short, Jeanne d'Arc rode out through the Porte de France, en route to Orléans.

GETTING HERE

Bus R410 runs from Nancy to Toul and takes around 35 minutes; from Toul, Bus R450 continues on to Vaucouleurs, but only on school days (€2.50 each leg).

WHERE TO STAY

$$ B&B/INN **Hostellerie de l'Isle en Bray.** A night in the fine Renaissance-style Château de Montbras—where grand public salons are crammed with antiques and spacious guest rooms are graced with period furniture elegantly offset by modern fabrics—is ideal for anyone indulging in Joan-of-Arc-related medieval musings. **Pros:** romantic and secluded; marvelous museum atmosphere; gentle prices with breakfast included. **Cons:** car indispensable. *Rooms from: €130* *3 rue des Erables, Montbras* *10 km (6 miles) south of Vaucouleurs on the D964* *03–29–90–49–90* *www.chateau-montbras.com* *5 rooms, 2 suites* *Breakfast.*

DOMRÉMY-LA-PUCELLE

19 km (12 miles) south of Vaucouleurs on D964.

Joan of Arc was born in a cottage here in either 1411 or 1412. You can see her birthplace, as well as the church where she was baptized, the actual statue of Ste-Marguerite before which she prayed, and the hillside where she tended sheep and first heard voices telling her to take up arms and save France from the English.

In the nearby forest of Bois-Chenu, perhaps an ancient sacred wood, Jeanne d'Arc gathered flowers. Near the village of Coussy, she danced with other children at country fairs attended by Pierre de Bourlémont, the local seigneur, and his wife Beatrice—the Château of Bourlémont may still be seen. Associated with Coussey and Brixey are Saints Mihiel and Catherine, who, with the Archangel Saint-Michael, appeared before Joan. In the Chapel of Notre-Dame at Bermont, where Joan vowed to save France, are the statues that existed in her time.

8

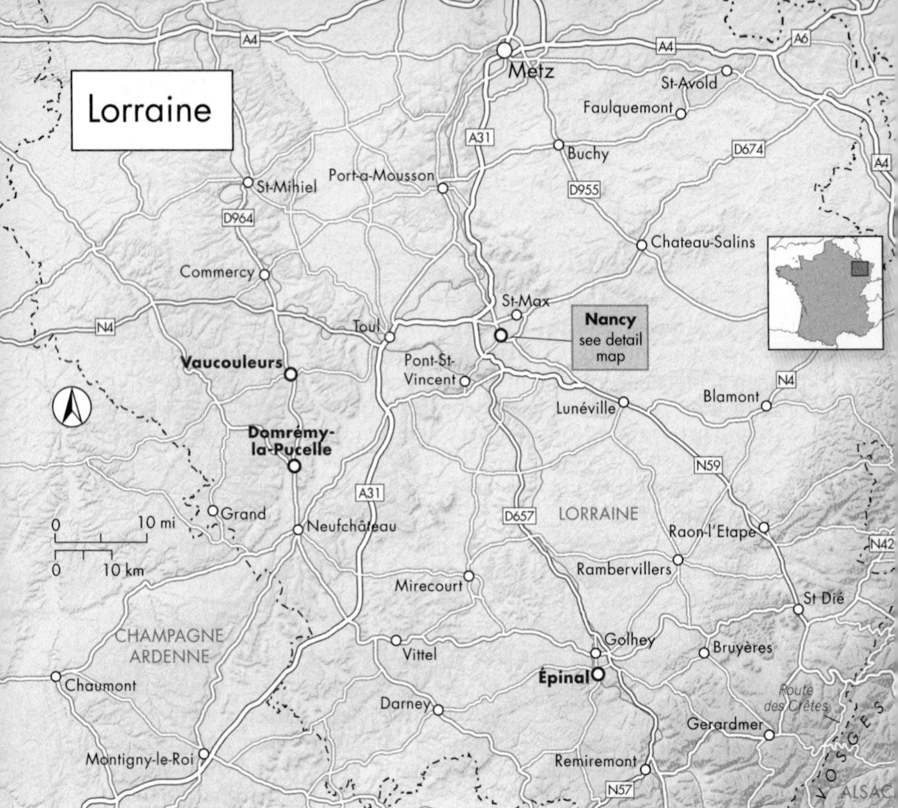

GETTING HERE

If you don't have your own car, you can come by taxi from Vaucouleurs for about €40.

EXPLORING

Basilique du Bois-Chenu (*Bois-Chenu Basilica*). The ornate late-19th-century Basilique du Bois-Chenu, high up the hillside above Domrémy, boasts enormous painted and mosaic panels expounding on Joan's legend in glowing Pre-Raphaelite tones. Outside lurk serene panoramic views over the emerald, gently rolling Meuse Valley. ✉ *Domrémy-la-Pucelle* 🌐 *www.basiliquedomremy.fr* ⏲ *Apr.–Oct., daily 8–7; Nov.–Mar., daily 8–5:30.*

Fodor's Choice ★ **Maison Natale de Jeanne d'Arc** (*Joan of Arc's Birthplace*). The humble stone-and-stucco Maison Natale de Jeanne d'Arc—an irregular, slope-roof, two-story cottage—has been preserved with style and reverence, although there is little to see inside. The modern museum alongside, the **Centre Johannique,** shows a film (French with English subtitles), while mannequins in period costume recount the Hundred Years War. After she heard mystical voices, Joan walked 19 km (12 miles) to Vaucouleurs. Dressed and mounted like a man, she later led her forces to lift the siege of Orléans, defeated the English, and escorted the unseated Charles VII to Reims, to be crowned king of France. Military missions after Orléans failed—including an attempt to retake Paris—and she was captured at Compiègne. The English turned her over to the Church, which sent her to be tried by the Inquisition for witchcraft and heresy. She was convicted and burned at the stake in Rouen. One of the latest theories is that Jeanne d'Arc was no mere "peasant" but was distantly connected to France's royal family—a controversial proposal that many historians discount. ✉ *2 rue de la Basilique, Domrémy-la-Pucelle* ☎ *03–29–06–95–86* 🌐 *www.vosges.fr* 🎫 *€4* ⏲ *Apr.–June, Wed.–Mon. 10–1 and 2–6:30; July–Sept., daily 10–1 and 2–6:30; Oct.–mid-Dec. and Feb.–Mar., Wed.–Mon. 10–1 and 2–5.*

ÉPINAL

74 km (44 miles) southeast of Domrémy-la-Pucelle, 72 km (45 miles) south of Nancy.

On the Moselle River at the feet of the Vosges, Épinal, a printing center since 1735, is famous throughout France for boldly colored prints, popular illustrations, and hand-colored stencils.

GETTING HERE

There are two direct TGVs from Paris's Gare de l'Est (2 hrs, 20 mins; €53–€68); 24 TER trains also arrive daily from Nancy, making the trip in just under an hour (€13.60).

EXPLORING

Basilique St-Maurice. The small but bustling Vieille Ville is anchored by the lovely old Basilique St-Maurice, a low gray-stone sanctuary blending Romanesque and Gothic styles. Note its sturdy belfry and deep, ornate, 15th-century entry porch. ✉ *Pl. St-Goëry, Épinal* ☎ *03–29–82–58–36* ⏲ *Daily 8–noon and 2–6.*

FAMILY **Musée de l'Image.** This is the private museum of the town's most famous printing workshop, L'Imagerie d'Épinal. Begun in 1796, L'Imagerie has produced woodcuts, lithographs, and other forms of printed imagery that are displayed here, offering a beautiful—and often critical—pictorial history of France. ✉ *42 quai de Dogneville, Épinal* ☎ *03–29–81–48–30* 🌐 *www.museedelimage.fr* 🎫 *€8 joint ticket for museum and workshop* ⏲ *Sept.–June, Mon. 2–6, Tues.–Thurs. and Sat. 9:30–noon and 2–6, Fri. 9:30–6, Sun. 10–noon and 2–6; July and Aug., Mon. 2–6, Tues.–Sat. 10–6:30, Sun.10–noon and 2–6.*

Fodor's Choice ★ **Musée Départemental d'Art Ancien et Contemporain** (*Museum of Antiquities and Contemporary Art*). A renovated 17th-century hospital on an island in the center of Épinal is home to the spectacular Musée Départemental d'Art Ancien et Contemporain. The crowning jewel here is *Job Lectured by His Wife,* one of the greatest works of Georges de la Tour, the painter whose candlelight scenes constitute Lorraine's most memorable artistic legacy. Works of other old masters on view (including Rembrandt, Fragonard, and Boucher) were once part of the famous collection of the Princes of Salm. The museum also contains one of France's largest collections of contemporary art, as well as Gallo-Roman artifacts, rural tools, and local faïence. ✉ *1 pl. Lagarde, Épinal* ☎ *03–29–82–20–33* 🎫 *€5* ⏲ *Wed.–Sat. and Mon. 9–12:30 and 1:30–6, Sun. 1:30–6.*

STRASBOURG

Although it's in the heart of Alsace, 490 km (304 miles) east of Paris, and draws appealingly on Alsatian *gemütlichkeit* (coziness), Strasbourg is a cosmopolitan French cultural center and the symbolic if unofficial capital of Europe. The Romans knew Strasbourg as Argentoratum before it came to be known as Strateburgum, or City of (Cross) Roads. After centuries as part of the Germanic Holy Roman Empire, it was united with France in 1681, but retained independence regarding legislation, education, and religion under the honorific title Free Royal City.

Against an irresistible backdrop of old half-timber houses, waterways, and the colossal single spire of its red-sandstone cathedral (which seems to insist imperiously that you pay homage to its majestic beauty), Strasbourg embodies Franco-German reconciliation and the wider idea of a united Europe. You'll discover an incongruously sophisticated mix of museums, charming neighborhoods like La Petite France, elite schools (including that notorious hothouse for blooming politicos, the École Nationale d'Administration, or National Administration School), international think tanks, and the European Parliament. The *Strasbourgeoisie* have a lot to be proud of.

GETTING HERE AND AROUND

Strasbourg is 2 hours, 20 minutes from Paris on any of the 14 daily direct TGVs (€75-€134). Frequent extra-regional trains also link the city to Nancy, Metz, Lyon, and Geneva. Because Strasbourg's train station (*20 pl. de la Gare*) is the hub of the regional TER system, direct trains run at least every 30–60 minutes to Colmar (€12.30) and Sélestat (€8.80), too. Buses head to Obernai from the Gare Routière (*03–88–23–43–23*) in Place des Halles. Within the city, you can take advantage of an extensive tram and bus network, operated by Companie des Transports Strasbourgeois (*03–88–77–70–70* ⊕ *www.cts-strasbourg.eu*). Trams and buses depart from the train station, and the same tickets can be used on both. If you want to sightsee on foot, audioguide walking tours of Strasbourg's Vieille Ville and other attractions are available through the tourist office for €5.50 per headset (plus €100 deposit).

If you're driving, keep in mind that the configuration of downtown streets makes it difficult to approach the center via the autoroute exit marked Strasbourg Centre. Instead, hold out for the exit marked Place de l'Étoile and follow signs to Cathédrale/Centre Ville. At Place du Corbeau, veer left across the Ill, and go straight to the Place Gutenberg parking garage, a block from the cathedral.

Visitor Information Strasbourg Tourist Office. ☎ *03–88–52–28–28* ⊕ *www.otstrasbourg.fr.*

THE HISTORIC HEART

The best of Old Strasbourg is concentrated in a central area that extends from the cathedral to picturesque Petite France. Effectively an island within two arms of the River Ill, it's known for twisting backstreets, flower-lined courts, tempting shops, and inviting winstubs.

A finalist by M. J. Glauber in Fodor's France contest, this stunning photo captures the Gothic grace of Strasbourg's cathedral in all its glory.

TOP ATTRACTIONS

FAMILY **Cathédrale Notre-Dame.** Dark pink, ornately carved Vosges sandstone masonry covers the facade of this most novel and Germanic of French cathedrals, a triumph of Gothic art begun in 1176. Not content with the outlines of the walls themselves, medieval builders lacily encased them with slender stone shafts. The off-center **spire,** finished in 1439, looks absurdly fragile as it tapers skyward some 466 feet; you can climb 330 steps to the base of the spire to take in sweeping views of the city, the Vosges Mountains, and the Black Forest.

The interior presents a stark contrast to the facade: it's older (mostly finished by 1275), and the nave's broad windows emphasize the horizontal rather than the vertical. Note Hans Hammer's ornately sculpted pulpit (1484–86) and the richly painted 14th- to 15th-century organ loft that rises from pillar to ceiling. The left side of the nave is flanked with richly colored Gothic windows honoring the early leaders of the Holy Roman Empire—Otto I and II, and Heinrich I and II. The **choir** is not ablaze with stained glass but framed by chunky Romanesque masonry. The elaborate 16th-century **Chapelle St-Laurent,** to the left of the choir, merits a visit; turn to the right to admire the **Pilier des Anges** (Angels' Pillar), an intricate column dating from 1230.

Just beyond the pillar, the Renaissance machinery of the 16th-century **Horloge Astronomique** whirs into action daily at 12:30 pm (but the line starts at the south door at 11:45 am): macabre clockwork figures enact the story of Christ's Passion. One of the highlights: when the apostles walk past, a likeness of Christ as a rooster crows three times. ✉ *Pl. de la Cathédrale, Strasbourg* 🌐 *www.cathedrale-strasbourg.fr* 🎫 *Clock €2;*

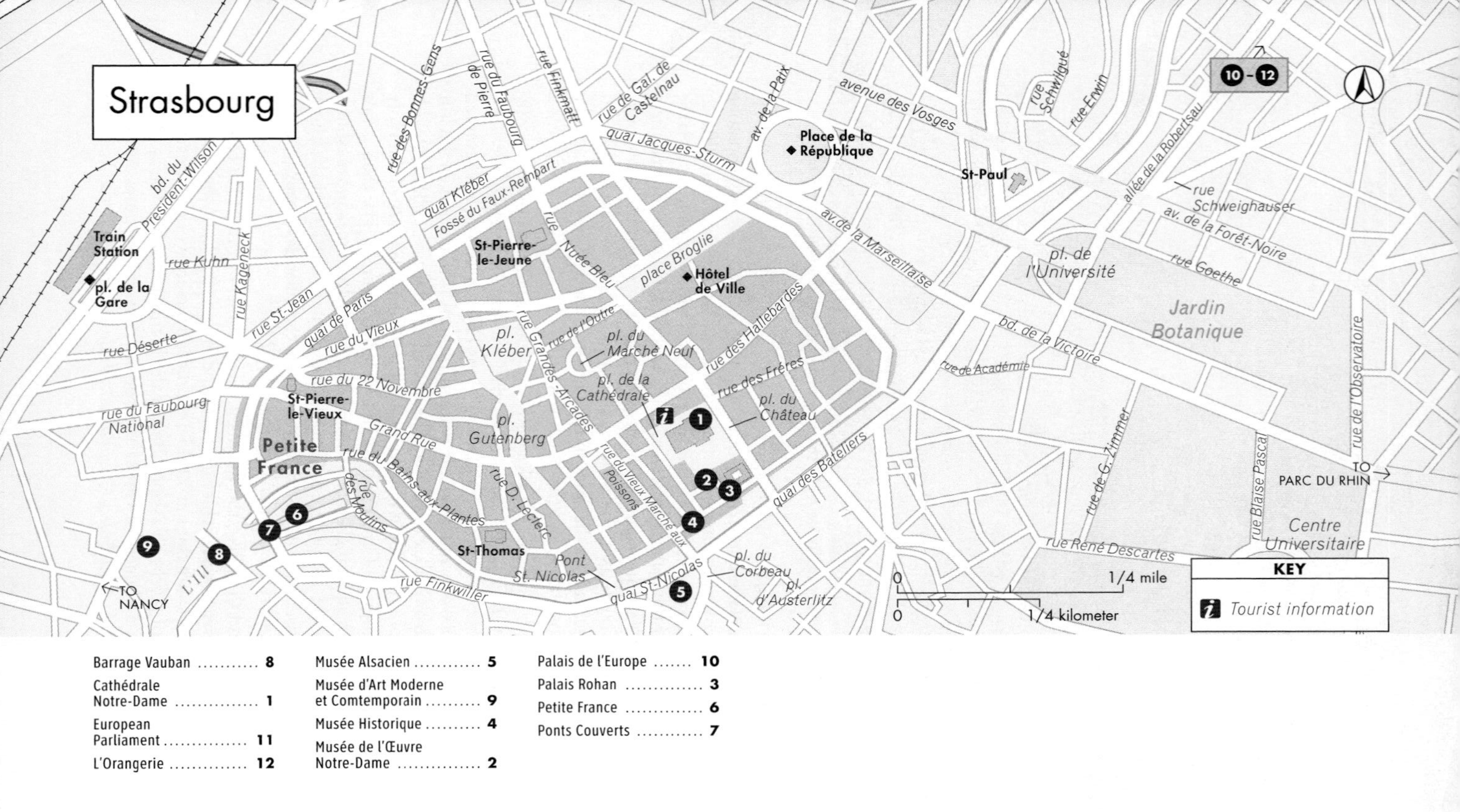
Strasbourg
KEY
Tourist information
0
1/4 mile
0
1/4 kilometer
TO PARC DU RHIN
TO NANCY
Train Station
pl. de la Gare
bd. du Président-Wilson
rue Kuhn
rue Kageneck
rue St-Jean
rue Déserte
rue du Faubourg National
quai de Paris
rue du Vieux
rue du 22 Novembre
St-Pierre-le-Vieux
Petite France
Grand Rue
rue du Bains-aux-Plantes
rue des Moulins
L'Ill
rue Finkwiller
rue des Bonnes-Gens
rue du Faubourg de Pierre
rue Finkmatt
rue de Gal. de Castelnau
quai Kléber
Fossé du Faux-Rempart
quai Jacques-Sturm
av. de la Paix
Place de la République
avenue des Vosges
St-Pierre-le-Jeune
rue Nuée Bleu
place Broglie
Hôtel de Ville
pl. Kléber
rue Grandes-Arcades
rue de l'Outre
pl. du Marché Neuf
pl. de la Cathédrale
pl. Gutenberg
rue D. Leclerc
St-Thomas
Pont St. Nicolas
quai St-Nicolas
rue du Vieux Marché aux Poissons
rue des Hallebardes
rue des Frères
pl. du Château
quai des Bateliers
pl. du Corbeau
pl. d'Austerlitz
av. de la Marseillaise
St-Paul
rue Schwilgué
rue Erwin
allée de la Robertsau
rue Schweighauser
av. de la Forêt-Noire
rue Goethe
pl. de l'Université
Jardin Botanique
bd. de la Victoire
rue de Académie
rue de G. Zimmer
rue Blaise Pascal
rue de l'Observatoire
rue René Descartes
Centre Universitaire
Barrage Vauban 8
Cathédrale Notre-Dame 1
European Parliament 11
L'Orangerie 12
Musée Alsacien 5
Musée d'Art Moderne et Comtemporain 9
Musée Historique 4
Musée de l'Œuvre Notre-Dame 2
Palais de l'Europe 10
Palais Rohan 3
Petite France 6
Ponts Couverts 7

spire platform €5 ⌚ Cathedral daily 7–11:20 and 12:40–7. Platform Apr.–Sept., daily 9:30–8; Oct.–Mar., daily 10–6.

Musée Alsacien (*Alsatian Museum*). In this labyrinthine half-timber home, with layers of carved balconies sagging over a cobbled inner courtyard, local interiors have been faithfully reconstituted. The diverse activities of blacksmiths, clog makers, saddlers, and makers of artificial flowers are explained with the help of old-time craftsmen's tools and equipment. ✉ *23 quai St-Nicolas, Strasbourg* ☎ *03–88–52–50–01* 🌐 *www.musees.strasbourg.eu* 🎫 *€6.50* ⌚ *Wed.–Mon.10–6.*

Musée d'Art Moderne et Contemporain (*Modern and Contemporary Art Museum*). At the city's modern and contemporary art museum, Adrien Fainsilber's stunning 1998 building sometimes outshines the displays inside. The latter includes a relatively thin collection of new, esoteric, and unsung 20th-century art. Downstairs, a permanent collection of Impressionists and Modernists up to 1950 is heavily padded with local heroes but happily fleshed out with some striking furniture; all are juxtaposed for contrasting and comparing, with little to no chronological flow. Upstairs, harsh, spare works must strive to live up to their setting; few contemporary masters are featured. Drawings, watercolors, and paintings by Gustave Doré, a native of Alsace, are enshrined in a separate room. ✉ *1 pl. Hans-Jean Arp, Strasbourg* ☎ *03–88–23–31–31* 🌐 *www.musees.strasbourg.eu* 🎫 *€7* ⌚ *Tues.–Sun. 10–6.*

Musée de l'Œuvre Notre-Dame (*Cathedral Museum*). There's more to this museum than the usual assembly of dilapidated statues rescued from the cathedral before they fell off (you'll find *those* rotting in the Barrage Vauban). Sacred sculptures stand in churchlike settings, and secular exhibits are enhanced by the building's fine old architecture. Subjects include a wealth of Flemish and Upper Rhine paintings, stained glass, gold objects, and massive, heavily carved furniture. ✉ *3 pl. du Château, Strasbourg* ☎ *03–88–52–50–00* 🌐 *www.musees.strasbourg.eu* 🎫 *€6.50* ⌚ *Tues.–Sun. 10–6.*

8

Palais Rohan (*Rohan Palace*). The exterior of this massive neoclassical palace (1732–42) by architect Robert de Cotte may be austere, but there's plenty of glamour inside. Decorator Robert le Lorrain's magnificent ground-floor rooms include the great **Salon d'Assemblée** (Assembly Room) and the book- and tapestry-lined **Bibliothèque des Cardinaux** (Cardinals' Library). The library leads to a series of less august rooms that house the **Musée des Arts Décoratifs** (Decorative Arts Museum) and its elaborate display of ceramics. This is a comprehensive presentation of works by Hannong, a porcelain manufacturer active in Strasbourg from 1721 to 1782; dinner services by other local kilns reveal the influence of Chinese porcelain. The **Musée des Beaux-Arts** (Fine Arts Museum), also in the château, includes masterworks of European painting from Giotto and Memling to El Greco, Rubens, and Goya. Downstairs, the **Musée Archéologique** (Archaeology Museum) displays regional finds, including gorgeous Merovingian treasures. ✉ *2 pl. du Château, Strasbourg* ☎ *03–88–52–50–00* 🌐 *www.musees.strasbourg.eu* 🎫 *€6.50 each museum* ⌚ *Wed.–Mon. 10–6.*

Fodor's Choice ★ **Petite France.** With gingerbread half-timber houses that seem to lean precariously over the canals of the Ill, plus old-fashioned shops and inviting little restaurants, "Little France" is the most magical neighborhood in Strasbourg. The district, just southwest of the center, is historically Alsatian in style and filled with Renaissance buildings that have survived plenty of wars. Wander up and down the tiny streets that connect Rue du Bain-aux-Plantes and Rue des Dentelles to Grande-Rue, and stroll the waterfront promenade. ✉ *Strasbourg.*

STRASBOURG BY WATER

Fluvial Strasbourg. Strasbourg is a big town, but the center is easily explored on foot, or, more romantically, by boat. Fluvial Strasbourg works with the company Batorama to organize 70-minute boat tours along the Ill. Tours depart four times a day in January and February, up to every hour in March, and every half hour from April through December; there are also nocturnal tours until 10:15 pm in July and August. Boats leave from behind the Palais Rohan, and tickets cost €12.50. ✉ *Strasbourg* ☎ *03-88-84-13-13* 🌐 *www.batorama.fr.*

WORTH NOTING

Barrage Vauban (*Vauban Dam*). Just beyond the Ponts Couverts is the grass-roofed Vauban Dam, built by its namesake in 1682. Climb to the top for wide-angle views of the Ponts Couverts and, on the other side, the Museum of Modern and Contemporary Art. Then meander through its echoing galleries, where magnificent cathedral statuary lies scattered among pigeon droppings. ✉ *Ponts Couverts, Strasbourg* 🎫 *Free* ⏲ *Daily 9–7:30.*

Musée Historique (*Local History Museum*). This museum, in a step-gabled slaughterhouse dating from 1588, contains a collection of maps, armor, arms, bells, uniforms, traditional outfits, printing paraphernalia, and two huge relief models of Strasbourg. The newer collection on the first floor covers civic history from the Napoleonic era to the present day. ✉ *3 pl. de la Grande-Boucherie, Strasbourg* ☎ *03–88–52–50–00* 🌐 *www.musees.strasbourg.eu* 🎫 *€6.50* ⏲ *Tues.–Sun. 10–6.*

Ponts Couverts (*Covered Bridges*). These three bridges, distinguished by their four stone towers, were once covered with wooden shelters. Part of the 14th-century ramparts that framed Old Strasbourg, they span the Ill as it branches into a quartet of fingerlike canals. ✉ *Strasbourg.*

BEYOND THE ILL

If you've seen the center and have time to strike out in new directions, head across the Ill to view an architectural landmark unrelated to Strasbourg's famous medieval past: the Palais de l'Europe.

EXPLORING

European Parliament. This sleek building testifies to the growing importance of the governing body of the European Union, which used to make do with rental offices in the Palais de l'Europe. Eurocrats continue to commute between Brussels, Luxembourg, and Strasbourg, hauling their staff and files with them. One week per month (August excepted), visitors can slip into the hemicycle and witness the tribune in debate, complete with simultaneous translation. Note: You must obtain a written appointment beforehand and provide a *pièce d'identité* (ID) before entering. ✉ *Behind Palais de l'Europe, Strasbourg* ☎ *03–88–17–40–01* 🌐 *www.europarl.europa.eu* 🎫 *Free* ⏲ *Call or write ahead for appointment.*

L'Orangerie. Like a private backyard for the Eurocrats in the Palais de l'Europe, this delightful park is laden with flowers and punctuated by noble copper beeches. It contains a lake and, close by, a small reserve of rare birds, including flamingos and noisy local storks. ✉ *Av. de l'Europe, Strasbourg.*

Palais de l'Europe. Designed by Paris architect Henri Bernard in 1977, this continental landmark is headquarters to the Council of Europe, founded in 1949 and independent of the European Union. A guided tour introduces you to the intricacies of its workings and may allow you to eavesdrop on a session. Arrange your tour by telephone in advance (a minimum of 15 people must sign up before one will be conducted); appointments are fixed according to language demands and usually take place in the afternoon. Note: You must provide ID before entering. ✉ *Av. de l'Europe, Strasbourg* ☎ *03–88–41–20–29 for appointment* 🎫 *Free* ⏲ *Tours weekdays by appointment.*

Place de la République. The spacious layout and ponderous architecture of this monumental *cirque* (circle) have nothing in common with the Vieille Ville except for the local red sandstone. A different hand was at work here—that of occupying Germans, who erected the former Ministry (1902), the Academy of Music (1882–92), and the Palais du Rhin (1883–88). The handsome neo-Gothic church of St-Paul and the pseudo-Renaissance Palais de l'Université (University Palace), constructed between 1875 and 1885, also bear the German stamp. Heavy turn-of-the-20th-century houses, some reflecting the whimsical curves of the Art Nouveau style, frame Allée de la Robertsau, a tree-lined boulevard that would not look out of place in Berlin. ✉ *Pl. de la République, Strasbourg.*

WHERE TO EAT

$$$$ FRENCH ✕ **Au Crocodile.** At one of the temples of Alsatian-French haute cuisine, you get a real taste of old Alsace with a nouvelle spin. Founded in the early 1800s, its grand salon is still aglow with skylights and a spectacular 19th-century mural showing the Strasbourgeoisie at a country fair continues to set the tasteful tone. Chef Philippe Bohrer, who worked privately for French presidents Valéry Giscard d'Estaing and François Mitterrand, presents some of the most dazzling dishes around. Delights include breast of guinea fowl stuffed with foie gras, grilled turbot with Champagne sauce, and warm gingerbread soufflé. Not surprisingly, the wine list is extensive. In case you're curious, Au Crocodile's name refers to a stuffed specimen brought back by a Strasbourg general from Napoléon's Egyptian campaign. $ *Average main: €50* ✉ *10 rue de l'Outre, Strasbourg* ☎ *03–88–32–13–02* 🌐 *www.au-crocodile.com* ⏲ *Closed Sun. and Mon.* ✍ *Reservations essential* 👔 *Jacket and tie.*

Medieval buildings that look airlifted in from Germany stunningly ornament Strasbourg's squares.

$
FRENCH

Chez Yvonne. Just around the corner from the cathedral is an eatery that is almost as exalted. Behind red-checked curtains you can find artists, tourists, lovers, and heads of state sitting elbow-to-elbow in this classic winstub, founded in 1873. All come to savor steaming platters of local specialties: the Munster cheese in puff pastry, the pike-perch on choucroute, and the braised ham hocks are all heartily recommended. Warm Alsatian fabrics dress tables, the china is regional, the photos historic—all making for chic, not kitsch. *Average main: €16* *10 rue du Sanglier, Strasbourg* *03–88–32–84–15* *www.restaurant-chez-yvonne.net* *Reservations essential.*

$$$$
MODERN FRENCH
Fodor's Choice ★

Le Buerehiesel. This lovely farmhouse, reconstructed in the Orangerie park, warrants a pilgrimage if you're willing to pay for the finest cooking in Alsace. Chef Eric Westermann focuses on the freshest of local-terroir specialties, supplemented by the best seafood from Brittany. Look for dishes like roast whiting fillet with scallop mousse or the chef's signature panfried frogs' legs served with *schniederspaetle* (onion- and potato-filled ravioli). The seasonal desserts are also a standout. Two small salons are cozy, but most tables are set in a modern annex made largely of glass and steel. In any event, plump European *parlementaires* come on foot; others might come on their knees. *Average main: €37* *4 parc de l'Orangerie, Strasbourg* *03–88–45–56–65* *www.buerehiesel.fr* *Closed Sun. and Mon., 2 wks in Jan., and 2 wks in Aug.* *Reservations essential.*

$$
GERMAN

Maison des Tanneurs. This half-timbered 16th-century landmark (one of oldest riverside buildings in Petite France) is draped with geranium-filled flower pots and perennially popular. Come for generous and delicious proportions of choucroute garnie, as well as other regional favorites such as goose foie gras, trout with almonds, and coq au Riesling. *Average main: €24* *42 rue Bain aux Plantes, Strasbourg* *03–88–32–79–70* *www.maison-des-tanneurs.com* *Closed Sun., Mon., and 3 wks in early Jan.*

$$ FRENCH **Maison Kammerzell.** This restaurant occupies what must be the most familiar house in Strasbourg—a richly carved, half-timber 15th-century building adorned with sumptuous allegorical frescoes. Fight your way through the crowds on the terrace and ground floor to one of the atmospheric rooms above, with their gleaming wooden furniture, stained-glass windows, and unrivaled views of the cathedral. Foie gras and choucroute are best bets, though you may want to try the chef's pet discovery, choucroute with freshwater fish. *Average main: €22* *16 pl. de la Cathédrale, Strasbourg* *03–88–32–42–14* *www.maison-kammerzell.com.*

$ BISTRO **Zum Strissel.** This rustic winstub near the cathedral has been in business since the 16th century. The charming decor provides a perfect backdrop for traditional Alsatian fare such as baeckeoffe and choucroute served with pike perch. To wash it down, you can choose from an extensive list of Alsace wines. Try for a room upstairs to admire the stained-glass windows with their tales depicting life in the vines, or opt for the outdoor terrace, which spills out over the square. *Average main: €17* *5 pl. de la Grande-Boucherie, Strasbourg* *03–88–32–14–73* *www.strissel.fr.*

WHERE TO STAY

$ HOTEL **Cathédrale.** Location and views, with windows framing the cathedral or 16th-century half-timber Maison Kammerzell, are what make these otherwise ordinary rooms so memorable. **Pros:** comfortable, clean, but not remarkable accommodations; across from the cathedral. **Cons:** some rooms are small; those with a cathedral view get some street noise (rooms that don't face the square are quieter). *Rooms from: €100* *13 pl. de la Cathédrale, Strasbourg* *03–88–22–12–12* *www.hotel-cathedrale.fr* *47 rooms* *No meals.*

$$ HOTEL **Hôtel Cour du Corbeau.** Opened as an inn in 1580 and magnificently restored to its half-timbered former glory, the "courtyard of the crow" retains its Middle Ages facade while the interiors are another thing completely: luxe design, crystal chandeliers, period furniture, and colorful fabrics are the essence of modern style, sumptuousness, and comfort. **Pros:** dazzling and luxurious; great location a short walk from the cathedral. **Cons:** has a tea salon, but no restaurant. *Rooms from: €145* *6–8 rue des Couples, Strasbourg* *03–90–00–26–26* *www.cour-corbeau.com* *38 rooms, 19 suites* *No meals.*

$ HOTEL **Hôtel Gutenberg.** In a 250-year-old mansion just off Place Gutenberg, this budget-priced urban hotel has colorful, modernized rooms with charming highlights from the past. **Pros:** excellent value; old-world style with modern amenities and design touches; picturesque location only a few blocks from the cathedral. **Cons:** some street noise; elevator doesn't reach the top floor. *Rooms from: €99* *31 rue des Serruriers, Strasbourg* *03–88–32–17–15* *www.hotel-gutenberg.com* *42 rooms* *Breakfast.*

8

$$$$ HOTEL Fodor'sChoice ★ **Régent-Petite France.** Surrounded by canals in the heart of the quaint La Petite France quarter, this centuries-old former ice factory—replete with noble pediment and mansard roofs—has been transformed into a boldly modern luxury hotel, where Philippe Starck–inspired sculptural furnishings contrast sharply with the half-timber houses and roaring river viewed from nearly every window. **Pros:** beautiful rooms; ideal location; great service; no skimping on the amenities—the beds and the bathrooms are divine. **Cons:** disappointing breakfast; restaurant closed Sunday and Monday. *Rooms from: €250* *5 rue des Moulins, Strasbourg* *03–88–76–43–43* *www.regent-petite-france.com* *55 rooms, 17 suites* *Some meals.*

NIGHTLIFE AND PERFORMING ARTS

Festival Musica (*Contemporary Music Festival*). The annual Festival Musica is held in September and October. *Cité de la Musique et de la Danse, 1 pl. Dauphine, Strasbourg* *03–88–23–46–46* *www.festivalmusica.org.*

Jazzdor (Jazz Festival). Strasbourg hosts its international jazz festival each November at venues both in and around the city. *25 rue des Frères, Strasbourg* *03–88–36–30–48* *www.jazzdor.com.*

La Laiterie. The Vieille Ville neighborhood east of the cathedral, along Rue des Frères, is the nightlife hangout for university students and twentysomethings; among a clutch of heavily frequented bars is La Laiterie, a multiplex concert hall showcasing art, workshops, and music ranging from electronic to post-rock and reggae. *16 rue Hohwald, Strasbourg* *03–88–23–72–37* *www.artefact.org.*

Opéra National du Rhin. A sizable repertoire makes the Opéra National du Rhin a popular—and accessible—choice. *19 pl. Broglie, Strasbourg* *03–88–75–48–00* *www.operanationaldurhin.eu.*

Orchestre Philharmonique. Classical concerts are presented by the Orchestre Philharmonique. Performances are staged mainly at the Palais de la Musique et des Congrès. *Palais des Congrès, Strasbourg* *03–69–06–37–06* *www.philharmonique-strasbourg.com.*

SHOPPING

The lively city center is full of boutiques, including chocolate shops and delicatessens selling locally made foie gras. Look for warm paisley linens and rustic homespun fabrics, Alsatian pottery, and local wines. Forming the city's commercial heart are **Rue des Hallebardes,** next to the cathedral; **Rue des Grandes Arcades,** with its shopping mall; and **Place Kléber.** An **antiques market** takes place behind the cathedral on Rue du Vieil-Hôpital, Rue des Bouchers, and Place de la Grande Boucherie every Wednesday and Saturday morning.

ALSACE

The Rhine River forms the eastern boundary of both Alsace and France. But the best of Alsace is not found along the Rhine's industrial waterfront. Instead it's in the Ill Valley at the base of the Vosges, southwest of cosmopolitan Strasbourg. Northwest is the beginning of the **Route du Vin,** the great Alsace Wine Road, which winds its way south through the Vosges foothills, fruitful vineyards, and medieval villages. Signs for the road help you keep your bearings on the twisting way south, and you'll find limitless opportunities to stop at wineries and sample the local wares. The Wine Road stretches 170 km (105 miles) between Thann and Marienheim, and is easily accessible from Strasbourg or Colmar. Many of the towns and villages have designated "vineyard trails" winding between towns (a bicycle will help you cover a lot of territory). Riquewihr and Ribeauvillé are connected by an especially picturesque route. Along the way, stop at any "Dégustation" sign for a tasting and pick up brochures on the Alsace Wine Road at any tourist office.

OBERNAI

30 km (19 miles) southwest of Strasbourg via A35/N422.

Many visitors begin their trip down the Route du Vin at Obernai, a thriving, colorful Renaissance market town named for the patron saint of Alsace. Head to the central town enclosed by the ramparts to find some particularly photo-friendly sites, including a medieval belfry, Renaissance well, and late-19th-century church.

GETTING HERE

You can reach Obernai from Strasbourg by bus (50 mins, €2) or train (30–40 mins, €6.20). Trains also connect Obernai and Sélestat (25–40 mins, €5.10).

Visitor Information Obernai Tourist Office. ☎ *03–88–95–64–13* 🌐 *www.tourisme-obernai.fr.*

EXPLORING

Kapelturm Beffroi (*Chapel Tower Belfry*). Place du Marché, in the heart of town, is dominated by the 13th-century Kapelturm Beffroi. The stout, square structure is topped by a pointed steeple that's flanked at each corner by frilly openwork turrets. ✉ *Obernai.*

Puits à Six-Seaux (*Well of Six Buckets*). An elaborate Renaissance well near the belfry, the Puits à Six-Seaux was constructed in 1579; its name recalls the six buckets suspended from its metal chains. ✉ *Obernai.*

St-Pierre–St-Paul. The twin spires of this parish church compete with the belfry for skyline preeminence. Like the rest of the sanctuary, they date from the 1860s, although the 1504 Holy Sepulchre altarpiece in the north transept is a survivor from the previous church. Other points of interest include the flower-bedecked **Place de l'Étoile** and the **Hôtel de Ville,** which is open to visitors the third weekend of September during *Les Journées du Patrimoine* (Heritage Days). ✉ *Obernai.*

8

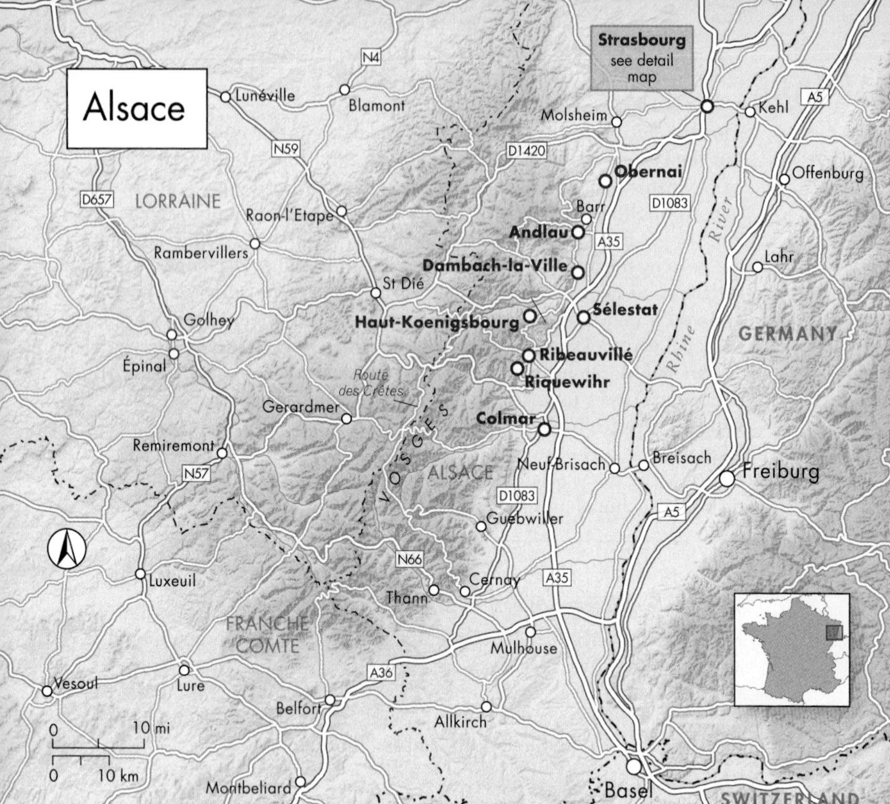

WHERE TO STAY

$$$ HOTEL **A La Cour d'Alsace.** In a quiet location just a few steps from the Kapelturm Beffroi, this smart hotel balances old-fashioned coziness with up-to-date guest rooms that are both comfortable and stylish; some overlook the garden and ramparts. **Pros:** dead-center location. **Cons:** no direct access from rooms to pool and spa—guests must cross the outdoor courtyard in their bathrobes. *Rooms from: €170* ✉ *3 rue de Gail, Obernai* ☎ *03–88–95–07–00* *www.cour-alsace.com* *Closed Christmas–late Jan.* *50 rooms, 4 suites* *Some meals.*

$ HOTEL **Hôtel Le Gouverneur.** Behind the photogenic facade of this half-timbered 17th-century house, you'll find comfy, clean-lined bedrooms that have recently been revamped; they're set around a geranium-festooned interior courtyard, and the quietest ones come with a view of the ramparts. **Pros:** good value; friendly staff; city-center location. **Cons:** small bathrooms; no air-conditioning. *Rooms from: €91* ✉ *13 rue de Sélestat, Obernai* ☎ *03–88–95–63–72* *www.hotellegouverneur.com* *32 rooms* *No meals.*

$ B&B/INN Fodor's Choice ★ **L'Ami Fritz.** A few miles west of Obernai, this white-shuttered, flower-bedecked, 18th-century house treats diners to fine meals and accommodates overnight guests in impeccable rooms with sleek contemporary furnishings (opt for one in the main building, not the adjacent annex). **Pros:** beautiful location; friendly staff; combines style, rustic warmth, and three generations of family tradition. **Cons:** a car is needed; uneven service. $ *Rooms from: €98* ✉ *8 rue des Châteaux, 5 km (3 miles) west of Obernai, Ottrott-le-Haut* ☎ *03–88–95–80–81* 🌐 *www.amifritz.com* ⌚ *Closed 2nd wk of July and 2 wks in mid-Jan.* *35 rooms, 7 suites* 🍴 *No meals.*

SHOPPING

Dietrich. Head to Dietrich for a varied selection of Beauvillé linens, locally handblown Alsatian wineglasses, and Obernai-pattern china. ✉ *74 rue du Général-Gouraud, Obernai* ☎ *03–88–95–57–58* 🌐 *www.dietrich-obernai.fr.*

ANDLAU

13 km (8 miles) southwest of Obernai.

This small, yet important, wine town in the Andlau River valley is surrounded by the Vosges mountains. Its historic center has several noteworthy houses dating from the 15th to 18th century; however Abbaye d'Andlau is the primary attraction.

GETTING HERE

By car, Andlau is 20 minutes from Obernai; if you don't have your own, expect to pay about €30 for cab fare.

EXPLORING

Abbaye d'Andlau. Built in the 12th century, the Abbaye d'Andlau has the richest ensemble of Romanesque sculpture in Alsace. Sculpted vines wind their way around the doorway as a reminder of wine's time-honored importance to the local economy. A statue of a female bear, the abbey mascot—bears used to roam local forests and were bred at the abbey until the 16th century—can be seen in the north transept. Legend has it that Queen Richarde, spurned by her husband, Charles the Fat, founded the abbey in AD 887 when an angel enjoined her to construct a church on a site to be shown to her by a female bear. ✉ *Andlau.*

8

WHERE TO STAY

$ HOTEL **Arnold.** Like Itterswiller—the cute wine village it overlooks—this yellow-walled, half-timbered hillside hotel exudes charm, from the wood-beam lobby with its wrought-iron staircase right through to the "country deluxe" lodgings with views across the nearby vineyards. **Pros:** all-around excellence; good half-board meal plan. **Cons:** no air-conditioning; inconsistent service. $ *Rooms from: €98* ✉ *98 rte. des Vins, Itterswiller* ⊕ *3 km (2 miles) south of Andlau on D253* ☎ *03–88–85–50–58* 🌐 *www.hotel-arnold.com* *37 rooms* 🍴 *Some meals.*

DAMBACH-LA-VILLE

8 km (5 miles) southeast of Andlau via Itterswiller.

Dambach-la-Ville—the largest wine-producing village along the Alsace Wine Road—is protected by ramparts and three imposing 13th-century gateways. It's particularly rich in half-timber, high-roof houses from the 17th and 18th centuries, clustered mainly around Place du Marché (Market Square). Also on the square is the 16th-century Hôtel de Ville.

CLOSE UP

A Tippler's Guide to Alsace

Threading south along the eastern foothills of the Vosges from Marienheim to Thann, the Alsatian Wine Road is home to delicious wines and beautiful vineyards. The 170-km (105-mile) Route du Vin passes through small towns, and footpaths interspersed throughout the region afford the opportunity to wander through the vineyards.

Buses from Colmar head out to the surrounding towns of Riquewihr, St-Hippolyte, Ribeauvillé, and Eguisheim; pick up brochures on the Wine Route from Colmar's tourist office. Although the route is hilly, bicycling is a great way to take in the countryside and avoid the parking hassle in the towns along this heavily traveled route.

Wine is an object of veneration in Alsace, and anyone traveling along the Route du Vin will want to become part of the cult. Just because Alsatian vintners use German grapes, don't expect their wines to taste like their counterparts across the Rhine.

German vintners aim for sweetness, creating wines that are best appreciated as an aperitif. Alsatian vintners, on the other hand, eschew sweetness in favor of strength, and their wines go wonderfully with knockdown, drag-out meals.

The main wines you need to know about are Gewurztraminer, Riesling, Muscat, Pinot Gris, and Sylvaner—all whites. The only red wine produced in the region is the light and delicious Pinot Noir. Gewurztraminer, which in Germany is an ultrasweet dessert wine, has a much cleaner, drier taste in Alsace, despite its fragrant bouquet. It's best served with the richest of Alsace dishes, such as goose.

Riesling is the premier wine of Alsace, balancing a hard structure with certain fruity roundness. With a grapy bouquet and clean finish, dry Muscat does best as an aperitif. Pinot Gris, also called "Tokay," is probably the most full-bodied of Alsatian wines.

Sylvaner falls below those grapes in general acclaim, tending to be lighter and a bit dull. You can discover many of these wines as you drive along the Route du Vin.

As you walk the charming streets, notice the wrought-iron signs and rooftop oriels.

GETTING HERE

Dambach-la Ville is 30 minutes from Colmar by TER train (€6.40); you can also arrive from Strasbourg directly (€8.90) or via Sélestat (€9.80), in under an hour.

WHERE TO STAY

$ B&B/INN **Le Vignoble.** Set in a beautifully restored 18th-century barn next to the village church, this unpretentious hotel offers real, rustic Alsatian charm; quiet, comfy guest rooms have functional dark-wood furnishings and, in some cases, balconies overlooking the street. **Pros:** wine-route location; warm Alsatian welcome. **Cons:** no air-conditioning; no restaurant; some rooms are on the small side. [$] *Rooms from:* €77 ✉ 1

Alsace's Wine Road passes a parade of "Hansel and Gretel" villages, each more picturesque than the last.

rue de l'Eglise, Dambach-la-Ville ☎ *03–88–92–43–75* 🌐 *www.hotel-vignoble-alsace.fr* ⊗ *Closed Jan.–mid-Feb.* 🛏 *7 rooms.*

SÉLESTAT

9 km (5½ miles) southeast of Dambach via D210 and N422, 47 km (29 miles) southwest of Strasbourg.

Sélestat, midway between Strasbourg and Colmar, is a lively, historic town with a Romanesque church and a library of medieval manuscripts (the latter of which will be closed for renovations until 2017). The fact that it has good transportation links is an added bonus. Head directly to the Vieille Ville and explore the quarter on foot.

GETTING HERE

TER trains depart Strasbourg every 30 minutes for Sélestat (€8.80). Frequent daily trains also connect the town to Colmar (€5.10), and buses run from here to Ribeauvillé (€2.50).

Visitor Information Sélestat Tourist Office. ☎ *03–88–58–87–20* 🌐 *www.selestat-haut-koenigsbourg.com.*

EXPLORING

St-Foy. The church of St-Foy dates from between 1155 and 1190; its Romanesque facade remains largely intact (the spires were added in the 19th century), as does the 140-foot octagonal tower over the crossing. Sadly, the interior was mangled over the centuries, chiefly by the Jesuits, whose most inspired legacy is the Baroque pulpit of 1733 depicting the life of St-Francis Xavier. Note the Romanesque bas-relief next to the baptistery, originally the lid of a sarcophagus. ✉ *Pl. du Marché-Vert,*

Sélestat ⏲ *Jan.–Mar., Nov., and Dec., daily 8–noon and 1:30–7; Apr.–Oct., daily 8–7.*

FLOWER POWERED

The colorful Corso Fleuri Flower Carnival takes place on the second Saturday in August, when Sélestat decks itself—and the floats in its vivid parade—with a magnificent display of dahlias.

WHERE TO EAT AND STAY

$$ FRENCH **La Vieille Tour.** Named for the 13th-century stone tower that flanks it, La Vieille Tour gives classic dishes a contemporary spin. Chefs Nicolas and Samy Ruhlmann seek inspiration from locally sourced seasonal produce, and their love for it shows in dishes such as terrine of foie gras with apple and ginger sauce, or bacon-wrapped scallops with creamed parsnips. Tantalizing desserts cap the menu. Take a table in the traditional dining room (complete with oak-beamed ceiling and fireplace), or opt for one on the more contemporary first floor. The fixed-price menus are an excellent value. *Average main: €24* ✉ *8 rue de la Jauge, Sélestat* ☎ *03–88–92–15–02* 🌐 *www.vieille-tour.fr* ⏲ *Closed Mon.*

$ HOTEL **Hôtel Vaillant.** More promising than you'd expect from the bland '70s exterior, this easy-to-find hotel near the train station has a distinct sense of style. **Pros:** air-conditioning, flat-screen TVs, and free Wi-Fi; large free car park in front of hotel. **Cons:** 10-minute walk to historic center. *Rooms from: €90* ✉ *7 rue Ignace Spies, Sélestat* ✣ *Pl. de la République* ☎ *03–88–92–09–46* 🌐 *www.hotel-vaillant.com* *47 rooms* *No meals.*

HAUT-KOENIGSBOURG

11 km (7 miles) west of Sélestat via D159.

One of the most popular spots in Alsace is the romantic, crag-top castle of Haut-Koenigsbourg, originally built as a fortress in the 12th century.

GETTING HERE

A shuttle bus provides transport from Sélestat to Orschwiller for €4 (return) daily from June to September and on weekends from March to December; from there it's a short walk to Haut-Koenigsbourg.

EXPLORING

FAMILY Fodor'sChoice ★ **Château du Haut-Koenigsbourg.** The ruins of the Château du Haut-Koenigsbourg were presented by the town of Sélestat to German emperor Wilhelm II in 1901. The château looked just as a kaiser thought one should, and he restored it with some diligence and no lack of imagination—squaring the main tower's original circle, for instance. The site, panorama, drawbridge, and amply furnished imperial chambers may lack authenticity, but they are undeniably dramatic. ✉ *Orschwiller* ☎ *03–69–33–25–00* 🌐 *www.haut-koenigsbourg.fr* *€9; free first Sun. of the month Nov.–Mar. only* ⏲ *Nov.–Feb., Tues.–Sun. 9:30–noon and 1–4:30; Mar. and Oct., daily 9:30–5; Apr., May, and Sept., daily 9:15–5:15; June–Aug., daily 9:15–6.*

RIBEAUVILLÉ

13 km (8 miles) south of Haut-Koenigsbourg via St-Hippolyte, 16 km (10 miles) southwest of Sélestat.

Fodor's Choice ★ The beautiful half-timber town of Ribeauvillé, surrounded by rolling vineyards and three imposing châteaux, produces some of the best wines in Alsace. (The Trimbach family has made Riesling and superb Gewurztraminer here since 1626.) Its narrow main street, crowded with winstubs, pottery shops, bakeries, and wine sellers, is bisected by the 13th-century **Tour des Bouchers,** or Butcher's Tower—a clock-belfry completed (gargoyles and all) in the 15th century.

GETTING HERE

Multiple daily buses let you reach Ribeauvillé via Colmar (€3.95) or Sélestat (€2.50).

Visitor Information Ribeauvillé Tourist Office. ☎ *03–89–73–23–23* 🌐 *www.ribeauville-riquewihr.com.*

EXPLORING

Place de l'Hôtel de Ville. Ignore the guides herding around French and German tour groups, and head straight for the place de l'Hôtel de Ville. Its town hall contains a famous collection of silver-gilt 16th-century tankards and chalices; and the *place* itself is a pretty place to perch. It is particularly lively the first Sunday in September, when the town hosts a grand parade to celebrate the Fête des Ménétriers (Festival of the Minstrels)—a day when at least one fountain here spouts free Riesling. Headlined by medieval musicians, the party begins mid-afternoon. Entrance tickets cost €8, and the best street seats go for €10 (contact the tourist office for details). ✉ *Pl. de l'Hôtel de Ville, Ribeauvillé* ☎ *No phone.*

WHERE TO EAT AND STAY

$$$$ MODERN FRENCH Fodor's Choice ★ ✕ **L'Auberge de L'Ill.** Marlene Dietrich and Spanish opera star Montserrat Caballé are just two of the famous guests who have feasted at this culinary temple, where Chef Marc Haeberlin marries Alsatian cuisine with Asian nuances. The impressive results include salmon soufflé, saddle of Aveyron lamb, and showstoppers like *le homard Prince Vladimir* (lobster with shallots braised in Champagne and crème fraîche). Japanese-Alsatian flair is particularly apparent in such dishes as steamed sole served with a creamy wasabi sauce. The kitchen's touch is incredibly light, so you'll have room left for masterful desserts like a dome of chestnut mousse with an Eglantine rose filling. $ *Average main: €90* ✉ *2 rue de Collonges au Mont d'Or, 10 km (6 miles) east of Ribeauvillé, Illhaeusern* ☎ *03–89–71–89–00* 🌐 *www.auberge-de-l-ill.com* ⊙ *Closed Mon., Tues., and Feb.*

$$ GERMAN ✕ **Zum Pfifferhüs.** This is a true-blue winstub, with yellowed murals, glowing lighting, and great local wines available by the glass. The cooking is pure Alsace, with German-scale portions of choucroute, ham hocks, and fruit tarts. Book ahead. $ *Average main: €21* ✉ *14 Grande-Rue, Ribeauvillé* ☎ *03–89–73–62–28* ⊙ *Closed Wed. year-round, Thurs. Nov.–July, mid-Feb.–mid-Mar., and 1st 2 wks in July* ✍ *Reservations essential.*

8

$ HOTEL **Hôtel de la Tour.** Guest rooms at this erstwhile family winery in the center of Ribeauvillé, with an ornate Renaissance fountain outside its front door, are modern, surprisingly spacious, and well positioned for experiencing the atmospheric town by night; those on the top floor have exposed timbers and wonderful views of ramshackle rooftops. **Pros:** family run; good amenities, including a sauna and Jacuzzi. **Cons:** no air-conditioning. *Rooms from: €83 1 rue de la Mairie, Ribeauvillé 03–89–73–72–73 www.hotel-la-tour.com Closed Jan.–early Mar. 31 rooms No meals.*

$$$$ B&B/INN **Hôtel des Berges.** If you want to enjoy the pleasant surroundings of the celebrated L'Auberge de L'Ill restaurant, with its terraced riverside lawns, book a night in the luxury annex. **Pros:** romantic and opulent; close to excellent restaurant. **Cons:** pricey; no meals included. *Rooms from: €350 4 rue de Collonges au Mont d'Or, Illhaeusern 10 km (6 miles) east of Ribeauvillé 03–89–71–87–87 www.hoteldesberges.com Closed Mon.,Tues., and Feb. 7 rooms, 6 suites No meals.*

$$$ B&B/INN **Seigneurs de Ribeaupierre.** On the edge of Ribeauvillé's old quarter, this gracious half-timber, 18th-century inn offers a warm welcome; a crackling fire greets you downstairs, while exposed timbers, sumptuous fabrics, and slick bathrooms await upstairs. **Pros:** tasteful and cozy; central location; gracious hosts; generous breakfast included. **Cons:** stuffy in summer (no air-conditioning). *Rooms from: €160 11 rue du Château, Ribeauvillé 03–89–73–70–31 www.ribeaupierre.com Closed Jan.–early Mar. 3 rooms, 2 suites Breakfast.*

RIQUEWIHR

5 km (3 miles) south of Ribeauvillé.

Fodor's Choice ★ With its unique once-upon-a-timeliness, Riquewihr is the Wine Route's pièce de résistance and a living museum of old Alsace's quaint architecture. Its steep main street, ramparts, and winding back alleys have scarcely changed since the 16th century, and could easily serve as a film set. Merchants cater to the sizable influx of tourists with a plethora of kitschy souvenir shops; bypass them and instead peep into courtyards with massive wine presses, study the ornately decorated houses, stand in the narrow old courtyard that was once the Jewish quarter, or climb up the Dolder Belfry for a stunning view of the town. You would also do well to settle into a winstub to sample some of Riquewihr's famous wines. Just strolling down the heavenly streets will reward your eye with half-timber houses, storybook gables, and storks'-nest towers. The facades of certain houses dating from the late Gothic period take pride of place, including the Maison Kiener (1574), the Maison Preiss (1686), and the Maison Liebrich (1535), but the Tower of Thieves and the Postal Museum, ensconced in the château of the duke of Württemberg, are also fascinating.

GETTING HERE

Riquewihr can be reached by bus from Colmar or Sélestat. From Colmar it is a 45-minute journey by bus (No. 106) from Mon.–Sat. (€4).

Visitor Information Riquewihr Tourist Office. *03–89–73–23–23 www.ribeauville-riquewihr.com.*

WHERE TO EAT AND STAY

$ FRENCH **Au Tire-Bouchon.** With its stone walls, wooden tables, and friendly waiters, "The Corkscrew" is the best place in town to sample Alsatian choucroute garnie—including unusual varieties like choucroute flavored with Pinot Noir and "Choucroute Royale." The menu also promises some seasonally changing innovations, plus a fine selection of medal-winning Pinot Blanc and Riesling wines. This winstub is recommended for that guaranteed touch of authenticity. *Average main: €17 29 rue du Général-de-Gaulle, Riquewihr 03-89-47-91-61 Closed mid-Jan.–early Feb., 1st wk in Mar., and Mon. year-round. No dinner Sun.*

$ HOTEL **Hôtel de la Couronne.** Looking like an illustration out of the Brothers Grimm, this hotel is set in a 16th-century house with a central tower, steep mansard roof, country shutters, and rusticated stone trim; inside, several guest rooms have grand timber beams and folkloric wall stencils, making this a truly charming base for touring a truly charming town. **Pros:** good location; outdoor dining in summer; old-world charm. **Cons:** no elevator; service can be inconsistent. *Rooms from: €65 5 rue de la Couronne, Riquewihr 03-89-49-03-03 www.hoteldelacouronne.com 41 rooms Some meals.*

$ B&B/INN **Le Sarment d'Or.** This little family-run hotel by the city walls, near the Dolder belfry, blends modern comforts with bare-stone walls, dark-timber ceilings, and a dining room that serves up firelit romance as well as delicious cuisine; the top-floor duplex suite is an exceptional value. **Pros:** pleasant, bright rooms; good food; you can drive through the town's car-free zone for luggage drop-off. **Cons:** no elevator; no air-conditioning. *Rooms from: €70 4 rue du Cerf, Riquewihr 03-89-86-02-86 riquewihr-sarment-dor.com Closed 1st wk in July 9 rooms Some meals.*

COLMAR TOURS

Les Circuits d'Alsace. For Colmar and its enchanting environs, take a highly recommended van tour with Les Circuits d'Alsace. Castles, villages, and vineyards make for an exhilarating itinerary. *8 pl. de la Gare, Colmar 03-89-41-90-88 www.alsace-travel.com.*

COLMAR

13 km (8 miles) southeast of Riquewihr via D3/D10, 71 km (44 miles) southwest of Strasbourg.

Forget that much of Colmar's architecture is modern (because of the destruction wrought by World Wars I and II): its Vieille Ville heart—an atmospheric maze of narrow streets lined with candy-color, half-timber Renaissance houses hanging over cobblestone lanes in a disarmingly ramshackle way—out-charms Strasbourg. Each shop-lined backstreet winds its way to the 15th-century customs house, the Ancienne Douane, and the square and canals that surround it.

GETTING HERE AND AROUND

Four daily direct TGVs run from Paris's Gare de l'Est to Colmar (€77.80), each taking 2 hours, 50 minutes. Twelve semi-direct, TGV/TER combos depart from the same station; these require a change at

DID YOU KNOW?

Colmar may be mostly modern, but it has an enchanting Old Town—head to the Lauch River to find La Petite Venise, a gorgeous district crammed with camera-ready buildings.

either Strasbourg or Mulhouse, which typically adds 10 minutes to the travel time. More than a dozen daily trains will take you from Colmar to Sélestat (€5.10), and nine daily buses (the last at 7:10 pm) make the 45-minute trip to Ribeauvillé (€3.95). The LK Groupe (🌐 *www.l-k.fr*) has regular bus service from the Gare SNCF to towns throughout the region. Within Colmar, TRACE buses (*03–89–20–80–80* 🌐 *www.trace-colmar.fr*) provide efficient public transit.

Visitor Information Colmar Tourist Office. ☎ *03-89-20-68-92* 🌐 *www.ot-colmar.fr.*

EXPLORING

Collégiale St-Martin. Built between 1235 and 1365, this beefy collegiate church is essentially Gothic (the Renaissance bell tower was added in 1572 following a fire). There are some interesting medieval sculptures on the exterior; and the interior, which was heavily vandalized during the Revolution, includes an ambulatory, a rare feature in Alsatian sanctuaries. ✉ *22 pl. de la Cathedrale* ☎ *03–89–41–27–20* ⏲ *Daily 8:30–6:30 (until 7 May–Sept.).*

Église des Dominicains (*Dominican Church*). The Flemish-influenced *Madonna of the Rosebush* (1473), noted German artist Martin Schongauer's most celebrated painting, hangs in the Église des Dominicains. Stolen from St-Martin's in 1972 and later recovered, the work has almost certainly been reduced in size from its original state but retains enormous impact. The grace and intensity of the Virgin match that of the Christ Child; yet her slender fingers dent the child's soft flesh (and his fingers entwine her curls) with immediate intimacy. Schongauer's text for her crown is: *Me carpes genito tuo o santissima virgo* ("Choose me also for your child, O holiest Virgin"). ✉ *Pl. des Dominicains, Colmar* ☎ *03–89–24–46–57* 🎫 *€1.30* ⏲ *Wed.–Mon. 9–noon and 2–5.*

La Petite Venise (*Little Venice*). To find Colmar at its most charming, wander along the calm canals that wind through La Petite Venise, an area of bright Alsatian houses with colorful shutters and window boxes that's south of the center of town. Here, amid half-timber buildings bedecked with flowers and weeping willow trees that shed their tears into the eddies of the Lauch River, you have the sense of being in a tiny village. ✉ *Colmar.*

Maison aux Arcades (*Arcades House*). Up the street from the Ancienne Douane on the Grande-Rue, the Maison aux Arcades was built in 1609 in High Renaissance style with a series of arched porches (arcades) anchored by two octagonal towers. ✉ *11 Grande-Rue, Colmar.*

Maison Pfister. Built in 1537, the Maison Pfister is the most striking of Colmar's many old dwellings. Note the decorative frescoes and medallions, carved balcony, and ground-floor arcades. ✉ *11 rue Mercière, Colmar.*

NEED A BREAK?

Au Croissant Doré. On the same street as Musée Bartholdi, this quaint, pink-fronted tearoom serves delicious pastries, cakes, and quiches. The zinc-topped counter, mismatched lamp shades, and a collection of ancient

coffeepots lend it a cozy, authentic feel. ✉ ***28 rue des Marchands, Colmar*** ☎ ***03–89–23–70–81*** ⏲ ***Closed Mon.***

Musée Bartholdi. The Bartholdi Museum is the birthplace of Frédéric-Auguste Bartholdi (1834–1904), the sculptor who designed the Statue of Liberty. Exhibits of his work claim the ground floor; a reconstruction of the artist's Paris apartment is upstairs; and, in adjoining rooms, the creation of Lady Liberty is explored. ✉ *30 rue des Marchands, Colmar* ☎ *03–89–41–90–60* 🎟 *€5* ⏲ *Mar.–Dec., Wed.–Mon. 10–noon and 2–6.*

Fodor's Choice ★ **Musée d'Unterlinden.** The cultural highlight of Colmar is the Musée d'Unterlinden, which is slated to reopen following an extensive multi-year renovation and construction project in late 2015. Once a Dominican convent and a hotbed of Rhenish mysticism, the building's star attraction is one of the greatest altarpieces of the 16th century, the *Retable d'Issenheim* (1512–16), by Matthias Grünewald, which is displayed in the convent's Gothic chapel. Originally painted for the convent at Issenheim, 22 km (14 miles) south of Colmar, the multipanel work is either the last gasp of medievalism or a breathtaking preview of modernism and all its neuroses. Framed with two-sided wings that unfold to reveal the Crucifixion and Incarnation, the masterpiece includes depictions of the Annunciation, the Resurrection, and scenes from the life of St. Anthony, including a Temptation involving monsters that even outdo those of Hieronymous Bosch. Replete with raw realism (note the chamber pots, boil-covered bellies, and dirty linen), Grünewald's altarpiece was believed to have miraculous healing powers over ergotism: widespread in the Middle Ages, this malady was produced by the ingestion of fungus-ridden grains and caused its victims—many of whom were being nursed at the Issenheim convent—to experience delusional, nearly hallucinogenic fantasies. Other treasures can be found around the enchanting 13th-century cloister, including arms and armor. Upstairs are fine regional furnishings and a collection of Rhine Valley paintings from the Renaissance, among them Martin Schongauer's opulent 1470 altarpiece painted for Jean d'Orlier. A new wing has three floors dedicated to modern and contemporary art (including the *Guernica* tapestry by Jacqueline de La Baume-Dürbach), as well as space for temporary exhibitions. ✉ *1 rue Unterlinden, Colmar* ☎ *03–89–20–15–50* 🌐 *www.musee-unterlinden.com* 🎟 *€8* ⏲ *May–Oct., daily 9–6; Nov.–Apr., Wed.–Mon. 9–noon and 2–5.*

WHERE TO EAT AND STAY

$ FRENCH ✕ **Au Koïfhus.** Not to be confused with the shabby little Koïfhus winstub on Rue des Marchands, this popular landmark (the name means "customhouse") serves huge portions of regional standards, plus changing specialties like coq au vin with spaetzle, and choucroute "Colmarienne" with six different meats. Appreciative tourists and canny locals contribute to the lively atmosphere. If you can cut a swath through this enthusiastic horde, choose between the big, open dining room, glowing with wood and warm fabric, and a shaded table on the broad, lovely square. 💲 *Average main: €17* ✉ *2 pl. de l'Ancienne-Douane, Colmar* ☎ *03–89–23–04–90* 🌐 *www.restaurant-koifhus-colmar.fr.*

8

$$ FRENCH **Chez Hansi.** Named after the Norman Rockwell–like illustrator whose clog-wearing folk children adorn most of the souvenirs of Alsace, this hyper-traditional beamed tavern serves excellent down-home classics such as quiche Lorraine, choucroute, and pot-au-feu. Offerings are prepared and presented with a sophisticated touch, despite the friendly waitresses' folksy dirndls; prices are surprisingly reasonable, too, given the quality of the food and the eatery's location in the Vieille Ville. *Average main: €18* *23 rue des Marchands, Colmar* *03–89–41–37–84* *Closed Wed., Thurs., and Jan.*

DESIGNATED DRINKING

During the first half of August, Colmar celebrates with its annual Foire Régionale des Vins d'Alsace, an Alsatian wine fair in the Parc des Expositions. Events include folk music, theater performances and, above all, the tasting and selling of wine.

$$$$ MODERN FRENCH **L'Atelier du Peintre.** This slick gastronomic restaurant in the historic center strikes a chord with in-the-know locals. Art-decked walls provide a fitting backdrop for the artful dishes prepared by chef-owner Loïc Lefebvre, who whips up creations like grilled scallops served with butternut squash mousse and a truffle-speckled fricassée of quince and hazelnuts, or roast partridge served with dandelion leaves—either of which can be washed down with a good selection of wines. Lefebvre's partner Caroline Cordier ensures service at the "atelier" is top-notch. *Average main: €34* *1 rue Schongauer, Colmar* *03–89–29–51–57* *www.atelier-peintre.fr* *Closed Sun. and Mon. No lunch Tues.*

$$$$ FRENCH Fodor's Choice ★ **Le Rendez-vous de Chasse.** The stellar cuisine of Julien Binz is as refined, elegant, and chic as the decor of this opulent Renaissance mansion. An extensive wine cellar perfectly accents dishes like lightly smoked pigeon with a spicy sauce or roast venison with fig-enriched polenta. Some of the region's finest dishes are prepared here with aplomb, so it's well worth the wrangle to secure a table. *Average main: €55* *7 pl. de la Gare, Colmar* *03–89–41–10–10* *www.grand-hotel-bristol.com/restaurant-gastronomique-colmar* *Reservations essential.*

$$$ B&B/INN **Le Maréchal.** Built in 1565 in the fortified walls that encircle the Vieille Ville, this romantic, riverside inn is made up of a series of Renaissance houses lavished with glossy rafters, rich brocades, four-poster beds, Jacuzzis, and other extravagant details; a vivid color scheme—scarlet, sapphire, candy pink—further enhances the Vermeer-like atmosphere (for the full experience, request the Wagner or Bach rooms). **Pros:** pretty location; good food; amiable staff. **Cons:** some rooms are small and unimpressive; parking is difficult to find. *Rooms from: €180* *4 pl. des Six-Montagnes-Noires, Colmar* *03–89–41–60–32* *www.hotel-le-marechal.com* *30 rooms* *Some meals.*

$$ HOTEL **Rapp.** In the Vieille Ville, just off the Champ de Mars, this solid, modern hotel has business-class comforts, a professional and welcoming staff, an extensive indoor pool complex, plus a good German-scale breakfast. **Pros:** good value; modern amenities; helpful staff. **Cons:** breakfast is extra; lacks historic character. *Rooms from: €111* *1–3–5 rue Weinemer, Colmar* *03–89–41–62–10* *www.rapp-hotel.com* *29 rooms, 10 suites* *No meals.*

BURGUNDY

WELCOME TO BURGUNDY

TOP REASONS TO GO

★ **Sip your way through Burgundy vineyards:** They are among the world's best, so take the time to stroll through Clos de Vougeot and really get a feel for the "terroir."

★ **Discover Dijon:** One of France's prettiest cities, with colorful banners and polished storefronts along narrow medieval streets, Dijon is perpetually being dolled up for a street fair.

★ **Relish the Romanesque:** Burgundy is home to a knee-weakening concentration of Romanesque churches, and Vézelay's Basilique has the region's greatest 12th-century sculptures.

★ **Get your viticultural and cultural fix in Beaune:** The "Capital of Caves" is famed for its wine caves and its 15th-century Flemish-style Hospices.

★ **Be inspired by Cluny, "Light of the World":** Erstwhile center of a vast Christian empire and today a ruin, the sheer volume of this Romanesque abbey still impresses.

1 Northwest Burgundy. The northern part of Burgundy came under the sway of the medieval Paris-based Capetian kings, and the mighty Gothic cathedrals they built are still much in evidence, notably St-Étienne at Sens. Thirty-two kilometers (20 miles) to the east is Troyes, its charming half-timber houses adding to the appeal of a town overlooked by most air-conditioned bus tours. Southeast lies Auxerre, beloved for its steep, crooked streets and magnificent churches; the wine village of Chablis; and two great Renaissance châteaux, Tanlay and Ancy-le-Franc. Closer to Dijon are the great Cistercian abbey at Fontenay and the noted Romanesque basilica at Vézelay, with a delightful hilltop setting.

2 Dijon. Burgundy's only real city, Dijon became the capital of the duchy of Burgundy in the 11th century, and acquired most of its important architectural and artistic treasures during the 14th and 15th centuries under four Burgundian dukes. The churches, the ducal palace, and one of the finest art museums in France are evidence of their patronage. Other treasures are culinary, including

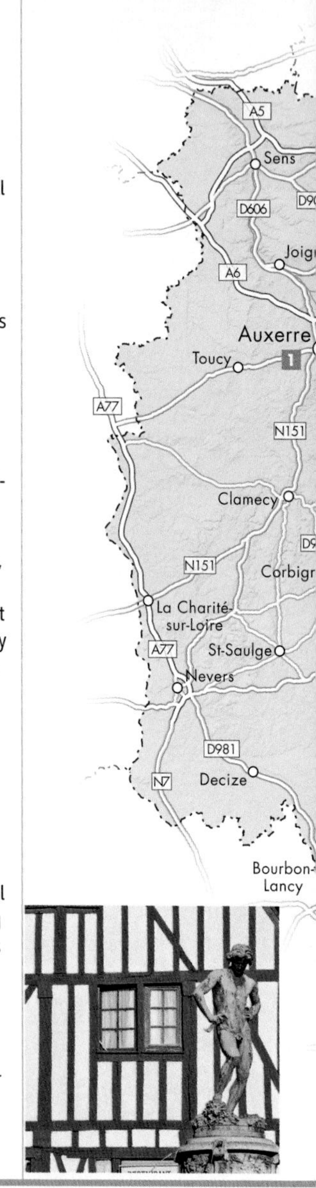

the world's best *bœuf bourguignonne.*

3 Wine Country. South of Dijon, follow the Côte d'Or, one of the most famous wine routes, as it heads down past the great wine villages of Clos de Vougeot and Nuits-St-Georges to Beaune, the heart of Burgundy's wine region. At the Hospices take in the great Rogier van der Weyden *Last Judgment* and the intimate *cour d'honneur*, the perfect postcard setting. Continuing south you'll find Autun, with renowned Roman ruins and the Romanesque landmark of Cluny, once the largest Christian church until Rome's St. Peter's was built.

GETTING ORIENTED

Burgundy, on the main route from Paris to both the Riviera and Switzerland/Italy, has always had an excellent fast train service, with Dijon serving as the region's Grand Central Station. This lively city makes the best hub, enabling travelers to discover Burgundy's many spokes, perhaps with the help of local bus stations (which often conveniently hook up with train stations).

EATING AND DRINKING WELL IN BURGUNDY

Bœuf bourguignonne is the ne plus ultra of Burgundian cuisine *(above)*; wake up those taste buds with a Kir (*right, top*); escargots are regional delights (*right, bottom*).

In a land where glorious wines define both lifestyle and cuisine, you'll find savory, soul-warming dishes, from garlicky escargots to coq au vin, both of which pair beautifully with the local wines.

While Burgundy's glittering wine trade imparts a sophisticated image to the region, Burgundy itself is basically prosperous farm country. Traditional cuisine here reflects the area's farm-centric soul, with lots of slow-cooked, wine-laced dishes. Distinctive farm-produced cheeses, such as the magnificent, odiferous Époisses, and the mild Cîteaux, made by Trappist monks, cap meals with rustic flourish. During a day of wine tasting in the Côte d'Or, dine at a traditional bistro to savor the *jambon persillé*, chunks of ham enrobed in a parsleyed aspic jelly, or a rich bœuf bourguignonne. In summer, be sure to spend a morning at one of the region's bountiful weekend markets—maybe Saulieu on Saturday. Afterward, enjoy a Charolais steak *à la moutarde* at a local café and raise a glass to the good life.

SOME LIKE IT HOT

Visit the 18th-century Maille mustard emporium at 32 rue de la Liberté to savor Dijon's world-famous mustards. Produced from stone-ground dried black or brown seeds macerated in *verjus* (the juice of unripe white grapes), these mustards accompany many dishes and heat up *lapin à la moutarde,* rabbit in mustard sauce. There is coarse-grained *à l'ancienne* or the classic, creamy, much hotter variety.

ESCARGOTS

Burgundy's plump snails, which grow wild in the vineyards, star on menus throughout the region. The signature preparation is *à la Bourguignonne*—simmered in white wine, stuffed with a garlicky parsley-shallot butter, and baked until bubbling. The delicacy is served in portions of six or eight on ceramic escargot dishes called *escargotières,* accompanied by tongs and a little fork.

Those immune to the true snail's charms may succumb to the luscious imposters made of solid chocolate and available at local candy shops and pâtisseries.

ÉPOISSES CHEESE

The greatest of Burgundian cheeses, the rich, earthy, cow's-milk Époisses is not for the faint of heart.

This assertive—yes, even odorous—cheese with the russet-hue rind develops its character from a daily scrubbing with marc-de-Bourgogne brandy as it ripens, a process that inhibits mold but encourages the growth of a particular bacteria necessary for the development of its creamy interior and distinctive flavor.

Go to the modest village of Époisses and buy your cheese from top producer Robert Berthaut. Caveat: transport in a tightly sealed container.

BŒUF À LA BOURGUIGNONNE

Burgundy is the birthplace of this beloved beef stew, aka bœuf bourguignonne, and no place on Earth makes it better.

A bottle or two of hearty red wine cooked down in the sauce is one secret to its success; the other is the region's prime Charolais beef.

The beef is braised with wine, onions, bacon, and mushrooms, turning tender as the sauce reduces and intensifies.

Other wine-soaked specialties here include coq au vin and *œufs en meurette*—eggs poached in red wine.

KIR

This rosy and refreshing aperitif, combining an inexpensive white wine called *aligoté* with a dose of crème de cassis (black-currant liqueur), was dubbed a "Kir" during World War II when the Resistance hero and mayor of Dijon, Canon Félix Kir, began promoting the drink to boost local sales of cassis liqueur.

Traditionally made, the Kir has four to five parts dry white wine to one part crème de cassis. In the Kir's aristocratic cousin, the Kir Royale, Champagne replaces the wine.

Updated By
Lyn Parry

Producing a rarefied concentration of what many consider the world's greatest wines and harboring a sigh-worthy collection of magnificent Romanesque abbeys, Burgundy hardly needs to be beautiful—but it is. Its green-hedge-rowed countryside, medieval villages, and stellar vineyards deserve to be rolled on the palate and savored. Like glasses filled with Clos de Vougeot, the sights here—from the stately city of Dijon to the medieval sanctuaries of Sens, Auxerre, Vézelay, and Cluny—invite us to tarry and partake of their mellow splendor.

Although you may often fall under the influence of extraordinary wine during a sojourn in Burgundy—called *Bourgogne* by the French—the beauty surrounding you is no boozy illusion. Passed over by revolutions, left unscarred by world wars, and relatively inaccessible thanks to circuitous country roads, the region still reflects the lovely pastoral prosperity it enjoyed under the Capetian kings. Those were the glory days, when self-sufficient Burgundy held its own against the creeping spread of France and the mighty Holy Roman Empire. This grand period was characterized by the expanding role of the dukes of Bourgogne. Consider these Capetians, history-book celebrities all: there was Philippe le Hardi (the Bold), with his power-brokered marriage to Marguerite of Flanders. There was Jean sans Peur (the Fearless), who murdered Louis d'Orléans in a cloak-and-dagger affair in 1407 and was in turn murdered, in 1419. And then there was Philippe le Bon (the Good), who threw in with the English against Joan of Arc.

Yet the Capetians couldn't hold a candle to the great Abbaye de Cluny: founded in 910, it grew to such overweening ecclesiastical power that it dominated the European Church on a papal scale for some four centuries. It was Urban II himself who dubbed it "*la Lumière du Monde*" ("the Light of the World"). But the stark geometry of Burgundy's Cistercian abbeys, such as Clairvaux and Cîteaux, stands in silent rebuke to Cluny's excess. The basilicas at Autun and Vézelay remain today in all their noble simplicity, yet manifest some of the finest Romanesque sculpture ever created; the tympanum at Autun rejects all time frames in its visionary daring.

It's almost unfair to the rest of France that all this history, all this art, all this natural beauty comes with delicious refreshments. As if to live up to the extraordinary quality of its Chablis, its Chassagne-Montrachet, its Nuits-St-Georges, its Gevrey-Chambertin, Burgundy flaunts some of the best plain food in the world. Once you taste a licensed and diploma'd *poulet de Bresse* (Bresse chicken) embellished by the poetry of one perfect glass of Burgundian Pinot Noir, you won't be surprised to see that food and drink entries will take up as much space in your travel diary as the sights you see.

PLANNER

WHEN TO GO

Whenever it's gray and cloudy in Paris, chances are the sun is shining in Burgundy. Situated in the heart of France, Burgundy has warm, dry summers. May here is especially lovely, as are September and October, when the sun is still warm on the shimmering golden trees, and the grapes, now ready for harvesting, scent the air with anticipation. This is when the vines are colorful and the *caves* (cellars) are open for business. Many festivals also take place around this time. The climate in early spring and late fall isn't quite as idyllic, with a mixture of sun and scattered showers. The winter months vary from year to year, and although snow is not common, freezing temperatures mean the bare vines and trees are covered with a soft white hue. Layers of clothing are always advisable, so you're ready for cooler mornings and hotter afternoons. Waterproof outer layers are wise on longer day trips if the weather forecast is changeable.

PLANNING YOUR TIME

France's prime preoccupations with food and wine are nowhere better celebrated than in Burgundy. Though it might sound glib, the best way to experience the region is to stay for as long as possible because there is so much to see and do here. If you want to go bike riding, the obvious place to set up is Beaune. If, on the other hand, you're an amateur medieval art historian or are interested in the lesser-known wines of Irancy, Chitry, and Tonnerre, base yourself at Auxerre or Vézelay in northern Burgundy. This will allow you to focus on these pursuits while also visiting vineyards, the cathedral of Sens, and (on a northward detour) the elegant, delightful town of Troyes. If you prefer the conveniences of modern cities but also want a taste of medieval Burgundy, then Dijon offers you the best of both worlds. Burgundy's capital has all the charm of another era and all the functionality of a major metropolis. It's the gateway to the Côte d'Or, as well as the perfect place to set off for exploring the back roads of Burgundy.

DID YOU KNOW?

Burgundy at its best is during harvest time; many head to such hallowed landmarks as the Château du Clos de Vougeot during mid-September so they can witness the famous *vendages* (grape harvests).

GETTING HERE AND AROUND

Burgundy, whose northern perimeter begins 75 km (50 miles) from Paris, is one of the largest regions in France. It's sliced in half by the north–south A6, so it's generally quicker to move in this direction than from west to east or vice versa. But a vast network of secondary roads makes travel from city to city or even village to village both practical and picturesque.

BUS TRAVEL

Local bus services are extensive; where the biggest private companies, Les Rapides de Bourgogne and TRANSCO, do not venture, the national SNCF network often does. One top choice is TRANSCO's No. 44 bus through the Côte d'Or wine region, which links Dijon to Beaune (1 hr) via Vougeot (40 mins) and Nuits-St-Georges (47 mins), with a €1.50 fare per leg. Popular Les Rapides de Bourgogne bus routes connect Auxerre to Chablis (45 mins) and Sens (2 hrs), with all trips priced at €2.50. Inquire at the local tourist office for timetables and ask your hotel concierge for further recommendations.

Bus Information Les Rapides de Bourgogne. ☎ *03–86–94–95–00* 🌐 *www.rapides-de-bourgogne-auxerre.fr.* **TRANSCO.** ☎ *03–80–42–11–00* 🌐 *www.mobigo-bourgogne.com.*

CAR TRAVEL

Although bus lines do service smaller towns, traveling through Burgundy by car allows you to explore its meandering country roads at leisure. A6 is the main route through the region; it heads southeast from Paris through Burgundy, past Sens, Auxerre, Chablis, Saulieu, and Beaune, continuing on to Lyon and the south. A38 links A6 to Dijon, 290 km (180 miles) from Paris; the trip takes around three hours. A31 heads down from Dijon to Beaune, a distance of 45 km (27 miles). D974 is a slower, more atmospheric option; but if it's scenery you want, D122 is the Route des Grands Crus, which reads like a wine list as it meanders through every wine village. The uncluttered A5 links Paris to Troyes, where the A31 segues south to Dijon.

TRAIN TRAVEL

Perhaps the most efficient way of arriving on Burgundy's doorstep is by rail. The TGV travels to Dijon from Paris's Gare de Lyon up to 17 times a day (1 hr, 30 mins); there's also daily TGV service direct from Paris's Charles De Gaulle Airport to Dijon (1 hr, 45 mins). Beaune is well served by trains arriving from Dijon, Lyon, and Paris; and Sens is on a main-line route from the capital (60–90 mins). The region has two local train routes as well: one linking destinations such as Sens, Dijon, Beaune, and Chalon, and the other connecting Auxerre and Autun. If you want to get to smaller towns or to vineyards, take a bus or car.

Train Information SNCF. ☎ *3635 €0.34 per min* 🌐 *www.voyages-sncf.com.* **TGV.** ☎ *3635 €0.34 per min* 🌐 *www.tgv.com.*

RESTAURANTS

For many French people, mention of Burgundy's capital, Dijon, conjures up images of round, rosy, merry men enjoying large suppers of *bœuf à la bourguignonne* and red wine. And admittedly, chances are that in any decent restaurant you can find at least one Dijonnais true to the stereotype.

Dijon ranks with Lyon as a gastronomic capital of France, and Burgundy's hearty traditions help explain why. It all began in the early 15th century when Jean, Duc de Berry, arrived here, built a string of castles, and proceeded to make food, wine, and art top priorities for his courtiers. Today, Parisian gourmands consider a three-hour drive a small price to pay for the cuisine of Burgundy's best restaurants, such as L'Espérance in Vézelay, Le Pré aux Clercs and Stéphane Derbord in Dijon, and Relais Bernard Loiseau in Saulieu.

Dijon is not quite the wine–mustard capital of the world it used to be, but the happy fact remains that mustard finds its way into many regional specialties, including the sauce that usually accompanies *andouillette,* a fabled sausage made with pork chitterlings (intestine). Other sausages—notably the *rosette du Morvan* and others served with a potato puree—are great favorites. Game, freshwater trout, coq au vin, *poulet au Meursault* (chicken in white wine sauce), snails, and, of course, bœuf à la bourguignonne (incidentally, this dish is only called bœuf bourguignonne when you are *not* in Burgundy) also number among the region's specialties.

The queen of chickens is the poulet de Bresse, which hails from east of the Côte d'Or and can be as pricey as a bottle of fine wine. Ham is a big item, especially around Easter, when garlicky jambon persillé—ham boiled with pig's trotters and served cold in jellied white wine and parsley—often tops the menu. Also look for *saupiquet des Amognes*—a Morvan delight of hot braised ham served with a spicy cream sauce. As for desserts, *pain d'épices* (gingerbread) is the dessert staple of the region. And, like every other part of France, Burgundy has its own cheeses. The Abbaye de Cîteaux, birthplace of Cistercian monasticism, has produced its mild cheese for centuries. Chaource and hearty Époisses also melt in your mouth—as do Bleu de Bresse and Meursault.

HOTELS

The vast range of lodging here includes everything from simple *gîtes d'étape* (bed-and-breakfasts) to four-star châteaux. But Burgundy is often overrun with tourists, especially in summer, so finding accommodations can be a problem. It's wise to make advance reservations—particularly if you're bound for wine country (from Dijon to Beaune). *Hotel reviews have been shortened. For full information, visit Fodors.com.*

WHAT IT COSTS IN EUROS

	$	$$	$$$	$$$$
Restaurants	under €18	€18–€24	€25–€32	over €32
Hotels	under €106	€106–€145	€146–€215	over €215

Restaurant prices are the average cost of a main course at dinner or, if dinner is not served, at lunch. Hotel prices are the lowest cost of a standard double room in high season.

VISITOR INFORMATION

Both the regional tourism board and the Dijon tourist office are invaluable sources of information. The numerous local tourist offices (listed under their respective towns) are also very helpful.

Comité Régional du Tourisme de Bourgogne. ✉ *5 av. Garibaldi, Dijon* ☎ *03–80–28–02–80* 🌐 *www.burgundy-tourism.com.*

Dijon Tourist Office. ✉ *11 rue des Forges, Dijon* ☎ *08–92–70–05–58 €0.34 per min* 🌐 *www.visitdijon.com.*

NORTHWEST BURGUNDY

If you're arriving from Paris by car, we suggest you grand-tour it from Sens to Autun. In northern Burgundy, the accents are thinner than around Dijon, and sunflowers cover the countryside instead of vineyards. Near Auxerre, many small, unheard-of villages boast a château or a once-famous abbey; they happily see few tourists, partly because public transportation is more than a bit spotty. Highlights of northern Burgundy include Sens's great medieval cathedral, historic Troyes, Auxerre's Flamboyant Gothic cathedral, the great Romanesque sculptures of the basilica at Vézelay, and the cathedral at Autun. Outside these major centers of northwest Burgundy, countryside villages are largely preserved in a rural landscape that seems to have remained the same for centuries. If you're driving down from Paris, we suggest you take the A6 into Burgundy (or alternatively the A5 direct to Troyes) before making a scenic clockwise loop around the Parc du Morvan, an imposing nature reserve—and the closest mountain range to Paris—dense with lush forests and laced with an extensive network of lakes and rivers.

SENS

112 km (70 miles) southeast of Paris on D606.

Pretty Sens enjoys a "four-leaf" ranking as a *ville fleurie,* or floral city—and you'll understand why when you see the Moulin à Tan (a gorgeous park with more than 35 acres of greenery), the excellently manicured square Jean-Cousin, and the municipal greenhouses. It finds full botanical expression on the second Sunday in September, when everything and everyone are festooned with flowers during the Fête de la Saint-Fiacre, a festival named after the patron saint of gardeners. But anytime during the year, the glorious **Cathédrale St-Étienne** makes a trip here worthwhile.

GETTING HERE

It makes sense for Sens to be your first stop in Burgundy, because it's only 90 minutes by car from Paris on the A6, a fast road that hugs the pretty Yonne Valley south of Fontainebleau. Training in and out of Sens is a breeze as it's on a major route with 27 direct TER trains (€19.70) leaving Paris's Gare de Bercy or Gare de Lyon station on weekdays and 12 on weekends. Regional trains also link Sens to Dijon, Beaune, and Chalon. Regional Bus service is available to Auxerre through Les Rapides de Bourgogne (€2.50).

9

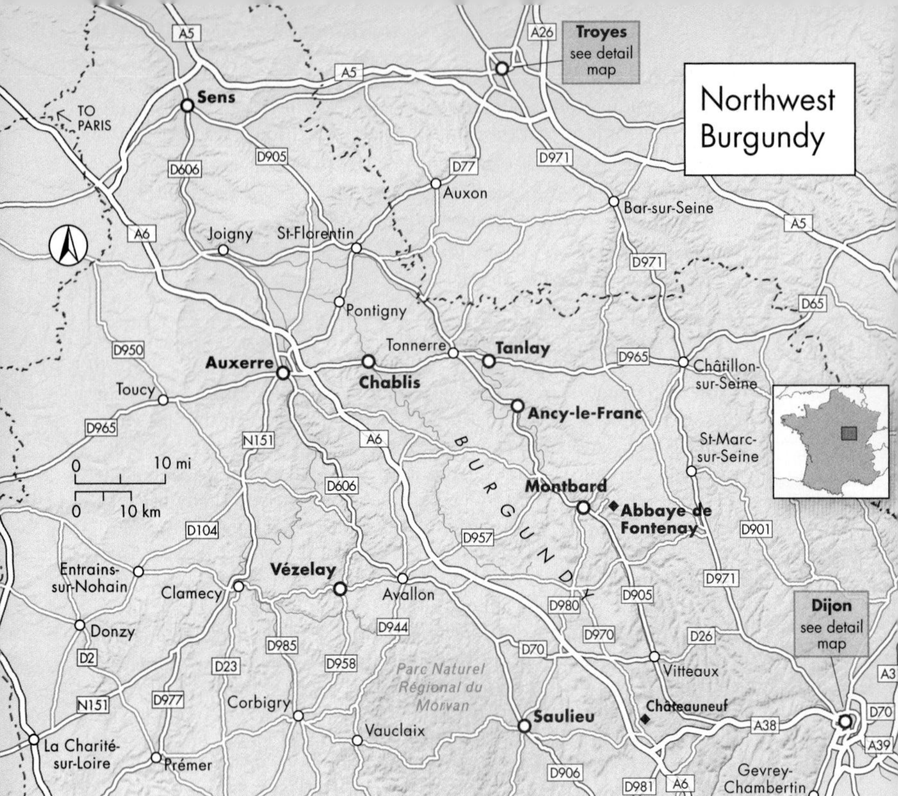

Visitor Information **Sens Tourist Office.** ☎ *03–86–65–19–49* 🌐 *www.tourisme-sens.com.*

EXPLORING

Fodor's Choice ★ **Cathédrale St-Étienne.** Historically linked more with Paris than Burgundy, Sens was the country's ecclesiastical center for centuries. Today it's still dominated by Cathédrale St-Étienne, once the French sanctuary for Thomas à Becket and a model for England's Canterbury Cathedral. You can see the 240-foot south tower from miles away. As you draw nearer, the pompous 19th-century buildings lining the town's narrow main street—notably the meringue-like Hôtel de Ville—can give you a false impression: the streets leading off it near the cathedral (notably Rue Abelard and Rue Jean-Cousin) are full of half-timber medieval houses. On Monday the cathedral square is crowded with merchants' stalls, and the beautiful late-19th-century market hall—a distant cousin of Baltard's former iron-and-glass Halles in Paris—throbs with people buying meat and produce. A smaller market is held on Friday morning.

Begun around 1140, the cathedral once had two towers; one was topped in 1532 by an elegant though somewhat incongruous Renaissance campanile that contained two monster bells; the other collapsed in the 19th century. Note the trefoil arches decorating the exterior of the remaining tower. The gallery, with statues of former archbishops of Sens, is a 19th-century addition, but the statue of St. Stephen (aka St-Étienne) between the doors of the central portal, is thought to date from late in the 12th century. The vast, harmonious interior is justly renowned for its stained-glass windows; the oldest (circa 1200) are in the north transept and include the stories of the Good Samaritan and the Prodigal Son; those in the south transept were manufactured in 1500 in Troyes and include a much-admired *Tree of Jesse*. Stained-glass windows in the north of the chancel retrace the story of Thomas à Becket: Becket fled to Sens from England to escape the wrath of Henry II before returning to his cathedral in Canterbury, where he was murdered in 1170. Below the window (which shows him embarking on his journey in a boat, and also at the moment of his death) is a medieval statue of an archbishop said to have come from the site of Becket's home in Sens. Becket's *aube* (vestment) is displayed in the annex to the Palais Synodal. ✉ *Pl. de la République, Sens* ☎ *03–86–65–06–57* ⏲ *Daily 8–6 (until 7 in summer).*

Musées des Sens. The roof of the 13th-century Palais Synodal, alongside Sens's cathedral, is notable for its yellow, green, and red diamond-tile motif—incongruously added in the mid-19th century by monument restorer Viollet-le-Duc. Six grand windows and the vaulted Synodal Hall are outstanding architectural features; the building now functions as an exhibition space. Annexed to the Palais is an ensemble of Renaissance buildings with a courtyard offering a fine view of the cathedral's Flamboyant Gothic south transept, constructed by master stonemason Martin Chambiges at the start of the 16th century (rose windows were his specialty, as you can appreciate here). Inside is a museum with archaeological finds from the Gallo-Roman period. The cathedral treasury, now on the museum's first floor, is one of the richest in France, comparable to that of Conques. It contains a collection of miters, ivories, the shrouds of St. Sivard and St. Loup, and sumptuous reliquaries. But the star of the collection is Thomas à Becket's restored brown-and-silver-edged linen robe. His chasuble, stole, and sandals are too fragile to display. ✉ *Pl. de la République, Sens* ☎ *03–86–64–46–22, 03–86–83–88–90 Museum info* 🎟 *€5* ⏲ *June–Sept., Wed.–Mon. 10–noon and 2–6; Oct.–May, Wed. and weekends 10–noon and 2–6, Mon., Thurs., and Fri. 2–6.*

9

WHERE TO EAT AND STAY

$$$ BISTRO FAMILY

✕ **Au Crieur de Vin.** Tucked away in a backstreet, this bijou bistro is one of the top-rated spots in town. Excellent in terms of both value and quality, its menus include modern, market-driven dishes with a splash of creativity. Choices like pheasant *à la plancha*or the fricassée of mushrooms and chestnuts in a creamy garlic sauce topped with a poached egg attest to the chef's flair. Au Crieur de Vin is always packed, so be sure to book ahead. 💲 *Average main: €29* ✉ *1 rue d'Alsace Lorraine, Sens* ☎ *03–86–65–92–80* 🌐 *www.restaurant-aucrieurdevin.fr* ⏲ *Closed Sun. and Mon. No lunch Tues.* ✍ *Reservations essential.*

$$$ MODERN FRENCH

✕ **Clos des Jacobins.** At this popular restaurant in the center of town, the balance between elegant and casual finds expression in the wide choice of dishes on offer. The upscale à la carte menu is replete with exceptional fish specialties, while La Tradition menu includes a *terrine de la mer tiède et sa crème de Chablis* (warm seafood terrine with a Chablis

Home to a famous cathedral, Sens also has many streets leading to atmospheric half-timber houses.

cream sauce) and *joues de boeuf à la bourguignonne* (beef cheeks cooked in a red wine sauce). *Average main: €28 ✉ 49 Grande-Rue, Sens ☎ 03–86–95–29–70 ⊕ www.restaurantlesjacobins.com ⏲ Closed Tues. and Wed. No dinner Sun.*

$ HOTEL **Paris & Poste.** At this inn, which began life as a canon's house in 1776, guest rooms are clean, spacious, and well equipped. **Pros:** unbeatable value; central location; great food; private parking. **Cons:** street-side rooms get some early-morning noise; not all rooms have a bath tub; some rooms lack space. *Rooms from: €95 ✉ 97 rue de la République, Sens ☎ 03–86–65–17–43 ⊕ www.hotel-paris-poste.com 30 rooms No meals.*

TROYES

64 km (40 miles) east of Sens, 150 km (95 miles) southeast of Paris.

The inhabitants of Troyes would be dismayed if you mistook them for Burgundians. After all, Troyes is the historic capital of the counts of Champagne, but we retain it here—closer to Burgundy's treasures—because it's some 80 km (50 miles) south of the heart of Champagne province. Troyes was also the home of the late-12th-century writer Chrétien (or Chrestien) de Troyes who, in seeking to please his patrons, Count Henry the Liberal and Marie de Champagne, penned the first Arthurian legends. Few, if any, other French town centers contain so much to see. In the Vauluisant and St-Jean districts, a web of enchanting pedestrian streets with timber-frame houses, magnificent churches, fine museums, and a wide choice of restaurants makes the Old Town—Vieux Troyes—especially appealing.

Keep an eye out for the delightful architectural accents that make Troyes unique: *essentes*, geometric chestnut tiles that keep out humidity and are fire resistant; and sculpted *poteaux* (in Troyes they are called *montjoies*), carvings at the joint of corner structural beams. There's a lovely one of Adam and Eve next door to the Comtes de Champagne hotel. GPS-equipped audioguides (€6), available from the Troyes tourist office, will help history buffs make the most of a visit here. There's enough to keep shoppers content, too. Along with its neighbors Provins and Bar-sur-Aube, Troyes was one of Champagne's major fair towns in the Middle Ages. The wool trade gave way to cotton in the 18th century when Troyes became the heartland of hosiery; today Troyes draws millions of shoppers from all over Europe, who come to scour its outlet clothing stores for bargains.

GETTING HERE

With the first train at 6:42 am, and then around one every hour until 8:42 pm, you can get to Troyes in about 90 minutes from Paris Gare de l'Est (€15–€20.50). Sens to Troyes is a little harder; there are seven daily trains, but they involve changing in Paris, Laroche Migennes, or Saint Florentin Vergigny. The journey takes just over three hours and costs €19.60–€31.60. Within Troyes, public transit is provided by TCAT buses (🌐 *wwww.tcat.fr*); single tickets cost €1.35.

Visitor Information Troyes Tourist Office. ☎ *08–92–22–46–09 €0.34 per min* 🌐 *www.tourisme-troyes.com.*

EXPLORING

TOP ATTRACTIONS

Basilique St-Urbain. Started in 1261 by Pope Urban IV (a native son) and eventually consecrated in 1389, St-Urbain is one of the most remarkable churches in France—a perfect culmination of the Gothic quest to replace stone walls with stained glass. Its narrow porch frames a 13th-century *Last Judgment* tympanum, whose highly worked elements include a frieze of the dead rising out of their coffins (witness the grimacing skeleton). Look for a carved crayfish on one of the statue's niches (a testament to the local river culture). Inside, a chapel on the south side houses the *Vièrge au Raisin* (*Virgin with Grapes*), clutching Jesus with one hand and a bunch of Champagne grapes in the other. ✉ *Pl. Vernie, Troyes* ☎ *03–25–73–37–13* ⏲ *May–Sept., Mon.–Sat. 10–12:30 and 2–7, Sun. 2–7; Oct.–Apr., Mon.–Sat. 9:30–12:30 and 2–5, Sun. 2–5.*

Cathédrale St-Pierre St-Paul. Dominating the heart of Troyes, this remarkable cathedral is a prime example of the Flamboyant Gothic style—regarded as the last gasp of the Middle Ages. Note the incomplete single-tower west front, the small Renaissance campaniles on top of the tower, and the artistry of Martin Chambiges, who worked on Troyes's facade (with its characteristic large rose window and flamboyant flames) around the same time as he did the transept of Sens. At night the floodlighted features burst into dramatic relief. The cathedral's vast five-aisle interior, refreshingly light thanks to large windows and the near-whiteness of the local stone, dates mainly from the 13th century. It has fine examples of 13th-century stained glass in the choir, such as the *Tree of Jesse* (a popular regional theme), and richly colored 16th-century

Basilique St-Urbain **6**
Cathédrale St-Pierre—St-Paul **4**
Hôtel-Dieu **1**
Hôtel de Vauluisant **9**
Hôtel de Ville ... **7**
Hôtel du Petit Louvre **2**
Musée d'Art Moderne **3**
Musée St-Loup .. **5**
Ste-Madeleine .. **8**

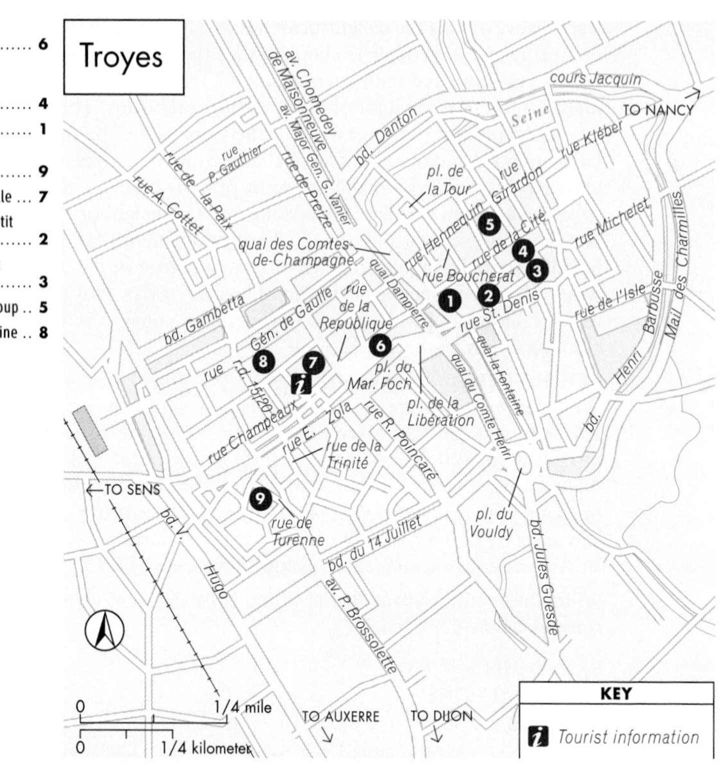

glass in the nave and west front rose window. ✉ *Pl. St-Pierre, Troyes* ☎ *03–25–76–98–18* ⏲ *May–Sept., Mon.–Sat. 10–1 and 2–7, Sun. 2–7; Oct.–Apr., Mon.–Sat. 9–noon and 1–5, Sun. 2–5.*

Musée d'Art Moderne (*Modern Art Museum*). Housed in the 16th- to 17th-century bishop's palace, this museum's magnificent interior features a wreath-and-cornucopia carved oak fireplace, ceilings with carved wood beams, and a Renaissance staircase. The jewel of the museum is the Lévy Collection (one of the finest provincial collections in France), which includes Art Deco glassware, tribal art, and an important group of Fauve paintings by André Derain and others. ✉ *Palais Épiscopal, Pl. St-Pierre, Troyes* ☎ *03–25–76–26–80* 🌐 *www.musees-troyes.com* 🎟 *Mar.–Oct. €5; Nov.–Feb. free* ⏲ *May–Sept., Tues.–Fri. 10–1 and 2–7, weekends 11–7; Oct.–Apr., Tues.–Fri. 10–noon and 2–5, weekends 11–6.*

Musée St-Loup. The former 18th-century abbey of St-Loup, to the side of the cathedral, now houses a superlative collection of paintings from the 15th to the 19th century—including works by Peter Paul Rubens, Anthony Van Dyck, Antoine Watteau, François Boucher, and Jacques-Louis David. Other highlights include an impressive assortment of birds and meteorites; medieval statuary; and local archaeological finds, most notably gold-mounted 5th-century jewelry and a bronze Gallo-Roman statue of Apollo. ✉ *1 rue Chrestien-de-Troyes, Troyes* ☎ *03–25–76–21–68* 🌐 *www.musees-troyes.com* 🎟 *Apr.–Oct. €5; Nov.–Mar. free* 🕓 *May–Sept., Mon. and Wed.–Fri. 10–1 and 2–7, weekends 11–7; Oct.–Apr., Mon. and Wed.–Fri. 10–noon and 2–5, weekends 11–6.*

A TOWN MADE FOR WALKERS

The tourist literature is quick to tell you that Troyes's Old Town resembles a Champagne cork: the Seine flows around what would be the top half and the train station is at the bottom. Though large for a cork, Troyes is small for a town. Everything is accessible by foot, but you can hop a TCAT bus (🌐 *www.tcat.fr*) to get around if you wish.

Ste-Madeleine. The oldest church in Troyes, Ste-Madeleine is best known for its elaborate triple-arch stone rood screen separating the nave and the choir. Only six other such screens still remain in France—most were dismantled during the French Revolution. This filigreed Flamboyant Gothic beauty was carved with panache by Jean Gailde between 1508 and 1517. The superbly tranquil Garden of the Innocents, established on the ancient "children's graveyard," symbolizes medieval spirituality. ✉ *Rue de la Madeleine, Troyes* ☎ *03–25–73–82–90* 🕓 *May–Sept., Mon.–Sat. 10–12:30 and 2–7, Sun. 2–7; Oct.–Apr., Mon.–Sat. 9:30–12:30 and 2–5, Sun. 2–5.*

WORTH NOTING

FAMILY **Hôtel de Vauluisant.** This charmingly turreted 16th- to 17th-century mansion contains two museums: the **Musée d'Art Champenois** (Regional Art Museum) and the **Musée de la Bonneterie** (Textile-Hosiery Museum). The former traces the development of Troyes and southern Champagne, with a particularly rich selection of religious sculptures and paintings of the late-Gothic era; the latter outlines the history and manufacturing procedures of the town's 18th- to 19th-century textile industry. ✉ *4 rue de Vauluisant, Troyes* ☎ *03–25–43–43–20* 🌐 *www.musees-troyes.com* 🎟 *Apr.–Oct. joint ticket to both museums €3; Nov.–Mar. free* 🕓 *May–Sept., Wed. 2–7, Thurs. and Fri. 10–1 and 2–7, weekends 11–1 and 2–7; Oct.–Apr., Wed. and Thurs. 2–5, Fri.–Sun. 10–noon and 2–5.*

Hôtel de Ville (*Town Hall*). Place du Maréchal-Foch, the main square of Troyes, is flanked by cafés, shops, and this delightful town hall. The central facade has black marble columns and a niche with a helmeted Minerva, which replaced a statue of Louis XIV that was destroyed during the French Revolution. In summer the square is filled with people from morning to night. ✉ *Pl. du Maréchal-Foch, Troyes.*

Hôtel-Dieu (*Hospital*). Across the Bassin de la Préfecture, an arm of the Seine, is this historic hospital, fronted by superb 18th-century wrought-iron gates topped with the blue-and-gold fleurs-de-lis emblems of the French monarchy. Around the corner is the entrance to the **Apothicairerie de l'Hôtel-Dieu,** a former medical laboratory and the only part of the Hôtel-Dieu open to visitors. Inside, time has been suspended: floral-painted boxes and ceramic jars containing medicinal plants line the antique shelves. ✉ *Quai des Comtes de Champagne, Troyes* ☎ *03–25–80–98–97* 🌐 *www.musees-troyes.com* 🎟 *Apr.–Oct. €3; Nov.–Mar.*

free ⏲ *May–Sept., Wed. 2–7, Thurs. and Fri. 10–1 and 2–7, weekends 11–1 and 2–7; Oct.–Apr., Wed. 2–5, Thurs.–Sun. 10–noon and 2–5.*

Hôtel du Petit Louvre. This former coaching inn is a handsome example of 16th-century architecture. ✉ *Pl. du Préau, Troyes.*

WHERE TO EAT AND STAY

$ FRENCH FAMILY ✕ **Aux Crieurs de Vin.** This popular bistro-cum-wineshop is often packed, and with good reason—in terms of both value and quality, Aux Crieurs de Vin really delivers. Modern dishes like a carpaccio of Sicilian octopus share the chalkboard menu with classic bistro choices, including homemade terrine and andouillette. The wine selection is excellent; natural wines and champagnes are a specialty, and you can taste them by the glass or buy a bottle from the wineshop to uncork with your meal. The lively atmosphere and spare decor (picture exposed brick walls and mismatched tables) make this more of a lunchtime spot than a romantic dinner venue. [$] *Average main: €16* ✉ *4 pl. Jean Jaurès, Troyes* ☎ *03–25–40–01–01* ⏲ *Closed Sun. and Mon.*

$ HOTEL **Comtes de Champagne.** In Vieux Troyes's topsy-turvy 16th-century former mint, this bargain find has a quaint inner courtyard and pleasant, refurbished rooms with iron bedsteads. **Pros:** affordable, old-fashioned charm; central location; suites have kitchenettes. **Cons:** bathrooms are a bit plain and small; no air-conditioning. [$] *Rooms from: €79* ✉ *54–56 rue de la Monnaie, Troyes* ☎ *03–25–73–11–70* 🌐 *www.comtesdechampagne.com* *44 rooms, 6 suites* 🍽 *No meals.*

$$$ HOTEL Fodor's Choice ★ **Le Champ des Oiseaux.** Tin chandeliers, Nantes silk and calico hangings, antique scrollwork panels, and other traditional luxe touches make lodgings in this trio of vine-clad, pink-and-yellow 15th- and 16th-century houses especially alluring. **Pros:** quiet, comfortable rooms; genial service; kid friendly. **Cons:** parking costs extra. [$] *Rooms from: €199* ✉ *20 rue Linard-Gonthier, Troyes* ☎ *03–25–80–58–50* 🌐 *www.champdesoiseaux.com* *9 rooms, 3 suites* 🍽 *No meals.*

$ HOTEL **Relais St-Jean.** This half-timber hotel, in the pedestrian zone near the church of St-Jean, has rooms that are refreshingly done in a sleek modern style; their white-and-pastel-color walls contrast tastefully with the sophisticated, multihued furnishings. **Pros:** good-size rooms; friendly service; interesting bar. **Cons:** rooms sometimes feel overheated and some get street noise. [$] *Rooms from: €98* ✉ *51 rue Paillot-de-Montabert, Troyes* ☎ *03–25–73–89–90* 🌐 *www.hotel-relais-saint-jean.com* *23 rooms* 🍽 *No meals.*

AUXERRE

58 km (36 miles) southeast of Sens.

Fodor's Choice ★ Auxerre is an evocative, architecturally interesting town with a trio of imposing churches perched above the Yonne River and an ample supply of antique houses. Yet it's an underappreciated place, perhaps because of its location, midway between Paris and Dijon. Fanning out from Auxerre's main square, Place des Cordeliers (just up from the cathedral), are a number of steep, crooked streets lined with half-timber and stone buildings. The best way to see them is to start from the riverside on Quai de la République, where you can find the tourist office (and pick up a handy local map); then continue along Quai de la Marine. The medieval arcaded gallery of the Ancien Evêché (Old Bishop's Palace), now an administrative building, is just visible on the hillside beside the tourist office. At 9 rue de la Marine (which leads off one of several riverside squares) are the two oldest houses in Auxerre, dating from the end of the 14th century. Continue up the hill to Rue de l'Yonne, which leads into Rue Cochois. Here, at No. 23, is the higgledy-piggledy home and shop of a maître verrier (lead-glass maker). Closer to the center of town, the most beautiful of Auxerre's many poteaux (the carved tops of wooden corner posts) can be seen at 8 rue Joubert. The building dates from the late 15th century, and its Gothic tracery windows, acorns, and oak leaves are an open-air masterpiece.

A MAP IS A MUST

Get a map from the tourist office because Auxerre's layout is confusing. The main part of the Old Town is west of the Yonne River and ripples out from Place des Cordeliers.

GETTING HERE

Seven direct trains arrive daily from Paris's Gare de Bercy (€28.30). Thirteen daily trains link Auxerre to Montbard (€18.20), mostly via Laroche-Migennes, with Dijon (€28.60) being at the end of the line. Train service to Beaune, via Laroche Migennes, is also available (€32.90). Les Rapides de Bourgogne buses link Auxerre to Sens (2 hrs, €2.50), Chablis (45 mins, €2.50), and other destinations. If you're driving, Auxerre is served by several major arteries, including the A6 (Autoroute of the Sun) and the D606/D906.

Visitor Information **Auxerre Tourist Office.** ☎ *03–86–51–03–26* 🌐 *www.ot-auxerre.fr.*

EXPLORING

Abbaye de St-Germain. North of Place des Cordeliers is the former Abbaye de St-Germain, which stands parallel to the cathedral some 300 yards away. The church's earliest aboveground section is the 12th-century Romanesque bell tower, but the extensive underground crypt was inaugurated by Charles the Bald in 859 and contains its original Carolingian frescoes and Ionic capitals. It's the only monument of its kind in Europe—a layout retaining the plan of the long-gone church built above it—and was a place of pilgrimage until Huguenots burned the remains of its namesake, a Gallo-Roman governor and bishop of Auxerre, in the 16th century. ✉ *Pl. St-Germain, Auxerre* ☎ *03–86–18–02–90* 🎫 *Crypt €6.70* ⏲ *May–Sept., Wed.–Mon. 9:45–6:45; Oct.–Apr., Wed.–Mon. 10–noon and 2–5.*

Cathédrale St-Étienne. The town's dominant feature is the ascending line of three magnificent churches—St-Pierre, St-Étienne, and St-Germain—with Cathédrale St-Étienne, in the middle, rising majestically above the squat houses around it. The 13th-century choir, the oldest part of the edifice, contains its original stained glass, dominated by brilliant reds and blues. Beneath the choir, the frescoed 11th-century Romanesque crypt keeps company with the treasury, which has a panoply of medieval enamels, manuscripts, and miniatures, plus a rare depiction

9

Presided over by Cathédrale St-Etienne, Auxerre is a medieval beauty filled with historic churches.

of Christ on horseback. A 75-minute son-et-lumière show focusing on Roman Gaul is presented every evening from June to September. ✉ *Pl. St-Étienne, Auxerre* ☎ *03–86–52–31–68* 🌐 *www.cathedrale-auxerre.com* 🎟 *Crypt €3, treasury €1.90* 🕑 *Easter–Nov., Mon.–Sat. 7:30–6, Sun. 2–5; Nov.–Easter, Mon.–Sat. 10–5.*

WHERE TO EAT AND STAY

$$$$ MODERN FRENCH

✕ **Le Jardin Gourmand.** This restaurant in a former manor house has a pretty garden (*jardin*) where you can dine on summer evenings, as well as an organic vegetable garden producing fresh herbs, gorgeous greens, and other foods that wind up on the table. The interior, accented by subtle-yellow panels and polished wood floors, is congenial and elegant, while the menu (which changes eight times a year) shows both flair and invention, drawing inspiration from the finest seasonal ingredients and an excellent cellar. The staff is discreet and friendly. $ *Average main: €40* ✉ *56 bd. Vauban, Auxerre* ☎ *03–86–51–53–52* 🌐 *www.lejardingourmand.com* 🕑 *Closed Mon. and Tues, 1 wk in Mar., last 2 wks of June, 1 wk in Sept., last 2 wks of Nov. No dinner Sun.*

$ B&B/INN

Château de Ribourdin. Retired farmer Claude Brodard began building his *chambres d'hôte* (bed-and-breakfast) in an old stable, bucolically enshrined just south of Auxerre, almost 20 years ago, and the cozy, comfortable, reasonably priced rooms overlook his fields. **Pros:** tasteful rooms; beautiful location; great complimentary breakfast; swimming pool. **Cons:** can feel a little isolated; no credit cards. $ *Rooms from: €90* ✉ *8 rte. de Ribourdin, 8 km (5 miles) southwest of Auxerre on D1, Chevannes* ☎ *03–86–41–23–16* 🌐 *www.chateauderibourdin.com* 💳 *No credit cards* 🛏 *5 rooms* 🍽 *Breakfast.*

$ HOTEL **Normandie.** Erected in the 19th-century, this rather grand, vine-covered mansion is close to the center of Auxerre, just a short walk from the cathedral. **Pros:** tidy rooms with nice bathrooms; helpful staff; on-site billiards room, gym, and garage. **Cons:** not in town center. *Rooms from: €88 ✉ 41 bd. Vauban, Auxerre ☎ 03–86–52–57–80 🌐 www.hotelnormandie.fr 47 rooms No meals.*

CHABLIS

16 km (10 miles) east of Auxerre.

The pretty village of Chablis is poised amid the hillside vineyards that produce its famous white wine on the banks of the River Serein and protected, perhaps from an ill wind, by the massive, round, turreted towers of the Porte Noël gateway. Although in America Chablis has become a generic name for cheap white wine, it's not so in France: here it's a bone-dry, slightly acacia-tasting wine of tremendous character, with the premier cru and grand cru wines standing head to head with the best French whites. Prices in the local shops tend to be inflated, so your best bet is to buy directly from a vineyard; keep in mind that most are closed Sunday. The town's tourist office will provide information on nearby cellars where you can take tours, enjoy tastings, and learn all you need to know about the region's illustrious wine tradition.

GETTING HERE

Les Rapides de Bourgogne buses from Auxerre run Monday through Saturday at 8:42 am and 1:44 pm (45 mins, both on request only—call ☎ *08–00–30–33–09*), and again at 4:35 pm (60 mins); tickets cost €2.50.

Visitor Information Chablis Tourist Office. ☎ *03–86–42–80–80* 🌐 *www.chablis.net.*

EXPLORING

Chablis Vititours. Personalized wine-themed excursions for two to six people are offered by Chablis Vititours. Choose a full- or half-day vineyards tour followed by a cellar visit and tasting opportunity (€140 and €65 respectively), or a 90-minute outing that includes a glass of wine (€25). Transportation is by air-conditioned minibus. ✉ *Chablis* ☎ *06–11–47–82–98* 🌐 *www.chablis-vititours.fr.*

WHERE TO STAY

$ HOTEL **Hostellerie des Clos.** Rooms at this moderately priced inn are simply, yet smartly, decorated; most people, however, come for Chef Michel Vignaud's cooking, which is some of the best in the region. **Pros:** newer rooms in the main building are large and well appointed; stellar food; great location. **Cons:** older rooms are a bit small; bathrooms in lower-grade lodgings have showers only. *Rooms from: €95 ✉ 18 rue Jules-Rathier, Chablis ☎ 03–86–42–10–63 🌐 www.hostellerie-des-clos.fr 26 rooms, 10 suites No meals.*

$$ HOTEL **Hôtel du Vieux Moulin.** Understated chic meets 18th-century authenticity at this boutique-style hotel in a converted water mill. **Pros:** central location; suites have two bathrooms. **Cons:** some rooms lack tubs.

$ Rooms from: €140 ✉ 18 rue des Moulins, Chablis ☎ 03–86–42–47–30 🌐 www.larochehotel.fr 5 rooms, 2 suites 🍴 No meals.

TANLAY

26 km (16 miles) east of Chablis.

Built along the banks of the Canal de Bourgogne, Tanlay is a sleepy village that's best known for the Renaissance-style château that sits slap bang in the center of it. A stopover for cruise boats, the tree-lined banks of the canal are also a pleasant place to stroll.

GETTING HERE

Buses operated by Les Rapides de Bourgogne run daily from Auxerre to Tonnerre (49 mins, €2); in summer, a second bus will take you the rest of the way to Château de Tanlay for €2 (4 daily, Wednesday–Sunday).

EXPLORING

Fodor's Choice ★ **Château de Tanlay.** Unlike most aristocrats who heeded the royal summons to live at Versailles and fled the countryside, the Marquis and Marquise de Tanlay opted to live here among their village retainers. As a result, the Château de Tanlay, built around 1550, never fell into neglect and is a masterpiece of early French Baroque. Spectacularly adorned with rusticated obelisks, pagoda-like towers, the finest in French Classicist ornamentation, and a "grand canal," the château is centered around a typical cour d'honneur . Inside, the Hall of Caesars vestibule, framed by wrought-iron railings, leads to a wood-panel salon and dining room filled with period furniture. A graceful staircase climbs to the second floor, which has the showstopper: a gigantic gallery frescoed in Italianate trompe l'oeil. A small room in the tower above was used as a secret meeting place by Huguenot Protestants during the 1562–98 Wars of Religion; note the cupola with its fresco of scantily clad 16th-century religious personalities. ✉ *Tanlay* ☎ *03–86–75–70–61* 🌐 *www.chateaudetanlay.fr* 🎫 *€8* ⏲ *Château tours Apr.–mid–Nov., Wed.–Mon. at 10, 11:30, 2:15, 3:15, 4:15, and 5:15; gardens Apr.–mid–Nov., Wed.–Mon. 9:45–6:30.*

ANCY-LE-FRANC

14 km (9 miles) southeast of Tanlay.

It may be strange to find a textbook example of the Italian Renaissance in Ancy-le-Franc, but in mid-16th-century France the court had taken up this import as the latest rage. So, quick to follow the fashion and gain kingly favor, the Comte de Tonnerre decided to create a family seat using all the artists François I (1515–47) had summoned from Italy to his court at Fontainebleau.

GETTING HERE

Les Rapides de Bourgogne has daily service from Auxerre to Tonnerre (49 mins, €2); in summer, you can take a second bus onward to Château d'Ancy-le-Franc for €2 (4 daily, Wednesday–Sunday).

EXPLORING

Fodor's Choice ★ **Château d'Ancy-le-Franc.** Built from Sebastiano Serlio's designs, with interior blandishments by Primaticcio, the Château d'Ancy-le-Franc is an important example of Italianism, less for its plain, heavy exterior than for its sumptuous rooms and apartments, many with carved or painted walls and ceilings plus original furnishings. Niccolò dell'Abate and other court artists created the magnificent Chambre des Arts (Art Gallery) and other rooms filled with murals depicting the signs of the zodiac, the Battle of Pharsala, and the motif of Diana in Her Bath (much favored by Diane de Poitiers, sister of the Comtesse de Tonnerre). Such grandeur won the approval of no less than the Sun King, Louis XIV, who once stayed in the Salon Bleu (Blue Room). The east wing of the ground floor, which housed Diane de Poitier's apartments, has recently been restored. Highlights here include Diane's bedroom with its 16th-century murals. ✉ *18 pl. Clermont-Tonnerre, Ancy-le-Franc* ☎ *03–86–75–14–63* 🌐 *www.chateau-ancy.com* 🎫 *Château €9; château and park €13* ⏲ *Apr.–mid-Nov., tours Tues.–Sun. at 10:30, 11:30, 2, 3, 4, and 5; Oct.–mid-Nov., no tour at 5.*

MONTBARD

45 km (28 miles) southeast of Tonnerre.

Attractions in this modest town on the banks of the Brenne River include an Ursuline convent that's been converted into a Musée des Beaux-Arts and lovely Parc Buffon. The gardens of the latter were planted on the site of an ancient château by Georges-Louis Leclerc de Buffon (the Count of Buffon), an important scientist and naturalist who influenced Charles Darwin. Just outside town, the work of another man—St. Bernard—draws visitors to the 12th-century Abbaye de Fontenay.

GETTING HERE

Frequent daily TER trains run to Montbard direct from Dijon (€13.30), and TGV service from Paris's Gare de Lyon is offered four times a day (€56). Abbaye de Fontenay—in Marmagne, a mere 6 km (3 miles) away—is easily reached by car; if you don't have your own, cab fare is about €10. Rental bikes are also available through the Montbard tourist office.

Visitor Information Montbard Tourist Office. ☎ *03–80–92–53–81* 🌐 *www.ot-montbard.fr.*

EXPLORING

Fodor's Choice ★ **Abbaye de Fontenay.** The best-preserved of the Cistercian abbeys, the Abbaye de Fontenay was founded in 1118 by St. Bernard. The same Cistercian criteria applied to Fontenay as to Pontigny: no-frills architecture and an isolated site—the spot was especially remote, for it had been decreed that these monasteries could not be established anywhere near "cities, feudal manors, or villages." The monks were required to live a completely self-sufficient existence, with no contact whatsoever with the outside world. By the end of the 12th century the buildings were finished, and the abbey's community grew to some 300 monks. Under the protection of Pope Gregory IX and Hughes IV, duke of Burgundy,

9

the monastery soon controlled huge land holdings, vineyards, and timberlands. It prospered until the 16th century, when religious wars and administrative mayhem hastened its decline. Dissolved during the French Revolution, the abbey was used as a paper factory until 1906. Fortunately, the historic buildings emerged unscathed. The abbey is surrounded by extensive, immaculately tended gardens dotted with the fountains that gave it its name. The church's solemn interior is lightened by windows in the facade and by a double row of three narrow windows, representing the Trinity, in the choir. A staircase in the south transept leads to the wooden-roof dormitory (spare a thought for the bleary-eyed monks, obliged to stagger down for services in the dead of night). The chapter house, flanked by a majestic arcade, and the scriptorium, where monks worked on their manuscripts, lead off from the adjoining cloisters. ✉ *6 km (3 miles) from Montbard TGV station, Marmagne* ☎ *03–80–92–15–00* 🌐 *www.abbayedefontenay.com* 🎫 *€10* ⏲ *Apr.–mid-Nov., daily 10–6; mid-Nov.–Mar., daily 10–noon and 2–5.*

VÉZELAY

48 km (30 miles) west of Abbaye de Fontenay.

In the 11th and 12th centuries Vézelay was one of the most important places of pilgrimage in the Christian world. Today the hilltop village is picturesque and somewhat isolated. Its one main street, Rue St-Étienne, climbs steeply and stirringly to the summit and its medieval basilica, world famous for its Romanesque sculpture. In summer you have to leave your car at the bottom and walk up. Off-season you can drive up and look for parking in the square.

In addition to the artistic treasures of Basilique Ste-Madeleine, Vézelay has other Romanesque-era delights. Hiding below its narrow ruelles (small streets) are several medieval cellars that once sheltered pilgrims. Sections of several houses have arches and columns dating from the 12th and 13th centuries: don't miss the hostelry across from the tourist office and, next to it, the house where Louis VII, Eleanor of Aquitaine, and the king's religious supremo Abbé Suger stayed when they came to hear St. Bernard preach the Second Crusade in 1146.

GETTING HERE

To reach Vézelay, you can take a TER train to Sermizelles from Paris's Gare de Bercy (about 2 hrs, 45 mins; €33); the remaining 10 km (6 miles) into town is covered by a shuttle bus twice daily (€3).

Visitor Information Vézelay Tourist Office. ☎ *03–86–33–23–69* 🌐 *www.vezelaytourisme.com.*

EXPLORING

Fodor's Choice ★ **Basilique Ste-Madeleine.** In the 11th and 12th centuries the celebrated Basilique Ste-Madeleine was one of the focal points of Christendom. Pilgrims poured in to see the relics of St. Mary Magdalene (in the crypt) before setting off on the great trek to the shrine of St. James at Santiago de Compostela, in northwest Spain. Several pivotal church declarations of the Middle Ages were made from here, including St. Bernard's

Continued on page 436

GRAPE EXPECTATIONS

A BURGUNDY WINE PRIMER

From the steely brilliance of Premier Cru Chablis in the north to the refined Pouilly-Fuissés in the south, Burgundy—Bourgogne to the French—is where you can sample deep-colored reds and full-flavored whites as you amble from one fabled vineyard to another along the **Route des Grands Crus**.

An oenophile's nirvana, Burgundy is accorded almost religious reverence, and with good reason: its famous chardonnays and pinot noirs, and the "second-tier" gamays and aligotés, were perfected in the Middle Ages by the great monasteries of the region.

The specific character of a Burgundy wine is often dependent on the individual grower or négociant's style. There are hundreds of vintners and merchants in this region, many of them producing top wines from surprisingly small parcels of land.

Get to know the *appellation d'Origine Protégée*, or AOP, wine classification system. In Burgundy, it specifies vineyard, region, and quality. The most expensive, top-tiered wines are called *monopole* and *grand cru*, followed by *premier cru*, *village*, and generic *Bourgogne*. Although there are 100 different AOP wines in the area, the thicket of labels and names is navigable once you learn how to read the road signs; and the payoff is tremendous, with palate-pleasing choices for all budgets.

By Christopher Mooney

GEOGRAPHY + CLIMATE = *TERROIR*

Soil, weather conditions, grapes, and savoir-faire are the basic building blocks of all great wines, but this is particularly true in Burgundy, where grapes of the same variety, grown a few feet apart, might have different names and personalities, as well as tremendously varying prices.

CHABLIS

Chablis' famous chardonnays are produced along both banks of the Serein River. The four appellations, in ascending order of excellence, are Petit Chablis AOP, Chablis AOP, Chablis Premier Cru AOP, and Chablis Grand Cru AOP. Flinty and slightly acidic, with citrus, pineapple, and green apple flavors and aromas, they age well (except the Petit Chablis, which are best drunk young) and are typically less intense than other burgundy whites, due to their colder northern climate.

CÔTE D'OR

The 30-mile long Côte d'Or contains two of the world's most gorgeous and distinguished wine regions: **Côte de Nuits** and **Côte de Beaune.**

The northern area, the **Côte de Nuits,** is sometimes called the "Champs-Elysées of Burgundy" as it is the site of Burgundy's top-rated grand cru wines. These Burgundian pinot noirs are ruby colored with red fruit and spice flavors. They tend to be richly textured with a full body. The wines develop savory, gamey notes with age, and are perfect matches for hearty Burgundian beef and game dishes. The best wines come from the grand cru appelations of Gevrey-Chambertin, Vougeot, Vosne-Romanée, and Nuits-St-Georges.

The **Côte de Beaune**, just to the south, is known for making the world's best dry whites, made from from chardonnay. These wines are green-gold in color and aromatically complex. They typically have a buttery texture and are medium- to full-bodied. Search out wines from the appelations of Aloxe-Corton, Beaune, and Pommard, then head south for the storied Montrachets, which are the most expensive chardonnay wines in the world. Renowned reds are also made here, though are lighter and less concentrated than their counterparts from the Côte de Nuits.

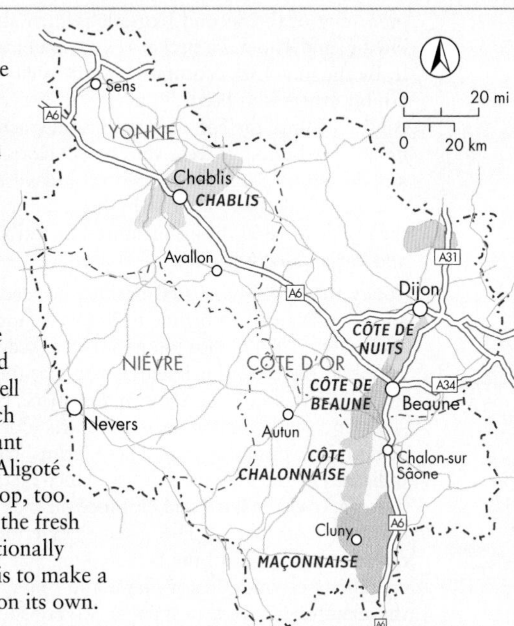

CÔTE CHALONNAISE

Farther south is the Côte Chalonnaise. Although not as famous, it produces chardonnays almost as rich as its northern neighbors. Pinot noirs with *villages* appellations Rully, Givry, and Mercurey are well-structured, with body, bouquet, and a distinction very similar to Côte de Beaune reds. Montagny and Rully whites are dry, light, well balanced, and fruity—much ends up in sparkling Crémant de Bourgogne. Bourgogne Aligoté de Bouzeron are worth a stop, too. Named after its grape, it is the fresh and lively white wine traditionally mixed with Crème de Cassis to make a Kir, but is just as delicious on its own.

CÔTE MAÇONNAISE

Next is the Côte Maçonnaise, the largest of the four Côtes, which brings its own quality dry whites to the market, particularly the distinctive and refined Saint Vérans, Virés and the more famous Pouilly-Fuissés. With lightly oaked aromas of toast and hazelnuts, these are three of France's best wines for seafood. Macon *villages* light and fruity reds are drinkable but hardly worth a detour. The best are found between Hurigny and Viré and, like the whites, should be drunk young while they still have their freshness.

LABEL KNOW—HOW

❶ SOCIETE CIVILE DU DOMAINE DE LA ROMANEE-CONTI
PROPRIÉTAIRE A VOSNE-ROMANÉE (COTE-D'OR) FRANCE
❷ MONTRACHET
APPELLATION MONTRACHET CONTROLÉE
❸ 1.718 Bouteilles Récoltées
LES ASSOCIÉS-GÉRANTS
❹ BOUTEILLE N° 01201
ANNÉE 1995
❺ Mise en bouteille au domaine

❶ The name and address of the proprietor.
❷ This wine was produced in the Montrachet region
❸ Number of bottles made
❹ Bottle number 1,201 and Vintage
❺ 'Made and bottled on the estate'—a great signifier of quality

FOR THE VINE INSPIRED

If you're going to spend a fortune on a bottle of Romanée-Conti and want to know how to savor it, sign up for one of the wine classes offered by Beaune's Ecole des Vins de Bourgogne, sponsored by the Bureau Interprofessionel des Vins de Bourgogne. They offer several choices, ranging from a two-hour intro to a full weekend jammed with trips to vineyards and cellars in Maçon and Chablis.

preaching of the Second Crusade (which attracted a huge French following) and Thomas à Becket's excommunication of English king Henry II. By the mid-13th century the authenticity of St. Mary's relics was in doubt; others had been discovered in Provence. The basilica's decline continued until the French Revolution, when the basilica and adjoining monastery buildings were sold by the state. Only the basilica, cloister, and dormitory escaped demolition, and were falling into ruin when ace restorer Viollet-le-Duc, sent by his mentor Prosper Merimée, rode to the rescue in 1840 (he also restored the cathedrals of Laon and Amiens and Paris's Notre-Dame).

Today the UNESCO-listed basilica has recaptured much of its glory and is considered to be one of France's most prestigious Romanesque showcases. The exterior tympanum was redone by Viollet-le-Duc (have a look at the eroded original as you exit the cloister), but the narthex (circa 1150) is a Romanesque masterpiece. Note the interwoven zodiac signs and depictions of seasonal crafts along its rim, similar to those at both Troyes and Autun. The pilgrims' route around the building is indicated by the majestic flowers, which metamorphose into full-blown blooms, over the left-hand entrance on the right; an annual procession is still held on July 22. The basilica's exterior is best seen from the leafy terrace to the right of the facade. Opposite, a vast, verdant panorama encompasses vines, lush valleys, and rolling hills. In the foreground is the Flamboyant Gothic spire of St-Père-sous-Vézelay, a tiny village 3 km (2 miles) away that is the site of L'Espérance, Marc Meneau's famed restaurant. ✉ *Pl. de la Basilique, Vézelay* ☎ *03–86–33–39–50* 🌐 *www.basiliquedevezelay.cef.fr* 🎟 *Guided tour by donation (phone for reservations)* ⏲ *Daily 8–8.*

Château de Bazoches. The former home of Sébastien de Vauban is just outside Vézelay in the small town of Bazoches-du-Morvan. Built during the 12th century in the stolid form of a trapezium with four towers and a keep, it was bought by Vauban in 1675 with the money Louis XIV awarded him for devising the parallel trenches successfully used in the siege of Maastricht. He transformed Château de Bazoches into a fortress and created many of his military engineering designs here. Vauban is considered the "father of civil engineering," and his innovations influenced innumerable forts throughout France. His designs and furnishings of his day are on display. ✉ *14 km (9 miles) south of Vezelay, Bazoches-du-Morvan* ☎ *03–86–22–10–22* 🌐 *www.chateau-bazoches.com* 🎟 *€8.50* ⏲ *Mar., daily 2–6; Apr.–June and Sept., daily 9:30–noon and 2:15–6; Oct.–mid-Nov., daily 9:30–noon and 2:15–5; July, Aug., and some holidays, daily 9:30–6.*

WHERE TO EAT AND STAY

$$$ FRENCH ✕ **Le Bougainville.** One of the few affordable restaurants in this well-heeled town occupies an old house with a fireplace in the dining room and the requisite Burgundian color scheme of brown, yellow, and ocher. Philippe Guillemard presides in the kitchen, turning out regional favorites like hare stew, crayfish, escargot ragout in Chardonnay sauce, and venison with chestnuts. He has also devised a vegetarian menu—a rarity in Burgundy—with such deeply satisfying dishes as vegetable *pot au feu.* 💲 *Average main: €30* ✉ *26 rue St-Étienne,*

Vézelay ☎ 03–86–33–27–57 ⊙ Closed Tues., Wed., and mid-Nov.–mid-Feb. ✍ Reservations essential.

$$$$ HOTEL FAMILY **Château de Vault de Lugny.** A bit off the beaten track, but only a short drive from Vézelay, this moated château with stellar period decor was built between the 13th and 16th centuries; its regal guest quarters are accented with high ceilings, wooden floors, open fireplaces, and toile de Jouy fabrics. **Pros:** old-style luxury; peaceful setting; great restaurant. **Cons:** car essential; pricey breakfast. *$ Rooms from: €295 ✉ 11 rue du Château, 13 km (8 miles) northeast of Vézelay at Vault de Lugny ☎ 03–86–34–07–86 ⊕ www.lugny.fr ⊙ Closed Nov.–Apr. 13 rooms, 1 suite No meals.*

$$ B&B/INN **La Cimentelle.** Originally part of the Vassy cement works, this elegant 19th-century manor offers comfortable guest rooms decorated with family heirlooms; even the bathrooms are inviting (the "Hippolyte" room, for instance, has an open-plan one with a freestanding tub near the fireplace). **Pros:** idyllic setting; friendly owners; outdoor pool; breakfast included. **Cons:** a car is essential. *$ Rooms from: €114 ✉ 4 rue de la Cimentelle, 21 km (13 miles) northeast of Vezelay, Vassy-Les-Avallon ☎ 03–86–31–04–85 ⊕ www.lacimentelle.com 3 rooms, 2 suites Breakfast.*

$$$ HOTEL Fodor's Choice ★ **L'Espérance.** Accommodations, which vary in price, form a delightful trinity: you can choose between pleasant rooms overlooking the garden; ones in the annex, the Pré des Marguerites; and full suites in a renovated mill, done up in a cozy *style Anglais.* Chef Marc Meneau heads one of the greatest kitchens in Burgundy, serving Breton lobster cooked in a salt crust, veal roasted with anchovies, and other creations next to a stream and in a large, statue-filled garden. **Pros:** spectacular restaurant; bucolic setting. **Cons:** uneven service; some rooms are uninspiring. *$ Rooms from: €185 ✉ St-Père-sous-Vézelay ☎ 03–86–33–39–10 ⊕ www.marc-meneau-esperance.com ⊙ Closed mid-Jan.–early Mar. 17 rooms, 8 suites No meals.*

$ HOTEL **L'Hôtel de la Poste et du Lion d'Or.** A terrace out front welcomes you to this rambling hotel, which features light, bright (if somewhat staid) rooms—most with private balconies. **Pros:** good-size rooms with balconies; good food; friendly staff; great location. **Cons:** some rooms get street noise; parking is difficult; some rooms are a bit worn; the bistro is very touristy and can be overcrowded. *$ Rooms from: €85 ✉ Pl. du Champ-de-Foire, Vézelay ☎ 03–86–33–21–23 ⊕ www.hoteldelaposteetduliondor.com ⊙ Closed Jan. and Feb. 40 rooms No meals.*

$$ B&B/INN **Manoir de Val en Sel.** Five classically decorated, color-coded rooms—all with private entrances and en-suite bathrooms—are set in a picturesque 18th-century country residence and surround a spectacular walled flower garden that's hailed as one of the world's finest. **Pros:** gardens are a fragrant haven of calm; comfortable, spacious rooms. **Cons:** car essential; credit cards aren't accepted. *$ Rooms from: €110 ✉ 1 Chemin de la Fontaine, St-Père-sous-Vézelay ☎ 03–86–33–26–95 ⊕ valensel.vezelay.free.fr No credit cards ⊙ Closed mid-Nov.–Apr. 3 rooms, 2 suites Breakfast.*

SAULIEU

48 km (30 miles) southeast of Vézelay.

Saulieu's reputation belies its size: it's renowned for good food (Rabelais, that roly-poly 16th-century man of letters, extolled its gargantuan hospitality) and for Christmas trees (a staggering million are packed and sent off from the area each year).

GETTING HERE

You can drive to Saulieu via the A6; otherwise, take a train to Montbard (a TGV stop), and then catch a bus into town (€1.50). Two buses also run from Beaune to Saulieu every day except Sunday, making the trip in two hours (€1.50).

EXPLORING

Basilique St-Andoche. The town's Basilique St-Andoche, one of Burgundy's finest Romanesque churches, is almost as old as that in Vézelay, though less imposing and much restored. Note the impressive Romanesque nave with 12th-century carved capitals. ✉ *4 rue Savot, Saulieu* ☎ *03–80–64–07–03* ⏲ *Nov.–Apr., Tues.–Sat. 9–noon and 2–4:30; May–Oct., Tues.–Sat. 9–noon and 2–6:30, Sun. 2–6:30.*

Musée François-Pompon. Beside the basilica, Musée François-Pompon is partly devoted to the work of animal-bronze sculptor Pompon (1855–1933), whose smooth, stylized creations seem contemporary but predate World War II. The museum also contains Gallo-Roman funeral stones, sacred art, and a room highlighting local gastronomic lore. ✉ *3 pl. Dr. Roclore, Saulieu* ☎ *03–80–64–19–51* 🎫 *€3* ⏲ *Apr.–Sept., Mon. 10–12:30, Wed.–Sat. 10–12:30 and 2–6, Sun. 10:30–noon and 2:30–5; Oct.–Dec. and Mar., Mon. 10–12:30, Wed.–Sat. 10–12:30 and 2–5:30, Sun. 10:30–noon and 2:30–5.*

WHERE TO STAY

$ HOTEL **Hostellerie La Tour d'Auxois.** The retro zinc-topped bar, stone floors, and log fire strike a perfect balance with the modern-day comforts of this handsome, family-run hotel. **Pros:** attractive budget option close to Relais Bernard Loiseau; the pool is a welcome amenity. **Cons:** rooms facing the busy road can be noisy; some look a bit worn. [$] *Rooms from: €99* ✉ *Sq. Alexandre Dumaine, Saulieu* ☎ *03–80–64–36–19* 🌐 *www.tourdauxois.com* ⏲ *Closed late Dec.–mid-Feb., and Mon. Oct.–Mar.* *23 rooms, 6 suites* 🍽 *No meals.*

$$$$ HOTEL Fodor's Choice ★ **Relais Bernard Loiseau.** At Relais Bernard Loiseau, lovely lodgings ooze rustic-chic with exposed beams, traditional red-clay tile floors, and elegantly understated furnishings. **Pros:** first-class facilities include a spa and pool; stellar food. **Cons:** restaurant prices are stratospheric; closed midweek. [$] *Rooms from: €255* ✉ *2 rue d'Argentine, off D906, Saulieu* ☎ *03–80–90–53–53* 🌐 *www.bernard-loiseau.com* ⏲ *Closed late Jan.–Feb., and Tues. and Wed.* *19 rooms, 13 suites* 🍽 *No meals.*

DIJON

38 km (23 miles) northeast of Châteauneuf, 315 km (195 miles) southeast of Paris.

You may never have been to Dijon but you've certainly tasted it. Many of the gastronomic specialties that originated here are known worldwide. They include snails (many now imported from the Czech Republic), mustard (although the handmade variety is becoming a lost art), and cassis (a black-currant liqueur often mixed with white wine—preferably Burgundy Aligoté—to make Kir, the popular aperitif). The city itself is also a feast for the eyes, with charming streets, chic shops, and an impressive array of medieval art. It has magnificent half-timber houses and *hôtels particuliers,*some rivaling those in Paris. There's also a striking trio of central churches, built one following the other for three distinct parishes—St-Bénigne, its facade distinguished by Gothic galleries; St-Philibert, Dijon's only Romanesque church (with Merovingian vestiges); and St-Jean, an asymmetrical building now used as a theater. On top of that, it has a tourist-friendly scale: indeed many travelers feel it is the perfect French community, possessing the charm of a village as well as the sophistication and liveliness you'd expect of a capital.

Dijon was a major player in the history of the region. Throughout the Middle Ages, Burgundy was a duchy that led a separate existence from the rest of France, culminating in the rule of the four "Grand Dukes of the West" between 1364 and 1477—Philippe le Hardi (the Bold), Jean Sans Peur (the Fearless), Philippe le Bon (the Good), and the unfortunate Charles le Téméraire (the Foolhardy, whose defeat by French king Louis XI at Nancy spelled the end of Burgundian independence). A number of monuments date from this period, including the Palais des Ducs (Ducal Palace), now largely converted into an art museum. Luckily, Dijon's fame and fortune outlasted the dukes, and it flourished under French rule from the 17th century on. It has remained the largest city in Burgundy—and the only one with more than 150,000 inhabitants; moreover, its location, on the major European north–south trade route and within striking distance of the Swiss and German borders, has helped maintain its economic importance. Dijon continues to be a thriving cultural center as well.

GETTING HERE AND AROUND

As the administrative capital of Burgundy, Dijon has most everything a city should, including fast train service. Up to 17 TGVs come from Paris daily (90 mins, €45–€65); once here, the TER network can take you virtually anywhere within the region by rail, with frequent connections to Sens (€31.40), Beaune (€7.80), and Auxerre (€28.60). Right next to the Dijon Ville train station is the Gare Routière from which the regional TRANSCO bus company operates 32 routes that crisscross the Côte d'Or. For wine lovers the No. 44 between Dijon and Beaune (€3) has an itinerary that reads like an oenologist's wish list; the 12:30 pm bus will get you to the cellar of your choice in time for an early afternoon tasting. Inside the city, Divia (🌐 *www.divia.fr*)—Dijon's public transit system—provides both regular bus and tram service (€1.20 for a 1-hour pass) and a free minibus shuttle in the historic center.

Visitor Information Dijon Tourist Office. ☎ *08–92–70–05–58 €0.34 per min* 🌐 *www.visitdijon.com.*

EXPLORING

TOP ATTRACTIONS

Cathédrale St-Bénigne. The chief glory of this comparatively austere cathedral is its atmospheric 11th-century crypt, in which a forest of pillars is surmounted by a rotunda. ✉ *Rue du Dr. Maret, Dijon* 🌐 *www.cathedrale-dijon.fr* 🎫 *Crypt €2* 🕙 *Crypt weekdays 10–noon and 2–6 (5 in winter), Sat. 10–noon and 2–4, Sun. 2–6:30 (5:30 in winter).*

THE ORIGINAL GREY POUPON

Dijon's legendary Maille shop at 32 rue de la Liberté (🌐 *www.maille.com*), established in 1777, still sells mustard in painted ceramic pots at outrageous prices, along with a huge selection of oils, vinegars, and spices.

Chartreuse de Champmol. All that remains of this former charter house—a half-hour walk from Dijon's center and now surrounded by a psychiatric hospital—are the exuberant 15th-century church porch and the *Puits de Moïse* (*Well of Moses*), one of the greatest examples of late-medieval sculpture. The well was designed by Flemish master Claus Sluter, who also created several other masterpieces during the late 14th and early 15th centuries, including one of the tombs of the dukes of Burgundy. If you closely study Sluter's six large sculptures, you will discover the Middle Ages becoming the Renaissance right before your eyes. Representing Moses and five other prophets, they are set on a hexagonal base in the center of a basin and remain the most compellingly realistic figures ever crafted by a medieval sculptor. ✉ *Centre Hospitalier Spécialisé de la Chartreuse, Av. Albert 1er, Dijon* 🎫 *Well of Moses €3.50* 🕙 *Jan.–Mar., Nov., and Dec., daily 9:30–12:30 and 2–5; Apr.–Oct., daily 9:30–12:30 and 2–5:30.*

Château de Marsannay. Situated a few kilometers south of Dijon at the beginning of the Route des Grands Crus, this domaine has vineyards that extend down to Vosne Romanée. It specializes in all three colors of Marsannay AOP (red, white, and rosé), but also produces Fixin, Gevrey-Chambertin, Vosne-Romanée, and Clos de Vougeot. Tours of its gleaming facilities (built in 1990 in traditional Burgundy-style) include a visit to the cellars and a tasting of either six wines, including one Premier Cru (€11), or seven wines, including two Premier Crus and one Grand Cru (€16). English is spoken. ✉ *2 rue des Vignes, Marsannay-la-Côte* ☎ *03–80–51–71–11* 🌐 *www.chateau-marsannay.com* 🕙 *May–Sept., daily 10–6:30; Oct.–Apr., daily 10–noon and 2–6.*

Hôtel de Vogüé. This stately 17th-century Renaissance mansion has a characteristic red, yellow, and green Burgundian tile roof—a tradition whose disputed origins lie either with the Crusades and the adoption of Arabic tiles or with Philip the Bold's wife, Marguerite of Flanders. ✉ *8 rue de la Chouette, Dijon.*

Musée de la Vie Bourguignonne et d'Art Sacré (*Museum of Burgundian Traditions and Religious Art*). Housed in the former Cistercian convent, one museum here contains religious art and sculpture; the other has crafts and artifacts from Burgundy—including old storefronts saved from the streets of Dijon that have been reconstituted, in Hollywood-studio style, to form an imaginary street. ✉ *17 rue Ste-Anne, Dijon* ☎ *03–80–48–80–90* 🎫 *Free* 🕒 *Wed.–Mon. 9:30–12:30 and 2–6.*

Musée Magnin. In a 17th-century mansion, this museum showcases a private collection of original furnishings and paintings from the 16th to the 19th century. ✉ *4 rue des Bons-Enfants, Dijon* ☎ *03–80–67–11–10* 🌐 *www.musee-magnin.fr* 🎫 *€3.50 (free 1st Sun. of month)* 🕒 *Tues.–Sun. 10–noon and 2–6.*

Notre-Dame. One of the city's oldest churches, Notre-Dame stands out with spindlelike towers, delicate arches gracing its facade, and 13th-century stained glass. Note the windows in the north transept tracing the lives of five saints, as well as the 11th-century Byzantine linden wood Black Virgin. Local tradition has it that stroking the small owl sculpted on the outside wall of the adjoining chapel with your left hand grants you a wish. ✉ *Rue de la Préfecture, Dijon* ☎ *06–42–47–55–23* 🕒 *Daily 9–6:30.*

Fodor's Choice ★ **Palais des Ducs** (*Ducal Palace*). The elegant, classical exterior of this former palace can best be admired from half-moon Place de la Libération and the cour d'honneur. The **kitchens** (circa 1450), with their six huge fireplaces and (for their time) state-of-the-art aeration funnel in the ceiling, catch the eye, as does the 15th-century **Salle des Gardes** (Guard Room), with its richly carved and colored tombs and late-14th-century altarpieces. The palace now houses one of France's major art museums, the **Musée des Beaux-Arts** (Fine Arts Museum). The magnificent tombs sculpted for dukes Philip the Bold and his son John the Fearless (note their dramatically moving mourners, hidden in shrouds) are just two highlights of a rich collection of medieval objects and Renaissance furniture gathered here as testimony to Marguerite of Flanders (Philip the Bold's wife). She brought to Burgundy not only her dowry, namely the rich province of Flanders, but also a host of distinguished artists—including Rogier van der Weyden, Jan van Eyck, and Claus Sluter. Their artistic legacy can be seen here, as well as at several of Burgundy's other museums and monuments. Among the paintings are works by Italian old masters and French 19th-century artists, such as Théodore Géricault and Gustave Courbet, plus their Impressionist successors, notably Édouard Manet and Claude Monet. ✉ *Cours de Flore, Dijon* ☎ *03–80–74–52–09* 🌐 *mba.dijon.fr* 🎫 *Free* 🕒 *May–Oct., Wed.–Mon. 9:30–6; Nov.–Apr., Wed.–Mon. 10–5.*

WORTH NOTING

Chambre des Métiers. This mansion with Gallo-Roman stelae incorporated into the walls (a remaining section of Dijon's 5th-century "Castrum" wall) was built in the 19th century. ✉ *Rue Philippe-Pot, Dijon.*

Musée Archéologique (*Antiquities Museum*). This museum, in the former abbey buildings of the church of St-Bénigne, outlines the history of the region through archaeological finds. ✉ *5 rue Dr. Maret, Dijon* ☎ *03–80–48–83–70* 🎫 *Free* 🕒 *Apr.–Oct., Wed.–Mon. 9:30–12:30 and 2–6; Nov.–Mar., Wed. and weekends 9:30–12:30 and 2–6.*

Museum Jardin des Sciences de l'Arquebuse (*Natural History Museum*). The natural history museum in the **Pavillon de L'Arquebuse** focuses on

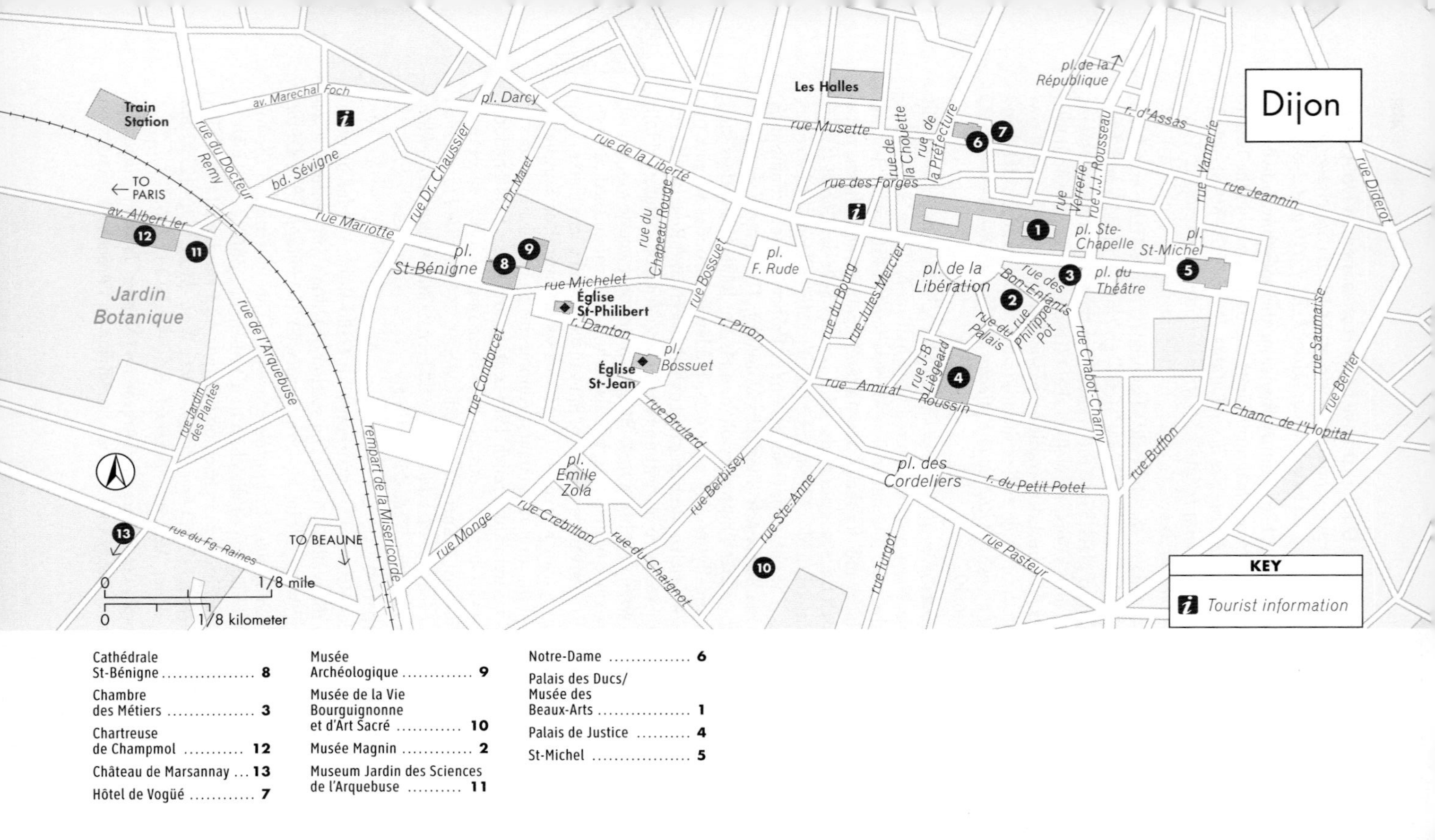
Dijon
KEY
Tourist information
Train Station
TO PARIS
av. Albert Ier
Jardin Botanique
rue du Docteur Remy
bd. Sévigne
av. Marechal Foch
pl. Darcy
rue Dr. Chaussier
r. Dr. Maret
rue Mariotte
rue de l'Arquebuse
rue Jardin des Plantes
rue du Fg. Raines
TO BEAUNE
0
1/8 mile
1/8 kilometer
rempart de la Misericorde
pl. St-Bénigne
rue Michelet
Église St-Philibert
r. Danton
rue Condorcet
rue Monge
rue de la Liberté
rue du Chapeau Rouge
rue Bossuet
pl. Bossuet
Église St-Jean
rue Brulard
pl. Emile Zola
rue Crebillon
rue du Chaignot
rue Berbisey
rue Ste-Anne
rue Turgot
pl. F. Rude
r. Piron
rue du Bourg
rue Jules Mercier
Les Halles
rue Musette
rue de la Chouette
rue de la Préfecture
rue des Forges
pl. de la Libération
rue des Bon-Enfants
rue du Palais
rue Philippe Pot
rue J-B Liégeard
rue Amiral Roussin
pl. des Cordeliers
r. du Petit Potet
rue Pasteur
rue Chabot-Charny
rue Buffon
r. Chanc. de l'Hopital
rue Berlier
rue Saumaise
pl. du Théâtre
pl. St-Michel
pl. Ste-Chapelle
rue Verrerie
rue J.J. Rousseau
r. d'Assas
rue Vannerie
rue Jeannin
rue Diderot
pl. de la République
Cathédrale St-Bénigne 8
Chambre des Métiers 3
Chartreuse de Champmol 12
Château de Marsannay ... 13
Hôtel de Vogüé 7
Musée Archéologique 9
Musée de la Vie Bourguignonne et d'Art Sacré 10
Musée Magnin 2
Museum Jardin des Sciences de l'Arquebuse 11
Notre-Dame 6
Palais des Ducs/ Musée des Beaux-Arts 1
Palais de Justice 4
St-Michel 5

current issues such as sustainable development. It is part of an impressive botanical garden, the **Jardin de l'Arquebuse,** which showcases local and exotic plant life. Strolling among the wide variety of trees and tropical flowers provides a pleasant break from sightseeing. ✉ *1 av. Albert 1er, Dijon* ☎ *03–80–48–82–00 museum* *Free* ⏲ *Museum Mon. and Wed.–Fri. 9–12:30 and 2–6, weekends 2–6; garden daily 7:30–7 (until 10 in summer).*

Palais de Justice. The meeting place for the old regional Parliament of Burgundy serves as a reminder that Louis XI incorporated the province into France in the late 15th century. ✉ *Rue du Palais, Dijon.*

St-Michel. This church, with its chunky Renaissance facade, fast-forwards 300 years from Notre-Dame. ✉ *Pl. St-Michel, Dijon* ☎ *03–80–63–17–81* 🌐 *www.saint-michel-dijon.com* ⏲ *Daily 9–6:30.*

WHERE TO EAT

As a culinary capital of France, Dijon has many superb restaurants, with three areas popular for casual dining: Place Darcy (a square catering to all tastes and budgets), Place Émile-Zola, and the old market (Les Halles), along Rue Bannelier.

$$$$ **MODERN FRENCH** ✕ **La Dame d'Aquitaine.** In the handsome stone cellar of a sumptuous 17th-century mansion, La Dame d'Aquitaine has long been a gastronomic mainstay on the Dijonaise scene. The talented owners, Sabine and Laurent Perriguey, prepare dishes like sole meunière with potato pasta in a seafood sauce, or tournedos of beef "Rossini" (that is, topped with warm fois gras) dusted with slivered truffle. The moderate prix-fixe menus are a great value. $ *Average main: €38* ✉ *23 pl. Bossuet, Dijon* ☎ *03–80–30–45–65* 🌐 *www.ladamedaquitaine.fr* ⏲ *Closed Sun. No lunch Mon.* *Reservations essential.*

$ **BISTRO** ✕ **Le Bistrot des Halles.** This eatery facing Les Halles marketplace caters to trendy locals, who are tempted by bistro dishes such as snail risotto or a fillet of cod with pistachio crust. Pull up a seat on the sidewalk or dine inside, where glass-topped wine casks serve as tables. A good choice of wines by the glass and prettily presented desserts are added bonuses. $ *Average main: €17* ✉ *10 rue Bannelier, Dijon* ☎ *03–80–35–45–07* ⏲ *Closed Sun. and Mon.*

$$$$ **FRENCH** ✕ **Le Pré aux Clercs.** This bright, beautiful Napoléon III–style restaurant is the perfect showcase for Chef Jean-Pierre Billoux's golden touch, which can turn the lowliest farmyard chicken into a palate-pleasing pièce de résistance—the roast *volaille* de Bresse with truffle puree is a case in point. Most house specialties are inventive, like panfried fillet of féra with orange marmalade, basil puree, and Bergamot lemon sauce, or, to finish, chocolate cannelloni filled with dulce de leche and served with caramel sauce. The welcome is always convivial, and the wine list features the region's best—though not necessarily best-known—winemakers. The lunch menu is a startling introduction to modern Burgundian cuisine. $ *Average main: €45* ✉ *13 pl. de la Libération, Dijon* ☎ *03–80–38–05–05* 🌐 *www.jeanpierrebilloux.com* ⏲ *Closed mid-Feb.–mid-Mar., 1 wk in Aug., and Sun. and Mon.* *Reservations essential.*

9

Making an entrance: Palais des Ducs' white-on-white exterior projects a regal elegance over the Cours de Flore.

$$$ MODERN FRENCH **Les Oenophiles.** A collection of superbly restored 17th-century buildings belonging to the Burgundian Company of Wine Tasters forms the backdrop to this pleasant restaurant. It's lavishly furnished but also quaint (candles sparkle in the evening), and the food is good, too. Vincent Bourdon juggles creativity and tradition to conjure sumptuous culinary surprises, including seared scallops with butternut squash and Chioggia beetroot. An excellent three-course menu is available for lunch or dinner. *Average main: €32* *18 rue Ste-Anne, Dijon* *03–80–30–73–52* *www.hotelphilippelebon.com* *Closed Sun.* *Reservations essential.*

$$$$ FRENCH **Stéphane Derbord.** The talented Derbord, this city's rising gastronomic star, ensures that dining in the restaurant that bears his name is an elegantly refined affair. Tempting prix-fixe menus range from a three-course lunch to an 11-dish dinner extravaganza and might include duck foie gras in a gingerbread crust, followed by saddle of hare with a cassis-juniper berry sauce, and, to cap things off, a chestnut dacquoise with tonka-bean cream and roast-chestnut ice cream. *Average main: €45* *10 pl. Wilson, Dijon* *03–80–67–74–64* *www.restaurantstephanederbord.fr* *Closed early Jan., last wk in Feb., first 2 wks in Aug., and Sun. and Mon.* *Reservations essential.*

WHERE TO STAY

$$$$ HOTEL **Grand Hôtel La Cloche.** At this luxurious, 19th-century grand hotel, ask for one of the large, plush guest rooms overlooking the tiny, tranquil back garden and its reflecting pool. **Pros:** very comfortable beds; attentive staff; imposing entry hall and smart bar. **Cons:** bad soundproofing;

ostentatious lobby. $ *Rooms from: €225* ✉ *14 pl. Darcy, Dijon* ☎ *03–80–30–12–32* 🌐 *www.hotel-lacloche.com* ⇨ *55 rooms, 10 suites* 🍴 *No meals.*

$$ HOTEL **Hostellerie du Chapeau Rouge.** Colorful, well-appointed rooms display charm and designer chic at the "Hotel of the Red Hat," a Best Western–branded property where the pleasant surroundings are complemented by the fine fare at William Frachot's on-site restaurant. **Pros:** fine restaurant; central location. **Cons:** breakfast is extra; staff can be gruff. $ *Rooms from: €120* ✉ *5 rue Michelet, Dijon* ☎ *03–80–50–88–88* 🌐 *www.chapeau-rouge.fr* ⇨ *28 rooms, 1 suite* 🍴 *No meals.*

$ HOTEL **Le Jacquemart.** In an 18th-century building in Old Dijon surrounded by antiques shops, a steep staircase leads up to high-ceilinged guest rooms of variable comfort, decorated with rustic furniture. **Pros:** cheerful; good value; nice bathrooms. **Cons:** far from the train station; no elevator or air-conditioning; some rooms don't have private bathrooms; might be too basic for some. $ *Rooms from: €65* ✉ *32 rue Verrerie, Dijon* ☎ *03–80–60–09–60* 🌐 *www.hotel-lejacquemart.fr* ⇨ *33 rooms* 🍴 *No meals.*

NIGHTLIFE AND PERFORMING ARTS

Bar Messire. Retro decor and a broad range of cocktails and whiskies lure an older crowd to Bar Messire. ✉ *3 rue Jules-Mercier, Dijon* ☎ *03–80–30–16–40.*

Bell-Ringing Festival. During the July Bell-Ringing Festival, St-Bénigne's bells chime and chime. ✉ *Rue du Dr. Maret, Dijon.*

Eden Bar. Catering to a broad clientele, Eden Bar features live sports coverage. ✉ *12 rue des Perrières, Dijon* ☎ *03–80–41–48–64.*

Festival International de Musiques et Danses Populaires (*Fêtes de la Vigne*). The city stages the Festival International de Musiques et Danses Populaires at the end of August in even-numbered years. ✉ *Dijon* 🌐 *www.fetesdelavigne.fr.*

International Gastronomy Fair. Dijon plays host to the International Gastronomy Fair the first two weeks in November. Each year a different country is invited to show off its produce and cuisine. ✉ *Dijon* 🌐 *www.foirededijon.com.*

Le Chat Noir. The popular "Black Cat" disco draws a huge crowd of dedicated groovers. Styles are eclectic and prices are high: €25 for a vodka and orange. Expect to pay a €6–€15 cover charge. ✉ *20 av. Garibaldi, Dijon* ☎ *03–80–73–39–57* 🌐 *www.lechatnoir.fr/dijon.*

WINE COUNTRY

Burgundy has given its name to one of the world's great wines. Although many people will allow a preference for Bordeaux, others for Alsace, Loire, or Rhône wines, some of the leading French gourmets insist that the precious red nectars of Burgundy have no rivals, and treat them with reverence. So, for some travelers a trip to Burgundy's Wine Country takes on the feel of a spiritual pilgrimage. East of the mountainous

Parc du Morvan, the low hills and woodland gradually open up, and vineyards, clothing the contour of the land in orderly beauty, appear on all sides. Their steeply banked hills stand in contrast to the region's characteristic gentle slopes. Burgundy's most famous vineyards run south from Dijon through Beaune to Mâcon along what has become known as the Côte d'Or. You can go from vineyard to vineyard tasting the various samples—both the powerfully tannic young reds and the mellower older ones. Purists will remind you that you're not supposed to actually drink what is offered but rather take a sip, then spit it into the little buckets discreetly provided. But who wants to be a purist?

While the "d'Or" in Côte d'Or doesn't mean "gold" (it's an abbreviation of orient, or east), the area does represent a golden opportunity for wine lovers as it branches out over the countryside in four great vineyard- *côtes* (slopes or hillsides). The northernmost, the Côte de Nuits, sometimes called the "Champs-Élysées of Burgundy," is the land of the unparalleled grand-cru reds from the Pinot Noir grape. The Côte de Beaune, just to the south, is known for both full-bodied reds and some of the best dry whites in the world. Even farther south is the Côte Chalonnaise. Although not as famous, it produces bottle after bottle of Chardonnay almost as rich as its northern neighbors. Finally, the Côte Mâconnaise, the largest of the four, brings its own quality whites to the market. There are hundreds of vintners in this region, many of them producing top wines from surprisingly small parcels of land. To connect these dots, consult the regional tourist offices for full information about noted wine routes. The 74-km (50-mile) Route des Grands Crus ranges from Dijon to Beaune and Santenay. You can extend this route southward by the Route Touristique des Grands Vins, which travels some 98 km (60 miles) in and around Chalon-sur-Saône. Coming from the north, you can tour the areas around Auxerre and Chablis on the Route des Vignobles de l'Yonne. Wherever you go in this killer countryside, you'll find that small towns with big wine names draw many travelers to their cellars.

CLOS DE VOUGEOT

16 km (10 miles) south of Dijon.

The reason to come to Vougeot is to see its *grange viticole* (wine-making barn) surrounded by its famous vineyard—a symbolic spot for all Burgundy aficionados.

GETTING HERE

TRANSCO's No. 44 bus connects Dijon to Vougeot (40 mins, €1.50); from there it's about a 10-minute walk from the town center to the château.

EXPLORING

Abbaye de Cîteaux. Robert de Molesmes founded the austere Cistercian order at this abbey near Clos de Vougeot in 1098, and the complex has housed monks ever since. Destroyed and rebuilt over the centuries, it is, understandably, a mix of styles and epochs: 13th-century cloisters, a 16th-century library, and a large, imposing 18th-century main building form an eclectic ensemble. From D996, follow signs pointing the way along a short country road that breaks off from the road to Château de Gilly, a four-star hotel. Call ahead for a guided tour. ✉ *St-Nicolas-lès-Cîteaux , Off D996, Vougeot* ☎ *03–80–61–32–58* 🌐 *www.citeaux-abbaye.com* 🎟 *Tour €7.50* ⏲ *Tours July and Aug., Tues.–Sat. at 10:30, 11:30, 2, 3, 4, and 5, Sun. 12:15, 1, 2, 3, 3:15, 4, 4:30, and 5; May, June, and Sept., Wed.–Sat. at 10:30, 11:30, 2:30, 3:30, and 4:30, Sun. 12:15, 1:30, 2:30, 3:30, and 4:30.*

Fodor's Choice ★ **Château du Clos de Vougeot.** Although it wasn't completed until the Renaissance, construction on Château du Clos de Vougeot was actually begun in the 12th century by Cistercian monks from neighboring Cîteaux who needed wine for Mass and wanted to make a diplomatic offering. It's best known as the seat of Burgundy's elite company of wine lovers, the Confrérie des Chevaliers du Tastevin, who gather here in November at the start of an annual three-day festival, Les Trois Glorieuses. You can admire the château's cellars, where ceremonies are held, and ogle the huge 13th-century grape presses, marvels of medieval engineering. There are regular photo exhibitions and concerts and an accompanied, 45-minute tour in English on request. ✉ *Clos de Vougeot* ☎ *03–80–62–86–09* 🌐 *www.closdevougeot.fr* 🎟 *€7* ⏲ *Apr.–Oct., daily 9–6:30; Nov.–Mar., daily 10–5.*

WHERE TO EAT AND STAY

$$$ FRENCH FAMILY ✕ **Restaurant Simon.** On the main square of Flagey-Echézeaux, a stellar wine village lying a few kilometers southeast of Clos de Vougeot, this inconspicuous culinary haven fills up with locals out for a quiet, French-inspired meal. Expect terroir-driven creations such as *poularde* (fattened hen) with a *vin jaune* and girolle mushroom sauce, or succulent lamb with a delicately flavored fresh thyme sauce. The wine list is, of course, excellent. $ *Average main: €28* ✉ *12 pl. de l'Eglise, 3.5 km (2 miles) southeast of Clos de Vougeot* ☎ *03–80–62–88–10* 🌐 *www.restaurant-simon.fr* ⏲ *Closed Wed. No dinner Sun.*

$$$ HOTEL **Château de Gilly.** Considered by some to be an obligatory stop on their tour of Burgundy's vineyards, this château retains glorious vestiges of bygone days: painted ceilings, a gigantic vaulted crypt-cellar (now the dining room), suits of armor, and (some) guest rooms with magnificent beamed ceilings and lovely views. **Pros:** beautiful location; friendly staff. **Cons:** pricey; heavily touristed; bathrooms could use a face-lift. $ *Rooms from: €175* ✉ *Gilly-lès-Cîteaux, Vougeot* ☎ *03–80–62–89–98* 🌐 *www.grandesetapes.fr* *37 rooms, 11 suites* 🍽 *No meals.*

NUITS-ST-GEORGES

21 km (13 miles) south of Dijon, 5 km (3 miles) south of Clos de Vougeot.

Wine has been made in Nuits-St-Georges since Roman times; its "dry, tonic, and generous qualities" were recommended to Louis XIV for medicinal use. But this is also the heart of currant country, where crops yield the wonderfully delicious ingredient known as cassis (the signature flavor in the famous Kir cocktail).

9

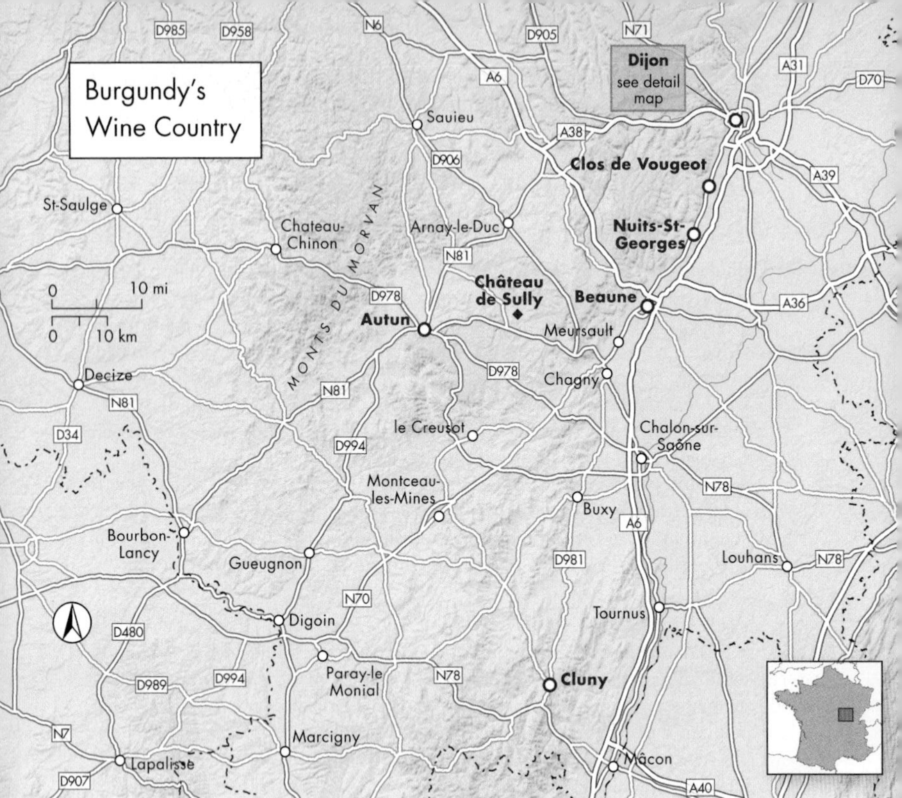

GETTING HERE

TRANSCO's No. 44 bus makes the trip from Dijon (47 mins, €1.50) and Beaune (26 mins, €1.50) to Nuits-St-Georges daily. TER train service is also available.

Visitor Information Nuits-St-Georges Tourist Office. ☎ *03–80–62–11–17* 🌐 *www.ot-nuits-st-georges.fr.*

EXPLORING

Cassissium. Inside the Cassissium's sparkling glass-and-steel building, the world of cassis is explored through films and interactive displays. A 90-minute tour of Védrenne's liqueur production ends (of course!) with a cassis tasting. ✉ *8 passage Montgolfier, Nuits-St-Georges* ☎ *03–80–62–49–70* 🌐 *www.cassissium.fr* 🎟 *€8.50* ⏲ *Apr.–mid-Nov., daily 10–1 and 2–7; mid-Nov.–Mar., Tues.–Sat. 10:30–1 and 2:30–5* ☞ *Last tour begins 1 hr, 45 mins before closing.*

WHERE TO EAT AND STAY

$$ BISTRO ✕ **La Cabotte.** If you're tired of hearty Burgundian classics, just follow savvy locals to this stylish little restaurant on the main street. Its creative market-inspired menus might include dishes such as wild garlic broth with mini-ravioli, asparagus, and snails or seared cod coupled with soba noodles in a spicy sauce. An impressive wine list includes a fine selection of Burgundy and Rhône producers. The three-course Menu Gourmand

(€28.50) is an excellent value. *Average main: €20* *24 Grand Rue, Nuits-St-Georges* *03–80–61–20–77* *www.restaurantlacabotte.fr* *Closed Sun. and Mon.*

$$$ BISTRO **La Toute Petite Auberge.** Vosne-Romanée, the greatest wine village on the côte, also entices with one of the most charming restaurants in Burgundy. The menu changes four times a year and is replete with succulent local dishes (picture a generous mound of frogs' legs, farm-reared capon, andouillette from Chablis, coq au vin, and crème brûlée). Everything is excellent and prices are more than reasonable. As you would expect, the wine list is top-notch. *Average main: €25* *Vosne-Romanée, Nuits-St-Georges* *03–80–61–02–03* *www.latoutepetiteauberge.fr* *Closed Tues. and Wed.* *Reservations essential.*

$ B&B/INN **Domaine Comtesse Michel de Loisy.** People who are serious about their wine flock here to stay in the eclectic guest rooms—memorably tempered with old-fashioned charm and furnished with fine antiques, tapestries, chintz-covered walls, and Oriental carpets. **Pros:** cultured hostess; large, comfortable rooms; breakfast included. **Cons:** no elevator; no air-conditioning in some rooms. *Rooms from: €100* *28 rue du Général-de-Gaulle, Rte. de Beaune, Nuits-St-Georges* *03–80–61–02–72* *www.domaine-de-loisy.com* *Closed late Dec.–early Jan.* *3 rooms, 2 suites* *Breakfast.*

$$ HOTEL FAMILY **La Gentilhommière.** Lush grounds, an outdoor pool complex, and a countryside location are the main lures at this peaceful property. **Pros:** peaceful setting; easy to park; cheery hosts. **Cons:** a car is essential; standard rooms get some noise from guests walking by; breakfast room fills up quickly. *Rooms from: €115* *13 Vallée de la Serrée, 3 km (2 miles) west of Nuits-St-Georges, Nuits-St-Georges* *03–80–61–12–06* *www.lagentilhommiere.fr* *20 rooms, 11 suites* *No meals.*

$$$ HOTEL **Le Richebourg.** Just north of town, Le Richebourg looks so ordinary from the outside that you wouldn't give it a second glance as you drive by on the busy thoroughfare through Vosne-Romanée, but the good-sized guest rooms inside are super-stylish; some come with a terrace facing the garden, and special "Cocoon" rooms have their own saunas. **Pros:** centrally located for visiting area vineyards. **Cons:** rooms on road side can be noisy. *Rooms from: €185* *Ruelle du Pont, 2 km (1 mile) north of Nuits-St-Georges, Vosne-Romanée* *03–80–61–59–59* *www.hotel-lerichebourg.com* *20 rooms, 4 suites* *No meals.*

9

BEAUNE

19 km (12 miles) south of Nuits-St-Georges, 40 km (25 miles) south of Dijon, 315 km (197 miles) southeast of Paris.

Beaune is sometimes considered the wine capital of Burgundy because it is at the heart of the region's vineyards, with the Côte de Nuits to the north and the Côte de Beaune to the south. It's also a popular spot for festivals, with top draws including the International Festival of Baroque Opera in July, Jazz à Beaune in September, and the wine-themed Les Trois Glorieuses in November. That combination makes Beaune one of Burgundy's most visited communities. Despite the hordes, however, it remains a very attractive provincial town, teeming with art aboveground and wine barrels down below.

GETTING HERE

Though only two direct TGVs leave Paris's Gare de Lyon daily for Beaune (at 6:53 am and 4:53 pm), there are 19 trains in all, with changes at Dijon. Travel times vary from 2 hours, 13 minutes to 4 hours, depending on transfers; fares range from €48.70 on the slower TER trains to €93.40 on the TGV. Beaune is 20 minutes from Dijon (€7.80) and gets plenty of train traffic from the through line to Lyon (€26.50). For those heading farther north, trains to Auxerre (€32.90), via Laroche Migennes, and a direct service to Sens (€35.80) are available. TRANSCO buses, departing from the SNCF station, run to Dijon via Nuits-St-Georges (No. 44, the wine-lovers line), and to Saulieu (the No. 72, no service Sunday).

Visitor Information Beaune Tourist Office. ☎ *03-80-26-21-30* 🌐 *www.beaune-tourisme.fr.*

EXPLORING

Bouchard Père et Fils Château de Beaune. Bouchard is one of the major domaines and négociants in Beaune. Its unparalleled legacy of 50,000 bottles from the Côte de Beaune and Côte de Nuits appellations includes a unique collection of rare vintages dating back to the 19th century. The museum and 15th-century cellar are accessible year-round, but call for the times of the guided tours in English; the extensive tasting (€19) is by appointment only. ✉ *Caveau Bouchard Père & Fils, 15 rue du Château, Beaune* ☎ *03-80-24-80-45* 🌐 *www.bouchard-pereetfils.com* 🕓 *Museum and cellar: Apr.–Nov., Mon.–Sat. 10–12:30 and 2:30–6:30, Sun. 10–12:30 (closed at 5:30 and all day Sun. Dec.–Mar.).*

Château de Meursault. A miraculous Meursault has been produced at this elegant spot since the 7th century. Walk up the Allée des Maronniers through the vines to the château's *cour d'honneur*. Visits to cellars dating from the 14th and 16th centuries and an art gallery are part of the free-range tour, which includes a sommelier-aided tasting of five wines (€18). More elaborate theme-based guided tours (€35) are available by appointment. English is spoken. ✉ *Château de Meursault, Rue du Moulin Foulot, Meursault* ☎ *03-80-26-22-75* 🌐 *www.chateau-meursault.com* 🕓 *Mar., Apr., Oct., and Nov., daily 10–noon and 2–6; May–Sept., daily 10–6:30; Feb., Mon.–Sat. 10–noon and 2–6, Sun. 10–1.*

Château de Santenay. This majestic 9th- to 16th-century castle is the former residence of Philippe le Hardi, son of the king of France. The surrounding estate—one of the largest in Burgundy—has 237 acres of vines, and a visit to it culminates with a tasting of four wines. The award-wining Saint-Aubin "En Vesvau," matured and aged in wooden casks, is a must-try, as is the Château Philippe le Hardi AOP Aloxe-Corton "Les Brunettes et Planchots." The tour and wine tasting (€6.80) is by appointment only. English is spoken. ✉ *1 rue du Chateau, Santenay* ☎ *03-80-20-61-87* 🌐 *www.chateau-de-santenay.com* 🕓 *Apr.–Nov., weekdays 10–12:30 and 1:30–6, weekends 10–6; Dec.–Mar., weekdays 9–noon and 2–5.*

Showing off its colorfully patterned roof tiles, medieval courtyard, and Rogier van der Weyden altarpiece, the Hôtel-Dieu is Beaune's most eye-popping edifice.

Collégiale Notre-Dame. A series of tapestries relating the life of the Virgin hangs in Beaune's main church, the 12th-century Romanesque Collégiale Notre-Dame. They are on public display from Easter to mid-November. ✉ *Pl. du General Leclerc, just off Av. de la République, Beaune* ☎ *03–80–24–77–95* 🎫 *Guided tour for tapestries €3* ⏲ *Oct.–May., Mon.–Sat. 9:30–12:30 and 2–5, Sun. 1–5; June–Sept., Mon.–Sat. 9:30–12:30 and 2–7, Sun. 1–7.*

9

Hospices de Beaune (*Hôtel-Dieu*). With its steep, gabled roof colorfully tiled in intricate patterns, the famed Hospices de Beaune is this city's top attraction—and one of Burgundy's most iconic sights. Better known to some as the Hôtel-Dieu, it was founded in 1443 as a hospital to provide free care for the poor after the Hundred Years' War. The interior looks medieval but was repainted by 19th-century restorer Ouradou (Viollet-le-Duc's son-in-law); it centers on the **grand salle,** more than 160 feet long, with the original furniture, a great wooden roof, and the super-picturesque **cour d'honneur.** The Hospices carried on its medical activities until 1971—its nurses still wearing their habit-like uniforms—and the hospital's history is retraced in the museum, whose wide-ranging collections contain some odd medical instruments from the 15th century. You can also see a collection of tapestries that belonged to the repentant founder of the Hospices, ducal chancellor Nicolas Rolin, who hoped charity would relieve him of his sins—one of which was collecting wives. Outstanding are both the tapestry he had made for Madame Rolin III, with its repeated motif of "my only star," and one relating the legend of St-Eloi and his miraculous restoration of a horse's leg.

But the showstopper at the Hôtel-Dieu is Rogier Van der Weyden's stirring, gigantic 15th-century masterpiece *The Last Judgment*, commissioned for the hospital's chapel by Rolin. The intense colors and mind-tripping imagery were meant to scare the illiterate patients into religious submission. Notice the touch of misogyny; more women are going to hell than to heaven, while Christ, the judge, remains completely unmoved. Note that the Hospices own around 150 acres of the region's finest vineyards, much of it classified as Grand and Premier Cru. ✉ *Pl. de la Halle, Rue de l'Hôtel-Dieu, Beaune* ☎ *03–80–24–45–00* 🌐 *www.hospices-de-beaune.com* 🎫 *€7.50* ⏲ *Late Mar.–late Nov., daily 9–6:30; late Nov.–late Mar., daily 9–11:30 and 2–5:30.*

Marché aux Vins (*Wine Market*). The liquid highlight of many Burgundian vacations is a visit to the Marché aux Vins, where you can sample a tongue-tingling, mind-spinning array of regional wines in an atmospheric setting made up of barrel-strewn cellars and vaulted passages. Opt for seven wines (with a *tastevin* as a souvenir) or 11 wines (with a free glass); no need to reserve. Other Beaune tasting houses include Cordelier on Rue de l'Hôtel-Dieu and the Caves Patriarche on Rue du Collège. ✉ *2 rue Nicolas-Rolin, Beaune* ☎ *03–80–25–08–20* 🌐 *www.marcheauxvins.com* 🎫 *€11–€45* ⏲ *Apr.–Oct., daily 10–6:30; Nov.–Mar., daily 10–noon and 2–6:30.*

WHERE TO EAT

$$$$ FRENCH

✕ **L'Écusson.** Don't be put off by its unprepossessing exterior: this friendly, oak-beamed restaurant offers good-value prix-fixe menus. Chef-owner Thomas Campagnon's sure-footed culinary mastery is evident in dishes like hare cooked three ways or pigeon breast with blackberries and crushed butternut squash. [$] *Average main: €36* ✉ *2 rue du Lieutenant-Dupuis, Beaune* ☎ *03–80–24–03–82* 🌐 *www.ecusson.fr* ⏲ *Closed Wed., Sun., and Feb.* ✍ *Reservations essential.*

$$ FRENCH Fodor's Choice ★

✕ **Le P'tit Paradis.** It's well worth squeezing into this tiny corner of paradise to experience the modern bistro fare of Beaune's most capable culinary couple. Charolais beef with an Époisses cream sauce and toasted slices of gingerbread topped with smoked duck breast, apple, and honey grace a menu fit for the angels. [$] *Average main: €20* ✉ *2 rue du Paradis, Beaune* ☎ *03–80–24–91–00* 🌐 *www.restaurantleptitparadis.fr* ⏲ *Closed Sun. and Mon., Aug., Dec., and Jan.* ✍ *Reservations essential.*

$$$$ FRENCH FUSION

✕ **Loiseau des Vignes.** Where else would you expect one of Burgundy's leading culinary establishments to open a wine bar? A massive range of 70 wines, all available by the glass, is the perfect accompaniment to a selection of Bernard Loiseau's famous regional dishes (along with some old-fashioned essentials). Lunch and dinner menus include such delights as *œufs meurette Bernard Loiseau* (poached eggs in red-wine sauce) and a ballotine of Bresse chicken. Indulge in the wine-tasting menu and sample five of Burgundy's best. [$] *Average main: €60* ✉ *31 rue Maufoux, Beaune* ☎ *03–80–24–12–06* 🌐 *www.bernard-loiseau.com* ⏲ *Closed Sun., Mon., and Feb.* ✍ *Reservations essential.*

Wine tastings abound in and around Beaune—check in with the tourist office to get a full list of vineyards and wine caves.

WHERE TO STAY

$$$ B&B/INN **Hostellerie de Levernois.** This idyllic Relais & Châteaux property—a gracious country manor, smartly run by Jean-Louis and Susanne Bottigliero—enchants on many levels, from its unique fleur-de-lys topiary to its superb restaurant to its wood-beam cathedral guest rooms. **Pros:** lovely, spacious rooms; personable staff; great food. **Cons:** pricey; no elevator; main restaurant only open for lunch on Sunday. *Rooms from: €188 Rue du Golf, 3 km (2 miles) east of Beaune, Levernois 03–80–24–73–58 www.levernois.com Closed Feb.–mid-Mar. 20 rooms, 6 suites No meals.*

9

$$$ HOTEL Fodor's Choice ★ **Hôtel Le Cep.** This stylish ensemble of buildings spanning the 14th to the 16th century oozes history from every arcade of its Renaissance courtyard, and, even better, all guest rooms—named for different Burgundy wines—have been luxuriously modernized and decorated with individual panache; some have wood beams, others canopied or four-poster beds. **Pros:** luxurious rooms; historical location; friendly staff. **Cons:** thin walls; pricey breakfast. *Rooms from: €195 27 rue Jean François Maufoux, Beaune 03–80–22–35–48 www.hotel-cep-beaune.com 36 rooms, 29 suites No meals.*

$$$$ HOTEL **La Cueillette.** Sitting pretty in the middle of manicured rows of Meursault vines, the Château de Citeaux provides a stately setting for this hotel and spa. **Pros:** excellent spa; vineyard setting. **Cons:** few rooms have bathtubs; a car is essential. *Rooms from: €240 Rue de Cîteaux, 9 km (5½ miles) southwest of Beaune, Meursault 03–80–20–62–80 www.lacueillette.com 17 rooms, 2 suites No meals.*

PERFORMING ARTS

Beaune Tourist Office. For festival information, contact Beaune's Office de Tourisme. ✉ *6 bd. Perpreuil, Beaune* ☎ *03–80–26–21–30* 🌐 *www.beaune-tourisme.fr.*

International Festival of Baroque Opera. In July Beaune stages its annual, monthlong International Festival of Baroque Opera, which draws big stars of the music world. ✉ *Beaune* ☎ *03–80–22–97–20* 🌐 *www.festivalbeaune.com.*

International Thriller Film Festival. Beaune plays host to the International Thriller Film Festival at the end of March and early April. ✉ *Beaune* ☎ *03–80–26–21–30 tourist office* 🌐 *www.beaunefestivalpolicier.com.*

Jazz à Beaune. International names and up-and-coming artists take to the stage in September during the city's jazz festival. ✉ *Beaune* ☎ *09–64–38–82–97* 🌐 *www.jazzabeaune.fr.*

Les Trois Glorieuses. Beaune holds its famous wine festival—Les Trois Glorieuses—on the third weekend in November. It starts with a public tasting on Saturday, continues with an auction on Sunday, and closes with a tipsy lunch for the wine elite at Château de Meursault on Monday. ✉ *Beaune.*

CHÂTEAU DE SULLY

16 km (10 miles) northeast of Autun, 75 km (47 miles) southwest of Dijon, 35 km (19 miles) west of Beaune.

This magnificent château is landmarked by four lantern-top corner towers that loom over a romantic moat filled with the waters of the River Drée. Birthplace of Maurice de MacMahon, the Duc de Magenta, Château de Sully is still home to the present Duchesse de Magenta and her family.

GETTING HERE

Take a local TER train to Autun, and then hop a bus for the 50-minute ride to Château de Sully (see 🌐 *www.destineo.fr* for times and prices).

EXPLORING

Château de Sully. "The Fontainebleau of Burgundy" was how Madame de Sévigné described this turreted Renaissance château with its Italianate inner court. Originally constructed by the de Rabutin family and once owned by Gaspard de Saulx-Tavannes—an instigator of the 1572 St. Bartholomew's Day Massacre, during which mobs attacked Huguenots in and around Paris—the château was partly reconstructed in elegant Régence style in the 18th century. Maurice de MacMahon, Napoléon III's field marshal, was born here in 1808; he went on to serve as the president of France's Third Republic from 1873 to 1879. Guided tours in English are available by reservation. ✉ *Sully* ☎ *03–85–82–09–86* 🌐 *www.chateaudesully.com* 🎫 *Guided tours of château and garden €8.70; gardens only €4.10, château only €4.60* 🕒 *Apr.–early Nov., tours daily at 10:30, 11:30, 1:30, 2:30, 3:30, and 4:30.*

The basilica of the Abbaye de Cluny was the world's largest church before St. Peter's in Rome took the title.

AUTUN

48 km (30 miles) west of Beaune.

One of the most richly endowed *villes d'art* in Burgundy, Autun is a great draw for fans of both Gallo-Roman and Romanesque art. The name derives from Augustodonum—city of Augustus—and it was Augustus Caesar who called Autun "the sister and rival of Rome itself." You can still see traces of the Roman occupation, dating from an era when this place was much larger and more important than it is now, in its well-preserved archways (Porte St-André and Porte d'Arroux) and Théâtre Romain (once the largest arena in Gaul). Parts of the Roman walls surrounding the town also remain. In addition to ancient ruins, Autun is home to a magnificent medieval cathedral and one of the region's best museums—Musée Rolin.

GETTING HERE

Some TGVs stop at Le Creusot, between Chalon and Autun—from here, you can catch a bus for the 45-minute ride to Autun. Local train lines also link Autun to Auxerre and Dijon.

Visitor Information Autun Tourist Office. ☎ *03–85–86–80–38* 🌐 *www.autun-tourisme.com.*

EXPLORING

Cathédrale St-Lazare. Autun's principal monument is the Cathédrale St-Lazare, a Gothic cathedral in Classical clothing. It was built between 1120 and 1146 to house the relics of St. Lazarus; the main tower, spire, and upper reaches of the chancel were added in the late 15th century. Lazarus's tricolor tomb was dismantled in 1766 by canons (vestiges of the exquisite workmanship can be seen in the neighboring Musée Rolin); and those same gentlemen did their best to transform the Romanesque-Gothic cathedral into a Classical temple, adding pilasters and other ornaments willy-nilly. Fortunately, the lacy Flamboyant Gothic organ tribune and some of the best Romanesque stonework, including the inspired nave capitals and the tympanum above the main door, emerged unscathed. Jean-Auguste-Dominique Ingres's painting *The Martyrdom of St. Symphorien* has been relegated to the dingy north aisle of the nave, partly masked by the organ. The *Last Judgment* carved in stone above the main door was plastered over in the 18th century, which preserved not only the stylized Christ and elongated apostles but also the inscription "*Gislebertus hoc fecit*" (Gislebertus did this). Christ's head, which had disappeared, was found by a local canon shortly after World War II. In summer, you can visit the cathedral's **Salle Capitulaire,** which houses Gislebertus's original capitals, distinguished by their relief carvings. If you come in late July, the cathedral provides a stunning setting for **Musique en Morvan**, a festival of choral music. ✉ *Pl. St-Louis, Autun* ☎ *03–85–52–12–37* 🌐 *www.art-roman.net/autun/autun.htm* 🎫 *Salle Capitulaire €2.50* ⏲ *Cathedral daily 8–7; Salle Capitulaire July and Aug. only, call for hrs.*

Musée Rolin. Built by Chancellor Nicolas Rolin, an important Burgundian administrator and famous art patron (he's immortalized in one of the Louvre's greatest paintings, Jan van Eyck's *Madonna and the Chancellor Rolin*), this museum across from the cathedral is noteworthy for its early Flemish paintings and sculpture. Among them is the magisterial *Nativity* painted by the Maître de Moulins in the 15th century, but the collection's star is a Gislebertus masterpiece, the *Temptation of Eve,* which originally topped one of the side doors of the cathedral. Try to imagine the missing elements of the scene: Adam on the left and the devil on the right. ✉ *5 rue des Bancs, Autun* ☎ *03–85–52–09–76* 🎫 *€5.20* ⏲ *Apr.–Sept., Wed.–Mon. 9:30–noon and 1:30–6; Oct.–mid-Dec. and Mar., Mon. and Wed.–Sat. 10–noon and 2–5, Sun. 2:30–5.*

FAMILY **Théâtre Romain.** The ancient theater, sitting at the edge of Autun on the road to Chalon-sur-Saône, makes an atmospheric picnic spot. Select lunch fixings in town; then settle in on the stepped seats, where as many as 15,000 Gallo-Roman spectators perched two millennia ago. On Friday and Saturday nights in the height of summer, a themed performance—the only one of its kind—is put on by locals wearing period costumes. The peak of a Gallo-Roman pyramid can be seen in the foreground. Elsewhere on the outskirts of town are the remains of a Roman Temple of Janus. ✉ *Autun.*

WHERE TO STAY

$ HOTEL Fodor's Choice ★ **Les Ursulines.** Placed above the Roman ramparts of the old city, this gorgeous 17th-century convent has been transformed into a delightful hotel, complete with spacious lodgings, an antiques-adorned restaurant, and a splendid, geometric French-style garden. **Pros:** historic setting; quiet yet central location. **Cons:** hodgepodge decor; limited elevator access. 💲 *Rooms from: €98* ✉ *14 rue de Rivault, Autun* ☎ *03–85–86–58–58* 🌐 *www.hotelursulines.fr* 🛏 *33 rooms, 5 suites* 🍽 *No meals.*

CLUNY

77 km (46 miles) southeast of Autun.

The village of Cluny is legendary for its medieval abbey, once the center of a vast Christian empire. Although most of the complex was destroyed in the French Revolution, a single, soaring transept of this church remains standing. It's one of the most magnificent sights of Romanesque architecture.

CIRCLING THE WAGONS À LA FRANÇAISE

On Friday and Saturday nights from late July to early August, time rewinds in Autun as its ancient Roman theater brings the Celtic and Gallo-Roman periods to life in a Busby Berkeley–esque extravaganza featuring Celtic fairies, Roman gladiators, and chariot races. Log on to 🌐 *www.autun-tourisme.com* for all the details.

GETTING HERE

Eight TGVs make the journey from Paris's Gare de Lyon daily (€84.20), though all require a 20-minute bus liaison from Mâcon. Regular buses also link Cluny to Chalon-sur-Saône, where you can connect to Autun and Le Creusot TGV railway stations. Driving to Cluny is a delight, as the surrounding countryside of the Mâconnais is among the most beautiful of France, with rolling fields and picturesque villages.

Visitor Information Cluny Tourist Office. ☎ *03–85–59–05–34* 🌐 *www.cluny-tourisme.com.*

EXPLORING

Fodor's Choice ★ **Ancienne Abbaye.** Founded in the 10th century, the Ancienne Abbaye was the largest church in Europe until the 16th century, when Michelangelo built St. Peter's in Rome. Art historians have written themselves into knots tracing the fundamental influence of its architecture in the development of early Gothic style. Cluny's medieval abbots were as powerful as popes; in 1098 Pope Urban II (himself a Cluniac) assured the head of his old abbey that Cluny was the "light of the world." That assertion, of dubious religious validity, has not stood the test of time—after the Revolution the abbey was sold as national property and much of it used as a stone quarry. Today Cluny stands in ruins, a reminder of the vanity of human grandeur. What remains, however, suggests the size and gorgeous glory of the abbey at its zenith, and piecing it back together in your mind is part of the attraction.

9

In order to get a clear sense of what you're looking at, start at the **Porte d'Honneur,** the entrance to the abbey from the village, whose classical architecture is reflected in the pilasters and Corinthian columns of the **Clocher de l'Eau-Bénite** (a majestic bell tower), crowning the only remaining part of the abbey church, the south transept. Between the two is the reconstructed monumental staircase, which led to the portal of the abbey church, and the excavated column bases of the vast narthex. The entire nave is gone. On one side of the transept is a national horse-breeding center (*haras*) founded in 1806 by Napoléon and constructed with materials from the destroyed abbey; on the other is an elegant pavilion built as new monks' lodgings in the 18th century. The gardens in front of it once contained an ancient lime tree (destroyed by a 1982 storm) named after Abélard, the controversial philosopher who sought shelter here in 1142. Off to the right is the 13th-century *farinier* (flour store), with its fine oak-and-chestnut roof and collection of exquisite Romanesque capitals from the vanished choir. The **Musée d'Art et d'Archéologie,** in the Palais Jean de Bourbon, contains Europe's foremost Romanesque lapidary museum. Vestiges of both the abbey and the village constructed around it are conserved here, as well as part of the Bibliothèque des Moines (Monks' Library). ✉ *Pl. de l'abbaye, Cluny* ☎ *03–85–59–15–93 Abbaye, 03–85–59–89–99 Palais de Bourbon* 🌐 *www.monuments-nationaux.fr* 🎟 *€9.50 for both sites, ticket valid for 2 days* ⏲ *Dec.–Mar., daily 9:30–5; Apr.–June and Sept., daily 9:30–6; July and Aug., daily 9:30–7.*

Hôtel des Monnaies (*Abbey Mint*). The village of Cluny was built to serve the abbey's more practical needs, and several fine Romanesque houses around Rue d'Avril and Rue de la République—including the so-called Hôtel des Monnaies—are prime examples of the period's different architectural styles. ✉ *6 rue d'Avril, Cluny* ☎ *03–85–59–05–56.*

Tour des Fromages. Parts of the town ramparts and the much-restored Tour des Fromages (or Cheese Tower, now home to the tourist office) also remain intact. You can ascend the 11th-century defensive tower to take in stellar views; an "augmented reality" gizmo at the top lets you picture the scene in all its former glory. ✉ *6 rue Mercière, Cluny* ☎ *03–85–59–05–34 Tourist Office* 🎟 *€2* ⏲ *Oct.–Mar., Mon.–Sat. 9:30–12:30 and 2:30–5; Apr., Mon.–Sat. 9:30–12:30 and 2:30–6:30; May, June, and Sept., daily 9:30–12:30 and 2:30–6:30; July and Aug., daily 9:30–6:30.*

WHERE TO STAY

$ HOTEL **Hôtel de Bourgogne.** Time-burnished if not time-stained, this old-fashioned hotel was built in 1817 on a site where parts of the abbey once stood. **Pros:** historic setting; good value; helpful staff; service comes with a no-holds-barred smile. **Cons:** no elevator; breakfast is extra but copious. $ *Rooms from: €98* ✉ *Pl. de l'Abbaye, Cluny* ☎ *03–85–59–00–58* 🌐 *www.hotel-cluny.com* ⏲ *Closed Dec. and Jan., and Tues. and Wed. in Feb.* *13 rooms, 3 suites* *No meals.*

PERFORMING ARTS

Grandes Heures de Cluny. The ruined abbey of Cluny forms the backdrop of the Grandes Heures de Cluny, a classical music festival held late July to mid-August. Free Burgundy wine-tastings are offered after concerts. ✉ *Hotel des Monnaies, 6 rue d'Avril, Cluny* ☎ *03–85–59–23–83.*

LYON AND THE ALPS

10

WELCOME TO LYON AND THE ALPS

TOP REASONS TO GO

★ **Vieux Lyon:** Lyon's Old Town *traboules*, or passageways, and 16th-century courtyards reveal a hidden trove of Renaissance architecture.

★ **Le Beaujolais Nouveau est arrivé!:** The third Thursday of November is a party like no other in France, when celebrations in honor of the new Beaujolais wine go around the clock.

★ **Mont Blanc:** Whether you brave the vertiginous slopes at Chamonix or enjoy the gentler skiing of Megève, you'll be singing "Ain't No Mountain High Enough" once you see Mont Blanc, France's tallest peak.

★ **Grenoble's market day:** Sunday morning offers a chance to walk miles through half a dozen different markets selling everything from herbs to haberdashery.

★ **Epic epicureanism:** There is no possible way to cite Lyon-Rhône Alps without mentioning Paul Bocuse, Mathieu Viannay, and the many other resident superstar chefs.

1 Lyon. This city is most famous for the Vieux Lyon district, with its Renaissance *traboules* (passageways), and the bustling Presqu'île, a peninsula between the two rivers. Lyon's historic industrial power has generated ample cultural resources and the energy to create first-rate music, cinema, theater, opera, dance, and cuisine.

2 Beaujolais. Follow the Saône River north from Lyon to the area around Villefranche and you will find the vineyards of Beaujolais, a moving pilgrimage for any wine lover. Diminutive villages with poetic names such as St-Amour, Fleurie, and Juliénas are surrounded by rolling hillsides bristling with grapevines. To the east lies Bourg-en-Bresse, famed for its church and its chickens.

GETTING ORIENTED

Lyon is France's natural hub, where the rivers Rhône and Saône meet and the mountainous wilderness of the Massif Central leans toward the lofty Alps. Lyon is a magnet for the surrounding region, including the vineyards of Beaujolais. South of Lyon is the quaint Rhône Valley. Along the southeastern border of France rises a mighty barrier of mountains that provides some of the most spectacular scenery in Europe: the French Alps, soaring to their climax in Western Europe's highest peak, Mont Blanc.

3 The Rhône Valley. Like predestined lovers, the Rhône joins the Saône to form a fluvial force rolling south to the Mediterranean. Their bounty includes hundreds of steep vineyards and small-town winemakers tempting you with samples. The ancient Roman ruins of Vienne and the Romanesque relics of Valence reflect the Rhône's importance as an early trade route.

4 Grenoble and the Alps. Grenoble, in the Dauphiné, is the gateway to the Alps at the nexus of rivers and highways connecting Marseille, Valence, Lyon, Geneva, and Turin. Literati will love its Stendahl sites and art-filled musée. To the east, rustic towns announce the Alps, none more idyllic than Annecy, thanks to its cerulean blue lake, covered lanes, and quiet canals. The region's natural Alpine splendors are showcased at Chamonix and Megève, ski resorts that buzz with life from December to April.

10

Updated By Jennifer Ladonne

Lyon and the Alps are as alike as chocolate and broccoli. Lyon is fast, congested, and saturated with culture. In the bustling city—often called the gateway to the Alps—it's hard to believe that those pristine peaks are only an hour's train ride away. Likewise, when you're in a small Alpine village you could almost forget France has any large cities at all, because everything you imagined about the Alps—soaring snowcaps, jagged ridges, refreshing lakes—is true. Culturally, Lyon and the Alps could well be on different continents but geographically they make for a great vacation combo.

Cheek by jowl, they share a patch of earth sculpted by the noble Rhône as it courses down from Switzerland, flowing out of Lake Geneva. And this soil, or as the French call it, the *terroir,* provides many tasty treasures, beginning with the region's saucy Beaujolais wines. Glinting purple against red-checked linens in a Lyonnais *bouchon* (tavern), pink-cheeked Beaujolais vintages flatter every item listed on those famous blackboard menus: a fat *boudin noir*bursting from its casing, a tangle of country greens in tangy mustard vinaigrette, or a taste of crackling roast chicken.

If you are what you eat, then Lyon itself is real and hearty, as straightforward and unabashedly simple as a *poulet de Bresse.* Yet the refinements of superlative opera, theater, and classical music also happily thrive in Lyon's gently patinated urban milieu, one strangely reminiscent of 1930s Paris—lace curtains in painted-over storefronts, elegant bourgeois town houses, deep-shaded parks, and low-slung bridges lacing back and forth over the broad, lazy Saône and Rhône rivers.

When you've had your fill of this, pack a picnic of victuals to tide you over and head for the hills—the Alps, to be exact. Here is a land of green-velvet slopes and icy mists, ranging from the modern urban hub of Grenoble and the crystalline lake of Annecy to the state-of-the-art ski resorts of Chamonix and Megève. Let your grand finale be Mont Blanc: at 15,700 feet, it's Western Europe's highest peak.

PLANNER

WHEN TO GO

Lyon and the Rhône-Alpes are so diverse in altitude and climate that the weather will depend mostly on where you are, when you're there, and which way the wind blows. Freezing gales have been known to turn Lyon's late September dance festival into a winter carnival, with icy blasts from the Massif Central sweeping down the Saône. As a rule, however, Lyon may be rainy and misty, but not especially cold. Conversely, Grenoble and the Alps can be bitter at any time of year, especially from December to April. The Beaujolais wine region is generally temperate, though a recent Beaujolais Nouveau fest (held on the third Thursday in November) froze vines and revelers alike. South of Lyon along the Rhône the sun beats down on the vineyards in full summer, but the winds howl in winter.

PLANNING YOUR TIME

Lyon, with its ample range of architecture, food, and culture, deserves several days—two at the very least. The wine country of the Beaujolais up the River Saône is another two-day visit, unless a drive-through directly to Bourg-en-Bresse is all that time constraints will allow. Medieval Pérouges is another good day's browse, with time left over for a late afternoon and evening drive into the Alps to Annecy, where the Vieille Ville (Old Town) is an eyeful by day or night.

The mountain resort of Megève is a place to settle in for a few days. Grenoble offers opportunities for perusing masterpieces in its superb museum or following the novelist Stendhal's footsteps through the old quarter.

HOW TO TALK WINE

The Beaujolais region has hundreds of village wine *caves* (cellars). Opt for those with signs that state *Dégustation, vente en direct* (sold directly from the property) or *Vente au détail* (sold by the bottle). Also look for the town's co-op *caveau*, where you can pay a few euros to taste all the wine you want. *À votre santé* (to your health).

GETTING HERE AND AROUND

Lyon is best explored on foot, with the occasional tramway or subway connection to get you across town, or to the train station or airport, in a hurry. Boat tours around the Presqu'île open up another perspective on this riverside metropolis, while bike rentals can also be handy. Consider taking advantage of the Lyon City Card, a one-, two-, or three-day pass (€22, €32, and €42 respectively) to museums, with discounts at boutiques, restaurants, and cultural events. Lyon is an important rail hub with three major stations. Trains from the Gare de la Part-Dieu connect easily with Villefranche-sur-Saône in the middle of the Beaujolais country, while the Gare de Perrache serves points south such as Valence and Vienne.

A car is probably the best way to get around the Beaujolais wine country and the rest of Rhône-Alpes, although bus routes, if infrequent, do usually extend to the far reaches of these regions.

AIR TRAVEL

The region's international gateway airport is Aéroport-Lyon-Saint-Exupéry, 26 km (16 miles) east of Lyon, in Satolas. There are domestic airports at Grenoble, Valence, Annecy, Chambéry, and Aix-les-Bains.

BUS TRAVEL

Buses from Lyon and Grenoble thoroughly and efficiently serve the region's smaller towns. Many ski centers, such as Chamonix, have shuttle buses connecting them with surrounding villages. As for Alpine villages, regional buses head out from the main train stations at Annecy, Chambéry, Megève, and Grenoble.

CAR TRAVEL

Regional roads are fast and well maintained, though smaller mountainous routes can be difficult to navigate and high passes may be closed in winter. A6 speeds south from Paris to Lyon—a distance of 463 km (287 miles). The Tunnel de Fourvière, which cuts through Lyon, is a classic hazard, and at peak times you may sit idling for hours. Lyon is 313 km (194 miles) north of Marseille on A7.

To make the 105-km (63-mile) trip southeast to Grenoble from Lyon, take A43 to A48. Coming from the south, take A7 to Valence and then swing east on A49 to A48 to Grenoble. From Grenoble to Megève and Chamonix through Annecy take A41–E712 to Annecy (direction Geneva), and then A40 (direction Montblanc-Chamonix). Turn off A40 at Sallanches for the 17-km (10½-mile) drive on the N212 to Megève.

TRAIN TRAVEL

High-speed TGV trains depart Paris's Gare de Lyon hourly and arrive in Lyon just two hours later. There are also two to eight TGVs daily between Paris's Charles de Gaulle Airport and Lyon. Two in-town train stations and a third at the airport (Lyon-Saint-Exupéry) make the city a major transportation hub. The Gare de la Part-Dieu (*Bd. Vivier-Merle*) is used for the TGV routes and links Lyon with many other cities, including Bordeaux, Montpellier and Marseilles, along with Grenoble. On the other side of town, the *centre-ville* station at Gare de Perrache (*Cours de Verdun, Pl. Carnot 04–72–56–95–30*) is the more crowded option and serves all the sights of the centre ville—many trains stop at both stations. The TGV station at Aéroport-Lyon-Saint-Exupéry serves Avignon, Arles, Valence, Annecy, Aix-les-Bains, and Chambéry, as well as Paris. The TGV also has a less frequent service to Grenoble, where you can connect to local SNCF trains headed for villages in the Alps. For the Beaujolais Wine Country, most people travel to Villefranche-sur-Saône's station on Place de la Gare; trains run to smaller towns from here.

SNCF. ☎ *3635* 🌐 *www.sncf.fr.*

RESTAURANTS

The food you'll find in the Rhône-Alps region is some of France's best—after all, this is considered the birthplace of the country's traditional cuisine, while also being the engine room of tomorrow's latest trends and gourmet styles. (⇨ *For the full scoop, see our special feature in this chapter, "Lyon: France's Culinary Cauldron."*) In Lyon's countless *bouchons* (taverns or eating houses), you'll find everything from *gras double* (tripe) to *boudin noir* (black sausage) to *paillasson* (fried hashed potatoes). If it's a light or vegetarian meal you're after, some of the newer wine bars or contemporary French restaurants are your best options.

HOTELS

Hotels, inns, *gîtes d'étapes* (hikers' way stations), and *chambres d'hôte* (bed-and-breakfasts) run the gamut from grand luxe to spartanly rustic in this multifaceted region embracing ultraurban chic in Lyon as well as ski huts in the Alps. Lyon accommodations range from guest rooms with panoramic views high in the hilltop Croix Rousse district to chic hotels in Vieux Lyon. The Alps, of course, are well furnished with top hotels, especially in Grenoble and the time-honored ski resorts such as Chamonix and Megève. Many hotels expect you to have at least your evening meal there, especially in summer; in winter they up the ante and hope travelers will take all three meals. *Hotel reviews have been shortened. For full information, visit Fodors.com.*

WHAT IT COSTS IN EUROS

	$	$$	$$$	$$$$
Restaurants	under €18	€18–€24	€25–€32	over €32
Hotels	under €106	€106–€145	€146–€215	over €215

Restaurant prices are the average cost of a main course at dinner or, if dinner is not served, at lunch. Hotel prices are the lowest cost of a standard double room in high season.

TOUR OPTIONS

The Lyon tourist office organizes walking tours of the city in English.

Lyon City Boat. This company arranges daily boat trips—with or without a meal—from Lyon's Quai des Célestins along the Saône and Rhône rivers. ✉ *Quai des Célestins, Lyon* ☎ *04–78–42–96–81* 🌐 *www.lyoncityboat.com.*

VISITOR INFORMATION

Comité Régional du Tourisme. ✉ *78 rte. de Paris, Charbonnières-les-Bains* ☎ *04–72–59–21–59* 🌐 *www.rhonetourisme.com.*

Local tourist offices are listed under their respective towns in this chapter.

10

LYON

The city's setting at the confluence of the Saône and the Rhône is a spectacular riverine landscape overlooked from the heights to the west by the imposing Notre-Dame de Fourvière church and from the north by the hilltop neighborhood of La Croix Rousse. Meanwhile, La Confluence Project at the southern tip of the Presqu'île (the land between the Saône and the Rhône) has reclaimed from the rivers nearly a square mile of center-city real estate that has become a neighborhood of parks, shops, restaurants, and cultural sites. Another attraction is Lyon's extraordinary dining scene—the city has more good restaurants per square mile than any other European city except Paris.

GETTING HERE AND AROUND

To get between the Aéroport-Lyon-Saint-Exupéry and the city center take the Rhone Express (*08–26–00–17–18* 🌐 *www.rhonexpress.fr* *€14.60*), a tramway that makes the 30-minute trip every quarter hour between 6 am and 9 pm, with various stops along the way—including the Lyon Part-Dieu train station. If you're coming by train, Lyon has three major stations so is easily reached by rail. To get here by car, take A6 south from Paris for 463 km (287 miles).

Visitor Information Lyon Tourist Information. ☎ *04–72–77–69–69* 🌐 *www.lyon-france.com.*

EXPLORING

Lyon's development owes much to its riverside site halfway between Paris and the Mediterranean, and within striking distance of Switzerland, Italy, and the Alps. Lyonnais are proud that their city has been important for more than 2,000 years. Under the Romans, who called it Lugdunum (meaning "hill or fortress of Lug," the supreme deity of Celtic mythology), it became the second-largest city in their empire and was named the capital of Gaul around 43 BC. The remains of the Roman theater and the Odéon, the Gallo-Roman music hall, are among the most spectacular Roman ruins in the world.

In the middle of the city is the Presqu'île (literally, "almost an island"), a fingerlike peninsula between the rivers where modern Lyon throbs with shops, restaurants, museums, theaters, and a postmodern Jean Nouvel–designed opera house. West of the Saône is Vieux Lyon (Old Lyon), with its peaceful Renaissance charm; above it is the old Roman district of Fourvière. To the north is the hilltop Croix Rousse district, where Lyon's silk weavers once operated their looms in lofts designed as workshop dwellings, while across the Rhône to the east are a mix of older residential areas, the famous Halles de Lyon market, and the ultramodern Part-Dieu business district with its landmark *gratte-ciel* (skyscraper) beyond.

VIEUX LYON AND FOURVIÈRE

Vieux Lyon—one of the richest groups of urban Renaissance dwellings in Europe—has narrow cobblestone streets, 15th- and 16th-century mansions, small museums, and a divine cathedral. When Lyon became an important silk-weaving town in the 15th century, Italian merchants and bankers built dozens of Renaissance-style town houses. Officially cataloged as national monuments, the courtyards and passageways are open to the public during the morning. The excellent Renaissance Quarter map of the traboules and courtyards of Vieux Lyon, available at the tourist office and in most hotel lobbies, offers the city's most gratifying exploring. Above Vieux Lyon, in hilly Fourvière, are the remains of two Roman theaters and the Basilique de Notre-Dame, visible from all over the city.

SECRET PASSAGEWAYS

Look for the quaint *traboules*, the passageways under and through town houses dating from the Renaissance (in Vieux Lyon) and the 19th century (in La Croix Rousse). Originally designed as shortcuts for silk weavers delivering their wares, they were used by the French Resistance during World War II to elude German street patrols.

TOP ATTRACTIONS

Basilique de Notre-Dame-de-Fourvière. The rather pompous late-19th-century basilica, at the top of the *ficelle* (funicular railway), is—for better or worse—the symbol of Lyon. Its mock-Byzantine architecture and hilltop site make it a close relative of Paris's Sacré-Coeur. Both were built to underline the might of the Roman Catholic Church after the Prussian defeat of France in 1870 gave rise to the birth of the anticlerical Third Republic. The excessive gilt, marble, and mosaics in the interior underscore the Church's wealth, although they masked its lack of political clout at that time. One of the few places in Lyon where you can't see the basilica is the adjacent terrace, whose panorama reveals the city—with the cathedral of St-Jean in the foreground and the glass towers of the reconstructed Part-Dieu business complex glistening behind. For a more sweeping view still, climb the 287 steps to the basilica observatory. ✉ *8 pl. de Fourvière, Fourvière, Lyon* ☎ *04–78–25–13–01* 🌐 *www.fourviere.org* 🎫 *Observatory €6* ⏲ *Basilica daily 9–noon and 2:30–6. Observatory Easter–Oct., daily 10–12:30 and 2–6; Nov.–Easter, weekends 2–6.*

Cathédrale St-Jean. Solid and determined—having withstood the sieges of time, revolution, and war—the cathedral's stumpy facade is stuck almost bashfully onto the nave. Although the mishmash inside has its moments—the fabulous 13th-century stained-glass windows in the choir and the varied window tracery and vaulting in the side chapels—the interior lacks drama and harmony. Still, it's an architectural history lesson. The cathedral dates from the 12th century, and the chancel is Romanesque, but construction on the whole continued over three centuries. The 14th-century astronomical clock, in the north transept, is a marvel of technology very much worth seeing. It chimes a hymn to St. John on the hour at noon, 2, 3, and 4 as a screeching rooster and other automatons enact the Annunciation. ✉ *70 rue St-Jean, Vieux Lyon, Lyon* ☎ *04–78–92–82–29* 🌐 *www.cathedrale-lyon.cef.fr* ⏲ *Weekdays 8:15–7:45, Sat. 8:15–7, Sun. 8–7.*

Hôtel Bullioud. This superb Renaissance mansion, close to the Hôtel Paterin, is noted for its courtyard, with an ingenious gallery built in 1536 by Philibert Delorme, one of France's earliest and most accomplished exponents of classical architecture. Delorme also worked on several spectacular châteaux in central France, including those at Fontainebleau and Chenonceaux. ✉ *8 rue Juiverie, off Pl. St-Paul, Vieux Lyon, Lyon* 🎫 *Free* ⏲ *Daily 10–noon and 2–6.*

Maison du Crible. This 17th-century mansion is one of Lyon's oldest. In the courtyard you can glimpse a charming garden and the original Tour Rose—an elegant pink tower. In those days, the higher the tower, the greater the prestige. This one was owned by a tax collector. ✉ *16 rue du Bœuf, off Pl. du Petit-Collège, Vieux Lyon, Lyon* 🎫 *Free* ⏲ *Daily 10–noon and 2–6.*

FAMILY **Musées Gadagne** (*Lyon Historical Museum and Puppet Museum*). These two museums are housed in the city's largest ensemble of Renaissance buildings, the Hôtel de Gadagne, built between the 14th and 16th century. The **Musée d'Histoire de Lyon** traces the city's history from its pre-Roman days onward, displaying sculpture, furniture, pottery, paintings, and engravings. The **Musée des Marionnettes du Monde** focuses on the history of puppets, beginning with Guignol and Madelon—Lyon's Punch and Judy—created by Laurent Mourguet in 1795. It includes two hanging gardens, a café, and a shop. ✉ *1 pl. du Petit-Collège, Vieux Lyon, Lyon* ☎ *04–78–42–03–61* 🌐 *www.gadagne.musees.lyon.fr* 🎫 *€6 one museum, €8 for both museums* ⏲ *Wed.–Sun. 11–6:30.*

Musée Gallo-Romain de Fourvière (*Gallo-Roman Museum*). Since 1933, systematic excavations have unearthed vestiges of Lyon's opulent Roman precursor. The statues, mosaics, vases, coins, and tombstones are excellently displayed in this partially subterranean museum next to the Roman theaters. The large, bronze Table Claudienne is inscribed with part of Emperor Claudius's address to the Roman Senate in AD 48, conferring senatorial rights on the Roman citizens of Gaul. ✉ *17 rue Clébert, Fourvière, Lyon* ☎ *04–72–38–81–90* 🌐 *www.musees-gallo-romains.com* 🎫 *€4* ⏲ *Tues.–Sun. 10–6.*

Place Bellecour. Shady, imposing Place Bellecour is one of the largest squares in France, and is Lyon's fashionable center, midway between the Saône and the Rhône. Classical facades erected along its narrower sides in 1800 lend architectural interest. The large, bronze equestrian statue of Louis XIV, installed in 1828, is the work of local sculptor Jean Lemot. ✉ *Pl. Bellecour, Presqu'île, Lyon.*

Fodor's Choice ★ **Rue du Bœuf.** Like parallel Rue St-Jean, Rue du Bœuf has traboules, courtyards, spiral staircases, towers, and facades. The traboule at No. 31 hooks through and out onto Rue de la Bombarde. At No. 19 is the standout Maison de l'Outarde d'Or, so named for the great bustard, a gooselike game bird, depicted in the coat of arms over the door. The late-15th-century house and courtyard inside have spiral staircases in the towers, which were built as symbols of wealth and power. No. 20 conceals one of the rare open-shaft spiral staircases allowing for a view all the way up the core. The Hotel Tour Rose at No. 22 has, indeed, a beautiful *tour rose* (pink tower) in the inner courtyard. At the corner of Place Neuve St-Jean and Rue du Bœuf is the famous sign portraying the bull for which Rue du Bœuf is named, the work of the Renaissance Italy–trained French sculptor Jean de Bologne. ✉ *Rue du Boeuf, Vieux Lyon, Lyon.*

Fodor's Choice ★ **Rue St-Jean.** Once Vieux Lyon's major thoroughfare, this street leads north from Place St-Jean to Place du Change, where money changers operated during medieval trade fairs. The elegant houses along it were

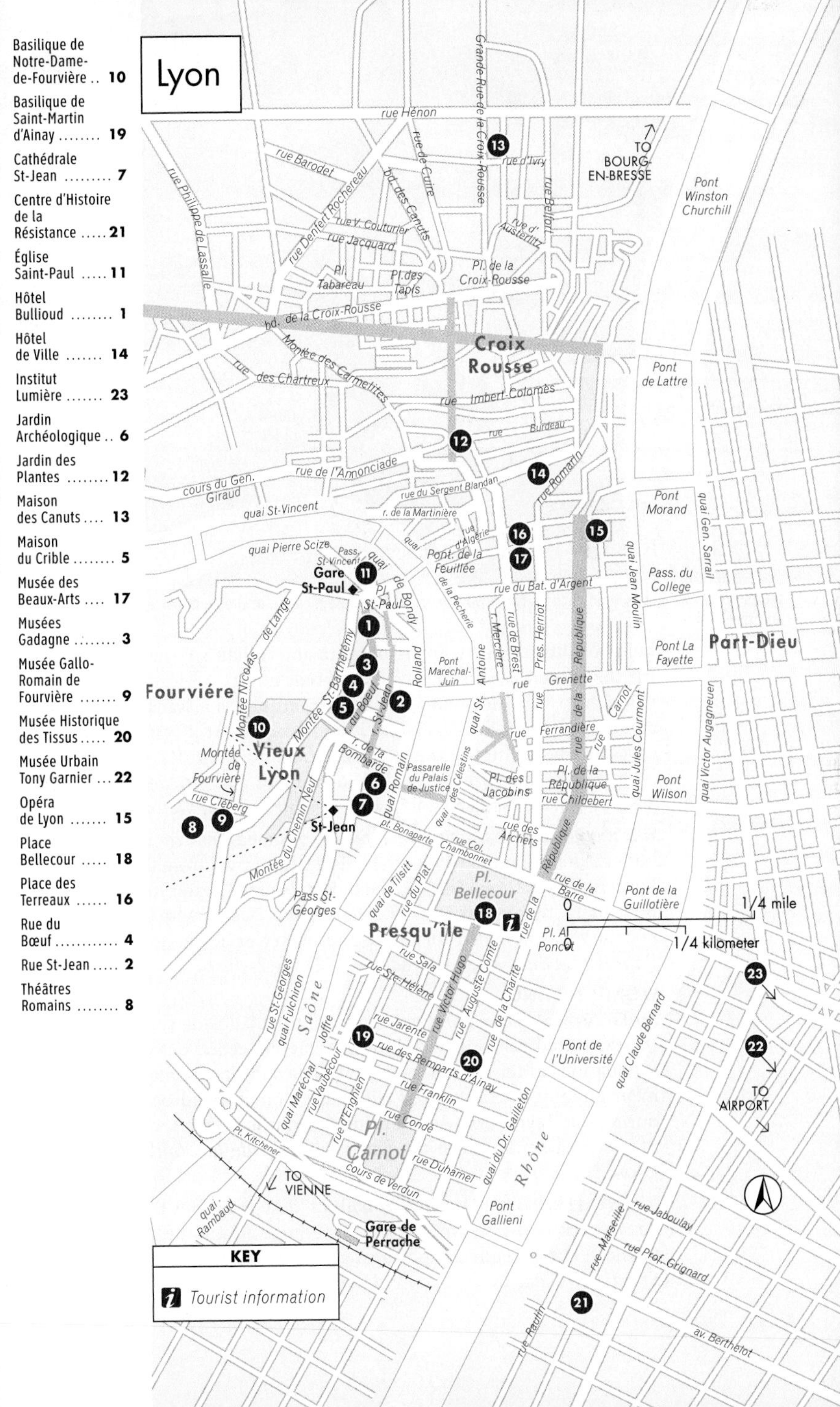

Basilique de Notre-Dame-de-Fourvière .. 10
Basilique de Saint-Martin d'Ainay 19
Cathédrale St-Jean 7
Centre d'Histoire de la Résistance 21
Église Saint-Paul 11
Hôtel Bullioud 1
Hôtel de Ville 14
Institut Lumière 23
Jardin Archéologique .. 6
Jardin des Plantes 12
Maison des Canuts 13
Maison du Crible 5
Musée des Beaux-Arts 17
Musées Gadagne 3
Musée Gallo-Romain de Fourvière 9
Musée Historique des Tissus 20
Musée Urbain Tony Garnier ... 22
Opéra de Lyon 15
Place Bellecour 18
Place des Terreaux 16
Rue du Bœuf 4
Rue St-Jean 2
Théâtres Romains 8
Lyon
rue Hénon
Grande Rue de la Croix-Rousse
rue d'Ivry
TO BOURG-EN-BRESSE
rue Barodet
rue de Cuire
bd. des Canuts
rue Denfert Rochereau
rue Philippe de Lassalle
rue V. Couturier
rue Jacquard
rue d'Austerlitz
rue Belfort
Pont Winston Churchill
Pl. Tabareau
Pl. des Tapis
Pl. de la Croix-Rousse
bd. de la Croix-Rousse
Montée des Carmelites
Croix Rousse
rue des Chartreux
rue Imbert-Colomès
rue Burdeau
Pont de Lattre
rue de l'Amonciade
cours du Gen. Giraud
rue du Sergent Blandan
rue Romarin
quai St-Vincent
r. de la Martinière
Pont Morand
quai Gen. Sarrail
quai Pierre Scize
Pass. St-Vincent
quai de Bondy
rue d'Algérie
Pont de la Feuillée
Gare St-Paul
Pl. St-Paul
rue de la Pecherie
rue du Bat. d'Argent
quai Jean Moulin
Pass. du College
Montée Nicolas de Lange
rue St-Barthélémy
Rolland
quai St-Antoine
r. Mercière
rue de Brest
Pres. Herriot
rue de la République
Pont La Fayette
Part-Dieu
Pont Marechal-Juin
rue Grenette
Carnot
quai Jules Courmont
quai Victor Augagneur
Fourviére
r. du Boeuf
r. St-Jean
Montée St-Barthélémy
rue Ferrandière
Vieux Lyon
Montée de Fourvière
r. de la Bombarde
quai Romain
Passarelle du Palais de Justice
quai des Célestins
Pl. des Jacobins
Pl. de la République
rue Childebert
Pont Wilson
rue Cléberg
St-Jean
Montée du Chemin Neuf
pt. Bonaparte
rue Col. Chambonnet
rue des Archers
Pass St-Georges
quai de Tilsitt
rue du Plat
Pl. Bellecour
rue de la Barre
Pont de la Guillotière
1/4 mile
1/4 kilometer
Presqu'île
Pl. A. Poncet
rue Sala
rue Ste-Hélène
rue Victor Hugo
rue Auguste Comte
rue de la Charité
rue St-Georges
rue Fulchiron
Saône
Joffre
rue Jarente
rue des Remparts d'Ainay
Pont de l'Université
quai Claude Bernard
quai Maréchal
rue Vaubecour
rue d'Enghien
rue Franklin
rue Condé
TO AIRPORT
Pl. Kitchener
Pl. Carnot
rue Duhamel
quai du Dr. Gailleton
Rhône
TO VIENNE
cours de Verdun
quai Rambaud
Pont Gallieni
rue Marseille
rue Jaboulay
rue Prof. Grignard
Gare de Perrache
KEY
Tourist information
rue Raulin
av. Berthelot

Lyon's economic and cultural success has always owed much to its location at the confluence of the Saône and the Rhône.

built for illustrious Lyonnais bankers and Italian silk merchants during the French Renaissance. The traboule at No. 54 leads all the way through to Rue du Bœuf (No. 27). Beautiful Renaissance courtyards can be visited at No. 50, No. 52, and No. 42. At 27 rue St-Jean, an especially beautiful traboule winds through to 6 rue des Trois Maries. No. 28 has a pretty courtyard, as do No. 18 and No. 24. Maison Le Viste at No. 21 has a splendid facade. ✉ *Rue St-Jean, Vieux Lyon, Lyon.*

Théâtres Romains (*Roman Theaters*). Two ruined, semicircular, Roman-built theaters are tucked into the hillside, just down from the summit of Fourvière. The **Grand Théâtre,** the oldest Roman theater in France, was built in 15 BC to seat 10,000. The smaller **Odéon,** with its geometric flooring, was designed for music and poetry performances. ✉ *Colline Fourvière, Fourvière, Lyon* 🎫 *Free* ⏲ *Daily 7–dusk.*

WORTH NOTING

Jardin Archéologique (*Archaeological Garden*). Inside this garden are the excavated ruins of two churches that succeeded one another. The foundations of the churches were unearthed during a time when apartment buildings—constructed here after churches had been destroyed during the Revolution—were being demolished. One arch forms part of the ornamentation in the garden. ✉ *Rue de la Bombarde, Vieux Lyon, Lyon.*

Jardin des Plantes (*Botanical Garden*). In these luxurious Botanical Gardens you'll find remnants of the once-huge Amphithéâtre des Trois Gaules (Three Gauls Amphitheater), built in AD 19. ✉ *Rue Lucien Sportisse, Vieux Lyon, Lyon* ⏲ *Daily dawn–dusk.*

Église Saint-Paul. The 12th-century church of St-Paul is noted for its octagonal lantern, its frieze of animal heads in the chancel, and its late-period Flamboyant Gothic chapel. ✉ *Pl. St-Paul, Vieux Lyon, Lyon* ☎ *04–78–29–69–58.*

PRESQU'ÎLE AND THE CROIX ROUSSE DISTRICT

Presqu'île, the peninsula flanked by the Saône and the Rhône, is Lyon's modern center, with fashionable shops, a trove of restaurants and museums, and squares graced by fountains and 19th-century buildings. This is the core of Lyon, and you'll be tempted to explore the entire stretch, from the southern point of the peninsula at La Confluence, up past the Gare de Perrache train station to Place Bellecour, and all the way up to Place des Terreaux.

TOP ATTRACTIONS

Institut Lumière. On the site where the Lumière brothers, Auguste and Louis, invented cinematography in their family home, this museum has daily showings of early film classics and contemporary movies as well as a permanent exhibit about the Lumières. ✉ *25 rue du Premier Film, Part-Dieu, Lyon* ☎ *04–78–78–18–95* 🌐 *www.institut-lumiere.org* *€6.50* ⏲ *Tues.–Sun. 10–6:30.*

Musée des Beaux-Arts (*Fine Arts Museum*). In the elegant 17th-century Palais St-Pierre, formerly a Benedictine abbey, this museum houses one of France's largest art collections after that of the Louvre. Byzantine ivories, Etruscan statues, Egyptian artifacts, and top-notch sculptures (most notably Rodin's *Walker*) are all on display; however, paintings remain the highlight. Amid old master, Impressionist, and modern paintings are works by the tight-knit Lyon School, characterized by exquisitely rendered flowers and overbearing religious sentimentality. Note Louis Janmot's *Poem of the Soul,* immaculately painted visions that are by turns heavenly, hellish, and downright spooky. A newer trove of treasures includes works by Manet, Monet, Degas, Bacon, Braque, and Picasso. ✉ *Palais St-Pierre, 20 pl. des Terreaux, Presqu'île, Lyon* ☎ *04–72–10–17–40* 🌐 *www.mba-lyon.fr* *€7 permanent collection; €9 temporary exhibits; €12 for both* ⏲ *Wed.–Mon. 10–6.*

Musée Historique des Tissus (*Textile Arts Museum*). A sister museum to the Musée des Arts Décoratifs, this one is dedicated to the woven-arts industries that were so crucial to Lyon's fame and fortune. Highlights include Asian tapestries from as early as the 4th century, Turkish and Persian carpets from the 16th to the 18th century, and 18th-century Lyon silks, so lovingly depicted in many portraits of the time. In the same building is the **Musée des Arts Décoratifs,** which has fine collections of silverware, furniture, porcelain, and tapestries. ✉ *34 rue de la Charité, Presqu'île, Lyon* ☎ *04–78–38–42–00* 🌐 *www.mtmad.fr* *€10 joint ticket with Musée des Arts Décoratifs* ⏲ *Tues.–Sun. 10–5:30.*

Opéra de Lyon. The barrel-vaulted Lyon Opera, a reincarnation of a moribund 1831 building, was designed by star French architect Jean Nouvel and built in the early 1990s. It incorporates a columned exterior, soaring glass vaulting, neoclassical public spaces, and an all-black interior. High above, looking out between the heroic statues lined up along the parapet, is a small but excellent restaurant, Les Muses de l'Opéra. ✉ *1 pl. de la Comédie, Presqu'île, Lyon* ☎ *04–72–00–45–00* 🌐 *www.opera-lyon.com.*

Place des Terreaux. The four majestic horses rearing up from a monumental 19th-century fountain in the middle of this large square are an allegory of the River Saône by Frédéric-Auguste Bartholdi, who sculpted New York Harbor's Statue of Liberty. The 69 fountains embedded in the wide expanse of the square are illuminated by fiber-optic technology at night. The notable buildings on either side are the Hôtel de Ville and the Musée des Beaux-Arts. ✉ *Pl. des Terreaux, Presqu'île, Lyon.*

WORTH NOTING

Basilique de Saint-Martin d'Ainay. This fortified church dates back to a 10th-century Benedictine abbey and a 9th-century sanctuary before that. The millenary energy field is palpable around the hulking structure, especially near the rear of the apse where the stained-glass windows glow richly in the twilight. In 1844 it became one of the first buildings in France to be classified a national monument; its interior murals and frescoes, though, are disappointingly plain and austere compared to the quirky, rough exterior. ✉ *Pl. de l'Abbaye d'Ainay, Presqu'île, Lyon* ☎ *04–72–40–02–50* 🎟 *Free* ⏲ *Daily 8:30–noon and 2:30–6.*

Centre d'Histoire de la Résistance et de la Déportation (*Museum of the History of the Resistance and the Deportation*). During World War II, Lyon played an important role in the Resistance movement against the German occupation of France. Newly renovated displays include equipment, such as radios and printing presses, photographs, and exhibits re-creating the clandestine lives and heroic exploits of Resistance fighters. ✉ *14 av. Berthelot, Part-Dieu, Lyon* ☎ *04–78–72–23–11* 🌐 *www.chrd.lyon.fr* 🎟 *€4, €7 guided tour* ⏲ *Wed.–Sun. 10–6.*

Hôtel de Ville (*Town Hall*). Architects Jules Hardouin-Mansart and Robert de Cotte redesigned the very impressive facade of the Town Hall after a 1674 fire. The rest of the building dates from the early 17th century. ✉ *Pl. des Terreaux, Presqu'île, Lyon.*

FAMILY **Maison des Canuts** (*Silk Weavers' Museum*). Old-time Jacquard looms are still in action at this historic house in the Croix Rousse, and the weavers are happy to show children how the process works. The boutique is a great place to stock up on a colorful range of silk, wool, and linen scarves all made in Lyon. ✉ *10–12 rue d'Ivry, La Croix Rousse, Lyon* ☎ *04–78–28–62–04* 🌐 *www.maisondescanuts.com* 🎟 *€7* ⏲ *Mon.–Sat. 10–6; guided tours at 11 and 3:30.*

Musée Urbain Tony Garnier (*Tony Garnier Urban Museum*). Built between 1920 and 1933, this project (also known as the Cité de la Création), was France's first attempt at low-income housing. Tenants have tried over the years to bring some art and cheerfulness to their environment: 22 giant murals depicting the work of Tony Garnier, the turn-of-the-20th-century Lyon architect, were painted on the walls. Artists from around the world, with the support of UNESCO, have added their vision to the creation of the ideal housing project. ✉ *4 rue des Serpollières, Quartier des États-Unis, Lyon* ✥ *Take the métro to Monplaisir-Lumière, then walk 10 mins south along Rue Antoine* ☎ *04–78–75–16–75*

Continued on page 476

LYON: FRANCE'S CULINARY CAULDRON

Rue Saint-Jean

No other city in France teases the taste buds like Lyon, birthplace of traditional French cuisine. Home to both the workingman's *bouchons* and many celebrity chefs, the capital of the Rhône-Alpes region has become the engine room for France's modern cooking canon.

Lyon owes much of its success as a gastronomic center to its auspicious location at the crossroads of several regional cuisines—the hearty cooking traditions and smoked meats of the mountainous east; the Massif Central cattle farms and Auvergne's lambs to the west; the tomato- and olive oil-kissed Mediterranean dishes to the south; and the excellent butters and cheeses of the north. Not to mention the Rhône-Alpes' own natural riches—fish from local lakes and rivers, apricots and cherries from hillside orchards, and dairy and pork products from valley farms.

Restaurants here offer a compelling juxtaposition between simple workingman's fare and sophisticated *haute* cuisine. Casual restaurants called *bouchons* offer classic everyday dishes like *gratinée lyonnaise* (onion soup) and *boudin noir* (pork blood) sausages. At the other end of the spectrum, über-chef Paul Bocuse—the original master of Nouvelle Cuisine—serves elevated preparations like black-truffle soup encased in pastry. And a coterie of creative young chefs like Anthony Bonnet have emerged, making it hard to go wrong in this food-focused city.

By George Semler

THE BOUCHON TRADITION

Lyon's iconic bouchons are casual bistro-like restaurants with modest décor along the lines of tiled walls, wooden benches, and zinc counters. In the late 19th-century, these informal eateries dished out hearty fare for working-class customers like pony express riders, stagecoach drivers, silk workers, and field laborers.

The term bouchon originated as a description for the bundles of straw that hung over the entrance of early bouchons, indicating the availability of food and drink for horses as well as humans. These friendly, family-run taverns were customarily run by female chefs, serving cuisine that relied heavily on humble pork and beef cuts, such as stomachs, brains, trotters, ears, cheeks, and livers.

Today many restaurants call themselves bouchons that would not fit the traditional definition. For the real thing, look for a little plaque at the door showing Gnafron, a drunken marionette with red nose and wine glass in hand. He signifies that the establishment is part of the official bouchon association. Bouchons are still a frugal dining choice: in many establishments, $25 will buy an appetizer, main course, salad, and dessert or cheese plate.

(top) Bouchons on Rue Merciere, (bottom) Ives Rivoiron, owner of Café des Fédérations

CLASSIC LYONNAIS FARE

At bouchons around the city, look for these traditional dishes:

Andouillette à la lyonnaise tripe sausages stuffed with veal and traditionally served with fried onions

Bavette skirt steak with shallots

Blanquette de veau veal stewed in cream, egg yolks, onions, and mushrooms

Boudin blanc sausage made from pork, onion, and eggs, without the blood

Boudin noir pork-blood sausage

Bresse chicken à la lyonnaise poached and stuffed chicken with truffles

Bugnes beignets of fried pork fat

Cervelas Lyonnais brioche filled with smoked sausage, truffles, and pistachio nuts

Frisée aux lardons curly leafed salad with bacon and eggs

Galette lyonnaise mashed potatoes with onions, browned in the oven and served in a gratin dish

Gâteau de foies blonds de volaille chicken liver mousse

Boudin noir sausages, the dark links at right, are just one of the area's famed pork products

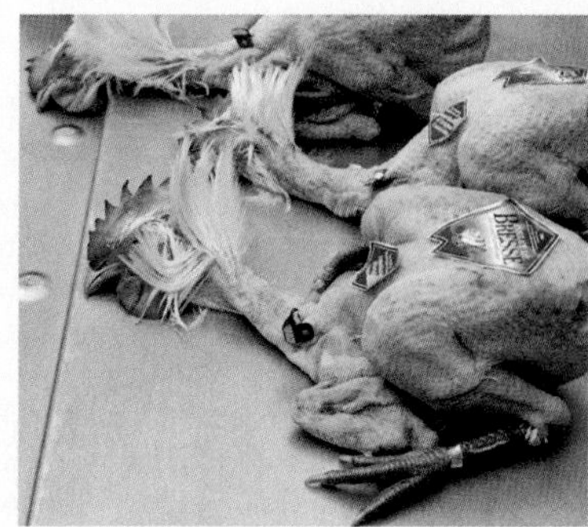

Lyon's famous blue-footed chickens, poulet de Bresse

Gras double breaded, fried tripe with onions and butter

Gratinée lyonnaise onion soup topped with bread and cheese

Paillasson fried hashed potatoes

Pot-au-feu vegetable and meat stew, a winter favorite

Pots de Lyon wine flagons, heavy-bottomed bottles originally conceived to satirize government attempts to limit silk workers' wine consumption in favor of increased labor productivity

Poularde demi-deuil chicken with black truffles sliced thinly under the skin

Quenelle de brochet velvety dumplings made from pike fish, flour, butter, and eggs, served with béchamel sauce

Rosette a garlicky pork sausage

Sabodet pig's-head sausage

Saucissons chauds slices of warm sausage with potatoes drizzled with oil and vinegar

Saucisson en brioche sausage encased in brioche

Tablier de sapeur breaded, fried tripe

www.museeurbaintonygarnier.com *€3* *Tours Tues.–Fri. 4:30, Sat. 2:30 and 4:30.*

WHERE TO EAT

$$$ MODERN FRENCH **Au 14 Février.** Cupid's arrows don't quite account for the rapturous reviews garnered by Tsuyoshi Arai in his tiny chocolate box of a restaurant. The young chef trained in French kitchens for over a decade, honing his natural genius before striking out on his own. A Michelin star later, the persnickety Lyonnais have fallen hard, waiting weeks to savor dishes that combine Japanese subtlety with rigorous French technique—like poached foie gras and creamy parsnip puree with caramelized carrot sauce, scallops rolled in sole and smoky bacon, verbena-infused lobster consommé with caviar, and salmon tartare in a gingery court bouillon with zucchini mousse. The quirky atmosphere (mirrored ceilings!) and excellent-value menu only add to its allure. *Average main: €32* *6 rue Mourguet, 5e, Vieux Lyon, Lyon* *04–78–92–91–39* *www.au14fevrier.com* *Closed Sun. and Mon. No lunch Sat.* *Reservations essential.*

$$$$ FRENCH **Auberge de l'Île.** If you're taking a walk along the River Saône, this enchanted eatery on leafy Île Barbe is the perfect place to refuel. Whether outside on the terrace or inside the graceful former 17th-century monastery refectory, it serves smart, contemporary cuisine based on fresh market products prepared with originality. Chef Jean-Christophe Ansanay-Alex is famous for his oral daily menu performance (listen for game in fall or winter), and the wine list is strong in local Condrieu and Côte-Rotie selections. Ordering a prix-fixe lunch menu (Tuesday to Friday, €40) will help you avoid a major economic hemorrhage. *Average main: €50* *L'Ile Barbe, Collonges au Mont-D'Or, Lyon* *04–78–83–99–49* *www.aubergedelile.com* *Closed Mon. No dinner Sun.* *Reservations essential.*

$$ FRENCH **Brasserie Georges.** This inexpensive brasserie at the south end of Rue de la Charité is one of the city's largest and oldest, founded in 1836 and housed in a palatial building dating from 1925. Meals range from hearty veal stew or sauerkraut and sausage to more refined fare. Cooking is less than creative—stick with the great standards, such as *saucisson brioché* (sausage in brioche stuffed with truffled foie gras)—and, like the vast room setting, service is a bit impersonal. Nevertheless, the Art Deco style is as delicious as it comes. *Average main: €21* *30 cours Verdun, Perrache, Lyon* *04–72–56–54–54* *www.brasseriegeorges.com.*

$ FRENCH **Café 203.** This happening spot near the opera is always teeming with young people and artists. Named for the Peugeot 203 parked in front of the terrace, the café-restaurant-chill-out is open daily from dawn to after midnight (but no Sunday breakfast). Its delicious cuisine is fresh, fast, original, and inexpensive. For a quick pre- or post-opera meal, this is the place. *Average main: €12* *9 rue du Garet, Presqu'île, Lyon* *04–78–28–66–65.*

$ FRENCH **Café des Fédérations.** For 80 years this sawdust-strewn café with homey red-check tablecloths has reigned as one of the city's leading bouchons; however, it may have overextended its stay by trading on past glory—some readers report a desultory hand in the kitchen, and native Lyonnais seem to head elsewhere since the legendary Raymond Fulchiron's recent retirement. Still, for a taste of classic Lyon gastronomy in a historic setting, the deftly prepared local classics like *boudin blanc* (white-meat sausage), *boudin noir* (black sausage), or *andouillettes* (veal and pork tripe sausage) are hard to beat. *Average main: €16 8 rue du Major-Martin, Presqu'île, Lyon 04–78–28–26–00 www.lesfedeslyon.com Closed Sun. and late Dec.–Jan.*

$$ FRENCH **Chez Hugon.** One of the city's top-rated insider spots, this typical bouchon with the de rigueur red-check tablecloths sits behind the Musée des Beaux-Arts. Practically a club, it's crowded with regulars who trade quips with the owner while the kitchen prepares the best *tablier de sapeur* (tripe marinated in wine and fried in bread crumbs) in town. Whether you order the hunks of homemade pâté, the stewed chicken in wine vinegar sauce, or the plate of *ris de veau* (sweetbreads), your dinner will add up to good, inexpensive food and plenty of it. *Average main: €18 12 rue Pizay, Presqu'île, Lyon 04–78–28–10–94 www.bouchonlyonnais.fr Closed weekends and Aug.*

$$$$ MODERN FRENCH **Christian Têtedoie.** Star chef Christian Têtedoie's rocked the culinary world when, after 20 years, he shuttered his Michelin-starred gastronomic temple to open this soaring art-filled aerie perched atop Lyon's Fourvière hill. The minimalist design and immense bay windows offering staggering views of the city signaled a new direction in the great chef's approach, breaking free of classicism in favor of a more audacious menu: roasted foie gras with bitter orange, pineapple, and onion in a duck reduction; roast pigeon stuffed with garlic, cabbage, and chestnuts; or the chef's signature pressed *tête de veau* (calf's head) served with a half lobster *en cocotte* (casserole). Le Phosphore wine bar downstairs offers lighter wine-focused "degustation" menus orchestrated by Têtedoie and a guest winemaker with a price-to-quality quotient that's hard to beat anywhere in town. *Average main: €36 Chemin Neuf, 1 rue de l'Antiquaille, Fourvière, Lyon 04–78–29–40–10 www.tetedoie.com Closed Sun. Reservations essential.*

$$ FRENCH Fodor's Choice ★ **Comptoir Abel.** About 400 years old, this charming house is one of Lyon's most frequently filmed and photographed taverns. Simple wooden tables in wood-panel dining rooms, quirky art on every wall, heavy-bottom *pot lyonnais* wine bottles—every detail is obviously pampered and lovingly produced. The *salade lyonnaise* (green salad with homemade croutons and sautéed bacon, topped with a poached egg) or the *rognons madère* (kidneys in a Madeira sauce) are standouts. *Average main: €22 25 rue Guynemer, Presqu'île, Lyon 04–78–37–46–18 www.cafecomptoirabel.fr No dinner Sun.*

10

$$ BISTRO **Daniel & Denise.** Among other honors, chef Joseph Viola has distinguished himself by creating a world-champion *pâté en croûte*—nothing to sneeze at, especially if you're at the helm of one of Lyon's best *bouchons* (taverns specializing in cuisine *populaire*). The traditional bouchon has come up in the world, and here you'll find a charming atmosphere, complete with checked tablecloths, lace curtains, and some of the city's most satisfying local specialties, including the *quenelles au brochet* (creamy fat sausages made from river pike). *Cervelle de veau*

Lyon's Place des Terreaux is a true spectacle, thanks to 69 Daniel Buren fountains and Bartholdi's centerpiece watery marvel.

(calf brains) is another standout, and the faint of heart can't go wrong with the excellent *boudin noir* (blood sausage) or the meltingly tender *foie gras en croûte*. Note: there are two Daniel & Denise outposts, but this one, in the Vieille Ville, is slightly more upscale. *Average main: €18 ✉ 36 rue Tramassac, 5e, Vieux Lyon, Lyon ☎ 04–78–42–24–62 🌐 daniel-et-denise.fr ⊙ Closed Sun., Mon., and 2 weeks in Jan. Reservations essential.*

$ FRENCH

Jura. The *gateau de foies de volaille aux raviolis* (chicken liver ravioli) is a masterpiece at this eatery founded in 1864. The game and steak dishes are robust, as is the *cassoulet des escargots* (stew of beans, mutton, and snails). For dessert, stick with the terrific cheese selection. The rows of tables, the mosaic-tile floor, and the absence of anything too decorative gives this place the feel of a men's club. *Average main: €16 ✉ 25 rue Tupin, Presqu'île, Lyon ☎ 04–78–42–20–57 🌐 www.bouchonlejura.fr ⊙ Closed Sun., Mon., and Aug.*

$$ FRENCH Fodor's Choice ★

La Famille. As the name would suggest, family photographs adorn the walls of this low-key bistro high on the Croix-Rousse hillside. The simple cuisine tends toward traditional recipes and authentic Lyon fare. From the *poulet fermier* (free-range chicken) to the grilled trout, the daily chalkboard announces the market specialties that Chef Gilles Mozziconacci has managed to cobble together on his early morning marketing tour through Les Halles de Lyon. In summer, opt for a table on the terrace. *Average main: €20 ✉ 18 rue Duviard, Croix Rousse, Lyon ☎ 04–72–98–83–90 🌐 www.la-famille-croix-rousse.fr ⊙ Closed Sun. and Mon. No dinner Thurs. Reservations essential.*

$$$$ FRENCH Fodor's Choice ★

La Mère Brazier. This is a legendary location in Lyon—even more so now that Mathieu Viannay, one of the top names in the city's contemporary cuisine scene, has honored food pioneer Eugénie Brazier by opening a restaurant in her former space. A winner of the coveted Meilleur Ouvrier de France prize, Viannay continues to experiment with taste, textures, and ingredients in this carefully restored traditional house. He describes the menu as "mixed" between completely modern cuisine and "Mère Brazier recipes revisited" such as the *poularde de Bresse demi-deuil* (Bresse poultry in "half mourning," that is, with black truffles under the breast skin). *Average main: €60 ✉ 12 rue Royale, Presqu'île, Lyon ☎ 04–78–23–17–20 🌐 lamerebrazier.fr ⏲ Closed weekends and Aug. ✍ Reservations essential.*

$ MODERN FRENCH
L'Ame Soeur. Just behind the Palais de Justice, this little *néo-bistrot* (think comfortable vibe but contemporary design) has a €20 prix-fixe *formule* that is nothing short of superb in terms of both value and quality. Artisanal terrine of free-range duck, *rillettes de maquereau en salade de chou chinois* (mackerel fillets in Chinese cabbage salad), and fillet of rockfish with peppers are just some of the interesting morsels at this innovative, affordable address. *Average main: €15 ✉ 209 rue Duguesclin, Vieux Lyon, Lyon ☎ 04–78–42–47–78 ⏲ Closed weekends. No dinner Mon. ✍ Reservations essential.*

$$$ MODERN FRENCH
La Table de Suzanne. Arnaud and Carine Leclercq racked up impressive successes from Zurich to Dubai before opening this 65-seat restaurant where good value and good cooking meet. The set menus at lunch (€23) and dinner (€48) both offer fine classic-contemporary French cuisine. The *soupe mousseuse de châtaignes et crème fermière* (soup-mousse of chestnuts and farmhouse cream) has a Corsican flavor, while the *tartine de canard séché* (crispy duck pie), steamed fish with sea algae, and jumbo shrimp tempura are all excellent. *Average main: €27 ✉ 39 rue Auguste Comte, Presqu'île, Lyon ☎ 04–78–37–49–83 🌐 www.latabledesuzanne.com ⏲ Closed Sun. and Mon. ✍ Reservations essential.*

$ CAFÉ
Le Café Mokxa. Watch the world go by on the street-side terrace at this small but lively café on a picturesque square at the foot of the hill leading to Croix-Rousse. Low-key and casual, the focus here is squarely on the java—every kind of caffeinated beverage can be conjured up here, and coffee aficionados are reassured by the fact that the meticulously sourced beans are roasted on the premises. Freshly baked carrot cake or cheesecake, tarte au citron, and warm chocolate fondant are irresistibly decadent alongside a luscious café crème. There's also a great choice of magazines and newspapers and free Wi-Fi access. *Average main: €5 ✉ 3 rue Abbé Rozier, Presqu'île, Lyon ☎ 04–27–01–48–71 🌐 www.cafemokxa.com.*

$$ FRENCH
Fodor's Choice ★
Le Garet. From *quenelles* (fish dumplings) to the house favorite, *andouillettes* (tripe sausage), this is the perfect primer course in bouchon fare. The cozy and joyful atmosphere is, perhaps even more than the food itself, what makes Lyon's version of the French bistro so irresistible. The *salade lyonnaise* (frisée lettuce, pork lardons, croutons, and a poached egg, with a Dijon vinaigrette) is an institution at this famous dining room near the Hôtel de Ville. The roast veal chop and ratatouille provide a welcome break from the standard porcine bouchon lineup.

Average main: €20 *7 rue Garet, Presqu'île, Lyon* *04–78–28–16–94* *Closed weekends and late July–late Aug.* *Reservations essential.*

$$ FRENCH **Le Nord.** The setting here is authentic turn-of-the-20th-century brasserie, with tiled floors, globe lamps, crisp white table linens, and a miles-long zinc bar. One of legendary chef Paul Bocuse's quartet of brasseries around the city, Le Nord has the feel of a traditional Lyonnais bouchon, with the classic fare to match—*ris de veau* (sweetbreads), *boudin noir* (blood sausage), creamed chicken, the local classic *quenelles* (fish sausage), and plenty of house-made charcuterie. *Average main: €24* *18 rue Neuve, Presqu'île, Lyon* *04–72–10–69–69* *www.nordsudbrasseries.com.*

$ FRENCH **Les Lyonnais.** Decorated with photographs of local celebrities, this popular bistro is particularly animated. The simple food—chicken simmered for hours in wine, meaty stews, and grilled fish—is served on bare wood tables. A blackboard announces plats du jour, which are usually less expensive than items on the printed menu. Try the *caille aux petits legumes* (quail with baby vegetables) for a change from heavier bouchon fare like the *bugnes* (beignets of fried pork fat). *Average main: €17* *19 rue de la Bombarde, Vieux Lyon, Lyon* *04–78–37–64–82* *www.restaurant-lyonnais.com* *Closed Mon. and 1st wk in Jan. No dinner Sun.*

$$ SEAFOOD **L'Est.** One of Lyon's Paul Bocuse four brasseries, the elegant L'Est is set in the 19th-century Belle Époque Brotteaux train station and cooks up a travel theme, thanks to a fish-centric menu that includes flavors from the world over—Cantonese rice with jumbo shrimp and squid, house-smoked Scottish salmon, curried cod with coconut milk and coriander, copious seafood platters—and a setting flavored with railroad memorabilia and a soupçon of nostalgia. *Average main: €24* *Gare des Brotteaux, 14 pl. Jules Ferry, Les Brotteaux, Lyon* *04–37–24–25–26* *www.nordsudbrasseries.com.*

$$ FRENCH **Le Sud.** The southern quadrant of Paul Bocuse's quartet, located in Lyon's central Bellecour neighborhood, this modern, sun-drenched eatery (with great people-watching potential) focuses on cooking from France's Mediterranean. Olive oil in all its glory takes front and center, whether spicy and green to complement fresh fish or vividly floral in a slow-cooked tagine of roasted eggplant, sweet onions, and preserved lemon. The wines of sunny Provence feature prominently of the excellent wine list, as do those of the Rhône. *Average main: €24* *11 pl. Antonin-Poncet, Presqu'île, Lyon* *04–72–77–80–00* *www.nordsudbrasseries.com.*

$$ FRENCH **L'Étage.** Hidden over Place des Terreaux, this semisecret upstairs dining room in a former silk-weaving loft prepares some of Lyon's finest and most daring cuisine. A place at the window (admittedly hard to come by), overlooking the facade of the Beaux Arts academy across the square, is a moment to remember—especially during December's Festival of Lights. *Average main: €22* *4 pl. des Terreaux, 3rd fl., Presqu'île, Lyon* *04–78–28–19–59* *www.letage-restaurant.com* *Closed Sun., Mon., and late July–late Aug.* *Reservations essential.*

$$ SEAFOOD **L'Ouest.** Set in a stylish industrial loft-style space in a quiet neighborhood on the banks of the River Saône, L'Ouest's sun-drenched interior

and beautiful outdoor terrace are the perfect backdrop for Bocuse's maritime culinary adventures in the islands of the Atlantic, Caribbean, and the South Seas. Dishes like turbot with wasabi-roasted vegetables, grilled crab cakes and garlicky aioli, or carpaccio of tuna served three ways celebrate the sea's briny best. The visible glassed-in wine cellar and excellent list of wines by the glass are your first clues that you won't go away thirsty. *Average main: €24* *1 quai du Commerce, Villefranche, Lyon* *04–37–64–64–64* *www.nordsudbrasseries.com.*

$$ FRENCH **M Restaurant.** Accomplished chef Julian Gautier struts his considerable stuff at this stylish upper-Brotteaux-district bistro east of the Rhône. Expect an inventive, market-driven cuisine, characterized by dishes like slow-cooked lamb with grilled eggplant, buffalo mozzarella and pine nuts; jumbo shrimp in a broth of garlic and tarragon; or succulent basque chicken with grilled chorizo and roasted red peppers to savor along with a fine selection of good-value wines by the bottle or glass. Consistently fabulous food, gentle prices, and a sleek contemporary design have made this bistro an exceedingly popular choice among fashionable foodies. *Average main: €20* *47 av. Foch, Les Brotteaux, Lyon* *04–78–89–55–19* *www.mrestaurant.fr* *Closed weekends and Aug.* *Reservations essential.*

$ WINE BAR Fodor's Choice ★ **Ô Vins d'Anges.** He's an indefatigable champion of small-producer wines, and you'd have to be a stone not to be swept up in Sébastien Milleret's passion. But if it's proof you need, you've come to the right place. A congenial atmosphere prevails at this wineshop and bar, and excellent small dishes—luscious burrata cheese served with fruity olive oil and capers, freshly shaved bresaola and lardo, or briny smoked eel—are complemented by reasonably priced wines by the glass. On Saturday afternoon, wine barrels are rolled out for tastings that draw a neighborhood crowd and often pour out onto the picturesque square. *Average main: €10* *2 pl. Bertone, Croix Rousse, Lyon* *09–51–88–20–99* *ovinsdanges.free.fr/ovinsdanges4* *Closed Sun. and Mon. No food Tues. and Wed.*

$$ BISTRO Fodor's Choice ★ **Palégrié.** A brilliant example of the *bistronomie* movement that's sweeping France, chef Guillaume Monjuré's sophisticated, fastidiously sourced cuisine is earning accolades from all quarters. Modest wooden tables and a spare decor belie a rich local fare rooted firmly in the bistro lexicon and imaginatively updated. Dishes like risotto perfumed with saffron and anise or luscious beef with wild *trompettes de la mort* mushrooms, black olives, and creamy rutabaga attest to this up-and-coming chef's flair with food. Spend just a few euros more for the *menu improviste* at dinner (€43), a perfect introduction to this ambitious cuisine. *Average main: €19* *8 rue Palais-Grillet, 2e, Presqu'île, Lyon* *04–78–92–94–84* *www.palegrie.fr* *Closed weekends. No lunch Mon.*

$$$$ FRENCH Fodor's Choice ★ **Paul Bocuse.** Whether Paul Bocuse—who kick-started the "new" French cooking back in the 1970s and became a superstar in the process—is here or not, the legendary black-truffle soup in pastry crust he created in 1975 to honor President Giscard d'Estaing will be. So will

the frogs'-leg soup with watercress; the green bean and artichoke salad with foie gras; and the "tripled" wood-pigeon, consisting of a drumstick in puff pastry, a breast roasted and glazed in cognac, and an aromatic dark pâté of the innards. For a mere €250 per person, the Menu Grand Tradition Classique includes the *volaille de Bresse truffée en vessie "Mère Fillioux"* (Bresse hen cooked in a pig bladder with truffles), which comes to the table looking something like a basketball. Like the desserts, the grand dining room is done in traditional style. *Average main: €62 ✉ 40 quai de la Plage, 10 km (6 miles) north of city center, Collongues au Mont d'Or, Lyon ☎ 04–72–42–90–90 🌐 www.bocuse.fr Reservations essential Jacket required.*

$$$ MODERN FRENCH Fodor's Choice ★ **Takao Takano.** After barely a year on his own, Takao Takano's eponymous restaurant earned off-the-charts accolades and a coveted Michelin star for his imaginative cuisine. Takano honed his craft during eight years as sous chef to Nicholas Le Bec (now in Shanghai), but he brings his own aesthetic to the fore in a warm, pared-down space outside the city center. Beautifully presented dishes, like tender Limousin lamb with artichokes and spicy olive oil; cucumber tarts with horseradish-inflected tarama and oyster-and-watercress gelée; roasted veal with bok choy, girolles mushrooms, and finely shaved lardo di Colonnata change according to the season. If you're pressed for time, or want to make one culinary splurge, you can't go wrong here. *Average main: €30 ✉ 33 rue Malesherbes, 6e, Part-Dieu, Lyon ☎ 04–82–31–43–39 🌐 takaotakano.com Closed Sun. and Mon. Reservations essential.*

WHERE TO STAY

$$$ HOTEL Fodor's Choice ★ **Collège.** A faithful reproduction of the owner's schoolboy days in Vieux Lyon, this charmingly nostalgic hotel ("taking us back to our dreams," as the owner puts it) offers public spaces decorated as antique classrooms, complete with polished wooden desks with inkwells and geography maps. **Pros:** in the heart of Vieux Lyon; reasonably priced; fun schoolboy theme. **Cons:** spartan interiors; rooms a bit short on space. *Rooms from: €165 ✉ 5 pl. St-Paul, Vieux Lyon, Lyon ☎ 04–72–10–05–05 🌐 www.college-hotel.com 40 rooms No meals.*

$ HOTEL **Dock Ouest.** The newest feather in Paul Bocuse's voluminous cap, Dock Ouest aims for a more youthful clientele that cares more about stylish comforts than an out-of-the-way location. **Pros:** excellent value; couldn't be quieter; underground parking. **Cons:** a 10-minute walk from the metro. *Rooms from: €97 ✉ 39 rue des Docks, 9e, Saint-Rambert, Lyon ☎ 04–78–22–34–34 🌐 www.dockouest.com 38 rooms, 5 suites No meals.*

$$ HOTEL **Hôtel des Artistes.** On an elegant square opposite the Théâtre des Célestins, this chic hotel has a sense of theatricality—logically enough because it has long been popular among stage and screen artists (many of whose photographs adorn the lobby walls). **Pros:** central location for Presqu'île; pretty view over square. **Cons:** slightly cluttered spaces; a few clicks behind cutting-edge technology. *Rooms from: €144 ✉ 8 rue Gaspard-André, Presqu'île, Lyon ☎ 04–78–42–04–88 🌐 www.hotel-des-artistes.fr 45 rooms No meals.*

$ HOTEL **Hôtel du Théâtre.** A friendly and enthusiastic owner, reasonable prices, and central location make this a recommendable address. **Pros:** sense of being at the center of the action; wallet friendly. **Cons:** small to tiny spaces in and around the hotel; street-side rooms can be noisy at night. *Rooms from: €69 ✉ 10 rue de Savoie, Presqu'île, Lyon ☎ 04–78–42–33–32 🌐 www.hotel-du-theatre.net 24 rooms No meals.*

$$$$ HOTEL Fodor's Choice ★ **La Cour des Loges.** King Juan Carlos of Spain, Céline Dion, and the Rolling Stones have all graced this former convent whose glowing fireplaces, Florentine crystal chandeliers, Baroque credenzas, and guest rooms swathed in antique Lyon silks now make monastic austerity a very distant memory. **Pros:** top Vieux Lyon location; cheerful service; extraordinary restaurant. **Cons:** hard on the budget. *Rooms from: €325 ✉ 6 rue du Bœuf, Vieux Lyon, Lyon ☎ 04–72–77–44–44 🌐 www.courdesloges.com 56 rooms, 4 suites No meals.*

$$$ HOTEL Fodor's Choice ★ **Phénix Hôtel.** This little hotel overlooking the River Saône has a winning combination of handy location, charming staff, tasteful rooms, and moderate prices. **Pros:** convenient to but not in the middle of Vieux Lyon; stylish but not stuffy; easy on the budget. **Cons:** interior rooms on the air shaft; a long walk to the middle of the Presqu'île. *Rooms from: €195 ✉ 7 quai Bondy, Vieux Lyon, Lyon ☎ 04–78–28–24–24 🌐 hotel-phenix-lyon.fr 36 rooms No meals.*

$$$$ HOTEL **Villa Florentine.** High above the Vieille Ville, this pristine hotel was once a 17th-century convent; glowing in its ocher-yellow exterior, it has vaulted ceilings, lovely terraces, and marvelous views, seen to best advantage from the Terrasses de Lyon restaurant. **Pros:** panoramic location above the Saône; wonderful restaurant; good access to Vieux Lyon. **Cons:** a hot climb up to the hotel in summer; tricky access by car; somewhat removed from the action. *Rooms from: €290 ✉ 25–27 montée St-Barthélémy, Fourvière, Lyon ☎ 04–72–56–56–56 🌐 www.villaflorentine.com 25 rooms, 4 suites No meals.*

NIGHTLIFE AND PERFORMING ARTS

Lyon is the region's liveliest arts center. Check the weekly *Lyon-Poche (🌐 www.lyonpoche.com)*for cultural events and goings-on at the dozens of discos, bars, and clubs.

NIGHTLIFE

Café Sevilla. This bar is salsa central on the Pentes de la Croix Rousse hillside. *✉ 7 rue Ste-Catherine, Presqu'île, Lyon ☎ 04–78–30–12–98.*

Hot Club. Live jazz has been played in the stone basement of the Hot Club since 1948, so they are obviously getting it right. *✉ 26 rue Lanterne, Presqu'île, Lyon ☎ 04–78–39–54–74 🌐 www.hotclubjazzlyon.com.*

La Cave des Voyageurs. Just below the St-Paul train station, La Cave des Voyageurs is a cozy place to sample some carefully selected wines. *✉ 7 pl. St-Paul, Vieux Lyon, Lyon ☎ 04–78–28–92–28 🌐 lacavedes-voyageurs.fr.*

Le Marché Gare. Live music from salsa to hip-hop rules at Le Marché Gare. *✉ 34 rue Casimir Périer, Presqu'île, Lyon ☎ 04–72–77–50–25 🌐 www.marchegare.fr.*

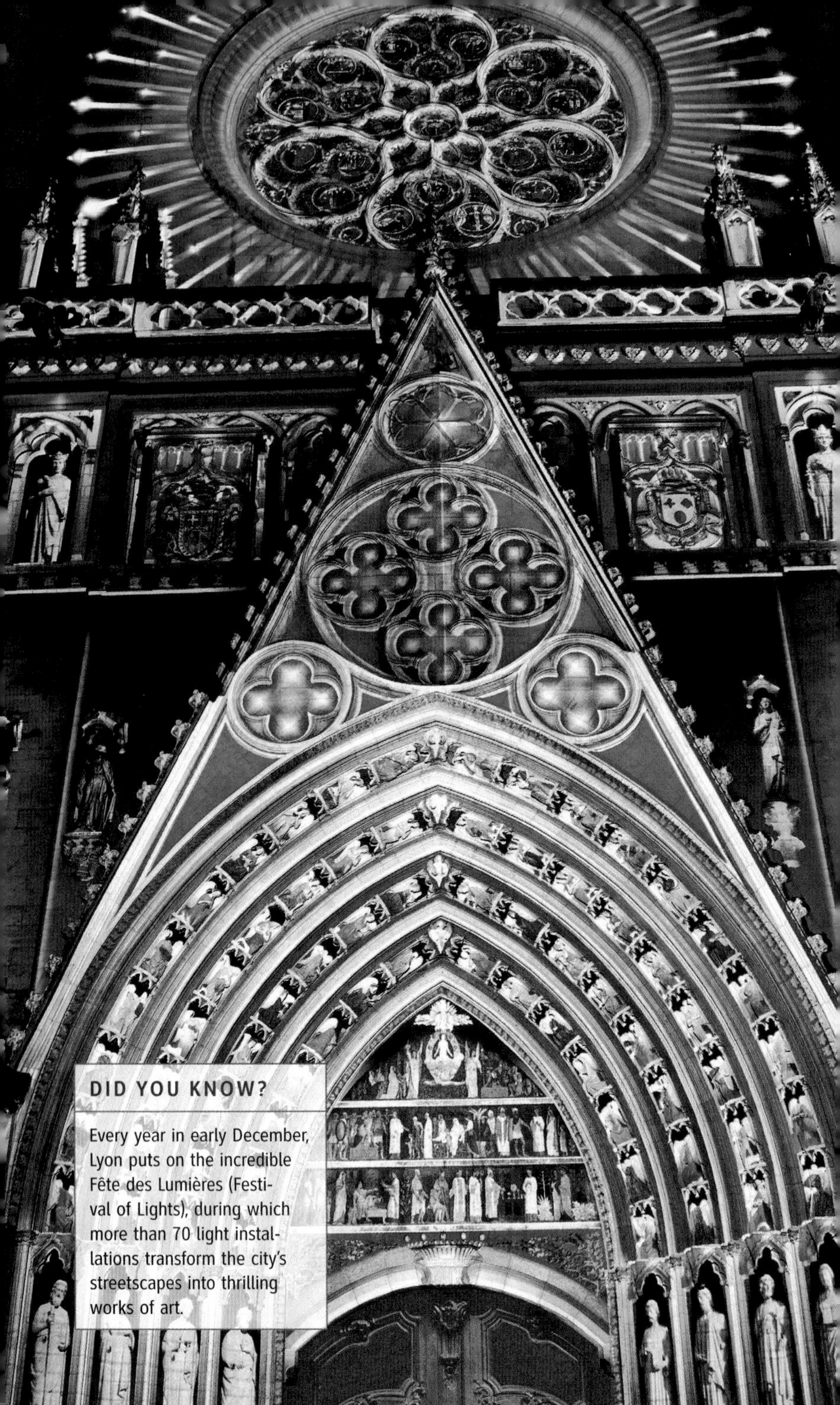

DID YOU KNOW?

Every year in early December, Lyon puts on the incredible Fête des Lumières (Festival of Lights), during which more than 70 light installations transform the city's streetscapes into thrilling works of art.

Smoking Dog. For the hottest English pub in Lyon, the Smoking Dog is the place to head. You can't miss the bright red awning out front. ✉ *16 rue Lainerie, Vieux Lyon, Lyon* ☎ *04–78–28–38–27.*

PERFORMING ARTS

Espace Gerson. The café-theater Espace Gerson presents revues and assorted stand-up shows. ✉ *1 pl. Gerson, Vieux Lyon, Lyon* ☎ *04–78–27–96–99* 🌐 *www.espacegerson.com.*

L'Accessoire Café-Théâtre. Here you can eat and drink while watching a comedy show. ✉ *26 rue de l'Annonciade, Presqu'île, Lyon* ☎ *04–78–27–84–84* 🌐 *www.accessoire-cafe-theatre.com.*

Le Complexe du Rire. Also known as the Minette Theatre, Le Complexe du Rire is a lively satirical café-theater above Place des Terreaux. ✉ *7 rue des Capucins, Presqu'île, Lyon* ☎ *04–78–27–23–59* 🌐 *www.complexedurire.com.*

SHOPPING

Lyon remains France's silk-and-textile capital, and all big-name designers have shops here. The 19th-century Passage de l'Argue (between Rue du Président Édouard-Herriot and Rue de la République in the center of town) is lined with traditional shops. The Carré d'Or district has more than 70 luxury ones between Place Bellecour and Cordeliers.

Food markets are held Tuesday to Sunday on Boulevard de la Croix-Rousse, at Les Halles on Cours Lafayette, on Quai Victor Augagneur, and on Quai St-Antoine. For antiques, wander down Rue Auguste-Comte. For secondhand books try the market along Quai de la Pêcherie near Place Bellecour, held every weekend 10–6.

À Ma Vigne. Popular with locals, this wineshop is known for its excellent selection. ✉ *18 rue Vaubecour, Presqu'île, Lyon* ☎ *04–78–37–05–29.*

Antic Wine. For great wines, tasting sessions, and up-to-the-minute information on local restaurants, don't miss the prize-winning "flying sommelier," Georges Dos Santos at Antic Wine. ✉ *18 rue du Bœuf, Vieux Lyon, Lyon* ☎ *04–78–37–08–96.*

Bernachon. Some say Bernachon is the best *chocolaterie* in France. It's a family business that proudly passes the torch from father to son. ✉ *42 cours Franklin-Roosevelt, Les Brotteaux, Lyon* ☎ *04–78–24–37–98* 🌐 *www.bernachon.com.*

Bouillet. With a stunning selection of artisanal chocolate, Bouillet is paradise for chocoholics. It also has stores at 14 rue des Archers and 3 rue d'Austerlitz. ✉ *15 pl. de la Croix Rousse, Croix Rousse, Lyon* ☎ *04–78–28–90–89* 🌐 *www.chocolatier-bouillet.com.*

Cha Yuan. The best tea shop in Lyon, Cha Yuan stocks more than 300 varieties from all over the world. You can also buy candies, gourmet goodies, and everything you need to brew the perfect cup of tea. ✉ *7–9 rue des Remparts d'Ainay, Presqu'île, Lyon* ☎ *04–78–41–04–60* 🌐 *www.cha-yuan.com.*

Diogène. Smelling of old leather and ancient paper, this shop sells rare and antique books. ✉ *29 rue St-Jean, Vieux Lyon, Lyon* ☎ *04–78–42-29–41* 🌐 *www.librairiediogene.fr*.

La Cave d'à Côté. This local favorite specializes in Côte du Rhône wines. Tucked away on a side street, the shop is distinguished by soaring stone arches. ✉ *7 rue Pleney, Presqu'île, Lyon* ☎ *04–78–28–31–46*.

La Maison des Canuts. In Lyon's old silk *quartier*, this boutique is replete with fine examples of locally made fabrics that you can wear or take home with you. ✉ *10–12 rue d'Ivry, La Croix Rousse, Lyon* ☎ *04–78–28–62–04* 🌐 *www.maisondescanuts.com* ⏲ *Closed Sun.*

L'Atelier de Soierie. To see how silk prints are made, and perhaps take home a piece of Lyon, visit L'Atelier de Soierie. ✉ *33 rue Romarin, Presqu'île, Lyon* ☎ *04–72–07–97–83* 🌐 *www.atelierdesoierie.com*.

Les Halles de Lyon. Take a cue from superstar chef Paul Bocuse and shop at the market stalls of Les Halles de Lyon. ✉ *102 cours Lafayette, Part-Dieu, Lyon* ☎ *04–78–62–39–33*.

Nicolas Fafiotte. This shop specializes in high-end evening wear, and you need an appointment to visit. ✉ *8 rue du Plat, Presqu'île, Lyon* ☎ *04–72–41–84–79* 🌐 *www.nicolasfafiotte.com*.

Part-Dieu. One of the biggest shopping centers in Europe is Part-Dieu, where you'll find more than 250 shops and boutiques. Galeries Lafayette, a major department store, brings Parisian flair to Lyon. ✉ *Rue du Dr-Bouchut, Part-Dieu, Lyon* ☎ *04–72–60–60–62* 🌐 *www.centrecommercial-partdieu.com*.

Pignol. This shop's pastries, meats, and wines are so good that it has expanded to become a mini-chain, with other locations at 8 place Bellecour, 48 rue Vendôme, and 42 rue de la République. ✉ *17 rue Émile-Zola, Presqu'île, Lyon* ☎ *04–78–92–43–92* 🌐 *www.pignol.fr*.

Printemps. This is the Lyon outpost of the famous Parisian department store specializing in fashions for men and women. ✉ *42 rue de la République, Presqu'île, Lyon* ☎ *04–72–41–29–29* 🌐 *www.printemps.com*.

Reynon. This is *the* place for charcuterie. Look for the wonderful array of sausages hanging in the front window. ✉ *13 rue des Archers, Presqu'île, Lyon* ☎ *04–78–37–39–08* 🌐 *www.reynonlyon.com*.

Fodor's Choice ★ **Village des Créateurs.** In the *quartier* Croix Rousse—once the heart of Lyon's silk trade and the traditional neighborhood for artists and craftspeople—this pleasant pedestrian street is a showplace for 70 talented young designers. Along with fashions for women (often using locally made silk), men, and children, you'll also find beautiful handmade ceramics, leather goods, and jewelry. ✉ *Passage Thiaffait, 19 rue René Leynaud, Croix Rousse, Lyon* ☎ *04–78–27–37–21* 🌐 *www.villagedescreateurs.com*.

Voisin. For the famous chocolate *coussins* (pillows), check out Voisin. The confections have become so popular that there are now eight shops in Lyon, including one at 11 place Bellecour, right next to the main tourist office. ✉ *28 rue de la République, Presqu'île, Lyon* ☎ *04–78–42–46–24* 🌐 *www.chocolat-voisin.com*.

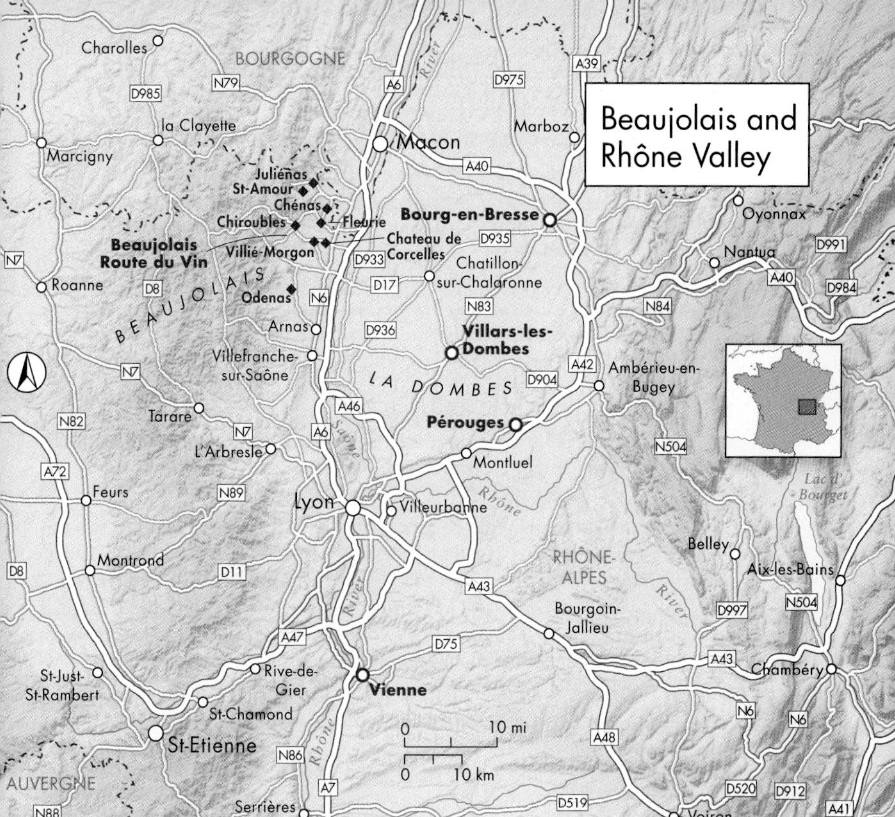

BEAUJOLAIS

North of Lyon along the Saône, the vineyards of Beaujolais are a thrill for any oenophile. In the area around Villefranche, small villages—perhaps comprising a church, a bar, and a boulangerie—pop up here and there out of the rolling vine-covered hillsides. The region's best wines are all labeled "grands crus," a more complex version of the otherwise light, fruity Beaujolais. Although these get better with age, many Beaujolais wines are drunk nearly fresh off the vine; every third Thursday in November marks the arrival of the Beaujolais Nouveau, a bacchanalian festival that also showcases regional cuisine. North of La Dombes region and east of the Beaujolais wine villages is Bourg-en-Bresse, famous for its marvelous church and a breed of poultry that impassions gourmands; it makes a good base after Lyon. South toward the Rhône, the great river of southern France, is the well-preserved medieval village of Pérouges.

BEAUJOLAIS WINE ROUTE

16 km (10 miles) north of Villefranche-sur-Saône, 49 km (30 miles) north of Lyon.

Not all Beaujolais wine is promoted as *vin nouveau* (new wine), despite the highly successful marketing campaign that has made Beaujolais Nouveau synonymous with French wine. Wine classed as "Beaujolais Villages" is higher in alcohol and produced from a clearly defined region northwest of Villefranche. Beaujolais is made from one single variety of grape, the *gamay noir à jus blanc*. However, there are 12 different appellations: Beaujolais, Beaujolais Villages, Brouilly, Chénas, Chiroubles, Côte de Brouilly, Fleurie, Juliénas, Morgon, Moulin à Vent, Régnié, and St-Amour. The Beaujolais Route du Vin (Wine Road), a narrow strip 23 km (14 miles) long, is home to nine of these deluxe Beaujolais wines, also known as *grands crus*.

GETTING HERE AND AROUND

For the Beaujolais wine country, most people take the train to the station on Place de la Gare in Villefranche-sur-Saône, 31 km (19 miles) north of Lyon, where trains to smaller towns are available. SNCF trains link Lyon Part-Dieu with Villefranche-sur-Saône (26 mins, €8.05). Cars du Rhône (Line 18) connects Lyon with Villefranche-sur-Saône with multiple connections to surrounding towns.

Visitor Information Beaujolais Tourist Office. ☎ *04–74–07–27–40* 🌐 *www.villefranche-beaujolais.fr.* **Cars du Rhône.** ☎ *08–00–10–40–36* 🌐 *www.carsdurhone.fr.*

EXPLORING

Château de Corcelles. The 15th-century Château de Corcelles is noted for its Renaissance galleries, canopied courtyard well, and medieval carvings in its chapel. The guardroom is now an atmospheric tasting cellar. ✉ *D9, 3 km (2 miles) east of Villié-Morgon via D9, Corcelles-en-Beaujolais* ☎ *04–74–66–00–24* 🌐 *www.chateaudecorcelles.fr* 🎫 *€5* ⏲ *Apr.–Sept., Mon.–Sat. 10–noon and 2:30–6:30.*

WHERE TO EAT AND STAY

$$$ FRENCH ✕ **Le Juliénas.** Since earning a Michelin star, this bright, contemporary dining room in the heart of the Beaujolais Wine Route has been busy reaching for ever new heights. Drawing from the area's exceptional seasonal bounty, Chef Fabrice Roche creates a virtuoso menu of meticulously prepared dishes that look as divine as they taste. French specialities like escargot, foie gras, and housemade gravlax are thrillingly reimagined with surprising accompaniments, including bananas, white currants, and roasted chestnuts. Main dishes like steamed cod with leek mousseline in a lemon-mint emulsion and pigs' feet with pickled beets and cumin are packed with flavor. Desserts are a house specialty, as is the superb wine list—a thrilling education in the best of Beaujolais. Come on a warm day to enjoy garden dining and an excellent prix-fixe menu: at lunch (€27) or dinner (€42). Hands down they're the region's best deals. 💲 *Average main: €32* ✉ *236 rue d'Anse, Villefranche-sur-Saône* ☎ *04–74–09–16–55* 🌐 *www.restaurant-lejulienas.com* ⏲ *Closed Sun. No lunch Sat., no dinner Mon.*

For a true Beaujolais blowout book a stay at Lady Hamlyn's Château de Bagnols, where even Louis XIV would feel right at home.

$$$$ HOTEL Fodor's Choice ★ **Château de Bagnols.** A destination in itself, Lady Hamlyn's dazzlingly elegant castle-hotel is one of the glories of the Beaujolais, as anyone can tell with one glance at the *fantastique* Grand Salon. **Pros:** grandly elegant; panoramic views; nonpareil dining. **Cons:** a little like living in a museum; very expensive rates. *Rooms from: €425* *D38, Bagnols* *15 km (9 miles) southwest of Villefranche* *04–74–71–40–00* *www.chateaudebagnols.fr* *Closed Jan. and Feb.* *27 apartments* *No meals.*

BOURG-EN-BRESSE

10

30 km (18 miles) east of St-Amour on N79, 81 km (49 miles) northeast of Lyon.

Cheerful, flower-festooned Bourg-en-Bresse is esteemed among gastronomes for its chickens—the striking-looking *poulet de Bresse,* with plump white bodies, bright blue feet, and red combs (adding up to France's *tricolore,* or national colors). The town's southeasternmost district, Brou, is its most interesting and the site of a singular church. This is a good place to stay before or after a trip along the Beaujolais Wine Road.

GETTING HERE

Baladain connects Lyon-Saint-Exupéry airport with Bourg-en-Bresse four times daily (1 hr, 20 mins; €26). SNCF trains link Lyon Perrache station with Bourg-en-Bresse (1 hr, 22 mins; €12.60).

Visitor Information Baladain. ☎ *04-74-45-19-29* ⊕ *www.baladain.fr.* **Bourg-en-Bresse Tourist Office.** ☎ *04-74-22-49-40* ⊕ *www.bourgenbresse tourisme.fr.*

EXPLORING

Église de Brou. A marvel of the Flamboyant Gothic style, the Église de Brou is no longer in religious use. The church was built between 1513 and 1532 by Margaret of Austria in memory of her husband, Philibert le Beau, Duke of Savoy, and their finely sculpted tombs highlight the rich interior. Outside, a massive restoration of the roof has brought it back to its 16th-century state, with the same gorgeous, multicolor, intricate patterns found throughout Burgundy. The museum in the nearby cloister stands out for its paintings: 16th- and 17th-century Flemish and Dutch artists keep company with 17th- and 18th-century French and Italian masters, 19th-century artists of the Lyon School, Gustave Doré, and contemporary local painters. ✉ *63 bd. de Brou, Bourg-en-Bresse* ☎ *04–74–22–83–83* ⊕ *brou.monuments-nationaux.fr* 🎫 *€7.50* ⏲ *Apr.–Sept., daily 9–12:30 and 2–6; Oct.–Mar., daily 9–noon and 2–5.*

WHERE TO EAT AND STAY

$$$$ FRENCH Fodor's Choice ★

✕ **Georges Blanc.** In the village of Vonnas, a simple 19th-century inn with 30 rooms full of antique country furniture doubles as one of the greatest gastronomic addresses in all of Gaul. *Poulet de Bresse*, truffles, and lobster are just some of the divine dishes featured on the legendary menu created by three-star chef Monsieur Blanc, whose culinary DNA extends back to innkeepers from the French Revolution. He serves his traditional-yet-nouvelle delights in a vast dining room, renovated—overly so, some might say—in a stately manner, replete with Louis Treize-style chairs, fireplace, and floral tapestries. Wine connoisseurs will go weak at the knees at the cellar here, overflowing with 130,000 bottles. The guest rooms range from (relatively) simple to luxurious. A block south you can repair to Blanc's cheaper, more casual restaurant, L'Ancienne Auberge, most delightfully set in a 1900s *Fabrique de Limonade* (soda-water plant) and now festooned with antique bicycles and daguerreotypes. $ *Average main: €95* ✉ *Pl. du Marché, Vonnas* ✢ *23 km (14 miles) from Bourg-en-Bresse* ☎ *04–74–50–90–90* ⊕ *www.georgesblanc.com* ⏲ *Closed Mon., Tues., and Jan. No lunch Wed. and Thurs.* ✍ *Reservations essential* 🍽 *No meals.*

$$$$ FRENCH

✕ **L'Auberge Bressane.** Overlooking the town's wonderful church, this modern, polished dining room is a good match for Chef Jean-Pierre Vullin's cuisine. Frogs' legs and Bresse chicken with a wild morel–cream sauce are the specialties, but also consider the *quenelles de brochet* (poached-fish dumplings). Jean-Pierre wanders through the dining room ready for a chat while his staff provides excellent service. Don't miss the house aperitif, a Champagne cocktail with fresh strawberry puree. The wine list has 300 vintages. $ *Average main: €34* ✉ *166 bd. de Brou, Bourg-en-Bresse* ☎ *04–74–22–22–68* ⊕ *www.aubergebressane.fr* ⏲ *Closed Tues.* ✍ *Reservations essential.*

$$ HOTEL

🏨 **Hôtel de France.** This centrally located and impeccably renovated hotel offers comfortable rooms equipped with the full range of modern amenities. **Pros:** convenient location for exploring the town; contemporary interior and equipment; close to good dining options. **Cons:** in the midst of the hustle and bustle. *Rooms from: €110 ✉ 19 pl. Bernard, Bourg-en-Bresse ☎ 04–74–23–30–24 🌐 www.bestwestern-hoteldefrance.com 42 rooms, 2 suites No meals.*

VILLARS-LES-DOMBES

29 km (18 miles) south of Bourg-en-Bresse, 37 km (23 miles) northeast of Lyon.

Villars-les-Dombes is the unofficial capital of La Dombes, an area once covered by a glacier. When the ice retreated, it left a network of lakes and ponds that draws anglers and bird-watchers today.

Parc des Oiseaux. The 56-acre Parc des Oiseaux, one of Europe's finest bird sanctuaries, is home-sweet-home to 400 species of birds from five continents. More than 400 aviaries house species from waders to birds of prey, and tropical birds in vivid hues fill the indoor birdhouse. Allow two hours for a visit. ✉ *D1083, Villars-les-Dombes* ☎ *04–74–98–05–54* 🌐 *www.parc-des-oiseaux.com* *€16* *Mar.–mid-Nov., daily 9:30–dusk.*

PÉROUGES

36 km (22 miles) northeast of Lyon.

With its medieval houses and narrow cobbled streets surrounded by ramparts, wonderfully preserved Pérouges is only 200 yards across. Handweavers first brought it prosperity; but the Industrial Revolution meant their downfall, and by the late 19th century the population had dwindled from 1,500 to 12. Now the government has restored the most interesting houses, giving the town a new lease on life. A number of restaurants make Pérouges a good lunch stop.

GETTING HERE

Park your car by the main gateway, Porte d'En-Haut, alongside the 15th-century fortress-church. Rue du Prince, the town's main street, leads to the Maison des Princes de Savoie (Palace of the Princes of Savoie), the erstwhile home of the influential Savoie family that once controlled the eastern part of France.

10

EXPLORING

Musée du Vieux Pérouges (*Old Pérouges Museum*). To one side of Place de la Halle, the Musée du Vieux Pérouges contains local artifacts and a reconstructed weaver's workshop. The medieval garden is noted for its array of rare medicinal plants. ✉ *Pl. du Tilleul, Pérouges* ☎ *04–74–46–70–84* *€4* *May–Sept., daily 10–noon and 2–6; Oct. and Apr., weekends 10–noon and 2–6.*

WHERE TO STAY

$$$$ HOTEL **Hostellerie du Vieux Pérouges.** If you want a sense of stepping back into medieval France, tarry a while at "The Old Man of Pérouges," a gorgeous complex of four ancient stone residences set around an extraordinary corbelled, 14th-century timber-frame house. **Pros:** age-old aura; graceful manor house surroundings; cheerful service. **Cons:** breakfast

is extra; no a/c (literally the "dog days" of summer); some bathrooms lack modern showers. 💲 *Rooms from: €220* ✉ *Pl. du Tilleul, Pérouges* ☎ *04–74–61–00–88* 🌐 *www.hostelleriedeperouges.com* 🛏 *26 rooms, 2 suites* 🍽 *No meals.*

THE RHÔNE VALLEY

At Lyon, the Rhône, joined by the Saône, truly comes into its own, plummeting south in search of the Mediterranean. The river's progress is often spectacular, as steep vineyards conjure up vistas that are more readily associated with the river's Germanic cousin, the Rhine. All along the way, small-town vintners invite you to sample their wines. Early Roman towns like Vienne and Valence reflect the Rhône's importance as a trading route. To the west is the rugged, rustic Ardèche *département*, where time seems to have slowed to a standstill.

VIENNE

27 km (17 miles) south of Lyon via A7.

Fodor's Choice ★ If you do nothing but head up to this town's famed Roman Theater and look out over the red-tile roofs of the Rhône Valley, you'll be happy you made the 20-minute trip from Lyon. Vienne is a historian's dream, and every street takes you to yet another ancient church, another austere Roman ruin, or another postcard-perfect view of crumbling walls and sloped roofs.

The €6 Billet Intermusée admits you to all local monuments and museums within a 48-hour period. Even better, the €5 Billet-Pass admits you to three museums and the Théâtre Roman. Both are available at the first site that you visit.

GETTING HERE

SNCF trains link Lyon Perrache or Lyon Part-Dieu stations with Vienne (18–32 mins, €7.40). From Lyon-Saint-Exupéry, the best connection to Vienne is to take the shuttle to Lyon Part-Dieu and the train to Vienne.

Visitor Information Vienne Tourist Office. ☎ *04–74–53–80–30* 🌐 *www.vienne-tourisme.com.*

EXPLORING

Cité Gallo-Romaine de St-Romain-en-Gal (*Gallo-Roman City*). Across the Rhône from the town center is the excavated Cité Gallo-Romaine, covering several acres. Here you can find villas, houses, workshops, public baths, and roads, all built by the Romans. Views of the site can be had from the stunning glassed-in museum, which houses temporary exhibitions, mosaics excavated at the site, a boutique, and a pleasantly bright café. ✉ *Rte. Départementale 502, Saint-Romain-en-Gal* ☎ *04–74–53–74–01* 🌐 *www.musees-gallo-romains.com* 🎟 *€4; €6 includes Théâtre Romain and St-André-le-Bas museums* ⏲ *Tues.–Sun. 10–6.*

St-André-le-Bas. Rue des Orfèvres (off Rue de la Charité) is lined with Renaissance facades and distinguished by the church of St-André-le-Bas, once part of a powerful abbey, with beautifully restored 12th-century capitals and a 17th-century wood statue of St. Andrew. It's best to see

One of the most important towns of Roman Gaul, Vienne is a historian's fantasyland famed for its ancient theater.

the cloisters during the music festival held here and at the cathedral from June through August. ✉ *Pl. du jeu de Paume, Vienne* ☎ *04–74–85–18–49* 🎫 *€2.80; €6 includes Cité Gallo-Romaine and Théâtre Romain museums* ⏲ *Apr.–Oct., Tues.–Sun. 9:30–1 and 2–6; Nov.–Mar., Tues.–Fri. 9:30–12:30 and 2–5, weekends 1:30–5:30.*

St-Maurice. Although religious wars deprived the cathedral of St-Maurice of many of its statues, much of the original decoration is intact; the portals on the 15th-century facade are carved with Old Testament scenes. The cathedral was built between the 12th and 16th century, with later additions, such as the splendid 18th-century mausoleum to the right of the altar. A frieze of the zodiac adorns the entrance to the vaulted passage that once led to the cloisters but now opens onto Place St-Paul. ✉ *Pl. St-Paul, Vienne* ☎ *04–74–85–60–28* ⏲ *Daily 10–6.*

St-Pierre. Beside the Rhône is the church of St-Pierre—note the rectangular 12th-century Romanesque bell tower with its arcaded tiers. The lower church walls date from the 6th century, and there is a collection of Gallo-Roman architectural fragments on display. ✉ *Quai Jean-Jaurès, Vienne.*

Temple d'Auguste et de Livie (*Temple of Augustus and Livia*). The remains of the Temple d'Auguste et de Livie, accessible via Place St-Paul and Rue Clémentine, probably date in part from Vienne's earliest Roman settlements (1st century BC). The Corinthian columns were walled in during the 11th century, when the temple was used as a church; in 1833 Prosper Mérimée intervened to have the temple restored. ✉ *Pl. du Palais, Vienne.*

Fodor's Choice ★ **Théâtre Romain** (*Roman Theater*). Measuring 143 yards across, the Théâtre Romain is one of the largest in Gaul. It held 13,000 spectators and is only slightly smaller than Rome's Theater of Marcellus. Rubble buried Vienne's theater until 1922; excavation has uncovered 46 rows of seats, some marble flooring, and the frieze on the stage. ✉ *7 rue du Cirque, Vienne* ☎ *04–74–85–39–23* *€2.80; €6, includes Cité Gallo-Romaine and St-André-le-Bas museums* ⏲ *Apr.–Aug., daily 9–1 and 2–6; Sept. and Oct., Tues.–Sun. 9:30–1 and 2–6; Nov.–Mar., Tues.–Fri. 9:30–12:30 and 2–5, weekends 1:30–5:30.*

WHERE TO EAT

$$$$ FRENCH Fodor's Choice ★ ✕ **La Pyramide.** Back when your grandmother's grandmother was making the grand tour, La Pyramide was *le must.* Fernand Point had perfected haute cuisine for a generation and became the first superstar chef, teaching a regiment of students who glamorize French dining the world over. Many decades later, La Pyramide has dropped its museum status and now offers contemporary classics by acclaimed Chef Patrick Henriroux, accompanied by a peerless selection of wines featuring local stars from the nearby Côte Rôtie and Condrieu vineyards. Both classical and avant-garde dishes triumph here, from *crème soufflée de crabe au croquant d'artichaut* (creamy crab soufflé with crunchy artichoke) to the *veau de lait aux légumes de la vallée* (suckling veal with vegetables from the Drôme Valley). For those who wish to sleep off the feast, there are graceful guest rooms at hand. $ *Average main: €65* ✉ *14 bd. Fernand-Point, Vienne* ☎ *04–74–53–01–96* 🌐 *www.lapyramide.com* ⏲ *Closed Tues., Wed., and Feb.–mid-Mar.*

$$$ FRENCH ✕ **Le Bec Fin.** With its understatedly elegant dining room and an inexpensive weekday menu, this unpretentious enclave opposite the cathedral is a good choice for lunch or dinner. Red meat, seafood, and both fresh- and saltwater fish are well prepared here. Try the turbot cooked with saffron, one of the specialties of the house. $ *Average main: €26* ✉ *7 pl. St-Maurice, Vienne* ☎ *04–74–85–76–72* ⏲ *Closed Mon. and 2 wks in Jan. No dinner Sun. and Wed.* *Reservations essential.*

GRENOBLE AND THE ALPS

In winter some of the world's best skiing is found in the Alps; in summer chic spas, shimmering lakes, and hilltop trails offer additional delights. The Savoie and Haute-Savoie regions occupy the most impressive territory; Grenoble, in the Dauphiné (so named for the dolphin in the coat of arms of an early noble family), is the gateway to the Alps and the area's only city, occupying the nexus of highways from Marseille, Valence, Lyon, Geneva, and Turin.

This is the region where Stendhal, the groundbreaking 19th-century novelist, was born and where the great 18th-century philosopher Jean-Jacques Rousseau lived out his old age. So, in addition to natural splendors, the traveler should also expect worldly pleasures: charming Annecy, set with arcaded lanes and quiet canals in the old quarter around the lovely 16th-century Palais de l'Isle, and old-master treasures on view at Grenoble's Musée are just some of the civilized enjoyments to be discovered here.

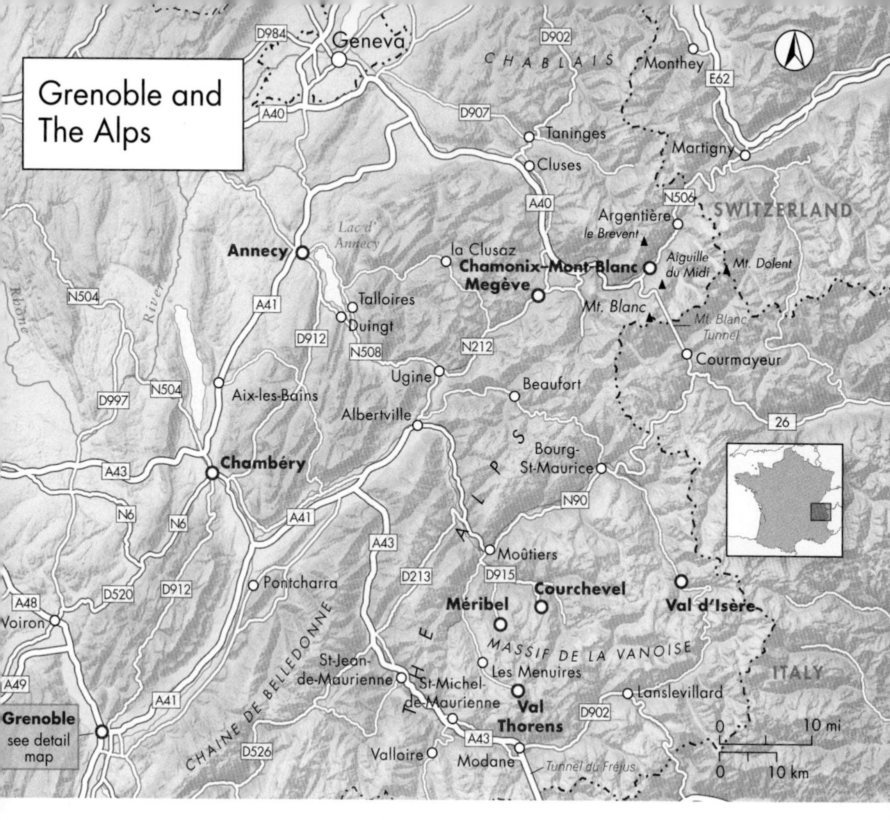

As for *le ski,* the season for most French resorts runs from December 15 to April 15. At the high-altitude resorts the skiing season lasts until May. In summer the lake resorts, as well as the regions favored by hikers and climbers, come into their own.

GRENOBLE

104 km (65 miles) southeast of Lyon, 86 km (52 miles) northeast of Valence.

Capital of the Dauphiné region, Grenoble sits at the confluence of the Isère and Drac rivers and lies within three *massifs* (mountain ranges): La Chartreuse, Le Vercors, and Belledonne. This cosmopolitan city's skyscrapers bear witness to the fierce local desire to move ahead with the times, and it's not surprising to find one of France's most noted universities here. Grenoble's main claim to fame is as the birthplace of the great French novelist Henri Beyle (1783–1842), better known as Stendhal, author of *The Red and the Black* and *The Charterhouse of Parma.* The native Grenoblois, known for their down-home friendliness, are delighted—and generally surprised—if you know of him.

GETTING HERE

Paris's Gare de Lyon dispatches more than a dozen trains daily (either direct or via Lyon Part-Dieu) to Grenoble (3 hrs, 3 mins; €84 or 3 hrs, 40 mins; €96 via Lyon). Six TGV trains daily connect Lyon-Saint-Exupéry airport with Grenoble (1 hr, 7 mins; €27). Faure buses connect Lyon-Saint-Exupéry with Grenoble every hour on the half hour (1 hr, 5 mins; €27.50). Altibus connects Grenoble with 60 ski stations and towns throughout the Alps.

Grenoble's layout is maddening: your only hope lies in the big, illuminated maps posted throughout town or the free map from the tourist office. The heart of the city forms a crescent around a bend of the Isère, with the train station at the western end and the university all the way at the eastern tip. As it fans out from the river toward the south, the crescent seems to develop a more modern flavor. The hub of the city is Place Victor Hugo, with its flowers, fountains, and cafés, though most sights and nightlife are near the Isère in Place St-André, Place de Gordes, and Place Notre-Dame

Altibus. ✉ *Grenoble* ☎ *08–20–32–03–68* 🌐 *www.altibus.com.*

Faure. ✉ *Grenoble* ☎ *04–76–88–08–80* 🌐 *www.faurevercors.fr.*

Visitor Information Grenoble Tourist Office. ☎ *04–76–42–41–41* 🌐 *www.grenoble-tourisme.com.*

EXPLORING

Cathédrale Notre-Dame. Despite its 12th-century exterior, the 19th-century interior of the Cathédrale Notre-Dame is somewhat bland. But don't miss the adjoining bishop's house, now a museum on the history of Grenoble; the main treasure is a noted 4th-century baptistery. ✉ *Pl. Notre-Dame, Grenoble* 🎫 *Free* ⏲ *Museum Wed.–Mon. 10–noon and 2–5.*

Centre National d'Art Contemporain. Contemporary art enthusiasts should check out the Centre National d'Art Contemporain. Behind the train station in an out-of-the-way district, it is noted for its distinctive warehouse space and avant-garde collection. ✉ *155 cours Berriat, Grenoble* ☎ *04–76–21–95–84* 🌐 *www.magasin-cnac.org* 🎫 *€4* ⏲ *Wed.–Sun. 2–7.*

FAMILY **La Bastille.** Starting at Quai St-Stéphane-Jay, this téléphérique (cable car) whisks you over the River Isère and up to the hilltop where there are splendid views and a good restaurant. Walk back down via the footpath through the Jardin Dauphinoise. ✉ *Quai Stéphane Jay, Grenoble* ☎ *04–76–44–89–65* 🌐 *www.bastille-grenoble.fr* 🎫 *€8 round-trip* ⏲ *May–Sept., daily; Oct.–Dec. and Feb.–Apr., Tues.–Sun. Hrs vary.*

Musée Archéologique St-Laurent. The church of St-Laurent, near the Musée Dauphinois, has a hauntingly ancient 6th-century crypt—one of the country's oldest Christian monuments—supported by a row of formidable marble pillars. A tour of the church traces the emergence of Christianity in the Dauphiné. ✉ *2 pl. St-Laurent, Grenoble* ☎ *04–76–44–78–68* 🌐 *www.musee-archeologique-grenoble.fr* 🎫 *Free* ⏲ *Wed.–Mon. 10–6.*

Musée Dauphinois. On the north side of the River Isère is Rue Maurice-Gignoux, lined with gardens, cafés, mansions, and a 17th-century

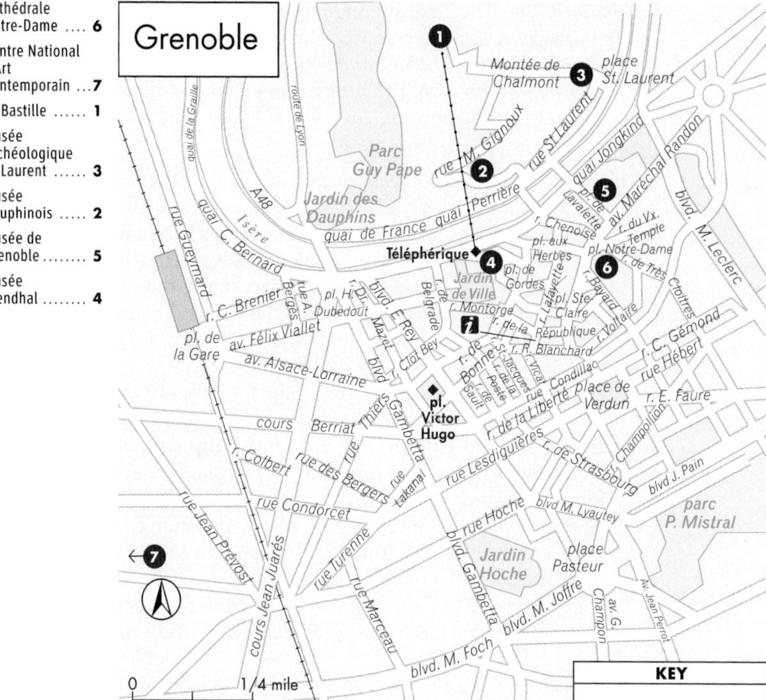

convent that contains the Musée Dauphinois, detailing the history of mountaineering and skiing. The Premiers Alpins section explores the evolution of the Alps and its inhabitants. ✉ *30 rue Maurice-Gignoux, Grenoble* ☎ *04–57–58–89–01* ⊕ *www.musee-dauphinois.fr* 🎟 *Free* ⏲ *Nov.–Apr., Wed.–Mon. 10–6; May–Oct., Wed.–Mon. 10–7.*

Musée de Grenoble. Place de Lavalette—on the south side of the river, where most of Grenoble is concentrated—is where you'll find the Musée de Grenoble. Founded in 1796, it's one of France's oldest museums and was the first to concentrate on modern art (Picasso donated his *Femme Lisant* in 1921). An addition incorporates the medieval Tour de l'Isle (Island Tower), a Grenoble landmark. The collection includes 4,000 paintings and 5,500 drawings, among them works by Impressionists such as Renoir and Monet, and 20th-century masters like Matisse, Signac, Derain, Vlaminck, Magritte, Ernst, Miró, and Dubuffet. Artists from the Italian Renaissance and Flemish School are also represented. ✉ *5 pl. de Lavalette, Grenoble* ☎ *04–76–63–44–44* ⊕ *www.museedegrenoble.fr* 🎟 *€8* ⏲ *Wed.–Mon. 10–6:30.*

Fodor's Choice ★

Musée Stendhal. Established in Stendhal's grandfather's house, this museum is a fascinating testament to the eminent author. It's one of three local landmarks where his legacy can be explored—the others being his birthplace and the Bibliothèque Municipale, which houses

10

his manuscripts. The English-language "Stendhal Itinerary," offered by the Grenoble Chamber of Commerce, recaps all the major sites associated with him. ✉ *20 Grande-Rue, Grenoble* ☎ *04–76–86–52–08* 🌐 *www.bm-grenoble.fr/1083-musee-stendhal.htm* 🎫 *€5 with audio guide* ⏲ *Tues., Wed., and Fri., 2–6, Sat. 10–noon and 2–6.*

WHERE TO EAT AND STAY

$ FRENCH ✕ **Café de la Table Ronde.** The second-oldest café in France, this was a favorite haunt of Henri Beyle (aka Stendhal) as well as the spot where Choderlos de Laclos sought inspiration for (or perhaps a rest from) his 1784 *Liaisons Dangereuses.* Traditionally known for gatherings of *les mordus* (literally, "the bitten," or passionate ones), the café still hosts poetry readings and concerts and serves dinner until nearly midnight. $ *Average main: €17* ✉ *7 pl. St-André, Grenoble* ☎ *04–76–44–51–41* 🌐 *www.restaurant-tableronde-grenoble.com.*

$$$$ FRENCH ✕ **L'Auberge Napoléon.** Frédéric Caby's culinary haven in a meticulously restored town house—once inhabited by Napoléon Bonaparte himself—is where Chef Agnès Chotin, one of France's top *cuisinières* (female chefs), puts together the best table in Grenoble. She specializes in dishes unique to the region, ranging from *daube de sanglier en aumonière croustillante* (wild boar stewed in port wine with lemon crust) to *crème de potiron* (cream of squash soup); and proposes a foie-gras menu that is nearly as wicked and wonderful as her regional *cru* chocolate dessert. $ *Average main: €37* ✉ *7 rue Montorge, Grenoble* ☎ *04–76–87–53–64* 🌐 *www.auberge-napoleon.fr* ⏲ *Closed Sun., early May, and late Aug. No lunch.*

$$$ HOTEL Fodor's Choice ★ **Chavant.** It's worth the drive 8 km (5 miles) south of Grenoble to this ivy-covered mansion-hotel, where elegant, spacious guest rooms overlook the meadows and forests that lie beyond the lush garden and pool. **Pros:** lovely village with pretty views and walks; classic cuisine and outstanding wine cellar; tasteful rooms. **Cons:** not handy to central Grenoble; tricky driving directions. $ *Rooms from: €165* ✉ *2 rue Emile Chavant, Bresson* ✣ *Leave Grenoble on Av. J. Perrot to Av. J. Jaurès, which becomes Rte. D269* ☎ *04–76–25–25–38* 🌐 *www.chavanthotel.com* *5 rooms, 1 suites* 🍽 *No meals.*

$ HOTEL **Europe.** This modest hotel, the region's oldest, is in a handy, central location at the edge of old Grenoble. **Pros:** location at Grenoble's center; good value; the feel of the Old Town. **Cons:** very small rooms; minimal creature comforts, such as tiny towels. $ *Rooms from: €87* ✉ *22 pl. Grenette, Grenoble* ☎ *04–76–46–16–94* 🌐 *www.hoteleurope.fr* *45 rooms* 🍽 *No meals.*

$ HOTEL **Grand Hotel Grenoble.** There's not much lacking in this handsome, centrally located hotel. **Pros:** valet parking; close to the area's best shopping. **Cons:** standard rooms can be on the small side. $ *Rooms from: €99* ✉ *5 rue de la Republique, Grenoble* ☎ *04–76–51–22–59* 🌐 *www.grand-hotel-grenoble.com* *56 rooms, 1 suite* 🍽 *No meals.*

NIGHTLIFE AND PERFORMING ARTS

Look for the monthly *Grenoble-Spectacles* for a list of events around town.

Starting at Quai St-Stéphane-Jay, Grenoble's *téléphérique* (cable car) helps visitors cross the Isère and ascend to the Fort de la Bastille.

Barberousse. Resembling a pirate ship, Barberousse is an always-popping rum mill. ✉ *3 rue Bayard, Grenoble* ☎ *04–76–51–14–53* 🌐 *www.barberousse.com.*

La Soupe aux Choux. The intimate La Soupe aux Choux is the prime spot for jazz in Grenoble. ✉ *7 rte. de Lyon, Grenoble* ☎ *04–76–87–05–67* 🌐 *www.jazzalasoupe.fr.*

Fodor's Choice ★ **Les Détours de Babel.** This festival is devoted to contemporary music. The first three weeks of April is prime time for 50 or more concerts of exceptional originality and cultural breadth. ✉ *Grenoble* 🌐 *www.detoursdebabel.fr.*

CHAMBÉRY

44 km (27 miles) northeast of Voiron, 40 km (25 miles) north of St-Pierre-de-Chartreuse.

As for centuries—when it was the crossroads for merchants from Germany, Italy, and the Middle East—elegant old Chambéry remains the region's shopping hub. Townspeople congregate for coffee and people-watching on pedestrians-only Place St-Léger.

Visitor Information Chambéry Tourist Office. ☎ *04–79–33–42–47* 🌐 *www.chambery-tourisme.com.*

EXPLORING

Château des Ducs de Savoie. Chambéry's premier sight, the 14th-century Château des Ducs de Savoie, features one of Europe's largest carillons. Its Gothic Ste-Chapelle has lovely stained glass and houses a replica of the Turin Shroud. At the moment, the chateau can be visited only by guided tour on weekends at 2:30 pm. The 90-minute tour includes a visit to Chambéry's historic center and ends at the château. Tours leave from 71 rue St-Réal in the *centre historique*. ✉ *Pl. du Château, Chambéry* ☎ *04–79–33–42–47* 🌐 *www.chambery-tourisme.com* €6 ⏲ *Weekends and school holidays (late Oct.—early Nov; late Dec.—early Jan.; late Feb.—early Mar.; mid-Apr.—early May, July, and Aug.) at 2:30.*

WHERE TO STAY

$$$ HOTEL **Château de Candie.** If you wish to experience *la vie Savoyarde* in all its pastel-hued glory, head to this towering 14th-century manor on a hill east of Chambéry. **Pros:** glorious views over the neighboring Chartreuse monastery and village; interesting antiques abound; personal service from host. **Cons:** not right in town, so a car is required; won't appeal to minimalists. $ *Rooms from: €170* ✉ *Rue du Bois de Candie, 6 km (4 miles) east of Chambéry, Chambéry-le-Vieux* ☎ *04–79–96–63–00* 🌐 *www.chateaudecandie.com* *23 rooms, 5 suites* *No meals.*

ANNECY

137 km (85 miles) east of Lyon, 43 km (27 miles) southwest of Geneva.

Fodor's Choice ★ Sparkling Annecy is on crystal-clear Lac d'Annecy, surrounded by snow-tipped peaks. Though the canals, flower-decked bridges, and cobbled pedestrian streets are filled with shoppers and tourists on market days—Tuesday and Friday—the town is still tranquil.

Does it seem that the River Thiou flows backward, that is, out of the lake? You're right: it drains the lake, feeding the town's canals. Most of the Vieille Ville (Old Town) is now a pedestrian zone lined with half-timber houses. Here is where the best restaurants are, so you'll probably be back in the evening.

GETTING HERE

There's a direct TGV train connection from Lyon-Saint-Exupéry airport to Annecy (1 hr, 55 mins; €37). TGV connects Paris's Gare de Lyon to Annecy (3 hrs, 42 mins; €86). Annecy Haute-Savoie Airport (🌐 *www.annecy.aeroport.fr*) receives flights from other French and some European destinations.

Crolard buses connect Lyon-Saint-Exupéry airport with Annecy (2 hrs, €34) and the main winter sport stations in the Alps year-round. Tickets must be purchased online or at the airport or bus station.

Visitor Information Annecy Tourist Office. ☎ *04–50–45–00–33* 🌐 *www.lac-annecy.com.* **Crolard.** ☎ *04–50–51–57–25* 🌐 *www.voyages-crolard.com.*

EXPLORING

The funky, asymmetrical, added-on, squished-in buildings of Annecy's Vieille Ville and the sheer limestone cliffs and jagged peaks of its mountain setting are impossibly picturesque. No matter that the paddleboat vendors try to outcharm each other for your business, you'll be tempted to stay here and dawdle awhile.

Just one of the scenic delights of Annecy, the photogenic Palais de l'Isle (Island Palace)

Fodor's Choice ★ **Château de Menthon-Saint-Bernard.** The exterior of the magnificent Château de Menthon-Saint-Bernard is the stuff of fairy tales (so much so that Walt Disney modeled Sleeping Beauty's castle on it); the interior is even better. The castle's medieval rooms—many adorned with tapestries, Romanesque frescoes, Netherlandish sideboards, and heraldic motifs—have been lovingly restored by the owner, who can trace his ancestry directly back to Saint-Bernard himself. All in all, this is one of the loveliest dips into the Middle Ages you can make in all of Europe. You can get a good view of the castle by turning onto the Thones road out of Veyrier. ✉ *Allée du Château, Annecy* ☎ *04–50–60–12–05* 🌐 *www.chateau-de-menthon.com* 🎫 *€8.50* ⏲ *July and Aug., daily noon–6; May, June, and Sept., Fri., weekends and holidays 2–6; Oct.–Apr., Thurs. and weekends 2–4:30.*

Fodor's Choice ★ **Musée-Château d'Annecy.** Crowning the city is one of France's most gorgeous castles, the medieval Musée-Château d'Annecy. High on a hill opposite the Palais and bristling with stolid towers, the complex is landmarked by the Tour Perrière, which dominates the lake, and the Tour St-Paul, Tour St-Pierre, and Tour de la Reine (the oldest, dating from the 12th century), which overlook the town. All provide storybook views over the town and countryside. Dwellings of several eras line the castle courtyard, one of which contains a small museum on Annecy history and how it was shaped by the Nemeurs and Savoie dynasties. ✉ *Pl. du Château, Annecy* ☎ *04–50–33–87–30* 🌐 *www.musees.agglo-annecy.fr* 🎫 *€5.20, with Palais de l'Ile €7.20* ⏲ *June–Sept., daily 10:30–6; Oct.–May, Wed.–Mon. 10–noon and 2–5.*

Palais de l'Isle (*Island Palace*). Meander through the Vieille Ville, starting on the small island in the River Thiou, at the 12th-century Palais de l'Isle, once site of law courts and a prison, now a landmark. Like a stone ship, the small islet perches in midstream, surrounded by cobblestone quays, and is easily one of France's most photographed sites. ✉ *Annecy.*

WHERE TO EAT AND STAY

$$$$ FRENCH Fodor's Choice ★

Auberge de Père Bise. For those who've never dined in one of France's grand old restaurants, this would be a fine start. In a century-old chalet-inn in the tiny village of Talloires, on the incomparably beautiful Lac d'Annecy, from start to finish you'll be pampered in the old style. Though the cuisine has been updated, dishes like veal carpaccio with white caviar and horseradish cream; *poulet de Bresse* stuffed with truffles and foie gras; and steamed lake fish with scallops, fennel, and ginger beurre blanc feature all the luxe ingredients that distinguish French cuisine. On a warm day, a seat on the gracious terrace overlooking the lake is a must. Prices are definitely not for the faint-hearted, but good memories are priceless. *Average main: €70* ✉ *303 rte. du Port, Annecy* ☎ *04–50–60–72–01* *www.perebise.com* *Closed Tues. and Wed.* *Reservations essential* *Jacket required.*

$ CAFÉ FAMILY

Le Barista Café. The fragrance of a perfect brew is your first clue that you've come to the right place for Annecy's best cup. This cozy café has a lot more going for it than just great coffee (although that's enough right there). Expect light and luscious cooking—inventive salads, sandwiches, quiches, and a delightful array of cookies, scones, and desserts—a charming outdoor terrace, friendly service, and a downstairs play area for the kids. Stop by for a yummy breakfast, not easy to come by in France. Tucked away on a small street in the city center, it's not the easiest place to find, but you'll be well rewarded for the effort. *Average main: €6* ✉ *2 passage Gruffaz, Annecy* ☎ *09–84–29–61–44* *www.barista-cafe.fr* *Closed Sun.* *Reservations not accepted.*

$$$$ HOTEL

L'Impérial Palace. Across the lake from the town center, Annecy's leading hotel has spacious, high-ceilinged guest rooms in subdued contemporary colors behind its Belle Époque exterior. **Pros:** beautiful location; splendid rooms; superior cuisine in La Voile. **Cons:** sluggish to haughty service; pricey; breakfasts expensive for what you get. *Rooms from: €330* ✉ *Allée de l'Impérial, Annecy* ☎ *04–50–09–30–00* *www.hotel-imperial-palace.com* *91 rooms, 8 suites* *No meals.*

$ HOTEL Fodor's Choice ★

Splendid Hotel. Just steps from crystalline Lac d'Annecy, overlooking a lovely canal running through Annecy's Old Town, this nicely renovated hotel has all the comfort and charm you could want plus the best location possible. **Pros:** delicious buffet breakfast included in price; hotel-subsidized parking nearby; package deals throughout the year. **Cons:** some noise due to hardwood floors. *Rooms from: €99* ✉ *4 quai Eustache Chappuis, Annecy* *www.hotel-annecy-lac.fr* *47 rooms* *Breakfast.*

CHAMONIX–MONT BLANC

94 km (58 miles) east of Annecy, 83 km (51 miles) southeast of Geneva.

Chamonix is the oldest and biggest of the French winter-sports resort towns and was the site of the first Winter Olympics, held in 1924. As a ski resort, however, it has its limitations. The ski areas are spread out, none is very large, and the lower slopes often suffer from poor snow conditions.

On the other hand, some runs are extremely memorable, such as the 20-km (12-mile) one through the Vallée Blanche or the off-trail area of Les Grands Montets. And the situation is getting better: many lifts have been added, improving access to the slopes as well as shortening lift lines. In summer it's a great place for hiking, climbing, and enjoying dazzling views. If you're heading to Italy via the Mont Blanc Tunnel, Chamonix will be your gateway.

GETTING HERE

TGV trains from Lyon-Saint-Exupéry airport take 1 hour, 55 minutes (€31.90). There's also TGV service from Paris's Gare de Lyon (3 hrs, 42 mins; €80). The required train ride from St-Gervais-Les-Bains to Chamonix is in itself an incredible trip, up the steepest railway in Europe. You'll feel your body doing strange things to adjust to the pressure change.

Alpybus transfers passengers from Geneva to Chamonix (1 hr, 10 mins; €27).

Visitor Information Alpybus. *www.alpybus.com.* **Chamonix Tourist Office.** ☎ *04–50–53–00–24* *www.chamonix.com.*

EXPLORING

Fodor's Choice ★ **Aiguille du Midi.** This 12,619-foot granite peak is topped with a needle-like observation tower, terrace, and restaurants. The world's highest cable car soars 12,000 feet up, almost to the top (an elevator completes the journey to the summit), providing positively staggering views of 15,700-foot Mont Blanc, Europe's loftiest peak. Be prepared for a lengthy wait, both going up and coming down—and wear warm clothing. ✉ *35 pl. de la Mer de Glace, Chamonix-Mont-Blanc* ☎ *33/04–51–53–22–75* *www.compagniedumontblanc.fr* *Cable car €57 round-trip* *May–Sept., daily 8–4:45; Oct.–Apr., daily 8–3:45.*

Fodor's Choice ★ **Mer de Glace.** Literally, the "sea of ice," the Mer de Glace glacier can be seen up close from the Train du Montenvers, a cogwheel mountain train that leaves from behind the main train station. At the top end of the track you can mount yet another transportation device—a mini- *téléphérique* (cable car) that suspends you over the glacier for five minutes. You can also venture into the *grotte de glace* (ice cave) and the new Glacorium, an interactive space recounting the glacier's formation and history. The hike back down is an easy two-hour ramble. ✉ *Chamonix* *www.compagniedumontblanc.fr* *€25 one-way* *Check website for train departure times.*

Musée Alpin. Chamonix was little more than a quiet mountain village until a group of Englishmen "discovered" the spot in 1741 and sang its praises far and wide. The town became forever tied to mountaineering

Even at the bottom of one of its ski runs, you'll feel on top of the world in stunning Chamonix.

when Horace de Saussure offered a reward for the first Mont Blanc ascent in 1760. Learn who took home the prize at the town's Musée Alpin, which documents the history of mountaineering; exhibits include handmade skis, early sleds, boots, skates, and mementos from every area of Alpine climbing lore. ✉ *89 av. Michel Groz, Chamonix* ☎ *04–50–53–25–93* 🎫 *€5.50* 🕒 *Late Dec.–mid-May, Wed.–Mon. 2–6.*

WHERE TO STAY

$$ HOTEL FAMILY **Auberge du Manoir.** For the feel of an authentic family-run mountain lodge—complete with wood paneling, flower-festooned balconies with delicious mountain views, and a resident golden retriever, this a great choice. **Pros:** centrally located; good breakfast; good value. **Cons:** management can be inflexible; people with allergies beware: cats and dogs at the hotel. $ *Rooms from: €112* ✉ *8 rte. du Bouchet, Chamonix* ☎ *04–50–53–10–77* 🌐 *www.chalethotelchamonix.fr* *18 rooms* *No meals.*

$$$$ HOTEL **Hameau Albert 1er.** At one of Chamonix's most desirable hotels, most of the beautifully furnished guest rooms have private balconies, with many (such as No. 33) offering unsurpassed views of Mont Blanc. **Pros:** dazzling panoramas; superb cuisine; polished and cheerful service. **Cons:** hard to get a reservation in season; the actual location is less than pristine. $ *Rooms from: €245* ✉ *119 impasse du Montenvers, Chamonix* ☎ *04–50–53–05–09* 🌐 *www.hameaualbert.fr* 🕒 *Closed 2 wks in May, 3 wks in Nov.* *33 rooms, 2 chalets* *No meals.*

$$$$ RESORT Fodor's Choice ★ **Hôtel Mont-Blanc.** In the center of town, this Belle Époque hotel has catered to an A-list clientele since it opened its doors in 1878. **Pros:** near shops and ski lifts; amazing cuisine; lovely pool and spa. **Cons:** staff could be more knowledgeable. $ *Rooms from: €270* ✉ *62 allée*

du Majestic, Chamonix ☎ *04–50–53–05–64* 🌐 *www.bestmontblanc.com* ⇆ *40 rooms* 🍽 *No meals.*

NIGHTLIFE

Casino de Chamonix. Besides games of chance like roulette and blackjack, the Casino de Chamonix has a bar and restaurant. Entrance is free with a passport or driver's license. ✉ *Pl. de Saussure, Chamonix* ☎ *04–50–53–07–65* 🌐 *www.lucienbarriere.com/fr/Casino/Chamonix/accueil.html.*

Chambre Neuf. Fabled landmark Chambre Neuf is a hot après-ski bar in the Hotel Gustavia. ✉ *Hotel Gustavia, 272 av. Michel Croz, Chamonix* ☎ *04–50–55–89–81.*

MEGÈVE

35 km (22 miles) west of Chamonix, 69 km (43 miles) southeast of Geneva.

The smartest of the Mont Blanc stations, idyllic Alpine Megève is not only a major ski resort but also a chic winter watering hole that draws royalty, celebrities, and fat wallets from all over the world. Because the slopes are comparatively easy, beginners and skiers of only modest ability will find Megève more to their liking than Chamonix: Megève, conveniently, also has one of France's largest ski schools. In summer the town is a popular spot for golfing and hiking.

GETTING HERE

Driving is by far the best way to get to Megève. From Grenoble to Megève the journey takes about 2½ hours whether via Annecy or Albertville. SNCF rail connections from Annecy to Megéve (1 hr, 17 mins; €14.80) are routed to Sallanches, 12 km (8 miles) away. Shuttle buses connect Sallanches and Megève (25 mins, €5.50).

Visitor Information Megève Tourist Office. ☎ *04–50–21–27–28* 🌐 *www.megeve.com.*

WHERE TO EAT AND STAY

$$$$ FRENCH Fodor's Choice ★

✕ **Flocons de Sel.** Emmanuel Renaut's three-star Flocons de Sel ("flakes of salt"), located in Leutaz, brings new meaning to the world of haute cuisine—and, even with the drive out of town, it's an excellent Megève dining option. Though the 10-course tasting menu is very expensive, it offers a rare taste experience from one of France's great chefs based on simple but carefully selected ingredients—freshwater crayfish, scallops en croute with sea salt, and roast wood pigeon are just a few of the creatively prepared specialties. The dining room is rustic-simple, allowing the food to take center stage. Surrounded by a series of chalets and much natural splendor, the establishment offers six exquisite guest rooms and three private chalets for crawl-away convenience. [$] *Average main: €60* ✉ *1775 rte. du Leutaz, Leutaz, Megève* ✥ *4 km (2½ miles) southwest of Megève* ☎ *04–50–21–49–99* 🌐 *www.floconsdesel.com* ⊗ *Closed Tues., Wed., and May and Nov.* ✍ *Reservations essential.*

10

$$$$ FRENCH Fodor'sChoice ★ **Le 1920.** Part of the beautiful Domaine du Mont d'Arbois, Le 1920 offers an ultra-refined menu of classics updated to reflect modern tastes and using only the freshest seasonal produce. It took Chef Julian Gatillon, veteran of top restaurants in France and Switzerland, two short years to earn his first Michelin star and gain the restaurant an avid following. Dishes like spaghetti with preserved quail egg, black truffles, and spinach; spit-roasted Bresse chicken with black truffles; or line-caught sole in salted butter with shrimp cream raise French cooking to new heights. The origin of everything you eat is listed on the menu, so you'll get a primer in local delicacies as well. *Average main: €60 447 chemin de la Rocaille, Megève 04–50–21–25–03 www.mont-darbois.fr Reservations essential.*

$$$$ HOTEL **Hôtel Mont-Blanc.** Wood predominates, as does artwork collected from all over Europe, in this hotel in the heart of Megève's pedestrian-only zone. **Pros:** walking distance from the gondolas up to the ski lifts; shares the clubby feel of the chic part of Megève town. **Cons:** in the thick of the crowds in high season; erratic service and upkeep. *Rooms from: €295 Pl. de l'Église, Megève 04–50–21–20–02 www.hotelmontblanc.com Closed mid-Apr.–early Dec. 38 rooms No meals.*

$$$$ B&B/INN **Les Cîmes.** This small, homey hotel, run by an English couple, offers cozy rooms and a pleasant little restaurant where simple dishes like roast lamb and grilled fish are served. **Pros:** friendly and comfortable; young and gregarious clientele; central location. **Cons:** smallish common areas; on a busy street. *Rooms from: €280 341 av. Charles Feige, Megève 06–31–04–74–18 www.hotellescimes.info Closed mid-Apr.–early June 8 rooms Some meals.*

$$$$ HOTEL FAMILY Fodor'sChoice ★ **Les Fermes de Marie.** By bringing a number of chalets and hay houses down from the mountains and decorating rooms with old Savoie furniture (including shepherds' tables, sculptured chests, and credenzas), Jocelyne and Jean-Louis Sibuet have created a luxury hotel with a delightfully rustic feel for both winter and summer getaways. **Pros:** ultra-comfortable quarters in authentic Alpine chalets; beautiful taste down to smallest detail; top Megève cuisine. **Cons:** somewhat isolated within the town; shuttle or car necessary to reach ski lifts. *Rooms from: €300 Chemin de Riante Colline, Megève 04–50–93–03–10 www.fermesdemarie.com Closed mid-Apr.–late June 61 rooms, 7 suites, 2 apartments No meals.*

NIGHTLIFE

Fodor'sChoice ★ **Jazz Club des Cinq Rues.** Hot both figuratively and literally (you'll probably end up stripping down to a T-shirt), this popular music bar near Plaza de l'Église packs in the après-ski party animals as soon as the sun is over the yardarm, which can be as early as 4 or 5 pm in December. *19 passage des Cinq Rues, Megève 04–50–89–65–68.*

VAL THORENS

131 km (81 miles) south of Chamonix, 153 km (95 miles) south of Geneva.

Skiing is this bustling resort town's raison d'être, so it's no surprise that lifts and gondolas fan out in every direction and that many of the trails pass over bridges and barrel through the main square. Just about anywhere in town you can strap on your skis and head downhill.

GETTING HERE

The best way to get to Val Thorens is by car. There are also shuttle buses that navigate the route from the airports in Lyon and Geneva.

Val Thorens Tourism Office. ✉ *Grand-Rue, Val Thorens* ☎ *04–70–00–08–08* 🌐 *www.valthorens.com.*

EXPLORING

Val Thorens. Europe's highest ski resort, Val Thorens has such a lofty position that you see nothing but snow-covered mountains in every direction. The landscape is so iconic that the three adjoining peaks that grace every bottle of Evian are found here. The season here lasts longer than at resorts down the mountain, often from mid-November to early May.

High-speed lifts of all types transport you up to 68 runs of various ski levels. More than 50 are best suited for intermediate-level skiers, but there is also a handful for beginners or experts. Val Thorens is connected to the Trois Vallées ski area, so you have access to more than 600 km (373 miles) of slopes in nearby Les Menuires and elsewhere.

It was first built in the 1970s, so Val Thorens isn't the loveliest resort in the French Alps. But it buzzes with energy day and night, thanks to a clientele of couples enjoying romantic getaways and groups of friends challenging the slopes and taking advantage of a wild après-ski scene. ✉ *D117, Val Thorens* 🎫 *€38 for 1-day Val Thoren pass, €47.17 for 1-day Trois Vallées pass.*

WHERE TO EAT AND STAY

$$ FRENCH

✕ **La Ruade.** The name refers to a horse kicking up its hind legs—a clue that this charming chalet serves hearty fare that could fortify a cowboy for a long ride on the trail. The tightly packed downstairs dining room of La Ruade is centered around an open fire where beef lovers can watch the expert staff grill up a côte de boeuf that's big enough for two. This is also a great place to sample regional specialties like raclette, in which a half-wheel of cheese is slowly melted onto a pile of perfectly seasoned potatoes. Getting here is half the fun; during the day you can ski to the door on an easy slope, while at night you hike across the snow. The twinkling lights on the edge of the gently sloped roof add a bit of evening magic. 💲 *Average main: €20* ✉ *Lieu-dit Preyerand, Les Menuires* ☎ *04–79–00–63–44.*

$$$$ HOTEL FAMILY Fodor's Choice ★

🏨 **Atlapura.** You can wave to skiers on the lifts that whiz past your sharply angled window at the Altapura, a ski-in, ski-out property on the edge of Val Thorens. **Pros:** easy access to the slopes; attentive staff; great choice of restaurants. **Cons:** uphill walk to the center of town. 💲 *Rooms from: €302* ✉ *Rue du Soleil, Val Thorens* ☎ *04–80–36–80–36* 🌐 *en.altapura.fr* 🛏 *72 rooms, 16 suites* 🍽 *No meals.*

$$$$ HOTEL

🏨 **Koh-I Nor.** Located on the edge of Val Thorens, this five-story hotel uses fur and other eye-catching materials in its design, including wooden walls with horizontal planks for a rough-hewn look, cream-color stone lining the bathroom's separate showers and soaking tubs, and furnishings upholstered in rich leather and suede. **Pros:** chic design; breakfast

10

and dinner for two included in price; head-spinning views. **Cons:** lots of traffic in the lobby. *Rooms from: €600 ✉ Rue de Gebroulaz, Val Thorens ☎ 04–79–31–00–00 🌐 www.hotel-kohinor.com 63 rooms Some meals.*

SPORTS AND THE OUTDOORS

Intersports. The staffers here are all expert skiers, so they really know their stuff. In minutes they'll set you up with a helmet, poles, skis, and boots (heated, of course). If you have a problem, there are many other locations in Val Thorens and around the region. *✉ Pl. du Péclet, Val Thorens ☎ 04–79–00–06–65 🌐 www.valthorens-intersport.com/en.*

SHOPPING

Fodor's Choice ★ **La Belle en Cuisse.** Hams cured right on the premises hang from the ceiling at this small gourmet shop, where you can sample just about any kind of regional meat or cheese. Looking for a pot of foie gras, or perhaps a bottle of the locally made liquor called *génépi*? This is the place. *✉ 1 rue de Caron, Val Thorens ☎ 04–79–00–04–30 🌐 www.la-belle-en-cuisse.fr.*

MÉRIBEL

111 km (69 miles) south of Chamonix, 178 km (110 miles) south of Geneva.

No building can be taller than the surrounding trees in this mountainside village, so Méribel feels tucked away in the forest. All the architecture must be typical of the region, down to the types of wood used for the graceful balconies and the color of the slate lined up on the gently sloped roofs. The result is one of the most gorgeous resorts in the French Alps.

GETTING HERE

A car is the most convenient way to get to Méribel, although if you're not used to driving in snowy conditions you might consider a shuttle from the airport in Lyon and Geneva. During ski season there's also daily train service to Méribel.

Visitor Information Méribel Tourism Office. *☎ 04–79–08–60–01 🌐 www.meribel.net.*

EXPLORING

Méribel. Méribel's first ski lift was built in 1938, and within a year construction had started on the accommodations that would turn this into a world-class ski resort. But because it sits inside Vanoise National Park, Méribel never experienced a period of rampant growth. Done up in the traditional Savoyard style, its rows of gorgeous chalets make Méribel feel like a village that's been here for centuries.

Back in 1992, the Winter Olympics were held in nearby Albertville. Méribel was the site for women's alpine skiing events, a testament to its world-class slopes. There are 150 km (93 miles) of ski trails, serviced by more than 50 lifts. There are some gentle green runs, but most of the slopes here are best for intermediate skiers. *✉ D90, Méribel €$49 for 1-day Méribel pass, €58 for 1-day Trois Vallées pass.*

WHERE TO EAT AND STAY

$$ BISTRO **Le Bistrot de l'Orée.** Done up in delectable shades of red and orange, hip Le Bistrot de l'Orée sits right across from the main slope that runs through the resort of Méribel. On a recent afternoon, a survey of the dining room revealed that nearly everyone in the well-dressed crowd had tottered in wearing their ski boots. On the lower level of the Hôtel L'Orée du Bois, this eatery is truly a family affair: The grandson of the hotel's original owner runs the kitchen, turning out modern takes on classics like cream of eggplant soup and veal chops flavored with brandy. Don't miss the baked *tartiflette*, a combination of potatoes, bacon, onions, and a local cheese called Reblochon. *Average main: €22* *Hôtel L'Orée du Bois, Rte. du Belvédère, Méribel* *04–79–00–31–29* *www.meribel-oree.com.*

$$$ FRENCH **Le Cèpe.** This place feels warm and welcoming even before you head through the front door, thanks to the rustic lanterns outside pointing the way. The wood-paneled dining room is hushed, as most patrons seem like couples out for a romantic evening. Good choice, as this is food you'll want to share: mushroom soup for a starter, perhaps, then crusty duck breast with roasted potatoes and a mushroom cream sauce. (If you're detecting a theme to the dishes, the restaurant's name refers to porcini mushrooms.) Desserts include blueberry tarts and waffles with salted butter and caramel ice cream. *Average main: €26* *Rte. D Plateau, Méribel Les Allues* *04–79–22–46–08* *No credit cards* *Reservations essential.*

$$$$ HOTEL **Le Savoy.** On the main drag running through Méribel, Le Savoy has a traditional stone-and-wood facade that leads to a rustic restaurant with wide-plank floors and rough-hewn beams that call to mind an old-time ski lodge. **Pros:** central location; refreshing design; staff that goes the extra mile. **Cons:** Wi-Fi connection isn't consistent; some noise from other rooms. *Rooms from: €350* *Pl. du Centre, Méribel Les Allues* *04–79–55–55–50* *www.hotel-savoy-meribel.com* *31 rooms, 5 suites* *Breakfast.*

NIGHTLIFE

Le Poste de Secours. If you'd rather avoid elbow-to-elbow crowds at the slope-side bars, head to Le Poste de Secours. Dispensing with the chalet-chic decor that's so popular in the region's watering holes, it has a futuristic feel. In the purple haze, spherical lighting fixtures float like planets while clusters of pod-like chairs sit low to the ground. This is the best place in town for classic cocktails, made by bartenders who know their stuff. *Immeuble Les Gentianes, Méribel* *04–79–00–74–31.*

SHOPPING

Farto. To sample a sensational *tartiflette,* the Savoie casserole made with potatoes, diced bits of salt pork, and locally produced Reblochon cheese, head to this tiny gourmet shop in Meribel Mottaret. It's made by hand in the spotless open kitchen, along with piles of *diots* (sausages) and other delicacies. *Centre Commercial Mottaret, Méribel* *04–79–04–27–93.*

COURCHEVEL

118 km (73 miles) south of Chamonix, 114 km (95 miles) southeast of Geneva.

Fodor'sChoice ★ The gondolas here are covered with ads for Chanel—your first clue that Courchevel caters to an upscale clientele. The gently curving streets are lined with beautiful boutiques offering the latest scarves from Hermès or bags from Louis Vuitton. And visitors take their dining seriously. There are more Michelin-starred restaurants here than in any other ski resort.

GETTING HERE

Driving is the best way to get to Courchevel. You can also take a taxi from the train station in Méribel or shuttle buses from the airports in Lyon and Geneva.

Visitor Information Courchevel Tourism Office. ☎ *04–79–08–00–29* 🌐 *www.courchevel.com.*

EXPLORING

Courchevel. It has a reputation as one of the most luxurious ski resorts in the French Alps, and Courchevel doesn't do much to dispel that notion. Ski shops glitter like designer boutiques, and ski valets place your skis and poles outside on the snow so you don't have to carry them.

But it turns out that Courchevel is also one of the area's most inviting towns. None of the locals seem stiff or snooty. The sommelier in the restaurant written up in all the food magazines is happy to give you a tour of the wine cellar, even when the dining room is crowded. Leave behind your voltage converter, and the front desk staff might just give you one for free.

And the skiing is amazing. There's a huge variety of slopes that cater to skiers of every skill level. It's heaven for intermediate skiers, and beginners will find plenty to keep them occupied (including one that has a great view of Courchevel's postage-stamp airport). The lifts are unusually speedy, keeping lines to a minimum. What's more, the scenery just doesn't get better than this in the French Alps. ✉ *D91A, Courchevel* 🎟 *€49 for 1-day Courchevel pass, €58 for 1-day Trois Vallées pass.*

WHERE TO EAT AND STAY

$$$$ FRENCH ✕ **L'Azimut.** This is hardly a jacket-and-tie kind of place, as the clientele often comes straight from the slopes. The laid-back atmosphere, the congenial staff, and the simple wood tables are among the joys of L'Azimut, where chef François Moureaux's cooking has earned the place a Michelin star. The dishes are updates of the classics, with some truly amazing flourishes, so look for panfried foie gras with passion-fruit foam, roasted breast of chicken with truffle cream, or turbot with a Champagne sauce. Don't pass up the cheese course; sample as many of the local favorites as you like, and they're all sliced for you tableside. [$] *Average main: €40* ✉ *Le Praz, Courchevel* ☎ *04–79–06–25–90* 🌐 *www.aubergedelapoutre.com/fr/restaurant-azimut.php* ⏲ *Closed May—Nov. No lunch Mon. and Wed.* ✍ *Reservations essential.*

$$$ FRENCH **La Cave des Creux.** An amazing view of Mont Blanc is yours at the Cave des Creux, opened by a couple of ski instructors on top of what was once a shelter for shepherds and their flocks. (You can still see some of the old cheese cellar and its equipment on the lower level.) On sunny days, the wraparound deck is packed elbow-to-elbow, even when temperatures drop below freezing. It's hard to resist the stone-trimmed dining room, where huge iron beams, industrial lighting, and a sleek fireplace give the place a modern feel. The menu is also forward-thinking—consider the pumpkin soup with foie gras shavings as a starter, then move on to lamb chops with wild garlic. Organic wines from the region make it hard to say no to a glass or two before heading back to the slopes. *Average main: €30 Courcehvel 1850, Courchevel 04–79–06–76–14 www.cavedescreux-courchevel.com Closed May–Nov.*

$$$$ HOTEL **Hotel Annapurna.** On the edge of the slopes, the ski-in, ski-out Hotel Annapurna could hardly have a better location if you plan on spending your days pounding the powder. **Pros:** slope-side location; free shuttle service; speedy Internet access. **Cons:** decor is a bit old-fashioned. *Rooms from: €715 Rte. de l'Altiport, Courchevel 04–79–08–04–60 www.annapurna-courchevel.com 44 rooms, 18 suites Breakfast.*

VAL D'ISÈRE

153 km (95 miles) southeast of Chamonix, 220 km (136 miles) southeast of Geneva.

Men's downhill racing was held in Val d'Isère during the 1992 Winter Olympics, and since then it's been a must-see for skiers wanting to challenge the impossibly steep slope called Bellevarde. But it has an incredible array of slopes, including an impressive number of easy green slopes at the top of the mountain.

GETTING HERE

To get to Val d'Isère, a car or taxi is your best option from the train station in Méribel or the airports in Lyon and Geneva.

Visitor Information **Val d'Isère Tourism Office.** *Pl. Jacques Mouflier, Val d'Isère 04–79–06–06–60 www.valdisere.com.*

EXPLORING

Val d'Isère. One of the joys of Val d'Isère is that the easy slopes aren't concentrated at the bottom of the mountains. Beginners can take the gondola to the top and ski for hours at the upper altitudes. Val d'Isère and neighboring Tinges form the Espace Killy, a massive ski area with 154 runs of various ski levels extending for a total of 300 km (186 miles).

Wish the ski season didn't have to end? Val d'Isère's Pissaillas Glacier and Tignes's Grand Motte Clacier both offer summertime skiing. And there are plenty of other activities in both resorts during warmer weather. *D902, Val d'Isère €38.50 for 1-day Val d'Isère pass, €52 for 1-day Espace Killy pass.*

10

WHERE TO EAT AND STAY

$$$$ FRENCH ✕ **La Fruitière.** Don't be fooled by the milky-white paint peeling from the rafters, the exposed zinc pipes, or the green tiles that look like they've been here for centuries—La Fruitière isn't really an old dairy, as the name suggests, but a newly built eatery that draws on the region's most hallowed traditions. Remarkably efficient waiters clad in blue coveralls strongly suggest regional specialties like the chestnut soup (which they serve with a flourish) or the breast of veal accompanied by endive and house-cured ham. La Fruitière is located on one of the mountain's more manageable slopes, so getting here is no trouble. And you might not want to leave, as next door is the local branch of the famous après-ski hangout La Folie Douce. *Average main: €35* ✉ *Top of La Daille gondola, Val d'Isère* ☎ *04–79–06–07–17* 🌐 *www.lafoliedouce.com* ✍ *Reservations essential.*

$$$$ HOTEL **Le Blizzard.** A pair of fireplaces flanks the double doors leading into Le Blizzard, and they'll warm you right up even on the most blustery evenings. **Pros:** center-of-it-all location; inviting bar and lounge; friendly staff. **Cons:** elevator is small and slow. *Rooms from: €360* ✉ *Av. Olympique, Val d'Isère* ☎ *04–79–06–02–07* 🌐 *www.hotelblizzard.com/en* *70 rooms* *Breakfast.*

PROVENCE

WELCOME TO PROVENCE

TOP REASONS TO GO

★ **See Vincent van Gogh's Arles:** Ever since the fiery Dutchman immortalized Arles in all its chromatic drama, this town has had a starring role in museums around the world.

★ **Experience unplugged Provence:** The marshy landscapes of the Camargue will swamp you with their strange beauty, white horses, pink flamingoes, and black bulls.

★ **Get hip-deep in lavender:** Tour the Lavender Route from the Abbaye de Sénanque (near Gordes) to a wide, blue-purple swath that ranges across the Drôme and the Vaucluse.

★ **Go fishing for Marseille's best bouillabaisse:** The version at Chez Fonfon will make your taste buds stand up and sing "La Marseillaise."

★ **Tour Cézanne Country:** Views of Mont Ste-Victoire, rising near the artist's hometown of Aix-en-Provence, may inspire you to pick up a brush.

1 Nîmes, Arles, and the Camargue. Still haunted by the genius of Van Gogh, Arles remains fiercely Provençal and is famed for its folklore events. A bus ride away and bracketed by the towns of Aigues-Mortes and Stes-Maries-de-la-Mer, the vast Camargue nature park is one of France's most remarkable terrains, complete with cowboys, horseback rides, and exclusive *mas* (converted farmhouse) hotels.

2 The Alpilles. These spiky mountains guard treasures like Les Baux-de-Provence, where the lively tangle of medieval streets and the atmospheric *ville morte* (dead town) are equally bewitching. Nearby is ritzy St-Rémy-de-Provence, Van Gogh's famous retreat.

3 Avignon and the Vaucluse. This area is the heart of Provençal delights. Presided over by its medieval Palais des Papes, Avignon is an ideal gateway for exploring the Roman ruins at Pont du Gard. About 16 km (10 miles) east of Avignon is the Sorgue Valley, where everybody goes "flea"-ing in the famous antiques market at L'Isle-sur-la-Sorgue. Just east are the Luberon's hilltop villages (globalized by Peter Mayle), such as picture-perfect Gordes. South lies Roussillon, set like a ruby in its red cliffs.

4 Aix-en-Provence and the Mediterranean Coast. For one day, join all those fashionable folk for whom café-sitting, people-watching, and boutique-shopping are a way of life in Aix-en-Provence. Enjoy the elegant 18th-century streets, then channel the spirit of Cézanne by visiting

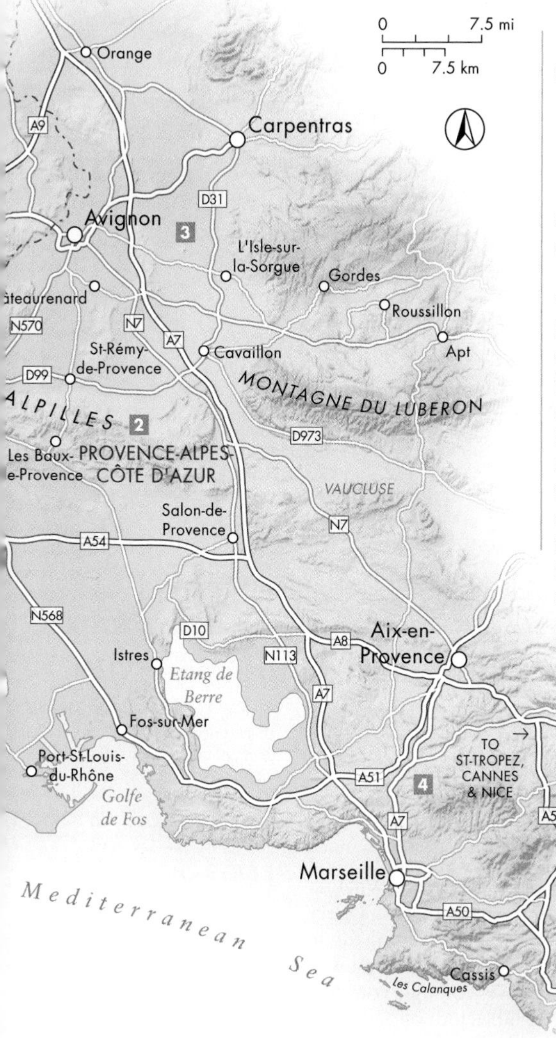

0 7.5 mi
0 7.5 km
Orange
A9
Carpentras
D31
Avignon
3
L'Isle-sur-la-Sorgue
Gordes
Roussillon
âteaurenard
N570
N7
A7
St-Rémy-de-Provence
Cavaillon
Apt
D99
MONTAGNE DU LUBERON
ALPILLES
2
D973
Les Baux-de-Provence
PROVENCE-ALPES-CÔTE D'AZUR
VAUCLUSE
Salon-de-Provence
N7
A54
N568
D10
Aix-en-Provence
A8
Istres
N113
Etang de Berre
A7
Fos-sur-Mer
TO ST-TROPEZ, CANNES & NICE
Port-St-Louis-du-Rhône
A51
4
Golfe de Fos
A7
A52
Marseille
Mediterranean Sea
A50
Cassis
Les Calanques

GETTING ORIENTED

What many visitors remember best about Provence is the light. The vibrant sun here bathes vineyards, olive groves, fields full of lavender, and tall stands of sunflowers with an intensity that captivated Cézanne and Van Gogh. Bordering the Mediterranean and flanked by the Alps and the Rhône River, Provence attracts hordes of visitors. Fortunately, many of them are siphoned off to the resorts along the Riviera, which is part of Provence but whose jet-set image doesn't fit in with the tranquil charm of the rest of the region.

his studio and nearby Mont Ste-Victoire, one of his favorite subjects. Head south to become a Calanques castaway before diving into Marseille, which ranks among France's most multicultural and vibrant cities.

PROVENCE'S VILLAGE MARKETS

In Provence, forget about the supermarket and head to the marketplace—an integral part of French culture anywhere in France, but even more so in this region.

Among the most prized gifts are Provençal *santon* figurines (above); less overhead means cheap prices (right, top); gourmet goodies for sale (right, bottom).

Provence is the equivalent of market heaven. Whether foodie, collectibles, antiques, or clothing, there is a (very often famous) street market in every Provençal town, each with an energy of its own and offering the best way to interact with the natives. So even though you may wonder if you should resist that tablecloth of pink-and-yellow Souleiado fabric, yield to the delight of puttering through a village market. Happily, they are a daily occurrence in Provence, passed from village to town—Sunday is for Isle-sur-la-Sorgue, Saturday for Arles, Wednesday for St-Rémy, Tuesday, Thursday, and Saturday for Aix. Remember to pick the wheat from the chaff. Provence lovers back home will appreciate those sunflower coasters much more than Day-Glo versions of Van Gogh masterpieces.

FEATS OF CLAY

Top gifts are the miniature figures called *santons,* or "little saints." When the French Revolution cracked down on Christmas reenactments, a crafty Marseillais decided to make terra-cotta figurines, which soon upstaged their human counterparts for good. Sold year-round, models include red-cheeked town drunks, lavender-cutters, and, wait, isn't that Gérard Depardieu and Carla Bruni-Sarkozy?

AIX-EN-PROVENCE

Aix has some delightful street markets. Unlike the more traditional fare of other markets, the one in Aix is more focused on food: you can find rare delicacies side by side with cured sausages bristling with Provençal spices, vats of olives, tapenade, and oils from the Pays d'Aix (Aix region), or bags of orange-spice shuttle-shape *navettes* (cookies). The food market takes place every day in Place Richelème, and just up the street in Place Verdun is a good all-purpose market Tuesday, Thursday, and Saturday morning.

ARLES AND THE CAMARGUE

Every Saturday morning over 2 km (1 mile) along Boulevard des Lices, which flows into Boulevard Clemenceau, Arles hosts one of the best textile markets in the area. Here you can find the famous *boutis* (cotton throws), textured fabrics in all styles and colors, and an endless array of brightly dyed and embroidered tablecloths, children's clothes, and Arlesian costumes. On the first Wednesday of every month, Boulevard Emile Combes converts into an antiques and collectibles market—all the more interesting because wares are mostly regional.

AVIGNON AND THE VAUCLUSE

Avignon has a great mix of French chains and youthful clothing shops, and Les Halles food stalls are a sight to see. Every Wednesday morning, St-Rémy-de-Provence hosts one of the most popular markets in France. Place de la République and the narrow town streets overflow with fresh produce, olives, tapenade by the vat, and a variety of other delicacies. In the Vaucluse area, you can find anything made from lavender.

MARSEILLE

The main shopping drag lies between La Canebière and the Préfecture, but Marseille offers up a large selection of quirky shops, urban youth boutiques, and brand-name stores all over the city. There is an assortment of street markets, from the daily fish market in the old port to the stamp market every Sunday morning in Cours Julien (which is also home to the Wednesday organic market). Probably the most famous item you'll find is the Savon de Marseille (Marseille soap).

THE SORGUE VALLEY

The best place to go trolling for time-burnished treasure is the famed antiques market held in lovely L'Isle-sur-la-Sorgue every weekend. Twice a year, around Easter and mid-August, in addition to the town's 250 art and antiques dealers, some 200 antiques merchants set up shop over four days for the *Grand Déballage*, or the "Great Unpacking."

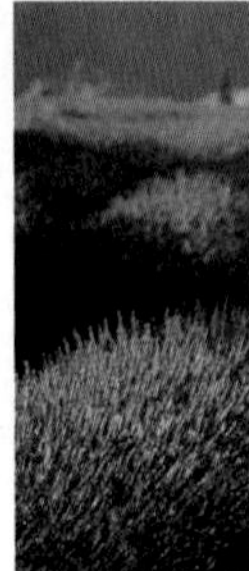

Updated By
Nancy Heslin

As you approach Provence there's a magical moment when you finally leave the north behind: cypresses and red-tile roofs appear; you hear the screech of cicadas and breathe the scent of wild thyme and lavender. Along the highway, oleanders bloom against a backdrop of austere, sun-filled landscapes, the very same that inspired the Post-Impressionists.

Ever since Peter Mayle abandoned the London fog and described with sensual relish a life of unbuttoned collars and espadrilles in his best-selling *A Year in Provence,* the world has beaten a path here. Now Parisians are heard in the local marketplaces passing the word on the best free-range rabbit and the lowest price on a five-bedroom *mas* (a traditional Provençal farmhouse). This *bon-chic-bon-genre* city crowd languishes stylishly at Provence's country inns and restaurants. Ask them, and they'll agree: when Princess Caroline of Monaco moved to St-Rémy, Provence became the new Côte d'Azur.

But chichi Provence hasn't eclipsed idyllic Provence, except that now every farmer and crafts vendor has an iPhone. Still, it's possible to melt into a Monday-morning market crowd, where blue-aproned *paysannes* scoop fistfuls of mesclun into willow baskets, matron-connoisseurs paw through bins containing the first Cavaillon asparagus, and a knot of *pépés* in workers' blues takes a pétanque break.

Relax, join them—and plan to stick around awhile. There are plenty of sights to see: great Roman ruins; the pristine Romanesque abbeys of Senanque and de Montmajour; weathered mas; the monolithic Papal Palace in old Avignon; the narrow streets in Arles immortalized on canvas by Van Gogh. Check out all these treasures but remember that highlights of any trip here are those hours spent dawdling at a sidewalk café, wandering aimlessly down narrow cobbled alleyways, and, after a three-hour lunch, taking a quick snooze in the cool shade of a 500-year-old olive tree. Allow yourself time to feel the rhythm of modern Provençal life, to listen to the pulsing *cigales*, smell the *parfum* of a tiny country path, and feel the night air on your skin.

PLANNER

WHEN TO GO

Spring and fall are the best months to experience the dazzling light, rugged rocky countryside, and fruited vineyards of Provence. Though the lavender fields show peak color in July, summertime here is beastly hot; worse, it's always crowded on the beaches and connecting roads. In winter (from November through February, even into March) you'll find many tourist services closed, including hotels and restaurants. Much of the terrace life is driven indoors by rain and wind, but around Easter the plane trees begin to leaf out and the café tables begin to sprout once more.

PLANNING YOUR TIME

The best place to start your trip is in Avignon. It's on a fast train link from Paris, but even if you arrive in record time, it's at exactly this moment that you need to slow down. As you step off the train and are confronted with all that magnificent architecture and art, breathe deeply. Provence is about lazy afternoons and spending "just one more day," and Avignon is a good place to have a practice run: it's cosmopolitan enough to keep the most energetic visitor occupied, while old and wise enough to teach the value of time.

GETTING HERE AND AROUND

Provence is home to one of France's largest airports (Aéroport de Marseille Provence), plus it has high-speed TGV train service from Paris. Departing from the Gare de Lyon, you can get to Nîmes, Aix-en-Provence, Marseille, or Avignon in three hours or less; you can even be whisked to Provence directly on arrival at Paris's Charles de Gaulle airport. Once in the region, well-organized public transport makes most towns accessible by train or bus. It's best to plan on combining the two—often smaller Provençal communities won't have their own train station, but rather a local bus connection to one in the nearest town over. Driving is also a good option, although for the first-time visitor negotiating the highways in Provence can be a scary experience. They're fast... regardless of the speed limit. Off the highway, however, on the national roads, or the district roads, driving can be the best and most relaxing way to get around.

AIR TRAVEL

Marseille has the fifth-busiest airport in France, the Aéroport de Marseille Provence in Marignane. Located about 20 km (12 miles) northwest of the city center, it receives flights from both major airlines—including Air France—and a broad range of budget carriers; airport shuttle buses regularly run to Marseille (€8.20) and Aix (€8.20). The smaller Aéroport de Nîmes-Alès-Camargue-Cévennes, 12 km (7½ miles) south of Nîmes, is served by Ryanair, which operates multiple weekly flights from Brussels, London, and Liverpool. A shuttle bus into Nîmes costs €6; if you're bound for Arles, cab fare for the 20-km (12-mile) trip is about €50 and takes about 20 minutes.

BUS TRAVEL

Buses, often working in tandem with trains, can get you almost anywhere you want to go. The official websites for individual communities (and even some attractions) typically include detailed bus-access information; a quick email or phone call will confirm it. Schedules and *trajets* (journeys) can also be found on the websites of the region's primary bus companies. Cartreize controls bus routes to and from the Bouches du Rhône; Lignes Express Régionales—the LER—operates between main hubs like Marseille, Aix, Arles, and Avignon, with some routes servicing smaller villages; while buses around the Nîmes area are the domain of Edgard Transport.

CAR TRAVEL

The A6–A7 toll road from Paris, known as the Autoroute du Soleil—the Highway of the Sun—takes you straight to Provence, dividing at Orange, 659 km (412 miles) from the capital; the trip can be done in a fast six or so hours. After Orange, the A7 continues southeast to Marseille, on the coast; the A9 heads west to Nîmes, while the A8 carries on to Aix-en-Provence and then to the Côte d'Azur and Italy.

TRAIN TRAVEL

The Marseille-St-Charles station—serving all parts of France, including Paris, Strasbourg, and Bordeaux—is at the northern end of Marseille's city center. Regional trains to Aix-en-Provence (40 mins), Arles (1 hr), Nîmes (1 hr, 20 mins), Avignon (1 hr, 10 mins), and other destinations run from there as well. Avignon itself is a major rail crossroads and a springboard for the Vaucluse. From Paris, you can make it to Avignon in 2 hours and 40 minutes aboard daily high-speed trains on the TGV *Méditerranée* line; these pull into a dedicated station a few miles southwest of the city. TGVs then connect with Nîmes (18 mins), Marseille (35 mins), and Nice (3 hrs). Many other locales within Provence can be reached by rail from Gare Avignon Centre, including Arles (20 mins) and Aix-en-Provence (100 mins with two connections).

RESTAURANTS

You'll eat later in the south, rarely before 12:30 for lunch, usually around 8 for dinner. In summer, shops and museums may shut down, after their morning hours, from noon until 3 or even 4 pm, as much to accommodate lazy lunches as for the crowds taking sun on the beach. But a late lunch works nicely with a late breakfast—and that's another southern luxury. As morning here is the coolest part of the day and the light is at its sweetest, hotels and cafés of every class take pains to make breakfast memorable and whenever possible serve it outdoors. Complete with tables in the garden with sunny-print cloths and a nosegay of flowers, accompanied by birdsong, it's one of the three loveliest meals of the day.

HOTELS

Accommodations in Provence range from luxurious villas to elegantly converted mas to modest city-center hotels. Reservations are essential for much of the year. Provence is more about charming bed-and-breakfasts and lovely expensive hideaways than big hotels, so space is at a premium—especially in summer. Book as far in advance as possible for high season (return guests often reserve next year's stay at the end of the current year's visit); even in low season, you should call ahead because many hotels close for the winter. Assume that all hotel rooms have TV, telephones, and private bath, unless otherwise noted. *Hotel reviews have been shortened. For full information, visit Fodors.com.*

	WHAT IT COSTS IN EUROS			
	$	$$	$$$	$$$$
Restaurants	under €18	€18–€24	€25–€32	over €32
Hotels	under €106	€106–€145	€146–€215	over €215

Restaurant prices are the average cost of a main course at dinner or, if dinner is not served, at lunch. Hotel prices are the lowest cost of a standard double room in high season.

NÎMES, ARLES, AND THE CAMARGUE

Sitting on the banks of the Rhône River, with a Vieille Ville where time seems to have stood still since 1888—the year Vincent van Gogh immortalized the city in his paintings—Arles remains both a vibrant example of Provençal culture and the gateway to the Camargue, a wild and marshy region that extends south to the Mediterranean. Arles, in fact, once outshone Marseille as the major port of the area before sea gave way to sand. Today it competes with nearby Nîmes for the title of "Rome of France," thanks to its magnificent Roman theater and Arènes (amphitheater). Just west and south of these landmarks, the Camargue is a vast watery plain formed by the sprawling Rhône delta and extending over 800 square km (309 square miles)—its landscape remains one of the most extraordinary in France.

NÎMES

35 km (20 miles) north of Aigues-Mortes, 43 km (26 miles) south of Avignon, 121 km (74 miles) west of Marseille.

If you've come to the south seeking treasures from antiquity, you need look no further than Nîmes (pronounced *neem*): with one of the best-preserved Roman amphitheaters in the world and a near-perfect Roman temple, Nîmes beats out Arles for the title of "French City Best Able to Cash In on the Roman Empire's Former Glory." But if you've come in search of a more modern mythology—of lazy, graceful Provence—give Nîmes a pass. It's a feisty, run-down rat race of a town, with jalopies and Vespas roaring irreverently around the ancient sites. Its medieval Vieille Ville lacks the grace of those in Arles or St-Rémy. Yet its rumpled and rebellious ways trace directly back to its Roman incarnation, when its population swelled with newly victorious soldiers flaunting arrogant behavior after their conquest of Egypt in 31 BC.

Already anchoring a fiefdom of pre-Roman *oppida* (elevated fortresses) before ceding to the empire in the 1st century BC, this ancient city grew to formidable proportions under the Pax Romana. Its next golden age bloomed under the Protestants, who established an anti-Catholic stronghold here and wreaked havoc on the iconic architecture—not to mention the papist minority. Their massacre of some 200 Catholic citizens in 1567 is remembered as the Michelade; many of those murdered were priests sheltered in the *évêché* (bishop's house), now the Museum of Old Nîmes.

GETTING HERE AND AROUND

A limited number of flights arrive at the Aéroport de Nîmes-Alès-Camargue-Cévennes. If you're coming by train, 10 TGVs daily make the three-hour trip from Paris; frequent trains also connect Nîmes with Avignon Centre (30 mins), Arles (30 mins), Marseille (about 1 hr, 20 mins), and other locales. Buses operate out of the gare routière, just behind the train station. Edgard runs several per day to Arles (1 hr); others go to Avignon every day. All sites within Nîmes are walkable, but if your feet get tired, the Tango bus does a loop from the station, passing many principal attractions en route; tickets cost €1.20.

VISITOR INFORMATION

Nîmes Tourist Office. ✉ *6 rue Auguste, Nîmes* ☎ *04–66–58–38–00* 🌐 *www.nimes-tourisme.com.*

EXPLORING

TOP ATTRACTIONS

Fodor's Choice ★ **Arènes.** The best-preserved Roman amphitheater in the world is a miniature of the Colosseum in Rome (note the small carvings of Romulus and Remus—the wrestling gladiators—on the exterior and the intricate bulls' heads etched into the stone over the entrance on the north side). More than 435 feet long and 330 feet wide, it had a seating capacity of 24,000 in its day. Bloody gladiator battles, criminals being thrown to animals, and theatrical wild-boar chases drew crowds to its bleachers—and the vomitoria beneath them. Nowadays the corrida (bullfight) transforms the arena (and all of Nîmes) into a sangria-flushed homage to Spain. Concerts are held here year-round, thanks to a high-tech glass-and-steel structure that covers the arena for winter use. ✉ *Bd. des Arènes, Nîmes* ☎ *04–66–21–82–56, 04–66–02–80–80 feria box office* 🌐 *www.arenes-nimes.com* 🎟 *€8.50; €11.70 joint ticket with Tour Magne and Maison Carrée* ⏲ *Mar. and Oct., daily 9–6; Apr., May, and Sept., daily 9–6:30; June, daily 9–7; July and Aug., daily 9–8; Nov.–Feb., daily 9:30–5.*

Carrée d'Art. The glass-fronted Carrée d'Art (directly opposite the Maison Carrée) was designed by British architect Sir Norman Foster as its neighbor's stark contemporary mirror. It literally reflects the Maison Carrée's creamy symmetry and figuratively answers it with a feather-light deconstructed colonnade. Homages aside, it looks like an airport terminal. It contains a library, archives, and the **Musée d'Art Contemporain** (Contemporary Art Museum). The permanent collection falls into three categories: French painting and sculpture; English, American, and German works; and Mediterranean styles, all dating from 1960 onward. There are often temporary exhibits of new work, too. But as lovely as the museum is, the facade suffers traffic pollution and could do with a

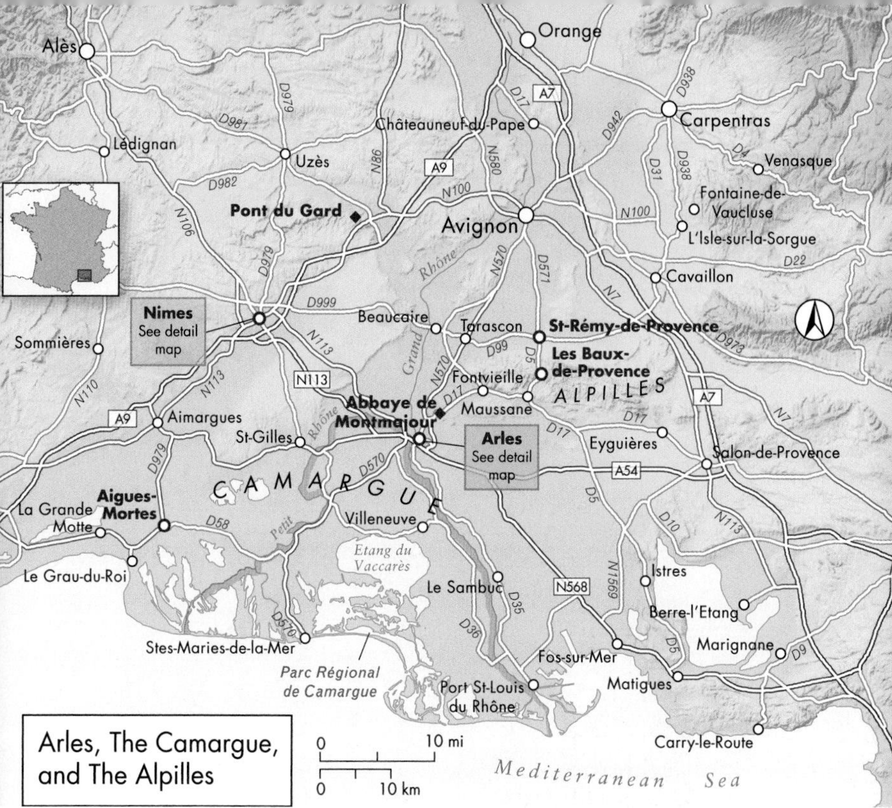

bit of a cleanup. ✉ *Pl. de la Maison Carrée, Nîmes* ☎ *04–66–76–35–70* 🌐 *carreartmusee.nimes.fr* 🎫 *€5* ⏲ *Tues.–Sun. 10–6.*

Maison Carrée (*Square House*). Lovely and forlorn in the middle of a busy downtown square, this exquisitely preserved temple strikes a timeless balance between symmetry and whimsy, purity of line and richness of decor. Modeled on the Temple to Apollo in Rome, adorned with magnificent marble columns and elegant pediment, the Maison Carrée remains one of the most noble surviving structures of ancient Roman civilization anywhere. Built around 5 BC and dedicated to Caius Caesar and his grandson Lucius, the temple has survived subsequent use as a medieval meeting hall, an Augustine church, a storehouse for Revolutionary archives, and a horse shed. Temporary art and photo exhibitions are held here, and among a permanent display of photos and drawings of ongoing archaeological work is a splendid ancient Roman fresco of Cassandra (being dragged by her hair by a hunter) that was discovered in 1992 and carefully restored. There's even a fun 3-D projection of the heroes of Nîmes. ✉ *Pl. de la Maison Carrée, Nîmes* ☎ *04–66–21–82–56* 🌐 *www.arenes-nimes.com* 🎫 *€5.80; €11.70 joint ticket with Arénes and Tour Magne* ⏲ *June, daily 10–7; July and Aug., daily 9:30–8; Apr., May, and Sept., daily 10–6:30; Mar. and Oct., daily 10–6; Nov.–Feb., daily 10–1 and 2–4:30.*

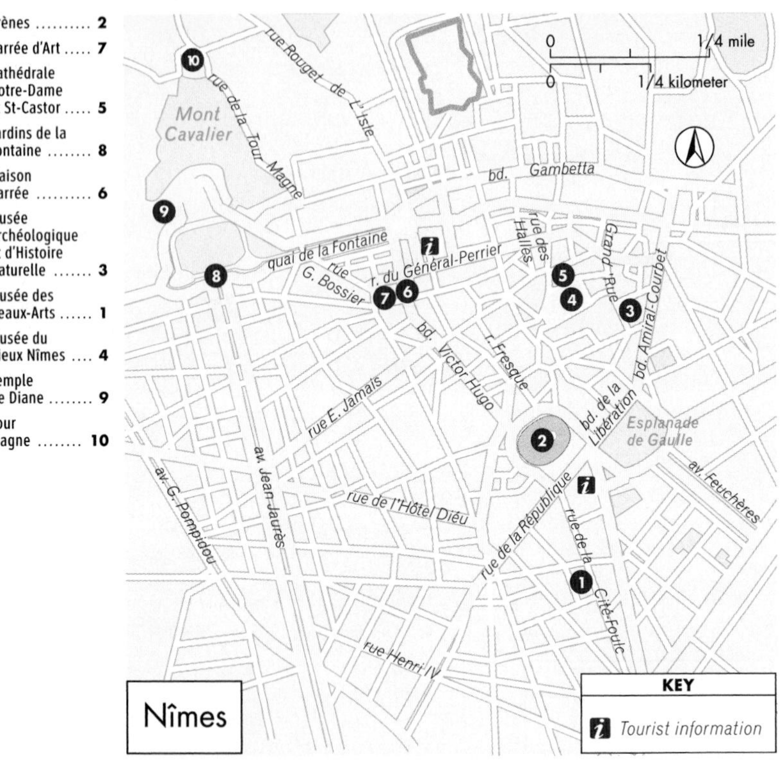

Musée Archéologique et d'Histoire Naturelle (*Museum of Archaeology and Natural History*). This old Jesuit college houses a wonderful collection of local archaeological finds, including sarcophagi, beautiful pieces of Roman glass, statues, busts, friezes, tools, coins, and pottery. Among the highlights are a rare pre-Roman statue called *The Warrior of Grezan* and the Marbacum Torso, which was dug up at the foot of the Tour Magne. ✉ *13 bd. Amiral Courbet, Nîmes* ☎ *04–66–76–74–80* 🌐 *www.nimes.fr* 🎟 *Free* ⏲ *Tues.–Sun. 10–6.*

Temple de Diane (*Temple of Diana*). This shattered Roman ruin dates from the 2nd century BC. The temple's function is unknown, though it's thought to have been part of a larger Roman complex that is still unexcavated. In the Middle Ages Benedictine nuns occupied the building before it was converted into a church. Destruction came during the Wars of Religion. ✉ *Jardins de la Fontaine, Nîmes.*

Tour Magne (*Magne Tower*). At the far end of the Jardins de la Fontaine, you'll find the remains of a tower the emperor Augustus had built on Gallic foundations; it was probably used as a lookout post. Despite losing 30 feet in height over the course of time, the tower still provides fine views of Nîmes for anyone energetic enough to climb the 140 steps. ✉ *Jardins de la Fontaine, Pl. Guillaume-Apollinaire, Nîmes* ☎ *04–66–21–82–56* 🎟 *€3.40; €11.70 joint ticket with Arènes and Maison Carrée*

Nov.–Feb., daily 9:30–1 and 2–4:30; Mar. and Oct., daily 9:30–1 and 2–6; Apr., May, and Sept., daily 9:30–6:30; June, daily 9–7; July and Aug., daily 9–8.

WORTH NOTING

Cathédrale Notre-Dame et St-Castor (*Nîmes Cathedral*). Destroyed and rebuilt in several stages, Nîmes Cathedral was damaged by Protestants during the 16th-century Wars of Religion but still shows traces of its original construction in 1096. A remarkably preserved Romanesque frieze portrays Adam and Eve cowering in shame, the gory slaughter of Abel, and a flood-wearied Noah. Inside, look for the 4th-century sarcophagus (third chapel on the right) and a magnificent 17th-century chapel in the apse. *Pl. aux Herbes, Nîmes 04–66–67–27–72 Mon. 9–noon and 2–6; Tues. and Thurs. 8:30–noon and 2–6; Wed. 9–1 and 3–4:30; Fri.–Sun. 8:30–noon.*

Jardins de la Fontaine (*Fountain Garden*). The Jardins de la Fontaine, an elaborate formal garden, was landscaped on the site of the Roman baths in the 18th century, when the Source de Nemausus, a once-sacred spring, was channeled into pools and a canal. It's a shady haven of mature trees and graceful stonework, and a testimony to the taste of the Age of Reason. It makes for a lovely approach to the Temple of Diana and the Tour Magne. *Corner of Quai de la Fontaine and Av. Jean-Jaurès, Nîmes 04–66–58–38–00 Free Mar. and Sept., daily 7:30–8; Apr.–Aug., daily 7:30 am–10 pm; Oct.–Feb., daily 7:30 am–6:30 pm.*

Musée des Beaux-Arts (*Fine Arts Museum*). The centerpiece of this early 20th-century building, stunningly refurbished by architect Jean-Michel Wilmotte, is a vast ancient mosaic depicting a marriage ceremony that provides intriguing insights into the lifestyle of Roman aristocrats. Also in the varied collection are seven paintings devoted to Cleopatra by 18th-century Nîmes-born painter Natoire Italian, plus some fine Flemish, Dutch, and French works (notably Rubens's *Portrait of a Monk* and Giambono's *The Mystic Marriage of St. Catherine*). *23 rue de la Cite Foulc, Nîmes 04–66–67–38–21 www.nimes.fr €5 Tues.–Sun. 10–6.*

Musée du Vieux Nîmes (*Museum of Old Nîmes*). Housed in the 17th-century bishop's palace opposite the cathedral, this museum shows off garments embroidered in the exotic and vibrant style for which Nîmes was once famous. Look for the 14th-century jacket made of blue serge de Nîmes—the famous fabric (now simply called denim) from which Levi-Strauss first fashioned blue jeans. *Pl. aux Herbes, Nîmes 04–66–76–73–70 www.nimes.fr Free Tues.–Sun. 10–6.*

WHERE TO EAT

$$$$ MODERN FRENCH

Alexandre. Michelin-starred Chef Michel Kayser adds a personal touch to both the gradual transformation of the restaurant's modern decor—the restoration of the dining room, a library sitting room—and to local specialties and change-with-the-season menus. Marinated rabbit traditionally cooked with a mustard dressing (€40) followed by a rich bull steak with pan-roasted Cantal potatoes and black olives served with a celery, caper, and anchovy "chausson" pastry, all drizzled in Camargue sauce (€62), may not leave room for dessert. The terrace opens to an extensive park with century trees, and often apricots and peaches plucked from the overhanging branches will appear on your plate, magically transformed into some delicious creation. *Average main: €56 2 rue Xavier Tronc, Rte. de l'Aeroport, Nîmes 04-66-70-08-99 www.michelkayser.com Closed Mon. and Tues. Sept.–June, Sun. and Mon. July and Aug., 3 wks in mid-Feb., and 2 wks in late Aug. No dinner Sun. Reservations essential.*

$$$ FRENCH **L'Enclos de la Fontaine.** Nîmes's fashionable post-corrida gathering spot is in the Art Deco Hotel Impérator, with warm-weather dining in an idyllic garden court. The food is hearty and delicious, with surprisingly Spanish touches. Chef Mathieu Groshenry carefully structures his menu, sprinkling in dishes such as almond duck, dried cod stuffed in red peppers, and roasted lamb cooked in wild mint. Have an after-dinner drink in the Bar Hemingway; after all, they named it for him because he loved to drink here. *Average main: €28 15 rue Gaston-Boissier, Nîmes 04-66-21-90-30 www.hotel-imperator.com Closed Mon. No lunch Sat., no dinner Sun.*

$$$$ FRENCH **Skab.** Don't be put off by the name, just a blend of the initials of owners Sébastien Kieffer and Alban Barbette. The seasonally changing menus of Chef Damien Sanchez will not disappoint, nor will the enchanting shaded garden terrace. Crispy Provençal lamb with seasonal vegetables makes for a great main dish, and for dessert there's poached apple sections on a crispy pastry with apple jelly, nougat, heavy cream, and gingerbread ice cream. Fixed-price menus range from €54 to $76, but the weekday lunch menu at €24 is a great value—if you can get a table. It's best to reserve ahead. *Average main: €35 7 rue de la République, Nîmes 04-66-21-94-30 www.restaurant-skab.fr Closed Wed. No lunch Sat., no dinner Sun.*

WHERE TO STAY

$ HOTEL **Amphithéâtre.** This old private home has fortunately fallen into the hands of a loving and very hospitable owner, who has refinished 18th-century double doors and fitted rooms with restored-wood details, white-tiled bathrooms, and antique bedroom sets. **Pros:** ideally located; good value for the price. **Cons:** underground parking is a few blocks away; amenities are limited. *Rooms from: €89 4 rue des Arènes, Nîmes 04-66-67-28-51 hoteldelamphitheatre.com 14 rooms No meals.*

$$$ HOTEL **Hotel Imperator.** Character-filled decor and a flavorful restaurant make this gracious old hotel near the Jardins de la Fontaine a local institution. **Pros:** richly atmospheric; excellent location. **Cons:** some rooms can be a little noisy, especially in summer; grandeur said to be fading. *Rooms from: €185 15 rue Gaston Boissier, Quai de la Fontaine, Nîmes 04-66-21-90-30 www.hotel-imperator.com 60 rooms Breakfast.*

SHOPPING

In Nîmes's Old Town you'll find the expected rash of chain stores mixed with fabulous interior-design boutiques and fabric shops selling the Provençal cottons that used to be produced here en masse (Les Indiennes de Nîmes, Les Olivades, Souleiado). Antiques and collectibles are found in

This photo by Mike Tumchewics, a Fodors.com member, captures Nîmes bathed in Provence's extraordinary light.

tiny shops throughout the city's backstreets, but there is a concentration of them in the Old Town.

Les Halles. This permanent covered market is at the heart of the city and puts on a mouthwatering show of olives, fresh fish, cheeses, and produce. ✉ *5 rue des Halles, Nîmes* ☎ *04–66–21–52–49* 🌐 *www.leshallesdenimes.com* ⏲ *Daily 8–1.*

PONT DU GARD

24 km (15 miles) northeast of Nîmes, 25 km (15½ miles) north of Arles, 25 km (15½ miles) west of Avignon.

No other ancient Roman sight in Provence rivals the Pont du Gard, a mighty, three-tiered aqueduct midway between Nîmes and Avignon and the highest bridge the Romans ever built. Erected some 2,000 years ago as part of a 48-km (30-mile) canal supplying water to Roman Nîmes, it is astonishingly well preserved. You can't walk across it anymore, but you can get close enough to see the amazing gigantic square blocks of stone (some weighing up to 6 tons) by traversing the 18th-century bridge built alongside it.

GETTING HERE AND AROUND

Edgard's B21 bus from Nîmes (35 mins, €1.50) and A15 bus from Avignon (45 mins, €1.50) both stop at Rond Point for the Pont du Gard. If you are coming by car, it's 14 km (9 miles) southeast of Uzès on the D981.

EXPLORING

Fodor's Choice ★ **Pont du Gard.** The ancient Roman aqueduct is shockingly noble in its symmetry, the rhythmic repetition of arches resonant with strength, testimony to an engineering concept that was relatively new in the 1st century AD, when the structure was built under Emperor Claudius. And, unsullied by tourists and by the vendors of postcards and Popsicles that dominate the site later in the day, nature is just as resonant, with the river flowing through its rocky gorge unperturbed by the work of master engineering that straddles it.

You can approach the aqueduct from either side of the Gardon River. If you choose the south side (Rive Droite), the walk to the *pont* (bridge) is shorter and the views arguably better. Although access to the spectacular walkway along the top of the aqueduct is now off-limits, the sight of the bridge is still a breathtaking experience. The nearby Espaces Culturels details the history of the bridge and includes an interactive area for kids. ✉ *400 rte. du Pont du Gard, Vers-Pont-du-Gard* ☎ *04–66–37–50–99* 🌐 *www.pontdugard.fr* 🎟 *€18 for up to 5 people, includes Espaces Culturels* ⏲ *Mar., Apr., and Oct., daily 8–8; May–Sept., daily 7:30–midnight; Nov.–Feb., daily 8:30–7.*

WHERE TO STAY

$$ HOTEL **La Bégude Saint Pierre.** A mere 2 km (1 mile) from Pont du Gard, this 17th-century coach house on 30 acres of greenery has been lovingly converted into a boutique hotel and gourmet restaurant. **Pros:** practical location; friendly staff; lovely pool. **Cons:** street-facing rooms can be noisy; can be difficult to find. [$] *Rooms from: €135* ✉ *295 chem des Bégudes, Vers-Pont-du-Gard* ☎ *04-66-02-63-60* 🌐 *www.hotel-begude-saint-pierre.com* *23 rooms* 💳 *No credit cards.*

ARLES

36 km (22 miles) southwest of Avignon, 31 km (19 miles) east of Nîmes, 92 km (57 miles) northwest of Marseille, 720 km (430 miles) south of Paris.

If you were obliged to choose just one city to visit in Provence, Arles would give Avignon and Aix a run for their money. It's too chic to become museumlike, yet the shuttered town houses and graceful squares of its Vieille Ville are still lovely enough to inspire modern-day Van Goghs, and its wealth of classical antiquities is undeniably impressive. A Greek colony since the 6th century BC, little Arles took a giant step forward when Julius Caesar defeated Marseille in the 1st century BC. The emperor-to-be designated Arles a Roman colony and lavished funds and engineering know-how on it. The settlement became an international crossroads by sea and land and a market to the world, with goods from Africa, Arabia, and the Far East. The emperor Constantine himself moved to Arles and brought Christianity with him.

The city's Roman and Romanesque architecture, listed as a UNESCO World Heritage Site, is sufficient reason to visit Arles, yet its character nowadays is as gracious and low-key as it once was cutting-edge. Seated in the shade of the plane trees on Place du Forum or strolling the rampart walkway along the sparkling Rhône, you can see what enchanted

Straddling the Gardon River and built during the rule of Emperor Claudius, the Pont du Gard was an aqueduct that brought water to nearby Nîmes.

Gauguin and drove Van Gogh to creative madness. Throughout the year, Arles hosts pageants, parades, and festivals like the prestigious Les Rencontres d'Arles, the international photography festival every July through September. The panoply of restaurants and small hotels make it the ideal headquarters for forays into the Alpilles and the Camargue. If you plan on doing a lot of sightseeing in Arles, buy either a a €9 *Pass Liberté* or a €13.50 *Pass Avantage*. They grant admission to most museums and monuments.

GETTING HERE

High-speed TGV rail service from Paris is available daily; trains also connect Arles's Gare Centrale with Avignon Centre (20 mins), Nîmes (30 mins), Marseille (1 hr), and Aix-en-Provence (around 2 hrs with connections). Buses from the gare routière (opposite the train station) run multiple times daily between Nîmes and Arles (1 hr), and between Avignon and Arles (1 hr); several buses per day also link Arles with Aix-en-Provence (90 mins).

Visitor Information Arles Tourist Office. ☎ *04–90–18–41–20* 🌐 *www.arlestourisme.com.*

EXPLORING

TOP ATTRACTIONS

Fodor's Choice ★ **Arènes** (*Arena*). Rivaled only by the even better-preserved version in Nîmes, the arena dominating old Arles was built in the 1st century AD to seat 21,000 people, with large tunnels through which wild beasts were forced to run into the center. Before being plundered in the Middle Ages, the structure had three stories of 60 arcades each; the four medieval towers are testimony to a transformation from classical sports arena to

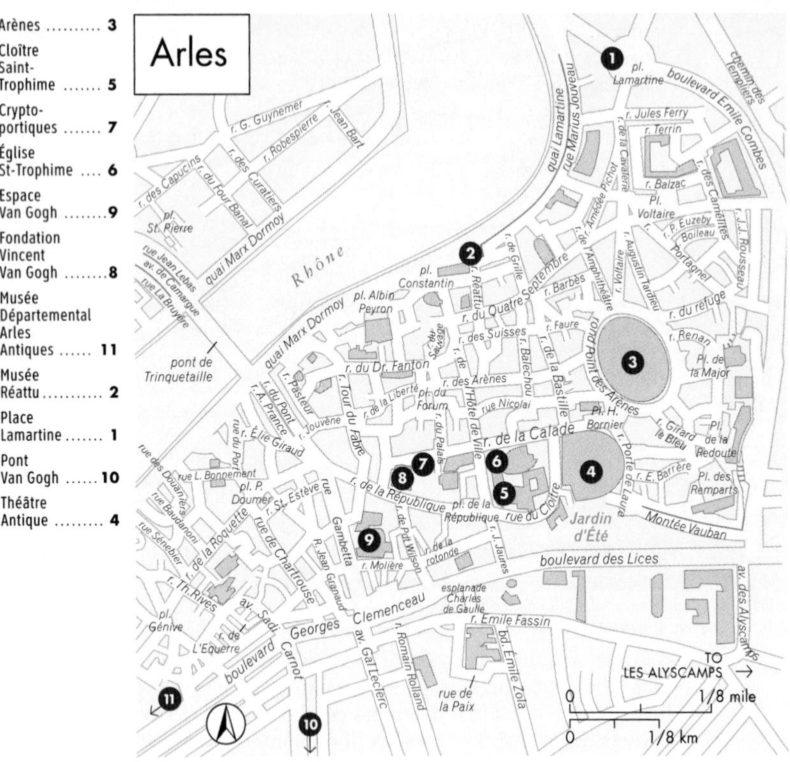

feudal fortification. Complete restoration of the arena, which originally held 12,500 people, began in 1825. Today it's primarily a venue for the traditional spectacle of the *corridas* (bullfights), which take place annually during the *féria pascale*, or Easter festival. The less bloodthirsty local variant *Course Carmarguaise* (in which the bull is not killed) also takes place here. Festivities start with the Fête des Gardians on May 1, when the Queen of Arles is crowned, and culminate in early July with the award of the Cocarde d'Or (Golden Rosette) to the most successful *raseteur*. Tickets are usually available, but make sure to book ahead. ✉ *24 bis, Rond Point des Arènes, Arles* ☎ *04–90–18–41–20 Info Arena, 08–91–70–03–70 Info Courses Carmarguaise* 🌐 *www.arlestourisme.com* 🎫 *€8, includes admission to Théâtre Antique* ⏲ *May–Sept., daily 9–7; Oct., Mar., and Apr, daily 9–6; Nov.–Feb., daily 10–5.*

Église St-Trophime. Classed as a world treasure by UNESCO, this extraordinary Romanesque church alone would justify a visit to Arles. The side aisles date from the 11th century and the nave from the 12th; the church's austere symmetry and ancient artworks (including a stunning early Christian sarcophagus) are fascinating. But it's the church's superbly preserved Romanesque sculpture on the 12th-century **portal**—the recently renovated entry facade—that earns international respect. Particularly remarkable is the frieze of the Last Judgment, with souls being dragged off to Hell in chains or, on the contrary, being lovingly delivered into the hands of the saints. Christ is flanked by his chroniclers, the evangelists: the eagle (John), the bull (Luke), the angel (Matthew), and the lion (Mark). ✉ *Pl. de la République, Arles* 🌐 *www.arlestourisme.com* 🎟 *Free* ⏲ *Weekdays 8–noon and 1:45–6:45, Sat. 8–noon and 2–6, Sun. 9–1 and 2–6* ⏲ *Not open to the public between noon and 2 pm.*

Fodor's Choice ★ **Espace Van Gogh.** A strikingly resonant site, this was the hospital to which the tortured artist repaired after cutting off his earlobe. Its courtyard has been impeccably restored and landscaped to match one of Van Gogh's paintings. The cloistered grounds have become something of a shrine for visitors, and there is a photo plaque comparing the renovation to some of the master's paintings, including *Le Jardin de la Maison de Santé*. The exhibition hall is open for temporary exhibitions; the garden is always on view. ✉ *Pl. Dr. Félix Rey, Arles* ☎ *04–90–18–41–20* 🌐 *www.arlestourisme.com* 🎟 *Free.*

OFF THE BEATEN PATH

Les Alyscamps. Though the romantically melancholic Roman cemetery lies 1 km (½ mile) southeast of the Vieille Ville, it's worth the hike—certainly Van Gogh thought so, as several of his famous canvases prove. This long necropolis amassed the remains of the dead from antiquity to the Middle Ages. Greek, Roman, and Christian tombs line the shady road that was once the main entry to Arles, the Aurelian Way. The finest of the stone coffins have been plundered over the centuries, thus no single work of surpassing beauty remains here (they're in the Musée Départmental Arles). Next to the ruins rise the Romanesque tower and ruined church of St. Honorat, where (legend has it) St. Trophimus fell to his knees when God spoke to him. ✉ *Allée des Sarcophages, Arles* ☎ *04–90–49–38–20* 🌐 *www.arlestourisme.com* 🎟 *€3.50* ⏲ *May–Sept., daily 9–7; Oct., Mar., and Apr., daily 9–noon and 2–6; Nov.–Feb., daily 10–noon and 2–5.*

Musée Départemental Arles Antiques (*Museum of Ancient Arles*). Though it's a hike from the center, this state-of-the-art museum is a good place to set the tone and context for your exploration of Arles. You can learn all about the city in its Roman heyday, from the development of its monuments to details of daily life. The bold, modern triangular structure (designed by Henri Ciriani) lies on the site of an enormous Roman *cirque* (chariot-racing stadium), and the permanent collection includes jewelry, mosaics, town plans, and carved 4th-century sarcophagi. ■ **TIP→ A new wing features a rare intact barge dating from AD 50 and a fascinating display illustrating how the boat was meticulously dredged from the nearby Rhône.** The quantity of these treasures gives an idea of the extent of Arles's importance. Seven superb floor mosaics can be viewed from an elevated platform, and you exit via a hall packed tight with magnificently detailed paleo-Christian sarcophagi. As you leave you will see the belt of St-Césaire, the last bishop of Arles, who died in AD 542 when the countryside was overwhelmed by the Franks and the Roman era met its end. Ask for an English-language guidebook. ✉ *Av. de la 1ère Division Française Libre, Presqu'île du Cirque Romain, Arles* ☎ *04–13–31–51–03* 🌐 *www.arles-antique.cg13.fr* 🎟 *€8, free 1st Sun. of the month* ⏲ *Wed.–Mon. 10–6.*

Van Gogh immortalized the courtyard of this former hospital—now the Espace Van Gogh, a center devoted to his works—in several masterpieces.

Musée Réattu. Three rooms of this museum, housed in a Knights of Malta priory dating to the 15th century, are dedicated to local painter Jacques Réattu. But the standouts are works by Dufy, Gauguin, and 57 drawings (and two paintings) done by Picasso in 1971—including one delightfully tongue-in-cheek depiction of noted muse and writer Lee Miller in full Arles dress. They were donated to Arles by Picasso himself, to thank the town for amusing him with bullfights. ✉ *10 rue Grand Prieuré, Arles* ☎ *04–90–49–37–58* 🌐 *www.museereattu.arles.fr* 🎟 *€8; free 1st Sun. of the month* ⏲ *Nov.–Feb., Tues.–Sun. 10–5; Mar.–Oct., Tues.–Sun. 10–6.*

WORTH NOTING

Cloître St-Trophime (*St.Trophime Cloister*). This peaceful haven, one of the loveliest cloisters in Provence, is tucked discreetly behind St-Trophime, the notable Romanesque treasure. A sturdy walkway above the Gothic arches offers good views of the town. ✉ *Off pl. de la République, Arles* ☎ *04–90–18–41–20* 🌐 *www.arlestourisme.com* 🎟 *€3.50* ⏲ *May–Sept., daily 9–7; Oct., daily 9–6; Nov.–Feb., daily 10–5; Mar. and Apr., daily 9–6.*

Cryptoportiques. Entering through the elegant 17th-century City Hall, you can gain access to these ancient underground passages dating from 30 BC to 20 BC. The horseshoe of vaults and pillars buttressed the ancient forum from below ground. Used as a bomb shelter in World War II, the galleries still have a rather ominous atmosphere. Yet openings let in natural daylight and artworks of considerable merit have been unearthed here, adding to the mystery of the site's original function. ✉ *Rue Balze, pl. de la République, Arles* ☎ *04–90–18–41–20* 🌐 *www.arlestourisme.com* 🎟 *€3.50* ⏲ *May–Sept., daily 9–noon and*

2–7; Oct., Mar., and Apr., daily 9–noon and 2–6; Nov.–Feb., daily 10–noon and 2–5.

Fondation Vincent Van Gogh. Van Gogh's 15-month stay in Arles represents a climax in the artist's career. Enchanted with Arles's limpid light, vibrant landscape, and scenic monuments, Van Gogh experienced here what was to be his greatest blossoming in a decade as a painter. The Fondation Vincent Van Gogh, originally conceived in the mid-80s in response to the 100th anniversary of the artist's arrival in Arles, pays homage to Van Gogh's legacy and monumental influence via an impressive range of artworks contributed by 90 contemporary artists. Opened in spring 2014 in the beautifully restored 15th-century Hôtel Léautaud de Donines, the Fondation houses a superb collection of contemporary art and provides a vital addition to Arles's cultural life with a revolving series of temporary art exhibitions, performance art, concerts, and happenings. ✉ *35 rue du Docteur Fanton, Arles* ☎ *04–90–93–08–08* 🌐 *www.fondation-vincentvangogh-arles.org* 🎫 *€9; €12 with Musée Réattu* 🕓 *Tues.–Sun. 11–6.*

Place Lamartine. Stand on the site of Van Gogh's residence in Arles—the now-famous Maison Jaune (Yellow House), destroyed by bombs in 1944. The artist may have set up his easel on the quais du Rhône, just off place Lamartine, to capture the view that he transformed into his legendary *Starry Night*. Eight other sites are included on the city's "Arles and Vincent van Gogh" (*www.arlestourisme.com*), linking sight to canvas, including place du Forum; the Trinquetaille bridge; rue Mireille; the Summer Garden on boulevard des Lices; and the road along the Arles à Bouc canal. ✉ *Arles.*

Pont Van Gogh (*Langlois Bridge*). Van Gogh immortalized many everyday objects and captured views still seen today, but his famous painting of this bridge—on the southern outskirts of Arles, about 3 km (2 miles) from the old city—seems to touch a particular chord among locals. Bombed in World War II, the bridge has been restored to its former glory. ✉ *Canal d'Arles à Bouc, Rte. de Port St-Louis, Arles.*

Théâtre Antique (*Ancient Theater*). Directly up Rue de la Calade from Place de la République, you'll find these ruins of a theater built by the Romans under Augustus in the 1st century BC. It's here that the noted Venus of Arles statue, now in the Louvre, was dug up and identified. The theater was once an entertainment venue that held 10,000 people, and is now a pleasant, park-like retreat. Only two columns of the amphitheater's stage walls and one row of arches remain; the fine local stone was used to build early Christian churches. Only a few vestiges of the original stone benches are left, along with the two great Corinthian columns. Today the ruins are a stage for the Festival d'Arles, in July and August, and site of Les Recontres d'Arles (Photography Festival) from early July to mid-September. During these festivals, check for early closing hours. ✉ *Rue de la Calade, Arles* ☎ *04–90–49–38–20* 🌐 *www.arlestourisme.com* 🎫 *€8 joint ticket with Arènes* 🕓 *May–Sept., daily 9–7; Oct., Mar., and Apr., daily 9–6; Nov.–Feb., daily 10–5.*

WHERE TO EAT

$ TAPAS ✕ **Bodeguita.** This popular institution near Place du Forum is known for excellent tapas at more than reasonable prices. Embrace the bullfighter within and try a range of morsels: spicy stuffed dumplings, roasted Camembert with chorizo bread, or sliced chicken Catalonia-style. Grilled bull steak with creamed garlic sauce and a few other entrées are also available. The warm reception by Chef Anthony (you're on a first-name basis here) is matched by the vivid yet simple interior. *Average main: €16 ✉ 49 rue des Arenes, Arles ☎ 04–90–96–68–59 🌐 www.bodeguita.fr ⏲ No lunch Sun.–Wed. Nov.–Apr.*

$$$$ FRENCH Fodor's Choice ★ ✕ **La Chassagnette.** Reputedly the original registered "organic" restaurant in Provence, this sophisticated yet down-home comfortable spot—located 12 km (7½ miles) south of Arles—is fetchingly designed and has a dining area that extends outdoors, where large family-style picnic tables await under a wooden-slate canopy overlooking the extensive gardens. Using ingredients that are grown right on the property, innovative master chef Armand Arnal serves prix-fixe menus that are a refreshing, though not inexpensive, mix of modern and classic French-country cuisine—you can expect to pay €85 to €125 per person. The à la carte options are equally admirable and much more affordable: sautéed Saucliéres pig with chopped parsley, garlic, and grated lemon zest for €38. Environmentally conscious oenophiles can wash it all down with a glass of eco-certified wine. *Average main: €37 ✉ Rte. du Sambuc, D36, Arles ☎ 04–90–97–26–96 🌐 www.chassagnette.fr ⏲ Closed Feb., 3 wks in Nov., and 2 wks in late Dec.; closed Tues. and Wed. Mar.–June and Sept.–Dec.; closed Mon.–Wed. in Jan. Reservations essential.*

$$$$ MODERN FRENCH ✕ **L'Atelier de Jean-Luc Rabanel.** Jean-Luc Rabanel is the culinary success story of the region, famous for fresh garden-inspired cuisine that he features in this stylish restaurant and cooking school, one of the few organic eateries in France to merit two Michelin stars. A super-chic Japanese-style reception area, which includes the five elements—water, fire, earth, air, and spirit—ensures that "guests will come into harmony with their cuisine." Menus are prix fixe only; the seven-dish tapas-style lunch (€65) is a treat not to be missed, and the "Emotion" dinner menu (€125) is unforgettable. Those keeping to a budget should try **A Côté** (*04–90–47–61–13* , *www.bistro-acote.com*), a few doors down, where you can more affordably experience the genius of this super-chef by sampling a tasty upmarket set menu (€29) and regional wines. *Average main: €125 ✉ 7 rue des Carmes, Arles ☎ 04–90–91–07–69 🌐 www.rabanel.com ⏲ Closed Mon. and Tues. Reservations essential.*

$$ BISTRO ✕ **L'Autruche.** This small contemporary bistro in central Arles provides cheerful, friendly service and innovative, affordable cuisine with modern leanings. The menu changes frequently depending on what's available in the market, but sumptuous dishes that are typical of this inventive chef's repertoire include fillet of cod with golden turnips, pumpkin puree, and wild mushrooms sprinkled with fresh chervil, and creamy risotto with beef bouillon and cheese crisps sprinkled with hazelnuts. On warm days, the terrace out front is a delightful place to while away an afternoon over a bottle of regional rosé and a good-value gourmet

CLOSE UP

Van Gogh in Arles and St-Rémy

It was the light that drew Vincent van Gogh to Arles. For a man raised under the iron-gray skies of the Netherlands and the gaslight pall of Paris, Provence's clean, clear sun was a revelation. In his last years he turned his frenzied efforts to capture the resonance of "... golden tones of every hue: green gold, yellow gold, pink gold, bronze or copper colored gold, and even from the yellow of lemons to the matte, lusterless yellow of threshed grain."

Arles, however, was not drawn to Van Gogh. Though it makes every effort today to make up for its misjudgment, Arles treated the artist badly during the time he passed here near the end of his life—a time when his creativity, productivity, and madness all reached a climax. It was 1888 when he settled in to work in Arles with an intensity and tempestuousness that first drew, then drove away, his companion Paul Gauguin, with whom he had dreamed of founding an artists' colony.

Frenziedly productive—he applied a pigment-loaded palette knife to some 200 canvases in that year alone—he nonetheless lived in intense isolation, counting his *sous*, and writing his visions in lengthy letters to his long-suffering, infinitely patient brother Theo. Often drinking heavily, occasionally whoring, Vincent alienated his neighbors, goading them to action. In 1889 the people of Arles circulated a petition to have him evicted, a shock that left him less and less able to cope with life and led to his eventual self-commitment to an asylum in nearby St-Rémy. The houses he lived in are no longer standing, though many of his subjects remain as he saw them. The paintings he daubed and splashed with such passion have been auctioned elsewhere.

Thus you have to go to Amsterdam or Moscow to view Van Gogh's work. But with a little imagination, you can glean something of Van Gogh's Arles from a tour of the modern town. In fact, the city has provided helpful markers and a numbered itinerary to guide you between landmarks. You can stand on Place Lamartine, where his famous Maison Jaune stood until it was destroyed by World War II bombs. *Starry Night* may have been painted from the Quai du Rhône just off Place Lamartine, though another was completed at St-Rémy.

The Café La Nuit on Place Forum is an exact match for the terrace platform, scattered with tables and bathed in gaslight under the stars, from the painting *Terrasse de café le soir*; Gauguin and Van Gogh used to drink here. (Current owners have determinedly maintained the Fauve color scheme to keep the atmosphere.) Both the Arènes and Les Alyscamps were featured in paintings, and the hospital where he broke down and cut off his earlobe is now a kind of shrine, its garden reconstructed exactly as it figured in *Le Jardin de l'Hôtel-Dieu.*

About 25 km (15½ miles) away is St-Rémy-de-Provence, where Van Gogh retreated to the asylum St-Paul-de-Mausolée. Here he spent hours in silence, painting the cloisters. On his ventures into town, he painted the dappled lime trees at the intersection of Boulevard Mirabeau and Boulevard Gambetta. And en route between the towns, you'll see the orchards whose spring blooms ignited his joyous explosions of yellow, green, and pink.

lunch. $ *Average main: €22* ✉ *5 rue Dulau, Arles* ☎ *04–90–49–73–63* ⏲ *Closed Sun.* ✍ *Reservations essential.*

$ FRENCH ✕ **Lou Caléu.** In a charming 16th-century building behind the Amphitheater, this popular, unpretentious place serves regional specialties cooked by the genial owner and chef Christian Gimenez—homemade salt-cod brandade, *jarret d'agneau* (lamb roasted with black olives), and *bourride* (Provençal soup)—at good prices. The pureed potatoes with truffled olives are a remarkable garnish, and make sure to order one of the many excellent Rhône Valley whites with the fish. Don't miss the terrific lunch deals. $ *Average main: €17* ✉ *27 rue Porte de Laure, Arles* ☎ *04–90–49–71–77* ⏲ *Closed Sun. and Mon.* ✍ *Reservations essential.*

$$$ FRENCH ✕ **Lou Marquès.** Whether you dine indoors, surrounded by glowing woodwork and rich Provençal fabrics, or amid the greenery of this former Carmelite cloister, atmosphere figures large in your evening at this Arles institution in the Jules César Hotel. Chefs Pascal Renaud and Joseph Kriz mix classical grandeur with Provençal rusticity: lobster risotto, roast pigeon with porcini, grilled bull steak, salsify with veal and tomato polenta, and strawberries in a pastry shell with fresh cream. The wine list is as ambitious as Caesar himself. $ *Average main: €30* ✉ *Jules César Hotel, 9 Bd. des Lices, Arles* ☎ *04–90–52–52–52* 🌐 *www.hotel-julescesar.fr* ✍ *Reservations essential.*

WHERE TO STAY

$$$ HOTEL Fodor's Choice ★ **Grand Hotel Nord-Pinus.** A richly atmospheric stage-set for literati (or literary poseurs), decor-magazine shoots, and people who prize ambience, this scruffy-chic landmark is not for everyone—but if Picasso once felt at home here, perhaps you will, too. **Pros:** transports you to a less complicated time; free mineral water in rooms; free Wi-Fi access. **Cons:** front rooms can be noisy, especially in summer; extra cost for parking. $ *Rooms from: €190* ✉ *Pl. du Forum, Arles* ☎ *04–90–93–44–44* 🌐 *www.nord-pinus.com* *25 rooms, 1 apartment* 🍽 *No meals.*

$$ HOTEL **Hôtel d'Arlatan.** Once home to the counts of Arlatan, this ideally located 15th-century stone house stands on the site of a 4th-century basilica, and a glass floor reveals the excavated vestiges under the lobby. **Pros:** the best French hospitality; warm welcome from staff; tasty foods. **Cons:** heated pool is quite small; drinks are pricier than at nearby cafés. $ *Rooms from: €130* ✉ *26 rue du Sauvage, Arles* ☎ *04–90–93–56–66* 🌐 *www.hotel-arlatan.fr* ⏲ *Closed Jan.* *39 rooms, 6 suites* 🍽 *No meals.*

$$$$ HOTEL Fodor's Choice ★ **L'Hôtel Particulier.** Once owned by the Baron of Chartrouse, this extraordinary 18th-century *hôtel particulier* (mansion) is delightfully intimate and decorated in sophisticated yet charming style, with gold-framed mirrors, white-brocade chairs, marble writing desks, artfully hung curtains, and hand-painted wallpaper. **Pros:** combines historical ambiance with high-tech conveniences; quiet and secluded atmosphere; only a short walk to town. **Cons:** nonrefundable deposit required when booking; small swimming pool; expensive breakfast. $ *Rooms from: €309* ✉ *4 rue de la Monnaie, Arles* ☎ *04–90–52–51–40* 🌐 *www.hotel-particulier.com* ⏲ *Closed Jan.–mid-Mar.* *18 rooms* 🍽 *No meals.*

$$ HOTEL **Le Cloître.** Built as the private home for the provost of the Cloisters, this grand old medieval building has luckily fallen into the hands of

a friendly, multilingual couple devoted to making the most of its historic details—with their own bare hands. **Pros:** lovely architecture made apparent with clever use of color; proud owners eager to talk about the history of hotel. **Cons:** rooms can be sparse to the point of being bare; can be noisy during Feria season. *Rooms from: €110 16 rue du Cloître, Arles 04–90–96–29–50 www.hotelcloitre.com Closed Nov.–Mar. 30 rooms No meals.*

$ HOTEL **Logis Hotel de la Muette.** This fabulous Old Town option has 12th-century exposed stone walls, a 15th-century spiral staircase, and weathered wood everywhere. **Pros:** excellent value; enthusiastic welcome; generous buffet breakfast. **Cons:** some rooms can be very noisy, especially in the summer; parking can be tricky; no elevator. *Rooms from: €81 15 rue des Suisses, Arles 04–90–96–15–39 www.hotel-muette.com Closed Jan. and Feb. 18 rooms No meals.*

NIGHTLIFE AND PERFORMING ARTS

To find out what's happening in and around Arles (even as far away as Nîmes and Avignon), check the free monthly *Journal Farandole* (*www.journal-farandole.com*) or *Arles Info* (*www.arles-agenda.fr*), which list films, plays, cabarets, and music events. Both can be picked up at the tourist office.

Association du Méjan. Founded in partnership with Actes Sud and housed in the beautiful Chapelle Saint-Martin du Méjan, this arts organization hosts a year-round program of classical and sacred music; a revolving series of exhibitions featuring painting, sculpture, and photography; and the superb Arles Jazz Festival, held every year in May. *Pl. Nina-Berberova, Arles 04–90–49–56–78 www.lemejan.com.*

Patio de Camargue. Though Arles seems like one big sidewalk café in warm weather, the best place to drink is at the hip bar-restaurant Patio de Camargue, with a great location on the banks of the Rhône. It serves great tapas and you can hear guitar music and watch traditional dance from Chico and Los Gypsies, led by a founding member of the Gypsy Kings. Reservations are a good idea in high season. *49 Chemin de Barriol, Arles 04–90–49–51–76 www.patiodecamargue.com.*

SHOPPING

Despite being chic and popular, Arles hasn't sprouted the rows of designer shops found in Aix-en-Provence and St-Rémy. Its stores remain small and eccentric and contain an overwhelming variety of Provençal goods.

Arles's colorful markets, with produce, regional products, clothes, fabrics, wallets, frying pans, and other miscellaneous items, take place every Saturday morning along Boulevard des Lices, which flows into Boulevard Clemenceau.

Christian Lacroix. You'll find Lacroix's exuberant scarves, accessories, and colorful sunglasses (Jackie O herself once bought a pair here) and a colorful selection of scented candles, stationery, and glassware in a range of gorgeous jewel colors, as well as some vintage items. *52 rue de la République, Arles 04–90–96–11–16 www.christian-lacroix.com.*

One of the centers of Provençal folklore, Arles is host to a bevy of parades featuring locals dressed in regional costume.

La Botte Camarguaise. If only to check out the bootmaster's moustache, pop 'round to this old-school workshop. Cowboys and country dancers have been coming to Patrick Vidal for 30 years, and you too can buy hand-stitched ready-to-wear or custom-made boots. ✉ *22 rue Jean Granaut, Arles* ☎ *04–90–96–20–87* 🌐 *labottecamarguaise.net.*

L'Occitane. Having put Provence on the worldwide fragrance map, it's fun to shop close to where it all began. The products here are still made in nearby Manosque using regional ingredients. Make sure to sniff Arlésienne, the newest women's fragrance, a floral tribute to the women of the South of France. ✉ *58 rue de la République, Arles* ☎ *04–90–96–93–62* 🌐 *www.loccitane.com.*

Pure Lavande. This boutique specializes in a huge range of pure, plant-based cosmetics from Le Château de Bois, one of Provence's oldest and most venerable producers of fine lavender oil. The range includes face creams, hand and body lotions, toning gels, massage oil, bath milk, hydrosol, and much more, all made with the purest essential oils produced nearby. ✉ *42 rue de la République, Arles* ☎ *04–90–52–01–35* 🌐 *www.lavandeandco.fr.*

ABBAYE DE MONTMAJOUR

6 km (4 miles) north of Arles.

Once the spiritual center of the region and a major 12th-century pilgrimage stop (it contained a small relic of the true cross), the haunting ruins of the Abbaye de Montmajour still dominate this romantic windswept landscape.

GETTING HERE

Cartreize's bus No. 29 runs from Arles daily (€1); by car, take the D17 in the direction of Fontvieille and follow the signs to the Abbaye.

EXPLORING

Fodor's Choice ★ **Abbaye de Montmajour.** This magnificent Romanesque abbey looming over the marshlands north of Arles stands in partial ruin. Begun in the 10th century by a handful of Benedictine monks, the abbey grew according to an ambitious plan of church, crypt, and cloister and, under the management of worldly lay monks in the 17th century, became more sumptuous. When the Church ejected those monks, they sacked the place, and what remained was eventually sold off as scrap. A 19th-century medieval revival spurred a partial restoration, but portions are still in ruins. What remains is a spare and beautiful piece of Romanesque architecture. The cloister rivals that of St-Trophime in Arles for its balance, elegance, and air of mystical peace: Van Gogh, drawn to its isolation, came often to the abbey to reflect, but the strong mistral winds kept him from painting there. The interior, renovated by contemporary architect Rudy Ricciotti, is used for world-class contemporary art exhibitions. ✉ *D17* ☎ *04–90–54–64–17* 🌐 *www.montmajour.monuments-nationaux.fr* 🎟 *€7.50* 🕑 *Apr.–June, daily 9:30–6; July–Sept., daily 10–6:30; Oct.–Mar., Tues.–Sun. 10–5.*

THE CAMARGUE

19km (12 miles) east of Aigues-Mortes, 15 km (9 miles) south of Arles.

Stretching to the horizon, the 800-square-km (328-square-mile) alluvial delta of the Rhône known as the Camargue is an austere, flat marshland, scoured by the mistral and swarmed over by mosquitoes. Between the endless flow of sediment from the Rhône and the erosive force of the sea, its shape is constantly changing. Even the Provençal poet Frédéric Mistral described it in bleak terms: *Ni arbre, ni ombre, ni âme* ("Neither tree, nor shade, nor a soul"). Yet its harsh landscape harbors a concentration of exotic wildlife unique in Europe, and its isolation has given birth to an ascetic and ancient way of life that transcends national stereotypes. People find the Camargue intriguing, birds find it irresistible. The protected marshes lure some 340 species and is the only place in France to see flamingos.

GETTING HERE

Bus No. 20 from Arles goes to Pont de Gau (46 mins, €1) and Stes-Maries-de-la-Mer (1 hr, €1). The strange region itself is worth discovering slowly, either on foot or on horseback—especially as its wildest reaches are inaccessible by car.

VISITOR INFORMATION

Camargue Tourist Office. ✉ *1 pl. Frédéric Mistral, Saint-Gilles* ☎ *04–66–87–33–75* 🌐 *tourisme.saint-gilles.fr/en.*

EXPLORING

Parc Régional de Camargue. As you drive the few roads that crisscross the Camargue, you'll usually be within the boundaries of the Parc Régional de Camargue. Unlike state and national parks in the United States, this area is privately owned and utilized within rules imposed by the state. The principal owners, the famous *manadiers* (the Camargue equivalent of a small-scale rancher), with the help of their *gardians*, keep it for grazing their wide-horned bulls and their broad-bellied, dappled-white horses. It is thought that these beasts are the descendents of ancient, indigenous wild animals, and though they're positively bovine in their placidity today, they still bear the noble marks of their ancestors. The strong, heavy-tailed Camargue horse has been traced to the Paleolithic period (though some claim the Moors imported an Arab strain) and is prized for its stolid endurance and tough hooves. The curved-horned *taureau* (bull), if not indigenous, may have been imported by Attila the Hun. When it's not participating in a bloodless bullfight (mounted players try to hook a ribbon from the base of its horns), a bull may well end up in the wine-rich regional stew, called *gardianne de taureau*. Riding through the marshlands in leather pants and wide-rimmed black hats and wielding long prongs to prod their cattle, the gardians themselves are as fascinating as the wildlife. Their homes—tiny whitewashed, cane-thatched huts with the north end raked and curved apse-like against the vicious mistral—dot the countryside. The signature wrought-iron crosses at the gable invoke holy protection, and if God isn't watching over this treeless plain, they ground lightning. ⊕ *www.parc-camargue.fr*.

WHERE TO STAY

$$$$ HOTEL **Mas de Peint.** Sitting on roughly 1,250 acres of Camargue ranch land, this exquisite 17th-century farmhouse may just offer the ultimate mas experience. **Pros:** isolated setting makes for a romantic getaway; staff offers a warm welcome; no detail is missed in service or style. **Cons:** make sure you confirm room has a shower; unheated pool is a tad chilly, even in September; not much to do once sun goes down. $ *Rooms from: €270* ✉ *D36, 20 km (12 miles) south of Arles, Le Sambuc* ☎ *04–90–97–20–62* ⊕ *www.masdepeint.com* ⏲ *Closed mid-Nov.–late Dec. and Jan.–late Mar.* *8 rooms, 5 suites* *No meals.*

THE ALPILLES

Whether approaching from the damp lowlands of Arles and the Camargue or the pebbled vineyards around Avignon, the countryside changes dramatically as you climb into the arid heights of the low mountain range called the Alpilles (pronounced ahl- *pee*-yuh). A rough-hewn, rocky landscape rises into nearly barren limestone hills, the fields silvered with ranks of twisted olive trees and alleys of gnarled *amandiers* (almond trees). It's the heart of Provence, and is appealing not only for the antiquities in St-Rémy and the feudal ruins in Les Baux, but also for its mellow pace when the day's touring is done.

LES BAUX-DE-PROVENCE

17 km (10 miles) west of Montmajour, 18 km (11 miles) northeast of Arles, 29 km (18 miles) south of Avignon.

When you first search the craggy hilltops for signs of Les Baux-de-Provence (pronounced lay- *bo-duh-pro-vance*), you may not quite be able to distinguish between bedrock and building, so naturally does the ragged skyline of towers and crenellations blend into the sawtooth jags of stone. This tiny château-village ranks as one of the most visited tourist sites in France, with natural scenery and medieval buildings of astonishing beauty. From this intimidating vantage point, the lords of Les Baux ruled over one of the largest fiefdoms in the south throughout the 11th and 12th centuries. In the 19th century Les Baux found new purpose: the mineral bauxite, valued as an alloy in aluminum production, was discovered in its hills and named for its source. A profitable industry sprang up that lasted into the 20th century before fading into history.

Today Les Baux offers two famous faces to the world: its beautifully preserved medieval village and the ghostly ruins of its fortress, once referred to as the *ville morte* (dead town). In the former, lovely 12th-century stone houses, even their window frames still intact, shelter the shops, cafés, and galleries that line the steep cobbled streets. At the edge of the village is a cliff that offers up a stunning view over the Val d'Enfer (Hell's Valley), said to have inspired Dante's *Inferno*.

GETTING HERE AND AROUND

June to September, Cartreize's No. 57 bus runs daily from Arles (€2.40). Otherwise, the easiest way to reach Les Baux is by car; take the A7 to exit 25, then the D99 between Tarascon and Cavaillon.

VISITOR INFORMATION

Les Baux-de-Provence Tourist Office. ✉ *Maison du Roy, Les Baux-de-Provence* ☎ *04–90–54–34–39* 🌐 *www.lesbauxdeprovence.com.*

EXPLORING

Carrières de Lumières. This vast old bauxite quarry has 66-foot-high stone walls that make a dramatic setting for a multimedia show in which thousands of images are projected onto the walls. Exhibitions change periodically, but recent showings have showcased the life and work of Monet, Renoir, and the "Renaissance Giants," Leonardo, Michelangelo, and Raphael. ✉ *Petite rte. de Mailliane, D27, Les Baux-de-Provence* ☎ *04–90–54–47–37* 🌐 *www.carrieres-lumieres.com* 🎫 *€10.50; €15.50 joint ticket with Château des Baux* ⏲ *Apr.–Sept., daily 9:30–7:30; Oct.–Dec. and Mar., daily 10–6.*

FAMILY **Château des Baux.** High above the Val d'Enfer, the 17-acre cliff-top sprawl of ruins is contained under the umbrella name the Château des Baux. At the entry, the Tour du Brau contains the **Musée d'Histoire des Baux,** a small collection of relics and models that shelters a permanent music-and-slide show called *Van Gogh, Gauguin, Cézanne au Pays de l'Olivier,* featuring artworks depicting olive orchards in their infinite variety. From April through September there are fascinating medieval exhibitions: people dressed up in authentic costumes, displays of medieval crafts, and even a few jousting tournaments with handsome knights carrying fluttering silk tokens of their beloved ladies, of which you can take part. Or fire the catapult or try the crossbow, it's up to medieval you. The exit gives access to the wide and varied grounds, where the tiny **Chapelle St-Blaise** and towers mingle with skeletal ruins. *Rue du Trencat, Les Baux-de-Provence 04–90–54–55–56 chateau-baux-provence.com €10; €15.50 joint ticket with Carrières de Lumières Mar. and Oct., daily 9:30–6:30; Apr.–June and Sept. daily 9–7:15; July and Aug., daily 9–8:15; Nov.–Feb., daily 10–5.*

WHERE TO EAT AND STAY

$$ MODERN FRENCH **Le Café des Baux.** For good-value gourmet cuisine, this intimate space in the heart of Les Baux, in view of the château walls, is your place. Well-presented and inventive dishes such as foie gras and sweet onion confit, apple-glazed lamb with crisped potato gratin and chanterelles, and salmon tartare with mango and green apple compare with those of pricier eateries. Don't miss the desserts: the chef's specialty. Popular and petite despite its terrace, you'll want to reserve in advance. *Average main: €23 Rue du Trencat, Les Baux-de-Provence 04–90–54–52–69 www.cafedesbaux.com Closed Nov.–Mar. Reservations essential.*

$$$ HOTEL Fodor's Choice ★ **L'Oustau de la Baumanière.** Spread over three historic buildings just outside the village of Les Baux, guest rooms at this fabled hotel are the last word in Provençal chic—breezy, private, and beautifully furnished with antiques yet done with a contemporary flair. **Pros:** one of the greatest restaurants in Provence; great for celebrity spotting; plenty of amenities. **Cons:** some rooms are far from the action; can be hit-or-miss with service. *Rooms from: €200 Val d'Enfer, Les Baux-de-Provence 04–90–54–33–07 www.oustaudebaumaniere.com Hotel and restaurant closed Jan. and Feb.; restaurant closed Wed. and Thurs. in Mar., and Oct.–mid-Dec. 17 rooms, 13 suites No meals.*

ST-RÉMY-DE-PROVENCE

8 km (5 miles) north of Les Baux, 24 km (15 miles) northeast of Arles, 19 km (12 miles) south of Avignon.

There are other towns as pretty as St-Rémy-de-Provence, and others in more dramatic or picturesque settings. Ruins can be found throughout the south, and so can authentic village life. Yet something felicitous has happened here in the heart of the Alpilles—a steady infusion of style, of art, of imagination—all brought by people with a respect for local traditions and a love of Provençal ways. As many of them have been gossip-column names or off-duty celebs, it is easy to understand why this pretty town has earned its nickname, the Hamptons of Provence. St-Rémy, more than anywhere, allows you to meditate quietly on antiquity, browse pungent markets with basket in hand, and also enjoy urbane galleries, cosmopolitan shops, and an abundance of chic dining and lodging choices. In short, St-Rémy has been gentrified through and through.

First established by an indigenous Celtic-Ligurian people who worshipped the god Glan, the village Glanum was adopted by the Greeks of Marseille in the 2nd and 3rd centuries BC. Under the Pax Romana there developed a veritable city, with temples and forum, luxurious villas, and baths. The Romans (and Glanum) eventually fell, but a village grew up next to their ruins, taking its name from their protectorate, the Abbey St-Remi, which was based in Reims. St-Rémy de Provence grew to be an important market town, and wealthy families built fine mansions in its center—among them the de Sades (whose black-sheep relation held forth in the Luberon at Lacoste). Perhaps the best known resident, though, was the ill-fated Vincent van Gogh. Shipped unceremoniously out of Arles at the height of his madness (and creativity), he committed himself to the asylum St-Paul-de-Mausolée, a tranquil spot that still draws devotees.

GETTING HERE AND AROUND

It's easiest to come by car; take the A7 until you hit exit 25, then the D99 between Tarascon and Cavaillon (direction St-Rémy). In summer, Cartreize has an Arles–St-Rémy–Les Baux bus (Monday–Saturday, €2.30). Local trains stop at nearby Tarascon, where you can board a bus bound for St-Rémy (20 mins, €1).

VISITOR INFORMATION

St-Rémy Tourist Office. ✉ *Pl. Jean-Jaurès, St-Rémy-de-Provence* ☎ *04–90–92–05–22* 🌐 *www.saintremy-de-provence.com.*

EXPLORING

TOP ATTRACTIONS

FAMILY **Glanum.** A slick visitor center prepares you for entry into the ancient village of Glanum, with scale models of the site in its various heydays. A good map and an English brochure guide you stone by stone through the maze of foundations, walls, towers, and columns that spread across a broad field; helpfully, Greek sites are noted by numbers, Roman ones by letters. Glanum is across the street from Les Antiques and set back from the D5, and the only parking is in a dusty roadside lot on the D5 south of town (in the direction of Les Baux). Hours vary, so check ahead. ✉ *Rte. des Baux de Provence, off the D5, direction Les Baux, St-Rémy-de-Provence* ☎ *04–90–92–23–70* 🌐 *www.glanum.monuments-nationaux.fr* 🎫 *€7.50* ⏲ *Apr.–Aug., daily 10–6:30; Sept., Tues.–Sun. 10–6:30; Oct.–Mar., Tues.–Sun. 10–5.*

Les Antiques. Two of the most miraculously preserved classical monuments in France are simply called Les Antiques. Dating from 30 BC, the **Mausolée** (mausoleum), a wedding-cake stack of arches and columns, lacks nothing but a finial on top, and is dedicated to a Julian, probably Caesar Augustus. A few yards away stands another marvel: the **Arc Triomphal,** dating from AD 20. ✉ *St-Rémy-de-Provence.*

St-Paul-de-Mausolé. This is the isolated asylum where Van Gogh spent the last year of his life (1889–90). Enter quietly: the hospital shelters psychiatric patients to this day, all of them women. You're free to walk up the beautifully manicured garden path to the church and its jewel-box Romanesque **cloister,** where the artist found womblike peace. ✉ *Chemin Saint-Paul, St-Rémy-de-Provence* ☎ *04–90–92–77–00* 🌐 *www.saintpauldemausole.fr* 🎫 *€4.65* ⏲ *Apr.–Sept., daily 9:30–6:45; Oct., Nov., and Mar., daily 10:15–5:15.*

DID YOU KNOW?

St-Rémy-de-Provence has more than its share of chic shops and restaurants; nevertheless, the town has succeeded in remaining true to its Provençal roots.

Vieille Ville. Within St-Rémy's fast-moving traffic loop, a labyrinth of narrow streets leads you away from the action and into the slow-moving inner sanctum of the Vieille Ville. Here trendy, high-end shops mingle pleasantly with local life, and the buildings, if gentrified, blend in unobtrusively. ✉ *St-Rémy-de-Provence.*

WORTH NOTING

Collégiale St-Martin. St-Rémy is wrapped by a lively commercial boulevard, lined with shops and cafés and anchored by its 19th-century church Collégiale St-Martin. Step inside to see the magnificent 5,000-pipe modern organ, one of the loveliest in Europe. If the main door is locked, the side door is always open. Rebuilt to 18th-century specifications in the early 1980s, it has the flexibility to interpret new and old music with pure French panache; you can listen for free Saturday afternoon at 5:30 from July through August (and sometimes September). ✉ *Pl. de la République, St-Rémy-de-Provence.*

Musée Estrine Présence Van Gogh. The 18th-century Hôtel Estrine is now the Musée Estrine Présence Van Gogh and has many reproductions of the artist's work, along with letters to his brother Theo and exhibitions of contemporary art, much of it inspired by Vincent. It also houses temporary exhibitions and a permanent collection dedicated to the father of Cubism, Albert Gleizes, who lived in St-Remy for the last 15 years of his life. ✉ *Hôtel Estrine, 8 rue Lucien Estrine, St-Rémy-de-Provence* ☎ *04–90–92–34–72* 🌐 *www.musee-estrine.fr* 🎟 *€8* ⏲ *Apr.–mid-June, Tues.–Sun. 10–noon and 2–6; mid-June–mid-Sept., Tues.–Sun. 10–6 (to 9 July and Aug.); Mar. and Nov., Tues.–Sun. 2–6.*

WHERE TO EAT

$$$ BISTRO

✕ **Bistrot Découverte.** Claude and Dana Douard were happy to collaborate with some of the greatest chefs of our time before getting away from the big city lights to open this bistro-wine bar hotspot in the center of St-Rémy. The wine selection is magnificent, and so is the simple food based on top-notch local ingredients. Try the grilled sea bass with chorizo, mashed potatoes, and seasonal vegetables, or the grilled Mont Ventoux spiced pork. $ *Average main: €25* ✉ *19 bd. Victor Hugo, St-Rémy-de-Provence* ☎ *04–90–92–34–49* 🌐 *www.bistrotdecouverte.com* ⏲ *Closed 2 wks mid-Feb.* ✍ *Reservations essential.*

$$$$ FRENCH

✕ **La Maison Jaune.** This 18th-century retreat with a Michelin star in the Vieille Ville draws crowds of summer people to its pretty roof terrace, with accents of sober stone and lively contemporary furniture both indoors and out. The look reflects the cuisine: with vivid flavors and a cool, contained touch, Chef François Perraud prepares fresh Mediterranean sea bream, bouillabaisse, grilled lamb from Provence, and other specialties on his seasonally changing menus. $ *Average main: €44* ✉ *15 rue Carnot, St-Rémy-de-Provence* ☎ *04–90–92–56–14* 🌐 *www.lamaisonjaune.info* 💳 *No credit cards* ⏲ *Closed Sun. and Mon., no lunch Tues. Mar.–June and Sept.–Feb.* ✍ *Reservations essential.*

$$$ HOTEL
Fodor's Choice ★

🏨 **Château des Alpilles.** Reached via a lane of majestic plane trees and set on 8 luxuriant acres of parkland, cypress groves, and gardens, this gracious mas and château date back to medieval times, yet underwent a complete face-lift when present owners bought the estate in the 1970s. **Pros:** service anticipates your every need; gorgeous Italian designer linens; spectacular grounds. **Cons:** outside the city center. $ *Rooms from: €215* ✉ *Rte. de Rougadou, St-Rémy-de-Provence* ☎ *04–90–92–03–33* 🌐 *www.chateaudesalpilles.com* ⏲ *Closed Jan.–mid-Mar.* *17 rooms, 4 suites* 🍽 *No meals.*

SHOPPING

Every Wednesday morning St-Rémy hosts one of the most popular and picturesque markets in Provence, during which Place de la République and narrow Old Town streets overflow with herbs and spices, olive oil by the vat, and tapenade by the scoop, as well as fabrics and *brocante* (collectibles). There's a smaller version Saturday morning.

Joël Durand Chocolatier. Known for his creamy ganaches, Joël Durand carries a range of gourmet chocolates, nut creams, toffee, and marmalades made in Provence from tree-ripened fruit. ✉ *3 bd. Victor Hugo, St-Rémy-de-Provence* ☎ *04–90–92–38–25* 🌐 *www.joeldurand-chocolatier.fr.*

Fodor's Choice ★ **Lilamand Confiseur.** Much more than just a sweet shop, this historical *confiseur* dates back to 1866 and is in its fifth generation of family ownership on the same St-Rémy premises. Makers of the famous Provençal *calisson*, an almond-shaped marzipan confection, as well as a gorgeous array of candied fruits—including everything from cherries and strawberries to kiwis, fennel, and even whole pumpkins—from a recipe credited to Nostradamus (a native son). There are also fruit syrups, jams, chocolates, and regional honey. A tour of the factory and a stop in the beautiful boutique make for a highly pleasurable hour or two. ✉ *5 av. Albert Schweitzer, St-Rémy-de-Provence* ☎ *04–90–92–11–08* 🌐 *www.lilamand.com.*

AVIGNON AND THE VAUCLUSE

Anchored by the magnificent papal stronghold of Avignon, the Vaucluse spreads luxuriantly east of the Rhône. Its famous vineyards seduce connoisseurs, and its Roman ruins draw scholars and art lovers alike. Arid lowlands with orchards of olives, apricots, and almonds give way to a rich and wild mountain terrain around the formidable Mont Ventoux and flow into the primeval Luberon, made a household name by Peter Mayle. The hill villages around the Luberon are as lovely as any you'll find in the south of France.

AVIGNON

82 km (51 miles) northwest of Aix-en-Provence, 98 km (59 miles) northwest of Marseille, 229 km (140 miles) south of Lyon.

Avignon is anything but a museum; it surges with modern ideas and energy and thrives within its ramparts as it did in the heyday of the popes—and, like those radical church lords, it's sensual, cultivated, and cosmopolitan, with a taste for worldly pleasures. Avignon remained papal property until 1791, and elegant mansions bear witness to the town's 18th-century prosperity. From its famous Palais des Papes (Papal Palace), where seven exiled popes camped between 1309 and 1377 after fleeing from the corruption and civil strife of Rome, to the long, low bridge of childhood-song fame, you can beam yourself briefly into 14th-century Avignon, so complete is the context, so evocative the setting.

Everything worth seeing (except the St. Bénézet Bridge) is confined within the medieval city walls. Most sights cluster around Place du Palais, with signs pointing the way. This is the Avignon of the visitors. To see Avignonnais leading their daily lives, however, turn off these tourist paths and get lost among the city's cobblestone streets. Note that the Avignon-Villeneuve PASSion (available free at the tourist office and cultural sites) gives 10% to 50% reductions on most museums and sites after you buy your first ticket at regular price.

GETTING HERE AND AROUND

High-speed *Méditerranée* line trains from Paris (2 hrs, 40 mins) and Nice (3 hrs) pull into the Gare Avignon TGV, 6 km (4 miles) southwest of the city, where Eurostar now arrives five times a week from London. To get to Avignon's central station, hop on a local train called Virgule. The bus terminal next door has connections to Arles (1 hr), Nîmes (1½ hrs), and more. Municipal buses operated by TCRA (🌐 *www.tcra.fr*) will zip you around the city itself for a €1.30 fare; alternately, you can rent a bike at one of 17 Vélopop stations (🌐 *www.velopop.fr*) and pedal away for €1 per hour (plus a €1 rental fee).

VISITOR INFORMATION

Avignon Tourist Office. ✉ *41 cours Jean-Jaurès, Avignon* ☎ *04–32–74–32–74* 🌐 *www.avignon-tourisme.com.*

EXPLORING

TOP ATTRACTIONS

Cathédrale Notre-Dame-des-Doms. Built in a pure Provençal Romanesque style in the 12th century, this cathedral was soon dwarfed by the extravagant palace that rose beside it. The 14th century saw the addition of a cupola, which promptly collapsed. As rebuilt in 1425, the cathedral is a marvel of stacked arches with a strong Byzantine flavor and is topped with a gargantuan Virgin Mary lantern—a 19th-century afterthought—whose glow can be seen for miles around. Closed for renovation of the nave and entrance, the museum was slated to reopen in late 2015. ✉ *Pl. du Palais, Avignon* ☎ *04–90–86–81–01* 🌐 *www.cathedrale-avignon.fr.*

Fodor's Choice ★ **Collection Lambert.** Known for the breadth of its collection as well as the scope of its exhibitions, the Lambert is a must-see for contemporary art lovers. Housed in an elegant 17th-century mansion, this impressive assembly of contemporary artworks came out of the private collection of Paris art dealer Yvon Lambert, who founded the museum in 2000 in honor of Avignon's designation as European Capital of Culture. Comprising more than 1,200 pieces dating from the 1960s to the present, the Lambert Collection also hosts an influential series of exhibitions, cultural events, lectures, and arts eduction programs independently or in conjunction with other arts institutions worldwide. The impressive bookshop carries dozens of original, limited-edition works by artists represented in the collection, including prints by Cy Twombly, Sol Lewitt, and Jenny Holzer, and the breezy courtyard café offers gourmet snacks, beverages, and light lunches under the shade of sleepy plane trees. ✉ *5 rue Violette, Avignon* ☎ *04–90–16–56–20* 🌐 *www.collectionlambert.fr* 🎫 *€15* ⏲ *Sept.–June, daily 11–6; July and Aug., daily 11–7.*

Musée Calvet. Worth a visit for the beauty and balance of its architecture alone, this fine old museum contains a rich collection of antiquities and classically inspired works. Acquisitions include neoclassical and Romantic pieces and are almost entirely French, including works by Manet, Daumier, and David. There's also a good modern section, with works by Bonnard, Duffy, and Camille Claudet (note Claudet's piece depicting her brother Paul, who incarcerated her in an insane asylum when her relationship with Rodin caused too much scandalous talk). The main building itself is a Palladian-style jewel in pale Gard stone dating from the 1740s; the garden is so lovely that it may distract you from the art. ✉ *65 rue Joseph-Vernet, Avignon* ☎ *04–90–86–33–84* 🌐 *www.musee-calvet-avignon.com* 🎫 *€6; €7 joint ticket with Musée Lapidaire* ⏲ *Wed.–Mon. 10–1 and 2–6.*

Musée du Petit Palais. This residence of bishops and cardinals before Pope Benedict built his majestic palace houses a large collection of old-master paintings, the majority of which are Italian works from the early-Renaissance schools of Siena, Florence, and Venice—styles with which the Avignon popes would have been familiar. Later works here include Sandro Botticelli's *Virgin and Child*, and Venetian paintings by Vittore Carpaccio and Giovanni Bellini. ✉ *Pl. du Palais, Avignon* ☎ *04–90–86–44–58* 🌐 *www.petit-palais.org* 🎫 *€6* ⏲ *Wed.–Mon. 10–1 and 2–6.*

Palais des Papes. This colossal palace creates a disconcertingly fortress-like impression, underlined by the austerity of its interior. Most of the original furnishings were returned to Rome with the papacy; others were lost during the French Revolution. Some imagination is required to picture the palace's medieval splendor, awash with color and with worldly clerics enjoying what the 14th-century Italian poet Petrarch called "licentious banquets." On close inspection, two different styles of building emerge at the palace: the severe **Palais Vieux** (Old Palace), built between 1334 and 1342 by Pope Benedict XII, a member of the Cistercian order, which frowned on frivolity, and the more decorative **Palais Nouveau** (New Palace), built in the following decade by the artsy, lavish-living Pope Clement VI. The Great Court, entryway to the complex, links the two.

The main rooms of the Palais Vieux are the **Consistory** (Council Hall), decorated with some excellent 14th-century frescoes by Simone Martini; the **Chapelle St-Jean,** with original frescoes by Matteo Giovanetti; the **Grand Tinel,** or Salle des Festins (Feast Hall), with a majestic vaulted roof and a series of 18th-century Gobelin tapestries; the **Chapelle St-Martial,** with more Giovanetti frescoes; and the **Chambre du Cerf,** with a richly decorated ceiling, murals featuring a stag hunt, and a delightful view of Avignon. The principal attractions of the Palais Nouveau are the **Grande Audience,** a magnificent two-nave hall on the ground floor, and, upstairs, the **Chapelle Clémentine,** where the college of cardinals once gathered to elect the new pope. To get the most out of the experience,

Avignon and the Vaucluse
Pont-St-Esprit
Vaison-la-Romaine
Crestet
Malaucène
Séguret
Gigondas
Le Barroux
Vacqueyras
Orange
MONT VENTOUX
Bédoin
Crillon-le-Brave
Caromb
Beaumes-de-Venise
DRÔME
ALPES DE HAUTE PROVENCE
Sault
Mormoiron
Carpentras
Châteauneuf-du-Pape
Bedarrides
Banon
GARD
Sorgues
Avignon
see detail map
VAUCLUSE
Lagarde-d'Apt
Venasque
Pernes-les-Fontaines
Vedène
PLATEAU DE VAUCLUSE
Simiane
Velleron
Pont du Gard
Remoulins
Villeneuve-lè-Avignon
Fontaine de Vaucluse
L'Isle-sur-la-Sorgue
Gordes
Le Thor
Roussillon
Viens
Barbentane
Lagnes
Caseneuve
Reillanne
Caumont
Apt
Châteaurenard
Noves
Coustellet
Saignon
Cavaillon
Graveson
Ménerbes
Buoux
Eyragues
BOUCHES-DU-RHÔNE
Lacoste
Bonnieux
Oppéde-le-Vieux
LUBERON
La Bastide-des-Jourdans
Beaucaire
Tarascon
St-Rémy-de-Provence
MONTAGNE DU LUBERON
Grambois
Lourmarin
Les Baux-de-Provence
Cadenet
La Tour-D'Aigues
Silvacane
Villelaure
Bellegarde
Fontvieille
Maussane-les-Alpilles
0 6 mi
0 6 km
A7
A9
N7
N86
N580
N100
N570
D538
D976
D8
D977
D7
D938
D950
D974
D542
D164
D1
D30
D942
D17
D4
D943
D28
D31
D2
D25
D51
D14
D973
D36
D35
D970
D571
D99
D561
D956

Avignon

KEY

Tourist information

- Cathédrale Notre-Dame-des-Doms **4**
- Collection Lambert **7**
- Les Halles **9**
- Musée Angladon **8**
- Musée Calvet **6**
- Musée de Petit Palais **2**
- Palais des Papes **5**
- Pont St-Bénézet **1**
- Rocher des Doms **3**

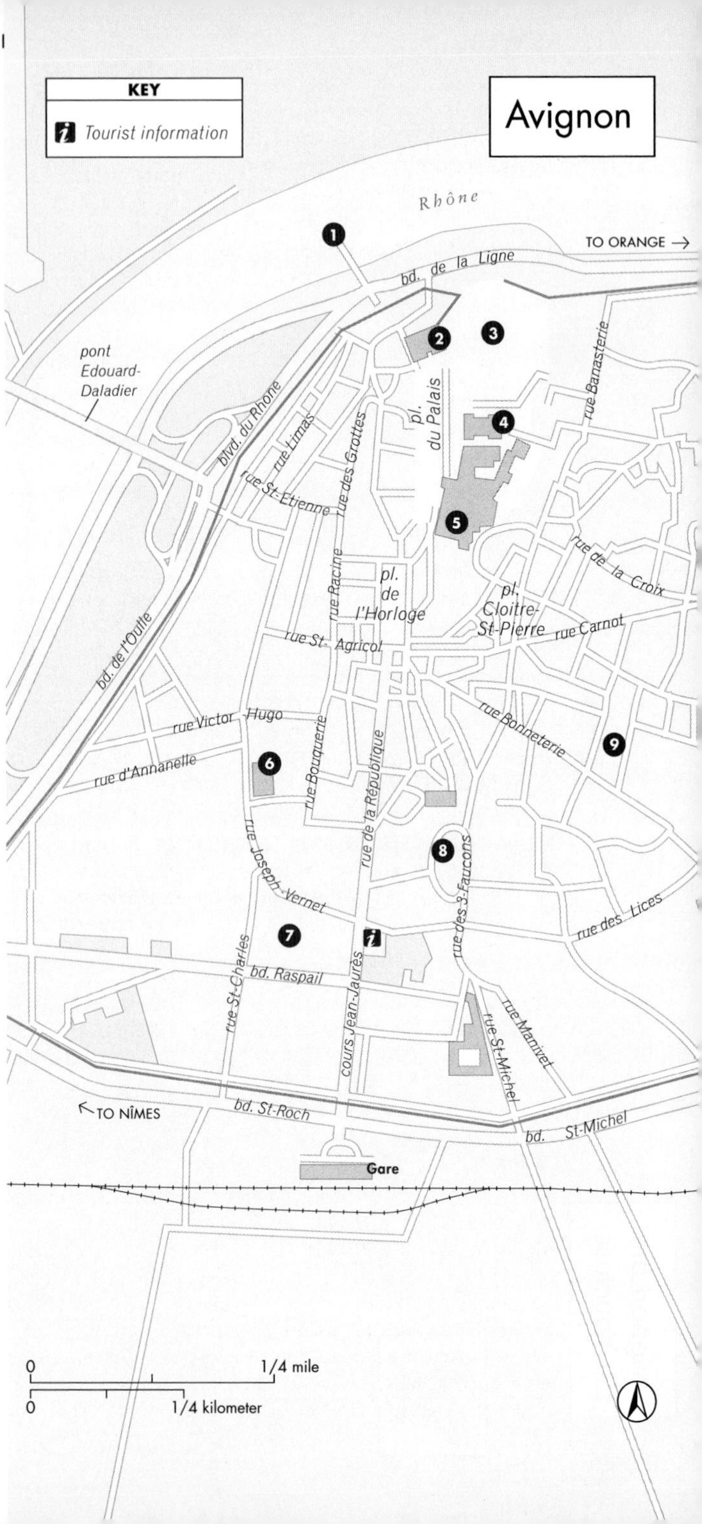

Rhône

TO ORANGE →

bd. de la Ligne

pont Edouard-Daladier

blvd. du Rhone

rue Limas

rue St-Etienne

rue des Grottes

pl. du Palais

rue Banasterie

rue de la Croix

rue Racine

pl. de l'Horloge

pl. Cloitre-St-Pierre

rue Carnot

rue St- Agricol

bd. de l'Oulle

rue Victor Hugo

rue d'Annanelle

rue Bouquerie

rue de la République

rue Bonneterie

rue Joseph-Vernet

rue des 3-Faucons

rue des Lices

rue St-Charles

bd. Raspail

cours Jean-Jaurès

rue Manivet

rue St-Michel

↖TO NÎMES

bd. St-Roch

bd. St-Michel

Gare

0 1/4 mile

0 1/4 kilometer

consider a €2 audio tour. ✉ *6 rue Pente Rapide, Avignon* ☎ *04–32–74–32–74* 🌐 *www.palais-des-papes.com* 🎫 *€11; €13.50 includes tour of Pont St-Bénéze* ⏲ *Mar., daily 9–6:30; Apr.–June, Sept., and Oct., daily 9–7; July, daily 9–8; Aug., daily 9–8:30; Nov.–Feb., daily 9:30–5:45.*

Pont St-Bénezet (*St. Bénezet Bridge*). "Sur le pont d'Avignon on y danse, on y danse . . ." Unlike London Bridge, this other fragment of childhood song (and UNESCO World Heritage site) still stretches its arches across the river, but only partway. After generations of war and flooding, only half remained by the 17th century. Its first stones allegedly laid with the miraculous strength granted St-Bénezet in the 12th century, it once reached all the way to Villeneuve. It's a bit narrow for dancing "tous en rond" (round and round) though the traditional place for dance and play was under the arches. For a fee, you can rent an audio guide and climb along its high platform for broad views of the Old Town ramparts. ✉ *Port du Rhône, Avignon* ☎ *04–32–74–32–74* 🌐 *www.avignon-pont.com* 🎫 *€5; €15.50 joint ticket with Palais des Papes* ⏲ *Apr.–June, daily 9–7; July, daily 9–8; Aug., daily 9–8:30; Sept. and Oct., daily 9–7; Nov.–Feb., daily 9:30–5:45; Mar., daily 9:30–6:30.*

THE AVIGNON PASSION PASS

A good investment is the *Avignon PASSion*: you pay full price for the first site/monument you visit and thereafter there are various reductions on all the other sites, depending on which of them you visit. The 15-day pass, available for free at the tourist office, as well as participating sites and monuments, gives discounts of 10%–50% on visits to every site in Avignon and Villeneuve-lez-Avignon for you and up to five people.

Fodor's Choice ★ **Rocher des Doms** (*Rock of the Domes*). Set on bluff above town, this lush hilltop garden has grand Mediterranean pines, a man-made lake (complete with camera-ready swans), plus glorious views of the palace, the rooftops of Old Avignon, the Pont St-Bénézet, and formidable Villeneuve across the Rhône. On the horizon loom Mont Ventoux, the Luberon, and Les Alpilles. The garden has lots of history as well: Often called the "cradle of Avignon," its rocky grottoes were among the first human habitations in the area. ✉ *Montée du Moulin off Pl. du Palais, Avignon* ☎ *04–32–74–32–74* 🌐 *www.avignon-tourisme.com* ⏲ *Nov., Jan., and Feb., daily 7:30–6; Dec., daily 7:30–5:30; Mar., daily 7:30–7; Apr., May, and Sept., daily 7:30–8; June–Aug., daily 7:30–9; Oct., daily 7:30—6:30.*

WORTH NOTING

Les Halles. By 6 every morning (except Monday) the merchants and artisans have stacked their herbed cheeses and arranged their vine-ripened tomatoes with surgical precision in pyramids and designs that please the eye before they tease the salivary glands. This permanent covered market is as far from a farmers' market as you can get, each booth a designer boutique of *haute de gamme* (top-quality) goods, from jewel-like olives to silvery mackerel to racks of hanging hares worthy of a Flemish still life. Even if you don't have a kitchen to stock, consider enjoying a cup of coffee or a glass of (breakfast) wine while you take in the sights and smells. Tuck into a plate of freshly shucked oysters and a *pichet* of the crisp local white, or, on Saturday from 11 to noon, September through July, watch a cooking demonstration, "La Petite Cuisine du Marché," by a well-known Provençal chef. ✉ *Pl. Pie, Avignon* ☎ *04–90–27–15–15* 🌐 *www.avignon-leshalles.com* ⏲ *Tues.–Sun. 6 am–1:30 pm, until 2 on Wed.*

Musée Angladon. This superb collection of major 18th- to 20th-century paintings and furnishings was assembled by the famous Parisian couturier Jacques Doucet (1853–1929), who counted many of the major painters and writers of his day among his close circle and purchased—or funded—some of the great works of the 20th century (he was the original owner of Picasso's *Desmoiselles d'Avignon*). With an unerring eye, this great appreciator of the arts created a collection that he then housed in this mansion, which he purchased toward the end of his life; it includes works by Degas, Van Gogh, Manet, Cézanne, Modigliani, and Picasso, along with important drawings, sculpture, photography, and furniture. The museum also hosts temporary exhibitions. ✉ *5 rue Laboureur, Avignon* ☎ *04–90–82–29–03* 🌐 *www.angladon.fr* 🎫 *€6* ⏲ *Nov.–Mar. Wed.–Sun. 1–6; Apr.–Oct. Tues.–Sun. 1–6.*

WHERE TO EAT

$$$ FRENCH Fodor's Choice ★

✕ **Christian Étienne.** Stellar period decor in a renovated 12th-century mansion makes for an impressive backdrop to innovative and delicious cuisine that has earned the chef a Michelin star. Try the pan-roasted medallion of veal with dried porcini blinis and thinly sliced mushrooms with chervil, or splurge for the whole lobster sautéed in olive oil, muscat grapes, and beurre blanc with verjuice. The seasonal truffle menu may be too rich for some (€150), but a €35 lunch menu offers nice balance for budget-conscious travelers. $ *Average main: €30* ✉ *10 rue de Mons, Avignon* ☎ *04–90–86–16–50* 🌐 *www.christian-etienne.fr* ⏲ *Closed Sun. and Mon.* ✍ *Reservations essential.*

$$ FRENCH Fodor's Choice ★

✕ **La Fourchette.** The food here is some of the best in town, as the bevy of locals clamoring to get in proves. It all smells so good that you may be tempted to rip one of the decorative forks off the wall and attack your neighbor's plate. Service is prompt and friendly, and you can dig in to heaping portions of escalope of salmon, chicken cilantro à l'orange , or what is likely the best Provençal daube (served with macaroni gratin) in France. $ *Average main: €20* ✉ *17 rue Racine, Avignon* ☎ *04–90–85–20–93* 🌐 *www.la-fourchette.net* ⏲ *Closed weekends and 1st 3 wks in Aug.* ✍ *Reservations essential.*

$$$$ FRENCH Fodor's Choice ★

✕ **La Vieille Fontaine.** Summer-evening meals around the old fountain and boxwood-filled oil jars in the courtyard of the Hôtel d'Europe would be wonderful with *filet de boeuf* alone, but combine this romantic backdrop with stellar southern French cuisine and you have a special event. Give yourself over to one of the most renowned restaurants in the Vaucluse, complete with the best regional wines and an army of urbane servers—and hope for moonlight. The €37 lunch menu, coffee and parking included, quickly refuels before tackling the afternoon's touring. $ *Average main: €45* ✉ *12 pl. Crillon, Avignon* ☎ *04–90–14–76–76* 🌐 *www.heurope.com* ⏲ *Closed Sun. and Mon.; 1st wk in Jan.; 1st 2 wks in Feb.; last 2 wks in Aug.* ✍ *Reservations essential.*

Beautiful town squares form the hub of Avignon's historic heart, as seen in this view from the roof of the famed Palais des Papes.

$$ FRENCH ✕ **L'Essentiel.** This chic hot spot, steps from the Palace des Papes, is part of the "bistronomy" movement that focuses on top-notch cooking, casual atmosphere, and more reasonable prices. Trained by Bardet and Senderens, chef-owner Laurent Chouviat makes his experience apparent with dishes like open ravioli with asparagus and small peas in a creamed basil sauce with garlic or roast cod with confit tomatoes, fresh coriander, and Arborio risotto. The quaint terrace on this side street will allure passersby, but the romantic 17th-century interior courtyard will keep them coming back. Choose from between two affordable set menus (€32 and €45). *Average main: €20* ✉ *2 rue Petite Fusterie, Avignon* ☎ *04–90–85–87–12* 🌐 *www.restaurantlessentiel.com* ⏲ *Closed Sun. and Mon.*

WHERE TO STAY

$$$$ HOTEL **Hôtel d'Europe.** This classic vine-covered 16th-century home once hosted Victor Hugo, Napoléon Bonaparte, and Emperor Maximilian; regally discreet, it is notable for its walled, tree-shaded courtyard and an interior filled with Aubusson tapestries, porcelains, and Provençal antiques. **Pros:** authentic historical setting; perfect romantic hideaway; close to everything. **Cons:** least expensive rooms are small; high season means noisy evenings. *Rooms from: €225* ✉ *12 pl. Crillon, Avignon* ☎ *04–90–14–76–76* 🌐 *www.heurope.com* *39 rooms, 5 suites* *No meals.*

$$$$ HOTEL Fodor's Choice ★ **Hôtel de la Mirande.** A designer's dream of a hotel, this *petit palais* permits you to step into 18th-century Avignon—enjoy painted coffered ceilings, sumptuous antiques, extraordinary handmade wall coverings, and other superb *grand siècle* touches (those rough sisal mats on the

floors were the height of chic back in the Baroque era). **Pros:** a step back in time to a more gracious era; luxurious Dr Hauschka toiletries; free bottled water. **Cons:** rooms can be a little stuffy; breakfast is expensive. *$ Rooms from: €450 ✉ Pl. de la Mirande, Avignon ☎ 04–90–14–20–20 ⊕ www.la-mirande.fr ⇨ 25 rooms, 1 suite, 1 apt ¶ No meals.*

$$ HOTEL **Hotel du Palais des Papes.** This third-generation family-run institution is a notably solid and comfortable place—all the better for its location just off Place du Palais. **Pros:** 40% reduction on Palais des Papes parking with hotel stamp; some rooms with double-glazed windows. **Cons:** can be stifling in summer; aspects of decor appear touristy kitsch. *$ Rooms from: €120 ✉ 3 pl. du Palais, Avignon ☎ 04–90–86–04–13 ⊕ www.hotel-palais-des-papes.fr ⇨ 26 rooms, 2 suites ¶ No meals.*

SHOPPING

Avignon has a cosmopolitan mix of French chains, hip clothing shops (it's a college town after all), and a few choice boutiques. The pedestrian area has a stretch of stores along Rue du Vieux Sextier, Rue des Fourbisseurs, and Rue des Marchands, where you'll find Hermès at the corner of Place de l'Horlage. But Rue de la République is the main shopping artery.

Les Délices du Luberon. For those with a taste for all things Provençal, this gourmet épicerie is a treasure trove of the many delicacies you'd find in the best local markets, all neatly packaged and suitcase ready—if they make it that far. There's everything from olive oils, tapenades, herbs, sweet and savory conserves, bottled soups, fruit jams, honey, pastries, lavender-based sweets and cosmetics, and much more. *✉ 20 rue du Changé, Avignon ☎ 04–90–84–03–58 ⊕ www.delices-du-luberon.fr.*

L'ISLE-SUR-LA-SORGUE

26 km (16 miles) east of Avignon.

Crisscrossed by lazy canals and alive with moss-covered waterwheels that once drove its silk, wool, and paper mills, this old valley town retains a gentle appeal—except on Sunday, when it transforms itself into a Marrakech of marketeers, its streets crammed with antiques and brocante stalls. There are also street musicians, food stands groaning under mounds of rustic breads, vats of tapenade, and cloth-lined baskets of spices, plus miles of café tables offering ringside seats to the spectacle. On a nonmarket day life returns to its mellow pace, with plenty of antiques dealers open year-round, as well as fabric and interior-design shops, bookstores, and food stores for you to explore.

GETTING HERE AND AROUND

There's a 40-minute bus (No. 6) from the Avignon train station that stops at Place Robert Vasse in Isle-sur-la-Sorgue (where the large Caisse d'Epargne bank is). It's €2 one-way or €1, if you return on the same day. By car the distance is 5 km (3 miles). The TER train line links Avignon and L'Isle-sur-la-Sorgue from the L'Isle-Fontaine train station.

VISITOR INFORMATION

L'Isle-sur-la-Sorgue Tourist Office. *✉ Pl. de la Liberté, L'Isle-sur-la-Sorgue ☎ 04–90–38–04–78 ⊕ www.oti-delasorgue.fr.*

EXPLORING

Collégiale Notre-Dame-des-Anges. L'Isle's 17th-century church, the Collégiale Notre-Dame-des-Anges, is extravagantly decorated with gilt, faux marble, and sentimental frescoes. The double-colonnade facade commands the center of the Vieille Ville. Visiting hours change frequently, so check with the tourist office. ✉ *L'Isle-sur-la-Sorgue.*

Campredon Centre d'Art. One of the finest of L'Isle's mansions, the 18th-century Hôtel de Campredon has been restored and reinvented as a modern-art gallery, mounting three temporary exhibitions per year. ✉ *20 rue du Docteur Tallet, L'Isle-sur-la-Sorgue* ☎ *04–90–38–17–41* 🎫 *€7* ⏲ *July–Oct., Tues.–Sun. 10–1 and 2:30–6:30; Feb.–June, Tues.–Sat. 10–12:30 and 2–5:30.*

WHERE TO EAT AND STAY

$$$$ FRENCH ✕ **Le Jardin du Quai.** This is where local antiques dealers come to eat, and the place feels so welcoming that it would be easy to linger for hours. Chef Daniel Hébet made his name at La Mirande in Avignon and Le Domaine des Andéols in St-Saturnin-lès-Apt before opening this bistro in his own image—young, jovial, and uncompromising when it comes to quality. Off a noisy street near the train station is the gate to this garden haven, with metal tables under the trees and an airy interior with a vintage tile floor. Hébet offers a single set menu at lunch and another at dinner, and the food is so good that no one is complaining at the lack of choice (though he has been known to substitute meat for fish on request): poached egg with truffles, Saint Pierre with a hint of green onion, lobster in delicate pastry, and cherry meringue are all delicious. $ *Average main: €35* ✉ *91 av. Julien Guigue, L'Isle-sur-la-Sorgue* ☎ *04–90–20–14–98* 🌐 *www.danielhebet.com* ⏲ *Closed Tues. and Wed. Oct.—Mar.*

$$$ B&B/INN Fodor's Choice ★ **La Prévôté.** Five beautifully decorated and freshly painted rooms, each styled with exquisite taste in soft colors and Provence chic, offer an ideal respite after a long day of antiques shopping. **Pros:** price includes breakfast; wonderful dining room; antiques-bedecked decor. **Cons:** a little tricky to find; parking may be difficult. $ *Rooms from: €165* ✉ *4 bis rue Jean Jacques Rousseau, L'Isle-sur-la-Sorgue* ☎ *04–90–38–57–29* 🌐 *www.la-prevote.fr* ⏲ *Closed 3 wks from end Feb. and from mid-Nov. Restaurant closed Wed. Sept.–June; no lunch Jul. and Aug. Closed Tues. year-round* 🛏 *5 rooms* 🍽 *Breakfast.*

SHOPPING

Throughout the pretty backstreets of L'Isle's Old Town (especially between Place de l'Église and Avenue de la Libération), there are boutiques spilling baskets full of tempting goods onto the sidewalk to lure you inside; most concentrate on home design and Provençal goods.

Passage du Pont. Of the dozens of antiques shops in L'Isle, one conglomerate—Passage du Pont (also known as L'Isle aux Brocantes)—concentrates some 40 dealers under the same roof. ✉ *7 av. des Quatre Otages, L'Isle-sur-la-Sorgue* ☎ *06–20–10–58–15.*

Un Jour. For more than 200 years, Brun de Vian-Tiran has been making wool blankets, cozy quilts, and other bed accessories. You can find their signature throws here among other home decor names like Nina

Ricci, Descamps, Yves Delormé, and Blanc les Vosges. ✉ *8 Pl. Ferdinand Buisson, L'Isle-sur-la-Sorgue* ☎ *04–90–38–50–19* 🌐 *www.unjourlingedemaison.fr.*

Xavier Nicod. Higher-end antiques are in plentiful supply at Xavier Nicod, which "pays tribute to eclecticism" in art and architecture. ✉ *9 av. des Quatre Otages, L'Isle-sur-la-Sorgue* ☎ *06–07–85–54–59* 🌐 *www.xaviernicod.com.*

GORDES

39 km (24 miles) east of Avignon.

This ancient stone village still rises above the valley in painterly hues of honey gold, and its cobbled streets—lined with boutiques, galleries, and real-estate offices—still wind steep and narrow to its Renaissance château, making this certainly one of the most beautiful towns in Provence.

GETTING HERE

There's no direct bus service from Avignon to Gordes, so you'll need to transfer in Cavaillon Gare Routière. It's a long ride, so consider a taxi, which costs about €80.

VISITOR INFORMATION

Gordes Tourist Office. ✉ *Le Chateau, Gordes* ☎ *04–90–72–02–75* 🌐 *www.gordes-village.com.*

EXPLORING

Fodor's Choice ★ **Abbaye de Sénanque.** If you've fantasized about Provence's famed lavender fields, head to the wild valley some 4 kilometers (2½ miles) north of Gordes (via D177), where this photogenic 12th-century Romanesque abbey seemingly floats above a redolent sea of lavender (in full bloom late June to August). Begun in 1150 and completed at the dawn of the 13th century, the **church** and adjoining **cloister** are without decoration but still touch the soul with their chaste beauty. Along with the abbeys of Le Thornet and Silvacane, this is one of a trio of "Three Sisters" built by the Cistercian Order in this area. Next door, the enormous vaulted **dormitory** contains an exhibition on Abbaye de Sénanque's construction, and the **refectory** shelters a display on the history of Cistercian abbeys. The few remaining monks here now preside over a cultural center presenting concerts and exhibitions. The bookshop has a huge collection of books about Provence (lots in English). ✉ *Gordes* ☎ *04–90–72–05–72* 🌐 *www.senanque.fr* 🎫 *€7.50* ⏲ *Daily services open to the public. Guided tour hrs vary.*

Village des Bories. Just outside Gordes, on a lane heading north from D2, you'll see signs leading to the Village des Bories. The bizarre and fascinating little stone hovels called *bories* are found throughout this region of Provence, and here they are concentrated some 20 strong in an ancient community. Their origins are provocatively vague: built as shepherds' shelters with tight-fitting, mortarless stone in a hive-like form, they may date to the Celts, the Ligurians, even the Iron Age—and were inhabited or used for sheep through the 18th century. A photo exhibition shows other structures, similar to bories, in countries around

Continued on page 564

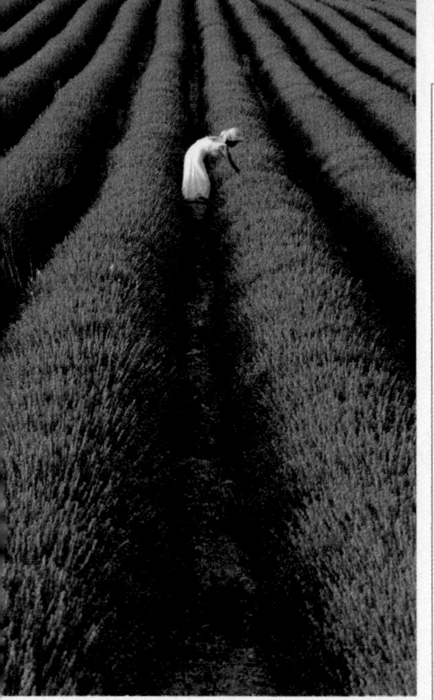

Van Gogh may have made the sunflower into the icon of Provence, but it is another flower—one that is unprepossessing, fragrant, and tiny—that draws thousands of travelers every year to Provence. They come to journey the famous "Route de la Lavande" (the Lavender Route), a wide blue-purple swath that connects over 2,000 producers across the south of France.

THE LAVENDER ROUTE

Once described as the "soul of Haute-Provence," lavender has colored Provence's plains since the days of the ancient Romans. Today it brings prosperity, as consumers are madly buying hundreds of beauty products that use lavender essence. Nostrils flared, they are following this route every summer. To help sate their lavender lust, the following pages present a detail-rich tour of the Lavender Route.

TOURING THE LAVENDER ROUTE

❶ Have your Nikon ready for the beautifully preserved Cistercian simplicity of the **Abbaye Notre-Dame de Sénanque**, a perfect foil for the famous waving fields of purple around it.

❷ No shrinking violet, the hilltop village of **Gordes** is famous for its luxe hotels, restaurants, and lavender-stocked shops.

❸ Get a fascinating A to Z tour—from harvesting to distilling to production—at the **Musée de la Lavande** near Coustellet.

❹ If you want to have a peak lavender experience—literally—detour 18 km (10 miles) to the northwest and take a spectacular day's drive up the winding road to the **summit of Mont Ventoux** (follow signs from Sault to see the lavender-filled valleys below).

❺ Even if you miss the biggest blow-out of the year, the Fête de la Lavande in **Sault** (usually on August 15), take in the charming *vieille ville* boutiques or the fabulous lavender fields that surround the hillside town.

❻ The awe-inspiring lavender fields around **Forcalquier** are one step away from perfection, and the Monday morning market is a treasure trove of local products.

❼ **Distillerie "Le Coulets"** on the outskirts of Apt has been a lavender farm for generations and offers free tours and products for sale at its boutique.

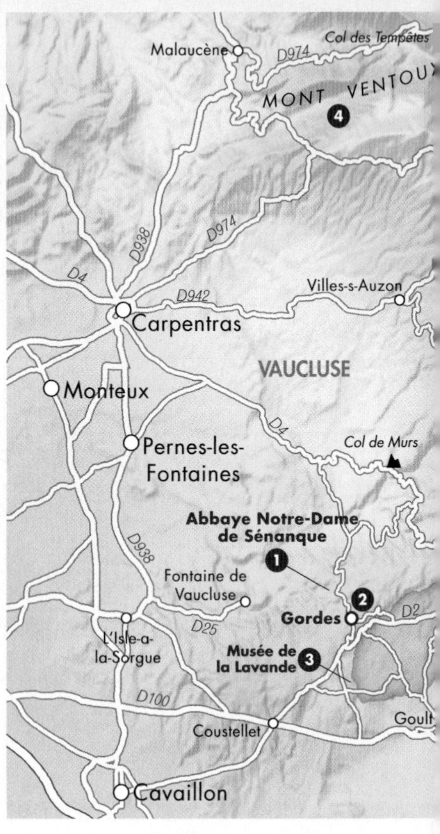

Provence is threaded by the "Routes de la Lavande" (the Lavender Routes), a wide blue-purple swath that connects over 2,000 producers across the Drôme, the plateau du Vaucluse, and the Alpes-de-Haute-Provence, but our itinerary is lined with some of the prettiest sights—and smells—of the region. Whether you're shopping for artisanal bottles of the stuff (as with wine, the finest lavender carries its own Appellation d'Origine Contrôlée), spending a session at a lavender spa, or simply wearing hip-deep purple as you walk the

Forcalquier Market

Purple haze

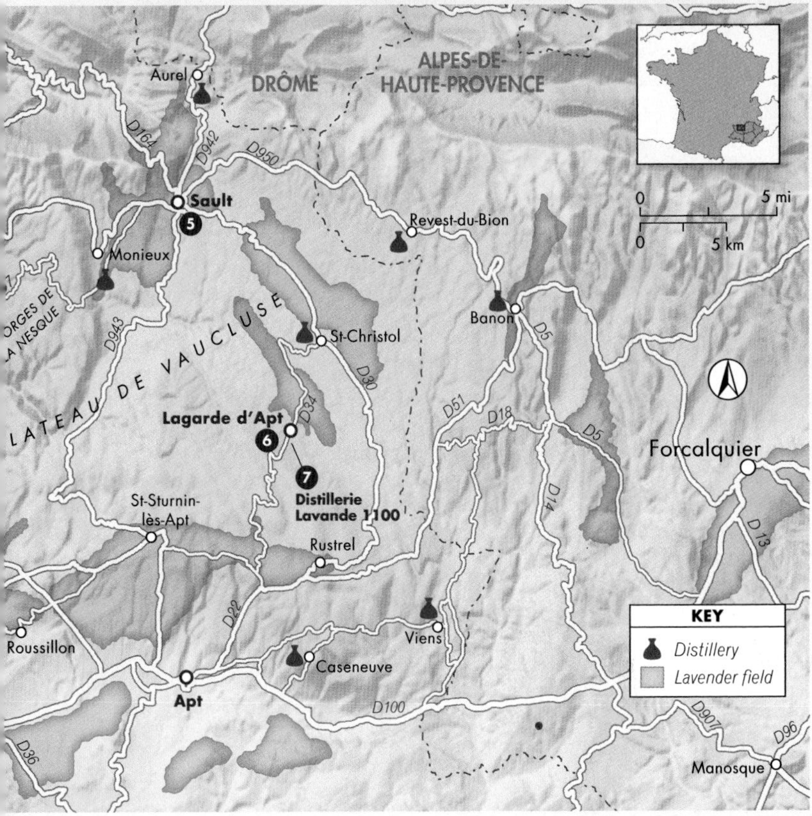

fields, the most essential aspect on this trip is savoring a magical world of blue, one we usually only encounter on picture postcards.

To join the lavender-happy crowds, you have to go in season, which (if you're lucky) runs from June to early August. Like Holland's May tulips, the lavender of Haute-Provence is in its true glory only once a year: the last two weeks of July, when the harvesting begins—but fields bloom throughout the summer months for the most part. Below, we wind through the most generous patches of lavender. Drive the colorful gambit southeastward (Coustellet, Gordes, Sault and Forcalquier), which will give you good visiting (and shopping) time in a number of the villages that are *fou de la lavande* (crazy for lavender).

Abbaye Notre-Dame de Sénanque

DAY 1

SÉNANQUE
A Picture-Perfect Abbey

An invisible Master of Ceremonies for the Lavender Route would surely send you first to the greatest spot for lavender worship in the world: the 12th-century Cistercian **Abbaye Notre-Dame de Sénanque,** which in July and August seems to float above a sea of lavender, a setting immortalized in a thousand travel posters. Happily, you'll find it via the D177 only 4 km (2½ miles) north of Gordes, among the most beautiful of Provence's celebrated perched villages. An architecture student's dream of neat cubes, cylinders, and pyramids, its pure Romanesque form alone is worth contemplating in any context. But in this arid, rocky setting the gray stone building seems to have special resonance—ancient, organic, with a bit of the borie about it. Along with the abbeys of Le Thornet and Silvacane, this is one of the trio of "Three Sisters" built by the Cistercian order in this area. Sénanque's **church** is a model of symmetry and balance. Begun in 1150, it has no decoration but still touches the soul with its chaste beauty.

The adjoining **cloister,** from the 12th century, is almost as pure, with barrel-vaulted galleries framing double rows of discreet, abstract pillars. Next door, the enormous vaulted dormitory and the refectory shelter a display on the history of Cistercian abbeys. The few remaining monks here now preside over a cultural center that presents concerts and exhibitions. The bookshop is one of the best in Provence, with a huge collection of Provençaliana (lots in English).

After spending the morning getting acquainted with the little purple flower at Sénanque, drive south along the D2 (or D177) back to **Gordes,** through a

THE ESSENCE OF THE MATTER

Provence and lavender go hand in hand—but why? The flower is native to the Mediterranean, and grows so well because the pH balance in the soil is naturally perfect for it (pH 6–8). But lavender was really put on the map here when ancient Romans arrived to colonize Provence and used the flower to disinfect their baths and perfume their laundry (the word comes from Latin *lavare,* "to wash"). From a small grass-roots industry, lavender proliferated over the centuries until the first professional distillery opened in Provence in the 1880s to supply oils for southern French apothecaries. After World War I, production boomed to meet the demand of the perfumers of Grasse (the perfume center of the world). Once described as the "soul of Haute-Provence," lavender is now farmed in England, India, and the States, but the harvest in the South of France remains the world's largest.

dry, rocky region mixed with deep valleys and far-reaching plains.

Wild lavender is already omnipresent, growing in large tracts as you reach the entrance of the small, unspoiled hilltop village, making for a patchwork landscape as finely drawn as a medieval illumination. A cluster of houses rises above the valley in painterly hues of honey gold, with cobbled streets winding up to the village's picturesque Renaissance château, making it one of the most beautiful towns in Provence.

Gordes has a great selection of hotels, restaurants, and B&Bs to choose from (see our listings under Gordes). Spend the early afternoon among tasteful shops that sell lovely Provençal crafts and produce, much of it lavender-based, and then after lunch, head out to Coustellet.

COUSTELLET

A Great Lavender Museum

Set 2 miles south of Gordes, Coustellet is noted for its **Musée de la Lavande** (take the D2 southeast to the outskirts of Coustellet). Owned by one of the original lavender families, who have cultivated and distilled the flower here for over five generations, this museum lies on the outskirts of more than 815 acres of prime lavender-cultivated land.

ON THE CALENDAR

If you plan to be at the Musée de la Lavande between July 1 and August 25 you can watch animations of workers swathing lavender with copper scythes.

Not only can you visit the well-organized and interesting museum (note the impressive collection of scythes and distilling apparatus), you can buy up a storm in the boutique, which offers a great selection of lavender-based products at very reasonable prices.

There are four main species. True lavender (*Lavandula angustifolia*) produces the most subtle essential oil and is often used by perfume makers and laboratories. Spike lavender (*Lavandula latifolia*) has wide leaves and long floral stems with several flower spikes. Hybrid lavender (*lavandin*) is obtained from pollination of true lavender and spike lavender, making a hybrid that forms a highly developed large round cluster. French lavender (*Lavendula stoechas*) is wild lavender that grows throughout the region and is collected for the perfume industry. True lavender thrives in the chalky soils and hot, dry climate of higher altitudes of Provence. It was picked systematically until the end of the 19th century and used for most lavender-based products. But as the demand for this remarkable flower grew, so did the need for a larger production base. By the beginning of the 20th century, the demand for the flower was so great that producers planted fields of lavender at lower altitudes, creating the need for a tougher, more resistant plant: the hybrid *lavandin*.

In many towns, Provence's lavender harvest is celebrated with charming folkloric festivals.

DAY 2

LAGARDE D'APT

A Top Distillerie

On the second day of your lavender adventure, begin by enjoying the winding drive 25 km (15 miles) east to the town of **Apt**. Aside from its Provençal market, busy with all the finest food products of the Luberon and Haute Provence, Apt itself is unremarkable (even actively ugly from a distance) but is a perfect place from which to organize your visits to the lavender fields of Caseneuve, Viens, and Lagarde d'Apt.

Caseneuve (east exit from Apt onto the D900 and then northwest on the D35) and Viens (16 km/10 miles east from Apt on the D209) are small but charming places to stop for a quick bite along the magnificent drive through the rows upon rows of lavender, but if you have to choose between the three, go to the minuscule village of Lagarde d'Apt (12 km/7 miles east from Apt on the D209).

Or for a closer look, take the D22 (direction Rustrel) a few kilometres outside of Apt to **Distillerie "Les Coulets."** From mid-July to mid-August you can take a free tour of the distillery, visit the farm and browse the gift shop.

SAULT

The Biggest Festival

To enjoy a festive overnight, continue northwest from Lagarde d'Apt to the village of **Sault**, 15 km (9 miles) to the northeast. Beautifully perched on a rocky outcrop overlooking the valley that bears its name, Sault is one of the key stops along the Lavender Route.

There are any number of individual distilleries, producers, and fields to visit—to make the most of your visit, ask the Office du Tourisme (☎ *04–90–64–01–21* 🌐 *www.saultenprovence.com*) for a list of events. Make sure to pop into the **Centre de Découverte de la Nature et du Patrimoine Cynégétique** to see the exhibitions on the natural history of the region, including some on lavender. Aim to be in Sault for the not-to-be-missed **Fête de la Lavande**, a day-long festival entirely dedicated to lavender, the best in the region, and usually held around August 15.

Village folk dress in traditional Provençal garb and parade on bicycles, horses leap over barrels of fragrant bundles of hay, and local producers display their wares at the market—all of which culminates in a communal Provençal dinner served with lavender-based products.

DAY 3

FORCALQUIER

The Liveliest Market

On your third day, the drive from Sault over 53 km (33 miles) east to Forcalquier is truly spectacular.

As you approach the village in early July, you will see endless fields of *Lavandula vera* (true wild lavender) broken only by charming stone farmhouses or discreet distilleries.

The epicenter of Haute-Provence's lavender cultivation, **Forcalquier** boasts a lively Monday morning market with a large emphasis on lavender-based products, and it is a great departure point for walks, bike rides, horse rides, or drives into the lavender world that surrounds the town.

In the 12th century, Forcalquier was known as the capital city of Haute-Provence and was called the *Cité des Quatre Reines* (City of the Four Queens) because the four daughters (Eleanor of Aquitaine among them) of the ruler of this region, Raimond Béranger V, all married royals.

Relics of this former glory can be glimpsed in the Vieille Ville of Forcalquier, notably its Cathédrale Notre-Dame and the Couvent des Cordeliers.

Plan on enjoying a fine meal and an overnight stay (reserve way in advance) at the town's most historic establishment, the **Hostellerie des Deux Lions**.

MAKING SCENTS

BLOOMING

Lavender fields begin blooming in late June, depending on the area and the weather, with fields reaching their peak from the end of July to early August. The first two weeks of July are considered the best time to catch the fields in all their glory.

HARVESTING

Lavender is harvested from July to September, when the hot summer sun brings the essence up into the flower. Harvesting is becoming more and more automated; make an effort to visit some of the older fields with narrow rows—these are still picked by hand. Lavender is then dried for two to three days before being transported to the distillery.

DISTILLING

Distillation is done in a steam alembic, with the dry lavender steamed in a double boiler. Essential oils are extracted from the lavender by water vapor, which is then passed through the cooling coils of a retort.

the world. ✉ *Gordes* ☎ *04–90–72–03–48* 🌐 *www.gordes-village.com* 🎫 *€6* ⏲ *Daily 9–dusk.*

WHERE TO EAT AND STAY

$$ FRENCH ✕ **Les Cuisines du Château.** This tiny but deluxe bistro across from the château may look like a tourist trap, but step inside and you'll find friendly service and wonderful home cooking like roast Luberon lamb, beef with truffle sauce, and the like. The '30s-style bistro tables and architectural lines are a relief from Gordes's ubiquitous rustic-chic, and there is a revolving array of paintings by local artists, many of which are for sale. There are only 26 seats, so book well in advance. 💲 *Average main: €20* ✉ *Pl. du Château, Gordes* ☎ *04–90–72–01–31* ⏲ *Closed Mon., Nov.–mid-Dec., and mid-Jan.–1st wk Mar. No dinner Sun.* ✍ *Reservations essential.*

$$$$ HOTEL 🏨 **La Bastide de Gordes.** Spectacularly perched on Gordes's hilltop, the 16th-century Bastide underwent a lengthy renovation in 2015 that returned its old-world charm. **Pros:** views are unmatched in the area; terrace is a great place to relax; sybaritic spa. **Cons:** hard to choose which restaurant to try. 💲 *Rooms from: €270* ✉ *Le Village, Rue de la Combe, Gordes* ☎ *04–90–72–12–12* 🌐 *www.bastide-de-gordes.com* ⏲ *Closed Jan. and Feb.* 🛏 *22 rooms, 18 suites* 🍽 *No meals.*

$$ B&B/INN 🏨 **Le Mas des Romarins.** This intimate inn atop a hill—the views are lovely—on the outskirts of Gordes is just a five-minute walk to the village. **Pros:** nights are incredibly peaceful; convenient location; reasonable rates. **Cons:** can be difficult to find; staff has a bit of an attitude. 💲 *Rooms from: €135* ✉ *Rte. de Sénanque, Gordes* ☎ *04–90–72–12–13* 🌐 *www.masromarins.com* ⏲ *Closed mid-Nov.–mid-Dec., Jan., and Feb.* 🛏 *13 rooms* 🍽 *Breakfast.*

ROUSSILLON

10 km (6 miles) east of Gordes, 45 km (28 miles) east of Avignon.

In shades of deep rose and russet, this quintessential cluster of hilltop houses blends into the red-ocher cliffs from which its stone was quarried. The ensemble of buildings and jagged, hand-cut slopes is equally dramatic, and views from the top look out over a landscape of artfully eroded bluffs that Georgia O'Keeffe would have loved. Roussillon is definitely one of the finalists in Provence's beauty contest. Unlike neighboring hill villages, though, it offers little of real historic significance; the pleasure of a visit lies in the richly varied colors that change with the light of day, and in the views of the contrasting countryside, where dense-shadowed greenery sets off the red stone with Cézanne-esque severity. There are pleasant *placettes* (tiny squares) to linger in nonetheless, and a Renaissance fortress tower crowned with a clock in the 19th century; just past it, you can take in expansive panoramas of forest and ocher cliffs. Since the village can get overcrowded with tourists in summer, the best time to visit is in spring or early fall.

GETTING HERE

The Cavaillon-Roussillon bus runs twice a day, but make sure to book ahead. The only other way to arrive is by car from the D4.

VISITOR INFORMATION

Point Info Roussilon. ✉ *Pl. de la Poste, Roussillon* ☎ *04–90–05–60–25* 🌐 *www.luberon-apt.fr.*

EXPLORING

Sentier des Ocres (*Ocher Trail*). This popular trail starts out from the town cemetery and allows you to wend your way through a magical, multicolor palette *de pierres* (of rocks) replete with eroded red cliffs and chestnut groves; the circuit takes about 45 minutes. The hours are complicated, so plan in advance. ✉ *Roussillon* 🎟 *€2.50, €7.50 joint ticket with Usine Mathieu Roussillon* ⏲ *Mar., daily 10–5; Apr., daily 9:30–5:30; May and Sept., daily 9:30–6:30; June, daily 9–6:30; July and Aug., daily 9–7:30; Oct., daily 10–5:30; early Nov., daily 10–4:30.*

Usine Mathieu de Roussillon (*Roussillon's Mathieu Ocher Works*). The area's famous vein of natural ocher, which spreads some 25 kilometers (16 miles) along the foot of the Vaucluse plateau, has been mined for centuries, beginning with the ancient Romans, who used it for their pottery. You can visit the old Usine Mathieu de Roussillon to learn more about ocher's extraction and its modern uses. Guided tours (50 mins) in English are on offer throughout the year. ✉ *On D104 southeast of town, Roussillon* ☎ *04–90–05–66–69* 🌐 *www.okhra.com* 🎟 *€6.50, €7.50 joint ticket with Sentier des Ochres* ⏲ *Apr.–Oct., daily 10–6; Nov., Dec., Feb., and Mar., daily 2–5.*

MÉNERBES

30 km (19 miles) southeast of Avignon.

Perched high on a rocky precipice, Ménerbes is designated one of the *plus beaux villages du France* for good reason. This picturesque community clings to a long, thin hilltop, looming over the surrounding forests like a great stone ship. At its prow juts the *Castellet,* a 15th-century fortress. At its stern looms the 13th-century *Citadelle.* These redoubtable fortifications served the Protestants well during the 16th-century Wars of Religion—until the Catholics wore them down with a 15-month siege. Ranking among the region's most visited villages, it's now besieged by peak-season tourists.

GETTING HERE AND AROUND

There is no direct bus service to Ménerbes. The only way to get here is by car.

EXPLORING

Fodor's Choice ★ **Festival Lacoste.** Seven kilometers (4 miles) east of Ménerbes is the eagle's-nest village of Lacoste, presided over by the once-magnificent Château de Sade, erstwhile retreat of the notorious Marquis de Sade (1740–1814). For some years, Paris couturier Pierre Cardin has been restoring the castle wall by wall, and under his generous patronage the Festival Lacoste takes place here over the last two weeks in July. A lyric, musical, and theatrical extravaganza, events (and their dates) change yearly, ranging from outdoor poetry recitals to ballet to colorful operettas. ✉ *Carrières du Château, Lacoste* ☎ *04–90–75–93–12* 🌐 *www.festivaldelacoste.com* 🎟 *€20–€140.*

Uniting natural and man-made beauty, ocher quarried from the surrounding painted-desert cliffs is applied directly to many roofs and facades in Roussillon.

Musée du Tire-Bouchon (*Corkscrew museum*). Don't miss the quirky Musée du Tire-Bouchon, which has an enormous selection of 1,200 corkscrews on display and interesting historical detail on various wine-related subjects. ✉ *Domaine de la Citadelle, Rte. de Cavaillon, Ménerbes* ☎ *04–90–72–41–58* 🌐 *www.domaine-citadelle.com* 🎟 *€4* 🕘 *Apr.–Oct., daily 9–noon and 2–7; Nov.–Mar., Mon.–Sat. 9–noon and 2–5.*

Place de l'Horloge (*Clock Square*). A campanile tops the Hôtel de Ville on pretty Place de l'Horloge, where you can admire the delicate stonework on the arched portal and mullioned windows of a Renaissance house. Just past the tower on the right is an overlook taking in views toward Gordes, Roussillon, and Mont Ventoux. ✉ *Pl. de l'Horloge, Ménerbes.*

WHERE TO STAY

$$$ B&B/INN **Le Mas du Magnolia.** A warm welcome—a little like visiting friends—and a relaxed atmosphere prevail at this small but spectacularly situated bed-and-breakfast close to villages and sites. **Pros:** plenty of added amenities; rates are reasonable; great views. **Cons:** not for those seeking solitude. 💲 *Rooms from: €159* ✉ *D103, Ménerbes* ☎ *04–90–72–48–00* 🌐 *www.masmagnolia.com* 🛏 *4 rooms* 🍽 *Breakfast.*

AIX-EN-PROVENCE AND THE MEDITERRANEAN COAST

The southeastern portion of this part of Provence, on the edge of the Côte d'Azur, is dominated by two major towns: Aix-en-Provence, considered the main hub of Provence and the most cultural community in the region; and Marseille, a vibrant port city that combines seediness with fashion and metropolitan feistiness with classical grace. To fully experience the dramatic contrast between the azure Mediterranean Sea and the rocky, olive tree–filled hills, take a trip along the coast east of Marseille and make an excursion to the Iles d'Hyères.

AIX-EN-PROVENCE

82 km (51 miles) southeast of Avignon, 176 km (109 miles) west of Nice, 759 km (474 miles) south of Paris.

Gracious, cultivated, and made all the more cosmopolitan by the presence of some 45,000 international university students, the old town of Aix (pronounced *ex*) was once the capital of Provence. The vestiges of its erstwhile power remain beautifully preserved today; however, individual museums and architectural marvels are overshadowed by the city itself, with its beautiful fountains, elegant *hôtels particuliers,*and time-burnished streets. Aix's centre ville is a maze of narrow roadways and it is difficult to keep your sense of direction. Happily, the main drag—the gorgeous tree-lined Cours Mirabeau—neatly divides old Aix in half, with the Quartier Ancien's narrow medieval streets to the north and the 18th-century houses and upscale restaurants of the Quartier Mazarin to the south. At the very center, and always photo-ready, are Place Richelme and Place de l'Hôtel de Ville, the main squares. You can't go wrong either ending up or beginning with them.

Romans were first drawn here by mild thermal baths, naming the town Aquae Sextiae (Waters of Sextius) in honor of the consul who founded a camp near the source in 123 BC. Just 20 years later some 200,000 Germanic invaders besieged Aix, but the great Roman general Marius pinned them against the mountain known ever since as Ste-Victoire. Marius remains a popular local first name to this day. Under the wise and generous guidance of *Roi* (King) René in the 15th century, Aix became a center of Renaissance arts and letters. At the height of its political, judicial, and ecclesiastic power in the 17th and 18th centuries, Aix profited from a building boom, each grand hôtel particulier vying to outdo its neighbor. Its signature courtyards and squares, punctuated by grand fountains and intriguing passageways, date from this time.

It was into this milieu that artist Paul Cézanne (1839–1906) was born, though he drew much of his inspiration from the surrounding countryside and often painted Ste-Victoire. A schoolmate of Cézanne's made equal inroads: the journalist and novelist Émile Zola (1840–1902) attended the Collège Bourbon with Cézanne and described their friendship as well as the city itself in several of his works. You can still sense something of the ambience that nurtured these two geniuses in the streets of modern Aix.

Atelier Cézanne **1**
Cathédrale St-Sauveur **2**
Cours Mirabeau **5**
Église de la Madeleine **9**
Église St-Jean-de-Malte **6**
Jas de Bouffan ... **8**
La Rotonde **4**
Musée Granet **7**
Pavillon de Vendôme **3**

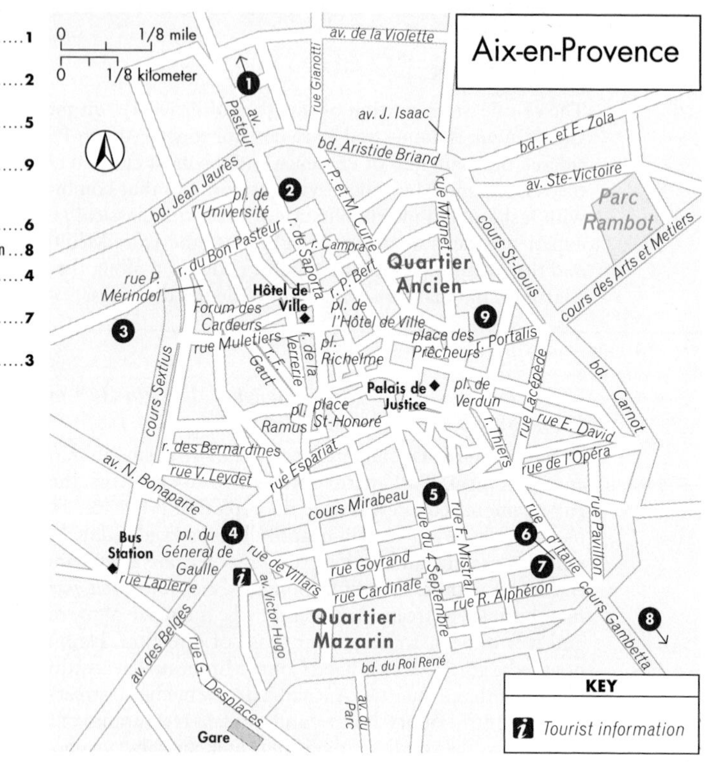

GETTING HERE AND AROUND

Aix's TGV station, 18 km (11 miles) west of the city, receives direct daily trains from Paris (3 hrs); a shuttle connects it with the central station on Place Victor Hugo. Arrivals at the latter include almost hourly trains from Marseille St-Charles (40 mins) and seasonal service from London (6 hours). The heart of Aix is best explored on foot, but municipal buses (€1) cover the city and outlying suburbs; most leave from La Rotonde in front of the tourism office. Regional buses depart from the gare routière on Rue Lapierre, one block west of La Rotonde, for destinations like Marseille (30 mins), Avignon (1 hr, 15 mins), Arles (1 hr, 30 mins), and Nice by the autoroute (2 hr, 30 mins).

VISITOR INFORMATION

Aix-en-Provence Tourist Office. ✉ *Les allées provençales, 300 av. Giuseppe Verdi, Aix-en-Provence* ☎ *04–42–16–11–61* 🌐 *www.aixenprovencetourism.com.*

EXPLORING

TOP ATTRACTIONS

Atelier Cézanne (*Cézanne's Studio*). Just north of the Vieille Ville loop you'll find Cézanne's studio. After the death of his mother forced the sale of the painter's beloved country retreat, Jas de Bouffan, he had this atelier built and some of his finest works, including *Les Grandes*

Baigneuses (*The Large Bathers*), were created in the upstairs workspace. But what is most striking is the collection of simple objects that once featured prominently in his portraits and still lifes—redingote, bowler hat, ginger jar—all displayed as if awaiting his return. The atelier is behind an obscure garden gate on the left as you climb Avenue Paul-Cézanne. ✉ *9 av. Paul-Cézanne, Aix-en-Provence* ☎ *04–42–21–06–53* 🌐 *www.atelier-cezanne.com* 🎫 *€6* ⏲ *Apr.–June and Sept., daily 10–noon and 2–6; July and Aug., daily 10–6; Oct.–Mar., daily 10–noon and 2–5.*

Cathédrale St-Sauveur. Many eras of architectural history are clearly delineated and preserved here. The cathedral has a double nave—Romanesque and Gothic side by side—and a Merovingian (5th-century) **baptistery,** its colonnade mostly recovered from Roman temples built to honor pagan deities. The deep bath on the floor is a remnant of total-immersion baptism. Shutters hide the ornate 16th-century carvings on the **portals,** opened by a guide on request. The guide can also lead you into the tranquil Romanesque **cloister** next door, with carved pillars and slender columns.

The extraordinary 15th-century *Triptyque du Buisson Ardent* (*Mary and the Burning Bush*) was painted by Nicolas Froment in the heat of inspiration following his travels in Italy and Flanders and depicts the generous art patrons King René and Queen Jeanne kneeling on either side of the Virgin, who is poised above a burning bush. To avoid light damage, it's rarely opened for viewing; check with the tourist office beforehand. ✉ *Pl. des Martyrs de la Résistance, Aix-en-Provence* ☎ *04–42–23–45–65* 🌐 *www.cathedrale-aix.net.*

Cours Mirabeau. Shaded by a double row of tall plane trees, the Cours Mirabeau is one of the most beautiful avenues anywhere, designed so its width and length would be in perfect proportion with the height of the dignified 18th-century *hôtels particuliers* lining it. You can view this lovely assemblage from one of the dozen or so cafés that spill onto the pavement. ✉ *Cours Mirabeau, Aix-en-Provence.*

OFF THE BEATEN PATH

Jas de Bouffan. Cézanne's father bought this lovely estate, whose name translates as "the sheepfold," in 1859 to celebrate his rise from hat-maker to banker. The budding artist lived here until 1899 and painted his first images of Mont Ste-Victoire—the founding seeds of 20th-century art—from the grounds. Today the salons are empty but the estate is full of the artist's spirit, especially the Allée des Marronniers out front. The Jas is a mile south of the center of town and can only be visited on tours organized through the central tourist office. ✉ *80 rte. de Valcros, Aix-en-Provence* ☎ *04–42–16–10–91* 🌐 *www.aixenprovencetourism.com* 🎫 *€6* ⏲ *English tours June—Sept., daily at 2; Oct., Tues., Thurs., and Sat. at 2.*

La Rotonde. If you've just arrived in Aix's center, this sculpture-fountain is a spectacular introduction to the town's rare mix of elegance and urban bustle. It's a towering mass of 19th-century attitude. That's Agriculture yearning toward Marseille, Art leaning toward Avignon, and Justice looking down on Cours Mirabeau. But don't study it too intently—you'll likely be sideswiped by a speeding Vespa. ✉ *Pl. de Gaulle, Aix-en-Provence.*

Fodor's Choice ★ **Musée Granet.** Once the École de Dessin (Art School) that granted Cézanne a second-place prize in 1856, the former priory of the Église St-Jean-de-Malte now showcases eight of Cézanne's paintings, as well as a nice collection of his watercolors and drawings. Also hanging in the galleries are 300 works by Bonnard, Picasso, Klee, Rubens, David, and Giacometti. ✉ *Pl. St-Jean-de-Malte, Aix-en-Provence* ☎ *04–42–52–88–32* 🌐 *www.museegranet-aixenprovence.fr* 🎫 *€5* ⏲ *Jan.–mid-July, Tues.–Sun. 10–6; mid-July–mid-Oct., Tues.–Sun. 10–7; mid-Oct.–Dec., Tues.–Sun. noon–6.*

Fodor's Choice ★ **Pavillon de Vendôme.** This extravagant Baroque villa was built in 1665 as a country house for the Duke of Vendome; its position just outside the city's inner circle allowed the duke to commute discreetly from his official home on Cours Mirabeau to this retreat, where his mistress, La Belle du Canet, was comfortably installed. The villa was expanded and heightened in the 18th century to draw attention to the classical orders—Ionic, Doric, and Corinthian—on parade in the row of neo-Grecian columns. Inside the cool, broad chambers you can find a collection of Provençal furniture and artwork. Note the curious two giant Atlantes that hold up the interior balcony. ✉ *32 rue Celony, Aix-en-Provence* ☎ *04–42–91–88–75* 🌐 *www.aixenprovence.fr* 🎫 *€3.50* ⏲ *Mid-Oct.–mid-Apr., Wed.–Mon. 1:30–5; mid-Apr.–mid-Oct., Wed.–Mon. 10–12:30 and 1:30–6.*

WORTH NOTING

Église de la Madeleine. Though the facade now bears 19th-century touches, this small 17th-century church still contains the center panel of the fine 15th-century *Annunciation Triptych*, attributed to the father of Jan Van Eyck, the greatest painter of the Early Netherlandish school. Some say the massive painting on the left side of the transept is a Rubens. The church is used regularly for classical concerts. ✉ *Pl. des Prêcheurs, Aix-en-Provence* ☎ *04–42–38–02–81* ⏲ *Daily 8–11:30 and 3–5:30.*

Église St-Jean-de-Malte. This 12th-century church served as a chapel of the Knights of Malta, a medieval order of friars devoted to hospital care. The church was Aix's first attempt at the Gothic style, and it was here that the counts of Provence were buried throughout the 18th century; their tombs (in the upper left) were attacked during the Revolution and have been only partially repaired. ✉ *Rue Cardinale and Rue d'Italie, Aix-en-Provence.*

WHERE TO EAT

$$$$ FRENCH ✕ **L'Esprit de la Violette.** Steps from the Cathédrale St-Sauveur, Michelin-starred L'Esprit de la Violette lets you watch Chef Marc de Passorio at work from a table d'hôte right in front of the kitchen. If you prefer, book the private dining lounge adorned with 400 bottles of wine. Despite the proximity to the Mediterranean, de Passorio turns inland for inspiration: vegetables come from the north of Aix or Châteaurenard (where his producer cultivates 80 different types of tomatoes), lamb from the Hautes-Alpes, and cheese from a small producer in Gap.

Crammed with elegant shops, chic cafés, and 18th-century houses, Aix-en-Provence is one of France's most charming towns.

From a subdued kitchen he creates tangy, colorful yet simple dishes like smoked beef tenderloin with thyme, parsnips, and sweet onions. The weekday lunch set menu at €39 is good value, as is the three-course weeknight menu for €49. More adventurous €79 and €128 set menus are for the true foodies at heart, to be appreciated with a very extensive wine list. *Average main: €42* ✉ *10 av. de la Violette, Aix-en-Provence* ☎ *04–42–23–02–50* 🌐 *lespritdelaviolette.com* ⏲ *Closed Sun. and Mon.* *Reservations essential.*

$$ **FRENCH** **La Fromagerie du Passage.** You can't sample all of France's 400 types of cheese at La Fromagerie du Passage, but there's a decadent selection of 20 or so, all *fait à la masion* by Laurent and Hervé Mons (Hervé won the prestigious Meilleurs Ouvriers award for outstanding cheese maker). The waiters lyrically—and patiently—explain the region or texture of each cheese, and suggest a wine with the right composition to bring out the subtle (and not so subtle) flavors. There's also an assortment of tapas, charcuterie, and desserts. While the setting is not the most romantic, it's an experience to be remembered. *Average main: €19* ✉ *55 cours Mirabeau, Passage Agard, Aix-en-Provence* ☎ *04–42–22–90–00* 🌐 *www.lafromageriedupassage.fr* *No credit cards.*

$$$ **FRENCH FUSION** **FAMILY** **Lavault.** Named for its vaulted stone cellar, where you can dine or enjoy your predinner apèro (a better choice decor-wise than the ordinary upstairs), this bistro has a frequently changing menu, but go for the foie gras club if you find it. You can't go wrong with anything on this menu, though: duck ravioli with foie gras and morels, or sea trout with saffron-mussel risotto are equally tempting. For dessert the white chocolate cheesecake or raspberries in lemon cream makes for a satisfying finish. A well-rounded wine list, plenty of wines by the glass, and a good children's menu make this a good choice for a family lunch. The three-course menu (€37) is the best deal. *Average main: €25 ✉ 24 rue Felibre Gaut, Aix-en-Provence ☎ 04–42–38–57–28 🌐 lavaultrestaurant.wix.com/fred ⊙ Closed Sun. and Mon. No lunch Tues. and Wed. Reservations essential.*

WHERE TO STAY

$$$$ HOTEL **Hôtel Cézanne.** Three blocks from Cours Mirabeau and the train station, this smart, spiffy, and cozily stylish hotel is a very handy option. **Pros:** breakfast buffet is one of the very best around; free in-room coffee, soda, and water; in the heart of things. **Cons:** some rooms get street noise; no pool. *Rooms from: €250 ✉ 40 av. Victor-Hugo, Aix-en-Provence ☎ 04–42–91–11–11 🌐 www.hotelaix.com 55 rooms, 12 suites No meals.*

$$$$ HOTEL Fodor's Choice ★ **Le Pigonnet.** Cézanne painted Ste-Victoire from what is now the large flower-filled terrace of this enchanting abode, and you can easily imagine former guests Princess Caroline, Iggy Pop, and Clint Eastwood swanning their way through the magnificent, pool-adorned, topiary-accented garden or relaxing in the spacious, light-filled guest rooms. **Pros:** unique garden setting; welcome is friendly; center of the city. **Cons:** reception area has been called old-fashioned; some of the antiques are a little threadbare; breakfast is extra. *Rooms from: €365 ✉ 5 av. du Pigonnet, Aix-en-Provence ☎ 04–42–59–02–90 🌐 www.hotelpigonnet.com 40 rooms, 4 suites No meals.*

$$$$ HOTEL Fodor's Choice ★ **Les Lodges Sainte-Victoire.** Set on a picture-perfect 10 acres of woods, olive groves, and vineyards just outside Aix, with Cézanne-immortalized Mont Ste-Victoire as a backdrop, this hotel raises the bar for lodging in the region. **Pros:** one of the city's top restaurants; Nespresso machines in rooms; modern vibe. **Cons:** outside the city center. *Rooms from: €330 ✉ 2250 rte. Cézanne, Le Tholonet ☎ 04–42–24–80–40 🌐 www.leslodgessaintevictoire.com 35 rooms, 4 lodges No meals.*

$$$$ HOTEL **Villa Gallici.** Hued in the lavenders, blues, ochers, and oranges of Aix, rooms here swim in the most gorgeous Souleiado and Rubelli fabrics: this all conjures up the swank 19th-century Provence that used to be colonized by Parisian barons and dukes. **Pros:** rich fabrics and dashing decor; beautiful garden spot; quick walk to town. **Cons:** breakfast is pricey; no elevator. *Rooms from: €395 ✉ Av. de la Violette, Aix-en-Provence ☎ 04–42–23–29–23 🌐 www.villagallici.com ⊙ Closed Jan. 22 rooms, 6 suites Breakfast.*

NIGHTLIFE AND PERFORMING ARTS

To find out what's going on in town, pick up a copy of the events calendar *L'Agenda Cuturel* at the tourist office.

Casino Aix en Provence. In between bouts at the roulette tables and slot machines of the Casino Aix en Provence, you can grab a bite at one of five restaurants or take in a floor show. *✉ 21 av. de l'Europe, Aix-en-Provence ☎ 04–42–59–69–00 🌐 www.casinoaix.com.*

Festival d'Aix. In late June and July, opera and music lovers descend on Aix for the internationally acclaimed Festival d'Aix to see world-class opera productions in the courtyard of the Palais de l'Archevêché and more of the city's most beautiful venues. The repertoire is varied and often offbeat, featuring works like Britten's Curlew River and Bartók's Bluebeard's Castle as well as the usual Mozart, Puccini, and Verdi. Most of the singers, however, are not celebrities, but rather an elite group of students who spend the summer with the Academie Européenne de Musique, training and performing under the tutelage of stars like Robert Tear and Yo-Yo Ma. ✉ *Aix-en-Provence* ☎ *04–34–08–02–17* 🌐 *www.festival-aix.com.*

Le Ballet Preljocaj. Angelin Preljocaj has created original ballets for the New York City Ballet and the Paris Opera Ballet, and his modern-dance troupe, Ballet Preljocaj, is based at the monolithic Pavillon Noir, designed by architect Rudy Ricciotti. The season runs September to May. The Pavillon hosts an annual series of contemporary ballet and modern dance performances featuring an international roster. There are also 6 pm rehersals free for the public. ✉ *530 av. Wolfgang Amadeus Mozart, Aix-en-Provence* ☎ *04–42–93–48–00* 🌐 *www.preljocaj.org.*

Le Scat Club. This is the place for live soul, funk, rock, blues, and jazz. ✉ *11 rue de la Verrerie, Aix-en-Provence* ☎ *04–42–23–00–23.*

SHOPPING

In addition to its old-style markets and jewel-box candy shops, Aix is a modern shopping town—perhaps the best in Provence. The winding streets of the Vieille Ville above cours Mirabeau—centered on Rue Clemenceau, Rue Marius Reinaud, Rue Espariat, Rue Aude, and Rue Maréchal Foch—have a head-turning parade of goods.

Béchard. The most picturesque shop specializing in calissons is the venerable bakery Béchard, founded in 1870. ✉ *12 cours Mirabeau, Aix-en-Provence.*

Santons Fouque. Established in 1936, Aix's most celebrated *santon*, or miniature statue, maker is Santons Fouque. ✉ *65 cours Gambetta, Aix-en-Provence* ☎ *04–42–26–33–38* 🌐 *www.santons-fouque.com.*

Weibel. An Aix institution since 1954, Maison Weibel is chock-full of sweets that look good enough to immortalize in a still life, let alone eat. Their version of the iconic Provençal calisson is hands down the best around. They make sublime gifts, packaged in lovely lavender boxes. ✉ *2 rue Chabrier, Aix-en-Provence* ☎ *04–42–23–33–21* 🌐 *maisonweibel.fr.*

MARSEILLE

31 km (19 miles) south of Aix-en-Provence, 188 km (117 miles) west of Nice, 772 km (483 miles) south of Paris.

Marseille is sometimes given a wide berth by travelers, but that's their loss. After all, it is vibrant enough to have been named 2013's European City of Culture; and the legacy of that honor lives on in a slew of new or renewed cultural attractions. Ten primary ones were inaugurated, either in formerly abandoned buildings (like the old tobacco factory) or purpose-built ones—most notably the glitzy, glassy National Museum of the Civilizations of Europe and the Mediterranean, otherwise known as MuCEM.

Moreover, the port area (Marseille is France's leading cruise port, attracting some 700,000 passengers per year) has become a pedestrian zone and benefited from a multimillion-dollar face-lift, which includes a seaside shopping center with 160 restaurants and shops. Even without such enhancements, Marseille's Cubist jumbles of white stone rising up over the waterfront, bathed in light of blinding clarity and crowned by larger-than-life neo-Byzantine churches, could still dazzle—and literally, too, as the city sees 300 days of sunlight a year.

TRIP TIP

If you plan on visiting many of the museums in Marseille, buy a City Pass (€24 for 24 hours, €31 for 48 hours, €39 for 72 hours) at the tourism office or online. It covers the entry fee for all the museums in Marseille as well as public transit, a ride on the petit train, and free guided tour of the city.

Neighborhoods here teem with multiethnic life, souklike African markets reek deliciously of spices and coffees, and the labyrinthine Vieille Ville is painted in broad strokes of saffron, cinnamon, and robin's-egg blue. Feisty and fond of broad gestures, Marseille is a dynamic city, as cosmopolitan now as when the Phoenicians first founded it, and with all the exoticism of the international shipping center it has been for 2,600 years. Vital to the Crusades in the Middle Ages and crucial to Louis XIV as a military port, Marseille flourished as France's market to the world—and still does today.

If you plan on visiting many attractions, consider buying a City-Pass (€24 for 1 day, €31 for 2) at the tourism office. It covers the entry fee into Marseille's museums and monuments, plus transport, a ride on the *petit train,* and a free, guided city tour.

GETTING HERE AND AROUND

Air travelers land at one of the country's largest airports, the Aéroport de Marseille Provence. The main train station—Gare St-Charles, on the TGV line—has frequent links with Paris, Nice, and Italy, as well as Aix, Avignon, Arles, and Nîmes. The new Eurostar train service from London arrives at Gare St-Charles. From the gare routière on Place Victor Hugo, Cartreize buses connect with the Bouches du Rhône; other coaches connect with Avignon and Nice via Aix-en-Provence. Within Marseille, you can take advantage of an efficient public transit system that includes buses, trams, subways, and water taxis (€1.50 for 90 mins), or hop the free César ferryboat, which crosses the Vieux Port every few minutes.

Marseille Tourist Office. ✉ *11 la Canebière, Marseille* ☎ *08–26–50–05–00 €0.15 per min* 🌐 *www.marseille-tourisme.com.*

EXPLORING

TOP ATTRACTIONS

Abbaye St-Victor. Founded in the 4th century by St-Cassien, who sailed into Marseille full of fresh ideas on monasticism that he acquired in Palestine and Egypt, this church grew to formidable proportions. With a Romanesque design, the structure would be as much at home in the Middle East as its founder was. The **crypt,** St-Cassien's original, is buried under the medieval church, and in the evocative nooks and crannies you can find the 5th-century sarcophagus that allegedly holds the martyr's remains. Upstairs, a reliquary contains what's left of St-Victor, who was ground to death between millstones, probably by Romans. There's also a passage into tiny **catacombs** where early Christians worshipped St-Lazarus and Mary Magdalene, said to have washed ashore at Stes-Maries-de-la-Mer. ✉ *3 rue de l'Abbaye, Rive Neuve, Marseille* ☎ *04–96–11–22–60* 🌐 *www.saintvictor.net* 🎟 *Crypt €2* ⏲ *Daily 9–7.*

La Vieille Charité (*Center of the Old Charity*). At the top of the Panier district you'll find this superb ensemble of 17th- and 18th-century architecture designed as a hospice for the homeless by Marseillais artist-architects Pierre and Jean Puget. Even if you don't enter the museums, walk around the inner court, studying the retreating perspective of triple arcades and admiring the Baroque chapel with its novel egg-peaked dome. Of the complex's two museums, the larger is the **Musée d'Archéologie Méditerranéenne** (Museum of Mediterranean Archaeology), with a sizable collection of pottery and statuary from classical Mediterranean civilization, elementally labeled (for example, "pot"). There's also a display on the mysterious Celt-like Ligurians who first peopled the coast, cryptically presented with emphasis on the digs instead of the finds themselves. The best of the lot is the evocatively mounted Egyptian collection—the second-largest in France after the Louvre's. There are mummies, hieroglyphs, and gorgeous sarcophagi in a tomblike setting. Upstairs, the **Musée d'Arts Africains, Océaniens, et Amérindiens** (Museum of African, Oceanic, and American Indian Art) creates a theatrical foil for the works' intrinsic drama: the spectacular masks and sculptures are mounted along a pure black wall, lighted indirectly, with labels across the aisle. ✉ *2 rue de la Charité, Le Panier, Marseille* ☎ *04–91–14–58–80* 🌐 *vieille-charite-marseille.com* 🎟 *€5* ⏲ *Tues.–Sun. 10–6.*

Le Panier. This is the heart of old Marseille, a maze of high-shuttered houses looming over narrow cobbled streets, *montées* (stone stairways), and tiny squares. Long decayed and neglected, the quarter is a principal focus of the city's efforts at urban renewal. In the last few years an influx of Bobos (bourgeois-bohemians) and artists have sparked the gentrification process, bringing charming B&Bs, chic boutiques, lively cafés, and artists' ateliers. Wander this picturesque neighborhood of pastel-painted town houses, steep stairways, and narrow streets at will, making sure to stroll along Rue du Panier, the montée des Accoules, Rue du Petit-Puits, and Rue des Muettes. ✉ *Marseille.*

Fodor's Choice ★ **Musée d'Histoire de Marseille** (*Marseille History Museum*). With the Port Antique in front, this modern, open-space museum illuminates Massalia's history with a treasure of archaeological finds and miniature models of the city as it appeared in various stages of history. Best by far is the presentation of Marseille's Classical halcyon days. There's a recovered wreck of a Roman cargo boat, its 3rd-century wood amazingly preserved, and the hull of a Greek boat dating from the 4th century BC. The model of the Greek city should be authentic—it's based on an eyewitness description by Aristotle. ✉ *2 rue Henri Barbrusse, Vieux Port, Marseille* ☎ *04–91–90–42–22* 🌐 *musee-histoire-de-marseille.marseille.fr* 🎟 *€5 joint ticket with Le Port Antique* ⏲ *Tues.–Sun. 10–6.*

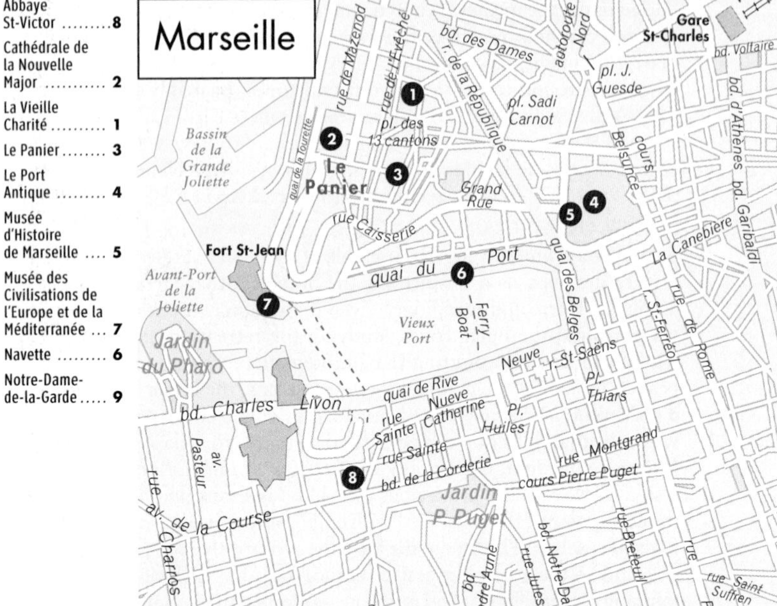

Fodor's Choice ★

Navette. In keeping with the Vieux Port's substantially spiffed-up image, the Marseille regional transport service now offers an efficient public ferry service. The nominal ticket charge of €3.10 (available only on board) is well worth it for the fun and convenience of crossing the port by boat. ⊠ *Pl. des Huiles on Quai de Rive Neuve side and Hôtel de Ville on Quai du Port, Vieux Port, Marseille* 🎟 *€3, free with métro pass.*

WORTH NOTING

Cathédrale de la Nouvelle Major. This gargantuan, neo-Byzantine 19th-century fantasy was built under Napoléon III—but not before he'd ordered the partial destruction of the lovely 11th-century original, once a perfect example of the Provençal Romanesque style. You can view the flashy decor (think marble and rich red porphyry inlay) in the newer of the two churches; the medieval one is being restored. ⊠ *Pl. de la Major, Le Panier, Marseille.*

OFF THE BEATEN PATH

Château d'If. In the 16th century, François I recognized the strategic advantage of an island fortress surveying the mouth of Marseille's vast harbor and built this imposing edifice. Its effect as a deterrent was so successful that the fortress never saw combat, and was eventually converted into a prison. It was here that Alexandre Dumas locked up his most famous character, the Count of Monte Cristo. Though the count was fictional, the hole through which Dumas had him escape

Continued on page 580

CUISINE OF THE SUN

Don't be surprised if colors and flavors seem more intense in Provence. It could be the hot, dry climate, which concentrates the essence of fruit and vegetables, or the sun beaming down on market tables overflowing with produce. Or maybe you're seeing the world anew through rosé-tinted wine glasses. Whatever the reason, here's how to savor Provence's *incroyable* flavors and culinary favorites.

Provence's rustic cuisine, based on local tomatoes, garlic, olive oil, anchovies, olives, and native wild herbs—including basil, lavender, mint, rosemary, thyme, and sage—has more in common with other Mediterranean cuisines than it does with most regional French fare. Everywhere you'll find sun-ripened fruit dripping with nectar and vegetables so flavor-packed that meat may seem like a mere accessory.

The natural bounty of the region is ample, united by climate—brilliant sunshine and fierce winds—and divided by dramatically changing landscapes. In the Vaucluse, scorched plains give way to lush, orchard-lined hills and gently sloped vineyards. The wild Calanques of Marseille, source of spiky sea urchins, ease into the tranquil waters of St-Tropez, home to gleaming bream and sea bass. Provence's pantry is overflowing with culinary treasures.

Simple preparations, like grilled vegetables with crusty bread, are best enjoyed with the region's famous rosé wine

PROVENCE'S TOP REGIONAL DISHES

Ratatouille

Fougasse

AÏOLI

The name for a deliciously pungent mayonnaise made with generous helpings of garlic, *aïoli* is a popular accompaniment for fish, meat, and vegetable dishes. The mayonnaise version shares its name with "grand aïoli," a recipe featuring salt cod, potatoes, hard-boiled eggs, and vegetables. Both types of aïoli pop up all over Provence, but they seems most beloved in Marseille. In keeping with Catholic practice, some restaurants serve grand aïoli only on Fridays. And it's a good sign if they ask you to place your order at least a day in advance. A grand aïoli is also a traditional component of the Niçois Christmas feast.

BOUILLABAISSE

Originally a humble fisherman's soup made with the part of the catch that nobody else wanted, bouillabaisse—the famous fish stew—consists of four or five kinds of fish: the villainous-looking *rascasse* (red scorpion fish), *grondin* (sea robin), *baudroie* (monkfish), *congre* (conger eel), and *rouget* (mullet). The fish are simmered in a stock of onions, tomatoes, garlic, olive oil, and saffron, which gives the dish its golden color. When presented properly, the broth is served first, with croutons and *rouille*, a creamy garlic sauce that you spoon in to suit your taste. The fish comes separately, and the ritual is to place pieces into the soup to enjoy after slurping up some of the broth.

BOURRIDE

This poached fish dish owes its anise kick to pastis and its garlic punch to aïoli. The name comes from the Provençal bourrido, which translates less poetically as "boiled." Monkfish—known as baudroie in Provence and lotte in the rest of France—is a must, but chefs occasionally dress up their bourride with other species and shellfish.

DAUBE DE BOEUF

To distinguish their prized beef stew from *boeuf bourguignon*, Provençal chefs make a point of not marinating the meat, instead cooking it very slowly in tannic red wine that is often flavored with orange zest. In the Camargue, daube is made with the local taureau (bull's meat), while the Avignon variation uses lamb.

Bourride

Bouillabaisse

FOUGASSE

The Provençal answer to Italian focaccia, this soft flatbread is distinguished by holes that give it the appearance of a lacy leaf. It can be made savory—flavored with olives, anchovy, bacon, cheese, or anything else the baker has on hand—or sweet, enriched with olive oil and dusted with icing sugar. When in Menton, don't miss the sugary *fougasse mentonnaise*.

LES PETITS FARCIS

The Niçois specialty called *les petits farcis* are prepared with tiny summer vegetables (usually zucchini, tomatoes, peppers, and onions) that are traditionally stuffed with veal or leftover *daube* (beef stew). Like so many Niçois dishes, they make great picnic food.

RATATOUILLE

At its best, *ratatouille* is a glorious thing—a riot of eggplant, zucchini, bell peppers, and onions, each sautéed separately in olive oil and then gently combined with sweet summer tomatoes. A well-made ratatouille, to which a pinch of saffron has been added to heighten its flavor, is also delicious served chilled.

SOUPE AU PISTOU

The Provençal answer to pesto, *pistou* consists of the simplest ingredients—garlic, olive oil, fresh basil, and Parmesan—ideally pounded together by hand in a stone mortar with an olivewood pestle. Most traditionally it delivers a potent kick to *soupe au pistou*, a kind of French minestrone made with green beans, white beans, potatoes, and zucchini.

SOCCA

You'll find *socca* vendors from Nice to Menton, but this chickpea pancake cooked on a giant iron platter in a wood-fired oven is really a Niçois phenomenon, born of sheer poverty at a time when wheat flour was scarce. After cooking, it is sliced into finger-lickin' portions with an oyster knife. Enjoy it with a glass of chilled rosé.

TIAN DE LÉGUMES

A *tian* is both a beautiful earthenware dish and one of many vegetable gratins that might be cooked in it. This thrifty dish makes a complete meal of seasonal vegetables, eggs, and a little cheese.

is real enough, on display in the cells. On the other hand, the real-life Man in the Iron Mask, whose cell is also erroneously on display, was not imprisoned here. The Frioul If Express boat ride (from quai des Belges, €10.50; for information call *04–96–11–03–50* or see frioul-if-express.com) and the views from the broad terrace are worth the trip. ✉ *Marseille* ☎ *08–26–50–05–00* 🌐 *if.monuments-nationaux.fr/en* 🎫 *€5.50* ⏲ *Apr.–mid-May., daily 9:30–4:45; mid-May–mid-Sept., daily 9:30–6:10; mid-Sept.–Mar., Tues–Sun. 9:30–4:45.*

Le Port Antique. This garden in front of the Musée d'Histoire de Marseille stands on the site of the city's classical waterfront and includes remains of the Greek fortifications and loading docks. Newly restored in 2013, the site, with several nearly intact boats (now exhibited in the museum), was discovered in 1967 when roadwork was being done next to the *Bourse* (Stock Exchange). ✉ *Centre Bourse, Vieux Port, Marseille* ☎ *04–91–90–42–22* 🎫 *€5 joint ticket with Musée d'Histoire de Marseille* ⏲ *Mon.–Sat. 10–6.*

Musée des Civilisations de L'Europe et de la Mediterranée. After a lengthy renovation, the Museum of the Civilizations of Europe and the Mediterranean (MuCEM) opened its doors to great fanfare in the summer of 2013. Made up of three sites designed by Rudy Ricciotti, MuCEM is all about new perspectives on Mediterranean cultures. Themes like "the invention of gods," "the treasures of the spice route," or "at the bazaar of gender" are explored in Ricciotti's virtuosic J4 (named for the esplanade). **■ TIP→ The museum's popular café, bistro, and restaurant (reservations required), overseen by star-chef Gérald Passédat, are great for refreshment and taking in the views.** You can access the 12th-century Fort St-Jean, built by Louis XIV with the guns pointing *toward* the city, in order to keep the feisty, rebellious Marseillais under his thumb. If you're not the queasy type, take a suspended footbridge over the sea; it provides spectacular photo ops and never-been-seen panoramas. On the other side, you can visit a new Mediterranean garden and a folk-art collection. A third building—the Center for Conservation and Resources, near the St-Charles train station—holds the museum's permanent collection of paintings, prints, drawings, photographs, and objects. ✉ *Quai du Port, Vieux Port, Marseille* ☎ *04–96–13–80–90* 🌐 *www.mucem.org* 🎫 *€8* ⏲ *May–Oct., Wed.–Mon. 11–7; Nov.–Apr., Wed.–Mon. 11–6.*

Notre-Dame-de-la-Garde. Towering above the city and visible for miles around, this overscaled neo-Byzantine monument was erected in 1853 by Napoléon III. The interior is a Technicolor bonanza of red-and-beige stripes and glittering mosaics, and the gargantuan *Madonna and Child* on the steeple (almost 30 feet high) is covered in real gold leaf. While the panoply of ex-votos, mostly thanking the Virgin for deathbed interventions and shipwreck survivals, is a remarkable sight, most impressive are the views of the seaside city at your feet. ✉ *Off Bd. André Aune, Rue Fort du Sanctuaire, Garde Hill, Marseille* ☎ *04–91–13–40–80* 🌐 *www.notredamedelagarde.com* ⏲ *Apr.–Sept., daily 7 am–7:15 pm; Oct.–Mar., daily 7–6:15.*

WHERE TO EAT

$$$$ FRENCH **AM by Alexandre Mazzia.**"There's Van Gogh, there's Picasso, but there's also Alexandre Mazzia. . . ." Architect, artist, creator, whatever you call him, one thing's for sure, you won't soon forget the master. Within nine months of opening his own restaurant, the chef was awarded a Michelin star. When you sit at one of the 24 seats in the minimalistic setting, a lone small card sits on the table. Your choice is simple, one of two set meals for lunch or dinner. After that, Mazza will serve a series of inspired dishes, and with a background in French, African, and Asian kitchens, the combinations are music to the mouth: charred satay tuna in tapioca speckled with bright green fish eggs, served with wasabi ice cream. *Average main: €69 9 rue François Rocca, Prado, Marseille 04–91–24–83–63 www.alexandremazzia.com Closed Sun. and Mon. Reservations essential.*

$$$$ BISTRO **Café des Épices.** Between the Old Port and Le Panier, this small, unpretentious restaurant with a large terrace is a popular choice for the kind of fresh, inventive cuisine representative of the best in contemporary bistro cooking. Though the choices are few on the Mediterranean-inspired menu (prix fixe only), they change daily according to what inspires Chef Arnaud Carton de Grammont at the market. Dishes like John Dory with pomegranate, white carrots, and tarragon-flecked mushrooms, or consomé-glazed foie gras with caramelized pear are hearty enough that dessert is optional. Best not to skip it, though. *Average main: €45 4 rue du Lacydon, Vieux Port, Marseille 04–91–91–22–69 cafedesepices.com Closed Sun. and Mon. No dinner Sat. Reservations essential.*

$$$$ PIZZA **Chez Etienne.** A well-known hole-in-the-wall, this small pizzeria is filled daily with politicos and young professionals who enjoy the personality of Chef Stéphane Cassero, who was famous at one time for having no printed menu and announcing the price of the meal only after he'd had the chance to look you over. Remarkably little has changed over the years, except now there is a posted menu (with prices). Brace yourself for an epic meal, starting with a large anchovy pizza from the wood-burning oven, then dig into fried squid, eggplant gratin, and a slab of rare grilled beef all served with the background of laughter, rich patois, and abuse from the chef. *Average main: €35 43 rue de Lorette, Le Panier, Marseille No credit cards Closed Sun.*

$$$$ SEAFOOD **Chez Fonfon.** Tucked into the tiny fishing port of Vallon des Auffes, this local landmark has one of the loveliest settings in greater Marseille. A variety of fresh seafood, impeccably grilled, steamed, or roasted in salt crust, is served in two pretty dining rooms with picture windows overlooking the fishing boats that supply your dinner. Try classic bouillabaisse served with all the bells and whistles—broth, hot-chili rouille, and flamboyant table-side filleting. For tapas or an apéro, head next door to Viaghji di Fonfon. *Average main: €50 140 rue du Vallon des Auffes, Vallon des Auffes, Marseille 04–91–52–14–38 www.chez-fonfon.com Reservations essential.*

$$$$ BRASSERIE **Chez Michel.** This beachside Michelin-starred brasserie near the Pharo gardens is considered the last word in bouillabaisse and draws a knowing local clientele willing to shell out a few extra euros for this authentic

classic (€72). Before dining, the fish are paraded by your table then ceremoniously filleted before being served with all the classic accompaniments: a spicy rouille, buttery croutons. Oysters, whole grilled fish (priced by the kilo), and an authentic garlic-steeped bourride are other fine choices—along with a good selection of great local wines. The bouillabaisse is well worth the splurge, but be sure to reserve in advance. *Average main: €70 ✉ 6 rue des Catalans, Vieux Port, Marseille ☎ 04–91–52–30–63 🌐 www.restaurant-michel-13.fr ⏲ No dinner Sun. ✍ Reservations essential.*

$$ TAPAS Fodor's Choice ★

Le Bistro d'Edouard. A big part of Marseille's allure is its Mediterranean multiculturalism, which is abundantly expressed at this popular neighborhood tapas restaurant. Red-checked tablecloths and a sunny outdoor terrace add to its low-key Provençal charm, but the food is the real draw here. Simple, flavorful dishes like artichokes drizzled with spicy olive oil, Iberian ham, grilled eggplant, and fresh sardines keep the local crowds coming back. *Average main: €20 ✉ 150 rue Jean Mermoz, Prado, Marseille ☎ 04–91–71–16–52 ⏲ Closed Sun., Mon., and 3 wks in July ✍ Reservations essential.*

$$$ BRASSERIE

Le Malthazar. This classic Mediterranean brasserie, with brightly tiled floors and a long zinc bar, is the home of two-star Michelin Chef Michel Portos, a native son who threw in the fancy chef's hat in favor of a more relaxed atmosphere and simpler fare. Portos makes spectacular use of the Old Port's fish market a few steps from his door, with dishes like shellfish lasagna with tomato confit; roasted sea bass in spicy fish bouillon with classic rouille; or fillet of sole with wild mushrooms, serrano ham, and hazelnut butter. For dessert the pineapple marmalade baba au rhum is a revelation. A well-priced selection of local wines makes everything go down just right. The three-course (€32) menu for lunch or dinner is an excellent value. *Average main: €25 ✉ 19 rue Fortia, Vieux Port, Marseille ☎ 04–91–33–42–46 🌐 www.malthazar.com ✍ Reservations essential.*

$$$$ SEAFOOD

L'Epuisette. Artfully placed on a rocky, fingerlike jetty surrounded by the sea, this seafood restaurant offers gorgeous views of crashing surf on one side and the port of Vallon des Auffes on the other. Chef Guillaume Sourrieu has acquired a big reputation (and a Michelin star) for sophisticated cooking—Atlantic turbot in citrus rind with oxtail ravioli, and slow-cooked sea bass baked in a salt butter crust and walnut oil are some top delights—matched with a superb wine list. Save room for dessert: the chocolate tart with bananas and pepper ice cream is amazing. *Average main: €45 ✉ 158 rue du Vallon des Auffes, Pharo, Marseille ☎ 04–91–52–17–82 🌐 www.l-epuisette.com ⏲ Closed Sun. and Mon. and last 2 wks in Aug. ✍ Reservations essential.*

WHERE TO STAY

$$ HOTEL

Alex Hotel. Breakfast is the most important meal of the day, and the Alex Hotel's pancakes, omelets, croissants, and freshly squeezed orange juice enjoyed in the inner courtyard should do the trick. **Pros:** free hospitality tray with coffee and tea; convenient location; lots of amenities. **Cons:** no restaurants nearby. *Rooms from: €120 ✉ 13-15 pl. des Marseillaises, Saint Charles, Marseille ☎ 04–13–24–13–25 🌐 www.alex-hotel.fr 21 rooms No meals.*

The heart of Marseille is its Vieux Port (Old Port), with its small boats and portside cafés, while the city's soul is hilltop Notre-Dame-de-la-Garde.

$$$$ HOTEL **C2 Hotel.** It took two years to transform this 19th-century home, previously occupied by a prominent Marseille family, into 20 exquisitely designed accommodations. **Pros:** a few minutes from the port; top destination for design fans. **Cons:** extra charge for breakfast in room. *Rooms from: €289 48 rue roux de Brignoles, Saint Charles, Marseille 04–95–05–13–13 www.c2-hotel.com 20 rooms No meals.*

$$$ HOTEL **Grand Hotel Beauvau Vieux Port.** Chopin spent the night and George Sand kept a suite in this historic hotel overlooking the Vieux Port. **Pros:** in the heart of the city; service is excellent; nice views. **Cons:** some rooms need freshening up. *Rooms from: €160 4 rue Beauvau, Vieux Port, Marseille 04–91–54–91–00 www.accorhotels.com 70 rooms, 3 suites No meals.*

$$$$ HOTEL Fodor's Choice ★ **Intercontinental Marseille Hôtel Dieu.** Housed in Marseille's majestic 18th-century Hôtel Dieu, a beloved landmark built according to plans by Jacques Hardouin-Mansart, architect to Louis XIV, this place has been transformed into a gleaming palace. **Pros:** a one-stop luxury spot; splendid views from open-air bar; rates include breakfast. **Cons:** only a fifth of rooms have a terrace; such indulgence does have a price. *Rooms from: €300 1 pl. Daviel, Vieux Port, Marseille 04-13-42–42–42 marseille.intercontinental.com 192 rooms No meals.*

$$$$ HOTEL **Le Petit Nice.** On a rocky promontory overlooking the sea, this fantasy villa was bought from a countess in 1917 and converted to a sleek hotel-restaurant; happily, the Passédat family has been getting it right ever since, especially in the famous restaurant. **Pros:** a memorable stay; breathtaking views; lovely pool area. **Cons:** leave your impatience at

the door when you dine here. $ *Rooms from: €260* ✉ *Anse de la Maldormé, Corniche J.-F.-Kennedy, Endoume, Marseille* ☎ *04–91–59–25–92* 🌐 *www.passedat.fr* ⏲ *Restaurant closed Sun. and Mon.* *13 rooms, 3 suites* *No meals.*

$ HOTEL **Mama Shelter.** Manufacturing hip is this urban chain hotel's claim to fame (no wonder, as it's the brainchild of designer Philippe Starck). **Pros:** breakfasts can't be beat; friendly service; cool vibe. **Cons:** not always a bargain; not to everyone's taste; iffy neighborhood. $ *Rooms from: €99* ✉ *64 rue de la Loubière, Cours Julien, Marseille* ☎ *04–84–35–20–00* 🌐 *www.mamashelter.com* *127 rooms* *No meals.*

NIGHTLIFE AND PERFORMING ARTS

With a population of nearly 860,000, Marseille is a big city by French standards, with all the nightlife that entails. Arm yourself with the monthly *In Situ* (a free guide to music, theater, and galleries) or *Sortir* (a weekly about film, art, and concerts in southern Provence). They're both in French.

La Caravelle. Restaurant by day, bluesy jazz club and tapas bar by night, La Caravelle hearkens back to prewar jazz clubs, but without the smoke. There are great views over the port and live jazz two nights a week. ✉ *Hotel Belle Vue, 34 quai du Port, Vieux Port, Marseille* ☎ *04–91–90–36–64* 🌐 *www.lacaravelle-marseille.com.*

Opéra Municipal de Marseille. Operas and orchestral concerts are held at the Opéra Municipal. ✉ *2 rue Molière, Vieux Port, Marseille* ☎ *04–91–55–11–10* 🌐 *opera.marseille.fr.*

Red Lion. This bar is a mecca for English-speakers, who pour onto the sidewalk, pints in hand, pub-style. There's live music, DJs on the weekend, and a lounge for the diehard rugby and football fans who can't go without watching a match. ✉ *231 av. Pierre Mendès France, Vieux Port, Marseille* ☎ *04–91–25–17–17* 🌐 *www.pub-redlion.com.*

SHOPPING

Savon de Marseille (Marseille soap) is a household standard in France, often sold as a satisfyingly crude and hefty block in odorless olive-oil green. But its chichi offspring are dainty pastel guest soaps in almond, lemon, vanilla, and other scents. You can never have too many Provençal gifts to take home, so peruse the market in the Old Port on weekdays in July and August and Thursday and Friday in June and the first half of September.

Four des Navettes. This famous bakery, up the street from Notre-Dame-de-la-Garde, has made orange-spice, shuttle-shape *navettes* in the same oven since it opened in 1781. These cookies are modeled on the little boat that, it is said, carried Lazarus and the "Three Marys" (Mary Magdalene, Mary Salome, and Mary Jacobe) to the nearby shore. ✉ *136 rue Sainte, Garde Hill, Marseille* ☎ *04–91–33–32–12* 🌐 *www.fourdesnavettes.com.*

La Maison du Pastis. Specializing in pastis, anisette, and absinthe, this smart little shop offers a dizzying range, but to really savor these unique delights, sign up (in advance) for one of the 90-minute tastings.

From Cassis be sure to take an excursion boat to the Calanques, the rocky finger-coves washed by emerald and blue waters.

✉ *108 quai du Port, Vieux Port, Marseille* ☎ *04–91–90–86–77* 🌐 *www.lamaisondupastis.com.*

Marianne Cat. A fashion magazine staple, Marianne Cat curates a choice of offbeat international designer clothing, jewelry, shoes, and accessories for women in this 18th-century town house . ✉ *53 rue Grignan, Belsunce, Marseille* ☎ *04–91–55–05–25* 🌐 *www.mariannecat.fr.*

Savonnerie Marseillaise Licorne. One of Marseille's oldest traditional manufacturers sells the fragrant *savon* in blocks, ovals, or fanciful shapes. This soap maker uses the highest olive oil content possible (72%) in the soaps, and only natural essential oils from Provence for the fragrances. Call ahead for a guided tour (in English) of this atmospheric factory—a great way to see the whole process done on traditional machines. ✉ *34 cours Julien, Cours Julien, Marseille* ☎ *04–96–12–00–91* 🌐 *www.savon-de-marseille-licorne.com.*

CASSIS

30 km (19 miles) southeast of Marseille.

Stylish without being too recherché, Cassis exudes pure, unadulterated charm. Back in the 19th century, famed author Colette raved about it, and many visitors understandably do the same today. Surrounded by vineyards and monumental cliffs, guarded by the ruins of a medieval castle, and nestled around a picture-perfect fishing port that's framed by pastel houses set at Cubist angles, this is the prettiest coastal town in Provence.

The Château de Cassis has loomed over the harbor since the invasions of the Saracens in the 7th century, evolving over time into a walled enclosure crowned with stout watchtowers. It's private property today and best viewed from a port-side café as you savor a bottle of cassis and a platter of sea urchins.

From Cassis, head east out of town and cut sharply right up Route des Crêtes. This road takes you along a magnificent crest over the water and up to the very top of Cap Canaille. Venture out on the vertiginous trails to the edge, where the whole coast stretches below.

GETTING HERE AND AROUND

Hourly trains between Marseille and Toulon stop at Cassis, but the station is about 3 km (2 miles) from the center. From the station, there is a local shuttle to the town center that runs at least once an hour. There is also the M06 Marseille-Cassis bus that takes an hour. By car, leave the A50 from Marseille and Toulon and take exit 8 for Cassis. The D559 from Marseille to Cassis is dramatically beautiful, continuing along the coast to Toulon, but it might be too curvy for motion-sickness sufferers.

VISITOR INFORMATION

Cassis Tourist Office. ✉ *Pl. Baragnon, Cassis* ☎ *08–92–39–01–03* 🌐 *www.ot-cassis.com.*

EXPLORING

Calanques. Touring the Calanques, whose fjord-like finger bays probe the rocky coastline, is a must. Either take a sightseeing cruise in a glass-bottom boat that dips into each Calanque in turn (tickets, sold at the eastern end of the port, are €16–€27, depending on how many Calanques you see) or hike across the cliff tops, clambering down the steep sides to these barely accessible retreats. Or do both, going in by boat and hiking back; make arrangements at the port. Of the Calanques closest to Cassis, **Port Miou** is the least attractive. It is also the only one fully accessible by car. It was a *pierre de Cassis* (Cassis stone) quarry until 1982 when the Calanques became protected sites, and now has an active leisure and fishing port. **Calanque Port Pin** is prettier, with wind-twisted pines growing at angles from white-rock cliffs. But with its tiny beach and jagged cliffs looming overhead, covered with gnarled pine and scrub and its rock spur known to climbers as the "finger of God," it's **Calanque En Vau** that's a small piece of paradise.

Icard Maritime. Note that boats make round-trips several times a day to the Calanques de Cassis from Marseille's Quai de la Fraternité (Quai des Belges). Tours are organized by various firms, including Icard Maritime, with a three-hour round-trip costing around €29. ✉ *1 quai Marcel Pagnol, Marseille* 🌐 *visite-des-calanques.com.*

WHERE TO EAT AND STAY

$$$ BISTRO ✕ **Le Chaudron.** Just off Cassis's picturesque port, locals and visitors alike flock to this welcoming bistro and terrace serving classic Provençal meals on one of the town's charming backstreets. Family-run since 1970, the owners have had plenty of time to perfect their game, and it shows. This being Cassis, fish is a mainstay on the menu; start with gratin of mussels followed by roasted John Dory with Provençal vegetables, or spicy fish soup, all to be savored with the local Cassis

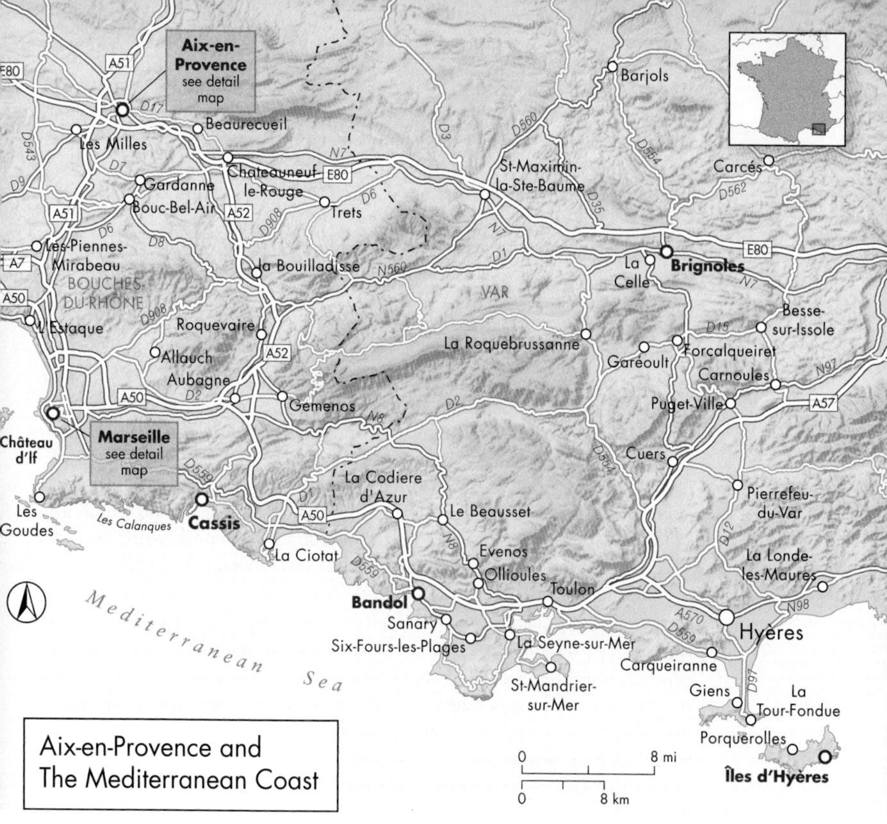

wines. The set menus (€26 and $35) serve generous portions, but you can also order à la carte. *Average main: €26* ✉ *4 rue Adolphe Thiers, Cassis* ☎ *04–42–01–74–18* ⏱ *Closed Tues. and mid-Dec.—Mar. No lunch* ✍ *Reservations essential.*

$$$$ FRENCH **La Villa Madie.** Don't expect to mosey into this seaside eatery wearing a cover-up and thongs. Chef Dimitri Droisneau may profess his cuisine to be humble, but his two-Michelin-star menu—studded with standouts like delicately grilled Mediterranean rouget with almonds and fennel and drizzled lightly with an urchin-and-saffron sauce—merits more than beachwear (plus closed-toe shoes are required). Droisneau and his wife Marielle took over La Villa Madie in 2014, and he earned the restaurant a second star within a year. Overseeing a cellar boasting 550 wines, regional and beyond, sommelier Lionel Legoina can suggest an accompaniment for the three menus (€75, €95, and €145) or the pricier route of à la carte orders. You cannot leave without sampling the exquisite Le Citron, and you may never be satisfied by any old lemon pie again. Give yourself time to linger over predinner cocktails by the waterfront Bar Bleu. *Average main: €62* ✉ *Av. de Revestrel-anse de Corton, Cassis* ☎ *04–96–18–00–00* 🌐 *lavillamadie.com* ⏱ *Closed Mon. and Tues. and Jan.—mid-Feb.* ✍ *Reservations essential.*

$$$ HOTEL **Les Roches Blanches.** First built as a private home in 1887, this cliff-side villa takes in smashing views of the port and the Cap Canaille, both

from the best rooms and from the panoramic dining hall. **Pros:** sweeping vistas are captivating; service is quick and friendly; most rooms have balconies. **Cons:** can be hard to find; breakfast is expensive. *Rooms from: €199 Rte. des Calanques, Cassis 04–42–01–09–30 www.roches-blanches-cassis.com Closed Nov.–Mar. 24 rooms No meals.*

ÎLES D'HYÈRES

32 km (20 miles) off coast south of Hyères.

Spanning some 32 km (20 miles), this southeastern archipelago could be a set for a pirate movie; in fact, it has been featured in several, thanks to a soothing microclimate and a wild, rocky coastline dotted with palms. Real pirates have made an appearance, too: in the 16th century the islands were seeded with convicts to work the land, but they soon ran amok and used their adopted base to ambush ships heading into Toulon. A more honest population claims the islands today, which are made up of three main areas. **Port-Cros** is a national park, with both its surface and underwater environs protected. **Levant** has been taken over, for the most part, by nudists.

Porquerolles is the largest and best of the lot—and a popular escape from the modern world. Off-season, it's a castaway delight of pine forests, sandy beaches, and vertiginous cliffs above rocky coastline. Inland, its preserved pine forests and orchards of olives and figs are crisscrossed with dirt roads to be explored on foot or on bikes; except for the occasional jeep or work truck, the island is car-free. In high season (April to October), day-trippers pour off the ferries and surge to the beaches.

GETTING HERE AND AROUND

To reach the islands, follow the narrow Giens Peninsula to La Tour-Fondue, at its tip. Boats leave every half hour in summer, every 60 or 90 minutes the rest of year, making a 20-minute beeline to Porquerolles (€119.50 round-trip). For Port-Cros and Levant, depart from Port d'Hyères at Hyères-Plages.

WHERE TO STAY

$$$$ B&B/INN **Les Glycines.** In soft shades of yellow-ocher and sky-blue, this sleekly modernized little bastide has an idyllic enclosed courtyard, as well as some lovely guest rooms with views over a jungle of mimosa and eucalyptus. **Pros:** quiet and simply elegant; in the village center. **Cons:** some rooms are small; church bells next door ring daily. *Rooms from: €260 Pl. d'Armes, Ile de Porquerolles 04–94–58–30–36 www.auberge-glycines.com 8 rooms, 3 suites Some meals.*

$$$$ HOTEL **Mas du Langoustier.** A fabled forgetaway, the Langoustier comes with a lobster-orange building, pink bougainvillea, a choice of California-modern- or old-Provençal-style guest rooms, and a secluded location at the westernmost point of the Ile de Porquerolles. **Pros:** a bastion of taste; can "upgrade" to dinner at L'Olivier; beach nearby and pool on-site. **Cons:** a hike to get here; no rooms have a sea view. *Rooms from: €420 Pointe du Langoustier, 3 km (2 miles) from the harbor, Ile de Porquerolles 04–94–58–30–09 www.langoustier.com Closed Oct.–Apr. 44 rooms, 5 apartments Some meals.*

STES-MARIES-DE-LA-MER

31 km (19 miles) southeast of Aigues-Mortes, 40 km (25 miles) southwest of Arles.

The principal town within the confines of the Parc Régional de Camargue, Stes-Maries became a pilgrimage town due to its fascinating history. Provençal legend has it that around AD 45 a band of the first Christians was rounded up and set adrift at sea in a boat without a sail and without provisions. Their stellar ranks included Mary Magdalene, Martha, and Mary Salome, mother of apostles James and John; Mary Jacoby, sister of the Virgin; and Lazarus, risen from the dead (or another Lazarus, depending on whom you ask). Joining them in their fate: a dark-skinned servant girl named Sarah. Miraculously, their boat washed ashore at this ancient site, and the grateful Marys built a chapel in thanks. Martha moved on to Tarascon to tackle dragons, and Lazarus founded the church in Marseille. But Mary Jacoby and Mary Salome remained in their old age, and Sarah stayed with them, begging in the streets to support them in their ministry. The three women died at the same time and were buried together at the site of their chapel.

A cult grew up around this legendary spot, and a church was built around it. When in the 15th century a stone memorial and two female bodies were found under the original chapel, the miracle was for all practical purposes confirmed, and the Romanesque church expanded to receive a new influx of pilgrims. But the pilgrims attracted to Stes-Maries aren't all lighting candles to the two St. Marys: the servant girl Sarah has been adopted as an honorary saint by the Gypsies of the world, who blacken the crypt's domed ceiling with the soot of their votive candles lighted in her honor.

To honor the presiding spirits of Stes-Maries-de-la-Mer, two extraordinary festivals take place every year in Stes-Maries, one May 24–25 and the other on the Sunday nearest to October 22. On May 24 Gypsy pilgrims gather from across Europe and carry the wooden statue of Sarah from her crypt, through the streets of the village, and down to the sea to be washed. The next day they carry a wooden statue of the two St. Marys, kneeling in their wooden boat, to the sea for their own holy bath. The same ritual is repeated by a less colorful crowd of non-Gypsy pilgrims on October 22, who carry the two Marys back to the sea.

GETTING HERE AND AROUND

The nearest train station is in Arles, and from here several buses a day run to Stes-Maries-de-la-Mer. The company serving this area is Envia, which runs buses up to five times a day. The trip takes about 45 minutes and costs €1 one-way. By car, take the A54 and at exit 4 take the D570 directly to Stes-Maries-de-la-Mer.

EXPLORING

As you enter this town's mammoth and medieval cathedral, the Église des Stes-Maries, you'll notice an oddity that wrenches you back to this century: a sign on the door forbids visitors to come *torse nu* (topless). For outside its otherworldly role as the pilgrimage center hallowed as the European landfall of the Virgin Mary, Stes-Maries is first and foremost a beach resort, dead-flat, whitewashed, and more than a little tacky. Unless you've made a pilgrimage to the sun and sand, you probably won't want to spend much time in the town center. And if you've chosen Stes-Maries as a base for viewing the Camargue, consider one of the discreet country inns outside the city limits.

Église des Stes-Maries. What is most striking to a visitor entering the damp, dark, and forbidding fortress-church Église des Stes-Maries is its novel character. Almost devoid of windows, its tall, barren single nave is cluttered with florid and sentimental ex-votos (tokens of blessings, prayers, and thanks) and primitive artworks depicting the famous trio. The sanctuary is open year-round from 8 am to 7 pm. For €2.50 you can climb up to the terrace for a panoramic view of the Camargue (hours vary depending on the season). ✉ *Stes-Maries-de-la-Mer* 🌐 *www.sanctuaire-des-saintesmaries.fr.*

WHERE TO STAY

$$ B&B/INN **Cacharel Hôtel.** A haven for nature lovers, this quiet, laid-back retreat is nestled in the middle of 170 acres of private marshland. **Pros:** screens on windows to keep out mosquitoes; a real taste of the Wild West with silent nights, wind blowing through long grass, animals rustling outside; perfect for those who want to de-urbanize. **Cons:** rooms are very sparse, almost monastery-like; not much to do in the way of socializing. *Rooms from: €144* ✉ *Rte. de Cacharel, Stes-Maries-de-la-Mer* ✣ *4 km (2½ miles) north of town on D85* ☎ *04–90–97–95–44* 🌐 *www.hotel-cacharel.com* *16 rooms* *No meals.*

$$$$ HOTEL **Mas de la Fouque.** With stylish rooms and luxurious balconies that look out over a beautiful lagoon, this upscale converted farmhouse, just 2 km (1 mile) from deserted beaches, is a perfect escape from the rigors of horseback riding and bird-watching. **Pros:** look for breakfast specials included; in the heart of nature. **Cons:** that means mosquitoes. *Rooms from: €346* ✉ *Rte. du Petit Rhone, Stes-Maries-de-la-Mer* ☎ *04–90–97–81–02* 🌐 *www.masdelafouque.com* ⊙ *Closed 2 wks in Jan.* *26 rooms* *No meals.*

THE FRENCH RIVIERA

WELCOME TO THE FRENCH RIVIERA

TOP REASONS TO GO

★ **Mingle with Picasso and company:** Because artists have long loved the Côte d'Azur, it's blessed with superb art museums, including the Fondation Maeght in St-Paul and the Musée Picasso in Antibes.

★ **Soak up the scene in St-Tropez:** Brave the world's most outlandish fishing port in high summer, but don't forget the sunglasses and sunblock.

★ **Experience "reel life" in Cannes:** Get your film fix during the glitzy Cannes International Film Festival, or put yourself in the picture by taking a selfie on the Allée des Étoiles (Stars' Walk).

★ **Take in the views from Èze:** An island in the sky, Èze has some of the most breathtaking views this side of a NASA space capsule.

★ **Get a sense of the Old Riviera in Nice:** With its bonbon-color palaces, blue chair–lined promenade, and time-stained Old Town, this is one of France's most colorful cities.

1 The Western French Riviera. Put on the map by Brigitte Bardot, St-Tropez remains one of France's flashiest vacation spots, small and laid-back. Conspicuous consumption characterizes the celluloid city of Cannes when its May film fest turns it into Oscar-goes-to-the-Mediterranean, but the Louis Vuitton set enjoys this city year-round. For the utmost in Riviera charm, head up the coast to Antibes: once Picasso's home, it has a harbor and an Old Town so dreamy you'll be reaching for your paintbrush.

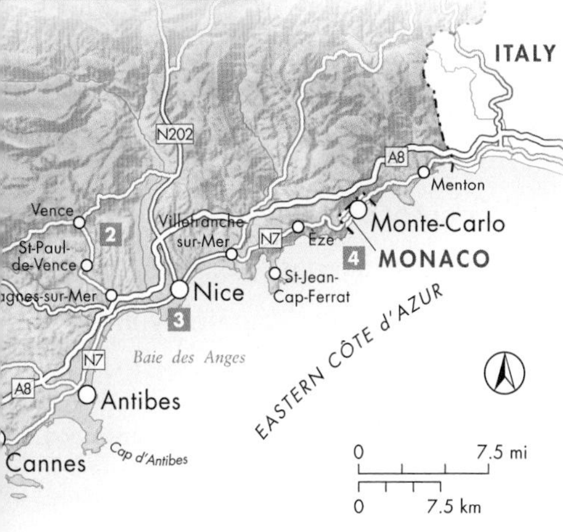

GETTING ORIENTED

The French Riviera can supply visitors with everything their hearts desire—and the purse can stand. Home to sophisticated resorts beloved by billionaires, remote hill villages colonized by artists, Mediterranean beaches, and magnificent views, the Côte d'Azur (to use the French name) stretches from Marseille to Menton. Thrust out like two gigantic arms, divided by the Valley of the Var at Nice, the peaks of the Alpes-Maritimes throw their massive protection, east and west, the length of the favored coast all the way from St-Tropez to the Italian frontier.

2 The Hill Towns. High in the hills overlooking Nice are the medieval walled villages of St-Paul-de-Vence and Vence, invaded by waves of artists in the 20th century. Today, you can hardly turn around without bumping into a Calder mobile, and top sights include the famous inn La Colombe d'Or, Matisse's sublime Chapelle du Rosaire, and the Fondation Maeght—probably the best museum this side of the Louvre.

3 Nice. Walking along the seaside promenade des Anglais is one of the iconic Riviera experiences. Add in top-notch museums, a charming old quarter, scads of ethnic restaurants, a world-class Carnaval, and the new 30-acre promenade du Paillon and you'll see why Nice is one of France's most rewarding cities.

4 The Eastern French Riviera. The 24-karat sun shines most brightly on the glamorous ports of Villefranche-sur-Mer and St-Jean-Cap-Ferrat. If you want to kiss the sky, head up to the charming, mountaintop village of Èze. To the east lies Menton, an enchanting Italianate resort where winters are so mild that lemon trees bloom in January.

Updated By Nancy Heslin

You may build castles in Spain or picture yourself on a South Sea island, but when it comes to serious speculation about how to spend that first $10 million and slip easily into the life of the idle rich, most people head for the French Riviera.

This is where the azure waters and indigo sky begin, where balustraded white villas edge the blue horizon, the evening air is perfumed with jasmine, and parasol pines are silhouetted against sunsets of ripe apricot. As emblematic as the sheet-music cover for a Jazz Age tune, the French Riviera seems to epitomize happiness, a state of being the world pursues with a vengeance.

But the Jazz Age dream confronts modern reality: on the hills that undulate along the blue water, every cliff bristles with cubes of hot-pink cement and balconies of ironwork, each skewed to catch a glimpse of the sea and the sun. Like a rosy rash, these crawl and spread, outnumbering the trees and blocking each other's views. But the Côte d'Azur (or Azure Coast) has always been exceedingly popular, starting with the ancient Greeks, who were drawn eastward from Marseille to market their goods to the natives. From the 18th-century English aristocrats who claimed the coast as one vast spa, to the 19th-century Russian nobles who transformed Nice into a tropical St. Petersburg, to the 20th-century American tycoons who cast themselves as romantic sheiks, the beckoning coast became a blank slate for their whims. Like the modern vacationers who followed, they all left their mark—villas, shrines, Moroccan-fantasy castles—temples all to the sensual pleasures of the sun and the sultry sea breezes. Artists, too, made the French Riviera their own, as museumgoers who have studied the sunny legacy of Picasso, Renoir, Matisse, and Chagall will attest.

Today's admirers can take this all in, along with the Riviera's textbook points of interest: animated St-Tropez; the Belle Époque aura of Cannes; the towns made famous by Picasso—Antibes, Vallauris, Mougins; the urban charms of Nice; and a number of spots where the per-capita population of billionaires must be among the highest on the planet, including Cap d'Antibes and Villefranche-sur-Mer.

But with just a little luck and a bus ride or two, you can find towns and villages far from the madding crowd, especially if you head to the low-lying mountains known as the *arriére-pays* (backcountry). Here, medieval stone villages cap rocky hills and play out scenes of Provençal life, with games of *boules*, slowly savored drinks of pastis (the anise-and-licorice-flavor spirit), and very little mobile phone coverage. Some of them—Èze, St-Paul, Vence—may have become virtual Provençal theme parks but even so you'll probably find a gorgeous and deserted Riviera alleyway hidden in one of their cobblestone mazes.

PLANNER

WHEN TO GO

Unless you enjoy jacked-up prices, traffic jams, and sardine-style beach crowds, avoid the coast like the plague in July and August. Many of the better restaurants simply shut down to escape the coconut-oil crew, and the Estérel—the rocky hillside that overlooks the Mediterranean—is closed to hikers during this flash-fire season. Cannes books up early for the film festival in May, so aim for another month (April, June, September, or October). Between Cannes and Menton, the Côte d'Azur's gentle microclimate usually provides moderate winters; it's protected by the Estérel from the mistral wind that razors through places like St-Raphaël.

Although the area is famous for having more than 340 days of sunshine per year, locals will say winter (November–early March) is cold, rainy, and miserable; in recent years, official snow days—complete with surging sea waves and road closures—have even hit parts of the coast at the end of January. This is a sign that Nice's Carnaval is around the corner.

PLANNING YOUR TIME

If you're settling into one town and making day trips, it's best to divide your time by visiting west and then east of Nice. Parallel roads along the corniches provide access into towns with different personalities, and the A8 main *autoroute* makes motoring from Monaco to St-Raphaël a breeze (just keep spare change handy, as there's a toll to use different parts of it—€3 between Cannes and Nice, for example). The coastal train is equally efficient. Tear yourself away from the coastal *plages* (beaches) at some point to visit the perched villages that this region is famed for. Reach them via Route Napoléon (N98), the D995, or the corniche roads, and plan on at least one overnight stop.

GETTING HERE AND AROUND

The less budget-conscious can consider buzzing around by helicopter (there are heliports in Nice, Cannes-Mandelieu, St-Tropez, and some of the hill towns) or by speedboat (providing service to all resort towns), but affordable transport along the Riviera translates to the train, the bus, or a rental car. Trains access major coastal areas, and most of the *gares* (train stations) are in town centers. Note that only a handful of hill towns have train stations, and St-Tropez is not on the rail line. The bus network between towns is fantastic, and a helpful website 🌐 *www.ceparou06.fr* allows you to calculate your route anywhere in the Alpes-Maritimes region. Renting a car is a good option, and the network of roads here is well marked and divided nicely into slow and very curvy (Bord de Mer Coast Road), faster and curvy (route National 98), and fast and almost straight (autoroute A8).

AIR TRAVEL

Nice, the main point of entry for the French Riviera, is home to France's second-largest airport—the Aéroport Nice-Côte d'Azur. Located 7 km (4 miles) southwest of the city, it's linked to Nice by the No. 98 and No. 99 Lignes d'Azur buses (*08–10–06–10–06* 🌐 *www.lignesdazur.com*), which loop to the bus and train station respectively (€6). Rapides Côtes d'Azur (*04–93–85–64–44* 🌐 *www.rca.tm.fr*) also provides regular airport shuttle service to Nice, Cannes, Antibes, and Menton (€10–€20). Avoid taxis, though, as they'll only rip you off.

Contact Aéroport Nice-Côte d'Azur. ☎ *08–20–42–33–33 €0.12 per min* 🌐 *www.nice.aeroport.fr.*

BOAT TRAVEL

The Côte d'Azur is one of the most beautiful coastlines in the world, and there are several companies that allow you to savor its scenery from the water. April through October, shuttle boats operated by Les Bateaux Verts make the trip between St-Tropez and Ste-Maxime in 15 minutes (return €13.50). Trans Côte d'Azur vessels, departing from Nice and Cannes, go to Corniche de l'Estérel (return €47), and St-Tropez (return €63); note that some routes are only available from May to early October.

Contacts Les Bateaux Verts. ☎ *04–94–49–29–39* 🌐 *www.bateauxverts.com.* **Trans Côte d'Azur.** ☎ *04–92–00–42–30* 🌐 *www.trans-cote-azur.com.*

BUS TRAVEL

Trains are quickest if you're traveling along the coast, but to reach backcountry spots not on the rail line—such as St-Paul-de-Vence and Vence—buses fill the gap. Lignes d'Azur runs to 24 communes in the Alpes-Maritimes for the bargain price of €1.50 (an exception is the Nice airport bus, which costs €6). The Envibus line, which originates in Antibes, covers that city before heading into the hills; going west to Cannes or east to Nice, for instance, you jump on the No. 200 (€1.50). From St-Tropez's station on Avenue du Général de Gaulle, VarLib buses travel to and from St-Raphaël, the town with the nearest railway station (1½ hrs, €3). In high season, traffic can lead to two-plus-hour bus rides, so if it may be wiser to take a Bateaux Verts shuttle boat between the two ports (⇨ *see Boat Travel*). Bus schedules are available at tourist offices and at the local *gare routière* (bus station).

Contacts Envibus. ☎ *04–89–87–72–00* 🌐 *www.envibus.fr.* **Lignes d'Azur.** ☎ *08–10–06–10–06* 🌐 *www.lignesdazur.com.* **VarLib.** ☎ *04–94–24–60–00* 🌐 *www.varlib.fr.*

■ TIP→ You must hail buses; don't presume the driver sees you. Drivers give change and hand you a ticket, which you must get stamped (composté) in the ticket validator and keep as proof of payment, as inspectors often board buses to check.

CAR TRAVEL

The best way to explore the secondary sights in this region is by car. Driving allows you the freedom to zip along A8 between the coastal resorts of St-Raphaël and Menton, and lets you enjoy the views provided by the three corniches that trace the shoreline from Nice to the Italian border. The scenic N98 follows the coast more closely, connecting Mediterranean towns in between, but it can be slow. If you're coming from Paris, the main southbound artery is A6/A7, known as the Autoroute du Soleil; it passes through Provence and joins the eastbound A8 at Aix-en-Provence.

TRAIN TRAVEL

Nice is the major rail crossroads for trains arriving from Paris, other northern cities, and from Italy, too. To reach Nice from Paris (with stops along the coast), you can take the TGV, though it only maintains high speeds to Valence.

You can easily move along the coast between Cannes, Nice, and Ventimiglia on the slick double-decker Côte d'Azur line, a dramatic and tourist-pleasing branch of the SNCF, with more than 40 trains a day. This line is also called the Marseille–Vintimille (Ventimiglia, in Italy). Some of its main stops from Nice are Antibes (30 mins), Cannes (40 mins), and Menton (30 mins); others include Villefranche-sur-Mer, Beaulieu, and Èze-sur-Mer.

For the western parts of the French Riviera, head to St-Raphaël, where the rail route begins its scenic crawl along the coast. There's no rail access to St-Tropez; St-Raphaël is the nearest stop. **■ TIP→ "Tarifs prem" are the cheapest train fares available from SNCF on a limited number of TGV tickets purchased 90 days before travel date, but there is no exchange. "Loisir" fares are flexible and offer peace of mind for the spontaneous traveler.**

Contacts SNCF. ☎ *3635 €0.34 per min* 🌐 *www.sncf.com.* **TGV.** ☎ *3635 €0.34 per min* 🌐 *www.tgv.com.*

RESTAURANTS

Even in tiny villages some haute-cuisine places can be as dressy as those in Monaco, if not more so, but restaurants on the Côte d'Azur are generally quite relaxed. At lunchtime, a decent T-shirt and shorts are fine in all but the fanciest spots; bathing suits, however, should be kept for the beach. Nighttime wear is casual, too—just be aware that for after-dinner drinks, many clubs and discos draw the line at running shoes. Food plays a crucial role in the south of France, and some of the best eateries aren't so easy to access; make sure to include taxi money in your budget to reach the more remote restaurants, or plan on renting a car. Try to come in truffle, lavender, or olive season.

HOTELS

It's up in the hills above the coast that you'll find the charm you expect from France, both in sophisticated hotels with gastronomic restaurants and in friendly mom-and-pop *auberges* (inns); the farther north you drive, the lower the prices. Of course, certain areas of the Riviera book up faster than others, but all hit overload from June to September. It's essential to reserve lodgings in advance; up to half a year for the summer season is not unheard of, and is, in fact, much appreciated. Festivals and good weather will also affect your chances. If you arrive without a reservation, try the tourist information centers, which can usually be of help. *Hotel reviews have been shortened. For full information, visit Fodors.com.*

	WHAT IT COSTS IN EUROS			
	$	**$$**	**$$$**	**$$$$**
Restaurants	under €18	€18–€24	€25–€32	over €32
Hotels	under €106	€106–€145	€146–€215	over €215

Restaurant prices are the average cost of a main course at dinner or, if dinner is not served, at lunch. Hotel prices are the lowest cost of a standard double room in high season.

VISITOR INFORMATION

For information on travel around St-Tropez, contact the Tourisme du Var. For Marseille to Cannes over to Menton, contact the Comité Regional du Tourisme de Provence-Alpes-Côte d'Azur. *Local tourist offices for major towns are listed under the towns covered in this chapter.*

Contacts Comité Regional du Tourisme de Provence-Alpes-Côte d'Azur. ☎ *04–91–56–47–00* 🌐 *www.tourismepaca.fr.* **Tourisme du Var (L'Agence de Développement Touristique).** ☎ *04–94–18–59–60* 🌐 *www.visitvar.fr.*

THE WESTERN FRENCH RIVIERA

Flanked at each end by subtropical capes and crowned by the red-rock Estérel, this section of the coast has a variety of waterfront landmarks. St-Tropez first blazed into fame when it was discovered by painters such as Paul Signac and writers like Colette, and since then it has never looked back. It remains one of the most animated stretches on the French Riviera, getting flooded at high season with people who like to roost at waterfront cafés to take in the passing parade. St-Tropez vies with Cannes for name recognition and glamour, but the more modest resorts—such as St-Raphaël—offer a more affordable Riviera experience. Historic Antibes and jazzy Juan-les-Pins straddle the peninsula of Cap d'Antibes.

ST-TROPEZ

73 km (45 miles) southwest of Cannes, 106 km (66 miles) southwest of Nice.

At first glance, St-Tropez really doesn't look all that lovely: there's a moderately pretty port full of bobbing boats, a picturesque Vieille Ville (Old Town) in candied-almond hues, sandy beaches, and old-fashioned squares with plane trees and *pétanque* players. So what made St-Tropez a household name? In two words: Brigitte Bardot. When this *pulpeuse* (voluptuous) teenager showed up in St-Tropez on the arm of the late

St-Tropez is absolutely gorgeous, but be aware that this is a playground for the rich, with prices to match.

Roger Vadim in 1956 to film *And God Created Woman,* the world snapped to attention. Neither the gentle descriptions of writer Guy de Maupassant (1850–93) nor the watercolor tones of Impressionist Paul Signac (1863–1935), nor even the stream of painters who followed him (including Matisse and Bonnard) could focus the world's attention on this seaside hamlet as could this one luscious female, in head scarf, Ray-Bans, and capri pants. With the film world following in her steps, St-Tropez became the hot spot it—to some extent—remains.

Although anything associated with the distant ages seems almost absurd here, the place does have a history that predates the invention of the bikini. In fact, people have been finding reasons to come since AD 68, when a Roman soldier named Torpes was beheaded for professing his Christian faith in front of Emperor Nero, transforming this spot into a pilgrimage site. To get a sense of the past, wake early (before the 11 am breakfast rush at portside spots lining Quai Suffern and Quai Jean Jaurès) and wander the narrow medieval backstreets by yourself—the rest of the town will still be sleeping off the Night Before. At this hour, you can experience what the artists found to love: the soft light, warm pastels, and the scent of the sea wafting in from the waterfront. Later, when you're tired, you can sit under a colored awning at an inviting café and simply watch the spectacle that is St-Trop (*trop* in French means "too much") saunter by.

GETTING HERE AND AROUND

You can only reach St-Trop by car, bus, or boat (from nearby ports like St-Raphaël). If you're driving, take the N98 coastal road (the longest route but also the prettiest, with great picnic stops along the way); once

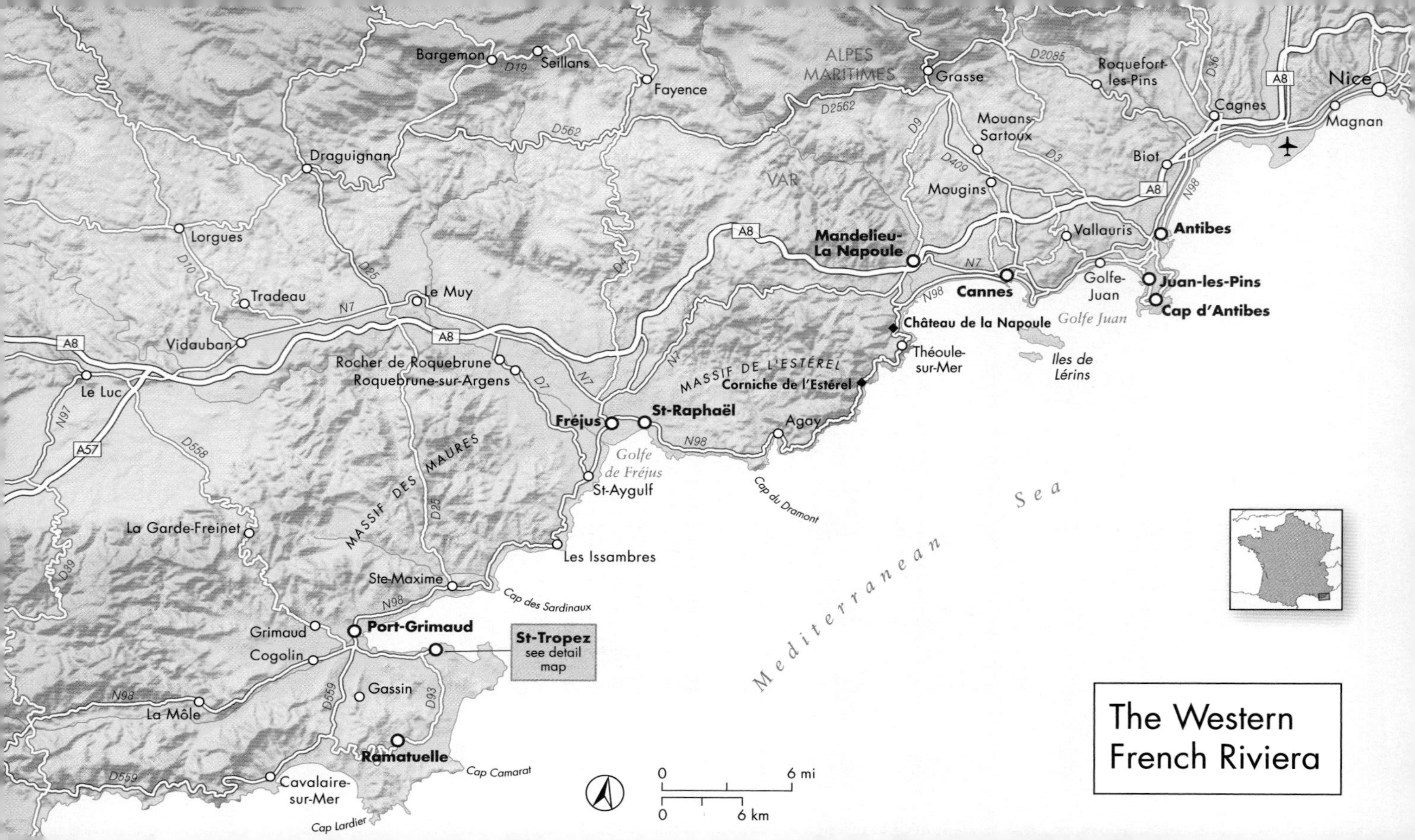

The Western French Riviera
Nice
Magnan
Cagnes
Biot
Roquefort-les-Pins
Antibes
Juan-les-Pins
Cap d'Antibes
Golfe-Juan
Golfe Juan
Vallauris
Iles de Lérins
Cannes
Mouans-Sartoux
Mougins
Grasse
ALPES MARITIMES
VAR
Mandelieu-La Napoule
Château de la Napoule
Théoule-sur-Mer
Corniche de l'Estérel
MASSIF DE L'ESTÉREL
Agay
Cap du Dramont
St-Raphaël
Fréjus
Golfe de Fréjus
St-Aygulf
Les Issambres
Cap des Sardinaux
Ste-Maxime
Port-Grimaud
St-Tropez
see detail map
Grimaud
Cogolin
Gassin
Ramatuelle
Cap Camarat
Cavalaire-sur-Mer
Cap Lardier
La Môle
La Garde-Freinet
MASSIF DES MAURES
Rocher de Roquebrune
Roquebrune-sur-Argens
Le Muy
Tradeau
Vidauban
Le Luc
Lorgues
Draguignan
Bargemon
Seillans
Fayence
Mediterranean Sea
A8
A57
N7
N97
N98
D2085
D36
D3
D409
D9
D2562
D562
D19
D25
D10
D4
D7
D558
D39
D559
D93
0
6 mi
6 km

here, paid parking is available at the Parking du Port lot (opposite the bus station on Avenue du Général de Gaulle) and the Parc des Lices (beneath Place des Lices in the center of town). A train-bus connection from Nice is another option; trains run from Nice's Centre-Ville station to St-Raphaël (€12), where you can catch a VarLib bus for the 90-minute ride onward (€3). From May to early October, Trans Côte d'Azur also has daily boat trips from Nice (2½ hrs, €63 return).

VISITOR INFORMATION

St-Tropez Tourist Office. ✉ *Quai Jean Jaurès, St-Tropez* ☎ *04–94–97–92–72, 08–92–68–48–28 €0.34 per min* 🌐 *sainttropeztourisme.com.*

EXPLORING

Citadelle. Head up Rue de la Citadelle to these 16th-century ramparts, which stand in a lovely hilltop park offering a fantastic view of the town and the sea. Amid today's bikini-clad sun worshippers it's hard to imagine St-Tropez as a military outpost, but inside the Citadelle's dungeon the modern **Musée de l'histoire maritime tropézienne** (St-Tropez Maritime Museum), which opened in 2013, resides a stirring homage to those who served the nation. ✉ *Rue de la Citadelle, St-Tropez* ☎ *04–94–97–59–43* 🎟 *€3 (includes museum entry)* ⏲ *Apr.–Sept., daily 10–6:30; Oct.–Mar., daily 10–12:30 and 1:30–5:30.*

FAMILY **La Maison des Papillons.** A block west of Rue Clémenceau, in a pretty house at the end of a typically Tropezien lane, the butterfly museum is a delight for children (and their parents). Sweetly aflutter, the 35,000 specimens can be toured by appointment with the collector, Dany Lartigue. ✉ *17 rue Étienne Berny, St-Tropez* ☎ *04–94–97–63–45* 🎟 *€2* ⏲ *Apr.–Oct., and 3 wks in Feb. and Dec., weekdays 10–noon and 2–6.*

Musée de l'Annonciade (*Annunciation Museum*). The legacy of the artists who loved St-Tropez has been carefully preserved in this extraordinary museum, housed in a 14th-century chapel just inland from the southwest corner of the Vieux Port. Cutting-edge temporary exhibitions featuring local talent and up-and-coming international artists keep visitors on their toes, while works by established artists line the walls. Signac, Matisse, Braque, Dufy, Vuillard, and Rouault are all here, and their pieces trace the evolution of painting from Impressionism to Expressionism. ✉ *Quai de l'Épi/Pl. Georges Grammont, St-Tropez* ☎ *04–94–17–84–10* 🎟 *€6* ⏲ *Dec.–Oct., Wed.–Mon. 10–1 and 2–6.*

Place des Lices. Enjoy a time-out in the social center of the Old Town, also called Place Carnot, just off the Montée G.-Ringrave as you descend from the Citadelle. A symmetrical forest of plane trees provides shade to rows of cafés and restaurants, skateboarders, children, and grandfatherly pétanque players. The square becomes a moveable feast (for both eyes and palate) on market days—Tuesday and Saturday—while at night a café seat is as coveted as a quayside seat during the day. Just as Deborah Kerr and David Niven once did in *Bonjour Tristesse,* watch the boule players under the glow of hundreds of electric bulbs. Heading back to the Vieux Port area, take in the boutiques lining rues Sibilli, Clemenceau, and Gambetta to help accessorize your evening look—you never know when that photographer from *Elle* will be snapping away at the *trendoisie.* ✉ *Av. Foch and Bd. Vasserot, St-Tropez.*

Quartier de la Ponche. Walk past Quai Suffern—where a statue of the Bailli de Suffren, an 18th-century customs official, stands guard—and streets lined with famous cafés to the Mole Jean Réveille, the harbor wall, where, if the wind isn't too strong, you can walk out for a good view of Ste-Maxime across the sparkling bay, the hills of Estérel, and, on a clear day, the distant Alps. Retrace your steps along the mole and quayside to the 15th-century **Tour du Portalet** and head past it to the old fishermen's quarter, the Quartier de la Ponche, just east of Quai Jean Jaurès. Here you can find the **Port des Pécheurs** (Fishermen's Port), on whose beach Bardot did a star-turn in *And God Created Woman*. Twisting, narrow streets, designed to break the impact of the mistral, open to tiny squares with fountains. Complete with gulf-side harbor, St-Tropez's Old Town maze of backstreets and old ramparts is daubed in shades of gold, pink, ocher, and sky-blue. Trellised jasmine and wrought-iron birdcages hang from the shuttered windows, and many of the tiny streets dead-end at the sea. The main drag here, Rue de la Ponche, leads into Place l'Hôtel de Ville, landmarked by a *mairie* (town hall) marked out in typical Tropezienne hues of pink and green. Head up Rue Commandant Guichard to the Baroque **Église de St-Tropez** to pay your respects to the bust and barque of St. Torpes, every day but May 17, when they are carried aloft in the Bravade parade honoring the town's namesake saint. ✉ *St-Tropez.*

Vieux Port. Bordered by Quai de l'Épi, Quai Bouchard, Quai Peri, Quai Suffren, and Quai Jean Jaurès, Vieux Port is a place for strolling and looking over the shoulders of artists painting their versions of the view on easels set up along the water's edge. Meanwhile, folding director's chairs at the famous port-side cafés Le Gorille (named for its late, exceptionally hirsute manager), Café de Paris, and Sénéquier are well placed for observing the cast of St-Tropez's living theater play out its colorful roles. ✉ *St-Tropez.*

WHERE TO EAT

$ FRENCH FAMILY

✕ **Basilic Burger.** Not every lunch in St-Tropez requires a platinum AmEx for payment. Basilic Burger serves up tasty gourmet burgers and copious salads at more than affordable prices. Just €15 gets you a meal and dessert; the kids' menu is only €10. $ *Average main: €15* ✉ *Pl. des Remparts, St-Tropez* ☎ *04–94–97–29–09* ⊙ *Closed Nov.–mid-May* ▭ *No credit cards.*

$$$ FRENCH

✕ **Dior des Lices.** What could be more fashionable than tucking into cuisine crafted by three-Michelin-star Chef Yannick Alléno in an enchanting sheltered garden designed by Peter Wirtz at the House of Dior? Dior des Lices serves a full breakfast, lunch, dinner, and snacks, with a range of reasonable prices, including set menus. Look for lobster and crunchy vegetable salad with garlic broth or linguine with cherry tomatoes, olive oil, and Parmesan shavings. Terrifically, the dessert selection is as long the rest of the menu; the D'Choux (delightful tiny round pastries), which come in salted caramel, pistachio, lemon zest, and more flavors, get rave reviews. By day the atmosphere is as playful as the outdoor ice-cream carousel and by sunset this magical oasis is perfect for a glass of Champagne (expect to pay €45 for *une verre* of Dom Pérignon 2004).

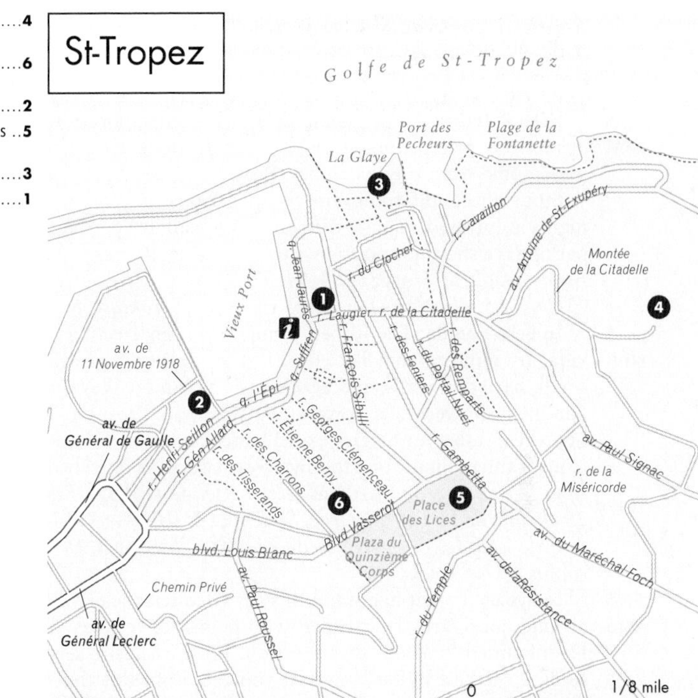

[$] *Average main: €26* ✉ *13 rue François Sibilli, St-Tropez* ☎ *04–98–12–67–65* 🌐 *www.yannick-alleno.com* 🕒 *Closed Oct.–May.*

$$$$ BISTRO ✕ **Le Bistrot à la Truffe.** "Emperor of the Truffle" Bruno Clément opened his truffle palace in a typical Provençal house, just down the street from the church in St-Tropez. Only he could revolutionize a simple oven-baked dish with cream of Tuber brumale (winter truffle), grated Tuber melanosporum (black truffle), and a dash of olive oil to create a meal of startling decadence. You can order à la carte or indulge in a full-on truffle feast by choosing set seasonal or traditional menus (€69, €89, and €146). The wine menu is as fabulous as the truffles, with bottles starting at €40; and if you're looking for the perfect picnic companion, Bruno can whip up a basket of truffles for four to five people for €295. [$] *Average main: €34* ✉ *2 rue de l'Église, St-Tropez* ☎ *04–94–43–95–18* 🌐 *www.bistrot-la-truffe.com* 🕒 *Closed Nov.–Mar.*

$$ BRASSERIE ✕ **Le Sporting.** You'll have to brace yourself for lively conversations at nearby tables and children not behaving as French children are reputed to; however, it's worth it when you pay just €14.60 for a lip-smacking *plat du jour*. Pizza, pasta, burgers, and lamb chops are served in generous portions and at reasonable prices, every day, all year long. The fixtures are nothing fancy—red awning, metal chairs, and typical café tables—but at least there's a place in St-Tropez that feels a little like an

American sports bar. Ⓢ *Average main: €24* ✉ *42 pl. des Lices, St-Tropez* ☎ *04–94–97–00–65.*

WHERE TO STAY

$$$ HOTEL **Hôtel B. Lodge.** All the small, delicately contemporary rooms of this attractively priced, four-story charmer overlook the Citadelle's green park, some from tiny balconies. **Pros:** good deal for location; rooms without air-conditioning are cheaper. **Cons:** minimum stay of four nights in July and August; with only two available parking spots, street parking is a sticky proposition; small rooms. Ⓢ *Rooms from: €200* ✉ *12 rue de l'Aïoli, St-Tropez* ☎ *04–94–97–06–57* 🌐 *www.hotel-b-lodge.com* ⏲ *Closed 5 wks Nov.–Jan.* *15 rooms* *Breakfast.*

$ HOTEL **La Belle Isnarde.** The Robert family has been greeting guests at this villa, just minutes from Place des Lices, since 1965, and while rooms are small, have thin walls, and are as basic as can be, they are clean, with handheld showerheads, towels, and shampoo. **Pros:** lots of free parking; cheap rates for St-Tropez; €11 breakfast well priced for St-Trop. **Cons:** a three-minute taxi to town costs €20; cash only; beds on the soft side. Ⓢ *Rooms from: €100* ✉ *Début Rte. de la Plage Tahiti, B.P. 39, 29 chemin de La Belle Isnarde, St-Tropez* ☎ *04–94–97–13–64* 🌐 *www.la-belle-isnarde.com* *No credit cards* ⏲ *Closed Oct. 15–Easter* *11 rooms* *No meals.*

$$$$ HOTEL **Le Byblos.** Forget five stars: this toy Mediterranean village grouped around courtyards landscaped with palms, olive trees, and lavender has obtained "Palace" classification. **Pros:** exquisite service, service, service; the best buffet breakfast you could imagine (but €40). **Cons:** glitz wears thin; some rooms are small for the price. Ⓢ *Rooms from: €855* ✉ *Av. Paul-Signac, St-Tropez* ☎ *04–94–56–68–00* 🌐 *www.byblos.com* ⏲ *Closed late-Oct.–Easter* *41 rooms, 50 suites* *No meals.*

$$$ HOTEL Fodor's Choice ★ **Lou Cagnard.** Set inside a lovely garden courtyard, this pretty little villa hotel is owned by an enthusiastic young couple, who have fixed it up room by room; recently added amenities include satellite TV and free Wi-Fi. **Pros:** fantastic value for your money (try room No. 17); walking distance to everything; free parking. **Cons:** a few of the older rooms share a bathroom, but at reduced rates. Ⓢ *Rooms from: €160* ✉ *18 av. Paul-Roussel, St-Tropez* ☎ *04–94–97–04–24* 🌐 *www.hotel-lou-cagnard.com* ⏲ *Closed Nov.–Feb.* *19 rooms* *No meals.*

NIGHTLIFE AND PERFORMING ARTS

Les Caves du Roy. Costing the devil and often jammed to the scuppers, this disco in the Byblos Hotel is *the* place to see and be seen; it's filled with svelte model types and their wealthy, silver-haired fans. When you hear the theme from *Star Wars*, take comfort while you sip your €27 glass of tap water that someone other than yourself has just spent €35,000 on a Methuselah of Champagne. There's a horrific door policy during high season; don't worry, it's *not* you. ✉ *Av. Paul-Signac, St-Tropez* 🌐 *www.lescavesduroy.com* ⏲ *July and Aug., nightly; Apr.–June, Sept., and Oct., weekends only.*

Les Nuits du Château de la Moutte. Every August, classical music concerts are given in the gardens of the Château de la Moutte. For ticket information, inquire at the tourist office. ✉ *Chemin de la Moutte, St-Tropez*

DID YOU KNOW?

Europe's upper crust flocked to La Croisette beach because they believed that lying on its white sands (instead of the beach pebbles of Nice) was enough to cure most ailments.

☎ *04–94–96–96–94 information* 🌐 *www.lesnuitsduchateaudelamoutte.com* 🎟 *€45.*

VIP Room. So notorious is the VIP Room for drawing flashy, gilded youths with deep pockets that it spawned a VIP Room Cannes expressly for those needing a dose of film festival before it opens for the summer. ✉ *Residence du Nouveau Port, St-Tropez* ☎ *06–38–83–83–83* 🌐 *st-tropez.viproom.fr.*

SHOPPING

There is something about St-Tropez that makes shopping simply irresistible—unlike Cannes, you'll be welcomed into the stores no matter what you look like or what you're wearing. **Rue Sibilli,** behind Quai Suffren, is lined with all kinds of trendy boutiques, many carrying those all-important sunglasses. Tuck in behind here to Place de la Garonne for some extra-hip purchases.

La Chemise Tropezienne. You'll turn more than a few heads wearing one of La Chemise Tropezienne's gorgeous beach kaftans or shirts, in all the colors of a Mediterranean rainbow—which for this circa 1960s boutique includes white. ✉ *35 rue Gambetta, St-Tropez* ☎ *04–94–79–59–75* 🌐 *lachemisetropezienne.com.*

La Vieille Mer. You probably will do more looking than buying here (unless you have a very large suitcase) but "The Old Sea" owner Walter Wolkowicz will put you in a time machine exploring navigational tools, lamps, and antique accoutrements of nautical yesteryear at his 100% marine shop. It's open daily from April to October, 10 am to 1 pm and 5 pm to midnight. ✉ *5 pl. de l'Ormeau, St-Tropez* ☎ *06–74–07–91–46* 🌐 *www.lavieillemer.com* 🕒 *Closed Nov.–Mar.*

Le Dépot. If you prefer traditional luxe, Le Dépot stocks castoffs by Chanel, Prada, Hermès, Vuitton, Gucci, et al. ✉ *6 bd. Louis-Blanc, St-Tropez* ☎ *04–94–97–80–10* 🌐 *www.ledepot-saint-tropez.com.*

Place des Lices. The aorta of the village, this congregational square overflows with produce and regional foods, as well as clothing and *brocantes* (secondhand items), every Tuesday and Saturday morning. ✉ *Pl. des Lices, St-Tropez.*

Rondini. You wear those strappy flip-flops back home, but are they the real *sandales Tropeziennes*? Here's your chance to pick up the genuine, handmade article at Rodini, St-Tropez's original cobbler, launched in 1927. Did we mention they Fed-Ex to the United States (€11.14 for a pair)? ✉ *16 rue Clemenceau, St-Tropez* ☎ *04–94–97–19–55* 🌐 *www.rondini.fr.*

Vilebrequin. In 1971 Fred Prysquel turned his swim-trunk designs, sketched on the tablecloth at his favorite St-Tropez café, into Vilebrequin, a brand that now sells "resort wear" in 54 countries. His Golden Turtle designs, 24-carat-gold-embroidered swim trunks, start at $8,000. ✉ *1 pl. de la Garonne, St-Tropez* ☎ *04–94–43–33–46* 🌐 *fr.vilebrequin.com.*

FRÉJUS

19 km (12 miles) northeast of Ste-Maxime, 37 km (23 miles) northeast of St-Tropez.

12

Turn your back on modern times—the gargantuan, pink, holiday high-rises that crowd the Fréjus–St-Raphaël waterfront—and head uphill to Fréjus-Centre with its maze of narrow streets lined with butcher shops, patisseries, and neighborhood stores barely touched by the cult of the lavender sachet.

Fréjus (pronounced fray- *zhooss*) has the honor of having some of the most important historic monuments on the coast. Founded in 49 BC by Julius Caesar himself and named Forum Julii, this quiet town was once a thriving Roman shipbuilding port with 40,000 citizens. In its heyday, Roman Fréjus had a theater, baths, and an enormous aqueduct that brought water all the way from Mons in the mountains, 45 km (28 miles) north of town. Today you can see the remains: a series of detached arches that follow the main Avenue du Quinzième Corps (leading up to the Old Town).

GETTING HERE AND AROUND

The direct bus to Fréjus from the Nice–Côte d'Azur airport takes about an hour and costs €20. By car, you are only 35 minutes from the airport on the A8 highway (take the No. 38 exit Fréjus/St-Raphaël). You can follow the N7 or N38 for a more scenic drive, but it takes a lot more time, particularly with summer traffic. Train travelers will pay €12.60 for the 80-minute journey from the Nice Ville station.

VISITOR INFORMATION

Fréjus Tourist Office. ✉ *Le Florus II, 249 rue Jean-Jaurès, Fréjus* ☎ *04–94–51–83–83* 🌐 *www.frejus.fr.*

EXPLORING

■ TIP→ The Fréjus Pass, available at various sites for €4.60, will save you money on entry fees if you plan to visit several monuments.

Arènes. The Arènes (often called the Amphithéâtre) is still used for concerts and bullfights, and can still seat up to 5,000. Back down on the coast, a big French naval base occupies the spot where ancient Roman galleys once set out to defeat Cleopatra and Mark Antony at the Battle of Actium. ✉ *Rue Henri Vadon, Fréjus* ☎ *04–94–51–34–31* 🎫 *€2* ⏲ *Oct.–Mar., Tues.–Sat. 9:30–noon and 2–4:30; Apr.–Sept., Tues.–Sun. 9:30–12:30 and 2–6.*

Chapelle Cocteau (*La Chapelle Notre-Dame de Jérusalem*). This eccentric chapel was designed by Jean Cocteau as part of an artists' colony that never happened. It's an octagon built around a glass atrium and is embellished with stained glass, frescoes depicting the mythology of the first Crusades, and a tongue-in-cheek painting of the apostles above the front door that boasts the famous faces of Coco Chanel, Jean Marais, and poet Max Jacob. ✉ *Av. Nicolaï, La Tour de la Mare, 5 km (3 miles) north of Fréjus on the RN7, Fréjus* ☎ *04–94–53–27–06* 🎫 *€2* ⏲ *Apr.–Sept., Tues.–Sun. 9:30–12:30 and 2–6; Oct.–Mar., Tues.–Sat. 9:30–noon and 2–4:30.*

Groupe Épiscopal. Fréjus is graced with one of the most impressive religious monuments in Provence: The Groupe Épiscopal is made up of an early Gothic **cathedral**, a 5th-century Roman-style **baptistery**, and an early Gothic **cloister**, its gallery painted in sepia and earth tones with a phantasmagoric assortment of animals and biblical characters. Off the entrance and gift shop is a small museum of finds from Roman Fréjus, including a complete mosaic and a sculpture of a two-headed Hermès. ✉ *58 rue de Fleury, Fréjus* ☎ *04–94–51–26–30* 🎫 *Cathedral free; cloister, museum, and baptistery €5.50* ⏲ *Cathedral daily 8:30–6:30. Cloister, museum, and baptistery June–Sept., daily 10–12:30 and 1:45–6:30; Oct.–May, Tues.–Sun. 10–1 and 2–5* ☞ *Closed 10 days early Nov.*

Théâtre Romain. Northeast of Old Town and near the Porte de Rome is the Roman theater (circa 1st century); its remaining rows of arches are mostly intact and much of its stage, including the orchestra and substructures, are still visible at its center. Today the site is known as the Philippe Léotard Theatre and hosts Les Nuits Auréliennes every July. ✉ *Rue du Théâtre Romain, Fréjus* 🎫 *Free* ⏲ *Oct.–Mar., Tues.–Sat. 9:30–noon and 2–4:30; Apr.–Sept., Tues.–Sun. 9:30–12:30 and 2–6.*

ST-RAPHAËL

38 km (24 miles) northeast of St-Tropez, 41 km (25½ miles) southwest of Cannes.

Once party central for F. Scott and Zelda Fitzgerald, who had a hideaway here, St-Raphaël is a now a sprawling resort town that essentially abuts neighboring Fréjus. Gamblers come for the downtown casino; golfers come to play a trio of nearby courses; and the weary (or just indulgent) come to revive in the seawater-based thalassotherapy spas. St-Raphaël is also a major sailing center, which is fitting because the port has a rich history: Napoléon landed here on his triumphant return from Egypt in 1799—it was also from here in 1814 that he cast off for Elba in disgrace. And it was here, too, that the Allied forces landed in their August 1944 offensive against the Germans, as part of Operation Dragoon (later known as the Champagne Campaign).

GETTING HERE

St-Raphaël, the western terminus of the SNCF's regional Riviera line, is easily reached by train. The gare routière (just behind the train station, on Rue Waldeck-Rousseau) offers bus links to destinations including Cannes and St-Tropez. Popular ferries to the latter depart from St-Raphaël's Vieux Port. If you're coming straight from Nice's airport, a shuttle bus is available (75 mins, €20).

VISITOR INFORMATION

St-Raphaël Tourist Office. ✉ *99 quai Albert 1er, St-Raphaël* ☎ *04–94–19–52–52* 🌐 *www.saint-raphael.com.*

EXPLORING

Vieille Ville (*Old Town*). St-Raphaël's Vieille Ville is a tiny enclave of charm crowned by the 12th-century **Église St-Pierre-des-Templiers**, a miniature-scale Romanesque church, and the intimate little **Musée**

Archéologique Marin (Marine Archaeology Museum), both located on Rue des Templiers. ✉ *St-Raphaël.*

WHERE TO EAT AND STAY

$$$ FRENCH ✕ **Le Bouchon Provençal.** *Trés sympa* in decor and ambience, this well-respected restaurant is a three-minute walk from the main strip to St-Raphaël's Old Town. A few years ago, it was profiled on the French TV show "Les escapades gourmandes," selected for its traditional *terroir* cuisine, as accentuated by the menu: cod crumble in a creamy chorizo sauce, lobster tail stew, and (on Friday) the *aioli façon Pastorel,* a famous mayonnaise dip. Lunch (€22) and dinner (€32–€40) menus change often and the wine list is heavy on the—you guessed it—Provençal side. *$ Average main: €32 ✉ 45 rue de la République, St-Raphaël ☎ 04–94–53–89–18 🌐 www.bouchon-provencal-st-raphael.fr ⊙ Closed Sun. and Mon., and 3 wks in Jan. Reservations essential.*

$$ FRENCH ✕ **Les Voiles Saint-Raphael.** Welcome to Les Voiles, a beach restaurant just east of the city center, where a three-course prix-fixe meal will set you back only €31 (if you're pressed for time at lunch, the weekday "express" special is €16). Diners can also order dishes like grilled entrecôte or white cod and risotto with coconut milk à la carte. The menu here isn't extensive, but the food is market-inspired and well-prepared. Selecting one of the divine desserts gives you an excuse to linger longer in front of the glorious azure backdrop. *$ Average main: €22 ✉ Port Santa Lucia, St-Raphaël ☎ 04–94–40–39–15 ⊙ Closed 3 wks in Jan. ▭ No credit cards.*

$ B&B/INN **Hôtel Thimothée.** This attractive 19th-century villa offers comfortable, well-priced rooms (the two on the top floor have poster-perfect sea views, worth the extra €30) as well as a lovely garden, where grand palms and pines shade the walk leading to a pretty little swimming pool. **Pros:** familial atmosphere and gentle hospitality; clean rooms and modern bathrooms. **Cons:** beach and waterfront cafés are a 20-minute walk away; really just an affordable place to lay your beach hat. *$ Rooms from: €80 ✉ 375 bd. Christian-Lafon, St-Raphaël ☎ 04–94–40–49–49 🌐 www.thimothee.com ▭ No credit cards ⊙ Closed 3 wks in Jan. 12 rooms No meals.*

SPORTS AND THE OUTDOORS

Club Nautique St-Raphaël. St-Raphaël is a serious sailing and boating center, with nautical complexes at four different sites along the coast: the Vieux Port, Santa Lucia (by Fréjus-Plage), Le Dramont (at the base of a dramatic little cape below the Estérel), and within Agay's quiet harbor. For information on boat rentals or sailing lessons, contact the Club Nautique St-Raphaël, founded in 1927. ✉ *Av. du Général de Gaulle, St-Raphaël* ☎ *04–94–95–11–66* 🌐 *www.cnsr.fr.*

MANDELIEU–LA NAPOULE

32 km (20 miles) northeast of St-Raphaël; 8 km (5 miles) west of Cannes.

La Napoule is the small, old-fashioned port village, Mandelieu the big-fish resort town that devoured it. You can visit Mandelieu for a golf-and-sailing retreat—the town is replete with many sporting facilities and hosts a bevy of sporting events, including sailing regattas, windsurfing contests, and golf championships (there are two major golf courses in Mandelieu right in the center of town overlooking the water). By the sea, a yacht-crammed harbor sits under the shadow of some high-rise resort hotels. La Napoule, on the other hand, offers the requisite quaintness, ideal for a port-side stroll, casual meal, beach siesta, or visit to its peculiar castle.

GETTING HERE

From the Aéroport Nice-Côte d'Azur, you can get here in 30 minutes by car (take the A8 to exit No. 40) or in 35 by airport shuttle (direction St-Raphaël, €20). The closest train stop is in Cannes; from there you can catch the No. 20 bus (€1.50) or a take a taxi (about €30).

Mandelieu–La Napoule Tourist Office. ✉ *806 av. de Cannes, Mandelieu–La Napoule* ☎ *04–93–93–64–64* 🌐 *www.ot-mandelieu.fr.*

EXPLORING

Château de la Napoule. Looming over the sea at Pointe des Pendus (Hanged Man's Point), the Château de la Napoule is a spectacularly bizarre hybrid of Romanesque, Gothic, Moroccan, and Hollywood cooked up by the eccentric American sculptor Henry Clews (1876–1937). Working with his architect-wife, Clews transformed the 14th-century bastion into something that suited his personal expectations and then filled the place with his own fantastical sculptures. The couple reside in their tombs in the tower crypt, its windows left slightly ajar to permit their souls to escape and allow them to "return at eventide as sprites and dance upon the windowsill." Today the château's foundation hosts visiting writers and artists, who set to work surrounded by Clews's gargoyle-ish sculptures. ✉ *Av. Henry Clews, Mandelieu–La Napoule* ☎ *04–93–49–95–05* 🌐 *www.chateau-lanapoule.com* 🎫 *€6, gardens only €3.50* ⏲ *Feb. 7–Nov. 7., daily 10–6, guided visits at 11:30, 2:30, 3:30, and 4:30; Nov. 8.–Feb. 6., weekdays 2–5, guided visits at 2:30 and 3:30; weekends 10–5, guided visits at 11:30, 2:30, and 3:30.*

WHERE TO EAT

$$$ SEAFOOD

✕ **Le Boucanier.** Wraparound plate-glass views of the marina and château make this low-ceilinged room a waterfront favorite. For 30-plus years locals have gathered here for mountains of oysters and whole fish, grilled simply and served with a drizzle of fruity olive oil, a pinch of rock salt, or a brief flambé in pastis. If you're not a fish fan but want to experience the scenery, you'll also find pasta, risotto, and steak on the menu. Ⓢ *Average main: €26* ✉ *273 av. Henry Clews, Port de La Napoule, Mandelieu–La Napoule* ☎ *04–93–49–80–51* 🌐 *www.restaurant-le-boucanier.fr* ⏲ *Closed 5 wks in Dec.–Feb.*

$$$$ MODERN FRENCH

✕ **L'Oasis.** A culinary landmark with two Michelin stars, this Gothic villa by the sea is home to Stéphane Raimbault—a master of Provençal cuisine who creates unexpected flavor collisions (think medallions of roasted blue lobster in a risotto of spaghetti *à la Puttanesca* or hazelnut venison with a pepper sauce and blueberries). A meal is accented with attentive service plus lots of extras in between courses; and few can quibble with the beauty of the famous garden terrace shadowed by gorgeous palm trees. The €98 menu shouldn't be dismissed. Le Bistro, upstairs, has earned a Michelin BIB designation for "good food at moderate prices" and offers excellent set menus Tuesday to Saturday for both lunch and dinner. Did we mention the cigar collection? $ *Average main: €80* ✉ *6 rue Jean Honoré Carle, Mandelieu–La Napoule* ☎ *04–93–49–95–52* 🌐 *www.oasis-raimbault.com* ⏲ *Closed Sun., Mon., and mid-Dec.–early Feb.* ✍ *Reservations essential.*

SPORTS AND THE OUTDOORS

Centre Nautique Municipal. Classified as a *station voile* (sailing resort), Mandelieu–La Napoule is a major water-sports center. Small sailboats and windsurfers can be rented from Centre Nautique Municipal, next to the restaurant La Plage. It's open daily all year round. ✉ *Av. du Général de Gaulle, Mandelieu–La Napoule* ☎ *04–92–97–07–70* 🌐 *www.mandelieu.fr.*

Golf Club de Cannes-Mandelieu. The Grand Duke Michael of Russia founded the Riviera's first golf course in 1891, known familiarly as The Old Course. Officially it's the International Golf Club Cannes-Mandelieu and has two courses—one with 18 holes (par 71) and one with 9 (par 33), which are the most visually stunning courses in the south of France. The €90 green fee for 18 holes drops nearly 40% if you tee off after 5 pm. ✉ *Rte. du Golf, Mandelieu–La Napoule* ☎ *04–92–97–32–00* 🌐 *www.golfoldcourse.com* 🏌 *Facilities: Driving range, golf carts, rental clubs, pro-shop, golf academy/lessons, restaurant.*

CANNES

8 km (5 miles) east of Mandelieu-La Napoule, 73 km (45 miles) northeast of St-Tropez, 33 km (20 miles) southwest of Nice.

Cannes is a sybaritic heaven for those who believe that life is short and sin has something to do with the absence of a tan. Backed by gentle hills and flanked to the southwest by the Estérel, warmed by dependable sun but kept bearable in summer by the cool Mediterranean breeze, Cannes is blessed with an ideal climate that has made it one of the most beloved (and bedazzled) resorts in Europe. The city's reputation as a top tourist destination has been further enhanced by the success of its glitzy international film festival.

It wasn't always this way—in fact, the bay only attracted fishermen until 1834. That was the year Lord Brougham, an English aristocrat, fell in love with the site during an emergency stopover with a sick daughter; he promptly had a home built and began returning every winter for a sun cure. The ritual was picked up by his peers. Today, glamour—and the perception of glamour—is self-perpetuating, and as long as Cannes enjoys its ravishing climate and setting, it will maintain its incomparable panache. If you love culture of the noncelluloid type, however, you should look elsewhere—there is only one museum here, devoted to history. Still, as his lordship instantly understood, this is a great place to pass the winter.

GETTING HERE

Cannes has one central train station, the Gare SNCF on Rue Jean Jaurès. All major trains pass through here—including TGVs that come direct from Paris (5 hrs)—but many of the trains run the St-Raphaël–Ventimiglia route. A network of buses connects Cannes with various locales, including Nice (90 mins) and Grasse (45 mins); the €1.50 fare to all destinations along the coast make these buses a bargain—be patient, though, as you may not get a seat. If you're flying into Nice, an airport shuttle to Cannes is available (50 mins, €20).

VISITOR INFORMATION

Cannes Tourist Office. ✉ *1 bd. de la Croisette, Cannes* ☎ *04–93–39–01–01* 🌐 *www.cannes-destination.com.*

EXPLORING

La Croisette. This is precisely the sort of place for which the verb *flâner* (to dawdle, saunter) was invented. Head to this famous waterfront promenade—which runs for 1.6 kilometers (1 mile) from its western terminus by the Palais des Festivals—and allow the *esprit de Cannes* to take over. Stroll among the palm trees and flowers and crowds of poseurs (fur coats in tropical weather, cell phones on Rollerblades, and sunglasses at night). Continue east past the broad expanse of private beaches, glamorous shops, and luxurious hotels (among them the wedding-cake Carlton, famed for its see-and-be-seen terrace-level brasserie). The beaches along here are almost all private, but it's worth forking out the money to get the total Cannes experience. ✉ *From Palais des Festivals, Bd. de Croisette, Cannes.*

Le Suquet. Climb up Rue St-Antoine into the picturesque Vieille Ville neighborhood known as Le Suquet, on the site of the original Roman *castrum*. Shops proffer Provençal goods, and the atmospheric cafés provide a place to catch your breath; the pretty pastel shutters, Gothic stonework, and narrow passageways are lovely distractions. In July, the "Nuits Musicales du Suquet" concerts mesmerize in front of Notre-Dame church. ✉ *Rue St-Antoine, Cannes.*

Malmaison. If you need a culture fix, check out the modern art and photography exhibitions held at the Malmaison, a 19th-century mansion that was once part of the Grand Hotel. ✉ *47 bd. La Croisette, La Croisette, Cannes* ☎ *04–97–06–44–90* 🎟 *Exhibit prices vary* ⏲ *July and Aug., daily 11–8; Sept., daily 11–7; Oct.–Apr., Tues.–Sun. 10–1 and 2–6.*

Musée de la Castre. The hill is topped by an 11th-century château, housing the Musée de la Castre, with its mismatched collection of weaponry, ethnic artifacts, and ceramics amassed by a 19th-century aristocrat. The imposing four-sided **Tour du Suquet** (Suquet Tower) was built in 1385 as a lookout against Saracen-led invasions. ✉ *Pl. de la Castre, Le Suquet, Cannes* ☎ *04–93–38–55–26* 🎟 *€6* ⏲ *Apr.–June and Sept., Tues.–Sun. 10–1 and 2–6; July and Aug., daily 10–7; Oct.–Mar., Tues.–Sun. 10–1 and 2–5* ☞ *Extended hrs until 9 on Wed., June–Sept.*

Palais des Festivals. Pick up a map at the tourist office in the Palais des Festivals; recently renovated to the tune of €22 million, the building sets the scene for the famous Festival International du Film, otherwise known as the Cannes Film Festival. As you leave the information center, follow the Palais to your right to see the 24 red-carpeted stairs that movie A-listers ascend every year. Set into the surrounding pavement, the **Allée des Étoiles** (Stars' Walk) enshrines some 375 autographed hand imprints—including those of Dépardieu, Streep, and Stallone (the clay imprints are sent to a potter in, where else, Vallauris before being cast in metal in Rhone). ✉ *Bd. de la Croisette, Cannes* 🌐 *www.palaisdesfestivals.com.*

NEED A BREAK?

Le 72 Croisette. Head down Boulevard de la Croisette and fight for a spot at Le 72 Croisette, the most French of all La Croisette bars. It offers great ringside seats for watching the rich and famous enter the Martinez hotel (home to the legendary two-Michelin-star Palm d' Or). From May to September it's open nearly 24 hours a day (7 am to 4 or 5 am) and in off-season from 7 am to 9 pm. ✉ ***71 bd. de la Croisette, Cannes*** ☎ ***04–93–94–18–30.***

Rue d'Antibes. Two blocks behind La Croisette lies Rue d'Antibes, Cannes's high-end shopping street. At its western end is **Rue Meynadier,** packed tight with trendy clothing boutiques and fine-food shops. Not far away is the covered **Marché Forville,** the scene of the animated morning food market. **Rue Houche**, behind Rue d'Antibes and down from Galleries Lafayette, has lots of boutiques and cafés; Volupté makes a fabulously creamy cappuccino and Chez Bruno is the stop for chocolate. ✉ *Rue d'Antibes, Cannes.*

Vieux Port (*Old Port*). Sparkling at the foot of Le Suquet, this narrow, well-protected port harbors a fascinating lineup of luxury yachts and slick little pleasure boats that creak and bob beside weathered-blue fishing barques. From the east corner, off La Pantiéro at Quai Laubeuf, you can catch a cruise to the Îles de Lérins. The port, as well as Quai St. Pierre (which runs alongside and hosts a plethora of restaurants), has emerged from its tattered and tired midlife crisis to become a smartly dressed, more energized version of its former self. ✉ *Vieux Port, Cannes.*

WHERE TO EAT

$$$ SEAFOOD ✕ **Astoux et Cie Brun.** A beacon to all fish lovers since 1953, Astoux et Cie Brun deserves its reputation for impeccably fresh *fruits de mer.* Well-trained staff negotiate cramped quarters to lay down heaping seafood platters, shrimp casseroles, and piles of oysters shucked to order. Open 365 days a year, it is noisy, cheerful, and always busy (so don't expect rapid service). Arrive early (noon for lunch, 6 pm for dinner) to get a table and avoid the line—reservations aren't accepted. $ *Average main: €30* ✉ *27 rue Félix Faure, La Croisette, Cannes* ☎ *04–93–39–21–87* 🌐 *www.astouxbrun.com* *Reservations not accepted.*

$$$$ FRENCH ✕ **L'Affable.** When Chef Battaglia decided to set up shop in Cannes, gastronomes were delighted—and the chef does not disappoint. The curried lobster is fantastic, the lamb rack succulent, and the risotto impossibly creamy. As for the Grand Marnier soufflé, well it's nothing short of grand. L'Affable is always packed (and often noisy), so reservations are essential. Note that dinner service is a fixed-price menu with lots of tempting choices. $ *Average main: €44* ✉ *5 rue Lafontaine, La Croisette, Cannes* ☎ *04–93–68–02–09* 🌐 *www.restaurant-laffable.fr* 🕒 *Closed Sun. and Aug. No lunch Sat.* *Reservations essential.*

$$$$ FRENCH **La Villa Archange.** You wouldn't expect to find a restaurant with two Michelin stars set in such a residential background, 10 minutes by car from La Croisette. But Bruno Oger, ex-chef at the Villa des Lys, promises you a rather unforgettable evening in this très cozy spot surrounded by centennial trees and gardens. Yes, it's pricey. Now that that's out of the way, concentrate on the selection (€98, €150, €210 menus or à la carte)—which features dishes like veal shank slow-cooked for 24 hours and served with truffle mashed potatoes, or Breton lobster and roasted squid served with chard ravioli. His creations have dazzled Tilda Swinton and Diane Kruger, and, frankly, a restaurant with its own app for the *plat du jour* in real time is surely in a league of its own. If this is beyond your means, opt for the three-course, €31 menu at the premise's Le Bistrot des Anges (Michelin BIB Gourmand). While waiting, sink into an armchair and watch the fashion parade at L'Ange Bar. *Average main: €85 15 bis rue Notre-Dame des Anges, Le Cannet 04–92–18–18–28 bruno-oger.com Closed Sun. and Mon. No lunch Tues.–Thurs.*

$$$$ FRENCH Fodor's Choice ★ **Le Park 45.** In the chic, retro-'60s Grand Hotel Cannes, this modern spot with sleek plate-glass windows to take in the views is the showcase for Chef Sébastien Broda's cooking. The local-boy-made-good (he trained at La Palme d'Or and at Roger Vergé's Mougins landmark) has piqued the curiosity of both far-flung foodies and plenty of trendy Cannoises, earning himself a Michelin star along the way. He continues to put on a real show: picture dishes like flaked crab with "Black River" caviar and Savora mustard ice cream. Order à la carte or opt for a set menu (€55, €80, and €120). *Average main: €38 45 bd. de la Croisette, Cannes 04–93–38–15–45 www.grand-hotel-cannes.com Closed Dec. and Jan.*

$$$$ FRENCH **Mantel.** In a city where style often wins out over substance, food lovers treasure this Suquet address, run by former chef and maître d' Noël Mantel, who started out at the Negresco before working with Ducasse at Louis XV in Monaco and then managing Les Muscadins in Mougins. In 2002 he opened this self-named eatery (now part of the Châteaux & Hôtels Collection), and he recently modernized the interior, choosing a more contemporary setting that's as appetizing as his cuisine. Find out for yourself with dishes à la carte or one of the seasonal prix-fixe menus (€35 or €44). Drawing on the finest Mediterranean produce, Mantel delivers simple yet eloquent dishes such as grilled local cuttlefish with parsley pesto, tomato jam, and candied lemon or braised veal shank (osso-buco style) with sun-dried tomatoes, big french fries, and black olives. *Average main: €41 22 rue St-Antoine, Cannes 04–93–39–13–10 www.restaurantmantel.com Closed Wed. No lunch Tues. and Thurs.*

$$$$ FRENCH **Sea Sens.** Occupying the fifth floor of a former post office, this trendy Michelin-star restaurant has a fabulous view over Le Suquet. Chef Arnaud Tabarec and world pastry champion Jérôme De Oliveira attempt to awaken all your senses either with à la carte dishes or two set menus—Signature (€55) and Degustation (€95), a series of surprise courses for those who live on the gastronomic edge. The wine selection can make even novices appreciate bouquet, taste, and texture. Sea Sens's new

Brasserie has a more limited menu but a broader price list, with choices ranging from risotto with taggiasche olives and confit tomatoes (€18) to grilled lobster with tarragon (€68). If you can't make if for a meal, sip a cocktail here at Cannes's best rooftop bar. *Average main: €45* ✉ *1 rue Notre-Dame, Cannes* ☎ *04–63–36–05–05* 🌐 *www.restaurant-seasens.com* ⏲ *Sea Sens: Closed most of Jan.; no dinner Mon., no lunch. Brasserie: no lunch weekends.*

WHERE TO STAY

$$$$ HOTEL **Five Hotel.** Housed in the town's old post office, steps from the Palais des Festivals, Five has a stylish decor that evokes voyages to the Far East: red fabrics blend with exquisite dark wood furniture against all-white linens and bathroom fixtures. **Pros:** excellent service, food, and location; complimentary minibar, in-room Nespresso machines and free Wi-Fi. **Cons:** who needs a scale in the bathroom when on holiday in France?. *Rooms from: €500* ✉ *1 rue Notre-Dame, Cannes* ☎ *04–63–36–05–05* 🌐 *www.five-hotel-cannes.com* ⏲ *Closed 3 wks in Jan.* *30 rooms, 15 suites* *Some meals.*

$$ HOTEL **Hotel Colette.** Facing the train station, this boutique hotel is suspiciously affordable, considering its proximity to the beach, particularly when you book in advance for rooms in the off-season (from mid-October until June); if you prepay online, even a room in July is only €127. **Pros:** not far from the Palais des Festivals; interior courtyard a bonus; l'Occitane toiletries provided. **Cons:** walls may be a bit thin; local parking is expensive. *Rooms from: €145* ✉ *5 pl. de la Gare, Cannes* ☎ *04–93–39–01–17* 🌐 *www.hotelcolette.com* *45 rooms* *No meals.*

$$$ HOTEL **Hôtel de Provence.** This affordable choice has a fabulous location and its very gracious owners, Julie and Jerry Duburcq, go the extra distance to ensure guests have the service and experience of a much-higher caliber hotel. **Pros:** all-day breakfast (€9); five-minute walk from Cannes center; cheaper rates if booking prepaid. **Cons:** only two parking places, so organize ahead of time with owners (street or paid garage otherwise). *Rooms from: €161* ✉ *9 rue Molière, Cannes* ☎ *04–93–38–44–35* 🌐 *www.hotel-de-provence.com* ⏲ *Closed Feb.* *30 rooms, 7 apartments* *No meals.*

$$$$ HOTEL **InterContinental Carlton Cannes.** Used by Hitchcock as a suitably glamorous frame for Grace Kelly in *To Catch a Thief*, this neoclassical landmark built in 1911 staked out the best position early on, sitting right on the sidewalk of La Croisette, radiating symmetrically from its figurehead waterfront site—the better for you to be seen on the popular brasserie's terrace. **Pros:** sense of history; five-star service. **Cons:** some rooms are lackluster; outrageous cost of extras, such as in-room Wi-Fi for €24 or €10 minibar Coke. *Rooms from: €935* ✉ *58 bd. de la Croisette, Cannes* ☎ *04–93–06–40–06* 🌐 *www.intercontinental-carlton-cannes.com* *343 rooms, 39 suites* *Some meals.*

$$$ HOTEL **Le Cavendish Boutique Hotel.** Lovingly restored by friendly owners Christine and Guy Welter, the giddily opulent former residence of Lord Cavendish is a true delight, playing up both contemporary decor and 19th-century elegance. **Pros:** genuine welcome is a refreshing change from the notoriously frosty reception at other Cannes palace hotels;

bar has complimentary drinks and snacks for guests each evening from 6 to 9; the only Cannes hotel that serves breakfast until the last client has eaten. **Cons:** even though rooms all have double-pane windows, the hotel is on the busiest street in Cannes, which means an inevitable amount of noise. *Rooms from: €195 ✉ 11 bd. Carnot, Cannes ☎ 04–97–06–26–00 🌐 www.cavendish-cannes.com ⏲ Closed mid-Dec.–mid-Mar. 34 rooms Breakfast.*

NIGHTLIFE AND PERFORMING ARTS

Cannes International Film Festival. The Riviera's cultural calendar is splashy and star-studded, and never more so than during the Cannes International Film Festival in May. The film screenings are not open to the public, so unless you have a pass, your stargazing will be on the streets or in restaurants (though if you hang around the back exits of the big hotels around 7 pm, you may bump into a few celebs on their way to the red carpet). *Cinéma de la Plage* shows Cannes Classics and Out of Competition films free at Macé beach at 8:30 pm. In addition, Cannes Cinéphiles (*www.cannes-cinema.com*) gives 4,000 film buffs a chance to view Official Selections; you can apply online in February. *✉ Cannes 🌐 www.festival-cannes.com.*

Casino Barrière. The famous Casino Barrière on La Croisette—open 10 am to 3 am (4 am on weekends and until 5 am during summer)—is said to draw more crowds to its slot machines than any other casino in France. *✉ Palais des Festivals, 1 La Croisette, Cannes ☎ 04–92–98–78–00 🌐 www.lucienbarriere.com.*

Le Bâoli. The biggest player on the Cannes nightlife scene is Le Bâoli, which attracts the likes of Kim and Kanye, Channing Tatum, and Jude Law. It's usually packed until dawn even outside of festival time. *✉ Port Canto, Bd. de la Croisette, La Croisette, Cannes ☎ 04–93–43–03–43 🌐 www.lebaoli.com ⏲ Closed Jan.–mid-Feb. and Sun.–Thurs. Nov.–mid-Apr.*

SPORTS AND THE OUTDOORS

Most of the beaches along La Croisette are owned by hotels and restaurants, and they rent out chaise loungers, mats, and umbrellas to the public and to hotel guests (who also have to pay). Public beaches are between the color-coordinated private beach umbrellas and offer simple open showers and basic toilets.

SHOPPING

Whether you're window-shopping or splurging on that little Raf Simons number in the Dior window, you'll find some of the best shopping outside Paris on the streets off La Croisette. For stores carrying designer names, try **Rond-point Duboys-d'Angers** off **Rue Amouretti, Rue des Serbes,** and **Rue des Belges,** all perpendicular to the waterfront. **Rue d'Antibes** is the town's main shopping drag, home base to every kind of clothing and shoe shop, as well as mouthwatering candy, fabric, and home-design stores. **Rue Meynadier** mixes trendy young clothes with high-end food specialties.

JUAN-LES-PINS

5 km (3 miles) southwest of Antibes, 10 km (6 miles) southwest of Cannes.

If Antibes is the elderly, historic parent, then Juan-les-Pins is the jazzy, younger-sister resort town. The scene along Juan's waterfront is something to behold, with thousands of international sunseekers flowing up and down the promenade or lying flank to flank on its endless stretch of sand. Yes, the **Plage de Juan-les-Pins** is made up of sand, not pebbles, and ranks among the Riviera's best (rent a beach chair from the nearby hotel concessions, the best of which is Les Belles Rives). Along with these white-powder wonders, Juan is famous for the quality—some pundits say quantity—of its nightlife. There are numerous nightclubs where you can do everything but sleep, ranging from casinos to discos to strip clubs. If all this sounds like too much hard work, wait for July's jazz festival—one of Europe's most prestigious—or simply repair to Les Belles Rives; if you're lucky enough to be a guest, you'll understand why F. Scott Fitzgerald set his *Tender Is the Night* in "Juantibes," as the place retains the golden glamour of the Riviera of yore and is surrounded by the last remnants of the pine forests that gave Juan its name. Elsewhere, Juan-les-Pins suffers from a plastic feel and you might get more out of Antibes.

GETTING HERE

Regional rail service connects Juan-les-Pins to Nice (€5.10), Cannes (€2.60), and other coastal towns; from the train station, Envibus No. 15 (€1) loops through town, stopping at the public beach. Juan-les-Pins can also be reached from either Nice or Cannes via the No. 200 Lignes d'Azur bus (75 mins, €1.50).

VISITOR INFORMATION

Juan-les-Pins Tourist Office. ✉ *60 chemin des Sables, Juan-les-Pins* ☎ *04–22–10–60–01* 🌐 *www.antibesjuanlespins.com.*

WHERE TO EAT AND STAY

$$$$ SEAFOOD ✕ **Les Pêcheurs.** In 1954 French resistance hero Camille Rayon built a restaurant on the Cap d'Antibes between two stone fishing huts. It wasn't long before La Maison des Pêcheurs became a fashionable address, though the site was abandoned in the 1990s before being transformed into the Relais & Chateau Cap d'Antibes Beach Hotel in 2009. If you have a hankering for a classy seaside experience, this Michelin-star restaurant will fit the bill. The seafood selection under Chef Nicolas Navarro is exquisite—sea bass, turbot, sole, and lobster grace the menu; however, the price per gram can bring on terrible post-meal indigestion. The set-price meals (€85 and €125) are more moderately priced. $ *Average main: €52* ✉ *10 bd. du Maréchal-Juin, Juan-les-Pins* ☎ *04–92–93–13–30* 🌐 *www.lespecheurs-lecap.com* ⏲ *Closed Nov.–Mar.*

$ HOTEL 🏨 **Hotel des Mimosas.** Situated in an enclosed hilltop garden studded with tall palms, mimosas, and tropical greenery, this is the sort of place where only the quiet buzzing of cicadas interrupts silent nights. **Pros:** nice garden and grounds (worth the extra money for room with terrace); easy 10-minute walk to train station. **Cons:** some rooms are small and dated; friendly service can be hit or miss; free Wi-Fi in common rooms but weak. $ *Rooms from: €99* ✉ *Rue Pauline, Juan-les-Pins* ☎ *04–93–61–04–16* 🌐 *www.hotelmimosas.com* ▬ *No credit cards* ⊙ *Closed Oct.–Apr.* *34 rooms* *No meals.*

$$$$ HOTEL Fodor's Choice ★ **Les Belles Rives.** Not far from the onetime villa of Gerald and Sara Murphy—those Roaring Twenties millionaires who devoted their lives to proving the maxim "living well is the best revenge"—the Belles Rives became the home-away-from-home for literary giant F. Scott Fitzgerald and his wife Zelda (chums of the Murphys). **Pros:** views are quite spectacular, but ask for a room with a frontal (not lateral) sea view; lots of water sports. **Cons:** restaurant is typically pricey; some rooms are on the small side. $ *Rooms from: €486* ✉ *33 bd. Édouard Baudoin, Juan-les-Pins* ☎ *04–93–61–02–79* 🌐 *www.bellesrives.com* ⊙ *Closed Jan. and Feb.* *43 rooms* *Breakfast.*

NIGHTLIFE AND PERFORMING ARTS

Eden Casino (*Casino Partouche Juan-les-Pins*). The glassed-in complex of the Eden Casino houses slot machines, roulette and blackjack tables, and a panoramic beach restaurant. Texas Hold'Em Poker is played every night. Players park for free. The casino is open until 4 am (5 am in summer). ✉ *17 bd. Baudoin, Juan-les-Pins* ☎ *04–92–93–71–71* 🌐 *www.casinojuanlespins.com.*

Festival International Jazz à Juan. Every July the world-renowned Jazz à Juan festival stages a stellar lineup in a romantic venue under ancient pines. Launched in 1960, this festival hosted the European debut performances of such stars as Miles Davis and Ray Charles. More recently, it spawned the fringier Jazz Off, with 200 musicians and free street concerts, as well as the Jazz Club at Les Ambassadeurs beach, where you can enjoy a drink with live music (headliners have been known to pop in for impromptu concerts here). Book online or buy tickets directly from the tourist office in Antibes or Juan-les-Pins. ✉ *Juan-les-Pins* ☎ *04–22–10–60–06 ticket information* 🌐 *www.jazzajuan.com.*

Kiss Club. The former Milk club has been glossed over with the sexiest decor and given a sound-system that will keep you shaking in your stilettos all night. ✉ *5 av. Georges Gallice, Juan-les-Pins* ☎ *06–30–71–46–18.*

Le Village. The cavernous Le Village sets the standard for cool in Juan-les-Pins, with thumping music played by the best DJs in town, but beware of the rudeness factor from staff. It's open from midnight to 5 am every day of the week. ✉ *1 bd. de la Pinède, Juan-les-Pins* ☎ *04–92–93–92–00.*

CAP D'ANTIBES

2 km (1 mile) south of Antibes.

This extravagantly beautiful peninsula, protected from the concrete plague infecting the mainland coast, has been carved up into luxurious estates shaded by thick, tall pines. Since the 19th century the wild greenery and isolation have drawn a glittering guest list of aristocrats, artists, literati, and the fabulously wealthy: Guy de Maupassant, Anatole France, Claude Monet, the Duke and Duchess of Windsor, the Greek shipping tycoon Stavros Niarchos, and the cream of the Lost

Generation, including Ernest Hemingway, Gertrude Stein, and Scott and Zelda Fitzgerald. Now the most publicized focal point is the Hôtel du Cap–Eden Roc, the preferred address of visiting film stars.

GETTING HERE

Envibus's No. 2 line (€1.50) connects Cap d'Antibes to downtown Antibes.

EXPLORING

Jardin Thuret (*Thuret Garden*). To fully experience the Riviera's heady hothouse exoticism, visit the glorious Jardin Thuret, established by botanist Gustave Thuret in 1856 as a testing ground for subtropical plants and trees. Thuret was responsible for the introduction of the palm tree, forever changing the profile of the French Riviera. On his death the property was left to the Ministry of Agriculture, which continues to dabble in the introduction of exotic species. The garden is in the middle of the Cap; from the Port Gallice, head up Chemin du Croûton, turn right on the Boulevard du Cap, then right again on Chemin Raymond. ✉ *90 chemin Raymond, Cap d'Antibes* ☎ *04–97–21–25–00* 🌐 *www6.sophia.inra.fr/jardin_thuret* 🎫 *Free* ⏲ *Winter, weekdays 8:30–5:30; summer, weekdays 8–6.*

Fodor's Choice ★ **Le Sentier du Littoral** (*Sentier Tire-poil*). Bordering the Cap's zillion-dollar hotels and over-the-top estates runs one of the most spectacular footpaths in the world. Nicknamed the Sentier Tire-poil (because the wind is so strong it "ruffles the hair"), the circuit was recently extended, bringing it "full circle" around the gardens at Eilenroc over to l'Anse de l'Argent Faux. It now stretches about 5 km (3 miles) along the outermost tip of the peninsula. The Sentier du Littoral begins gently enough at the pretty Plage de la Garoupe (where Cole Porter and Gerald Murphy used to hang out), with a paved walkway and dazzling views over the Baie de la Garoupe and the faraway Alps. Round the far end of the cap, however, and the paved promenade soon gives way to a boulder-studded pathway that picks its way along 50-foot cliffs, dizzying switchbacks, and thundering breakers (*Attention Mort*—"Beware: Death"—read the signs, reminding you this path can be very dangerous in stormy weather). Continue along the new portion of the path to the cove l'Anse de l'Argent Faux, where you can stop and catch your breath before heading up to entrance of Eilen Roc. Then follow Avenue Beaumont impasse tangent until it touches the Cap's main road RD 2559. On sunny days, with exhilarating winds and spectacular breakers, you'll have company, although for most stretches all signs of civilization completely disappear—except for a yacht or two. The walk takes about two hours to complete, but it may prove to be two of the more unforgettable hours of your trip (especially if you tackle it at sunset). By the way, if you come across locked gates blocking your route it's because storm warnings have been issued and you are not allowed to enter. ■ **TIP→ From the bus station in town take the No. 2 bus to the "Fontaine" stop. To return, follow the Plage de la Garoupe until Boulevard de la Garoupe, where you'll make a left to reconnect with the bus.** ✉ *Cap d'Antibes.*

Phare de la Garoupe (*Garoupe Lighthouse*). You can sample a little of what draws famous people to this part of the world by walking up Chemin de Calvaire from the Plage de la Salis in Antibes—a distance of about 1 km (½ mile)—and taking in the extraordinary views from the hill surmounted by this old *phare* (lighthouse). Next to it, the 16th-century double chapel of **Notre-Dame-de-la-Garoupe** contains ex-votos and statues of the Virgin, all in memory of and for the protection of sailors. ✉ *Chemin de Calvaire, Cap d'Antibes* ☎ *04–22–10–60–10* ⏲ *Chapel, Mon. and Fri. 2:30–6; Mass daily at 11:30.*

Fodor's Choice ★ **Villa Eilenroc.** The Sentier du Litterol passes along the beach at the Villa Eilenroc, designed by Charles Garnier, who created the Paris Opéra—which should give you some idea of its style. It commands the tip of the peninsula from a grand and glamorous garden. Over the last decade an ecomuseum was completed and a scented garden created at the entrance to the rose garden. On Wednesday from September to June, visitors are allowed to wander through the reception salons, which retain the Louis Seize-Trianon feel of the noble facade. The Winter Salon still has its *1,001 Nights* ceiling mural painted by Jean Dunand, the famed Art Deco designer; display cases are filled with memorabilia donated by Caroline Groult-Flaubert (Antibes resident and goddaughter of the great author); and the boudoir has boiseries from the Marquis de Sévigné's Paris mansion. As you leave, be sure to detour to La Rosaerie, the rose garden of the estate—in the distance you can spot the white portico of the Château de la Cröe, another legendary villa (now reputedly owned by a syndicate of Russian billionaires). It has a host of big names attached to it—singer Helene Beaumont built it; and King Leopold II of Belgium, King Farouk of Egypt, Aristotle Onassis, and Greta Garbo all rented here. ✉ *460 av. L.D. Beaumont, at the peninsula's tip, about 3.75 km (2.5 miles) from Garoupe Bay, Cap d'Antibes* ☎ *04–93–67–74–33* 🌐 *www.antibesjuanlespins.com* 🎫 *Free Oct–Mar.; €2 Apr.–Sept.* ⏲ *Oct.–Mar., Wed. and Sat. 1–4; Apr.–June, Wed. and Sat. 10–5; July–Sept., Wed., Sat., and Sun. 3–7.*

WHERE TO EAT AND STAY

$$$$ SEAFOOD ✕ **Restaurant de Bacon.** Since 1948, under the careful watch of the Sordello brothers, Restaurant de Bacon has been *the* spot for seafood on the French Riviera; its Michelin star dates back to 1979. The catch of the day may be minced in lemon ceviche (€38), floating in a top-of-the-line bouillabaisse (€125), or simply grilled with fennel and crisped with hillside herbs (€80). The dreamy terrace over the Baie des Anges, with views of the Antibes ramparts, justify extravagance, even if the service sometimes falls short of pricey expectations. Many of the à la carte fish dishes are expensive, but a €55 lunch menu and an €85 dinner menu are available in July and August. (Note that there are very few nonfish alternatives.) $ *Average main: €85* ✉ *664 bd. de Bacon, Cap d'Antibes* ☎ *04–93–61–50–02* 🌐 *www.restaurantdebacon.com* ⏲ *Closed Mon. and Nov.–Feb. No lunch Tues.* ✍ *Reservations essential.*

$$$$ HOTEL 🏨 **Hôtel du Cap–Eden Roc.** In demand by celebrities from De Niro to Madonna, this extravagantly expensive hotel looking out on 22 acres of immaculate gardens bordered by rocky shoreline has long catered to the world's fantasy of a subtropical idyll on the French Riviera. **Pros:**

no other hotel in Southern France has the same reputation or style; specially designed children's summer programs. **Cons:** if you're not a celebrity, tip big to keep the staff interested; don't even try to book a room during the Cannes Film Festival in early May. *Rooms from: €950 Bd. J.F. Kennedy, Cap d'Antibes 04–93–61–39–01 www.hotel-du-cap-eden-roc.com Closed Oct.–mid-Apr. 104 rooms, 14 suites Breakfast.*

12

$$ HOTEL **La Garoupe-Gardiole.** Cool, simple, and accessible to non–movie stars, this pair of partnered hotels offers a chance to sleep on the hallowed Cap peninsula and bike or walk to the pretty Garoupe beach. **Pros:** location among million-dollar mansions; spacious rooms available for families but the area is pretty quiet; free parking; free Wi-Fi; fitness room. **Cons:** buffet breakfast costs €13; towels €2/day; some rooms are small, but ask for ones facing pool. *Rooms from: €140 60–74 chemin de la Garoupe, Cap d'Antibes 04–92–93–33–33 www.hotel-lagaroupe-gardiole.com Closed mid-Oct–mid-Apr. 37 rooms No meals.*

ANTIBES

11 km (7 miles) east of Cannes, 15 km (9 miles) southeast of Nice.

No wonder Picasso once called this home: Antibes (pronounced Awn-*teeb*) is a stunner. Broad stone ramparts and bright tile roofs help make it one of the Riviera's most enchanting towns. The waterside location doesn't hurt either. Port Vauban harbor (gateway to the Cap d'Antibes) has some of the largest yachts in the world tied up at its berths—and their millionaire owners won't find a more dramatic spot to anchor, with the tableau of the snowy Alps looming in the distance and the formidable medieval block towers of the Fort Carré guarding entry to the port. Stroll promenade Amiral-de-Grasse along the crest of Vauban's seawalls, and you can understand why the views inspired Picasso to paint on a panoramic scale. A few steps inland, you enter a souk-like maze of old streets that are relentlessly picturesque. To visit Old Antibes, pass through the Porte Marine, an arched gateway in the rampart wall. Follow Rue Aubernon to Cours Masséna, where the little sheltered market sells the freshest produce, cheese, and hand-stuffed sausages. Along the way, wander the back alleys, check out the shops, and relax at one of the dawdle-and-dine cafés before paying homage to Picasso at the château-cum-museum that bears his name.

GETTING HERE

Antibes receives high-speed TGV service from Paris, as well as other cities—including Avignon and Aix in neighboring Provence. If you're flying into Nice, the No. 250 bus will bring you in from the airport for €10 (40 mins). The Lignes d'Azur No. 200 bus connects Antibes to Cannes, Nice, Cagnes-sur-Mer, and Juan-les-Pins for €1.50; going west to Cannes or east to Nice, you board it at the Briand stop behind Place de Gaulle, but note that buses heading in different directions depart from different streets due to one-way traffic.

VISITOR INFORMATION

Antibes Tourist Office. *42 ave Robert Soleau, Antibes 04–22–10–60–10 www.antibesjuanlespins.com.*

EXPLORING

Fodor's Choice ★ **Commune Libre du Safranier** (*Free Commune of Safranier*). A few blocks south of the Château Grimaldi is the Commune Libre du Safranier, a magical little neighborhood with a character (and mayor) all its own even though it's technically part of Antibes. Not far off the seaside promenade, Rue de la Touraque is the main street to get here, and you can amble around Place du Safranier, where tiny houses hang heavy with flowers and vines, and neighbors carry on conversations from window to window across the stone-stepped Rue du Bas-Castelet. ✉ *Rue du Safranier, rue du Bas-Castelet, Antibes.*

Eglise de l'Immaculée-Conception (*Cathédrale Notre-Dame*). This sanctuary served as the region's cathedral until the bishopric was transferred to Grasse in 1244. The church's 18th-century facade, a marvelously Latin mix of classical symmetry and fantasy, has been restored in stunning shades of ocher and cream. Its stout medieval watchtower was built in the 11th century with stones "mined" from Roman structures. Inside is a Baroque altarpiece painted by the Niçois artist Louis Bréa in 1515. ✉ *Rue du Saint Esprit, Antibes* ⏲ *Daily 8:30—noon and 3—6.*

Musée Archéologique (*Archaeology Museum*). Promenade Amiral-de-Grasse—a marvelous spot for pondering the mountains and tides—leads directly to the Bastion St-André, a squat Vauban fortress that now houses the Musée Archéologique. In its glory days this 17th-century stronghold sheltered a garrison; the bread oven is still visible in the vaulted central hall. The museum collection focuses on Antibes's classical history, displaying amphorae and sculptures found in local digs as well as in shipwrecks from the harbor. ✉ *Bastion St-André, Av. Général-Maizières, Antibes* ☎ *04–22–10–60–10* 🎫 *€3* ⏲ *Sept. 16–June 15, Tues.–Sun. 10–1 and 2–5; June 16–Sept. 15., Tues.–Sun. 10–noon and 2–6.*

Musée Picasso. Rising high over the water, Musée Picasso is set in the stunning medieval Château Grimaldi. As rulers of Monaco, the Grimaldi family lived here until the revolution; this fine old castle, however, was little more than a monument until its curator offered use of its chambers to Picasso in 1946, when that extraordinary genius was enjoying a period of intense creative energy. The result was a bounty of exhilarating paintings, ceramics, and lithographs inspired by the sea and by Greek mythology—all very Mediterranean. The château, which became the **Musée Picasso** in 1966, houses some 245 works by the artist, as well as pieces by Miró, Calder, and Léger; the first floor displays more than 100 paintings by Russian-born artist Nicholas de Staël. Even those who are not great Picasso fans should enjoy his vast paintings on wood, canvas, paper, and walls, alive with nymphs, fauns, and centaurs. ✉ *Château Grimaldi, Pl. Mariejol, Antibes* ☎ *04–22–10–60–10* 🎫 *€6* ⏲ *Sept. 16–June 15, Tues.–Sun. 10–noon and 2–6; June 16–Sept. 15, Tues.–Sun. 10–6.*

WHERE TO EAT

$$$$ FRENCH Fodor's Choice ★ ✕ **Le Figuier de Saint-Esprit.** After 18 years performing in the kitchens of others, acclaimed Chef Christian Morrisset opened one of the best restaurants in the Old Town of Antibes and earned himself a Michelin star. It's in a contemporary setting with dark wood tables and is gorgeously shaded by a 40-year-old fig tree and a canopy of vines—the shady street

Along with its time-burnished alleys and cul-de-sacs, Antibes is packed with little squares that offer the perfect chance to chill out and get to know the locals.

is one of the most picturesque in town. The former chef of Juana has kept his prices democratic at lunchtime, when a two-course meal costs around €39; you can easily spend twice as much at dinner. Typical of his style, which focuses on local ingredients, is a saddle of lamb from the Alpilles cooked in a crust of Vallauris clay with gnocchi and truffles, zucchini, eggplant, and thyme jus. *Average main: €45* *14 rue Saint-Esprit, Antibes* *04–93–34–50–12* *www.christianmorisset.fr* *Closed Tues. and most of Nov. No lunch Mon. and Wed.*

$$$ FRENCH **Taverne le Safranier.** Part of a tiny Old Town enclave determined to resist the press of tourism, this casual tavern is headquarters for the *tables* scattered across the sunny terrace on Place Safranier. Install yourself at one and tuck into dishes like zucchini beignet, Saint Jacques and lobster cassoulet, thick handmade ravioli, or whole *dorade,* a delicate Mediterranean fish that is unceremoniously split, fried, and garnished with lemon. A laid-back staff shouts your order into the nautical-decor bar. There's a €16 lunch option, and the homemade blackboard specials are reasonably satisfying, but it's the location that brings out the best flavors here. *Average main: €31* *1 pl. Safranier, Antibes* *04–93–34–80–50* *Closed Mon. and Jan.*

NIGHTLIFE

Blue Lady Pub. Located next to Geoffrey's British food shop, this pub is frequented by French and foreigners alike (and their kids and dogs). It's a great little spot to collect your thoughts over a drink after a long day, or to hear some live music. The Blue Lady has daytime appeal, too. Beginning at 7:30 am you can grab a latté, smoothie, and even an English breakfast (there are newspapers on deck). If you stick around for lunch, you can order homemade burgers, potpies, and fresh salads. Friendly service and free Wi-Fi are bonuses. ✉ *L Galerie du Port, Rue Lacan, Antibes* ☎ *04–93–34–41–00* 🌐 *www.blueladypub.com.*

La Siesta. This is an enormous summertime entertainment center and the largest beach club in France—some 15,000 revelers pack in every Friday and Saturday from mid-June to early September. The casino has 193 slot machines, English roulette and blackjack tables, a bistro, and a terrace overlooking the sea. ✉ *Rte. du Bord de Mer, Antibes* ☎ *04–93–33–31–31* 🌐 *www.joa-casino.com.*

THE HILL TOWNS

The hills behind the coast are often called the *arrière-pays,* or backcountry, and this particular wedge of backcountry—between Cannes and Antibes—has a character all its own that is deeply, unselfconsciously Provençal. Its undulating fields of lavender are watched over by villages perched on golden stone, creating vignettes and vistas that inspired Picasso, Matisse, and other art icons. Not surprisingly, one of the highlights here is St-Paul de Vence, home to the Maeght Foundation (which ranks among France's leading modern art museums) and La Colombe d'Or (an incomparable, painting-covered inn); another is neighboring Vence, where you'll find the Chapelle du Rosaire, entirely designed and decorated by Matisse. Although it's possible to get a small taste of this backcountry on a day trip out of Cannes or Antibes, you may want to settle in for a night or two: after dark the scent of the boutiques' strawberry potpourri is washed away by the natural perfume of bougainvillea and jasmine wafting from terra-cotta jars. **■ TIP→ One of the best Provençal markets is held on Friday morning in the delightful 16th-century Valbonne village, about 7 km (4 miles) north of Mougins. There are no museums in this English-friendly spot, but you'll find endless restaurants and cafés around Place des Arcades for post-shopping hunger. There's plenty of free parking if you're driving; otherwise take a €1.50 bus from Nice (No. 230), Cannes (No. 630), or Antibes (No. 10).**

VALLAURIS

6 km (4 miles) northeast of Cannes, 6 km (4 miles) northwest of Antibes.

In the low hills over the coast, dominated by a blocky Renaissance château, this ancient village was ravaged by waves of the plague in the 14th century, and then rebuilt in the 16th century by 70 Genoese families imported to repopulate the abandoned site. They brought with them a taste for Roman planning—hence the grid format in the Old Town—but, more important in the long run, a knack for pottery making as well. Their skills and the fine clay of Vallauris proved to be a marriage made in heaven, and the village thrived as a pottery center for hundreds of years. Even Picasso made clay creations during his seven-year residency here.

GETTING HERE

Trains from Nice (€5.70) and Cannes (€2) arrive at the SNCF Golfe-Juan train station; from there Envibus No. 8 makes the drive into Vallauris proper about every 15 minutes (45 minutes on Sunday). Envibus

Vauban's Fort Carré and the seawalls he designed guard Antibes's harbor, home to some of the most envy-inducing yachts in the world.

No. 5 also connects Vallauris to Antibes directly (€1), while the Lignes d'Azur No. 200 links it with Nice and Cannes (€1.50).

■ TIP→ The Riviera has been suffering from an influx of petty crime, so keep your car doors locked at all times, with bags stashed out of view. Also keep close tabs on your wallet, handbag, and phone when exploring the streets on foot.

EXPLORING

Musée National Picasso. In the late 1940s Picasso settled here in a simple stone house, creating pottery art from the malleable soil with a single-minded passion. But he returned to painting in 1952 to create one of his masterworks in the château's Romanesque chapel, the vast multi-panel oil-on-wood composition called *La Guerre et la Paix* (*War and Peace*). Today the chapel is part of the Musée National Picasso, where several of Picasso's ceramic pieces are displayed. ✉ *Pl. de la Libération, Vallauris* ☎ *04–93–64–71–83* 🌐 *musees-nationaux-alpesmaritimes.fr/picasso* 🎫 *€4* ⏲ *July and Aug., daily 10–7; Sept.–June, Wed.–Mon. 10–12:15 and 2–5.*

MOUGINS

6 km (4 miles) northwest of Valluris, 8 km (5 miles) north of Cannes, 11 km (7 miles) northwest of Antibes.

Passing through Mougins, a popular summerhouse community convenient to Cannes and Nice and famously home to a group of excellent restaurants, you may perceive little more than suburban sprawl. But in 1961 Picasso found much to admire and settled into a *mas* (farmhouse) that verily became a pilgrimage spot for artists and art lovers; he died here in 1973. More recently, Picasso's electrician, Pierre Le Guennec, came forward in 2010 with a box of 271 Picasso works, apparently given to him 40 years prior. The handyman only discovered the trove (valued at €50 million) when cleaning out his garage. Soon after, he was charged with handling stolen goods. The case is ongoing.

GETTING HERE

The No. 600 and No. 630 buses (€1.50) from Cannes stop in Mougins; from there it's a 15-minute uphill walk to the Vieux Village. Alternately, you can opt for a taxi from Cannes (around €35).

VISITOR INFORMATION

Mougins Tourist Office. ✉ *39 pl. des Patriotes, Mougins* ☎ *04–93–75–87–67* 🌐 *www.mougins.fr/tourisme.*

EXPLORING

Les Étoiles de Mougins. This festival transformed the medieval village of Mougins into a vast "open-air theater of gastronomy." Over three days in September, hundreds of the greatest chefs from around the globe converge to share their passion for cooking with equally enthusiastic audiences. Demonstrations, workshops, and competitions dazzle 25,000 spectators annually. And yes, there are glorious tastings, too. ✉ *Vieux Village, Mougins* ☎ *04–93–75–87–67* 🌐 *www.lesetoilesdemougins.com* 🎟 *€5–€15.*

Musée d'Art Classique de Mougins. Opened in 2011, this hidden gem "highlights the dialogue between the old and the new" with Roman, Greek, and Egyptian art rubbing shoulders with pieces by Picasso, Matisse, Cézanne, Warhol, and Dali. Expect to come across a sarcophagi alongside a Cocteau or a Hirst sculpture next to an ancient bust. Spread over four floors, the museum also houses antique jewelry and the world's largest armory collection. This is as hip as classic will ever be. ✉ *32 rue Commandeur, Mougins* ☎ *04–93–90–00–91* 🌐 *www.mouginsmusee.com* 🎟 *€12* ⏲ *May–Sept., daily 10–8; Oct.–Apr., daily 10–6.*

Notre-Dame-de-Vie. You can find Picasso's final home, where he lived for 12 years until 1973, by following D35 2 km (1 mile) south of Mougins to the ancient ecclesiastical site of Notre-Dame-de-Vie. From his room, he could see the 13th-century bell tower and arcaded chapel, a pretty ensemble once immortalized in a painting by Winston Churchill. The chapel, listed as a historical monument since 1927, is said to date back to 1655. Approached through an allée of ancient cypresses, the former priory house Picasso shared with his wife, Jacqueline, overlooks the broad bowl of the countryside (now blighted with modern construction). Unfortunately, his residence was bought by a private investor and is closed to the public. ✉ *Chemin de la Chapelle, Mougins.*

WHERE TO EAT

$$$$ FRENCH Fodor's Choice ★

✕ **Daniel Desavie.** Judging by the crowd of regulars at his restaurant, located 7 km (4½ miles) from Mougins village, Daniel Desavie has built quite a reputation. That's hardly surprising given that he was trained for 23 years by Roger Vergé at the famous Moulins de Mougins. His engaging wife Chantal, who speaks English, makes diners feel very welcome, as does the lovely French Provençal decor. When you're ready to order,

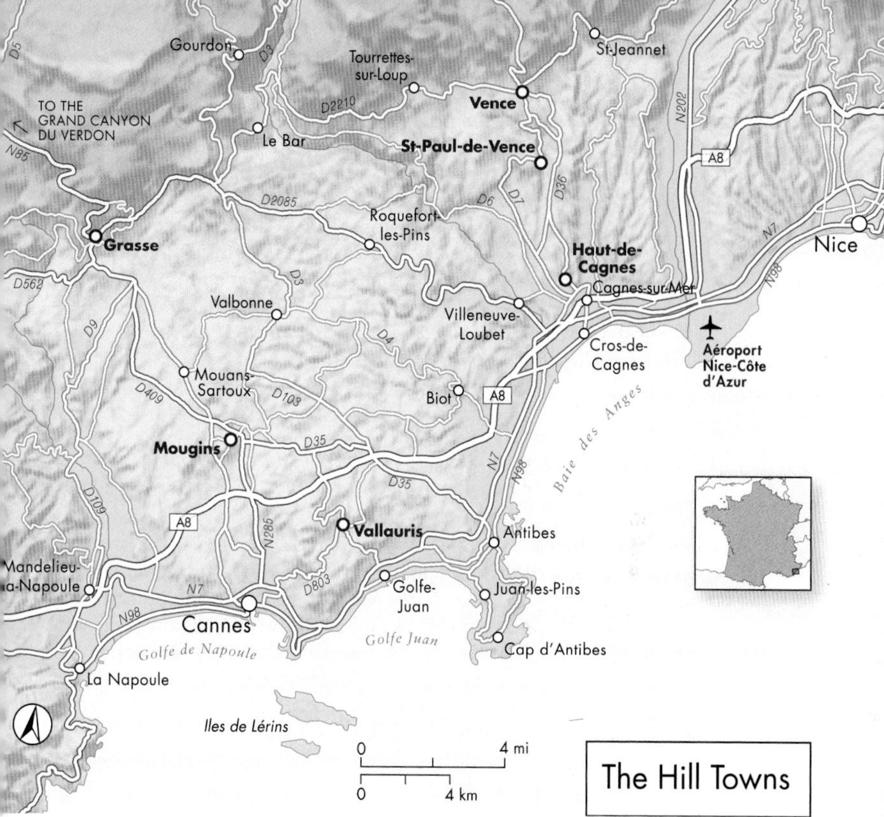

try the lobster with tabbouleh and orange-mango vinaigrette before digging into the braised lamb shoulder fricassee. If you want to add wine, there's a sommelier on hand to help you turn your classic meal into a masterful one. *Average main: €37* *1360 rte. d'Antibes, Valbonne* *From Mougins village, follow the D3 toward Valbonne, then take a right at the Forum roundabout along the D103* *04–93–12–29–68* *www.restaurantdanieldesavie.fr* *Closed Sun. and Mon.*

$$$$ FRENCH **Paloma.** Young Nicolas Decherchi has already had a stellar career: since starting out at age 16, he's worked at five Michelin-star restaurants, and his own gastronomic eatery earned a star in 2014, only one year after opening. Occupying a stone villa, Paloma has been designed to re-create the serenity of a Provençal farmhouse, complete with distant views (in this case, of the sea and the Lerins Islands off Cannes). The service is flawless, from the valet to the sommelier; and the food combines time-honored southern cooking techniques with a hefty dollop of imagination—picture delicate pin-wheeled hare with foie gras and truffles, cooked for 36 hours, and served with black radish, celery root, and cinnamon ravioli. Portions aren't copious, so à la carte diners will probably have room for dessert. Set menus are available at both lunch (from €39) and dinner (from €79). *Average main: €60* *47 av. du Moulin de la Croix, Mougins* *04–92–28–10–73*

www.restaurant-paloma-mougins.com *Closed Sun. and Mon., 1 wk in Feb., and after film festival.*

$$$$ HOTEL **Le Mas Candille.** Nestled in a 10-acre private park, this 19th-century *mas* (farmhouse) has been cleverly transformed into an ultraluxurious Relais & Chateaux hotel with antique wallpapers, "reissued" vintage furniture, and many other high-gloss touches that make the place *Elle Decor*–worthy. **Pros:** award-winning service; beautiful views; parking included in price. **Cons:** tricky to find; pay extra for a room with a view. *Rooms from: €470* *Bd. Clément-Rebuffel, Mougins* *04–92–28–43–43* *www.lemascandille.com* *Closed most of Jan.* *38 rooms, 7 suites* *Breakfast.*

GRASSE

10 km (6 miles) northwest of Mougins, 17 km (10½ miles) north of Cannes, 22 km (14 miles) northwest of Antibes, 42 km (26 miles) west of Nice.

High on a plateau over the coast, this busy, modern town is usually given a wide berth by anyone who isn't interested in its most prized industry, the making of perfume. But its unusual art museum features works of the 18th-century artist Fragonard, while the famed perfume museum and the picturesque backstreets of its very Mediterranean Vieille Ville round out a pleasant day trip from the coast. You can't visit the laboratories where the great blends of Chanel, Dior, and Guerlain are produced, but to accommodate the crowds who come here wanting to know more, Grasse has three functioning perfume factories that create simple blends and demonstrate production techniques for free.

GETTING HERE

The No. 500 bus from Nice has daily service to Grasse, and the No. 610 comes from Cannes; both cost €1.50.

VISITOR INFORMATION

Grasse Tourist Office. *Pl. de la Buanderie, Grasse* *04–93–36–66–66* *www.grasse.fr.*

EXPLORING

Fragonard. Built in 1782, this perfume factory is open to the public daily for guided tours. *20 bd. Fragonard, Grasse* *04–93–36–44–65* *www.fragonard.com* *Free* *Mid-Dec.–mid-Nov., daily 9–6; mid-Nov.–mid-Dec., daily 9–12:30 and 2–6.*

Galimard. Tracing its pedigree back to 1747, Galimard has a factory that is open to visitors 365 days a year. **TIP→ For €45 you can create and name your own perfume in a two-hour workshop. They're held Monday to Saturday at 10, 2, and 4 in Galimard's Studio des Fragrances, around the corner at 5 route de Pegomas; Sunday workshops are added from April to October.** *73 rte. de Cannes, Grasse* *04–93–09–20–00* *www.galimard.com* *Free* *Apr.—Oct., daily 9–6:30; Nov.–Mar., daily 9–noon and 2–6.*

Molinard. Established in 1849, Molinard offers an extensive tour that includes visits to the Soap Factory, the Distillery (witness "the nose" at work concocting new fragrances), and the Cream Room, where the packaging team hand-labels each bottle or pump. ✉ *60 bd. Victor Hugo, Grasse* ☎ *04–92–42–33–28* 🌐 *www.molinard.com* 🎟 *Free* 🕓 *Early Jan.–Christmas, daily 9:30–6:30.*

Musée d'Art et d'Histoire de Provence (*Museum of the Art and History of Provence*). Just down from the Fragonard perfumery, the Musée d'Art et d'Histoire de Provence has a large collection of *faïence* from the region, including works from the famous pottery towns of Moustiers, Biot, and Vallauris. ✉ *2 rue Mirabeau, Grasse* ☎ *04–93–36–80–20* 🌐 *www.museesdegrasse.com* 🎟 *Free* 🕓 *Apr.–Sept., daily 10–7; Oct.–Mar., Wed.–Sun. 10:30–5:30* ☞ *Closed last 3 wks of Nov.*

Musée International de la Parfumerie (*International Museum of Perfume*). This is one of the more sleekly spectacular museums along the coast. Housed in a soaring structure of steel, glass, and teak, the museum traces the 3,000-year history of perfume making; highlights include a fascinating collection of 4,000 antique perfume bottles. In the rooftop greenhouse you can breathe in the heady smells of different herbs and flowers, while the expert and amusing guide crushes delicate petals under your nose to better release the scents. ✉ *2 bd. du Jeu de Ballon, Grasse* ☎ *04–97–05–58–00* 🌐 *www.museesdegrasse.com* 🎟 *€4; €6 for temporary expositions* 🕓 *Apr.–Sept., daily 10–7; Oct.–Mar., Wed.–Mon. 10:30–5:30* ☞ *Closed last 3 wks of Nov.*

Vieille Ville (*Old Town*). Go down the steps to Rue Mirabeau and lose yourself in the dense labyrinth of the Vieille Ville, where steep, narrow streets are thrown into shadow by shuttered houses five and six stories tall. The studio of native Grassois and perfume creator extraordiniare Didier Galgeweski (at 12 rue de l'Oratoire) is steps from the International Perfumery Museum. ✉ *12 rue de l'Oratoire, Grasse.*

Villa Musée Fragonard. This museum headlines the work of Grasse's own Jean-Honoré Fragonard (1732–1806), one of the great French "chocolate-box" artists of his day (these artists were known for their maudlin style that stemmed from the type of artwork found on boxes of chocolate). The lovely villa contains a collection of Fragonard's drawings, engravings, and paintings; also on display are works by his son Alexandre-Evariste and his grandson, Théophile. ✉ *23 bd. Fragonard, Grasse* ☎ *04–93–36–93–10* 🌐 *www.museesdegrassse.com* 🎟 *Free* 🕓 *Apr.–Sept., daily 10–7; Oct.–Mar., Wed.–Sun. 10:30–5:30* ☞ *Closed last 3 wks of Nov.*

WHERE TO STAY

$$$$ B&B/INN **La Bastide Saint-Antoine.** This ocher mansion, once the home of an industrialist who hosted the Kennedys and the Rolling Stones, is now the domain of celebrated Chef Jacques Chibois, who welcomes you with old stone walls, shaded walkways, an enormous pool, and guest rooms that glossily mix Louis Seize, Provençal, and high-tech delights. **Pros:** a bastion of culinary excellence; perks like iPod docks, 1,000 TV channels, and coffee/organic tea in each room; seasonal deals on Bastide's website. **Cons:** rooms are a touch too Provençal for some tastes; breakfast (€29) not included. $ *Rooms from: €350* ✉ *48 av. Henri-Dunant, Grasse* ☎ *04–93–70–94–94* 🌐 *www.jacques-chibois.com* *9 rooms, 7 suites* 🍽 *No meals.*

VENCE

20 km (12 miles) east of Grasse, 4 km (2½ miles) north of St-Paul, 22 km (14 miles) northwest of Nice.

Encased behind stone walls inside a thriving modern market town, the historic part of Vence dates from the 15th century. Though its back-streets and alleys have been colonized by crafts stores and "art galleries," La Vieille Ville remains conscious of its history—plaques guide you through the age-old *portes* (gates) and around atmospheric little squares, like Place du Peyra. The area is especially lively on Tuesday when a Provençal market sets up near the cathedral.

GETTING HERE

You can catch the No. 400 bus from Nice (1 hr, €1.50) or take the train as far as Cagnes-sur-Mer, and then cover the remaining 10 km (6 miles) by bus or taxi. Motorists should take the Cagnes-sur-Mer highway exit (No. 47 or 48, depending on the direction you come from) and look for signs on the RD 436 to La Colle sur Loup/Vence.

VISITOR INFORMATION

Vence Tourist Office. ✉ *8 pl. du Grand Jardin, Vence* ☎ *04–93–58–06–38* 🌐 *www.vence-tourisme.com.*

EXPLORING

Cathédrale de la Nativité de la Vierge (*Cathedral of the Birth of the Virgin*). In the center of the Vieille Ville, the Cathédrale de la Nativité de la Vierge was built on the Romans' military drilling field in the 11th and 12th centuries and is a hybrid of Romanesque and Baroque styles. The cathedral has been expanded and altered many times over the centuries. Note the rostrum added in 1499—its choir stalls are carved with particularly vibrant and amusing scenes of daily life in the Middle Ages. In the baptistery is a ceramic mosaic of Moses in the bulrushes by Chagall. ✉ *Pl. Godeau, Vence* 🌐 *vence.fr/our-lady-of-nativity?lang=fr* ⏲ *Daily 9–6.*

Fodor's Choice ★ **Chapelle du Rosaire** (*Chapel of the Rosary*). On the outskirts of "new" Vence, toward St-Jeannet is the Chapelle du Rosaire, better known to the world-at-large as the Matisse Chapel. The artist decorated it with beguiling simplicity and clarity between 1947 and 1951 as his gift to nuns who had nursed him through illness. It reflects the reductivist style of the era: walls, floor, and ceiling are gleaming white, and the small stained-glass windows are cool greens and blues. "Despite its imperfections I think it is my masterpiece . . . the result of a lifetime devoted to the search for truth," wrote Matisse, who designed and dedicated the chapel when he was in his 80s and nearly blind. ✉ *466 av. Henri-Matisse, Vence* ☎ *04–93–58–03–26* 🎟 *€6* ⏲ *Dec.–mid-Nov., Tues. and Thurs. 10–11:30 and 2–5:30; Mon., Wed., and Sat. 2–5:30; Sun. Mass at 10.*

WHERE TO EAT AND STAY

$$$$ FRENCH ✕ **Les Bacchanales.** Michelin-star Chef Christophe Dufau's weekly changing menu puts an inventive spin on traditional local ingredients; the suckling pig with onion, fresh walnut, and pumpkin is a must when it's available. Meals are served in a sun-filled, beautifully decorated garden villa, a mere 10 minutes by foot from Vence. In summer, the terrace is an idyllic place to linger over a four-, five-, or seven-course set menu

(from €32 for lunch, €65 for dinner). *Average main: €65 ✉ 247 av. de Provence, Vence ☎ 04–93–24–19–19 🌐 www.lesbacchanales.com ⏲ Closed Wed. year-round and Tues. Sept.–June. No lunch weekdays in July and Aug. Reservations essential.*

12

$$$$ HOTEL **Château du Domaine St. Martin.** Occupying the site of an ancient Knights Templar fortress and set amid acres of greenery designed by Jean Mus, this hilltop domain with its noteworthy restaurant, ecological spa, and helicopter pad welcomes you with light, airy public salons (where afternoon tea and rare Champagnes are offered) and luxurious guest quarters that include two- and three-bedroom villas accented with beautiful antiques. **Pros:** stunning views; possible celebrity sightings; Martin's Club for kids in summer. **Cons:** restaurant prices steep (€26 for a starter soup); nothing really within walking distance. *Rooms from: €600 ✉ 2490 av. des Templiers, Vence ☎ 04–93–58–02–02 🌐 www.chateau-st-martin.com ⏲ Closed mid-Oct.–mid-Apr. 40 suites, 6 villas Breakfast.*

$ B&B/INN **L'Auberge des Seigneurs et du Lion d'Or.** Dating to the 17th century and the only hotel set within Vence's old walls, this former stagecoach inn has an ambience *à la François Premier*. **Pros:** lovely family atmosphere; parking vouchers available; affordable breakfast (€10). **Cons:** front rooms with views are noisy (especially in summer) while quieter back rooms lack view; no air-conditioning (but fans). *Rooms from: €90 ✉ Pl. du Frêne, Vence ☎ 04–93–58–04–24 🌐 www.auberge-seigneurs.com ⏲ Closed mid-Dec.–mid-Jan. 6 rooms Some meals.*

PERFORMING ARTS

Nuits du Sud. Since 1997, world-music lovers have taken over Place du Grand Jardin in Vence from mid-July for four weeks, with up to 9,000 revelers a night gyrating to various beats. Even if you don't want to buy concert tickets, come for the atmosphere and share a picnic—the music will find you no matter where you are. *✉ 39 rue de 8 Mai 1945, Vence ☎ 04–93–58–40–17 🌐 www.nuitsdusud.com.*

ST-PAUL-DE-VENCE

4 km (2½ miles) south of Vence, 18 km (11 miles) northwest of Nice.

The famed medieval village of St-Paul-de-Vence can be seen from the coast, standing out like its companion, Vence, against the skyline. Basically a city-state in the Middle Ages, it controlled its own political destiny for centuries. But by the early 20th century St-Paul had faded to oblivion, overshadowed by the growth of Vence and Cagnes—until it was rediscovered in the 1920s when a few penniless artists began paying for their drinks at the local auberge with paintings. Those artists turned out to be Signac, Modigliani, and Bonnard, who met at La Colombe d'Or, now a sumptuous inn, where the walls remain covered with their ink sketches and daubs. Today, art of a sort continues to flourish in local tourist traps. The most commercially developed of Provence's hilltop villages, St-Paul is nonetheless a magical place when the crowds thin. Artists are still lured by its light, its pure air, its wraparound views, and its honey-color stone walls, soothingly cool on a hot afternoon. Film stars still love its lazy yet genteel ways, and they might be spotted lingering on the garden-bower terrace of the Colombe d'Or or playing a game of pétanque with the natives under shady plane trees. To enjoy the timeless aura of St-Paul, arrive early in the day (cars and tour buses can clog the main D36 departmental road by noon) or plan on staying the night. Either way, consider dining beneath the Picassos at the Colombe d'Or (reserve in advance), even if the menu prices seem almost as fabulous as the collection.

GETTING HERE

If you're coming by bus from Nice, take the No. 400 (1 hr, €1.50). If you're driving, exit the highway at Cagnes-sur-Mer and look for signs on the RD 436 to La Colle sur Loup/Vence. (GPS users should type in "St Paul" without "de Vence," and then the street name.)

VISITOR INFORMATION

St-Paul-de-Vence Tourist Office. ✉ *2 rue Grande, St-Paul-de-Vence* ☎ *04–93–32–86–95* 🌐 *www.saint-pauldevence.com.*

EXPLORING

Fondation Maeght. Many people come to St-Paul just to visit the Fondation Maeght, founded in 1964 by art dealer Aimé Maeght. High above the medieval town, the small modern art museum attracts 200,000 visitors a year. It's an extraordinary marriage of the arc-and-plane architecture of Josep Sert; the looming sculptures of Miró, Moore, and Giacometti; the mural mosaics of Chagall; and the humbling hilltop setting, complete with pines, vines, and flowing planes of water. On display is an intriguing and ever-varying parade—one of the most important in Europe—of works by modern masters, including Chagall's wise and funny late-life masterpiece *La Vie* (Life). On the extensive grounds, fountains and impressive vistas help to beguile even those who aren't into modern art. Café F, should you need time to reflect, is open year-round. For a guided visit in English, contact the tourist office (€7 plus admission). ✉ *623 Chemin des Gardettes, St-Paul-de-Vence* ☎ *04–93–32–81–63* 🌐 *www.fondation-maeght.com* 🎟 *€15* ⏲ *July–Sept., daily 10–7; Oct.–June, daily 10–6.*

WHERE TO STAY

$
B&B/INN

Hostellerie les Remparts. With original stone walls, coved ceilings, and a perfect location in the center of the Vieille Ville, this small medieval hotel is an uncut gem, even if it's in need of a little polishing. **Pros:** clean; loaded with charm; affordable (most expensive room is €130, breakfast included). **Cons:** must book at least two months in advance for summer stays; village shuts down at night. $ *Rooms from: €105* ✉ *72 rue Grande, St-Paul-de-Vence* ☎ *04–93–24–10–47* 🌐 *www.hostellerielesremparts.com* *9 rooms* 🍴 *Breakfast.*

$$$$
B&B/INN
Fodor's Choice ★

La Colombe d'Or. Often called the most beautiful inn in France, "the golden dove" occupies a rose-stone Renaissance mansion just outside the walls of St-Paul and is so perfect overall that some contend you haven't really been to the French Riviera until you've stayed or dined here. **Pros:** you can have an aperitif under a real Picasso or wander in the garden, glass of wine in hand, and stare at a real Rodin. **Cons:** some rooms in the adjoining villa have blocked views; menu often outshone by the art; service not always a work of art. $ *Rooms from: €310* ✉ *Pl. Général-de-Gaulle, St-Paul-de-Vence* ☎ *04–93–32–80–02* 🌐 *www.la-colombe-dor.com* ⏲ *Closed Nov.–Christmas* *13 rooms, 12 suites* 🍴 *Breakfast.*

HAUT-DE-CAGNES

6 km (4 miles) south of St-Paul-de-Vence, 21 km (13 miles) northeast of Cannes, 10 km (6 miles) north of Antibes, 14 km (9 miles) west of Nice.

From the N7 you might think about skipping **Cagnes-sur-Mer**, with its congested sprawl of freeway overpasses and beachfront pizzerias—think again. Following the brown signs inland touting "Bourg Médiéval," you'll find one of the Riviera's most beautiful *villages perchés* (perched villages): Haut-de-Cagnes. Alice, of Wonderland fame, would adore this steeply cobbled Old Town, honeycombed as it is with tiny piazzas, winding streets that abruptly morph into stairways, and return-to-your-starting-point-twice alleys that pass under vaulted arches draped with bougainvillea. Many of the pretty residences are dollhouse size (especially the hobbit houses on Rue Passebon), and most date from the 14th and 15th centuries. There's nary a shop, so the commercial horrors of Mougins or St-Paul-de-Vence are left far behind. It's little wonder the rich and literate—Soutine, Modigliani, and Simone de Beauvoir, among them—have long kept Haut-de-Cagnes a secret hideaway. Or almost: enough cars now arrive that a garage (Parking du Planastel) has been excavated out of the hillside.

GETTING HERE

Frequent daily trains from Nice and Cannes stop at Cagnes-sur-Mer (get off at Cros-de-Cagnes if you're heading to the beach); from Cagnes-sur-Mer you can catch a free shuttle to Haut-de-Cagnes. Lignes d'Azur's bus No. 200 (€1.50) also stops in Cagnes-sur Mer.

VISITOR INFORMATION

Cagnes-sur-Mer Tourist Office. ✉ *6 bd. Maréchal Juin, Cagnes-sur-Mer* ☎ *04–93–20–61–64* 🌐 *www.cagnes-tourisme.com.*

EXPLORING

■ TIP→ The Côte d'Azur Card covers 100-plus activities and sites from St-Raphaël to Menton, including the Château-Museé Grimaldi. Valid for three or six consecutive days (€39 or €54), they're available from tourist offices along the Riviera. See www.cotedazurcard.com.

Château-Museé Grimaldi. Crowning Haut-de-Cagnes is the fat, crenellated Château-Museé. Built in 1310 by the Grimaldis and reinforced over the centuries, this imposing fortress lords over the coastline, banners flying from its square watchtower. You are welcomed inside by a grand balustraded stairway and triangular Renaissance courtyard with a triple row of classical arcades infinitely more graceful than the exterior. Filling nearly the entire courtyard is a mammoth, 200-year-old pepper tree—a spectacular sight. Beyond lie vaulted medieval chambers, a vast Renaissance fireplace, and a splendid 17th-century trompe-l'oeil fresco of the fall of Phaëthon from his sun chariot. The château also contains three highly specialized museums: the **Musée de l'Olivier** (Olive Tree Museum), an introduction to the history and cultivation of this Provençal mainstay; the obscure and eccentric **Collection Suzy-Solidor,** a group of portraits of the cabaret chanteuse painted by her artist friends, including Cocteau and Dufy; and the **Musée d'Art Moderne Méditerranéen** (Mediterranean Museum of Modern Art), which contains paintings by some of the 20th-century devotees of the Côte d'Azur, including Chagall, Cocteau, and Dufy. If you've climbed this far, continue to the **tower** and look over the coastline views in the same way that the guards once watched for Saracens. ✉ *Pl. du Château, Haut de Cagnes, Cagnes-sur-Mer* ☎ *04–92–02–47–30* 🎫 *€4; €8 with Renoir Museum* ⏲ *Oct.–Mar., Wed.–Mon. 10–noon and 2–5; Apr. and May, Wed.–Mon. 10–noon and 2–6; June–Sept., daily 10–1 and 2–6.*

Musée Renoir. After staying up and down the coast, Auguste Renoir (1841–1919) settled into a house in Les Collettes, just east of the Vieille Ville, which is now the Musée Renoir. He passed the last 12 years of his life here, painting the landscape around him, working in bronze, and rolling his wheelchair through the luxuriant garden tiered with roses, citrus groves, and spectacular olive trees. You can view this sweet and melancholic villa as it has been preserved by Renoir's children, and admire 11 of his last paintings. In 2013, after an 18-month renovation, the museum opened the kitchen and rooms by the garden, which include a set of 17 plaster sculptures donated by Renoir and Guion families, as well as two additional original paintings. Although up a steep hill, Les Collettes is walkable from Place du Général-du-Gaulle in central Cagnes-Ville. ✉ *Chemin des Collettes, Cagnes-sur-Mer* ☎ *04–93–20–61–07* 🎫 *€6; €8 joint ticket with Château-Musée Grimaldi* ⏲ *Oct.–Mar., Wed.–Mon. 10–noon and 2–5; Apr. and May, Wed.–Mon. 10–noon and 2–6; June–Sept., daily 10–1 and 2–6.*

WHERE TO STAY

$$$$ HOTEL Fodor's Choice ★ **Château Le Cagnard.** There is no better way to experience Old Haut-de-Cagnes's grand castle views than to stay in an acclaimed 13th-century manor that is perched on the ramparts of the Grimaldi fortress. **Pros:** free shuttle bus to Cagnes-sur-Mer; service is friendly and prompt; romantic. **Cons:** there's not tons to do in village; better suited if you have a car. $ *Rooms from: €230* ✉ *54 rue Sous Barri, Cagnes-sur-Mer* ☎ *04–93–20–73–21* 🌐 *www.lecagnard.com* ⏲ *Closed Nov.–mid-Dec.* *12 rooms, 14 suites* 🍽 *No meals.*

NICE

15 km (9 miles) northwest of Antibes, 23 km (14 miles) southwest of Monaco.

Some people think of France's fifth-largest city as a distended urban tangle that's best avoided—if you are one of them, you'll want to reconsider. Nice, in fact, strikes an engaging balance between historic Provençal grace, port-town exotica, urban energy, and high culture. You could easily spend your entire vacation here, attuned to Nice's quirks, its rhythms, its very multicultural population, and its Mediterranean tides. The high point of the year falls in mid-February, when the city hosts one of the world's most spectacular Carnaval celebrations (🌐 *www.nicecarnaval.com*). But at any time of year you can appreciate the 10-km-long (6-mile-long) waterfront, paralleled by the fabled promenade des Anglais and lined by gorgeous grand hotels.

Back in the 4th century BC, Greeks founded a market-port here and named it Nikaia. Celts and Romans followed—as did Saracen invaders; by the Middle Ages, however, Nice had developed into an important port and was ready to flex its muscles. In 1388, under Louis d'Anjou, Nice, along with the hill towns behind, effectively seceded from the county of Provence and allied itself with Savoie as the Comté de Nice (Nice County). Thus began a relationship that lasted some 500 years, adding a rich Italian flavor to the city's culture, architecture, and dialect.

Nice, of course, has continued to evolve. In the 19th century it emerged as a tourist destination when first the English, and then the Russian nobility discovered its extraordinary climate and superb waterfront position. Now it's being transformed into the "the Green City of the Mediterranean." For proof, witness the Promenade de Paillon: a new 30-acre park in the middle of town. The redevelopment of Nice's port is another enhancement, making it easier for amblers who want to take in the area's Genoese architecture or peruse the antiques at the Puces de Nice along Quai Papacino.

GETTING HERE AND AROUND

TGV trains can link Paris to Nice in 5½ hours. Air travelers can reach town from the airport using Bus No. 98 or No. 99 (€6). The No. 98 stops along the promenade and at the port; get off at the J.C. Bermond stop for connections to buses up and down the Riviera. The No. 99 turns off the promenade just before the Hôtel Negresco and goes to the main train station; from there you can access all major coastal locales by rail. If you're using Nice as a base for exploring by car, consider renting one through Greenrent (☏ *09–83–80–98–16* 🌐 *www.greenrent.fr*), at the corner of Rue de France and Rue Meyerbeer: a first in France, it specializes in electric or hybrid vehicles. Within Nice, the modern tramway (☏ *08–10–06–10–06* 🌐 *tramway.nice.fr*) is a boon to aching feet; tickets are €1.50 per or €5 for a 24-hour pass. Alternately, you can rent a Vélo Bleu bike (☏ *04–93–72–06–06* 🌐 *www.velobleu.org*) at any of 90 stations for €1 a day or €5 a week; sign up online in advance (you'll need your mobile phone with you to activate once in Nice) or use your credit card at the city's main docking stations.

VISITOR INFORMATION

Nice Tourist Office. ✉ *5 promenade des Anglais, Nice* ☏ *08–92–70–74–07* 🌐 *www.nicetourism.com.*

EXPLORING

VIEUX NICE

Framed by the "château"—really a rocky promontory—and Cours Saleya, Nice's Vieille Ville is the city's strongest drawing point and the best place to capture historic atmosphere. Its main core leading to the famous market has been converted into a very attractive pedestrian zone, while the grid of narrow streets, rimmed by houses five and six stories high with bright splashes of laundry fluttering overhead and jewel-box Baroque churches on every other corner, creates a magic that seems utterly removed from the French Riviera fast lane.

TOP ATTRACTIONS

Chapelle de la Miséricorde. A superbly balanced *pièce-montée* (wedding cake) of half-domes and cupolas, this chapel is decorated within an inch of its life with frescoes, faux marble, gilt, and crystal chandeliers. A magnificent altarpiece by Renaissance painter Ludivico Brea crowns the ensemble. ✉ *7 cours Saleya, Vieux Nice, Nice* ⏲ *Tues. 2:30–5:30.*

Cours Saleya. This long pedestrian thoroughfare—half street, half square—is the nerve center of Old Nice, the heart of the Vieille Ville, and the stage-set for the daily dramas of marketplace and café life. Framed with 18th-century houses and shaded by plane trees, the narrow square bursts into a fireworks-show of color Tuesday through Sunday until 1 pm, when flower-market vendors roll armloads of mimosas, roses, and orange blossoms into *cornets* (paper cones) and thrust them into the arms of shoppers, who then awkwardly continue forward to discover a mix of local farmers and stallholders selling produce (try the fresh figs), spices, olives, and little gift soaps. Cafés and restaurants, all more or less touristy (don't expect friendly service) fill outdoor tables with onlookers who bask in the sun. At the far east end, antiques and *brocantes* (collectibles) draw avid junk-hounds every Monday morning. At this end you can also find Place Charles Félix. From 1921 to 1938, Matisse lived in the imposing yellow stone building at Number 1, and you don't really need to visit the local museum that bears his name to understand this great artist: simply stand in the doorway of his former home and study Place de l'Ancien Senat 10 feet away—the scene is a classic Matisse. ✉ *Cours Saleya, Vieux Nice, Nice.*

Palais Lascaris. The aristocratic Lascaris Palace was built in 1648 for Jean-Baptiste Lascaris-Vintimille, *marechal* to the duke of Savoy. The magnificent vaulted staircase, with its massive stone balustrade and niches filled with classical gods, is surpassed in grandeur only by the Flemish tapestries (after Rubens) and the extraordinary trompe-l'oeil fresco depicting the fall of Phaëthon. With a little luck, you'll be in time for one of the many classical concerts performed here. ✉ *15 rue Droite, Vieux Nice, Nice* ☎ *04–93–62–72–40* 🌐 *www.palais-lascaris-nice.org* 🎟 *€10* ⏲ *Wed.–Mon. 10–6.*

WORTH NOTING

Cathédrale Ste-Réparate. An ensemble of columns, cupolas, and symmetrical ornaments dominates the Vieille Ville, flanked by an 18th-century bell tower and glossy ceramic-tile dome. The cathedral's interior, restored to a bright palette of ocher, golds, and rusts, has elaborate plasterwork and decorative frescoes on every surface. ✉ *3 pl. Rossetti, Vieux Nice, Nice* 🌐 *cathedrale-nice.com* ⏲ *Weekdays 9–noon and 2–6, Sat. 9–noon and 2–7:30, Sun. 9–1 and 3–6.*

Chapelle Sainte-Rita (*Église de l'Annonciation*). This 17th-century Carmelite chapel, officially known as the Église de l'Annonciation, is a classic example of pure Niçoise Baroque, from its sculpted door to its extravagant marble work and the florid symmetry of its arches and cupolas. ✉ *1 rue de la Poissonerie, Vieux Nice, Nice* 🌐 *www.sainte-rita.net* ⏲ *Daily 9–noon and 2:30–6.*

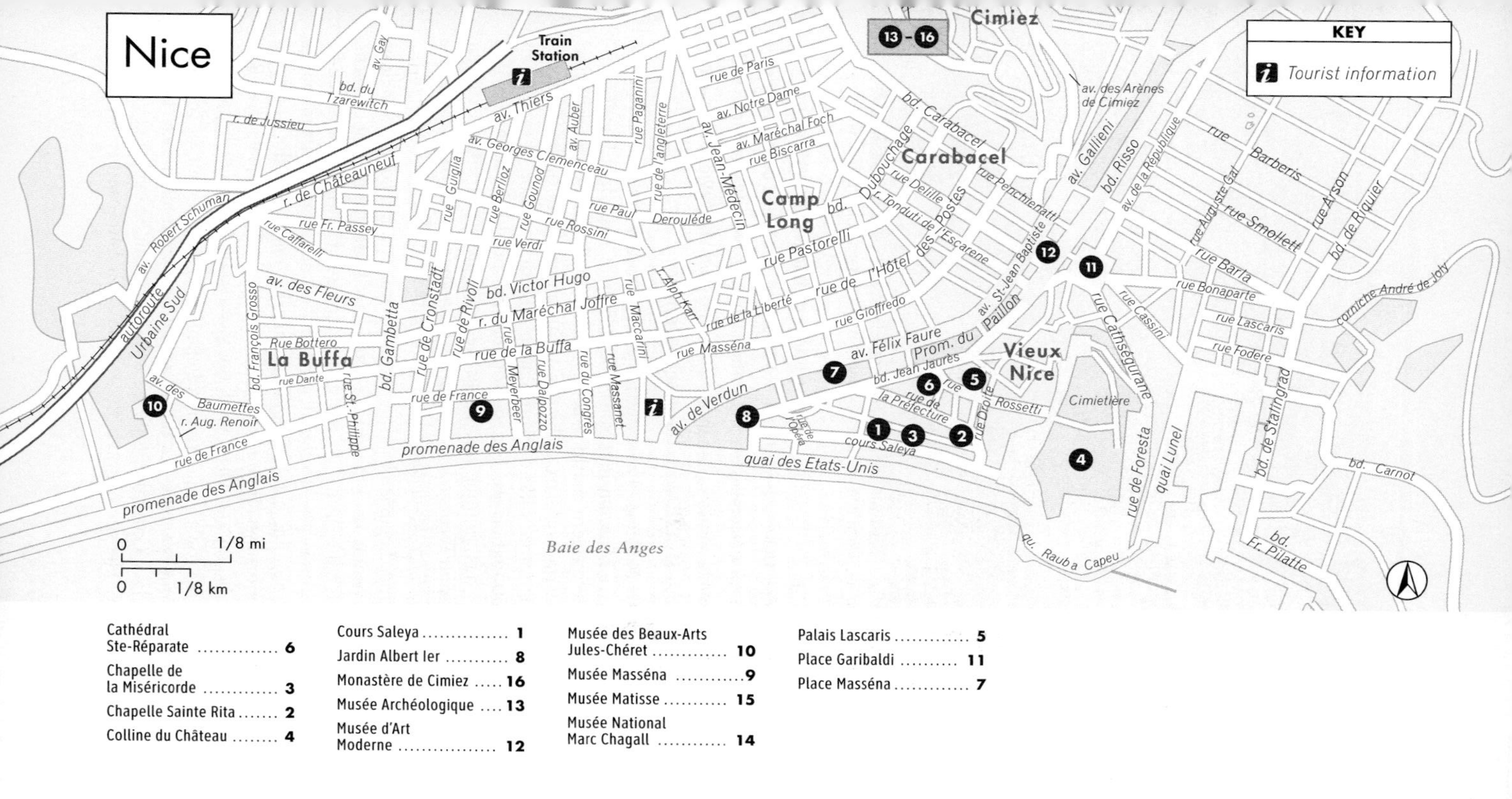

Nice
KEY
Tourist information
Train Station
Cimiez
13 - 16
Carabacel
Camp Long
Vieux Nice
La Buffa
Baie des Anges
Cimetière
av. Thiers
r. de Châteauneuf
autoroute Urbaine Sud
av. Robert Schuman
bd. du Tzarewitch
r. de Jussieu
av. Gay
rue Fr. Passey
rue Caffarelli
av. des Fleurs
bd. François Grosso
Rue Bottero
rue Dante
av. des Baumettes
r. Aug. Renoir
rue de France
promenade des Anglais
rue St.-Philippe
bd. Gambetta
rue de Cronstadt
rue de Rivoli
bd. Victor Hugo
r. du Maréchal Joffre
rue de la Buffa
rue Meyerbeer
rue Dalpozzo
rue du Congrès
rue Massanet
rue Maccarini
r. Alph.Karr
rue Masséna
av. de Verdun
av. Georges Clemenceau
rue Guiglia
rue Berlioz
rue Gounod
rue Verdi
rue Rossini
rue Paul Deroulède
av. Auber
rue Paganini
rue de l'angleterre
av. Jean-Médecin
rue de Paris
av. Notre Dame
av. Maréchal Foch
rue Biscarra
bd. Carabacel
bd. Dubouchage
rue Delille
r. Tonduti de l'Escarene
rue Pastorelli
rue de l'Hôtel des Postes
rue de la Liberté
rue Gioffredo
av. Félix Faure
Prom. du Paillon
bd. Jean Jaurès
rue de la Préfecture
rue de l'Opéra
cours Saleya
quai des Etats-Unis
rue Droite
rue Rossetti
rue Penchienatti
av. St-Jean Baptiste
av. Gallieni
bd. Risso
av. des Arènes de Cimiez
av. de la République
rue Barberis
rue Auguste Gal
rue Smollett
rue Barla
rue Arson
bd. de Riquier
rue Bonaparte
rue Cassini
rue Cathséguranе
rue Lascaris
rue Fodere
corniche André de Joly
bd. de Stalingrad
rue de Foresta
quai Lunel
qu. Rauba Capeu
bd. Carnot
bd. Fr. Pilatte
0 1/8 mi
0 1/8 km
Cathédral Ste-Réparate 6
Chapelle de la Miséricorde 3
Chapelle Sainte Rita 2
Colline du Château 4
Cours Saleya 1
Jardin Albert Ier 8
Monastère de Cimiez 16
Musée Archéologique 13
Musée d'Art Moderne 12
Musée des Beaux-Arts Jules-Chéret 10
Musée Masséna 9
Musée Matisse 15
Musée National Marc Chagall 14
Palais Lascaris 5
Place Garibaldi 11
Place Masséna 7

Our vote for France's most beautiful *village perché*, Haut-de-Cagnes is an enchanting place filled with tiny piazzas, winding alleys, and staircase streets.

NEED A BREAK?

Les Causeries de Blandine. Nothing brings on hunger like walking on cobblestones. Down the road from Ste-Réparate, you'll find Les Causeries de Blandine, a welcoming tea and coffee shop with homemade quiche and tarts to provide a little sustenance. ✉ ***8 rue du Pont Vieux, Vieux Nice, Nice*** ☎ ***04–93–80–41–12*** 🌐 ***www.lescauseriesdeblandine.com.***

Musée d'Art Moderne. The assertive contemporary architecture of the Modern Art Museum makes a bold statement regarding Nice's presence in the modern world. The collection inside focuses intently and thoroughly on works from the late 1950s onward, but pride of place is given to sculptor Nikki de Saint Phalle's recent donation of more than 170 exceptional pieces. The rooftop terrace, sprinkled with minimalist sculptures, has stunning views over the city. Guided tours (€6) are given by reservation Wednesday at 3 pm. ✉ *Promenade des Arts, Nice* ☎ *04–97–13–42–01* 🌐 *www.mamac-nice.org* 🎫 *€10* 🕒 *Tues.–Sun. 10–6.*

Place Garibaldi. Encircled by grand vaulted arcades stuccoed in rich yellow, the broad pentagon of this square could have been airlifted out of Turin. In the center, the shrine-like fountain sculpture of Garibaldi seems to be surveying you as you stroll under the very attractive arcades and lounge in the surrounding cafés. An antiques market takes over the square on Saturday mornings. If you hear jackhammers, look no further than Rue Catherine-Séguarane where work on Nice's second tram line has started.

If you're up for an underground excursion, take a tour of **La crypte archéologique de Nice**—a half-acre underground chamber, located beneath Place Garibaldi. Opened in 2012, it can be explored via steel walkways. The site contains the remains of a 14th-century tower and aqueduct that were hidden underground for hundreds of years. When Nice's tram system was being built at the beginning of this century, excavators discovered medieval structures that had been razed by Louis XIV in 1706 and promptly forgotten. The Centre du Patrimoine (Heritage Center) offers 55-minute tours (€5), which must be booked at 1 place Pierre Gautier (*04–92–00–41–90*). Place Jacques Toja, the meeting point, is just before Place Garibaldi. Bring "sensible shoes," as heels can't be worn in the crypt. Tours run Tuesday–Sunday at 2, 3, and 4. ✉ *Pl. Garibaldi, Vieux Nice, Nice.*

ALONG THE PROMENADE DES ANGLAIS

Nice takes on a completely different character west of Cours Saleya, with broad city blocks, vast neoclassical hotels and apartment houses, and a series of inviting parks dense with palm trees, greenery, and splashing fountains. From the Jardin Albert Ier the famous promenade des Anglais, symbol of Nice, stretches the length of the city's waterfront. The original promenade was the brainchild of Lewis Way, an English minister in the then-growing community of British refugees drawn to Nice's climate. Nowadays it's a wide multilane boulevard thick with traffic—in fact, it's the last gasp of the N98 coastal highway. Beside it runs its charming parallel, a wide, sun-washed pedestrian walkway with intermittent steps leading down to the smooth-rock beach. A daily parade of *promeneurs,* rollerbladers, joggers, and sun baskers traverse it, looking out over the hypnotic blue expanse of the sea. Take note of the green-painted bike path that shares parts of the promenade. The sea can be mesmerizing, so be sure not to veer over into the path of oncoming bell-ringing cyclists. Only in the wee hours is it possible to enjoy the waterfront stroll as the cream of Nice's international society once did, when there were nothing more than hoofbeats to compete with the roar of the waves.

Colline du Château (*Château Hill*). Although nothing remains of the once-massive medieval stronghold but a few ruins left after its 1706 dismantling, the name "château" still applies to this high plateaulike park, from which you can take in extraordinary views of the Baie des Anges, the length of promenade des Anglais, and the red-ocher roofs of the Old Town. Children can let off steam at the playground, while you enjoy a picnic with panoramic views and a bit of shade. You can take the 213 steps up to it, or the free elevator next to the Hotel Suisse; alternatively, ascend the hill slower from the port side, near Place Garibaldi, which is a more gentle climb. ✉ *At east end of promenade des Anglais, Nice* ⏲ *Apr., May, and Sept., daily 8–7; Jun.–Aug., daily 8–8; Oct.–Mar., daily 8–6.*

Jardin Albert Ier (*Albert I Garden*). Along promenade des Anglais, this luxurious garden stands over the delta of the River Paillon, underground since 1882. Every kind of flower and palm tree grows here, thrown into exotic relief by night illumination. Home base for many city festivals with its Théâtre de Verdure and also Ciné Prom in the summer (screenings of box office hits at 9:30 pm), the garden is the starting point for Nice's promenade du Paillon. ✉ *2–16 av. de Verdun, Nice* 🎫 *Free* ⏲ *24 hrs daily.*

Like the Rio of France, Nice is lined with a gigantic crescent beach whose prime spot, promenade des Anglais, is home to many palace-hotels.

Musée des Beaux-Arts (*Jules-Chéret Fine Arts Museum*). Originally built for a member of Nice's Old Russian community, the Princess Kotschoubey, this Italianate mansion is a Belle Époque wedding cake, replete with one of the grandest staircases on the coast. After the *richissime* American James Thompson took over and the last glittering ball was held here, the villa was bought by the municipality as a museum in the 1920s. Unfortunately, much of the period decor was sold; but in its place are paintings by Degas, Boudin, Monet, Sisley, Dufy, and Jules Chéret, whose posters of winking *damselles* distill all the *joie* of the Belle Époque. From the Hôtel Negresco area the museum is about a 15-minute walk up a gentle hill. ✉ *33 av. des Baumettes, Centre Ville, Nice* ☎ *04–92–15–28–28* 🌐 *www.musee-beaux-arts-nice.org* 🎟 *€10* 🕑 *Tues.–Sun. 10–6.*

Musée Masséna (*Masséna Palace*). This spectacular Belle Époque villa houses the **Musée d'Art et d'Histoire** (Museum of Art and History), where familiar paintings from French, Italian, and Dutch masters line the walls. A visit to the palace gardens set with towering palm trees, a marble bust of the handsome General Masséna, and backdropped by the ornate trim of the Hôtel Negresco, is a delight; this is one of Nice's most imposing oases. ✉ *Entrance at, 65 rue de France, Centre Ville, Nice* ☎ *04–93–91–19–10* 🎟 *€10* 🕑 *Wed.–Mon. 10–6.*

Place Masséna. As Cours Saleya is the heart of the Vieille Ville, so this impressive and broad square is the heart of the entire city. It's framed by early 17th-century, Italian-style arcaded buildings, their facades stuccoed in rich red ocher. On the west flank sits the city's Belle Époque icon, the Hôtel Negresco. This enticing space hosts an event at least once a month, from Carnaval to the Christmas market; promenade du Paillon runs through it. ✉ *Pl. Masséna, Centre Ville, Nice.*

Promenade de Paillon. Running parallel behind the Old Town, from the Museum of Modern Art to the Théâtre de Verdure, is Nice's emerald jewel—the Promenade de Paillon, a €40-million, 30-acre park. Inaugurated in 2013, it serves as a playground for kids, a refuge for adults (who take advantage of the free Wi-Fi), and a venue for many of the city's one-off events, like April Fool's Day (in French, *Poisson d'Avril*, or fish day). No matter when you arrive, there's plenty to photograph here. At the east end of the Prom, you'll find Nice's own Statue of Liberty (look carefully, she's only 4½-feet tall!). Towards the west, construction of the city's controversial second tram line (T2) is underway, parts of which run parallel to the sea; disruptions and partial closures of the Prom are inevitable until 2017. ✉ *Promenade de Paillon, Nice* ⏲ *Apr.–Sept., daily 7 am–11 pm; Oct.–Mar., daily 7 am–9 pm.*

CIMIEZ

Once the site of the powerful Roman settlement Cemenelum, the hilltop neighborhood of Cimiez—4 km (2½ miles) north of Cours Saleya—is Nice's most luxurious quarter (use Bus No. 15 from Place Masséna or Avenue Jean-Médecin to visit its sights).

Monastère de Cimiez. This fully functioning monastery is worth the pilgrimage. You can find a lovely **garden,** replanted along the lines of the original 16th-century layout; the **Musée Franciscain,** a didactic museum tracing the history of the Franciscan order; and a 15th-century **church** containing three works of remarkable power and elegance by Bréa. ✉ *Pl. du Monastère, Cimiez, Nice* ☎ *04–93–81–00–04* 🎟 *Free* ⏲ *Church Thurs.–Tues. 9–6 and Sun. after 10:30 Mass–6; museum Mon.–Sat. 10–noon and 3–5:30.*

Musée Archéologique (*Archaeology Museum*). This museum, next to the Musée Matisse, has a dense collection of objects extracted from digs around the Roman city of Cemenelum, which flourished from the 1st to the 5th century. Among the fascinating ruins are an amphitheatre, frigidarium, gymnasium, baths, and sewage trenches, some dating back to the 3rd century. **■ TIP→ It's best to avoid midday visits on warm days.** ✉ *160 av. des Arènes-de-Cimiez, Cimiez, Nice* ☎ *04–93–81–59–57* 🌐 *www.musee-archeologique-nice.org* 🎟 *€10* ⏲ *Wed.–Mon. 10–6.*

Fodor's Choice ★ **Musée Matisse.** In the '60s the city of Nice bought this lovely, light-bathed 17th-century villa, surrounded by the ruins of Roman civilization, and restored it to house a large collection of Henri Matisse's works. Matisse settled along Nice's waterfront in 1917, seeking a sun cure after a bout with pneumonia, and remained here until his death in 1954. During his years on the French Riviera, Matisse maintained intense friendships and artistic liaisons with Renoir, who lived in Cagnes, and with Picasso, who lived in Mougins and Antibes. He eventually moved up to the rarefied isolation of Cimiez and took an apartment in the Hôtel Regina (now an apartment building, just across from the museum), where he lived out the rest of his life. Matisse walked often in the parklands around the Roman remains and was buried in an olive grove outside the Cimiez cemetery. The collection of artworks includes several pieces the artist donated to the city before his death; the rest were donated by his family. In every medium and context—paintings, gouache cutouts, engravings, and book illustrations—the collection represents the evolution of his art, from Cézanne-like still lifes to exuberant dancing paper dolls. Even the furniture and accessories speak of Matisse, from the Chinese vases to the bold-printed fabrics with which he surrounded himself. A series of black-and-white photographs captures the artist at work, revealing telling details. ✉ *164 av. des Arènes-de-Cimiez, Cimiez, Nice* ☎ *04–93–81–08–08* 🌐 *www.musee-matisse-nice.org* 🎫 *€10; €16 with guided tour in English* 🕙 *Wed.–Mon. 10–6.*

Musée National Marc Chagall (*Marc Chagall Museum of Biblical Themes*). Inaugurated in 1973, this museum has one of the finest permanent collections of Chagall's late works (1887–1985). Superbly displayed, 17 vast canvases depict biblical themes, each in emphatic, joyous colors. Chamber music and classical concert series also take place here, though admission fees may apply. The No. 15 and 22 buses stop at the museum. ✉ *Av. du Dr-Ménard, Cimiez, Nice* ☎ *04–93–53–87–20* 🌐 *www.musee-chagall.fr* 🎫 *€8; €9.50 with temporary exhibtion* 🕙 *May–Oct., Wed.–Mon. 10–6; Nov.–Apr., Wed.–Mon. 10–5.*

■ TIP→ Nice Greeters are volunteers who passionately share their interests in the form of a free guided tour. You can book an outing with a preferred theme—such as a cycling around the city, shopping, or discovering a neighborhood—online at en.nice-greeters.com.

WHERE TO EAT

$ ITALIAN ✕ **Attimi.** Specializing in salads, pizzas, and pastas—prepared on the spot from local produce—this place offers a refreshing, light alternative to all those heavy French dishes. But Attimi is as hot as the lasagna Bolognese it serves, so you'll need to reserve or eat early. A seat on the terrace next the fountain at the end of Place Masséna lets you dine with a side order of people-watching. [$] *Average main: €16* ✉ *10 pl. Masséna, Nice* ☎ *04–93–62–00–22* 🌐 *www.attimi.fr* *Reservations essential.*

$ FRENCH ✕ **Chez René Socca.** This back-alley landmark is the most popular dive in town for *socca,* the chickpea-pancake snack food unique to Nice. Rustic olive-wood tables line the street, and curt waiters splash down your drink order. Then you get in line, choose your plate, and carry it steaming to the table yourself. It's off Place Garibaldi on the edge of the Vieille Ville, across from the old bus station. If you're looking for a veritible Niçois memory, this is it. [$] *Average main: €4* ✉ *2 rue Miralheti, Vieux Nice, Nice* ☎ *04–93–92–05–73* 💳 *No credit cards* 🕙 *Closed Mon. and Jan.*

$ FRENCH ✕ **Co-t-Café.** This brightly colored and vibrant local café, one block from the promenade and Hôtel Negresco, has the best coffee in Nice. Expect creamy lattés, iced coffees, cappuccinos, plus teas and smoothies, in all sizes, to stay or to go. Sandwiches, salads, and wraps—superbly priced and made fresh each morning—are perfect for the beach (look for Winestar, wine in a can, also ideal for a beach picnic). [$] *Average main: €8* ✉ *11 bis rue Meyerbeer, New Town, Nice* ☎ *04–93–16–09–84* 🌐 *coffeeshop.co-t-cafe.com* 🕙 *Closed Dec.–Feb.*

$$$$ MODERN FRENCH ✕ **Flaveur.** Run by a young threesome (two chefs and a maître d') with a haute cuisine background, this modern Michelin-star bistro is perpetually packed—which means you should book at least a week ahead for dinner and several days ahead for lunch. The key to the trio's success is the heart that goes into their cooking: the limited menu changes often, and the chefs like to experiment with historical recipes such as *petits farcis* (stuffed vegetables) from a 19th-century cookbook. Their hand-cut steak tartare with chickpea fries and thick gazpacho has become a classic. You can sample the *plat du moment* at lunch for €34; at dinner, you'll pay €60 to €95 for a three-, five- or six-course menu. *Average main: €60 ✉ 25 rue Gubernatis, New Town, Nice ☎ 04–93–62–53–95 🌐 www.flaveur.net ⏲ Closed Sun. and Mon., and last 2 wks in Aug. No lunch Sat. ✍ Reservations essential.*

$$$ FRENCH ✕ **La Merenda.** The back-to-bistro boom climaxed here when Dominique Le Stanc retired his crown at the Negresco to take over this tiny, unpretentious landmark of Provençal cuisine. Now he works in the miniature open kitchen creating ultimate versions of stuffed sardines, tagliatelle with pistou, slow-simmered daubes (beef stews), and the quintessential stockfish (the local lutefisk), while his wife whisks the dishes into the dining room. There are two sittings at both lunch and dinner. You'll have to stop by in person to reserve entry to the inner sanctum as there's no phone—note that there are no credit cards accepted either. *Average main: €26 ✉ 4 rue Raoul Bosio, Vieux Nice, Nice ☎ No credit cards ⏲ Closed weekends, 1st 2 wks in Aug., and holidays.*

$$ FRENCH ✕ **La Part des Anges.** This wineshop with a few tables and chairs at the back is really about *vins naturels*—unfiltered, unsulfured, hand-harvested wines from small producers—but the often-simple food it serves also happens to be excellent. Whether you choose a charcuterie or cheese plate or one of the handful of hot dishes (like spaghetti with razor clams or octopus cooked in red wine), you can expect it to be generous and fresh. No corkage fee is charged for wines off the shelf, a rarity for a wine bar. Reservations are best for Friday and Saturday nights. It's worth noting that bilingual owner Olivier has opened a second wine bistro, La Mise en Verre, at 17 rue Pastorelli. *Average main: €18 ✉ 17 rue Gubernatis, New Town, Nice ☎ 04–93–62–69–80 🌐 www.la-part-des-anges-nice.fr ⏲ Closed Sun.*

$$ BISTRO ✕ **Le Bistrot d'Antoine.** You won't find any "concept" cooking here, just pure French bistro fare at its finest—beef salad with anchovy dressing, butter risotto with truffles, sliced leg of lamb, and traditional pork casserole. Leave room for the day's dessert, such as the wonderfully warm peach-and-frangipane tart. The prices here are as appealing as the menu. If you can't score a reservation, try one of Chef Antoine Crespo's other eateries: the Comptoir du Marché (at 8 rue du Marché) has affordable market-fresh cuisine, and the Bar des Oiseaux (at 5 rue Saint-Vincent) is a charming pasta place with a €20 set menu. *Average main: €18 ✉ 27 rue de la Préfecture, Vieux Nice, Nice ☎ 04–93–85–29–57 ⏲ Closed Sun., Mon., 3 wks in Aug., 10 days at Christmas, and at Easter ✍ Reservations essential.*

$$$$ BISTRO ✕ **Le Bistrot Gourmand.** Chef David Vaqué received the Maître Cuisinier title in 2013 for his preservation of French cuisine at Le Bistrot

Gourmand, a local favorite since it opened in 2011. The setting is convenient—just steps away from the Hotel Beau Rivage and with an outdoor terrace—but the focus in on the food and the wine. Menu options include black risotto, panfried European lobster and Iberian chorizo, and a cappuccino of peppers and ginger, plus a soufflé that may actually leave you *à bout de souffle* (breathless). The sommelier amazingly seems to know your order before you do; a bottle will set you back around €55. Don't expect a warm and cheery interior; while the service is friendly enough, the stark white setting with a few dashes of color is meant to keep your eye on the plate. One can only hope that the prices stay as humble as the staff. *Average main: €35 3 rue Desboutin, Vieux Nice, Nice 04–92–14–55–55 www.lebistrogourmand.fr Closed Sun. and Wed.*

$$$ FRENCH **Luc Salsedo.** Young Luc Salsedo, who trained at the Louis XV in Monaco, has a hit on his hands with this little ocher-wall bistro. His brief dinner menu, which changes completely every 10 days, often involves modern twists on traditional Niçois dishes, such as socca (a chickpea flour pancake, which he wraps around stir-fried spring vegetables) or *pain perdu aux pommes* (French toast with apples and cinnamon served with salted caramel ice cream). Servings are generous—expect a big appetizer plate and *mignardises* in addition to the set menu's three copious courses (€45)—and the dining room staff, led by Luc's wife Christine, is stellar. The word is out about this place, so reservations are recommended. *Average main: €26 14 rue Maccarani, Nice 04–93–82–24–12 www.restaurant-salsedo.com Closed Wed. and 2 wks late Jan. No lunch.*

WHERE TO STAY

$ HOTEL **Hotel Felix Beach.** This practical hotel sits a block from the beach on popular Rue Masséna—and, if you choose one of the four rooms that features a tiny balcony, you'll have a ringside seat over the pedestrian thoroughfare. **Pros:** prime location makes perfect touring sense; owners are so nice that you feel right at home. **Cons:** rooms can be noisy, especially those facing the street; there's no elevator and rooms are on upper floors. *Rooms from: €98 41 rue Masséna, Place Masséna, Nice 04–93–88–67–73 www.hotel-felix.com No credit cards 14 rooms No meals.*

$$$$ HOTEL Fodor's Choice ★ **Hôtel Negresco.** This white-stucco slice of old-fashioned Riviera extravagance accommodates well-heeled guests in elegant, uniquely decorated rooms replete with swagged drapes and fine antiques (plus a few unfortunate "with-it" touches like those plastic-glitter bathtubs). **Pros:** like staying in a museum; attention and service from the moment you arrive; food at the famed Chantecler is as glorious as the hotel is fascinating. **Cons:** mediocre buffet breakfast is expensive (€30). *Rooms from: €330 37 promenade des Anglais, Nice 04–93–16–64–00 www.hotel-negresco-nice.com 96 rooms, 21 suites No meals.*

$ HOTEL **Nice Garden Hotel.** It's hard to believe that this little gem of a hotel, with its own courtyard garden, is smack in the middle of Nice, next to the pedestrian shopping streets and a five-minute walk from the Old Town. **Pros:** breakfast (extra) with homemade jam in the garden; extremely helpful owner; check-in from 2 to 9 pm. **Cons:** parking is down the street at public garage. *Rooms from: €100 ✉ 11 rue du Congrès, New Town, Nice ☎ 04–93–87–35–62 🌐 www.nicegardenhotel.com 9 rooms No meals.*

$ HOTEL **Solara.** One block from the beach and two from Place Masséna, this tiny budget hotel perches on the fourth and fifth floors, high above the main shopping street. **Pros:** fabulous location, near the beach; top-floor terraces overlooking pedestrian street; soundproof windows. **Cons:** rooms on the smallish size, but worth it for the rates. *Rooms from: €85 ✉ 7 rue de France, New Town, Nice ☎ 04–93–88–09–96 🌐 www.hotelsolara.com 14 rooms No meals.*

$$ HOTEL **Windsor.** This is a memorably eccentric hotel—most of its white-on-white rooms either have frescoes of mythological themes or are works of artists' whimsy—but the real draw at this otherworldly place is its astonishing city-center garden, a tropical oasis of lemon, magnolia, and palm trees, only outdone by the excellent service. **Pros:** private pool and garden in heart of city; enthusiastic welcome; you can print your boarding pass for free in the lobby. **Cons:** artist-inspired decor isn't for everyone (look online before booking!); street rooms can be noisy; Ultra-Violet elevator is cool the first time but annoying by the end of the week. *Rooms from: €145 ✉ 11 rue Dalpozzo, Nice ☎ 04–93–88–59–35 🌐 www.hotelwindsornice.com 57 rooms Some meals.*

NIGHTLIFE AND PERFORMING ARTS

Acropolis. Classical music, ballet performances, and traditional French pop concerts take place at Nice's convention center, the Acropolis. *✉ Palais des Congrès, Esplanade John F. Kennedy, Nice ☎ 04–93–92–83–00 🌐 www.nice-acropolis.com.*

Bar Le Relais. If you're all dressed up and have just won big, invest in a drink in the intimate walnut-and-velour Bar Le Relais in the iconic Hôtel Negresco. It's worth the price just to get a peek at the washrooms (just don't trip over the owner's lounging cat Carmen). *✉ 37 promenade des Anglais, Promenade Nice, Nice ☎ 04–93–16–64–00 🌐 www.hotel-negresco-nice.com.*

Casino du Palais de la Méditerranée. In the 1920s, the swanky Palais de la Méditerranée drew performers like Charlie Chaplin and Edith Piaf; however, the establishment lost its glory and was demolished in 1990, save for the facade you see today. Reopened with hotel service in 2004, the contemporary version has 200 slot machines, plus electric roulette, blackjack, and Texas Hold 'Em Poker tables. It's open weekdays from 10 am to 3 am, until 4 am on weekends; table play starts at 8 pm. *✉ 15 promenade des Anglais, Promenade, Nice ☎ 04–92–14–68–00 show reservations 🌐 www.casinomediterranee.com.*

Glam. The city's most colorful gay club has DJs who compel you to dance to the best mixes around. It's open to all clubbers in the know, with only one criterion: be cool. *✉ 6 rue Eugène Emmanuel, Nice ☎ 06–60–55–26–61 🌐 www.leglam.org.*

High Club. Nice was a sleepy city until High came along (just ask the neighbors). Right across from the sea, its three designated floors should fill up your dance card. Expect to pay a €20 cover and another €120 for a table (four people/one bottle); a VIP magnum will set you back €400. Don't show up unless you're here to be seen. ✉ *45 promenade des Angais, New Town, Nice* ☎ *07–81–88–42–04* 🌐 *www.highclub.fr.*

Nice Jazz Festival. For five days in July, the Nice Jazz Festival draws performers from around the world to Place Masséna and Théâtre de Verdure. Tickets begin around €35 per show and can be purchased online or from FNAC and Carrefour. Enter at Place Masséna. ✉ *Pl. Masséna and Théâtre de Verdure, Espace Jacques Cotta, Nice* ☎ *08–92–68–36–22* 🌐 *www.nicejazzfestival.fr.*

Opéra de Nice. A half block west of Cours Saleya stands a flamboyant Italian-style theater designed by Charles Garnier, architect of the Paris Opéra. It's home today to the Opéra de Nice, with a permanent chorus, orchestra, and ballet corps. The season runs from mid-November to June, and tickets cost anywhere from €8 to €85. ✉ *4 rue St-François-de-Paule, Vieux Nice, Nice* ☎ *04–92–17–40–40* 🌐 *www.opera-nice.org.*

Seven Blue Bar. Don't forget your camera when heading up to this panoramic bar on the seventh floor of the Clarion Grand Aston Hotel. The views of old Nice and the new Promenade du Paillon across to the airport are spectacular, and drink prices are more than reasonable. In the summer, the bar moves to the rooftop, where there's a pool (for guests) and 360-degree views. Note that there are 23 steps from the hotel lobby to the bar's elevator. ✉ *12 av. Felix Faure, Centre Ville, Nice* ☎ *04–93–17–53–00* 🌐 *www.hotel-aston.com.*

SPORTS AND THE OUTDOORS

Nice's beaches extend all along the Baie des Anges. Free public stretches alternate with posh private concessions that have restaurants. You're expected to buy any food or drink from the restaurant that controls the beach.

Beau Rivage. Across from Cours Saleya, Beau Rivage Plage—which claims to be the Riviera's largest private beach—has a split personality. On the Zen side, topless sunseekers can rent a cushy lounge chair with umbrella for €19; on the scene-y Trend side, bathers can enjoy cocktails and tapas. The beach itself is stone, so water shoes are advisable. If there are jellyfish sightings, you'll see a written warning of "méduse" on a beach board; ditto for strong winds. **Amenities:** food and drink; toilets; showers. **Best for:** swimming; sunset; service; scene. ✉ *107 quai des États-Unis, Nice* ☎ *04–92–00–46–80* 🌐 *www.plagenicebeaurivage.com* ⏲ *Closed Nov.–Mar.*

Castel Plage. At the east end of the promenade, near Hotel Suisse, there is both a large public beach and a private one, where the water is calm and clear (you can rent a lounger at the latter for about €18). The public beach is composed of large stones, which are more comfortable to walk on than pebbles. Jellyfish are also less of a problem in this corner than they are a little farther west, and lifeguards at the neighboring beach are on duty mid-June to mid-September. **Amenities:** none. **Best for:** sunrise; sunset; snorkeling; swimming. ✉ *8 quai des États-Unis, Nice.*

Hi Beach. A stone strand packed with rows of loungers (you'll pay €22 a day to rent one with an umbrella), Hi Beach has three different zones: Hi Energy, Hi Relax, and, for the kids, Hi Play. On-site perks include a beach bar and tons of food, Hi Body for those in need of a massage, plus English-language yoga sessions on summer Saturdays from 9 to 11 am (€15); the funkiest of Nice's private beaches also has designs by Philippe Starck protégé Matali Crasset. If there are any water warnings—jellyfish or strong winds—sign boards will keep you informed. **Amenities:** food and drink; showers; toilets. **Best for:** swimming; sunrise; sunset. ✉ *47 promenade des Anglais, Promenade, Nice* ☎ *04–97–14–00–83* 🌐 *www.hi-beach.net.*

SHOPPING

Nice's main shopping street, **Avenue Jean-Médecin,** runs inland from Place Masséna; all needs and most tastes are catered to in its big department stores (Galeries Lafayette, Monoprix, and the split-level Étoile mall). The tramway, launched in late 2007, has made this mini–Champs-Elysées all the more accessible, so expect crowds on Saturday (the majority of shops are still closed on Sunday). Luxury boutiques, such as Emporio Armani, Kenzo, Chanel, and Sonia Rykiel, line Rue du Paradis, while Rue de France and the Old Town have more affordable offerings.

Alziari. Tiny Alziari sells olive oil by the gallon in the famous blue and yellow cans with old-fashioned labels. ✉ *14 rue St-François-de-Paule, Vieux Nice, Nice* 🌐 *www.alziari.com.fr.*

Confiserie Florian du Vieux Nice. Open every day except Christmas, this spot is a good source for crystallized fruit (a Nice specialty). It's located on the west side of the port. ✉ *14 quai Papacino, Vieux Nice, Nice* 🌐 *www.confiserieflorian.com.*

Henri Auer. Open Tuesday through Saturday, the venerable Henri Auer has been selling crystallized fruit since 1820. ✉ *7 rue St-François de Paule, Vieux Nice, Nice* 🌐 *www.maison-auer.com.*

La Promenade des 100 Antiquaires. France's third largest *regroupment* of antiques collectors forms a triangle from Place Garibaldi to the port (Quai Papacino) and along Rue Catherine Ségruane at the bottom of the château. There's a helpful map on the website, which includes side streets like Rue Antoine Gautier and Rue Emmanuel Philibert. Les Puces de Nice has 30 stalls under one roof in Quai Lunel, and Place Garibaldi hosts a morning antiques market on the third Saturday of the month. ✉ *Vieux Nice, Nice* 🌐 *nice-antic.com.*

Mademoiselle. You have to hand it to the French: they even do second-hand fashion right. Steps away from the Hôtel Negresco, Mademoiselle has quickly become a must-stop shop in Nice. Chanel, Dior, Louis Vuitton, Hermès . . . you name it, the gang's all here, at least in vintage terms. You'll find lots of luxury brand clothes, shoes, bags, and belts to rummage through—all of it excellently priced and gorgeously displayed. ✉ *41 rue de France, New Town, Nice.*

Star Dog Boutique. For the jet-set pet, Star Dog Boutique has iPawds (a plush toy with FaceBark, DogTube, and Bark Street Journal apps), Doggle sunglasses, and Oh My Dog! cologne to get Fido's tail wagging. ✉ *40 rue de France, New Town, Nice* ☎ *04–97–03–27–40* 🌐 *jophicotedazur.com.*

THE EASTERN FRENCH RIVIERA

With the mistral-proof Alps and Pre-Alps playing bodyguard against inland winds, this part of the Riviera is the most renowned and glamorous stretch of coastline in Europe. Here, coddled by mild Mediterranean breezes, waterfront resorts—Villefranche and Menton—draw energy from the thriving city of Nice and serenity from jutting tropical peninsulas including Cap Ferrat. Here the corniche highways snake above sparkling waters, their pink-and-white villas turning faces toward the sun. Cliffs bristle with palm trees and parasol pines, and a riot of mimosa, bougainvillea, jasmine, and even cactus blooms in the hothouse climate. Crowded with sunseekers and billionaires, the Riviera still reveals quiet corners with heart-stopping views of sea, sun, and mountains—all within one memorable frame.

The lay of the land east of Nice is nearly vertical, as the coastline is one great cliff, terraced by three parallel highways—the **Basse corniche**, the **Moyenne corniche**, and the **Grande corniche**—that wind along its graduated crests. The lowest (*basse*) is the slowest, following the coast and crawling through the main streets of resort towns—including Beaulieu and Villefranche-sur-Mer. The highest (*grande*) is the fastest, but its panoramic views are blocked by villas, and there are few safe overlooks. The middle (*moyenne*) runs from Nice to Menton and offers views down over the shoreline and villages—plus it passes through a few picturesque towns, most notably Èze.

VILLEFRANCHE-SUR-MER

10 km (6 miles) east of Nice.

The character of Villefranche was subtly shaped by the artists and authors who gathered at the Hôtel Welcome. Among them were Diaghilev and Stravinsky, taking a break from the Ballet Russe in Monaco; Somerset Maugham and Evelyn Waugh; and, above all, Jean Cocteau, who came here to recover from the excesses of Paris life. Luckily, this pretty port retains a restorative vibe—despite being flanked by the big city of Nice and the assertive wealth of Monaco. The streets of the Vieille Ville tilt downhill just as they did in the 13th century; and whether it's just the force of gravity, or the fact that it remains so picturesque, the deep harbor here continues to attract visitors. Set in the caldera of a volcano, it was once filled with yachts belonging to royals and assorted Greek tycoons. Today you're more likely to spot cruise ships, whose passengers take over the town's tiny streets, but genuine fishermen still skim up to its docks in weathered-blue barques. Guided tours of the village (sometimes in English) depart every Friday morning at 10 from the tourist office (€5). Just remember to wear flat shoes—there are lots of cobblestone streets and slope-y climbs.

No wonder Matisse lived on the top floor of the golden yellow building seen here at the end of Cours Saleya—this marketplace is one of the most colorful in France.

GETTING HERE

Villefranche is a major stop on the Marseilles–Ventimiglia coastal rail route, and more than 40 trains daily make the six-minute trip from Nice. Lignes d'Azur buses also connect it with Nice and Monaco (€1.50). If you're driving, be advised that public parking typically costs €1.70 per hour and can be hard to find.

VISITOR INFORMATION

Villefranche-sur-Mer Tourist Office. ✉ *Jardin François Binon, Villefranche-sur-Mer* ☎ *04–93–01–73–68* 🌐 *www.villefranche-sur-mer.com.*

EXPLORING

Chapelle St-Pierre. So enamored was Jean Cocteau of this painterly fishing port that he decorated the 14th-century Chapelle St-Pierre with images from the life of St. Peter and dedicated it to the village's fishermen. ✉ *Quai de l'Amiral Courbet Courbet, Villefranche-sur-Mer* ☎ *04–93–76–90–70* 🎫 *€3* ⏲ *Apr.–Sept., Wed.–Mon. 10–noon and 3–7; Oct.–Mar., Wed.–Mon. 10–noon and 2–6.*

Citadelle St-Elme. Restored to perfect condition, the stalwart 16th-century Citadelle St-Elme anchors the harbor with its broad, sloping stone walls. Beyond its drawbridge lie the city's administrative offices and a group of minor gallery-museums, with a scattering of works by Picasso and Miró. Whether or not you stop into these private collections (all free of charge), you're welcome to stroll around the inner grounds and circle the imposing exterior. ✉ *Harbor, Villefranche-sur-Mer* 🎫 *Free* ⏲ *Museums: June and Sept., Wed.–Sat. 9–noon and 3–6, Sun. 3–6; July and Aug., Tues.–Sat. 10–noon and 3–7, Sun. 3–6; Oct. and Dec.–May, Tues.–Sat. 10–noon and 2–5, Sun. 2–5.*

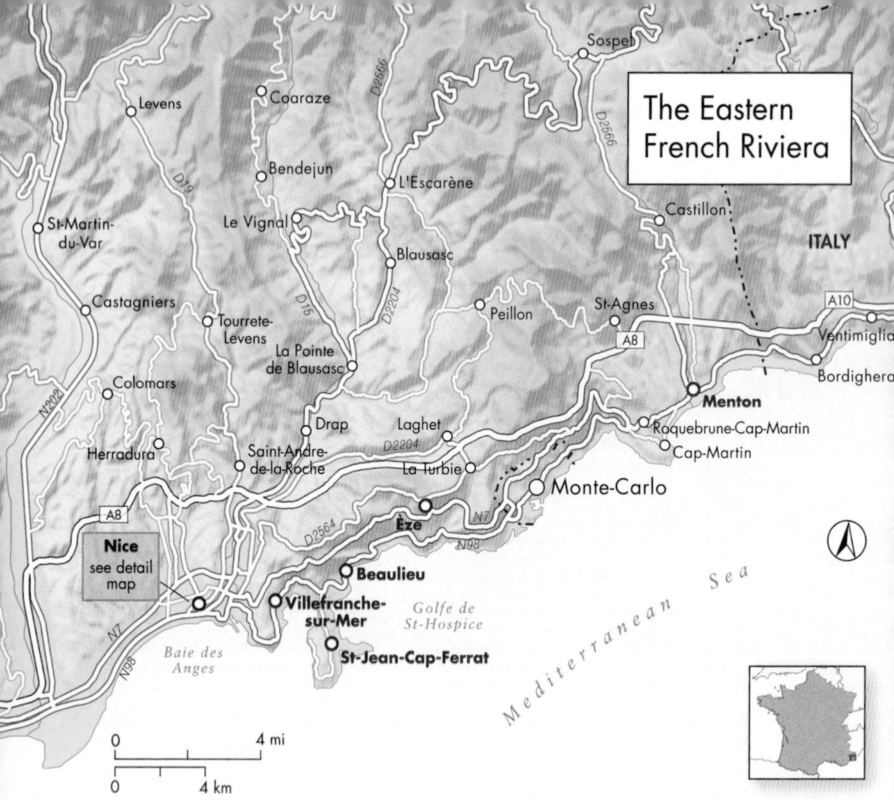

Rue Obscure. Running parallel to the waterfront, the extraordinary 14th-century Rue Obscure (literally, "Dark Street") is entirely covered by vaulted arcades; it sheltered the people of Villefranche when the Germans fired their parting shots—an artillery bombardment—near the end of World War II. ✉ *Rue Obscure, Villefranche-sur-Mer.*

WHERE TO EAT AND STAY

$$$ MEDITERRANEAN

✕ **Cosmo Bar.** Once you've discovered Cosmo, you're likely to come back again and again. Facing the Cocteau chapel with an enviable view of the sea from its terrace, this modern brasserie could easily get away with being merely mediocre. Instead, it serves fresh, colorful Mediterranean food ranging from an addictive *anchoïade*—crudités with anchovy dip—to Moroccan-inspired monkfish tagine. It's a favorite of English-speaking expats in Villefranche and it's easy to understand why, since it brings together all the ingredients that make for a casual yet memorable meal on the French Riviera. Call ahead to be sure of securing a coveted terrace table. $ *Average main: €30* ✉ *11 pl. Amélie Pollonnais, Villefranche-sur-Mer* ☎ *04–93–01–84–05* ⏲ *Closed 3 wks in Jan.* ✍ *Reservations essential.*

$$$$ FRENCH

✕ **La Mère Germaine.** This is an ideal place to linger over warm lobster salad or sole meuniere in butter with almonds while watching the world go by. The seaside restaurant opened in 1938, and proprietor Germaine

Halap soon became a second mother to American naval officers and sailors who came into port. A movie has been made about "Mère Germaine," and excerpts from the book *Mother of the Sixth Fleet* were published in *Readers Digest*. The food is tasty, but the fabulous setting of this veritable institution is reflected in the prices. Valet parking is available from April to October. *Average main: €45 Quai Corbert, Villefranche-sur-Mer 04–93–01–71–39 www.meregermaine.com Closed late Nov.–Christmas.*

$$$$ HOTEL **Hôtel Welcome.** Somerset Maugham holed up in one of the tiny crow's-nest rooms at the top, Jean Cocteau lived here while writing *Orphée*, and Elizabeth Taylor and Richard Burton used to tie one on in the bar (now nicely renovated) at this waterfront landmark—which remains a comfortable and noteworthy retreat. **Pros:** excellent service; artistic heritage makes for a nostalgic trip into the Roaring Twenties. **Cons:** decor, especially on the top floor, is distinctly nautical in flavor; some rooms are oddly shaped—narrow and long—so they feel smaller; parking is €45/day but public parking (limited) costs approx €42/24 hours. *Rooms from: €235 3 quai Amiral Courbet, Villefranche-sur-Mer 04–93–76–27–62 www.welcomehotel.com Closed mid-Nov.–Christmas 32 rooms, 3 suites Breakfast.*

BEAULIEU-SUR-MER

4 km (2½ miles) east of Villefranche, 14 km (9 miles) east of Nice.

With its back pressed hard against the cliffs of the corniche and sheltered between the peninsulas of Cap Ferrat and Cap Roux, this once-grand resort basks in a tropical microclimate that earned its central neighborhood the name *Petite Afrique*. The town was the pet of 19th-century society, and its hotels welcomed Empress Eugénie, the Prince of Wales, and Russian nobility. Beaulieu is still a posh address, but if you're a picky atmosphere-hunter, you may find the town center too built up with apartment buildings.

GETTING HERE

Being one of the main stops on the Marseille–Ventimiglia coastal train line, Beaulieu has frequent arrivals and departures. Bus No. 81 (€1.50) connects it with neighboring St-Jean-Cap-Ferrat, while the No. 100 (€1.50) connects it with Nice and Monaco.

VISITOR INFORMATION

Beaulieu Tourist Office. *Pl. Georges Clemenceau, Beaulieu 04–93–01–02–21 www.beaulieusurmer.fr.*

EXPLORING

Fodor's Choice ★ **Villa Kerylos.** One manifestation of Beaulieu's Belle Époque excess is the eye-knocking Villa Kerylos, a 1902 mansion built in the style of classical Greece (to be exact, of the villas that existed on the island of Delos in the 2nd century BC). It was the dream house of amateur archaeologist Théodore Reinach, who hailed from a wealthy German family, helped the French in their excavations at Delphi, and became an authority on ancient Greek music. He commissioned an Italian architect from Nice, Emmanuel Pontremoli, to surround him with Grecian delights: cool Carrara marble, rare fruitwoods, and a dining salon where guests reclined to eat *à la grecque*. Don't miss this—it's one of the most unusual houses in the south of France. Not far away is the **promenade Maurice-Rouvier,** an enchanting coastal path that leads to St-Jean-Cap-Ferrat. Note that a combination ticket allows you to also visit Villa Ephrussi del Rothschild in St-Jean-Cap-Ferrat within the same week. ✉ *Impasse Gustave-Eiffel, Beaulieu* ☎ *04–93–01–01–44* 🌐 *www.villa-kerylos.com* 🎫 *€11.50; €20 for both villas* ⏲ *Mar.–June, Sept., and Oct., daily 10–6; July and Aug., daily 10–7; Nov.–Feb., weekdays 2–6, weekends 10–6.*

ST-JEAN-CAP-FERRAT

2 km (1 mile) south of Beaulieu.

This luxuriously sited pleasure port moors the peninsula of Cap Ferrat. Yachts purr in and out of its sparkling blue harbor, their passengers scuttling into cafés for take-out drinks to enjoy on their private decks. If you're not invited to join them, you can still take advantage of the waterside walkways and crescent beach with the graceful green bulk of the corniches behind. Unfortunately, Cap Ferrat is a vast peninsula and hides its secrets—except for the Villa Ephrussi, most estates are well hidden behind iron gates, towering hedges, and tropical gardens.

GETTING HERE AND AROUND

Ironically, €1.50 in bus fare brings you to one of the most exclusive patches of land on the planet; the No. 81 accesses the cape from Nice.

VISITOR INFORMATION

St-Jean-Cap-Ferrat Tourist Office. There are two tourist offices: one at the entrance to the village and a second near Place Clémenceau. ✉ *5 and 59 av. Denis Semeria, St-Jean-Cap-Ferrat* ☎ *04–93–76–08–90* 🌐 *www.saintjeancapferrat-tourisme.fr.*

EXPLORING

Coastline Promenade. While Cap Ferrat's villas are sequestered for the most part in the depths of tropical gardens, you can nonetheless walk its entire coastline promenade if you strike out from the port; from the restaurant Capitaine Cook, cut right up Avenue des Fossés, turn right on Avenue Vignon, and follow Chemin de la Carrière. The 11-km (7-mile) walk passes through rich tropical flora and, on the west side, follows white cliffs buffeted by waves. When you've traced the full outline of the peninsula, veer up Chemin du Roy past the fabulous gardens of the **Villa des Cèdres,** owned by King Leopold II of Belgium at the turn of the last century. The king owned several opulent estates along the French Riviera, undoubtedly paid for by his enslavement of the Belgian Congo. Past the gardens, you can reach the **Plage de Passable,** from which you cut back across the peninsula's wrist. A shorter loop takes you from town out to the **Pointe de St-Hospice,** much of the walk shaded by wind-twisted pines. From the port, climb Avenue Jean Mermoz to Place Paloma and follow the path closest to the waterfront. At the point are an 18th-century prison tower, a 19th-century chapel, and unobstructed views of Cap Martin. You can arrange a visit to the Villa des Cèdres by faxing 04–93–76–17–61, "Attention: Sécrétariat."✉ *St-Jean-Cap-Ferrat.*

Villa Ephrussi de Rothschild. Between the port and the mainland, the floridly beautiful Villa Ephrussi de Rothschild bears witness to the wealth and worldly flair of the baroness who had it built. Constructed in 1905 in neo-Venetian style (its flamingo-pink facade was thought not to be in the best of taste by the local gentry), the house was baptized "Ile-de-France" in homage to the Baroness Bétrice de Rothschild's favorite ocean liner. In keeping with that theme, her staff used to wear sailing costumes and her ship travel kit is on view in her bedroom. Precious artworks, tapestries, and furniture adorn the salons—in typical Rothschildian fashion, each is given over to a different 18th-century "époque." Upstairs are the private apartments of Madame la Baronne, which can only be seen on a guided tour offered around noon. The grounds are landscaped with no fewer than seven gardens and topped off with a Temple of Diana. Be sure to allow yourself time to wander here, as this is one of the few places on the coast where you'll be allowed to experience the lavish pleasures characteristic of the Belle Époque Côte d'Azur. Tea and light lunches, served in a glassed-in porch overlooking the grounds and spectacular coastline, encourage you to linger. **■ TIP→ A combination ticket allows you to also visit Villa Kerylos in nearby Beaulieu in the same week.** ✉ *Av. Ephrussi, St-Jean-Cap-Ferrat* ☎ *04–93–01–33–09* 🌐 *www.villa-ephrussi.com* 🎟 *€13; 20 for both villas* ⏲ *Mar.–June, Sept., and Oct., daily 10–6; July and Aug., daily 10–7; Nov.–Feb., weekdays 2–6, weekends 10–6.*

WHERE TO EAT AND STAY

$$$ SEAFOOD ✕ **Le Sloop.** Catering to the yachting crowd, this sleek port-side restaurant has outdoor tables surrounding a tiny "garden" of potted palms. The focus is fish, of course: *soupe de poisson* (fish soup), *St-Pierre* (John Dory) steamed with asparagus, and roasted whole sea bass. Chef Alain Therlicocq has manned the kitchen here for 30 years, and his five-course fixed menu—which includes a fish and meat dish—is one of the best values on the coast. Reservations are necessary in the summer, but if you arrive without, ask with a smile for a table and Alain's wife, Regine, will find you *une p'tite place.* 💲 *Average main: €25* ✉ *Port de St Jean Cap Ferrat, St-Jean-Cap-Ferrat* ☎ *04–93–01–48–63* 🌐 *www.restaurantsloop.com* ⏲ *Closed mid-Nov.–mid-Dec. No lunch Wed. in summer.*

$$$ HOTEL 🏨 **Brise Marine.** With a glowing Provençal-yellow facade, bright blue shutters, a balustraded sea terrace, and pretty pastel guest rooms, Brise Marine fulfills most desires for that perfect, picturesque Cap Ferrat hotel. **Pros:** nighttime quiet interrupted only by gently breaking waves; excellent value for location; short walking distance to beach. **Cons:** some rooms are small; only seven available parking spots (paid), and they must be reserved in advance. 💲 *Rooms from: €178* ✉ *58 av. Jean Mermoz, St-Jean-Cap-Ferrat* ☎ *04–93–76–04–36* 🌐 *www.hotel-brisemarine.com* ⏲ *Closed Nov.–Feb.* 🛏 *16 rooms* 🍽 *No meals.*

$$$$ HOTEL 🏨 **Grand Hôtel du Cap-Ferrat.** Just this side of paradise, this extravagantly expensive hotel has always been the exclusive playground for Hollywood's elite; now, after a grand refurbishment, it is *the* new standard for discreet Cap-Ferrat moneyed luxury. **Pros:** epitome of wealth and luxury; every detail is well thought out and promptly attended to; acres of sculpted gardens. **Cons:** forget it if you're on a budget; two-night

minimum in July and August (but is that a bad thing?). *Rooms from: €750 71 bd. du Charles du Gaulle, St-Jean-Cap-Ferrat 04–93–76–50–50 www.ghcf.fr Closed mid-Dec.–mid-Mar. 49 rooms, 24 suites (8 with private pools).*

$$$$ HOTEL **Royal Riviera.** Completely revamped by Parisian designer guru Grace Leo Andrieu, this former *residence hôtelière* for British aristocrats now invites visitors on an intimate voyage into neo-Hellenic style, complete with an admiring wink at the nearby Villa Kerylos. **Pros:** excellent service and concierge; gorgeous property; free parking. **Cons:** noise from rooms facing railway, which is near hotel; €38 breakfast. *Rooms from: €445 3 av. Jean Monnet, St-Jean-Cap-Ferrat 04–93–76–31–00 www.royal-riviera.com Closed mid.-Nov.–Jan. 90 rooms, 3 suites No meals.*

ÈZE

2 km (1 mile) east of Beaulieu, 12 km (7 miles) east of Nice.

Towering above the coast and crowned with ramparts and the ruins of a medieval château, preposterously beautiful Èze (pronounced *ehz*) is the most spectacularly sited of all coastal promontories and the most accessible of all the perched villages. This translates into hordes of tourists, many of whom come to browse the boutique-lined staircase-streets (happily most shops are quite stylish, and there's a nice preponderance of bric-a-brac and vintage fabric dealers). If you manage to shake the midday crowds and duck off to a quiet overlook, you'll be rewarded with a sublime view of the coast. It's long been a draw for distinguished visitors—including Georges Sand, Friedrich Nietzsche, and lots of crowned heads. Some have even established local residences: Consuelo Vanderbilt, for one, traded Blenheim Palace for a custom-built home in Èze when she tired of being duchess of Marlborough; more recently U2's Bono and the Edge acquired houses down by the coast in Èze-sur-Mer.

GETTING HERE

Motorists should use the Moyenne Corniche, which deposits you near the gateway to Èze Village. The No. 112 and No. 82 buses from Nice also use this road; the No. 100 goes by the sea, while the No. 116 heads up the Grande Corniche (€1.50). Trains arrive at the station in Èze-sur-Mer, and a shuttle bus (€1.50) from there takes you to the hilltop; the trip, with its 1,001 switchbacks, takes 15 minutes. Hikers can follow the Nietzsche Path up; the ascent takes at least 90 minutes (proper footwear required). Èze's tourist office, on Place du Général-de-Gaulle, can direct you to numerous other footpaths.

TIP→ If you want to fully enjoy the magnificence of the village's arched passages, stone alleyways, and ancient fountains, come at dawn or after dusk. If you have the means, spend the night.

VISITOR INFORMATION

Èze Tourist Office. *Pl. du Général de Gaulle, Èze 04–93–41–26–00 www.eze-tourisme.com.*

12

EXPLORING

Jardin Exotique. Set 1,310 feet above sea level, the Jardin Exotique is one of the Riviera's most visited sites. Full of rare succulents and Jean-Philippe Richard sculptures, the botanical garden is also blessed with superlative views: from this crest-top locale you can pan all the way from Italy to St-Tropez (on a clear day, you can even see Corsica). In 2014, it expanded on the northern slope, where you can now stroll amidst typical Mediterranean vegetation. Just a few feet from the entrance, take a time-out lunch at the Nid d'Aigle, an inexpensive eatery featuring focaccias and salads, quaintly set on stone levels rising up around a tall tree. ✉ *20 rue du Château, Èze* ☎ *04–93–41–10–30* *€6* *Feb. and Mar., daily 9–5; Apr. and May, daily 9–6; June and Sept., daily 9–7; July and Aug., daily 9–7:30; Oct., 9–5:30; Nov.–Jan., 9–4:30.*

WHERE TO EAT AND STAY

$$$$ FRENCH

✕ **Cap Estel–La Table de Patrick Raingeard.** For over 50 years celebs have holidayed and dined at Cap Estel along Èze's *bord de mer*. Little wonder: it's poised on a private 5-acre peninsula with all-encompassing views of the Med. Chef Patrick Raingeard's Michelin-star cuisine is worthy of the setting. Start with six oysters "Pearls Monte-Carlo," followed by the Charolais beef fillet with chard cannelloni, and finish it all off with "the all-chocolate tube." Vegetarian options also available, and the produce used often comes directly from the hotel's garden. $ *Average main: €48* ✉ *1312 av. Raymond-Poincaré, Charbonnières-les-Bains* ☎ *04–93–76–29– 29* *www.capestel.com* *Closed Jan.–Mar.* *Reservations essential.*

$$$ FRENCH

✕ **Troubadour.** Amid the clutter and clatter of the nearby coast, Troubadour is a wonderful find (and has been for more than 30 years), earning high ratings for charm and decor. This old family house provides pleasant service and excellent dishes like roasted scallops with chicken broth and squab with citrus zest. Choose the €40 set menu at lunch and dinner, or order à la carte. $ *Average main: €30* ✉ *4 rue du Brec, Èze* ☎ *04–93–41–19–03* *Closed Sun., Mon., and Nov. 20–Dec. 20.*

$$$$ HOTEL Fodor's Choice ★

Château de la Chèvre d'Or. The "Château of the Golden Goat" is actually an entire stretch of the village, streets and all, bordered by gardens that hang from the mountainside in nearly Babylonian style; in addition to divine accommodations, it delivers some of the most breathtaking Mediterranean views—at a price. **Pros:** unique setting; fabulous infinity pool; faultless service. **Cons:** €61 cancellation fee in all cases; no elevator; bit of cobblestone walking involved to reach hotel. $ *Rooms from: €420* ✉ *Rue du Barri, Èze* ☎ *04–92–10–66–66* *www.chevredor.com* *Closed Dec.–Feb.* *30 rooms, 7 suites* *No meals.*

MENTON

14 km (9 miles) east of Èze, 9 km (5½ miles) east of Monaco.

Modesty makes Menton—the most Mediterranean and least pretentious of the French Riviera resorts—all the more alluring. Rubbing shoulders with the Italian border, the town owes its balmy climate to the protective curve of the Ligurian shore. Its picturesque harbor skyline seems to beg artists to immortalize it, while its Cubist skew of

The "eagle's-nest" village of the Riviera, Èze perches 1,300 feet above the sea; travelers never fail to marvel at the dramatic setting.

terra-cotta roofs and yellow-ocher houses, Baroque arabesques capping the church facades, and ceramic tiles glistening on their steeples all evoke the villages of the Italian coast. Menton acquaints you with its rich architectural heritage by offering regular *visites du patrimoine* (heritage tours) to its villas, museums, and gardens; tours start at €6. Details are available at the tourist office.

GETTING HERE AND AROUND

Trains run here all day from Monaco and Nice; the latter also has links to Menton via Lignes d'Azur's No. 100 bus (1 hr, €1.50).

VISITOR INFORMATION

Menton Tourist Office. ✉ *Le Palais de l'Europe, 8 av. Boyer, Menton* ☎ *04–92–41–76–76* 🌐 *www.tourisme-menton.fr.*

EXPLORING

Basilique St-Michel. This majestic basilica dominates the skyline of Menton. Beyond the beautifully proportioned facade—a 19th-century addition—the richly frescoed nave and chapels contain several works by Genovese artists plus a splendid 17th-century organ. Volunteers man the doors here, so you may have to wait for the church to open before visiting. ✉ *Parvis St-Michel, 22 rue St-Michel, Menton* ⏲ *Weekdays 10–noon and 2–5.*

Chapelle de l'Immaculée-Conception. Just above the main church, the smaller Chapelle de l'Immaculée-Conception answers St-Michel's grand gesture with its own pure Baroque beauty. The sanctuary, dating from 1687, is typically closed to the public; however, you can try and slip in to see the graceful trompe l'oeil over the altar and the ornate gilt lanterns early penitents carried in processions. ✉ *Menton.*

Hôtel de Ville. The 19th-century Italianate Hôtel de Ville conceals a treasure by painter Jean Cocteau: he decorated the **Salle des Mariages** (Marriage Room) with vibrant allegorical scenes; today it is used for civil marriages. ✉ *17 av. de la République, Menton* 🎫 *€2* ⏲ *Weekdays 8:30–noon and 2–4:30.*

■ **TIP→ A couple of blocks from the Hôtel de Ville, at 2 rue Vieux Collège, you'll stumble upon the decadent Central Park Café, which serves creamy lattés, mouthwatering burgers, chunky-filled bagels, and desserts that you'll walk off later.**

Marché Couvert (*Covered Market*). Between the lively pedestrian Rue St-Michel and the waterfront, the marvelous Marché Couvert (Les Halles) sums up Menton style with its Belle Époque facade decorated in jewel-tone ceramics. It's equally appealing inside, with merchants selling chewy bread and mountains of cheese, oils, fruit, and Italian delicacies daily in Caravaggesque disarray (on Saturday, clothing is also sold). ✉ *Quai de Monléon, Menton.*

Fodor's Choice ★ **Musée Jean Cocteau.** On the waterfront opposite the market, a squat medieval bastion crowned with four tiny watchtowers houses the extraordinary Musée Jean Cocteau, France's memorial to the eponymous artist-poet-filmmaker (1889–1963). Cocteau spotted the fortress, built in 1636 to defend the port, as the perfect site for a group of his works. While the museum has nearly 1,800 *ouevres graphic*, about 990 are original Cocteaus, a donation from the late California businessman and Holocaust survivor Severin Wunderman's personal collection. This is a must-see. ✉ *2 quai Monléon, Vieux Port, Menton* ☎ *04–89–81–52–50* 🌐 *museecocteaumenton.fr* 🎫 *€8* ⏲ *Wed.–Mon. 10–6.*

Palais Carnolès (*Musée de Beaux-Arts*). At the far west end of town stands the 18th-century Palais Carnolès in vast gardens luxuriant with orange, lemon, and grapefruit trees. This was once the summer retreat of the princes of Monaco; nowadays it contains a sizable collection of European paintings from the Renaissance to the present day, plus some interesting temporary exhibits. ✉ *3 av. de la Madone, Menton* ☎ *04–93–35–49–71* 🎫 *Free* ⏲ *Wed.–Mon. 10–noon and 2–6.*

Serre de la Madone. With a temperate microclimate created by its southeastern and sunny exposure, Menton attracted a great share of wealthy horticultural hobbyists, including Major Lawrence Johnston, a gentleman gardener best known for his Cotswolds wonderland, Hidcote Manor.

He wound up buying a choice estate in Gorbio—one of the loveliest of all perched seaside villages, 10 km (6 miles) west of Menton—and spent the 1920s and 1930s making the Serre de la Madone a masterpiece. Johnston brought back exotica from his many trips to South Africa, Mexico, and China, and planted them in a series of terraces, accented by little pools, vistas, and stone steps. While most of his creeping plumbago, pink belladona, and night-flowering cacti are now gone, his garden has been reopened by the municipality. If you don't have a car, you can reach it from Menton via bus No. 7 (get off at Serre de la Madone stop). ✉ *74 rte. de Gorbio, Menton* ☎ *04–93–57–73–90* 🌐 *www.serredelamadone.com* 🎫 *€8* ⏲ *Apr.–Oct., Tues.–Sun. 10–6; Dec.–Mar., Tues.–Sun. 10–5.*

Val Rahmeh Botanical Garden. Green-thumbers will want to visit Menton's Val Rahmeh Botanical Garden. Planted by Maybud Campbell in the 1910s and much prized by connoisseurs, it's bursting with rare ornamentals and subtropical plants, and adorned with water-lily pools and fountains. The tourist office can also give you directions to other gorgeous gardens around Menton, including the Fontana Rosa, the Villa Maria Serena, and the Villa Les Colombières. ✉ *Av. St-Jacques, Menton* ☎ *04–93–35–86–72* 🌐 *www.mnhn.fr/fr/visitez/lieux/jardin-botanique-exotique-menton* 🎫 *€6* ⏲ *May–Aug., daily 10–12:30 and 3:30–6:30; Sept.–Apr., daily 10–12:30 and 2–5.*

WHERE TO EAT

$$$$
MODERN FRENCH
Fodor's Choice ★

✕ **Mirazur.** Avant-garde French cuisine by an Argentinian-Italian chef? At Mirazur—an innovative restaurant on the border of France and Italy that's earned two Michelin stars—it makes complete sense. Chef Mauro Colagreco learned his craft in Latin America before acquiring a solid French base with the likes of Bernard Loiseau in Burgundy and both Alain Passard and Alain Ducasse in Paris. Now he is a perfect example of the wave of young chefs whose style has been dubbed *la jeune cuisine*; for Colagreco, the plate is a palette and each ingredient has its precise place and significance. Overlooking a cascading tropical garden and the sea, his airy dining room on Menton's outer edge makes the ideal setting for this expressive cooking. Set menus start at €70 (€47 at lunch) and go up to €140. $ *Average main: €49* ✉ *30 av. Aristide Briand, Menton* ☎ *04–92–41–86–86* 🌐 *www.mirazur.fr* ⏲ *Closed Mon. and Tues. mid-Feb.–Oct. No lunch Mon.–Wed. mid-July–Aug.* ✍ *Reservations essential.*

FESTIVALS

Fête du Citron (*Lemon Festival*). The Fête du Citron, running from the end of February through the first week of March, is a full-blown lemon love-in: citrus floats and sculptures, all made of real fruit, glide through town, and musicians are on hand with entertainment. Think of it as France's answer to the Rose Bowl Parade. ✉ *Menton* ☎ *04–92–41–76–95* 🌐 *www.fete-du-citron.com.*

MONACO

WELCOME TO MONACO

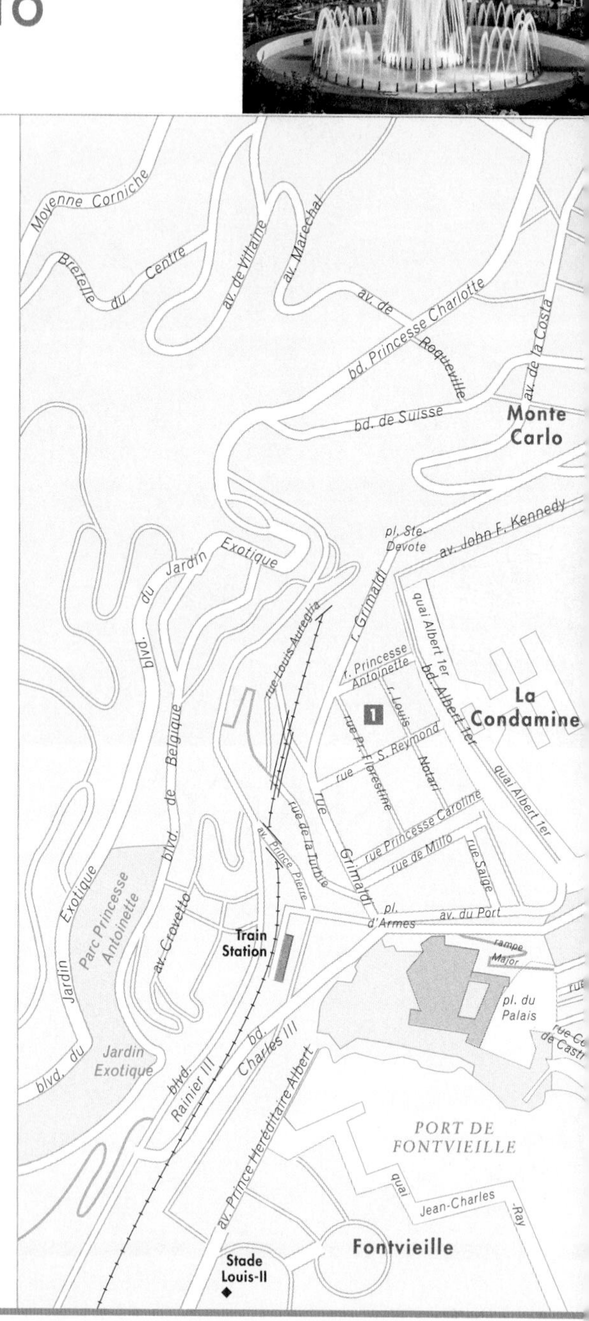

TOP REASONS TO GO

★ **High stakes and high style:** Even if you aren't a gambler, the gold leaf and over-the-top rococo in the casino are definitely worth a long look.

★ **Princess for a day:** Follow in Grace Kelly's footsteps with a visit to the Palais Princier, the official residence of the royal family, including heir apparent Prince Jacques.

★ **Walk in the park:** Yes, Virginia, you can afford to visit Monte Carlo—that is, if you head to its magnificent Jardin Exotique de Monaco.

★ **The Undersea World:** One of the world's best oceanography museums, the Musée Océanographique is an architectural masterpiece in its own right.

★ **Hit the beach:** The chicest spot on the entire French Riviera, Monte Carlo is well known for its underwater diving and its people-watching.

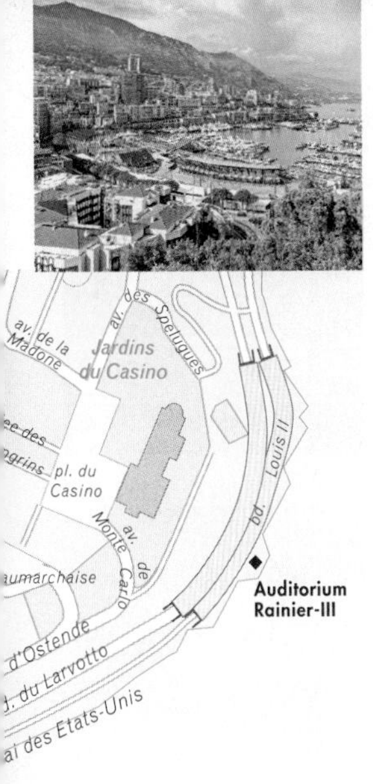

1 Monaco. The principality's exceptional position on the Mediterranean seduces the rich and famous, and those who want to see how the other 1% lives. It bristles with gleaming glass-and-concrete corncob-towers 20 and 30 stories high and with vast apartment complexes, their terraces, landscaped like miniature gardens, jutting over the sea. These literally fall in the shadow of the new 50-story, 56-foot Tour Odéon, where the five-floor penthouse would set you back a mere $440 million—but you can slide from the upper dance floor down to one of the unit's multiple pools, so definitely worth the investment.

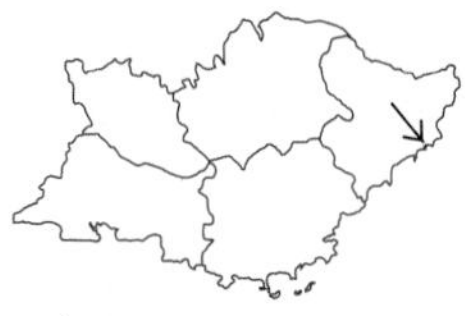

GETTING ORIENTED

Monaco covers just 473 acres and would fit comfortably inside New York's Central Park. (That said, it also reaches a height of 528 feet, so bring some walking shoes.) Despite its compact nature, everybody drives here, whether from the Palais Princier perched on the Rock down to the port or up to Casino Gardens at the eastern tip.

PORT HERCULE

The Rock (Le Rocher)

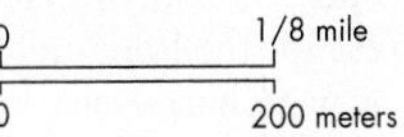

Updated By Nancy Heslin

On one of the best stretches of the Mediterranean, this classic luxury destination is one of the most sought-after addresses in the world. With all the high-rise towers you have to look hard to find the Belle Époque grace of yesteryear. But if you head to the town's great 1864 landmark Hôtel de Paris—still a veritable crossroads of the buffed and befurred Euro-gentry—or enjoy a grand *bouffe*at its famous Louis XV restaurant, or attend the opera, or visit the ballrooms of the casino, you may still be able to conjure up Monaco's elegant past.

Reigning monarch Prince Albert II, a political science graduate from Amherst College, traces his ancestry to Otto Canella, who was born in 1070. The Grimaldi dynasty began with Otto's great-great-great-grandson, Francesco Grimaldi, also known as Frank the Rogue. Expelled from Genoa, Frank and his cronies disguised themselves as monks and in 1297 seized the fortified medieval town known today as Le Rocher (the Rock). Except for a short break under Napoléon, the Grimaldis have been here ever since, which makes them the oldest reigning family in Europe.

In the 1850s a Grimaldi named Charles III made a decision that turned the Rock into a giant blue chip. Needing revenue but not wanting to impose additional taxes on his subjects, he contracted with a company to open a gambling facility. The first spin of the roulette wheel was on December 14, 1856. There was no easy way to reach Monaco then—no carriage roads or railroads—so no one came. Between March 15 and March 20, 1857, one person entered the casino—and won two francs. In 1868, however, the railroad reached Monaco, and it was filled with Englishmen who came to escape the London fog. The effects were immediate. Profits were so great that Charles eventually abolished all direct taxes. Almost overnight, a threadbare principality became an elegant watering hole for European society. Dukes (and their mistresses) and duchesses (and their gigolos) danced and dined their way through a world of spinning roulette wheels and bubbling Champagne—preening themselves for nights at the opera, where such artists as Vaslav Nijinsky, Sarah Bernhardt, and Enrico Caruso came to perform.

Prince Rainier III, who reigned from 1949 to 2005, worked hard to regain Monaco's glitz and glamour. He married 26-year-old Hollywood legend Grace Kelly in 1956, after the Kelly family paid a $2 million dowry (of which Grace paid half herself). They had three children, Caroline, Albert, and Stephanie, who was a passenger in her mother's Rover when it plummeted 120 feet off a cliff in nearby La Turbie. Some 100 million people watched Grace Kelly's funeral on September 18, 1982.

Before Prince Albert II married Charlene Wittstock in 2011, Monaco residents were nervous that there might not be a legitimate heir to the throne. Finally, on December 10, 2014, Princess Gabriella was born, followed two minutes later by her brother Jacques. When 45 cannon shots rang out, Monaco residents knew they had their heir.

Monaco's sensational position on a broad, steep peninsula that bulges into the Mediterranean—its harbor and new yacht club sparkling with luxury cruisers, its posh mansions angling awnings toward the nearly perpetual sun—continues to draw the rich and famous. One out of every three people in Monaco is a millionaire, and many celebrities want to become naturalized "Monégasques," including superchef Alain Ducasse, who said that he gave up his French passport out of affection for Monaco rather than for its status as a tax haven.

Monaco residents themselves add to the sense of flossy, flashy self-contentment. Nearly everything is dyed-to-match here, even the lap dog in the Vuitton bag, and fur coats flourish from September through May. Police officers dress in ice-cream–colored uniforms worthy of an operetta, and along the port you might catch a glimpse of exclusive birthday parties for little-rich-girls in couture party dresses. Pleasure boats vie with luxury cruisers in their brash beauty and *Titanic* scale, and teams of handsome young men—themselves dyed blond and tanned to match—scour and polish every gleaming surface. Only in Monaco would you find *La Belle*, a 262-foot megayacht for women only, complete with Swarovski crystal chandeliers, gold mosaics, and a snow room with ice fountains, designed by Monaco-based Lidia Bersani.

As you might expect, all this glitz doesn't come cheap. Eating is expensive, and even the most modest hotels cost more here than in nearby Nice or Menton. As for taxis, they don't even have meters so you are completely at the driver's mercy (with prices skyrocketing during events such as the Grand Prix). For the frugal, Monaco is the ultimate day trip, although parking is as coveted as a room with a view. At the very least you can afford a coffee at the very friendly Starbucks (where you'll also find free Wi-Fi).

The harbor district, known as La Condamine, connects the new quarter, officially known as Monte Carlo, with Monaco-Ville (or Le Rocher), a medieval town on the Rock, topped by the palace, the cathedral, and the Oceanography Museum. Have no fear that you'll need to climb countless steps to get to Monaco-Ville, as there are plenty of elevators and escalators climbing the steep cliffs. But shuttling between the lovely casino grounds of Monte Carlo and Old Monaco, separated by a vast port, is a daunting proposition for ordinary mortals without wings, so hop on the No. 1 bus from the Jardin Exotique and the No. 2, which stops at Place du Casino—both come up to Monaco Ville (€2 on board or €1.50 at ticket machines).

PLANNER

WHEN TO GO

The area is at its hottest in July and August, and the beaches are at their best in June or September. To avoid the shiploads of travelers during high season, visit in the fall or winter. The temperatures may not be as high, but you'll still get color from reflecting diamonds.

FESTIVALS

Printemps des Arts. Monte Carlo's monthlong spring arts festival, Printemps des Arts, brings together the world's top ballet, operatic, symphonic, and chamber-music performers at venues across Monaco (Opéra de Monte-Carlo, Oceanography Museum, Grimaldi Forum, and the Yacht Club Monte Carlo) as well as in Cap d'Ail and Beaulieu. ☎ *377/98–06–28–28* 🌐 *www.printempsdesarts.com.*

Top Marques Monaco. What can you say about a four-day exhibition where you could buy anything from an AgustaWestland helicopter to a Rolex Submariner to a $55,000 bed? So much more than just an exclusive car show, Top Marques takes place in the third week of April at Grimaldi Forum. ✉ *10 av. Princesse Grace* ☎ *377/97–70–12–77* 🌐 *www.topmarquesmonaco.com* 🎫 *€50.*

GETTING HERE AND AROUND

From Nice's train station, Monaco is serviced by regular trains along the Cannes–Ventimiglia line; from Nice the journey costs €3.90 one way and takes 20 minutes. A taxi from Nice will cost around €90, depending on the season and the time of day.

BUS TRAVEL

Compagnie des Autobus de Monaco operates a bus line that threads the avenues of Monaco. Purchase your ticket on board for €2; or save 50 cents a ticket by buying in advance from an agent, a machine, or online. The company also operates a solar electric boat from Quai des États-Unis to the casino; it runs daily from 8 to 8 and costs €2.

If you're headed here from Nice, the Conseil Général Alpes-Martimes runs the 100X express bus from Vauban Station in Nice to Place des Armes in Monaco. It's only available on weekdays, however. Lignes d'Azur's bus 100 costs €1.50 and departs from promenade des Arts in Nice.

Bus Information Compagnie des Autobus de Monaco. ☎ *377/97–70–22–22* 🌐 *www.cam.mc.*

HOTELS

Hotel prices skyrocket during the Monaco Grand Prix, so reserve as far ahead as possible. That goes for festivals like the Printemps des Arts as well. *Hotel reviews have been shortened. For full information, visit Fodors.com.*

WHAT IT COSTS IN EUROS				
	$	$$	$$$	$$$$
Restaurants	under €18	€18–€24	€25–€32	over €32
Hotels	under €106	€106–€145	€146–€215	over €215

Restaurant prices are the average cost of a main course at dinner or, if dinner is not served, at lunch. Hotel prices are the lowest cost of a standard double room in high season.

VISITOR INFORMATION

Monaco Tourist Office. Before starting off, arm yourself with a map and a bus schedule or an excellent pair of walking shoes and start at the tourist office, just north of the casino gardens. ✉ *2a bd. des Moulins, Monte Carlo* ☎ *377/92–16–61–16* 🌐 *www.visitmonaco.com.*

EXPLORING MONACO

TOP ATTRACTIONS

Casino Monte-Carlo. Place du Casino is the center of Monte Carlo and a must-see, even if you don't like to bet. Into the gold-leaf splendor of the casino, the hopeful descend from tour buses to tempt fate beneath the gilt-edge rococo ceiling—and some spend much more than planned here, as did the French actress Sarah Bernhardt, who lost 100,000 francs. Jacket and tie are required in the private back rooms, which open at 4 pm. Bring your passport (under-18s not admitted). Note that there are special admission fees to get into any of the period gaming rooms. For €10 you can also visit the casino daily in the off-hours, from 9 am to 12:30, with access to all rooms. ✉ *Pl. du Casino, Monte Carlo* ☎ *377/98–06–21–21* 🌐 *www.casinomontecarlo.com* ⏲ *Tours daily 9–12:30.*

Jardin Exotique de Monaco (*Tropical Garden*). Six hundred varieties of cacti and succulents cling to a sheer rock face at Monaco's magnificent Tropical Garden, a brisk half-hour walk west from the palace. The garden traces its roots to days when Monaco's near-tropical climate nurtured unheard-of exotica, amazing visitors from the northlands as much as any zoo. The plants are of less interest today, especially to Americans familiar with southwestern flora. The views over the Rock and coastline, however, are spectacular. Also on the grounds, or actually under them, are the **Grottes de l'Observatoire** —spectacular grottoes and caves adrip with stalagmites and spotlit with fairy lights. The **Musée d'Anthropologie** showcases two rooms: Albert I covers general prehistory while Ranier III unearths regional Paleolithic discoveries. ✉ *62 bd.*

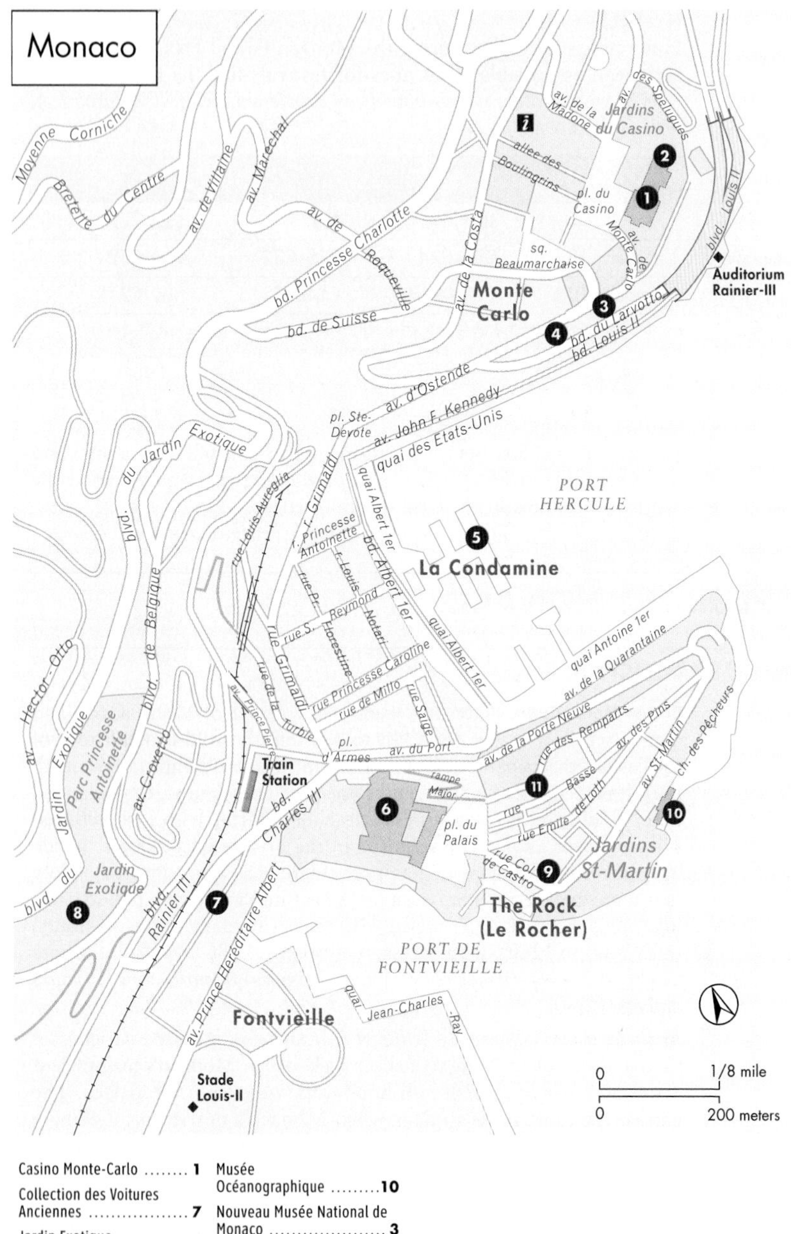

Casino Monte-Carlo 1
Collection des Voitures Anciennes 7
Jardin Exotique de Monaco 8
Les Thermes Marins de Monte-Carlo 4
Monaco Cathedral 9
Musée Océanographique 10
Nouveau Musée National de Monaco 3
Opéra de Monte-Carlo 2
Palais Princier 6
Port 5
The Rock 11

du Jardin Exotique 🌐 *www.jardin-exotique.mc* 🎫 *€7.20* ⏲ *Nov.–Jan., daily 9–5; Feb.–Apr. and Oct., daily 9–6; May–Sept., daily 9–7.*

Les Thermes Marins de Monte-Carlo (*Sea Baths of Monte-Carlo*). Added to the city in the 1990s, this sea-water-therapy treatment center stretches between the landmark Hôtel de Paris and its sister, the Hermitage, and can be accessed directly from either hotel. Within its sleek, multilevel complex you can pursue every creature comfort, from underwater massage to seaweed body wraps to light, elegant spa-style lunches, in one of the 37 treatment rooms—almost all with views over the port. After all that walking in the principality, you may need the 50-minute Monte-Carlo Foot Cocooning Massage (€160). ✉ *2 av. de Monte-Carlo* ☎ *377/98–06–69–00* 🌐 *www.thermesmarinsmontecarlo.com* ⏲ *Daily 8–8.*

POP-UP SHOPPING

It would be hard not to notice the five pebble-shaped pavilions that have invaded the Boulingrins Gardens in front of Place du Casino. There are temporary shops for luxury brands like Miu Miu, Bottega Alexander McQueen, Piaget, and Chopard. Erected in 2014, they'll be around until about 2020 when the iconic Sporting d'Hiver, the last of the principality's Art Deco buildings, is replaced by seven new residential and commercial buildings.

13

Monaco Cathedral. Follow the crowds down the last remaining streets of medieval Monaco to the 19th-century Cathédrale de l'Immaculée-Conception, which contains the tomb of Princess Grace and Prince Rainier III, as well as a magnificent altarpiece, painted in 1500 by Louis Bréa. ✉ *Av. St-Martin* ☎ *377/93–30–87–70* 🌐 *www.cathedrale.mc* ⏲ *Oct.—Apr., daily 8:30—6; May—Sept., daily 8—7.*

FAMILY Fodor's Choice ★ **Musée Océanographique** (*Oceanography Museum*). Perched dramatically on a cliff, this museum is a splendid Edwardian structure, built under Prince Albert I to house specimens collected on amateur explorations. Jacques Cousteau (1910–97) led the missions from 1957 to 1988. The main floor displays skeletons and taxidermy of enormous sea creatures; early submarines and diving gear dating from the Middle Ages; and a few interactive science displays. The main draw is the famous **aquarium,** a vast complex of backlighted tanks containing more than 6,000 species of fish, crab, and eel in pools ranging from 100 to 450,000 liters. ✉ *Av. St-Martin* ☎ *377/93–15–36–00* 🌐 *www.oceano.mc* 🎫 *€14; €19 combined ticket includes Palais Princier* ⏲ *Apr.–June and Sept., daily 10–7; July and Aug., daily 10–8:30; Oct.–Mar., daily 10–6.*

Opéra de Monte-Carlo. In the true spirit of the town, it seems that the Salle Garnier Opera House, with its 18-ton gilt-bronze chandelier and extravagant frescoes, is part of the casino complex. The designer, Charles Garnier, also built the Paris Opéra, so we are talking one fabulous jewel box. On display are some of the coast's most significant performances of dance, opera, and orchestral music. ✉ *Pl. du Casino* ☎ *377/98–06–28–28* 🌐 *www.opera.mc* ⏲ *Ticket office Tues.–Sat. 10–5:30.*

Palais Princier. The famous Rock, crowned by the palace where the royal family resides, stands west of Monte Carlo. An audio guide leading you

Monaco's Belle Époque opulence is epitomized by its Opéra House Monte Carlo, designed in 1879 by Garnier.

through this sumptuous chunk of history, first built in the 13th century and expanded and enhanced over the centuries, reveals an extravagance of 16th- and 17th-century frescoes, as well as tapestries, gilt furniture, and paintings on a grand scale. Note that the **Relève de la Garde** (Changing of the Guard) is held outside the front entrance of the palace most days promptly at 11:55 am. Les Grands Appartements are open to the public from late March through October, and you can buy a joint ticket with the Muséé Océanographique. Beginning in mid-July, a summer concert series can be enjoyed at 9:30 pm in the palace's glorious courtyard. Tickets can be purchased through the Orchestre Philharmonique de Monte-Carlo (www.opmc.com). ✉ *Pl. du Palais* ☎ *377/93–25–18–31* 🌐 *www.palais.mc* 🎫 *€8, €19 combined ticket includes Musée Océanographique* ⏲ *Apr.–Oct., daily 10–6.*

Port. It's a hike or a ride on bus No. 6 from Monte Carlo to the port along Boulevard Albert Ier, where pleasure boats of every shape flash white and blue. It's here that they erect the stands for fans of the Grand Prix. And it's from the far corner of the port that the Institut Océanographique launches research boats to study aquatic life in the Mediterranean, as its late director Jacques Cousteau did for some 30 years.

The Rock. On the broad plateau known as Le Rocher, or the Rock, the majority of Monaco's touristic sights are concentrated with tidy, self-conscious charm. This is the medieval heart of Monaco, and where its cathedral, palace, and Musée Océanographique can be found. You can either climb up the Rampe Majeur from Place d'Armes, behind the right corner of the port, or approach it by elevator from the seafront at the port's farthest end.

WORTH NOTING

FAMILY **Collection des Voitures Anciennes** (*Collection of Vintage Cars*). In this impressive assemblage of Prince Rainier's vintage cars, you'll find everything from a De Dion Bouton to a Lamborghini Countach. Also on the Terrasses de Fontvieille is the **Jardin Animalier** (Animal Garden), a mini-zoo housing the Grimaldi family's animal collection—an astonishing array of wild beasts that includes monkeys and exotic birds. Admission to this mini-menagerie is €5. ✉ *Terrasses de Fontvieille* ☎ *377/92–05–28–56, 377/93–25–18–31* 🎟 *€6.50* ⏲ *Daily 10–6.*

GRACE'S KINGDOM

Thanks in part to the pervasive odor of money to burn, Monaco remains the playground of royalty, wealthy playboys, and glamorous film stars. One of the loveliest of the latter, Hollywood darling Grace Kelly, became Monaco's princess when she married Prince Rainier in 1956; their wedding, marriage, and her tragic death in a car accident—eerily presaged in scenes filmed in Alfred Hitchcock's *To Catch a Thief*—have only added to the mythology of this fairy-tale mini-principality.

Nouveau Musée National de Monaco. To get here take the elevator down from Place des Moulins. NMNM houses two museums, each of which hosts two exhibitions a year. One of the surviving buildings from the Belle Époque, Villa Sauber, with its rose garden, is in the Larvotto Beach complex, which has been artfully created with imported sand. The Villa Paloma (next door to the Jardin Exotique) was recently restored with fabulous stained-glass windows. ✉ *Villa Sauber, 17 av. Princesse Grace* ☎ *377/98–98–91–26* 🌐 *www.nmnm.mc* 🎟 *€6* ⏲ *June–Sept., daily 11–7; Oct.–May, daily 10–6.*

WHERE TO EAT

$$$$ BRASSERIE ✕ **Café de Paris.** The landmark Belle Époque "La Brasserie 1900"—better known as Café de Paris—offers the usual classics (shellfish, steak tartare, matchstick frites, and fish boned table-side). Supercilious, superpro waiters fawn gracefully over titled preeners, jet-setters, and tourists alike. Open daily beginning at 8 am, there's good hot food until 2 am. To claim "I've been there," grab a chair outside in Place du Casino, order an €8 coke or €15 sundae and sit back to watch the show. $ *Average main: €34* ✉ *Pl. du Casino* ☎ *377/98–06–76–23* 🌐 *www.casinocafedeparis.com.*

$$$$ FRENCH ✕ **Elsa.** Paoli Sari is not the first chef to earn a cherished Michelin star, but he is the first to be awarded the honor for an all-organic restaurant. The Venetian-born chef uses the produce of 30 local growers from around France and Italy, and just as many winemakers. The seafood on his menu comes from small inshore fishermen, and he chooses the best fair-trade coffee and chocolate and makes his own mozzarella. Breads made with organic flour are baked daily before lunch and dinner. Elsa—named after Elsa Maxwell, the American writer and high-society hostess from the 1930s—offers two set menus at €98 and €115, but you can order also order individual items. Start with assorted summer

vegetables from the chef's own garden, finished with extra-virgin olive oil and fleur de sel from Camargue. Great main dishes include gold risotto with black cuttlefish ragout, roasted langoustine with saffron, or roasted rack of lamb coated with honey celeriac and licorice puree. If your pocketbook permits dessert, the soufflé with almonds or the mille-feuille with gingerbread will leave you smiling. The terrace views are cruise-worthy, but don't let the nautical casualness deceive you; the first-rate service and inspired food is first-rate. *Average main: €60 Monte-Carlo Beach, Av. Princesse Grace, Roquebrune-Cap-Martin 377/98–06–50–05 monte-carlo-beach.com Closed Nov.—early Mar. Reservations essential.*

$$$$ FRENCH **Hostellerie Jérôme.** Prince Albert's country home Roc Angel is located about 10 kilometers (6 miles) behind Monaco in La Turbie, so it's no wonder a top-notch dinner restaurant (read: expensive, expensive, expensive) is situated here as well. In addition to the regular menu, the prix-fixe four-course menu is €78, while the famous 10-course extravaganza is €138. Chef Bruno Cirino's scampi Mediterranean in an almond crust with dates or roasted white local figs, sugared black olives, and buffalo milk sherbet has become a signature dish for a reason. Too rich for your blood? Try Cirino's bistro next door, Le Café de la Fontaine, open year-round for lunch and dinner with €18 main courses. *Average main: €55 20 rte. Comte de Cessole 04–92–41–51–51 www.hostelleriejerome.com Closed Nov.–Mar. and Mon. and Tues. except July and Aug. No lunch.*

$$$$ FRENCH **La Trattoria.** Set in the entertainment complex Le Sporting d'Été (an expensive cab ride from the center of town), La Trattoria restaurant overlooks Jimmyz and the Med, and is only open during summer months, but an Alain Ducasse window of opportunity must never be overlooked. Take the advice of the enthusiastic waiters and order the Milan-style risotto or the roasted sea bass with sun-dried vegetables—either of which could prove as much of a revelation as the conversation at the next table (you may overhear something like: "I have 52 million in my bank account"). Gluten-free dishes are available. *Average main: €42 Le Sporting, Av. Princesse Grace 377/98–06–71–71 www.alain-ducasse.com Closed late Sept.–mid-May. No lunch Reservations essential.*

$$$$ FRENCH Fodor's Choice ★ **Le Louis XV.** This extravagantly showy restaurant stuns with neo-Baroque details, yet it manages to be upstaged by its product: the superb cuisine of Alain Ducasse, one of the world's most respected chefs. He leaves the Louis XV kitchen, for the most part, in the more-than-capable hands of Chef Franck Cerutti, who draws much of his inspiration from the Cours Saleya market in Nice. Glamorous iced lobster with chestnuts and Alba white truffles slum happily with stockfish (stewed salt cod) and tripe. The decor is magnificent—a surfeit of gilt, mirrors, and chandeliers—and the waitstaff seignorial as they proffer a footstool for madame's handbag. In Ducasse fashion, the Baroque clock on the wall is stopped just before 12—Cinderella should have no fears. The 400,000 bottles in the wine cellar should offer you enough of a selection to accompany the €230 and €330 fixed-menu dinners. If your wallet is willing, this is a must. *Average main: €100 Hôtel de Paris, Pl. du*

Casino ☎ *377/98–06–88–64* 🌐 *www.alain-ducasse.com* ▭ *No credit cards* ⏲ *Closed Tues., Wed., and Nov. No lunch weekdays* ✍ *Reservations essential* *Jacket required.*

$$$ FRENCH ✕ **Quai des Artistes.** Packing well-heeled diners shoulder-to-shoulder at banquettes lined up for maximum people-watching, this warehouse-scale neo-Deco bistro on the port is the chicest of the chic with Monégasque residents. Rich brasserie classics (lamb shank on the bone, potato puree with rosemary, spicy gravy) are counterbalanced with high-flavor international experiments (salmon served sushi-rare with warm potatoes, pickled ginger, wasabi sauce). There's a fabulous terrace with a palatial view that you can enjoy year-round. [$] *Average main: €32* ✉ *4 quai Antoine Ier* ☎ *377/97–97–97–77* 🌐 *www.quaidesartistes.com* ✍ *Reservations essential.*

$$ AMERICAN ✕ **Stars'n'Bars.** This American-style port-side bar/restaurant/entertainment center is like the Monégasque version of the Hard Rock Café, and it's owned by a childhood friend of the prince. Sports jerseys and photos hang on the wall, while fat and juicy burgers, cookie sundaes, real iced tea in thick glasses, and (gasp!) pitchers of ice water draw in homesick expats and quesadilla-starved backpackers (so much so that they're willing to pay €12 for onion rings or €24 for a Big Star cheeseburger). Upstairs, the open-air Star Deck cocktail lounge has panoramic views and a DJ to keep things lively. [$] *Average main: €20* ✉ *6 quai Antoine I* 🌐 *www.starsnbars.com.*

WHERE TO STAY

$$$$ HOTEL **Hermitage.** They've all been here—kings, queens, Pavarotti in jeans—among the riot of frescoes and plaster flourishes embellished with gleaming brass in this landmark yet relatively low-profile 1900 hotel set back a block from the casino scene. **Pros:** terraces overlooking casino; Bvlgari toiletries. **Cons:** public spaces not very lively; rooms on street side may have some traffic noise; watch out for €35 breakfast and €38/day parking charges. [$] *Rooms from: €715* ✉ *Sq. Beaumarchais* ☎ *377/98–06–40–00* 🌐 *www.hotelhermitagemontecarlo.com* *192 rooms, 86 suites* *Some meals.*

$$$$ HOTEL Fodor's Choice ★ **Hôtel Métropole.** This Belle Époque hotel, set on land that once belonged to Pope Leon XIII, has pulled out all the stops in its decoration—famed Paris designer Jacques Garcia has given the rooms his signature hyper-aristocratic look and Karl Lagerfield is the architect behind The Odyssey pool and lounge. **Pros:** flawless and attentive service; free newspapers and Hermès products; impeccable design. **Cons:** food is so superb you won't want to eat anywhere else. [$] *Rooms from: €640* ✉ *4 av. de la Madone* ☎ *377/93–15–15–15* 🌐 *www.metropole.com* *62 rooms, 64 suites* *Some meals.*

$$$$ HOTEL **Monte-Carlo Bay Hotel.** Perched on a 10-acre peninsula, with 75% of its rooms offering sea views, this highly acclaimed luxury resort—which immodestly bills itself as "a natural Eden reinvented"—seeks to evoke the Côte d'Azur's 1920s heyday with its neoclassical columns and arches, exotic gardens, lagoon swimming pool, casino, and concert hall. **Pros:** ultra-luxurious rooms; sofas on balconies; never need

to leave the hotel. **Cons:** later check-in time than other hotels; pool area can become crowded. $ *Rooms from: €670* ✉ *40 av. Princesse Grace* ☎ *377/98–06–20–00* 🌐 *www.montecarlobay.com* *312 rooms, 22 suites* *No meals.*

NIGHTLIFE

There's no need to go to bed before dawn in Monte Carlo when you can go to the grand casino or swanky nightspots.

CASINOS

Casino de Monte-Carlo. The bastion and landmark of Monte Carlo gambling is, of course, the gorgeously ornate Casino de Monte-Carlo. The main gambling hall is the Salle Européene (European Room), where you can play roulette, craps, or blackjack, while the slot machines stand apart in the Salle des Amériques and the Salon Renaissance. Like these rooms, the Salons Touzet (Trente et Quarante and Texas Hold'Em poker) also opens at 2 pm, but it has a €10 admission fee (whereas the others are free). Bring your passport (under-18s not admitted). ✉ *Pl. du Casino* ☎ *377/98–06–23–00* 🌐 *www.casinomontecarlo.com* *Hrs vary depending on season.*

Sun Casino. Described as the "most American" of all the casinos in the principality thanks to a more extensive range of gaming tables, the Sun Casino is part of the Fairmont Monte-Carlo. While you can't hit the tables until 5 pm (4 pm on weekends), slot machines open daily from noon and entry is free (you must be over 18 and snappily dressed). Don't be surprised to cross paths with women's poker champion Isabelle Mercier, a true fan of Sun Casino. ✉ *12 av. des Spélugues* ☎ *377/98–06–12–12* 🌐 *www.montecarlosuncasino.com.*

CONCERTS

Salle des Etoiles. SBM's Le Sporting, a summer-only entertainment complex on the waterfront that celebrated 40 years in 2014, has a roof that opens up to the stars and fireworks, perhaps justifying the €150 ticket for the Monte-Carlo Sporting Summer Festival or the €1,000 Red Cross Gala—although the celebs are also part of the draw. Where else can you see Lady Gaga and Tony Bennett, Elton John, Rod Stewart, or Duran Duran in a sit-down dinner venue for 700 people? The Salles des Etoiles is open year-round, but hosts music and events May through September. ✉ *Le Sporting, Av. Princesse Grace* ☎ *377/92–16–21–25* 🌐 *en.sportingsummerfestival.com.*

DANCE CLUBS

Jimmyz. Dominating the club scene, Jimmyz boasts an edgy reputation that reaches far beyond Monaco. The legendary disco at Sporting Monte-Carlo is not for lightweights: the year-round partying is as serious as the need to be seen, so if surgically enhanced faces and body parts upset you, then stay at your hotel. ✉ *Sporting Monte-Carlo,*

Av. Princesse Grace ☎ *377/98–06–70–68* 🌐 *fr.jimmyzmontecarlo.com* ⏲ *Closed mid-Sept.–mid-Oct.*

SPORTS AND THE OUTDOORS

AUTO RACING

Grand Prix de Monaco. When the filmmakers depart, the auto racing begins: the Grand Prix de Monaco takes place the last Sunday of the Cannes Film Festival in May. To watch live, it's €10,000 a person to stand on a balcony overlooking the course. If that's more than you want to spend but you still want to watch action on the same track, two weeks earlier is the Historic Grand Prix of Monaco (but only every other even year); tickets range from €25 to €55. ☎ *377/93–15–26–00 for information* 🌐 *www.monaco-grand-prix.com.*

13

BEACHES

FAMILY **La Note Bleu.** Probably the best of the private beaches is La Note Bleu, which has something for everyone with activities for kids, jazz concerts, and an excellent beach restaurant serving Mediterranean-Asian food (and a lounge with Wi-Fi, if you must!). It's also a jellyfish-free zone, with nets that keep their tentacles at bay. **Amenities:** food and drink; toilets; showers. **Best for:** swimming; sunrise. ✉ *Plage du Larvotto, Av. Princesse Grace* ☎ *377/93–50–05–02* 🌐 *www.lanotebleue.mc* ⏲ *Closed Dec.–Mar.*

FAMILY **Larvotto Beach.** The sandy Larvotto Beach just off Avenue Princess Grace, said to be the world's most costly street to live on, is the only free public beach in Monaco, and it has the added bonus of being protected by jellyfish nets. Access by the No. 4 or 6 bus, you can rent loungers or just bring your own umbrella. There's a mini-club for kids; dogs are not permitted but that doesn't stop some owners. SkiVol operates from the Larvotto public beach during the summer season with a great range of water sports including wake boarding, doughnuts, and fly-fishing. **Amenities:** water sports; lifeguards; toilets; showers. **Best for:** swimming. ✉ *Av. Princesse Grace.*

Plage Mala. This lovely stretch of sandy, shaded land is easily one of the most stylish of the Riviera beaches, and despite its proximity to Monaco—half an hour by foot—Plage Mala's public area never gets crowded. Another upside is that the coves under the impressive cliffs produce the best area for snorkeling along the coast. But there are also numerous bare tops. Private beach restaurants are close by where you can rent loungers. The 3.5-kilometer (2.2-mile) Mala footpath that stretches to Plage Marquet in Fontvieille in Monaco is relatively easy to walk, with the most challenging leg being the access to Mala beach itself. Walking to Monte Carlo generally take less than an hour, however, avoid the path during stormy conditions. **Amenities:** none. **Best for:** snorkeling; swimming; walking. ✉ *Av. Raymond Gramaglia, Cap d'Ail.*

14

CORSICA

WELCOME TO CORSICA

TOP REASONS TO GO

★ **Island hiking:** From a stroll in the countryside to an overnight hike in the mountains, Corsica offers more than 100 peaks and scenic trails, including the famous 201-km (125-mile) "GR20" trek across the island.

★ **Water adventures:** The warm and crystal waters here are ideal for snorkeling, diving, boating, and windsurfing.

★ **Rich cuisine:** Blending French specialties with Italian cuisine, Corsica tempts the palate with the rich flavors of honey, chestnuts, wine, and Brin d'Amour cheese.

★ **Coastal drives:** These curvy mountain roads, skirted by turquoise waters, are not to be missed.

★ **Cultural exploration:** Dotting the island are chapels, towers, and more than 350 villages framed by fields of grazing goats and sheep. Corsica's cultural treasures, preserved through centuries of tradition, find expression in the island's art, music, food, and festivals.

1 Corse du Sud. Southern Corsica prides itself on its picturesque coastline, ancient hilltop villages, fortified cities, prehistoric sites, and breathtaking natural wonders. The regional capital of Ajaccio, Napoléon's birthplace, remains the island's modern commercial hub. Famous for its dramatic white limestone cliff-top setting, historic Bonaficio is the stunning backdrop to the postcard-perfect marine reserve surrounding the Lavezzi Islands—a UNESCO World Heritage Site.

2 Haute Corse. The natural savage beauty that defines northern Corsica begins in the lush promontory of Cap Corse with its mountain ridges running down the peninsula's center to traditional fishing villages and picturesque harbors. The north is also renowned as an important wine-producing region where some of the finest vineyards benefit from the area's fertile soil and perfect temperatures.

GETTING ORIENTED

The northern half of the island (Haute Corse) is generally wilder than the southern half (Corse du Sud), which is hotter and more barren. Southern Corsica's archaeological sites at the Col de Bavella and its majestic Laricio pine forest, and the ancient towns of Bonifacio all rank indisputably among the island's finest treasures. One of the prettiest drives is the tour around the northward-pointing finger of Cap Corse. Don't hesitate to drive into the interior highlands, the true Corsica; if you spend too much time at sea level you'll be missing the remote villages and dramatic heights for which the island is famous.

Centuri
Tomino
Baragogna
D80
Nonza
Erbalunga
Santa-Maria-di-Lota
Bastia
Patrimonio
Saint-Florent
Furiani
D81
D62
Biguglia
L'Ile-Rousse
Losari
N1197
N193
Algajola
Pigna
Sorio
Murato
Lama
Calvi
N197
Cateri
D151
Calenzana
Ponte Leccia
Morosaglia
Suare
D71
La Porta
D81
Asco
N147
N193
Haut-Asco
Castirla
Piedicroce
Monte Cinto
Cervione
Soveria
Albertacce
Corscia
Valle-d'Alesani
Osani
D84
Corte
HAUTE CORSE
Alistro
Porto–Les Calanches
Ota
Lugo
2
N198
D70
N200
D81
Vivario
Vico
Aleria
Ghisoni
Cargèse
Sagone
Tavera
Tiuccia
Acciani
Carbuccia
D69
D81
N193
Bastelica
Mignataja
Palneca
Chisa
Travo
Ajaccio
Bastelicaccia
Zicavo
Porticcio
Grosseto
Solenzara
1
CORSE DU SUD
N196
D69
D268
Col de Bavella
Verghia
Bicchisano
Favone
Casalabriva
Zérubia
Zonza
N198
Marmontaja
Filitosa
Capiniellu
Sainte-Lucie-de-Tallano
Pinarellu
Porto-Vecchio
Sartène
Sotta
Precojo
Tizzano
N196
Pianottoli-Caldarello
Chiova-d'Asino
Bonifacio
Ile Cavallo
0
10 mi
0
10 km
ITALY

Updated By Sean Hillen

"The best way to know Corsica," according to Napoléon, "is to be born there." Not everyone has had his luck, so chances are you'll be arriving on the overnight ferry from Marseille or flying in from Paris or Rome to discover "the Isle of Beauty." This vertical chalky granite world of its own, rising in the Mediterranean between Provence and Tuscany, remains France's very own Wild West: a powerful natural setting and, literally, a breath of fresh air.

Corsica's strategic location 168 km (105 miles) south of Monaco and 81 km (50 miles) west of Italy made Corsica a prize hotly contested by a succession of Mediterranean powers, notably Genoa, Pisa, and France. Their vestiges remain: the city-state of Genoa ruled Corsica for more than 200 years, leaving impressive citadels, churches, bridges, and nearly 100 medieval watchtowers around the island's coastline. The Italian influence is also apparent in village architecture and in the Corsican language: a combination of Italian, Tuscan dialect, and Latin.

Corsica gives an impression of immensity, seeming far larger than its 215-km (133-mile) length and 81-km (50-mile) width, partly because its rugged, mountainous terrain makes for very slow traveling and partly because the landscape and the culture vary greatly from one microregion to another. Much of the terrain of Corsica that is not wooded or cultivated is covered with a dense thicket of undergrowth, which along with chestnut trees makes up the maquis, a variety of wild and aromatic plants including lavender, myrtle, and heather that gave Corsica one of its sobriquets, "the perfumed isle."

PLANNER

WHEN TO GO

The best time to visit Corsica is fall or spring, when the weather is cool. Most Corsican culinary specialties are at their best between October and June. Try to avoid July and August, when mostly French and Italian vacationers fill hotels, crowd beaches, and jam roads. Prices soar and the Corsican temperament is at its most volatile. In winter the island has the best weather in France, but a majority of the hotels and restaurants are closed.

Travelers enjoying Corsica's laid-back vibe might be surprised to hear that it has the highest homicide rate per capita in France. Organized crime is the reason, and a spate of bombings and shootings has not helped improve the island's reputation. The good news is that none of the violence has targeted visitors, and the government of France is so confident that things are under control that it allowed the Tour de France to pass through the island for the first time in 2013.

GETTING HERE AND AROUND

AIR TRAVEL

Air France has daily service connecting Paris and Lyon with Ajaccio and Bastia. Air Corsica connects Ajaccio and Bastia to Nice and Marseille with several flights a day.

AIRPORTS Corsica has four major airports: Ajaccio, Bastia, Figari, and Calvi. The airports at Ajaccio and Bastia run regular shuttle-bus services to and from town. Taxis are also available in front of the terminals. Expect to pay around €25 to €30 to go from Campo dell'Oro to Ajaccio; €37 from Poretta Airport to Bastia. At Figari a bus during summer months meets all incoming flights and will take passengers as far as Bonifacio and Porto-Vecchio for about €9.

Contacts Ajaccio Napoleon Bonaparte Airport (*AJA*). ☎ *04-95-23-56-56.* **Bastia-Poretta Airport** (*BIA*). ☎ *04-95-54-54-54* 🌐 *www.bastia.aeroport.fr.* **Calvi Sainte Catherine Airport** (*CLY*). ☎ *04-95-65-88-88.* **Figari-Sud Corse Airport** (*FSC*). ☎ *04-95-71-10-10.*

BOAT AND FERRY TRAVEL

Regular car ferries run from Marseille, Nice, and Toulon to Ajaccio and Basta. These crossings take from 5 to 10 hours, with sleeping cabins available. The high-speed ferry from Nice to Bastia takes about three hours. Package deals, which include making the crossing with a car, an onboard cabin, and a hotel in Corsica, are available from SNCM, the Société Nationale Maritime Corse-Méditérranée. Connections from the Italian mainland are run by Corsica Ferries and Moby Lines. Sardinia can be reached by ferry from Bastia or Bonifacio on Moby Lines. Saremar also runs ferries to Sardinia. La Méridionale runs a service from Marseille to Ajaccio, Bastia, and Propriano in Corsica and Porto Torres in Sardinia.

Contacts CMN (*Compagnie Meridionale de Navigation*). ☎ *04-91-99-45-09* 🌐 *www.lameridionale.fr.* **Corsica Ferries.** ☎ *08-25-09-50-95* 🌐 *www.corsica-ferries.fr.* **La Méridionale.** ☎ *04-95-11-01-15* 🌐 *www.lameridionale.fr.* **Moby Lines.** ☎ *04-95-34-84-94* 🌐 *www.mobylines.fr.* **Saremar.** ☎ *04-95-73-00-96* 🌐 *www.saremar.it.* **SNCM** (*Société Nationale Maritime Corse-Méditérranée*). ☎ *04-95-29-66-65* 🌐 *www.sncm.fr.*

CAR TRAVEL

Though driving is undoubtedly the best way to explore the island's scenic stretches, note that winding, mountainous roads, uneven surfaces, and microclimates with fog or precipitation can actually double or triple your expected travel time. A good map is essential. Drive defensively: you'll find that others on the road tend to move at terrifying speeds, even at curves. Night driving, especially in the mountains, is not recommended since many areas are poorly lighted.

CRUISE TRAVEL

Ships dock in Ajaccio port, a short walk from the town of Ajaccio. Cafés and shops can be found immediately outside the port gates.

Renting a car allows you to explore several towns and surrounding attractions during your stay on the island. Be aware that travel times may be longer than map distances suggest, because the mountain roads can be narrow and winding.

TRAIN TRAVEL

The main line of Corsica's simple rail network runs from Ajaccio, in the west, to Corte, in the central valley, then divides at Ponte Leccia. From here one line continues to L'Ile Rousse and Calvi, in the north, and the other to Bastia, in the northeast. Another service runs four times daily between Ajaccio and Bastia.

Contacts SNCF. ☎ *04–95–23–11–03* 🌐 *www.sncf.com/en/passengers.*

RESTAURANTS

Corsican cuisine has been called a "winter cuisine," better between October and May, when game like sanglier (wild boar) as well as brocciu are well represented on all menus. The Corsican maquis grows some of Europe's wildest flora and fauna, ranging from free-range pigs to woodcock and pigeon. Chestnuts are a Corsican staple not to miss, whether in pastries, *pulenta,* or beer, while cheeses, especially the characteristic *brocciu* fresh cheese, are omnipresent upland delicacies.

HOTELS

Corsica's *fermes-auberges* (farmhouse-inns) have had a healthy dose of restoration, and tastefully designed hotels are still being built. During the peak season (from July to mid-September) prices are significantly higher, and some hotels insist that charges for breakfast and dinner be tacked onto the price. The best seaside hotels are priced only marginally lower than on the Riviera, but lodgings in the interior villages remain substantially cheaper. *Hotel reviews have been shortened. For full information, visit Fodors.com.*

WHAT IT COSTS IN EUROS

	$	$$	$$$	$$$$
Restaurants	under €18	€18–€24	€25–€32	over €32
Hotels	under €106	€106–€145	€146–€215	over €215

Restaurant prices are the average cost of a main course at dinner or, if dinner is not served, at lunch. Hotel prices are the lowest cost of a standard double room in high season.

VISITOR INFORMATION

The Agence du Tourisme de la Corse can provide practical and in-depth information about the whole island. The Parc Naturel Régional de la Corse, Corsica's wildlife and natural-resource management authority, controlling well over a third of the island, can provide trail maps, booklets, and a wide variety of information.

Contacts Agence du Tourisme de la Corse. ☎ *04-95-51-77-77* 🌐 *www.visit-corsica.com.*

TOURS

BOAT TOURS

Colombo Line Cruises. Most of Corsica's spectacular scenery is best viewed from the water. This company organizes whole-day glass-bottom boat tours. ✉ *Quai Landry, Calvi* ☎ 🌐 *www.colombo-line.com.*

Nave Va Promenades en Mer. In Ajaccio, Nave Va Promenades en Mer organizes twice-daily trips to the stunning Iles Sanguinaires. ✉ *Résidence L'Orée du Bois, Bloc A, Rte. de Mezzavia, Ajaccio* ☎ *04–95–51–31–31* 🌐 *www.naveva.com.*

BUS TOURS

Ollandini Voyages. This company arranges whole- and half-day bus tours of the island, leaving from Ajaccio. ✉ *1 rue Paul Colonna d'Istria, Ajaccio* ☎ 🌐 *www.groupencorse.com.*

14

CORSE DU SUD

Corse du Sud includes the French administrative capital of Ajaccio, the more mountainous zones, and the fortressed towns of Bonifacio and Porto-Vecchio. A beautiful combination of natural beauty and ancient history, the region is known as Napoléon's birthplace and visited for its exceptional sandy beaches, dramatic promontories, and stunning coves.

AJACCIO

40 mins by plane, 5–10 hrs by ferry from Marseille, Nice, or Toulon.

Considered Corsica's primary commercial and cultural hub, the largest city and regional capital of Ajaccio is situated on the west coast of the island, approximately 644 km (400 miles) southeast of Marseille, France. Founded in 1492, vestiges of ancient Corsica in this ville impériale revolve around the city's most famous son, Napoléon Bonaparte, whose family home—now the national museum Maison Bonaparte—pays tribute to the emperor's historical influence.

Remnants from what was originally a 12th-century Genoese colony are still visible around the Old Town near the imposing citadel and watchtower. Perfect for exploring, the luminous seaside city surrounded by snowcapped mountains and pretty beaches offers numerous sites, eateries, side streets, and a popular harbor, where sailboats and fishing vessels moor in the picturesque Tino Rossi port lined with well-established restaurants and cafés serving fresh local fare.

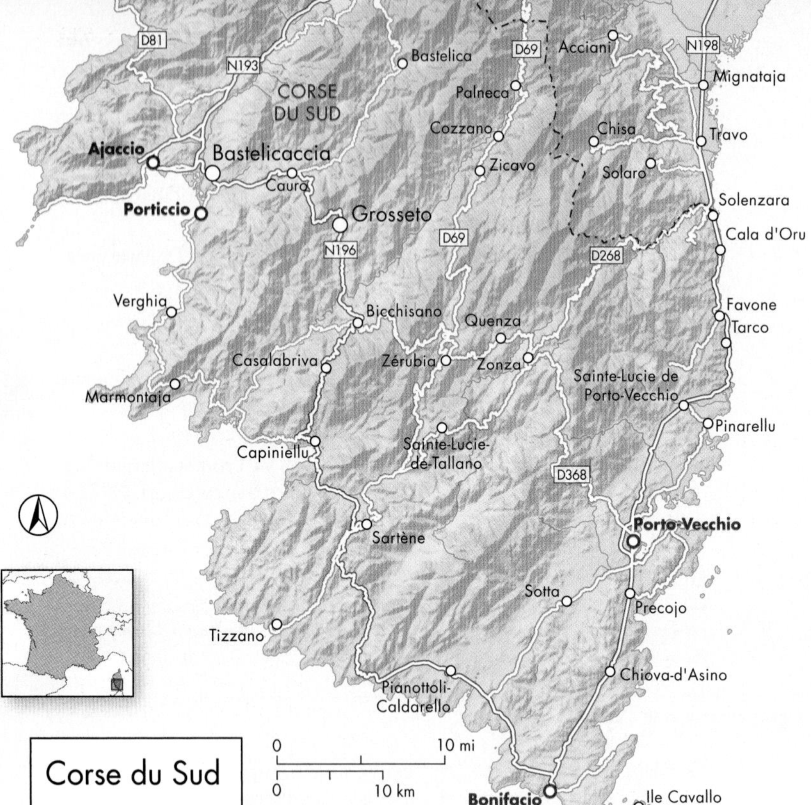

GETTING HERE

Flights into Aéroport d'Ajaccio Napoléon Bonaparte arrive regularly. To travel the short 5-km (3-mile) distance into the city center, take a shuttle bus to the main Gare Routière station that operates Monday to Saturday (€4.50). Alternatively, a taxi (€15) will take approximately 20 minutes. Ferries from Nice, Toulon, and Marseilles in France connect directly to Ajaccio and operate up to eight times daily. The average ferry crossing time is six hours.

Visitor Information Office de Tourisme d'Ajaccio. ☎ *04–95–51–53-03* 🌐 *www.ajaccio-tourisme.com.*

EXPLORING

Cathédrale Notre-Dame de L'Assomption. The 16th-century Baroque cathedral where Napoléon was baptized sits at the end of Rue St-Charles. The interior is covered with trompe-l'oeil frescoes, and the high altar, from a church in Lucca, Italy, was donated by Napoléon's sister Eliza after he made her princess of Tuscany. Eugène Delacroix's *The Triumph of Religion* hangs above the Virgin of the Sacred Heart marble altar from the 17th-century. ✉ *Rue Forcioli Conti, Ajaccio* ☎ 🌐 *www.ajaccio-tourisme.com* 🎫 *Free.*

Chapelle Impériale. In the south wing of the Palais Fesch, the neo-Renaissance-style Imperial Chapel was built in 1857 by Napoléon's nephew,

CLOSE UP

La Cuisine Sauvage

Authentic Corsican fare is based on free-range livestock, game (especially *sanglier*, or wild boar), herbs, and wild mushrooms best found between October and May in the villages of the mountainous interior. *Civets* (meaty stews) headline menus, as do the many versions of the proto-typical, hearty Corsican soup (*soupe paysanne, soupe corse*, or *soupe de montagne*) made from herbs and vegetables simmered for hours with a ham bone. Seafood dishes available on the coast include *aziminu*, a rich bouillabaisse.

Excellent *charcuterie* (pork products) include *lonzu* (shoulder), *coppa* (fillet), and *figatelli* (liver sausage), along with *prizuttu* (ham). Corsica's most emblematic cheese is really not a cheese at all: *brocciu* (pronounced broach), similar to ricotta, is used in omelets, *fiadone* (cheesecake), *fritelli* (chestnut-flour doughnuts), and as stuffing for trout or rabbit. Cheeses from Corsica's microregions include *bastelicaccia*, a soft, creamy sheep cheese, and the harder and sharper *sartenais*. Many of the most power-ful cheeses are simply designated as *brebis* (sheep) or *chèvre* (goat).

Chestnuts and chestnut flour, major players in Corsican gastronomy, are found in *castagna* (Corsican for chestnut), a cake; *panetta*, a kind of bread; *canistrelli*, dry cookies; beignets; *pulenta*, a doughy bread; and *Pietra*, chestnut beer. Corsica's best wines include the Arenas, Orenga de Gaffory, and Gentile cellars from the Patrimonio vineyards; Domaine Peraldi, Clos de Capitoro, or Clos Alzeto, from Ajaccio; Fiumicicoli, from Sartène; or Domaine de Torracia, from Porto-Vecchio.

14

Napoléon III, to accommodate the tombs of the Bonaparte family (Napoléon Bonaparte himself is buried in the Hôtel des Invalides in Paris). The Coptic crucifix over the altar was taken from Egypt during the general's 1798 campaign. Renovated in 2012, the somber chapel officially classified as a historic monument is constructed from the white calcified stone of St. Florent and worth a visit to view its neoclassi-cal cupola and ecclesiastical iconography. ✉ *50-52 rue Cardinal Fesch, Ajaccio* ☎ *04–95–21–48–17* 🌐 *www.ajaccio.fr/La-Chapelle-Imperiale_a353.html* 🎫 *€1.50* ⏲ *Apr.—end of June, Tues.—Sun 9:15—12:15 and 2:15—5:15, Mon. 1—5:15.*

Eglise St-Jean Baptiste. At the intersection of Rue du Roi-de-Rome and Rue Saint-Charles, you can visit the *confrérie*, or religious brother-hood, of St-Jean Baptiste. On June 24, the patron saint is honored with a solemn mass conducted by the city's bishop and Corsican music concert. ✉ *Rue du Roi-de-Rome, Ajaccio* ☎ *04–95–22–27–38* 🌐 *www.ajaccio.fr* 🎫 *Free.*

Hôtel de Ville (*Town Hall*). Ajaccio's town hall has an Empire-style grand salon hung with portraits of a long line of Bonapartes. You'll find a fine bust of Letizia, Napoléon's formidable mother, a bronze death mask of the emperor himself, and a frescoed ceiling depicting Napoléon's mete-oric rise. ✉ *Av. Antoine Serafini, Ajaccio* ☎ *04–95–51–52–53* 🌐 *www.*

The birth of an empire: Napoléon's birthplace and childhood home are on display in Ajaccio.

ajaccio.fr 🎫 *€2.30* ⏱ *June 15–Sept. 15, daily 9–11:45 and 2–5:45; Sept. 16–June 14, daily 9–11:45 and 2–4:45.*

Fodor's Choice ★ **Maison Bonaparte** (*Bonaparte House*). One of four national historic museums dedicated to Napoléon, the multilevel house where the emperor was born on August 15, 1769, contains memorabilia and paintings of the extended Bonaparte family. History aficionados can tour bedrooms, dining rooms, and salons where Charles and Letitzia Bonaparte raised their eight children. Period furnishings and antiques in Corsican and Empire styles are scattered about and pay tribute to the family's bourgeoisie upbringing. Head downstairs to see the cellars and granite oil pressing mill acquired by Napoléon III in 1860, which depict the importance of rural industry for the Bonaparte's income. Visit the trapdoor room and find the opening next to the door through which Napoléon allegedly escaped in 1799. The building itself changed hands multiple times through Bonaparte heirs until 1923, when it was donated to the state of France by Prince Victor, elder son of Prince Jérôme Napoléon. ✉ *Rue St-Charles, Ajaccio* ☎ *04–95–21–43–89* 🌐 *www.musees-nationaux-malmaison.fr/musee-maisonbonaparte* 🎫 *€7* ⏱ *Oct.–Mar., Tues.–Sun. 10:30–12:30 and 1:15–4:30; Apr.–Sept., Tues.–Sun. 10:30–12:30 and 1:15–6.*

FAMILY **Marché Central.** For an authentic view of daily Corsican life, tour this wonderful open-air food market brimming with gastronomic delights. There is an array of local cheeses, charcuterie, breads, pastries, olives, condiments, and aromatic meats for sale. Traditional indulgences like chestnut-infused beignets can be savored in an atmosphere guaranteed to be lively and local. Bring your euros—cash is the preferred method of payment. ✉ *Pl. Foch, Ajaccio* 🌐 *www.ajaccio-tourisme.com* ⏲ *Tues.–Sun. 8–noon.*

FAMILY Fodor's Choice ★ **Musée des Beaux-Arts–Palais Fesch.** This internationally recognized museum houses one of the most important collections from the Napoleonic era; it's undoubtedly one of the most significant displays in France of ancient Italian masterpieces spanning the 14th to 20th century. There are nearly 18,000 items, all part of an astounding inventory that belonged to Napoléon's uncle, Cardinal Fesch. Thanks to his nephew's military conquests, the cardinal was able to amass (steal, some would say) many celebrated old master paintings, the most famous of which are now in Paris's Louvre. The museum's beautiful vaulted corridors showcase 700 paintings, portraits, still lifes, and sculptures from the First and Second Empire from the French school. Don't miss the new gallery with engravings and drawings depicting historic Corsica. The building itself, constructed by the cardinal as the Institute of Arts and Sciences, dates back to 1837. ✉ *50-52 rue Cardinal Fesch, Ajaccio* ☎ *04–95–26–26–26,* 🌐 *www.musee-fesch.com* 🎟 *€8* ⏲ *Oct.–Apr., Mon., Wed., and Sat. 10–5, Thurs. and Fri. noon–5; May–Sept., Mon., Wed., and Sat. 10:30–6, Thurs., Fri., and Sun. noon–6.*

Place Maréchal-Foch. Surrounded by a row of stately palm trees, Place Maréchal-Foch is easily recognizable by its fountain of four Corsican granite lions encircling a commanding statue of Napoléon, the work of sculptor Jérôme Maglioli. Popular as a spot to people-watch on a sunny day, this triangle is surrounded by cafés and opens up to the Ajaccio port. ✉ *Pl. Marechal Foch, Ajaccio.*

WHERE TO EAT

$$$$ FRENCH ✕ **20123.** The tables are always full at this popular establishment known for its traditional cuisine, fresh daily catches, and, in season, game specials such as *civet de sanglier* (wild boar stew), served in a bubbling earthenware casserole with cheese-infused polenta. The rustic interior has a starry sky above, antique lanterns, and a stone fountain where guests pour their own water into ceramic jugs. In keeping with the familial style of service and food presentation, cutting boards with fresh-baked loaves of wheat bread are provided to start your copious meal. Three-course fixed menus are offered in two seatings at 7:30 and 9:30, and include an exquisite cheese platter with homemade fig confiture. $ *Average main: €35* ✉ *2 rue Roi-de-Rome, Ajaccio* ☎ *04–95–21–50–05* 🌐 *www.20123.fr* ⏲ *Closed Mon. and mid-Jan.–mid-Feb. No lunch mid-June–mid Sept.*

$$ SEAFOOD ✕ **Le Cabanon Bleu.** With an attractive terrace at the edge of the sea granting wonderful views across Ajaccio Bay, Le Cabanon Bleu serves mainly fresh fish and seafood dishes like John Dory in a creamy aioli sauce. The seafood platter is generous, mixing shellfish and saffron rice, and the fresh lobster dish is another good option. Located beside Hotel Les Mouettes, it is reached off the main coast road about a mile outside Ajaccio. $ *Average main: €20* ✉ *65 Cours Lucien Bonaparte, Ajaccio* ☎ *04–95–51–02–15* 💳 *No credit cards.*

14

$$$$ MEDITERRANEAN FAMILY **Le Week End.** About 10 minutes from downtown Ajaccio is this eatery where white rattan furniture and blue tablecloths are overshadowed by a spectacular ocean view and fine seafood menu. Here you'll find everything from marinated octopus and tuna spring rolls to rockfish soup and grilled red sea bream. Family-run since 1956, this restaurant flourishes with secret recipes handed down from generations. History can still be found in the fireplace lounge, where velvet chairs and family paintings date back to 1920. *Average main: €60 Rte. des Iles Sanguinaires, Ajaccio 04–95–52–01–39 www.leweekend-plage.com.*

WHERE TO STAY

$$$ HOTEL **Hôtel San Carlu.** On the edge of the Old Town, this friendly hotel overlooking the ramparts and sea was once the home of Napoléon's nanny. **Pros:** convenient location; clean rooms; free Wi-Fi. **Cons:** no parking; some rooms are old-fashioned; ordinary breakfast buffet. *Rooms from: €175 8 bd. Danielle Casanova, Ajaccio 04–95–21–13–84 www.hotel-sancarlu.com Closed mid-Dec.–early Feb. 39 rooms Breakfast.*

$$$$ HOTEL FAMILY **La Dolce Vita.** Spread out over whitewashed terraces at the edge of the Golfe d'Ajaccio, this hotel has a spectacular swimming pool that overlooks the sea. **Pros:** splendid sea views; good amenities. **Cons:** rocky beach; pricey rooms. *Rooms from: €380 Rte. des Iles Sanguinaires, 8 km (5 miles) from center of town, Ajaccio 04–95–52–42–42 www.hotel-dolcevita.com Closed mid-Oct.–late Apr. 30 rooms, 2 suites Some meals.*

$$$ HOTEL **Les Mouettes Hotel Demeure.** With a charming garden overlooking the glistening waters of the bay, this hotel offers great views of the picturesque town of Porticcio. **Pros:** spacious rooms; picturesque views; lovely swimming pool. **Cons:** restaurant only serves a snack menu. *Rooms from: €195 9 Cours Lucien Bonaparte, Ajaccio 04–95–50–40–40 www.hotellesmouettes.fr Closed Nov. 21–Apr. 1 26 rooms, 2 suites Breakfast No credit cards.*

$$$ B&B/INN **Palazzu u Domu.** Steps away from the house where Napoléon was born, this lodging once served as the ancestral residence of Duke Charles-Andre Pozzo di Borgo of the notable Ajaccio family. **Pros:** comfortable beds; central location; outdoor terrace. **Cons:** unreliable Internet connection; inconsistent service. *Rooms from: €189 17 rue Bonaparte, Ajaccio 04–95–50–00–20 www.palazzu-domu.com 45 rooms, 1 suite Breakfast.*

NIGHTLIFE AND PERFORMING ARTS

La Place. A well-known *boîte du nuit* (nightclub), La Place draws both young clubbers and older locals looking for a good, loud time. Dance away the hours to techno and house music. *Pl. du Diamant, Ajaccio 06–18–86–74–30.*

Le Privilège. In a low-key part of Old Town, Le Privilège is a local gathering place featuring music and themed party nights. *7 rue Eugène Macchini, Ajaccio 04–95–50–11– 80.*

SHOPPING

Art'Insula. A large selection of leather, pottery, and beautiful jewelry crafted by local artisans is available at Art'Insula. For the gourmand, there's an assortment of honeys, vinegars, and liqueurs. ✉ *57 rue Fesch, Ajaccio* ☎ *04–95–50–54–67* 🌐 *www.artisula.com*.

Casa Napoléon. This well-stocked boutique sells organic jams, olives oils, wines, and traditional dishes. It belongs to Charles Antona, who's been in business for more than 30 years. ✉ *3 rue Fesch, Ajaccio* ☎ *04–95–21–47–88* 🌐 *www.casanapoleon.com*.

U Stazzu. Known for its high-quality cheese and wine, this award-winning shop offers some of the best hams on the island, including the waist-busting Coppa and Lonzu. Tasting is encouraged. ✉ *1 rue Bonaparte, Ajaccio* ☎ *04–95–51–10–80* 🌐 *www.ustazzu.com*.

PORTICCIO

17 km (11 miles) south of Ajaccio on N196.

Between the sea and mountain, this upscale resort town a short scenic drive from the capital benefits from unforgettable views and a palette of nautical activities perfect for the clear, calm waters of the Ajaccio Gulf. It's an oasis, dotted with a number of luxury resorts, notable for its beaches, verdant countryside, and ancient Tower of Capitello.

GETTING HERE

Découvertes Naturelle and other companies shuttle passengers between Ajaccio and Porticcio throughout the summer season (one-way €5, round-trip €8). Buses leave Ajaccio's Gare Routière and stop at Porticcio Mare e Monti Sud and Mare a Mare Centre (€3 one-way). The 19-km (11-mile) drive by taxi (€28) or car takes approximately 30 to 40 minutes from downtown Ajaccio.

TOURS

FAMILY **Découvertes Naturelle.** Discover the stunning landscape with boat excursions from Ajaccio, Porticcio, and Propriano offered by Découvertes Naturelle. The company also runs shuttles between Ajaccio and Porticcio costing €5 each way. ✉ *1 rue Emmanuel Arene, Ajaccio* ☎ *06–03–13–46–80* 🌐 *www.promenades-en-mer.org*.

VISITOR INFORMATION

Office Municipal de Tourisme de Porticcio. ✉ *Les Echoppes, BP 125, Porticcio* ☎ *04–95–25–10–09* 🌐 *www.porticcio-corsica.com*.

WHERE TO EAT AND STAY

$$$$ MEDITERRANEAN ✕ **Le Caroubier.** Inside the Sofitel Golfe d'Ajaccio, Le Caroubier presents a sedate ambience with a dining room featuring contrasting shades of black, white, and crimson. Floor-to-ceiling pillars, a pianist tickling the ivories, and candlelit tables add a touch of class. Wraparound windows offer terrific views of the coastline. The kitchen prides itself on incorporating Corsican flavors into modern cuisine in such dishes as roasted veal blended with tender chicory and mountain rosemary, as well as poached eggs Corsican-style: a blend of local cheeses, including brocciu, make it a tasty combination indeed. $ *Average main: €40*

✉ *Sofitel Golfe d'Ajaccio Thalassa Sea & Spa, Domaine de la Pointe Golfe d'Ajaccio, Porticcio* ☎ *04–95–29–40–40* 🌐 *www.sofitel.com.*

$$$$ HOTEL FAMILY Fodor's Choice ★ **Le Maquis.** One of the island's finest *hôtels de charme,* this graceful ivy-covered Genoese-style retreat rambles down through terraced gardens to a private beach overlooking the Golfe d'Ajaccio. **Pros:** excellent restaurant; exceptional service; indoor pool. **Cons:** loud plane noise from airport; no gym or spa; outdoor pool isn't heated. $ *Rooms from: €520* ✉ *Bd. Marie-Jeanne Bozzi, Porticcio* ☎ *04–95–25–05–55* 🌐 *www.lemaquis.com* ⊙ *Closed Jan.–Mar.* *18 rooms, 7 suites* *No meals.*

$$$$ RESORT **Sofitel Golfe d'Ajaccio Thalassa Sea & Spa Hotel.** Leave your door ajar and the rhythmic ebb and flow of the sea over rocks outside your bedroom provides perfect accompaniment to sleep—that sums up the ideal location of the 5-star Sofitel Golfe d'Ajaccio Thalassa Sea & Spa, a 15-minute drive from Ajaccio airport. **Pros:** luxurious seawater spa; great views over Ajaccio and the mountains beyond; attentive service. **Cons:** small, rocky beach; transport required to Ajaccio. $ *Rooms from: €368* ✉ *Sofitel Golfe d'Ajaccio Thalassa Sea & Spa Hotel, Domaine de la Pointe, Porticcio* ☎ *04–95–29–40–40* 🌐 *http://www.sofitel.com/gb/hotel-0587-sofitel-golfe-d-ajaccio-thalassa-sea-spa/index.shtml* ⊙ *Closed Jan.–Feb. 13* *98 rooms* *No meals.*

BONIFACIO

110 km (68 miles) southeast of Porticcio.

The ancient fortress town of Bonifacio occupies a spectacular cliff-top aerie above a harbor carved from limestone cliffs. It's 13 km (8 miles) from Sardinia, and the local speech is heavily influenced by the accent and idiom of that nearby Italian island. Established in the 12th century as Genoa's first Corsican stronghold, Bonifacio remained Genoese through centuries of battles and sieges. As you wander the narrow streets of the **Haute Ville** (Upper Village), inside the walls of the citadel, think of Homer's *Odyssey.* It's here, in the harbor, that scholars place the catastrophic encounter (Chapter X) between Ulysses's fleet and the Laestrygonians, who hurled lethal boulders down from the cliffs.

GETTING HERE

Bonifacio is approximately 20 km (12 miles) south of Figari airport (Figari-Sud Corse), with transfers by taxi (€45) or seasonal shuttle bus (€10). In summer months, expect congested streets in and around Bonifacio, delaying journey times.

Visitor Information Office Municipal de Tourisme Bonifacio. ☎ *04–95–73–11–88* 🌐 *www.bonifacio.fr.*

EXPLORING

Bastion de l'Étendard (*Bastion of the Standard*). From Place d'Armes at the city gate, enter the 13th-century Bastion de l'Étendard, where you can still see the system of weights and levers used to raise the drawbridge. The former garrison, the last remaining part of the original fortress, houses life-size dioramas of the bombardment of the bastion in the 16th-century Franco-Turkish war. Climb the steep steps for an incredible panoramic view of the white-chalk cliffs along the coastline. ✉ *Av.*

Charles de Gaulle, Bonifacio ☎ *04–95–73–11–88* 🌐 *www.bonifacio.fr/site-historique-bastion-de-letendard.html* 🎟 *€2.50* ⏲ *Mid-June–mid-Sept., weekdays 9–8, weekends 10–7.*

FAMILY **Dragon Grottoes.** Boats from Bonifacio bring you to see the blue Dragon Grottos, a spectacular geological site. Tours typically venture to Venus's Bath, sea caves at Sdragonatto and St-Angoine, and the Lavezzi Islands. Boats set out every 15 minutes during July and August. ✉ *Bonifacio* 🌐 *www.bonifacio.fr.*

Eglise Sainte Marie Majeure. The oldest structure in the city, the 12th-century church with buttresses attaching it to surrounding houses is located in the center of the citadel's maze of cobblestone streets. Inside the Pisan-Genoese church, look for the 3rd-century white-marble Roman sarcophagus and the Renaissance baptismal font. Walk around the back to see the loggia built above a huge cistern that stored water for use in times of siege. The 14th-century bell tower rises 82 feet. ✉ *Rue du Saint Sacrement, Bonifacio* ☎ *04–95–73–11–88* 🌐 *www.visit-corsica.com/en/infotour/evenmts_manifs/id/143.*

14

WHERE TO EAT

$$$$ BISTRO FAMILY ✕ **Kissing Pigs.** For traditional Corsican meat, cheese, and wine, head to this cozy eatery where aged salamis hang from the rafters. Adding rustic authenticity are stone walls, terra-cotta tile floors, and illuminated alcoves holding books, bottles, and baskets. Start with the selection of farmers' cheese served with chestnut bread, fig jam, dried fruit, and purple grapes. The summer menu features gourmet salads like La Basse Cour (duck, bacon, and apples on a bed of greens) and open-faced sandwiches like the Pertusato *tartine* (foie gras with muscat-marinated macerated figs). Organic pork is the specialty here, since it comes directly from the owner's pig farm. Save room for the homemade ice cream that comes in flavors of fig, myrtle, and chestnut. [$] *Average main: €35* ✉ *5 quai Banda del Ferro, Bonifacio* ☎ *04–95–73–56–09* ⏲ *Closed Sun. Nov.—Apr.* ✍ *Reservations essential.*

$$$ SEAFOOD ✕ **Les 4 Vents.** This friendly restaurant near the boat terminal is popular with the yachting crowd. In winter the kitchen serves up such Alsatian specialties as sauerkraut and sausages. In summer the focus is on grilled fish and meats, as well as typical Corsican dishes. Try a perfectly prepared risotto, bouillabaisse, or pasta with succulent *langouste* (lobster). Fresh ingredients, upscale presentation, and friendly service are consistent draws. [$] *Average main: €75* ✉ *29 quai Banda di Ferro, Bonifacio* ☎ *04–95–73–07–50* ⏲ *Closed Nov.—Feb.* ✍ *Reservations essential.*

$$$ SEAFOOD FAMILY ✕ **Le Voilier.** Chef Jean Paul Bartoli and his wife make this year-round restaurant at the port a popular dining spot with their warm smiles and attentive service. The couple serves carefully selected and prepared seafood, along with fine Corsican sausage and traditional cuisine from soup to *fiadone* (cheesecake). Try the affordably priced set menus. [$] *Average main: €30* ✉ *81 quai Jerome Comparetti, Bonifacio* ☎ *04–95–73–07–06* 🌐 *www.restaurant-levoilier-bonifacio.com* ⏲ *Closed Dec. 1—15.*

WHERE TO STAY

$$$$ B&B/INN **Hôtel le Genovese.** This intimate *hotel de charme* is built into the ramparts of the upper town's citadel, with stone elements reflecting the surrounding architecture. **Pros:** stylish hotel; excellent seafood; central location. **Cons:** expensive breakfast; curt staff. *Rooms from: €270* ✉ *Haute Ville, Pl. de l'Europe, Haute Ville, Bonifacio* ☎ *04–95–73–12–34* 🌐 *www.hotel-genovese.com* *12 rooms, 6 suites* *No meals* *Free Wi-Fi.*

NIGHTLIFE

B'52. For an evening of clubbing, head to this popular nightspot filled with the rich but not necessarily famous during summer. During off-season, the club is a weekend haunt for young locals who enjoy DJ theme nights. ✉ *35 quai Comparetti, Bonifacio* ☎ *06–32–82–18–69* 🌐 *www.b52bonifacio.com* *June—Sept.*

PORTO-VECCHIO

29 km (18 miles) north of Bonifacio, 140 km (87 miles) southeast of Ajaccio.

With a compact Old Town of cobblestone streets lined with charming buildings, a modern marina teeming with yachts, and white-sand beaches lapped by turquoise water, Porto-Vecchio is most attractive. Place de République, the main square, is filled with lively restaurants and cafés, as is the neighboring Cours Napoléon. There are more along the harbor area, where you can purchase tickets for boat trips to Bonifacio or the nature preserve on the Lavezzi Islands. Walking the Old Town is easy with the tourist office's free map of historic sights, including well-maintained fortresses. For great views, walk along the top of the ancient wall, especially near the the Porte Genoise Gate.

GETTING HERE AND AROUND

Porto-Vecchio is reached by air and sea. Figari Sud Corse Airport, 24 km (15 miles) south of Porto-Vecchio, receives flights from Paris, Marseille, and Nice, as well as other European cities in high season. Buses connect Porto-Vecchio to Figari airport for around €10. Taxi fares from Porto-Vecchio to the airport are around €50. In season, buses also go from Porto-Vecchio to different area beaches and connect with ferries that head to Marseille and Toulon in France and Civitavecchia, Italy.

Visitor Information Office Municipal de Tourisme Porto Vecchio. ☎ *04–95–70–09–58* 🌐 *www.ot-portovecchio.com.*

EXPLORING

Col de Bavella. There's no better place to enjoy this region's raw, beautiful scenery than Col de Bavella, a mass of towering, rippling rock formations shaped like a huge church organ. Numerous walks here cater to people of all fitness levels. There's a small information point at the parking lot that describes options. A three- to four-hour circuit to the Trou de la Bombe—-an 8 meter-hole in the rock—-is a popular choice. Other activities include rock-climbing and canyoning. ✉ *D268, Zonza.*

WHERE TO EAT AND STAY

$$$$ MEDITERRANEAN **La Table de Cala Rossa.** The cuisine at La Table mixes Corsican and Japanese influences with products from the well-regarded eatery's own garden. A three-course menu with two options for each course changes daily and ranges from squares of piglet roasted in their own skin with Asian spices to lightly grilled scallops in a soup of pumpkin with hazelnut oil. Meals are served with wine from Clos Canarelli, a vineyard just outside Figari belonging to the same family who own the hotel. *Average main: €45 Grand Hotel de Cala Rossa, Cala Rossa, Porto Vecchio 04–95–71–61–51 www.hotel-calarossa.com.*

$$$$ HOTEL Fodor's Choice ★ **Grand Hotel de Cala Rossa.** Partially hidden by the thick foliage out front, the Grand Hotel Calla Rossa has the feel of a tropical retreat. **Pros:** easy access to sandy beach; excellent amenities; superb restaurant. **Cons:** need a car to get around; expensive rates. *Rooms from: €530 Rte. de Cala Rossa, Porto Vecchio 04–95–71–61–51 www.hotel-calarossa.com Closed Nov.—Apr. 42 rooms Some meals.*

14

HAUTE CORSE

Haute Corse (Upper Corsica) is the northeastern end of the island and is, indeed, higher in mean altitude than Corse du Sud, topped by the 8,876-foot Monte Cinto. Most Corsica enthusiasts agree that Haute Corse is the island's finest trove of highland forests, remote villages, hidden cultural gems, vineyards, beaches, and alpine lakes and streams. In the center of Haute Corse is the city of Corte, Corsica's historic heart. To the east is the forested region of La Castagniccia, named for its *châtaigniers* (chestnut trees), one of Corsica's treasures, especially in the fall, when fallen leaves and chestnuts blanket the ground. The forest's tiny roadways go through villages with stunning Baroque churches and houses still roofed in traditional blue-gray slate.

CORTE

83 km (51 miles) northeast of Ajaccio.

Set amid spectacular cliffs and gorges at the confluence of the Tavignano, Restonica, and Orta rivers, Corte is the spiritual heart and soul of Corsica. Capital of Pasquale Paoli's government from 1755 to 1769, it was also where Paoli established the Corsican University in 1765. Closed by the victorious French in 1769, the university, always a symbol of Corsican identity, was reopened in 1981. To reach the upper town and the 15th-century château overlooking the rivers, walk up the cobblestone ramp from Place Pasquale-Paoli. Stop in lovely Place Gaffori at one of the cafés or restaurants. Note the bullet-pocked house where the Corsican hero Gian Pietro Gaffori and his wife, Faustina, held off the Genoese in 1750.

GETTING HERE

Public transport is quite poor in Corsica, so to access stunning views of interior Corsica, your best bet is to rent a car or take a local minibus. The shortest distance to Corte is from Bastia. Count on at least an hour

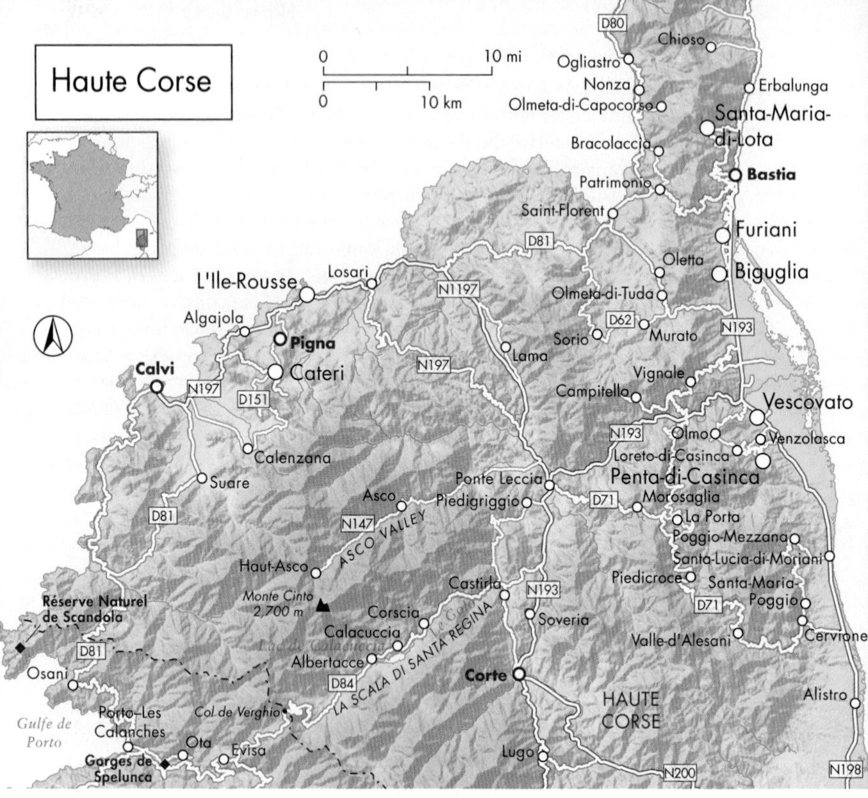

to negotiate the 68-km (42-mile) drive. From Ajaccio, a distance of 80 km (49 miles) will take at least 90 minutes.

The Corsican train called the *trinighellu* is infrequent and slow, and the journey from Ajaccio to Corte takes about one hour and 40 minutes; from Bastia, it's 90 minutes. A main bus line connects Bastia to Corte (90 minutes).

Visitor Information Office de Tourisme Corte. ☎ *04–95–46–26–70* 🌐 *www.corte-tourisme.com.*

EXPLORING

FAMILY **Citadelle.** One of six island fortifications of its kind, the Citadelle, a Vauban-style fortress (1769–78), is built around the original 15th-century bastion at the highest point of the cliff, with the river below. In 1769, after the defeat of Ponte Novu, Corsica came under French rule. Count de Vaux, who held Corte, undertook the construction of the citadel's second reconstruction to strengthen the defense system of the city. The building contains the **Musée de la Corse** (Corsica Museum), dedicated to the island's history and ethnography. ✉ *Rue de Donjon, Corte* ☎ *04–95–45–25–45* 🌐 *www.musee-corse.com* 🎫 *€5.30* 🕒 *Apr.–mid-June and late Sept.–Oct., daily 10–6; mid-June–late Sept., daily 10–8; Nov. and mid-Jan.–Mar., daily 10–5.*

FAMILY **Gorges de la Restonica** (*Restonica Gorges*). Put on your hiking boots—the Gorges de la Restonica make a spectacular day tour, 10 km (6 miles) southwest of Corte. At the top of the Restonica Valley, leave your car in the parking area. A two-hour climb will take you to Lac de Mélo, a trout-filled mountain lake 6,528 feet above sea level. Another hour up is the usually snow-bordered Lac de Capitello. Information on trails is available from the Parc Naturel Régional. Light meals are served in the stone shepherds' huts at the Bergeries de Grotelle. ✉ *Off D623, Corte* ☎ *04–95–50–59–04, 04–95–51–79–00* 🌐 *www.parc-corse.org.*

La Scala di Santa Regina. The Stairway of the Holy Queen is one of Corsica's most spectacular roads—one of the most difficult to navigate, especially in winter. About 20 km (12 miles) northwest of Corte, it traces the twisty path of the Golo River, which has carved its way through layers of red granite, forming dramatic gorges and waterfalls. Follow the road to the Col de Verghio (Verghio Pass) for superb views of Tafunatu, the legendary perforated mountain, and Monte Cinto. On the way up you'll pass through the Valdo Niello Forest, Corsica's most important woodlands, filled with pines and beeches. As you descend from the Verghio Pass through the Forêt d'Aitone (Aitone Forest), note how well manicured it is—the pigs, goats, and sheep running rampant through the tall Laricio pines keep it this way. As you pass the village of Evisa, with its orange roofs, look across the impressive Gorges de Spelunca (Spelunca Gorge) to see the hill village of Ota. A small road on the right will take you across the gorge, where there's an ancient Genoese-built bridge. ✉ *D84, Corte.*

Palais National (*National Palace*). The Palais National, just outside the citadel and above Place Gaffori, is the ancient residence of Genoa's representatives in Corsica and was the seat of the Corsican parliament from 1755 to 1769 where Paoli set up his government for independent Corsica. Today it is part of Corte University. ✉ *3 rue du Palais National, Corte* ☎ *04–95–45–00–00* 🌐 *www.univ-corse.fr/presentation-carte-de-la-corse-palazzu-naziunale_4192.html.*

WHERE TO EAT

$$$ ITALIAN ✕ **L'Annexe.** This eatery's modern decor, ambient music, and young staff dressed in jeans and black T-shirts make it a hip spot. Funky artwork covers the walls, and chilled wine bottles come in fluorescent bags rather than champagne buckets. Popular with the locals are the brick-oven pizzas, grilled hamburgers, and gourmet salads. For something more traditional, try the meat-and-cheese platter of prosciutto, Brie, smoked salmon, roasted peppers, and fig jam before moving on to the *magret de canard.* $ *Average main: €25* ✉ *Rampe Sainte Croix, Corte* ☎ *04–95–38–37–59* 🌐 *www.restaurant-lannexe.fr* ⏲ *Closed Sun.*

$$$$ MODERN FRENCH ✕ **Le 24 Restaurant.** Rough-hewn archways, stone walls, and atmospheric lighting give this chic restaurant a cavernous feel. The chalkboard-menu, brought to each table, features shrimp tempura, seafood pasta, and sautéed dorado, among other favorites. Grilled to perfection is the filet mignon, topped with foie gras and served with a baked potato and artichoke. Portions are large, and the presentation is extraordinary. Definitely try one of the decadent desserts like the chocolate soufflé

or homemade sorbet. $ *Average main: €50* ✉ *24 cours Paoli, Corte* ☎ *04–95–46–02–90.*

$$ FRENCH FAMILY **Le Nicoli.** The mouthwatering aroma of rotisserie chicken wafting from the open kitchen seals the deal for most newcomers, but there are plenty of other options like veal tournedos with potatoes, mushroom risotto, and salmon tartare served with scallops and pistachio oil. The restaurant is extremely modern, down to the stone plates. In summer, ask for a table on the terrace and nibble tapas to your heart's—and stomach's—content. Try the affordable Corsican menu for only €19.50, including appetizer, main course, and dessert. $ *Average main: €20* ✉ *4 av. Jean Nicoli, Corte* ☎ *04–95–33–27–17* ⏲ *Closed Sun. Oct.–Mar.*

WHERE TO STAY

$$$ B&B/INN **Hôtel Dominique Colonna.** This modern hotel is full of delightful surprises, including sliding doors leading directly out to breakfast nooks beside a stream. **Pros:** incredible breakfast; enchanting location; gracious staff. **Cons:** hard mattresses; no shade at the pool; a bit outside town. $ *Rooms from: €160* ✉ *Vallee de la Restonica, BP 83, Corte* ☎ *04–95–45–25–65* 🌐 *www.dominique-colonna.com* ⏲ *Closed Nov. 5–Mar. 14* *29 rooms and suites* 🍽 *Some meals.*

CALVI

85 km (53 miles) north of Piana, 164 km (100 miles) north of Ajaccio, 92 km (57 miles) west of Bastia.

Corsica's slice of the Riviera, Calvi has been described as "an oasis of pleasure on an otherwise austere island." Today Calvi sees a summertime invasion of tourists, drawn to the 6-km (4-mile) stretch of sandy white beach, impressive citadel overlooking the Old Town, and lively restaurants. Calvi is a city for strolling, whether in search of bars, picturesque coastline views, or simply a bit of retail therapy.

GETTING HERE

From Bastia, follow D81 until you cross Saint Florent. Continue on D81 toward Saint Florent for 52 km (32 miles), then go right onto N197. Follow the N197 for 40 km (24 miles) to reach Calvi. The drive will take approximately 2½ hours. Trains arrive from the main cities. Coach buses and boats are also available to access and tour the popular resort promontory.

Visitor Information Office de Tourisme Calvi. ☎ *04–95–65–16–67* 🌐 *www.balagne-corsica.com/calvi-ile-rousse-corse.html.*

EXPLORING

Cathédrale St-Jean-Baptiste. The austere facade of the 13th-century catehdral of John the Baptist is worth a visit to see its alabaster Renaissance baptismal font decorated with angel heads and rows of pews where the city's chaste upper-class women used to pray. ✉ *Pl. d'Armes, Calvi* ☎ *04–95–65–16–67* 🌐 *www.balagne-corsica.com/cathedrale-saint-jean-baptiste-de-calvi.html.*

FAMILY **Citadelle.** This Genoese citadel is perched on a rocky promontory at the tip of the bay. An inscription above the drawbridge—*civitas calvi* *semper fidelis* ("The citizens of Calvi are always faithful")—reflects the town's unswerving allegiance to Genoa. At the welcome center, just inside the gates, you can watch the video on the city's history, book an English-language guided tour, or follow the self-guided walking tour. ✉ *Rte. de la Citadelle, Calvi* ☎ *04–95–65–36–74* 🌐 *www.balagne-corsica.com/visite-de-la-citadelle-avec-christophe-colomb.html.*

WHERE TO EAT

$$$$ FRENCH ✕ **Emile's.** With an open terrace offering panoramic views of the port, you're lucky if you find a table at Emile's during summer. This elegant restaurant serves prix-fixe menus for lunch and dinner. Prices run from steep to splurge for the classic French cuisine paired with local wines—the seasonal degustation menu runs €140. [$] *Average main: €70* ✉ *Quai Landry, Calvi* ☎ *04–95–65–09–60* 🌐 *www.restaurant-emiles.fr* ✍ *Reservations essential.*

14

$$$$ MEDITERRANEAN ✕ **La Palmeraie.** Part of La Signoria Hotel, La Palmeraie has two dining options: a bistro-style room with circular tables, colorful chairs, and photographs depicting various celebrities who have visited the property, and a beautiful conservatory emanating an art-nouveau style in a spectrum of colors ranging from terra-cotta to olive green to sky blue. Dinner highlights include a starter of pressed duck foie gras with local figs and sautéed veal with wild mushrooms. Indulge in cheese heaven: this place stocks 40 different Corsican varieties. [$] *Average main: €40* ✉ *Rte. de la Foret de Bonifato, Calvi* ☎ *04–95–65–93–00* 🌐 *www.hotel-la-signoria.com.*

$$$$ MEDITERRANEAN ✕ **La Table by La Villa.** Perched high amid rambling hills overlooking the ocher-colored Old Citadel, La Table by La Villa is the proud recipient of a Michelin star. Memorable dining highlights include *oeuf mollet frit* (poached eggs with celery, mushrooms, and black truffles); carpaccio of John Dory and spider crab with fennel, fresh coriander, and shiso leaves; and braised pigeon breast with confit of pigeon leg, porcini mushrooms, and dried fruits. [$] *Average main: €45* ✉ *Chem. Notre-Dame de la Serra, Calvi* ☎ *04–95–65–10–10* 🌐 *www.hotel-lavilla.com* ⏲ *Closed mid-Oct.—mid Apr.*

WHERE TO STAY

$$$ B&B/INN 🏨 **Calvi Mariana Hotel.** On a hillside overlooking Calvi Bay, this hotel sits just five minutes from the center of town. **Pros:** in-room massages; good facilities; convenient to town. **Cons:** small bathrooms; extra fee for Wi-Fi access; on busy roundabout. [$] *Rooms from: €155* ✉ *Av. Santa Maria, Calvi* ☎ *04–95–65–31–38* 🌐 *www.hotel-mariana.com* 🛏 *50 rooms, 4 suites* 🍽 *Breakfast.*

$$$$ HOTEL 🏨 **Hotel La Signoria.** From the minute you step onto the honeycombed terra-cotta tiles of this historic 17th-century country manor—a former Genoese estate bestowed by King Louis XV—you'll see why it's part of the luxurious Relaix & Chateaux collection. **Pros:** tranquil location; excellent buffet breakfast; spa and fitness center have natural products. **Cons:** expensive rates; transport required to visit Calvi. [$] *Rooms from: €510* ✉ *Rte. de la Forêt de Bonifato, 5 km (3 miles) from Calvi, Calvi* ☎ *04–95–65–93–00* 🌐 *www.hotel-la-signoria.com* ⏲ *Closed Nov.–Easter* 🛏 *27 rooms and suites* 🍽 *No meals.*

$$ B&B/INN **Hotel Le Magnolia.** In this pretty 19th-century former mansion between the church and the market, cozy rooms are named after French literary figures. **Pros:** central location; discreet service; comfortable rooms. **Cons:** very thin walls; old-fashioned decor. *Rooms from: €120 Rue Alsace Lorraine, Calvi 04–95–65–19–16 www.hotel-le-magnolia.com No credit cards Closed Nov.—Apr. 10 rooms Multiple meal plans.*

$$$$ HOTEL FAMILY Fodor's Choice ★ **La Villa Hotel & Spa.** A piece of paradise awaits—this Relais & Châteaux hotel on a manicured hill with marvelous views of the town and the citadel feels like a private Mediterranean villa. **Pros:** spectacular views; outstanding restaurant; two swimming pools. **Cons:** expensive; 30-minute walk from downtown. *Rooms from: €450 Chemin de Notre-Dame de la Serra, Calvi 04–95–65–10–10 www.hotel-lavilla.com Closed mid-Oct.—mid-Apr. 22 rooms, 24 suites, 5 apartments and 4 villas Breakfast.*

NIGHTLIFE

L'Eden Port. A popular nightspot, this centrally located disco offers expensive drinks, electronic music, and enthusiastic crowds. *Quai Landry, Port de Plaisance, Calvi 04–95–60–57–44 www.facebook.com/leden.calvi/info?tab=page_info Daily 7 pm—2 am.*

PIGNA

25 km (15 miles) northeast of Calvi.

The village of Pigna is dedicated to bringing back traditional Corsican music and crafts. Here you can listen to folk songs in cafés, visit workshops, and buy handmade musical instruments. During the first half of July, the Casa Musicale hosts a Festivoce featuring international vocal groups.

GETTING HERE

From Calvi, follow N197 toward L'Ile Rousse, take a right on D313 at Curso and another right on to D151 in Casaposa. Continue on D151 until you reach Pigna.

WHERE TO STAY

$ B&B/INN **Casa Musicale.** This enchanting locale has traditional home-style cuisine and music of all kinds—often authentic Corsican polyphonic chanting—and a commanding view of La Balagne. **Pros:** rooms overlooking Algajola Bay; make your own kind of music; relaxed bohemian ambience. **Cons:** tiny rooms; thin walls; uninspiring decor. *Rooms from: €88 Pl. de l'Eglise, Pigna 04–95–61–77– 31 www.casa-musicale.org Closed Jan. 1–Feb. 14 9 rooms Breakfast.*

SHOPPING

Casa di l'Artigiani. Created to showcase local artisans, Casa di l'Artigiani is the perfect place to find handmade crafts, from traditionally forged knives, leather items, and musical instruments, to hand-knit sweaters. There are also locally produced culinary treasures like olive oils, jams, honeys, and *canistrelli* biscuits. *Rte. des Artisans, Pigna 04–95–61–77–29 www.balagne-corsica.com.*

A microcosm of mountains, beaches, fishing ports, wilderness, Corsica is the purest strain of proto-Mediterranean culture.

BASTIA

170 km (105 miles) north of Bonifacio, 153 km (95 miles) northeast of Ajaccio.

Notably more Italianate than the French-influenced Ajaccio, Bastia is quintessentially Corsican. The Baroque coastal town has a historic center that retains the timeless, salty flavor of an ancient Mediterranean port. Its name is derived from the word "bastion," in reference to the fortress the Genoese built here in the 14th century as a stronghold against rebellious islanders. The **Terra Vecchia** (Old Town) is best explored on foot. Start at the wide, palm-filled Place St-Nicolas, bordered on one side by docked ships looming large in the port and on the other by two blocks of popular cafés along Boulevard Général-de-Gaulle.

GETTING HERE

You can reach Bastia by air or sea. Flights arrive regularly from main cities in Europe at the Aéroport de Bastia-Poretta situated in Lucciana, southeast of the city. From here, Autobus Bastiais shuttle bus lines run from 6:30 am to 10 pm (depending on season) to downtown in 40 minutes for €8. Expect to pay €30 to €40 for a taxi.

Ferries cross from France (Nice, Toulon, Marseilles) and Italy (Livorno, Genova, Verde Ligure). The average crossing time is around five hours. Train services link Bastia to Ajaccio and Calvi. The station is only a short distance from Bastia's ferry port, on Rond-point Maréchal Leclerc.

Visitor Information Office de Tourisme Bastia. ☎ *04–95–54–20–40* 🌐 *www.bastia-tourisme.com.*

EXPLORING

FAMILY **Cathédrale Ste-Marie.** A network of cobbled alleyways rambles across the citadel to the 15th-century Cathédrale Ste-Marie, one of the town's prettiest churches. Inside, classic Baroque style abounds in an explosion of gilt decoration. Numerous works of art from the 18th and 19th centuries, forged metalwork, sculptures, and statues that were generous gifts from the bishops of Mariana, residents of the cathedral from 1600 to 1622, are showcased. ✉ *12 rue Notre-Dame, Bastia* ☎ *04–95–31–01–80* 🌐 *www.bastia-tourisme.com.*

Chapelle Ste-Croix (*Chapel of the Holy Cross*). The sumptuous rococo style of the Chapelle Ste-Croix, behind the cathedral, makes it look more like a theater than a church. The chapel owes its name to a blackened oak crucifix, dubbed "Christ of the Miracles," discovered by fishermen at sea in 1428 and venerated to this day by Bastia's fishing community. The most ancient church of the town, this chapel has officially been classified as a historic monument since 1931. ✉ *4 rue de l'Evêché, Bastia.*

Église de la Conception (*Church of the Conception*). The 16th-century Église de la Conception occupies a cobblestone square. Step inside the Baroque portal to admire the church's ornate 18th-century interior, requiring a bright day to see much detail as interior lighting is quite dim. The walls are covered with wood carvings, gold, marble, and velvet fabric. Check out the altar's interpretation of the Assumption of Murillo, whose original version sits in Madrid's El Prado Museum. ✉ *Rue Napoléon, Bastia* 🌐 *www.bastia-tourisme.com.*

Musée de Bastia. The vaulted, colonnaded galleries of the Palais des Nobles Douzes houses the Musée de Bastia. Don't miss the *Casablanca,* a French submarine used by the Resistance with swastikas on the turret representing downed Nazi aircraft. The building itself has been undergoing modifications since the 18th century, when it was used as the meeting place for rural commune leaders. ✉ *Pl. du Donjon, La Citadelle, Bastia* ☎ *04–95–31–09–12* 🌐 *www.musee-bastia.com* 🎫 *€5 plus €1 for the garden* ⏲ *May and Sept., Tues.–Sun. 10–6:30; July and Aug., daily 10–6:30; Oct.–Apr., Tues.–Sat. 9–noon and 2–5.*

FAMILY **Terra Nova** (*New Town*). The city's more modern quarter of the city is well worth a promenade. Climb the Escalier Romieu steps beside the leafy Jardins Romieu for a sweeping view of the Italian islands of Capraia, Elba, and Montecristo. ✉ *Citadelle, Bastia.*

Vieux Port (*Old Port*). The picturesque Vieux Port, along Quai des Martyrs de la Libération, is dominated by the hilltop citadel. Take a stroll along the harbor, which is lined with excellent seafood restaurants. You can still find many bright red-and-blue fishing boats with tangles of old nets and lines. ✉ *Quai des Martyrs de la Libération, Bastia* ☎ *04–95–31–31–10 Capitainerie* 🌐 *www.bastia.fr.*

WHERE TO EAT

$$$ SEAFOOD ✕ **A Scaletta.** Enjoy the view of the Vieux Port from this popular spot with friendly service. Expect traditional Corsican fare made from fresh local ingredients, including an array of fish and seafood. Three-course menus (€18 to €29) may include *beignets de fromage* (fried cheese),

ravioli in tomato sauce, or sautéed sardines with eggplant. *$ Average main: €30 ✉ 4 rue St-Jean, Bastia ☎ 04–95–32–28–70 No credit cards ⊙ Closed Sun. Reservations essential.*

$$$$ BISTRO **La Citadelle.** This rustic and intimate spot, built in an ancient oil press, has great views of the port and a perfect location near the Governor's Palace. Serving trendy cuisine in nouvelle Corsican style, the restaurant offers elegantly prepared and presented dishes featuring veal, lobster, and fresh fish. Especially popular are the swordfish garnished with wild mint and roasted eggplant, the caramelized suckling pig, and the sea bass fillet draped in panzetta. *$ Average main: €60 ✉ 6 rue du Dragon, Bastia ☎ 04–95–31–44–70 ⊙ Closed Sun. and Mon. Nov.–Dec. No lunch Sat.*

$$ BRASSERIE **L'Imperial.** A perfect place to people-watch as you enjoy a quick lunch, this busy restaurant has ample outdoor seating right in the center of Place Saint Nicolas. Thin-crust pizzas and salads are a bargain, but for something more substantial, try the risotto with shrimp, beef fillet with foie gras, or wok-sautéed salmon with fresh vegetables. *$ Average main: €20 ✉ 9–11 bd. Général De Gaulle, Bastia ☎ 04–95–31–04–42.*

14

WHERE TO STAY

$$$ HOTEL **Hôtel Castel Brando.** More a walled château than a medieval fortress, Hôtel Castel Brando sits near the harbor town of Erbalunga. **Pros:** two swiming pools; helpful staff; stunning location. **Cons:** no restaurant. *$ Rooms from: €179 ✉ Brando, Erbalunga ☎ 04–95–30–10–30 ⊕ www.castelbrando.com ⊙ Closed early Nov.–mid-Mar. 37 rooms, 6 suites Breakfast.*

$ HOTEL **Hotel Posta Vecchia.** At the end of a quiet promenade near the water's edge, this former post office puts you close to Place St-Nicolas and the Citadelle. **Pros:** central location; spic-and-span rooms; friendly staff. **Cons:** tiny bathrooms; overpriced breakfast; noisy rooms on boulevard side. *$ Rooms from: €62 ✉ Quai des Martyrs-de-la-Libération, 8 rue Posta Vecchia, Bastia ☎ 04–95–32–32–38 ⊕ www.hotel-postavecchia.com ⊙ Closed mid-Dec.–early Jan. 50 rooms Breakfast.*

SHOPPING

Cap Corse Mattei. The most legendary Corsican distillery, founded in 1917, sells the Mattei family's special grape-based Cap Corse liqueur. Other products include aromatic honeys, jams, chutneys, and oils. *✉ ID Resignani, Borgo ☎ 04–95–59–17–17 ⊕ capcorsemattei.com.*

Marché Traditionnel. In front of the town hall, meander through myriad stalls selling everything from local cheeses to charcuterie, oils, and other fine Corsican gastronomic products every Saturday and Sunday. *✉ Pl. de l'Hôtel de Ville behind St-Jean-Baptiste, Bastia ⊕ www.bastia-tourisme.com.*

15

THE MIDI-PYRÉNÉES AND LANGUEDOC-ROUSSILLON

WELCOME TO THE MIDI-PYRÉNÉES AND LANGUEDOC-ROUSSILLON

TOP REASONS TO GO

★ **Matisse madness:** Captivating Collioure, the main town of the Vermilion Coast, was where Matisse and Derain went crazy with color and created the Fauvist art movement in the early 20th century.

★ **Fairy-tale Carcassonne:** Complete with towers, turrets, and battlements, Carcassonne's fortified upper town is a UNESCO World Heritage Site that feels like a medieval theme park.

★ **Tumultuous Toulouse:** With rosy roofs and red-brick mansions, the "Pink City" is a place where high culture is an evening at an outdoor café.

★ **Albi's Toulouse-Lautrec:** Presided over by the fortresslike Cathédrale Ste-Cécile, Albi honors its most famous native son, Toulouse-Lautrec, with the largest museum of his works.

★ **Abbey in the sky:** At an altitude of nearly 3,600 feet, the picture-postcard medieval Abbaye St-Martin du Canigou enjoys a perch that (literally) takes your breath away.

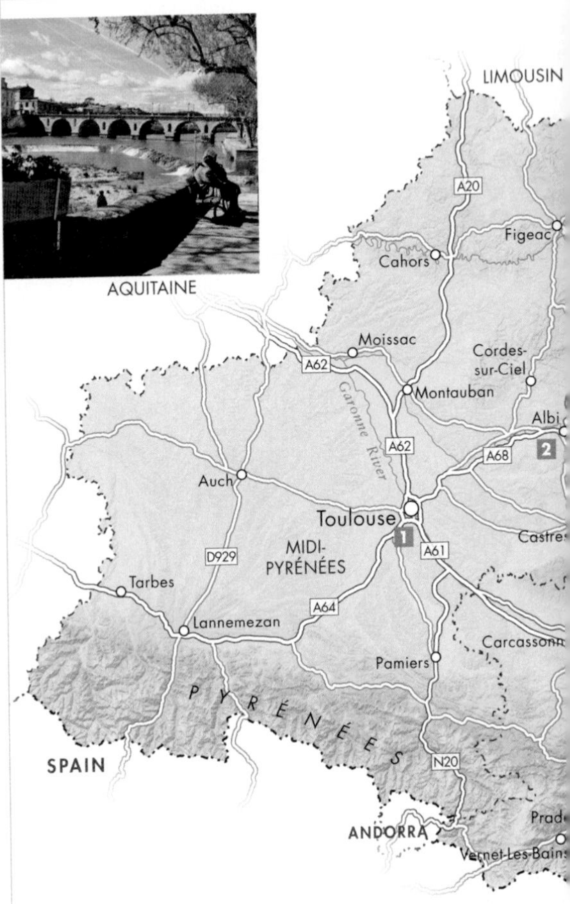

1 Toulouse. Now the center of Europe's high-tech aerospace industry (Airbus is made here), the city sees itself as the modern gateway to the south. Happily, Toulouse's new forward-looking attitude hasn't infringed on the well-preserved *centre ville* (city center), a veritable museum of mansions, where the brick-paved streets make you feel as if you're in a small town and aerospace engineers own Renaissance houses.

2 Albi and the Gers. Some 75 km (47 miles) northeast of Toulouse, Albi sits on the Tarn River and was once a major center of the Cathars, a medieval Christian sect; the huge Cathédrale Ste-Cécile was a symbol of the Roman Catholic Church's victory over these heretics. Art lovers make a pilgrimage to the famed Musée Toulouse-Lautrec.

AUVERGNE
RHÔNE-ALPES
0 30 mi
0 30 km
A75
Mende
Rodez
N88
Millau
Alès
LANGUEDOC-ROUSSILLON
3
D999
A75
A7
Nîmes
A9
Avignon
A54
Mazamet
Montpellier
A9
A75
PROVENCE-ALPES-CÔTE D'AZUR
Béziers
A61
Golfe du Lion
Narbonne
VERMILION COAST
A9
Salses
D117
N116
Perpignan
Ceret
Collioure
SPAIN

3 Languedoc-Roussillon. Studded with vineyards and ghosts of famed artists, Languedoc is a vast province that ranges from Carcassonne in the Black Mountains eastward to aristocratic Montpellier on the Mediterranean. Included in the region are famous sights like Carcassonne's La Cité—the largest medieval town extant—and *le littoral Languedocien* (the Languedoc coast), where France's "second Riviera" draws both artists and sun worshippers to Collioure and other towns along the Côte Vermeille (Vermilion Coast).

GETTING ORIENTED

Spend some time in the Midi-Pyrénées, the country's largest region, and the term "the south of France" takes on new meaning. This western half of France's true south is less glamorous (and much less expensive) than the Riviera and Provence but has an array of must-sees, beginning with lively Toulouse. East lies Languedoc, a province of contrasts—of rolling sun-baked plains around Carcassonne, of stone-and-shrub-covered hills spiked with ruins of ancient civilizations. Stretching south along the Mediterranean is the southernmost province of Roussillon, home to that artists' paradise, the Vermilion Coast.

Updated By
Avery Sumner

Like the most celebrated dish of this area, cassoulet, the southwestern region of France is made up of diverse ingredients. Just as it would be a gross oversimplification to refer to cassoulet merely as a mixture of baked beans, southwestern France is much more than just Toulouse, the peaks of the Pyrénées, and the fairy-tale ramparts of Carcassonne.

For here you'll also find, like so many raisins sweetening up a spicy stew, the pretty seaside town of Collioure, the famed Côte Vermeille (where Matisse, Picasso, and Braque first vacationed to paint), and Albi, a hilltop town that honors its hometown hero, Toulouse-Lautrec, with a great museum. But in most cases, every traveler heading to this area begins with the regional gateway: "La Ville Rose," so-called for Toulouse's redbrick buildings.

Big enough to be France's fourth-largest city and yet with the look and vibe of a gorgeous small town, Toulouse is all that more famous regional capitals would like to have remained, or to become. The cultural hub of this corner of France, the city has a vibrancy that derives from its large student population and lively music scene, plus a rich heritage of sculpture and architectural gems. Snaking along the banks of the Garonne as it meanders north and west from the Catalan Pyrénées on its way to the Atlantic, romantic Toulouse has a Spanish sensuality unique in all of Gaul. The city began as the ancient capital of the province called Languedoc, so christened when it became royal property in 1270, langue d'oc meaning the country where *oc* replaced the *oui* of northeastern France for "yes."

If you head out in any direction from Toulouse you'll enjoy a feast for the eyes. Albi, with its Toulouse-Lautrec legacy, is a star attraction, while Céret is the gateway to a fabled "open-air museum" prized by artists and poets, the Côte Vermeille. The Vermilion Coast is centered around Collioure, the lovely fishing village where Matisse, Derain, and the Fauvists—the "wild beasts" of the early-20th-century art world—threw out the pretty pastel rule book, drawing inspiration instead from the savage tones found in Mother Nature hereabouts. When you see picturesque Collioure's stunning Mediterranean setting, you can understand why Matisse went color-mad. Sheer heaven for painters, the town's magic did not go unnoticed, and it soon drew vacationers by the boatload, who quickly discovered that everything around here seems to be asking to be immortalized on canvas: the Mediterranean, smooth and opalescent at dawn; villagers dancing Sardanas to the music of the raucous and ancient woodwind *flavioles* and *tenores*; and the flood of golden light so peculiar to the Mediterranean.

PLANNER

WHEN TO GO

You can expect pleasantly warm weather as early as April and as late as October, but be prepared for rainstorms and/or heat waves at almost any time. The weather is especially unpredictable in the Pyrénées: a few passing clouds can rapidly turn into a full-blown storm. Needless to say, during July and August towns high on tourist lists—like Albi, Carcassonne, and Collioure—are packed, so perhaps opt for April and May, which are delightful months on the Côte Vermeille and also the time when the Pyrénéan flowers are at their best. June and September (grape-picking season, or *vendange*) are equally good for both inland and coastal areas. As October draws near, the chilly winds of winter begin to blow and frenzied mushroom hunters ferret amid the chestnut and pine trees. Olive harvesters set to work in November.

No matter the season, there's plenty here to occupy those who love the outdoors, whether it be hiking the Grandes Randonnées (GRs), scaling lofty peaks, or skiing sun-dappled snowfields.

PLANNING YOUR TIME

Getting to know this vast region would take several weeks, or even years. But it's possible to sample all of its finest offerings in nine days, if that's all the time you have. Begin by practicing your "Olé's" in Spanish-soul Toulouse; after two days and two nights in this vibrant city, veer west to the Gers *département* to spend Day 3 in Albi and take a virtual art class with Toulouse-Lautrec at the famous museum here devoted to his masterworks. On Day 4, continue some 112 km (70 miles) south to once-upon-a-timefied Carcassonne to introduce your kids to the Puss-in-Boots fantasy of this castellated wonder. After a night filled with medieval history and glamour, travel southeast on Day 5 to the Vermilion Coast. It's time to pack your crayons for a trip to Matisse Country and head to the Roussillon's coastal town of Collioure to channel the spirits of the famous Fauve painters. Spend all of Day 6 here. Then on Day 7, drive north past Perpignan, the historic hub city of the Roussillon, and head to marvelous Montpellier. After your seventh night, enjoy Day 8 by touring this city's fascinating Vieille Ville (Old Town), steeped in culture, history, and young blood (a famous university is based here). Add on a Day 9 to chill out before returning to reality.

GETTING HERE AND AROUND

AIR TRAVEL

Flying here is easy because the region has four airports—Toulouse-Blagnac being the largest. They're served by major airlines, like Air France (🌐 *www.airfrance.com*), as well as budget carriers, including Ryanair (🌐 *www.ryanair.com*), easyJet (🌐 *www.easyjet.com*), and Hop! (🌐 *www.hop.com*).

Airport Information Aéroport Montpellier-Méditerranée. ☎ *04-67-20-85-00* 🌐 *www.montpellier.aeroport.fr.* **Aéroport Sud de France-Carcassonne.** ☎ *04-68-71-96-46* 🌐 *www.aeroport-carcassonne.com.* **Aéroport Sud de France-Perpignan.** ☎ *04-68-52-60-70* 🌐 *www.aeroport-perpignan.com.* **Aéroport Toulouse-Blagnac.** ☎ *08-25-38-00-00 €0.15 per min* 🌐 *www.toulouse.aeroport.fr.*

BUS TRAVEL

Many public and private bus companies thread through the Midi-Pyrénées, including the Conseil Général buses from Toulouse and Perpignan; Cars Teissiers from Carcassonne; and Herault Transport from Montpellier. It's wise to check with the pertinent local tourist office regarding your best options, as bus stops and schedules can be confusing even for native commuters. Generally speaking, Toulouse's bus routes run to and from Albi and Carcassonne; Albi connects with Cordes-sur-Ciel, while Montpellier connects with Narbonne. From Perpignan, the Conseil General's extensive network of buses links almost all towns and villages in the department for €1. (All destinations on the train line from Perpignan to Villefranche are also just €1.) Note that if you are coming from Spain, Eurolines (*www.eurolines.fr*) and Perpicat (*www.perpicat.com*) run cross-border buses to Perpignan.

Bus Information Cars Teissiers. ☎ *04-68-25-85-45* 🌐 *www.teissier.fr.* **Conseil Général Buses.** ☎ *05-61-61-67-67 Toulouse, 04-68-80-80-80 Perpignan* 🌐 *www.haute-garonne.fr (for Toulouse) or www.cg66.fr (for Perpignan).* **Herault Transport.** ☎ *04-34-88-89-99* 🌐 *www.herault-transport.fr.*

CAR TRAVEL

The fastest route from Paris to Toulouse, 677 km (406 miles) south, is via Limoges on A20, then A62; the journey time is about six hours. If you choose to head south over the Pyrénées to Barcelona, the Tunnel du Puymorens saves half an hour of switchbacks between Hospitalet and Porta; but in good weather—and with time to spare—the drive over the Puymorens Pass is spectacular. Plan on taking three hours between Toulouse and Font-Romeu and another three to Barcelona. The fastest route from Toulouse to Barcelona is the under-three-hour, 391-km (235-mile) drive via Carcassonne and Perpignan on A61 and A9, which becomes AP7 at Le Perthus. A62/A61 slices through the region on its way through Carcassonne to the coast at Narbonne, where A9 heads south to Perpignan. At Toulouse, where A62 becomes A61, various highways fan out in all directions. A9 (La Languedocienne) is the main highway artery that connects Montpellier with Beziers to the south and Nîmes to the north.

TRAIN TRAVEL

At least 10 high-speed TGVs per day leave Paris's Gare Montparnasse and Gare Austerlitz bound for Toulouse; depending on which one you choose, the journey can take between 5½ and 7 hours. There are also 15 daily departures from Paris to Narbonne and 13 to Perpignan. Most of these trips take 6 to 7 hours, but if you get a TGV from the Gare de Lyon you can be in Narbonne in 4½ hours. A TGV line from Paris also serves Montpellier 18 times a day, departing from the Gare de Lyon. The regional French rail network provides regular service to many towns, though not all. Within the Midi-Pyrénées, Toulouse is the biggest hub, with a major line linking Carcassonne (1 hr), Narbonne (1½ hrs, change here for Perpignan), and Montpellier (2 hrs); trains link up with Albi (1 hr), too. Toulouse trains also connect with Biarritz (5 hrs), Pau (3 hrs), and Bordeaux (3 hrs). Montpellier connects with Carcassonne (2 hrs), Perpignan (2 hrs), and other towns. From Perpignan, take one of the dozen or so daily trains to Collioure (20 mins).

Train Information Gare SNCF Carcassonne. ✉ *1 av. Marechal Joffre, Carcassonne* ☎ *3635 €0.34 per min.* **Gare SNCF Montpellier.** ✉ *Rue Jules Ferry, Montpellier* ☎ *3635 €0.34 per min.* **Gare SNCF Narbonne.** ✉ *1 bd. Frédéric Mistral, Narbonne* ☎ *3635 €0.34 per min.* **Gare SNCF Perpignan.** ✉ *Av. du Général de Gaulle, Perpignan* ☎ *3635 €0.34 per min.* **Gare SNCF Toulouse-Matabiau.** ✉ *64 Bd. Pierre Semard, Toulouse* ☎ *3635 €0.34 per min.* **SNCF.** ☎ *3635 €0.34 per min* 🌐 *www.voyages-sncf.com.* **TGV.** 🌐 *www.tgv.com.*

RESTAURANTS

As a rule, the closer you get to the Mediterranean coast, the later you dine and the more you pay for your seafood platter and bottle of iced rosé. The farther you travel from the coast, the higher the altitude, the more rustic the setting, and the more reasonable the prices will be. During the scorching summer months in sleepy mountain villages, lunches are light, interminable, and *bien arrosé* (with lots of wine). Here you can also find that small personal restaurant where the chickens roasting on spits above the open fire have first names and the cheese comes from the hippie couple down the road who arrived here in the '60s and love their mountains, their goats, and the universe in general.

HOTELS

Hotels range from Mediterranean modern to medieval baronial to Pyrénéan chalet, and most are small and cozy rather than luxurious and sophisticated. Toulouse has the usual range of big-city hotels, for which you need to make reservations well in advance if you plan to visit in spring or fall. Look for *gîtes d'étape* (hikers' way stations) and *chambres d'hôtes* (bed-and-breakfasts), which offer excellent value, a chance to meet local and international travelers, and, perhaps, to sample life on a farm, as well as the delights of *cuisine du terroir* (country cooking). As for off-season—if there is such a thing, since chic Parisians often arrive in November in their SUVs with a hunger for the authentic—call ahead and double-check when hotels close for their annual hibernation. This usually starts sometime in winter, either before, or right after, the Christmas holidays. *Hotel reviews have been shortened. For full information, visit Fodors.com.*

WHAT IT COSTS IN EUROS

	$	$$	$$$	$$$$
Restaurants	under €18	€18–€24	€25–€32	over €32
Hotels	under €106	€106–€145	€146–€215	over €215

Restaurant prices are the average cost of a main course at dinner or, if dinner is not served, at lunch. Hotel prices are the lowest cost of a standard double room in high season.

VISITOR INFORMATION

The regional tourist office for the Midi-Pyrénées is the Comité Régional du Tourisme Midi-Pyrénées. For Languedoc-Roussillon, contact the Comité Régional du Tourisme du Languedoc-Roussillon.

Contacts Comité Régional du Tourisme du Languedoc-Roussillon. ☏ *04-67-20-02-20* 🌐 *www.sunfrance.com.* **Comité Régional du Tourisme Midi-Pyrénées.** ☏ *05-61-13-55-55* 🌐 *www.tourisme-midi-pyrenees.com.*

Handy websites for this region are 🌐 *www.audetourisme.com,* 🌐 *www.tourisme-pyreneesorientales.com,* and 🌐 *www.tourisme-tarn.com.*

TOULOUSE

Ebullient Toulouse is the capital of the Midi-Pyrénées and the fourth-largest city in France. Just 100 km (60 miles) from the border with Spain, Toulouse is in many ways closer in flavor to southern European Spanish than to northern European French. Weathered redbrick buildings line sidewalks, giving the city its nickname, "La Ville Rose" (the Pink City). Downtown, the sidewalks pulse late into the night with tourists, technicians from the giant Airbus aerospace complex, and, since this is the country's second-largest university center, loads of students. Despite Toulouse's bustling, high-tech attitude, its well-preserved *centre ville*—the brick-paved streets between the Garonne River and the Canal du Midi—retains the feel of a small town, where food, Beaujolais nouveau, and the latest rugby victory are the primary concerns. So be prepared to savor the city's Mediterranean pace, southern friendliness, and youthful spirit.

Toulouse was founded in the 4th century BC and quickly became an important part of Roman Gaul. In turn, it was made into a Visigothic and Carolingian capital before becoming a separate county in 843. Ruling from this Pyrénéan hub, the counts of Toulouse held sovereignty over nearly all of the Languedoc and maintained a brilliant court known for its fine troubadours and literature. In the early 13th century, Toulouse was attacked and plundered by troops representing an alliance between the northern French nobility and the papacy, ostensibly to wipe out the Albigensian heresy (Catharism), but more realistically as an expansionist move against the power of Occitania, the French southwest. The counts toppled, but Toulouse experienced a cultural and economic rebirth thanks to the *woad* (blue dye) trade, and, consequently, wealthy merchants' homes constitute a major portion of Toulouse's architectural heritage.

You can learn more about the city's past and present by visiting the tourist office for details about guided tours (self-guided itineraries can be downloaded directly from its website). The office also sells So Toulouse passes, valid for 24, 48 or 72 hours (€18, €25, or €32), that admit you to 30 tourist sites free or at a reduced rate and give you free transport on the tram, bus, *métro*, and airport shuttle. For a personalized introduction to the city, contact Toulouse Greeters; the complimentary program can link you up with a local volunteer who'll show you around (🌐 *www.toulousegreeters.fr*).

GETTING HERE AND AROUND

Aéroport Toulouse-Blagnac is served by a range of airlines, including Air France and easyJet; a shuttle (🌐 *www.tisseo.fr*) runs every 20 minutes between 5:30 am and 12:15 am from the airport to Toulouse's combined train-bus station on Boulevard Pierre Sémard (€5.50). If you're coming by train, there are at least 10 high-speed TGVs a day from Paris; the travel time for a direct one is about 5 hours, 30 minutes (€84). There are now two daily TGVs from Barcelona, too; they take 3 hours, 30 minutes (€83). Toulouse is also a regional rail hub, so train links to other locales within the Midi-Pyrénées are widely available.

The main square of Toulouse's *centre ville*, Place du Capitole, is a 15-minute walk from the train station but only a few blocks away from the city's other focal points—Place Wilson, Place Esquirol, and the Basilique St-Sernin. (If you've driven into town, there's a huge parking garage beneath Place du Capitole, too.) Within Toulouse, the public transit system (🌐 *www.tisseo.fr*) includes a *métro* (subway), which conveniently connects the Gare Matabiau with Place du Capitole and Place Esquirol, as well as a tram line and an efficient bus network. If you're interested in getting to know Toulouse's cycle-friendly side, you can rent bikes at conveniently placed Vélô Toulouse stations; be sure to drop into La Maison du Vélo de Toulouse (🌐 *www.maisonduvelotoulouse.com*) by the train station for information about cyclotourism in and around the city.

Visitor Information Toulouse Tourist Office. ☎ *08–92–18–01–80* 🌐 *www.toulouse-tourisme.com.*

EXPLORING

OLD TOULOUSE

The area between the boulevards and the Garonne forms the historic nucleus of Toulouse. Originally part of Roman Gaul and later the capital for the Visigoths and then the Carolingians, Toulouse was one of the artistic and literary centers of Europe by AD 1000. Although defeated by the lords of northern France in the 13th century, it quickly reemerged as a cultural and commercial power and has remained so ever since. Religious and civil structures bear witness to this illustrious past, even as the city's booming student life mirrors a dynamic present. This is the heart of Toulouse, with Place du Capitole at its center.

TOP ATTRACTIONS

Fodor's Choice ★ **Basilique St-Sernin.** Toulouse's most famous landmark and the world's largest Romanesque church once belonged to a Benedictine abbey, built in the 11th century to house pilgrims on their way to Santiago de Compostela in Spain. Inside, the aesthetic high point is the magnificent central apse, begun in 1080, glittering with gilded ceiling frescoes, which date from the 19th century. When illuminated at night, St-Sernin's five-tier octagonal tower glows red against the sky. Not all the tiers are the same: the first three, with their rounded windows, are Romanesque; the upper two, with pointed Gothic windows, were added around 1300. The ancient crypt contains the relics and reliquaries of 128 saints, but the most famous item on view is a thorn that legend says is from the Crown of Thorns. ✉ *Pl. Saint-Sernin, Toulouse* ☎ *05–61–21–80–45* 🌐 *www.basilique-saint-sernin.fr* 🎫 *Basilica free; crypt €2* ⏲ *Oct.–May, Mon.–Sat. 8:30–6, Sun. 8:30–7:30; June–Sept., Mon.–Sat. 8:30–7, Sun. 8:30–7:30.*

Capitole/Hôtel de Ville (*Capitol/Town Hall*). The 18th-century Capitole is home to the Hôtel de Ville and the city's highly regarded opera company; the reception rooms are open to the public when not in use for official functions or weddings. Halfway up the **Grand Escalier** (Grand Staircase) hangs a large painting of the *Jeux Floraux*, the "floral games" organized by a literary society created in 1324 to promote the local Occitanian language, Langue d'Oc. The festival continues to this day: poets give public readings here each May, and the best are awarded silver- and gold-plated violets, one of the emblems of Toulouse. At the top of the stairs is the **Salle Gervaise,** a hall adorned with a series of paintings inspired by the themes of love and marriage. The mural at the far end of the room portrays the Isle of Cythères, where Venus received her lovers, alluding to a French euphemism for getting married: *embarquer pour Cythères* (to embark for Cythères). More giant paintings in the **Salle Henri-Martin,** named for the artist (1860–1943), show the passing seasons set against the eternal Garonne. Look for Jean Jaurès (1859–1914), one of France's greatest socialist martyrs, in *Les Rêveurs* (*The Dreamers*); he's wearing a boater-style hat and a beige coat. At the far left end of the elegant **Salle des Illustres** (Hall of the Illustrious) is a large painting of a fortress under siege, portraying the women of Toulouse slaying Simon de Montfort, leader of the Albigensian crusade against the Cathars, during the siege of Toulouse in 1218. ✉ *Pl. du Capitole, Toulouse* ☎ *05–61–22–34–12* 🎫 *Free* ⏲ *Mon.–Sat. 8:30–7, Sun. 10—7.*

Ensemble Conventuel des Jacobins. An extraordinary structure built in the 1230s for the Dominicans (renamed Jacobins in 1216 for their Parisian base in Rue St-Jacques), this church is dominated by a single row of seven columns running the length of the nave. The easternmost column (on the far right) is one of the finest examples of palm-tree vaulting ever erected, the much-celebrated *Palmier des Jacobins,* a major masterpiece of Gothic art. Fanning out overhead, its 22 ribs support the entire apse. The original refectory site is used for temporary art exhibitions. The cloister is one of the city's aesthetic and acoustical gems, and in summer hosts piano and early music concerts. ✉ *69 rue Pargaminières, Toulouse*

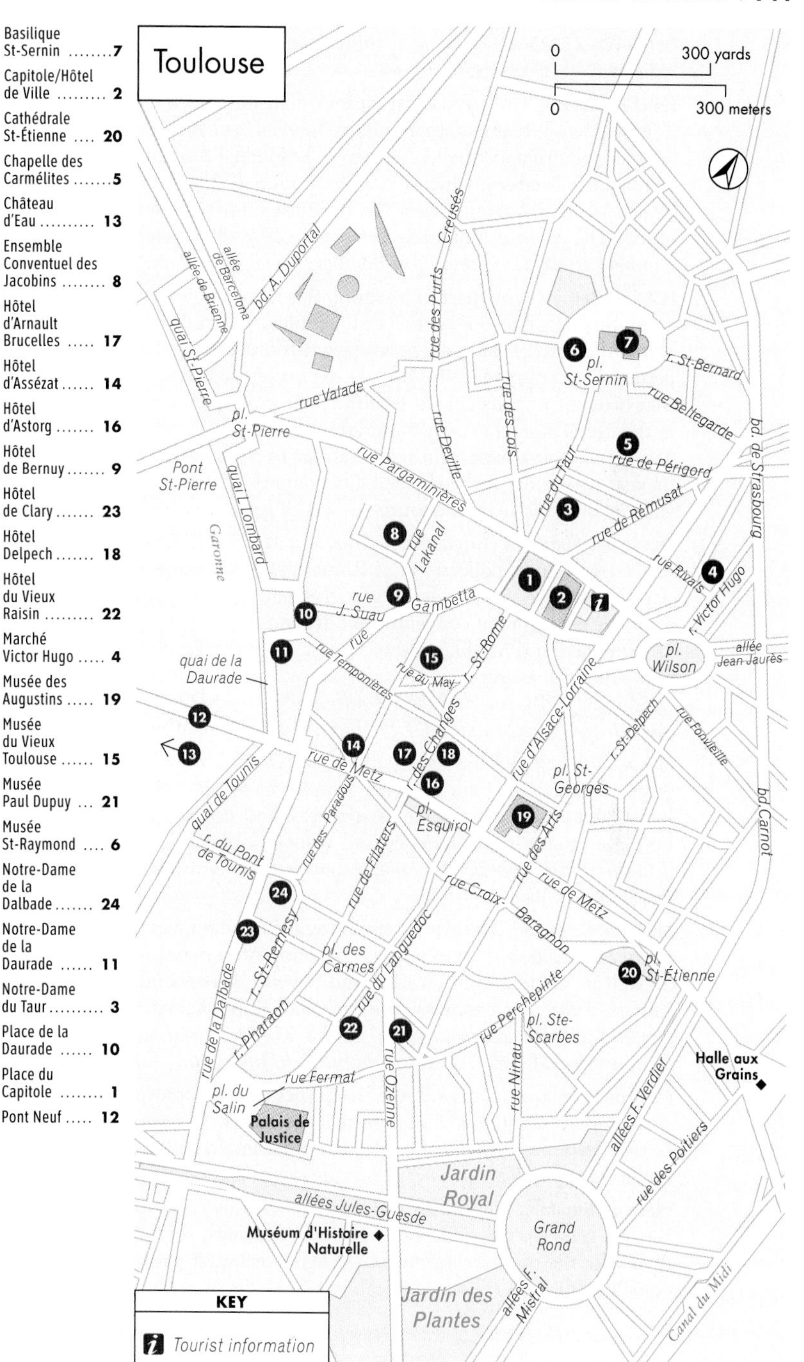
Basilique St-Sernin 7
Capitole/Hôtel de Ville 2
Cathédrale St-Étienne 20
Chapelle des Carmélites 5
Château d'Eau 13
Ensemble Conventuel des Jacobins 8
Hôtel d'Arnault Brucelles 17
Hôtel d'Assézat 14
Hôtel d'Astorg 16
Hôtel de Bernuy....... 9
Hôtel de Clary 23
Hôtel Delpech 18
Hôtel du Vieux Raisin 22
Marché Victor Hugo 4
Musée des Augustins 19
Musée du Vieux Toulouse 15
Musée Paul Dupuy ... 21
Musée St-Raymond 6
Notre-Dame de la Dalbade....... 24
Notre-Dame de la Daurade 11
Notre-Dame du Taur.......... 3
Place de la Daurade 10
Place du Capitole 1
Pont Neuf 12
Toulouse
0 300 yards
0 300 meters
allée de Brienne
allée de Barcelona
bd. A. Duportal
quai St-Pierre
rue des Purts
Creusés
rue Valade
pl. St-Pierre
rue des Lois
rue Deville
pl. St-Sernin
r. St-Bernard
rue Bellegarde
rue de Périgord
rue du Taur
bd. de Strasbourg
Pont St-Pierre
quai L Lombard
rue Pargaminières
rue de Rémusat
Garonne
rue Lakanal
rue Rivals
r. Victor Hugo
rue J. Suau
Gambetta
r. St-Rome
pl. Wilson
allée Jean Jaurès
quai de la Daurade
rue Temponières
rue du May
rue d'Alsace-Lorraine
r. St-Delpech
rue Fonvielle
quai de Tounis
rue de Metz
r. des Changes
pl. St-Georges
rue des Paradoux
pl. Esquirol
bd. Carnot
r. du Pont de Tounis
rue des Filatiers
rue des Arts
rue Croix-Baragnon
r. St-Remesy
pl. des Carmes
rue du Languedoc
pl. St-Étienne
rue Perchepinte
rue de la Dalbade
r. Pharaon
pl. Ste-Scarbes
Halle aux Grains
rue Fermat
rue Ozenne
rue Ninau
allées F. Verdier
pl. du Salin
Palais de Justice
rue des Poitiers
Jardin Royal
allées Jules-Guesde
Grand Rond
Muséum d'Histoire Naturelle
Jardin des Plantes
allées F. Mistral
Canal du Midi
KEY
Tourist information

☎ *05–61–22–23–82* 🌐 *www.jacobins.mairie-toulouse.fr* 🎫 *Church free; cloister €3* 🕘 *Daily 10–6.*

Hôtel d'Assézat. The city's most elegant mansion was built in 1555 by Toulouse's top Renaissance architect, Nicolas Bachelier. Notable for its arcades and ornately carved doorways, the Hôtel d'Assézat is now home to **Fondation Bemberg**, which has an exceptional collection of paintings by artists ranging from Tiepolo to Toulouse-Lautrec, Monet, and Bonnard. ✉ *Pl. Assézat, Toulouse* ☎ *05–61–12–06–89* 🌐 *www.fondation-bemberg.fr* 🎫 *Free; Fondation Bemberg €8* 🕘 *Tues.–Sun. 9–7.*

Hôtel de Bernuy. Now part of a school, this mansion, around the corner from the Ensemble Conventuel des Jacobins, was built for Jean de Bernuy in the 16th century, the period when Toulouse was at its most prosperous. De Bernuy made his fortune exporting woad, the dark-blue dye that brought unprecedented wealth to the city; his success is reflected in the use of stone (a costly material in this region of brick) and by the octagonal stair tower. You may wander freely around the courtyard or visit it on one of the themed city tours (€7.50—€9.50) offered at various times daily by the tourist office. ✉ *1 rue Gambetta, Toulouse.*

Musée des Augustins (*Augustinian Museum, Musée des Beaux-Arts*). One of Europe's finest collections of Romanesque sculpture and religious paintings can be seen inside the sacristy, chapter house, and cloisters of a former Augustinian convent. Built around the same time as the Louvre, the medieval Mediterranean-Gothic architectural complex is vast, and—like the Louvre—it contains many treasures from Napoléon's conquests. ✉ *21 rue de Metz, Toulouse* ☎ *05–61–22–21–82* 🌐 *www.augustins.org* 🎫 *Museum €4* 🕘 *Thurs.–Tues. 10–6, Wed. 10–9.*

Musée du Vieux Toulouse (*Museum of Old Toulouse*). This museum is worthwhile for the building itself as much as for its collection of Toulouse memorabilia, paintings, sculptures, and documents. Be sure to note the ground-floor fireplace and wooden ceiling. ✉ *7 rue du May, Toulouse* ☎ *05–62–27–11–50* 🎫 *€2.50* 🕘 *Apr.–Nov., Mon.–Sat. 2–6; guided tours Wed. and Fri.*

Musée St-Raymond. The city's archaeological museum, next to the Basilica of St-Sernin, has an extensive collection of imperial Roman busts, as well as ancient coins, vases, and jewelry. It's second only to the Louvre in the richness of its sculptures and Gallo-Roman vestiges. ✉ *1 Ter Pl. St-Sernin, Toulouse* ☎ *05–61–22–31–44* 🌐 *www.saintraymond.toulouse.fr* 🎫 *€4* 🕘 *Oct.–June, daily 10–6; July–Sept., daily 10–7.*

Place de la Daurade. Set beside the river, Place de la Daurade ranks among the city's nicest squares. The corner of the quay offers a romantic view of the Garonne, the Hôtel Dieu on the other bank, and the pretty Pont Neuf. A stop at Café des Artistes is almost obligatory. ✉ *Toulouse.*

Place du Capitole. Lined with shops and cafés, this vast, open square in the city center is a good spot to get your bearings, soak up some sun, or peruse the outdoor markets held here weekly. A parking garage is conveniently underneath. ✉ *Toulouse.*

WORTH NOTING

Chapelle des Carmélites. All that remains of the Carmelite convent that once stood here is its chapel, begun in 1622 by King Louis XIII and Anne of Austria. Look up to admire the remarkable painted vaulted ceiling. ✉ *1 rue de Périgord, Toulouse* ☎ *05–61–21–27–60* 🎫 *Free* ⏲ *Tues.–Sun. 10–noon and 2–6.*

Château d'Eau. This 19th-century water tower at the far end of the Pont Neuf, originally used to store water and build water pressure, is now the oldest public institution in France dedicated to photographic exhibits. It was built in 1822, the same year Nicéphore Nièpce created the first permanent photographic images. ✉ *1 pl. Laganne, Toulouse* ☎ *05–61–77–09–40* 🎫 *€2.50* ⏲ *Tues.–Sun. 1–7.*

Hôtel d'Arnault Brucelles. One of the tallest and best of Toulouse's 49 towers can be found at this 16th-century mansion. ✉ *19 rue des Changes, Toulouse.*

Hôtel d'Astorg et St-Germain. This 16th-century mansion is notable for its lovely Romanesque wooden stairways and galleries and for its top-floor *mirande,* a wooden balcony. ✉ *16 rue des Changes, Toulouse.*

Hôtel Delpech. Look for the 17th-century biblical inscriptions carved in Latin in the stone under the windows. ✉ *20 rue des Changes, Toulouse.*

Marché Victor Hugo (*Victor Hugo Market*). This hangarlike indoor market, where you're sure to find the ingredients for almost any French recipe, is always a refreshing stop. Consider eating lunch at one of the seven upstairs restaurants. **Chez Attila,** just to the left at the top of the stairs, is among the best. ✉ *Pl. Victor Hugo, Toulouse* ☎ *05–61–22–76–92* 🌐 *www.marchevictorhugo.fr* ⏲ *Tues.–Sun. sunrise–1.*

Notre-Dame de la Daurade. The 18th-century Notre-Dame de la Daurade overlooks the Garonne. The church's name—derived from *doré* (gilt)—refers to the golden reflection given off by mosaics decorating the 5th-century temple to the Virgin Mary that once stood on this site. ✉ *1 pl. de la Daurade, Toulouse* ☎ *05–61–21–38–32* ⏲ *Daily 8:30–7.*

Notre-Dame du Taur. Built on the spot where St-Saturnin (or Sernin), the martyred bishop of Toulouse, was dragged to his death in AD 250 by a rampaging bull, this church is famous for its *cloche-mur,* or wall tower. The wall looks like an extension of the facade and has inspired many similar versions throughout the region. ✉ *12 rue du Taur, Toulouse* ☎ *05–61–21–80–45* ⏲ *Weekdays 2–7, Sat. 10–7:30, Sun. 9:45–12:45* ☞ *Closed Sun. in July and Aug.*

Pont Neuf (*New Bridge*). Despite its name, the graceful span of the Pont Neuf is hardly new: it opened to traffic in 1632. Remains of the old bridge—one arch and the lighter-color outline on the brick wall of the **Hôtel-Dieu** (hospital)—are visible across the river. The 16th-century hospital was used for pilgrims on their way to Santiago de Compostela. Just over the bridge, on a clear day in winter, the snowcapped peaks of the Pyrénées can often be seen in the distance. ✉ *Toulouse.*

SOUTH OF RUE DE METZ

South of Rue de Metz you'll discover the Cathédral St-Étienne, the antiques district along Rue Perchepinte, and town houses and palaces on Rue Ninau, Rue Ozenne, and Rue de la Dalbade—all among the top sights in Toulouse.

Cathédrale St-Étienne. The cathedral was erected in stages between the 13th and the 17th century, though the nave and choir languished unfinished because of a lack of funds. A fine collection of 16th- and 17th-century tapestries traces the life of St. Stephen. In front of the cathedral is the city's oldest fountain, dating from the 16th century. ✉ *Pl. St-Étienne, Toulouse* ☎ *05–61–52–03–82* ⏲ *Mon.–Sat. 8–7, Sun. 9–7.*

Hôtel de Clary. One of the finest mansions on Rue de la Dalbade is also known as the Hôtel de Pierre because of its unusually solid *pierre* (stone) construction, which was considered a sign of great wealth at the time. The ornately sculpted facade was designed by Nicolas Bachelier in the 16th century. ✉ *25 rue de la Dalbade, Toulouse.*

Hôtel du Vieux Raisin. Officially the Hôtel Beringuier Maynier, this building was dubbed the Vieux Raisin (Old Grape) after the early name of the street and even earlier inn. Built in the 15th and 16th centuries, the mansion has an octagonal tower, male and female figures on the facade, and allegorical sculptures of the three stages of life—infancy, maturity, and old age—over the windows to the left. ✉ *36 rue de Languedoc, Toulouse.*

Musée Paul Dupuy. This museum, dedicated to medieval applied arts, is housed in the Hôtel Pierre Besson, a 17th-century mansion. ✉ *13 rue de la Pleau, Toulouse* ☎ *05–61–14–95–40* 🎫 *€3* ⏲ *Oct.–May, Wed.–Mon. 10–5; June–Sept., Wed.–Mon. 10–6.*

Notre-Dame de la Dalbade. Originally called Sancta Maria de Ecclesia Alba in Langue d'Oc and Ste-Marie de l'Église Blanche in French (*alba* and *blanche* both meaning "white"), the name of this church evolved into "de Albata" and later "Dalbade." Ironically, one of its outstanding features today is the colorful 19th-century ceramic tympanum over the Renaissance door. ✉ *Pl. de la Dalbade, Toulouse* ☎ *05–61–25–58–05.*

WHERE TO EAT

$$ BISTRO ✕ **Bistrot de l'Étoile.** Don't let the dismal backstreet exterior put you off: Bistrot de l'Étoile is a delightfully retro 1960s pub that promises fast service, a smiling staff, and a great choice of dishes on the blackboard menu (including excellent grilled meats cooked on the fire in the center of the restaurant). The homemade desserts are great, too. [$] *Average main: €23* ✉ *6 rue de l'Étoile, Toulouse* ☎ *05–61–63–13–43* 🌐 *www.bistrotdeletoile.fr* ⏲ *Closed weekends, 3 wks in Aug., 1 wk in May* ✍ *Reservations essential.*

$$$ BRASSERIE ✕ **Brasserie Flo "Les Beaux Arts".** Overlooking the Pont Neuf, this elegant brasserie is idyllic at sunset, as artists Ingres and Matisse—who were regulars—knew all too well; watch the colors change over the Garonne from a quayside window or a sidewalk table while enjoying seafood sauerkraut with Champagne or wild sea bass with salmon tartare. The

Seat of the municipal government, Place du Capitole is an elegant square that's often transformed into an open market.

kitchen is open until 11:30 pm on Friday and Saturday (a rarity in France), which is perfect if you want to eat out after a show. $ *Average main: €27* ✉ *1 quai de la Daurade, Toulouse* ☎ *05–61–21–12–12* 🌐 *www.brasserielesbeauxarts.com.*

$$$ FRENCH ✕ **Chez Emile.** With a great location and lovely summer terrace, this is the place to savor such regional specialties as cassoulet—the locals love it, which speaks volumes here in the heart of cassoulet country. $ *Average main: €30* ✉ *13 pl. St-Georges, Toulouse* ☎ *05–61–21–05–56* 🌐 *www.restaurant-emile.com* ⏲ *July and Aug., closed Sun., no lunch Mon.; Sept.–June, closed Sun. and Mon.; closed 2 wks at Christmas.*

$$$$ FRENCH ✕ **Jardins de l'Opéra.** Stéphane Tournié's elegant restaurant next to the Grand Hôtel de l'Opéra is a perennial favorite. Intimate rooms and a covered terrace around a little pond give it an undeniable allure, though some may find the grand flourishes—glass ceilings and mammoth chandeliers—a little too, well, operatic. Inspired by the seasons, the food is gastronomical local fare with added nouvelle and Gascon touches. Seductive four-course prix-fixe menus are available, with prices starting at €30. If you're looking for something a little lower key, consider the adjacent Grand Café de l'Opera. $ *Average main: €33* ✉ *1 pl. du Capitole, Toulouse* ☎ *05–61–23–07–76* 🌐 *www.lesjardinsdelopera.com* ⏲ *Closed Sun., Mon., and 1 wk in Jan.* ✍ *Reservations essential.*

$$ FRENCH ✕ **Le Bon Vivre.** This bustling bistro, brightened with Jean Vier-designed striped Basque tablecloths, fills up at lunch and dinner every day. Quick, unpretentious, and always good, the house specialties include such dishes as cod, cassoulet, and wild boar in season (September–March). If you forgot to book, ask if you can wait for a table with a drink at

EATING WELL

Dining in France's Southwest is a rougher, heartier, and more rustic version of classic Mediterranean cooking—the peppers are sliced thick, the garlic and olive oil used with a heavier hand, the herbs crushed and served au naturel.

Expect *cuisine du marché* (market-based cooking), savory seasonal dishes based on the culinary trinity of the south—garlic, onion, and tomato—straight from the village market.

Garlic and goose fat are generously used in traditional recipes. Be sure to try some of the renowned foie gras (goose or duck liver) and *confit de canard* (preserved duck). The most famous regional dish is cassoulet, a succulent white-bean stew with *confit d'oie* (preserved goose), duck, lamb, or a mixture of all three.

Keep your eyes open for festive *cargolades*—Catalan for huge communal barbecues starting off with thousands of buttery-garlic snails roasted on open grills and eaten with your fingers, followed by cured bacon and lamb cutlets and vats (and vats) of local wine. In the Roussillon and along the Mediterranean coast from Collioure up through Perpignan to Narbonne, the prevalent Catalan cuisine features olive-oil-based cooking and sauces such as the classic *aioli* (crushed and emulsified garlic and olive oil). When you're on the coast, it's fish, of course, often cooked over a wood fire.

the bistro's salon next door. $ *Average main: €20* ✉ *15 bis pl. Wilson, Toulouse* ☎ *05–61–23–07–17* 🌐 *www.lebonvivre.com.*

$$$ VIETNAMESE **✕ L'Empereur de Huê'.** Occupying a sleek contemporary space on a bohemian backstreet, this Vietnamese eatery is helmed by a hip female chef who has drawn national attention for her style in and out of the kitchen. Banana flower and duck salad, citronella beef, and ginger-orange *macaroons* are just a few of her novel creations—but you can only enjoy them at dinner (lunch isn't served). Annual closure varies year to year, so call first if you're coming in winter. $ *Average main: €26* ✉ *17 rue Couteliers, Toulouse* ☎ *05–61–53–55–72* 🌐 *www.empereurdehue.com* ⏲ *Closed Mon. No lunch.*

$ BAKERY **✕ Les curieux gâteaux de Tata Bidule.** If you need a pick-me-up, head to this gourmet cupcake-and-coffee shop with Wi-Fi and a choice of inside or street-side tables. The homage to pastel pastries is run by three crafty women who claim their traveling great-aunt discovered the Anglo-Saxon cupcake after her circus act won her an invitation to tea with Queen Elizabeth. Try the violette, black tea, and royal icing cupcake or the chocolate and hot red pepper with your espresso. Hot chocolate and fresh-squeezed seasonal juices are also available. Though old-school in style, this shop is *au courant* in that it uses no additives or preservatives and has gluten-free options. Best news: it's open on Sunday. You can also get these cakes at Slow Concept, a new art boutique and café on rue Saint Ursule (*www.slowconcept.fr*). $ *Average main: €5* ✉ *14 rue Temponières, Toulouse* ☎ *05–81–60–14–32* 🌐 *www.tatabidule.com.*

$$$$ MODERN FRENCH Fodor's Choice ★ **Michel Sarran.** The post-nouvelle haven for what is arguably Toulouse's finest dining departs radically from the traditional stick-to-your-ribs cuisine of southwest France, instead favoring Mediterranean formulas suited to the rhythms and reasons of modern living. The ambience is contemporary sophistication expertly blended with warmth, and the food is light but flavorful. Delicacies like foie gras soup with Belon oysters or wild salmon in green curry sauce prove that Chef Michel Sarran's two Michelin stars are well deserved . Don't count on a Saturday night *fête* here. The restaurant is closed weekends—the obvious mark of a sought-after chef who is free to choose his own hours. *Average main: €50 21 bd. A. Duportal, Toulouse 05–61–12–32–32 www.michel-sarran.com Closed weekends and Aug. No lunch Wed. Reservations essential.*

WHERE TO STAY

$$$ HOTEL **Grand Hôtel de l'Opéra.** Little wonder the likes of Deneuve, Pavarotti, and Aznavour favored this downtown doyen: its keynote grandeur is obvious the moment you step into the lobby, complete with soaring columns, Second Empire bergères, and sofas of blue tasseled velvet. **Pros:** ideally situated on main square; within five minutes of the train station. **Cons:** splendor and a certain reserved professionalism rank higher than intimacy. *Rooms from: €195 1 pl. du Capitole, Toulouse 05–61–21–82–66 www.grand-hotel-opera.com 44 rooms, 6 suites No meals.*

$ HOTEL **Grand Hôtel d'Orléans.** Although it's in a slightly sketchy neighborhood, this picturesque former stagecoach relay station—built in 1867—still retains a certain 19th-century charm and is home to a good restaurant. **Pros:** fine restaurant; close to train and bus stations. **Cons:** surrounding neighborhood is a little dicey. *Rooms from: €75 72 rue Bayard, Toulouse 05–61–62–98–47 www.grand-hotel-orleans.fr 54 rooms No meals.*

$ HOTEL **Hôtel Albert I.** The building may seem undistinguished, but its cheerful guest rooms are spacious (especially the older ones with giant fireplaces), and the location is central to everything; it's the personable owner, however, who really sets this hotel apart. **Pros:** ideal location; warm and helpful service. **Cons:** parking can be arranged but the lot is difficult to find; some rooms are small. *Rooms from: €95 8 rue Rivals, Toulouse 05–61–21–17–91 www.hotel-albert1.com 47 rooms No meals.*

$$$ HOTEL **Hôtel Garonne.** In the thick of the most Toulousain part of town, next to the Pont Neuf and the former fish market (although somewhat far from the city center), this is a small but hyper-stylish spot with contemporary perks—like gourmet takeout delivered to your room on request. **Pros:** hip design; chic bohemian neighborhood with eclectic shops and restaurants nearby; helpful staff. **Cons:** a hike to the city center; lobby and rooms feel a bit small. *Rooms from: €180 22 descente de la Halle aux Poissons, Toulouse 05–34–31–94–80 www.hotelgaronne.net 11 rooms, 3 suites No meals.*

$ HOTEL **Hôtel Royal Wilson.** With a quiet city-center location across from the Théâtre National, this two-star hotel—one of the best deals in

Toulouse—attracts theater professionals, business travelers, and garden-variety tourists. **Pros:** great central location; good value. **Cons:** some bathrooms don't have wall-mounted showerheads; though unobtrusive, some color schemes might not appeal (think pink). *Rooms from: €61 ✉ 6 rue Labéda, Toulouse ☎ 05–61–12–41–41 ⊕ www.hotelroyalwilson-toulouse.com 27 rooms No meals.*

$$ HOTEL **Le Grand Balcon.** You can dream in the clouds with Toulouse's famous aviators in this 1930s hotel tucked into a corner of Place du Capitol—popular with pioneering pilots back in the glory days, it's been playfully retrofitted with a smart design that pays homage to Toulouse's high-flying heritage. **Pros:** A+ location next to Place du Capitol; stylish design; congenial staff. **Cons:** lower level rooms get street noise; no on-site parking; some rooms feel small. *Rooms from: €115 ✉ 8–10 rue Romiguières, Toulouse ☎ 05–34–25–44–09 ⊕ www.grandbalconhotel.com 47 rooms No meals.*

NIGHTLIFE AND PERFORMING ARTS

Toulouse is jammed with small, independent concert halls and theaters, most of them covered in the mini-mag *Clutch*, which can be found in any hotel lobby. As for cultural highlights, so many opera singers perform at the Théâtre du Capitole and the Halle aux Grains that the city is known as the *capitale du bel canto*. The opera season lasts from October until late May, with occasional summer presentations as well. A wide variety of dance companies also perform in Toulouse: the Ballet du Capitole stages classical ballets, while Ballet-Théâtre Joseph Russillo and Compagnie Jean-Marc Matos put on modern-dance performances. The Centre National Chorégraphique de Toulouse, in the St-Cyprien quarter, welcomes international companies each year.

Bar Basque. You'll find Bar Basque among the many watering holes around Place St-Pierre. *✉ 7 pl. St-Pierre, Toulouse ☎ 05–61–21–55–64.*

Chez Ton Ton. A somewhat raucous crowd is drawn to this very popular Place St-Pierre dive. *✉ 14 pl. St-Pierre, Toulouse ☎ 05–61–21–89–54.*

Cosmopolitain. You can dine, sip, or dance at this industrial-chic restaurant, wine bar, and cocktail lounge combo. *✉ 1 rue des 3 Journées, Toulouse ☎ 05–61–29–89–33 ⊕ cosmopolitain-toulouse.fr.*

Halle Aux Grains. Home of l'Orchestre du Capitole, the hexagonal-shaped Halle Aux Grains ranks among the best music auditoriums in Europe. *✉ Pl. Dupuy, Toulouse ☎ 05–61–63–13–13 ⊕ www.onct.mairie-toulouse.fr.*

La Bonita. Brazilian guitarists perform at La Bonita, a festive *restaurant musical*. *✉ 112 Grand-Rue St-Michel, Toulouse ☎ 05–62–26–36–45 ⊕ www.labonita.fr.*

L'Atelier de l'Echarpe. Good food, fine wine, classic cocktails, and a retro-cool aesthetic make this spot popular among young (but not university young) Toulousains. *✉ 8 rue de l'Echarpe, Toulouse ☎ 05–34–30–93–35 ⊕ latelierdelecharpe.fr.*

Le Bijou. If you don't mind a short bus ride across the Garonne, take Line 12 to the front of a small concert hall and restaurant filled with an eclectic, all-ages crowd; most are regulars who come for the great bistro menu and a musical lineup featuring top Toulouse acts. ✉ *123 av. de Muret, Toulouse* ☎ *05–61–42–95–07* 🌐 *www.le-bijou.net.*

Le Mandala. Be sure to stop by Le Mandala for a bit of the bubbly and some of the best jazz in town. ✉ *23 rue des Amidonniers, Toulouse* ☎ *05–61–28–36–41* 🌐 *www.lemandala.com.*

Le Purple. Ready to dance? Le Purple is a hot multispace disco. ✉ *2 rue Castellane, Toulouse* ☎ *05–62–73–04–67* 🌐 *www.purepurple.fr.*

Les Terrasses de Saint-Rome. If you're looking for a pretty terrace for a late dinner (served until 11), try Les Terrasses de Saint-Rome. ✉ *39 rue St-Rome, Toulouse* ☎ *05–62–27–06–06* 🌐 *terrasses.saint.rome.free.fr.*

Melting Pot. This pub lives up to its name, with young people from around the world crowding the bar. ✉ *26 bd. de Strasbourg, Toulouse* ☎ *05–61–62–82–98* 🌐 *www.toulouseweb.com/meltingpot.*

No. 5 Wine Bar. At this stylish wine bar, epicurians can choose from 32 wines by the glass and more than 800 bottles accompanied by gourmet tapas. ✉ *5 rue de la Bourse, Toulouse* ☎ *05–61–38–44–51* 🌐 *www.n5winebar.com.*

Père Louis. Begin your night on the town at Père Louis, an old-fashioned winery (and restaurant), with barrels used as tables. ✉ *45 rue des Tourneurs, Toulouse* ☎ *05–61–21–33–45.*

15

SHOPPING

Toulouse is a chic design center for clothing and artifacts of all kinds. Rue St-Rome, Rue Croix Baragnon, Rue des Changes, and Rue d'Alsace-Lorraine are all good shopping streets. For artful vintage finds look for the word *friperie* on store fronts along Rue Peyrolières.

ALBI AND THE GERS

Along the banks of the Tarn to the northeast of Toulouse, Albi rivals Toulouse in rose colors. West from Albi, along the river, the land opens up to the rural Gers *département,* home of the heady brandy, Armagnac, and heart of the former dukedom of Gascony. Studded with châteaux—from simple medieval fortresses to ambitious classical residences—and with tiny, isolated village jewels like Cordes-sur-Ciel, the Gers is an easy place to fall in love with, or in.

ALBI

75 km (47 miles) northeast of Toulouse.

Toulouse-Lautrec's native Albi is a busy, beautifully preserved provincial market town. In its heyday Albi was a major center for the Cathars, members of a dualistic and ascetic religious movement critical of the hierarchical and worldly ways of the Catholic Church.

GETTING HERE

About 18 trains daily (1 hr, €15) run between Toulouse and Albi's main station on Place Stalingrad (in a somewhat isolated part of town). Buses also make the trip from Toulouse (1½ hrs, €13) and adjoining towns to the Albi bus station on Place Jean Jaurès.

Visitor Information Albi Tourist Office. ☎ *05–63–36–36–00* ⊕ *www.albi-tourisme.fr.*

MY WAY OR THE HIGHWAY

Beneath Ste-Cécile's organ is an impressive 15th-century mural depicting punishments for the seven deadly sins in the Last Judgment. The scenes of torture and hellfire give an indication of how the Vatican kept its Christian subjects in line during the crusade against the Cathars and subsequent Inquisition trials.

EXPLORING

Fodor's Choice ★ **Cathédrale Ste-Cécile.** One of the most unusual and dazzling churches in France, the huge Cathédrale Ste-Cécile, with its intimidating clifflike walls, resembles a cross between a castle and an ocean liner. It was constructed as a symbol of the Church's return to power after the 13th-century crusade that wiped out the Cathars. The interior is an astonishingly ornate contrast to the massive austerity of the outer walls. Maestro Donnelli and a team of 16th-century Italian artists (most of the Emilian school) covered every possible surface with religious scenes and brightly colored patterns—it remains the largest group of Italian Renaissance paintings in any French church. On the west wall you can find one of the most splendid organs in the world, built in 1734 and outfitted with 3,500 pipes, which loom over a celebrated fresco of the Last Judgment. ✉ *Pl. Ste-Cécile, Albi* ☎ *05–63–43–23–43* ⏲ *May–Oct., Mon.–Sat. 9:30–6:15, Sun. 9:30–10:45 and 2–5:45; Nov.–Apr., Mon.–Sat. 9–1 and 2–6:30, Sun. 9:30–10:45 and 2–5:45.*

Cloître St-Salvi. From the central square and parking area in front of the Palais de la Berbie, walk to the 11th- to 15th-century college and Cloître de St-Salvy. ✉ *Rue Maries, Albi* ⏲ *Daily 7 am–8 pm.*

Maison du Vieil Albi (*Old Albi House*). Take a look at Albi's finest restored traditional house, the Maison du Vieil Albi. ✉ *Corner of Rue de la Croix-Blanche and Puech-Bérenguer, Albi* ☎ *05–63–54–96–38* 🎫 €2 ⏲ *Oct.–Mar., Mon.–Sat. 2–5; Apr.–June and Sept., Mon.–Sat. 2–5:30; July and Aug., Mon.–Sat. 10:30–12:30 and 2–6.*

Maison Natale de Toulouse-Lautrec (*Hôtel du Bosc*). Real fans of Toulouse-Lautrec may want to snap a photo of his birthplace, the Maison Natale de Toulouse-Lautrec, which remains a private residence. ✉ *14 rue Henri de Toulouse-Lautrec, Albi.*

Fodor's Choice ★ **Musée Toulouse-Lautrec.** In a garden designed by the renowned André Le Nôtre, creator of the "green geometries" at Versailles, the landmark **Palais de la Berbie** (Berbie Palace), between the cathedral and the Pont Vieux (Old Bridge), is the setting for this exceptional museum. Built in 1265 as a residence for Albi's archbishops, the fortresslike structure was transformed in 1922 into a museum to honor Albi's most celebrated son, Belle Époque painter Henri de Toulouse-Lautrec (1864–1901). Toulouse-Lautrec left Albi for Paris in 1882 and soon became famous for his colorful, tumultuous evocations of the lifestyle of bohemian glamour found in and around Montmartre. Son of a wealthy and aristocratic family (Lautrec is a village not far from Toulouse), the young Henri suffered from a genetic bone deficiency and broke both legs as a child, which stunted his growth. But it was the artist's fascination with the decadent side of life that led him to an early grave at the age of 37. The museum's collection of artworks—more than a thousand, representing the world's largest Toulouse-Lautrec corpus—has been deftly organized into themed rooms, including galleries devoted to some of his greatest portraits and scenes from Paris's *maisons closées* (brothels), with paintings stylishly hung amid the palace's brick ogival arches. There are other masterworks here, including paintings by Georges de la Tour and Francesco Guardi. ✉ *Palais de la Berbie, Off Pl. Ste-Cécile, Albi* ☎ *05–63–49–48–70* 🌐 *www.museetoulouselautrec.net* 🎫 *€8; gardens free* ⏲ *June 21–Sept., daily 9–6; Oct.–Dec., Wed.–Mon. 10–noon and 2–5:30; Jan., Wed.–Mon. 10–noon and 2–5; Feb. and Mar., Wed.–Mon. 10–noon and 2–5:30; Apr. and May, daily 10–noon and 2–6; June 1–20, daily 9–noon and 2–6.*

15

Place du Vigan. Rue de l'Hôtel de Ville, two streets west of the Maison Natale, leads past the Mairie (City Hall), with its hanging globes of flowers, to Albi's main square, Place du Vigan. Take a break in one of the two main cafés, Le Pontie or Le Vigan. ✉ *Pl. du Vigan, Albi.*

WHERE TO EAT AND STAY

$ FRENCH ✕ **Le Jardin des Quatre Saisons.** A good-value menu and superb fish dishes are the reasons for this restaurant's excellent reputation. Chef-owner Georges Bermond's house specialties—which change seasonally—include *pot au feu* (stew) of the sea and *suprême de sandre* (a freshwater fish cooked in wine). Though the traditional setting could use some spunk, the warm service and *correcte* (fair) bill make up for any old-fashioned ambience. $ *Average main: €17* ✉ *5 rue de la Pompe, Albi* ☎ *05–63–60–77–76* 🌐 *www.le-jardin-des-quatre-saisons.com* 💳 *No credit cards* ⏲ *Closed Mon. No dinner Sun.*

$$$ HOTEL 🏨 **Hostellerie St-Antoine.** Founded in 1734, this eminently comfortable hotel in the center of town is one of the oldest in France and has been run by the same family for five generations (note the Toulouse-Lautrec sketches given to the owner's great-grandfather, a friend of the painter). **Pros:** slightly off the beaten path in a quiet area; friendly staff. **Cons:** breakfast is very expensive; overall, doesn't quite live up to its four-star rating. $ *Rooms from: €147* ✉ *17 rue St-Antoine, Albi* ☎ *05–63–54–04–04* 🌐 *www.hotel-saint-antoine-albi.com* ⏲ *Closed 2 wks in Dec.* 🛏 *41 rooms, 3 suites* 🍽 *No meals.*

$ HOTEL 🏨 **Hôtel Chiffre.** A former stagecoach inn, this centrally located town house has fairly lackluster rooms and a hearty restaurant all overlooking a cozy garden. **Pros:** restaurant is good and a great value. **Cons:** foyer and rooms are sparsely decorated; some beds need to be replaced. $ *Rooms from: €78* ✉ *50 rue Séré-de-Rivières, Albi* ☎ *05–63–48–58–48* 🌐 *www.hotelchiffre.com* ⏲ *Closed mid-Dec.–mid-Jan.* 🛏 *39 rooms* 🍽 *No meals.*

Albi honors native son Toulouse-Lautrec with a museum crammed with his masterpieces, including *Salon in the rue des Moulins*.

SHOPPING

Around **Place Ste-Cécile** are numerous clothing, book, music, and antiques shops.

Alby Foie Gras. The finest foie gras in town is found at Alby Foie Gras. ✉ *29 rue Mariès, Albi* ☎ *05–63–38–21–33.*

Flea and antiques market. A Saturday-morning flea and antiques market is held in the Halle du Castelviel. ✉ *Pl. du Castelviel, Albi.*

L'Artisan Chocolatier (*Chocolatier Michel Belin*). Michel Belin's chocolate delights are deservedly famous. ✉ *4 rue Dr-Camboulives, on Pl. du Vigan, Albi* ☎ *05–63–54–18–46.*

Produce markets. Albi has many produce markets: one takes place Tuesday to Sunday in the market halls near the cathedral; another is held on Tuesday and Saturday mornings at Place Fernand Pelloutier. An all-organic market runs Tuesday afternoons at Place Fernand Pelloutier. ✉ *Albi.*

CORDES-SUR-CIEL

25 km (15½ miles) northwest of Albi, 80 km (50 miles) northeast of Toulouse.

A must-stop for many travelers, the picture-book hilltop town of Cordes-sur-Ciel appears to hover in midair when mists steal up from the Cérou Valley below, hence the name—*sur-ciel* means "in the sky/heaven." It was established in 1222 by Count Raymond VII of Toulouse as a redoubt after the Occitan wars waged against the region's Cathars; and its conical hill is riddled with caves that served as granaries

CLOSE UP

Crusading Cathars

Scorched by the southern heat, the dusty ruins high atop cliffs in southern Languedoc were once the refuges of the Cathars, the notoriously ascetic religious group persecuted out of existence by the Catholic Church in the 12th and 13th centuries. The Cathars inhabited an area ranging from present-day Germany all the way to the Atlantic Ocean. Adherents to this dualistic doctrine of material abnegation and spiritual revelation abstained from fleshly pleasures in all forms, forgoing procreation and the consumption of animal products. In some cases, they even committed suicide by starvation; diminishing the amount of flesh in the world was the ultimate way to foil the forces of evil. However, not thrilled by a religion that did not "go forth and multiply" (and that saw no need to pay taxes to the Church), Pope Innocent III launched the Albigensian Crusade (Albi was one of the major Cathar strongholds), and Pope Gregory IX rounded up the stragglers during a period of inquisition starting in 1233. All these forces had been given scandalously free rein by the French court, which allowed dukes and counts from northern France to build *bastides* (fortified medieval towns built along a strict grid plan) through the area to entrap the peasantry.

The counts were more than happy to oblige the pope with a little hounding, an inquisition or two, and some burnings at the stake. Entire towns were judged to be guilty of heresy and inhabitants by the dozens were thrown to their deaths from high town walls. The persecuted "pure" soon took refuge in the Pyrénées Mountains, where they survived for 100 years. Now all that remains of this unhappy sect are their former hideouts, with tour groups visiting the vacant stone staircases and roofless chapels of haunted places like Peyrepertuse and Quéribus. For more information, log on to 🌐 *www.cathar.info* or go hiking with medievalist Ingrid Sparbier (🌐 *www.guide-sud-france.com*).

15

during times of siege. Today you may find Cordes-sur-Ciel besieged by summertime tourists, who come to admire well-preserved buildings (like the 14th-century St-Michel church) and to peruse plentiful shops and markets. The town is particularly busy during the annual Fêtes Médiévales du Grand Fauconnier (🌐 *www.grandfauconnier.com*) in mid-July—a three-day blowout, replete with an artisanal fair and costumed Bal Médiéval.

GETTING HERE

Tarnbus (🌐 *tarnbus.tarn.fr*) makes the 34-minute trip from Albi to the bottom of Cordes at least five times daily (€2). If you're driving, note that traffic is banned in the upper town in summer, and parking nearby is virtually impossible.

Visitor Information Cordes-sur-Ciel Tourist Office. ☎ *05–63–56–00–52* 🌐 *www.cordessurciel.fr.*

EXPLORING

Grande-rue Haute. When peace arrived in the late Middle Ages, the town prospered and many rich residents built pink-sandstone Gothic-style houses—a sizable number of which still line the main street, Grande-rue Haute (also called Rue Droite). Today, many are occupied by painters, sculptors, weavers, leatherworkers, and even creators of illuminated manuscripts, whose ateliers and stores lure the summer crowds. ✉ *Grande-rue Haute, Cordes-sur-Ciel.*

Musée Charles-Portail. The small Musée Charles-Portail has relics from the town's medieval past, plus items uncovered during excavations of the 372-foot-deep Cordes Well. ✉ *1 rue St-Michel, Cordes-sur-Ciel* ☎ *05–63–80–51–72* €2.50 ⏲ *July and Aug., Wed.–Mon. 2–6; Easter–June, Sept., and Oct., weekends 2–6.*

Musée Les Arts du Sucre et du Chocolat. For proof that life is indeed sweet in Cordes-sur-Ciel, visit this two-room museum dedicated to sugar and chocolate. It showcases the confectionary creations of noted chef Yves Thuriès. ✉ *33 Grand-Rue Raimond VII, Cordes-sur-Ciel* ☎ *05–63–56–02–40* 🌐 *artdusucre.fr* *€4* ⏲ *Late Mar.–early June and early Sept.–Oct., Wed.–Sun. 10–7; early June–early Sept., daily 10–7.*

WHERE TO STAY

$ HOTEL **L'Hostellerie du Vieux Cordes.** One of famed chocolatier Yves Thuriès's lovely Cordes hotels, this 13th-century house, built around a spectacular courtyard dotted with tiny tables and shaded by a magnificent 300-year-old wisteria, has stylishly decorated guest rooms and a fine on-site eatery. **Pros:** some rooms have views of the valley (book well in advance). **Cons:** cramped Room 4 should be avoided; uphill hike to the hotel from parking area. $ *Rooms from: €68* ✉ *Rue St-Michel, Cordes-sur-Ciel* ☎ *05–63–53–79–20* 🌐 *www.vieuxcordes.fr* ⏲ *Closed Jan.–mid-Feb.* *19 rooms* *No meals.*

LANGUEDOC-ROUSSILLON

One of the most diverse backdrops in France, Languedoc-Roussillon skirts the Mediterranean coast southward toward Spain where the Pyrénées plunge dramatically into the sea. The southern half of the region, Roussillon was long dominated by Spanish Catalonia's House of Aragon—which explains why the area is also known as French Catalonia. Historically rooted in agricultural pursuits, Roussillon's varied landscape allows for citrus and cherry trees, while the snowcapped Pic du Canigó towers over palm trees in the valley. Olive groves and vineyards thrive on arid hillsides inland and earthy cheeses come from herds in the bordering high mountains. Beaches stretch down the coast to Cerbère at the Spanish border. Immortalized by Matisse and Picasso, this strip is known as the Côte Vermeille and attracts droves of European sun worshippers (plus aspiring painters) to its craggy shoreline. Heading northward, Languedoc begins around the ancient Roman capital of Narbonne and extends to the region's hub, the elegant city of Montpellier. The Canal du Midi flows through the vineyard-laden region to Le Littoral Languedocien (the Languedoc Coast), famous for fresh

Bouzigues oysters and resident flamingos. Life in Languedoc-Roussillon is distinctly relaxed and casual, so you'll probably be taking afternoon siestas before you know it.

CARCASSONNE

88 km (55 miles) southeast of Toulouse, 105 km (65 miles) south of Albi.

Poised atop a hill overlooking lush green countryside and the Aude River, Carcassonne's fortified upper town, known as La Cité, looks lifted from the pages of a storybook—literally, perhaps, as its circle of towers and battlements is said to be the setting for Charles Perrault's classic tale *Puss in Boots*. With its turrets and castellated walls, it appeals to children and those with a penchant for the Middle Ages. The lower, newer part of the city is the *ville basse*, where you'll find the train station and a smattering of sights (most notably the Musée des Beaux-Arts).

GETTING HERE

Ryanair operates regular flights from London, Dublin, and several other European cities; a €5 airport shuttle transports passengers to the rail station (on Avenue du Maréchal Joffre, beside the Canal du Midi), stopping at La Cité en route. Arriving by boat or barge via the historic canal is a romantic alternative, but trains are more reliable—there are six per day from Narbonne and 15 from Toulouse alone; from the station you can take a cab, hop a *navette* shuttle, or make the 30-minute walk up to La Cité. Bus service is available, too (a trip from Toulouse takes two hours and costs €12). If you're driving, be advised that unless you're staying at a hotel in La Cité, you are not allowed to enter it with your vehicle. Paid parking is available in a lot across the road from the drawbridge.

Visitor Information Carcassonne Tourist Office. ☎ *04–68–10–24–30* 🌐 *www.tourisme-carcassonne.com.*

EXPLORING

FAMILY Fodor'sChoice ★ **La Cité.** Legend has it that Charlemagne laid siege to the original settlement here early in the 9th century, only to be outdone by one Dame Carcas—a clever woman who boldly fed the last of the city's wheat to a pig in full view of the would-be conqueror. Thinking this indicated endless food supplies, Charlemagne promptly decamped, and the exuberant townsfolk named their city after her. During the 13th century, Louis IX (Saint Louis) and his son Philip the Fair strengthened Carcassonne's fortifications—so much so that the town came to be considered inviolable by marauding armies and was duly nicknamed "the virgin of Languedoc."

A town that can never be taken in battle is often abandoned, however, and for centuries thereafter Carcassonne remained under a Sleeping Beauty spell. It was only awakened during the 19th-century craze for chivalry and the Gothic style, when, in 1835, the historic-monument inspector (and poet) Prosper Mérimée arrived. He was so appalled by the dilapidated state of the walls that he commissioned the architect,

Languedoc -
Roussillon
Toulouse
see detail
map
Montpellier
see detail
map
Cordes-
sur-Ciel
Albi
MIDI-
PYRÉNÉES
LANGUEDOC-
ROUSSILLON
Gimont
l'Isle Jourdain
Samatan
Garonne River
Lacaune
Lodeve
Castres
Bédarieux
Gignac
Mazamet
Revel
St-Pons-de-Thomieres
Auterive
St Sulpice
Castelnaudary
Puisserguier
Frontignan
Sete
Golfe d'Aigues Mortes
Béziers
Agde
Carcassonne
Lézignan-
Corbieres
Pamiers
Mirepoix
Narbonne
Limoux
Gruissan
St-Girons
Foix
Lavelanet
Massat
Couiza
Grotte
de Niaux
Tarascon-
sur-Ariège
Quillan
Ax-les-
Thermes
Salses
Estagel
SPAIN
ANDORRA
ANDORRA
Villefranche-
de-Conflent
Prades
Vernet-
les-Bains
Perpignan
Font
Romeu
Mount-Louis
le Boulou
Céret
Amélie-les-Bains
Argeles
Collioure
Port Vendres
Portbou
SPAIN
VERMILION COAST
Mediterranean Sea
0
15 mi
0
15 km
A62
A68
D999
A75
D986
D32
D612
D112
D622
D17
N124
D4
N126
D2
D11
A9
N109
D28
A61
D2
A75
D626
D612
D61
D909
N20
D907
D919
D118
A64
N9
A9
N112
A66
D628
D627
D117
A61
D626
D117
D618
D625
D618
D613
D117
D611
A9
D625
N20
D117
D118
N116
CG2
N114
N320
CG1
N116
D115
N260
C14

painter, and historian Viollet-le-Duc (who found his greatest fame restoring Paris's Notre-Dame) to undertake repairs. Today the 1844 renovation is considered almost as much a work of art as the medieval town itself. No matter if La Cité is more Viollet than authentic; it still remains one of the most romantic sights in France.

THE POSTCARD COMES TO LIFE

Carcassonne usually goes medieval in mid-August with Les Médiévales (🌐 *www.carcassonne-tourisme.com*), a festival of troubadour song, rich costumes, and jousting performances (some years the event isn't held; check with the tourist office). And don't forget the Bastille Day (July 14) fireworks over La Cité—spectacular!

There's no mistaking the fact that 21st-century tourism has taken over here. La Cité's streets are lined with souvenir shops, crafts boutiques, restaurants, and tiny "museums" (a Cathars Museum, a Hat Museum), all out to make a buck and rarely worth that. But you should still plan on spending at least a couple of hours exploring the walls and peering over the battlements across sun-drenched plains toward the distant Pyrénées. Staying overnight within the ancient walls lets you savor the timeless atmosphere after the daytime hordes are gone. ✉ *La Cité, Carcassonne.*

Musée des Beaux-Arts (*Fine Arts Museum*). The real draw in the ville basse, this museum houses a nice collection of porcelain, 17th- and 18th-century Flemish paintings, and works by local artists—including some stirring battle scenes by Jacques Gamelin (1738–1803). ✉ *1 rue de Verdun, Ville Basse, Carcassonne* ☎ *04–68–77–73–70* 🎫 *Free* ⏲ *Mid-Sept.–mid-June, Tues.–Sat. 10–noon and 2–6; mid-June–mid-Sept., daily 10–6.*

WHERE TO EAT

$$ MODERN FRENCH

✕ **Bloc G.** Just outside the upper city walls, this all-white urbanesque restaurant and wine bar, run by three food-and-design-savvy sisters, offers a reality check after the touristic, turreted streets of La Cité. The blackboard menu highlights experimental touches to classic dishes (like sautéed foie gras in a Thai broth) and helps attract a sophisticated, casual clientele. If returning to the crowds leaves you feeling claustrophobic, consider one of the five loft-style guest rooms in the upstairs inn—each with enough space for a full-on yoga practice. Also ask about sister Delphine's B&B not far away. $ *Average main: €18* ✉ *112 rue Barbacane, Carcassonne* ☎ *04–68–47–58–20* 🌐 *www.bloc-g.com* ⏲ *Closed Sun. and Mon. in winter.*

$$$$ MODERN FRENCH

✕ **Le Puits du Tresor.** At the foot of the famous Cathar castle of Lastours, in an old textile factory above the Orbiel River, this Michelin-starred treat comes as something of a surprise. Headed by the talented Jean-Marc Boyer, the restaurant serves inventive and artistic *néo-classique* meals inspired by the seasons and based on local ingredients. Strapped for cash? You can always eat at Boyer's Auberge du Diable au Thym, right next door, for a fraction of the price. $ *Average main: €45* ✉ *Rte. des Châteaux, Lastours, 12 km (8 miles) north of Carcassonne,*

Carcassonne ☎ *04–68–77–50–24* 🌐 *www.lepuitsdutresor.fr* ⏲ *Closed Mon., Tues., and Mar. No dinner Sun. Nov.–May.*

$ FRENCH ✕ **Sire de Cabaret.** Nestled beneath the château of Roquefère, an unspoiled *village fleuri* in the Cabardés region of the Montagne Noire, this regional favorite dishes up amazing steaks *à la Languedocienne* and bottomless plates of homemade pâté and charcuterie. Cooked over wood fires, many of the meat-centered dishes are accompanied by mushrooms picked from nearby mountains by the genial chef. This place is worth visiting as much for its rustic charm as for its great food. In warm weather, ask for a table on the terrace amid hills cloaked with oak and chestnut trees. The owners have a lovely B&B cottage next door, but make sure to reserve well in advance as it is nearly always booked. *Average main: €15* ✉ *Roquefère, 25 km (11 miles) north of Carcassonne, Carcassonne* ☎ *04–68–26–31–89* 🌐 *www.auberge-siredecabaret.fr* ⏲ *Closed Jan.–mid-Feb.; mid-Feb–Easter, closed Mon.–Wed. and no dinner Sun.; Easter–June and Sept.–Nov., closed Wed. and no dinner Sun.; July and Aug., closed Wed.; Nov. and Dec., closed Mon.–Wed. and no dinner Sun.*

WHERE TO STAY

$ B&B/INN **Château La Villatade.** On a sprawling wine estate, far from Carcassonne's madding crowd, this serene retreat is owned by ever-hospitable (and English speaking) vintners from Toulouse, who happily share their best vintages and fine countryside lifestyle with guests. **Pros:** real French living amid vineyards; natural swimming pool; breakfast included. **Cons:** somewhat isolated—a car is essential; no on-site restaurant. *Rooms from: €95* ✉ *15 km (10 miles) north of Carcassonne, Salleles, Carcassonne* ☎ *04–68–77–57–51* 🌐 *www.villatade.com* *No credit cards* *2 rooms, 1 villa, 1 cottage* *Breakfast.*

$$$ HOTEL **Domaine d'Auriac.** Minutes away from Carcassonne, this seriously elegant 19th-century manor has one of the best restaurants in the region, and the entire building oozes grace and old-world charm; rooms vary in size, with the largest of them offering views over a magnificent park and vineyards. **Pros:** excellent 18-hole golf course; personalized service; stately interiors. **Cons:** a few miles from Carcassonne's center; classic French luxury may grate on guests seeking a low-key ambience. *Rooms from: €200* ✉ *Rte. de St-Hilaire, 4 km (2½ miles) southwest of Carcassonne, Carcassonne* ☎ *04–68–25–72–22* 🌐 *www.domaine-d-auriac.com* ⏲ *Closed Jan., 2nd wk of Feb., and 2nd wk of Nov.; Oct.–Apr* *19 rooms, 5 suites* *No meals.*

$$$$ HOTEL Fodor's Choice ★ **Hôtel de la Cité.** Enjoying the finest location within the walls of the old city, this ivy-covered former Episcopal palace provides a high level of creature comfort, which the ascetic Cathars would most definitely have deprived themselves of. **Pros:** no better location in Carcassonne; vintage luxury. **Cons:** must coordinate parking behind the city walls in advance; small pool. *Rooms from: €325* ✉ *Pl. August-Pierre Pont, La Cité, Carcassonne* ☎ *04–68–71–98–71* 🌐 *www.hoteldelacite.com* *47 rooms, 13 suites* *No meals.*

$ HOTEL **Hôtel Montségur.** With its central lower city location, this hotel isn't only handy to Carcassonne's shops, restaurants, and nightlife; it also has special touches that belie the sweet prices here—many guest rooms

An entry to Fodor's "Show Us Your France" contest, this view of Carcassonne's ramparts was sent in by seeyourworld, a Fodors.com member.

feature Louis XV and Louis XVI furniture, some of it genuine. **Pros:** the Faugras family has been in the hospitality business for over a century, so they know how to take care of their guests; convenient location. **Cons:** lends itself to street noise; may be disappointing to those wishing to sleep inside the walls of La Cité. *Rooms from: €97* *1 av. Bunau Varilla, Ville Basse, Carcassonne* *04–68–25–31–41* *www.hotelmontsegur.com* *Closed Dec. 22–Feb. 1* *18 rooms* *No meals.*

PERFORMING ARTS

Festival de Carcassonne. Carcassonne hosts a major arts festival in July that includes dance, theater, and circus performances. Concerts are also on the lineup, featuring musicians like Elton John, James Blunt, and Lana Del Rey. *Carcassonne* *04–68–11–59–15* *www.festivaldecarcassonne.fr.*

PERPIGNAN

118 km (71 miles) southeast of Carcassonne, 27 km (17 miles) northwest of Collioure.

Salvador Dalí once called Perpignan's train station "the center of the world." That may not be true, but the city certainly is the capital hub of Roussillon. Perpignan tends to echo its surrounding agricultural landscape, rough around the edges and full of yet-unrealized potential that attracts a kind of bold spirit. Scratch the surface of Perpignan and you'll find gypsy music, deep Catalonian pride, loud Spanish influences, and the occasional classic crêpe. It's just as varied as the region's dynamic winemakers, who might hail from the Loire Valley or South Africa. Center of the world? Could be.

GETTING HERE

Ryanair flies daily to Aéroport Sud de France-Perpignan from London and Brussels, while planes operated by HOP! arrive from Paris; a shuttle between the airport and the train station (at the end of Avenue du Général de Gaulle) is available for incoming and outgoing passengers. If you're arriving from Paris by rail, the TGV takes about six hours and costs about €95. Plenty of trains connect Perpignan with Montpellier (2 hrs, €27) and Narbonne (45 mins, €11.90), as well as many other communities. Bus links operate out of a terminal on Boulevard St-Assicle, next to the TGV station.

Visitor Information **Perpignan Tourist Office.** ☎ *04–68–66–30–30* 🌐 *www.perpignantourisme.com.*

EXPLORING

Castillet. Perpignan's alluring town center is lined with rosemary bushes and landmarked by a medieval monument, the 14th-century Castillet, with its tall, crenellated twin towers. Originally this hulking brick building was the main gate to the city; later it was used as a prison. Now the **Casa Pairal,** a museum devoted to Catalan art and traditions, is housed here. ✉ *Pl. de Verdun, Perpignan* ☎ *04–68–35–42–05* 🎫 €2 🕙 *Tues.–Sun. 10:30–6.*

Cathédrale St-Jean. Note the frilly wrought-iron campanile and dramatic medieval crucifix on the Cathédrale St-Jean. ✉ *Pl. Gambetta, Perpignan.*

Palais des Rois de Majorque (*Kings of Majorca Palace*). The Spanish influence is evident in Perpignan's leading monument, the fortified Palais des Rois de Majorque, begun in the 13th century by Jacques II of Majorca. Highlights here are the majestic **Cour d'Honneur** (Courtyard of Honor), the two-tier Flamboyant Gothic chapel of **Ste-Croix Marie-Madelene,** and the **Grande Salle** (Great Hall), with its monumental fireplaces. ✉ *Rue des Archers, Perpignan* ☎ *04–68–34–64–93* 🎫 *€4* 🕙 *June–Sept., daily 10–6; Oct.–May, daily 9–5.*

Petite Rue des Fabriques d'En Nabot. To see some interesting medieval buildings, walk along the Petite Rue des Fabriques d'En Nabot—near Le Castillet—to the adjacent Place de la Loge, the town's nerve center. ✉ *Perpignan.*

Promenade des Plantanes. Across Boulevard Wilson from Le Castillet, this is a cheerful place to stroll among flowers, plane trees, and fountains. ✉ *Perpignan.*

WHERE TO EAT

$ FRENCH ✕ **Crêperie du Théâtre.** Walk past the pubs and bars on this narrow alley for the best crêperie in Perpignan. Owned by a young couple from Brittany, it prepares authentic buckwheat crêpes with a modern twist and relies heavily on organic ingredients. Top picks include a galette stuffed with endive, smoked duck, pine nuts, cheese, and a honey-cream sauce, which can be gobbled down in the colorful, casual dining room. Two outside tables are good for enjoying coffee and a dessert crêpe. Gluten-free travelers will be pleased to know buckwheat is not a wheat—*bon appetit.* *Average main: €8* *12 rue du Théâtre, Perpignan* *04–68–34–29–06* *www.creperie-du-theatre.fr* *No credit cards* *Closed Sun., Mon., and 10 days in Jan.*

$$$$ INTERNATIONAL **Garriane.** Foodies appreciate Garriane's direct approach to eating and drinking well. Here a plain-Jane decor and a dim neighborhood spectacularly contrast with immaculate plates presented by the Aussie-bred chef (who incidentally shook up Perpignan's sleepy food scene with a strictly seasonal menu emphasizing local produce boldly prepared for an exotic outcome). Wine is the only choice you'll need make; after that the nine-course *degustation* (€35) begins, with dishes like citrusy wild partridge and butternut squash mousse promptly appearing one after the other, ending with three separate desserts (picture chocolate gazpacho garnished with ultrafresh peppery olive oil). For a quick rendition, book a table at lunch for half the price and half the time. *Average main: €35* *15 rue Valette, Perpignan* *04–68–67–07–44* *Closed Sun. and Mon. No lunch Sat.*

15

$ BISTRO **Le France.** Occupying a 15th-century former stock market with exposed beams and arcades, this café-restaurant in the center of Perpignan is a perfect place to enjoy an easy meal under the umbrellas as you watch the world go by. Although the menu isn't extraordinary, a broad array of well-presented, well-priced choices makes it popular. Options include scallop salad, foie gras with green beans and raisins, and grilled duck breast with apples. Forgoing the typical break between lunch and dinner, Le France offers all-day service. *Average main: €15* *1 pl. de la Loge, Perpignan* *04–68–51–61–71.*

$$ FRENCH **Les Antiquaires.** In a corner of old Perpignan, this friendly spot serves traditional Roussillon specialties in a rustic setting. Duck à l'orange, a house favorite, has appeared on the menu by popular demand for decades. Foie gras in a Banyuls (sweet red wine) sauce is another staple. Les Antiquaires is known for unpretentious yet refined cuisine, but let's be clear: this is an old-school Catalan eatery, so trend seekers may want to consider going elsewhere. *Average main: €20* *Pl. Joseph Desprès, Perpignan* *04–68–34–06–58* *Closed Mon., last 2 wks in Jan., last wk in June, and 1st 2 wks in July. No dinner Sun.*

$ WINE BAR Fodor's Choice ★ **Les Indigènes.** You'll find a well-rounded crowd at this wine-and-tapas bar where Rousillon's top *vignerons* often mingle. Owned by two musicians with lots of friends, its walls are lined with bottles and long oak tables filled with locals who spill out into the alley. If you've had one too many drawn-out French meals, this is the place to savor flavorful salads and small bites (like pesto and mozzarella *entre pains*) washed down with an excellent glass *du sud*. Just don't count on this address in August because the bar is closed when everyone's at the beach. Order wine by the bottle and pay the cellar rate plus corking fee—by the glass can get expensive. *Average main: €12* *26 rue de la Cloche d'Or, Perpignan* *04–68–35–65–02* *Closed 1st wk in Jan. and several wks in summer. No lunch.*

WHERE TO STAY

$$ HOTEL Fodor's Choice ★ **Casa 9.** Among the orchards and vineyards in the countryside surrounding Perpignan sits Casa 9—a 15th-century *mas* (farm) with a barn that's been converted into lavish lodgings. **Pros:** all rooms look onto a patio or garden; property shaded by lush palms and 100-year old trees; stylish interiors. **Cons:** no on-site restaurant; a car is essential. *Rooms from: €135 Mas Petit, Rte. de Corbère, 17 km (10½ miles) west of Perpignan, Perpignan 07–78–80–54–35 www.casa9hotel.fr Closed Jan. 9 rooms No meals.*

$$$ B&B/INN **Château la Tour Apollinaire.** This Belle Époque château—turned—postmodern B&B was once the mayor's residence and surrounded by sprawling vineyards. **Pros:** great location; lovely grounds with pool and gardens; multiroom suites are extra spacious. **Cons:** you pay for the spacious suites; laminate flooring in places seems out of sync with other stately attributes. *Rooms from: €160 5 rue Guillaume Apollinaire, Perpignan 04–68–92–43–02 www.latourapollinaire.com 7 suites No meals.*

$$$ HOTEL **La Villa Duflot.** In a large park filled with olive and cypress trees, this hotel-restaurant complex prepares some of the best meals in one of the calmest settings just outside the city center. **Pros:** restaurant is a local favorite; trees screen the property from the road. **Cons:** located in a commercial zone on the outskirts of town; though very comfortable, rooms and lobby lack character. *Rooms from: €210 Rond Point Albert Donnezan, Perpignan 04–68–56–67–67 www.villa-duflot.com 24 rooms, 1 suite No meals.*

SHOPPING

Rue des Marchands, near Le Castillet, is thick with chic shops.

Maison Quinta. This multilevel Catalan design shop has an attic studio where custom orders are cut from the area's famously colorful fabric. *3 rue Grande des Fabriques, Perpignan 04–68–34–41–62 www.maison-quinta.com.*

Sant Vicens Crafts Center. Excellent local ceramics can be found at the picturesque Sant Vicens Crafts Center. Crowds flock here over Christmas to see the tiny—and extremely detailed—Nativity scenes made with ceramic figurines called *santons*. *Rue Sant Vicens, off D22 east of town center, Perpignan 04–68–50–02–18 www.santvicens.fr.*

PRADES

45 km (27 miles) west of Perpignan.

It may be easy to bypass Prades en route to the region's high peaks, but to do so would mean missing out on this authentic market town. Farmers, artists, vendors, and loyal shoppers descend from the tiny surrounding villages each Tuesday to sustain the vibrant stalls. Serenely positioned at the foot of the imposing north face of Mont Canigou, Prades is also a great jumping-off spot for mountain excursions.

GETTING HERE

To reach Prades, take a regional train or Conseil General bus from Perpignan (€1 each). A second €1 bus will take you onward to Abbaye de St-Michel de Cuxa; if you'd rather walk, pick up a map of "Le Tour de l'Abbaye de St-Michel de Cuxa" from the tourist office and follow the easy-rated trail through the woods.

Visitor Information Prades Tourist Office. ☎ *04–68–05–41–02* 🌐 *www.prades-tourisme.fr.*

ORGANIC OLIVE OIL OBSESSION

Historically, Roussillon was France's leader in olive oil production—that is, until the crippling winter of 1956 persuaded growers to abandon their trees for more lucrative crops. But the biblical fruit regained popularity with the Mediterranean diet buzz of the 1980s, once again making olive oil a profitable endeavor. Today, high-quality, aromatic, organic ones are the most sought after. Visit Domaine Les Fonts, about 14 km (8½ miles) west of Perpignan, for a detailed tasting and olive-grove tour with passionate producers Carmen and Didier Lamirand (*04–68–92–82–05* 🌐 *www.olivesbiolesfonts.fr*).

EXPLORING

Abbaye de St-Michel de Cuxa. One of the gems of the Pyrénées, this medieval abbey's sturdy, crenellated bell tower is visible from afar. The remains of its cloisters are divine in every sense of the word—if they seem familiar, it may be because you've seen the missing pieces in New York City's Cloisters Museum. A hauntingly simple, six-voice Gregorian vespers service held (somewhat sporadically) at 7 pm in the monastery is medieval in tone and texture; next door, the 10th-century pre-Romanesque church (France's largest) has superb acoustics that make it an unforgettable concert venue. ✉ *3 km (2 miles) south of Prades and Codalet on D27, Prades* ☎ *04–68–96–15–35* 🌐 *abbaye-cuxa.com* 🎫 *€5* ⏲ *May–Sept., daily 9:30–11:50 and 2–6; Oct.–Apr., daily 9:30–11:50 and 2–5.*

Festival Pablo Casals. World-renowned Catalan cellist Pablo Casals, who took refuge in Prades during the Spanish Civil War, gave his name to the international music festival that's held here each year from late July to mid-August. ✉ *Prades* ☎ *04–68–96–33–07* 🌐 *www.prades-festival-casals.com.*

WHERE TO EAT AND STAY

$$ MODERN FRENCH Fodor's Choice ★

El Taller. Run by four entrepreneurial friends in the small village of Taurinya (just down the road from the famous Abbaye de St-Michel de Cuxa), this hip bistro serves fine locally sourced fare. Like the food, the setting is modern and stylish: its sleek glass-walled building and steel-framed terrace were constructed by the village specifically to house this *Bistrot de Pays* (a government-subsidized network of village restaurants promoting commerce in rural areas). The contemporary air of the place, complete with art exhibits, concerts, and theater nights, makes El Taller a popular out-of-the-way gathering place for locals and travelers. $ *Average main: €24* ✉ *5 km (3 miles) south of Prades, Taurinya, Prades* ☎ *04–68–05–63–35* ⏲ *Closed Wed. and Jan. 9–22.*

15

$$$$ FRENCH **Les Loges du Jardin d'Aymeric.** In a quiet mountain village just outside Prades, this semisecret *gourmand* restaurant serves five-course meals that locals swear by. The ambience is refined yet relaxed, and the market-inspired menu changes seasonally. If you get carried away with the wine you can always stay in one of three rooms at the attached B&B (though the old-fashioned room decor doesn't match the restaurant's haute cuisine). *Average main: €38 7 rue du Canigou, Prades 8 km (5 miles) south of Prades 04–68–96–08–72 www.logesaymeric.com Closed Jan. and Wed. Sept.–June. No dinner Tues.*

$$ B&B/INN **Castell Rose.** Original hardwood floors, conservatively fine interiors, and a well-educated adolescent greeting you at the door make a night at Castell Rose feel like staying with a modern-day French bourgeois family. **Pros:** warm and welcoming hosts; beautiful view of Mont Canigou. **Cons:** interiors might be too traditional for some tastes. *Rooms from: €110 Chemin de la Litera, Prades 04–68–96–07–57, 06–32–68–72–26 cell phone www.castellrose-prades.com No credit cards 5 rooms, 1 villa Breakfast.*

$$$ HOTEL Fodor's Choice ★ **Le Château de Riell.** An eccentric late-19th-century castle that blends Baroque style and English elements, this Relais & Châteaux property welcomes guests who want to enjoy its tranquil mountain setting or soak in the healing waters of Molitg-les-Bains. **Pros:** rooftop swimming pool; spectacular views of Mont Canigou; superb restaurant. **Cons:** though a bus connects Molitg to Prades, a car is more practical; odd accents may be a bit much for some (but the zebra-print carpet on the stairs somehow works). *Rooms from: €155 9 km (5½ miles) north of Prades, Molitg-les-Bains, Prades 04–68–05–04–40 www.chateauderiell.com Closed mid-Nov.–Mar. 19 rooms No meals.*

$ B&B/INN **Maison 225.** Don't let the bland street-front facade of this late 1800s town house deter you—inside, the renovated interior mixes stately original attributes with contemporary edges, and natural light spills in from the quiet gardens and terrace that give front-row views of snow-capped Mont Canigou. **Pros:** attentive hosts; casual yet cultivated service; swimming pool with mountain views. **Cons:** breakfast is included but tables are shared; rooms book up fast. *Rooms from: €70 225 av. du General de Gaulle, Prades 04–68–05–52–79, 06–42–91–79–21 cell phone www.225prades.com No credit cards 4 rooms Breakfast.*

VERNET-LES-BAINS

12 km (7 miles) southwest of Prades, 55 km (34 miles) west of Perpignan.

Many notables—including English writer Rudyard Kipling—have come to take the cure at this long-established spa town, which is dwarfed by imposing Mont Canigou.

GETTING HERE

Take a direct Conseil General bus (€1) from Perpignan to Vernet-les-Bains. To access the Abbaye St-Martin du Canigou, stay on the same bus to the end of the line at Casteil, and then be prepared to proceed on foot.

Visitor Information Vernet-les-Bains Tourist Office. 04-68-05-55-35 www.vernet-les-bains.fr.

EXPLORING

Fodor's Choice ★ **Abbaye St-Martin du Canigou.** Visitors, tackling a steep, half-hour climb from the parking area, come to make a pilgrimage—esthetic or spiritual—to this celebrated medieval abbey. It's one of the most photographed in Europe thanks to its sky-kissing location atop a triangular promontory at an altitude of nearly 3,600 feet. St-Martin du Canigou's breathtaking mountain setting was due, in part, to an effort to escape the threat of marauding Saracens from the Middle East. Constructed in 1009 by Count Guifré of Cerdagne, then damaged by an earthquake in 1428 and abandoned in 1783, the abbey was diligently (perhaps too diligently) restored by the Bishop of Perpignan early in the 20th century. The oldest parts are the cloisters and the two churches, of which the lower church, dedicated to Notre-Dame-sous-Terre, is the most ancient. Rising above is a stocky, fortified bell tower. Although the hours vary, Masses are sung daily; call ahead to confirm. Easter Mass here is especially joyous and moving. ✉ *Casteil, 2 km (1 mile) south of Vernet-les-Bains, Vernet-les-Bains* ☎ *04–68–05–50–03* 🌐 *www.stmartinducanigou.org* *€6* ⏲ *Feb.–May and Oct.–Dec., tours Tues.–Sat. at 10, 11, 2, 3, 4, Sun. and holidays at 10, 12:30, 2, 3, 4; June–Sept., tours Mon.–Sat. at 10, 11, noon, 2, 3, 4, 5, Sun. and holidays at 10, 12:30, 2, 3, 4, 5.*

CÉRET

68 km (41 miles) southeast of Prades, 35 km (21 miles) west of Collioure, 31 km (19 miles) southwest of Perpignan.

The "Barbizon of Cubism," Céret achieved immortality when leading artists found the small Catalan town irresistible at the beginning of the 20th century. Here in this medieval enclave set on the banks of the Tech River, Picasso and Gris developed a vigorous new way of visualizing that would result in the fragmented forms of Cubism, a thousand years removed from the Romanesque sculptures of the Roussillon chapels and cloisters. The town famously grows the first and finest crop of cherries in France.

GETTING HERE

Buses to Céret (35 mins, €1) leave from Perpignan's Gare Routiére, next to the train station.

Visitor Information Céret Tourist Office. 04–68–87–00–53 www.ot-ceret.fr.

EXPLORING

Fodor's Choice ★ **Musée d'Art Moderne** (*Modern Art Museum*). Some of the town landscapes captured in paintings by Picasso, Gris, Dufy, Braque, Chagall, Masson, and others are on view in the fine Musée d'Art Moderne. ✉ *8 bd. Maréchal-Joffre, Céret* ☎ *04–68–87–27–76* 🌐 *www.musee-ceret.com* *€8* ⏲ *July–mid-Sept., daily 10–7; mid-Sept.–June, Wed.–Mon. 10–6.*

As color-splashed as a Matisse or Braque painting, Collioure's harbor once inspired those masters and continues to seduce today's artists.

Vieux Céret (*Old Céret*). Place Picasso is the heart of Old Céret, and the sardana dancers and *castellers* (human tower troops) who perform here are evidence of the pride locals take in their Catalan heritage. While in this pretty quarter, stroll around **Place de la Fontaine des Neuf Jets** (Nine Fountains Square). Drop into the church, wander out to the lovely fortified **Porte de France** gateway, then leave the historic town center and head toward the single-arched medieval **Pont du Diable** (the Devil's Bridge) on the perimeter of town, said to have been built by the devil himself in a single night. ✉ *Céret.*

WHERE TO EAT AND STAY

$$$ FRENCH ✕ **Del Bisbe.** Located in the old bishop's quarters, Del Bisbe earned its reputation by promptly serving authentic, well-presented Catalan dishes (such as roasted red peppers and fresh anchovies with grilled summer vegetables), along with classic French fare (including foie gras with apple-pear chutney). Reserve ahead for a table on the hidden, vine-covered terrace upstairs; otherwise ask for one in the clay-tiled dining room with open air views of Céret's main street. $ *Average main: €25* ✉ *4 pl. Soutine, Céret* ☎ *04–68–87–00–85* 🌐 *www.hotelceret.com* ⏲ *Closed Nov. and 1 day per wk Apr.–Oct. (day varies, call ahead to confirm).*

$$$ HOTEL **La Terrasse au Soleil.** Although guest rooms here don't quite live up to the high prices, this hostelry—set high above Céret—has terrific terrace views of Mont Canigou and its verdant valley. **Pros:** outdoor pool; on-site spa with Turkish bath perfumed by organic essential oils. **Cons:** not in town center; somewhat flat ambience. $ *Rooms from: €165* ✉ *Rte. de Fontfrede, Céret* ☎ *04–68–87–01–94* 🌐 *www.terrasse-au-soleil.com* ⏲ *Closed Dec. 15–Feb. 15* *37 rooms, 2 suites* *No meals.*

$ **Les Arcades.** This comfortable, well-priced spot in mid-Céret looks
HOTEL and feels exactly the way an inn ensconced in the heart of a provincial French town should, and having both the world-class collection of paintings of the Musée d'Art Moderne and the top-rated Restaurant del Bisbe just next door further elevates it as a desirable place to stay. **Pros:** family-run business with great customer service; superior art in the public areas. **Cons:** some rooms are small; walls are thin. *Rooms from: €59 ✉ 1 pl. Picasso, Céret ☎ 04–68–87–12–30 🌐 www.hotel-arcades-ceret.com 30 rooms.*

COLLIOURE

35 km (21 miles) east of Céret, 27 km (17 miles) southeast of Perpignan.

Fodor's Choice ★ The fishing village where famed painters Henri Matisse, André Derain, and the Fauvists committed chromatic mayhem in the early 20th century, Collioure is still the jewel of the Vermilion Coast. A town of espadrille merchants, anchovy packers, and lateen-rigged fishing boats in the shadow of a 13th-century Château Royal, it is now as much a magnet for travelers (beware the crowds in July and August) as it once was and remains a lure for artists.

15

Matisse set up shop here in the summer of 1905 and was soon inspired by the colors of the town's terra-cotta roofs *(see "Matisse Country")*. André Derain, Henri Martin, and Georges Braque—who were dubbed Fauves for their "savage" (*fauve* means "wild beast") approach to color and form—quickly followed. To discover tomorrow's Matisses and Derains, head to the streets behind the Place du 18-Juin and to the old Le Mouré neighborhood, beneath Fort Miradou—the studios here are filled with contemporary artists at work; or visit the streets behind the Vieux Port to find former fishermen's quarters now occupied by smart boutiques and restaurants. Other dining delights await on the café-terraces overlooking the main beach and the fashionable Rue Camille Pelletan by the harbor, where you can feast on Collioure's tender, practically boneless anchovies and the fine Banyuls and Collioure AOC wines coming from the impeccably cultivated vineyards surrounding the town. Although nearby villages are apparently only rich in quaintness, Collioure is surprisingly prosperous, thanks to the cultivation of *primeurs,* early ripening fruit and vegetables, shipped to the markets of northern France.

GETTING HERE

About a dozen daily trains from Perpignan (20 mins, €6) pull into Collioure's rail station at the end of Avenue Aristide Maillol. But the subsidized Conseil General bus network, which gets you anywhere in the département for €1, is the most economical (and thus popular) mode of transportation.

Visitor Information Collioure Tourist Office. *☎ 04–68–82–15–47 🌐 www.collioure.com.*

CLOSE UP

Matisse Country

The little coastal village of Collioure continues to play muse to the entire Côte Vermeille—after all, it gave rise to the name of the Vermilion Coast, because the great painter Henri Matisse daringly painted Collioure's yellow-sand beach using a bright red terra-cotta hue. For such artistic daredevilry, he was branded a "fauve." Considered, along with Picasso, to be one of the most influential artists of the modern period, Matisse (1869–1954) and fellow painter André Derain (1880–1954) discovered Fauvism *en vacances* in Collioure in 1905.

Holed up here during that summer, the friends were seduced by its pink and mauve houses, ocher rooftops, and the dramatic combination of sea, sun, and hills. Back then, further touches of color were added by the red and green fishing boats. With nature's outré palette at hand, Matisse was inspired to passionate hues and a brash distortion of form.

Today Matisse's masterpieces grace the walls of the greatest museums in the world. In a sense, Collioure has something better: a host of virtual Matisses, 3-D Derains, and pop-up Dufys. Realizing this, the mayor decided to create the Chemin du Fauvisme (Fauvist Way) more than a decade ago, erecting 20 reproductions of Matisse's and Derain's works on the very spots where they were painted.

Matisse could return today and find things little changed: the Château Royal still perches over the harbor, the Fort Saint-Elme still makes a striking perspectival point on its hilltop, and the plage Boramar still looks like a 3-acre "Matisse."

Pick up the Chemin's trail at the town's Espace Fauve by going to Quai de l'Amiraute (*04–68–98–07–16*) or check out its history at *www.collioure.com*.

EXPLORING

Château Royal. A slender jetty divides the Boramar Beach, beneath Notre-Dame-des-Anges, from the small landing area at the foot of the Château Royal. The castle served as the summer residence of the kings of Majorca from 1276 to 1344 and was remodeled by Vauban 500 years later. *Collioure* *04–68–82–06–43* *€4* *June and Sept., daily 10–6; July and Aug., daily 10–7; Oct.–May, daily 9–5.*

Chemin du Fauvisme. Composed of narrow, cobbled streets and pretty houses, Collioure today is a living museum, as evidenced by the Chemin du Fauvisme (Fauvist Way), a pedestrian trail winding through town with 20 points where you can compare reproductions of noted Fauvist canvases with the actual scenes that were depicted in them. The information center, behind the Plage Boramar, has an excellent map. Viewfinder picture frames let you see how delightfully little of what the artists once admired has changed in the ensuing century. To the north, the rocky Îlot St-Vincent juts out into the sea, a modern lighthouse at its tip, and inland the Albères mountain range rises to connect the Pyrénées with the Mediterranean. The town harbor is a painting unto itself, framed by a 13th-century castle and a 17th-century church fortified with a tower. *Collioure.*

Musée d'Art Moderne Fonds Péské. No Matissses hold pride of place at the town's Musée d'Art Moderne Fonds Péské, but the collection of 180 works deftly sums up the influence the painter had on this *cité des peintures* (city of artists). Works by Cocteau, Valtat, and others are impressively housed in a picturesque, ivy-shrouded villa on a beautiful hillside site. ✉ *Rte. de Porte-Vendres, Collioure* ☎ *04–68–82–10–19* *€3* ⏲ *July and Aug., daily 10–noon and 2–6; Sept.–June, Wed.–Mon. 10–noon and 2–6.*

Notre-Dame-des-Anges. At the end of Boulevard du Boramar is the 17th-century church of Notre-Dame-des-Anges. It has exuberantly carved, gilded Churrigueresque altarpieces by celebrated Catalan master Joseph Sunyer and a pink-dome bell tower that doubled as the original lighthouse. ✉ *Pl. de l'Église, Collioure.*

15

WHERE TO EAT AND STAY

$$ SEAFOOD **Au Casot.** Locals and tourists alike come here for fresh Catalan and seafood dishes, like sea bass simply prepared with lemon, sea salt, and *herbes de Provence.* The casual-cool beach vibe is an added draw: dining tables cover a boardwalk in front of the artful kitchen shack, and low round bar tables (usually occupied by one or two philosopher types) are perched in the sand. Au Casot's pricey prices reflect its prime location beneath the picturesque Chapelle St-Vincent, but the food, wine, and atmosphere are all authentically pleasing. $ *Average main: €24* ✉ *Plage St-Vincent, Collioure* ☎ *04–68–22–42–46.*

$$ FRENCH FUSION **Le 5eme Péché.** On one of Collioure's quieter cobblestoned streets you'll find Le 5eme Péché, where the clean-lined decor seems in synch with simple yet innovative dishes like tempura shrimp with chestnut cream and apple crisps. Iijima Masashi, the young Japanese chef who dared open this tiny French-fusion bistro, is more than just tolerated among local traditional French gourmets—he's celebrated. With only 18 seats and an open kitchen plan, you'll feel like you know him personally by the time dinner is done. The limited menu may not please finicky eaters. $ *Average main: €22* ✉ *18 rue de la Fraternité, Collioure* ☎ *04–68–98–09–76* 🌐 *www.le5peche.com.*

$$ HOTEL **Casa Païral.** This idyllic, palm-shaded 19th-century town house surrounded by a leafy garden feels like an oasis in often-tumultuous Collioure. **Pros:** in the center of Collioure; very helpful staff. **Cons:** closed in winter; rooms vary in terms of size and decor. $ *Rooms from: €141* ✉ *Impasse des Palmiers, Collioure* ☎ *04–68–82–05–81* 🌐 *www.hotel-casa-pairal.com* ⏲ *Closed Nov.–Mar.* *27 rooms* *No meals.*

$ HOTEL **Les Templiers.** Matisse, Maillol, Dalí, Picasso, and Dufy used to hang out here, and today owner Jojo Pous (son of the driving force behind Collioure's art colony) is proud to show off the 2,500-plus original works hanging from every nook and cranny of this celebrated inn and restaurant—universally considered the "soul" of Collioure. **Pros:** in the center of town; short walk to beaches, shops, and restaurants. **Cons:** on a pedestrian alley, so no access for cars; noisy during the hustle and bustle of August. $ *Rooms from: €70* ✉ *12 quai de l'Amirauté, Collioure* ☎ *04–68–98–31–10* 🌐 *www.hotel-templiers.com* ⏲ *Closed Jan. and last wk of Nov.* *45 rooms* *No meals.*

$$$ HOTEL Fodor's Choice ★ **Relais des Trois Mas.** With a perfect perch overlooking the harbor from the cliffs south of town, this hotel enjoys vistas that are priceless—which is the main reason why staying here is pricey. **Pros:** breathtaking views of Collioure; welcoming service; fine restaurant. **Cons:** some standard rooms are very small; lodgings are basic for the price; no lobby, sitting area, or bar. *Rooms from: €170 ✉ Rte. de Port-Vendres, Collioure ☎ 04–68–82–05–07 🌐 www.relaisdes3mas.com ⏲ Closed Nov. 15–Feb. 4 19 rooms, 4 suites No meals.*

NARBONNE

61 km (38 miles) north of Perpignan, 60 km (37 miles) east of Carcassonne, 94 km (58 miles) south of Montpellier.

In Roman times, bustling, industrial Narbonne was the second-largest town in Gaul (after Lyon) and an important port, though today little remains of its Roman past, except an impressive underground warehouse (*horreum*in Latin) once used to store the wines and goods shipped through its harbor. Until the sea receded during the Middle Ages, Narbonne prospered. Today, the city center would be considered sleepy in comparison, but it has an elegant feel more in tune with Montpellier's classy shops than with the streets of gypsy-influenced Perpignan.

GETTING HERE

There are 15 daily departures from Paris to Narbonne, and TGVs leaving the Gare de Lyon can cover the distance in 4½ hours (€105). Narbonne is also an important rail junction for the region, with frequent trains departing for Perpignan (45 mins, €11.90), Montpellier (1 hr, €16.90), Carcassonne (30 mins, €11.20), and Toulouse (1½ hrs, €21). The train station is on Boulevard Frédéric Mistral, north of the city center and adjacent to the Gare Routière (bus station) on Avenue Carnot.

Visitor Information Narbonne Tourist Office. ☎ *04–68–65–15–60* 🌐 *www.narbonne-tourisme.com.*

EXPLORING

Cathédrale St-Just-et-St-Pasteur. The town's former wealth is evinced by the 14th-century Cathédrale St-Just-et-St-Pasteur—its vaulting rises 133 feet from the floor, making it the tallest cathedral in southern France. Only Beauvais and Amiens (both in Picardy) are taller, and, as at Beauvais, the nave here was never completed. The "Creation" tapestry is the cathedral's finest treasure. Enter from the back side (Rue Gustave Fabre) for an especially impressive look at the unfinished nave and insight into the construction process. ✉ *Rue Armand-Gauthier, Narbonne.*

Palais des Archevêques (*Archbishops' Palace*). Richly sculpted cloisters link the cathedral to the former Palais des Archevêques, now home to museums of archaeology, art, and history. Note the late-13th-century keep, the Donjon Gilles-Aycelin; climb the 180 steps to the top for a view over the town and surrounding region. ✉ *Pl. de l'Hôtel de Ville, Narbonne* ☎ *04–68–90–30–65* *€4; €9 includes admission to seven town sites* ⏲ *Apr.–July 14, Wed.–Mon. 10–noon and 2–5; July 15–Oct., daily 10–1 and 2:30–6; Nov.–Mar., Wed.–Mon. 2–5.*

WHERE TO STAY

$$ HOTEL Fodor'sChoice ★ **Château L'Hospitalet.** A stay at this sprawling family-owned wine estate, located between Narbonne's city center and its beaches, is like a course in the art of Mediterranean living complete with surrounding vineyards, sea breezes, an immense wine-tasting cellar, organic kitchen garden, and resident artist studios. **Pros:** a good sampling of wine, art, and lifestyle; close to beaches and town. **Cons:** guest rooms lack character; property has a somewhat commercial undertone. *Rooms from: €145 ✉ Rte. de Narbonne Plage, Narbonne ☎ 04–68–45–28–50 ⊕ www.chateau-lhospitalet.com ⊗ Closed 3 wks in Jan. 38 rooms No meals.*

$ HOTEL **Hôtel La Résidence.** One block from the Canal de la Robine and another block from Place Salengro and the cathedral, Hôtel La Résidence has housed French arts icons like singer Georges Brassens and actor Michel Serrault; the 19th-century building is itself charming, and rooms combine old-fashioned warmth with modern comforts. **Pros:** centrally located for shops, restaurants, and museums. **Cons:** parking area can be difficult to navigate and can fill up. *Rooms from: €105 ✉ 6 rue Premier Mai, Narbonne ☎ 04–68–32–19–41 ⊕ www.hotel-laresidence-narbonne.fr 26 rooms No meals.*

$$ HOTEL **Le Relais du Val d'Orbieu.** This pretty spot west of town is a viable solution to Narbonne's scarcity of good hotels—rooms are grouped around a courtyard and most are reached through covered arcades; the better ones are pleasantly simple, with bare tile floors and large French doors leading onto terraces, while the standard ones are slightly smaller and do not have terraces or views. **Pros:** English-speaking owner is extremely helpful. **Cons:** some rooms don't have window screens—and get very buggy in summer. *Rooms from: €120 ✉ D24, 14 km (8 miles) west of Narbonne, Ornaisons, Narbonne ☎ 04–68–27–10–27 ⊕ www.relaisduvaldorbieu.com ⊗ Closed Dec. and Jan. 14 rooms, 2 suites, 4 apartments No meals.*

MONTPELLIER

140 km (87 miles) northeast of Perpignan, 42 km (26 miles) southwest of Nîmes.

The vibrant capital of the Languedoc-Roussillon region Montpellier (pronounced monh-pell- *yay*) has been a center of commerce and learning since the Middle Ages, when it was both a crossroads for pilgrims on their way to Santiago de Compostela, in Spain, and an active shipping center trading in spices from the East. Along with exotic luxuries, Montpellier imported Renaissance learning, and its university—founded in the 13th century—has nurtured a steady influx of ideas through the centuries. Though the port silted up by the 16th century, the city never became a backwater. A student population of some 75,000 keeps things lively, especially on Place de la Comédie; and, as a center of commerce and conferences, Montpellier keeps its focus on the future. An imaginative urban planning program has streamlined the 17th-century Vieille Ville, and monumental perspectives dwarf passersby on the promenade du Peyrou. An even more utopian venture in urban planning is the

TOURING MONTPELLIER

Montpellier Tourist Office. English-language walking tours organized by the Montpellier Tourist Office depart on Saturday from Place de la Comédie (€9, reserve online or at the office). If you prefer to explore independently, a free mobile app guides you through three different walking itineraries. You can also purchase a City Card, good for 24, 48, or 72 hours (€13.50, €19.80, or €25.20), which provides you with free public transport, plus free entry into one tourist site and reduced admission at the others. ✉ *30 allée Jean de Lattre de Tassigny, Esplanade Comédie, Montpellier* ☎ *04-67-60-60-60* 🌐 *www.ot-montpellier.fr.*

Tourist train. Mid-February through October, a small tourist train with broadcast commentary leaves from Place de la Comédie daily at 11, noon, 2, 3, and 4 (extra runs are added in high season). Tickets cost €7. ✉ *Montpellier* ☎ *04-67-66-24-38 information* 🌐 *www.ot-montpellier.fr/en/little-train.*

Antigone district, a vast, harmonious 100-acre complex designed in 1984 by Barcelona architect Ricardo Bofill.

GETTING HERE AND AROUND

Air France, easyJet, and Ryanair all serve the Aéroport Montpellier-Méditerranée, southeast of the city; from the airport, you can reach Montpellier via shuttle (€2.60). Multiple TGV rail options will get you here from Paris's Gare de Lyon in 3 hours, 30 minutes (about €109). Regional rail lines connect the city with destinations like Narbonne (1 hr, €16.90), Toulouse (2 hrs, €39), Carcassonne (2 hrs, €27), and Perpignan (2 hrs, €27); there are also direct trains as far afield as Avignon, Nice, and Marseille. If you're trying to get to the sea, hail bus No. 131 (which passes every half hour for Palavas).

Montpellier's historic *centre ville*, with its labyrinth of stone paths and alleys leading from courtyard to courtyard, is well suited to walkers. Hotels, restaurants, and sights can all be reached on foot from Place de la Comédie; however, the city also has a comprehensive public transit system—TAM (🌐 *www.tam-voyages.com*)—which includes brightly painted tram cars. The Gare Routière bus and tram stations are by the train terminal on Rue Jules Ferry. If you like to cycle, TAM also operates the Vélomagg' bike rental program, with 50 automated stations accessible around the clock.

Visitor Information Montpellier Tourist Office. ☎ *04-67-60-60-60* 🌐 *www.ot-montpellier.fr.*

EXPLORING

TOP ATTRACTIONS

Arc de Triomphe. Looming majestically over the peripheral highway that loops around the city center, this enormous arch is the centerpiece of the Peyrou. Designed by d'Aviler in 1689, it was finished by Giral in 1776. Together, the noble scale of these harmonious stone constructions and the sweeping perspectives they frame make for an inspiring

Antigone 8
Arc de Triomphe 2
Cathédrale St-Pierre 4
Faculté de Médecine 5
Jardin des Plantes 3
Musée Fabre 7
Place de la Comédie 6
Promenade du Peyrou 1

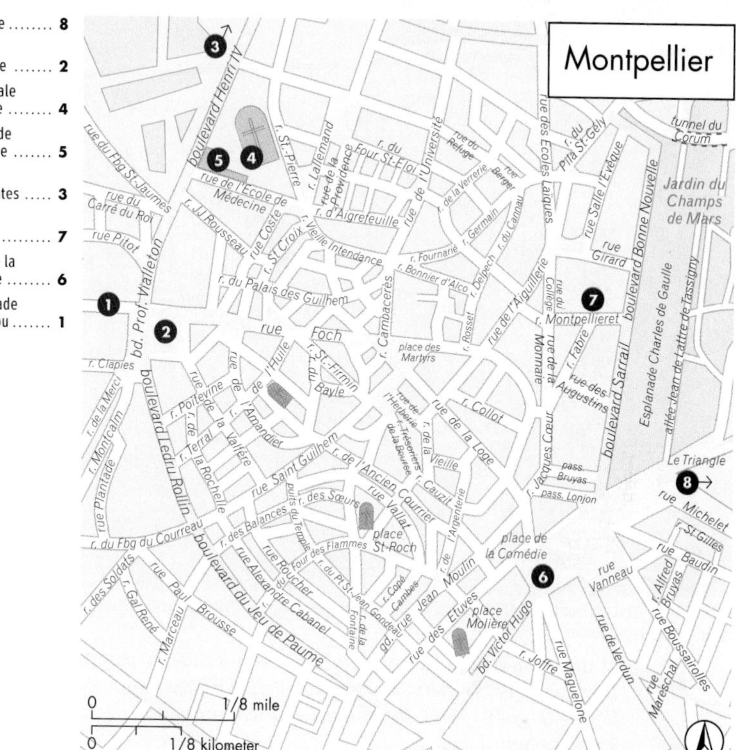

stroll through this upscale stretch of town. At the end of the park is the historic **Château d'Eau,** a Corinthian temple and the terminal for **les Arceaux,** an 18th-century aqueduct; on a clear day the view from here is spectacular, taking in the Cévennes Mountains, the sea, and an ocean of red-tile roofs (it's worth coming back at night to see the entire promenade illuminated). ✉ *Montpellier.*

Musée Fabre. From crowd-packed Place de la Comédie, Boulevard Sarrail leads north past the shady Esplanade Charles de Gaulle to this rich, renowned art museum. The building—combining a 17th-century *hôtel,* a vast Victorian wing with superb natural light, and a remnant of a Baroque Jesuit college—is a mixed bag of architectural styles. The collection inside is surprisingly big, thanks to the museum's namesake, a Montpellier native. François-Xavier Fabre, a student of the great 18th-century French artist David, established roots in Italy and acquired a formidable collection of masterworks—which he then donated to his hometown, supervising the development of this fine museum. Among his gifts were the *Mariage Mystique de Sainte Catherine,* by Veronese, and Poussin's coquettish *Venus et Adonis.* Later contributions include a superb group of 17th-century Flemish works (Rubens, Steen), a collection of 19th-century French canvases (Géricault, Delacroix, Corot, Millet) that inspired Gauguin and Van Gogh, and a growing group of

Both the Three Graces fountain and the Opéra Comédie theater anchor Place de la Comédie, the social and cultural hub of Montpellier.

20th-century acquisitions that buttress a legacy of paintings by early Impressionist Frédéric Bazille. ✉ *39 bd. Bonne Nouvelle, Montpellier* ☎ *04–67–14–83–00* 🌐 *museefabre.montpellier-agglo.com* 🎫 *€8* 🕒 *Tues.–Sun. 10–6.*

Place de la Comédie. The number of bistros and brasseries increases as you leave the Vieille Ville to cross Place des Martyrs, and if you veer right down Rue de la Loge, you emerge onto the festive gathering spot known as Place de la Comédie. Anchored by the neoclassical 19th-century **Opéra-Comédie,** this broad square is a beehive of leisurely activity, a cross between Barcelona's Ramblas and a Roman *passeggiata* (afternoon stroll, en masse). Eateries and entertainment venues draw crowds, but the real pleasure is getting here and seeing who came before, wearing what, and with whom. ✉ *Montpellier.*

Promenade du Peyrou. Montpellier's grandest avenue was built at the end of the 17th century and dedicated to Louis XIV. ✉ *Montpellier.*

WORTH NOTING

Antigone. At the far-east end of the city loop, Montpellier seems to transform itself into a futuristic metropolis designed in one smooth, low-slung postmodern style. This is the Antigone district, the result of city planners' efforts (and local industries' commitment) to pull Montpellier up out of its economic doldrums. It worked. This ideal neighborhood, designed by the Catalan architect Ricardo Bofill, covers 100-plus acres with plazas, esplanades, shops, restaurants, and low-income housing constructed out of stone-color, pre-stressed concrete. Don't miss Place du Nombre d'Or—symmetrically composed of curves—and the long vista that stretches down a mall of cypress trees to the glass-fronted Hôtel de Region. ✉ *Montpellier.*

Cathédrale St-Pierre. After taking in the broad vistas of the promenade de Peyrou, cross over into the Vieille Ville and wander its maze of narrow streets full of pretty shops and intimate restaurants. At the northern edge of the Vieille Ville, visit this imposing cathedral. Its fantastical 14th-century entry porch alone warrants the detour: two cone-top towers—some five stories high—flank the main portal and support a groin-vaulted shelter. The interior, despite 18th-century reconstruction, maintains the formal simplicity of its 14th-century origins. ✉ *Pl. St-Pierre, Montpellier.*

WHERE TO EAT

$$$$ MODERN FRENCH

Cellier Morel (*La Maison de la Lozère*). Dine under a medieval vaulted ceiling or in a shaded courtyard at Cellier Morel, arguably the finest restaurant in Montpellier's historic center. Some of the region's best bottles are featured on the wine list, and regional specialties are served in haute-cuisine fashion starting with an *amuse bouche* (bite-sized hors d'oeuvre) and ending with a house-made *douceur* (sweet). In between, everyone is served the restaurant's signature *aligot* (a mass of potatoes, garlic, and cheese from the Lozère region), done table-side. *Average main: €35 ✉ 27 rue de l'Aiguillerie, Montpellier ☎ 04–67–66–46–36 www.celliermorel.com Closed Sun. No lunch Mon., Wed., and Sat.*

$$$ MODERN FRENCH

Chistera. Expect to eat well at this upscale pub–restaurant combo hidden on a backstreet near Place de la Comèdie. It's owned by Montpellier rugby star François Trinh-Duc, and smartly dressed locals gather on the pub side to watch matches and socialize into the night. The restaurant side is a fashionable steakhouse *á la francaise*, where cuts of duck and beef are grilled over a wood fire and artfully served. The beer list is expansive, and the wine list's nice regional selection doesn't disappoint. *Average main: €25 ✉ 2 bis rue d'Obilion, Montpellier ☎ 04–67–55–39–51 www.la-chistera.com Closed Sun.*

$$$ FRENCH

Le Chat Perché. People flock here for the warm bistro ambience, the terrace overlooking the square below, the carefully selected regional wines, and the traditional dishes served with flair. The cuisine varies with the seasons, the markets, and the humor of the chef, but *everything* is homemade and reasonably priced. *Average main: €25 ✉ Pl. de la Chapelle Neuve, 10 rue college Duvergier, Montpellier ☎ 04–67–60–88–59 Closed Sun. No lunch Reservations essential.*

$ MEDITERRANEAN

Le Petit Mickey. Since 1885 this eatery—the oldest in the city, known historically as Casimir—has been feeding locals fine Mediterranean fare such as bull stew and fish of the day *à la plancha* (grilled with olive oil, garlic, and herbs) at great prices. You might have to endure the crowds and a sometimes irascible owner, but when the copious traditional plates hit the table you'll quickly forget the wait. *Average main: €15 ✉ 15 rue du Petit Jean, Montpellier ☎ 04–67–60–60–41 Closed Mon. and Aug.*

$ WINE BAR

Little Red Café. Montpellier's vino scene has been on the upswing ever since Languedoc's vineyards and vintages made it onto the world wine map—thereby insuring the success of wine bars like Little Red Café. A middle-aged crowd tends to gather here for live music, well-prepared tapas, and, of course, great wine. *Average main: €11* *15 rue des Soeurs Noires, Montpellier* *04–99–65–63–48* *littleredcafe.com* *Closed Sun.*

WHERE TO STAY

$$$ B&B/INN Fodor's Choice ★ **Baudon de Mauny.** The finest rooms in Montpellier (and quite possibly the whole region) can be found at this chic guesthouse on one of the historic district's nicest streets. **Pros:** architectural success; extra-spacious rooms; flawless service. **Cons:** no on-site parking. *Rooms from: €180* *1 rue de la Carbonnerie, Montpellier* *04–67–02–21–77* *www.baudondemauny.com* *8 rooms, 1 apartment* *Breakfast.*

$$$$ HOTEL **Domaine de Verchant.** A five-year renovation project transformed this 14th-century wine-producing estate into a posh retreat, where stylish rooms are intended for serious comfort and relaxation; walls are encased in old stone, and the decor is supplied by Italian designers. **Pros:** tranquillity in the countryside; close to Mediterranean beaches; fine on-site dining. **Cons:** no elevator; far from town center; far from cheap. *Rooms from: €290* *1 bd. Philippe Lamour, Castelnau le Lez, 9 km (5½ miles) northeast of Montpellier* *04–67–07–26–00* *www.domainedeverchant.com* *23 rooms, 2 apartments, 1 cottage* *No meals.*

$ HOTEL **Le Guilhem.** On the same quiet backstreet as the restaurant Le Petit Jardin, this *hôtel de charme* is actually a series of 16th-century houses rebuilt from ruins, replete with an extraordinary old garden. **Pros:** location close to Cathedrale St-Pierre, Jardin des Plantes, and promenade du Peyrou. **Cons:** it's a long walk from Place de la Comédie. *Rooms from: €97* *18 rue Jean-Jacques-Rousseau, Montpellier* *04–67–52–90–90* *www.leguilhem.com* *35 rooms* *No meals.*

$$ B&B/INN **Les 4 Etoiles.** In the owner's family for five generations, this 1930s manor features four stylish guest rooms; comfortably equipped with large beds, crisp linens, and grand walk-in showers, they exemplify modern design while still maintaining original features like colorful antique cement tiles and big French windows. **Pros:** personalized service; communal kitchen available; tranquillity in the city. **Cons:** 10-minute walk from city center; only four rooms. *Rooms from: €125* *3 rue Delmas, Montpellier* *04–67–02–47–69* *www.les4etoiles.com* *4 rooms* *Breakfast.*

NIGHTLIFE AND PERFORMING ARTS

Orchestre National de Montpellier. This young, energetic orchestra performs regularly in the Salle Molière and in the Opéra Berlioz at the Corum conference center. *Montpellier* *www.opera-orchestre-montpellier.fr.*

16

THE BASQUE COUNTRY, GASCONY, AND HAUTES-PYRÉNÉES

WELCOME TO THE BASQUE COUNTRY, GASCONY, AND HAUTES-PYRÉNÉES

TOP REASONS TO GO

★ **Bask in Biarritz:** This former fishing village has been trumped by a glitzy Second Empire aura, but you won't find the bathing beauties and high rollers complaining.

★ **Be charmed by Basque chic:** The camera-ready villages of Ainhoa, Sare, and St-Jean-de-Luz show off quirky, colorful, and asymmetrical Basque architecture.

★ **Indulge yourself in Michel Guérard's Les Prés d'Eugénie:** The co-father (with Paul Bocuse) of nouvelle cuisine still creates glorious meals in tucked-away Eugénie-les-Bains.

★ **Gasp at gorgeous Gavarnie:** Victor Hugo called the 1,400-foot-high waterfall here "the greatest architect's greatest work."

★ **Take in the view from pretty Pau:** With views of the Pyrénées, Pau is the historic capital of Béarn—and regal monuments recall its royal past as the birthplace of King Henri IV.

1 The Basque Coast. Colorful villages and golden-sand beaches punctuated with brightly painted fishing boats keep your eyes busy with their competing palettes on the lush Basque Coast, where world-class chefs make the most of local produce. Bayonne as the graceful French provincial city, Biarritz as the imperial beach domain, and St-Jean-de-Luz as the vibrant fishing port all play their parts to perfection along this southwestern coastline backed by the soft green pastures of the Basque hills.

2 The Atlantic Pyrénées. From the first important height at La Rhune, towering 2,969 feet over the edge of the Atlantic, the Basque Pyrénées rise eastward through picturesque valleys and villages to the Iparla Ridge above Bidarrai and the range's first major peak, the 6,617-foot Orhi. The hills cosset cozy villages like Sare and Ainhoa.

3 Hautes-Pyrénées. The Hautes-Pyrénées include the most spectacular natural wonders in the cordillera. Although mountains soar in this region, making travel difficult, the area has always attracted cultural luminaries including Victor Hugo, Montaigne, and Rossini, who came to marvel at the Cirque de Gavarnie, a natural mountain amphitheater. Millions of others are lured here by the healing holy waters of Lourdes.

GETTING ORIENTED

This is the southwestern corner of France's sprawling "Southwest." The rolling hills of the Basque provinces stretch from the Atlantic beaches of glittering Biarritz to the first Pyrenean heights: the hills and highlands of Gascony around the city of Pau. These are mere stepping-stones compared to the peaks of the Hautes-Pyrénées, which lie to the east and sit in the center of the towering barrier historically separating the Iberian Peninsula from continental Europe.

Colorful architecture and flower-festooned balconies help preserve St-Jean-Pied-de-Port's charm. Gateway to the Pyrénées, Pau is the most culturally vibrant city in Gascony, with elegant *hôtels particuliers* and a royal château.

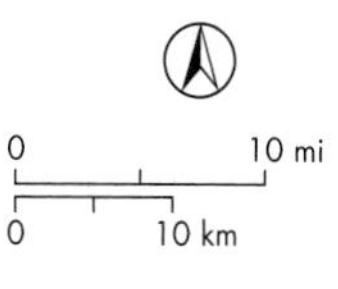

Updated By Avery Sumner

Several years back, a mayor in the province of Soule welcomed a group of travelers with the following announcements: the Basque Country is the most beautiful place in the world; the Basque people are very likely direct descendants of Adam and Eve via the lost city of Atlantis; his own ancestors fought in the Crusades; and Christopher Columbus was almost certainly a Basque. There, in brief, was a composite picture of the pride, dignity, and humor of the Basques.

And if Columbus was not a Basque (a claim very much in doubt), at least historians know that whalers from the regional village of St-Jean-de-Luz sailed as far as America in their three-mast ships, and that Juan Sebastián Elkano, from the Spanish Basque village of Getaria, commanded the completion of Magellan's voyage around the world after Magellan's 1521 death in the Philippines. The distinctive culture—from berets and pelota matches to Basque cooking—of this little "country" has cast its spell over the corners of the Earth.

The most popular gateway to the entire region is Biarritz, the "king" of France's Atlantic coast resorts, whose refinements once attracted the crowned heads of Europe. It was Empress Eugénie who gave Biarritz its coming-out party, transforming it, in the era of Napoléon III, from a simple bourgeois town into an international glitterati favorite. Today, after a round of sightseeing, you can still enjoy the Second Empire trimmings from a perch at the roulette table in the town's casino. Then work on your suntan at Biarritz's famous beach or, a few miles away, really bask under the Basque sun at the picturesque port of St-Jean-de-Luz. As for the entire Pays Basque (Basque Country), it's happily compact: the ocher sands along the Bay of Biscay are less than an hour from the emerald hills of St-Jean-Pied-de-Port in the Basque Pyrénées.

Heading eastward toward the towering peaks of the central Pyrenean cordillera lies the Béarn region, with its splendid capital city of Pau, while northward lies a must-detour for lovers of the good life: Eugénie-les-Bains, where you can savor every morsel of a Michel Guérard feast at one (or all!) of his magnificently stylish restaurants and hotels. East through the Aubisque Pass, at the Béarn's eastern limit, is the heart of the Hautes-Pyrénées, where the mountains of Vignemale and Balaïtous compete with the Cirque de Gavarnie, the world's most spectacular natural amphitheater, centered around a 1,400-foot waterfall. Whether you finish up with a vertiginous Pyrenean hike or choose to pay your respects to the religious shrine at Lourdes, this region will lift your spirits.

PLANNER

WHEN TO GO

The Basque Country is known for its wet climate, but when the skies clear the hillsides are so green and the air so clean that the weather gods are immediately forgiven. Late fall and winter are generally rainier than early autumn or late spring. The Pyrenean heights such as Brèche de Roland and Gavarnie, on the other hand, may only be approached safely in midsummer. Treacherous ice and snow plaques can be present even in mid-June, and summer blizzards remain a risk. Climate change may be shrinking glaciers and extending the safety period in the high Pyrénées, but freak conditions—the reverse side of the same coin—may be creating even more unpredictable and dangerous weather patterns. Beach weather is from May through September, and sometimes lasts until mid-October's *été de la Saint-Martin* (Indian summer). Skiing conditions are reliable from December through March and, on occasion, into April.

PLANNING YOUR TIME

Traveling west to east, with the sun behind you as the shadows lengthen, is the best way to approach this part of the Pyrénées. Bayonne is the natural starting point, at the mouth of the Atlantic Pyrenean watershed, with the Basque Museum as an instructive primer for the culture of the villages you are about to go through. Biarritz and St-Jean-de-Luz offer opportunities for beach time and glamour. The picturesque villages of Sare and Ainhoa guide you into the mountains and valleys, threaded by rivers flowing into the Nive. St-Jean-Pied-de-Port is a Pyrenean hub from which Eugénie-les-Bains is a short detour before continuing east to Pau, the Hautes-Pyrénées, and their crowning glory, Gavarnie.

Wherever you head, take your time: this region's proximity to Spain comes to life in its architecture, in the expressive Midi accent, which turns the word *demain* (tomorrow) into "demaing," and the slow-paced lifestyle.

GETTING HERE AND AROUND

A car is best for getting around the Basque Coast and the Pyrénées. The mountain roads are good, albeit slow—60 kph to 70 kph (37 mph to 43 mph) on average. But the A64 highway from Bayonne to Pau is fast and has spectacular views of the Pyrénées. Train and bus connections will get you from Bayonne to Biarritz and up to St-Jean-Pied-de-Port easily; moving east, Pau and Lourdes are readily accessible as well.

Public transportation to less pivotal destinations, however, can entail much waiting and loss of valuable time.

AIR TRAVEL

Air France (*www.airfrance.com*) serves the Aéroport de Biarritz-Anglet-Bayonne with six direct daily flights from Paris; easyJet (*www.easyjet.com*) also operates one flight per day from the capital, and Ryanair (*www.ryanair.com*) offers a London link three times per week. Once you arrive, Chronoplus buses will take you to train stations in Biarritz (10 mins) or Bayonne (30 mins) for €1. Air France lands another six direct daily flights from Paris at the Aéroport Pau-Pyrénées; the airport is also connected to Lyon, Marseille, and several other cities each day by HOP! (*www.hop.com*). You'll pay €1 for the half-hour ride from the airport into town.

Aéroport de Biarritz-Anglet-Bayonne. *Anglet* *05–59–43–83–83* *www.biarritz.aeroport.fr.*

Aéroport Pau-Pyrénées. *05–59–33–33–00* *www.pau.aeroport.fr.*

BUS TRAVEL

Numerous private bus companies are consolidated into regional bus networks. Key ones include Transports-64 (covering the Pyrénées-Atlantiques department from Lourdes to the coast), Chronoplus (covering the Bayonne-Anglet-Biarritz greater metropolitan area), and R.D.T.L. (covering the Landes department). Where the regional network buses don't go, the trusty SNCF national bus lines occasionally do (*www.voyages-sncf.com*). Local tourist offices and train stations can provide you with schedules and network maps. When traveling by bus in summer, beware of peak-hour traffic on roads, which can mean both delays and fewer seats on buses.

Bus Information Chronoplus. *05—59—52—59—52* *www.chronoplus.eu.* **R.D.T.L. Buses.** *05–59–55–17–59* *www.rdtl.fr.* **Transports-64.** *08–00–64–24–64* *www.transports64.fr.*

CAR TRAVEL

The A64 connects Pau and Bayonne in less than an hour, and the A63 runs up and down the Atlantic coast. The N134-E7 connects Bordeaux, Pau, and Spain via the Col de Somport and Jaca. The D918 along the Nive River from Saint-Jean-de-Luz to St-Jean-Pied-de-Port is a pretty drive, continuing on (as the D918, D919, and D933) through the Béarn countryside to Pau. Roads are occasionally slow and tortuous in the more mountainous areas, but valley and riverside roads are generally quite smooth and fast.

TRAIN TRAVEL

High-speed TGV trains link Paris to Bayonne (4 hrs, 30 mins), to Biarritz (5 hrs, 15 mins), and to Pau (5 hrs, 34 mins). Biarritz's La Négresse station has trains connecting with Bayonne, Bordeaux, St-Jean-de-Luz, and many other destinations. Bayonne and Toulouse are connected by SNCF trains via Pau, Tarbes, and Lourdes. Bayonne also has links to other popular locales (like St-Jean-de-Luz), and local trains from here travel into the Atlantic Pyrénées, a slow but picturesque trip. Hendaye is connected to Bayonne and to San Sebastián via the famous *topo* (mole) train, so called for the number of tunnels it passes through.

Train Information **Gare Ville Bayonne.** *www.gares-sncf.com.* **Gare Ville Biarritz La Négresse.** *www.gares-sncf.com.* **SNCF.** *3635 €0.34 per minute* *www.voyages-sncf.com.* **TGV.** *www.tgv.com.*

RESTAURANTS

Dining in the regions of the Basque Country is invariably a feast, whether it's seafood, local lamb, or the famous migratory *palombes* (wood pigeons). Dishes to keep in mind include *ttoro* (hake stew), *pipérade* (tomatoes and green peppers cooked in olive oil, and often scrambled eggs), *bakalao al pil-pil* (cod cooked in oil "al pil-pil"—the bubbling sound the fish makes as it creates its own sauce), *marmitako* (tuna and potato stew), and *zikiro* (roast lamb). Home of the eponymous *sauce béarnaise,* Béarn is also famous for its *garbure*, a thick vegetable soup with *confit de canard* (preserved duck) and *fèves* (broad beans).

Civets (stews) made with *isard* (wild goat) or wild boar are other specialties. La Bigorre and the Hautes-Pyrénées are equally dedicated to garbure, though they may call their version *soupe paysanne bigourdane* (Bigorran peasant soup) to distinguish it from that of their neighbors. The Basque Coast's traditional fresh seafood is unsurpassable every day of the week except Monday, the fleet having stayed in port on Sunday. The inland Basque Country and upland Béarn are famous for game in fall and winter and lamb in spring. In the Hautes-Pyrénées, the higher altitude makes power dining attractive and thick bean soups and wild-boar stews come into their own.

HOTELS

From palatial beachside splendor in Biarritz to simple mountain auberges in the Basque country to Pyrenean refuges in the Hautes-Pyrénées, the gamut of lodging in southwest France is conveniently broad. Be sure to book summertime accommodations on the Basque Coast well in advance, particularly for August. In the Hautes-Pyrénées, Lourdes presents the greatest challenge. Pilgrims pack the place between Easter and All Saint's Day (November 1), with August 15 being especially busy, so make reservations as far ahead as possible. *Hotel reviews have been shortened. For full information, visit Fodors.com.*

WHAT IT COSTS IN EUROS

	$	$$	$$$	$$$$
Restaurants	under €18	€18–€24	€25–€32	over €32
Hotels	under €106	€106–€145	€146–€215	over €215

Restaurant prices are the average cost of a main course at dinner or, if dinner is not served, at lunch. Hotel prices are the lowest cost of a standard double room in high season.

VISITOR INFORMATION

The Atlantic and Hautes Pyrénées region has three main tourist offices. For Biarritz and France's Big Sur in the southwest corner of the country, contact the Comité Régional du Tourisme d'Aquitaine. For Pau and the Basque and Béarnaise Pyrénées, contact the Comité Départemental du Tourisme Béarn Pays Basque in Pau. For Gavarnie and the Hautes Pyrénées contact the Hautes Pyrénées Tourist Office in Tarbes. ⇨ *For specific local tourist offices, see the town entries in this chapter.*

Contacts Comité Départemental du Tourisme Béarn Pays Basque. ☎ *05–59–30–01–30* 🌐 *www.tourisme64.com.* **Comité Régional du Tourisme d'Aquitaine.** ☎ *05–56–01–70–00* 🌐 *www.tourisme-aquitaine.fr.* **Hautes Pyrénées Tourisme.** ☎ *05–62–56–70–65* 🌐 *www.tourisme-hautes-pyrenees.com.*

THE BASQUE COAST

La Côte Basque—a world unto itself with its own language, sports, and folklore—occupies France's southwest corner along the Spanish border. Inland, the area is laced with rivers: the Bidasoa River border with Spain marks the southern edge of the region, and the Adour River, on its northern edge, separates the Basque Country from neighboring Les Landes. The Nive River flows through the heart of the verdant Basque littoral to join the Adour at Bayonne, and the smaller Nivelle River flows into the Bay of Biscay at St-Jean-de-Luz. Bayonne, Biarritz, and St-Jean-de-Luz are the main towns along the coast, all less than 40 km (25 miles) from the first peak of the Pyrénées.

BAYONNE

184 km (114 miles) south of Bordeaux, 295 km (183 miles) west of Toulouse.

Located at the confluence of the Adour and Nive rivers, Bayonne was a Roman *castrum* (fort) in the 4th century and an English colony from 1151 to 1451: today it is the proud capital of the Pays Basque. Even though its port is spread out along an estuary some 5 km (3 miles) inland from the sea, two rivers and five bridges lend this small city a definite maritime feel. From the elegant 18th-century homes along Rue des Prébendés to the 17th-century ramparts and the market stalls of Place des Halles, it is a city worth wandering. If you want an overview, the Bayonne tourist office leads two-hour, English-language tours of the city every Saturday at 10 am in July and August (€6).

GETTING HERE

Air France, Ryanair, and easyJet planes land at the Aéroport de Biarritz-Anglet-Bayonne; a shuttle bus runs from there to the central train station (30 mins, €1). Four daily TGVs connect Bayonne and Paris (4 hrs, 30 mins; €69). Train connections from Bayonne include St-Jean-de-Luz (28 mins, €6), St-Jean-Pied-de-Port (1 hr, 26 mins; €10.10), Pau (1 hr, 33 mins; €18.60), Lourdes (1 hr, 44 mins; €24), Bordeaux (1 hr, 39 mins; €31.90), and Toulouse (3 hrs, 21 mins; €47). Frequent daily trains also

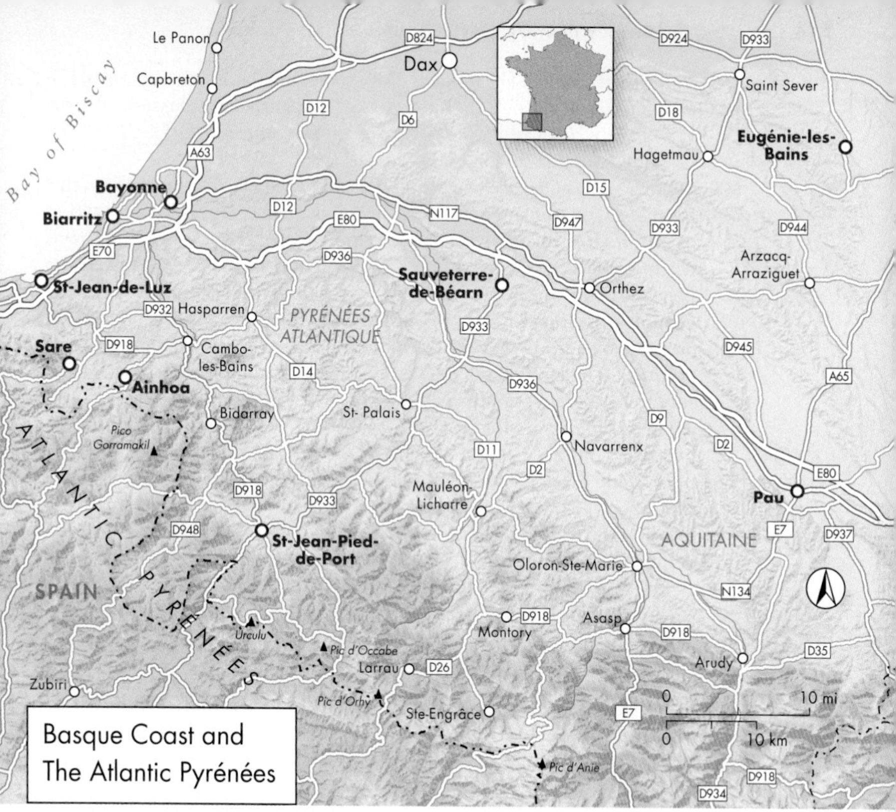

Basque Coast and The Atlantic Pyrénées

make the short jaunt to Biarritz (8 mins, €2.90). The Chronoplus bus network connects Bayonne with towns on the French Basque Coast, notably Biarritz (15 mins, €1) and Anglet (20 mins, €1).

Visitor Information Bayonne Tourist Office. ☎ *08–20–42–64–64* 🌐 *www.bayonne-tourisme.com.*

EXPLORING

Cathédrale. Built mainly in the 13th century, the Cathédrale (called both Ste-Marie and Notre-Dame) is one of France's southernmost examples of Gothic architecture. Its 13th- to 14th-century cloisters are among its best features. ✉ *Pl. de la Cathédrale, Bayonne* ☎ *05–59–59–17–82* 🌐 *www.cathedrale-bayonne.fr* 🎫 *Free* 🕒 *Daily 8–12:30 and 3–7.*

Musée Basque. The handsomely designed and appointed Musée Basque on the right bank of the Nive offers an ethnographic history of the Basque Country and culture. ✉ *37 quai des Corsaires, Bayonne* ☎ *05–59–59–08–98* 🌐 *www.musee-basque.com* 🎫 *€6.50* 🕒 *July and Aug., daily 10–6:30 (until 8:30 Thurs.); Sept.–June, Tues.–Sun. 10:30–6.*

WHERE TO EAT AND STAY

$$ BISTRO ✕ **Bayonnais.** Next to the Musée Basque, with a dining terrace over the River Nive just short of its confluence with the Adour, this unassuming and unpretentious local favorite serves honest Basque cuisine in a

traditional setting. The *agneau de lait* (suckling lamb) and *chipirons en persillade* (cuttlefish in chopped parsley and garlic) are classics. *Average main: €20 ✉ 38 quai des Corsaires, Bayonne ☎ 05–59–25–61–19 ⏲ Closed Sun. and Mon. Sept.–mid-July.*

$$$ FRENCH **L'Auberge du Cheval Blanc.** Run by the Tellechea family since 1715, this former stagecoach inn in the Petit Bayonne quarter serves a combination of *cuisine du terroir* (home-style regional cooking) and original recipes in contemporary surroundings. Michelin-starred chef Jean-Claude Tellechea showcases fresh fish as well as upland specialties from the Basque hills, sometimes joining the two in dishes such as the *merlu rôti aux oignons et jus de volaille* (hake roasted in onions with essence of poultry). The Irouléguy wines offer the best value on the wine list. Be sure to be there on time: lunch *ends* at 1:30. *Average main: €30 ✉ 68 rue Bourgneuf, Bayonne ☎ 05–59–59–01–33 🌐 www.cheval-blanc-bayonne.com ⏲ Closed Mon. No lunch Sat., no dinner Sun.*

$$ HOTEL **Le Grand Hôtel.** Just down the street from the Château-Vieux, this reasonably priced Best Western property offers an old-world feel in a great location. **Pros:** prime location; triple and quad rooms good for families; helpful staff. **Cons:** pricey breakfast; vintage elevator not everyone's cup of tea. *Rooms from: €124 ✉ 21 rue Thiers, Bayonne ☎ 05–59–59–62–00 🌐 www.legrandhotelbayonne.com 57 rooms No meals.*

BIARRITZ

8 km (5 miles) south of Bayonne; 190 km (118 miles) southwest of Bordeaux; 50 km (31 miles) north of San Sebastián, Spain.

Biarritz may no longer lay claim to the title "the resort of kings and the king of resorts," but there's no shortage of deluxe hotel rooms or bow-tied gamblers ambling over to the casino. The city first rose to prominence when rich and royal Carlist exiles from Spain set up shop here in 1838. Unable to visit San Sebastián—just across the border on the Basque Coast—they sought a summer watering spot as close as possible to their old stomping ground. Among the exiles was Eugénie de Montijo, destined to become empress of France. As a child, she vacationed here with her family, fell in love with the place, and then set about building her own palace once she married Napoléon III. During the 14 summers she spent here, half the crowned heads of Europe (including Queen Victoria and Edward VII) were guests in Eugénie's villa: a gigantic wedding-cake edifice, now the Hôtel du Palais, on Biarritz's main seaside promenade. Whether you consider the bombastic architectural legacies of that era an eyesore or an eyeful, the builders at least had the courage of their convictions. If you want to rediscover yesteryear Biarritz, start by exploring the narrow streets around the cozy 16th-century church of St-Martin.

GETTING HERE AND AROUND

The Aéroport de Biarritz-Anglet-Bayonne receives flights from Air France, Ryanair, and easyJet; a shuttle bus from the airport takes 10 minutes and costs €1. TGV trains connect Paris and Biarritz six times daily (5 hrs, 15 mins; €88). Biarritz's La Négresse train station has rail connections with St-Jean-de-Luz (11 mins, €3.50), Bordeaux (1 hr, 50

Continued on page 761

BASQUE SPOKEN HERE

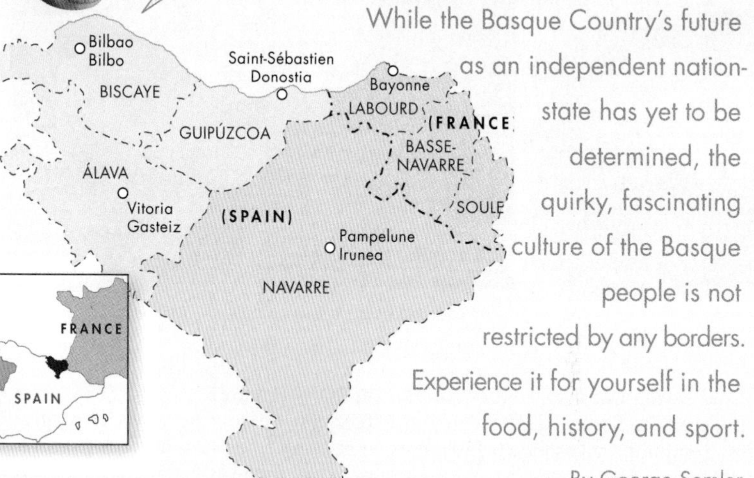

While the Basque Country's future as an independent nation-state has yet to be determined, the quirky, fascinating culture of the Basque people is not restricted by any borders. Experience it for yourself in the food, history, and sport.

By George Semler

Basque solar cross

The cultural footprints of this tiny corner of Europe, which straddle the Atlantic end of the border between France and Spain, have already touched down all over the globe. The sport of jai-alai has come to America. International magazines give an ecstatic thumbs-up to Basque cooking. Historians are pointing to Basque fishermen as the true discoverers of North America. And bestsellers, not without irony, proclaim *The Basque History of the World*. As in the ancient 4 + 3 = 1 graffiti equation, the three French (Labourd, Basse Navarre, and Soule) and the four Spanish (Guipúzcoa, Vizcaya, Alava, and Navarra) Basque provinces add up to a single people with a shared history. Although nationless, Basques have been Basques since Paleolithic times.

Stretching across the Pyrénées from Bayonne in France to Bilbao in Spain, the New Hampshire-sized Basque region retains a distinct culture, neither expressly French nor Spanish, fiercely guarded by its three million inhabitants. Fables stubbornly connect them with Adam and Eve, Noah's Ark, and the lost city of Atlantis, but a leading genealogical theory points to common bloodlines with the Celts. The most tenable theory is that the Basques are descended from aboriginal Iberian peoples who successfully defended their unique cultural identity from the influences of Roman and Moorish domination.

It was only in 1876 that Sabino Arana—a virulent anti-Spanish fanatic—proposed the ideal of a "pure" Basque independent state. That dream was crushed by Franco's dictatorial reign (1939–75, during which many Spanish Basques emigrated to France) and was immortalized in Pablo Picasso's *Guernica*. This famous painting, which depicts the catastrophic Nazi bombing of the Basque town of Gernika stands not only as a searing indictment of all wars but as a reminder of history's brutal assault upon Basque identity.

"THE BEST FOOD YOU'VE NEVER HEARD OF"

(left) Zurrukutuna, garlic soup with codfish. (right) Preparing canapes.

So says *Food & Wine* magazine. It's time to get filled in.

An old saying has it that every soccer team needs a Basque goaltender and every restaurant a Basque chef. Traditional Basque cuisine combines the fresh fish of the Atlantic and upland vegetables, beef, and lamb with a love of sauces that is rare south of the Pyrénées. Today, the *nueva cocina vasca* (new Basque cooking) movement has made Basque food less rustic and much more nouvelle. And now that pintxos (the Basque equivalent of tapas) have become the rage from Barcelona to New York City, Basque cuisine is being championed by foodies everywhere. Even superchef Michel Guérard up in Eugénie-les-Bains has, though not himself a Basque, influenced and been influenced by the master cookery of the Pays Basque.

WHO'S THE BEST CHEF?

Basques are so naturally competitive that meals often turn into comparative rants over who is better: Basque chefs based in France or in Spain. Some vote for Bayonne's Jean-Claude Tellechea (his L'Auberge du Cheval Blanc is famed for groundbreaking surf-and-turf dishes like hake roasted in onions with essence of poultry) or St-Jean-Pied-de-Port's Firmin Arrambide (based at his elegant Les Pyrénées inn). Others prefer the postmodern lobster salads found over the border in San Sebastián and Bilbao, created by master chefs Juan Mari Arzak, Pedro Subijana, and Martin Berasategui, with wunderkind Andoni Aduriz and the Arbelaitz family nipping at their culinary heels.

SIX GREAT DISHES

Angulas. Baby eels, cooked in olive oil and garlic with a few slices of guindilla pepper.

Bacalao al pil-pil. Cod cooked at a low temperature in an emulsion of olive oil and fish juices, which makes a unique pinging sound as it sizzles.

Besugo. Sea bream, or besugo, is so revered that it is a traditional Christmas dish. Enjoy it with sagardo, the signature Basque apple cider.

Marmitako. This tuna stew with potatoes and pimientos is a satisfying winter favorite.

Ttoro. Typical of Labourd fishing villages such as St-Jean-de-Luz, this peppery Basque bouillabaisse is known as *sopa de pescado* (fish soup) south of the French border.

Txuleta de buey. The signature Basque meat is ox steaks marinated in parsley and garlic and cooked over coals.

BASQUE SPORTS: JAI-ALAI TO OXCART-LIFTING

Sports are core to Basque society, and virtually no one is immune to the Basque passion for competing, betting, and playing.

Over the centuries, the rugged physical environment of the Basque hills and the rough Cantabrian sea traditionally made physical prowess and bravery valued attributes. Since Basque mythology often involved feats of strength, it's easy to see why today's Basques are such rabid sports fans.

PELOTA

A Basque village without a frontón (pelota court) is as unimaginable as an American town without a baseball diamond. "The fastest game in the world," pelota is called *jai-alai* in Basque (and translated officially as "merry festival"). With rubber balls flung from hooked wicker gloves at speeds up to 150 mph—the impact of the ball is like a machine-gun bullet—jai-alai is mesmerizing. It is played on a three-walled court 175 feet long and 56 feet wide with 40-foot side walls.

Whether singles or doubles, the object is to angle the ball along or off of the side wall so that it cannot be returned. Betting is very much part of pelota and courtside wagers are brokered by bet makers as play proceeds. While pelota is the word for "ball," it also refers to the game. There was even a recent movie in Spain entitled *La Pelota Vasca*, used metaphorically to refer to the greater "ball game" of life and death.

HERRIKIROLAK

Herrikirolak (rural sports) are based on farming and seafaring. Stone lifters (*harrijasotzaileak* in Euskera) heft weights up to 700 pounds. *Aizkolari* (axe men) chop wood in various contests, *Gizon proba* (man trial) pits three-man teams moving weighted sleds; while *estropadak* are whaleboat rowers who compete in spectacular regattas (culminating in the September competition off La Concha beach in San Sebastián). *Sokatira* is tug of war, and *segalariak* is a scything competition. Other events include oxcart-lifting, milk-can carrying, and ram fights.

SOCCER

When it comes to soccer, Basque goaltenders have developed special fame in Spain, where Bilbao's Athletic Club and San Sebastián's Real Sociedad have won national championships with budgets far inferior to those of Real Madrid or FC Barcelona. Across the border, Bayonne's rugby team is a force in the French national competition; the French Basque capital is also home to the annual French pelota championship.

PARLEZ-VOUS EUSKERA?

Although the Basque people speak French north of the border and Spanish south of the border, they consider Euskera their first language and identify themselves as the *Euskaldunak* (the "Basque speakers"). Euskera remains one of the great enigmas of linguistic scholarship. Theories connect it with everything from Sanskrit to Japanese to Finnish.

What is certain is where Euskera did not come from, namely the Indo-European family of languages that includes the Germanic, Italic, and Hellenic language groups.

Currently used by about a million people in northern Spain and southwestern France, Euskera sounds like a consonant-ridden version of Spanish, with its five pure vowels, rolled "r," and palatal "n" and "l." Basque has survived two millennia of cultural and political pressure and is the only remaining language of those spoken in southwestern Europe before the Roman conquest.

The Euskaldunak celebrate their heritage during a Basque folk dancing festival.

A BASQUE GLOSSARY

Aurresku: The high-kicking *espata danza* or sword dance typically performed on the day of Corpus Christi in the Spanish Basque Country.

Akelarre: A gathering of witches that provoked witch trials in the Pyrénées. Even today it is believed that *jentilak* (magic elves) inhabit the woods and the Olentzaro (the evil Basque Santa Claus) comes down chimneys to wreak havoc—a fire is kept burning to keep him out.

Boina: The Basque beret or *txapela*, thought to have developed as the perfect protection from the siri-miri, the perennial "Scotch mist" that soaks the moist Basque Country.

Eguzki: The sun worship was at the center of the pagan religion that, in the Basque Country, gave way only slowly to Christianity. The Basque solar cross is typically carved into the east-facing facades of ancient *caserios* or farmhouses.

Espadrilles: Rope-soled canvas Basque shoes, also claimed by the Catalans, developed in the Pyrénées and traditionally attached by laces or ribbons wrapped up the ankle.

Etxekoandre: The woman who commands all matters spiritual, culinary, and practical in a traditional Basque farmhouse. Basque matriarchal inheritance laws remain key.

Fueros: Special Basque rights and laws (including exemption from serving in the army except to defend the Basque Country) originally conceded by the ancient Romans and abolished at the end of the Carlist Wars in 1876 after centuries of Castilian kings had sworn to protect Basque rights at the Tree of Guernika.

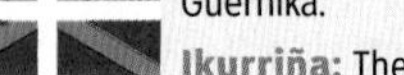

Ikurriña: The Basque flag, designed by the founder of Basque nationalism, Sabino Arana, composed of green and white crosses over a red background and said to have been based on the British Union Jack.

Lauburu: Resembling a four-leaf clover, lau (four) buru (head) is the Basque symbol.

Twenty: Basques favor counting in units of twenty (*veinte duros*—20 nickels—is a common way of saying a hundred pesetas, for example).

Txakolí: A slightly fizzy young wine made from grapes grown around the Bay of Biscay, this fresh, acidic brew happily accompanies tapas and fish.

mins; €33.80), and many other places, including San Sebastián, Spain, via Hendaye (50 mins, €21.50). Multiple trains also arrive daily from Bayonne (8 mins, €2.90) and Pau (1½ hrs, €21). The station is 3 km (2 miles) southeast of the city core, so catch bus No. 2 to reach the centrally located Hôtel de Ville, near the main beach. Chronoplus buses serve the Biarritz-Anglet-Bayonne area (€1); Transports-64 buses travel regularly to and from other Basque towns, including St-Jean-de-Luz.

Visitor Information Biarritz Tourist Office. ☎ *05–59–22–37–10* 🌐 *www.biarritz.fr.*

EXPLORING

Église Orthodoxe Russe. Eugénie and her Carlist compatriots weren't the only exiled royals to arrive in Biarritz. White Russians found refuge, too, turning the city into their Yalta-by-the-Atlantic. Witness the Église Orthodoxe Russe, a Byzantine-style church they built adjacent to the Grand Plage in the early 1890s. ✉ *8 rue de l'Impératrice, Biarritz* ☎ *05–59–24–16–74* 🌐 *www.eglise-orthodoxe-biarritz.com* ⏲ *Sat., Sun., and Thurs. 3:30–6.*

La Chapelle Impériale. If you wish to pay your respects to the Empress Eugénie, visit La Chapelle Impériale, which she had built in 1864 to venerate a figure of a Mexican Black Virgin from Guadalupe (and perhaps to expiate her sins for furthering her husband's tragic folly of putting Emperor Maximilian and Empress Carlotta on the "throne" of Mexico). The style is a charming hybrid of Roman-Byzantine and Hispano-Mauresque. ✉ *Rue Pellot, Biarritz* ☎ *05–59–22–37–10* ⏲ *July and Aug., Tues., Thurs., and Sat. 3–7; Sept.–June, call for hrs.*

La Grande Plage. Biarritz's urban beaches are understandably popular—particularly the fine, sandy strands of La Grande Plage and the neighboring Plage Miramar, both set amid craggy natural beauty. A walk along the seaside promenade gives a view of the foaming breakers that beat constantly upon the sands, giving the name Côte d'Argent (Silver Coast) to this part of France's Basque Coast. As you drink in that view, try to imagine the gilded days when the fashionable set used to stroll here in Worth gowns and picture hats. ✉ *Biarritz.*

Place Ste-Eugénie. During Biarritz's original heyday, the elite often repaired to the terraced restaurants of festive Place Ste-Eugénie, still considered the social center of town. ✉ *Pl. Ste-Eugénie, Biarritz.*

WHERE TO EAT

$$ SEAFOOD
✕ **Chez Albert.** The Port des Pêcheurs (Fishing Port) provides a tantalizing glimpse of old Biarritz, plus some tantalizing dining options. Water views and salty harborside aromas make Chez Albert's hearty fish and seafood offerings all the more irresistible. But beware, this easygoing eatery is definitely on the tourist radar—it's nearly impossible to find a seat on the terrace in summer. $ *Average main: €24* ✉ *51 bis Allée Port des Pêcheurs, Biarritz* ☎ *05–59–24–43–84* 🌐 *www.chezalbert.fr* ⏲ *Closed Nov. 25–Feb. 10, and Wed. except in July and Aug.*

$$$ FRENCH
✕ **L'Atelier.** Alexandre Bousquet and Isabelle Caulier's hot restaurant in the Quartier Saint-Charles, a few steps from the Grande Plage, is the *dernier cri* in a town surrounded by, but not known for, great cuisine.

Meals are stunningly presented in a setting that is at once classic and contemporary—expect dishes like tuna *tartare et croustillant* (raw and crunchy) with mustard sauce, and specialties like *pigeonneau* (young pigeon). The wine list includes selections from Bordeaux and Spain's Ribera de Duero, exemplifying the couple's *savoir faire* in the art of food and wine pairing. The lunch menu (served Thursday and Friday in summer) is one of the best bargains in Biarritz. But culinary experimentation is the catchword here, so traditionalists may prefer the crêpes and pizza elsewhere. *Average main: €28 18 rue Bergerie, Biarritz 05–59–22–09–37 www.latelierbiarritz.com Closed Sun. July and Aug.; rest of year closed Sun. and Mon. No lunch Mon.–Wed. or Sat.*

WHERE TO STAY

$$$$ HOTEL **Château de Brindos.** Take Jazz Age glamour, Renaissance stonework, and the most luxe of guest rooms, add fine dining, and you have this Pays Basque Xanadu—a large, rambling, white-stone manor topped with a Spanish belvedere tower set 4 km (2½ miles) east of Biarritz in Anglet. **Pros:** flawless performance by staff; excellent dining; ultimate comfort. **Cons:** fitness facilities limited; addictively grande luxe; difficult to leave. *Rooms from: €350 1 allée du Château, Anglet 05–59–23–89–80 www.chateaudebrindos.com Closed 2 wks in Feb. and Mar. 24 rooms, 5 suites No meals.*

$$$$ HOTEL **Hôtel du Palais.** Set on the beach, this majestic, colonnaded redbrick hotel with an immense driveway, lawns, and a grand semicircular dining room still exudes an opulent, aristocratic air, no doubt imparted by Empress Eugénie who built it in 1855 as her Biarritz palace. **Pros:** historic grounds; gastronomical nirvana; perfect location. **Cons:** staff obsessed with hotel rules; slightly stuffy; magisterially expensive. *Rooms from: €560 1 av. de l'Impératrice, Biarritz 05–59–41–64–00 www.hotel-du-palais.com 122 rooms, 30 suites No meals.*

$ B&B/INN **La Ferme de Biarritz.** For those in search of rustic and affordable quarters near swank Biarritz, this beautifully restored 17th-century farmhouse offers the best of both worlds—particularly delightful are the guest rooms' antique furnishings, which might have been used by Empress Eugénie herself. **Pros:** near the beach; cute dormered rooms with antique furniture; breakfast in the garden or in front of the fire. **Cons:** small rooms; no restaurant. *Rooms from: €90 15 rue Harcet, Biarritz 05–59–23–40–27 www.fermedebiarritz.com No credit cards Closed Jan. 5 rooms, 1 studio, 1 apartment No meals.*

$$ HOTEL **Maïtagaria.** This typical Basque town house 400 yards from the beach is a handy and comfortable family operation that makes you feel more like a guest in a private home than a hotel patron. **Pros:** good price and location; intimate yet friendly; leafy garden. **Cons:** somewhat cramped quarters; limited soundproofing (and thus privacy). *Rooms from: €110 34 av. Carnot, Biarritz 05–59–24–26–65 www.hotel-maitagaria.com Closed 3 wks around Christmas 15 rooms No meals.*

$$$ HOTEL **Windsor.** Built in the 1920s, close to the casino and overlooking the Grand Plage, this service-oriented hotel has crisp, contemporary accommodations with light walls and linens offset by bright splashes of color; rooms with sea views cost about twice as much as the larger ones facing

the inner courtyard and street. **Pros:** central beachfront location; sea views if you can get them; excellent restaurant; expert service. **Cons:** sea views cost double; street rooms get some noise. *Rooms from: €148* ✉ *19 bd. du Général-de-Gaulle, Biarritz* ☏ *05–59–24–08–52* 🌐 *www.hotelwindsorbiarritz.com* *44 rooms, 4 suites* *No meals.*

NIGHTLIFE AND PERFORMING ARTS

Casino de Biarritz. At the glitzy Casino de Biarritz you can play the slots and blackjack or just chill while channeling your inner James Bond. It's open daily from 10 am until 4 am. ✉ *1 av. Edouard-VII, Biarritz* ☏ *05–59–22–77–77* 🌐 *www.lucienbarriere.com/fr/casino/biarritz/accueil.html.*

L'Arena Café. This pretty pizzeria at the edge of the beach serves fine dinners and morphs into a late-night dance club around 11 pm. ✉ *Esplanade du Port Vieux, Biarritz* ☏ *05–59–24–88–98* 🌐 *dolce-arena.com.*

Le Carré Coast. Sip cocktails while listening to soul, jazz, and house music in a glamorous design setting close to the surf. ✉ *24 av. Édouard-VII, Biarritz* ☏ *05–59–24–64–64* 🌐 *www.lecarrecoast.com.*

Le Caveau. There's guaranteed action every night at Le Caveau—a mythical Biarritz dance club. ✉ *4 rue Gambetta, Biarritz* ☏ *05–59–24–16–17* 🌐 *www.caveau-biarritz.com.*

16

Le Playboy. In season, the surfing crowd fills Le Playboy. ✉ *15 pl. Georges Clémenceau, Biarritz* ☏ *05–59–24–38–46.*

Le Temps d'Aimer. In September the three-week Le Temps d'Aimer festival presents dance performances, from classical to hip-hop, in a range of venues throughout the city. They're often held at the Théâtre Gare du Midi, a renovated railway station. Troupes such as the Ballets Biarritz, Les Ballets de Monte-Carlo, and leading *étoiles* from other companies take to the stage in an ambitious schedule of events, with admission generally costing about €20. ✉ *Biarritz* 🌐 *www.letempsdaimer.com.*

Newquay. This midtown Irish pub is popular with surfers. ✉ *20 pl. Georges Clemenceau, Biarritz* ☏ *05–59–22–19–90.*

SPORTS AND THE OUTDOORS

Biarritz Athletic Club. Instruction in every type of Basque pelota—including *main nue* (bare-handed), *pala* (paddle), *chistera* (with a basketlike racquet), and *cesta punta* (another game played with the same curved basket)—is available at the Biarritz Athletic Club. It also organizes the Biarritz Masters Jai-Alai tournament in July, as well as Golden Glove boxing competitions. ✉ *Parc des Sports d'Aguilera, Fronton Euskal Jai, Biarritz* ☏ *05–59–23–91–09* 🌐 *www.cesta-punta.com.*

Golf de Biarritz Le Phare. Greens fees at the 18-hole, par-69 Golf de Biarritz Le Phare course start at €75 in the height of summer. ✉ *2 av. Edith-Cavell, Biarritz* ☏ *05–59–03–71–80* 🌐 *www.golfbiarritz.com.*

Parc des Sports d'Aguilera. This stadium is the fiefdom of the champion rugby club Biarritz Olympique, winner of the 2012 European Challenge. Call for information or check the website for scheduled matches. ✉ *Biarritz* ☏ *05–59–01–64–79* 🌐 *www.bo-pb.com.*

CLOSE UP

Le Surfing

For wave action in Europe's hot-cool surfing center, head to the coast north of Biarritz and the towns of Anglet and Hossegor. La Barre beach doubles as the hangout for dedicated surfers who live out of their vans. On the southern end (by the Anglet-Biarritz border) are surf shops, snack bars, and one boulangerie. These give the main beach drag, Chambre d'Amour, a decidedly California flair. If you're coming by train, get off in Bayonne or Biarritz and transfer to a Chronoplus bus bound for Anglet. The main tourist office (1 av. de la Chambre d'Amour ☎ *05–59–03–77–01* 🌐 *www.anglet.fr*) is closed off-season. Hossegor, 20 km (12 miles) north of Bayonne, hosts the Rip Curl Pro and the ASO Junior Surf Tour Championships every August as well as the ASP World Tour competition in September.

ST-JEAN-DE-LUZ

23 km (16 miles) southwest of Bayonne, 54 km (32 miles) northwest of St-Jean-Pied-de-Port.

Back in 1660, Louis XIV chose this tiny fishing village as the place to marry the Infanta Maria Teresa of Spain. Ever since, travelers have journeyed here to enjoy the unique charms of St-Jean. Along the coast between Biarritz and the Spanish border, it remains memorable for its colorful harbor, old streets, curious church, and elegant beach. Its iconic port shares a harbor with its sister town Ciboure, on the other side of the Nivelle River. The glorious days of whaling and cod fishing are long gone, but some historic multihued houses around the docks are evocative enough.

GETTING HERE

Frequent train service is available from Biarritz (11 mins, €3.50) and Bayonne (28 mins, €6). Regional Transports-64 buses also arrive at Place Maréchal Foch by the tourist office. Though slower than the train and only slightly less expensive, buses give you more beach-town options.

Visitor Information St-Jean-de-Luz Tourist Office. ☎ *05–59–26–03–16* 🌐 *www.saint-jean-de-luz.com.*

EXPLORING

Église St-Jean-Baptiste. The marriage of the Sun King and the Infanta took place in 1660 in the church of St-Jean-Baptiste. The marriage tied the knot, so to speak, on the Pyrénées Treaty signed by French chief minister Mazarin on November 7, 1659, ending Spanish hegemony in Europe. Note the church's unusual wooden galleries lining the walls, creating a theaterlike effect. Fittingly, St-Jean-Baptiste hosts a "Musique en Côte Basque" festival of early and Baroque music during the first two weeks of September. ✉ *Pl. des Corsaires, St-Jean-de-Luz* 🕐 *Daily 9–noon and 2–6.*

Maison de l'Infante (*Princess's House*). The Louis XIII–style Maison de l'Infante, between the harbor and the bay, is where Maria Teresa of Spain—accompanied by her mother, Queen Anne of Austria, and a healthy entourage of courtiers—stayed prior to her marriage to Louis XIV. ✉ *Quai de l'Infante, St-Jean-de-Luz* 🎫 *€2.50* ⏲ *June–Oct. 15 and Oct. 25–Nov. 11, Tues.–Sat. 11–12:30 and 2:30–6:30.*

Maison Louis-XIV. Take a tour of the twin-tower Maison Louis-XIV. Built as the Château Lohobiague, it housed the French king during his nuptials and is austerely decorated in 17th-century Basque fashion. ✉ *Pl. Louis XIV, St-Jean-de-Luz* ☎ *05–59–26–27–58* 🌐 *www.maison-louis-xiv.fr* 🎫 *€6* ⏲ *July and Aug., Wed.–Mon. 10:30–12:30 and 2:30–6:30; June and Sept., Wed.–Mon. 11–3 and 4–5; check website for off-season openings.*

Place Louis-XIV. Tree-lined Place Louis-XIV, alongside the Hôtel de Ville, with its dainty statue of Louis XIV on horseback, is the hub of the town. In summer, concerts are offered on the square, as well as the famous "Toro de fuego" festival, which honors the bull with a parade and a papier-mâché beast. ✉ *St-Jean-de-Luz.*

WHERE TO EAT AND STAY

$$$ SEAFOOD **Chez Pablo.** The catch of the day determines the offerings here. Long tables covered with red-and-white tablecloths, benches, and plaster walls give off a casual vibe, but the dishes are often excellent. $ *Average main: €27* ✉ *Rue Mme. Etxeto, St-Jean-de-Luz* ☎ *05–59–26–37–81* 🌐 *www.restaurant-chez-pablo.com* 💳 *No credit cards* ⏲ *Closed Wed. and several wks between Sept. and June.*

$$ BISTRO **La Taverne Basque.** This well-known midtown standard is one of the old-faithful dining emporiums, specializing in Basque cuisine with a pronounced maritime emphasis. Try the ttoro (a rich fish, crustacean, potato, and vegetable soup). Perhaps the best stamp of approval is that locals eat here often. $ *Average main: €18* ✉ *5 rue République, St-Jean-de-Luz* ☎ *05–59–26–01–26* 🌐 *www.latavernebasque.com* ⏲ *Closed Mon. No dinner Sun.*

$$ SEAFOOD **Txalupa.** The name is Basque for "skiff" or "small boat," and you feel like you're in one when you are this close to the bay—yachts and fishing vessels go about their business just a few yards away. The mixed seafood platter here is legendary, and daily nonstop service from noon to midnight makes it a hard meal to miss. $ *Average main: €22* ✉ *Pl. Louis-XIV, St-Jean-de-Luz* ☎ *05–59–51–85–51.*

$$$$ HOTEL **Le Grand Hôtel.** Built in the 1920s and traditionally considered to be St-Jean-de-Luz's premier hotel, Le Grand offers ocean views, intimacy, plus a general sense of being where the action is; redesigned rooms in pastels, wood, and marble, and the unbeatable location at the northern end of the St-Jean-de-Luz beach, seal the deal. **Pros:** views; comforts; action center. **Cons:** expensive; not too relaxing unless your pockets are deep; slightly self-absorbed staff. $ *Rooms from: €345* ✉ *43 bd. Thiers, St-Jean-de-Luz* ☎ *05–59–26–35–36* 🌐 *www.luzgrandhotel.fr* ⏲ *Closed 1 wk around Jan 1.* 🛏 *49 rooms, 3 suites* 🍽 *No meals.*

Biarritz's main beach, the Grande Plage, is the town's focal point, especially for those who don't have money to lose in the resort casinos.

THE ATLANTIC AND HAUTES-PYRÉNÉES

The Atlantic Pyrénées extend eastward from the ocean to the Col du Pourtalet, and encompass Béarn and the mountainous part of the Basque Country. Watching the Pyrénées grow from rolling green foothills in the west to jagged limestone peaks in the Béarn to glacier-studded granite massifs in the Hautes-Pyrénées makes for a dramatic progression of scenery. The Atlantic Pyrénées' first major height is at La Rhune (2,969 feet), known as the Balcon du Côte Basque (Balcony of the Basque Coast). The highest Basque peak is at Orhi (6,617 feet); the Béarn's highest is Pic d'Anie (8,510 feet). Not until Balaïtous (10,375 feet) and Vignemale (10,883 feet), in the Hautes-Pyrénées, does the altitude surpass the 10,000-foot mark. Starting east from St-Jean-de-Luz up the Nivelle River, a series of villages—including Sare, Ainhoa, and Bidarrai—are picturesque stepping-stones leading to St-Jean-Pied-de-Port and on into the Hautes-Pyrénées.

This journey ends in Pau, in the Béarn region, far from the Pays Basque. The Béarn is akin in temperament to the larger region that enfolds it, Gascony. Gascony may be purse-poor, but it is certainly rich in scenery and lore. Its proud and touchy temperament is typified in literature by the character d'Artagnan in Dumas's *The Three Musketeers*, and in history by the lords of the château of Pau. An inscription over the château's entrance, *Touchez-y, si tu l'oses*—"Touch this if you dare"—was left by the golden-haired Gaston Phoebus (1331–91), 11th count of Foix and viscount of Béarn, a volatile arts lover with a nasty temper who murdered his brother and his only son.

Farther east, past Lourdes, the Hautes-Pyrénées include the highest and most spectacular natural wonders in the cordillera: the legendary Cirque de Gavarnie (a natural mountain amphitheater), the Vignemale and Balaïtous peaks, and the Brèche de Roland are the star attractions. Trans-Pyrenean hikers (and drivers) generally prefer moving from west to east for a number of reasons, especially the excellent light prevailing in the late afternoon and evening during the prime months of May to October.

SARE

14 km (8 miles) southeast of St-Jean-de-Luz, 9 km (5½ miles) west of Ainhoa.

The much-prized and picturesque village of Sare, described by author Pierre Loti in his *Ramuntxo* as a virtually autonomous Eden, is built around a large *fronton*, or backboard, where a pelota game rages around the clock. Not surprisingly, the Hôtel de Ville offers a permanent exhibition on Pelote Basque (*July and Aug., daily 9–1 and 2–6:30; Sept.–June, daily 3–6*). Sare was a busy smuggling hub throughout the 19th century, but today's visitors are drawn by lovely sights, not illicit activities: chief among them are a collection of wood-beam and whitewashed Basque houses, and the late-Romanesque church with its triple-decker interior. There are also more than a dozen tiny chapels sprinkled around Sare that were built as ex-votos by seamen who survived Atlantic storms.

16

GETTING HERE

Buses leaving from the train station in St-Jean-de-Luz travel to Sare (30 mins, €3.50) and neighboring villages.

Visitor Information Sare Tourist Office. ☎ *05–59–54–20–14* 🌐 *www.sare.fr.*

EXPLORING

Église Saint-Martin de Sare. One of the Labourd province's prettiest churches, Église Saint-Martin de Sare was built in the 16th-century and enlarged in the 17th with a triple-decker set of galleries. Parish priest Pierre Axular ranks among the great early authors in the Basque language. His tomb is under the bell tower with an epitaph by Prince Bonaparte: "Every hour wounds; the last sends you to your tomb."✉ *Le Bourg, Sare* 🎫 *€3* 🕒 *Tours Tues. at 2:30.*

Grottes de Sare. Follow the Sare Valley up to the panoramic Col de Lizarrieta and the Grottes de Sare. Just outside these huge caves, you can learn about the Basque region's culture and millennia-long history at the **Musée Ethnographique** (Ethnographic Museum); then take a multilingual guided tour that leads 1 km (½ mile) underground to see a subterranean son-et-lumière (sound-and-light) show. ✉ *Sare* ☎ *05—59—54—21—88* 🌐 *www.grottesdesare.fr* 🎫 *€8.50* 🕒 *Nov.–mid-Apr., weekdays 2–5, weekends 1–5; mid-Apr.–July and Sept., daily 10–6; Aug., daily 10–7; Oct., daily 10–5.*

Musée du Gâteau Basque. This sweet museum traces the evolution of the most famous of all Basque pastries; call ahead for a schedule of workshops and baking classes. ✉ *Maison Haranea, Quartier Lehenbiscay,*

CLOSE UP

Getting On Top of Things

Supping on hearty regional cuisine makes perfect sense after a day of hiking the Pyrénées, which are best explored on foot. Day trips to La Rhune overlooking Biarritz and the Basque Coast and the walk up to Biriatou from the beach at Hendaye are great ways to get to know the countryside. Hiking the Pyrénées end-to-end is a 43-day trip. The GR (Grande Randonnée) 10, a trail signed by discreet red-and-white paint markings, runs from the Atlantic at Hendaye to Banyuls-sur-Mer on the Mediterranean, through villages and mountains, with refuges along the way.

The HRP (Haute Randonnée Pyrénéenne, or High Pyrenean Hike) follows terrain in France and Spain irrespective of borders. Local trails are well indicated, with blue or yellow markings. Some classic walks in the Pyrénées include the Iparla Ridge walk between Bidarrai and St-Étienne-de-Baïgorry, the Santiago de Compostela Trail's dramatic St-Jean-Pied-de-Port to Roncesvalles walk over the Pyrénées, and the Holçarté Gorge walk between Larrau and Ste-Engrâce. Get trail maps at local tourist offices.

Sare ☎ 05–59–54–22–09 ⊕ www.legateaubasque.com ✉ €7.50 ⊙ Daily 9–1 and 2–6:30.

Ortillopitz. Take a guided tour of Ortillopitz, a vintage Basque country manor. Its typical architecture and traditional furnishings give a glimpse into 17th-century farm life. The rural vistas are especially lovely. *✉ Sare ☎ 05–59–85–91–92 ⊕ www.ortillopitz.com ✉ €9 ⊙ Tours: Apr. 13–July 11, weekdays 2:15, 3:30, and 4:45, Sun. 3:30; July 13–Aug. 22, weekdays 10:45, noon, 2:15, 3:30, 4:45, and 6, Sun. 2:15, 3:30, 4:45, and 6; Aug. 24–Sept. 19, weekdays 2:15, 3:30, and 4:45, Sun. 2:15, 3:30, and 4:45; Sept. 21–Oct. 17, Sun.–Fri. 3:30.*

FAMILY
Fodor's Choice ★

Petit Train de la Rhune. Not much on the Petit Train has changed since its inaugural voyage to the peak of La Rhune on June 30, 1924. Today, passengers still ride in the original varnished cars made of pine and chestnut from Pyrenean forests at the less-than-dizzying speed of 8 kph (5 mph); and, as they ascend, present-day passengers are just as enthralled by the incredible views of the Bay of Biscay and the grassy Basque farmlands below. You can board this high-climbing cogwheel train (one of only three in France) at the Col de St-Ignace, 3.5 km (2.2 miles) west of Sare. *✉ West of Sare on the D4, Col de St-Ignace, Sare ☎ 05–59–54–20–26 ⊕ www.rhune.com ✉ €18 ⊙ July and Aug., daily 8:30–5:30; Sept.–June, daily 9:30–11:30 and 2–4 (departures every 35 mins).*

WHERE TO STAY

$ B&B/INN

Baratxartea. This little inn, located 1 km (½ mile) from the center of Sare in one of the town's prettiest and most ancient *quartiers*, is a beauty—a 16th-century town house complete with exposed wood-beam framework. **Pros:** upland location 20 minutes from beach; personalized family service; two splendid meals included. **Cons:** can get steamy in August; annex rooms are less charming and rustic; open windows in farm country attract insects. *Rooms from: €100* ✉ *Quartier Ihalar, Sare* ☎ *05–59–54–20–48* 🌐 *www.hotel-baratxartea.com* ⏲ *Closed mid-Nov.–mid-Mar.* *14 rooms* *Some meals.*

AINHOA

9 km (5½ miles) east of Sare, 31 km (19 miles) northwest of St-Jean-Pied-de-Port.

The Basque village of Ainhoa, officially selected by the national tourist ministry as one of the prettiest in France, is a showcase for the Labourd region. Established in the 13th century, its little streets are lined with lovely 16th- to 18th-century houses featuring whitewashed walls, flower-filled balconies, brightly painted shutters, and carved master beams.

GETTING HERE

Exploring Ainhoa on foot is a pleasure, but you'll need your own wheels to get to here.

Visitor Information Ainhoa Tourist Office. ☎ *05–59–29–93–99* 🌐 *www.ainhoa-tourisme.com.*

16

EXPLORING

Notre-Dame de l'Assomption. The village's most noteworthy building is the Romanesque church of Notre-Dame de l'Assomption. Founded in the 13th century by Premonstratensian monks, it has a traditional Basque three-tier wooden interior with carved railings and ancient oak stairs; women sat on the ground floor, while men occupied the first balcony, and the choir sang in the loft above. ✉ *Ainhoa* ⏲ *Daily 10–6.*

WHERE TO STAY

$$ HOTEL Fodor's Choice ★ **Ithurria.** A registered historic monument, this 17th-century Basque-style building was once a staging post on the fabled pilgrims' route to Santiago de Compostela, and today it still makes a fitting resting spot if you're doing a modern version of the pilgrimage or just need a stopover on your way deeper into the mountains. **Pros:** country charm; pretty grounds and pool; cheery family service. **Cons:** you'll understand why they call it luggage while hauling your gear from car to room; some room decor undistinguished. *Rooms from: €145* ✉ *Rue Principale, Ainhoa* ☎ *05–59–29–92–11* 🌐 *www.ithurria.com* ⏲ *Closed Nov.–Apr.* *26 rooms, 2 apartments* *No meals.*

$ B&B/INN **Oppoca.** This 17th-century *relais,* or stagecoach relay station, on Ainhoa's main square and pelota court is one of the loveliest Basque houses in town, with small but adequate guest rooms. **Pros:** helpful service; superb fare; historic site. **Cons:** cramped spaces in some rooms; center of town can be noisy on weekends and holiday eves. *Rooms from: €97* ✉ *Pl. du Fronton, Ainhoa* ☎ *05–59–29–90–72* 🌐 *www.oppoca.com* ⏲ *Closed mid-Nov.–Feb.* *10 rooms* *No meals.*

ST-JEAN-PIED-DE-PORT

31 km (19 miles) southeast of Ainhoa.

St-Jean-Pied-de-Port, a fortified town on the Nive River, got its name from its position at the foot (*pied*) of the mountain pass (*port*) of Roncevaux (Roncesvalles). The pass was the setting for *La Chanson de Roland* (*The Song of Roland*), the anonymous 11th-century epic poem considered the true beginning of French literature; and the town itself remains a major stop for pilgrims en route to Santiago de Compostela. After a tour through the quiet villages of the Béarn countryside, it feels like a frenzied metropolis—even in winter. In summer, the bustling center is filled to the gills, and the tone is something between exciting and unbearable.

GETTING HERE

SNCF trains between Bayonne and St-Jean-Pied-de-Port depart six times daily in each direction (1 hr, 26 mins; €10.10).

Visitor Information St-Jean-Pied-de-Port Tourist Office. ☎ *05–59–37–03–57* 🌐 *www.saintjeanpieddeport-paysbasque-tourisme.com.*

EXPLORING

Notre-Dame-du-Bout-du-Pont (*Our Lady of the End of the Bridge*). Walk into the old section of St-Jean-Pied-de-Port through the Porte de France, just behind and to the left of the tourist office; climb the steps on the left up to the walkway circling the ramparts, and stroll around to the stone stairway down to the Rue de l'Église. The church of Notre-Dame-du-Bout-du-Pont, known for its magnificent Gothic Rayonnant doorway, is at the bottom of this cobbled street. Built in the 12th century and designated a church in the 13th century, it is a characteristically Basque three-tier structure. ✉ *Rue de l'Église, St-Jean-Pied-de-Port.*

Pont Notre-Dame (*Notre-Dame Bridge*). From the Pont Notre-Dame you can watch the wild trout in the Nive (also an Atlantic salmon stream) as they pluck mayflies off the surface. Note that fishing is forbidden in town. Upstream, along the left bank, is another wooden bridge. Cross it and then walk around and back through town, returning to the left bank on the main road. ✉ *St-Jean-Pied-de-Port.*

Rue de la Citadelle. Several sights of interest line Rue de la Citadelle, including the **Maison Arcanzola** (Arcanzola House), at No. 32 (1510); the **Maison des Évêques** (Bishops' House), at No. 39; and the famous **Prison des Évêques** (Bishops' Prison), next door to it. Continuing up you'll reach the **Citadelle** itself—a classic Vauban fortress built between 1625 and 1627, now occupied by a school. The views from the top, complete with maps identifying the surrounding heights and valleys, are panoramic. ✉ *Rue de la Citadelle, St-Jean-Pied-de-Port.*

WHERE TO EAT AND STAY

$$$$ FRENCH Fodor's Choice ★

✕ **Les Pyrénées.** A former stagecoach inn on the route to Santiago de Compostela now houses the best restaurant in the Pyrénées. Directed by renowned master chef Firmin Arrambide and his son Philippe, this haute-cuisine address is characterized by refined interpretations of Pays Basque cooking with a focus on Pyrenean delicacies, like trout from the Nive and local wood pigeon. For dessert, the elder Arrambide's recipe for gâteau Basque has circled the world. After dining, you can bed down in one of the inn's 14 rooms and four suites; needless to say, you'll want to invest in one of the board plans. *Average main: €44 19 pl. Charles-de-Gaulle, St-Jean-Pied-de-Port 05–59–37–01–01 www.hotel-les-pyrenees.com Closed Mon., Jan. 5–28, and Nov. 20–Dec. 22 Reservations essential.*

$ HOTEL **Central Hôtel.** This family-run hotel and restaurant over the Nive is a vintage venue (note the 200-year-old oak staircase)—it's also the best value in town. **Pros:** central location, as suggested by the name; personal family service; river sounds and views. **Cons:** creaky bedsprings; can be hot in midsummer; village life starts early and you're at the heart of it. *Rooms from: €64 1 pl. Charles-de-Gaulle, St-Jean-Pied-de-Port 05–59–37–00–22 Closed Dec.–Feb. 13 rooms No meals.*

EUGÉNIE-LES-BAINS

151 km (94 miles) northeast of St-Jean-Pied-de-Port, 56 km (35 miles) north of Pau.

Empress Eugénie popularized the region's thermal baths at the end of the 19th century, and in return the villagers named this town after her. Then, in 1973, Michel and Christine Guérard made the village world famous by putting together one of France's most fashionable thermal retreats, which became one of the birthplaces of nouvelle cuisine, thanks to the great talents of Chef Michel. Their empire now includes restaurants serving three types of cuisine (*minceur, gourmand,*and *terroir*), four places to stay, a cooking school, and a spa.

16

GETTING HERE

Neither buses nor trains serve Eugénie-les-Bains. If you haven't rented a car, contact the local tourist office for a list of taxi companies; the fare from Pau (an hour away) is about €100.

Visitor Information Eugénie-les-Bains Tourist Office. *05–58–51–13–16 www.tourisme-aire-eugenie.fr.*

EXPLORING

Thermes d'Eugénie-les-Bains. This therapeutic *station thermale* is certified by the French Ministry of Health to treat digestive, urinary, and metabolic problems, as well as rheumatism. Three-week "cures" are prescribed by doctors and covered by national health insurance. But foreign visitors can sign up for weight-loss retreats or simply enjoy a restorative stint in healing baths filled with 39°C (102°F) water that comes from nearly 1,300 feet below the surface. *Eugénie-les-Bains 05–58–05–06–06 www.chainethermale.fr.*

WHERE TO STAY

$$$ HOTEL **La Maison Rose.** A (relatively) low-cost, low-calorie alternative to famed Les Prés d'Eugénie, Michel and Christine Guérard's "Pink House" spa beckons with a renovated, super-stylish 18th-century farmhouse adorned with old paintings, rustic antiques, and Pays Basque handicrafts. **Pros:** much easier on the wallet; a sybaritically simple spa approach; more relaxed; superb dining without stuffing. **Cons:** cravings for the full foie-gras treatment next door. *Rooms from: €200*

The Hautes-Pyrénées have some of the best hiking trails in Europe, especially those found on the way to the Cirque de Gavarnie.

✉ Rue René Vielle, Eugénie-les-Bains ☎ 05–58–05–06–07 🌐 www.michelguerard.com 🛏 25 rooms, 5 suites 🍴 No meals.

$$$$ B&B/INN **Le Logis des Grives.** With four superb suites for the lucky first-comers, the Guérards' delightfully re-created old coaching inn, set at one end of their Prés d'Eugénie fiefdom, is meant to be a more rustic alternative to their main flagship. **Pros:** the rusticity is more relaxing than the full-on Guérard treatment; finest country cooking in the land a few yards away. **Cons:** slight sense of gated community overprotection; isolated from village life; only for those on an elite budget. *$ Rooms from: €600 ✉ Rue René Vielle, Eugénie-les-Bains ☎ 05–58–05–06–07 🌐 www.michelguerard.com ⏲ Closed Jan. 4–Feb. 12 🛏 4 suites 🍴 No meals.*

$$$$ HOTEL Fodor's Choice ★ **Les Prés d'Eugénie.** Ever since Michel Guérard's restaurant fired the first shots of the nouvelle revolution in the late 1970s, the excellence of this suave culinary landmark has been a given (so much so that breakfast here outdoes dinner at most other places); hence a visit to Les Prés d'Eugénie remains an important notch on any gourmand's belt. **Pros:** Guérard in full; magical cuisine; intelligent and attentive service; range of recreational options. **Cons:** too beautiful to close your eyes and go to sleep (fortunately, Bacchus comes to your rescue). *$ Rooms from: €360 ✉ Rue René Vielle, Eugénie-les-Bains ☎ 05–58–05–06–07, 05–58–05–05–05 restaurant reservations 🌐 www.michelguerard.com 🛏 38 rooms 🍴 No meals.*

PAU

56 km (35 miles) south of Eugénie-les-Bains, 106 km (63 miles) southeast of Bayonne and Biarritz, 41 km (27 miles) northwest of Lourdes.

The stunning views, mild climate, and elegance of Pau—the historic capital of Béarn, a state annexed to France in 1620—make it a lovely place to visit and a convenient gateway to the Pyrénées. The birthplace of King Henri IV, Pau was "discovered" in 1815 by British officers returning from the Peninsular War in Spain, and it soon became a prominent winter resort town. Fifty years later English-speaking inhabitants made up one-third of Pau's population, many of them believing in the medicinal benefits of mountain air (later shifting their loyalties to Biarritz for the sea air). While here, the Brits not only introduced fox hunting and popularized tea drinking—they started the Pont-Long Steeplechase (still one of the most challenging in Europe) in 1841, and created France's first golf course in 1856.

GETTING HERE

The Pau-Pyrénées airport, 12 km (7 miles) north of town, receives daily flights from Paris, Lyon, and other points; a shuttle bus into Pau runs hourly from 7:40 am to 7:40 pm (30 mins, €1). The TGV connects Pau and Paris with four trains daily (5 hrs, 34 mins; €67.50). Overnight sleeper trains from Paris run via Bayonne or Toulouse (7 hrs, 45 mins; €107). Trains connect with Biarritz five times daily (1½ hrs, €21). You can also take the train to Lourdes (28 mins, €8.30), Bayonne (1 hr, 33 mins; €18.60), and Toulouse (2 hrs, 52 mins; €34.20). To reach the center of Pau from the train station on Avenue Gaston-Lacoste, cross the street and take the funicular up the hill to Place Royale. If you prefer the bus, Transports-64 connects Pau with Bayonne.

Visitor Information Pau Tourist Office. ☎ *05–59–27–27–08* 🌐 *www.pau-pyrenees.com.*

EXPLORING

Musée des Beaux-Arts. For some man-made splendors, head to the Musée des Beaux-Arts and ogle works by El Greco, Degas, Sorolla, and Rodin. ✉ *Rue Mathieu-Lalanne, Pau* ☎ *05–59–27–33–02* 🎫 *€5* ⏲ *Weekdays 10–noon and 2–6, weekends 10–12:30.*

Fodor's Choice ★ **Musée National du Château de Pau.** Pau's regal past is commemorated at its Musée National du Château de Pau, begun in the 14th century by Gaston Phoebus, the flamboyant count of Béarn. The building was transformed into a Renaissance palace in the 16th century by Marguerite d'Angoulême, sister of François I. A woman of diverse gifts, she wrote pastorals, many performed in the château's sumptuous gardens. Her bawdy *Heptameron*—written at age 60—furnishes as much sly merriment today as it did when read by her doting kingly brother. Marguerite's grandson, the future king of France Henri IV, was born in the château in 1553. Exhibits connected to Henri's life and times are displayed regularly, along with portraits of the most significant of his alleged 57 lovers and mistresses. His cradle, a giant turtle shell, is on exhibit in his bedroom, one of the sumptuous, tapestry-lined royal apartments. ✉ *Rue du Château, Pau* ☎ *05–59–82–38–00* *chateau-pau.fr* *7€* *Mid-June–mid-Sept., daily 9:30–12:30 and 1:30–6:45; mid-Sept.–mid-June, daily 9:30–11:45 and 2–5.*

Sentiers du Roy. The "King's Path" is a marked trail just below Boulevard des Pyrénées. When you reach the top, look for the large map identifying the main peaks of the Hautes Pyrénées in the distance. *Pau.*

WHERE TO EAT AND STAY

$$ FRENCH **Henri IV.** On a quiet pedestrian street near the château, this dining room with its open fire is a cozy find for a cold, wet winter night, and the terrace is a shady place to cool off in summer. Traditional Béarn dishes here include *magret de canard* (duck breast) cooked over coals, and *cuisses de grenouille* (frogs' legs) sautéed dry and crispy in parsley and garlic. *Average main: €22* *18 rue Henri IV, Pau* *05–59–27–54–43* *Closed Wed. and Thurs.*

$ HOTEL **Hôtel de Gramont.** This 17th-century stagecoach stop is a convenient base that's frequented by a mixed bag of travelers seeking respectable lodgings at reasonable prices. **Pros:** a short walk from the Château de Pau and overlooking the oldest part of town; relaxing and unpretentious; easy on the wallet. **Cons:** breakfast (at extra charge) is to be avoided; small rooms. *Rooms from: €89* *3 pl. de Gramont, Pau* *05–59–27–84–04* *www.hotelgramont.com* *No credit cards* *32 rooms, 3 suites* *No meals.*

$$$$ HOTEL **Hôtel Parc Beaumont.** If you're craving New World efficiency and unquestionable comfort, this place has definite appeal. **Pros:** plush rooms and polished service; contemporary style. **Cons:** a longish walk to the historic center of town; comfort takes precedence over charm. *Rooms from: €270* *1 av. Edouard VII, Pau* *05–59–11–84–00* *www.hotel-parc-beaumont.com* *70 rooms, 10 suites* *No meals.*

$$$ HOTEL Fodor's Choice ★ **Hôtel Villa Navarre.** In the 1800s Pau became home to a colony of elite British expats (including famed climber Henry Russell), who were drawn here by the mountains and climate. **Pros:** views of the Pyrénées; beautiful gardens; well-preserved English heritage. **Cons:** 15-minute walk to town; caters to business travelers (like all of Pau's hotels). *Rooms from: €189* *59 rue Trespoey, Pau* *05–59–14–65–65* *www.villanavarre.fr* *30 room* *No meals.*

NIGHTLIFE AND PERFORMING ARTS

Festival de Pau. During the Festival de Pau, theatrical and musical events take place almost every evening from mid-July to late August, nearly all of them *gratuit* (free). The Tango Festival erupts in early October. *Pau* *www.festivaltangopau.com.*

LOURDES

41 km (27 miles) southeast of Pau, 30 km (19 miles) north of Cauterets.

The mountain town of Lourdes is arguably the most famous Catholic pilgrimage site in the world, but its origins are decidedly humble and its renown relatively recent. In February 1858, a 14-year-old miller's daughter named Bernadette Soubirous claimed she saw the Virgin Mary in the Grotte de Massabielle (in all, she had 18 visions). Bernadette dug in the grotto, releasing a gush of water from a spot where no spring had flowed before. From then on, pilgrims thronged the Massabielle rock for the water's supposed healing powers. Today, more than 6 million visitors come each year from every corner of the globe—not all of them are Christian, but most are bound by their common hope for a miracle cure.

GETTING HERE AND AROUND

With direct rail service from Pau (28 mins, €8.30), Bayonne (1 hr, 44 mins; €24), and Toulouse (2 hrs, 4 mins; €26.50), Lourdes's train station on Avenue de la Gare is one of the busiest in the country. In fact, so many pilgrim trains arrive between Easter and All Saint's Day (November 1) that the station has a separate entrance to accommodate them; and dedicated local buses shuttle passengers to the grotto every 20 minutes. Regional Transports-64 and SNCF-run TER buses also serve the area.

Visitor Information Lourdes Tourist Office. ☎ *05–62–42–77–40* 🌐 *www.lourdes-infotourisme.com.*

EXPLORING

Basilique Souterraine St-Pie X. Lourdes celebrated the centenary of Bernadette Soubirous's visions by building the world's largest underground church, the Basilique Souterraine St-Pie X, with space for 20,000 people—more than the town's permanent population. The Basilique Supérieure (1871), tall and white, hulks nearby. ✉ *Lourdes.*

Cachot. The cachot, a tiny room where, in extreme poverty, Bernadette and her family took refuge in 1856, can be visited. ✉ *15 rue des Petits-Fossés, Lourdes* ☎ *05–62–94–51–30* 🎫 *Free* ⏲ *Easter–mid-Oct., daily 9:30–11:45 and 2:30–5:30; mid-Oct.–Easter, daily 2:30–5:30.*

Grotte de Massabielle. Lourdes wouldn't even be on the map if it weren't for this deep grotto near the Gave de Pau where 14-year-old Bernadette Soubirous first claimed to see visions of the Virgin Mary in 1858. Church authorities initially reacted with skepticism: it took four years for the miracle to be authenticated by Rome and a sanctuary erected over the grotto. But in 1864 the first organized procession was held. Now there are six official annual pilgrimages between Easter and All Saints' Day, the most important being on August 15. In fall and winter there are far fewer visitors, but that will be a plus for those in search of peace and tranquillity. ✉ *Lourdes.*

Moulin de Boly (*Boly Mill*). Across the river is the Moulin de Boly, where Bernadette was born on January 7, 1844. ✉ *12 rue Bernadette-Soubirous, Lourdes* 🎫 *Free* ⏲ *Easter–mid-Oct., daily 9–noon and 2–6:30.*

Fodor's Choice ★ **Musée Pyrénéen.** The **château** on the hill above town can be reached by escalator, by 131 steps, or by the ramp up from Rue du Bourg (from which a small Basque cemetery with ancient discoidal stones can be seen). Once a prison, the castle now contains the Musée Pyrénéen, one of France's best provincial museums, devoted to the popular customs, arts, and history of the Pyrénées. ✉ *25 rue du Fort, Lourdes* ☎ *05–62–42–37–37* 🌐 *www.chateaufort-lourdes.fr* 🎫 *€7* ⏲ *June–Sept., daily 9–6:30; Oct.–May, daily 9–noon and 2–6.*

Musée Sainte-Bernadette. Bernadette's life story is chronicled through mementos and more at the museum that bears her name; information

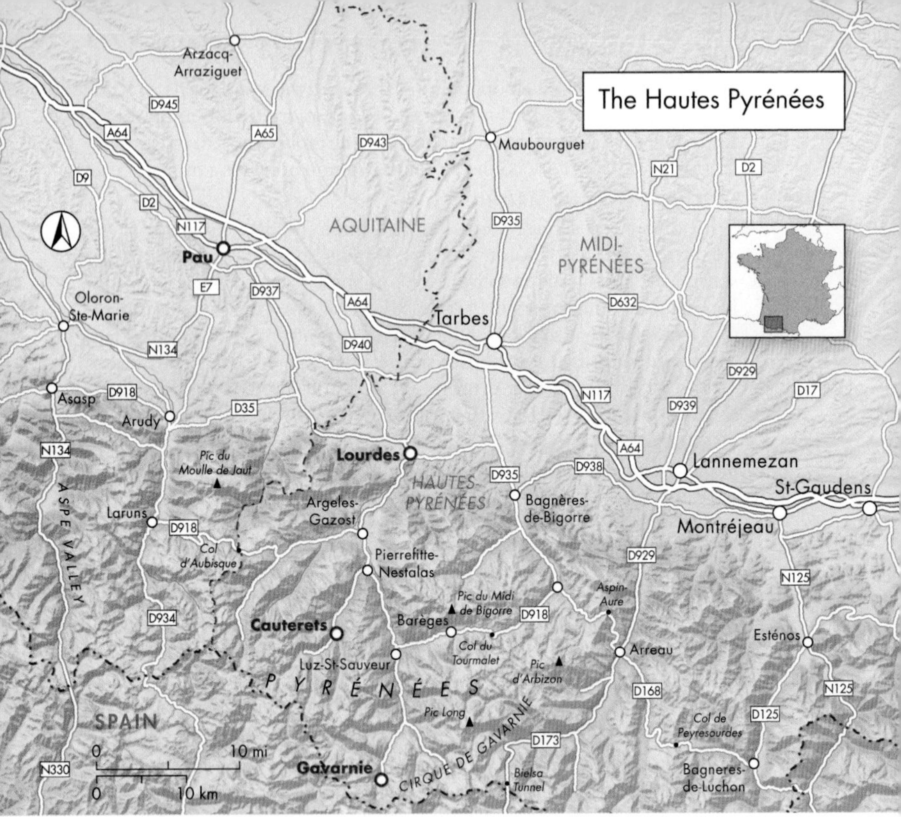

about the construction of the nearby sanctuaries is also provided. ✉ *Bd. Rémi Sempé, Lourdes* ☎ *05–62–42–78–78* 🌐 *www.lourdes-france.com* 🎟 *Free* ⏲ *July–Nov., daily 9–noon and 2:30–7; Dec.–June, Wed.–Mon. 9–noon and 2:30–5:45.*

WHERE TO STAY

$$$ HOTEL **Grand Hôtel Gallia et Londres.** A feel of traditional France in the Louis XVI furniture and the general ambience of the place makes the pretty Gallia, not far from the sanctuaries and the grotto, something of a retreat within a retreat. **Pros:** traditional French hotel; near the sanctuaries; maintains a certain dignity in the midst of the prevailing commercial vibe of Lourdes. **Cons:** some rooms are on the small side; closed during the winter; breakfast is extra. $ *Rooms from: €180* ✉ *26 av. B. Soubirous, Lourdes* ☎ *05–62–94–35–44* 🌐 *www.hotelsvinuales.com* ⏲ *Closed Oct. 20–Apr. 11* *88 rooms, 3 suites* *No meals.*

$$$ HOTEL Fodor's Choice ★ **Grand Hôtel Moderne.** After braving the pilgrim-packed streets, this hotel—built in 1896 by one of Bernadette's nephews—may seem like the answer to your prayers; after all, it promises comfortable rooms, attentive service, and an excellent restaurant right in the center of everything. **Pros:** premier location across from the Grotto; warm service; good restaurant. **Cons:** attracts large groups (you can't avoid that in Lourdes); driving into the heart of town is tricky (can't avoid that

either). *Rooms from: €160 ✉ 21 av. Bernadette Soubirous, Lourdes ☎ 05–62–94–12–32 🌐 www.grandhotelmoderne.com 110 rooms No meals.*

CAUTERETS

30 km (19 miles) south of Lourdes, 30 km (19 miles) north of Gavarnie.

Cauterets—which derives from the word for hot springs in the local *bigourdan* dialect—is a spa resort town set high in the Pyrénées. It has been revered since Roman times for thermal baths thought to cure maladies ranging from back pain to infertility. Novelist Victor Hugo (1802–85) womanized here, and Lady Aurore Dudevant—better known as the writer George Sand (1804–76)—is said to have discovered her feminism here. Other famous visitors include Chateaubriand, Sarah Bernhardt, King Edward VII of England, and Spain's King Alfonso XIII.

GETTING HERE

Unless you're coming to Cauterets from a hiking path, only one road leads into town. SNCF buses travel to and from Lourdes on it seven times a day (1 hr, €7).

Visitor Information Cauterets Tourist Office. *☎ 05–62–92–50–50 🌐 www.cauterets.com.*

16

EXPLORING

Les Bains du Rocher. The naturally heated sulfur water here was particularly popular among 19th-century aristocrats who arrived in Cauterets to "take the cure." Today, it's still used to alleviate rheumatism and respiratory maladies (three-week treatments can even be covered by national health insurance). In keeping with modern trends, however, the *station thermale* now caters to guests who simply want to indulge as well. Opened in 2010, Les Bains du Rocher has a genuine spa aesthetic. It offers massages, facials, aqua-gym sessions, and, of course, soaks in hot healing pools both inside and outside. *✉ Ave. du Dr. Domer, Cauterets ☎ 05–62–92–14–20 🌐 www.bains-rocher.fr.*

GAVARNIE

30 km (19 miles) south of Cauterets.

Geologists point to the natural wonder that is the Cirque de Gavarnie as one of the world's most formidable examples of the effects of glacial erosion; the cliffs were worn away by the advancing and retreating ice sheets of the Pleistocene epoch. Seeing it, one can understand its irresistible appeal for mountain climbers—appropriately, the village has a statue honoring one of the first of them, Count Russell.

GETTING HERE

Conseil Général and SNCF buses from Lourdes will take you as far as Luz-St-Sauveur (34 mins, €5); you can cover the last 20 km (12 miles) by taxi or, from June to September, connect to another bus that travels onward to Gavarnie (30 mins, €5).

Visitor Information Gavarnie Tourist Office. *☎ 05–62–92–49–10 🌐 www.gavarnie.com.*

EXPLORING

Fodor's Choice ★ **Brèche de Roland.** One dramatic sight is 12 km (7 miles) west of the village of Gavarnie. Take D921 up to the Col de Boucharo, where you can park and walk five hours up to the Brèche de Roland glacier (you cross it during the last two hours of the hike). For a taste of mountain life, have lunch high up at the Club Alpin Français's **Refuge la Brèche de Roland–Sarradets.** This is a serious climb, only feasible from mid-June to mid-September, for which you need (at least) good hiking shoes and sound physical conditioning. Crampons and ice axes can be rented in Gavarnie. ✉ *Gavarnie.*

Fodor's Choice ★ **Cirque de Gavarnie.** A spectacular natural amphitheater, the Cirque de Gavarnie has been dubbed the "Colosseum of Nature" and inspired many writers, including Victor Hugo. At its foot is the village of Gavarnie, a good base for exploring the mountains in the region. Thanks to glacial erosion, the Cirque is a Cinerama wall of peaks and a daunting challenge to mountaineers. Horses and donkeys, rented in the village, are the traditional way to reach the head of the valley (though walking is preferable). When the upper snows melt, numerous streams tumble down from the cliffs to form spectacular waterfalls; the greatest of them, the **Grande Cascade,** drops nearly 1,400 feet. ✉ *Gavarnie.*

WHERE TO EAT AND STAY

$ FRENCH Fodor's Choice ★ ✕ **Hôtel du Cirque.** With its legendary views of the Cirque de Gavarnie, this spot, which opened at the head of the valley in 1848, is well worth the one-hour hike up from the village. Despite its name, the hôtel is a restaurant, but not just any old one: the *garbure* here is as delicious as the view is grand. Seventh-generation owner Pierre Vergez claims his recipe using water from the Cirque and *cocos de Tarbes,* or *haricots tarbais* (Tarbes broad beans) is unique. [$] *Average main: €15* ✉ *1-hr walk above village of Gavarnie, Gavarnie* ☎ *05–62–92–48–02* ⏲ *Closed Nov.–May.*

$$$ HOTEL **Hotel Vignemale.** Built in 1902, this spacious château-like hotel has an imposing granite facade with steep rooflines reflecting the towering Hautes Pyrénées to the south; sunny guest rooms with floor-to-ceiling windows overlook the rushing Gave (river) de Gavarnie, and the breakfast terrace out front is an ideal place to start a day in the mountains. **Pros:** rushing water music provided by the stream; a sense of space; historic mountaineer's haven. **Cons:** small balconies; decor somewhat dated; bathrooms not as splendid as the facade might suggest. [$] *Rooms from: €150* ✉ *Chemin du Cirque, Gavarnie* ☎ *05–62–92–40–00* 🌐 *www.hotel-vignemale.com* ⏲ *Closed mid-Oct.–mid-May* *10 rooms* *No meals.*

17

BORDEAUX AND THE WINE COUNTRY

WELCOME TO BORDEAUX AND THE WINE COUNTRY

TOP REASONS TO GO

★ **La Route de Médoc:** With eight appellations (districts) in this small area alone, and names like Rothschild, Latour, and Margaux on its bottles, the route will fulfill your grape expectations.

★ **Bordeaux:** 18th-century wine merchants endowed this city with an almost regal elegance—for proof, see their gracious mansions and the city's sublime squares.

★ **The Rothschild legacy:** Although the family's Château Lafite is often locked, oenophiles will be welcomed with open arms at Château Mouton-Rothschild's visitor center and museum.

★ **St-Émilion:** With its 13th-century ramparts, cobblestone streets, and rock-face hermitage, this hilltop town presides over one of the region's richest wine districts.

★ **Bordeaux bacchanal:** Wine-themed festivals—most notably the Fête du Vin extravaganza, held in Bordeaux's biggest *place*at the end of June—keep corks popping.

1 Bordeaux. Dominated geographically by the nearby Atlantic Ocean and historically by great wine merchants and shippers, Bordeaux has long ranked among France's largest cities. There is considerable, if concentrated, affluence, which hides behind 18th-century facades. Showing off may not be a regional trait but, happily, the city fathers did provide a bevy of cultural riches to discover, including the spectacular Place de la Bourse, the Grand Théâtre, and the Musée des Beaux-Arts.

2 The Médoc. Northwest of Bordeaux, this triangulated peninsula extends from the Garonne River to the Atlantic coast. Dutch engineers drained its marshy landscape in the 18th century to expose the gravelly soil that is excellent for growing grapes, and today the Médoc is home to several of the *grands crus classés*, including Château Margaux, Château Latour, Château Lafite-Rothschild, and Château Mouton-Rothschild. Public buses run here but stops are sometimes in the middle of nowhere—a car, bike, or guided tour may be the best option.

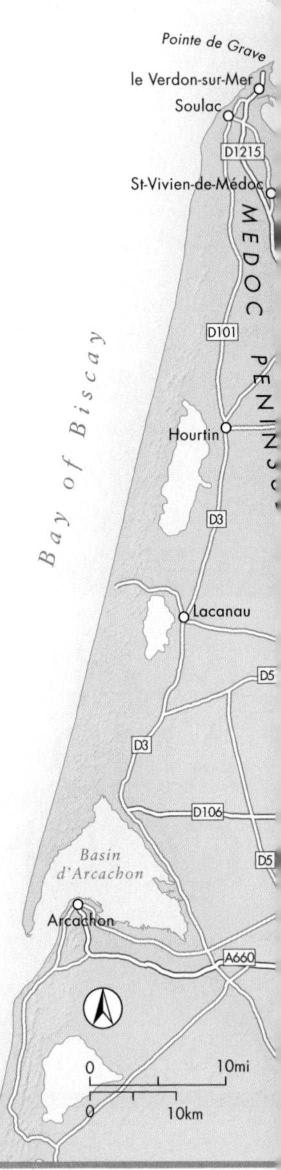

3 The Libournais. On the right bank of the Dordogne, this region was put on the map by two great wine districts—St-Émilion and Pomerol. Crowds head here because the town of St-Émilion looks as delicious as its wines taste: a UNESCO World Heritage Site, this open-air museum was constructed out of a limestone plateau honeycombed with vast caves and passageways, the source for the golden stonework of its 19th-century houses and steep streets. During summer, the small town is often swamped with visitors, so plan your parking and hotels carefully.

Royan
Cozes
D730
Gironde
Route du Medoc
Lesparre-Médoc
Château de Loudenne
Mirambeau
St-Ciers-sur-Gironde
D730
2
D2
A10
Montendre
Château Mouton Rotschild
Pauillac
Montlieu-la-Garde
POITOU CHARENTES
Blaye
D1215
D137
N10
Margaux
Bourg
AQUITAINE
Ste-Hélène
D2
Isle
D1
D215
D18
A89
N89
Banquefort
A10
Libourne
Pomerol
3
Bordeaux
St-Émilion
Pessac
1
D936
Gradignan
D10
Léognan
A63
Langoiran
Labrède
Haut-Bénauge
A62
Cadillac
Barsac
Loupiac
Sauternes
Langon

GETTING ORIENTED

Along with Burgundy and Champagne, Bordeaux is one of the great wine regions of France. As the capital of the Gironde *département* and of the historic province of Aquitaine, the city of Bordeaux is both the commercial and cultural center of southwest France and an important transportation hub. It is smack-dab in the middle of one of the finest wine-growing areas in the world: Sauternes lies to the south, flat and dusty Médoc to the northwest, and Pomerol and St-Émilion to the east.

VISITING THE VINEYARDS

Château Smith Haut Lafitte is a famous name in Bordeaux *(above)*; the tower of Château Latour *(right, above)*; Château Margaux has Bordeaux's greatest house *(right, bottom)*.

Touring a region with more than 1,555 square km (600 square miles) of wine-growing country, 5,000 châteaux, and 100,000 vineyards producing around 70 million gallons of wine annually, you'll find it hard to resist sampling Bordeaux's liquid bounty—but where to start?

The best bet is to head north for the Route de Médoc (also called the Route des Châteaux or the Route des Grands-Crus), armed with maps and pointers from Bordeaux's helpful Office of Tourism (the *tourisme de viticole* desk is the place for this)—it's at 12 cours du XXX-Juillet in the city center of Bordeaux. Or check out the "Wine Tours" section of the official Bordeaux tourism website before you travel: 🌐 *www.bordeaux-tourisme.com*. A map is essential, as signage is poor and many "châteaux" are small manors hidden in the hills. Three main wine regions surround the city: Médoc to the northwest, St-Émilion to the east, and Graves-Sauternes to the south. Each boasts big-name vineyards, but remember that Baron Philippe de Rothschild, owner of Mouton-Rothschild, drank *vin ordinaire* at most meals.

I HEARD IT THROUGH THE GRAPEVINE

For more tips go to the Forums at 🌐 *www.fodors.com*. "Remember that almost all châteaux are closed from noon to 2 pm for lunch." —at. "We had a 3-hour private tour at Latour, with a movie, a tour, and a tasting. Everything was first-class—especially the wine! We also made same-day reservations at beautiful Pichon-Longeville." —oforparis!

BY APPOINTMENT ONLY

If you're planning on visiting any of the famous growers (or some of the lesser known ones for that matter), make sure to contact them ahead of time to arrange a *dégustation* (wine tasting)—many of the labels are "by appointment only" because they're too small to have full-time guides. Even the famous Château Mouton-Rothschild—visited by thousands—requires reservations, at least a week in advance for a regular tour and several weeks for a tour that includes the cellars. Conveniently, you can create your agenda online by booking your visits through the tourism office's website—it also supplies you with a printable map for your personalized itinerary.

VINEYARD TOURS

The staff at Bordeaux's tourism office is very helpful, and because many vineyards are inaccessible without a car or bike, the easiest way to reach those of the Route de Médoc and Gironde is to join one of the themed bus tours it sponsors.

Here's the main scoop: These tours depart from (and return to) the Office de Tourisme at 12 cours XXX-Juillet. In the off-season, same-day reservations can be had; in high season, make them in advance. There are daylong trips and also half-day versions (the latter usually from 2 to 6 in the afternoon).

In high season there's a tour every day; otherwise a few run per week. Most tours stop at two châteaux only—for instance, in the Médoc, you can visit the Château Palmer (Troisième Cru Classé) and the Château Lanessan (Cru Bourgeois)—but there are so many diverse tours that you could go on a different one each day for a week and not see the same domains. Tours are offered in several languages, including English, and usually a bus holds 40 participants.

You can view information regarding each tour (including availability) at 🌐 *www.bordeaux-tourisme.com*; then book your choice online.

THE GRAPE ESCAPE

Want to play *vigneron* (vintner) for a night? Some great vineyards welcome guests: here are two top options.

The 14th-century estate of Château Smith Haut Lafitte (*05–57–83–11–22* 🌐 *www.smith-haut-lafitte.com*) houses the very successful Les Sources de Caudalie hotel as well as a spa offering wine-based treatments (*05–57–83–83–83* 🌐 *www.sources-caudalie.com*).

Wine king Bernard Magrez has two rooms available at his 17th-century Château Fombrauge; book through his big Luxury Wine Tourism company (*05–57–26–43–06* 🌐 *www.luxurywinetourism.fr*).

Updated By Avery Sumner

When travelers arrive here, Bordeaux's countryside enchants them without their quite knowing why: what the French call *la douceur de vivre* (the sweetness of living) may have something to do with it.

To the east, extending their lush green rows to the rising sun, the renowned vineyards of the Route de Médoc entice visitors to discover magical medieval wine towns like St-Émilion. To the north, the Atlantic coast offers elite enclaves with white-sand beaches. In between is the metropolis of Bordeaux, replete with 18th-century landmarks and 20-year-old college students. Some complain that Bordeaux is like Paris without the good stuff, but if you're a wine lover it's still the doorway to paradise. And things are on the move in Bordeaux these days; it's consistently voted one of the top three French cities for young people to live in.

From the grandest *premiers grands crus*—the Lafite-Rothschilds, the Margaux—to the modest *supérieur* in your picnic basket, Bordeaux wines command respect around the world. So much so that oenophiles by the thousands come here to pay homage: to gaze at the noble symmetries of estate châteaux, whose rows of green-and-black vineyards radiate in every direction; to lower a nose deep into a well-swirled glass, inhaling the heady vapors of oak and almond and leather; and, finally, to reverently pack a few bloodline labels into a trunk or a suitcase for home.

The history, economy, and culture of Bordeaux have always been linked to the production and marketing of wine. The birth of the first Bordeaux winery is said to have occurred between AD 37 and 68, when the Romans called this land Burdigala. By the Middle Ages a steady flow of Bordeaux wines was headed to England, where it's still dubbed "claret," after *clairet,* a light red version from earlier days. During these centuries the region was also put on the tourist radar because it had become a major stopping-off point on the fabled Santiago de Compostela pilgrimage road. With all these allurements, it's no wonder the English fought for it so determinedly throughout the Hundred Years' War. This coveted corner of France became home to Eleanor of Aquitaine, and when she left her first husband, France's Louis VII, to marry Henry II of Normandy (later king of England), both she and the land came under English rule. Henry Plantagenet was, after all, a great-grandson of William the Conqueror, and the Franco-English ambiguity of the age exploded in a war that defined much of modern France and changed its face forever. Southwestern France was the stage upon which much of the war was conducted—hence the region's many castles and no end of sturdy churches dedicated to the noble families' cause.

What they sought, the world still seeks. The wines of Bordeaux set the standard against which other wines are measured, and to truly savor them you should drink them on-site—from the mouthful of golden Graves that eases the oysters down to the syrupy sip of Sauternes that civilizes the smooth gaminess of the foie gras to the last glass of Médoc paired with the salt-marsh lamb that leads to pulling the cork on a Pauillac—because there is the cheese tray yet to come. With a smorgasbord of 57 wine appellations to choose from, the revitalized city of Bordeaux, and the wine country that surrounds it with a veritable army of varietals, the entire region is intoxicating.

PLANNER

WHEN TO GO

Southwestern France can have bad storms even during the summer because of the nearby Atlantic. Happily, inclement weather doesn't hang around for long. French people usually vacation within their own national borders, so that means mid-July to the end of August is when you'll have company—lots of it—especially in the more famous destinations. Spring and fall are the best times to visit, when there aren't as many tourists and the weather is still pleasant. The *vendanges* (grape harvests) usually begin about mid-September in the Bordeaux region (though you can't visit the wineries at this time), and two weeks later in the Cognac region, to the north.

PLANNING YOUR TIME

How do you find the best vineyards (also referred to as *crus, clos,* and *domaines*) if you're based in Bordeaux? Easy—just head in any direction. The city is at the hub of a patchwork of vineyards: the Médoc peninsula to the northwest; Bourg and Blaye across the estuary; St-Émilion inland to the east; then, as you wheel around clockwise, Entre-Deux-Mers, Sauternes, and Graves.

The nearest vineyard to Bordeaux itself is one of the best: Haut-Brion, on the western outskirts of the city, and one of the five châteaux to be officially recognized as a *premier cru*, or first growth. There are only five premiers crus in all, and Haut-Brion is the only one not in the Médoc (Château Mouton-Rothschild, Château Margaux, Château Latour, and Château Lafite-Rothschild complete the list). The Médoc is subdivided into various appellations, or wine-growing districts, with their own specific characteristics and taste. Pauillac and Margaux host premiers crus; St-Julien and St-Estèphe possess many domaines of almost equal quality, followed by Listrac and Moulis; wines not quite so good are classed as Haut-Médoc or, as you move farther north, Médoc, pure and simple.

The Médoc wine region begins at the meeting point of the Dordogne and Garonne rivers, just north of the city. The D2 (aka the Route des Châteaux) cuts northwest through the majority of the wine country along the Gironde all the way to Talais, and the D1215 farther west runs through the other side of the region entering appellations like Listrac and Moulis.

Eastward lies the Libournais and St-Émilion regions, with Libourne being the main transportation (train) hub if you're heading to the stunning Vieille Ville (Old Town) of St-Émilion, which deserves at least a day, if not two. The surrounding vineyards see the merlot grape in control, and wines here often have more immediate appeal than those of the Médoc. There are several small appellations apart from St-Émilion itself, the most famous being Pomerol, whose Château Pétrus is the world's most expensive wine. South of St-Émilion is the region known as Entre-Deux-Mers ("between two seas"—actually two rivers, the Dordogne and Garonne), whose dry white wine is particularly flavorsome. This region is famed for its sweet wines, including the world's best, which hail from legendary Sauternes.

GETTING HERE AND AROUND

Bordeaux is one of France's main transportation hubs. However, once you get out into the surrounding Gironde—the "Wine Country"—you may find its seven regions (divided according to geography and the types of wine produced) difficult to reach without a car. Public buses run frequently through the countryside, but they don't necessarily stop in convenient places. The Conseil Général's comprehensive TransGironde website outlines your options in English. If you have access to a car, you'll find life much easier, particularly if you purchase a Michelin map; Map No. 234 covers a large portion of the southwest. Another option is to go on a bus tour organized by the Bordeaux tourism office.

AIR TRAVEL

Daily flights on Air France (🌐 *www.airfrance.com*) link Bordeaux and Paris; the Bordeaux airport is also served by several budget carriers—including easyJet (🌐 *www.easyjet.com*) and Ryanair (🌐 *www.ryanair.com*).

Airport Information Aéroport de Bordeaux-Mérignac. ☎ *05–56–34–50–50* 🌐 *www.bordeaux.aeroport.fr.*

BUS TRAVEL

The Conseil Général's TransGironde network of buses covers towns in the wine country and beach areas not well served by rail. The main Gare Routière (bus terminal) in Bordeaux is on Allées de Chartres (by Esplanade des Quinconces), near the Garonne River and Stalingrad Square.

Contacts TransGironde. ☎ *09–74–50–00–33* 🌐 *transgironde.gironde.fr.*

CAR TRAVEL

As the capital of southwest France, Bordeaux has superb highway links with Paris, Spain, and even the Mediterranean (the A62 expressway via Toulouse links up with the A61 to Narbonne). The A10 is the Paris–Bordeaux expressway, and the A63 south brings you past Bayonne. The

A20 south is the main route from Paris to just before Cahors, but it's an hour quicker to go south on the A10 through Tours and Poitiers.

TRAIN TRAVEL

The superfast TGV Atlantique service links Paris's Gare Montparnasse to Bordeaux, 585 km (364 miles) away, in 3½ hours. Trains link Bordeaux to Lyon (6½ hrs) and Nice (9 hrs) via Marseille as well. At least a dozen trains leave Bordeaux most days bound for St-Émilion, arriving 37 minutes later. If you're heading north to Pauillac (75 mins), there are also at least a dozen trains daily from Bordeaux.

Contacts Gare de Bordeaux St-Jean. ☎ *05–47–47–10–00.* **SNCF.** ☎ *3635 €0.34 per min* 🌐 *www.sncf.fr.* **TGV.** 🌐 *www.tgv.com.*

RESTAURANTS

Although countryside Médoc eateries are few, the city of Bordeaux is jammed with restaurants, especially around Place du Parlement; plus it has many cafés (notably in the Quartier St-Pierre) and bars (Place de la Victoire and Cours de la Somme). Not surprisingly, the wines of the region are often used as a base for regional food specialties. Lamprey, a good local fish, is often served in a red wine sauce as *lamproie à la Bordelaise*; and sturgeon is cooked in a white wine sauce, as *esturgeon à la Libournaise* (Libourne-style). As for meat, the lamb from Pauillac and the beef from Bazas and Aquitaine are rightly famous, as is the wood pigeon (*palombe*). And Bordeaux has spectacular desserts, such as *fanchonnette Bordelaise* (puff pastry in custard covered with meringue), *cannelé de Bordeaux* (small cakes, made in fluted molds, that can only be found here), and the famed *macarons* from St-Émilion, invented there by the town's Ursuline nuns in the 17th century.

HOTELS

Countryside hotels can be gorgeous—not to mention convenient for touring the region's famed vineyards—but basing yourself in Bordeaux city is definitely worth considering, because pickings for rural inns can be slim in summer months and nonexistent in winter, when most of them close. And don't fret about missing the vineyards. Many of the city hotels can create tours for you. *Hotel reviews have been shortened. For full information, visit Fodors.com.*

WHAT IT COSTS IN EUROS

	$	$$	$$$	$$$$
Restaurants	under €18	€18–€24	€25–€32	over €32
Hotels	under €106	€106–€145	€146–€215	over €215

Restaurant prices are the average cost of a main course at dinner or, if dinner is not served, at lunch. Hotel prices are the lowest cost of a standard double room in high season.

VISITOR INFORMATION

The Office de Tourisme in Bordeaux is the first place to head for further information on local and regional sights, including wine tours and tastings; a round-the-clock phone service in English is available. The office also organizes coach tours of the surrounding vineyards every

17

day in high season and nearly every Wednesday and weekends in the off-season. In addition to the main office (at 12 cours du XXX-Juillet), there are branches at the Gare de Bordeaux train station and the airport.

Contact Office of Tourism of Bordeaux. ☎ *05–56–00–66–00* 🌐 *www.bordeaux-tourisme.com.*

BORDEAUX

Bordeaux as a whole, rather than any particular points within it, is what you'll want to visit in order to understand why Victor Hugo described it as Versailles plus Antwerp, and why the painter Francisco de Goya, when exiled from his native Spain, chose it as his last home (he died here in 1828). The capital of southwest France and the region's largest city, Bordeaux remains synonymous with the wine trade: wine shippers have long maintained their headquarters along the banks of the Garonne, while buyers from around the world arrive for the huge biennial Vinexpo show (held in odd-number years).

Bordeaux is, admittedly, a less exuberant city than many others in France, but lively and stylish elements are making a dent in its conservative veneer. The cleaned-up riverfront is said by some, after a bottle or two, to exude an elegance reminiscent of St. Petersburg, and that aura of 18th-century élan also permeates the historic downtown sector—"le vieux Bordeaux"—where fine shops invite exploration. To the south of the city center are old docklands undergoing renewal—one train station has now been transformed into a big multiplex movie theater—but the area is still a bit shady. To get a feel for the historic port of Bordeaux, take the 90-minute boat trip that leaves Quai Louis-XVIII every weekday afternoon, or the regular passenger ferry that plies the Garonne between Quai Richelieu and the Pont d'Aquitaine in summer. A nice time to stroll around the city center is the first Sunday of the month, when it's pedestrian-only and vehicles are banned.

GETTING HERE AND AROUND

Served by both national airlines and budget carriers, the Aéroport de Bordeaux-Mérignac is 10 km (7 miles) west of Bordeaux; the airport's Jet'Bus loops between it and the city center every 45 minutes for €7.20 one-way, €12.30 return. You can also come by rail from Paris, with high-speed TGVs making the 3½-hour trip at least 16 times a day; the train deposits you at one of the country's major hubs, the Gare de Bordeaux St-Jean, about 3 km (2 miles) from downtown. Bordeaux's urban TBC buses (Nos. 7 and 8) will take you from the train station to the city center for less than €1.50; other buses, augmented by trams and commuter boats, help you get around the city itself with ease (🌐 *www.infotbc.com/en*). The TransGironde network of regional buses goes farther afield in the Gironde, and even to other nearby *départements*.

CLOSE UP

Red Gold: The Wines of Bordeaux

Everyone in Bordeaux celebrated the 2000 vintage as the "crop of the century," a wine that comes along once in a lifetime. But bringing everything down to earth are some new sour grapes: the increasingly loud whispers that Bordeaux may be "over."

In this world of nouvelle cuisine and uncellared wines, some critics feel the world has moved away from pricey, rich, red wines and more people are opting for younger choices from other lands. Be that as it may, if you have any aspirations to being a wine connoisseur, Bordeaux will always remain the bedrock of French viticulture.

It has been considered so ever since the credentials of Bordeaux wines were traditionally established in 1787. That year, Thomas Jefferson went down to the region from Paris and splurged on bottles of 1784 Château d'Yquem and Château Margaux, for prices that were, he reported, "indeed dear." Jefferson knew his wines: in 1855, both Yquem and Margaux were officially classified among Bordeaux's top five. And two centuries later, some of his very bottles (the authenticity of their provenance has since been disputed, as well as documented in the controversial book *The Billionaire's Vinegar*) fetched upward of $50,000 when offered in a high-flying auction in New York City.

As it turns out, Bordeaux's reputation dates from the Middle Ages. From 1152 to 1453, along with much of what is now western France, Bordeaux belonged to England. The light red wine then produced was known as *clairet*, the origin of our word "claret." Today no other part of France has such a concentration of top-class vineyards.

The versatile Bordeaux region yields sweet and dry whites and fruity or full-bodied reds from a huge domain extending on either side of the Gironde (Blaye and Bourg to the north, Médoc and Graves to the south) and inland along the Garonne (Sauternes) and Dordogne (St-Émilion, Fronsac, Pomerol) or in between these two rivers (Entre-Deux-Mers).

At the top of the government-supervised scale—which includes, in descending order, Appellation d'Origine Contrôlée (often abbreviated AOC), Vins de Pays, and Vin de France—are the fabled vintages of Bordeaux, leading off with Margaux. Sadly, the vineyards of Margaux are among the ugliest in France, lost amid the flat, dusty plains of the Médoc.

Other towns better represent Bordeaux's wine country. St-Émilion, with its cascading cobbled streets, is more beautiful; and even humble Sauternes is more interesting, though nothing in the latter would suggest the mind-boggling wealth lurking amid the picturesque vine-laden slopes and hollows. The village has a wineshop where bottles gather dust on rickety shelves, next to handwritten price tags demanding small fortunes.

Making Sauternes is a tricky business. Autumn mists steal up the valleys to promote *Botrytis cinerea*, a fungus known as *pourriture noble* or noble rot, which sucks moisture out of the grapes, leaving a high proportion of sugar. Sauternes's liquid gold is harvested in *vendanges* beginning in September and lasting to December. *Santé!*

EXPLORING

TOP ATTRACTIONS

Cathédrale St-André. This may not be one of France's finer Gothic cathedrals, but the intricate 14th-century chancel makes an interesting contrast with the earlier nave. Excellent stone carvings adorn the facade of the hefty edifice. You can climb the 15th-century, 160-foot **Tour Pey-Berland** for a stunning view of the city; it's open Tuesday–Sunday, 10–1:15 and 2–5. ✉ *Pl. Pey-Berland, Bordeaux* ☎ *05–56–81–26–25* *Tower €5.50.*

BORDEAUX'S BIG WINE BLOWOUT

The four-day Fête du Vin (Wine Festival) at the end of June sees glass-clinking merriment along the banks of the Garonne. The city's grandest square gets packed with workshops, booths, and thousands of wine lovers. Log on to 🌐 *www.bordeaux-fete-le-vin.com* for all the heady details.

École du Vin de Bordeaux. On tree-lined Cours du XXX-Juillet, not far from the banks of the Garonne and the main artery of the Esplanade des Quinconces, you'll find the École du Vin. Run by the CIVB (Conseil Interprofessionnel des Vins de Bordeaux, which oversees the Bordeaux wine trade), this school offers two-hour wine appreciation workshops (€39) as well as intensive programs and summer courses for professionals. The on-site Le Bar à Vin is a good place to sample reds (like Pauillac or St-Émilion), dry whites (like an Entre-Deux-Mers, Graves, or Côtes de Blaye), and sweet whites (like Sauternes or Loupiac). This can be particularly useful when trying to decide which of the 57 wine appellations to focus on during your trip. You can also make purchases at the school's **Vinothèque**. Further info is available right across the street at the city tourist office. ✉ *8 cours du XXX-Juillet, Bordeaux* ☎ *05–56–00–22–85* 🌐 *www.bordeaux.com/us/wineschool; www.vinotheque-bordeaux.com* ⏲ *Bar Mon.–Sat. 11–10; see school website for workshop schedules.*

Grand Théâtre. One block south of the École du Vin is the city's leading 18th-century monument: the Grand Théâtre, designed by Victor Louis and built between 1773 and 1780. It's the pride of the city, with an elegant exterior ringed by graceful Corinthian columns and a dazzling foyer with a two-winged staircase and a cupola. The theater hall has a frescoed ceiling with a shimmering chandelier composed of 14,000 Bohemian crystals. Contact the Bordeaux tourist office to learn about guided tours. ✉ *Pl. de la Comédie, Bordeaux* ☎ *05–56–00–85–95* 🌐 *www.opera-bordeaux.com.*

Haut-Brion. One of the region's most famous wine-producing châteaux is actually within the city limits: follow N250 southwest from central Bordeaux for 3 km (2 miles) to the district of Pessac, home to Haut-Brion, producer of the only non-Médoc wine to be ranked a *premier cru* (the most elite wine classification). It's claimed the very buildings surrounding the vineyards create their own microclimate, protecting the precious grapes and allowing them to ripen earlier. The white château looks out over the celebrated pebbly soil. The wines produced at **La Mission–Haut Brion (Domaine Clarence Dillon)**, across the road, are almost as sought-after. ✉ *135 av. Jean-Jaurès, Pessac* ☎ *05–56–00–29–30* 🌐 *www.*

Bordeaux

KEY
Tourist information

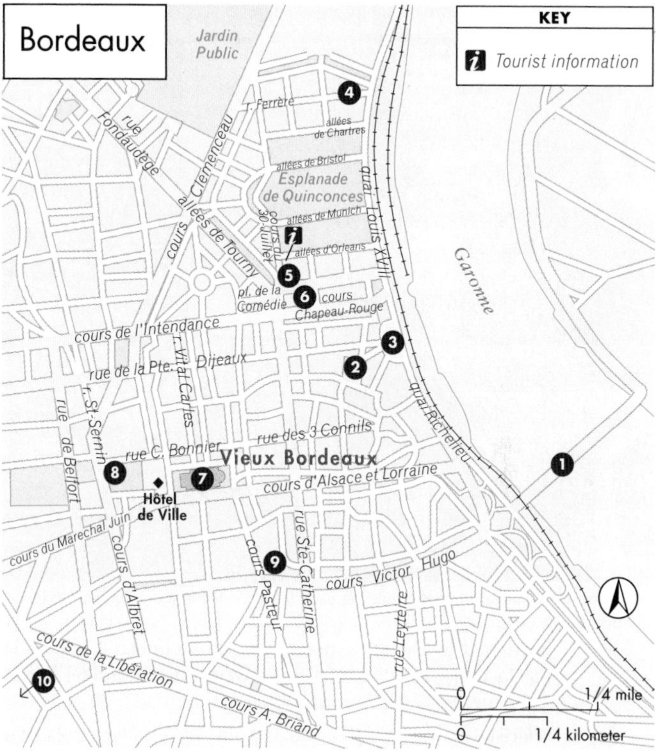

haut-brion.com *Free 1-hr visits with tasting, weekdays by appointment* *Closed mid-July–mid-Aug.*

Musée d'Aquitaine. Two blocks south of the Cathédrale St-André, this excellent museum takes you on a trip through Bordeaux's history, with emphasis on Roman, medieval, Renaissance, colonial, and 20th-century daily life. The detailed prehistoric section almost saves you a trip to Lascaux II, which is reproduced here in part. ✉ *20 cours Pasteur, Bordeaux* ☎ *05–56–01–51–00* *www.musee-aquitaine-bordeaux.fr* *Free* *Tues.–Sun. 11–6.*

Musée des Beaux-Arts. Bordeaux was one of 15 French cities chosen by Napoléon to showcase his war-acquired works (most notably from Italy) along with bits of existing royal art, so this museum has a fetching collection. Expanded to include pieces from the 15th century to the present, it now displays important paintings by Paolo Veronese (*St. Dorothy*), Camille Corot (*Bath of Diana*), and Odilon Redon (*Apollo's Chariot*), plus sculptures by Auguste Rodin. Located near the Cathédrale St-André and ornate Hôtel de Ville, the Museé des Beaux-Arts is flanked by tidy gardens. ✉ *20 cours d'Albret, Bordeaux* ☎ *05–56–10–20–56* *www.musba-bordeaux.fr* *Free* *Wed.–Mon. 11–6.*

Place de la Bourse. The centerpiece of the left bank is this open square built in 1729–33. Ringed with large-windowed buildings, it was beautifully

At the end of June, Bordeaux becomes one big party thanks to the four-day Fête du Vin (Wine Festival).

designed by the era's most esteemed architect, Jacques Gabriel, father of Jacques-Ange Gabriel (who went on to remodel Paris's Place de la Concorde). ✉ *Bordeaux*.

Place du Parlement. A few blocks southeast of Place de la Bourse, Place du Parlement is also ringed by elegant 18th-century structures and packed with lively outdoor cafés. ✉ *Bordeaux*.

WORTH NOTING

Musée d'Art Contemporain (*Contemporary Art Center*). Just north of the Esplanade des Quinconces (a sprawling square), this two-story museum is imaginatively housed in a converted 19th-century spice warehouse—the Entrepôt Lainé. Many expositions here showcase cutting-edge artists who invariably festoon the huge expanse of the square with hanging ropes, ladders, and large video screens. ✉ *7 rue Ferrère, Bordeaux* ☎ *05–56–00–81–50* 🎟 *Free, €5 for temporary expositions* ⏲ *Tues. and Thurs.–Sun. 11–6, Wed. 11–8.*

Pont de Pierre. For a view of the picturesque quayside, stroll across the Garonne on this bridge, built on the orders of Napoléon between 1810 and 1821, and until 1965 the only bridge across the river. ✉ *Bordeaux*.

WHERE TO EAT

$$$ FRENCH ✕ **Baud et Millet.** With a cellar full of *fromage*—and a vast wine stock that you peruse in lieu of a list—Baud et Millet is a good place to get acquainted with some of the 246 different French cheeses that Charles de Gaulle famously blamed for making this such a complex, and thus difficult, country to govern. You must buzz to gain entry, and that's just the first element of the unique experience here. Order from the cheese buffet and serve yourself from the downstairs cellar, or start with a cherry tomato and Roquefort *clafoutis*, then move on to Camembert flambéed in Calvados. For €45 you can try a *dégustation* of nine cooked cheese dishes. Genuine stinky cheese lovers should know some cheeses here aren't as potent as can be had elsewhere in France. *Average main: €25* ✉ *19 rue Huguerie, Bordeaux* ☎ *05–56–79–05–77* ⏲ *Closed late Dec.–early Jan.*

$$ BRASSERIE

Café Français. Situated on a *grande place* in the Vielle Ville, with cathedral views and a traditional menu of solid sustenance, this venerable bistro attracts those looking for an all-day mixture of café and restaurant. It's the quintessential spot to people-watch over a coffee or meal. Try for a table on the terrace. The view over Place Pey-Berland is never less than diverting; however, some say you end up paying for the *place* more than the plate. *Average main: €20* ✉ *5–6 pl. Pey-Berland, Bordeaux* ☎ *05–56–52–96–69* *No credit cards.*

$$$ FRENCH

La Tupina. Under the eye of flamboyant owner Jean-Pierre Xiradakis, *cuisine de terroir* is served up at this classic restaurant (the name means "kettle") on one of Bordeaux's oldest streets. Dried herbs hang from the ceiling, a Provençal grandfather clock ticks off the minutes, and an antique fireplace sports a grill bearing sizzling morsels of duck and chicken. Like the room itself, the menu aspires to *nostalgie,* and it succeeds. On the same street (No. 34) is the owner's fetching—and cheaper—Bar Cave de la Monnaie. You can also dine or shop at his *épicerie*, Le Comestible (No. 3), which is lined with bistro tables and jars of foie gras, cassoulet, and other regional sundries. Copies of this business-savvy chef's southwestern cuisine cookbook are sold at the épicerie. *Average main: €31* ✉ *6 rue Porte-de-la-Monnaie, Bordeaux* ☎ *05–56–91–56–37* 🌐 *www.latupina.com* *Reservations essential.*

17

$$$$ FRENCH Fodor's Choice ★

Le Chapon-Fin. Some say you haven't really been to Bordeaux if you haven't been to Le Chapon-Fin—an epicurean indulgence, housed in one of Bordeaux's most historically esteemed establishments, where guests once included wealthy wine merchants, elite transatlantic travelers, and cultural icons such as Sarah Bernhardt and Toulouse-Lautrec. Founded in 1825, this was one of the first 33 restaurants crowned by Michelin in 1933. Reopened in 1987, guests are now served from Chef Nicolas Nguyen Van Hai's refined menu in the extraordinary, original rococo grotto *salle* (room). Expect offerings like civet of hare (a kingly, 500-year-old dish of whole jackrabbit cut into pieces and then cooked for days in fine wine thickened with blood and liver). The wine list, not surprisingly, boasts the region's best vintages. *Average main: €38* ✉ *5 rue Montesquieu, Bordeaux* ☎ *05–56–79–10–10* 🌐 *www.chapon-fin.com* ⏲ *Closed Sun., Mon., and Aug.* *Reservations essential.*

$$$ MODERN FRENCH

L'Estacade. *Le tout Bordeaux* comes to this trendy glass-encased restaurant, which hangs spectacularly over the Garonne River, for its privileged views of Bordeaux proper and the 18th-century Place de la Bourse on the opposite bank. The setting is sleek modern with a casual, sometimes noisy crowd. The cuisine is creative but not edgy (imagine sesame-and-soy-marinated veal, or mullet tartare with cream and fish eggs), while the wine list focuses on young Bordeaux. The city lights

Bordeaux doesn't have many grand châteaux-hotels, but the Grand Barrail Château Hôtel & Spa is a winner.

make views better at night. *Average main: €29* *Quai de Queyries, Bordeaux* *05–57–54–02–50* *www.lestacade.com.*

$ CAFÉ **l'Oiseau Cabosse.** This straight-up organic restaurant and coffee bar is a good option for a light meal. With its kind and spunky service, chic outside terrace, and interesting location in the bourgeois-bohemian Quartier de la Grosse Cloche (Big Clock neighborhood), it's a welcome find in the city. Try the duck confit parmentier, curry-and-leek quiche, or a fresh baked dessert. Don't miss the organic, artisanal cola or 100% pure cocoa hot chocolate. *Average main: €12* *30 rue Ste-Colombe, Bordeaux* *05–57–14–02–07* *Closed Mon.*

WHERE TO STAY

$ HOTEL **Acanthe Hotel.** Just steps from Place de la Bourse, this budget hotel is an extremely convenient choice if you're looking for something less than grand; renovated rooms have air-conditioning, double-paned windows, environmentally friendly wall paint, and freshened bathrooms—top-floor rooms also have views over the neighboring rooftops. **Pros:** genial staff; breakfast (extra charge) includes an organic option. **Cons:** some rooms feel a bit claustrophobic; gets a lot of street noise. *Rooms from: €76* *12 rue Saint Remi, Bordeaux* *05–56–81–66–58* *www.acanthe-hotel-bordeaux.com* *20 rooms* *No meals.*

$$$ HOTEL **Burdigala.** The modern exterior may be bland, but the interior of this five-star M Gallery Collection hotel dispels any risk of dullness. **Pros:** soundproof rooms; in the heart of Bordeaux, close to Gambetta Square. **Cons:** if you want old-world charm, this is not the place; room styles vary. *Rooms from: €205* *115 rue Georges-Bonnac, Bordeaux*

☏ *05–56–90–16–16* 🌐 *www.burdigala.com* *68 rooms, 15 suites* 🍴 *No meals.*

$$$$ HOTEL **Grand Hôtel de Bordeaux & Spa.** Festooned in luxury fabrics and 18th-century furnishings, this posh extravaganza, designed by France's über-chic Jacque Garcia, put Bordeaux back on the world scene with its veritable army of restaurants and bars along with a swanky Roman bath–inspired spa—all just steps from the city's Golden Triangle shopping district. **Pros:** marble bathrooms and loads of in-room amenities; deluxe service; superb central location. **Cons:** some rooms lack natural light; superior rooms are small (but executive rooms let you sprawl out). $ *Rooms from: €395* ✉ *2-5 pl. de la Comédie, Bordeaux* ☏ *05–57–30–44–44* 🌐 *www.ghbordeaux.com* *121 rooms, 27 suites* 🍴 *No meals.*

$$ HOTEL **Quality Hôtel Bordeaux Centre.** At the heart of Bordeaux's pedestrian center, this fully modernized hotel—in a 19th-century building in the old part of town—has compact, deep-toned rooms, and a helpful reception staff; it's the place to stay if you want businesslike contemporary comfort without original character. **Pros:** convenient location beside the Grand Théâtre; functional rooms. **Cons:** somewhat generic furnishings; parking is five minutes away. $ *Rooms from: €135* ✉ *27 rue du Parlement-Ste-Catherine, Bordeaux* ☏ *05–56–81–95–12* 🌐 *www.qualityhotelbordeauxcentre.com* *84 rooms* 🍴 *No meals.*

17

NIGHTLIFE AND PERFORMING ARTS

Aux Quatre Coins du Vin. This sleek wine and tapas bar has dispensing machines that allow you to taste as many wines as you want in a single sitting. ✉ *8 rue de la Devise, Bordeaux* ☏ *05–57–34–37–29.*

Comptoir du Jazz. Near the station, this is the place not only for jazz, but also blues, soul, and funk. Log on to the website for the latest lineup. ✉ *58–59 quai Paludate, Bordeaux* ☏ *05–56–49–15–55* 🌐 *portdelalune-comptoirdujazz.com.*

Grand Théâtre. Arguably one of the most beautiful historic theaters in Europe, the Grand Théâtre puts on performances of French plays and, occasionally, operas. The venue (which can be visited on guided tours) is an 18th-century showpiece studded with marble muses. ✉ *Pl. de la Comédie, Bordeaux* ☏ *05–56–00–85–95* 🌐 *www.opera-bordeaux.com.*

l'Apollo. Named after Harlem's Apollo Theater, this casual, friendly pub comes to life around aperitif hour. Once the night gets going, prepare for some serious funk and soul music. ✉ *19 pl. Fernand-Lafargue, Bordeaux* ☏ *05–56–01–25–05* 🌐 *www.apollobar.fr.*

Le Bistrot. This is *the* all-night club for hip-hop, disco, and theme nights like "mother funk-in" and "prohibition"—but come dressed up, as there's no admittance without a *tenue correcte* (avoid running shoes). ✉ *50 quai de Paludate, Bordeaux* ☏ *06–70–71–02–25.*

SHOPPING

Between the cathedral and the Grand Théâtre are numerous pedestrian streets (Rue Ste-Catherine being the biggest), where stylish stores and clothing boutiques abound. Bordeaux may favor understatement, but there's no lack of elegance in and around its Golden Triangle shopping district.

Bear in mind that the *soldes* (sales) start in France at the height of summer, especially just before the Bastille (July 14) weekend.

Baillardran. With five stores in Bordeaux alone, Baillardran is going to be hard to walk by without at least looking in its windows at those indigenous sweet delights, *cannelés de Bordeaux*. Much like a Doric column in miniature, the small indented, caramelized cakes, made with vanilla and a dash of rum, are a delicious regional specialty. ✉ *55 cours de l'Intendance, Bordeaux* ☎ *05–56–52–92–64* 🌐 *www.baillardran.com.*

Fromagerie Deruelle. For a grand selection of cheeses—along with raw milk, smoked-sea-salt butter, bulk honey, and all things creamy and tasty—stop in at Elodie Deruelle's shop, Fromagerie Deruelle. ✉ *66 rue du Pas-Saint-Georges, Bordeaux* ☎ *05–57–83–04–15.*

Grand Déballage de Brocante. Within the shadow of the church of Saint Michel, a few blocks south of the Pont de Pierre and just off the river, one of the country's largest flea markets operates every second Sunday during the months of March, June, September, and December—all day long. Year-round, a weekly Sunday flea market is also held here, which is just the ticket if you're looking for real bargains away from the storefronts or need a nice excuse to explore the historic St-Michel quarter. ✉ *Pl. St-Michel, Bordeaux.*

Jean d'Alos Fromager-Affineur. For an exceptional selection of cheeses, go to Jean d'Alos Fromager-Affineur. ✉ *4 rue Montesquieu, Bordeaux* ☎ *05–56–44–29–66.*

La Fabrique Pains et Bricoles. Want Bordeaux's best bread to go with your cheese? Get in line. Apparently, the word's out about La Fabrique Pains et Bricoles because the queue is out the door at this fine bakery—and that's always a good sign. ✉ *47 rue du Pas-Saint-Georges, Bordeaux* ☎ *05–56–44–84–26.*

Vinothèque. Inside the École du Vin, Vinothèque sells top-ranked Bordeaux wines. ✉ *8 cours du XXX-Juillet, Bordeaux* ☎ *05–57–10–41–41* 🌐 *www.vinotheque-bordeaux.com.*

ROUTE DU MÉDOC AND THE WINE COUNTRY

All along the western side of the Gironde estuary south, until you hit the meeting point of the Dordogne and Garonne rivers just north of Bordeaux city, you will encounter the almost mythical Médoc wine region. Farthest north is the Médoc appellation itself. To the south of this, the Paulliac appellation surrounds the Saint-Estéphe and St-Julien appellations, which lie nearer to the estuary. Closer to Bordeaux, and just south of the Paulliac region, is the conglomeration of the Listrac, Moulis, Margaux, and (nearest to the city along the Garonne) the Haut-Médoc appellations.

Above the city, the D2—or Route des Châteaux—veers northwest through most of the wine country along the Gironde all the way to Talais, and the D1215 (farther west) runs through the other side of the region, giving access to appellations like Listrac and Moulis, which the D2 bypasses.

Wines from the Médoc are made predominantly from the Cabernet Sauvignon grape, and can taste dry, even austere, when young. The better ones often need 15 to 25 years before "opening up" to reveal their full spectrum of complex flavors. More celebrated vintages are found 35 km (22 miles) to the east of the city in the medieval region of St-Émilion. Here, vineyards that are family owned and relatively small—on average, just 17 acres each—are divided into two appellations, St-Émilion and St-Émilion Grand Cru. At the region's heart lies the beautiful wine town of St-Émilion.

TIP→ If you want to get into the Médoc from Bordeaux by car make sure to get off the road that encircles Bordeaux (the "Rocade") using Sortie (Exit) 7.

MARGAUX

30 km (18.6 miles) north of Bordeaux.

Margaux is home to the eponymous appellation that landed more châteaux in the original wine classification of 1855 than any other in Bordeaux. The appellation was a favorite of Thomas Jefferson, who supposedly ordered several cases of the 1784 Château Margaux during a visit to the region. But the unexciting village of Margaux itself still wouldn't be much without the famed terroir that surrounds it.

17

GETTING HERE

TransGironde buses connect Bordeaux with Margaux (90 mins, €2.50) three times a day. The more expensive TER train (€7.50) runs roughly every hour and gets you here in 45 minutes.

EXPLORING

Château Lascombes. This classically elegant 17th-century château is actually a facade for a sleek and modern operation. Historically considered an underperformer according to its second grand cru classification, Château Lascombes welcomes novices, wine lovers, and professionals to take a free guided tour of the vineyards and cellars followed by a tasting (by appointment only). ✉ *Margaux* ☎ *05–57–88–70–66* 🌐 *www.chateau-lascombes.com.*

Château Margaux. Housed in a magnificent neoclassical building from 1810, Château Margaux is recognized as a producer of premiers crus, and its wine ranks with Graves's Haut-Brion as one of Bordeaux's five finest reds. As with most of the top Bordeaux châteaux, visits and tastings are by appointment only. While there's no charge for these, appointments are reserved for serious seekers accompanied by professionals in the trade. ✉ *Margaux* ☎ *05–57–88–83–83* 🌐 *www.chateau-margaux.com.*

Château Palmer. It is said that in some years the wines of Château Palmer (classified as a third cru) can rival those of neighboring Château Margaux (a premier cru). Since 2004, the estate has been under the direction of a young agronomist-oenologist who has overseen a revitalization of the operation; it accepts visitors at no charge, Monday through Friday

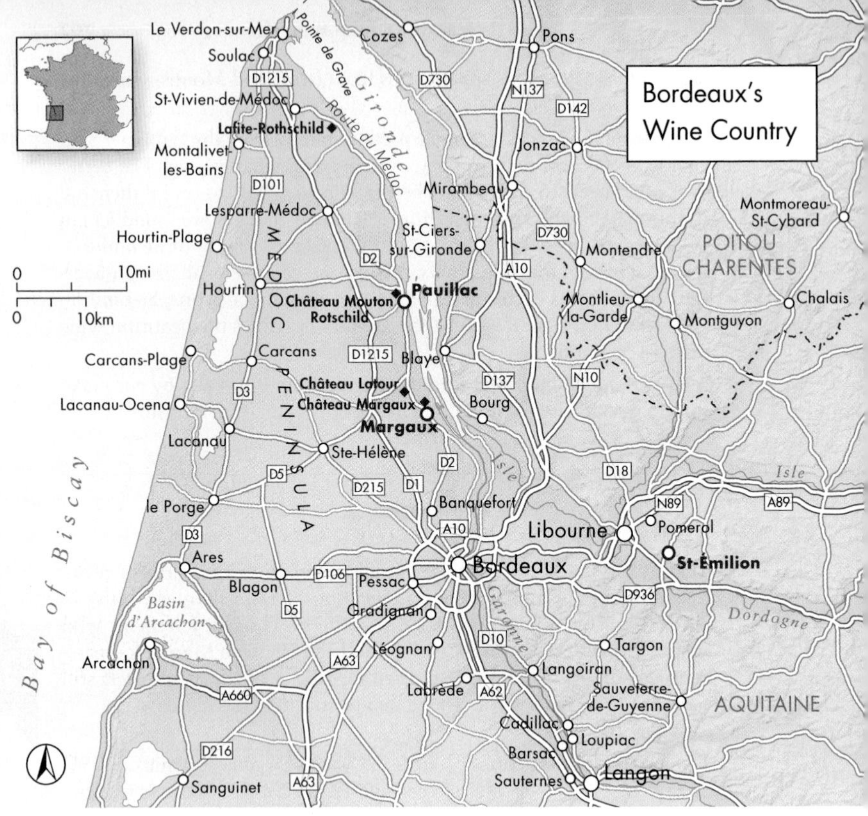

by appointment. ✉ *Margaux* ☎ *05–57–88–72–72* 🌐 *www.chateau-palmer.com.*

WHERE TO STAY

$$ B&B/INN **Villa St. Simon.** If you want a convenient base for exploring all of the Médoc, it's worth taking a 15-minute ferry ride across the Gironde estuary to Blaye, a pretty waterfront town that provides a refreshing change of pace in an otherwise drab area. **Pros:** town is home to an UNESCO-designated citadel; quality on-site bistro; personalized service; access to value-for-money wines. **Cons:** not the place for chichi châteaux seekers; must cross river to access Médoc vineyards. $ *Rooms from: €120* ✉ *8 cours du Generale De Gaulle, Blaye, Margaux* ✣ *16 km (10 miles) north east of Margaux* ☎ *05–57–42–99–66* 🌐 *villastsimon.com* *5 rooms, 10 apartments* *No meals* *No credit cards.*

PAUILLAC

90 km (56 miles) north of Bordeaux.

Pauillac lays claim to three of the five Bordeaux grand crus—Lafite-Rothschild, Latour, and Mouton-Rothschild. It's said that Pauillac wines are textbook Bordeaux in style, with the ability to age and evolve for decades. But if the posh prices of these top reds aren't for you, ask about bike rentals at the town's tourist office and pedal off to visit any of the slightly less expensive wineries nearby. Pauillac is the prettiest of all the towns and villages in the Médoc, so just strolling the riverfront or lingering at a waterside restaurant has its own rewards.

GETTING HERE

If you're heading north, you'll have to make your way to or through Pauillac. TransGironde runs buses from Bordeaux three times a day (2 hrs, €2.50). TER trains cost extra (€10.20), but they're faster (1 hr, 15 mins) and more frequent; at least 12 from Bordeaux arrive daily at the Gare de Pauillac on 2 bis, place Verdun.

Visitor Information **Pauillac Tourist Office.** ☎ *05–56–59–03–08* 🌐 *www.pauillac-medoc.com.*

17

EXPLORING

Château Lafite-Rothschild. Lafite-Rothschild is among the most resonant names in the wine world. Even by the giddy standards of the Médoc, Lafite—owned by the Rothschild family since 1868 and a recorded producer since 1234—is a temple of wine making at its most memorable. Prices may be sky-high, but no one fortunate enough to sample one of the classic vintages will forget the experience in a hurry. Too bad you can't visit the family château on the grounds—its rooms are the defining examples of *le style Rothschild,* one of the most opulent styles of 19th-century interior decoration. ✉ *Pauillac* ☎ *05–56–59–26–83* 🌐 *www.lafite.com* 🎫 *Free* ⏲ *Nov.–July, by appointment only at 2 and 3:30; reserve at least 2 wks in advance.*

Château Latour. Tastings and tours at the renowned Château Latour are typically free, but very selective—you have to be a serious taster, accompanied by a guide or professional in the wine trade, and you will be expected to make a purchase. Reservations are also required, and these must sometimes be made a month in advance. ✉ *Saint-Lambert, Pauillac* ☎ *05–56–73–19–80* 🌐 *www.chateau-latour.com.*

Château Mouton-Rothschild. Most of the great vineyards in this area are strictly private, although owners are usually receptive to inquiries from bona fide wine connoisseurs. One, however, has long boasted a welcoming visitor center: Mouton-Rothschild, whose eponymous wine was brought to perfection in the 1930s by that flamboyant figure Baron Philippe de Rothschild. The baron's daughter, Philippine, continues to lavish money and love on this growth, so wine fans flock here for either the one-hour visit, which includes a tour of the cellars, *chai* (wine warehouse), and museum, or the slightly longer version that's topped off with a tasting. ✉ *Le Pouyalet, Pauillac* ☎ *05–56–73–21–29* 🌐 *www.chateau-mouton-rothschild.com* 🎫 *€6.50; €16 with tasting* ⏲ *Mon.–Thurs. 9:30–11 and 2–4, Fri. 9:30–11 and 2–3, by appointment only; reserve at least 2 wks in advance.*

WHERE TO STAY

$$$ HOTEL **Château Cordeillan-Bages.** Though the clean-lined, contemporary interior of this 17th-century, stone-faced, wine-producing mansion may not speak to everyone, the vines growing right up to the property, the luxury rooms, the sommelier's dream of a wine cellar (with over 200 different Champagnes alone), and the celebrated restaurant are definite inducements. **Pros:** lovely marble building; tranquil location; top chef in residence; expert wine-tasting and discovery courses offered. **Cons:** somewhat faded modern decor; remote with airport 45 km (27 miles) away—but you could ask to use the château's helipad. *Rooms from: €203 ✉ Rte. des Châteaux, 1½ km (1 mile) south of town, Pauillac ☎ 05–56–59–24–24 🌐 www.cordeillanbages.com ⏲ Closed late Dec.–mid-Mar. 24 rooms, 4 suites No meals.*

$ HOTEL **France & Angleterre.** Occupying a low-slung, 19th-century building that overlooks the quaint waterfront and Gironde estuary, this low-key spot is a convenient choice if you wish to explore Pauillac's winding streets. **Pros:** central location; estuary views. **Cons:** small, generic rooms; budget furnishings. *Rooms from: €77 ✉ 3 quai Albert-Pichon, Pauillac ☎ 05–56–59–01–20 🌐 www.hoteldefrance-angleterre.com ⏲ Closed mid-Dec.–mid-Jan. 28 rooms No meals.*

ST-ÉMILION

74 km (41 miles) southeast of Pauillac, 35 km (22 miles) east of Bordeaux.

Suddenly the sun-fired flatlands of Pomerol break into hills and send you tumbling into St-Émilion. This jewel of a town has old buildings of golden stone, ruined town walls, well-kept ramparts offering magical views, and a church hewn into a cliff. Sloping vineyards invade from all sides, and thousands of tourists invade down the middle, many thirsting for the red wine and *macarons* that bear the town's name. The medieval streets, delightfully cobbled (though often very steep), are filled with craft shops, bakeries, cafés, restaurants, and—of course—wine stores (St-Émilion reaches maturity earlier than other Bordeaux reds and is often better value for the money than Médoc or Graves). For the best export prices try Ets Martin (*25 rue Guadet 🌐 www.martinvins.com*), or climb the stairs to the *cremant* (sparkling wine) specialist and its *bar a bulles* (bubbles bar) Les Cordaliers (*🌐 www.lescordeliers.com*), where you can buy a glass or bottle of Bordeaux's bubbly to sip in a lovely courtyard beneath 13th-century cloister ruins. Note that the town's Office de Tourisme organizes tours of the pretty local vineyards, as well as assorted wine-theme classes and workshops. It also rents bikes (€15 per day) if you'd prefer to explore the surrounding area independently.

GETTING HERE

Direct TER trains from Bordeaux depart at least a dozen times daily during the week and six times daily on weekends and holidays (37 mins, €9.50). It will cost you €2.50 if you opt to take a TransGironde bus from Bordeaux to St-Émilion, the trip being a two-pronged affair with a changeover in Libourne and a total travel time of about an hour.

Visitor Information St-Émilion Tourist Office. *☎ 05–57–55–28–28 🌐 www.saint-emilion-tourisme.com.*

A Fodor's.com member, t56gf, captured the medieval beauty of cobblestoned St-Émilion in this photo.

EXPLORING

Château Angelus. Named for the prayer-signaling church bells that can be heard from its vineyards, this fabled château is a premier grand cru property. ✉ *St-Émilion* ☎ *05–57–24–71–39* 🌐 *www.angelus.com.*

Château Ausone. Just south of the town walls, Château Ausone is an estate that is ranked with Château Angelus as a producer of St-Émilion's finest wines. ✉ *St-Émilion* ☎ *05–57–24–24–57* 🌐 *chateau-ausone.fr.*

Château du Roi (*King's Castle*). A stroll along the 13th-century ramparts takes you to the Château du Roi. To this day nobody knows whether it was Henry III of England or King Louis VIII of France who chose the site and ordered its building. ✉ *St-Émilion.*

Église Monolithe (*Monolithic Church*). One of Europe's largest underground churches, the Église Monolithe was hewn out of the rock face between the 9th and 12th century by monks faithful to the memory of St-Émilion, an 8th-century hermit and miracle worker. Its spire-top *clocher* (bell tower) rises out of the bedrock, dominating the center of town. The church may only be visited on a guided tour. ✉ *Pl. du Marché, St-Émilion* 🎫 *€ 7* ⏲ *July–Aug., hourly tours daily 10:30–5; Sept.–June, tours daily at 11:30, 2:30, and 4.*

Place du Marché. From the castle ramparts, cobbled steps lead down to Place du Marché, a leafy square where cafés remain open late into the balmy summer night—just be prepared for the inflated prices they charge. ✉ *St-Émilion.*

WHERE TO EAT

$ BISTRO **Chai Pascal.** This cozy yet stylish restaurant and wine bar is popular with locals in the wine trade. Wood tables, lounge chairs, and understated artwork on the original stone walls give it a casual, intellectual vibe. The menu is limited, but made fresh and very good value compared to the generally elevated prices of St-Émilion. Free Wi-Fi is available. *Average main: €17 37 rue Guadet, St-Émilion 05–57–24–52–45 www.chai-pascal.com Closed Sun. Nov.–June. No dinner Mon.*

$ BRASSERIE **Chez Germaine.** Family cooking and regional dishes are the focus at this central St-Émilion eatery, which serves lunch only. The upstairs dining room and the terrace are both pleasant places to enjoy reasonably priced set menus. Grilled meats and fish are house specialties; for dessert, order the almond *macarons*. *Average main: €16 13 pl. du Clocher, St-Émilion 05–57–74–49–34 Closed mid Nov.–mid Feb. No dinner.*

WHERE TO STAY

$ HOTEL **Auberge de la Commanderie.** Close to the ramparts, this 19th-century hotel has a gorgeous, white-shuttered facade that blends in beautifully with St-Émilion's stonework. **Pros:** free parking; inside the village. **Cons:** some rooms are bare-bones and very small; mod color scheme may be too bold for some tastes. *Rooms from: €90 Rue des Cordeliers, St-Émilion 05–57–24–70–19 www.aubergedelacommanderie.com Closed mid-Dec.–mid-Feb. 17 rooms No meals.*

$$$$ HOTEL Fodor's Choice ★ **Grand Barrail Château Hôtel & Spa.** Presiding over the picturesque vineyards encircling St-Émilion, this fairy-tale Belle Époque château has gorgeous guest rooms that are at once classic and contemporary (for the full storybook experience, ask for one in the main 19th-century building rather than the modern luxury annex). **Pros:** expansive vineyard views; special spa packages; golf and hot-air balloon rides nearby. **Cons:** pricey; ambience so fairytale-esque it borders on unoriginal. *Rooms from: €340 Rte. de Libourne, St-Émilion 4 km (2½ miles) northwest of St-Émilion on D243 05–57–55–37–00 www.grand-barrail.com 41 rooms, 5 suites No meals.*

$$$ HOTEL **Le Relais de Franc Mayne.** Once a relay station for weary travelers on an ancient Gallo-Roman path, this luxury boutique hotel in the vineyards surrounding St-Émilion today provides considerably more comfort with its eclectic-chic rooms and elegant dining and lounge areas. **Pros:** walking or biking distance to town through quintessential vineyards; chemical-free natural swimming pool. **Cons:** room designs are themed (African lodge, pop art, Indian fusion, . . .); overly shiny welcome center distracts. *Rooms from: €200 14 la Gomerie, St-Émilion 05–57–24–62–61 www.relaisfrancmayne.com 12 rooms No meals.*

$$$$ HOTEL Fodor's Choice ★ **L'Hostellerie de Plaisance.** Flaunting a unique interior design masterminded by Alberto Pinto and an elite location in the upper part of town, just across the way from the famous Église Monolithe, this stunning Italianate mansion has long been considered the top hotel in St-Émilion. **Pros:** superstar style; ideally located in St-Émilion proper. **Cons:** certain rooms are small; pricey (breakfast alone is €30 per person). *Rooms from: €390 3 pl. du Clocher, St-Émilion 05–57–55–07–55 www.hostelleriedeplaisance.com Closed mid-Dec.–Feb. 14 rooms, 3 suites No meals.*

18

THE DORDOGNE

WELCOME TO THE DORDOGNE

TOP REASONS TO GO

★ **Fantastic food:** Périgord truffles, foie gras, walnuts, plums, and myriad species of mushrooms jostle for attention on restaurant menus here—and the goose-liver pâté is as good as it gets.

★ **Rock stars:** Lascaux is like the Louvre of Paleolithic art, and millions have witnessed prehistory writ large on its spectacularly painted cave walls.

★ **Religious Rocamadour:** Climb toward heaven up the towering cliff to place St-Amadour's seven chapels and you might be transported to a better place.

★ **Sarlat's Cité Médiévale:** Feast your eyes on Sarlat's honey-color houses and 16th-century streets, and then just feast at the hundred or so wine and foie gras shops.

★ **Versailles in the sky:** A dizzying 400 feet above the Dordogne River, the Jardin de Marqueyssac is a glorious garden with a 3-km (2-mile) maze of topiaries, parterres, and hedges.

1 Western Dordogne. The western part of the Dordogne is rife with castles, like those at Monbazillac and Biron; and lands cultivated by peasant farmers for centuries ring *bastide*towns, such as Monpazier, which were once heavily fortified. Heading southeast, the Lot Valley—a 50-km (31-mile) gorge punctuated by medieval villages—is anchored by the lively town of Cahors. Nearby St-Cirq-Lapopie is like a Renaissance-era time machine, while Rocamadour's sky-touching Cité Religieuse is one of France's most famous pilgrimage shrines.

GETTING ORIENTED

Just northeast of Bordeaux, the region of Périgord is famed for its prehistoric art, truffle-rich cuisine, and once-upon-a-time villages. The best of these delights are found in the beloved *département* (province) called the Dordogne. Part of the Aquitaine region, this living postcard is threaded by the Dordogne River, which, after its descent from the mountainous Massif Central, weaves westward past prehistoric sites like Lascaux. Astounding, too, are the medieval cliff-hewn villages like Rocamadour—provided that you manage to peer through the crowds in high season.

2 Eastern Périgord. You'll have a tough time figuring out which sector of the Dordogne is the most beautiful, but many give the prize to the Périgord Noir. Immerse yourself in the past at Sarlat-la-Canéda, a regional capital so beautifully preserved that film crews flock here for its 16th- and 17th-century turrets and towers. Nearby are the riverside village of La Roque-Gageac and the hilltop castle at Beynac. To the north is the Vézère Valley, the prehistoric capital of France, home to fabled Lascaux. Beyond lies the thriving little city of Périgueux.

EATING AND DRINKING WELL IN THE DORDOGNE

The Dordogne, or as the French like to call it, the Périgord, is considered by those in the know to have one of the best regional cuisines in the country. Local chefs celebrate the area's natural abundance in epicurean preparations and simple peasant dishes alike.

The best pâté de fois gras comes from the Dordogne *(above)*; this region is truffle heaven *(right, top)*; top wines hail from Cahors. *(right, bottom)*

The rich resources of the Périgord are legendary: forests and fields are alive with wild game feasting on the nuts and leaves of chestnut, walnut, and oak trees, which encourages the growth of rare mushrooms and coveted truffles. The picturesque, winding rivers are home to trout and crayfish. Rolling fields are filled with grains and vegetables, running alongside orchards of stone fruit.

Few regions in France can boast such a wide selection of local meats (particularly the famed Dordogne foie gras and equally famous pork, duck, and goose dishes); cheeses like Cabécou, Cujassous, Dubjac, Thieviers, and Échougnac; and distinctive wines, liqueurs, and brandies. This amazing variety of ingredients enables chefs here to create nearly everything from local products.

REGIONAL SPECIALTIES

Many well-known French meat dishes are named after surrounding villages and towns. Don't miss steak *à la Sarladaise* (stuffed with pâté de foie gras) or chicken *à la mode de Sorges* (stuffed with a mixture of chicken liver, mustard, bacon, and herbs). And for a sure dose of truffles, try any dish with *sauce Périgueux* or *à la périgourdine* in its name.

FOIE GRAS

Goose liver may not sound too enticing, but once you've had it there's no denying this delicious delicacy. The region has numerous farms with advertisements for foie gras everywhere you go, in shop windows and on road signs, portraying plump geese and ducks happily meandering toward you. At any food shop, you'll find containers of fresh and frozen foie gras, and it is an ever-present restaurant offering, prepared *pôelé* (pan-fried, usually accompanied by a sweet side), in a terrine (pâté), or otherwise added to your salads and main courses.

WALNUTS

The importance of noix (walnuts) in the Dordogne—and the rest of this country—cannot be overstated because the walnut is *the* nut here (the translation of noix is simply "nut"). The French make walnut oil for cooking and drizzling on salads, incorporate walnut meat into savory and sweet dishes, and even make alcoholic beverages infused with walnut flavor. In fact, the aperitif of choice in the Dordogne is a sweet dark wine made from green walnuts picked in summer. The immature nuts impart a unique flavor to the wine.

TRUFFLES

Between November and March, the region's black gold—a fungus called *tuber melanosporum*—is unearthed and sold for exorbitant prices.

Found at the roots of oak trees by trained dogs and pigs, truffles contribute to the local economy, and to the region's celebrated cuisine. Their earthy perfume and delicate flavor have inspired countless dishes prepared by home cooks and restaurant chefs alike.

WINE AND LIQUOR

If you are dining on the region's fabulous bounty, the best accompaniment is a local wine, liqueur, or brandy.

Bergerac is known for its white wines made from Sémillon and Sauvignon Blanc grapes, and for its reds made from Merlot, Cabernet Sauvignon, and Cabernet Franc varieties. The area also produces excellent white dessert wines from the Sémillon grape.

The *fait maison*, or homemade, liqueurs are made from many fruits, including plum, quince, and black currant.

Fruit is also favored here for distilling brandies, with some of the best known made from cherries, grapes, pears, and plums.

Updated By Jennifer Ladonne

Want to smile happily ever after? Linger in a fantasyland full of castles, cliff-top châteaux, and storybook villages? Join the club. Since the 1990s the Dordogne region has ranked among the hottest destinations in France. Formerly one of those off-the-beaten-path areas, it's now in danger of getting four-starred, boutiqued, and postcarded to death, but scratch the surface and you can still find one of the most authentic and appealing regions of rural France.

What's more—and unlike the Loire Valley, for example, where attractions are often far apart—you can discover romantic riverside château after château with each kilometer traveled. Factor in four troglodyte villages, numerous natural *gouffres* (chasms), the sky-kissing village of Rocamadour, and the most famous prehistoric sights in the world, and you can see why all these attractions have not gone unnoticed: in July and August even the smallest village is often packed with sightseers.

The Dordogne *département* (province) is in the Aquitaine region of southwest France, where, above the river valleys and oak and chestnut forests crowd in on about 1,200 châteaux, most from the 13th and 14th centuries. The area is marked by rich, luxuriant valleys, through which flow clear-water rivers such as the Dordogne, Isle, Dronne, Vézére, and Lot. Separating the valleys are rugged plateaux of granite and limestone, sharp outcroppings of rock, and steep, sheer cliffs. Offering a nice contrast to the region's rugged physiognomy and *nature sauvage* (wilderness) are hyperpicturesque villages such as La Roque-Gageac, wedged between rocky cliffs and the Dordogne River.

The region is centered on Sarlat, and its impeccably restored medieval buildings make it a great place to use as a base. Even better, the area around this town is honeycombed with dozens of *grottes* (caves) filled with Paleolithic drawings, etchings, and carvings. Just north of Sarlat is Lascaux, the "Louvre" of Cro-Magnon man and perhaps the most notable prehistoric sight.

Fast-forward 30,000 years. The modern era dawns as the region comes under Merovingian rule in the 9th century. Subsequently divided up by the dukes of Aquitaine, it later came under English rule and was returned to the French crown around 1370. The crown complicated matters further by giving the area to the Spanish house of Bourbon in 1574, which meant Henry of Navarre inherited it . . . but in 1589 Henry became Henri IV, king of France, so the region returned to the French crown once again. Well, history is repeating itself, at least from an English perspective, as over the last several decades the British have moved back here in droves. They see the Dordogne as the quintessential French escape—and now the rest of the world is following in their footsteps.

PLANNER

WHEN TO GO

The Dordogne has a temperate climate, but it's not Provence. Because this is France's third-largest département, local differences abound—winds blow in from the Atlantic along the western borders, and varying topographic and continental weather conditions affect the eastern and northern areas. Sarlat, in the southeast, tends to get a lot more winter sun than other locales. As you move westward toward the Atlantic conditions get foggier, cloudier, and colder; however, in summer the southwestern Dordogne is sunnier than the rest of the region. All in all, spring and autumn are the best times to visit since there aren't as many tourists around, and the weather is still pleasant.

PLANNING YOUR TIME

From a practical perspective, staying in Sarlat or thereabouts would be your best plan if you want to really appreciate this diverse region. Not only is the historic town a worthwhile destination in its own right, it's also near the top sights: Lascaux and Les Eyzies de Tayac lie to the north; Beynac-et-Cazenac, La Roque-Gageac, and Domme are immediately south; Rocamadour is a little farther to the southeast. Sarlat is also just off the A20 highway, which brings you south to Cahors and north to the regional airport in Brive La Gaillarde (the Bergerac airport to the west is a bit farther afield).

After getting yourself situated, you can explore the camera-ready villages, imposing châteaux, and captivating caves that sprinkle this part of France like so much historical and cultural confetti. If you prefer solitude and unspoiled scenery you won't have any trouble finding them in the vast, sparsely populated countryside. All you have to do is head for the hills—literally. Wherever you go, just be sure to leave plenty of time for dining. The Dordogne's edible delights (foie gras and truffles being chief among them) are as famous as the region's varied sights.

VISITING THE PREHISTORIC WONDERS

Perhaps the Dordogne's most famous sights are its prehistoric caves and grottos, with the legendary Lascaux topping the list. It's been closed to the public since 1963, but many others are open for viewing. Lascaux II—a near perfect replica—can accept up to 2,000 visitors a day; on the other hand, the Grotte des Combarelles takes only 40 in total and no more than six on any given tour, thereby guaranteeing an intimate look.

Either because demand far outstrips supply, or because tickets are so limited, it's recommended that you call or email to prebook tickets whenever possible. For places like Lascaux II, reserve as far ahead as you can (up to a year). For less popular sights, a couple of days should suffice. Alternately, you can try signing up for a day-of tour first thing in the morning.

The main tourist offices in the region, such as the one at Les Eyzies-de-Tayac, have the lowdown on all the caves and prehistoric sights in the area. If you can't secure tickets in advance, it's worth stopping by the cave of your choice even if the office says they are sold out as space often opens up. Be forewarned: you might get signed onto a tour that starts in a couple of hours, leaving you with time to kill, so have a game plan handy for other places to visit nearby.

GETTING HERE AND AROUND

AIR TRAVEL

The closest major airport is in Bordeaux, 88 km (55 miles) west of Bergerac, but the Dordogne has regional airports in Bergerac itself as well as in Brive La Gaillarde. The former, Aéroport de Bergerac-Périgord-Dordogne, receives regular flights from Paris Orly, operated by Twin Jet (🌐 *www.twinjet.fr*), plus two-dozen flights per week from the United Kingdom, operated by budget carriers Flybe (🌐 *www.flybe.com*) and Ryanair (🌐 *www.ryanair.com*). Ryanair also lands farther east at Aéroport de Brive–Vallée de la Dordogne, as does the low-cost airline HOP! (🌐 *www.hop.fr*), thereby providing links with Paris and select other European cities.

Airport Information Aéroport de Bergerac-Périgord-Dordogne. ☎ *05-53-22-25-25* 🌐 *www.bergerac.aeroport.fr.* **Aéroport de Bordeaux-Mérignac.** ☎ *05-56-34-50-50* 🌐 *www.bordeaux.aeroport.fr.* **Aéroport de Brive–Vallée de la Dordogne.** ☎ *05-55-22-40-00* 🌐 *www.aeroport-brive-vallee-dordogne.com.*

BIKE TRAVEL

The Dordogne is prime biking territory. In particular, the hour-long ride between Rocamadour and the Gouffre de Padirac might just be one of your fondest experiences in France; and let's not forget daylong bike trips through the neighboring Célé Valley and the 35-km (22-mile) trip to the prehistoric Grotte du Pech Merle outside the town of Cabrerets. Happily, there are plenty of *cyclotourisme* operators who rent bikes in assorted styles and sizes. Electric bicycles are increasingly available, too.

Contacts Atout Loc. ☎ *05-53-28-18-33.* **Bike Bus.** ☎ *06-08-94-42-01* 🌐 *www.bike-bus.com.*

BOAT TRAVEL

One popular way to see the Dordogne's landscape is by canoe or kayak. Rental depots spring up frequently along the rivers of the region, especially near campgrounds. The curving and winding Vézère River is a very boat-friendly stretch, while the valley of the Lot River is famous for its dreamy dawn mists. Single-person boats go for about €10 to €20 an hour, double that for two-person boats. Some rental companies will take you by car to a departure point upstream, and some will even provide tents and waterproof casings for overnight trips. For more information, pick up boating brochures at any tourist office in the region.

BUS TRAVEL

The regional bus operator in the Dordogne is CFTA. It connects the main towns with 14 bus lines, operated by eight different outfits. The maximum fare is €2, and there are reduced rates if you buy 10 passes (€15), so traveling by bus in the Dorgdogne could save you a lot of money. For urban transport in Périgueux use Peribus; in Bergerac use TUB (Transports Urbains Bergeracois).

Bus Information CFTA. ☎ *05–53–08–43–13* 🌐 *www.cftaco.fr.* **Peribus.** ☎ *05–53–53–30–37* 🌐 *peribus.agglo-perigueux.fr.* **TUB** (*Transports Urbains Bergeracois*). ☎ *05–53–63–96–97* 🌐 *www.bergerac.fr/Cadre-de-vie/Deplacements/Transports-Urbains-Bergeracois.*

CAR TRAVEL

The Dordogne has a surplus of memorable sights, many of them off the beaten path; the public transport system here, however, is limited. So you'll want a car to maximize touring opportunities and minimize frustration. The A20 is the main route for motorists, extending from Paris almost all the way to Cahors. It connects with the N21 at Limoges, which brings you down into Périgueux and Bergerac. A89 links Bordeaux to Périgueux and D936 runs along the Dordogne Valley from Libourne to Bergerac continuing as D660 toward Sarlat.

TRAIN TRAVEL

The superfast TGV Atlantique service links Paris's Gare Montparnasse to Bordeaux—the major rail hub in this part of France—covering 585 km (365 miles) in 3 hours, 30 minutes. From Bordeaux, 15 trains daily run to Bergerac (1 hr, 23 mins), at least a dozen serve Périgueux (1 hr, 30 mins), and another six go to Sarlat (2 hrs, 45 mins). If you're bound for Cahors, in the southern Dordogne, you can get there direct from Paris's Gare d'Austerlitz in just over 5 hours.

Train Information SNCF. ☎ *3635 €0.34 per min* 🌐 *voyages-sncf.fr.* **TGV.** 🌐 *www.tgv.com.*

RESTAURANTS

If you're traveling in the Dordogne between October and March, it's essential to call restaurants ahead of time to avoid disappointment, as some shut down for the slow season. Closing times, too, can be variable. When you do snag your table, scan the menu for listings of dishes *à la périgourdine,*which usually mean you're about to enjoy truffles or foie gras, or perhaps even both.

HOTELS

Advance booking is recommended in the highly popular Dordogne, where hotels fill up quickly, particularly in midsummer. Many country or small-town hotels expect you to have at least one dinner with them, and if you have two meals a day with your lodging and stay several nights, you can save money. Prices off-season (October to May) often drop as much as 20%, but note that some hotels close from the end of

October through March. *Hotel reviews have been shortened. For full information, visit Fodors.com.*

WHAT IT COSTS IN EUROS				
	$	$$	$$$	$$$$
Restaurants	under €18	€18–€24	€25–€32	over €32
Hotels	under €106	€106–€145	€146–€215	over €215

Restaurant prices are the average cost of a main course at dinner or, if dinner is not served, at lunch. Hotel prices are the lowest cost of a standard double room in high season.

VISITOR INFORMATION

The main tourist office for the region, the Comité Départemental du Tourisme de la Dordogne, is in Périgueux. Its multilingual website is a great resource (to access English info, simply click the Union Jack icon). Specific areas—including Périgord Noir and the Lot Valley—also have their own helpful websites, as do many of the local tourist offices (⇨ *listed under town names below*). Note that in the small villages a lot of the tourist offices have unusual opening hours.

Contacts Comité Départemental du Tourisme de la Dordogne. ☎ *05-53-35-50-24* 🌐 *www.dordogne-perigord-tourisme.fr.* **Comité Départemental du Tourisme de Lot-et-Garonne.** ☎ *05-53-66-14-14* 🌐 *www.tourisme-lotetgaronne.com.* **Les Offices de Tourisme du Périgord Noir.** ☎ *05-53-31-45-45* 🌐 *www.perigordnoir.com.* **Tourisme dans le Lot.** ☎ *05-65-35-07-09* 🌐 *www.tourisme-lot.com.*

WESTERN DORDOGNE

From a bird's-eye perspective the geographic area in this region is known in France by four colors: the Périgord Noir, Blanc, Pourpre, and Vert. Sarlat and its environs are known as the Périgord Noir, or Black Périgord, for the precious black truffles found there; Périgueux to the north is based in the Périgord Blanc (white) region, named for its vertiginous white-limestone cliffs; wine-producing Bergerac to the southwest is the Périgord Pourpre (purple); and lush, forested Brantôme in the far north is in the Périgord Vert (green). With more than 2 million visitors every year, the Périgord Noir is the most frequented. But the entire Dordogne relies heavily on travelers, so the local tourist offices have plenty of informative guides and maps to help you enjoy whatever "color" you choose. Many first opt for "purple," since Bergerac is the main hub for flights (after Bordeaux). Thus we kick things off in Western Dordogne and then head southwest down to the lovely Lot Valley, where dramatic Rocamadour lures throngs of tourists and pilgrims annually.

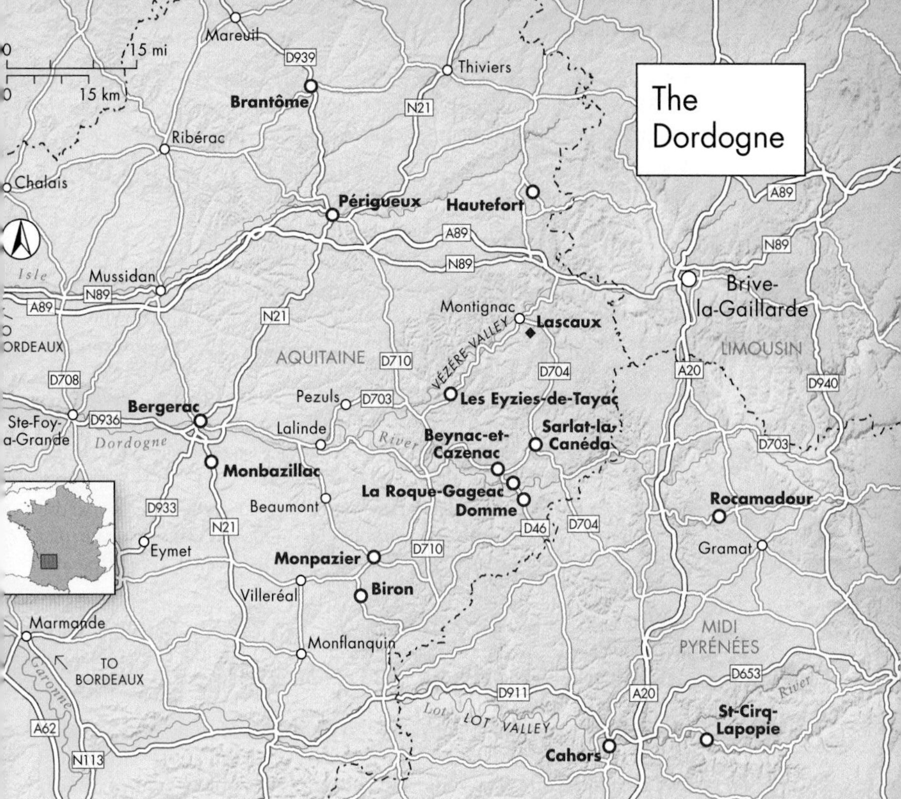

BERGERAC

57 km (36 miles) east of St-Émilion via D936, 112 km (70 miles) east of Bordeaux.

Yes, this is the Bergerac of Cyrano de Bergerac fame—but not exactly. The real satirist and playwright Cyrano (1619–55), who inspired Edmond Rostand's long-nosed swashbuckler, was born in Paris and never set foot anywhere near here. That hasn't prevented his legend from being preempted by the town fathers, who erected an exceedingly ugly statue of Cyrano and plastered his schnoz all over Bergerac's promotional materials. Frankly, they needn't have bothered. The town's gorgeous old half-timber houses, narrow alleys, riverside setting, and gastronomic specialties are more than enough to attract tourists from Bordeaux or Sarlat. If you're only coming for the day, try to arrive on Wednesday or Saturday, when colorful farmers' markets are held (the latter being the larger of the two).

GETTING HERE

About 5 km (8 miles) south of town, the Aéroport Bergerac-Périgord-Dordogne is served by budget carriers that fly passengers in from Paris (Orly), London (Stansted), and a handful of other cities. There is no airport shuttle yet, so you have to take a taxi (*05–53–23–32–32*) into the town center. Fifteen trains daily link Bergerac with Bordeaux (1 hr,

23 mins) and Sarlat (1 hr, 20 mins); regular buses from Périgueux (1 hr, 35 mins) also pull in at the train station on Avenue du 108e. Within Bergerac, the TUB urban bus service will help you get around (€1).

Visitor Information **Bergerac Tourist Office.** ☎ *05–53–57–03–11* 🌐 *www.bergerac-tourisme.com.*

EXPLORING

Cloître des Récollets. This former convent is now in the wine business, and its stone-and-brick buildings, dating from the 12th to the 15th century, include galleries, a large vaulted cellar, and a cloister where the **Maison des Vins** (Wine Center) provides information on—and samples of—local vintages of sweet whites and fruity young reds. ✉ *1 rue des Récollets, Bergerac* ☎ *05–53–63–57–55* 🌐 *www.bergerac-tourisme.com/Le-Cloitre-des-Recollects-Maison* 🎟 *€5* ⏲ *Feb.–Apr. and Oct.–Dec., Tues.–Sat. 10:30–12:30 and 2–6; May, June, and Sept., Tues.–Sat. 10–12:30 and 2–7; July and Aug., daily 10–7.*

Périgord Gabarres. From Easter to October, you can cruise along the Dordogne in an old wooden sailboat operated by Périgord Gabarres; an hour-long trip costs €9. ✉ *Bergerac* ☎ *05–53–24–58–80* 🌐 *www.gabarres.fr* ⏲ *Easter–Oct., daily 11–6.*

WHERE TO EAT AND STAY

$$ FRENCH FUSION

✕ **L'Imparfait.** In the heart of old Bergerac, this characterful restaurant has beamed ceilings, openwork stone, brick walls, large lamps, and cane-back chairs. The lunch and dinner menu, which changes with the seasons, is good value, considering you can start with such delights as warm oysters with saffron or a skewer of langoustine with honey and rosemary, and then move on, perhaps, to ravioli in a citron sauce. [$] *Average main: €24* ✉ *8–10 rue des Fontaines, Bergerac* ☎ *05–53–57–47–92* 🌐 *www.imparfait.com.*

$ HOTEL

Bordeaux. Although it's been in business since 1855 and has occasionally played host to some famous guests (Francis Bacon and François Mitterand among them), the Bordeaux of today has contemporary furnishings and simple, tidy rooms—the best of which look out on the garden courtyard. **Pros:** good location close to the market (held Wednesday and Saturday), the Old Town, and the train station. **Cons:** rooms are a little too understated and are in need of some updating. [$] *Rooms from: €83* ✉ *38 pl. Gambetta, Bergerac* ☎ *05–53–57–12–83* 🌐 *www.hotel-bordeaux-bergerac.com* *40 rooms* *No meals.*

MONBAZILLAC

6 km (4 miles) south of Bergerac via D13.

The hilltop village of Monbazillac provides spectacular views of the sweet-wine–producing vineyards tumbling toward the Dordogne River.

GETTING HERE

TUB buses on the Bergerac–Bouniagues route travel to Monbazillac three times a day—but the 6-km (4-mile) journey takes 40 minutes, so you're better off driving.

EXPLORING

Château de Monbazillac. The storybook corner towers of the beautifully proportioned, 16th-century, gray-stone château pay tribute to the fortress tradition of the Middle Ages, but the large windows and sloping roofs reveal a Renaissance influence. Regional furniture and an ornate early-17th-century bedchamber enliven the interior. A wine tasting is included to tempt you into buying a case or two of the famous but expensive bottles. ✉ *Le Bourg, Monbazillac* ☎ *05–53–63–65–00* 🌐 *www.chateau-monbazillac.com* 🎟 *€7.50* ⏲ *June–Sept., daily 10–7; May and Oct., daily 10–12:30 and 2–6; Nov., Dec., Feb., and Mar., Tues.–Sun. 10–noon and 2–5; Apr. daily 10–noon and 2–6.*

MONPAZIER

45 km (28 miles) southeast of Bergerac via D660.

Built in ocher-color stone by English king Edward I in 1284 to protect the southern flank of his French possessions, Monpazier, on the tiny Dropt River, ranks among "Les Plus Beaux Villages de France" ("the most beautiful villages of France"). With three of its original six stone gateways still standing, it is also one of the country's best-preserved bastide (fortified) communities.

GETTING HERE

Monpazier is a drive-to destination.

Visitor Information Monpazier Tourist Office. ☎ *05–53–22–68–59* 🌐 *www.pays-des-bastides.com/gb/monpazier.asp.*

EXPLORING

Église Saint-Dominique. This austerely beautiful medieval church dates back to 1284 and the founding of Monpazier, but it was extensively rebuilt in 1450. A new bell, still in use today, was added in 1476. The gorgeous gothic-style wooden choir stalls were added in 1506. ✉ *Pl. des Cornières, Monpazier* 🌐 *www.pays-des-bastides.com.*

Maison du Chapître (*Chapter House*). Opposite the church, this chapter house is the finest medieval building in town. Once used as a barn for storing grain, its wood-beam roof is constructed of chestnut to repel insects. ✉ *Monpazier.*

WHERE TO STAY

$ HOTEL **Hôtel de France.** Once an outbuilding on the estates of the Château de Biron, the Hôtel de France has never capitalized on its 13th-century heritage but today remains a small, modest, family-run hotel that caters less to tourists than to locals—especially at its bar and restaurant, which serves rich regional food. **Pros:** central location; great restaurant ($$); helpful staff. **Cons:** rooms are not nearly as impressive as the restaurant; no Internet service. $ *Rooms from: €48* ✉ *21 rue St-Jacques, Monpazier* ☎ *05–53–22–60–06* 🌐 *www.hoteldefrancemonpazier.fr* ⏲ *Closed mid-Nov.–Mar.* *10 rooms* 🍽 *No meals.*

BIRON

8 km (5 miles) south of Monpazier via D2/D53.

Dominated by the graceful Château de Biron, this time-burnished town offers a glimpse of life in the past lane.

GETTING HERE

You'll want your own wheels to reach Biron.

EXPLORING

Fodor's Choice ★ **Château de Biron.** Stop in Biron to see its massive hilltop castle, the highlights of which include a keep, square tower, and chapel, dating from the Renaissance, and monumental staircases. In addition to the period apartments and the kitchen, with its huge stone-slab floor, there's a gigantic dungeon, complete with a collection of scarifying torture instruments. The classical buildings were completed in 1760. The Gontaut-Biron family—whose ancestors invented great typefaces centuries ago—has lived here for 14 generations. The château has been undergoing renovations on a room-by-room basis since 2013, but these interfere only minimally with the viewing. It's well worth renting an audioguide (€3) to get a detailed history, plus specifics about the architecture and decor. ✉ *Biron* ☎ *05–53–05–65–65* 🌐 *semitour.com* 🎟 *€8.10* ⏲ *Mid-Feb.–Mar., Tues.–Sun. 10–12:30 and 2—5; Apr.–June, Sept., and Oct., daily 10–1 and 2–6; July and Aug., daily 10–7; Nov. and Dec., Tues.–Sun. 10–12:30 and 2—5.*

CAHORS

60 km (38 miles) southeast of Monpazier via D811.

Fodor's Choice ★ Just an hour north of Toulouse (southwestern France's main city), Cahors makes a fine base for exploring the Lot River valley. Less touristy and populated than most of the Dordogne, this valley has a subtler charm. The clustered towns lining the eponymous river and smaller waterways that cut through the dry, vineyard-covered plateau have a magical, abandoned feel. After visiting them, Cahors (the area's largest community) offers a pleasant change of pace—especially if you're an oenophile. Once an opulent Gallo-Roman town, it's famous for *vin de Cahors*, a tannic red known to the ancients as "black wine." Caesar is said to have taken a supply with him when he returned to Rome; another booster was the local bishop who went on to become Pope John XXII—in the 14th century he made his hometown libation the communion wine of the Avignon church. Malbec is the most common grape used here; there's also a sizable amount of Merlot in the region, with other vintners specializing in the local Jurançon Noir grape. Many small estates offer tastings, and the town tourist office on Place François-Mitterrand can direct you to some of the more notable vineyards, including the Domaine de Lagrezette (in Caillac) and the Domaine de St-Didier (in Parnac).

GETTING HERE

Multiple direct trains per day from Paris's Gare d'Austerlitz pull into the Cahors station on Place Jouinot Gambetta (5 hrs, 10 mins; €62). As in the rest of the Dordogne, buses serving regional routes can be erratic, but they cost only €2 a trip.

Visitor Information Cahors Tourist Office. ☎ *05–65–53–20–65* 🌐 *www.tourisme-cahors.com.*

EXPLORING

Cathédrale St-Étienne. The fortresslike cathedral is in Byzantine style and its cloisters connect to the courtyard of the archdeaconry, awash with Renaissance decoration and thronged with townsfolk who come to view art exhibits. ✉ *Off Rue du Maréchal-Joffre, Cahors.*

Fodor's Choice ★ **Pont Valentré.** The town's finest sight is this 14th-century bridge, its three elegant towers constituting a spellbinding feat of medieval engineering. ✉ *Cahors.*

WHERE TO STAY

$$$$ HOTEL **Château de Mercuès.** Set on a rocky spur just outside town, the former home of the count-bishops of Cahors has older rooms in baronial splendor (ask for one of these), as well as unappealing modern ones (which tend to attract midges); others have a mix of French Moderne and medieval-esque furniture that can be jarring, but the ambitious restaurant and great views make up for a lot of sins. **Pros:** unbeatable view; great pool. **Cons:** odd mix of furnishings; lunch served on Saturday and Sunday only. $ *Rooms from: €380* ✉ *8 km (5 miles) northwest of Cahors on road to Villeneuve-sur-Lot, Mercuès* ☎ *05–65–20–00–01* 🌐 *www.chateaudemercues.com* ⏲ *Closed Nov.–Mar.* *24 rooms, 6 suites* 🍽 *No meals.*

ST-CIRQ-LAPOPIE

32 km (20 miles) east of Cahors via D653, D662, and D40.

Poised on the edge of a cliff 330 feet up, sublime St-Cirq (pronounced san- *seer*) looks as though it could slide right into the Lot River. Traversing steep paths and alleyways among flower-filled balconies, you'll realize it deserves its reputation as one of the most beautiful villages in France. Pretty boutiques, artisan workshops, and tempting eateries invite lingering. But if you feel energetic, the tourist office will direct you to the mostly ruined 13th-century château—it's a stiff walk away along a path that starts near the Hôtel de Ville. Morning hikes in the misty gorges of the valley are beyond breathtaking.

GETTING HERE

If you're driving, there's plenty of parking up a steep winding hill above the town. Otherwise, the easiest way to access St-Cirq-Lapopie is by taking the Figeac-bound bus from Cahors's train station (20 mins); St-Cirq is a 25-minute hike from where the bus drops you. From the Tour de Faure bus stop, go back to the D181 (sign says "St-Cirq 2 km"), cross the bridge, and walk uphill. It's a haul, but worth the effort.

Visitor Information St-Cirq-Lapopie Tourist Office. ☎ *05–65–31–31–31* 🌐 *www.saint-cirqlapopie.com.*

CLOSE UP

Dordogne's Indulgent Eats

The Dordogne is a land of foie gras and cognac, so travelers get to eat (and quaff) like the royals who once contested this coveted corner of France, staking it out with châteaux-forts and blessing it with Romanesque churches.

Begin by following the winding sprawl of the Dordogne River into the realm of the *gavée* goose, where force-fed birds with extravagantly plump livers produce one of the world's most renowned delicacies.

The fat glistens on potatoes, on salty confits, and on *rillettes d'oie,* a spread of potted goose that melts on the tongue as no mere butter ever could.

Wild mushrooms and truffles (referred to locally as "black diamonds") weave their musky perfume through dense game pâtés.

Although truffle production is nothing like it used to be, this subterranean edible fungus continues to beguile chefs and foodies.

The truffle forms a symbiotic relationship with the roots of certain trees and plants (in the Périgord region they are mainly found growing from green oaks) to form a part that is technically known as the *ascoma,* the fruiting body of a fungus.

Mysteriously appearing anytime from November to mid-March in the forests of Périgord (and other areas of Western Europe), the more famous *truffes* (truffles) are black, but there are also white varieties—hundreds of species in all.

Truffles are savory, zesty, and extremely aromatic, and because of this they have been glorified as a delicacy for thousands of years (if we are to believe old Greek and Roman writings on the subject). They can be canned for export and are often infused into oils.

Traditionally, pigs were used to hunt for truffles; but nowadays dogs are more commonly employed because canines can be taught to point for truffles and, unlike the avaricious piglets, don't want to eat them when they find them.

Cultivation of the famous fungus by way of inoculating the roots of a host plant seedling with fungal spores has had success, although the manufactured truffles are still thought to taste inferior to the ones naturally found in the forests.

To stand up to such an onslaught of earthy textures and flavors, the best Dordogne wines—like Bergerac and Cahors—have traditionally been coarser vintages.

However, since the 1970s the winegrowers around Cahors have succeeded in mellowing those coarser edges.

And to round it all off? A snifter of amber cognac—de rigueur for the digestion.

Dining thus, in a vine-covered stone *ferme auberge* (farmhouse inn) deep in the green wilds of the Dordogne, replete with a feast of pâtés, truffles, and cognacs, you begin to see what the 13th-century Plantagenet invaders from England were fighting for.

Draped on a cliff 1,500 feet over the Alzou River gorge, Rocamadour is one of the most dazzling towns of the Dordogne.

18

EXPLORING

Croisières de St-Cirq-Lapopie. This cruise line offers popular 75-minute boat rides on a picture-perfect 8-km (5-mile) stretch of the Lot River that meanders below St-Cirq-Lapopie past dramatic cliffs, grottoes, and forest. Adventurous types can rent smaller vessels (€40 per hour for a four-person boat; €140 per day) to explore river and grottos on their own. ✉ *St-Cirq-Lapopie* ☎ *05–65–31–72–25* 🌐 *www.lot-croisieres.com.*

Grotte du Pech Merle. Discovered in 1922, the Grotte du Pech Merle displays 4,000 square feet of prehistoric drawings and carvings. Particularly known for its peculiar polka-dot horses, impressions of the human hand, and footprints, this is the most impressive "real" Cro-Magnon cave that is open to the public in France. The admission charge includes a 20-minute film, an hour-long tour, and a visit to the adjacent museum. Tickets are at a premium, with a daily limit of 700 visitors, so for peak summer days book at least one week in advance. If you like cycling, it's lovely to arrive by bike from St-Cirq-Lapopie. ✉ *10 km (6 miles) north of St-Cirq-Lapopie, St-Cirq-Lapopie* ☎ *05–65–31–27–05* 🌐 *www.pechmerle.com* 🎫 *€11* 🕘 *Early Apr.–early Nov., daily 9:30–5; select days in winter (see website).*

WHERE TO STAY

$ B&B/INN **L'Auberge du Sombral.** If location and views are your top priorities, then you've come to the right place. **Pros:** can't beat the location. **Cons:** things could be spiffed up a bit. 💲 *Rooms from: €72* ✉ *St-Cirq-Lapopie* ☎ *05–65–31–26–08* 🌐 *www.lesombral.com* 🕘 *Closed Nov. 15–Apr. 1* 🛏 *8 rooms* 🍽 *No meals.*

ROCAMADOUR

72 km (45 miles) north of St-Cirq via Labastide-Murat.

A medieval village that seems to defy the laws of gravity, Rocamadour surges out of a cliff 1,500 feet above the Alzou River gorge—an awe-inspiring sight that makes this one of the most-visited tourist spots in France. Rocamadour got its name after the thousand-year-old body of St. Amadour was discovered "quite whole" in 1166. Legend has it that Amadour was actually a publican named Zacheus, who entertained Jesus in his home and, after the crucifixion, came to Gaul, eventually establishing a private chapel in the cliff here. In any case, his saintly remains soon began working miracles, and the sanctuary that housed them began attracting pilgrims who'd ascend the 216 steps to the church on their knees. Making the climb on foot is a sufficient reminder of the medieval penchant for agonizing penance; today two elevators lift weary souls. Unfortunately, the summer influx of a million tourists can itself be agonizing.

GETTING HERE

Brive–Vallée de la Dordogne—the nearest airport, 54 km (34 miles) north of Rocamadour—receives regular flights from Paris and select other European cities. Direct trains run from Toulouse (2 hrs, 30 mins; €33) and Brive (40 mins, €9.50); keep in mind, however, that the Rocamadour–Padirac station is 4 km (3 miles) outside the village. Walking takes about an hour, biking 15 minutes, or you can call Taxi Pascal Herbert (*06–81–60–14–60*). Motorists should note that cars are not allowed in Rocamadour; you must park in the lot below it.

Visitor Information Rocamadour Tourist Office. ☎ *05–65–33–22–00* 🌐 *www.vallee-dordogne-rocamadour.com.*

EXPLORING

Fodor's Choice ★ **Cité Religieuse.** The Basse Ville's Rue Piétonne, the main pedestrian street, is crammed with crêperies, tea salons, and hundreds of tourists, many of whom are heading heavenward by taking the **Grand Escalier** (staircase) or elevator (€2.60) from Place de la Carreta up to the Cité Religieuse, set halfway up the cliff. If you walk, pause at the landing 141 steps up to admire the fort. Once up, you can see tiny Place St-Amadour and its seven chapels: the basilica of **St-Sauveur** opposite the staircase; the **St-Amadour crypt** beneath the basilica; the chapel of **Notre-Dame,** with its statue of the Black Madonna, to the left; the chapels of **John the Baptist, St-Blaise,** and **Ste-Anne** to the right; and the Romanesque chapel of **St-Michel** built into an overhanging cliff. St-Michel's two 12th-century frescoes—depicting the Annunciation and the Visitation—have survived in superb condition. ✉ *Rocamadour.*

Hôtel de Ville. The town is split into four levels joined by steep steps. The lowest level is occupied by the village of Rocamadour itself, and mainly accessed through the centuries-old Porte du Figuier (Fig Tree Gate). Past this portal, the **Cité Médiévale,** also known as the **Basse Ville,** though in parts grotesquely touristy, is full of beautifully restored structures, such as the 15th-century Hôtel de Ville, near the Porte Salmon, which houses the **tourist office** and an excellent collection of tapestries. ✉ *Rocamadour*

☎ 05–65–33–22–00 ⊕ *www.vallee-dordogne-rocamadour.com* €2 ⊙ *July and Aug., daily 9:30–7; Jan., Feb., Nov., and Dec., daily 2–5; Mar.–June, Sept., and Oct., daily 10:30–noon and 2–6.*

WHERE TO STAY

$$$ HOTEL Fodor's Choice ★ **Château de la Treyne.** Certainly the most spectacular château-hotel in the Dordogne, this Relais & Châteaux outpost sits amid Baroque gardens perched over the Dordogne River. **Pros:** sparklingly renovated; modern amenities like Jacuzzis and minibars. **Cons:** restaurant is pricey ($$$$). $ *Rooms from: €200* ✉ *15 km (9 miles) northwest of Rocamadour, Lacave* ☎ *05–65–27–60–60* ⊕ *www.chateaudelatreyne.com* ⊙ *Closed Jan. 2–Mar. 21* *12 rooms, 5 suites* *No meals.*

$ HOTEL **Lion d'Or.** In the center of Rocamadour, this simple, bargain-price, family-run hotel has a restaurant with panoramic views of the valley, where genial owners Emmanuel and Sally Vernillet serve up delicious truffle omelets and homemade foie gras *au Noilly*. **Pros:** location in the Old Town; amazing views from restaurant. **Cons:** rooms have floral wallpaper and linens that might not be to everyone's taste. $ *Rooms from: €55* ✉ *Cité Médiévale, Rocamadour* ☎ *05–65–33–62–04* ⊕ *www.liondor-rocamadour.com/?lang=en* ⊙ *Closed Jan. and Feb.* *75 rooms* *No meals.*

$$$ B&B/INN **Manoir de Malagorse.** Using local materials and furnishings, Anna and Abel (a Franco-British husband-and-wife team) have spent more than a dozen years gracefully restoring the 19th-century stone farm buildings on their 10-acre parcel of quietude; in the process, they've brought this refined, family-friendly manor into the 21st century—soothing earth tones set the scene, with light oak floors matching the sand-colored stone walls, which in turn match the blond house dogs. **Pros:** hosts who know great food and wine but keep it simple; lovely breakfast included. **Cons:** reservations essential for July and August; somewhat remote. $ *Rooms from: €160* ✉ *26 km (16 miles) northwest of Rocamadour, Rignac, Cuzance* ☎ *05–65–27–14–83* ⊕ *www.manoir-de-malagorse.fr* ⊙ *Closed Nov.–Mar.* *4 rooms, 2 suites, 1 self-contained apartment* *Breakfast.*

EASTERN PÉRIGORD

Entering the Périgord Noir, a trifecta of top Dordogne sights awaits: the cliff-face village of La Roque-Gageac, the prehistoric grotto in Domme, and the storybook castle at Beynac. Just eastward lies Sarlat, a regional center famed for its half-timber medieval vibe. Northward lies the Vézère Valley: known as the prehistoric capital of France, it is home to celebrated locales like Lascaux, which were settled by primitive man. Continuing north, you arrive at the bustling little city of Périgueux and numerous riverside towns, including historic Brantôme. For three centuries during the Middle Ages, this entire region was a battlefield in the wars between the French and the English. Of the châteaux dotting the area, those at Hautefort and Beynac are among the most spectacular.

LA ROQUE-GAGEAC

55 km (36 miles) west of Rocamadour via Payrac, 10 km (6 miles) southwest of Sarlat via D703.

Across the Dordogne from Domme, in the direction of Beynac, one of the best-restored villages in the valley is huddled romantically beneath a cliff. Crafts shops line its narrow streets, dominated by the outlines of the 19th-century mock-medieval Château de Malartrie and the Manoir de Tarde, with its cylindrical turret. If you leave the main road and climb one of the steep cobblestone paths, you can check out the medieval houses on their natural perches and even hike up the mountain for a magnificently photogenic view down to the village.

GETTING HERE

No buses serve La Roque-Gageac, so you'll have to come by car.

WHERE TO STAY

$ B&B/INN **La Plume d'Oie.** Famed for its eatery, this small inn overlooking the river and limestone cliffs welcomes weary guests with rooms that flaunt some fabulous views. **Pros:** great view; top eatery. **Cons:** hotel is noisy; expected to have breakfast (€12). *Rooms from: €75 ⊠ La Roque-Gageac ☎ 05–53–29–57–05 ⊕ www.aubergelaplumedoie.com ⊗ Closed late Nov.–early Mar. 4 rooms No meals.*

DOMME

5 km (3 miles) east of La Roque-Gageac.

Stunning views aside, the cliff-top village of Domme offers a hefty dose of history. Some of its fortified walls and doors, dating back to 1280, are still standing; and the Porte des Tours still harbors graffiti from the Knights Templar, who were imprisoned here from 1306 to 1318 awaiting trial. Most visitors, however, come to see something much older—Domme's renowned grotto.

GETTING HERE

Like La Roque-Gageac, Domme isn't covered by public transit; hence a car is required.

Visitor Information Domme Tourist Office. *⊠ Pl. de la Halle, Domme ☎ 05–53–31–71–00.*

EXPLORING

Grotte de Domme. Beneath the fortified city lies the largest natural cave in the Périgord Noir. You won't see wall drawings, but prehistoric bison and rhinoceros bones have been discovered here, and you can visit the 500-yard-long illuminated galleries, which are lined with impressive stalactites. The view of the countryside upon exiting the dark cave is stellar. *⊠ Pl. de la Halle, entrance opposite City Hall, Domme ☎ 05–53–31–71–00 €8.50 ⊗ Mid-Feb.–mid-Nov., daily 10–noon and 2–6; mid-Dec.–early Jan., daily 10–noon and 2–5.*

BEYNAC-ET-CAZENAC

11 km (7 miles) west of La Roque-Gageac via D703.

One of the most picturesque sights in the Dordogne is the medieval castle that sits atop the wonderfully restored town of Beynac.

GETTING HERE

You'll want a car to reach Beynac and its châteaux-dotted environs.

Visitor Information Beynac-et-Cazenac Tourist Office. ☎ *05–53–29–43–08* ⊕ *www.sarlat-tourisme.com/beynac-et-cazenac.*

EXPLORING

Castelnaud. With a fabulous mountaintop setting, the now-ruined castle of Castelnaud, containing a large collection of medieval arms, is just upstream from Beynac across the Dordogne. Make sure to give yourself at least an hour to visit. In summer the castle comes to life with demonstrations, reenactments, and opportunities to try out some of the medieval weapons yourself. ✉ *Beynac* ☎ *05–53–31–30–00* ⊕ *www.castelnaud.com* 🎫 *€9.60* ⏲ *Apr.–June and Sept., daily 10–7; July and Aug., daily 9–8; mid-Nov.–Jan., daily 2–5 (10–5 during Christmas holidays); Oct., Feb., and Mar., daily 10–6.*

Château de Beynac. Perched above a sheer cliff face beside an abrupt bend in the Dordogne River, the muscular 13th-century Château de Beynac has unforgettable views from its battlements. Thanks to its camera-ready qualities, it frequently doubles as a film set. During the Hundred Years' War, this castle often faced off with forces massed directly across the way at the fort of Castelnaud. ✉ *Beynac* ☎ *05–53–29–50–40* ⊕ *www.beynac-en-perigord.com* 🎫 *€8* ⏲ *Mar.–May, daily 10–6; June–Sept., daily 10–6:30; Oct. and Nov., daily 10–sunset; Dec.–Feb., daily 11–sunset.* 18

Château des Milandes. Five kilometers (3 miles) from Castelnaud, the turreted Château des Milandes was built around 1489 in Renaissance style, and has lovely terraces and gardens. It was once owned by the American-born cabaret star of Roaring '20s Paris, Josephine Baker, and it was here that she housed her "rainbow family"—a large group of adopted children from many countries. An on-site museum is devoted to her memory. Falconry displays (April to October) are another attraction. From here D53 (via Belvès) leads southwest to Monpazier. ✉ *Beynac* ☎ *05–53–59–31–21* ⊕ *www.milandes.com* 🎫 *€9.20* ⏲ *Apr. and May, daily 10–6:30; June–mid-July and Sept., daily 10–7; mid-July–Aug., daily 9:30–7:30; Oct.–Nov., daily 10–6:15.*

Fodor's Choice ★ **Jardins de Marqueyssac.** For Périgord Noir at its most enchanting, head to the heavenly heights of this hilltop garden in Vézac, just south of Beynac. Founded in 1682, its design—including a parterre of topiaries—was greatly influenced by André le Nôtre, the "green geometer" of Versailles. Shaded paths bordered by 150,000 hand-pruned boxwoods are graced with breathtaking viewpoints, rock gardens, waterfalls, and verdant glades. From the belvedere 400 feet above the river, there's an exceptional view of the Dordogne Valley. For a unique and romantic perspective, the garden stays open until midnight under candlelight each Thursday in July and August. You can drink in panoramic views from the terrace of the tea salon, from March to mid-November. ✉ *Belvédère de la Dordogne, Vézac* ⊕ *3 km (2 miles) south of Beynac-et-Cazenac* ☎ *05–53–31–36–36* 🌐 *www.marqueyssac.com* 🎫 *€8.80* ⊙ *July and Aug., daily 9–8 (also 7–midnight Thurs. by separate ticket); Feb., Mar., and Oct.–mid-Nov., daily 10–6; mid-Nov.–Jan., daily 2–5; Apr.–June and Sept., daily 10–7.*

VERSAILLES IN THE SKY

Perched on their cliff top, the topiaries of Marqueyssac seem like a mirage. This style of landscaping first made its mark at Versailles, where the king's eye could stretch along nearly 3 km (2 miles) of manicured gardens before finally coming up against a wall of trees, resulting in the feeling that the entire world was within his grasp. Here, on the contrary, gorgeous views extend for miles over the Dordogne Valley below.

WHERE TO EAT

$$ FRENCH ✕ **Hostellerie Maleville.** At this highly regarded waterside eatery, you'll want to forego a table in the modern wood-beam dining room for a blissful perch on the riverbank itself. Here umbrellas and willow trees shade diners happily tucking into such fare as goose neck stuffed with truffles and Beynacoises potatoes, or Landes hen with a rich sauce of house-made foie gras sauce and wild morels. If you need a nap afterwards, the owner's vintage stone Hôtel Pontet offers 13 sweet and simple guest rooms in the heart of this adorably Dordognesque town, just a stone's throw from the restaurant. $ *Average main: €19* ✉ *Beynac-et-Cazenac* ☎ *05–53–29–50–06* 🌐 *www.hostellerie-maleville.com* ⊙ *Closed Mon. No dinner Sun.* ✍ *Reservations essential.*

SARLAT-LA-CANÉDA

10 km (6 miles) northeast of Beynac via D57, 74 km (46 miles) east of Bergerac.

Tucked among hills adorned with corn and wheat, Sarlat is a well-preserved medieval town that has managed to retain some of its true character, despite the hordes of visitors. The end of the Hundred Years' War in 1453 led to the construction of beautiful urban buildings in the Dordogne, and Sarlat was especially favored: when the English handed the region back to the French king, he rewarded loyal townspeople here with royal privileges. Before long, a new merchant class sprang up, building sublime stone mansions in the latest French Renaissance style. To do justice to Sarlat, meander through its Cité Médiévale in the late afternoon or early evening, aided by the tourist office's walking map. The tourist office also organizes English-language walking tours that give you an in-depth look at the town's architecture; they depart every Thursday at 11 from mid-May through July and again from September to mid-October (€5.50). If you're planning a trip to the many prehistoric caves and perched villages nearby, the capital of the Périgord Noir makes an ideal base for exploring, too.

GETTING HERE

Regular flights from Paris, London, and Amsterdam land at Brive–Vallée de la Dordogne, 51 km (32 miles) northeast of Sarlat. Trains make the trip from Paris in six hours, with a change in Souillac. Fifteen trains daily link Bergerac with Sarlat. Multiple trains per day also arrive from Les Eyzies and Périgueux, with connections in Le Buisson, or direct from Bordeaux. Note that the station is 1½ km (1 mile) northeast of Sarlat's center. Buses connect the town to Périgueux and other area communities.

Visitor Information **Sarlat-la-Canéda Tourist Office.** ☎ *05–53–31–45–45* 🌐 *www.sarlat-tourisme.com.*

EXPLORING

Cathédrale St-Sacerdos. The elaborate turreted tower of the Cathédrale St-Sacerdos, begun in the 12th century, is the oldest part of the building and, along with the choir, all that remains of the original Romanesque structure. ✉ *Pl. du Peyrou, Sarlat-la-Canéda.*

Eco-Musée de la Noix. If you're nuts about nuts, Sarlat is your town—the Périgord is the second-biggest producer of walnuts in France, and those from the Sarladais region are prized. The nuts are sold in the markets in October and November and walnut wood (often preferred here to oak) is used to make beautiful furniture. Visit the Eco-Musée de la Noix, just south of Sarlat in Castelnaud-la-Chapelle, to learn more. ✉ *La Ferme de Vielcroze, Castelnaud La Chapelle ✣ 12 km (7 miles) southwest of Sarlat via D57* ☎ *05–53–59–69–63* 🌐 *ecomuseedelanoix.voila.net* 🎫 *€5* ⏲ *Apr.–Nov., daily 10–7.*

Jardin des Enfers. The sloping garden behind the cathedral, the Jardin des Enfers, contains a strange, conical tower known as the Lanterne des Morts (Lantern of the Dead), which was occasionally used as a funeral chapel. ✉ *Sarlat-la-Canéda.*

Place du Peyrou. Sarlat's Cité Médiévale has many beautiful photo ops. Of particular note is Rue de la Liberté, which leads to Place du Peyrou, anchored on one corner by the steep-gabled Renaissance house where writer-orator Étienne de la Boétie (1530–63) was born. ✉ *Sarlat-la-Canéda.*

Rue des Consuls. The church of Ste-Marie points the way to Sarlat's most interesting street, Rue des Consuls. Among its medieval buildings are the Hôtel Plamon, with broad windows that resemble those of a Gothic church, and, opposite, the 15th-century Hôtel de Vassal. ✉ *Sarlat-la-Canéda.*

Rue Montaigne. Running the length of the Enfer gardens is Rue Montaigne, where the great 16th-century philosopher Michel de Montaigne once lived. Some of the half-timber houses that line it cast a fairy-tale spell. Rue d'Albusse (adjoining the garden behind the cathedral) and Rue de la Salamandre are narrow, twisty streets that head to Place de la Liberté and the 18th-century Hôtel de Ville. ✉ *Sarlat-la-Canéda.*

Ste-Marie. Opposite the town hall and overlooking Place du Marché aux Oies, the deconsecrated Gothic church of Ste-Marie was redesigned by star architect Jean Nouvel to become the town's covered food hall.

DID YOU KNOW?

Sarlat's tourist office has seasonal walking tours that enable you to fully savor the town's golden-stone splendor—heading out from Rue Tourny, these walks include charming nooks wanderers might otherwise miss.

Open daily until 8 pm from April to November (every day but Thursday other months), it overflows with everything you'll need for a gourmet picnic or mouthwatering memento. Try to come on Saturday when a farmers' market winds all the way here from the entrance to the evocative Cité Médiévale. All the (liverless) ducks and geese on sale are proof of the local addiction to foie gras; and you'll have the opportunity to stock up on homemade confiture, everything walnut—pastry, oil, liqueur—plus truffles galore. ✉ *Sarlat-la-Canéda.*

REEL LIFE

It's no surprise to learn that only Nice and Paris have had more movies shot on-site than Sarlat. Many of the 45-plus films that have used it as a backdrop are historical epics, but others—most notably Lasse Hallstrom's *Chocolat* (2000) with Johnny Depp and Juliette Binoche—highlight Sarlat's romantic side. The town even has its own annual film festival; each November, stars, producers, and film technicians arrive to host an informational get-together for 500 students (🌐 *www.festivaldufilmdesarlat.com*).

WHERE TO STAY

$ HOTEL **Hostellerie La Couleuvrine.** Sarlat is not overly blessed with beautiful historic hotels, so this one stands out—literally—thanks to its massive crenellated tower (an imposing structure that held off besieging forces during the Wars of Religion) and an interior that includes a magically medieval restaurant. **Pros:** like a Relais & Chateaux property at one-quarter the price. **Cons:** a few blocks east of the Cité Médiévale. *Rooms from: €80* ✉ *1 pl. de la Bouquerie, Sarlat-la-Canéda* ☎ *05–53–59–27–80* 🌐 *www.la-couleuvrine.com* *25 rooms, 3 suites* *No meals.*

$ HOTEL FAMILY Fodor's Choice ★ **La Villa des Consuls.** On a meandering cobbled street in the heart of Sarlat's Cité Médiévale, La Villa des Consuls lets you bed down in either guest rooms or self-service apartments; some are on two floors, and all boast soaring beamed ceilings, modern bathrooms, plus charming views over the Old City's rooftops. **Pros:** exemplary service; extremely reasonable rates; clean, quiet, air-conditioned rooms. **Cons:** staircases in duplex rooms aren't for everyone. *Rooms from: €95* ✉ *3 rue Jean-Jacques Rousseau, Sarlat* ☎ *05–53–31–90–05* 🌐 *www.villaconsuls.fr* *4 rooms, 9 apartments* *No meals.*

$$ HOTEL Fodor's Choice ★ **Plaza Madeleine.** Constructed in the 19th-century, this elegant stone building, just to the north of the Old Town, has been extensively renovated by owners Monsieur and Madame Florent. **Pros:** spacious lounge to relax in; nice outdoor terrace. **Cons:** very hard to find parking nearby. *Rooms from: €139* ✉ *1 pl. de la Petite-Rigaudie, Sarlat-la-Canéda* ☎ *05–53–59–10–41* 🌐 *www.plaza-madeleine.com* *39 rooms* *No meals.*

LES EYZIES-DE-TAYAC

21 km (13 miles) northwest of Sarlat via D47.

Sitting comfortably under a limestone cliff, Les Eyzies is the doorway to the prehistoric capital of France. Early *Homo sapiens* (the species to which we humans belong) lived about 40,000 years ago, and skeletal

18

remains of Cro-Magnon man—along with other artifacts of Aurignacian culture—were first found here in 1868. Today a number of excavated caves and grottoes are open for public viewing. The tourist office can give you the lowdown on all of them; it also sells tickets for most sites, and you should reserve here because a surprising number of tours sell out in advance.

GETTING HERE

Five trains arrive from Sarlat daily (€9.80); the trip can take anywhere from 50 minutes to two hours, 30 minutes.

Visitor Information Eyzies-de-Tayac Tourist Office. ☎ *05–53–06–97–05* 🌐 *www.lascaux-dordogne.com.*

EXPLORING

Fodor's Choice ★ **Grotte de Combarelles.** Want an up-close look at Cro-Magnon cave drawings? Those at les Combarelles are considered among the best in the world. Although traces of pigments have been found, the colors have long since vanished, leaving the sinuous graven outlines of woolly mammoths, cave bears, lions, and astonishingly lifelike reindeer. There are well over 600 drawings all told, and seeing them is an almost mystical experience, especially since only 40 people are admitted per day. Hour-long tours are available in English on Monday at 10, 11:30, and 2:30; guides on other tours *may* speak English (but it's basically the luck of the draw). This is not a spot for the claustrophobic—the winding 1,000-foot long cavern is 6½ feet tall and, at most, 3 feet wide. ✉ *1 km (½ mile) from Les Eyzies-de-Tayac, Les Eyzies-de-Tayac* ☎ *05–53–06–86–00* 🌐 *eyzies.monuments-nationaux.fr* 🎫 *€7.50* ⏲ *Mid-May—mid-Sept., daily 9:30–5:30; mid-Sept.—mid-May, Sun.–Fri. 9:30–12:30.*

Grotte du Grand-Roc. Amid the dimness of the Grotte du Grand-Roc you can view weirdly shaped crystalline stalactites and stalagmites. At the nearby **Abri Préhistorique de Laugerie,** you can visit caves that were once home to prehistoric man. ✉ *Av. de Laugerie, Les Eyzies-de-Tayac* ☎ *05–53–05–65–60* 🌐 *www.semitour.com* 🎫 *€7.50* ⏲ *July and Aug., daily 10–7; Sept. and Oct., daily 10–1 and 2–6; Nov., Dec., and mid-Feb.–Apr., Sun.–Thurs. 10–12:30 and 2–5; Apr.–June, daily 10–12:30 and 2–6.*

Fodor's Choice ★ **Grotte-Font-de-Gaume.** Font-de-Gaume is the last French cave with polychrome paintings that remains open to the public. Though discovered in the late 1800s, it wasn't until the early 20th century that the importance of the artwork (dating back to around 17,000 BC) was recognized by archaeologists. Astonishingly graceful animal figures, many at eye level, include woolly mammoths, horses, reindeer, rhinos, and more. The cave's masterpiece is a grouping of five large superimposed bison in vivid color that was uncovered in 1966 during a routine cleaning. Like similar representations in Lascaux, the sophisticated shading techniques used for their bellies and thighs create a stunning impression of dimensionality and movement. Guided tours run every 40 minutes, but only 80 visitors are admitted each day—down from 160 in 2012. The cave is destined to close, so see it while you can! ✉ *1 km (½ mile) from Les Eyzies-de-Tayac, Les Eyzies-de-Tayac* ☎ *05–53–06–86–00*

The Raphaels, Leonardos, and Picassos of prehistoric art are on view in the amazing caves of Lascaux II.

eyzies.monuments-nationaux.fr *€7.50* *Mid-May—mid-Sept., daily 9:30–5:30; mid-Sept.–mid-May, Sun.–Fri. 9:30–12:30.*

Fodor's Choice ★ **La Madeleine.** As you head north from Les Eyzies-de-Tayac toward Lascaux, stop off near the village of Tursac to discover the mysterious troglodyte "lost village" of La Madeleine, found hidden in the Valley of Vézère at the foot of a ruined castle. Human settlement here dates to 15,000 BC, but what is most eye-catching today is its picturesque cliff-face chapel; seemingly half Cro-Magnon, half Gothic, it was constructed during the Middle Ages. The site, abandoned in the 1920s, can be visited on guided tours (call ahead, English available). *7 km (4 miles) north of Les Eyzies-de-Tayac, Les Eyzies-de-Tayac* *05–53–46–36–88* *www.la-madeleine-perigord.com* *€6* *Mid-Feb.—mid-Mar., daily 11–5; mid-Mar.—June, daily 10–6; July and Aug., daily 9:30–8; Sept. and Oct., daily 10–6.*

Musée National de Préhistoire (*National Museum of Prehistory*). To truly enhance your understanding of the paintings at Lascaux and other caves in the Dordogne, visit the Musée National de Préhistoire. Its renowned collection of prehistoric artifacts—including primitive sculpture, furniture, and tools—attracts large crowds. You can also get ideas at the museum about which excavation sites to visit in the region. *1 rue du Musée, Les Eyzies-de-Tayac* *05–53–06–45–45* *musee-prehistoire-eyzies.fr* *€6* *June and Sept., Wed.–Mon. 9:30–6; July and Aug., daily 9:30–6:30; Oct.–May, Wed.–Mon. 9:30–12:30 and 2–5:30.*

Pole International de la Prehistoire (*Prehistory Welcome Center*). This well-equipped welcome center, opened in 2011, provides a solid introduction to the region's important prehistoric sites. Its exhibits, slide shows, and time lines (all free of charge) help you wrap your brain around the immensity of the archaeological riches in the Dordogne. ✉ *30 rue du Moulin, Les Eyzies-de-Tayac* ☎ *05–53–06–06–97* 🌐 *www.pole-prehistoire.com* 🎟 *Free* 🕑 *May–Sept., daily 9:30–6:30; Oct.–Dec. and Feb.–May, Sun.–Fri. 9:30–5:30.*

WHERE TO STAY

$$$ HOTEL **Le Vieux Logis.** Built around the most gorgeous dining room in the Dordogne, this vine-clad manor house in Trémolat is one of the region's top hotels. **Pros:** breathtaking grounds; Le Bistrot de la Place ($$) offers a value version of the restaurant's delectable food. **Cons:** swimming pool is small. 💲 *Rooms from: €200* ✉ *24 km (15 miles) west of Les Eyzies, Le Bourg, Trémolat* ☎ *05–53–22–80–06* 🌐 *www.vieux-logis.com* 💳 *No credit cards* 🛏 *14 rooms, 9 suites* 🍽 *No meals.*

LASCAUX

27 km (17 miles) northeast of Les Eyzies via D706.

Named a UNESCO World Heritage Site in 1979, Lascaux is one of the world's great galleries of Paleolithic art, a mysterious remnant that scientists still debate the meaning of. Although the actual cave has been closed to the public for more than 50 years, visiting Lascaux II—a near perfect replica—is an awe-inspiring experience that shouldn't be missed. Nearby, the Château de Losse puts a different spin on this area's rich history.

GETTING HERE

Lascaux II is best reached by car. If you're driving from Sarlat, head toward Montignac, 26 km (16 miles) north on route D704; the cave is 1 km (½ mile) south of Montignac. If you're relying on public transport, Sarlat has early buses to Montignac (7 and 9 am), leaving from Place de la Petite Rigandie.

Visitor Information Lascaux Tourist Office. ☎ *05–53–51–82–60* 🌐 *www.lascaux-dordogne.com.*

EXPLORING

FAMILY **Château de Losse.** There are more grandiose castles in France, but few can offer a more intimate a look at how 16th-century nobles lived than the Château de Losse. Built in 1576 on the site of the family's original 11th-century stronghold, the graceful Renaissance-style structure retains the furnishings, artwork, and other authentic trappings of daily life during the Wars of Religion. The beautiful wooded grounds and formal gardens overlooking the Vézère River make for a lovely stroll, and a charming café with a grassy terrace is the perfect place for a gourmet lunch. Although tours of the interior are offered in French only, a detailed text in English is provided. ✉ *8 km (5 miles) southwest of Montignac-Lascaux, Thonac* ☎ *05–53–50–80–08* 🌐 *www.chateaudelosse.com* 🎟 *€9* 🕑 *May–Sept., Sun.—Fri. noon–6.*

Fodor's Choice ★ **Grotte de Lascaux** (*Lascaux Caves*). Just south of Montignac, the famous Grotte de Lascaux contain hundreds of prehistoric wall paintings between 15,000 and 20,000 years old. The horses, cow, black bulls, and unicorn on their walls were discovered by chance by four schoolkids looking for their dog in 1940. Over time, the original Lascaux cave paintings began to deteriorate due to the carbon dioxide exhaled by thousands of visitors. To make the colorful mosaic of animals accessible to the general public, the French authorities built Lascaux II, a formidable feat in itself. They spent 12 years perfecting the facsimile, duplicating every aspect of two of the main caves to such a degree that the result is equally awesome. Painted in black, purple, red, and yellow, the powerful images of stags, bison, and oxen are brought to life by the curve of the stone walls; many of them appear pregnant, and historians think these caves were shrines to fertility rather than living quarters—no tools or implements were ever found. Unlike caves marked with authentic prehistoric art, Lascaux II is completely geared toward visitors, and you can watch a fancy presentation about cave art or take a 40-minute tour in the language of your choice. This is one of the most visited sites in the Dordogne and, in summer, tickets can be at a premium. To be sure of admittance, arrive early, as tickets can sell out by midday. During the winter season, you are permitted to purchase tickets at the site, but from April to October tickets are available only at a booth beside the tourist office in Montignac (*Pl. Bertran-de-Born*). Even better, make reservations via email as soon as you know you're heading to the Dordogne. ✉ *Rte. de la Grotte de Lascaux, Lascaux* ☎ *05–53–05–65–60* 🌐 *www.lascaux-dordogne.com* 🎫 *€10* 🕓 *Mid-Feb.–early Apr. and mid-Nov.–Dec., Tues.–Sun. 10–12:30 and 2–5:30; mid-Apr.–early July, and Sept.–mid-Nov., daily 9:30–12:30 and 2–6; early July–Aug., daily 9–7.*

WHERE TO STAY

$ RENTAL **Manoir d'Hautegente.** Originally a forge, this old, ivy-covered edifice occupies a pastoral nook by the Coly River—a lovely vista to enjoy from your guest room or the impressive restaurant and less expensive bistro. **Pros:** cozy family feel; close to Sarlat. **Cons:** bathrooms need updating; rooms suffer somewhat from an attack of French Moderne style. 💲 *Rooms from: €105* ✉ *12 km (7 miles) east of Lascaux, Haute Gente, Coly* ☎ *05–53–51–68–03* 🌐 *www.manoir-hautegente.com* 🕓 *Closed mid-Oct.–Apr.* 🛏 *11 rooms, 6 suites* 🍽 *No meals.*

18

HAUTEFORT

25 km (15½ miles) north of Lascaux via D704.

The reason to come to Hautefort is its castle, which presents a forbiddingly arrogant face to the world.

GETTING HERE

Weekdays, CFTA's Line 9 bus from Périgueux makes two round-trips per day (1 hr, €2); otherwise, you'll have to come by car.

Visitor Information Hautefort Tourist Office. ☎ *05–53–50–40–27* 🌐 *www.ot-hautefort.com.*

EXPLORING

Château de Hautefort. The silhouette of the Château de Hautefort bristles with high roofs, domes, chimneys, and cupolas. The square-line Renaissance left wing clashes with the muscular, round towers of the right wing, and the only surviving section of the original medieval castle—the gateway and drawbridge—plays referee in the middle. Adorning the inside are 17th-century furniture and tapestries. ✉ *Hautefort* ☎ *05–53–50–51–23* 🌐 *www.chateau-hautefort.com* 🎫 *€8.50* 🕓 *Apr. and May, daily 10–12:30 and 2–6:30; June–Aug., daily 9:30–7; Sept., daily 10–6; Oct., daily 2–6; Mar. and early Nov., weekends 2–6.*

PÉRIGUEUX

46 km (27 miles) west of Hautefort via D5, 120 km (75 miles) northeast of Bordeaux.

For anyone tired of bucolic delights, even a short visit to the region's capital can provide a restorative urban fix. Since Périgueux is the commercial center of the Périgord, the shops here are stylish and sophisticated—some consider them the best reason for visiting this thriving little city. Specialty-food purveyors proliferate (pâtés are the chief export), as do fashionable clothing boutiques—and don't forget Périgueux's appetite-inducing open-air markets.

GETTING HERE

Air travelers from Paris and London can fly into Bergerac, 48 km (29 miles) south, or Brive–Vallée de la Dordogne, 81 km (50 miles) west. By rail, you can get from Paris's Gare d'Austerlitz to Périgueux's train station on Rue Denis Papin in five hours, with a connection in Bordeaux (€73). CFTA buses link the gare routiere (also on Rue Denis Papin) with Brantôme, Hautefort, and Bergerac for €2 per trip. Peribus provides public transit within Périgueux itself (€1.25).

Visitor Information Périgueux Tourist Office. ☎ *05–53–53–10–63* 🌐 *www.tourisme-perigueux.fr.*

EXPLORING

Cathédrale St-Front. Périgueux's history reaches back more than 2,000 years, yet the community is best known for this odd-looking church, which was associated with the routes to Santiago de Compostela. Finished in 1173 and fancifully restored in the 19th century, Cathédrale St-Front seems like it might be on loan from Istanbul, given its shallow-scale domes and the elongated conical cupolas sprouting from the roof like baby minarets. You may be struck by similarities between it and the Byzantine-style Sacré-Coeur in Paris; that's no coincidence—architect Paul Abadie (1812–84) had a hand in the design of both. After a mandatory visit to the cathedral, you can make for the cluster of tiny pedestrian-only streets that run through the heart of Périgueux. ✉ *Périgueux.*

Farmers' Markets. A farmers' market is open daily on Place du Coderc from 8 am to 12.30 pm; on Wednesday and Saturday bigger versions spill over the square to the front of the Hôtel de Ville (Town Hall). If you love your *gras* (fat) as much as the locals do, you'll also want to witness one of the many *marchés de gras* that run on Wednesday and Saturday, November through March. The Saturday *marchés aux truffes* (truffle markets)—held December through February on Place Saint-Louis—are tempting, too. ✉ *Périgueux* 🌐 *perigueux.fr/perigueux-au-quotidien/commerces-marches-et-emplois/679-les-marches-de-perigueux.html.*

Sorges Truffle Museum. If it's truffles you're after, take a guided tour of the truffle groves in Sorges, a picturesque village northeast of Périgueux. Organized by the Sorges Truffle Museum (L'écomusée de la Truffe), the hour-long outings run every Tuesday and Thursday in July and August, beginning at 3:30. The rest of the year, guided tours are only available, by reservation, for groups of more than 20 people. ✉ *Le Bourg, Sorges* ✣ *20 km (12.5 miles) northeast of Périgueux via the N21* ☎ *05–53–05–90–11* 🌐 *www.ecomusee-truffe-sorges.com* 🎫 *€5* ⏲ *Mid-June–late Sept., weekdays 9:30–6:30, weekends 9:30–12:30 and 2:30–6:30; late Sept.—mid-June, Tues.–Sun. 10–noon and 2–5.*

WHERE TO EAT

$$ FRENCH ✕ **Un Parfum de Gourmandise.** Outside the city center, but well worth the detour, Un Parfum de Gourmandise is where natives go for inventive seasonal cuisine. This tiny eatery makes excellent use of the local bounty and has a flair for introducing surprising ingredients: think guinea fowl with tonka-bean-flecked endive or roasted veal with hazelnut oil and sweet potatoes perfumed with bitter orange. Dishes are beautifully presented, and the wine list is excellent. Best of all, three-course dinner menus are just €32, so you'll spend a fraction of what you would in many lesser restaurants. $ *Average main: €24* ✉ *67 cours St. Georges, Périgueux* ☎ *05–53–53–46–33* 🌐 *www.unparfumdegourmandise.com* ⏲ *Closed Mon. No dinner Wed. and Sun.* ✍ *Reservations essential.*

BRANTÔME

27 km (17 miles) north of Périgueux via D939.

When the reclusive monks of the abbey of Brantôme decided the inhabitants of the village were getting too inquisitive, they dug a canal between themselves and their nosy neighbors, setting the *brantômois* adrift on an island in the middle of the River Dronne. How happy for them—or at least for us. Brantôme has been unable to outgrow its small-town status and remains one of the prettiest villages in France. Today it touts itself as the "Venice of Périgord." Enjoy a walk along the river or through the old, narrow streets. The meandering river follows you wherever you stroll. Cafés and small shops abound.

GETTING HERE

If you don't have your own car, CFTA's Line 1A bus makes a single weekday circuit between Périgueux and Brantôme (45 mins, €2).

Visitor Information Brantôme Tourist Office. ☎ *05–53–05–80–63* 🌐 *www.perigord-dronne-belle.fr.*

EXPLORING

Abbaye Bénédictine. Possibly founded by Charlemagne in the 8th century, Abbaye Bénédictine has none of its original buildings left, but its bell tower has been hanging on since the 11th century (the secret of its success is that it's attached to the cliff rather than the abbey, and so withstood waves of invaders). Fifth-century hermits carved out much of the abbey and some rooms have sculpted reliefs of the Last Judgment. Also here is a small museum devoted to the 19th-century painter Fernand-Desmoulin. At night the abbey is romantically floodlighted.

⊠ Bd. Charlemagne, Brantôme ☎ 05–47–45–30–12 €5 ⊙ July and Aug., Wed.–Mon. 10–7; Apr.–June and Sept., Wed.–Mon. 10–6; Oct.–Dec. and mid-Feb.–Mar., Wed.–Mon. 10–noon and 2–5.

WHERE TO STAY

$$ HOTEL FAMILY Fodor's Choice ★ **Les Jardins de Brantôme.** Although it's within easy walking distance of the town, this intimate spot is pleasantly removed from the hustle and bustle of the main tourist center. **Pros:** attentive hosts; tranquil, tasteful setting. **Cons:** pool is on the small side. *Rooms from: €145 ⊠ 33 rue de Mareuil, Brantôme ☎ 05–53–05–88–16 ⊕ lesjardinsdebrantome.com ⊙ Closed mid-Dec.–mid-Jan. 7 rooms No meals.*

FRENCH VOCABULARY

One of the trickiest French sounds to pronounce is the nasal final *n* sound (whether or not the n is actually the last letter of the word). You should try to pronounce it as a sort of nasal grunt—as in "huh." The vowel that precedes the *n* will govern the vowel sound of the word, and in this list we precede the final *n* with an *h* to remind you to be nasal.

Another problem sound is the ubiquitous but untransliterable eu, as in bleu (blue) or deux (two), and the very similar sound in je (I), ce (this), and de (of). The closest equivalent might be the vowel sound in "put," but rounded. The famous rolled *r* is a glottal sound. Consonants at the ends of words are usually silent; when the following word begins with a vowel, however, the two are run together by sounding the consonant. There are two forms of "you" in French: vous (formal and plural) and tu (a singular, personal form). When addressing an adult you don't know, vous is always best.

ENGLISH	FRENCH	PRONUNCIATION

BASICS

ENGLISH	FRENCH	PRONUNCIATION
Yes/no	Oui/non	wee/nohn
Please	S'il vous plaît	seel voo play
Thank you	Merci	mair- **see**
You're welcome	De rien	deh ree- **ehn**
Excuse me, sorry	Pardon	pahr- **don**
Good morning/ afternoon	Bonjour	bohn- **zhoor**
Good evening	Bonsoir	bohn- **swahr**
Good-bye	Au revoir	o ruh- **vwahr**
Mr. (Sir)	Monsieur	muh- **syuh**
Mrs. (Ma'am)	Madame	ma- **dam**
Miss	Mademoiselle	mad-mwa- **zel**
Pleased to meet you	Enchanté(e)	ohn-shahn- **tay**
How are you?	Comment allez-vous?	kuh-mahn-tahl-ay **voo**
Very well, thanks	Très bien, merci	tray bee-ehn, mair- **see**
And you?	Et vous?	ay voo?

NUMBERS

ENGLISH	FRENCH	PRONUNCIATION
one	un	uhn
two	deux	deuh
three	trois	twah

ENGLISH	FRENCH	PRONUNCIATION
four	quatre	**kaht**-ruh
five	cinq	sank
six	six	seess
seven	sept	set
eight	huit	wheat
nine	neuf	nuf
ten	dix	deess
eleven	onze	ohnz
twelve	douze	dooz
thirteen	treize	trehz
fourteen	quatorze	kah- **torz**
fifteen	quinze	kanz
sixteen	seize	sez
seventeen	dix-sept	deez- **set**
eighteen	dix-huit	deez- **wheat**
nineteen	dix-neuf	deez- **nuf**
twenty	vingt	vehn
twenty-one	vingt-et-un	vehnt-ay- **uhn**
thirty	trente	trahnt
forty	quarante	ka- **rahnt**
fifty	cinquante	sang- **kahnt**
sixty	soixante	swa- **sahnt**
seventy	soixante-dix	swa-sahnt- **deess**
eighty	quatre-vingts	kaht-ruh- **vehn**
ninety	quatre-vingt-dix	kaht-ruh-vehn- **deess**
one hundred	cent	sahn
one thousand	mille	meel

COLORS

black	noir	nwahr
blue	bleu	bleuh

ENGLISH	FRENCH	PRONUNCIATION
brown	brun/marron	bruhn/mar- **rohn**
green	vert	vair
orange	orange	o- **rahnj**
pink	rose	rose
red	rouge	rouge
violet	violette	vee-o- **let**
white	blanc	blahnk
yellow	jaune	zhone

DAYS OF THE WEEK

Sunday	dimanche	dee- **mahnsh**
Monday	lundi	luhn- **dee**
Tuesday	mardi	mahr- **dee**
Wednesday	mercredi	mair-kruh- **dee**
Thursday	jeudi	zhuh- **dee**
Friday	vendredi	vawn-druh- **dee**
Saturday	samedi	sahm- **dee**

MONTHS

January	janvier	zhahn-vee- **ay**
February	février	feh-vree- **ay**
March	mars	marce
April	avril	a- **vreel**
May	mai	meh
June	juin	zhwehn
July	juillet	zhwee- **ay**
August	août	ah- **oo**
September	septembre	sep- **tahm**-bruh
October	octobre	awk- **to**-bruh
November	novembre	no- **vahm**-bruh
December	décembre	day- **sahm**-bruh

ENGLISH	FRENCH	PRONUNCIATION
USEFUL PHRASES		
Do you speak English?	Parlez-vous anglais?	par-lay **voo** ahn- **glay**
I don't speak . . .	Je ne parle pas . . .	zhuh nuh parl pah . . .
French	français	frahn- **say**
I don't understand	Je ne comprends pas	zhuh nuh kohm- **prahn** pah
I understand	Je comprends	zhuh kohm- **prahn**
I don't know	Je ne sais pas	zhuh nuh say **pah**
I'm American/ British	Je suis américain/ anglais	zhuh sweez a-may-ree- **kehn** /ahn- **glay**
What's your name?	Comment vous appelez-vous?	ko-mahn vooz a-pell-ay- **voo**
My name is . . .	Je m'appelle . . .	zhuh ma- **pell** . . .
What time is it?	Quelle heure est-il?	kel air eh- **teel**
How?	Comment?	ko- **mahn**
When?	Quand?	kahn
Yesterday	Hier	yair
Today	Aujourd'hui	o-zhoor- **dwee**
Tomorrow	Demain	duh- **mehn**
Tonight	Ce soir	suh **swahr**
What?	Quoi?	kwah
What is it?	Qu'est-ce que c'est?	kess-kuh- **say**
Why?	Pourquoi?	poor- **kwa**
Who?	Qui?	kee
Where is . . .	Où est . . .	oo ay
the train station?	la gare?	la gar
the subway station?	la station de métro?	la sta- **syon** duh may- **tro**
the bus stop?	l'arrêt de bus?	la-ray duh booss
the post office?	la poste?	la post
the bank?	la banque?	la bahnk
the . . . hotel?	l'hôtel . . .?	lo- **tel**

ENGLISH	FRENCH	PRONUNCIATION
the store?	le magasin?	luh ma-ga- **zehn**
the cashier?	la caisse?	la **kess**
the . . . museum?	le musée . . .?	luh mew- **zay**
the hospital?	l'hôpital?	lo-pee- **tahl**
the elevator?	l'ascenseur?	la-sahn- **seuhr**
the telephone?	le téléphone?	luh tay-lay- **phone**
Where are the . . .	Où sont les . . .	oo sohn lay
restrooms?	toilettes?	twah- **let**
(men/women)	(hommes/femmes)	(**oh**-mm/ **fah**-mm)
Here/there	Ici/là	ee- **see** /la
Left/right	A gauche/à droite	a goash/a draht
Straight ahead	Tout droit	too drwah
Is it near/far?	C'est près/loin?	say pray/lwehn
I'd like . . .	Je voudrais . . .	zhuh voo- **dray**
a room	une chambre	ewn **shahm**-bruh
the key	la clé	la clay
a newspaper	un journal	uhn zhoor- **nahl**
a stamp	un timbre	uhn **tam**-bruh
I'd like to buy . . .	Je voudrais acheter . . .	zhuh voo- **dray ahsh**-tay
cigarettes	des cigarettes	day see-ga- **ret**
matches	des allumettes	days a-loo- **met**
soap	du savon	dew sah- **vohn**
city map	un plan de ville	uhn plahn de **veel**
road map	une carte routière	ewn cart roo-tee- **air**
magazine	une revue	ewn reh- **vu**
envelopes	des enveloppes	dayz ahn-veh- **lope**
writing paper	du papier à lettres	dew pa-pee- **ay** a **let**-ruh
postcard	une carte postale	ewn cart pos- **tal**
How much is it?	C'est combien?	say comb-bee- **ehn**
A little/a lot	Un peu/beaucoup	uhn peuh/bo- **koo**

ENGLISH	FRENCH	PRONUNCIATION
More/less	Plus/moins	plu/mwehn
Enough/too (much)	Assez/trop	a-say/tro
I am ill/sick	Je suis malade	zhuh swee ma- **lahd**
Call a . . .	Appelez un . . .	a-play uhn
doctor	docteur	dohk- **tehr**
Help!	Au secours!	o suh- **koor**
Stop!	Arrêtez!	a-reh- **tay**
Fire!	Au feu!	o fuh
Caution!/Look out!	Attention!	a-tahn-see- **ohn**

DINING OUT

A bottle of . . .	une bouteille de . . .	ewn boo- **tay** duh
A cup of . . .	une tasse de . . .	ewn tass duh
A glass of . . .	un verre de . . .	uhn vair duh
Bill/check	l'addition	la-dee-see- **ohn**
Bread	du pain	dew panh
Breakfast	le petit-déjeuner	luh puh- **tee** day-zhuh- **nay**
Butter	du beurre	dew burr
Cheers!	A votre santé!	ah **vo**-truh sahn- **tay**
Cocktail/aperitif	un apéritif	uhn ah-pay-ree- **teef**
Dinner	le dîner	luh dee- **nay**
Dish of the day	le plat du jour	luh plah dew **zhoor**
Enjoy!	Bon appétit!	bohn a-pay- **tee**
Fixed-price menu	le menu	luh may- **new**
Fork	une fourchette	ewn four- **shet**
I am diabetic	Je suis diabétique	zhuh swee dee-ah-bay- **teek**
I am vegetarian	Je suis végétarien(ne)	zhuh swee vay-zhay-ta-ree- **en**
I cannot eat . . .	Je ne peux pas manger de . . .	zhuh nuh puh pah mahn- **jay** deh

ENGLISH	FRENCH	PRONUNCIATION
I'd like to order	Je voudrais commander	zhuh voo- **dray** ko-mahn- **day**
Is service/the tip included?	Est-ce que le service est compris?	ess kuh luh sair- **veess** ay comb- **pree**
It's good/bad	C'est bon/mauvais	say bohn/mo- **vay**
It's hot/cold	C'est chaud/froid	say sho/frwah
Knife	un couteau	uhn koo- **toe**
Lunch	le déjeuner	luh day-zhuh- **nay**
Menu	la carte	la cart
Napkin	une serviette	ewn sair-vee- **et**
Pepper	du poivre	dew **pwah**-vruh
Plate	une assiette	ewn a-see- **et**
Please give me . . .	Donnez-moi . . .	doe-nay- **mwah**
Salt	du sel	dew sell
Spoon	une cuillère	ewn kwee- **air**
Sugar	du sucre	dew **sook**-ruh
Waiter!/Waitress!	Monsieur!/ Mademoiselle!	muh- **syuh** / mad-mwa- **zel**
Wine list	la carte des vins	la cart day vehn

MENU GUIDE

FRENCH	ENGLISH
GENERAL DINING	
Entrée	Appetizer/Starter
Garniture au choix	Choice of vegetable side
Plat du jour	Dish of the day
Selon arrivage	When available
Supplément/En sus	Extra charge
Sur commande	Made to order
PETIT DÉJEUNER (BREAKFAST)	
Confiture	Jam
Miel	Honey

FRENCH	ENGLISH
Oeuf à la coque	Boiled egg
Oeufs sur le plat	Fried eggs
Oeufs brouillés	Scrambled eggs
Tartine	Bread with butter

POISSONS/FRUITS DE MER (FISH/SEAFOOD)

Anchois	Anchovies
Bar	Bass
Brandade de morue	Creamed salt cod
Brochet	Pike
Cabillaud/Morue	Fresh cod
Calmar	Squid
Coquilles St-Jacques	Scallops
Crevettes	Shrimp
Daurade	Sea bream
Ecrevisses	Prawns/Crayfish
Harengs	Herring
Homard	Lobster
Huîtres	Oysters
Langoustine	Prawn/Lobster
Lotte	Monkfish
Moules	Mussels
Palourdes	Clams
Saumon	Salmon
Thon	Tuna
Truite	Trout

VIANDE (MEAT)

Agneau	Lamb
Boeuf	Beef
Boudin	Sausage
Boulettes de viande	Meatballs

FRENCH	ENGLISH
Brochettes	Kebabs
Cassoulet	Casserole of white beans, meat
Cervelle	Brains
Chateaubriand	Double fillet steak
Choucroute garnie	Sausages with sauerkraut
Côtelettes	Chops
Côte/Côte de boeuf	Rib/T-bone steak
Cuisses de grenouilles	Frogs' legs
Entrecôte	Rib or rib-eye steak
Épaule	Shoulder
Escalope	Cutlet
Foie	Liver
Gigot	Leg
Porc	Pork
Ris de veau	Veal sweetbreads
Rognons	Kidneys
Saucisses	Sausages
Selle	Saddle
Tournedos	Tenderloin of T-bone steak
Veau	Veal

METHODS OF PREPARATION

A point	Medium
A l'étouffée	Stewed
Au four	Baked
Ballotine	Boned, stuffed, and rolled
Bien cuit	Well-done
Bleu	Very rare
Frit	Fried
Grillé	Grilled
Rôti	Roast

FRENCH	ENGLISH
Saignant	Rare

VOLAILLES/GIBIER (POULTRY/GAME)

FRENCH	ENGLISH
Blanc de volaille	Chicken breast
Canard/Caneton	Duck/Duckling
Cerf/Chevreuil	Venison (red/roe)
Coq au vin	Chicken stewed in red wine
Dinde/Dindonneau	Turkey/Young turkey
Faisan	Pheasant
Lapin/Lièvre	Rabbit/Wild hare
Oie	Goose
Pintade/Pintadeau	Guinea fowl/Young guinea fowl
Poulet/Poussin	Chicken/Spring chicken

LÉGUMES (VEGETABLES)

FRENCH	ENGLISH
Artichaut	Artichoke
Asperge	Asparagus
Aubergine	Eggplant
Carottes	Carrots
Champignons	Mushrooms
Chou-fleur	Cauliflower
Chou (rouge)	Cabbage (red)
Laitue	Lettuce
Oignons	Onions
Petits pois	Peas
Pomme de terre	Potato
Tomates	Tomatoes

TRAVEL SMART FRANCE

GETTING HERE AND AROUND

AIR TRAVEL

Direct flying time to Paris is 7½ hours from New York, 9 hours from Chicago, 11 hours from Los Angeles, and 1½ hours from London. Flying time between Paris and Nice is also about 1½ hours.

As one of the world's most popular destinations, Paris is served by many international carriers. Air France, the French flag carrier, offers many direct flights to Paris's Charles de Gaulle Airport (CDG, also known as Roissy) from New York City's JFK Airport, as well as ones from Chicago, Cincinnati, Dallas-Fort Worth, Houston, Los Angeles, Miami, Montréal, San Francisco, Toronto, and Washington, D.C. Most other North American cities are served through Air France partnerships with Delta, either directly or via connecting flights. Another popular carrier is United, with nonstop flights to Paris from Chicago, Newark, San Francisco, and Washington, D.C. American Airlines operates daily nonstop flights (some seasonally) to Charles de Gaulle from numerous cities, including Boston, Chicago, Miami, and New York City's JFK Airport.

Airline Security Issues Transportation Security Administration. 🌐 *www.tsa.gov.*

AIRPORTS

There are two major gateway airports to France, both just outside the capital: Orly, 16 km (10 miles) south of Paris, and Charles de Gaulle, 26 km (16 miles) northeast of the city. Orly mostly handles flights to and from destinations within France and the rest of Europe, while Charles de Gaulle is France's leading international gateway. The smaller Beauvais Airport, 88 km (55 miles) north of Paris, is used by European budget airlines, most notably Ryanair. Many carriers have flights to Biarritz, Bordeaux, Lourdes, Lyon, Marseille, Nantes, Nice, Perpignan, and Toulouse. If you're going onward by rail, there is a TGV station at Charles de Gaulle's Terminal 2, where you can connect to trains heading all over the country.

Airport Information Beauvais. ☎ *08-92-68-20-66 €0.34 per min* 🌐 *www.aeroportbeauvais.com.* **Charles de Gaulle/Roissy.** ☎ *3950 €0.34 per min* 🌐 *www.aeroportsdeparis.fr.* **Orly.** ☎ *3950 €0.34 per min* 🌐 *www.aeroportsdeparis.fr.*

GROUND TRANSPORTATION

From Charles de Gaulle (CDG), the fastest and least expensive way to get into Paris is on the RER-B line, the suburban express train, which runs daily from 5 am to 11 pm. The free CDGVal light-rail connects each terminal (except 2G) to the Roissypôle RER station in less than 8 minutes; for Terminal 2G, take the free N2 "navette" shuttle bus outside Terminal 2F. Trains to central Paris (Gare du Nord, Les Halles, St-Michel, Luxembourg) depart every 10–15 minutes. The fare (including métro connection) is €9.75, and the journey time is 30–35 minutes.

The Air France shuttle service is a comfortable alternative, and you don't need to have flown the carrier to use it. The buses cost €17 if you pay on board or €15.50 if you buy your ticket online; the approximate travel time is 75 minutes. Line 2 goes from CDG to Paris's Charles de Gaulle Étoile and Porte Maillot from 5:45 am to 11 pm daily. Buses leave every 30 minutes until 9:45 pm, with two further services at 10:20 pm and 11 pm. Line 4 goes to Montparnasse and the Gare de Lyon from 6 am to 10 pm. Buses run every 30 minutes. Passengers arriving in Terminal 1 should use Exit 32 on the Arrivals level; Terminals 2A and 2C, Exit C2; 2B and 2D, Exit B1; Terminals 2E and 2F, Exit E8; Terminal 2G, take the N2 shuttle to Terminal 2F, and then use Exit 3.

Another option is to take Roissybus, operated by the Paris Transit Authority (RATP), which runs between CDG and the Opéra every 15–20 minutes from 6 am to 12:30 am; the cost is €11, and you can pay on board. The trip takes about 45 minutes in regular traffic, about 90 minutes in rush-hour traffic.

Taxis are your least desirable mode of transportation into the city. If you're traveling at peak times, you may have to stand in a long line with many other disgruntled travelers. Journey times, and, as a consequence, prices, are unpredictable. At best, the trip takes 30 minutes, but it can take as long as 90 minutes during rush hour. Count on a €50–€70 fare (add 15% between 7 pm and 7 am), plus €1 for a second bag in the trunk. Beware of unauthorized taxi drivers who solicit customers near baggage carousels and airport exits; only choose a cab from the designated areas outside the terminal, where official taxis have both an illuminated roof sign and a meter.

SuperShuttle Paris and Parishuttle are two van companies that serve both Charles de Gaulle and Orly airports. Prices are set, so it costs the same no matter how long the journey takes. To make a reservation, call or email your flight details several days in advance to the shuttle company and an air-conditioned van with a bilingual chauffeur will be waiting for you on arrival. Note that these shuttle vans pick up and drop off other passengers, which can add significant time to the journey.

From Orly, the most economical way to get into Paris is to take the RER-C or Orlyrail line. Catch the shuttle bus from the terminal to the Pont de Rungis train station. Trains to Paris leave every 15 minutes. Passengers arriving in South Terminal use Exit F; for West Terminal use Exit G on the Arrivals level. The total fare is €6.70, and journey time is about 35 minutes. Another slightly faster option is to take the 8-minute monorail service, Orlyval, which runs between the Antony RER-B station and Orly Airport every 8–15 minutes from 6 am to 11 pm. Passengers arriving in the South Terminal should look for Exit K; those arriving in the West Terminal, Exit A on the Departures level. The fare to central Paris is €12.05, including the RER transfer.

You can also take the Air France bus service from Orly to Les Invalides, Montparnasse, and Etoile; it runs every 20 minutes from 6 am to 11:40 pm. (You need not have flown on Air France to use this service.) The fare is €12.50 if you pay on board, €11 if you buy your ticket online, and the trip takes 45–60 minutes, depending on traffic. Passengers arriving in Orly South need to look for Exit K; those arriving in Orly West, Exit D. The Paris Transit Authority's Orlybus is yet another option; buses leave every 8–15 minutes for the Denfert-Rochereau métro station in Montparnasse, and tickets cost €7.50. You can economize further by using RATP Bus 183, which shuttles you from the South Terminal to the Porte de Choisy métro station (Line 7). It runs every 30–40 minutes from 6 am to 12:20 am (frequency may be reduced on Sunday and holidays); tickets cost €2, and the travel time is about 40 minutes.

There are several options for traveling between Paris's airports. The RER-B travels from CDG to Orly with Paris in the middle, so to transfer, just stay on. Travel time is 50–70 minutes, and tickets cost €20.90. The Air France Bus Line 3 also runs between the airports every 30 minutes for €21 one-way; the trip takes 50–75 minutes. Taxis are available but expensive (€60–€80, depending on traffic).

Contacts Air France Bus. ☎ *08-92-35-08-20 (recorded information in English) €0.34 per min* 🌐 *www.lescarsairfrance.com.* **Parishuttle.** ☎ *01-82-28-38-70* 🌐 *www.parishuttle.com.* **RATP.** ☎ *3246 €0.34 per min* 🌐 *www.ratp.fr.* **SuperShuttle.** ☎ *08-11-70-78-12 at least €.06 per min* 🌐 *en.supershuttle.fr.*

BOAT TRAVEL

A number of ferry routes link the United Kingdom and France, with fares depending on the length of the crossing and the number of passengers in your party. Ferries on the most popular route—Dover/

Calais—cross the Channel in about 90 minutes. Driving distances from the French ports to Paris are as follows: from Calais, 290 km (180 miles); from Cherbourg, 358 km (222 miles); from Caen, 233 km (145 miles); from St-Malo, 404 km (250 miles). Trains also connect these ports with the capital. It's best to book directly through the ferry providers rather than from third-party websites offering cheap rates.

Dover–Calais DFDS Seaways. ☎ *02-32-14-68-50* 🌐 *www.dfdsseaways.co.uk.* **P&O European Ferries.** ☎ *03-66-74-03-25* 🌐 *www.poferries.com.*

Portsmouth and Poole–Cherbourg, Caen and St-Malo Brittany Ferries. ☎ *08-25-82-88-28 €0.15 per min* 🌐 *www.brittany-ferries.com.*

BUS TRAVEL

If you're traveling to or from another country, train service can be just as economical as bus travel, if not more so. The largest international bus operator is Eurolines France, whose main terminal is in the Parisian suburb of Bagnolet (a ½-hour métro ride from central Paris, at the end of métro Line 3). Terminals are also located at Charles de Gaulle Airport, Porte de Clichy, and Porte de Charenton. Eurolines links scores of European destinations, with fares that vary greatly depending on where and when you travel. It will take you about 8½ hours to get from London to Paris, and a round-trip ticket will cost €34 to €49. Other Eurolines routes to or from Paris include: Amsterdam (7½ hrs, €76); Barcelona (15 hrs, €117); and Berlin (14 hrs, €91). Economical passes are available—a 15-day version costs €215–€355, and a 30-day one costs €320–€465. These offer unlimited coach travel to all of Eurolines's European destinations.

France's excellent train service means that long-distance bus routes within France are rare; regional buses are found mainly where train service is spotty. The service can be unreliable in rural areas, and schedules can be incomprehensible for those who don't speak French. Your best bet is to contact local tourism offices.

Bus Information Eurolines. ☎ *08-92-89-90-91 €0.34 per min, 01-41-86-24-21 outside France* 🌐 *www.eurolines.fr.*

CAR TRAVEL

Driving in France can be a leisurely experience. Autoroutes are well maintained, and there are ample service-oriented rest areas along major highways; smaller roads wind through scenic landscapes and quaint villages. An International Driver's Permit isn't required, but it can prove useful in emergencies—particularly when a foreign language is involved (check with your local Department of Motor Vehicles to obtain one at nominal cost). Drivers in France must be over 18 years old; however, there is no top age limit, provided your faculties are intact. If you're driving from the United Kingdom to the Continent, you have a choice of ferry services or the Channel Tunnel (aka the Chunnel) via the Eurotunnel Shuttle. Reservations are essential at peak times.

GASOLINE

Gas is expensive, especially on expressways and in rural areas. The main types of gas available are *essence super* (leaded), *sans plomb* (unleaded), and *gazole* (diesel), so make sure you know what type your car takes. When possible, buy gas before you get on the expressway and keep an eye on pump prices as you go. These vary—anywhere from €1.10 to €2 per liter. The cheapest gas can be found at *hypermarchés* (large supermarkets). In rural areas it's possible to drive for miles without passing a gas station, so don't let your tank get too low.

PARKING

Parking is a nightmare in Paris and many other metropolitan areas. "Pay and display" metered parking is usually limited to two hours in city centers. Parking is free on Sunday, national holidays, and after 7 pm. In residential areas, parking meters showing a dense yellow circle indicate a free parking zone during the month of August. In smaller towns, parking may be permitted on one side of the street only—alternating every two weeks—so pay attention to signs. In France, illegally parked cars are likely to be impounded, especially those blocking entrances or fire exits. Parking tickets start at €17, topping out at €175 in a handicapped zone for a first offense, and there's no shortage of blue-uniformed parking police. Parking lots, indicated by a blue sign with a white "P," are usually underground and generally expensive.

ROAD CONDITIONS

Metropolitan France has 11,465 km (7,124 miles) of expressways and 1,054,092 km (654,982 miles) of main roads. For the fastest route between two points, look for roads marked *autoroute*. A *péage* (toll) must be paid on most expressways: the rate varies but can be steep. The N (*route nationale*) roads—which are sometimes divided highways—and D (*route départementale*) roads are usually also wide and fast.

There are excellent links between Paris and most French cities, but poor ones between the provinces (the principal exceptions are A26 from Calais to Reims, A62 between Bordeaux and Toulouse, and A9/A8 the length of the Mediterranean coast).

Though routes are numbered, the French generally guide themselves from city to city and town to town by destination name. When reading a map, keep one eye on the next big city toward your destination as well as the next small town; most snap decisions will have to be based on town names, not road numbers. Look for signage pointing you in the right direction; this is especially useful in roundabouts, which can be rather confusing.

ROADSIDE EMERGENCIES

All highways also have special phones you can use in the event of a roadside emergency; you'll see them every few kilometers—just pick up the bright orange phone and dial the free number (*112*). If you have car trouble anywhere else, find the nearest garage or contact the police. No matter where you are, make sure to turn on your hazard lights. Note that each rental car should also be equipped with a mandatory high-visibility vest and a warning triangle.

Emergency Services Police. ☎ *112*.

RULES OF THE ROAD

The general rule is to drive on the right and yield to drivers coming from streets to the right; however, this does not necessarily apply at traffic circles, where you should watch out for just about everyone. Do not expect to find traffic lights in the center of the road, as French lights are usually on the right- and left-hand sides; and do not make right turns at red lights unless you have a blinking arrow. Do not use a cell phone—or even a hands-free headset—while driving; it's illegal and could incur a €135 fine. But do make sure to buckle up; seat belts are mandatory for all passengers, and those under age 12 must be in the backseat.

Speed limits are designated by the type of road you're driving on: 130 kph (80 mph) or 110 kph (70 mph) on expressways (*autoroutes*); 90 kph (55 mph) on divided roads (*routes nationales*), which could soon be reduced to 80 kph (50 mph); 50 kph (30 mph) on departmental roads (*routes*); and 35 kph (22 mph) in some cities and towns (*villes et villages*). Drivers are expected to know these limits, so signs are usually posted only when there are exceptions to these rules. French drivers break speed limits all the time, and police dish out on-the-spot fines with equal abandon. So don't feel pressure from Jean-Pierre honking behind you to speed up: in addition to the 2,173 fixed speed cameras across the country, there are now 150 unmarked police vehicles that can flash a car in either direction. Within the first 15 months of operation, some 270,000 speeding tickets were issued.

You might be asked by the Police National to pull over at busy intersections. You will have to show your papers (*papiers*)—including car insurance—and may be submitted to a *l'éthylotest* (Breathalyzer test). The rules in France have become stringent because of the high incidence of accidents on the roads; anything above a 0.05% blood alcohol level—which, according to your size, could simply mean two or three glasses of wine—and you are over the limit. For new drivers, having passed their test within three years, the limit is only 0.02%.

Some important traffic terms and signs to note: *sortie* (exit); *sens unique* (one-way); *stationnement interdite* (no parking); and *impasse* (dead end). Blue rectangular signs indicate a highway; green rectangular signs indicate a major direction; triangles carry illustrations of a particular traffic hazard; speed limits are indicated in a circle with the maximum limit circled in red. If you see a red triangle with an "X" or with a line through a straight arrow, be careful to give priority to the next right, even if it doesn't seem like a main road: in these cases, you do not have the right of way.

CRUISE SHIP TRAVEL

Canal and river cruises are popular in France, particularly along the picturesque waterways of Brittany, Burgundy, and the Midi.

Cruise Ship Companies Abercrombie & Kent. ☎ *800/554–7016 in U.S. and Canada* 🌐 *www.abercrombiekent.com.* **AmaWaterways.** ☎ *800/626–0126 in U.S. and Canada* 🌐 *www.amawaterways.com.* **En-Bateau.** ☎ *04–67–13–19–62* 🌐 *www.en-bateau.com.* **European Waterways.** ☎ *877/879–8808 in U.S., 877/574–3404 in Canada* 🌐 *www.gobarging.com.* **France Passion Plaisance.** ☎ *03–85–53–76–70* 🌐 *www.france-passion-plaisance.fr.* **French Country Waterways.** ☎ *800/222–1236 in U.S. and Canada* 🌐 *www.fcwl.com.* **Viking River Cruises.** ☎ *877/668–4546 in U.S. and Canada* 🌐 *www.vikingrivercruises.com.*

TRAIN TRAVEL

The French national train agency, the Sociète Nationale de Chemins de Fer, or SNCF, is fast, punctual, comfortable, and comprehensive . . . when it's not on strike. Traveling across France, you have various options: local trains, overnight trains with sleeping accommodations, and the high-speed Trains à Grande Vitesse, known as the TGV.

TGVs are the best and the fastest domestic trains, averaging 255 kph (160 mph) on the Lyon–southeast line and 320 kph (200 mph) on the Lille and Bordeaux–southwest lines. They operate between Paris and Lille/Calais, Paris and Brussels, Paris and Amsterdam, Paris and Lyon–Switzerland–Provence, Paris and Angers–Nantes, Paris–Avignon and Tours–Poitiers–Bordeaux. As with other main-line trains, a small supplement may be assessed at peak hours.

It's usually fast and easy to cross France without traveling overnight, especially on TGVs, which are generally affordable, efficient, and equipped with creature comforts, such as Wi-Fi. Be aware that trains fill up quickly on weekends and holidays, so purchase tickets well in advance for these times. Otherwise, you can take a slow overnight train, which often costs more than a TGV, with the option of reclining in your assigned seat or bedding down in a *couchette* (bunk, six to a compartment in second class, four to a compartment in first, or private cabins).

In Paris there are six international rail stations: Gare du Nord (northern France, northern Europe, and England via Calais or Boulogne); Gare St-Lazare (Normandy and England via Dieppe); Gare de l'Est (Strasbourg, Luxembourg, Basel, and central Europe); Gare de Lyon (Lyon,

Marseille, Provence, Côte d'Azur, Switzerland, and Italy); Gare d'Austerlitz (Loire Valley and central France, overnight to Nice and Spain); and Gare Montparnasse (southwest France and Spain).

BOOKING AND BUYING TICKETS

There are two classes of train service in France; first (*première*) or second (*deuxième*). First-class seats offer more legroom, plusher upholstery, private reading lamps, computer plugs on the TGV, and wireless connectivity, not to mention a hushed, no-cell-phone environment for those who want to sleep. The price can be nearly double, though there are often deals online.

It is best—and in many cases, essential—to prebook your train tickets. This requires making a reservation online, by phone, or in person at the train station. Rail Europe does an excellent job providing train tickets to those in the United States. It offers a service, and the higher prices reflect that. If you want to save money, however, book directly with the SNCF.

RAIL PASSES

There are two kinds of rail passes: those you must purchase at home (including the France Rail Pass and Eurail Pass) and those available in France from SNCF.

If you plan to travel outside Paris by train, consider purchasing a France Rail Pass through Rail Europe; it allows for 1, 3, 4, 5, 6, 7, 8, or 9 days of unlimited train travel in a one-month period. If you travel solo for three days, first class will run you $283 and second class $230; you can add up to six days on this pass for $40 a day in first class, $31 a day in second class. For two people traveling together on a Saver Pass, the first-class cost is $248 per person, and in second class it's $201.

France is one of 28 countries in which you can use Eurail passes, which provide unlimited rail travel for a set amount of time. If you plan to rack up the miles, get a Global Pass; it's valid for first-class rail trail in all member nations for periods ranging from five days ($581) to three months ($2,037). The Regional Pass, which covers rail travel in and between pairs of bordering countries over a two-month period, is an alternative. Unlike most Eurail passes, Regional passes are available for first- or second-class travel; prices begin at $395 (first class) and $317 (second class) for four days of travel. Whichever pass you choose, remember that you must buy it before leaving for France.

Reduced fares are available for seniors (over 60), children (under 12), and passengers under 26. The Senior+ railcard costs €60, is valid for one year, and entitles you to up to a 50% reduction on full-fare TGV and intercité trains, with a guaranteed minimum reduction of 25% on all other train fares (including last-minute ones). With the Carte Enfant Plus (€60), children 4 to 11 years old accompanying adults can get up to 50% off most trains for an unlimited number of trips; valid for a year, this card is perfect if you're planning to spend a lot of time traveling *en famille*. You can also opt for the Enfant+: when you buy your ticket, simply show a valid ID with your child's age and you can get a significant discount for your child and a 25% reduction for up to four accompanying adults.

If you purchase an individual ticket from SNCF in France and you're under 26, you automatically get a 25% reduction when you flash a valid ID. If you're under 26 and plan to ride the train quite a bit, consider buying the Carte 12–27 (€50), which offers unlimited 50% reductions for one year. If you don't benefit from any of these reductions but plan on traveling at least 200 km (132 miles) round-trip and don't mind staying over a Saturday night, look into the CarteWeek-end (€75); it gives you and your traveling companion a 25% reduction.

BOARDING THE TRAIN

Get to the station at least an hour before departure to ensure you'll have time for ticketing and, in some cases, seat

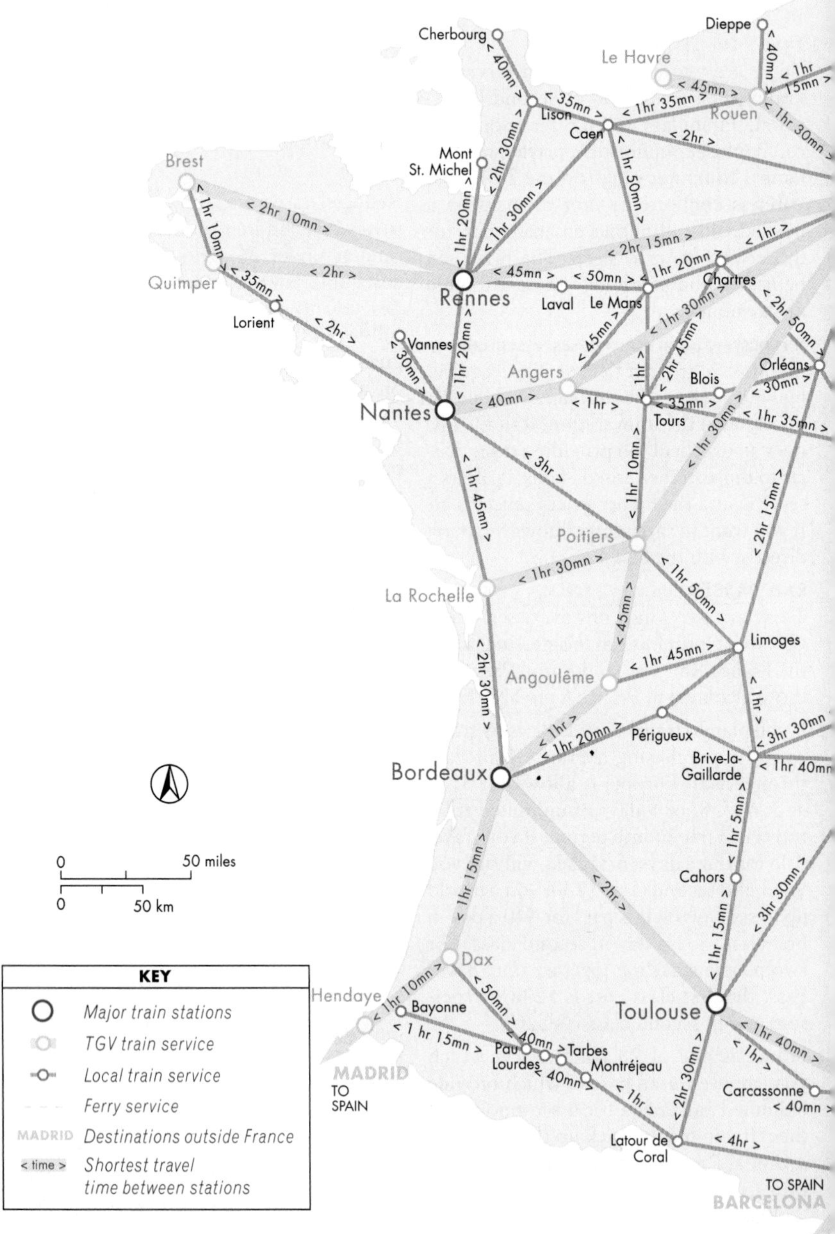

TO U.K.
LONDON
Boulogne
Dieppe
Le Havre
Rouen
Cherbourg
Lison
Caen
Mont St. Michel
Brest
Quimper
Lorient
Rennes
Laval
Le Mans
Chartres
Vannes
Angers
Nantes
Blois
Orléans
Tours
Poitiers
La Rochelle
Limoges
Angoulême
Périgueux
Brive-la-Gaillarde
Bordeaux
Cahors
Dax
Hendaye
Bayonne
Pau
Lourdes
Tarbes
Montréjeau
Toulouse
Carcassonne
Latour de Coral
MADRID
TO SPAIN
TO SPAIN
BARCELONA
< 40mn >
< 45mn >
< 1hr 15mn >
< 35mn >
< 1hr 35mn >
< 1hr 30mn >
< 2hr >
< 2hr 30mn >
< 1hr 50mn >
< 2hr 10mn >
< 1hr 20mn >
< 1hr 30mn >
< 1hr 10mn >
< 2hr 15mn >
< 1hr >
< 2hr >
< 45mn >
< 50mn >
< 1hr 20mn >
< 35mn >
< 2hr >
< 2hr 50mn >
< 1hr 30mn >
< 45mn >
< 30mn >
< 1hr 20mn >
< 1hr >
< 2hr 45mn >
< 40mn >
< 1hr >
< 35mn >
< 30mn >
< 1hr 35mn >
< 1hr 30mn >
< 3hr >
< 1hr 10mn >
< 1hr 45mn >
< 2hr 15mn >
< 1hr 30mn >
< 1hr 50mn >
< 45mn >
< 1hr 45mn >
< 2hr 30mn >
< 1hr >
< 1hr >
< 1hr 20mn >
< 3hr 30mn >
< 1hr 40mn >
< 1hr 5mn >
< 1hr 15mn >
< 2hr >
< 3hr 30mn >
< 1hr 15mn >
< 1hr 10mn >
< 50mn >
< 1 hr 15mn >
< 40mn >
< 40mn >
< 1hr >
< 2hr 30mn >
< 1hr 40mn >
< 1hr >
< 40mn >
< 4hr >
0
50 miles
0
50 km
KEY
Major train stations
TGV train service
Local train service
Ferry service
MADRID Destinations outside France
< time > Shortest travel time between stations

Travel Times by Train
TO BELGIUM
BRUSSELS
TO BELGIUM
GHENT
FRANKFURT
TO GERMANY
KARLSRUHE
TO GERMANY
STUTTGART
TO GERMANY
ZURICH
TO SWITZERLAND
LAUSANNE
TO SWITZERLAND
GENEVA
SWITZERLAND
TURIN
TO ITALY
GENOA
TO ITALY
LUXEMBOURG
Dunkerque
Calais
Lille
Arras
Amiens
Cambrai
Charleville-Mézières
Reims
Châlons-en-Champagne
PARIS
Metz
Lorraine
Strasbourg
Nancy
Troyes
Chaumont
Colmar
Mulhouse
Belfort
Auxerre
Dijon
Besançon
Bourges
Nevers
Beaune
Frasne
Vichy
Mâcon
Bourg-en-Bresse
Clermont-Ferrand
Lyon
Chambéry
Modane
Aurillac
Grenoble
Gap
Nîmes
Avignon
Montpellier
Narbonne
Perpignan
Cerbère
Aix-en-Provence
Marseille
Toulon
Nice
MONACO
Monte Carlo
Antibes
Cannes
St-Raphaël
Bastia
Calvi
CORSICA

selection. If you're taking a TGV, your seat is reserved by car and seat number. Before boarding, you must punch your ticket (*composter le billet*) in one of the yellow machines at the entrance to the platforms (*quais*) or else risk a €10–€25 fine (*amende*) plus a processing fee of €30–€38. Tickets printed by the SNCF must be validated; Eurail passes and tickets printed at home don't need validation. If you board your train on the run and don't have time to punch it, look for a conductor (*contrôleur*) as soon as possible and get him to sign it. Once you're aboard, note that smoking is forbidden on all public transportation in France. Even lighting up in the bathrooms or connecting compartments will land you an on-the-spot fine of €68.

OTHER SERVICES

With an advance arrangement, SNCF will pick up and deliver your bags at a given time. For instance, if you're planning on spending a weekend in Nice, SNCF will collect your luggage at your hotel in Paris in the morning before checkout and deliver it to your hotel in Nice, where it will be awaiting your arrival. The cost within France is €38 for the first bag (up to 30 kg), and €20 per additional bag. Be advised that luggage service is only available Monday to Saturday mornings in mainland France, Germany, Luxembourg, and Switzerland.

You can also book a driver to take you to or pick you up from the station. Rates are fixed, and pickup is guaranteed; even if your train is late, your driver (who carries a sign with your name) will wait for you at no extra cost. With prices starting at €9.90, it's much more economical than a taxi, and the same rate applies for up to four people per car (maximum four pieces of luggage). See 🌐 *www.idcab.sncf.com* for details.

TO AND FROM THE UNITED KINGDOM

When you factor in travel time to and from the airport, not to mention flight delays, taking the Channel Tunnel is the fastest and easiest way to travel between France and the United Kingdom. The high-speed Eurostar train from Paris's Gare du Nord to London's St. Pancras Station takes 2 hours, 15 minutes. Eurostar prices vary widely—round-trip tickets range from €620 for first class to €175 for second class—but depending on when and where you travel and how far in advance you book, you should be able to find discounted rates; there are special ones available for early-bird purchasers, children, seniors, and multiple-fare buyers. If you wish to drive most of the route, you can put your car on the train (either through Eurotunnel or Eurostar) for the 35-minute Chunnel crossing between Calais and Folkestone. Britain's National Rail also has daily departures from London that link up with the Dover–Calais–Boulogne ferry services through to Paris, and there's an overnight service on the Newhaven–Dieppe ferry.

Information **Britain's National Rail.** ☎ *0845/748–4950 in U.K., 44/0207–278–5240 from U.S.* 🌐 *www.nationalrail.co.uk.* **Eurail.** 🌐 *www.eurail.com.* **Eurostar.** ☎ *08–92–35–35–39 €0.34 per min, 0343/218–6186 in U.K.* 🌐 *www.eurostar.com.* **Eurotunnel.** ☎ *08–10–63–03–04* 🌐 *www.eurotunnel.com.* **Rail Europe.** ☎ *800/622–8600 in U.S. and Canada* 🌐 *www.raileurope.com.* **SNCF.** ☎ *3635 €0.34 per min* 🌐 *www.sncf.com.* **TGV.** ☎ *3635 €0.34 per min* 🌐 *www.tgv.com.*

ESSENTIALS

ACCOMMODATIONS

Most hotels and other lodgings require you to give your credit-card details before they will confirm your reservation. If you don't feel comfortable emailing this information, ask if you can fax it. However you book, get confirmation in writing and have a copy of it handy when you check in.

Be sure you understand the hotel's cancellation policy. Some places allow you to cancel without any kind of penalty—even if you prepaid to secure a discounted rate—provided you do so at least 24 hours in advance. Others require you to cancel a week in advance or penalize you the cost of one night. Most hotels allow children under a certain age to stay free in their parents' room, but others charge for them as extra adults; so always ask about cutoff ages. Also note that the *taxe de séjour*—a local tax which, depending on the type and location of your accommodation, can range from €0.20 to €4 per person per night—is not included in the quoted rates.

APARTMENT AND HOUSE RENTALS

Individual tourist offices often publish lists of *locations meublés* (furnished rentals) that have been inspected and rated. Usually they're booked directly through the property owner, which may require some knowledge of French. The French-based Fédération Nationale des Gîtes is another good place to start house hunting.

Vacation rentals in France typically book from Saturday to Saturday. Always check on policies regarding pets and children and specify if you want an enclosed garden for toddlers, a washing machine, a fireplace, a pool, and so on. If you plan to have overnight guests during your stay, let the owner know; there may be additional charges (insurance restrictions prohibit loading in guests beyond the specified capacity). Occasionally, further fees apply: these might include an end-of-stay cleaning, or even bed linen and towel rentals because French vacationers tend to bring their own. Be sure to plan early: apartment and house rentals are quite popular, especially during the summer.

Contacts **Fédération Nationale des Gîtes de France.** ☎ *01/49–70–75–75* 🌐 *www.gites-de-france.com.*

BED-AND-BREAKFASTS

Small inns and B&Bs are among the most charming lodgings in France. Take care when booking, as many require you to cancel far in advance.

Reservation Services **Chambres Hôtes France.** 🌐 *www.chambres-hotes.fr.* **Hôtes Qualité Paris.** 🌐 *www.hotesqualiteparis.fr.*

HOME EXCHANGES

With a direct home exchange you stay in someone else's house while they stay in yours. Some outfits also deal with vacation homes, so you're not actually staying in someone's full-time residence, just their vacant weekend place.

Exchange Clubs **Home Exchange.com.** ☎ *800/877–8723 in U.S. and Canada* 🌐 *www.homeexchange.com.* **HomeLink International.** ☎ *800/638–3841 in U.S. and Canada* 🌐 *www.homelink.org.* **Intervac U.S.** ☎ *866/884–7567 in U.S.* 🌐 *www.intervacus.com.*

HOTELS

According to industry statistics, there are around 17,350 hotels in France. These range from luxury properties to budget lodgings. The quality of accommodations, particularly in older properties and even in luxury hotels, can vary greatly from room to room; if you don't like the room you're given, ask to see another.

Meal plans, which are usually an option offered in addition to the accommodations, are generally only available with a minimum two- or three-night stay and are, of course, more expensive than the basic room rate. Inquire about meal plans when making reservations; details and prices are often stated on hotel websites. Sometimes breakfast is included in the stated price automatically. This is France, though, and most hotels will be within walking distance of a café or bakery.

It's always a good idea to make hotel reservations in Paris and other major tourist destinations as far in advance as possible, especially in late spring, summer, or early fall. Most hotels allow you to book online. If you wish to communicate further, email is the easiest way to proceed—the hotel staff is probably more likely to read English than to understand it spoken over the phone long-distance. Whether by email, phone, or fax you should notify your hotel of a possible late check-in (to prevent your room from being given away) and to make any special requests (such as the location or the size of the room you want). Ask that the hotel provide written confirmation of your reservation and requests.

If you arrive without a reservation, the tourist offices in major train stations and most towns can probably help you find a room. You can also check at the airport for accommodation listings.

Many hotels in France are small, family-run establishments. Some are affiliated with hotel groups, such as Logis de France (🌐 *www.logishotels.com*), which can be relied on for comfort, character, and regional cuisine. Three prestigious international groups with numerous converted châteaux, manor houses, and boutique properties are Châteaux & Hotels Collection (🌐 *www.chateauxhotels.com*), Relais & Châteaux (🌐 *www.relaischateaux.com*), and Small Luxury Hotels of the World (🌐 *www.slh.com*): check the websites for property listings. France also has numerous hotel chains. Examples in the upper price bracket are Novotel and Sofitel as well as InterContinental, Marriott, Hilton, Hyatt, Westin, and Sheraton. The Best Western, Holiday Inn, Campanile, Climat de France, Mercure, and Timhotel chains are more moderate. If you simply need a place to crash for one night (and aren't claustrophobic), the ubiquitous Ibis, Hotel Kyriad, and Formule FI brand fits the bill. Typically, chains offer a consistently acceptable standard of comfort (modern bathrooms, TVs, etc.) but tend to lack atmosphere. One notable exception is Best Western: its properties are independently owned and most try to maintain the local character.

COMMUNICATIONS

INTERNET

Most hotels have in-room *haut-débit* wireless access, although some only offer Wi-Fi in the lobby or ground-floor rooms; if being connected from your room is important, be sure to confirm in advance. Also, if you need to spend a lot of time online, make sure to ask when you book if there's a charge for the service. These days it's usually included in the room rate except at some high-end hotels; but, if not, hourly rates can add up quickly. Remember to bring an adapter for European-style plugs, too.

Wi-Fi hot spots can be found at many cafés, and the civic government offers no-cost access at hundreds of public places in Paris; check 🌐 *www.paris.fr* for "How to access the Wi-Fi free of charge." In other major cities, like Bordeaux, you'll find free access but will need to sign up online. Major airports also offer complimentary Wi-Fi, though sessions may be limited to 30 minutes. In smaller towns, ask at the local tourism office where you can get connected. Note: if you capture a wireless network called "Free," don't be misled—it's the name of the carrier used in France and is not free of charge.

■ TIP→ Check 🌐 *www.wificafespots.com* for the nearest hot spot. Worse-case scenario—head to the Golden Arches for unlimited access with any purchase.

PHONES

The country code for France is 33. The first two digits of French numbers are a prefix determined by zone: Paris and Ile-de-France, 01; the northwest, 02; the northeast, 03; the southeast, 04; and the southwest, 05. Pay close attention to numbers beginning with 08; some—but not all—are toll-free (when you dial one with a fee attached, a recorded message will tell you how much it will cost to proceed with the call, usually €0.15 or €0.34 per minute). Numbers beginning with 09, connected to DSL and Internet lines, are generally free when calling in France. Numbers that begin with 06 and 07 are reserved for cell phones.

Note that when dialing France from abroad, you drop the initial 0 from the number. For instance, to call a telephone number in Paris from the United States, dial 011–33 plus the phone number minus the initial 0 (phone numbers *in this book* are listed with the full 10 digits, which you use to make local calls).

CALLING WITHIN FRANCE

The French are very fond of their mobile phones (*portables*), meaning that telephone booths are on their way to becoming obsolete. But French telecom giant Orange does maintain some 40,000 nationwide, and the majority will accept a *ticket téléphone*, a prepaid calling card, which can be purchased through Orange boutiques (🌐 *www.orange.fr*). The cards work on any phone (including your hotel phone). To use one, you dial a free number, and then punch in a code indicated on the back of the card. For telephone information in France, you need to call one of the dozen or so six-digit *renseignement* numbers that begin with 118. (For Les Pages Jaunes—the French Yellow Pages—you dial 118–008.) The average price for one of these calls is €0.34 per minute.

CALLING OUTSIDE FRANCE

Telephoning from a hotel is almost always the priciest option because hotels usually add huge surcharges to all calls, particularly international ones. Calling cards can help lower costs. Then there are mobile phones (⇨ *below*), which are sometimes more prevalent than landlines. To make a direct international call out of France, dial 00 and wait for the tone; then dial the country code (1 for the United States and Canada), the area code (minus any initial 0), and the number.

MOBILE PHONES

If you have a multiband phone (some countries use different frequencies from what's used in the United States) and your service provider uses the world-standard GSM network (as do T-Mobile and AT&T), you can probably use your phone abroad. But be warned: this can be expensive, with toll charges on incoming and outgoing calls sometimes as high as $4 per minute. Roaming fees can be steep, too: 99¢ a minute is considered reasonable. Sending an international text message is usually a cheaper option, but be aware that fees abroad vary greatly (from 15¢ to 50¢ and up), and there's usually a charge for incoming messages. When using a cell phone abroad, it's advisable to turn off your data services function to avoid exorbitant, unexpected fees.

If you just want to make local calls, consider buying a prepaid SIM card (your provider may have to unlock your phone for you to use it); you can purchase one through Le French Mobile (🌐 *www.lefrenchmobile.com*), a service catering to English-speaking visitors. An alternative is to buy a cheap, disposable "BIC" prepaid phone; they're available from Orange outlets, tabacs, magazine kiosks, and some supermarkets. You can then have a local number and make local calls at local rates.

ONLINE CALLS

A cost-effective alternative is to use Skype (🌐 *www.skype.com*), Google Hangouts (🌐 *www.google.com/hangouts*), or Apple FaceTime (🌐 *www.apple.com*), which allow you to make calls online. After downloading free software, you can place no- or low-cost calls anywhere in the world with an Internet connection from your smartphone, tablet, or laptop.

EATING OUT

All establishments must post their menus outside, so take a look before you enter. Most restaurants have two basic types of menu: à la carte and fixed-price (*un menu* or prix-fixe). The prix-fixe menu is usually the best value, though choices are more limited. Many of these include three courses; however, it's increasingly common to see set menus with two—either a starter and main course (*entrée et plat*) or a main course and dessert (*plat et dessert*).

FAST FOOD, FRENCH STYLE

Many say that bistros served the world's first fast food. After the fall of Napoléon, the Russian soldiers who occupied Paris were known to bang on zinc-top café bars, crying "*bistro*"—"quickly"—in Russian. In the past, bistros were simple places with minimal decor and service. Nowadays many are upscale and trendy, but you can still find cozy, low-key establishments serving straightforward, frequently gutsy cooking.

Brasseries—ideal places for quick, one-dish meals—originated when Alsatians, fleeing German occupiers after the Franco-Prussian War, came to Paris and opened restaurants serving specialties from home. Pork-based dishes, *choucroute* (sauerkraut), and beer (*brasserie* also means brewery) remain the mainstays here. The typical brasserie is convivial and keeps late hours. Some are open 24 hours a day, a good thing to know since many restaurants stop serving at 10 or 10:30 pm.

Like bistros and brasseries, cafés come in a variety of styles and sizes. Often informal neighborhood hangouts, cafés may also be veritable showplaces attracting chic, well-heeled crowds. At most cafés the regulars congregate at the bar, where coffee and drinks are cheaper than at tables. At noon tables are set, and a limited lunch menu is served. Sandwiches, usually with *jambon* (ham), *fromage* (cheese), or *mixte* (ham and cheese), are served throughout the day. Sometimes snacks are also for sale. Cafés are for lingering, for people-watching, and for daydreaming. If none of these options fit the bill, head to the nearest *traiteur* (deli) for picnic fixings.

Breakfast is usually served from 7:30 am to 10 am, lunch from noon to 2 pm, and dinner from 7:30 or 8 pm to 10 pm. Restaurants in Paris usually serve dinner until 10:30 pm. Many restaurants close on Sunday—head to the Latin Quarter, the Champs Élysées, or Montmartre for the greatest choice of eateries open then.

PAYING

By French law, prices must include tax and tip (*service compris* or *prix nets*), but pocket change left on the table to round up the bill in basic places, or an additional 5% in better restaurants, is always appreciated. (Don't expect the dangling generous tip to guarantee friendly service, though: customer service is practically nonexistent in France.) Beware of bills stamped *service not included* in English. The prices given in this book are per person for a main course at dinner, including tax (10%) and service; note that if a restaurant offers only prix-fixe (set-price) meals, it is given a price category that reflects the full prix-fixe price.

ELECTRICITY

The electrical current in France is 220 volts, 50 cycles alternating current (AC); electrical outlets take Continental-type plugs, with two round prongs. So you may need to use both an adapter (which enables you to plug your appliance into the different style of socket) and a converter (which allows it to run on the different voltage). Most laptops and mobile phone chargers are dual voltage (i.e., they operate equally well on 110 and 220 volts); hence they require only an adapter. These days the same is true of many small appliances, but you should always check labels and manufacturer instructions to be sure. Don't use 110-volt outlets marked "for shavers only" for high-wattage appliances such as hair dryers.

Contacts Adaptelec. 🌐 *www.adaptelec.com.*

EMERGENCIES

France's emergency services are conveniently streamlined. Every town and village has a *médecin de garde* (on-duty doctor) for flus, sprains, tetanus shots, and similar problems. Larger cities also have a remarkable house-call service called SOS Médecins (☎ *01–47–07–77–77*); for dental emergencies, contact SOS Dentistes (☎ *01–43–37–51–00*). The cost is minimal, compared to the United States—about €65 for a house call. If you need an X-ray or emergency treatment, call an ambulance (☎ *15*). The easiest number to remember in case of emergency is 112, the European equivalent of 911; the call is free from any land line or cell phone.

Most hotels will be able to help you find assistance in the event of a health crisis. Note that outside Paris it may be difficult to locate English-speaking doctors.

You may be able to get a list of ones—along with info on nearby hospitals, private clinics, and medical centers—from a pharmacy. Bear in mind that pharmacists themselves are authorized to administer first aid and recommend over-the-counter drugs, and hence can be very helpful when health problems are minor. *Pharmacies de garde* are designated dispensaries that remain open overnight, on Sunday and holidays, or 24/7. These rotate, but a list of locations is posted at the entrance of every pharmacy; you can also find one by calling 3915 (€0.34/min), though the operator may not speak English.

On the street the French phrases that may be needed in an emergency are: *Au secours!* (Help!), *urgence* (emergency), *samu* (ambulance), *pompiers* (firefighters), *préfecture de police* (police station), *médecin* (doctor), and *hôpital* (hospital).

HOLIDAYS

With 11 national *jours feriés* (holidays) and at least five weeks of paid vacation, the French have their share of repose. In May there's a holiday nearly every week, so be prepared for stores, banks, and museums to shut their doors for days at a time. Be sure to call museums, restaurants, and hotels in advance to make sure they'll be open.

Note that these dates are for the calendar year 2016: January 1 (New Year's Day); March 27 and 28 (Easter Sunday and Monday); May 1 (Labor Day); May 5 (Ascension Day); May 8 (V.E. Day); May 16 (Pentecost Monday); July 14 (Bastille Day); August 15 (Assumption); November 1 (All Saints Day); November 11 (Armistice Day); December 25 (Christmas Day).

MAIL

Post offices, found in every town, are recognizable by a yellow La Poste sign. They're usually open weekdays from 9 or 9:30 am to 5 pm, and Saturday from 9 am to noon.

SHIPPING PACKAGES

Letters and postcards to the United States and Canada cost €1.20 for 20 grams. Stamps can be bought in post offices and in cafés displaying a red tabac sign outside. It takes, on the average, four days for letters to arrive in Europe, and five days to reach the United States.

If you're uncertain where you'll be staying, have mail sent to the local post office, addressed as *poste restante*. The French postal service has a €0.58 per item service charge.

Sending overnight mail from major cities in France is relatively easy. Besides DHL, Federal Express, and UPS, the French post office has overnight mail service, called Chronopost, which is much cheaper for small packages. Keep in mind that certain things cannot be shipped from France to the United States, such as perfume, fresh food, or any meat products.

MONEY

The following prices are for Paris; other areas are often cheaper (with the notable exception of the Côte d'Azur). Keep in mind that it's less expensive to eat or drink standing at a café or bar counter than sitting at a table. Two prices are listed, *au comptoir* (at the counter) and *à salle* (at a table). Sometimes orders cost even more if you're seated at a terrace table. Coffee in a bar: €1.50–€2.50 (standing), €2–€7 (seated); beer in a bar: €3 (standing), €3.50–€7 (seated); Coca-Cola: €3–€5 a bottle; ham sandwich: €3–€6; 2-km (1-mile) taxi ride: €7–€10; movie-theater seat: €11.40 (morning shows are always cheaper); foreign newspaper: €3–€6.

Prices throughout this guide are given for adults. Substantially reduced fees are almost always available for children, students, and senior citizens.

ATMS AND BANKS

Readily found throughout France, ATMs (*guichets*) are the easiest ways to get euros. Your own bank will probably charge a fee for using one abroad; the foreign bank you choose may also charge a fee. Nevertheless, you can usually get a better rate of exchange at an ATM than you will at a currency-exchange office or even when changing money in a bank. Extracting funds as you need them is also a safer option than carrying around a large amount of cash. Just be sure to know your withdrawal limit before taking money out, and be advised that French ATMs sometimes restrict how much you can get, regardless of your bank balance.

TIP→ PINs with more than four digits are not recognized at ATMs in many countries. If yours has five or more, remember to change it before you leave.

You'll find lots of ATMs on the street, but it's best to use ones inside the bank's doors. Even then, cover the key pad with one hand while you type your PIN in with the other. If anyone tries to speak to you during your transaction, ignore them. Note that the ATM will give you two chances to enter the correct PIN; if you make a mistake on the third try, your card will be held, and you'll have to go into the bank to retrieve it (this may mean returning during open hours).

CREDIT CARDS

Credit cards—MasterCard and Visa in particular—are widely accepted here, so a business would have to be extremely small or very remote not to have some credit-card capability. Some smaller restaurants and stores, however, do have a credit-card minimum (usually around €15); this should be clearly indicated, but ask if you're in doubt. After using your card, remember to take your receipt, as fraudulent use of credit-card numbers gleaned from receipts is on the rise.

It's a good idea to inform your credit-card company before you leave home, especially if you don't travel internationally very often. Otherwise, they might put a hold on your card due to unusual activity—not a good thing halfway through your trip. Record all your credit-card numbers—as well as the phone numbers to call if your cards are lost or stolen—in a safe place, like a USB stick, so you're prepared should something go wrong. MasterCard and Visa have general numbers you can call (collect if you're abroad) if your card is lost, but you're better off calling the number of your issuing bank, since MasterCard and Visa typically just transfer you to your bank anyway; your bank's number is usually printed on your card.

If you plan to use your credit card for cash advances, you'll need to apply for a PIN at least two weeks before your trip. Although it's generally cheaper (and safer) to use a credit card abroad for large purchases (so you can cancel payments or be reimbursed if there's a problem), note that some credit-card companies *and* the banks that issue them add substantial percentages to all foreign transactions, whether they're in a foreign currency or not. Check on these fees before leaving home, so there won't be any surprises when you get the bill.

Also be warned that many non-European cards lack the *puce* microchip typically found in French credit cards. While waiters and store vendors will have no problem swiping your card, buying métro passes from a machine is impossible without a chip-enhanced card.

CURRENCY AND EXCHANGE

The advent of the euro makes any whirlwind European tour all the easier. From France you can glide across the borders of Austria, Germany, Italy, Spain, Holland, Ireland, Greece, Belgium, Finland, Luxembourg, and Portugal with no pressing need to run to the local exchange booth to change to yet another currency before you even had the time to become familiar with the last. You'll be able to do what drives many tourists crazy—to assess the value of a purchase (for example, to realize that eating a three-course meal in a small restaurant in Lisbon is cheaper than that ham sandwich you bought on the Champs Élysées).

At this writing, one euro equals U.S. $1.14 and $1.42 Canadian. These days, the easiest way to get euros is through ATMs; you can find them in airports, train stations, and throughout cities and towns. ATM rates are excellent because they're based on wholesale rates offered only by major banks. Remember, though, that you may be charged an added exchange fee when withdrawing euros from your account. It's a good idea to bring some euros with you from home and always to have some cash on hand as backup.

Currency Conversion **XE.com.** *www.xe.com.*

PASSPORTS

All Canadian, U.K., and U.S. citizens, even infants, need only a valid passport to enter France for stays of up to 90 days. You must apply in person if you're getting a passport for the first time; if your previous passport was lost, stolen, or damaged; or if your previous passport has expired and was issued more than 15 years ago or when you were under 16. All children under 18 must appear in person to apply for or renew a passport. Both parents must accompany any child under 14 (or send a notarized statement with their permission) and provide proof of their relationship to the child.

SAFETY

Beware of petty theft—purse snatching, cell phone grabbing, pickpocketing, and the like—throughout France, particularly in Paris and along the Côte d'Azur. Use common sense: keep your expensive jewelry at home, avoid pulling out a lot of money in public, and avoid darkly lit areas in the evening. Women should carry a handbag with zippered compartments for money and passports, plus long straps that can be slung across the body, bandolier style. Men should keep their wallets in front pockets. When withdrawing money from cash machines, be especially aware of your surroundings and anyone standing too close. If you feel uneasy, press the cancel button (*annuler*) and walk to an area where you feel more comfortable. Credit-card fraud is increasing in France, especially in urban areas; be sure to collect your receipts, as these have recently been used by thieves to make online purchases. Car break-ins, especially in central Paris, inner suburbs, and isolated parking lots, are definitely on the rise. Don't leave valuables, luggage, phones, computers, or other electronics in your car; if you must, make sure they are out of view in the glove compartment or trunk.

TIP→ Distribute your cash, credit cards, IDs, and other valuables between a deep front pocket, an inside jacket or vest pocket, and a hidden money pouch. Don't reach for the money pouch once you're

in public. Be especially vigilant on public transportation and in crowded areas.

TAXES

Taxes must be included in affixed prices in France. Prices in restaurants and hotels must by law include taxes and service charges. **TIP→ If these appear as additional items on your bill, you should complain.** There is, however, one exception: don't be shocked to find the *taxe de séjour* (tourist tax) on your hotel tab when you check out. Ranging from €0.20 to €4 per person per day, it is applied to all types of lodging. Even if you prepaid your accommodation online through a third-party travel website, you'll still have to cough up the coins.

The standard rate of the V.A.T. (Value-Added Tax, known in France as T.V.A.) is now 20%, with luxury goods taxed at a higher rate (up to 33%) and restaurant food taxed at a lower one (10%). The V.A.T. for services (restaurants, theaters, etc.) is not refundable, but foreigners are often entitled to a V.A.T. refund on goods they buy. To be eligible for one, the item (or items) that you purchased must have been bought in a single day in a participating store (look for the "Tax-Free" sticker on the door) and must equal or exceed €175.01.

A new procedure for obtaining this refund—the PABLO system—was launched in 2014. Participating retailers will provide you with a computer-generated PABLO Value-Added Tax (V.A.T.) refund form containing a bar code and the PABLO logo. You then scan the code before checking in at the airport for your outbound flight. PABLO machines at CDG and Orly provide service in English and can credit the refunded amount directly to your bank account.

At the airport, be sure to have your passport, your ticket, and your PABLO form for items purchased. Go to the La Détaxe/tax refund machine, scan the form's bar code and you'll receive a message "*OK bordereau confirmé*" ("OK, form approved"). An electronic confirmation will be sent directly to the retailer for your reimbursement to be processed. Remember, this must be done *before* checking-in your luggage.

TIME

The time difference between New York and Paris is 6 hours: when it's 1 pm in New York, it's 7 pm in Paris. France, like the rest of Europe, uses the 24-hour clock, which means that after noon you continue counting forward: 13h00 is 1 pm, 22h30 is 10:30 pm. The European format for abbreviating dates is day/month/year, so 7/5/13 means May 7, not July 5.

Time Zones Timeanddate.com. 🌐 *www.timeanddate.com/worldclock.*

TIPPING

The French have a clear idea of when they should be tipped. Bills in bars and restaurants include a service charge incorporated into the price, but it's customary to round out your bill with some small change unless you're dissatisfied. The amount varies: anywhere from €0.20, if you've merely bought a beer or coffee, to €1–€3 (or more) after a meal. Tip taxi drivers and hair stylists 5–10%. In some theaters and hotels, coat-check attendants may expect nothing (if there's a sign saying "*pourboire interdit*"—tips forbidden); otherwise give them €1. Washroom attendants usually get €0.50, though the sum is often posted.

If you stay in a hotel for more than two or three days, it's customary to leave something for the chambermaid—€1–€2 per day. In expensive hotels you may well use the services of a parking valet, doorman, bellhop, and concierge. All expect a tip. Expect to pay €2 (€1 in a moderately priced hotel) to the person who carries your bags or hails a taxi for you; if the concierge has been helpful, leave a tip of €5–€20 depending on the service;

in hotels that provide room service, give €1–€2 to the waiter (this does not apply to breakfast served in your room).

Museum guides should get €1–€1.50 after a tour. For other kinds of tours, tip the guide or excursion leader 10% of the tour cost; it's standard practice to tip long-distance bus drivers about €2 after an excursion, too. Other tips will depend on how much you've used a person's services—common sense must guide you here.

VISITOR INFORMATION

All major cities and most small towns have tourism offices that can provide information on accommodation and sightseeing as well as maps.

France Tourism Information **France Tourism.** *int.rendezvousenfrance.com.*

ONLINE TRAVEL TOOLS

All About France **Centre des Monuments Nationaux.** *www.monuments-nationaux.fr.*
French Ministry of Culture. *www.culture.fr.*
French National Museums. *www.rmn.fr.*

INDEX

A

B

C

L

M

N

Q

R

S

PHOTO CREDITS

Front cover: JLImages / Alamy [Description: Abbey de Senanque viewed over lavander fields, Provence, France.] Back cover, from left to right: Rrrainbow / Shutterstock; abadesign/Shutterstock; Dominik Michalek/Shutterstock. Spine: Ron van Elst/Shutterstock. 1, Lane Clark, Fodors.com member. 2-3, iStockphoto. 5, alohaspirit/iStockphoto. Chapter 1: Experience France: 8-9, SIME / eStock Photo. 10, Lisa Ferguson, Fodors.com member. 11 (left), Michael Gwyther-Jones/Flickr. 11 (right), Betty H, Fodors.com member. 12, Bob Lawson, Fodors.com member. 13, Doug Pearson/Agency Jon Arnold Images/age fotostock. 14 (left), Chris Christensen, Fodors.com member. 14 (right), AJ Kersten, Fodors.com member. 15, SGM/age fotostock. 18 (left), Pete Labrozzi, Fodors.com member. 18 (center), Tiffany Weir, Fodors.com member. 18 (bottom), Claudio Giovanni Colombo/Shutterstock. 18 (right), elaine, Fodors.com member. 19 (left), Elena Elisseeva/Shutterstock. 19 (center), Holly McKee, Fodors.com member. 19 (bottom), Tangata, Fodors.com member. 19(right), james incorvaia, Fodors.com member. 20, basingstoke2, Fodors.com member. 21 (left), smugman, Fodors.com member. 21 (right), Judy J. Potrzeba, Fodors.com member. 22, Stefano Ember / Shutterstock. 23, Anna McClain, Fodors.com member. 24, Le Buerehiesel. 25 (left), GLong2027, Fodors.com member. 25 (right), dthomasdupont, Fodors.com member. 26, Shannon McShane, Fodors.com member. 27 (left and right), Robert Fisher. 28, Zyankarlo/Shutterstock. 29 (left), LadyofHats/wikipedia.org. 29 (right), Elizabeth A. Miller, Fodors.com member. 30, dspiel, Fodors.com member. 31 (left), nfldbeothuk, Fodors.com member. 31 (right), schlegal1, Fodors.com member. 34, Juan Carlos Muñoz/age fotostock. Chapter 2: Paris: 35, ajkarlin, Fodors.com member. 36, equiles28, Fodors.com member. 37 (left), Andrea Schwab, Fodors.com member. 37 (right), Ann Forcier, Fodors.com member. 38, christinaaparis, Fodors.com member. 47, Shoutforhumanity Dreamstime.com. 48, Fabien1309/wikipedia.org. 49, Renaud Visage/age fotostock. 50 (left), Frank Peterschroeder / Bilderberg/Aurora Photos. 50 (right), ostill/Shutterstock. 53, Directphoto.org / Alamy. 59, fabio chironi/age fotostock. 64, P. Narayan/age fotostock. 69, Elizabeth A. Miller, Fodors.com member. 71, Kevin George / Alamy. 74, rfx/Shutterstock. 78, Marisa Allegra Williams/iStockphoto. 87 (top), Paul Hahn/laif/Aurora Photos. 87 (bottom), SuperStock/age fotostock. 88 (left), Renaud Visage/ age fotostock. 88 (right), Ivan Vdovin/Shutterstock. 89 (top left), Stevan Stratford/iStockphoto. 89 (bottom), Gideon/Flickr, [CC BY 2.0]. 89 (top right), Robert Haines / Alamy. 90 (left), Renaud Visage/age fotostock. 90 (right), Carsten Madsen/iStockphoto. 91 (top left), xc/Shutterstock. 91 (top right), Corbis. 91 (bottom), Mehdi Chebil / Alamy. 105, Roger Salz/Flickr. 114, P. Narayan/age fotostock. 139, Cezary Piwowarski/wikipedia.org. Chapter 3: Side Trips from Paris: 145, Wojtek Buss/age fotostock. 146, Judith Nelson, Fodors.com member. 147 (top), elaine, Fodors.com member. 147 (bottom), TravelChic10, Fodors.com member. 148, Ivan Bastien/iStockphoto. 156-57, AM Corporation / Alamy. 158 (first), Elias H. Debbas II/Shutterstock. 158 (second), Jason Cosburn/Shutterstock. 158 (third), Public Domain. 158 (fourth), Michael Booth /Alamy. 158 (fifth), Michael Booth / Alamy. 159 (left), Jens Preshaw/age fotostock. 159 (top right), Public Domain. 159 (bottom right), The Print Collector / Alamy. 160 (top), michel mory/iStockphoto. 160 (center), Mike Booth/Alamy. 160 (bottom), Tommaso di Girolamo/age fotostock. 161, Hemis/Alamy. 162 (first), Public Domain. 162 (second), Jason Cosburn/Shutterstock. 162 (third), Guy Thouvenin/age fotostock. 162 (fourth), Visual Arts Library (London) / Alamy. 163 (top), Guy Thouvenin/age fotostock. 163 (bottom), Public Domain. 169, Jose Ignacio Soto/Shutterstock. 174, ShutterbugBill, Fodors.com member. 185, bobyfume/wikipedia.org. 188, Jean-Luc Bohin / age fotostock. Chapter 4: The Loire Valley: 195, Kevin Galvin/age fotostock. 196, P. Narayan/age fotostock. 197 (top left), P. Narayan/age fotostock. 197 (top right), Michael McClain, Fodors.com member. 197 (bottom), Connie28, Fodors.com member. 198, Per Karlsson - BKWine.com / Alamy. 199 (left), J.Bilic/age fotostock. 199 (right), Kelly Cline/iStockphoto. 200, caspermoller/Flickr. 210, vittorio sciosia / age fotostock. 212 (top), SuperStock/age fotostock. 212 (bottom), David Lyons / Alamy. 214 (top left), P. Narayan/age fotostock. 214 (top right), Public Domain. 214 (bottom), P. Narayan/age fotostock. 215 (top left), Duncan Gilbert/iStockphoto. 215 (bottom left), Public Domain. 215 (top right), S. Greg Panosian/iStockphoto. 215 (bottom center), Public Domain. 215 (bottom right), Visual Arts Library (London) / Alamy. 220-21, Travel Pix Collection / age fotostock. 231, Edyta Pawlowska/Shutterstock. 238, PHB.cz (Richard Semik)/Shutterstock. Chapter 5: Normandy: 245, San Rostro/age fotostock. 246, Anger O./age fotostock. 247, paolo siccardi/age fotostock. 248, Sylvain Grandadam/age fotostock. 249 (left), Robert Fried / Alamy. 249 (right), JTB Photo/age fotostock. 250, Barbs44, Fodors.com member. 261, JTB Photo / age fotostock. 271, Renaud Visage / age fotostock. 275, Matz Sjöberg / age fotostock. 284, S Tauqueur / age fotostock. 285, iStockphoto. 286, impact productions / Alamy. 287 (top left), Sylvain Grandadam/age fotostock. 287 (bottom left), Martin Florin Emmanuel / Alamy. 287 (top right), Wojtek Buss/age fotostock. 287 (bottom right), Visual Arts Library (London) / Alamy. Chapter 6: Brittany: 291, danilo donadoni/age fotostock. 292, iStockphoto. 293 (top), Chris Marlow, Fodors.com member. 293 (bottom), Poendl, Dreamstime.com.

294, SGM / age fotostock. 295 (left), SUDRES Jean-Daniel / age fotostock. 295 (right), psd/Flickr. 296, Guillaume Dub./iStockphoto. 298, GUIZIOU Franck / age fotostock. 305, MATTES René / age fotostock. 312, Guy Thouvenin / age fotostock. 318, Christophe Boisvieux / age fotostock. 324, clu/iStockphoto. 326, Elena Elisseeva/iStockphoto. Chapter 7: Champagne Country: 333, Doug Pearson/age fotostock. 334, Jean-Pierre Lescourre/age fotostock. 335, teresaevans, Fodor.com member. 336, Claudio Giovanni Colombo/Shutterstock. 343, Michel de Nijs/iStockphoto. 348, David W Hughes/Shutterstock. 349, John Miller / age fotostock. 350 (left), Cephas Picture Library / Alamy. 350 (right), Eric Baccega/age fotostock. 351 (top left), Public Domain. 351 (center left), Gryffindor/Wikimedia Commons. 351 (top right), Public Domain. 351 (bottom), Ray Roberts / Alamy. 351 (center right), PlatinumSunlight/Wikimedia Commons. 356, Sylvain Grandadam / age fotostock. 359, Yann Guichaoua / age fotostock. Chapter 8: Alsace-Lorraine: 365, SGM/age fotostock. 366 (left), Mary Jane Glauber, Fodors.com member. 366 (right), busterx, Fodors.com member. 367, Mary Jane Glauber, Fodors.com member. 368, klondike, Fodors.com member. 369 (top), Joerg Beuge/Shutterstock. 369 (bottom), Robert Harding Picture Library Ltd / Alamy. 370, Brian Ferrigno, Fodors.com member. 372, David Hughes / age fotostock. 380, Kevin O'Hara / age fotostock. 387, Mary Jane Glauber, Fodors.com member. 392, ARCO/G Lenz / age fotostock. 399, RIEGER Bertrand/age fotostock. 404-05, BODY Philippe / age fotostock. Chapter 9: Burgundy: 409, Sylvain Grandadam/age fotostock. 410 (top), R. Matina/age fotostock. 410 (bottom), Tristan Deschamps/age fotostock. 411, Christopher Redo, Fodors.com member. 412, Simon Reddy / Alamy. 413 (left), beltsazar/Shutterstock. 413 (right), Per Karlsson - BKWine.com / Alamy. 414, Cynthia Stalker, Fodors.com member. 416, RIEGER Bertrand / age fotostock. 422, RIEGER Bertrand / age fotostock. 428, lynnlin/Shutterstock. 433, Clay McLachlan/IPN/Aurora Photos. 434 (left), Alain DOIRE - CRT Bourgogne. 434 (right), Ernst Fretz/iStockphoto. 444, Tomasz Parys/iStockphoto. 451, Steve Vidler/SuperStock. 453, Austrophoto / age fotostock. 455, R. Matina / age fotostock. Chapter 10: Lyon and the Alps: 459, AJ Kersten, Fodors.com member. 460, Boyer/age fotostock. 461, wug, Fodors.com member. 462, Minerva Bloom, Fodors.com member. 470, MOIRENC Camille / age fotostock. 473, Matz Sjöberg / age fotostock. 474 (top), Hemis / Alamy. 474 (bottom), Cesar Lucas Abreu / age fotostock. 475 (left), Homer W Sykes / Alamy. 475 (right), Lourens Smak / Alamy. 478, Saillet Erick / age fotostock. 484, CHICUREL Arnaud / age fotostock. 489, von Essen Hotels. 493, GUIZIOU Franck / age fotostock. 499, Lazar Mihai Bogdan/Shutterstock. 501, Lazar Mihai-Bogdan/Shutterstock. 504, Walter Bibikow / age fotostock. Chapter 11: Provence: 513, Sylvain Grandadam /age fotostock. 514, Earl Eliason/iStockphoto. 515 (left), Carson Ganci/age fotostock. 515 (right), xms, Fodors.com member. 516, Guillaume Piolle/wikipedia.org. 517 (left), anj*f* či/Flickr. 517 (right), Andy Hawkins/Flickr. 518, SGM/age fotostock. 527, Mike Tumchewics, Fodors.com member. 529, Zyankarlo/Shutterstock. 532, JTB Photo / age fotostock. 538, JTB Photo/age fotostock. 544, JACQUES Pierre / age fotostock. 553, Minerva Bloom, Fodors.com member. 557 (top), Chad Ehlers/ age fotostock. 557 (bottom), Renaud Visage/age fotostock. 558 (left), David Barnes/age fotostock. 558 (right), Tramont_ana/Shutterstock. 559 (left), Bruno Morandi/age fotostock. 559 (right), David Buffington/age fotostock. 560 (top), Susan Jones/age fotostock. 560 (bottom), Plus Pix/age fotostock. 561 (top), DWPhoto/Shutterstock. 561 (bottom), Plus Pix/age fotostock. 562, Doug Scott/age fotostock. 563 (top), David Hughes/Shutterstock. 563 (center), SGM/age fotostock. 563 (bottom), Doug Scott/age fotostock. 566, Peter Adams/age fotostock. 571, MOIRENC Camille /age fotostock. 577, Owen Franken. 578 (left), Susana Guzmán Martínez/iStockphoto. 578 (right), Colin & Linda McKie/iStockphoto. 579 (left), Le Jardin du Quai. 579 (right), Alain Llora- Le Moulin de Mougins. 583, Brasil2/iStockphoto. 585, Johan Sjolander/iStockphoto. Chapter 12: The French Riviera: 591, mkinct, Fodors.com member. 592, Kathy Jensen, Fodors.com member. 593 (bottom left), Walter Bibikow/age fotostock. 593 (top), annerev, Fodors.com member. 593 (bottom right), flauta, Fodors.com member. 594, Perov Stanislav/Shutterstock. 599, Priamo Melo/iStockphoto. 605, Alan Copson / age fotostock. 623, GARDEL Bertrand / age fotostock. 625, MOIRENC Camille / age fotostock. 638, Renaud d'Avout d'Auerstaedt/ wikipedia.org. 640, Jose Fuste Raga / age fotostock. 649, Richard L'Anson / age fotostock. 656, Giancarlo Liguori/Shutterstock. Chapter 13, Monaco: 659, ostill/Shutterstock. 660, Matej Kastelic/ Shutterstock. 661 (top), StevanZZ/Shutterstock. 661 (bottom), Bertl123/Shutterstock. 662, Boris Stroujko/Shutterstock. 668, Britrob/Flickr. Chapter 14: Corsica: 675, Boris Buschardt/iStockphoto. 676 (top), Bouvier Ben/Shutterstock. 676 (center), Claudia Dewald/iStockphoto. 676 (bottom), Pixachi/ Shutterstock. 678, Bouvier Ben/Shutterstock. 684, Christophe Boisvieux / Alamy. 697, Oleksiy Drachenko/Shutterstock. Chapter 15: The Midi-Pyrénées and Languedoc-Roussillon: 701, Javier Larrea/age fotostock. 702, dcazalet, Fodors.com member. 703, wikipedia.org. 704, Mike Tumchewics, Fodors.com member. 715, FELIX Alain / age fotostock. 722, wikipedia.org. 729, seeyourworld, Fodors.com member. 736, Christian Musat/iStockphoto. 744, Jos. Antonio Moreno / age fotostock. Chapter 16: The Basque Country, Gascony, and Hautes-Pyrénées: 747, Josu Altzelai / age fotostock. 749 (left),

Botond Horvath/Shutterstock. 749 (right), Jens Buurgaard Nielsen/wikipedia.org. 750, Roger Bruton, Fodors. com member. 757, BERNAGER E./age fotostock. 758 (left), Javier Larrea/age fotostock. 758 (right), Javier Larrea/age fotostock. 759 (left), Le Naviose/age fotostock. 759 (center right), Mark Baynes /Alamy. 759 (top right), Robert Fried / Alamy. 759 (bottom), Mark Baynes / Alamy. 760, Mark Baynes/Alamy. 766, Gonzalo Azumendi / age fotostock. 772, GUIZIOU Franck / age fotostock. Chapter 17: Bordeaux and the Wine Country: 779, J.D. Dallet / age fotostock. 780, salciccioli, Fodors.com member. 781, The BORDEAUX WINE FESTIVAL /Laurent WANGERMEZ. 782, Benjamin Zingg/ wikipedia.org. 783 (top), Benjamin Zingg/wikipedia.org. 783 (bottom), Benjamin Zingg/wikipedia.org. 784, The BORDEAUX WINE FESTIVAL / Jean-Bernard NADEAU. 792, The BORDEAUX WINE FESTIVAL /Jean-Bernard NADEAU. 794, Fabrice RAMBERT. 801, t56gf, Fodors.com member. Chapter 18: The Dordogne: 803, P. Narayan/age fotostock. 804, Public Domain. 805 (top), Lagui/Shutterstock. 805 (bottom), S. Greg Panosian/iStockphoto. 806, aleske/Flickr. 807 (left), titanium22/Flickr. 807 (right), wikipedia.org. 808, deanh, Fodors.com member. 819, Peter Garbet/iStockphoto. 826, BODY Philippe/ age fotostock. 829, CINTRACT Romain / age fotostock.

About Our Writers: All photos are courtesy of the writers except for the following: Lyn Parry, courtesy of Brett Jones; Avery Sumner, courtesy of André Bizard.

NOTES

ABOUT OUR WRITERS

Nancy Heslin is editor-in-chief of the English-language *Riviera Reporter* magazine and a professor at the École de Journalisme in Nice. Since swapping Canada for the Côte d'Azur in 2001, she's distinguished herself as a "go-to" authority on the region, being interviewed by the likes of CBS, BBC, and APF. Nancy became a French citizen in 2010; she works her baguette butt off with endurance sports like the Nice Ironman (no, she didn't win). For this edition, she updated the Provence, French Riviera, Monaco, and Travel Smart chapters.

Writer **Sean Hillen** updated the Corsica chapter for this edition.

When writer-editor **Jennifer Ladonne** decided it was time to leave her longtime home of Manhattan, there was only one place to go: Paris. Her insatiable curiosity—which earned her a reputation in New York for knowing just the right place to go for just the right anything—has found the perfect home in the inexhaustible streets of Paris. An avid cook and wine lover, she's a frequent contributor on wine, culture, and travel and a monthly columnist for the magazine *France Today*. For this book she updated the Day Trips from Paris, Lyon and the Alps, and Dordogne chapters.

British travel writer and editor **Lyn Parry** has lived in France for almost 20 years. In Britain her Masters in Hotel and Catering Management, and a stint in a luxury four-star hotel, gave her a taste for fine French food and wine. After working for the wine trade in London her nose led her to Bordeaux. Since then she has lived near Paris, and latterly in the Rhône Valley. For this edition of France, she updated the Alsace-Lorraine chapter, the Burgundy chapter, and the Champagne Country chapter.

In 2007 **Avery Sumner** sold her café in the Florida Everglades and moved to France. Since then she's walked and cycled across the country perfecting the art of slow travel. Her current project, Real Travel France (*realtravel-france.com*), is an organic food and wine bike tour company in the southernmost region of France where she now lives, writes, and rides. For this edition, Avery updated our Midi-Pyrénées and the Languedoc-Roussillon; Basque Country, Gascony, and Hautes-Pyrénées; and Bordeaux and the Wine Country chapters.

Jack Vermee is a Canadian screenwriter, film critic, festival programmer, university lecturer, and freelance writer and editor who happily exchanged nature for culture by moving from Vancouver to Paris six years ago. Starting in the pre-video days of the early 1980s when he first visited the city to watch classic films at the old Cinémathèque Française, he has carried on a shameless love affair with *la ville-lumière* and its innumerable charms. He suspects the love affair will never run its course—with 6,100 city streets to explore and new adventures just around the next corner, how could it? Jack brought his knowledge to the Brittany, Normandy, and the Loire Valley chapters. He has no regrets. You can reach him at jvermee@gmail.com.

Updating our Paris chapter was our team of crack writers from *Fodor's Paris 2016*: **Jennifer Ladonne, Linda Hervieux, Nancy Heslin, Virginia Power,** and **Jack Vermee.**

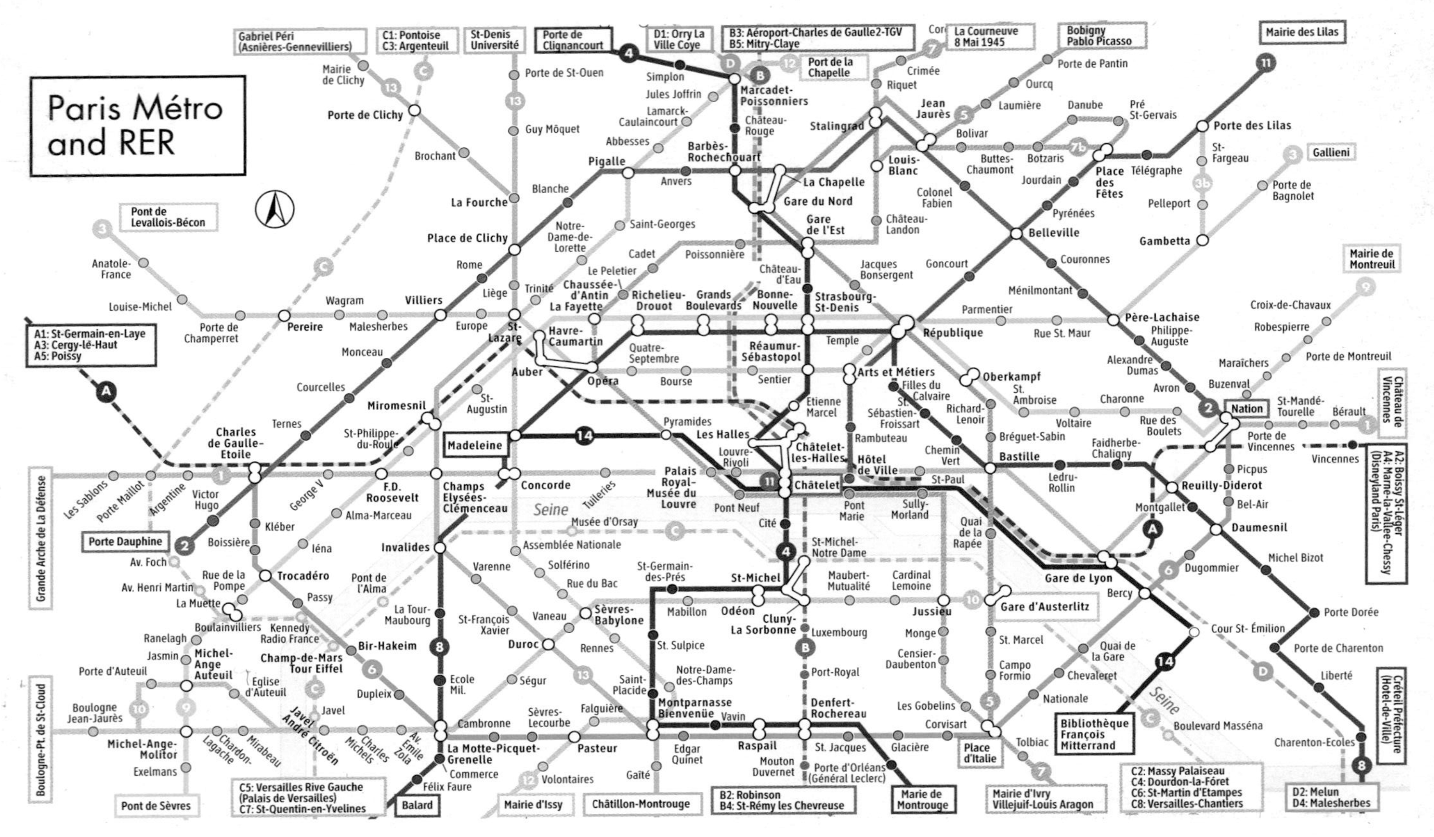

Paris Métro and RER
Gabriel Péri (Asnières-Gennevilliers)
C1: Pontoise
C3: Argenteuil
St-Denis Université
Porte de Clignancourt
D1: Orry La Ville Coye
B3: Aéroport-Charles de Gaulle2-TGV
B5: Mitry-Claye
Port de la Chapelle
La Courneuve 8 Mai 1945
Bobigny Pablo Picasso
Mairie des Lilas
Gallieni
Mairie de Montreuil
Château de Vincennes
A2: Boissy St-Léger
A4: Marne-la-Vallee-Chessy (Disneyland Paris)
Créteil Préfecture (Hotel-de-Ville)
D2: Melun
D4: Malesherbes
C2: Massy Palaiseau
C4: Dourdon-la-Fôret
C6: St-Martin d'Etampes
C8: Versailles-Chantiers
Mairie d'Ivry
Villejuif-Louis Aragon
Marie de Montrouge
B2: Robinson
B4: St-Rémy les Chevreuse
Châtillon-Montrouge
Mairie d'Issy
Balard
C5: Versailles Rive Gauche (Palais de Versailles)
C7: St-Quentin-en-Yvelines
Pont de Sèvres
Boulogne-Pt. de St-Cloud
Grande Arche de La Défense
Porte Dauphine
A1: St-Germain-en-Laye
A3: Cergy-lé-Haut
A5: Poissy
Pont de Levallois-Bécon
Mairie de Clichy
Porte de Clichy
Brochant
La Fourche
Porte de St-Ouen
Guy Môquet
Simplon
Jules Joffrin
Lamarck-Caulaincourt
Abbesses
Marcadet-Poissonniers
Château-Rouge
Barbès-Rochechouart
Pigalle
Anvers
Blanche
La Chapelle
Gare du Nord
Gare de l'Est
Stalingrad
Riquet
Crimée
Jean Jaurès
Louis-Blanc
Colonel Fabien
Château-Landon
Porte de Pantin
Ourcq
Laumière
Bolivar
Danube
Pré St-Gervais
Buttes-Chaumont
Botzaris
Place des Fêtes
Télégraphe
Porte des Lilas
St-Fargeau
Pelleport
Gambetta
Porte de Bagnolet
Jourdain
Pyrénées
Belleville
Couronnes
Ménilmontant
Père-Lachaise
Philippe-Auguste
Alexandre Dumas
Avron
Nation
Buzenval
Maraîchers
Porte de Montreuil
Robespierre
Croix-de-Chavaux
St-Mandé-Tourelle
Bérault
Porte de Vincennes
Vincennes
Picpus
Bel-Air
Reuilly-Diderot
Montgallet
Daumesnil
Michel Bizot
Porte Dorée
Porte de Charenton
Liberté
Charenton-Ecoles
Dugommier
Bercy
Cour St- Émilion
Gare de Lyon
Quai de la Gare
Chevaleret
Nationale
Bibliothèque François Mitterrand
Boulevard Masséna
Seine
Place d'Italie
Tolbiac
Corvisart
Glacière
Les Gobelins
Campo Formio
St. Marcel
Gare d'Austerlitz
Quai de la Rapée
Jussieu
Monge
Censier-Daubenton
Cardinal Lemoine
Maubert-Mutualité
St-Michel-Notre Dame
Cluny-La Sorbonne
Luxembourg
Port-Royal
Denfert-Rochereau
St. Jacques
Porte d'Orléans (Général Leclerc)
Mouton Duvernet
Raspail
Vavin
Montparnasse Bienvenüe
Edgar Quinet
Gaîté
Notre-Dame-des-Champs
St. Sulpice
Saint-Placide
St-Michel
Odéon
Mabillon
St-Germain-des-Prés
Cité
Châtelet
Châtelet-les-Halles
Les Halles
Louvre-Rivoli
Pont Neuf
Pont Marie
Sully-Morland
St-Paul
Hôtel de Ville
Rambuteau
Etienne Marcel
Arts et Métiers
Filles du Calvaire
St. Sébastien-Froissart
Chemin Vert
Bastille
Ledru-Rollin
Faidherbe-Chaligny
Rue des Boulets
Charonne
Voltaire
Bréguet-Sabin
Richard-Lenoir
St. Ambroise
Oberkampf
République
Parmentier
Rue St. Maur
Goncourt
Jacques Bonsergent
Temple
Strasbourg-St-Denis
Château-d'Eau
Réaumur-Sébastopol
Sentier
Bonne-Nouvelle
Grands Boulevards
Richelieu-Drouot
Bourse
Quatre-Septembre
Poissonnière
Cadet
Le Peletier
Saint-Georges
Notre-Dame-de-Lorette
Chaussée-d'Antin La Fayette
Trinité
Liège
Place de Clichy
Rome
St-Lazare
Havre-Caumartin
Opéra
Auber
Pyramides
Palais Royal-Musée du Louvre
Madeleine
Concorde
Tuileries
Musée d'Orsay
Assemblée Nationale
Solférino
Rue du Bac
Sèvres-Babylone
Vaneau
Duroc
Rennes
St-François Xavier
Varenne
Invalides
Champs Elysées-Clémenceau
St-Augustin
Miromesnil
St-Philippe-du-Roule
F.D. Roosevelt
Alma-Marceau
Europe
Villiers
Malesherbes
Wagram
Pereire
Porte de Champerret
Louise-Michel
Anatole-France
Monceau
Courcelles
Ternes
Charles de Gaulle-Etoile
George V
Victor Hugo
Argentine
Porte Maillot
Les Sablons
Kléber
Boissière
Iéna
Trocadéro
Pont de l'Alma
Passy
Av. Foch
Av. Henri Martin
Rue de la Pompe
La Muette
Boulainvilliers
Kennedy Radio France
Ranelagh
Jasmin
Michel-Ange Auteuil
Porte d'Auteuil
Eglise d'Auteuil
Champ-de-Mars Tour Eiffel
Bir-Hakeim
Dupleix
La Tour-Maubourg
Ecole Mil.
Ségur
La Motte-Picquet-Grenelle
Cambronne
Sèvres-Lecourbe
Pasteur
Falguière
Volontaires
Commerce
Félix Faure
Av. Emile Zola
Charles Michels
Javel
Javel André Citroën
Mirabeau
Chardon-Lagache
Michel-Ange-Molitor
Exelmans
Boulogne Jean-Jaurès